Handbook of
North American Indians

Handbook of North American Indians

WILLIAM C. STURTEVANT
General Editor

VOLUME 12

Plateau

DEWARD E. WALKER, JR.

Volume Editor

SMITHSONIAN INSTITUTION

WASHINGTON

1998

For sale by the Superintendent of Documents,
U.S. Government Printing Office, Washington, D.C. 20402.

Library of Congress Cataloging in Publication Data

Handbook of North American Indians.

    Bibliography.
    Includes index.
    CONTENTS:

               v. 12. Plateau.

    1. Indians of North America.
I. Sturtevant, William C.

E77.H25   970´.004´97   77-17162

For sale by the U.S. Government Printing Office
Superintendent of Documents, Mail Stop: SSOP, Washington, DC 20402-9328
ISBN 0-14-049514-8

Contents

This map is a diagrammatic guide to the coverage of this volume; it is not an authoritative depiction of territories for several reasons. Sharp boundaries have been drawn and no area is unassigned. The groups mapped are in some cases arbitrarily defined, subdivisions are not indicated, no joint or disputed occupations are shown, and different kinds of land use are not distinguished. Since the map depicts the situation at the earliest periods for which evidence is available, the ranges mapped for different groups often refer to different periods, and there may have been intervening movements, extinctions, and changes in range. Not shown are groups that came into separate existence later than the map period for their areas. The simplified ranges shown are a generalization of the situation in the early to mid-19th century, with those of the Nicola and Flathead showing earlier traditional locations. For more

specific information see the maps and text in the appropriate chapters.

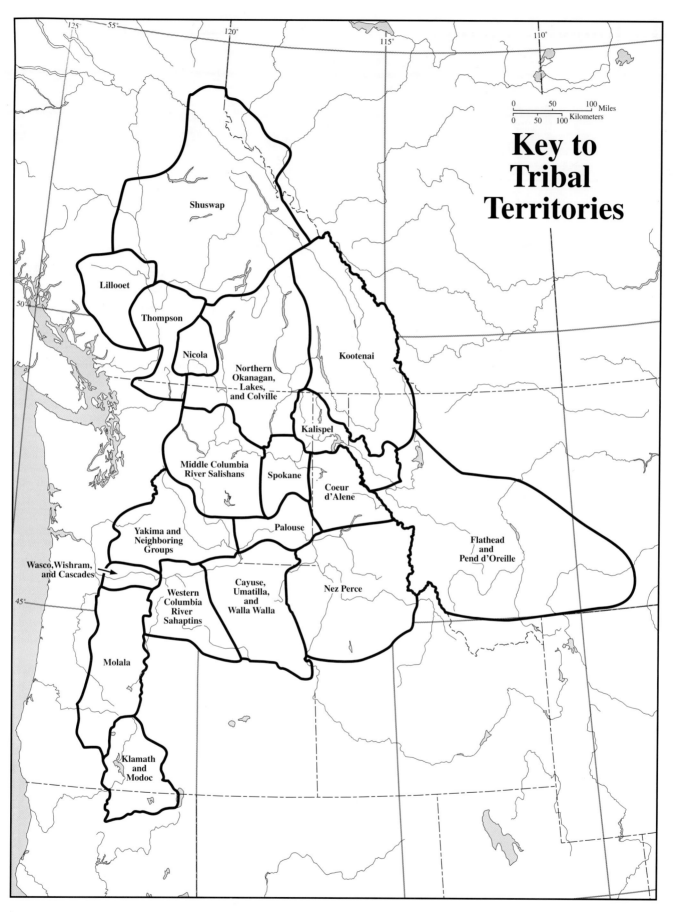

0   50   100 Miles
0   50   100 Kilometers

Key to Tribal Territories

Shuswap

Lillooet

Thompson

Nicola

Kootenai

Northern
Okanagan,
Lakes,
and Colville

Kalispel

Middle Columbia
River Salishans

Spokane

Coeur
d'Alene

Palouse

Yakima and
Neighboring
Groups

Flathead
and
Pend d'Oreille

Wasco, Wishram,
and Cascades

Western
Columbia
River
Sahaptins

Cayuse,
Umatilla,
and
Walla Walla

Nez Perce

Molala

Klamath
and
Modoc

Technical Alphabet

Consonants

		bilabial	labiodental	dental	alveolar	alveopalatal	velar	back velar	glottal
stop	vl	p		t	t		k	q	ʔ
	vd	b		d	d		g	ġ	
affricate	vl			θ̂	c	č			
	vd			δ̂	ʒ	ǯ			
fricative	vl	φ	f	θ	s	š	x	x̣	h
	vd	β	v	δ	z	ž	γ	γ̇	
nasal	vl	M		N			Ṇ		
	vd	m		n			ŋ	ŋ	
lateral	vl				ł				
	vd				l				
semivowel	vl	W				Y			
	vd	w				y			

vl=voiceless; vd=voiced

Vowels

	front	central	back
high	i (ü)	ɨ	u (ɨ)
	ɪ		ʊ
mid	e (ö)	ə	o
	ɛ		ɔ
		ʌ	
low	æ	a	a

Other symbols include λ (voiced lateral affricate), ƛ (voiceless lateral affricate), ʕ(pharyngeal stop, ḥ (voiceless pharyngeal fricative), r (medial flap, trill, or retroflex approximant), ẏ or ÿ (unrounded velar glide).

Unparenthesized vowels are unrounded if front or central, and rounded if back; ü and ö are rounded; ɨ is unrounded. The special symbols for lax vowels (ɪ, ʊ, ɛ, ɔ) are generally used only where it is necessary to differentiate between tense and lax high or mid vowels. i and a are used for both central and back vowels, as the two values seldom contrast in a given language.

Modifications indicated for consonants are: glottalization (t̓, k̓, etc.), fronting (x̟, etc.), retroflexion (ṭ), palatalization(tʸ, kʸ, nʸ, lʸ), labialization (kʷ), aspiration (tʰ), length (t·). For vowels: length (a·), three-mora length (a:), nasalization (ą), voicelessness (A). The commonest prosodic markings are, for stress: á (primary) and à (secondary), and for pitch: á (high), à (low), â (falling), ǎ (rising); however, the details of prosodic systems and the uses of accents differ widely from language to language.

Words in Indian languages cited in italics in this volume are with one set of exceptions in phonemic transcription. That is, the letters and symbols are used in specific values defined for them by the structure of the sound system of the particular language. However, as far as possible, these phonemic transcriptions use letters and symbols in generally consistent values, as specified by the standard technical alphabet of the *Handbook*, displayed on this page. Deviations from these standard values as well as specific details of the phonology of each language (or references to where they may be found) are given in an orthographic footnote in each tribal chapter. Exceptionally, italics are used for Chinook Jargon words, which appear in the conventional English-based spellings of the sources. Phonetic transcriptions, even if available, would be variable, and a unified phonemic transcription impossible, since speakers of Chinook Jargon tended to pronounce it using the sounds of their respective languages.

No italicized Indian word is broken at a line end except when a hyphen would be present anyway as part of the word. Words in italicized phonemic transcription are never capitalized. Pronunciations or phonetic values given in the standard technical alphabet without regard to phonemic analysis are put in brackets rather than in italics. The glosses, or conventionalized translations, of Indian words are enclosed in single quotation marks.

Indian words recorded by nonspecialists or before the phonemic systems of their languages had been analyzed are often not written accurately enough to allow respelling in phonemic transcription. Where phonemic retranscription has been possible the citation of source has been modified by the label "phonemicized" or "from." A few words that could not be phonemicized have been "normalized"—rewritten by mechanical substitution of the symbols of the standard technical alphabet. Others have been rationalized by eliminating redundant or potentially misleading diacritics and substituting nontechnical symbols. Words that do not use the standard technical alphabet occasionally contain some letters used according to the values of other technical alphabets or traditional orthographies. The most common of these are c for the *Handbook* [š]; ch for [x]; E (sometimes printed as E) for [ə]; h for [x]; H (sometimes printed as H) for [x]; hl, ˈl for [ł]; k̲ for [q]; k· for [kʸ]; q for [x], [x̣]; Q (sometimes printed as Q) for [x]; r for [ʕ]; tc for [č]; tl and L (sometimes printed as L) for [ł], [λ], [ƛ]; ᵘ for ʷ; x̲ for [x]; x for [x̣]; χ for [x] or [x̣]; z for [c]; ˀ for [ʔ] and for glottalization (e.g., t' for [t̓]); and ʿ(sometimes printed as ʿ or ʾ) for [h].

All nonphonemic transcriptions give only incomplete, and sometimes imprecise, approximations of the correct pronunciation.

Nontechnical Equivalents

Correct pronunciation, as with any foreign language, requires extensive training and practice, but simplified (incorrect) pronunciations may be obtained by ignoring the diacritics and reading the vowels as in Italian or Spanish and the consonants as in English. For a closer approximation to the pronunciation or to rewrite into a nontechnical transcription the substitutions indicated in the following table may be made. The orthographic footnote for some languages contains a practical alphabet that may be used as an alternative by substituting the letters and letter groups for their correspondents in the list of technical symbols in the same footnote.

Technical	Nontechnical		Technical	Nontechnical		Technical	Nontechnical
æ	ae		M	mh		Y	yh
β	bh		N	nh		$\check{z}$	zh
c	ts		η	ng		$\mathfrak{z}$	dz
$\check{c}$	ch		$\mathcal{N}$	ngh		$\check{\mathfrak{z}}$	j
δ	dh		$\mathfrak{o}$	o		$\mathfrak{\gamma}$	'
ϵ	e		θ	th		$\acute{k}, \acute{p}, \acute{t}$, etc.	k', p', t', etc.
γ	gh		ϕ	ph		$a\cdot, e\cdot, k\cdot, s\cdot$, etc.	aa, ee, kk, ss, etc.
$\bar{t}$	lh		$\check{s}$	sh		$ą, ę$, etc.	an, en, etc.
λ	dl		W	wh		k^y, t^y, etc.	ky, ty, etc.
$\check{\lambda}$	tlh		x	kh		k^w	kw

English Pronunciations

The English pronunciations of the names of tribes and a few other words are indicated parenthetically in a dictionary-style orthography in which most letters have their usual English pronunciation. Special symbols are listed below, with sample words to be pronounced as in nonregional United States English. Approximate phonetic values are given in parentheses in the standard technical alphabet.

ŋ: thi<u>ng</u> (ŋ)
θ: <u>th</u>in (θ)
o: <u>th</u>is (δ)
zh: vi<u>s</u>ion (ž)

ă: b<u>a</u>t (æ)
ä: f<u>a</u>ther (a)
ā: b<u>ai</u>t (ey)
e: b<u>e</u>t (ε)
ē: b<u>ea</u>t (iy)

ə: <u>a</u>bout, gall<u>o</u>p (ə)
ĭ: bit (I)
ī: b<u>i</u>te (ay)
ô: b<u>ou</u>ght (ɔ)

ō: b<u>oa</u>t (ow)
o͝o: b<u>oo</u>k (ᴜ)
o͞o: b<u>oo</u>t (uw)
u: b<u>u</u>t (ʌ)

ˈ(primary stress), ˌ(secondary stress): elevator (ˈelə͵vātər) (ɛ́ləvèytər)

Conventions for Illustrations

- • Native settlement
- ○ Abandoned settlement
- ■ Non-native or mixed settlement
- □ Abandoned settlement
- ▲ Modern reservations or archeological sites
- × Battlefield
- ⍦ Rapids
- / Dam
- + Mountain peak
- ⟋⟨ Mountain pass
- 🐟 Fishery

Colville Tribe

Penticton Settlement

Lower Arrow Lake Geographic feature

 Movement/migration

 Drainage

―――――――― Reservation border

―――――――― National border

――――――――― State border

├―┼―┼―┼―┼―┤ Railroad

 Indian reservations and reserves

 Precontact territory

 Water

 Marsh

Credits and Captions

Credit lines give the source of the illustrations or the collections where the artifacts shown are located. The numbers that follow are the catalog or negative numbers of that repository. When the photographer mentioned in the caption is the source of the print reproduced, no credit line appears. "After" means that the *Handbook* illustrators have redrawn, rearranged, or abstracted the illustration from the one in the cited source. All maps and drawings not otherwise credited are by the *Handbook* illustrators. Measurements in captions are to the nearest millimeter if available; "about" indicates an estimate or a measurement converted from inches to centimeters. The following abbreviations are used in the credit lines:

Amer.	American	Instn.	Institution
Anthr.	Anthropology, Anthropological	Lib.	Library
Arch.	Archives	Mt.	Mount
Arch(a)eol	Arch(a)eology, Arch(a)eological	Mus.	Museum
		NAA	National Anthropological Archives
Assoc.	Association		
Co.	County	Nat.	Natural
Coll.	Collection(s)	Natl.	National
Dept.	Department	neg.	Negative
Div.	Division	opp.	opposite
Ethnol.	Ethnology, Ethnological	pl(s).	plate(s)
fol.	folio	Prov.	Provincial
Ft.	Fort	Res.	Reservation (U.S.) Reserve (Canada)
Hist.	History		
Histl.	Historical	Soc.	Society
Ind.	Indian	St.	Saint
Inst.	Institute	U.	University

Preface

This is the eleventh volume to be published of a 20-volume set planned to give an encyclopedic summary of what is known about the prehistory, history, and cultures of the aboriginal peoples of North America north of the urban civilizations of central Mexico. Volumes 5-11 and 13-15 treat the other major culture areas of the continent.

Some topics relevant to the Plateau area are excluded from this volume because they are more appropriately discussed on a continent-wide basis. Readers should refer to volume 1, Introduction, for general descriptions of anthropological and historical methods and sources and for summaries for the whole continent of certain topics regarding social and political organization, religion, and the performing arts. Volume 2 contains detailed accounts of the different kinds of Indian and Eskimo communities in the twentieth century, especially since 1950, and describes their relations with one another and with the surrounding non-Indian societies and nations. Volume 3 gives the environmental and biological backgrounds within which Native American societies developed, summarizes the early and late human biology or physical anthropology of Indians and Eskimos, and surveys the earliest prehistoric cultures. (Therefore the Paleo-Indian or Early Man period in the Plateau receives major treatment in volume 3 rather than in this volume.) Volume 4 contains details on the history of the relations between Whites and Native American societies. Volume 16 is a continent-wide survey of technology and the visual arts—of material culture broadly defined. Volume 17 surveys the Native languages of North America, their characteristics and historical relationships. Volumes 18 and 19 are a biographical dictionary; included in the listing are many Plateau Indians. Volume 20 contains an index to the whole, which will serve to locate materials on Plateau Indians in other volumes as well as in this one; it also includes a list of errata found in all preceding volumes.

Preliminary discussions on the feasibility of the *Handbook* and alternatives for producing it began in 1965 in what was then the Smithsonian's Office of Anthropology. (A history of the early development of the whole *Handbook* and a listing of the entire editorial staff will be found in volume 1.) As the *Handbook* was originally conceived, the Plateau and Great Basin areas were to be treated together; the General Editor's preliminary mapping for the coverage of the various *Handbook* volumes showed one large region labeled "Great Basin–Plateau." The decision to differentiate the two areas more sharply, made in 1968, was based on the advice of consultants with a continental comparative perspective. George Peter Murdock and Harold E. Driver especially

urged that a boundary be drawn between the two areas. As "Introduction," this volume, makes clear, recognition of the Plateau as a distinct culture area is well established in Americanist anthropology. Following a planning meeting for the *Handbook* as a whole that was held in Chicago in November 1970, separate editors were appointed for the Plateau and the Great Basin. However, it still seemed then that a single volume would suffice to cover the available knowledge of the two areas at a level of detail comparable to that of the other areas of North America (except the two volumes for the Southwest). Accordingly, a joint meeting to plan the detailed contents of such a volume was held in Reno, Nevada, March 19-20, 1971, which was attended by the separate editors and planning committees for the two areas, and the General Editor. That meeting resulted in the decision to treat the two areas in separate volumes.

During the March 1971 planning meeting a tentative table of contents for this volume was drawn up. Participating in planning for the Plateau volume during that meeting were Richard D. Daugherty and William W. Elmendorf, in addition to the Volume Editor and the General Editor. Soon thereafter Verne F. Ray was added as a consultant to the planning committee, and at later dates others were added; the full planning committee is listed on p.[v]. At the Reno meeting and soon thereafter a list was compiled of 46 chapters by 27 authors (many authors responsible for more than one chapter). Of the original chapters planned, 24 survived into the present volume; of the 29 authors of these chapters proposed in 1971, 12 contributed to the same chapters in the present volume. During the early 1970s important changes in the chapter topics and the authors resulted from consultations with a somewhat enlarged planning committee, and with authors and potential authors. Some problems regarding the boundaries of the Plateau were resolved; in particular, after consultation with volume editors and some authors, the General Editor decided that the Modoc should be treated in this volume rather than in the California volume, and the Chilcotin should be considered as Subarctic rather than Plateau. The reverse assignments would have been almost as well justified.

The Volume Editor began inviting contributions in August 1971, and the first draft manuscript was received in the General Editor's office on May 4, 1972. After a few other manuscripts were submitted, in about 1977 it became necessary to change the publication schedules for the *Handbook* volumes. Editorial attention then focused on one after another of the 10 volumes that were published first (see the list on p. [i]).

During 1985-1989 the Volume Editor led a revision of the plans for this volume, enlarging the Planning Committee to 10 members (in addition to himself) and consulting on the contents and coverage of tribal chapters with tribal historians and other members of more than eight of the tribal groups covered here. In November 1990 intensive work to complete the *Plateau* volume began. The Volume Editor sent each author a brief description of the desired contents of the chapter, and he sent suggestions for updating to authors of the chapters already received. Also sent was a "Guide for Contributors" prepared by the General Editor, which described the general aims and methods of the *Handbook* and the editorial conventions. One convention has been to avoid the present tense, where possible, in historical and cultural descriptions. Thus a statement in the past tense, with a recent date or approximate date, may also hold true for the time of writing. The contents of this volume reflect the state of knowledge in the 1990s, rather than in the early 1970s when planning first began.

As they were received, the manuscripts were reviewed by the Volume Editor, the General Editor and his staff, and usually one or more referees, who frequently included a member of the Planning Committee and often authors of other chapters. Suggestions for changes and additions often resulted. The published versions frequently reflect more editorial intervention than is customary for academic writings, since the encyclopedic aims and format of the *Handbook* made it necessary to attempt to eliminate duplication, avoid gaps in coverage, prevent contradictions, impose some standardization of organization and terminology, and keep within strict constraints on length. Where the evidence seemed so scanty or obscure as to allow different authorities to come to differing conclusions, authors have been encouraged to elaborate their own views, although the editors have endeavored to draw attention to alternative interpretations published elsewhere.

The first editorial acceptance of an author's manuscript was on September 11, 1995, and the last on August 15, 1997. Edited manuscripts were sent from the Washington office to authors for their final approval between November 18, 1996, and September 23, 1997. These dates for all chapters are given in the list of Contributors.

Linguistic Editing

As far as possible, all cited words in Indian languages were referred to consultants with expert knowledge of the respective languages and rewritten by them in the appropriate technical orthography. In some cases a chapter author served as the linguist consultant. The consultants and the spelling systems are identified in the orthographic footnotes, drafted by the Linguistic Editor, Ives Goddard.

Statements about the genetic relationships of Plateau languages have also been checked with linguist consultants, to ensure conformity with recent findings and terminology in comparative linguistics and to avoid conflicting statements

within the *Handbook*. In general, only the less remote genetic relationships are mentioned in the individual chapters. The chapter "Languages" discusses the wider relationships of those languages, and further information is in volume 17.

The Linguistic Editor served as coordinator and editor of these efforts by linguist consultants. A special debt is owed to these consultants, who provided advice and assistance without compensation and, in many cases, took time from their own research in order to check words with native speakers. The Linguistic Editor is especially grateful to M. Dale Kinkade, Haruo Aoki, Barry Carlson, Scott DeLancey, Ivy G. Doak, Jan van Eijk, Catherine S. Fowler, Anthony Mattina, John McLaughlin, Douglas Parks, Robert L. Rankin, Bruce Rigsby, Noel Rude, Michael Silverstein, Sarah G. Thomason, Timothy Jon Thornes, Janne Underriner, and three anonymous consultants.

In the case of words that could not be respelled in a technical orthography, an attempt has been made to rationalize the transcriptions used in earlier anthropological writings in order to eliminate phonetic symbols that are obsolete and diacritics that might convey a false impression of phonetic accuracy.

Synonymies

Toward the end of ethnological chapters is a section called Synonymy. This describes the various names that have been applied to the groups and subgroups treated in that chapter, giving the principal variant spellings used in English and sometimes in French, self-designations, and often the names applied to the groups in neighboring Indian languages. For the major group names, an attempt has been made to cite the earliest attestations in English.

Many synonymies have been expanded or reworked by the Linguistic Editor, who has added names and analyses from the literature and as provided by linguist consultants. Where a synonymy is wholly or substantially the work of the Linguistic Editor or a linguist consultant, other than the chapter author, a footnote specifying authorship is given.

These sections should assist in the identification of groups mentioned in the earlier historical and anthropological literature. They should also be examined for evidence on changes in the identifications and affiliations of groups, as seen by their own members as well as by neighbors and by outside observers.

Radiocarbon Dates

Authors were instructed to convert radiocarbon dates into dates in the Christian calendar. Such conversions have often been made from the dates as originally published, without taking account of changes that may be required by developing research on revisions of the half-life of carbon 14, long-term changes in the amount of carbon 14 in the atmosphere, and other factors that may require modifications of absolute dates based on radiocarbon determinations.

Binomials

The scientific names of animal and plant genera and species, printed in italics, have been checked and revised by Eugene S. Hunn and Nancy J. Turner, respectively, to ensure that they reflect modern usage by biological taxonomists. Especially the plant names (but also most of the animal names) submitted in the chapter "Ethnobiology and Subsistence" were taken as standard. Binomials in other chapters have been brought into agreement with those in that chapter.

Bibliography

All references cited by contributors have been unified in a single list at the end of the volume. Citations within the text, by author, date, and often page, identify the works in this unified list. Wherever possible the *Handbook* Acting Bibliographer, Cesare Marino, has resolved conflicts between citations of different editions, corrected inaccuracies and omissions, and checked direct quotations against the originals. The bibliographic information has been verified by examination of the original work or from standard reliable library catalogs (especially the National Union Catalog, the published catalog of the Harvard Peabody Museum Library, and the OCLC/PRISM on-line catalog). The unified bibliography lists all the sources cited in the text of the volume, except personal communications, and works consulted but not cited in the chapters. In the text, "personal communications" to an author are distinguished from personal "communications to editors." The sections headed Sources at the ends of most chapters provide general guidance to the most important sources of information on the topics covered.

Illustrations

Authors were requested to submit suggestions for illustrations: photographs, drawings, maps, and lists and locations of objects that might be illustrated. Although many responded with suggestions, considerations of space, balance, reproducibility, and availability often required modifications in what was submitted. Much original material was provided by editorial staff members from research they conducted in museums and other repositories and in the published literature. Locating suitable photographs, drawings, and paintings was the responsibility of the Illustrations Researcher, Joanna Cohan Scherer. Selection of and research on suitable artifacts to be photographed or drawn

was the responsibility of the Artifact Researcher Christine A. Jirikowic; Barbara Watanabe provided some research in the final stages of production. All uncredited drawings are by the Scientific Illustrators, Karen B. Ackoff and Marcia Bakry, with contributions from Tamara L. Clark.

Maps for the chapters "Molala" and "Demographic History Until 1990" were produced by Daniel G. Cole of the Smithsonian Automatic Data Processing office while all others were by Alex Tait and David Swanson of Equator Graphics. Maps were created using information from the chapter manuscripts, from their authors, and from other sources.

Layout and design of the illustrations were the responsibility of the Scientific Illustrator, Karen B. Ackoff (until May 1997), and thereafter Marcia Bakry assisted in carrying the project to completion. Captions for illustrations were usually composed by Scherer, Jirikowic, and Watanabe and for maps by Tait and Swanson. Native place-names in map captions were supplied by authors and edited by the Linguistic Editor and his consultants. All illustrations, including maps, and all captions, have been approved by the authors of the chapters in which they appear, the Volume Editor, and the Technical Editor.

The list of illustrations was compiled by Carin Cobb and Joanna Cohan Scherer.

Acknowledgements

During the first few years of this project, the Handbook editorial staff in Washington worked on materials for all volumes of the series. Since intensive preparation of this volume began in 1990, especially important contributions were provided by: the Editorial Liaison and (since October 1996) Staff Coordinator, Paula Cardwell; the Production Manager and Manuscript Editor, Diane Della-Loggia; the Researcher and Acting Bibliographer, Cesare Marino; the Scientific Illustrator, Karen B. Ackoff (until May 1997); the Illustrations Researcher, Joanna Cohan Scherer; the Assistant Illustrations Researchers, Rebecca Dobkins (April-August 1996) and Carin Cobb (1996-1997); the Artifact Researchers, Christine A. Jirikowic (1994-1997) and Barbara Watanabe (June-September 1997); the Administrative Specialist, Melvina Jackson; and the Managing Editor, Karla Billups (through 1995). Peter Yiotis served as the bibliographic assistant during the initial period of volume preparation and Alexander Young during the later stages. Martha Arcos served as the volunteer assistant for the Acting Bibliographer. The Illustrations Researcher was assisted by Leslie Taylor Davol, Mercy McDonald, Margo Rosingana, Jerome Saltzman, and Meg Strawbridge as interns; illustrations production for a number of chapters was provided by Tamara L. Clark, Catherine Spencer, Peter Mundel, and Editorial Experts, Inc. Phillip E. Minthorn, Jr. of the Office of Repatriation, National Museum of Natural History, assisted at different times in documenting illustrations. The index was compiled by L. Pilar Wyman. The music was set by Kent Ashcraft.

Beginning in January 1996 Carolyn Rose served in effect as Managing Editor in addition to her other duties as Deputy Chairman of the Department of Anthropology, National Museum of Natural History. She was particularly helpful in guiding the *Handbook* staff to work within an accelerated production schedule.

Throughout, Ives Goddard was of particular assistance on matters of historical and geographical accuracy. He served as Technical Editor as well as the *Handbook* Linguistic Editor and advisor to the General Editor.

Beyond the members of the Planning Committee and those individuals acknowledged in appropriate sections of the text, the Volume Editor would like to thank tribal members that helped to make his research possible. Among these individuals he would like particularly to cite the aid of Joe Antastite (Kootenai); Lawrence Aripa (Coeur d'Alene); Clarence Burke (Walla Walla); William Burke (Umatilla); Rudy Clements (Warm Springs); Lucy Covington (Colville); Delbert Frank (Warm Springs); Ozzie George (Coeur d'Alene); Alphonse Halfmoon (Umatilla–Nez Perce); Richard A. Halfmoon (Nez Perce); Ross Hillary (Colville); Tony Incashola (Bitterroot Salish); Mary Jim (Yakama); Robert Jim (Yakama); Alex Lefthand (Kootenai); Pat Lefthand (Kootenai); Chris Luke (Kootenai); Adeline Mathias (Kootenai); Wilson Meanus (Warm Springs); Joe Meninick (Yakama); Antone Minthorn (Cayuse-Umatilla); Harvey Moses, Sr. (Colville–Nez Perce); George Nanamkin (Colville); Shirley Palmer (Colville); Ike Patrick (Umatilla); Alex Pinkham (Nez Perce); Joe Pinkham (Nez Perce); Alec Saluskin (Yakama); Ellen Saluskin (Yakama); Eagle Selatsee (Yakama); Alex Sherwood (Spokane); Alice Shotnana (Kootenai); Bearhead Swaney (Bitterroot Salish); Agnes Vanderburg (Bitterroot Salish); Nelson Wallulatum (Warm Springs); Sam Watters (Nez Perce); Basil White (Kootenai); Elizabeth Wilson (Nez Perce); David Wynkoop (Spokane); Bruce Wynne (Spokane); and William Yallup (Yakama). He extends special thanks to Carl Borgman, Lawson Crow, David Greene, Evelyn Hu-DeHart, Jack Kelso, Milton Lipetz, Roderick Sprague, and Barbara Voorhies who assisted in securing special funding and other support during various stages of volume preparation.

Acknowledgement is due to the Department of Anthropology, National Museum of Natural History, Smithsonian Institution (and to its other curatorial staff), for releasing Sturtevant and Goddard from part of their curatorial and research responsibilities so that they could devote time to editing the *Handbook* and for supporting the participation of Deputy Chair Carolyn Rose and Scientific Illustrator Marcia Bakry. Walker thanks the Departments of Anthropology and Ethnic Studies, University of Colorado, Boulder, for financial support and released time from teaching, which enabled him to devote time to editing this volume.

Preparation and publication of this volume have been supported by federal appropriations made to the Smithsonian Institution.

December 8, 1997   William C. Sturtevant
                                        Deward E. Walker, Jr.

Introduction

DEWARD E. WALKER, JR.

A simple definition of the Plateau culture area is that it is the region drained by the Columbia and Fraser rivers excepting certain portions of the northern Great Basin drained by the Snake River, itself a tributary of the Columbia River (fig.1). The culture areas that border it are the Great Basin on the south, the Subarctic on the north, the Northwest Coast on the west, and the Plains on the east. The Plateau culture area includes the Interior Salishan peoples, the Sahaptian peoples, and several cultural isolates, Athapaskan outliers, and the Kootenai and Cayuse whose exact linguistic affiliations remain unclear.

While Plateau tribes may have undergone some territorial realignments over the last several millennia, they appear not to have moved very much in recent centuries. Their ancient occupation of their current homelands is evidenced in both place-names and highly localized creation epics. Despite this apparent ancient stability, it is still possible that ancestral Salishans came into the northern Plateau from the Fraser delta after Sahaptians had already occupied the region. Possible ancient links of Sahaptians with Uto-Aztecans of the northern Great Basin have been suggested but remain unclarified.

Boundaries of the Culture Area*

The Plateau has been recognized as a distinct culture area ever since Otis T. Mason (1896, improved in 1907) first suggested that there were 12 "ethnic environments" or "culture areas" in North America. Although he did not list the cultures in each of his 12 regions, or map them, his "Columbia-Fraser region" corresponds quite well with the area defined in this volume. It differs mainly by including the coast, evidently from about the mouth of the Columbia River to about the California border (this region is here assigned to the Northwest Coast, vol. 7). The map provided by Holmes (1914, 1919:96, 117–118) shows "the Columbia-Fraser area" essentially as defined by Mason. Although again no tribes are listed or mapped, the Flathead-Pend d'Oreille area seems to be assigned to "the Great Plains and Rocky Mountain area." Wissler's (1914) "Plateau Area" is similar but excludes the Oregon coast and includes the Flathead–Pend d'Oreille. He includes the Chilcotin (here in the Subarctic, vol. 6) but places the Molala in the Northwest

Coast, the Klamath and Modoc in California, and the Shoshone (here in the Great Basin, vol. 11) overlapping the Plateau and the Plains. When Wissler's general textbook, *The American Indian*, appeared (1917, 1938) he did not map the Plateau area but revised his earlier map by indicating that the Kootenai, Flathead, and Nez Perce overlapped into the Plains. In 1923 Kroeber presented a map of culture areas "modified from Wissler," where the Plateau extends farther north, apparently including the Carrier and Sekani (in the Subarctic, vol. 6, here). By 1939 Kroeber was more specific, although by then his "Columbia-Fraser" was a subarea of the larger "Intermediate and Intermountain areas," which included the Great Basin and much of California. This subarea included all those in the Plateau as defined in this volume, with the exception of the Klamath and Modoc (in Kroeber's Great Basin subarea), and the Wasco, Wishram, and Cascades (in Kroeber's Northwest Coast). It also included the Chilcotin and, more doubtfully, the Carrier (both placed in the Subarctic by this *Handbook*). Verne Ray's (1936) "Plateau Culture Area" included those treated in this volume, except that the following were omitted: Klamath and Modoc, Molala, Wasco-Wishram-Cascades, Flathead and Pend d'Oreille, and in the north the Thompson, Lillooet, Shuswap, and Kootenai. Later Ray (1939) added the last six and the Molala, and probably also the Sekani, Carrier, and Chilcotin. Ray (1942) certainly included the Carrier and Chilcotin in the Plateau. For G.P. Murdock (1941; also map in Murdock and O'Leary 1975, 3:212) the Plateau included the same groups as those included in this volume, with the exception of the Klamath and Modoc, which he placed in the California culture area. Driver and Massey (1957) defined the Plateau to include all the groups included in this volume, plus the Takelma and Kalapuya, which are here in volume 7, Northwest Coast. A statistical study of Driver and Massey's culture-trait distributions (Driver and Coffin 1975:16–17) resulted in a Plateau culture area that excluded the Klamath and Modoc, and probably the Wasco-Wishram-Cascades and Tolowa (placed in a Southern Northwest Coast area), but included the Chilcotin. Somewhat later a statistical study of the distribution of 292 "cultural variables" among Western tribes (Jorgensen 1980:89–91) identified a Plateau area much like that in this volume, except that it extended north to include the Carrier and Chilcotin.

The definition of the Plateau area for the *Handbook* is the result of the General Editor's mapping, following especially

*This section was written by William C. Sturtevant.

1

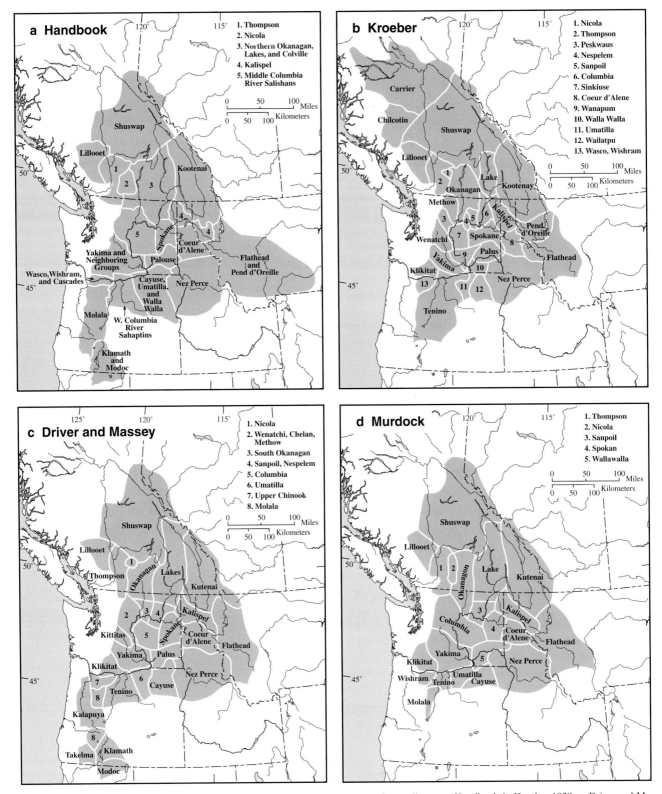

a Handbook

120° 115°

1. Thompson
2. Nicola
3. Northern Okanagan, Lakes, and Colville
4. Kalispel
5. Middle Columbia River Salishans

0   50   100 Miles
0   50   100 Kilometers

Shuswap
Lillooet
1
2 3
Kootenai
4
5 Spokane 4
Coeur d'Alene
Yakima and Neighboring Groups
Palouse
Flathead and Pend d'Oreille
Wasco,Wishram, and Cascades
Cayuse, Umatilla, and Walla Walla
Nez Perce
Molala
W. Columbia River Sahaptins
Klamath and Modoc

50°
45°

b Kroeber

120° 115°

1. Nicola
2. Thompson
3. Peskwaus
4. Nespelem
5. Sanpoil
6. Columbia
7. Sinkiuse
8. Coeur d'Alene
9. Wanapum
10. Walla Walla
11. Umatilla
12. Wailatpu
13. Wasco, Wishram

0   50   100 Miles
0   50   100 Kilometers

Carrier
Chilcotin
Shuswap
Lillooet
1
2 Okanagan Lake
Methow Kootenay
3 4 5 6 Kalispel
7 Spokane Pend d'Oreille
Wenatchi 8
9 Palus
Yakima 10 Flathead
Klikitat Nez Perce
13 11 12
Tenino

50°
45°

c Driver and Massey

125° 120° 115°

1. Nicola
2. Wenatchi, Chelan, Methow
3. South Okanagan
4. Sanpoil, Nespelem
5. Columbia
6. Umatilla
7. Upper Chinook
8. Molala

0   50   100 Miles
0   50   100 Kilometers

Shuswap
Lillooet
1
Thompson Okanagan Lakes
Kutenai
2 3 4 Kalispel
Kittitas 5 Spokane Coeur d'Alene Flathead
Yakima Palus
Klikitat Nez Perce
7 2 6 Cayuse
8 Tenino
Kalapuya
8
Takelma Klamath
Modoc

50°
45°

d Murdock

120° 115°

1. Thompson
2. Nicola
3. Sanpoil
4. Spokan
5. Wallawalla

0   50   100 Miles
0   50   100 Kilometers

Shuswap
Lillooet
1 2 Okanagn Lake
Kutenai
3 Kalispel
Columbia 4 Coeur d'Alene
Yakima Flathead
Klikitat 5 Nez Perce
Wishram Umatilla Cayuse
Tenino
Molala

50°
45°

Fig. 1. Definitions of the Plateau culture area. Area and component groups are mapped according to a, *Handbook*; b, Kroeber 1939; c, Driver and Massey 1957; and d, Murdock 1941 (as redrawn in Murdock and O'Leary 1975, 3:212).

Driver and Massey (1957), Kroeber (1939), and Murdock (1941), and then modifying his map following the advice of several specialists consulted by mail, and taking into account discussions by the *Handbook* volume editors and volume planning committees. The results, for this volume and for others, reflect compromises as well as reasoned arguments. These discussions, as also the previous literature, demonstrated both general agreement as to the practicality of treating together the cultures assigned to this volume, and the arbitrariness of defining precise boundaries for this and all the other culture areas of the continent.

Culture Pattern

Among the distinguishing features of the Plateau are:
- riverine (linear) settlement patterns.
- reliance on a diverse subsistence base of anadramous fish and extensive game and root resources.
- a complex fishing technology similar to that seen on the Northwest Coast.
- mutual cross-utilization of subsistence resources among the various groups comprising the populations of the area.
- extension of kinship ties through extensive inter-marriage throughout the area.
- extension of trade links throughout the area through institutionalized trading partnerships and regional trade fairs.
- limited political integration, primarily at the village and band levels, until adoption of the horse.
- relatively uniform mythology, art styles, and religious beliefs and practices focused on the vision quest, shamanism, life-cycle observances, and seasonal celebrations of the annual subsistence cycle.

Until adoption of the horse, Plateau peoples maintained close connections with the Northwest Coast, but afterward also with the Plains. Hostile relationships tended to occur with Shoshone and Paiute groups to the south, but there were also substantial trade and other interactions between Sahaptian groups and Northern Shoshone and Northern Paiute. After adoption of the horse, composite band political organization emerged in response to growing conflict with both Plains and northern Great Basin, especially in the eastern and southern Plateau. After adoption of the horse, limited forms of social stratification appeared, based especially on wealth in horses.

The Plateau culture area is located in a complex physiographic unit, bounded on the west by the Cascade Range, on the south by the Blue Mountains and the Salmon River, on the east by the Rocky Mountains, and on the north the low extensions of the Rocky Mountains and the northern reach of the Columbia River. In the south the Plateau gradually merges with the Great Basin, the boundaries between them being especially vague and subject to differing interpretations.

The climate of the Plateau can be harsh and continental, but it is normally moderated by Pacific weather influences. Temperatures range from -50ºF in winter to 100ºF+ in summer. Precipitation is low, except for snow during the winter. There are three vegetation provinces: the Middle Columbia area, a steppe of sagebrush and bunchgrass fringed by yellow pine at higher elevations, the territory of the Sahaptian groups with a few Salishan outliers; the Upper Columbia area, a forested region area with grasslands and river valleys, which is the home territory of the Northern Okanagan, Flathead, and Kootenai; and the Fraser area, with a semi-open coniferous forest interspersed with grasslands, home of northern Salishan groups. Overall the Plateau contains numerous tributary streams, lakes, and rivers that contain an abundance of both resident and anadromous fish that have provided a secure subsistence base for millennia.

A village settlement pattern with semipermanent longhouses and temporary subsistence camps in the higher elevations emerged as early as two millennia ago in the Plateau and changed little until adoption of the horse about 1700. Thereafter villages increased in size and were located so as to both protect and feed the large herds of horses that flourished especially in the southern Plateau, an area ideal for horses, with some families owning large herds exceeding 1,000 head in cases. The lush grasses, protected valleys, and abundant water made the Southern Plateau a primary center of American Indian equestrian development in North America (fig. 2).

Plateau permanent winter villages had semisubterranean earth lodges along the main rivers, but the summer camps had mat-covered lodges located in the higher elevations. The Plateau groups shared many cultural traits with their more affluent Northwest Coast neighbors. With adoption of the horse there were more influences from the east. The Northern Shoshone had acquired horses and furnished their neighbors on the Plains and Plateau with a ready supply acquired through trade and raiding. From the beginning of the nineteenth century, Nez Perce, Cayuse, Walla Walla, and Flathead possessed more horses than most tribes of the northern Plains, helping create an extensive trade in horses with Plains groups like the Crow who routinely met to trade horses and other items with Plateau groups.

Other elements of Plains culture adopted with the horse included beaded dresses, feathered warbonnets, and skin-covered tepees. In contrast to eastern Sahaptians such as the Nez Perce, the northwestern Salishan groups retained more of the prehorse Plateau culture patterns. Due to pressure from the Blackfoot, the Flathead and Kootenai withdrew from central Montana by 1800. Resettled west of the continental divide, they made occasional buffalo hunts onto the Plains in the company of other Plateau tribes, such as the Coeur d'Alene and Nez Perce (Anastasio 1972).

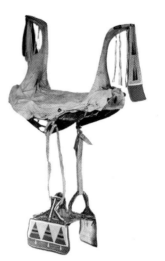

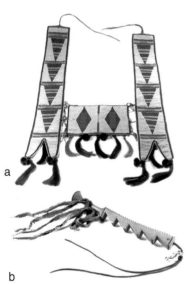

a

b

4

Eastern Wash. State Histl. Soc., Cheney Cowles Mus., Spokane: top left and bottom left; Smithsonian, Dept. of Anthr.: top right, 277655 (neg. 95–2078I), bottom right, 23873 (neg. 88–15546); Smithsonian, Natl. Mus. of the Amer. Ind.: top center: 14/3518; center left, a, 14/3524; b, 13/8451; center right, U. of Mont., K. Ross Toole Arch., Missoula.

Fig. 2. Horse transportation. The adoption of the horse allowed not only for greater mobility but also for access to a more diverse economy including the hunting of buffalo on the Plains. The importance of horses in Plateau culture is demonstrated by the elaborate material culture associated with them. top left, Mrs. John (Minnie) Stevens, Spokane, wearing a cloth wing dress decorated with beads and a breastplate of tubular hollow bones and large beads. The horse is equipped with a high-horned woman's saddle including a fur saddle drape and beaded horse blankets and collar. Photograph by Thomas W. Tolman, 1903–1915. top center, Flathead woman's saddle covered with buckskin and decorated with beadwork on the stirrups and pommels. Collected by William Wildschut on the Jocko Res., Mont., in 1925. Length 104 cm. top right, Southern Okanogan side-fringed rawhide case made from a single piece of hide and painted with red and green designs. These cases were lightweight, sturdy, and easily packed on a horse. While Plains peoples used this type of bag to store mainly religious objects, Plateau peoples used it for both ceremonial and secular materials, including medicines. In the late 20th century these bags were used in dressing the horse for parades (Torrence 1994:239). Collected by Louis C. Fletcher before 1913. Width without fringe 27 cm. center left, a, Flathead horse collar of red wool decorated with bells, horsehair tassels, and glass beads. The beaded geometric designs are green, orange, yellow, and pink on a light blue background. Collected by William Wildschut on the Jocko Res., Mont., 1925. Length 96 cm. center b, Umatilla quirt made of hide and wood decorated with red pigment, brass tacks, and fur strips. Collected by F.W. Skiff before 1925. Length of handle 45.5 cm. center right, Big Pielle and wife, Flathead. Her native horse is painted with both hand and hoof marks, the hoofs enumerating how many horses were stolen in raids. Photograph by Edward H. Boos, Flathead Indian Res., Mont., 1899–1910. bottom left, Flathead Indians herding small Indian horses. Photographed about 1898. bottom right, Yakima beaded saddle pouch, actually 2 complete beaded bags joined together at the top. It was probably placed over the saddle horn (R.K. Wright 1991:66). The side shown has a floral design in yellow, red, black, and blue. The opposite side shows a three-part floral design on a blue and white background. Collected by Agent James H. Wilbur, at Ft. Simcoe, Wash. Terr., before 1876. Height without fringe 29 cm.

Social Organization

In the prehorse period, the village appears to have been the primary political unit. Informal village meetings were held for decision making, and in matters of general interest the consent of all villagers had to be obtained. Plateau bilateral kinship helped shape the extended family groups that formed the core of most villages. Villages generally had a formal political structure with a headman, and a village council in which every adult had a vote. In some cases the position of village headman was semihereditary. Sometimes groups from several villages would band together at fishing sites and camas meadows resulting in formation of intervillage band councils. Likewise, intervillage groups emerged in the bison-hunting task groups. The emergence of composite bands and chiefs of considerable power followed the horse-based bison hunting after 1700. It was not until missionary and Bureau of Indian Affairs influence that tribal head chiefs were appointed, although there were prominent warriors who led large war parties before the head chiefs were appointed.

Plateau marriages were normally forbidden between first cousins, and newly wedded couples preferred to live with the husband's group but occasionally resided with the bride's family. Marriage tended to be informal but sometimes involved betrothal and exchange of property between families in more formal marriages. Divorce, like marriage, was a family matter, and in the case of death a surviving spouse often married a person drawn from the same family as the deceased. An anticipatory levirate and sororate custom was reflected in joking relationships and occasional sexual contact between a man and his sister-in-law. Throughout the Plateau, marriages between one man and several wives (polygyny) were permitted but not common. Slaves, who were occasionally seen, for the most part acquired their status from being captured in warfare.

The individual life cycle was marked by a series of rituals beginning before birth with rituals designed to guarantee a healthy baby and a healthy delivery for the mother. The newborn spent his first months in a cradleboard, and at about age one the child was ceremonially given his first name. Child rearing was the responsibility of various relatives, especially grandparents, uncles, and aunts. Grandparents saw to it that the child was toughened by practices such as bathing in cold streams and sweatbathing. Whipping was periodically administered by a family relative or friend. At puberty boys (and some girls) were sent on vision quests to receive spiritual guides. If successful, upon returning to the community, boys gradually took their place among adult men.

Girls at their first menstruation were secluded in menstrual lodges. Their hair was bound up, and they were required to use only scratching sticks to touch their body. They were painted, dressed, and required to use drinking tubes until they left their menstrual hut.

Various forms of burial were found in the Plateau. Pit burials took place in sand or gravel near riverbanks and were often marked with piles of boulders. Rockslide burials were also located close to rivers, sometimes with a wooden stake as a marker. Cremation burials occurred in the Yakima valley and at The Dalles but also in the Lillooet-Thompson area. Evidence of other types of burials diffused from the Northwest Coast, such as canoe burials; and scaffold burials from the Plains have been reported. The bereaved observed various taboos, such as having the widow or widower dress poorly, cutting one's hair, and with women, wailing at the grave. Mourning for a year or more before remarriage was considered. There are reports that the house of the deceased was torn down or even burned so that the dead would not reappear. Elaborate giveaways of the deceased's personal effects occurred widely with annual memorials of the death being celebrated, especially for prominent families.

Intergroup relations in the Plateau have been the subject of analysis (Walker 1967; Anastasio 1972; Brunton 1968). It is clear that Plateau peoples were and remain highly interactive maintaining extensive intergroup connections as well as extensive linkages with the Plains, Northwest Coast, and Great Basin groups. Connections with Subarctic groups are evident in the northern reaches of the Plateau in Canada. Two major Plateau ritual congregations have been identified, one primarily composed of Salishan groups in the U.S. and Canada and the other primarily of Sahaptian groups in the U.S. These extend into neighboring culture areas and seem to function in part as a basis for political alliance as well as serving various ceremonial and other functions. Their antiquity has not been determined, but they date from at least protohistoric times.

Structures, Clothing, and Property

Plateau villages were generally located near the conjunctions of tributary waterways, particularly where fish were abundant and easily caught. Permanent and semipermanent camps for hunting and root gathering were located in the uplands, but riverine villages were the permanent winter quarters and could temporarily accommodate up to several hundred people. Winter dwellings were of two main types, the semisubterranean earth lodge and the mat-covered longhouse. The longhouse may have been more recent and was focused mostly in the southern Plateau where it probably replaced the older earth lodge in late prehistoric times. The average earth lodge was circular, with a flat roof, supported by poles fastened to central posts. The smokehole in the top was the entrance, the floor being reached by an inside ladder or notched log. The mat-covered tepee was replaced by the Plains skin-covered tepee.

In historic times Plateau peoples used tailored skin garments of the type well-known from the Plains. During winter men wrapped their legs with fur, and women used leggings of hemp. Rabbit-fur robes and other skin robes were also worn. Sahaptian women wore twined basket hats, whereas men generally wore headbands. Caps of fur and feathered headdresses appeared later with Plains influence. Both sexes braided their hair.

Household tools, clothing, weapons, traps, snares and similar items were the personal property of individuals, but the larger fish weirs were communal property. Food resources were in most places distributed according to need through kinship networks and trade. In the northern Plateau, where gift-giving ceremonies were conducted reminiscent of the potlatches of the Northwest Coast, gifts were distributed to guests who reciprocated by giving presents to their hosts. Although wealth was valued in many parts of the Plateau, the Klamath paid greater attention to social status based on wealth than most other groups, an orientation probably deriving from Northwest Coast influences.

Belief and Aesthetic Systems

Major Plateau rituals included the guardian-spirit quest, the first-foods rituals, and the Winter Spirit Dances. The guardian-spirit quest was required for most boys, recommended for girls, and usually conducted at puberty. Vision quest spirits were specialized and granted powers to be hunters, warriors, shamans, root diggers, fishermen, and other roles. Shamans were much feared and politically influential. Generally wealthy, they cured diseases by extracting malignant spirits that were thought to invade the patient's body, causing illness. Shamans also retrieved lost souls in more northerly Plateau groups. The first-foods ceremonies celebrated the first salmon and first roots and berries of the spring and early summer. The First Salmon ceremony celebrated the arrival of the spring salmon run and called for ritual eating of the first fish in a manner reminiscent of the Northwest Coast, including return of the bones to the river so as to ensure a continuation of the run. Some groups had a salmon chief who supervised construction of weirs, fishing, and distribution of the catch. The Winter or Spirit Dance was a ceremonial in which participants celebrated their respective guardian spirits in song, dance, and costume. These dramatic performances and associated songs were also conducted in order to bring warm weather, plentiful game, and successful hunts.

Plateau mythology and folklore revolved around the culture hero and transformer, mostly Coyote but also Bluejay among some groups. Coyote is a beloved character in the myths but is also both a creator and trickster. The Plateau Coyote myth cycle is similar to that found in adjacent culture areas, and the tales are generally similar among all Plateau peoples. Plateau art styles share much with both the Plains and Northwest Coast. Decorative art consisted of pictographic designs with symbolic content, but there were many geometric designs, as well, especially in basketry and in beadwork, with the horse becoming a highly decorated animal among some groups. Distinctive basketry, bone, and wood carving were also well developed.

During the protohistoric period it is generally agreed that various religious cults emerged in the Plateau. Whether these were responses to epidemics or were similar to cargo cults is undecided. What is clear is that they form the basis of contemporary nativistic religions in the Plateau such as the Washat religion of the mid-Columbia region. The much older vision quest, the shamanic complex and the ceremonial cycle of rituals have been merged with those syncretic cults so that they are now viewed as the "traditional religion" of many tribes. The Plateau continues to be a center of religious activity; Sun Dances, the Native American church, the Indian Shaker church, and the Feather cult were in evidence in the 1990s. Newer Pentecostal and Holiness churches were established on most reservations in both the U.S. and Canada, but many of the mainline Christian churches were in decline. A new-found respect for what is termed Indian religion was growing in strength as part of neotraditionalist movements in both the Canadian and U.S. portions of the Plateau.

6

History

The period beginning in 1846 with division of the Oregon Country between Canada and the U.S. ushered in a new phase in the acculturation of Plateau peoples. Up to 1846 they were under the administration primarily of the Hudson's Bay Company and were guided by their policies, which did not involve massive immigration and settlement of the region by Euro-Americans. By 1846, and especially thereafter, this changed for the U.S. portion of the Oregon Country as thousands of emigrants settled in the Northwest.

By 1855 treaty making began in the U.S. Northwest and ultimately created very different conditions for U.S. tribes from those encountered in Canada. The U.S. treaties, especially those negotiated by Gov. Isaac I. Stevens, reserved large land areas for the tribes and contained reserved rights language and guarantees that continue to be of great political and legal significance for the U.S. tribes. This is especially true for the reserved, off-reservation hunting, fishing, and gathering rights where the tribes continue to play a major role. Following the Indian Reorganization Act of 1934 and the Indian Claims Commission decisions of the 1950s and 1960s tribal governments in the U.S. portion of the Plateau initiated numerous legal actions to clarify and affirm their reserved treaty rights. These have concerned not only fishing, hunting, and gathering on traditional tribal lands but also affirmation of their rights to tax, legal jurisdiction, and other expressions of the sovereignty still retained by the U.S. tribes.

In British Columbia, tribal governments have operated under provincial authority rather than under the federal authority. This situation does not allow for tribal challenges to regulatory authority that have so often been seen in Washington, Oregon, Idaho, and Montana. Overall it seems clear that U.S. Indian policy in the Northwest has allowed for creation of much stronger tribal governments than has been the case in Canada. As part of this, most tribal groups in the U.S. Plateau were engaged in the 1990s in various long-term economic development programs. Gambling, forest enterprises, tourism, small-scale manufacturing, recreation, and contracting with the federal government for various services (Public Law 93–638) are examples of economic development activities. Plateau tribes acted in political concert to secure their legislative, political, and other goals. An indication of this revitalization throughout the region was a general population increase, improved economic conditions, higher levels of education, and improved health conditions.

History of Research

E.S. LOHSE AND RODERICK SPRAGUE

The history of anthropological research in the Plateau culture area is best defined within a broad perspective encompassing the development of academic anthropology in North American museums and universities and within the broader regional perspective of research in northwestern North America. Observations on Plateau aboriginal societies were first made by interested explorers, traders, missionaries, and settlers. Trained ethnologists began work in this region only in the late nineteenth century. Throughout the twentieth century, Plateau anthropology matured, with creation of regional universities and development of consistent, systematic research programs, particularly in archeology, as part of culture resource management and cultural heritage programs in the United States and Canada.

Early Contact and Acculturation

Europeans first came into direct contact with Plateau tribes as fur trapping companies and exploring expeditions traveled the drainages of the Fraser and Columbia river systems. The Meriwether Lewis and William Clark expedition of 1804–1806 traveled down the Clearwater River to the lower Snake River and along the lower Columbia River to its mouth on the Pacific Ocean at Astoria. Captains Lewis and Clark, and other members of the expedition, left reports, letters, and diaries that offer insights into the lifeways of the aboriginal societies they met (Gass 1807; Jackson 1978; Moulton 1983–; Quaife 1916; Thwaites 1904–1905). References to Plateau tribes occur in the accounts of other explorers, fur trappers, and fur trading company administrators from the end of the eighteenth century until the middle of the nineteenth. Fur traders like David Thompson (1914, 1916, 1917, 1920), Simon Fraser (1889), John Work (1909, 1912, 1912a, 1913, 1914, 1914a, 1914b, 1915, 1923, 1971), Alexander Ross (1849, 1913), Ross Cox (1831), David Douglas (1904–1905, 1914; Harvey 1947), Peter Skene Ogden (1909–1910, 1933, 1950, 1961, 1971), and George Simpson (1847, 1931) offer descriptions of Plateau tribes in the precontact setting and in the earliest stages of acculturation. The journals of Fathers Pierre Jean de Smet (1863, 1905; Peterson and Peers 1993) and Nicolas Point (1967) are good sources on the Flathead, Coeur d'Alene, and Colville tribes in the middle nineteenth century, as dislocation of aboriginal societies intensified. Accounts by

Washington Irving (1836) describing the Nez Perce, John K. Townsend (1839) on the Cayuse, Joel Palmer (1847), Daniel Lee and J.H. Frost (1844), and Samuel J. Parker (1838) on the Nez Perce and Klikitat, and Meredith Gairdner (1841), Horatio Emmons Hale (1946), John Scouler (1848), Henry Warre (1848), and Paul Kane (1856, 1859; Harper 1971) describing several tribes each, have left invaluable accounts of tribes as traditional lifeways began to fragment.

Valuable as these early insights are for understanding traditional aboriginal lifeways, they lag far behind the effects of earliest European contact. Earliest influences came into the Pacific Northwest–Plateau region 100 years before these first accounts were written. Trade items traveled from village fairs on the Middle Missouri through the Crow on the northwestern Plains, and then on to Nez Perce traders in the Clearwater River drainage. Ewers (1955:7–11) describes English and French trade items and perhaps North West Company guns as reaching Plateau tribes on horseback before any of the tribes had direct contact with White traders (cf. Gunther 1950). Anastasio (1972:127–130) notes that horses and Spanish goods moved north with Plateau traders who had attended Shoshone trading rendezvous in the Rocky Mountains.

The earliest accounts provide glimpses of aboriginal societies already heavily impacted in many areas by Euro-American contact. The North West Company and Hudson's Bay Company established posts on the Columbia River and the Fraser River. These became focuses for economic change (A.J. Ray 1978, 1980, 1984).

Anthropological Research

Victorian America came to emphasize the museum as an institution geared to preserving and ordering information. The late nineteenth century was a time of unsettling social and economic changes propelled by developing technologies and markets. Interest in how and why American society was changing led to fascination with the lives of others, and in particular, with saving elements of the Native American lifeway (Hinsley 1981). Early anthropologists found intellectual bases in museums before the birth of academic departments in universities. The earliest systematic anthropological work on the Plateau came at the behest of major museums like the Smithsonian Institution,

Washington, D.C., and the American Museum of Natural History in New York.

Culture history was the driving force in these early anthropology museums. A major intellectual proponent was Otis Tufton Mason, curator of the department of ethnology in the U.S. National Museum, Smithsonian Institution. The goal was to collect as much information as possible on the lifeway of nonindustrial cultures in order to facilitate comparative study. Mason and other early American ethnologists were following the lead of Gustav Klemm of the Museum of Ethnology in Leipzig, Germany, who argued for a composite history of human development through progressive stages of savagery, barbarism, and civilization. Mason devotedly collected comparative data on Native American tribes, writing particularly on material inventions and technology of subsistence, and emphasizing similar developments in similar environments. A major critic of this approach was Franz Boas, a champion for studying the uniqueness of specific cultural patterns, and diametrically opposed to Mason's natural science model of ethnology (Boas 1887; Mason 1887). Boas urged early American ethnologists to study special industries and lifeways of individual cultures.

The primary force in anthropological research in this period was the Bureau of (American) Ethnology, founded by John Wesley Powell in 1879. Based in the Smithsonian Institution, the Bureau was dedicated to producing systematic, simultaneous, coordinated study of all aspects of aboriginal culture. Studies based on the Bureau's ethnographic surveys of Native American tribes were published in the United States Geographical and Geological Survey Series *Contributions to North American Ethnology* (until 1893) and in the Bureau's *Annual Reports* and *Bulletins*. Hinsley (1981:151) argues that the founding of the Bureau set the context, force, and direction of late nineteenth-century American anthropology. This was a development only curtailed by the rise of "Boasian anthropology" in the 1920s and 1930s. Powell's overriding emphasis became an authoritative study of linguistic diversity in North America. Observers were recruited and sent out to different parts of the continent.

Albert Gatschet, a Swiss linguist, joined the Bureau in 1879. His work among the Klamath (Gatschet 1890; "Languages," fig. 7, this vol.) was judged by Boas as the best grammar for any American Indian language in its day. Gatschet, like many of the Bureau surveyors, declared frustration in following Powell's mandate to study as many tribes as possible and would have preferred more intense study of specific cultures.

Powell's emphasis on linguistic study followed Henry Rowe Schoolcraft's admonition to the Smithsonian Regents in 1846 that the study of language held the most promise in solving puzzles about Native American origins and histories. By 1847 Schoolcraft had issued a comparative vocabulary list for missionaries, government agents, soldiers, and other data collectors (Schoolcraft 1847). The American Eth-

nological Society issued its own circular in 1852. In 1863, George Gibbs, stationed in the Pacific Northwest, expanded his "Instructions" to include directions for philological observations, rules for recording speech sounds, and a short vocabulary list (Gibbs 1865). Gibbs (1855) had published on the tribes of Washington Territory and had supplied a preface on Yakima Sahaptin (Gibbs 1862). His circular of 1865 served as the basis for Powell's (1877) *Introduction to the Study of Indian Languages*. Responses from Powell's field observers varied widely in quality and frustrated the ultimate goal of complete compilation.

The vitality of the Bureau of American Ethnology program was tied closely to the dominant personality and position of Powell. Between 1890 and 1900, researchers left or retired, and the level of activity stepped back. The Smithsonian reviewed the situation in 1903, and testimony from leading researchers like Franz Boas made it clear that greater rigor in fieldwork was necessary. Few of the planned collaborative projects had come to fruition, and most publications emerged through individual effort. Jesse Walter Fewkes, who had joined the staff in 1897, pointed to the Jesup North Pacific Expedition, funded through the American Museum of Natural History, as a much better model for collection of ethnological data on the American Indian (Hinsley 1981:266). Franz Boas had, by this time, emerged as the most influential advocate for a professional anthropology in the United States. He had taken charge of Bureau linguistics and had conducted joint expeditions with the American Museum. Boas trained his own students to collect specimens, information in the native language, and grammatical information necessary to explain their texts.

Boasian Anthropology

The first systematic work on the Plateau occurred as part of the Jesup North Pacific Expedition. Morris K. Jesup, president of the American Museum, financed a six-year research project in northwestern North America and northeast Asia, under the direction of Franz Boas. The expedition involved work in ethnology, physical anthropology, linguistics, and archeology. James A. Teit and Livingston Farrand were recruited to work on interior British Columbia tribes under Boas's direction from 1897 to 1900.

James A. Teit (fig. 1), born in the Shetland Islands, Scotland, had settled at Spence's Bridge, British Columbia, near a village of Thompson Indians. Boas met Teit in 1895 and was deeply impressed with Teit's thorough knowledge of Thompson language and customs. Teit was fluent in Thompson, at ease in Shuswap and Lillooet. Boas (1922:490) declared that his collaborator had a "whole knowledge of the material culture, social organization, customs, beliefs and tales of Salish tribes of the interior of British Columbia." Teit worked with the Geological Survey of Canada on natural history and ethnology and assembled ethnographic collections for the National Museum, Ottawa,

Fig. 1. James A. Teit (b. 1864, d. 1922) and his first wife, Lucy Artko, a Thompson Indian. Photograph by Harlan I. Smith, Spence's Bridge, B.C., 1897.

and the Field Museum, Chicago. He produced ethnographic studies of the Thompson (Teit 1900, 1912), Lillooet (Teit 1906), and Shuswap (Teit 1909) as part of the Jesup North Pacific Expedition series. Two overviews of the Middle Columbia River Salishans (Teit 1928) and Salishan tribes of the Plateau (Teit 1930) were published. Teit co-authored a volume on Salishan and Sahaptian folktales with Marian K. Gould, Livingston Farrand, and Herbert J. Spinden, and a study of Salish basketry with H. Haeberlin. An ardent spokesman for British Columbia tribes, Teit served as the secretary for the first native rights organization.

Charles Hill-Tout was another productive early ethnologist, with a career devoted to the tribes of British Columbia. He wrote his first ethnographic report on the Thompson (Hill-Tout 1900) and his last on the Northern Okanagan (Hill-Tout 1911). Hill-Tout settled in Vancouver, British Columbia, where he served as housemaster at Whetham College, principal at Trinity College, and then opened his own school, Buckland College. A close friend and informant was Thompson Chief Mischelle of Lytton, British Columbia. Boas met Hill-Tout in 1897 but developed an

immediate dislike for this ardent fieldworker, declining his services for the Jesup North Pacific Expedition (Maud 1978). Hill-Tout produced reports for the Ethnological Survey of Canada on the archeology of Lytton, folklore from Lytton, Thompson speech and grammar, Squamish vocabulary and grammar, and descriptions of tribal divisions and place-names. From 1896 to 1906, Hill-Tout covered most of the Salishan tribes, emphasizing collection of stories and tales.

The work of the Jesup North Pacific Expedition set the stage for development of a "Boasian anthropology" that was to emphasize complete data collection and intensive knowledge of the language, customs, and lifeways of specific tribal groups. Boas made a conscious effort to rid anthropology of its amateurs and armchair specialists. His avowed aim was to make ethnographic research in the field the central experience and minimum measure of professional standing (Lesser 1935). Boas trained a long and distinguished list of students who transformed the discipline of anthropology, many of whom worked in the Pacific Northwest and on the Plateau. Boas took a lead in founding the American Folk-Lore Society in 1888, the transformation of the professional journal *American Anthropologist* in 1898, the founding of the American Anthropological Association in 1900, and the reformation of the American Ethnological Society in 1900. Alfred Kroeber, foremost among Boas's students, argued that there was no "Boas school," but Boas's influence on North American anthropology and on the work done on the Plateau in the early twentieth century was undeniable (Kroeber 1935:540).

The Report of the Committee for Investigating and Publishing Reports on the Physical Characters, Languages, and Industrial and Social Conditions of the North-Western Tribes of the Dominion of Canada was published in the annual reports of the British Association for the Advancement of Science from 1886 to 1899. The work of the committee was largely directed by Boas who wrote the general annual reports, the final conclusions, the physical anthropology, most of the Northwest Coast material, and some material for the Interior including Athapaskan groups and the Shuswap. A.F. Chamberlain (1893) wrote on the British Columbia branch of the Kootenai and Livingston Farrand (1899) on the Chilcotin. These scattered but important works were collected and reprinted in 1974 as *Northwest Anthropological Research Notes*, Volume 8.

Other important ethnographic work included James Mooney (1896) working for the Bureau of American Ethnology describing the Washat religion of Smohalla of the Wanapam; Merton L. Miller collecting ethnographic specimens on the Nez Perce, Umatilla, Yakima, and Warm Springs reservations in 1901 (Sprague 1971); Stewart Culin (1901) working for the University of Pennsylvania Museum on the Umatilla and Warm Springs reservations; Albert B. Lewis (1906) with the first tribal distribution study to include the Plateau; Spinden (1908) working with the Nez

Perce in 1907 and 1908; and the classic study of Edward S. Curtis (1907–1930, 7, 8).

Every Boasian fieldworker aimed at full reconstruction of aboriginal culture. But by the early twentieth century it was increasingly difficult to find informants with the requisite knowledge of traditional lifeways. As the number of knowledgeable informants dwindled, the aims of fieldwork shifted to reflect the historical context of acculturation, and emphasis came to be placed on relations between culture and the individual, processes of cultural change, and the character of contemporary Indian societies.

The Culture Area Concept

As information accumulated, anthropologists recognized the need for organizational frameworks to enable synthesis over broader regions. Earlier anthropologists like Mason had struggled to order the building ethnographic collections of the late nineteenth century in evolutionary typologies (Mason 1896, 1907). Mason's 18 American Indian environments or cultural areas were used by ethnographers throughout the early twentieth century. W.H. Holmes (1914) refined the number and extent of areas of culture characterization. Wissler (1917, 1938) used Mason's conception as the basis for his landmark study of American Indian ethnology. It was Alfred Kroeber, however, who was to pioneer the culture-area concept (Kroeber 1931, 1939).

The utility of accurate ethnographic maps showing tribal territories and the distribution of important cultural traits related to features of the physical environment was obvious and seductive. The practical problem was accurate definition of these boundaries. Driver (1969:17) noted the practical utility of the culture area concept for cataloguing cultural elements or traits that highlight common cultural histories and define typical goups. Mapping of tribal areas and drawing of accurate boundaries are usually held to be based on the first observations recorded for a tribal group. Tribal names applied are based on convention, most often drawn from anglicized and hispanicized names applied to tribes by missionaries, federal and state agents, and early anthropologists. "Tribes" in general are designations derived from research showing that groups are related by language and community. Appropriate coverage is held to entail identification of the tribe and its neighbors, description of geographic location, inclusion of relevant prehistoric and historic data, description of language and comparison of linguistic relations, listing of ecological adaptations and material culture, and discussion of socioeconomic organization.

Kroeber (1939:49, 55) defined the Columbia-Fraser Plateau area as one of three "Intermediate and Intermountain" cultural areas. The others were the Great Basin and California cultural areas. All three were seen to be similar in some respects and yet retained unique cultural characteristics, characteristics related in greater or lesser degree to adaptation to distinctive physical environments. Archeolog-

ically and ethnographically, the Plateau has been separated into two major divisions based on the Columbia and Fraser rivers. The Snake River, Clearwater River, and Salmon River drainages constitute another important subunit of study to the east and south. Kroeber (1939:56–59) defined the Fraser area, the Middle Columbia area, and the Upper Columbia area.

Ethnographers described the Plateau cultural area as a transition zone, where the cultures of most tribes resembled those of groups in neighboring cultural areas. The Plateau was characterized as transitional physiographically as well, lying between the Rocky Mountains on the east and and the Cascade Range on the west. The northern boundary is generally marked by the great northern bend of the Fraser River, and the southern extent by the heads of the Columbia and Snake river tributaries. Sharp cultural distinctions were judged to be rare, though language boundaries can be cited, with the Plateau separated from the Great Basin cultural area to the south by the ethnographic boundary between the Plateau Sahaptins and the Great Basin Shoshonean groups. On the north, Plateau Interior Salish tribes are bordered by ones speaking Subarctic Athapaskan languages.

Environmental differences, and distinctive arrays of resources, notably the anadromous salmon, were held to form a distinctive economic focus for Plateau tribes. Historical connections to other cultural areas were acknowledged to account for significant cultural changes. Kroeber (1939:56) highlighted the Middle Columbia River and its open sagebrush-grassland environment as the most receptive to Plains influences accompanying adoption of the horse. Here, adopted aspects of Plains culture include the coup system, societies, and the Sun Dance. Distinctive adopted traits of material culture include horse equipment, tepees, the parfleche, and floral beadwork designs. Kroeber noted that this Plains influence stopped at The Dalles, an obvious boundary between Plateau and Northwest Coast culture areas. Further, Kroeber speculated that the pronounced connection between Plains and Plateau was only a recent one, and clearly tied to adoption of the horse. The horse was probably brought into the Plateau cultural area via contact with the Lemhi Northern Shoshone or Bannock on the Snake River drainage or directly across the Rocky Mountains through the Nez Perce. Kroeber pointed out that the Columbia River must have been a broad channel of communication from coast to interior throughout the prehistoric and historic records.

Inclusion of the northern Plateau tribes was debated somewhat, and researchers argued that perhaps the Kootenai and Flathead, located just east of the Rocky Mountains, were better assigned to the Plains cultural area. Spinden (1908) noted the same imprinting of Plains culture on the Nez Perce of the Clearwater River drainage of the Rockies. Many researchers accepted lack of a clear boundary and emphasized the transitional nature of Plateau culture with lack of any dominant cultural focus.

Ind. U., William Hammond Mathers Mus., Bloomington, top and bottom.
Fig. 2. The Rodman Wanamaker Expeditions of Citizenship. The 3 Wanamaker expeditions from 1908 to 1913 created several thousand photographs, including many leaders of Native American tribes. top, Joseph K. Dixon interviewing chiefs. left to right: Leo Sampson, Umatilla and Cayuse interpreter; Umpanine or Heyoohapima, Cayuse; Tin-Tin-Meet-Sa, Umatilla; Joseph K. Dixon and Roland Dixon. Photograph possibly by Joseph Cline, Crow Res., Montana, 1909. bottom, Nez Perces listening to President Woodrow Wilson's speech on the phonograph, an obligatory part of the patriotic ceremony promoted by the expedition. Roland Dixon has his hand on the phonograph. Behind Dixon, left to right, standing, are: Peo-peo tholekt, David Williams, Yellow Wolf, unidentified man, and Crow Blanket. Photograph by Joseph Dixon, Lapwai Res., Idaho, 1913.

A singular part of the cultural area concept was measurement of cultural strength or intensity in a defined cultural area. Kroeber (1935:5) identified a "cultural climax" that entailed fluorescence of cultural growth, and "cultural centers" that were districts of greatest cultural productivity and richness. The climax was considered a regional expression of a culmination at a specified time. This was the concept pioneered by Wissler (1917, 1922) in culture-classification maps. Kroeber worked to clarify these by identifying con-

stellations of shared traits and drawing boundaries where two culture climaxes or focuses meet in equal strength.

Mason (1896) had suggested "Northern Pacific Coast," "Columbia drainage," and "Interior Basin" cultural areas based on distributions of cultural traits and flora and fauna associations. Wissler (1922) placed the Plateau tribes in a salmon area with the Northwest Coast as part of Mason's "Columbia-Fraser" ethnic environment. Plateau tribes were thus placed on resource maps, though boundaries were hard to define and debatable. Kroeber's (1939:89) series of maps correlating tribal, cultural, and physiographic maps were drawn on transparent paper to a uniform scale. His boundaries were defined with weight given to natural features, principally watersheds. Tribal areas thus defined were argued to indicate boundaries at the time of European contact. Kroeber concluded that there was significant correlation between cultural distributions and "life zones" but he acknowledged that the correlation was not absolute, just as Powell and others had demonstrated that language families flowed across environmental boundaries. Tribal economies were portrayed as adaptations designed for taking specific resources in specific environments.

In Kroeber's (1939:222–228) assessment of cultural intensity and climax, the Plateau graded #2, above the Great Basin cultural area to the south at #1, but beneath the Northwest Coast cultural areas at #3 and #4 (#5–7 were the highest levels of intensity reserved for cultural complexes with elements indicative of higher development such as agriculture, calendrical systems, and social stratification). Kroeber's seminal study grew out of an attempt in the 1920s and 1930s to define culture areas systematically in terms of comprehensive lists of traits. These lists were used to develop coefficients of similarity. The University of California, Berkeley, under Kroeber's supervision, sent students to western tribes to fill out extensive culture element surveys (Kroeber and Driver 1932), including Ray (1942) for the Plateau. Difficulties in accumulating comparable data sets involving thousands of items led Kroeber to abandon massive trait compilations in preference for the more impressionistic assessments of "cultural centers" or "cultural climaxes."

The culture area concept championed by Kroeber is still considered a useful heuristic device by many researchers, though the utility of measures of cultural intensity and cultural climax has been questioned. For example, an overview of North American Indian culture by Spencer and Jennings (1977:168) evokes this view when it states that the Plateau lacks culture focus, and emphasizes that relations of life mode of native peoples to their natural surroundings account for much of the defined Plateau character. These authors noted that Plateau tribes all depended on salmon to a greater or lesser extent, fishing by a variety of methods during the spawning runs. Differences in water distribution, vegetation, and landscape produced differences in cultural organization and character. Following Anastasio (1972), they conclude that there was sufficient basic cultural unity in the Plateau to permit "diagnostic descriptions." These descriptions focused on tribal groups held to be characteristic of the Plateau area or what Kroeber had called "climax groups." Spencer and Jennings (1977) following the lead of Ray (1933, 1939) highlight the Sanpoil-Nespelem of the middle Columbia River and the Klamath as climax tribes characteristic of the Plateau pattern as a whole. Their summaries are based on the ethnographic work of Verne F. Ray (1933, 1939, 1942) among the Sanpoil and Nespelem, and Leslie Spier and Edward Sapir (Spier 1930; Spier and Sapir 1930) and Theodore Stern (1965) among the Klamath (fig. 3). General references for Plateau culture cite the work of James A. Teit (1928, 1930) and H.H. Turney-High (1937, 1941). Garbarino and Sasso (1994:iii) state that the culture area framework is the clearest and simplest means for understanding the relationship between culture and adaptation as well as an excellent mnemonic device for characterizing the diversity of North American Indian culture. Critical variables in research entail the timing, nature, and extent of Euro-American contact, academic and national agendas, and contemporary political and social contexts.

After World War II

By World War II, anthropology on the Plateau had matured. Indian tribes had been identified and their tribal distributions mapped, a heuristic framework had been adopted for study of the tribes, histories of Euro-American entry and subsequent development had been developed, and anthropologists struggled to move from a simple descriptive approach of gathering ethnographic information on traditional Indian cultures to examining how native groups had survived hundreds of years of acculturation. Interest shifted from compilations of traits to understanding of Indian societies in contemporary American and Canadian society.

Fig. 3. Theodore Stern (b. 1917) and Jesse Kirk (b. 1894, d. 1962; Klamath). Jesse Lee Kirk was the Vice-Chairman of the Executive Committee of the Tribal Council. Stern who worked with the Klamath and Modoc from 1949 until the 1960s collected many myths from the Kirk family, especially from Jesse's brother Sheldon Kirk. Photographed at Beatty, Oreg., Klamath Indian Res., before 1962.

Studies of contemporary cultural expressions were more compelling, and issues of language retention, art expression, ethnobiology (fig. 5), and legal and political standing of tribes came strongly to the fore. Suttles and Jonaitis (vol. 7:80–87) characterized the period of post-Boasian field research in the Pacific Northwest as the time when anthropologists recognized that Indians were not losing all their traditional culture but were retaining many institutions, modifying others, and developing new forms.

Much of the energy and interest of anthropologists in the period preceding and extending beyond the World War II was invested in the Northwest Coast area rather than on the Plateau, as Northwest Coast societies were seen to exemplify highly stratified, complex, hunting and gathering societies. From the 1920s through the 1950s, the neighboring Plateau cultural area sparked little research interest as a hinterland of the more complex development to the west.

Some anthropologists did bridge from a focus on Northwest Coast culture to the neighboring Plateau. For example, Gunther's (1928) work on the First Salmon ceremony traced that ritual from coast to interior tribes, and her analysis of the westward movement of Plains traits into the Plateau did much to clarify historic changes noted in Middle Columbia River tribes (Gunther 1950). But in both instances, the Plateau was merely a transitional area between two better developed or defined cultural areas. Allan H. Smith had performed ethnographic field research among the Kalispel, and produced an overview of the Indians of Washington (A.H. Smith 1953). Turney-High wrote overviews on the Flathead and the Kootenai (Turney-High 1937, 1941), the accuracy of which has been questioned by some tribal members. Claude E. Schaeffer (1937) compiled notes on the Kootenai in this period. Melville Jacobs had produced a brief description of Northern Sahaptin grammar (Jacobs 1931), followed by development of a historical perspective on the Indian languages of Oregon and Washington (Jacobs 1937). Archie Phinney, a Nez Perce who studied anthropology under Boas at Columbia University, transcribed stories told by his mother (Phinney 1934; "History Since 1846," fig. 2, this vol.). Gladys A. Reichard published on Coeur d'Alene mythology (Reichard 1934, 1947) and summarized Salishan languages (Reichard 1958–1960). Walter Cline, Rachel S. Commons, May Mandelbaum, Richard H. Post, and L.V.W. Walters, under the direction of Leslie Spier, wrote an ethnography of the Southern Okanogan (Cline et al. in Spier 1938). Work on the prophet dance (Spier 1935) and Feather cult (1938) as well as on tribal distribution (Spier 1936) were all in *General Series in Anthropology*.

William W. Elmendorf worked among the northern Plateau tribes from 1935–1936 (Elmendorf 1965). Alfred W. Bowers's (1952) fieldwork among Coeur d'Alene was presented to the Indian Claims Commission.

Ethnomusicology includes Merriam's (1967) work on Flathead (fig. 4) and Olsen's (1972, 1979) and M. Williams's (1967) thesis.

Fig. 4. The Merriams among the Flathead. The research of the Merriams, from 1950 to 1958, included both field recordings and the transcription and analysis of Flathead music. The comparative musicological reports that resulted from this fieldwork were some of the first in the field of ethnomusicology. left, Barbara W. Merriam (b. 1927) and Agnes Vanderburg (b. 1901, d. 1989). In addition to assisting the Merriams in their study of music, Vanderburg recorded data on Flathead ethnobiology, which is preserved in Salish in the archives of the Salish Culture Committee. right, Sophie Moiese (b. 1867, d. 1960) and Alan P. Merriam (b. 1923, d. 1980). Moiese contributed about 20 songs to the Merriams' study (Merriam and Merriam 1950:52). Photographs by Barbara and Alan Merriam, near Arlee, Mont., 1950.

By the 1950s, anthropological departments were thriving at regional universities, and more students studied Plateau Indian societies, with research in ethnology, linguistics, physical anthropology, and archeology, and an increasing emphasis on contemporary Indian societies. Angelo Anastasio described intergroup relations in the Southern Plateau (Anastasio 1955, 1972). Haruo Aoki began study of Nez Perce language ("Mythology," fig. 2, this vol.) and its ties to Proto-Sahaptian (Aoki 1962, 1966, 1970). The Shuswap language, including grammar, texts, and a dictionary, was summarized by Aert H. Kuipers (1974). Bill Brunton's study outlined characteristics of ceremonial integration in the Plateau (Brunton 1968). Legends of the Pacific Northwest were the focus of Ella Clark (1966). George Coale compiled ethnohistoric sources for the Nez Perce (Coale 1956) and published his notes on the guardian-spirit concept of the Nez Perce (Coale 1958). Clifford Drury compiled the diaries and letters of Henry H. Spalding and Asa B. Smith regarding their mission among the Nez Perce (Drury 1958). M. Gidley wrote of contemporary reservation life for the Nez Perce (Gidley 1985). Francis Haines published a definitive volume on the Nez Perce (Haines 1955) and outlined litigation between the Nez Perce and the United States (Haines 1964a). Alvin Josephy included accounts of the origins and role of the Nez Perce in the westward expansion of Euro-Americans (Josephy 1955, 1962, 1965, 1983). Henry P. Lundsgaarde (1967) has supplied a structural analysis of Nez Perce kinship. Alice Fletcher's ethnographic work among the Nez Perce (fig. 6) has been summarized by Joan

Mark (Mark 1988; Sappington and Carley 1995). Allen Slickpoo and Deward E. Walker collaborated to produce a tribal history of the Nez Perce (Slickpoo and Walker 1973). Walker has studied Nez Perce contemporary culture, focusing on maintenance of cultural heritage in the face of strong forces for acculturation (Walker 1964, 1964a, 1966, 1967, 1967a, 1967b, 1968, 1970, 1970a).

Eugene Hunn's (1990) contemporary study of the Middle Columbia tribes is excellent. Hunn's (1990) synthesis of the Plateau culture area is the most complete overview, emphasizing the contemporary social, political, and legal status of Indian societies. Cohen (1986) presents a comprehensive overview of issues surrounding Indian fishing rights in Washington and Oregon, an arena in which Columbia River tribes have played a determined role. A bibliographic essay on the Yakima by Helen H. Schuster (1982), based on her dissertation (1975), is the most complete such work for a Plateau tribe. Rodney Frey (1995) assembled an excellent collection of myths. Stern (1993), concentrating on Fort Nez Perces, is vital to understanding the background of the Cayuse, Umatilla, and Walla Walla, as is Gunkel (1978) on the Walla Walla. Material culture research was revitalized by the impressive work on baskets by Mary Dodds Schlick (1994). Christopher Miller (1985) has written a seminal treatise on Plateau Indian prophecy and describes interactions between native religious belief and the missionaries of the nineteenth century. Haruo Aoki and Deward E. Walker (1989) have produced a volume on Nez Perce oral narratives. Caroline James (1996) explores the changing role of

Fig. 5. David French (b. 1918, d. 1994) and Eva Winishut (b. 1898, d. 1974, Wasco; speaker of Warm Springs Sahaptin, English, and Wasco), on a berry-picking and plant-collecting trip. David French's fieldwork, primarily on the Warm Springs Res., Oreg., involved ethnobiology and linguistics. Eva Winishut and her husband, Linton Winishut, a Sahaptin-English interpreter, were colleagues of David and Kathrine French, sharing knowledge of the traditional cultures. In 1989 the Confederated Tribes of Warm Springs recognized David French's contributions with a Certificate of Appreciation. Photograph by Kathrine French, Multorpor Mt., south of Mt. Hood, Oreg., 1952.

women in contemporary Nez Perce society. Nancy J. Turner (1978, 1979) and her collaborators produced authoritative volumes on traditional plant use of Plateau societies: Turner, Randall T. Bouchard, and Dorothy I.D. Kennedy (1980) on the ethnobotany of the Okanogan-Colville and Turner et al. (1990) on Thompson ethnobotany (cf. Steedman 1930 on Thompson ethnobotany); Turner (1974) on plant taxonomies of the Northwest Coast and Lillooet; Palmer (1975) on Shuswap ethnobotany. Welch and Striker's (1994) bibliography on ethnobotany contains over 400 sources. Kennedy and Bouchard have developed research into Thompson fishing and hunting practices as part of the British Columbia Indian Language Project (Kennedy 1975–1976, 1976, 1976a; Kennedy and Bouchard 1984). Brian Hayden (1992) studied Shuswap and Lillooet subsistence.

The major contributions to Plateau ethnography have been made by only a few researchers and their students. The work of James A. Teit is significant not only because of the early date of his research but also because of the publication of his extensive knowledge. Teit's library, notes, and many of the artifacts he collected are housed in the Nicola Valley Museum in Merritt, British Columbia.

The first major work of Verne F. Ray (1933) was his thesis on the Sanpoil and Nespelem, which has served as representative of the culture climax of the ethnographic

Plateau. Attempts by archeologists to discredit Ray's thesis of the Plateau being characterized by pacifistic tendencies have not been successful. These works suggested that the archeological evidence shows burials with projectiles in the bodies and mesa tops used as defensive areas and lookouts. Such evidence can just easily be used as evidence that these people were the victims of aggression not the aggressors. Ray also published on the location and distribution of Plateau groups (Ray 1936, 1938), work that was to be vital to his later Indian Claims Commission work.

Ray's dissertation (1939) and Anastasio's dissertation (1972) represent the two major Plateau ethnographic overviews. Ray's is the first and still the major synthesis of the Plateau, using a series of traits for culture-area-wide comparisons. Ray (1942) also worked with Kroeber in the preparation of the Culture Element Distribution study for the Plateau. This basic study is important for the completeness of the survey and because in several cases it represents the only data available for specific tribal groups. He produced monographs on the Klamath and Chinook. His later work was largely devoted to the preparation of expert testimony for several tribes before the Indian Claims Commission. He made a study of the contribution of Lewis and Clark to Nez Perce ethnography (Ray 1971a; Ray and Lurie 1954).

Angelo Anastasio's dissertation (1955) from the University of Chicago was published in *Northwest Anthropological Research Notes* (1972). The concept of the "task group" has proved to be an important one in the understanding of the rapidly changing structure of Plateau social and political organization. Anastasio's (1972) work stands as the basic ecological and political study of the Plateau.

Beginning in the early 1960s, Deward E. Walker, Jr., and his students conducted ethnographic research on the Nez Perce, Umatilla, Yakima, Spokane, Colville, Coeur d'Alene, Kootenai, Warm Springs, and Flathead Indian reservations. Walker (1964, 1964a) worked on religion, politics, and acculturation and was a strong advocate for ethnographic, ethnohistorical, and contemporary research in the Plateau and especially Idaho. He continued the Indian claims work begun by Ray, Stern, Malouf, Bowers, and A.H. Smith. In over 25 cases he served as an expert witness involving treaty rights, water rights, religious freedom, fishing and hunting, and taxation. Walker has produced an impressive body of ethnohistoric and ethnologic knowledge including extensive information on territoriality, intergroup relations, fishing and hunting activity (Walker 1967), settlement patterns, and relationships with the Great Basin and northern Plains groups.

In 1967 Walker and Sprague established *Northwest Anthropological Research Notes* as the only serial publication devoted solely to all aspects of anthropology in the Pacific Northwest. Walker has contributed to tribally based research on ethnohistory and mythology through his efforts with Nez Perce author Allen P. Slickpoo, Sr. (Slickpoo and Walker 1972, 1973), and Yakama author Virginia Beavert (Beavert and Walker 1974; Beavert,

Smithsonian, NAA: top, 55021-B and C; bottom right, 55020; bottom left, Idaho State Histl. Soc., Boise.
Fig. 6. Alice Fletcher (b. 1838, d. 1923), ethnologist among the Nez Perce and one of her consultants Billy Williams (b. 1819, d. 1896) (Kew-kew-lu-yah or Jonathan Williams). Fletcher worked for the Peabody Museum of Harvard University starting in 1886 and was the first anthropologist to do serious research on American Indian music (vol. 4:61, 643–644). As a special agent in the allotment of Nez Perce lands, she worked with various native consultants. top, Map of Nez Perce lands, made by Billy Williams showing geographical features covering roughly 250 miles north and south and 180 miles east and west, with their Nez Perce names, as well as 78 Nez Perce villages and village sites dating back to about 1800 (Fletcher 1891a). bottom left, Camp near Craig Mt., Idaho Terr., where Fletcher (center) was working on land allotment for the Nez Perce Res. At right is Anson "Joe" Briggs, the surveyor (Gay 1981:10). Photograph by E. Jane Gay, 1889. bottom right, Billy Williams, native cartographer. He was present at the treaties of 1854–1855 and 1863 and understood firsthand the problems caused by the abandonment of villages and territory long used by the Nez Perce. When allotment of lands began, Williams was the first person among the Nez Perce to take his allotment (Fletcher 1891a:17). Photographed in 1891.

Martin, and Walker 1992). Walker has popularized Plateau anthropological research books (1973, 1980) and a film on Umatilla (Walker and Johnson 1994). Other major areas of his research have included sacred geography (Walker 1991, 1996), Nez Perce and Umatilla demography (Walker 1967b, 1997a; Walker and Leonhardy 1967), the impacts of hydroelectric and nuclear radiation on fishing resources (Walker 1992, 1997), and ethnographic assessment of the Native American Graves Protection and Repatriation Act. Additional major works include witchcraft and sorcery (Walker 1989), acculturation (Walker 1985), Nez Perce myth with Haruo Aoki (1989), and an innovative work on the character of Coyote in Nez Perce mythology (Walker and Matthews 1994). His emphasis on the training of ethnographers in the Plateau area has also been an important contribution and includes Daniel N. Matthews, Rodney Frey, John Schultz, John Ross, Bill Brunton, Madge Schwede, John Tockle, Michael Burney, Alan Marshall, and others.

The emphasis on understanding changes in Native American societies has clear antecedents in the work of Franz Boas and his students in the pre-World War II era. With the development of professional anthropology and regional academic departments, research on the Plateau as elsewhere on the North American continent has come to emphasize contemporary Native American societies and the continued stresses of acculturation and fit within the dominant societies of the United States and Canada.

Archeological Research

Archeological research in the Plateau region has a long and complex history, extending from the cursory observations of early explorers and traders and government officials, through tentative early twentieth-century efforts at systematic work, through amateur efforts, and then careful professional work beginning about World War II. Archeology, properly defined, is a historical study of human behavior emphasizing scientific methods. It is anthropology, but an anthropology of the past, where artifacts and patterns of artifacts replace living informants. It is done conscientiously, carefully monitored by professional standards and federal and state regulations. Many groups claim an intense interest in archeology: federal and state managers as part of culture resource management, academics as a research area into human behavior, the public as a fascinating entry into past times and lifeways, and Native Americans as an intimate part of their cultural heritage.

Detailed overviews for archeological research in the Plateau are not available, though there are a number of good, if limited, discussions of specific phases of research and of the programs or individuals involved. Roderick Sprague (1965, 1967, 1973, 1993) has produced summaries of research in prehistoric and historical archeology and physical anthropology. His publication series offer detailed insights into the development and continuation of Plateau research (Sprague 1967a; Pavesic, Plew, and Sprague 1979, 1981). Aikens (1993), Butler (1968, 1978), and Kirk and Daugherty (1978) have written state summaries. James Chatters and his coworkers (Chatters 1987, 1995; Chatters and Hoover 1992; Butler and Chatters 1994; Chatters et al. 1995) have produced challenging syntheses on selected aspects of Plateau prehistory.

Early Exploration

Archeology, as a hybrid discipline of history and science, relies heavily on written accounts documenting aboriginal societies in the earliest phases of contact with Euro-Americans. For example, Lewis and Clark made wonderful ethnographic observations on the daily life of aboriginal societies along the Clearwater, Lower Snake, and Lower Columbia River drainages in 1804–1806 and many of these observations have been confirmed by professional excavations and have stimulated archeological research models.

Archeologists also try to understand impacts on the archeological record and to study or characterize early attempts at excavation and collection. Sprague (1973) attributes the first "archeological excavations" in the Pacific Northwest to pillaging of Chinook graves on the Columbia River by Ross Cox in 1811, John Scouler in 1825, and John K. Townsend in 1835. Informal, nonsystematic digging continued throughout the nineteenth century as intellectuals, hobbyists, and ardent amateur archeologists approached prehistory. Daugherty (1956) presented an overview of early archeology in this region. George Gibbs described Oregon antiquities as an appendix in Schoolcraft's (1847) synthesis of Native American culture. John K. Lord traveled through Washington and British Columbia in 1866, describing surface scatters of artifacts and burial sites on the Columbia River drainage near Fort Walla Walla and Fort Colville. Edwin A. Barber and Charles H. Sternberg, in the 1880s and 1890s, described Early Man discoveries of artifacts and fossil elephants (Daugherty 1959). Rev. Myron Eells's discoveries were first summarized in Bancroft (1874–1876). Garrick Mallery (1886, 1893) was the first to describe Plateau rock art. Within the region, the first publication was *The Antiquarian*, a journal created by Albany, Oregon, schoolteacher George L. Howe, that included archeology and ethnography.

Culture-Historical Research Before World War II

The period of culture-historical research is defined as an overwhelming interest in description of finds in time and space (Willey and Phillips 1958). The research emphasis in this early period was to define prehistoric cultures as constellations of types and type assemblages. Cultural chronologies or sequences of assemblages and phases over time was the goal. Archeologists were explicitly working within the culture area concept that dominated anthropological thinking in the early part of the twentieth century.

Kroeber's (1939) culture-area study was a landmark synthetic approach to Native American ethnography and archeology. Primary goals were to examine the articulation of a historic aboriginal culture with its physical environment and to examine historic relations between known cultures and the archeological record. The culture-area concept was considered a means to an end, the end being a better understanding of cultural processes or historic events in cultural perspective. This framework focused much of the early archeological work, as it did ethnographic work. The avowed aim was to link historic aboriginal cultures and prehistoric cultures.

Harlan I. Smith directed the archeological work of the Jesup North Pacific Expedition. Though flawed by the antiquated methods employed, Smith's work is invaluable because it represents the only published material on excavations in Plateau areas of British Columbia and Washington. Summaries of this work were issued as *Publications of the Jesup North Pacific Expedition* between 1900 and 1907.

Other excavations during this period included the work of Merton L. Miller for the Field Museum, Chicago, in 1901 (Sprague 1971). Charles Hill-Tout began work in British Columbia at about the same time, and Carlson (1970:11) dubs Hill-Tout's (1895) report as the beginning of scientific archeology in that region. Sprague (1973:256) cites Spinden's (1908) work on the ethnography of the Nez Perce as valuable for the inclusion of archeological observations, and applauds Harlan I. Smith's summary of archeological work in the Yakima Valley as extraordinary for its detailed descriptions of artifacts and collections.

Amateurs were also active during this period. Oluf L. Opsjon's work suggesting that aboriginal rock art in the Spokane region were Norse runes received broad play in almost daily newspaper accounts in 1924 (Sprague 1973). They reached review by eastern archeologists in 1926 in the *New York Times*, where Opsjon's views were soundly trounced. Speculation again emerged in the writing of Karl H. Isselstein (1965).

Theoretical archeological research on the Plateau or within the broader region of the Pacific Northwest is said to begin with A.L. Kroeber (1923a); only then were archeologists knowledgeable enough to begin to test broad cultural hypotheses (Sprague 1973:257). Following Smith's work for the Jesup expedition, and until World War II, most archeological research was on the Columbia River drainage below the Canadian border. A long period of work was initiated by Strong and Schenck (1925) in a study of petroglyphs and artifact collections found near The Dalles. Strong, Schenck, and Steward (1930) published the first comprehensive site survey and excavation report for the Pacific Northwest. This summary of work in The Dalles-Deschutes region is an acceptable descriptive report by later standards, though taxonomic schemes and conclusions have been greatly modified.

In 1934, Herbert W. Krieger, curator of ethnology at the U.S. National Museum, surveyed and tested burial and housepit sites on the Columbia River. This investigation was the first of many large-scale archeological investigations prior to reservoir development in the Plateau.

Academic archeology in the Plateau begins with the hiring of Luther S. Cressman at the University of Oregon in 1933. Cressman established the first university-based archeological program in the Pacific Northwest, and his field-

work continued over 40 years. Cressman (1937) conducted the first state-wide study of petroglyphs in the region. Robin A. Drews, a Cressman student, wrote the first thesis on archeology in 1938. This was followed by Alex D. Krieger's master's thesis in 1939. Cressman coordinated salvage excavations for Lake Roosevelt, behind Grand Coulee Dam (Collier, Hudson, and Ford 1942). This work was supported by the Eastern Washington State Historical Society, Spokane, and labor provided by the National Youth Administration, with fieldwork directed by the Department of Anthropology at the University of Washington and the Department of Sociology and Anthropology at the State College of Washington, now Washington State University, Pullman.

During World War II, archeological activity dropped markedly. Cressman confined his research largely to the Willamette Valley. Overviews and summaries were written, with Robert F. Heizer (1941) publishing a review of Oregon prehistory and Melville Jacobs (1945) writing on Pacific Northwest anthropological research. Thomas Cain (1950) published a thesis on Pacific Northwest rock art. Amateurs continued to be active with work on pictographs in the Wenatchee area (Cundy 1938) and cist burials on the Middle Columbia and Lower Snake (Perry 1939) were published. N.G. Seaman (1940) published his memoirs on archeological work in the *Oregon Historical Society Quarterly* and produced a book that remains popular with the amateur community (Seaman 1946).

Culture-Historical Research After World War II

Reservoir construction, and correlative work in archeology and physical anthropology, accelerated at the end of World War II. Thirty-five different mimeographed reports of the Columbia Basin Project, River Basin Surveys, Smithsonian Institution, were published from 1947 to 1953 (Sprague 1984). Philip Drucker was the field director initially, with survey reports authored by Richard D. Daugherty, Francis A. Riddell, and Franklin Fenenga. Douglas Osborne became field director in October 1948. In May 1950, Osborne joined the Department of Anthropology, University of Washington, Seattle, and Joel Shiner became acting field director. Frequent articles were published in *American Antiquity*, regional journals, and *Bureau of American Ethnology, River Basin Survey Reports*. Osborne and Shiner coauthored site excavation reports until June 1951. Publications in this series continued until December 1953. The Columbia Basin Project produced over 40 surveys of reservoirs and nine significant site excavation reports. The Survey office was maintained in cooperation with the University of Oregon, Eugene. The River Basin Surveys, while issuing reports and monographs of variable quality (Osborne 1957), marked a turning toward large-scale systematic research on the Plateau.

Fig. 7. Roadcut site at Fivemile Rapids (35–WS–4), The Dalles, Oreg. Photograph by Luther S. Cressman, 1955.

Academic departments were focused on archeology by the River Basin Survey. The University of Washington worked in the McNary and Chief Joseph Dam reservoirs, the University of Oregon at The Dalles (fig. 7) and John Day reservoirs, and Washington State University in the Lower Snake River region. The data derived from the early work is flawed in some respects, as site survey, testing, and excavation methodologies were questionable by later standards (Sprague 1973:262). Coordination improved with direction of the program by Paul J.F. Schumacher, Chief for Archeological Investigations, the U.S. National Park Service.

Archeology expanded to focus on historical sites during this same period. Louis R. Caywood, from 1947–1955, conducted excavations at Fort Vancouver, Fort Clatsop, Spokane House, and Fort Okanogan. Thomas R. Garth excavated Waiilatpu Mission and Fort Walla Walla.

Archeology was expanding in British Columbia, with research by A.E. Pickford and Marian W. Smith (1950) on the Fraser River drainage, and the important contributions beginning to be made by Charles E. Borden of the University of British Columbia, Vancouver (Borden 1950). Borden began salvage archeology in British Columbia with his work in Tweedsmuir Park. Borden (1952a) set up the Canadian site designation system. Douglas Leechman, at about the same time, was publishing archeological reports in regional journals. A survey by Riddell and Daugherty in the Lind Coulee of central Washington in the summer of 1947 located the first documented Early Man site in the Plateau region. Daugherty (1956) published the descriptive material, and this publication became the basis of Daugherty's (1959) summary of Washington prehistory. Daugherty moved to the faculty of the State College of Washington in 1949, where he built a strong archeological program that dominated work in the eastern Plateau region for the next 30 years. The first Washington State University fieldschool ran in the summer of 1953 at McGregor Cave in eastern Washington.

The 1950s saw increased development of archeology programs. Sprague (1973:264–265) refers to the problem-oriented archeology that went beyond the confines of reservoir construction. Interest focused on the Northwest Coast, though questions arose over the relationship of the Plateau culture area to the more complex Northwest Coast cultures. Borden (1954) was influential in shaping questions on coastal-interior relationships. Osborne, Caldwell, and Crabtree (1956) challenged the notion that cultural flows were consistently from the coast to the interior.

During this period, the number of regional publications expanded in proportion to the emergent debates. Up until the 1950s, publications in the Pacific Northwest were limited almost entirely to occasional papers or reports in national journals or to the two established regional publication series, the *University of Oregon Monographs, Studies in Anthropology* and the *University of Washington Publications in Anthropology*. *Anthropology in British Columbia* was published 1950 through 1956. A *Memoir* series was attached, which ran until 1964. In 1955, the *Davidson Journal of Anthropology* began publication at the University of Washington. This excellent, professional journal was presented in mimeographed form for only three and one-half years. *Research Studies of the State College of Washington* issued a Northwest archeology volume in March 1956, edited by Daugherty (see Daugherty et al. 1956). This single issue became a significant chapter in Plateau archeology, with articles by Daugherty, Warren A. Snyder, Douglas Osborne, Carling Malouf, Herbert Taylor, Wilson Duff, and Charles Borden. Coverage included both Plateau and Northwest Coast archeology. The paper by Carling Malouf describing cultural connections between the upper Missouri and the Columbia River was especially influential (Sprague 1973:268). Gillett G. Griswold (1954) expanded on this issue. Daugherty, in an effort to encourage synthesis, promoted and expanded upon the Krieger typological concept, using the terms "form" and "style" in characterizations of Plateau cultures.

A singular development was creation of the Northwest Anthropological Conference, which held its first meeting on May 8, 1948, in Portland, Oregon. By 1955 the Northwest Anthropological Conference had largely supplanted the Western States Branch of the American Anthropological Association (Sprague 1973:266), which had briefly published a *Newsletter* and *News Bulletin* and a series entitled *Western Anthropology* under the editorship of Carling Malouf. An informal organization, without dues, officers, or constitution, the conference is organized by committees at the year's host institution. The meetings have been balanced across anthropological subdisciplines since the conference's inception (Sprague 1968).

Activities of amateur societies increased during the 1950s. The Oregon Archaeological Society formed in 1951, and began publication of its series *Screenings* in March 1952. The society was influenced by Emory Strong, a serious amateur archeologist, in its early formation. The Washington Archaeological Society was formed in Seattle in 1955 (Sprague 1973:267; C.G. Nelson 1957). The Society formed a satellite chapter at Washington State University under the direction of Richard Daugherty (Palus Chapter), and another at Ephrata (Columbia Basin Chapter) under the guidance of Washington State Sen. Nat Washington. These chapters folded, but the Society continued to be a strong

advocate with publication of *The Washington Archaeologist* beginning in 1957 and ceasing in 1982. The Columbia Archaeological Society, formed in the late 1950s in Seattle, conducted excavations on Fishhook Jim Island in the Snake River.

Highway salvage archeology began in 1957 in the State of Washington, with a program directed by Daugherty and Bruce Stallard, whose work (1958) was the first overall review on archeology of the entire state and the first organized bibliography of archeological work (Sprague 1973:270). Stallard authored the first issue of the *Washington State University. Laboratory of Anthropology. Report of Investigations* in 1957. This series was not formally established until 1962.

The University of Washington and the University of Oregon were conducting programs of excavation at The Dalles during this period. The University of Oregon covered its side of the river in field seasons from 1952 through 1956. Cressman et al. (1960) produced an extensive report of two major sites at either end of Fivemile Rapids. This report was seminal in supplying the first Plateau stratigraphic sequence extending from the terminal Pleistocene to the historic period. It also gained importance because it speculated on coast-interior relationships at The Dalles, which was known as an important travel and trade nexus. The University of Oregon expanded archeological investigations, at first under the impetus of Luther S. Cressman and later under David L. Cole, into the John Day Reservoir. Work continued from 1958 through 1968. The University of Washington established an archeological project with the Priest Rapids Reservoir during the 1950s under the direction of Robert E. Greengo.

B. Robert Butler issued a compelling report in 1958 that attempted to establish a theoretical framework for the increasing body of archeological data being produced for the Plateau (Butler 1958). Butler (1961, 1965) presented his notion of an Old Cordilleran culture, outlining possible cultural connections and developments in the Pacific Northwest.

Washington State University, under the direction of Daugherty, conducted archeological research in Sun Lakes State Park from 1958 through 1961. Other Washington State University projects included historical excavations by John D. Combes at Spokane House and military Fort Spokane.

By the late 1950s and into the 1960s, the focus of Washington State University archeology shifted to the Lower Snake River, beginning with work at Ice Harbor Reservoir and moving up through Lower Monumental and Little Goose reservoirs. In the same period, University of Washington work focused on Wanapum Reservoir, again under the direction of Greengo (1986, 1986a). Results of these projects were slow in being published, since most of the research was done as student theses and dissertations. The University of Washington's archeological program in the 1960s accelerated with surveys of state parks and investigations required as part of reservoir development. A major archeological project was begun at Wells Reservoir, under the direction of Garland F. Grabert (1968, 1971, 1974).

Archeological programs on the southern Plateau began to develop in the 1960s at Oregon State University with Wilbur A. Davis and at Portland State University with Thomas M. Newman at Cascadia Cave (Newman 1966).

Passage of the British Columbia Archeological and Historic Site Protection Act in 1960 spurred archeological research to the north. Charles Borden directed University of British Columbia projects on the Fraser River throughout the 1960s. A number of archeologists authored reports on British Columbia archeology during this period, for example, Donald H. Mitchell (1970, 1970a) and David Sanger (1967, 1969). Knut Fladmark has authored a number of informative reviews of British Columbia prehistory (Fladmark 1982, 1986).

Attempts at synthesis began to emerge in the 1960s, with Cressman's (1962) popular account of Oregon archeology. Daugherty (1962) published his theoretical framework for Pacific Northwest archeology. Frank Leonhardy and David G. Rice (1970) produced one of the most influential syntheses in their proposed culture typology for the Lower Snake River. Earl Swanson (1962) added to the debates.

The Washington highway salvage program was divided between the University of Washington and Washington State University in 1966. Washington State University was involved in an intensive program in the Lower Granite Reservoir, and reports of investigations were being written by graduate students. Sprague had taken over direction of the salvage archeology program in 1965 and was succeeded by Leonhardy in 1968. Construction of powerhouse facilities at Grand Coulee Dam and corresponding lowering of Lake Roosevelt prompted archeological investigation by first the University of Washington and then the University of Idaho, especially at Fort Colville. The University of Idaho also conducted historical archeology at Cataldo Mission, Spalding Mission, Fort Lapwai, and Lewis and Clark Canoe Camp, all in Idaho. Collections of historical archeological research were published in *Northwest Anthropological Research Notes* 1975, and 1977 (Sprague 1994).

Increasing archeological work focused attention on syntheses, bibliographies, and publication series for dissemination of results. The years 1967 through the early 1970s saw an expansion in research, as archeologists began to focus on ordering the archeological record.

Important summary articles on Plateau archeology include Caldwell and Mallory (1967) on the Upper Snake River, Sanger (1967) on interior British Columbia, and Sprague's (1967) summary of burial practices. Another achievement was initiation of the journal *Northwestern Anthropological Research Notes,* which issued bibliographies (Sprague 1967a; Swartz 1967; Pavesic, Plew, and Sprague 1979, 1981).

Butler (1968, 1978) published *A Guide to Understanding Idaho Archeology*, which characterized the Upper Snake River region in terms of both the Plateau and Great Basin

culture areas. Three new publication series were also initiated in 1968. The University of Washington published *Reports in Archeology*, whose first two issues were a report on the work in Wells Reservoir by Grabert. The Washington Archaeological Society issued an *Occasional Paper* series as a supplement to the *Washington Archaeologist*. The British Columbia Provincial Museum published *Syesis*, a broad-content journal with articles on archeology.

David L. Browman and David A. Munsell (1969; Swanson 1970) published on prehistoric cultural development. Charles M. Nelson's (1969) work stands as one of the most important and exhaustive descriptive summaries of Plateau prehistory. Nelson presented complete descriptions and illustrations of artifact types as part of a thorough culture historical sequence that would be cited for 20 years.

Another important development in this period was the beginning professionalization of federal agencies. David H. Chance (1968) was hired by the Oregon Bureau of Land Management and housed at the University of Oregon. Federally funded work continued on the Plateau, with Washington State University working in the Lower Granite Reservoir under the direction of Leonhardy, and David Rice directing projects in Asotin Reservoir, Lake Roosevelt, and the Cascade Mountains. Harvey S. Rice directed highway salvage projects in the eastern portion of the state, and Munsell ran work in the west. Max G. Pavesic replaced Dan Morse as the Idaho highway archeologist, excavating the important Lenore site on the Clearwater River. Sprague replaced the retiring Alfred W. Bowers at the University of Idaho and began a program emphasizing historical archeology. David Rice was hired at the University of Idaho in 1969 and supplied emphasis on the prehistoric archeology. The University of Idaho concentrated work at Fort Colville in Lake Roosevelt.

A comparable spurt of activity was occurring in British Columbia during the late 1960s. Fieldwork was initiated by the University of Calgary's Knut R. Fladmark, Jason W. Smith, A.H. Stryd, and Christopher Turnbull. Other workers included James Baker from Vancouver City College, Paul G. Sneed from the University of British Columbia, James Hester from the University of Colorado, Cay Calert from the Vancouver Centennial Museum, Philip M. Hobler and Roy L. Carlson of Simon Fraser University, and Donald Mitchell and Bjorn O. Simonsen of the University of Victoria and Archeological Sites Advisory Board of the Province of British Columbia. Roscoe Wilmeth directed a large National Museum of Canada project in the Carrier-speaking area of British Columbia, involving Paul Donahue and Kenneth M. Ames.

Professionals based in academic institutions and federal and state agencies, who acknowledged a common history of work, tried to organize and synthesize an increasingly complex body of information on Plateau prehistory, history, and ethnology. University programs were expanding and archeologists worked to form close associations with other programs, federal and state agencies, and the public. In Washington, Astrida R. Onat of Seattle Community College directed archeological work. William C. Smith began a successful program at Central Washington State College, Ellensburg. Garland F. Grabert conducted work from Western Washington State College, Bellingham. Washington and Oregon amateur archeological societies continued their emphasis, while a number of new societies were formed in Canada. The Archaeological Society of British Columbia was founded in Vancouver in 1966. In Washington, David Rice promoted founding of the Mid-Columbia Archeological Society in 1967.

Public perceptions of Plateau archeology were expanding as archeologists exposed more of the region's prehistory at significant sites. Marmes Rockshelter in eastern Washington attracted attention to the interior of the Plateau ("Prehistory of the Southern Plateau," fig. 3, this vol.). The Marmes Rockshelter was first reported by an archeological survey party during excavation of McGregor Cave in 1953. Daugherty at that time felt that the rockshelter probably had been scoured out by Palouse River floods and that there was probably no significant cultural stratigraphy. It was only when excavations at the nearby Palus Village site proved unrewarding in 1962 that attention was focused on the excavation of Marmes Rockshelter. Excavation continued during the field seasons of 1963–1964. In 1965 a crew returned for two weeks to verify that culturally sterile, basal deposits had been reached. In that same summer, geologist Roald Fryxell found skeletal material exposed in a bulldozer trench being cut at the base of the rockshelter. C.E. Gustafson, a zoologist in the Department of Anthropology, Washington State University, discovered "Marmes Man" in 1967 upon identifying human bone in the sample recovered by Fryxell. Additional human skeletal material was found in the bulldozer cut by a graduate class in April 1968. The significance of the Marmes Rockshelter site was demonstrated, and an earthen dike was built to save the site from the rising water of the Lower Monumental Reservoir. Unfortunately, the dike failed and the site was flooded. At about 10,000 years old, the rockshelter is not the oldest site in the Pacific Northwest, but it was the best publicized archeological site on the Plateau during these formative years (Washington Archaeological Society 1969).

Leonhardy and Rice (1970), in their authoritative synthesis, ascribed the earliest occupations at Marmes Rockshelter to the Windust phase, dated 8500–5500 B.C. Diagnostic artifacts included large leaf-shaped and stemmed stone projectile points, lanceolate and ovate stone knives, large stone scrapers and choppers, polyhedral stone cores and prismatic blades, bone awls, bone needles, and bone atlatl spurs. Broken food bone showed that aboriginal inhabitants were taking and eating deer, elk, pronghorn antelope, jackrabbit, cottontail rabbit, and beaver. Freshwater mussels from the Palouse River had been gathered and eaten as well. Olivella shells from a cremation pit containing human bones were evidence of trade contacts with the Pacific coast. The Marmes Rockshelter became the type site anchoring the earliest well-dated assemblage in the cultural sequence defined for the Plateau.

Leonhardy and Rice's synthesis marks maturation of Plateau archeology and reflects methodological and theoretical concerns current in the discipline. Phases were defined based on distinctive types of artifacts with dated temporal distributions. Usual earmarks were changing styles of stone projectile points. Leonhardy and Rice defined six cultural phases for the archeological record of the lower Snake River: Windust phase, Cascade phase, Tucannon phase, Harder phase, Piqúnin phase, and Numípu phase. This synthesis revised the work of Daugherty (1962) and complemented Nelson's (1969) synthesis from the Sunset Creek site on the Middle Columbia River. Leonhardy and Rice's synthesis and that of Nelson (1969) formed the descriptive basis for continuing archeological work up to the present time.

By the early 1970s, archeological research had progressed to the point that the Plateau cultural area was recognized as historically distinct from the surrounding Plains, Great Basin, California, Northwest Coast, and Subarctic cultural areas (Aikens 1978; Spencer and Jennings 1977; Jennings 1968, 1989). Opportunities for archeology, largely through salvage operations associated with construction of dams and reservoirs up and down the Columbia River drainages, prompted development of substantial academic programs at regional universities. A hundred years of archeology, from the 1870s–1970s, saw progression from amateur and hobbyist interest to professionalization, and deposited thousands of artifacts from hundreds of archeological sites in the collections of academic departments, private museums, university museums, and federal and state repositories.

Archeological theory during this same transformational period of the 1960s came to emphasize attempting more than simply describing archeological finds in time and space. Imperatives were issued that cried out for archeologists to go beyond collection and description and begin to focus on understanding human behavior. Cultural ecological studies became the norm, where projects would have interdisciplinary teams of researchers with specialties in related natural sciences, who would examine how prehistoric Plateau societies organized themselves to exploit their environments over the span of the Late Pleistocene to the Holocene. Reliably dated chronological sequences of archeological types and cultures were still required, but research since the 1970s focused on research problems: settlement pattern, subsistence organization, social organization, and ethnicity. Preoccupation with static description turned to emphasis on cultural changes over time, and models and explanations of how and why these significant shifts in prehistoric socioeconomic organization occurred.

The signal syntheses of Cressman et al. (1960), Daugherty (1962), Browman and Munsell (1969, 1972), Nelson (1969, 1973), and Leonhardy and Rice (1970) guided descriptive chronological studies and supply raw material for more contemporary problem-oriented research. The rough temporal sequences found general acceptance, though debate continued on the areal extent of distinctive assemblages and on overriding issues of accurate interpretation. A schism emerged between the fractious field of competing academic researchers and the relatively consensual culture resource management field, where managers and contractors agree to standards and employ generally accepted culture-historical narratives and type sequences (Dunnell 1979:441; Lohse 1994). In part, this difference is attributable to the relative freedom granted the academic researcher, who can pursue a wide gamut of perceived problems and lacunae in knowledge, and the constraints placed on archeologists engaged in salvage archeology. Most archeological work on the Plateau in the 1990s was the direct result of mandated mitigation projects, largely focused on dam and reservoir development. As a result, samples of the prehistoric record tend to be tightly clustered along the Columbia, Snake, Clearwater, and Fraser river drainages. Further, managing federal and state and provincial agencies demand that archeological contractors assess archeological resources within the two primary dimensions of time (site depth) and space (surface extent), with the primary aim to assess significance of the resource base: deeply stratified equating with significant and shallow with less significant. Unfortunately, pigeonholing of project data into established cultural sequences has become the norm. Problems with dissemination of results are comparable to those present earlier, principally the inevitable lag resulting from dependence upon students for analysis and reporting as theses and dissertations.

Chatters (1995:346) has characterized problems of adequate temporal and areal coverage in archeological samples and argued for correcting the bewildering character of culture historical sequences on the Plateau. Dammed stretches of rivers have been studied and restudied, by different academic institutions and within varying theoretical frameworks. There has been a tendancy for archeologists to avoid synthesis by imposing new phase names at the subregion and local sequence levels. The result has been a confusing array of culture-historical sequences and overlays of more problem-oriented research without integration of contemporary work with that body of information and knowledge developed over the past century. Often, contemporary results are seen to be incompatible with prior work because of changing methods and theories. This observation is not new or unique to the Plateau. Willey and Phillips (1958) admonished that archeologists must surmount the inevitable problem of lack of correlation between archeological types and prehistoric social contexts. Binford (1967:235) posited

that the standard goal of culture-historical interpretation could only play a role in public education (cf. Dunnell's 1979 notion of consensual description in culture resource management; Lohse 1994).

Contemporary archeological research and resulting syntheses are often limited to consideration of principal study areas generated by culture resource management directed research, university involvement, and the individual agendas. Research histories create discrete areas with internal consistency in culture historical schemes, interpretation, and problem orientations. On the Plateau, these study areas coincide with stretches of rivers: the Lower Columbia, Middle Columbia, lower Snake River, Hells Canyon section of the Snake River, the middle and upper sections of the Snake River, the Clearwater River, the Salmon River, the lower and middle reaches of the Fraser River.

After the early 1970s, historical developments shifted from individual researchers and particular finds or discoveries, to roles of academic programs, federal and state legislation, significance of large- and small-scale projects, and the schisms between academic and culture resource management archeologies. Archeology on the Plateau since the developmental period of post-World War II culture-historical description has matured as a discipline. Legislation has created myriad job opportunities for archeologists, supplied massive infusions of funding, and at the same time, frozen many of the goals of archeological research to the descriptive character of culture-historical research of the 1950s–1970s. Contemporary archeology must operate within the defined culture resource management structure monitoring work in an area, must secure permits, and must cooperate and mediate between forces of academic research interest, government requirements, and Native American and general public demands. In the 1990s Plateau archeology was synonymous with culture resource management, the Native American Graves Protection and Repatriation Act, grants, and refereed publication.

The change of focus in Plateau research can be seen in the simple observation that Sprague's (1973) overview remains the standard reference for the history of research. Articles emphasize dissemination of work as unpublished contract reports or as unpublished theses and dissertations. Overviews and syntheses in refereed articles and monographs are rare indeed, and probably a direct reflection of the practical difficulties of obtaining unpublished reports and of relating project-specific culture historical reconstructions (cf. Chatters 1995; Lohse 1994). Selected examples are presented here to emphasize the character of contemporary research since the 1970s.

During the late 1960s-early 1970s the most intensive excavation on the southern Plateau occurred along the lower Snake River between its confluence with the Columbia River and the vicinity of Lewiston, Idaho. Along this stretch of about 160 kilometers, five reservoirs were constructed. Results of preinundation archeology were disseminated in theses, dissertations, descriptive reports, and the rare published refereed article by Washington State University graduate students and faculty (Adams 1972; Bense 1972; Brauner 1976; Combes 1968; Daugherty, Purdy, and Fryxell 1967; Fryxell and Daugherty 1962, 1963; Grater 1966; Gustafson 1972; Hammatt 1977; Kenaston 1966; Leonhardy 1970; Leonhardy and Rice 1970; Nelson 1966; Rice 1965; Schroedl 1973; Sprague 1965, 1967; Rice 1972; Yent 1976).

Other major projects since the early 1970s include McNary Reservoir (Thoms 1983), Chief Joseph Dam (Campbell 1985, 1985a, 1985b, 1985c), Wells Reservoir (Chatters 1986), and Lake Roosevelt (Chance and Chance 1985). The Chief Joseph Dam Project is perhaps the most characteristic of trends in research. The project was begun the late 1970s to determine impacts of operation of the Rufus Woods Lake Reservoir below Grand Coulee Dam on archeological resources. Inundation and subsequent raising and lowering of reservoir levels behind Chief Joseph Dam was known to have dramatic impact on hundreds of archeological sites spanning at least the last 8,000 years. Work on the Chief Joseph Dam Project was within the tradition of reservoir salvage archeology prevalent on the Plateau for the preceding two decades, but it was also a unique and important development in several respects. It was a systematic, problem-oriented investigation that attempted to draw upon past research. It was a staged project that would extend over a period of years, from 1976–1984, and would progress from survey to testing to excavation to analysis and on to reporting. The U.S. Army Corps of Engineers, Seattle District, made a conscious effort to fund this project to a reasonable level that would enable adequate professional standards to be employed in all aspects of the work. Envisioned was a project that emphasized state-of-the-art field methodology and theory in design, analysis, and interpretation. The contract required that the project select a number of sites believed to be representative of site variability, and that these samples be used as the basis for defining a chronological framework for the region. Research emphasis was strongly geared to characterizing cultural adaptations over the span of the archeological record. The project was also a pioneer in attempting to work carefully and profitably with a Native American tribe, in this case, the Colville Confederated Tribes.

The Chief Joseph Dam Project was administered through the Office of Public Archeology, University of Washington, with Robert C. Dunnell as principal investigator and Jerry Jermaine and, later, Manfred W. Jaehnig as field project directors. Intensive field and laboratory work took place between July 31, 1978, and December 31, 1984. Eighteen prehistoric habitation sites were excavated, analyzed, and reported on. The project had its own resident team, including botanists and computer programmers. Jermann et al. (1980) presented a management plan for cultural resources in the project area. Leeds et al. (1981) reported on testing at 79 prehistoric habitation sites. Reports were issued in four series. Series I includes the project research design (Camp-

bell 1984b) and a preliminary report authored by Jaehnig (1983a). Series II consists of descriptive reports on excavated prehistoric habitation sites (Campbell 1984a; Jaehnig 1984, 1984a; Lohse 1984, 1984a, 1984b, 1984c, 1984d, 1984e; Miss 1984, 1984a, 1984b, 1984c), on prehistoric nonhabitation sites and burial relocation sites (Campbell 1984b), and a report on the survey and excavation of historic sites (Thomas, Larson, and Hawkes 1984). Campbell (1985c) presents the summary of project results.The report series was carefully reviewed and printed in large numbers for dissemination.

Campbell (1984b), in the research design summary, notes that project designs for data recovery varied considerably over the project history. She notes that until the initial reconnaisance was completed in 1978, Corps of Engineers policy was not to fund "research." Explicit study goals, data recovery decisions, and plans for systems analyses were presented in a plan of action for site testing (Jermann and Whittlesey 1978) and in a management plan (Jermann et al. 1980). When Corps policy changed, and research was allowable, a draft research design was presented (Jermann et al. 1980) that guided much of the project. The draft was designed to investigate activity areas at sites and test a subsistence model based on ethnographic Sanpoil-Nespelem subsistence and settlement (Leeds, Leeds, and Whittlesey 1985). Campbell (1984b) notes that flaws in the research design centered on the lack of specific expectations derived from the model that could be tested in the archeological record. Strong points include systematic site sampling, thorough faunal analysis, and computerized artifact analyses. Project completion required a shift from full implementation of the modeling exercise to a pragmatic focus on descriptive report writing.

The Chief Joseph Project remains the largest, most comprehensive and systematic archeological project done within a proscribed time frame on the Plateau. The summary of results volume for the project (Campbell 1985) includes articles by Leeds, Leeds, and Whittlesey (1985) on model building, Dennis M. Hibbert (1985) on the geology, Rinita Dalan (1985) and Nickman and Leopold (1985) on Goose Lake core pollen analyses, Campbell (1985a, 1985b) on sedimentary sequences and selected aspects of the artifact assemblage, Lawr V. Salo (1985, 1985a) on chronological periods and artifact types and site clusters, Leeds (1985) on prehistoric adaptation, Christian J. Miss (1985) on site frequency reflecting intensity of use over time, Lohse (1985) on projectile point chronology, Stephanie Livingston (1985) on fauna recovered, Nancy A. Stenholm (1985) on the botanical assemblage, and Dorothy Sammons-Lohse (1985) on cultural features and site interpretation. Innovations include construction of the computer data base for the project and various spin-offs from the automated analyses pursued as part of analysis. Lohse (1985), for example, created a computerized projectile point classification system for the project that assigned over 1,500 recovered projectile points to established Plateau types. These were arranged in a well-defined sequence based on careful site excavations and a radiocarbon ladder of over 100 dates on Rufus Woods Lake site components (Sappington 1994:37). The Rufus Woods Lake Project also produced a dissertation authored by Sarah Campbell (1989), which offers a summary of the very late period of Plateau prehistory, 1500–1900.

A direct continuation of the Chief Joseph Dam Project was the work of James Chatters from 1982–1984 (Chatters 1984), and his work on the nearby Wells Reservoir, from 1983–1986 (Chatters 1986). This work was used as the basis for a number of fine papers and reports in which Chatters has attempted synthesis for southern Plateau prehistory (Chatters 1987, 1989, 1989a, 1995).

Contemporary syntheses are often done for specific areas of federal and state management responsibility (Arnold 1984; Boreson 1976, 1976a; Bright 1980; Chance 1980; Chatters 1989; Draper 1990; Galm et al. 1981; Galm and Masten 1985; Hudson et al. 1978; Knudson, Sappington, and Pfeiffer 1977; Leen 1988; McLeod and Melton 1986; Rice 1980a; Rice et al. 1974; Sisson 1983, 1984a, 1985a; Stratton and Lindeman 1978). These reports summarize past work, attempt integration of findings with local and regional syntheses, and identify problems or goals for any future mitigation work or planning. These planning documents or overviews often provide stimulus for directed research that brings the latest theory and method to bear on archeological problems. Other significant syntheses are by graduate students and exist as unpublished theses and dissertations (Sappington 1994; Hackenberger 1988; Hackenberger, Sisson, and Womack 1989; Hammatt 1977). One outlet for such work are the various regional report series on university campuses.

The practical problem is adequate synthesis when research designs, typological frameworks, and reporting conventions are not comparable (Bicchieri 1975; Lyman 1985a). Attempts at standardization are invaluable but limited in scope usually to good chronological indicators and culture-historical sequences (Leonhardy and Rice 1970; Lohse 1985; Nelson 1969). There have been no successful attempts to link the northern and southern Plateau, and approaches on the Fraser River and Columbia River remain unlinked methodologically and theoretically.

Chatters (1995) has constructed a culture history sequence for the southern Plateau and has suggested an interpretive model for changes in adaptive strategy from about 4000 B.C. to A.D. 1. He bases his study on the large regional-scale excavation projects along the upper Columbia River (Campbell 1985; Chatters 1984, 1986), augmented by smaller-scale data recovery projects on the Lower Snake and Clearwater rivers. He cites Kroeber (1939) that ethnographic adaptations in this region were variants on a single theme: collector strategy emphasizing logistical mobility focused on base villages, supported by intensive harvest and storage of roots, berries, salmon, and large game (Chatters 1987:344). Variants involve differences in the availability and acquisition of resources. For instance, populations on the lower Columbia River may have been near-

ly sedentary while those in mountainous uplands would have been highly mobile.

One solution for assembling the bewildering array of typological schemes is to lump regional and areal schemes into general periods of Early, Middle, and Late. Divisions are based on the temporal and areal distribution of diagnostic artifact types and correlation with inferred climatic changes, major technological innovations, and general shifts in adaptive patterns for prehistoric societies. A major emphasis in these culture history reconstructions is assessment of the age of the observed ethnographic pattern (cf. Palmer 1975; Ray 1939; Teit 1900, 1909). Ethnographers recorded Plateau societies that had a seminomadic settlement pattern, with subsistence centered on harvest and storage of salmon, ungulates, and roots (Ames 1985, 1988; Ames and Marshall 1980). Typically, large winter housepit villages occupied major river valleys. The chronological extent of this pattern has not been systematically examined. Archeological study regions have been confined to environmental zones impacted by reservoir development, and little systematic work has taken place that would explore a range of environments indicative of the ethnographic subsistence pattern. Extent is most often gauged simply by observation and inference. For example, salmon has been present in the Fraser and Columbia river drainages throughout the greater part of the Holocene. Yet, archeological evidence for intensive exploitation is found no earlier than perhaps 3,000 years ago. Antiquity for intensive gathering and storage of roots is similarily only about 6,000–5,000 years. Housepits, another important element of the ethnographic pattern are only documented at about 5,500 years ago. So, evidence for the ethnographic Plateau pattern is on the order of 5,000–2,500 years old over the Plateau region (Lohse and Sammons-Lohse 1986; Ames 1988).

The first summary of rock art (pictographs and petroglyphs) in the Plateau is the work of Boreson (1976) covering the Pacific Northwest south of the international border. This was accompanied by a very complete bibliography (Boreson 1976a), including even newspaper articles. A review article (Sprague 1983) of the major works by Loring and Loring (1982) and Woodward (1982) included a list of major references to that period. Work since then has included work by Thomas H. Lewis (1985) concentrating on the Plateau in Montana, an overview of Washington by McClure (1978), and a synthetic work by James D. Keyser (1992).

A compelling issue spanning the 1980s and 1990s has been identification of Plateau ethnic groups in the archeological record. Legislation, under the Native American Graves Protection and Repatriation Act (Public Law 101–601), has introduced the need for identification of archeological remains to contemporary tribes whenever practicable (Collins and Andrefsky 1995). Sprague (1993), in an overview of burial and repatriation in the southern Plateau, states that modern descendents should be able to determine what is done with related archeological remains, 25 and that human remains with clear historic associations should be excavated only if that is the only alternative to impending destruction.

Reburial issues are a controversial issue for Native American and anthropological communities in the Plateau (cf. Isham 1974; Sloss 1995). Archeologists who have addressed the ethical issues include Adams (1984), Cheek and Keel (1984), Ferguson (1984), and Meighan (1984). Meighan has been adamant in arguing against repatriation of Native American remains. Zimmerman (1992) and McGuire (1992) offer reviews of reburial issues. Sprague (1993:4) notes that, in practice, reburial is far from a simple issue and that Native American remains are commonly not reburied without prolonged debate. He also explores the differing tribal attitudes toward removal of human remains, scientific study, and reburial. There is certainly no consensus among Plateau tribes. The Colville Confederated Tribes may demand radiocarbon assays on prehistoric burials. The Yakima, conversely, abhor destruction of the human remains and assert that all human remains and grave goods must be returned to the earth. The Colville will often keep the artifacts recovered for later study and display after appropriate purification ceremonies. The Nez Perce argue that grave goods from historic or known burials must be reinterred, while prehistoric burials and associated artifacts should be discussed as a different issue (cf. Walker 1967a).

Traits assigned to the ethnographic pattern are often used to identify tribal or ethnic groups in the past. Many of these assignments in fact simply link traits of the ethnographic pattern with region, and then region to historic tribal occupation. Federal and state managers will, for practicality, assign disposition of uncovered Native American burials to the tribe recognized to have held the region of concern in the historic period. General changes in assemblages over the span of the archeological record are often suggested to represent recent inferred movements of ethnic groups (Magne and Matson 1987; Reid 1991).

Archeology and Government

The spurt of archeological fieldwork in the 1970s and 1980s on both the northern and southern Plateau was a direct reflection of the need for culture resource mitigation. The archeological record was a significant part of cultural heritage management, and archeologists and Native Americans struggled over how to address issues of proper assessment, testing, excavation, and preservation. By the late 1980s and the early 1990s, tribes became vociferous over control of archeological research. Federal and state agencies responded to political pressure and sought tribal inclusion in the planning and implementation process. Funds have been directed to increase tribal involvement, and internship programs with federal agencies have been developed to speed training of tribal archeologists.

Chatters (1992) published a history of cultural resources management at the U.S. Department of Energy's Hanford site in Washington State. First acquired by the federal government in 1943, the site history is typical of shifting culture resource management frames applied to the Plateau as whole. The earliest research was that of Herbert Krieger, Smithsonian Institution, who excavated the village site of Wahluke during 1926 and 1927 (Krieger 1928a). Artifacts and human remains are at the National Museum of Natural History, Smithsonian Institution. This was the first and last instance of research at Hanford, with all later work directed by pragmatic culture resource management concerns. In 1947, Philip Drucker conducted surveys of the McNary Dam reservoir pool at Hanford as part of the River Basin Surveys program (Drucker 1948a), which had been initiated after the Reservoir Salvage Act of 1935 mandated funds for identification and excavation of archeological sites to be inundated by federal water control projects. In 1951, Puck Hyah Toot, Wanapam chief at Priest Rapids, requested fencing from the Atomic Energy Commission to protect grave sites in Priest Rapids Canyon and at Wanawisha Cemetery in Richland from looting. The Atomic Energy Commission declined. Puck then passed his request on to the Bureau of Indian Affairs, which also declined to construct the fencing. In 1953 the Atomic Energy Commission consented to assess damage at the sites, and government and Wanapam representatives marked the locations of five cemeteries on maps. In 1955, with more looting of Wanawisha Cemetery, the Commission cited Washington State Law RCW 27.44, the Indian Graves and Records Act, and urged police patrols and signs posted to read "Indian Burial Ground, Digging is Prohibited by State and Federal Law." The Wanawisha Cemetery was sold to the Yakima Indian Nation, fenced, and legally designated as a cemetery.

Passage of the National Historic Preservation Act in 1967 prompted initiation of the first large-scale surveys of the Hanford site as part of mitigation study for the Ben Franklin Dam (Rice 1968). Rice, a student at Washington State University, conducted the fieldwork with assistance from members of the Mid-Columbia Archeological Society. The Interagency Archeological Service of the National Park Service suggested that Rice conduct another survey to cover the rest of the Hanford site (Rice 1968a). First priority was given to areas scheduled for proposed construction and radioactive waste disposal. Sites found during these surveys constituted the primary data base for Hanford cultural resource management into the 1980s. From 1968 to 1971, the Atomic Energy Commission used the Interagency Archeology Service as its consultant, and the Service referred issues to Rice, who was then at the University of Idaho. The primary issue during this period was opening of the Columbia River to public access, plans Rice castigated as potentially threatening to the archeological resources. All cemeteries were marked to forestall looting.

From 1972 to 1981, the Washington Public Power Supply System sponsored surveys and test excavations at Hanford in compliance with federal statutes and Atomic Energy Commission and Energy Facilities Site Evaluation Council Guidelines (Rice 1983). Other surveys touching on Hanford at this time included U.S. Army Corps of Engineers survey of the McNary pool (Cleveland et al. 1976), a Washington State Department of Transportation survey of a potential bridge corridor (V. Morgan 1981), and surveys for rights of way by the Bonneville Power Association (Lynch 1976; J.B. Jackson and Hartmann 1977; W.C. Smith et al. 1977) and Puget Power (ERTEC 1982).

In 1973 David Rice persuaded Commission officials to nominate Hanford archeological sites to the National Register of Historic Places by citing Executive Order 11593. This led to a culture resource management program at Hanford and training of Hanford employees to recognize archeological resources. Chatters (1989:79), while commending the efforts, notes that recording was lax in some instances, and that a number of archeological sites were leveled as development proceeded. Rice (1980a) suggested guidelines for culture resource management at Hanford, including a 10 percent stratified sampling design, intensive surveys of lands to undergo signficant ground altering undertakings, prepare case studies for significant sites and submit National Register nominations, increase surveillance, note places of importance to Native American groups to conform to the American Indian Religious Freedom Act, and consider alternative protection strategies for historic structures.

After 1980, cultural resource management at Hanford was delegated to contractors, with the Department of Energy's Richland Office in an oversight role. Plant locations and waste disposal sites were closely monitored as construction work progressed. The U.S. Army Corps of Engineers and Washington State Department of Transportation continued conducting surveys for small development projects. Control was again centralized in the mid-1980s, prompted by increasing concern on the part of Indian tribes, the Washington State Historic Preservation Officer, and professional archeologists. Elevation of treaty Indian tribes and the state of Washington to "Affected Party" status under the Nuclear Waste Policy Act and selection of the Hanford site as a nuclear waste repository were what moved Hanford officials to centralize archeological management. Department of Energy initiated a cultural resources management program under the Site Management Division in autumn 1986. At this same time, the Sitewide Service Assessment Program allocated funds to the Pacific Northwest Laboratory to create a Hanford Cultural Resources Center, which would maintain an archeological data base and provide technical support for Department of Energy.

A full-time staff of cultural resource specialists were hired in 1987 as the Hanford Cultural Resources Laboratory, which established procedures for compliance with cultural resource laws prior to any earth-disturbing activity. Procedures were developed for treatment of human remains, and consultation with Indian tribes was made mandatory for the Richland Office pursuant to the American Indian Reli-

gious Freedom Act, Archaelogical Resources Protection Act, and 36 CFR 800. The Hanford Laboratory developed the Hanford Cultural Resources Management Plan in consultation with the Wanapam, Yakima, Umatilla, Nez Perce, Palouse, and Confederated Colville Tribes, the Washington State Historic Preservation Officer, and the Advisory Council for Historic Preservation (Chatters 1989). The plan made explicit procedures and guidelines for resource identification, evaluation, protection, and preservation, and for interaction with Indian tribes over issues of traditional importance.

Consultation with Native American groups became an integral part of the Hanford site cultural resources program (Chatters 1992:84). Reports that show potential impact to cultural resources are sent to tribal organizations and councils for review and comment. Efforts are made to elicit information on traditional uses of the area and sites. Such interaction has demonstrated the importance of the Hanford area for local Native American groups. The area plays a significant part in the origin mythology of the Washat religion. From the 1960s through the 1970s most initiatives for protection of archeological resources came from outside Hanford. It was only with passage of the Nuclear Waste Policy Act and subsequent directives from Department of Energy that compliance procedures were formally put in place.

This overview of archeology at the Hanford site is informative for understanding the changing nature of archeological research since the 1980s. Passage of significant legislation and established precedents dictating implementation of procedures set up to comply with federal and state mandates has transformed the character of archeology and placed Native American groups in the political spotlight. The single, overriding piece of legislation that served as a political hammer in the 1990s was the Native American Graves Protection and Repatriation Act, passed as federal law in 1990. It establishes Native American rights to claim and secure culturally affiliated human remains and objects of special cultural patrimony or sacredness, as legislatively defined. This law also requires that inventories be made of human remains and sacred objects in federal agencies and federally funded museums and institutions. An oversight committee was established to monitor and review the implementation of the inventory and identification process and repatriation required under this law.

Archeological research on the Plateau in the 1990s was subject to political factors. Laws have been passed and precedents established that concretely link Native Americans, archeologists, and anthropologists. Archeological research and Native American interests were the subject of anthropological study. Heritage programs have become the principal focus, and archeological fieldwork is mostly confined to compliance work for culture resource management. "Research" has for several decades been a poor term seen to be underpowered compared to compliance and management. Many of these management summaries and mitigation reports fail at synthesis. Most contemporary archeological studies cite synthetic work of years before (Nelson 1969; Leonhardy and Rice 1970 for the southern Plateau). Knowledge from work in mitigation is held to be incremental and additive in nature, with archeologists and anthropologists merely adding positive bits to the building knowledge base, a base laid out in the culture-historical framework of the 1960s (cf. Lohse 1994).

Anthropology in the 1990s

Most work at Simon Fraser University, Burnaby, British Columbia; the University of Idaho, Moscow; and Washington State University, Pullman, was aimed at retrieving information in the wake of developments impacting the archeological resource base and at assessing the character of Native American societies within American society. Four dissertations and theses have examined acculturation processes on the northern Plateau: Winter (1996) on archeological and ethnological collections in Canadian repositories; Beram (1990) on the management of archeological resources in the Canadian Capital Regional District Parks system; Spurling (1986) on archeological resource management in western Canada; Nelles (1984) on the sociology of archeological knowledge or the fit of archeology, myth, and oral tradition. Masters' theses aimed at understanding the contemporary include: Kawamura (1995) on Nez Perce determination of ethnic identification, Owens (1976) on the historical and theoretical examination of nativism, Shawley (1975) on changes in Nez Perce dress, Woolums (1972) on the history of Indian education programs, and Tokle (1970) on motifs in Idaho Indian myths. Other graduate work included: Fortier (1995) on Coeur d'Alene interaction with Jesuit priests; Tanimoto (1994) on Nez Perce elders and enculturation; Dahl (1990) on issues of sovereignty and ethnicity on the Colville Reservation; Ackerman (1982) on Plateau sexual equality; Giniger (1977) on female status within Plateau tribes; Marshall (1977) on Nez Perce social

groups related to ecology; Pembroke (1976) on conflict and confrontation in Lower Kootenai society; Coburn (1975) on Plateau pictographs and myth; Johnson (1975) on the role of phonetic details in Coeur d'Alene language; Brunton (1974) on the Kootenai stick game; Finster (1973) on Nez Perce beadwork; Blaundau (1972) on Nez Perce on the Colville Reservation from 1885–1968; Clark (1971) on the public image of Washington State archeology; Schultz (1971) on acculturation and religion on the Colville Reservation; Brunton (1968) on Plateau ceremonial integration; Ross (1967) on factionalism on the Colville Reservation; Schwede (1966) on Nez Perce settlement patterns; Baenen (1965) on Nez Perce fishing rights; and Harbinger (1964) on Nez Perce food plants important in cultural identification.

Unfortunately, far too few of these dissertations and theses are developed in publication for broader distribution, and often they are left uncited in the papers, books, and monographs developed for Plateau ethnology and archeology. The Plateau culture area sees considerable archeological research as part of normal mitigation in heritage resource management. Issues of development, site destruction, control of excavation and testing, and rights of ownership and access to collections are at stake. Resource management is such a concern that it oftentimes overwhelms other research efforts. Ethnologists are heavily engaged in the contemporary legal and political setting and often find more impetus for applied projects focused on Native American treaty rights or issues of acculturation like poor education than on preservation of traditional lifeways simply for the sake of enhancing knowledge. Both ethnologists and archeologists have had to become more creative in developing research opportunities in decades when the political and social mandates are so overwhelming, and in sociopolitical contexts where many potential Native American informants remain hostile and suspicious of the 'intent of outsiders. Tribal education programs, tribal museums, and tribal law offices all find uses for anthropological research.

Environment

JAMES C. CHATTERS

The hunting and gathering populations of the Plateau were strictly dependent on the products of the natural world. Sometimes they were able to manage that production to increase the distribution or yield of key foods (Marshall 1977), but the timing and potential habitat of even managed resources were largely constrained by the environment. Productivity was cyclic in both time and space, different food, material and medicinal resources becoming available at different seasons in distinct parts of the landscape. Physiography—the relief, slope, aspect, geology and elevation of the environment—soil characteristics, and climate constrained the hydrology and vegetation. All affected the distribution of terrestrial and aquatic faunas. Climatic variation also affected resources in the long term. As temperatures cooled, productive seasons became more seasonally restricted, with the opposite occurring when temperatures increased. Thus the Plateau can be thought of as an ever-changing mosaic of habitats for human beings and the resources upon which they depended for food, shelter, clothing, implements, medicine, and ceremony.

Physiography and Climate

The Plateau is a region of high relief, varying from lowland plains only 100 meters above sea level to precipitous peaks over 3,000 meters high. In general terms, it is a broad, open troughlike feature; the Cascade and Coast ranges form the west wall and the high Rocky Mountain ranges the east wall. The southern wall is the low crest of the Blue-Ochoco mountains. South of the Blue-Ochoco mountains, outside the trough, lie the Lava Plains and the Basin and Range physiographic provinces, the northwestern corners of which make up the homeland of the Klamath-Modoc people. From the Blue Mountains northward, forming the floor of the trough, and sloping upward from west to east, are the open, expansive Columbia Basin, the low mountains of the Okanogan Highlands, the rugged Thompson Plateau, and the high, rolling Fraser Plateau. Cultural and ecological transitions, rather than physiographic barriers, distinguish the northern limit of the region.

Plateau climate is a mix of continental and maritime influences. Moist maritime air moves inland from the North Pacific, often as cyclonic storms driven by the Aleutian Low pressure system, and is responsible for most of the precipitation the region receives. The Aleutian Low moves in a north-south axis with the seasons as the Subtropical Pacific High expands with summer warmth and contracts in winter. Therefore, most storms move through and precipitation falls in winter in southerly parts of the region, but the farther north one proceeds, the more frequent cyclonic storms become at other times of year. Continental air masses, which move south out of the arctic, tend to be drier and more often associated with high pressure systems. They bring fair weather and give the region its extreme temperatures both summer and winter. Occasionally, in summer, the Pacific Subtropical High will shift unusually far northward, deflecting marine air into southern parts of the Plateau and generating frontal storms.

The mountains that form the east and west edges of the Plateau block these various air masses and affect the local distribution of precipitation. As moist marine air encounters the Cascade and Coast ranges, it rises, cools, and releases moisture as rain and snow (orographic effect). As the air passes over the crest and loses altitude, it warms and its moisture retention capacity increases. The lower the elevation it sinks to, the drier the air becomes, creating a rain shadow effect to the east of all the highest mountain chains. Each time the air encounters another mountain chain, the orographic effect occurs. As a result, mountain peaks, particularly the Cascade Range and the highest ranges of the Rocky Mountains, receive the most precipitation, typically over 250 centimeters a year, and lower elevations receive progressively less. Where mountain ranges are adjacent and parallel, the rain shadow effect is minimized, and even low elevations receive the benefit of the moisture releasing effect of the mountain masses.

Ten physiographic areas comprise the Plateau: Coast Range, Cascade Range, Rocky Mountains, Fraser Plateau, Thompson Plateau, Okanogan Highland, Columbia Basin, Blue-Ochoco mountains, Lava Plains, and Basin and Range (fig. 1). Each area has unique topographic and geologic characteristics and exerts its own influence on local climates.

The Cascade and Coast mountains are series of north-south trending tectonic ridges 50 to 100 kilometers wide and ranging from 1,800 to 2,500 meters high in the north to 1,500 to 1,800 meters in the south. Rock types vary from sedimentary and metamorphic to extrusive igneous on a north-south axis; slopes are often precipitous and valleys are deep and narrow. Passes below 1,200 meters are common from 41° to 47°30′ and 49° to 51° north latitude, making possible frequent interaction between peoples of the Plateau and North-

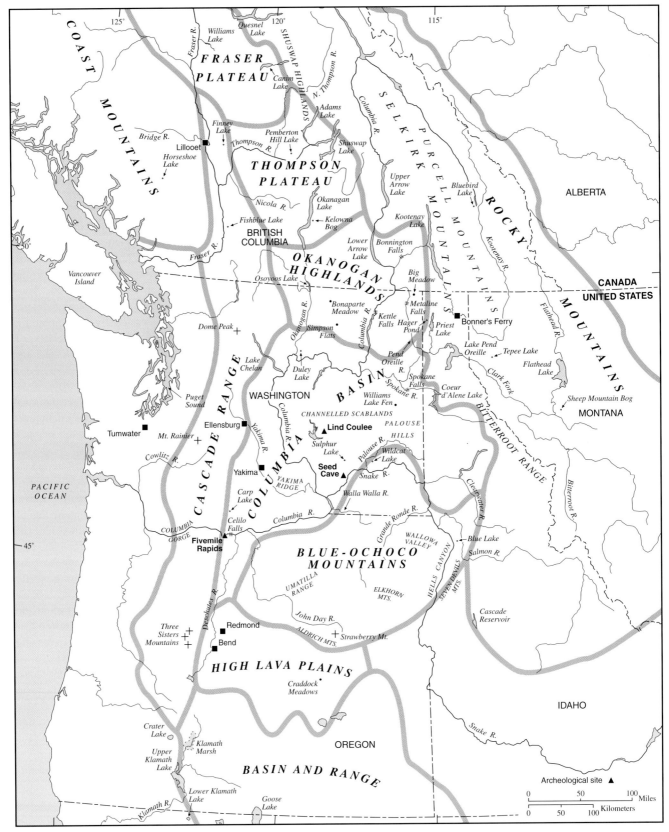

Fig. 1. Selected physiographic features of the Plateau.

Fig. 2. The Blue Mts. of Oreg. And Wash. left, Grand Ronde River, southeastern Wash. Deeply incised canyons characterize much of the Plateau creating a complex of habitats and a diverse, productive environment. right, Wallowa Lake in northeastern Oreg. Located in the bunchgrass steppe-forest interface, it is one of the most productive areas for deer, elk, plant resources, and sockeye salmon. Balsamroot is in the foreground. Photographs by John Clement, left, 1989; right, 1993.

west Coast. These mountain masses form a nearly continuous barrier to moist maritime air and receive precipitation in proportion to their elevation. Typically, northerly peaks receive over 250 centimeters of precipitation annually and the most southerly ridges less than 150. Moisture drops off sharply east of the crest, particularly south of 49° north latitude, such that foothills of the Cascade Mountains receive less than 40 centimeters. Areas with the heaviest precipitation receive it as snow, which mantles the middle to high elevations, impedes travel for people and game animals, and fills raging south and east-flowing streams when it melts in late spring and early summer. Two low areas, each below 1,200 meters and approximately one-half degree latitude wide, breach this barrier, one between 49° and 49°30′ and the other between 45°30′ and 46° north latitude. Marine air, warm in winter, cool in summer, passes eastward through each gap; waters of the Fraser and Columbia rivers pass westward at near sea level through gorges bearing their names.

The Columbia Basin, Okanogan Highland, and Fraser and Thompson plateaus that floor the intermountain trough differ in topography and climate. The Blue Mountains are a complex highland of folded and faulted uplifts of various ages and orientations, between which lie broad, structural basins. Included among them are the Elkhorn, Umatilla, Ochoco, Aldrich, Strawberry, Wallowa, and Seven Devils mountains; the largest valleys are the Grand Ronde and Wallowa (fig. 2). Most mountains are of moderate slope and rise to 1,800 to 2,100 meters. The Wallowas reach 2,900 meters, and peaks of the Seven Devils are even higher. Valley elevations are typically 750–900 meters. Orographic effects in summer and winter bring high precipitation to the mountains and relief from surrounding aridity for the valleys. Precipitation over the upland is 40 to 80 centimeters, and most areas are freeze free for 90 to 150 days. Unlike the

rest of the region, the Blue-Ochoco mountains receive a significant amount of precipitation in late spring and summer owing to the development of convection storms from moist marine air crossing the southern Cascade Mountains and passing through the Columbia Gorge. The most striking feature about this landform is Hells Canyon (fig. 3), an over 2,000-meter deep defile eroded by the northward course of the Snake River. At approximately 200-meter elevation, the floor and walls of this gorge are intensely hot in summer but provide an oasis of warmth in the winter from the colder conditions of the surrounding mountains.

The Columbia Basin is the lowest landform of the region, rising from 100 meters near the confluence of the Snake and Columbia rivers to 600 meters along the mountain fronts. Aside from a series of low ridges (Yakima Folds) near west center, this sequence of horizontally stratified basalts tends to be a gently rolling to level plain that rises gradually in all directions. Much of the surface is mantled by windblown loess, which has been deeply eroded in the northeast by catastrophic glacial floods released up to 40 times from Glacial Lake Missoula (Waitt 1980). These floods eroded deep, vertical-walled coulees called the Channelled Scablands, and river entrenchment has carved sheer-walled canyons, often over 150 meters high, around the north, west, and south edges of the plain. Petrified wood and vitrified diatomaceous earth exposed in the interbeds between basalt flows are the primary tool stone of this area. Lying in the rain shadow of the Cascade Mountains, the Columbia Basin receives only 16 to 30 centimeters of precipitation. Most areas receive their precipitation as winter rain and snow, but the Palouse Hills, which lie just north of the Blue Mountains, receive a secondary peak of spring and summer moisture from thunder storms that form along the Blue Mountains. The Columbia Basin is the warmest part of the Plateau; mean temperatures range from above -5°C in January to above 20°C in July. The freeze-free period is over 120 days throughout the area, and 150 to 210 days in the southwestern half. A band that stretches along the north edge of the Blue-Ochoco mountains, including the canyons of the middle Columbia and lower Snake rivers, averages above 0°C in January due to the passage of warm maritime air through the Columbia Gorge.

The Okanogan Highland is a series of north-south ridges and narrow plateaus that separate the Columbia and Thompson plateaus. These ancient highlands of metamorphic and granitic rock (sometimes referred to as Cascadia) were overridden by glacial ice during the Pleistocene, leaving them low, rounded, and often bare of soil. Although higher peaks occur, elevations are typically below 1,500 meters, which minimizes the orographic influence on precipitation and keeps temperatures relatively high. Although temperature and precipitation vary with altitude, western parts of the highland have 90–120 freeze-free days per year and less than 40 centimeters of precipitation, higher eastern ridges receive up to 40 centimeters of precipitation and have fewer than 90 freeze-free days. The valley of the Okanogan River, which flows southward along the western edge of the Highland, lies below 200 meters and is drier and warmer than the surrounding upland.

The Thompson Plateau is similar, although deeply incised stream valleys increase vertical relief and climatic variability. Repeated glaciation and millions of years of erosion have reduced multiple tectonic ridges into low, gently sloping mountains and broad, till-filled valleys and upland basins. Elevations are typically between 600 and 1,500 meters; a few higher summits reach above 1,800 meters. The forks of the Thompson River follow ancient courses through glacial till and sedimentary and granitic rocks in valleys below 600 meters. Long reservoir-like lakes fill upper valleys of the Thompson River basin and the upper Okanogan River basin, including the Shuswap Lakes and Lake Okanogan. The rain shadow effect of the Coast and Cascade mountains combines with low elevation to make this the warmest, driest area north of the Columbia Basin ("Shuswap," fig. 2, this vol.). Precipitation is less than 40 centimeters over much of the area, increasing with elevation as one moves west or up the mountain slopes. The Thompson River valley and areas around the Shuswap and Okanogan lakes are freeze free for over 140 days of the year, and much of the surrounding upland has over 100 freeze-free days. July temperatures are 16° to over 22°C; January means range from -5 to -15°C.

The level to rolling lowland between the Coast and Rocky Mountains is known as the Fraser Plateau. Almost entirely below 600 meters, it lies in the rain shadow of the Coast Range and precipitation is typically 30 to 40 centimeters annually. However, because of its latitude temperatures are cooler summer and winter. Except along the canyon of the Fraser River, the Fraser Plateau experiences fewer than 100 frost-free days. January and July means are below -10°C and above 18°C, respectively.

The Rocky Mountains are a broad series of uplands and valleys made up of two landform types. In their south and west extent, and including the Clearwater and Salmon rivers, the Rocky Mountains consist of irregular ridges and narrow stream valleys eroded from the granitic rocks of the domelike Idaho Batholith. To the north and east are northwest-southeast trending folded and faulted ridges, including the Selkirk, Shuswap, Purcell, and Rocky Mountain ranges. Elevations often reach over 3,000 meters. Principal ridges are separated by structural troughs forming valleys like the Rocky Montain Trench, and the Flathead, Bitterroot, and Kalispel valleys, which are 10–40 kilometers at their widest. All contain large streams, and many contain extensive reservoir-type lakes such as Flathead, Kootenay, Arrow, and Pend Oreille. As air crossing the interior plateaus rises against the Rocky Mountain ridges, it cools and releases

Fig. 3. Rugged Plateau terrain. left, Imnaha Canyon, with Hells Canyon in the distance, northeastern Oreg. In the foreground is the lithosolic habitat, which produces a wide variety of root sources. right, Shrub steppe in the central Columbia Basin, the most arid part of the Plateau with about 15 cm of precipitation per year. Photographs by John Clement, left, 1987; right, winter 1979.

150–250 centimeters of precipitation, most of it in winter as snow. Valleys in the rain shadow of the highest ridges, such as the Clark Fork and Flathead, can receive as little as 30 centimeters. Temperatures are highly variable with altitude, but overall this area is cold. Only the Flathead Valley and portions of the Kootenay Valley have over 100 frost-free days per year. Most of the area north of 49° north latitude receives fewer than 60 frost-free days.

Sources on physiography and climate are Barry and Chorley (1968), Farley (1979), Jackson (1985), Phillips (1965), Rosenfeld (1985), and U.S. Geological Survey (1968).

Surface Water

Surface water runoff in the region results primarily from snow melt. Most precipitation that falls in the warmer seasons of the year is either evaporated or trapped and immediately transpired by plants. Consequently, the waters that coalesce into the Plateau rivers derive from the areas of deepest snow cover: the North Cascades, Coast Range, and, most important, the many high ridges of the Rocky Mountains. Because of their origin in snowmelt, nearly all streams have an annual flow distribution with a strong peak between May and July. The Fraser River, for example, has a minimum flow near its mouth of around 2,500 cubic meters per second between December and April, rises swiftly to nearly 12,500 in June, and declines to 3,500 by September. This snowmelt peak, or freshet, is even more pronounced in smaller Rocky Mountain rivers, such as the South Thompson and Kootenay, the flows of which rise by factors of 10 to 18 during the freshet. Only the Deschutes and Klamath rivers, which drain the Lava Plains south of the Blue Mountains, deviate from this pattern, having their highest flows in winter and early spring.

Forested watersheds and a snowmelt origin keep the waters clean and cold and the stream beds lined primarily with gravel. Grass or steppe watersheds permit faster, often-catastrophic runoff and allow fine sediment to be carried into stream beds (Schumm and Brakenridge 1987). The absence of woodland borders (figs. 4–5) allows the sun to raise water temperatures.

The Columbia and Fraser rivers drain over 95 percent of the land surface. Each begins in the Rocky Mountain Trench, deriving its flow from the snow packs and ice fields of the Rocky and Purcell mountains. Each flows north, then exits the Rocky Mountains, and flows on southward across drier lowlands. The Columbia and its largest upper tributaries, the Kootenay (fig. 5), Pend Oreille-Clark Fork, and Spokane rivers flow through immense oligotrophic lakes, the largest of which, Arrow and Kootenay lakes, are over 200 kilometers long. Smaller lakes occur on upper and middle reaches of the Quesnel and Thompson rivers (the major eastern tributaries of the Fraser), and on the Okanogan River. The Snake River, from the Idaho Batholith region and Central Rocky Mountains, and streams from the Blue-Ochoco mountains add their

Fig. 4. Yakima River between Yakima and Ellensburg, Wash. Note the sparse vegetation. Photograph by Jill Sabella, 1993.

flows before the Columbia turns west toward the sea. The Columbia's mean flow is over 5,600 cubic meters per second; the Fraser's, 3,600.

Numerous falls and cataracts punctuate the flows of the Columbia and Fraser river systems. Some of the highest falls, Metaline on the Pend Oreille River, Bonnington on the Kootenai River, and Spokane on the Spokane River block anadromous fish from much of the eastern Columbia River basin. The largest of the less limiting cataracts on the Columbia are Fivemile Rapids and Celilo Falls (fig. 6) near the Columbia Gorge, and Kettle Falls below the confluence of the Columbia and Pend Oreille rivers.

The Klamath River drains the southwestern part of the Klamath-Modoc country flowing through the deeper Upper Klamath Lake and draining shallower Lower Klamath Lake en route to the Pacific. Unlike the reservoir lakes of the northern systems, the Klamath Lakes, and nearby basin-type Goose Lake are shallow, warm, and productive, with extensive marshes.

Water, readily available throughout the mountainous regions where numerous small perennial streams occur, was not a limit to human settlement there. However, the Columbia Basin contains little surface water away from the Columbia and Snake rivers, and what is present after late spring is largely restricted to seeps and potholes. Human activities were thus restricted to the vicinity of these water sources, which would vary with changes in the ground water table.

Sources on surface water are Farley (1979) and Muckleston (1985).

Vegetation

Temperature and the amount of precipitation, both mean annual and seasonal, and whether precipitation falls primarily as rain or snow determine the distribution of plant species and communities. The driest and coldest terrestrial environments support steppe and meadow communities,

Fig. 5. Columbia River and its tributary the Kootenay. left, Panoramic view of the section of the Columbia River that is the spawning habitat of the fall chinook salmon. right, Kootenay River, east of Bonner's Ferry, Idaho. This area of dense hemlock forests is the least productive for hunter-gatherers. Photographs by James Chatters, left, 1989; right, 1995.

Fig. 6. Celilo Falls, Oreg., with Wash. on the far side. On the right is the Spokane, Portland, and Seattle Railway train coming from Bend, Oreg. In the center is Tumwater fishwheel owned by the Seufert Bros. Co. The canal, highway, and railroad were all on Seufert Bros. Co. land. Photograph by Gladys Seufert, early 1950s.

which consist of grasses, herbs, and shrubs, while conifer-dominated forests inhabit moister environments. Ecologists recognize scores of habitat types (Daubenmire and Daubenmire 1968; Daubenmire 1970; Franklyn and Dyrness 1973; Krajina 1976), which can be simplified into seven groups: shrub steppe, bunchgrass steppe, woodland transition, xeric montane forest, mesic montane forest, subalpine forest, and montane meadows (fig. 7).

Shrub Steppe

An association of shrubs and bunch grasses inhabits most of the western Columbia Basin, Lava Plains, and Basin and Range provinces. The most common association is the big sagebrush-bluebunch wheatgrass (*Artemisia tridentata* and *Agropyron spicatum*) habitat type (Daubenmire 1970), which occupies the most arid settings (fig 3). Cooler, more mesic areas in the northern Columbia Basin and lower flanks of the Cascade Range support a three-tip sagebrush/Idaho fescue (*Artemisia tripartita/Festuca idahoensis*) habitat type, which contains a wide variety of perennial forbs, notably the culturally important yellowbells (*Fritillaria pudica*) and balsamroot (*Balsamorhiza* spp.).

Distinct communities occur on sandy, rocky, or wet soils. Bitterbrush (*Purshia tridentata*), Indian ricegrass (*Oryzopsis hymenoides*), and needle and thread grass (*Stipa comata*) inhabit stabilized and partially active sand dunes. Shallow and stony soils have either wild buckwheats (*Eriogonum* spp.) or stiff sagebrush (*Artemisia rigida*), in association with Sandberg bluegrass (*Poa sandbergii*) and an array of edible-rooted forbs, including bitterroot (*Lewisia rediviva*), wild onions (*Allium* spp.), and various members of the genus *Lomatium* (*L. canbyi, L. farinosum, L. macrocarpum, L. grayi*). Saltbrush (*Atriplex nuttallii*), shadscale (*A. confertifolia*), and spiny hopsage (*A. spinosa*) occupy saline and alkaline soils in the driest parts of the region. Garlands of serviceberry (*Amelanchier alnifolia*), mock orange (*Philadelphus lewisii*), wax currant (*Ribes cereum*), and chokecherry (*Prunus virginiana*) grow around the edges of talus slopes, where they tap water condensed and trapped by the openwork rock. In periodically moist soils with moderate salinity the giant wildrye (*Elymus cinereus*) occurs with greasewood (*Sarcobatus vermiculatus*) and halophytic grasses. Moist, more neutral soils along stream channels and marshes are inhabited by willows (*Salix* spp.), black cottonwood (*Populus balsamifera* ssp. *trichocarpa*), water hemlock (*Cicuta douglasii*) and, from the Okanogan basin southward, Indian hemp (*Apocynum cannabinum*). Marshes, in this and other warmer zones, contain sedges (*Carex* spp.), rushes (*Juncus* spp.)(fig. 8), cattail (*Typha latifolia*), and tule (*Scirpus acutus*); the last two were important construction and bedding materials.

Bunchgrass Steppe

Two common bunchgrass communities occur. The bluebunch wheatgrass–Idaho fescue type occurs in the regions with higher late spring precipitation, around the Blue-Ochoco mountains, north into the southeastern Columbia Basin, and in a few valleys of the Thompson Plateau and Fraser River valley. Species diversity is low; secondary plants include the rabbitbrush (*Chrysothamnus nauseosus*), and a few perennial forbs, such as yellowbells and balsam-

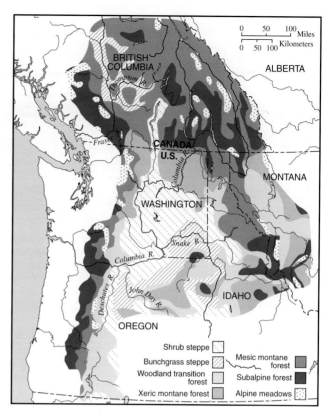

Fig. 7. Vegetation regions of the Plateau.

root. Nearly pure stands of hackberry (*Celtis douglasii*) occur on alluvial fans and along streams.

In the northeastern Columbia Basin are communities dominated by Idaho fescue and common snowberry (*Symphoricarpos albus*) or wild roses (*Rosa* spp.). These communities are known as meadow steppes due to their diverse assortment of perennial forbs, such as lupines (*Lupinus* spp.), asters (*Aster* spp.), and balsamroot (Daubenmire 1970). Moist slopes and stream bottoms (riparian zone) support an association of black hawthorn (*Crataegus douglasii*), quaking aspen (*Populus tremuloides*), red osier dogwood (*Cornus stolonifera*), serviceberry, and chokecherry.

Moist, grassy meadows in the higher portions of these communities and the drier forests contain a variety of edible forbs. In the Rocky Mountains and in western parts of the Plateau from the Okanogan Highland southward, common camas (*Camassia quamash*) (fig. 9) often occurs in dense concentrations along with wild onions (Statham 1975). In the Thompson Plateau, the waterleaf (*Hydrophyllum capitatum*), chocolate lily (*Fritillaria lanceolata*), tiger lily (*Lilium columbianum*), and spring beauty (*Claytonia lanceolata*) are the common edibles (Pokotylo and Froese 1983).

Woodland Transition

Throughout most of the Plateau, the woodland transition zone consists of an open forest of ponderosa pine (*Pinus ponderosa*) with a shrubby or herbaceous understory. Other

Fig. 8. Klamath Marsh, Winema Natl. Forest, south-central Oreg. In the foreground are bullrushes, an important resource. Photograph by John Jones, 1995.

conifer and deciduous species are often associated, including the garry oak (*Quercus garryana*) along the east flank of the southern Cascade Range, and lodgepole pine (*Pinus contorta*) and Douglas fir (*Pseudotsuga menziesii* var. *glauca*) elsewhere. Typical understories consist of low diversity associations dominated by common snowberry, bitterbrush, big sagebrush, Idaho fescue, blue wildrye (*Elymus glaucus*), or bluebunch wheatgrass. Edible forbs such as balsamroot, salsifies (*Tragopogon* spp.), triteleias (*Triteleia* spp.), yellowbells, and wild onion are found in the more open understories. Stands of quaking aspen, serviceberry, chokecherry, hawthorn, and dogwood grow in the riparian zone. The steppe-forest ecotone is often deeply convoluted. Ponderosa pine stands occur preferentially on stony soils, along streams (fig. 10), or on north facing slopes, whereas steppe floras extend deep into the forests on drier south facing slopes or wind-dried ridges (fig. 11). On the Lava Plains between the Deschutes and Klamath basins, western juniper (*Juniperus occidentalis*) occurs below and intermingled with the ponderosa pine.

A community known as the Cariboo Aspen (*Populus* spp.)–Lodgepole Pine biogeoclimatic zone (Krajina 1976) occurs as a species-poor forest over most of the Fraser Plateau. This plant community occurs where winters are severe and summers are hot and dry and is a more northerly zonal equivalent to the montane transition.

Xeric Montane Forest

Coniferous forests (fig. 12 left) found in mountainous areas with lower amounts of precipitation and light snowpacks are dominated by Douglas fir. The most commonly associated tree species are ponderosa and lodgepole pines on dry and burned-over sites, and western larch (*Larix occidentalis*) and white fir (*Abies concolor*) in moister areas. At higher elevations, particularly in the

north, quaking aspen, western birch (*Betula occidentalis*), paper birch (*B. papyrifera*), and rocky mountain maple (*Acer glabrum*) often occur. Dominant understory species in moister sites are common snowberry and Oregon boxwood (*Pachystima myrsinites*). Sedges and pinegrass (*Calamagrostis rubescens*) or Idaho fescue and bluebunch wheatgrass are typical understories along with big sagebrush or northern sage (*Artemisia frigida*) in more open forests on drier sites. Most edible species associated with this forest type occur in the herbaceous parks and are largely the same as those described for steppe zones. Wetlands and riparian habitats are typically inhabited by quaking aspen, paper birch, and alders (*Alnus* spp.).

In the southern parts of the Plateau, grand fir (*Abies grandis*) becomes a dominant tree in higher or cooler parts of the Douglas fir forest. The understory that occurs near the upper edge of this forest is much richer than that found elsewhere. Oregon boxwood and black huckleberry (*Vaccinium membranaceum*) occur with baldhip rose (*Rosa gymnocarpum*), prickly currant (*Ribes lacustre*), and dwarf bramble (*Rubus lasiococcus*).

Fig. 9. Camas meadow in the Cascade Mts., Wash. For camas preparation see "Ethnobiology and Subsistence," fig. 2, this vol. Photograph by James Chatters, 1986.

Fig. 10. Three Sisters Mountains in the distance with the Deschutes River in the foreground near Redmond, Oreg. Ponderosa pines follow the stream bed where trout flourish. Photographer and date not recorded.

Mesic Montane Forest

A forest of western hemlock (*Tsuga heterophylla*) and western red cedar (*Thuja plicata*) occurs in lower mountain slopes and valleys where maritime winter climate and high moisture trapped by the western crests of the Rockies create a warm, wet habitat like that of the northwest coast. This forest type also contains Douglas fir, lodgepole pine, western white pine (*Pinus monticola*), western larch, and grand fir, particularly in drier habitats or as successional species. The dense, diverse understories include dominants such as Oregon boxwood, devil's club (*Oplopanax horridum*), black huckleberry, lady fern (*Athyrium felix-femina*), and queen-cup beadlily (*Clintonia uniflora*).

Subalpine Forest

Subalpine forests are divisible into two groups, one found on the wetter eastern slopes of the Cascade and Coast mountain crests and wetter western slopes of the Rockies, and the other in the drier parts of those ranges. In the moister areas, dominant forest trees are mountain hemlock (*Tsuga mertensiana*) and Pacific silver fir (*Abies amabilis*), often associated with the trees of the upper montane forests. Understories consist of

Fig. 11. High steppe-covered terraces above the Fraser River near Lillooet, B.C. Douglas fir trees are in the foreground. Photograph by James Chatters, 1989.

woody shrubs, notably the big huckleberry. In dry areas the dominant trees are subalpine fir (*Abies lasiocarpa*) and Engelmann spruce (*Picea engelmannii*). Two common understory associations are beargrass (*Xerophyllum tenax*) (fig. 12 right) with big huckleberry (fig. 13), and grouseberry (*Vaccinium scoparium*) with common juniper (*Juniperus communis*), other huckleberry species, and sedges. These understory species are also the fire-successional species in the subalpine zone.

Montane Meadows

Herbaceous communities can occur at any elevation as part of a mosaic with any of the forest communities. They are found in dry and perennially moist sites at lower elevation and are the only floras above the timberline. Dry sites or balds, where soil moisture is reduced by slope, shallow soil depth, or exposure, consist of grasses and perennial shrubs and can occur at any elevation. In the subalpine and alpine zones, extensive grassy meadows interfinger with forest clumps or stands of huckleberries and other shrubs.

Mammals

The region supported a typical north temperate mammalian fauna, plus a few species more common to the Subarctic. The composition and behavior of the mammalian fauna varied widely.

Nine species of ungulate occurred in the Plateau (table 1), of which the most widely distributed were the elk and mule deer. These deer were most abundant in areas with a vegetation mosaic, where patches of forest alternate with grass or shrub land, particularly the woodland transition and drier portions of the xeric montane forest. Both species tend to occur in groups, particularly in winter when they move to lower elevations to avoid deep snow (Wallmo 1981). The mountain sheep, which was once common in rugged mountains and the canyon lands at lower elevations, is not only gregarious but also habitual in its movements, making mass kills possible. Pronghorn, found only in drier parts of the region, are also continuously gregarious and vulnerable to mass harvest. Mountain bison, which are less gregarious than their plains relatives, were common only in the Clark Fork and Flathead basins of the Rockies. Archeological finds (Schroedl 1973) and historical reports (Van Vuren 1987) also place them in the southeastern Columbia Basin and the Blue-Ochoco mountains. Other species are either solitary or occur at high elevations. Notably, the only species likely to frequent the western hemlock–western red cedar forest is the moose.

Other herbivorous mammals with economic potential were larger rodents and logomorphs. Hares and rabbits are active year-round and include snowshoe hare (*Lepus americanus*) in mountain forests, white-tailed jackrabbit (*L. townsendii*) in open grassland, and black-tailed jackrabbit (*L. californicus*) in shrub steppes. Various species of cottontail rabbit (*Sylvilagus* spp., *S. idahoensis*) occur in shrub steppe, riparian zones, and woodlands. Three species of marmot are present: the yellow-bellied marmot (*Marmota flaviventris*) in all drier vegetation zones of all but the most arid parts of the shrub steppe, the hoary marmot (*M. caligata*) in the alpine zone, and the woodchuck (*M. monax*) in the forested valleys between the Rocky and Purcell mountains. These and other members of the squirrel family hibernate and are available only from early spring to late summer or early fall. Also found are the red squirrel (*Tamiasciurus hudsonicus*), Douglas squirrel (*T. douglasii*), western gray squirrel (*Sciurus griseus*), and the flying squirrel (*Glaucomys volans*) in the evergreen forests, and various colonial ground squirrels (*Spermophilus* spp.) in steppe, grassland, and transitional forest. Muskrat (*Ondatra*

zibethicus) and beaver (*Castor canadensis*) occupy streams, lakes, and marshes throughout the region.

Most carnivores are found throughout the region, including the mountain lion (*Felis concolor*), lynx (*F. canadensis*), bobcat (*F. rufus*), river otter (*Lutra canadensis*), ermine (*Mustela erminea*), mink (*M. vison*), longtailed weasel (*M. frenata*), gray wolf (*Canis lupus*), and coyote (*C. latrans*). The wolverine (*Gulo luscus*) and red fox (*Vulpes vulpes*) occur in forest and alpine tundra. The badger (*Taxidea taxus*) is restricted to steppe and open forest environments, whereas fisher (*Martes pennanti*) and pine marten (*M. americana*) are restricted to denser forests.

Black bears (*Ursus americanus*), grizzly bears (*U. horribilis*), and raccoons (*Procyon lotor*) are omnivorous and can occur at higher densities than other carnivores. Raccoons occur in warmer forests and steppes south of 50° north latitude. Grizzlies are found primarily in alpine meadows and subalpine parklands and move to lower elevations in winter. The ubiquitous black bears are more social than most carnivores, congregating seasonally at salmon streams and berry patches (Jonkel 1967), where they constitute both a resource and a threat to human foragers.

Sources on mammals are Dalquest (1948), Farley (1979), Cowan and Guiguet (1973), Hall (1981), Ingles (1965), Matzke (1985), Schmidt and Gilbert (1978), and Thomas and Toweill (1982).

Birds

Over 300 bird species occur in the Plateau region at one season or another (Udvardy 1977, 1997). The ground birds, migratory

Fig. 12. The influence of fire on the forest. left, Xeric montane forest in northwestern Mont., showing how dense and restrictive mature forest can be without the intervention of fire. right, A recent burn in the hemlock forest of northwestern Mont. has allowed beargrass, shown in the foreground, and edible berries to flourish. Photographs by James Chatters, left, 1995; right, 1993.

Fig. 13. Blanche Tohet, Warm Springs Sahaptin, picking big huckleberries (*Vaccinium membranaceum*). They are abundant in open areas, especially previously burned areas. In the 1950s the location where she picked was a productive picking area; by the 1990s, the trees had grown back to such an extent that berries were few. Photograph by David and Kathrine French, 1951.

waterfowl, and birds of prey were of some significance to human inhabitants, although only the Klamath-Modoc made extensive use of them as a food source (Spier 1930).

Millions of ducks and geese stop during seasonal migrations at the Klamath Lakes and lakes in the southern Rockies (table 2). Klamath lakes are a bottleneck in the Pacific Flyway and receive the greatest concentrations of waterfowl in western North America (Bellrose 1976). The Klamath Basin and Fraser Plateau are also important breeding habitats for waterfowl. The Columbia Basin is of lesser significance for migration and breeding but is the region's most important wintering area.

Ground birds are divisible into steppe, forest, and alpine types. Sage grouse (*Centrocercus urophasianus*), sharp-tailed grouse (*Tympanuchus phasianellus*), and California quail (*Callipepla californica*) are limited to the shrub steppes and grasslands, and they form large flocks in winter and smaller flocks in summer. Sage and sharp-tailed grouse concentrate at traditional breeding grounds or leks in spring. Spruce (*Dendragrapus canadensis*) and blue grouse (*D. obscurus*) occupy subalpine and montane forests, respectively. Both are relatively solitary birds that frequent berry patches in summer and conifer groves in winter. Ruffed grouse (*Bonasa umbellus*) inhabit the forest transition of the entire region, while the mountain quail (*Oreortyx pictus*) is found in that habitat in only the Klamath Basin and Blue-Ochoco mountains. The white-tailed ptarmigan (*Lagopus leucurus*) occurs in alpine meadows.

Sources on birds are Bellrose (1976), Godfrey (1986), Johnsgard (1973), Larrison (1981), and Udvardy (1977, 1997).

Fishes

The cold, clear waters of the Columbia and Fraser river systems do not produce high populations of resident fishes, but they are rich in anadromous species. Exploitation of anadromous fish, notably salmonids, was a primary subsistence pursuit of many Plateau peoples and may have influenced their cultural development (Schalk 1977).

The principal anadromous fishes of the Columbia and Fraser systems are the chinook (*Oncorhynchus tschawytscha*) and sockeye salmon (*O. nerka*) and steelhead trout (*O. mykiss*). Chum salmon (*O. keta*) occurred prehistorically in the middle Fraser (Berry 1991) and coho (*O. kisutch*), which enter the rivers in summer and spawn in the early fall, occur to the middle reaches of the Columbia and Fraser rivers. Spring, summer, and fall races of chinook salmon occur, spawning during the fall in upper tributaries, and upper and lower reaches of major streams, respectively. Sockeye migrate from mid-summer to early fall, entering small streams above lakes to spawn and rearing in the lakes. Steelhead, which spawn in streams of all sizes and can tolerate low flows and warm temperatures, typically run between December and April in the Fraser system and in both winter and mid-summer in the Columbia and Snake rivers. Salmonids are impeded by falls and rapids, such as Celilo and Kettle Falls on the Columbia River. Natural falls, most notably Bonnington Falls on the Kootenay and Metaline Falls on the Pend Oreille-Clark Fork, prevent anadromous salmonids from reaching the Eastern Plateau. Runs become smaller and less reliable in an upstream direction as progressively fewer stocks pass through; fisheries of the lower reaches are thus the most productive and predictable, and fisheries of the upper tributaries the least. Salmon have adapted to the flow patterns of Plateau streams, requiring cold, clear, gravel-bottomed streams for hatching and rearing, and the annual pulse of snowmelt to wash young to the sea.

Other anadromous species are the white sturgeon (*Acipenser transmontanus*) and Pacific lamprey (*Entosphenus tridentatus*), both of which were found in the rivers during winter and early spring. Lamprey were important food fish on the middle and lower Columbia and Snake rivers (Hunn 1990), but sturgeon were of little importance to most people.

Larger resident fishes include the ubiquitous bridgelip (*Catostomus columbianus*) and largescale (*C. macrocheilus*) suckers, the northern squawfish (*Ptychocheilus oregonensis*), peamouth (*Meilocheilus caurinus*), chiselmouth (*Acrocheilus alutaceus*), mountain whitefish (*Prosopium williamsoni*), burbot (*Lota lota*), Dolly Varden trout (*Salvelinus malma*), and cutthroat trout (*Oncorhynchus clarki*). Longnose suckers (*C. catostomus*) occur in the Fraser and upper Columbia systems only; chiselmouth are limited to the Columbia system; and lake trout (*Salvelinus namaykush*) occur only in lakes of the northernmost Rocky Mountains in the Fraser and Thompson systems. The Tui chub (*Gila bicolor*) and endemic species of sucker are found only in the Klamath Basin. Landlocked species of sockeye salmon occur naturally in some lakes, and landlocked steelhead (rainbow trout) are ubiquitous. All resident species aggregate seasonally to spawn, all but the whitefish in shallow water gravel beds. Burbot spawn beneath winter ice at the shores of their lake homes; the rainbow trout, squawfish, chub, chiselmouth, and peamouth spawn in streams or lake shores in spring or early summer. Cutthroat trout spawn in early fall. Sucker runs, which occur from April through June, can be particularly productive and were an important source of protein in many parts of the Plateau (Hunn 1990; Spier 1930).

A source on fish is Wydoski and Whitney (1979).

Invertebrates

Mollusks and crustaceans are often abundant in parts of the region. Three large bivalves occupy Plateau rivers, each with a preferred habitat (Ingram 1948; Lyman 1980a). The freshwater pearl mussel (*Margaritifera falcata*) occurs in often-dense concentrations in swift, clear, cold, gravel-to-sand-bottomed streams and gravel or sand-bottomed oligotrophic lakes (Roscoe and Redelings 1964). *Gonidea angulata* prefers warmer temperatures and tolerates slower,

Table 1. Habitat and Behavior of Plateau Ungulates

Species	Habitat	Behavior	Distribution
Elk or wapiti (*Cervus elaphus*)	Grassland, open Ponderosa pine and Douglas fir forests using meadows and balds	Seasonal movements to lowlands; gregarious, forming especially large groups in winter pastures	Rocky Mts., Blue-Ochoco Mts., east flank of Cascade Range and adjacent grasslands; formerly on Fraser Plateau
Moose (*Alces alces*)	Montane forests, especially old burns, riparian zones, marshes	Solitary, seasonal moves only to avoid deepest snow	Common north of 50°N, also present in the Rockies and northern Cascades
Caribou (*Rangifer tarandus*)	Alpine tundra and subalpine parklands	Occur in small herds, may move into subalpine forests in winter	Rocky Mountain Ranges south to 51°N; Purcell Mts.
Mule deer (*Odocoileus hemionus*)	Any area with forbs, woody browse and nearby cover	Dispersed in summer, tend to concentrate at lower elevations in winter	Ubiquitous; most common in areas with forest-grass or shrub mosaic
White-tailed deer (*Odocoileus virginianus*)	Riparian zones in grassland, and montane and transitional forest	Territorial and solitary, may become concentrated in yards by deep snow	Ubiquitous in lowlands, most common in eastern parts of the Plateau
Bison (*Bison bison*)	Grasslands	Gregarious, forming small herds	Valleys of N. Rocky Mts., formerly in southeast Columbia Basin and Blue Mts.
Mountain sheep (*Ovis canadensis*)	Grassy slopes adjacent to steep terrain at any elevation	Gregarious at all seasons, make seasonal migrations on habitual routes	Ubiquitous where suitable habitat occurs
Mountain goat (*Oreamnos americanus*)	Roughest terrain generally at or above timberline	Females and young gregarious; males solitary	Cascade and Rocky Mts.
Pronghorn (*Antilocapra americana*)	Open shrub steppe and grassland	Form huge herds in winter; disperse into smaller groups in summer	Columbia Basin, Basin and Range, Lava Plains

more turbid flows and sand to silt bottoms (Vannote and Minshall 1982). Species of thin-shelled *Anodonta* species inhabit still waters and grow particularly rapidly in warm, algae-laden lakes and marshes. Large terrestrial snails are found in many areas. Crayfish are ubiquitous in rivers and lakes, and a wide variety of insects are found, most notably the grasshoppers. Grasshoppers can be abundant in the steppe zones during dry years.

Key Resource Environments

All vegetation types offer some edible medicinal or technologically useful plants and are habitat to some prey species. Even the dense, largely food-poor western hemlock–western red cedar forest offers the cedar bark, which is used for clothing, mats, and basketry, and light, strong, easily shaped wood. Closed forests are generally unproductive in both vegetable and animal resources; the majority of useful plants come from herbaceous and shrubby communities, which are also of the greatest importance to prey species, particularly ungulates. The most important of these are the stony soil, riparian, and talus garland communities of the steppe, wet meadows and marshes of lower elevation forests and steppe, the steppe or meadow forest ecotone, and the seral communities of the subalpine zone.

The perennial herbs that inhabit stony soils in the shrub steppe become green in early spring, then flower, go to seed, and die back in the span of two to three months. They are most efficiently collected in the later part of their active period, when skins slip easily from edible roots. For many this is after the seeds are set. Other species, like yellowbells, have vegetatively reproducing rootlets that are easily dis-

lodged. In the act of digging, gatherers dislodge and replant the seeds and vegetatively regenerating parts.

Moist meadows produce many large roots, particularly tiger lily, camas, wild onions (all members of the lily family), wild carrot, and thistle. The lilies and wild carrot grow in stands of multiple ages and are also best collected after seeds have set. This occurs at different times, depending on elevation and latitude, making it possible to gather roots from late spring well into summer. Root diggers will selectively remove larger plants and replant smaller individuals, ensuring future harvests and often enhancing a site's productivity. Where these meadows interfinger with forest, they provide both food and cover to deer.

Riparian floras in the steppe and forest transition zones, and the talus garlands of the steppe include numerous late-summer ripening, fruiting shrubs, including the hawthorn, serviceberry, chokecherry, dogwood, and currant. Wood of other species, particularly the mock orange and serviceberry have strong, straight, resilient stems that can be used for arrow shafts and other constructions. Riparian patches are home to white-tailed deer and cover for elk and mule deer.

Marshes and marsh edges offer Indian hemp, the fibers of which make a strong string used for nets, bowstrings, baskets, and mats. Hemp fiber was one of the most important trade commodities between the Plateau and Northwest Coast. Cattail has edible roots, seeds, and shoots and was used to make strong, durable mats for housing and bedding. Tules were used throughout the southern parts of the Plateau for the light, insulating mats that walled and lined the floors of dwellings. Willows were made into bows, baskets, traps, and the infrastructure of houses. Water parsnip (*Sium suave*) and cinquefoils (*Potentilla* spp.) have edible roots. Marshes are the most important resting and feeding areas for water-

Table 2. Waterfowl in the Plateau

	Klamath Basin	Columbia Basin	Southern Rocky Mt. lakes and rivers	Fraser Plateau
Transitory species	snow goose (*Chen cerulescens*) Canada goose (*Branta canadensis*) northern pintail (*Anas acuta*) northern shoveler (*Anas clypeata*) American wigeon (*Anas americana*)	northern pintail mallard (*Anas platyrhynchos*)	northern pintail	
Breeding species	Canada goose gadwall (*Anas strepera*) cinnamon teal (*Anas cyanoptera*) redhead (*Aythya americana*)	mallard cinnamon teal redhead canvasback (*Aythya valisineria*)		American wigeon gadwall Canada geese mallard redhead lesser scaup (*Aytha affinis*)
Wintering species		Canada goose American wigeon	American wigeon	

41

fowl and can be critical sources of drinking water for people and game animals.

The steppe-forest ecotone, whether at the lower forest border or in dry or seral patches of montane and transitional forests, is the most productive game habitat. Ponderosa pine woodlands and dry, open Douglas fir forests are historically the highest producers of deer and elk. Indigenous peoples periodically burned these areas to prevent the encroachment of closed forest and maintain prey populations.

Above the montane forests are seral communities of the subalpine zone with huckleberry and beargrass, and concentrations of bears, elk, and mule deer. People took advantage of the fact that understory species take over burned sites, maintaining extensive stands of huckleberries and beargrass in some mountainous areas by periodic burning, and at the same time maintaining forage for large prey (Franklin and Dyrness 1973). Huckleberries, which ripen in late summer and early fall, were collected in massive quantities; beargrass was used for the weft of coiled baskets by many Plateau peoples.

Clear, cold, gravel-bedded streams were also critically important. Although they contain some food directly available in mussels and resident fishes, such habitats are essential to the life cycle of salmon. Clean gravel beds on lake shores or streams are also necessary for spawning and rearing of most resident species.

Sources on plant uses are Hunn (1990), Turner (1979), and Turner, Bouchard, and Kennedy (1980).

Resource Variation in Space

The Plateau is divisible into four parts with different resource potentials and patterning. These are the Southern, Eastern, and Northern Plateau and the Klamath Basin. The southern Plateau, which is the Columbia River basin below Arrow and Osoyoos lakes and the falls of the Kootenay, Pend Oreille, and Spokane rivers, is a bowllike feature of lowland steppe traversed by immense rivers and surrounded by the forested Cascade, Rocky, and Blue-Ochoco mountains. As one moves in any direction from the lowest point in the bowl, the land rises, temperatures tend to decline, precipitation increases, and shrub steppe gives way to grassland, then to ponderosa pine forest, mixed conifer forest, subalpine forest, and occasionally alpine tundra. The resource year begins in the lowlands with the greening of the steppe and flowering of the root species of stony soils. Greening and ripening of vegetable foods then proceeds upslope into camas meadows in grassland and forest and finally to the berry fields of the subalpine zone in late summer. Salmon runs also begin in the lowlands and move upstream in successive waves beginning in April and ending at spawning grounds from September through November. Snow in the highlands brings big game down-slope, concentrating them in lowland meadows and along the forest

edge for the winter. The Blue-Ochoco mountains are the most productive of game (Matzke 1985) because their islandlike character and multiple ridges create deeply involuted, and thus extensive, steppe-forest ecotones.

The Northern Plateau includes the upper Okanogan River and the lower parts of the Fraser River system, an area of moderate relief with deeply incised valleys. Narrow bands of grassland and pine woodland follow lowland streams, but most of the region is covered by evergreen forests. Unlike the Southern Plateau, with its concentric rings of steppe and forest zones, this region consists of multiple sets of forested ridges and woodland or grassy valleys. Thus, no spot on the Fraser or Thompson river is far removed from the full range of resource habitats. This happy circumstance is counteracted by the colder northern climate, which shortens the productive seasons and lengthens the resource-poor winter portion of the annual cycle, and by the fact that dense forest covers a far greater part of the landscape here than on the southern Plateau. Modern wildlife counts show that large game production in this region is far exceeded by that of the Blue-Ochoco mountains (Matzke 1985; Farley 1979). Fisheries are similar to those of the Columbia system, although the majority of the run occurs in late summer and early fall and consists in the greater part of lake-rearing sockeye salmon.

Upstream of the falls on the Columbia River system is the Eastern Plateau, with its high, precipitous mountain ridges and broad valleys, including the upper reaches of the Columbia and Kootenay rivers and the Clark Fork and Spokane River basins. Precipitation on the mountains, most of it snow, is the highest in the Plateau. The high altitude and continental influence make the climate the coldest; productive seasons are short. Southern parts of this region have extensive moist meadows and ponderosa pine forests. Production of game and roots is high, but anadromous fish are absent. Subalpine zones, with their fruiting shrubs, cover large areas, especially to the north. As on the Northern Plateau, extreme relief brings most resources into close proximity.

The Klamath Basin is distinct from the rest of the Plateau. Consisting of large lakes and an extensive pine woodland bordering the vast steppes of the Great Basin, the area offers extensive deer and elk populations, spring runs of large suckers, seasonal migrations and the eggs and young of waterfowl, and the roots of meadows and stony soils. Its low latitude is offset by a high altitude, making the unproductive seasons comparable in length to the Eastern Plateau.

Paleoenvironments

Evidence for changing environmental conditions throughout the Holocene is available from numerous sources. Reconstructions of vegetation patterns presented here come from fossil pollen and plant macrofossil deposits (summarized in Baker 1983; Barnosky, Anderson, and

Bartlein 1987; Hebda 1982; Mathewes and King 1989; Mehringer 1985), subfossil mammal bone deposits (Chatters 1986; Gustafson 1972; Livingston 1985; Lyman and Livingston 1983; Schroedl 1973; R.S. Thompson 1985), and rates of surface erosion (which indicate variations in plant cover) (Mehringer 1985a; Fryxell 1963). Changing temperatures are inferred from glacial geology (Osborn and Luckman 1988; Davis 1988; Burke and Birkeland 1983), fossil timberline reconstructions (Luckman and Kearney 1986; Clague and Mathewes 1989), rates of rock spall deposition in caves (Fryxell 1963; Thompson 1985), and indirectly from vegetation distributions. Glaciers respond to changes in the temperature-precipitation balance; timberlines rise with summer temperatures at a rate of approximately 170 meters per degree Centigrade; and rock spalling occurs when winter temperatures lie for long periods between -5 and -15°C (Walder and Hallet 1985). Oxygen isotope ratios from basin-type lake sediments indicate the balance between runoff and evaporation (Forbes 1986), from which wet and dry intervals are distinguished. Shifts in levels of pothole lakes in the Plateau (Mathewes and King 1989; Mehringer 1985) and nearby Northern Great Basin (Wigand 1985) and radiocarbon ages of confined ground water (Silar 1969) are similarly used, but they also are indicative of the timing of precipitation. Precipitation falling in cooler months, when plants are inactive and evaporation is at a minimum, is more likely than warm season precipitation to recharge ground water. Rising water levels and increased ground water recharge rates also mean more water reached the surface as springs in arid parts of the Plateau. Surface water hydrology has been interpreted from geomorphology and characteristics of anthropogenic assemblages of freshwater mussels (Chatters and Hoover 1992; Cochran 1988; Hammatt 1977). Taxonomic composition of bivalve faunas varies with stream bed structure (see Lyman 1980a) and the frequency of bed aggradation (Vannote and Minshall 1982); the timing of mussel collection is evidence for periods of low stream flow (Chatters 1986), and growth rates are closely correlated with water temperatures. Surface water hydrology affects the productivity of anadromous fisheries (see Chatters et al. 1991) and is indirectly used here to estimate potential salmon productivity. Models of the solar energy reaching the earth have been developed based on reconstructed variations in the earth's orbital cycles (Kutzbach and Geuter 1986; Kutzbach 1987) and are used in support of climatic interpretations made from environmental data.

Although climates were continually changing, marked, approximately synchronous transitions occur throughout the region at 7500–7000 B.C., 4300 to 4500 B.C., 2500 B.C., and 800 B.C. to A.D. 1. Less widespread or less pronounced changes occur at approximately 5800 B.C. and 3400 to 3000 B.C. Environmental reconstructions for these periods are based on the aforementioned sources, unless otherwise noted.

9,000–7500 B.C.

For much of the Plateau, this period is the warmest and driest of the Holocene. By 9000 B.C., glacial ice had melted from all but a few of the highest mountains and by 8200 B.C. it was gone (Clague 1981). Timberlines in the Coast Range and northern Rockies, as indicated by fossil wood and percentages of pollen in highland sites, had risen above modern levels by 8600 B.C. They were elevated 200 meters by the end of the period, showing summer temperatures were approximately 1.2°C higher than during the mid-twentieth century. Oxygen isotope ratios from Duley Lake, near the confluence of the Columbia and Okanogan rivers, reached their maximum, indicating the greatest rates of evaporation, highest temperatures of precipitation, or both. Few of the aquifers sampled in the Columbia Basin contained water of this age. High summer temperatures and rates of evaporation are consistent with Kutzbach's (1987) estimate that insolation reached its highest mid-summer levels during this period. During times when summer insolation is at a maximum in the northern hemisphere, winter insolation is at a minimum. Peak rates of rock spall deposition in Columbia Basin caves confirm that winters were intensely cold.

Grasses and other steppe plants dominated the regional flora. As far north as 51° north latitude (Hebda 1982) and as far east as Tepee Lake, Montana (Mack, Rutter, and Valastro 1983), grasses dominated the flora below 1,300 meters; at Craddock Meadow, near the southern edge of the Blue-Ochoco mountains, shrub steppe occupied land well above 1,650 meters (Wigand 1989). Low arboreal pollen percentages in the rugged Okanogan Highland indicate that few patches of forest existed, even on the highest ridges. Forests that were present, at least as high as 1,950 meters at Sheep Mountain Bog (Mehringer 1985) in the Clark Fork drainage, consisted of Douglas fir; high percentages of sagebrush pollen at that location probably indicate steppe at lower elevations. The driest parts of the region appear to have been the central and southwestern Columbia Basin, where sagebrush and chenopods were a major part of the steppe flora. Wettest conditions existed along the Coast Range, where open pine and Douglas fir forests existed at low elevations around Horseshoe and Fishblue lakes (Mathewes and King 1989), and as low as 1,000 meters near the Columbia and Kootenay headwaters, which had an open pine-juniper woodland (Hebda 1981). Only Kelowna Bog, on Lake Okanagan (Alley 1976), deviates from a general picture of warmth and drought. Dating problems, or perhaps the existence of a stagnant block of ice, may account for the anomalous low elevation occurrence of a spruce-fir forest. A reconstruction of the steppe forest boundary based on these observations indicates extensive steppes with forests confined to higher elevations.

Terrestrial fauna of the Columbia Basin was typical of early Holocene steppes, including elk, bison, deer, mountain sheep, and pronghorn. The ratio of elk to pronghorn along the lower Snake River was relatively high (Gustafson 1972), which is consistent with a grass rather than shrub-dominated steppe. *Bison antiquus* has been dated at about 7700 B.C. at the Lind Coulee site (Irwin and Moody 1978), but the similarity of associated artifacts to the much earlier Marmes horizon assemblages (Fryxell and Keel 1969) contradicts the late date.

The Fraser and upper Columbia rivers were still eroding through thick glacial outwash deposits. The Snake and lower Columbia rivers had begun aggrading floodplains by 9000 B.C., but geologic evidence from the Clearwater River (Ames, Green, and Pfoertner 1981) and a high frequency of *Gonidea* species among mussels found on the lower Palouse River (Lyman 1980a) indicate sandy, shifting river beds. Finds of salmon at Fivemile Rapids (Cressman et al. 1960) and the Milliken site (Borden 1975) show that some anadromous fish runs were viable in the Columbia and Fraser systems.

The occurrence of grass, high evaporation rates, cold winters, and lack of ground water recharge are evidence that atmospheric flow patterns may have differed from subsequent periods. Cold, dry winters and hot, moist springs and summers can account for this pattern (Chatters 1991), which resembles the more continental climate of the northern Plains (Petersen 1990).

7500 to 4400 B.C.

For the Thompson Plateau and northern Rocky Mountain ranges, 7500 to 7000 B.C. marks the beginning of an increase in effective precipitation. In the Columbia Basin and Okanogan Highland, however, conditions became more arid.

To the north, lower forest boundaries began a downslope shift. On the Thompson Plateau, Hebda (1982) estimates that the boundary between grassland and transitional woodland stood between 1,100 and 1,200 meters. Deer are the primary ungulates recorded (Rosseau et al. 1991). Hemlock pollen appeared sporadically in pollen sites west of the Fraser River, perhaps blown in from the west. Open ponderosa pine and Douglas fir forests replaced grasslands at sites in the western Rockies between 48 and 49° north latitude, which now stand in hemlock–red cedar forest. Ponderosa pine woodland expanded down the Cascade mountain slopes and engulfed Carp Lake (Barnosky 1985).

While an apparent rise in moisture occurred in the uplands, grasses were replaced by sagebrush steppe in the Okanogan Highland and eastern Columbia Basin, where conifers were still too far off to impact the pollen counts. Conditions in the Clark Fork basin remained unchanged. In the central Columbia Basin the proportions of sagebrush and ragweed (*Ambrosia* spp.), a colonizer of open soil, increased at Wildcat Lake (Mehringer 1991); the small mammal fauna from nearby Seed Cave contained high frequencies of Great Basin pocket mice (*Perognathus parvus*) (Thompson 1985), which thrive on open ground. Pronghorn increased at the expense of elk.

Timberlines remained high throughout this period, reaching elevations 300 meters above modern limits. Rock spalls became a less common component of Columbia Basin rockshelters, being replaced by windblown loess. Extensive tracts of sand dunes formed. Ground-water recharge increased in Columbia Basin aquifers, and oxygen isotope ratios declined at Duley Lake. Mountain glaciers were absent.

The coincident expansion of forests, lowering of oxygen isotope ratios, and ground-water recharge, indicating moister climates, seem to contradict expansion of the shrub steppe and dune formation, elevated tree lines, and the decline in rock spalling, which evince drought, warm summers and warmer winters, respectively. These disparities are accounted for by a change from continental to maritime climatic patterns, which include warmer, wetter winters. Such conditions have two effects. First, they promote xeric-adapted conifers and sagebrush, which have root systems capable of reaching water that infiltrates the soil while plants are dormant, over grasses, which have shallow root systems and can better use precipitation reaching them in the growing season (Petersen 1990). Second, they increase rates of ground-water recharge. No change in the amount of precipitation need be invoked.

Southern rivers underwent a brief episode of aggradation prior to 7000 B.C., but flows declined and generally high frequencies of *Gonidea* species mussel indicate channels remained sandy. Wind replaced water as a primary agent of deposition after 7000 B.C. The seasonality of mussel assemblages from the middle Columbia, which were collected as early in summer as mid-June (Chatters 1986), indicates the spring freshet was abbreviated and occurred as much as a month earlier than in modern times. Growth rates in the same assemblages were nearly double those found in later prehistoric specimens, showing much longer periods of warm water (Chatters 1992a). Vegetation cover indicates a reduction in probable runoff of at least 30 percent. Modeling of the impact of reduced stream flows on chinook salmon in the Yakima subbasin of the Columbia system indicates that fish runs would have been severely reduced from historic levels (Chatters et al. 1991).

Some analysts (Barnosky, Anderson, and Bartlein 1987; Mathewes and King 1989) see the major change in flora occurring at 5800 to 5500 B.C., at about the time of the Mount Mazama ashfall. Changes discernible at this time are often the second step in the apparent moistening of the northern highlands and drying of the lowlands. Among the changes indicating moistening at this time are a return of water to Simpson Flats and Bonaparte Meadows in the Okanogan Highland (Mack, Rutter, and Valastro 1978, 1979), the increase in hemlock, and the appearance of cedar pollen at sites along the Fraser Canyon, the appearance of low frequencies of Douglas fir in Finney and Pemberton Hill lakes on the Thompson Plateau, establishment of a lodgepole pine–birch forest at the Columbia-Kootenay headwaters (Hebda 1981), and the arrival of pine nearer 1,650 meters at Craddock Meadow in the Blue-Ochoco mountains (Wigand 1989). Sagebrush and other open-ground flora became more dominant at Williams Lake; the proportion of pocket mice increased at Seed Cave (R.S. Thompson 1985); and pronghorn increased relative to elk along the Lower Snake River. Dune activity and eolian deposition in rockshelters and lake basins intensified. There was a brief episode of erosion in small stream basins along the Columbia and Clearwater rivers coinciding with aggradation along the lower Okanogan River (Chatters and Hoover 1992).

4500–2500 B.C.

Evidence for cooling is widespread beginning between 4300 and 4500 B.C. Timberlines began to descend and there was an apparent development of a small glacier on Mount Garibaldi in the Coast Range (Ryder and Thompson 1986). Cooling brought an increase in effective moisture and vegetation density in the steppe zone at Williams Lake, occasioning a reduction in wind-deposited sediment in Wildcat Lake (Mehringer 1985) and permitting development of a paleosol on floodplains of the Snake and Columbia rivers (Cochran 1991; Hammatt 1977; Chatters 1984a). The grass understory disappeared from Douglas fir forests in the Fraser Valley, and forests farther west on the Thompson Plateau encroached farther downslope. Ponderosa pine forest invaded the upper Okanogan Valley around Kelowna Bog and slopes above Simpson Flats in the Okanogan Highland; pine pollen began to increase in other sites in the vicinity, reflecting the forest's presence. An increase in rates of ground-water recharge began in the Columbia Basin.

Effective moisture increased again sharply between 3400 and 3000 B.C. under continued cooler conditions. Alpine glaciers advanced shortly after this time on Dome Peak in the North Cascade Range, overriding a 5,000-year-old stump, but extended little beyond the twentieth-century ice margin (Miller 1969). Rock spalling increased slightly in Seed Cave, indicating occasional cold winters, and the timberline approached modern levels. Ground-water recharge rates rose rapidly on the Columbia Plateau. Pollen influx rates, which may result from higher plant productivity, increased at in several Okanogan Highland lakes as pine forests approached elevations of 400–600 meters around the rim of the Columbia Basin and encroached on former steppe land in the Blue-Ochoco mountains. At Sheep Mountain Bog, Douglas fir forest was invaded by spruce and fir of the subalpine zone. Forests of the Thompson Plateau closed, eliminating the last of the northern grasslands.

An episode of aggradation on the Columbia and Snake rivers began around 5000 B.C., coinciding with this rise in moisture availability. Growth rates in mussels from the middle Columbia River remained high and times of mussel har-

vest were restricted compared to the period before 4400 B.C. Together these data indicate increased frequencies of flooding, continued high water temperatures, and a later freshet. The timing of the freshet was comparable to the historic period, but water temperatures remained warmer.

Despite expansion of the forest, the climate of this period remained relatively warm. Evidence of this can be found in the existence of trees typical of the upper montane forest and the more xeric subalpine forests on the southwest flank of Mount Rainier where a mountain hemlock forest now grows (Dunwiddie 1986).

2500 to 800 B.C.

The climate cooled abruptly at between 2500 and 2100 B.C. and remained unusually wet. Rock spalls again dominated cave deposits; alpine glaciers advanced in all higher mountain ranges; mussel growth rates show a sharp decline in river temperature, which remained low thereafter. Ground water recharge reached maximum Holocene levels at around 2000 B.C., and oxygen isotope ratios declined, showing reduced temperature and/or lower evaporation rates. Subalpine forests moved downslope to 1,300 meters on Mount Rainier, near Simpson's Flat, and to as low as 1,100 meters in the three sites in what is now a hemlock-cedar forest. Douglas fir forests in the Fraser Valley and Thompson Plateau reached their maximum densities, and Douglas fir, hemlock, and red cedar pollen became more important at Carp Lake in the southwestern Columbia Basin (Barnosky 1985). Hemlock pollen reached Kelowna Bog and Bluebird Lake for the first time as the tree invaded the region east of the Fraser River. Pollen influx rates remained high in the Okanogan Highland and rose at Williams Lake, which had become enclosed by ponderosa pine forest. Pine marten and flying squirrel occur at 3,000-year-old Columbia River sites between the Spokane and Okanogan rivers (Chatters 1986; Livingston 1985), historically an area of artemisia steppe. Because this is the only time in the Holocene that these animals occur in that reach, it may indicate encroachment of conifer forest beyond historic limits and onto the lowlands to the south. Open pine–Douglas fir forests moved into the southeast corner of the Columbia Basin around Blue Lake, where fire frequencies were at a minimum (Smith 1983).

Mehringer (1985a) interprets the shrub-steppe vegetation around lakes in the central Columbia Basin as a three-tip sagebrush and Idaho fescue habitat type. The abundance of the vole (*Microtus* spp.), which requires dense cover, and paucity of the open-ground-dwelling pocket mouse in the microfauna of this era at Seed Cave (R.S. Thompson 1985) corroborate his conclusion.

Severe floods became uncommon in the Columbia system. A general rarity of *Gonidea* in mussel assemblages and the decline in growth rates indicates clear, cold, gravel-bottomed streams. Collection dates for mussels became further restricted, beginning as late as August, evidence the spring freshet began later or lasted longer than at any other time in the Holocene. Conditions were optimal for salmonid production, but the later freshet and colder waters would have meant abbreviated, intense, fish runs, at least in the Columbia system.

The climate of this period can be interpreted as the coldest and wettest of the Holocene. The continued existence of shrub steppe, further expansion of the evergreen forests, and high rates of ground-water recharge indicate that precipitation remained winter dominant; low timber lines, reduced evaporation rates, and rock spalling show that both summer and winter temperatures were low. Mehringer (1985a) calculates that the effective moisture required for the three-tip sage and Idaho fescue steppe at Sulphur Lake would be at least 25–30 percent above historic averages.

After 800 B.C.

Glaciers receded as temperatures warmed between 800 B.C. and A.D. 100, and modern vegetation distributions appeared. Subalpine forests again moved upslope at Hager Pond, Big Meadow, and Tepee Lake in the northern Rockies (Mack, Bryant, and Valastro 1978; Mack et al. 1978; Mack, Rutter, and Valastro 1983) and were replaced by western hemlock and western red cedar; grass again invaded the ponderosa pine woodland on floors of valleys, and probably dry slopes of the Thompson Plateau. Forests on the eastern fringe of the Columbia Basin also thinned, and the dense shrub steppe of the southeast Columbia Basin was replaced by bunchgrass. From 400 B.C. to A.D. 200 bison became common for the only time during the Holocene, but all faunal assemblages containing over 10 percent bison remains lie within the bunchgrass habitat type or less than 50 kilometers to the west of it.

Geologic evidence in the form of erosion in alluvial fans and small basins throughout the Columbia Basin and surrounding highlands (Chatters and Hoover 1992; Cochran 1988) and an absence of ground-water dates for the period between 800 B.C. and A.D. 400 are indicative of severe drought and summer-dominant precipitation. Rivers began aggrading a final Holocene floodplain, and *Gonidea* increased in the Columbia River, indicating a finer-textured bed. A decline in salmon productivity may have occurred under these conditions.

Where fire frequencies have been considered, such as at Blue Lake (Smith 1983) and sites in the eastern Rockies (Hemphill 1983; Mehringer, Arno, and Petersen 1977), fires are more frequent, but less severe in the past 1,000–2,000 years than at other times in forest histories. Human efforts to maintain the seral vegetation and promote production of game and fruits are the probable cause of this phenomenon.

There is little evidence for major environmental change in the last 2,000 years. The Little Ice Age, which caused alpine glaciers to advance worldwide between A.D. 1400 and 1850, although evident in all higher mountain ranges, had little impact on the flora of the Northwest. A drought occurred in the central Columbia Basin around A.D. 1400 (Bartholomew 1982), and severe floods were more frequent on the middle Columbia River 1000–1400 and less frequent after 1400. Otherwise, published paleoecological records show no other coincident changes.

Resource Variation Through Time

Resource productivity of the Plateau environment varied according to two dimensions of climate: effective moisture and temperature. Typically warmth and drought and cold and dampness coincided, but at least one warm wet period and several cooler, drier intervals occurred, demonstrating the relative independence of these variables.

In the temperature dimension, the primary issue is the relative length of warm and cold seasons. If the year is thought of as a circle, consisting of a productive arc for the warm seasons and a relatively unproductive arc for cool seasons, cooling expands the unproductive part of the year at the expense of the productive one. This change in productivity affects other animals as well as people.

With cooling, salmon, whose migrations from the sea and spawning behavior are triggered by the temperature of their natal rivers, will enter the rivers later and spawn earlier. Conversely, warming extends the duration of salmon residency. The result is that cooling focuses the fish resource in time, whereas warming disperses it (V.L. Butler and Schalk 1986). The same is true of other resources, such as roots or fruits, that are accessible to foragers for only part of the year. The effect on large game is to extend the period of concentration in lowlands, and hence the interval of greatest vulnerability to hunters. Long winters, however, can cause animals to deplete their pastures, reducing overall numbers of animals. For foragers who lack a well-developed strategy of food harvest and storage, winter has the same population-limiting effect.

Warm climate will expand the productive arc, extending the availability of plant foods but also allowing game animals longer tenure in the highlands. In the absence of accompanying drought, this can result in increased numbers of large mammals and their predators. Salmon may be negatively affected, however, since prolonged residency in warm water increases the probability of infection in adults and a shorter, warmer winter permits fungal attacks on spawned eggs. It also reduces the snow pack and brings on an earlier freshet, which will diminish the out-migration success of the young. High summer temperatures allow subalpine forest species to colonize higher elevations and montane forest to replace subalpine. Because mountains' surface area declines with altitude, the extent of subalpine and alpine floras would decline, even disappear from lower peaks. Warmer climates, therefore, adversely affect the extent of berry fields in the subalpine habitat, even though the productive season may be longer.

Changes in moisture, in the absence of temperature fluctuation, primarily affect the density and extent of steppe and lower forest zones and the resource patches within them. As moisture declines below that suitable for tree growth, the forests retract upslope, and bare patches appear within the forest on exposed slopes or shallow soils. This creates openings in the forest for deer and elk, but may either increase or decrease suitable habitat at the forest border, depending on the effect of upslope migration on the involution of the forest edge. Retraction of the forest and a decrease in moisture at lower elevation can also mean a change in the location of the root-bearing steppes of stony soils and a decline in the number and extent of wet meadows. In the steppe, drying means a decline in terrestrial productivity, although exposure of soil to erosion and dune formation increase the habitat suitable for large-seeded grasses. As steppes expand, particularly up mountain slopes, the watershed deteriorates; flash floods and stream siltation occur. Disappearance of large areas of forest can expose rivers to warming from the sun over more of their length, warming the waters. The overall result, as with warming, is a decline in fish productivity.

An increase in moisture will have much the opposite effect. It raises the water table, making more surface water available in the steppe zone and enlarging the area suitable for camas and other wet meadow resources. It allows forests to expand downslope and enclose internal bare patches of the forest, and it reduces fire frequencies and the creation of seral habitats so important to game species and people. Depending on the shape of the landscape, this may have disparate effects on deer and elk populations. The elimination of bare patches in highlands would reduce mountain sheep populations at higher elevations, but improved pastures at low elevations might compensate. Enclosing of the forest improves the watershed and shades streams, providing cleaner, cooler water and enhanced salmon productivity.

Changes in temperature and moisture during the Holocene affected the resource productivity of the Plateau's subregions differently. Often, conditions that improved the productivity of one area diminished the productivity of another, or changed the balance between terrestrial and aquatic resources.

In the early Holocene, before 7500 B.C., forests were confined to land above 1,300 meters in the Northern Plateau and above 1,650 meters in the Blue Mountains. This meant that in the north, forests that now carpet the landscape except for small, linear strips in the valley bottoms were then islands in a sea of grass. Many of the forests that did exist were open pine, fir, and juniper. The same was true of the Eastern Plateau. The forests of the Blue-Ochoco mountains could occur only on a few high ridges. Subalpine floras probably were confined, if in fact they had developed yet, to only the highest peaks. Rivers drained a largely open watershed. In terms of resources this means the Thompson Plateau and Clark Fork and Kootenay basins, with greater edge area, would have resembled today's Blue-Ochoco

mountains in high deer and elk productivity, while the then Blue-Ochoco mountains would have been less productive. Berries of the subalpine zone would have been confined to rare patches or remote mountains, while the fruiting talus garlands and riparian zones of the steppe should have been relatively more abundant. Hot summers and a watershed largely in steppe meant warm, sediment-laden waters and poor salmon productivity, although both major basins supported viable populations. Sucker and other resident fishes more tolerant of these conditions would have thrived. Low ground water levels in the Columbia Basin meant wet meadows dispersed to the periphery and an absence of drinking water in many parts of the lowlands. The marked seasonality of the time meant good summer productivity, but long, harsh winters.

Between 7500 and 4400 B.C., forests encroached progressively on northern grasslands, ultimately reducing them to nearly their modern extent. This change does not appear to have been accompanied by a decline in summer temperatures, but winters were warmer as the maritime climatic patterns became established. The productive arc of the annual circle thus expanded. As the forest islands in the north and east grew and coalesced, the forest edge habitat became first more, then less extensive. Forests in the Blue-Ochoco mountains expanded but did not reach their modern size or productivity until much later. Steppes of the Southern plateau changed from grass to shrub dominated, becoming less productive of game but more productive of dune-inhabiting grasses. Watersheds in the Columbia system seem to have remained poor, with the warm, sediment-laden water and early freshets probably depressing salmon populations. As in the early Holocene, the Northern and Eastern Plateau remained more productive than the Southern Plateau.

Between 3000 and 2500 B.C. moisture had increased in the south and forests reached closure in the north. This warm, moist interval would have been characterized by an increase in steppe productivity in the Southern Plateau, but by an increased forest density in the north and east. Improved watersheds, slightly cooler water, and a later spring freshet may have enabled salmon populations to increase some, particularly in the Fraser system. Between 4400 and 3000 B.C., subalpine floras and accompanying berry resources probably appeared or expanded in some northern mountains as summer temperatures began to decline.

Between 2500 and 800 B.C., the terrestrial game productivity of the Northern and Eastern Plateau would have been at their minimum. The productive season was short due to cold temperatures both summer and winter, and the forests had closed even the valley bottoms. There was little or no forest edge north of 48° north latitude or east of the Rocky Mountains' west flank. Fires were few, keeping seral habitats at a minimum. Deer and elk would have become much less common in these areas, although mountain sheep, mountain goats, and possibly caribou might have partially offset this loss due to an expanded, altitudinally depressed

47

alpine zone. In the north, an enclosed watershed, heavy snow pack, and late freshet would have made conditions ideal for salmon production in short, spectacular runs. The Eastern Plateau, lacking salmon, had no compensation for the forest closure. Subalpine zones also reached their maximum extent and lowest elevation, making berry fields more accessible, although depressed fire frequencies would have damped the effects of this change. Steppes to the south reached their maximum productivity. Ground water there was high, probably enabling development of extensive camas meadows; forest edges lay along or near the principal streams, bringing game into close proximity to hunters during long winters. Like the Fraser, Columbia River waters were conducive to peak salmon production. Despite improved terrestrial and aquatic productivity, the south also experienced an abbreviated productive season. Winter would again have limited game numbers and could have limited human populations lacking a well-developed storage technology.

Warming and partial drought between 800 B.C. and A.D. 200 again allowed mountain forests to open up and expanded the year's productive season. Increased fires and greater edge area would have elevated game populations in the north and east, but some species may have declined along edges of the steppe zone. Subalpine zones moved upslope, but increasing fire frequency would have increased the size of berry patches. Opening of the watershed and increased flooding again reduced the suitability of salmon habitat in many parts of the region. Bison moved into the southeastern Columbia Basin, temporarily raising terrestrial game productivity at the same time fish were less productive.

After A.D. 1–200 although significant temperature changes occurred worldwide, the paleoenvironmental record of the Plateau shows little sign of change. There is evidence in the forests of frequent, small fires, which are unrelated to known climatic variations. People, it appears, were managing their habitat to maintain a balance of steppe, forest, and meadow that suited the needs of their populations. The Plateau had become a managed environment.

Languages

M. DALE KINKADE, WILLIAM W. ELMENDORF, BRUCE RIGSBY, AND HARUO AOKI

Wider Classification

The Plateau area contained two large and territorially extensive language groupings and six smaller ones. Most of the region was occupied by languages of the Salishan family in the north and the Sahaptian family in the south. There was also one Athapaskan language (Nicola), one dialect of a Chinookan language (Wasco-Wishram, a dialect of Kiksht), and four linguistic isolates (Kootenai, Molala, Cayuse, Klamath), languages without close or clearly demonstrable relationships to others (fig. 1). Of these, only Salishan, Athapaskan, and Chinookan have non-Plateau members in the Northwest Coast area to the west.

Salishan is the most diversified of these groupings, comprising seven languages in the northern Plateau. It also occupies the largest territory, extending through southern interior British Columbia to northwestern Montana, and south through a large part of eastern Washington and northern Idaho. Plateau Salishan forms a distinct Interior Salish subgroup within the family. Its distinction from other Salishan subgroupings is clear (Boas and Haeberlin 1927).

The Sahaptian family includes just two languages, Sahaptin and Nez Perce, bordering Interior Salish languages on the south. The extinct Nicola language, in the Nicola Valley in southern interior British Columbia, was a member of the widespread Athapaskan family (Boas 1895, 1924). It was certainly intrusive in Interior Salish territory, from the north, and was replaced by dialects of Salishan Thompson, Shuswap, and Okanagan during the nineteenth century. Of the remaining Plateau languages, Kootenai held territory along the northeastern border of the area, between the easternmost Interior Salish and the Algonquian Blackfoot in the Alberta plains. Plateau Upper Chinook, Molala, Cayuse, and Klamath were all to the south in contact with Sahaptian.

Languages are listed in table 1 in generally north to south order. Phyla are groupings of language families hypothesized, but not proven, to be remotely related. Language families are groups of languages that can be shown to be genetically related, using techniques developed by comparative linguistics; branches are subdivisions of families. Dialects are different, but mutually intelligible, varieties of a language. Before 1930 the term "dialect" was often used to emphasize the fact of genetic linguistic relationship, so that the term sometimes is applied to what later would be called distinct languages.

Two notable features of speech community contacts between the Plateau and adjoining regions are the obvious cultural influences from Plains tribes to the east, and the consistently hostile relations with Numic (Shoshonean) groups to the south. Plateau-Plains contacts were often hostile also but did not preclude heavy borrowing of Plains traits during the eighteenth and early nineteenth centuries, particularly by eastern and southern Plateau peoples. These cultural borrowings seem to have been accompanied by relatively little linguistic influence. Hostility between all southern Plateau groups and the Numic-speaking Paiute, Bannock, and Shoshone to their south may reflect recent northward expansion of these Great Basin peoples and consequent territorial pressures on Plateau peoples. Despite this, Aoki (1975) has noted what may be earlier linguistic influence of some Numic language on Nez Perce.

Languages and Language Families

Nicola Athapaskan

The descendants of a small Athapaskan-speaking group lived positioned along the border between the Thompsons and the Okanagans. Both they and their original language are named after their main area of residence in the upper Nicola Valley in British Columbia, although they also occupied the Upper Similkameen area. Both J.W. McKay (Dawson 1892:24) and Mrs. S.S. Allison (1892:305) reported a "tradition" that the Nicola Indians were the descendants of a Chilcotin war party that had entered the area 150 years earlier. Their accounts seem improbable for several reasons, not the least of which is the statement that the Chilcotins had brought their women along. When James Teit talked with several old Nicola Indians in 1895, they had no traditions of foreign origin, recent or not. They told Teit that their people had intermarried in recent generations with the Thompsons and Okanagans and had since given up their earlier language for a Thompson Salish dialect. An Okanagan Salish dialect evidently replaced Nicola speech in the Upper Similkameen area.

The Nicola linguistic evidence (Boas 1895, 1924) is fragmentary and of poor quality. Though adequate to show that the language was indeed Athapaskan, the data do not permit

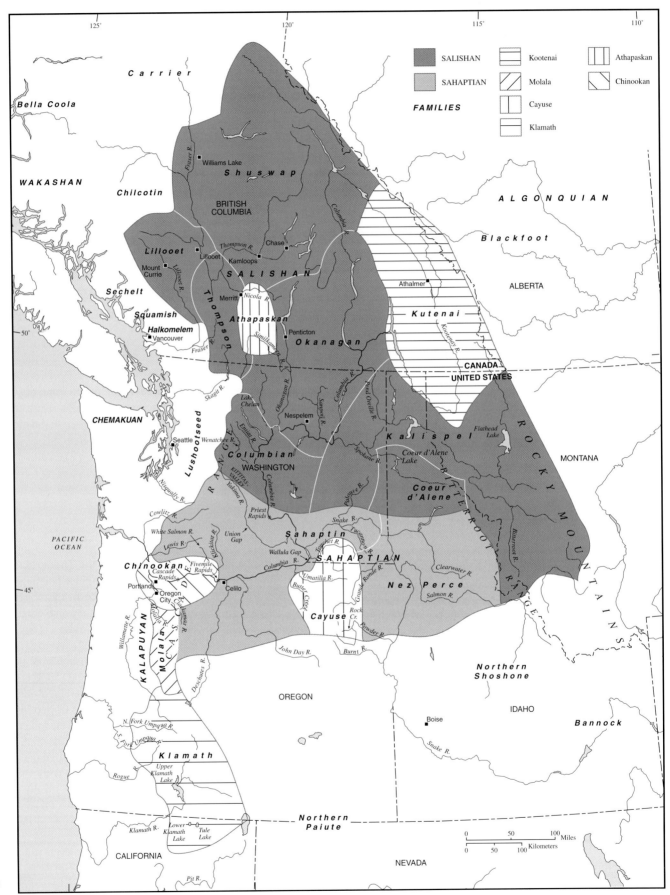

SALISHAN

SAHAPTIAN

FAMILIES

Kootenai

Molala

Cayuse

Klamath

Athapaskan

Chinookan

Carrier

Bella Coola

WAKASHAN

Chilcotin

Williams Lake

Shuswap

BRITISH
COLUMBIA

Lillooet

Lillooet

Kamloops

Sechelt

Squamish

Halkomelem
Vancouver

Mount
Currie

Thompson R.

Chase

Columbia R.

ALGONQUIAN

Blackfoot

ALBERTA

Merritt   Nicola R.

SALISHAN

Athabaskan

Okanagan

Simikameen R.

Penticton

Athalmer

Kutenai

Kootenay R.

CANADA

UNITED STATES

Fraser

CHEMAKUAN

Seattle

Skagit R.

Wenatchee R.

Lake
Chelan

Okanogan R.

Nespelem

Sanpoil R.

Columbia R.

Pend Oreille R.

Kalispel

Flathead
Lake

Coeur d'Alene
Lake

Spokane R.

Columbian

WASHINGTON

Entiat R.

Columbia R.

Palouse R.

MONTANA

*Coeur
d'Alene*

PACIFIC
OCEAN

Nisqually R.

Cowlitz R.

White Salmon R.

Lewis R.

Klickitat R.

Priest
Rapids

*KITTITAS
VALLEY*

Yakima R.

Union
Gap

Wallula Gap

Sahaptin

Snake R.

Tucannon R.

Touchet R.

SAHAPTIAN

Clearwater R.

Bitterroot R.

ROCKY MOUNTAINS

BITTERROOT RANGE

Chinookan

Cascade
Rapids

Fivemile
Rapids

Portland

Oregon
City

Celilo

Columbia R.

Umatilla R.

Butter Creek

Cayuse

Rock
Cr.

Grande Ronde R.

Nez Perce

Salmon R.

Powder R.

*Northern
Shoshone*

KALAPUYAN

Willamette R.

Molala

Molalla R.

CASCADE RANGE

Deschutes R.

John Day R.

Burnt R.

OREGON

IDAHO

Boise

Bannock

N. Fork Umpqua R.

S. Fork Umpqua R.

Klamath

Rogue

Upper
Klamath
Lake

Snake R.

Klamath R.

Lower
Klamath
Lake

Tule
Lake

*Northern
Paiute*

NEVADA

CALIFORNIA

Pit R.

0   50   100 Miles

0   50   100 Kilometers

50

KINKADE, ELMENDORF, RIGSBY, AND AOKI

Fig. 1. Native languages and language families of the Plateau.

Table 1. Language Classification

Phylum	Family	Subfamily	Branch	Language	Dialect
Na-Dene Phylum	Eyak-Athapaskan	Athapaskan		Nicola	
Kootenai Language Isolate				Kootenai	Upper Kootenai
					Lower Kootenai
Salishan			Interior Salish	Lillooet	Upper Lillooet
					Lower Lillooet
				Thompson	
				Shuswap	Eastern
					Western
				Okanagan	Northern Okanagan
					Lakes
					Colville
					Sanoil-Nespelem
					Southern Okanogan
					Methow
				Kalispel	Flathead
					Kalispel
					Spokane
				Coeur d'Alene	
				Columbian	Sinkayuse
					Wenatchee
					Chelan
Penutian Phylum	Sahaptian			Sahaptin	Northeast/Northwest Columbia River
				Nez Perce	Upper Nez Perce
					Lower Nez Perce
	Cayuse Language Isolate			Cayuse	
	Molala Language Isolate			Molala	
	Chinookan			Kiksht[a]	Wasco
					Wishram
	Klamath Language Isolate			Klamath	Klamath
					Modoc

[a] Includes additional dialects in the Northwest Coast area (vol. 7:6).

the determination of its exact relationship to other Athapaskan languages or subgroupings, although Krauss concedes that "Harrington is far more likely to be correct in considering . . . Nicola . . . a branch of Chilcotin" (Krauss 1973:919). J.P. Harrington (1943; Stirling 1943:50–51) claimed to have gathered more extensive Nicola materials in 1942, but an examination of his field notes (Harrington 1941) does not support his enthusiastic reports of the relationships of the language (Krauss 1973:919). Thus Nicola remains a problematic case in comparative Athapaskan linguistics.

Kootenai

The historical territory of the Kootenai Indians centered upon the Kutenai River drainage system along the eastern margins of the Plateau area in parts of modern Idaho, Montana, Alberta, and British Columbia (Turney-High 1941:23–25). In prehorse times, the Kootenais also occupied the eastern slopes of the Rockies and portions of the adjacent High Plains (Turney-High 1941:10–14), but they were forced westward into the mountains by the Blackfoot (Ewers 1955:300).

The ethnographic division of the Kootenais into Upper (with respect to position in the Kutenai drainage system) and Lower groups is paralleled by a linguistic division into Upper and Lower Kootenai dialects (Garvin 1948:37). The dialectal differences are not marked. In 1990 there were fewer than 250 speakers of Kootenai.

Powell (1891:85) classified Kootenai as the sole member of the Kitunahan language family. Sapir placed Kootenai as one of three coordinate branches of a "Macro-Algonkian" stock in his 1929 classification (Sapir 1929). C.F. Voegelin and F.M. Voegelin (1964:93–105) listed Kootenai as one of four language isolates in the Algonquian-Wakashan phylum, which also includes the Algonquian, Chemakuan, Salishan, and Wakashan families. Haas (1965) reviewed the history of Kootenai linguistic classification and provided preliminary comparisons of Kootenai with Algonquian and Salishan. She regarded her comparisons as suggestive, but not conclusive. Kootenai grammar is described in Canestrelli (1894) (fig. 2) (and in Canestrelli 1926 as annotated by Boas; also Boas 1926), Garvin (1948, 1948a, 1948b, 1951, 1951a), Dryer (1991, 1992, 1994, 1996), and Morgan (1991). Texts collected by Boas and Chamberlain and a dictionary are in Boas (1918); additional texts are in Garvin (1953, 1954). The Kootenai kinship system is described in Sapir (1918). A plant taxonomy and terminology can be found in Hart (1974).

Salishan

Almost half the languages of the Plateau culture area belong to the Salishan language family. The majority of the languages of this diverse family are found in the Northwest Coast culture area, but the Interior branch, consisting of seven languages, is entirely on the Plateau. Lexical evidence suggests that the Interior Salish languages reflect an old (proto-Interior) dialect chain, in which closest relations ran from what became Lillooet in the northwest to Coeur d'Alene in the southeast, in a relationship order Lillooet-Thompson–Shuswap-Okanagan-Kalispel-Coeur d'Alene (Elmendorf 1965). Columbian appears to link equally with Okanagan and Kalispel and thus to have developed to the south of the main chain sequence.

On the basis of structural and lexical similarities, these seven languages can be divided into two groups: a northwestern group comprising Lillooet, Thompson, and Shuswap, and a southeastern group comprising Okanagan, Columbian, Kalispel, and Coeur d'Alene. Nevertheless, the Interior branch of Salishan has much less diversity than is found in the large Central Salish branch on the coast; the diversity of Interior Salish is on the order of Slavic languages within Indo-European. All the Interior Salish languages have been studied extensively. Published dictionar-

---

Linguae Ksanka

(Kootenai)

Elementa Grammaticae

AUCTORE

PHILIPPO CANESTRELLI

e

Societate Jesu.

TYPIS N. H. DOWNING,
Santa Clara, Cal.
1894.

26

Quando actu aliqua multitudo numeratur, usurpantur non participia, sed ipsa themata verborum numeralium, quae themata dici possunt numeri cardinales. Accipe schema numerorum cardinalium.

1. ukwi	11. yitwum-la-ukwi	10. yitwu
2. as	12. yitwum-la-as	20. aiwu
3. kalsa	13. yitwumlakalsa	30. kalsanwu
4. gatsa	14. yitwumlagatsa	40. gatsanwu
5. yikwu	15. yitwumlayikwu	50. yikwunwu
6. inmisa	16. yitwumlainmisa	60. inmisanwu
7. wistala	17. yitwumlawistala	70. wistalanwu
8. wugatsa	18. yitwumlawugatsa	80. wugatsanwu
9. kaikitu	19. yitwumlakaikitu	90. kaikitunwu
10. yitwu	20. aiwu	100. yitwunwu
	21. aiwumlaukwi	
	22. aiwumlaas	

100. yitwunwu	1000. yitwulyitwunwu
200. as-l-yitwunwu	2000. aslyitwulyitwunwu
300. kalsa-l-yitwunwu	3000. kalsalyitwulyitwunwu
400. gatsalyitwunwu	4000. gatsalyitwulyitwuwu
500. yikwulyitwunwu	5000. yikwulyitwulyitwunwu
600. inmisalyitwunwu	6000. inmisalyitwulyitwunwu
700. wistalalyitwunwu	7000. wistalalyitwulyitwunwu
800. wugatsalyitwunwu	8000. wugatsalyitwulyitwunwu
900. kaikitulyitwunwu	9000. kaikitulyitwulyitwunwu
1000. yitwulyitwunwu	10000. yitwulyitwulyitwunwu

In istis vocabulis literae *m* ut in *yitwu-m-la-ukwi*, *l* ut in *as-l-yitwunwu* sunt phonicae sive conglutinativae; particula vero *la* ut in *yitwum-la-ukwi* est particula iterationis, quae proinde idem valet ac *iterum*. Ista particula usurpari debet quoties enuntiatur numerus qui pluribus decadibus constat. Sic si vis pronuntiare e. g. numerum 1894 dices: *yitwulyitwunwu la wugatsalyitwunwu la kaikitunwu la gatsa*.

Nomina numeralia modo considerata, praecipue inserviunt, ut diximus, ad aliquam multitudinem numerandam, ac praescindunt a

---

Fig. 2. Kootenai grammar, title p. and p. 26, which discusses cardinal numbers 1 to 10,000 (Canestrelli 1894). The grammar was written in Latin so that it could be used by missionaries of various nationalities. An estimated 300 copies were printed in 1894 by the *Santa Clara Journal*. Philip Canestrelli (b. 1839, d. 1918) was a Jesuit from Rome who served in missions at Ft. Colville and at St. Francis Regis. He was at St. Ignatius Mission in western Mont. from 1887 to 1893; while there he published works in both Kootenai and Flathead. He returned to Rome in 1894.

ies are available for Thompson, Shuswap, Okanagan, Kalispel (fig. 3) (as well as for its Spokane dialect), and Columbian (the last in the form of a short lexicon), and short text collections in the native languages have been published in Shuswap and Kalispel. Kinkade (1994) surveys textual material in both English and the native languages from the Plateau and Northwest Coast in terms of source and quantity, genres, form, stylistic features, and setting. Because Interior Salish languages have retained some consonants lost elsewhere in Salishan, they are of particular importance for comparative studies. For comparative Salishan studies see Boas and Haeberlin (1927), Vogt (1940a), Swadesh (1950, 1952), Reichard (1958–1960), Kuipers (1970, 1978, 1981, 1982), Kinkade and Thompson (1974), Haeberlin (1974), and Newman (1976). Haeberlin (1918) is an early study of reduplication in Salishan languages. Newman (1979, 1979a, 1980) and Hoard (1971) compare and reconstruct pronominal systems in Salish. P.D. Kroeber (1991) compares the syntax of subordinate clauses in Salishan and contains much information on Interior Salish syntax, Elmendorf (1961) compares kinship systems, Elmendorf (1962) compares numerals, Kinkade (1988) compares and reconstructs color terms, and Kinkade (1993) compares and reconstructs words referring to people. Palmer (1997) is a general study of semantic domains. Kinkade and Sloat (1972) compare Interior Salish vowels. A general discussion of Salishan languages (with extensive references) is found in L.C. Thompson (1979) and Czaykowska-Higgins and Kinkade (1997) and a survey of the study of languages of the Northwest in L.C. Thompson (1973). Additional bibliography can be found in Adler (1961); earlier materials are listed in Pilling (1885, 1893a).

Interior Salish languages, like all Salishan languages, express grammatical categories such as aspect, transitivity, control (vol. 7:33; vol. 17:619; Thompson 1985), voice, person, and causation. These categories are expressed primarily through elaborate systems of suffixation. Prefixes are much less frequent but are used for aspect and for locational concepts. Reduplication is used regularly to indicate the categories of diminutive, distributive, and out-of-control; in the three northwestern languages, diminutive reduplication copies the stressed vowel and the following consonant, allowing the typologically unusual phenomenon of reduplicating across morpheme boundaries or in affixes. As elsewhere in Salish, lexical suffixes are used extensively for derivation (see Haeberlin 1974); they refer to body parts, common objects in nature or the native cultures (as in Columbian sk̓əmcín 'mouth', with the suffix -cin 'mouth'), or in abstract extensions of these basic concepts (as in Columbian nk̓ʷ ancíntn 'song' from nk̓ʷ nám 'sing'). Tense is an optional category and is expressed by particles. Number is also largely optional, but different kinds of number categories (collective, distributive) may be expressed in different ways—by stem changes, by reduplication, by affixation, or by particles. A category of gender, basic to all other Salishan languages, is absent from Interior Salish. In transitive

forms, objects and subjects are suffixes (in that order); in intransitive forms, subjects are marked by clitics. This person marking system is partly ergative (Gardiner and Saunders 1991), with third-person objects and third-person intransitive subjects unmarked, and third-person transitive subjects marked by a suffixed -s. Possessive markers are a mixed set of prefixes and suffixes or, arguably, clitics, with first and second singulars marked by prefixes (only first-person singular in Lillooet), and all other persons by suffixes. Third-person plural is an optional category throughout the pronominal system, expressed by a clitic in Columbian and elsewhere by a (cognate) suffix. Aspect is marked by prefixes, suffixes, and particles, and minimally a perfective/imperfective contrast is expressed. Aspectual and aspectlike categories, especially stative, are widely used and expressed either by a prefix or by particles. Characteristic of Interior Salish languages is the common use of -t 'durative' and -ilx 'autonomous' (used particularly to mark predicates indicating motion); reflexes of both suffixes can be found elsewhere in Salish, but only residually. Unique to the Interior is an unusual marking of the category 'inchoative', where -ʔ- is infixed into strong roots (those requiring primary stress) while a suffix -p is added to weak roots. Interior Salish languages have modified an original system of passive marking where passives in independent clauses were marked by -t-m and dependent clauses by -t; the Interior languages still have these suffixes but have integrated them into the regular active transitive subject marking system, particularly to mark first-person plural (with -t-m still used for 'passive' as well, but resulting in ambiguity with active forms with a third-person object and first-person plural subject). The three northwestern Interior languages differ from the others by having a special set of intransitive subject clitics for dependent clauses. All words except the numerous particles have a primarily predicative function (see Kinkade 1983a; for an alternate analysis see van Eijk and Hess 1986); any primary word may occur with appropriate affixes in a secondary role of argument (subject, object, instrument, etc.) or in a variety of subordinate clauses.

Several affixes, marking a variety of grammatical concepts, occur in Interior Salish languages, and, along with the features just discussed, help to distinguish this branch of Salishan from other branches. The differences in occurrence of these affixes within Interior Salish help to distinguish the interior languages from each other. The distribution of several of these affixes is summarized in table 2. Besides these differences each language has several affixes and grammatical particles unique to that language.

Interior Salish phonological systems are unusual in a number of ways. Consonant systems have the usual Northwest elaboration, with plain and rounded velars and uvulars, a full series of ejective stops, a full series of glottalized resonants, and several kinds of laterals (an ejective lateral affricate, a voiceless lateral fricative, plain and glottalized lateral continuants, and sometimes retracted or dark ver-

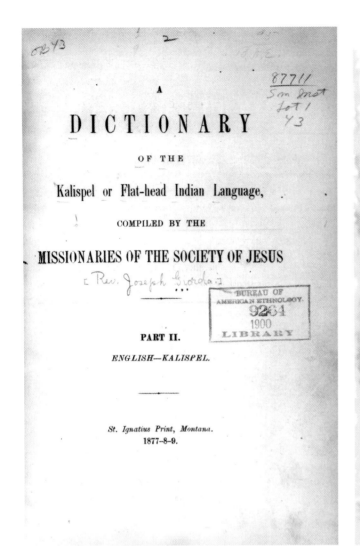

A

DICTIONARY

OF THE

Kalispel or Flat-head Indian Language,

COMPILED BY THE

MISSIONARIES OF THE SOCIETY OF JESUS

[Rev. Joseph Giorda]

PART II.

ENGLISH—KALISPEL.

St. Ignatius Print, Montana.
1877-8-9.

Ł, Is a sign of diminutive prefixed to nouns, verbs and adverbs. Usually, but not always, the verb or noun, reduplicates the first syllable up to the accent, and then the same syllable is repeated, dropping the accented vowel, in the repeated syllable. But by practice only, can one find out the way; even Indians make it in different ways. 'Sípi.' Rope. 'Lsìspi.' Small rope. 'Guist.' He went away. 'Łguigust.' He went away for awhile.

ŁAÁKO,—[*root of,*]

Łaàko, It got uncovered, it appeared, it got manifest. 'Tle łaàko łu supùlegu.' Already the grass appears after the snow disappeared. 'Tas łaàko.' It did not come to light.

Chines-laàkomi, chines-łaàko, łaàkosh, *v. pass.* (5) I am being uncovered, appearing, I am uncovered, open to sight, [not stripped,] I appear, not by a voluntary action, but simply being being exposed to view, not being concealed.

Chines-laakomì, chin-lakòm łakòish, *v. act. ind.* (7) I show manifest, expose to view something, reveal, declare.

Ies-łakomìm, łakomistèn, łakomisku, or, łakomistèku, *v. tr. r.* (10) I manifest that, reveal, expose it.

" łakomìłtèm, łakomìłtèn, łakomìłt, *v. rel.* (17) I manifest his... or it to him. 'Łakomìłtèn łu téie i-szkuèn łu kuiálks.' I declared my sins to the Priest.

" łakoshìtem, łakoshìten, łakoshìt, *v. rel.* (15) I show something to him. 'Ko-łakoshìt.' Show me something. 'Kae-łakoshìłis.' He showed us something.

" łakomshìshem, łakomshìshemen, łakomshìshement, *v. rel.* (9) I show that......[not mine,] to others *indef.*

" łakomshishemłtem, *v. rel.* (16) I show to others his......'Taks-lakomshisbemłtgu łu téie szkuèis łu a-snkuskéligu.' Do not tell others the sins of your fellow beings.

Chines-łakomshìshi, *v. rel.* (6) I show something to somebody.

Kaes-łakoshituègui, [from łakoshìtem,] We show something to one another.

Chines-łakomìsti, *v. ref.* I become exposed to view.

Chines-łakomenzùti, *v. ref.* I expose myself to view, I reveal myself, I appear to somebody by voluntary action. 'Łaàko łu spakani.' The sun appeared was seen, after the clouds scattered away. 'Łakomenzùt łu Jesu Kli.' Our Lord appeared,

Fig. 3. The Kalispel-English (part 1) and English-Kalispel (part 2) dictionary (Giorda et al. 1877–1879), title p. from part 2 and p. 351 from part 1. P. 351 is the first page for the letter *ł*. Although often ascribed to Joseph Giorda, the superior of the mission, it was based on a manuscript by Gregory Mengarini and, after his departure for California in 1852, was completed by Giorda, Joseph Bandini, Leopold Van Gorp, and Joseph Guidi. It was printed at St. Ignatius Mission, Mont.

sions of the latter pair). More unusual features of these consonant systems are a tapped *r* in four languages, a *γ* in four languages, and the contrast between a retracted and unretracted *l* in at least two languages; such sounds are found infrequently throughout North America. The most striking feature of Interior Salish consonants is the presence of pharyngeal or uvular approximants or resonants (Kinkade 1967a); these occur both rounded and unrounded and plain and glottalized. Bessell (1992, 1997) and Bessell and Czaykowska-Higgins (1992) examine pharyngeal and uvular consonants in Interior Salish languages. In addition, Lillooet, Thompson, Shuswap, and Columbian distinguish plain and retracted coronal consonants (minimally *c, s,* articulated with the blade of the tongue against the alveolar ridge, versus retracted *ç, ṣ,* with the tip of the tongue touching the same position), where it is the body of the tongue that is retracted, not the point of articulation. It is not surprising that these special coronal consonants are absent

from Kalispel and Coeur d'Alene, because these two languages have shifted the unrounded velar stops and fricative (*k, ḱ, x*) to a palato-alveolar position (*č č̓ š*); this shift results in the articulation of *c* and *s* with the tongue tip at the alveolar ridge, leaving little room for a retracted third set of coronals. It is unexpected, then, that Okanagan, which retains *k ḱ x* unshifted, also lacks the distinctive set of retracted coronals. Another striking feature of Interior Salish is the sheer number of resonants. There may be up to 10 pairs (plain and glottalized); some of their developments are shown in table 3. In addition, these resonants often become vowels (especially *y* and *w*, including the Thompson *y* from *l* or the *y* from *γ* in the southeastern languages). A very striking development is the frequent change of nasals to vowels when they occur between consonants or word-finally after an obstruent; this is pervasive in Eastern Shuswap, and a regular process in Thompson and Kalispel. It occurs in more limited environments in Columbian and sporadical-

54

Table 2. Comparison of Selected Interior Salishan Affixes

	Lillooet	Thompson	Shuswap	Okanagan	Kalispel	Coeur d'Alene	Columbian
1. *kaɬ 'unrealized'	+	[+]	[+]	+	(+)	+	+
2. -mix 'imperfective'	(+)	(+)	—	+	+	+	+
3. -í-ablaut 'plural'	—	+	(+)	+	(+)	+	+
4. *-a-ʔ/C₁- 'repetitive'	—	(+)		+	+	—	+
5. *-xa 'intr. sg. imperative'	—	+	+	+	+	+	—
6. *-ámn 'desiderative/habitual'	+	+	+	+	+	+	—
7. *-ilx '3d plural'	—	+	—	+	—	+	+
8. -xíx 'indef. object'	—	—	—	+	+	+	+
9. -ɬ(t)- 'indirective'	—	—	—	+	+	+	+
10. -tuɬ(t) - 'indirective'	—	—	—	+	—	+	+
11. *-y- (pl.), *-ákʷ (sg.) 'trans. imperative'	—	—	+	+	+	—	—
12. -ɬ 'diminutive'	—	—	—	+	+	—	—

NOTE: Parentheses indicate limited use or altered function of the affix; brackets indicate that the shape of the affix is reduced in that language. Blanks are left where relevant information is unavailable or unclear. The label "applicative" is often used in place of "indirective."

ly elsewhere in Interior Salish. This change is documented for Spokane (B.F. Carlson 1976) and Shuswap (Kuipers 1989).

Interior Salish vowel systems are also unusual. Each language has a basic set of three or four vowels, but this number is doubled by the same tongue-root retraction noted above for coronal consonants. Further mergers then may reduce the total number of vowels, although Lillooet, Thompson, and Columbian retain a full component of eight vowels (see table 4). Underlying vowels are usually lost in unstressed syllables, leaving long clusters of consonants (4, 5, and 6 being common). These clusters are often broken up by excrescent vowels before resonants or by resonants turning into vowels. Stress patterns are complex; it is necessary to distinguish strong and weak roots and suffixes—strong elements taking stress from other elements, and weak elements taking stress only when nothing stronger is present. Suffixes may also occur with variable stress, and then stress assignment depends on the presence and location of strong, weak, and other variable elements.

• LILLOOET   Two dialects can be recognized within Lillooet: Upper Lillooet (or Fountain), spoken along the Fraser River around Lillooet, British Columbia (200 miles up the Fraser River from Vancouver), and Lower Lillooet (or Mount Currie), spoken to the west along the Lillooet River (northwest of Vancouver). Because of its location at the western edge of the Interior Salish area, Lillooet shows a fair amount of influence from the Salishan languages of the Northwest Coast, especially neighboring Sechelt, Squamish, and Mainland Halkomelem. This influence is most noticeable in vocabulary and in the pronominal systems. Elsewhere in Interior Salish, transitive subjects are indicated by suffixes following the object suffixes; Lillooet follows this pattern in subjunctive (dependent)

forms, but in indicative (independent) forms, it follows the coast pattern of using the same enclitics that are used with intransitive forms to mark transitive subjects (except for forms with a third-person subject, where the pattern is entirely like other Interior Salish languages). For an extensive grammar of Lillooet see van Eijk (1997a). Swoboda (1971), a discussion of the phonology of the language, includes a short lexicon and limited textual material. Remnant (1990) treats specific problems in the phonology of Lillooet (i.e., retraction of vowels and consonants). Van Eijk (1993) examines reduplication and infixation in Lillooet. Roberts (1994) treats the relationship between subjects and topics. Matthewson (1996) examines determiners in Lillooet. Van Eijk and Williams (1981) present a number of texts for school use. Extensive lessons and vocabulary for elementary school use are found in Joseph et al. (1979), van Eijk (1978a), and Williams (1979)("Lillooet," fig. 11, this vol.).

• THOMPSON   The Thompson people are also known as Ntlakyapamuk (nɬeʔképmx), and the language is sometimes given this designation as well (see the synonymy in "Thompson," this vol.). The language is spoken in the Nicola Valley, along the Thompson, and part of the Fraser. Dialect differences within Thompson are slight; they involve some minor variations in pronunciation, distribution of sounds, and grammar, in addition to the expected diversity in lexicon. For example, some speakers, especially from downriver, have an ejective i contrasting with ƛ̓ in a few loanwords from neighboring languages, while others have only the latter sound. Thompson differs from other Interior Salishan languages in having undergone a sound shift of *y, *l, and *r to z, y, and l, respectively (Lillooet and Shuswap share the *r to l shift, and Lillooet has changed many cases of Proto-Salishan *y to z). The z of Thompson and Lillooet is an unusual sound, resembling English z, but with less friction and stridency, and is often produced with some retroflexion and sometimes with some lateral articulation. For a grammar of Thompson see L.C. Thompson and M.T. Thompson (1992) and volume 17:609–643; Hill-Tout (1900) has earlier notes and vocabulary on the language. See also Thompson and Thompson (1996), Howett (1993), and Jimmie (1994). Egesdal (1992) is a study of speech styles in Thompson narrative (see also M.T. Thompson and Egesdal 1993; Egesdal and M.T. Thompson 1994). The ethnobotany of Thompson has been studied extensively; two major treatments are Steedman (1930, based on Teit 1896–1918) and Turner et al. (1990).

• SHUSWAP   There are two distinct dialects of Shuswap, with the dividing line occurring between the Kamloops and Chase reserves. The most striking difference is the replacement of the nasals *m ṁ n ṅ* in the east with vowels when they occur between consonants or word-finally. The changes are in general as follows: *m ṁ* remain unchanged after the labials *p ṗ m ṁ*, become *u uʔ* after labialized consonants (including *w ẇ*), and otherwise become *e eʔ; n ṅ* remain unchanged after the coronals *t ƛ̓ t̓ n ṅ l l̓*, become *i iʔ* after *c c̓ s y y̓*, and otherwise become *e eʔ* (except in the Kinbasket dialect spoken at Athalmer, where they become

i iʔ here as well). For example, 'Indian potato' is *skʷnkʷínm* in the west and *skʷekʷíne* in the east, and 'pebbles' is *sxnxéxnx* in the west and *sxexéxex* in the east (Kuipers 1989:17–18). A distinctive feature of all Shuswap is the deglottalization of all but the last glottalized (ejective) obstruent in a root; this shows up clearly under reduplication, as in *cəqcqéq̓ƚp* 'young fir growth' from *cq̓éƚp* 'fir tree'. Shuswap is the only Salishan language to distinguish first-person inclusive and exclusive, inclusive being indicated by the subject enclitic *kt*, exclusive by *kʷəxʷ*; in transitive and possessive forms, the particle *kʷəxʷ* is combined with third-person forms for first plural exclusive objects and possessors. Gibson (1973) is a grammar based on the speech of the westernmost reserve of the southeastern dialect. Kuipers (1974) is a grammar of northwestern Shuswap; it includes texts and a dictionary. Kuipers (1989) supplements this, giving additional grammatical, textual, and lexical information and adds southeastern dialect vocabulary. Kuipers (1975) is a classified word list, and Kuipers (1983) another dictionary. Palmer (1975) and Turner et al. (1997) are ethnobotanical studies of Shuswap. See Gardiner (1993, 1997), Idsardi (1991), and Kuipers (1993).

Table 3. Correspondences of Resonants in Interior Salishan Languages

Proto–Interior Salish	*m	*n	*l	*r	*y	*ɣ	*w	*ʕ	*ʕʷ
Lillooet	m	n	l	ḷ	z,y	ɣ	w	ʕ	ʕʷ
Thompson	m	n	y	ḷ	z	ɣ	w	ʕ	ʕʷ
Shuswap	m	n	l	ḷ	y	ɣ	w	ʕ	ʕʷ
Okanagan	m	n	l	r	y	ɣ,y[a]	w	ʕ	ʕʷ
Kalispel	m	n	l	l	y	y	w	ʕ	ʕʷ
Spokane	m	n	l	r	y	y	w	ʕ	ʕʷ
Coeur d'Alene	m	n	l	r	y,d	y,ǰ	w,gʷ	ʕ	ʕʷ
Columbian	m	n	l	r	y	y	w	ʕ	ʕʷ

[a] Northern Okanagan dialects retain ɣ, whereas Southern dialects replace it with *y*.

Table 4. Interior Salishan Stressed Primary Vowel Developments

			Before back consonants		Elsewhere			
Proto-Interior Salish	*i	*u	*a	*ə	*i	*u	*a	*ə
Lillooet	i	u	a	ə	i	u	e	ə
Thompson	i	u	e	ə	i	u	e	ə
Western Shuswap	i	u	e	ə	i	u	e	ə,e
Eastern Shuswap	i	u	e	ə	i	u	e	ə,e
Okanagan	i	u	a	a	i	u	i	ə,a
Kalispel	i	o	a	a	i	u	e	i
Coeur d'Alene	e	o	a	a	i	u	i	e
Columbian	i	u	a	ə	i	u	a	ə

NOTE: The symbols in this table are phonemic; the symbol *e* represents a lower mid to low front vowel ([ɛ] to [æ]). The vowels represented by *i* and *u* vary from high to higher mid vowels. On the left, *i* is lowered to approximately [ɛ], *u* to approximately [ɔ], and *ə* to approximately [ʌ]; other vowels have roughly the same value as those on the right, resulting in some overlapping between *i* before back consonants and *e* elsewhere. This represents the development of the four primary vowels; an additional set of retracted vowels, with tongue-root retraction, often merges with those given here before back consonants.

• OKANAGAN Okanagan is spoken in several dialects, the differences among which are not great; nevertheless, it is possible to distinguish the following: Northern Okanagan (with Head of the Lake, Douglas Lake, Similkameen, and Penticton subvarieties; Watkins 1970), Lakes, Colville, Sanpoil-Nespelem, Southern Okanogan, and Methow. Methow has often been considered a dialect of Columbian, but Kinkade (1967) shows that it is best considered a slightly divergent dialect of Okanagan. One consistent distinction between the northern dialects (Northern Okanagan and Lakes) and the southern is the retention of γ in the north and its replacement by y in the south. Northern Okanagan dialects have lost the rounded series of pharyngeals by merging them with the plain series. Okanagan has only one series of coronal consonants, unlike Columbian to the south and Shuswap, Thompson, and Lillooet to the north, which contrast a retracted set with a nonretracted set. Nevertheless, Okanagan does share the phenomenon of vowel retraction with most other Interior Salishan languages; it differs from them in that all basic vowels retract to a, rather than each vowel having its own retracted counterpart. In many respects Okanagan appears more conservative than the other Interior Salishan languages; or else its central location has resulted in its sharing features with languages both to the northwest and the southeast. This conservatism can be seen in the consonant inventory, which is relatively unchanged from Proto–Interior Salish, and in having all of the affixes listed in table 2. Grammars of Northern Okanagan are Watkins (1970, from Head of the Lake) and Hébert (1982, from Nicola Lake); A. Mattina (1973) is a grammar of the Colville subdialect of Okanagan. Pattison (1978) is a study of the phonology and morphology of the Okanagan spoken in the Nicola Valley. Somday (1980) and A. Mattina (1987) are extensive dictionaries of Okanagan, and Doak (1983) is an appraisal, reproduction, and retranscription of Okanagan word lists collected by James Teit in 1908. A long Okanagan text of European origin is given in A. Mattina (1985); three texts in Okanagan can be found in Hill-Tout (1911) and another in A. Mattina (1994). Turner, Bouchard, and Kennedy (1980) provide extensive ethnobotanical information on Okanagan. See N. Mattina (1996), A. Mattina (1993), and A. Mattina and Jack (1992).

• KALISPEL Kalispel is recognized as consisting of a dialect chain and is usually considered to comprise three distinct dialects, representing points along this chain: Spokane along the Spokane River, Kalispel along the Pend Oreille River from northeastern Washington into western Montana, and Flathead in Montana west of the Rocky Mountains. The most noticeable difference is between Spokane and the others; Spokane retains r from Proto-Salishan, while the dialects to the east have changed it to l. Kalispel as a whole is marked by a tendency to lose that part of a word following the stressed vowel; this tendency increases from west to east in the dialect chain. Kalispel

and Coeur d'Alene are the only Interior Salish languages to have shifted the velar obstruents k k̓ x to palato-alveolars č č̓ š, a change that otherwise occurred in all coast Salishan languages except Bella Coola. Kalispel is like Okanagan in having only one series of coronal consonants. Kalispel makes regular use of an unusual nested reduplication found only sporadically in neighboring languages. All Interior Salish languages mark 'out-of-control' (where an agent has no control over an action) by reduplicating C_2 of a root; but in Kalispel in weak roots of shapes other an CVC (i.e., weak CVCC, CCVC, or CVCV´C roots) both the second and third consonants are repeated with the stressed vowel between them: šlič 'turn' becomes šlličč 'it got turned by accident'. Grammars for all three dialects of Kalispel exist, although the ones for Flathead are old and inadequate; for Flathead see Mengarini (1861) and Post (1904; given in modern transcription in Speck 1980), for Kalispel see Vogt (1940), and for Spokane see B.F. Carlson (1972). Vogt (1940) includes texts and a dictionary; more comprehensive dictionaries are Carlson and Flett (1989) and Giorda et al. (1877–1879; vol. 17:39)(fig. 3); although old, this dictionary contains much valuable information. Other vocabulary lists are Weisel (1952) and Krueger (1960, 1961, 1961a, 1967a). A taxonomy of Flathead plants and plant terminology can be found in Hart (1974, 1979). Additional grammatical information can be found in B.F. Carlson (1976, 1980, 1980a, 1989, 1990, 1993) and Carlson and Thompson (1982). For a Spokane text see B.F. Carlson (1978). One of the earliest language works on the Plateau was a Spokane primer (vol. 17:38) (E. Walker and Eells 1842). See Bates and Carlson (1992, 1997), Orser (1993), C. Smith (1991), and Flemming, Ladefoged, and Thomason (1994).

• COEUR D'ALENE Coeur d'Alene is a rather homogeneous language originally spoken in a broad area around Coeur d'Alene Lake in northern Idaho. Dialect variations have not been noted. Like Kalispel, Coeur d'Alene has shifted the velar obstruents k k̓ x to č č̓ š and has only one series of coronal obstruents. Distinctive to Coeur d'Alene is a change of many instances of y, γ, and w to, respectively, d, ǰ, and gʷ, making it the only Interior language to have contrastive voiced stops. Coeur d'Alene has also shifted stress forward in words to a much greater degree than any other Interior language, and it has merged the glottalized (ejective) stops t̓ and ƛ̓ as t̓ (note that this merger is in the opposite direction from the merger in Lillooet, Thompson, and Shuswap, where they merged to ƛ̓). Coeur d'Alene has developed a number of locative prefixes beyond what is usually found in Interior Salish to a total of seven or eight. Reichard (1933–1938), long the standard grammar of Coeur d'Alene, is expanded by Doak (1997). Studies of the phonology of the language are Sloat (1966, 1972, 1980), Doak (1992), and Johnson (1975). Reichard (1939) is a comprehensive stem list. Nicodemus (1975) is a lengthy but erratic dictionary of Coeur d'Alene; this work evidently began as a direct translation of an English-language dictionary, but the project diminished part way into the alphabet, so that entries under *a* through *d* are much more extensive than those following. Nicodemus (1975a) is a set of lessons in Coeur d'Alene. See Palmer (1990) and Doak (1991, 1993).

• COLUMBIAN Columbian (also called Moses Columbian; the native name for the language is *nxaʔamxcín*, meaning 'language of the local people') was originally spoken along the middle portion of the Columbia River in Washington, but the few remaining speakers in 1990 resided mainly to the north on the Colville Reservation. Dialect differences from south to north were very slight, involving only a few grammatical differences and some lexical items. Columbian differs from its neighbors in a number of striking respects. It has lost Proto-Salishan *γ, merging it with *y*; but it is one of four Salishan languages to preserve *r*; and it has developed two voiceless pharyngeal fricatives. Columbian (like Coeur d'Alene) has innovated a number of locative prefixes; other Interior Salish languages have only one or two, but Columbian has eight. It also has prefixes for translocative (away from the speaker) and cislocative (toward the speaker), possibly under the influence of Sahaptin to the south, where such categories are expressed by suffixes. Columbian, along with Coeur d'Alene and Okanagan, has more indirective suffixes (which change the valence of direct and oblique objects) than other Salishan languages, distinguishing three or four varieties. It has developed a second reciprocal suffix alongside the one derived from Proto-Salishan (although the two do not appear to contrast semantically) by interpreting the ending of *-waxʷ* 'reciprocal' as a second-person singular marker; the new form is *-wap lx* also 'reciprocal', with *-p* as if it were second-person plural, and adding the third-person plural clitic. Columbian is the only Interior Salish language to retain from Proto-Salishan a suffix to mark a topic when it has become a direct object (the cognate in Coeur d'Alene appears to have merged with the causative suffix; Doak 1993); this suffix is otherwise found only in Coast Salishan languages from Lushootseed south (Kinkade 1990), and in Lillooet, where it has a related but different function. For a short lexicon of Columbian see Kinkade (1981), while Kinkade (1975) is a semantic study of Columbian anatomical terminology; Krueger (1967) also contains a limited amount of vocabulary. For grammatical information see Kinkade (1980, 1982, 1982a, 1983 and in part 1981, 1981a). For a Columbian text see Kinkade (1978). See Czaykowska-Higgins (1991, 1993, 1993a, 1997), and Bessell and Czaykowska-Higgins (1993).

Sahaptian

In historic times, Sahaptian speech extended from west of the Cascade Divide in Washington State to the Bitterroot Range of Idaho, a distance of about 375 miles. The two Sahaptian languages, Sahaptin in the west and Nez Perce in the east, thus were spoken throughout most of the Southern Plateau.

Sahaptin is the linguists' and anthropologists' name for the complex of mutually intelligible dialects that by 1990 were spoken by about 100 Indian people who lived on the Yakima, Warm Springs, and Umatilla reservations, as well as in several smaller communities at Celilo, Oregon, and at Rock Creek, Priest Rapids, and Nespelem, all in Washington. The name Sahaptin had no popular currency among its speakers, who generally referred to it as Yakima, Warm Springs, Umatilla, Walla Walla, or the like. There is no single native term for the language. Sahaptin is an anglicization of the name for the Nez Perce Indians that occurs in several Interior Salish languages, for instance, Columbian Salish *sháptnəxʷ*.

The Sahaptin dialects fall into two main divisions: Northern and Southern Sahaptin. The Northern division comprises the dialects of two clusters, Northwest and Northeast Sahaptin, while the Southern division is made up of the dialects of the Columbia River cluster.

The Northwest Sahaptin cluster includes dialects from the Klikitat, Yakima, Taitnapam (Upper Cowlitz), and Upper Nisqually (Mishalpam) areas. They were concentrated primarily, but not exclusively, in the Yakima drainage system. The main Klikitat villages were found on the Lewis, White Salmon, and Klickitat rivers, but some Klikitat also lived in villages on the north bank of the Columbia below The Dalles. The Taitnapam and Mishalpam dialects were located west of the Cascade Divide, while the Yakima proper occupied the lower part of the Yakima Valley, the Kittitas dialect being spoken above Union Gap. The Yakima, Kittitas, and Taitnapam dialects all share some lexical resemblances with the neighboring Salishan languages and thus evidence contact with them. The Yakimas and Kittitas were missionized by French Roman Catholic priests in the past century and have more French loanwords than the other Sahaptin dialects.

The dialects of the Northeast Sahaptin cluster were spoken on the Columbia River from above Wallula Gap to the head of Priest Rapids and along the Snake River to a point somewhere east of the mouth of the Palouse River, as well as in the extreme lower Yakima system, the lower Walla Walla system, and much of the Palouse system. Northeast Sahaptin dialect names are Walla Walla (Waluulapam), Lower Snake, (Naxiyampam, including Chamna and Wauyukma villages), Wanapam, and Palouse. The Northeast dialects all evidence strong grammatical, lexical, and phonological influences from Nez Perce.

The dialects of the Columbia River cluster were spoken along the Columbia River from the head of Fivemile Rapids (east of The Dalles) eastward to Wallula Gap, as well as in large parts of the Deschutes, John Day, and Umatilla river systems. They include the Tygh Valley, Tenino, Celilo (Wayampam), John Day, Rock Creek, and Umatilla dialects. The westernmost Columbia River dialects show strong lexical borrowing from Northwest Sahaptin, probably from

Klikitat and Yakima, while the Umatilla dialect shows much lexical borrowing from Nez Perce.

Most speakers of the Nez Perce language resided in 1997 on the Nez Perce Reservation, but there was a small community of speakers on the Colville Reservation, and a handful on the Umatilla Reservation. In total, there were fewer than 100 fluent speakers by 1990, and perhaps twice that number who had some knowledge of the language.

The traditional territories of the Nez Perce spanned the Clearwater drainage basin and the northwestern part of the Salmon system (Walker 1973:55). The lack of dialectal diversity in Nez Perce is in striking contrast to that within Sahaptin. There are but two groupings, the Upper (or Eastern) and the Lower (or Western). The Snake River served as the boundary between the two. The dialectal contrast suggests that Nez Perce speech has occupied its territory for a shorter period of time than has Sahaptin, according to Sapir's (1916:76–78) principle that the area of greatest linguistic differentiation is the area of longest occupation. Nez Perce dialect differences comprise a few phonological and a very small number of lexical features.

The genetic relationship of Sahaptin and Nez Perce is close and was apparent even to Meriwether Lewis and William Clark in 1805–1806. Several dimensions of the relationship have been explored and features of Proto-Sahaptian reconstructed (Aoki 1962, 1966, 1966a; Rigsby 1965, 1965a, 1969, 1971, 1996; Rigsby and Silverstein 1969; Rude 1996, 1997). Proto-language reconstructions have included both consonantal and vocalic features, the development of their reflexes in the modern languages, characteristics of the Proto-Sahaptian kinship terminology, and a number of semantic taxonomies involving age, sex, and status terms, numerals, and color designations.

The consonants were first treated by Aoki (1962). Major features of consonantal develoment are the loss of glottalized sonorants and the addition of a velar palatalization rule in Sahaptin and the loss of the Proto-Sahaptian lateral obstruents *ƚ, ƛ λ/ in Nez Perce. The Sahaptin velar palatalization rule is similar in effect to velar palatalization rules

that operated historically in Coeur d'Alene and Kalispel, the easternmost Interior Salish languages.

The vowels have been discussed in several places (Aoki 1962, 1966a; Jacobsen 1968; Rigsby and Silverstein 1969) and have a wider relevance to general phonological theory (Aoki 1968; Chomsky and Halle 1968:377–379; Kiparsky 1982; Zwicky 1971).

There are basically two types of numeral systems found among the Sahaptian peoples that involve the numerals 'six', 'seven', 'eight', and 'nine' (see table 5). The two patterns are clearly seen in the Yakima and Nez Perce columns and may be so designated. The comparative evidence indicates that those Sahaptin dialects whose speakers had the greater amount of contact and interaction with the Nez Perces through their proximity have borrowed the Nez Perce pattern of numeral formation, either in whole or in part (Rigsby 1965:Chap. IV). The greater complexity and arbitrariness of the Yakima type, as well as its dialectal distribution, make it the likely candidate for Proto-Sahaptian status.

There are other obvious historically significant resemblances in numerals among the Plateau languages, but it is difficult, if not impossible, to discriminate those that may derive from common genetic ancestry from those that reflect borrowing. Note the resemblances in the forms for 'two' in Sahaptin (nápt, níipt), Nez Perce (lepít), Cayuse (líplint), Molala (lépkeʔ), and Klamath (laʹp). They involve lVp- or nVp- shape, which may be a metathesized form of the pVn- shape that is found in some of the California Penutian languages, indeed the 'Pen-' of 'Penutian'. The ethnographic ethnohistorical, and archeological data (Brunton 1968; Butler 1958–1959; Desmond 1952) all indicate the presence of gambling and trade relations that would have provided suitable sociocultural contexts for the borrowing of numerals and patterns of numeral formation in the prehistoric period.

Nez Perce has a tradition and literature of practical and theoretical linguistic scholarship that dates back to 1839–1840, when H.H. Spalding (1839, 1840) printed a short Nez Perce primer (Rigsby 1972:737; vol. 17:38, 40), the first book print-

Table 5. Sahaptian Numeral Systems

	Nez Perce	Yakima Sahaptin	Celilo Sahaptin	Umatilla Sahaptin	Walla Walla Sahaptin
'1'	*náʹqc*	*náx̣s*	*náx̣s*	*náx̣š*	*náx̣s, láx̣s*
'2'	*lepít*	*níipt*	*nápt*	*nápt*	*nápt*
'3'	*mitáʹt*	*mítaat*	*mítaat*	*mítaat*	*mítaat*
'4'	*píʹlept*	*píniipt*	*pínapt*	*pínapt*	*pínapt*
'5'	*páx̣at*	*páx̣aat*	*páx̣at*	*páx̣at*	*páx̣at*
'6'	*ʔoyláʹqc*	*ptáx̣ninš*	*ptáx̣ninš*	*uyláx̣s*	*uyláx̣s*
'7'	*ʔuynéʹpt*	*túskaas*	*túskaski*	*uynáapt*	*uynápt*
'8'	*ʔoymátat*	*páx̣aƚumáat*	*páx̣aƚumaat*	*uymátat*	*uymítaat*
'9'	*ḱúyc*	*čimíst*	*čimíst*	*ḱuyc*	*čimst*
'10'	*púːtimt*	*pútimt*	*pútimt*	*pútimt*	*pútimt*

MATTHEWNIM TAAISKT.

PRINTED AT THE PRESS OF THE
OREGON MISSION, UNDER
THE DIRECTION OF
THE AMERICAN
BOARD, C. F.
MISSIONS.
CLEAR WATER:
M. G. FOISY, PRINTER.

1845.

MATTHEWNIM TAAISKT.

WANAHNA I.

TIMASH hiwash Jesus Christpkinih wiautsath kuph. Davidnim miahs awaka Jesus Christ, Abrahamnim miahs a-waka David.

2 Abrahamnim miahs autsama Isaac; Isaacnim miahs aut-sama Jacob; Jacobnim mamai-as autsama Judas wak aska-ma;

3 Judasnim autsama mamai-as Phares wah Zara, Tharma-pkinih; Pharesnim miahs aut-sama Esrom; Esromnim miahs autsama Aram;

4 Aramnim miahs autsama Aminadab; Aminadabnim mi-ahs autsama Naason; Naasonm miahs autsama Salmon;

5 Salmonm miahs autsama Booz Rachabkinih; Booznim miahs autsama Obed Ruthpki-nih; Obednim miahs antsama Jesse;

6 Jessenim miahs autsama David, Miohat; Davidnim Mio-hatom miahs autsama Solomon, ka yoh awaka iwapna Urianm, kunimpkinih;

7 Solomon miahs autsama Roboam; Roboamnim miahs

autsama Abia; Abianm miahs autsama Asa;

8 Asanm miahs autsama Jo-saphat; Josaphatom miahs aut-sama Joram; Joramnim miahs autsama Ozias;

9 Oziasnim miahs antsama Joatham; Joathamnim miahs autsama Achaz; Achaznim miahs autsama Ezekias;

10 Ezekiasnim miahs autsa-ma Manases; Manasesnmi mi-ahs autsama Amon; Amonnim miahs autsama Josias;

11 Josiasnim mamaias aut-sama Jechonias wak askama, ka kaua Babylonpa panahnas-ankika immuna.

12 Ka kaua panahpaiksan-kika Babylonpa immuna, kaua Jekoniasnim miahs autsama Salathiel; Salathielm miahs autsama Zorobabel;

13 Zorobabelm miahs aut-sama Abiud; Abiudnim miahs autsama Azor;

14 Azornm miahs autsama Sadoc; Sadocnim miahs autsa-ma Achim, Achimnim miahs autsama Eliud;

15 Eliudnim miahs autsama Eleazar, Eleazarnim miahs

Fig. 4. The Gospel According to St. Matthew in Nez Perce (Spalding 1845), title p. and p. 1, Matthew 1:1–15. Henry H. Spalding was a Presbyterian missionary at Lapwai, Idaho (vol. 4:686).

ed in the Oregon Territory (Ballou 1922). Sound symbolism is described in Aoki (1994a). Modern grammars of Nez Perce are Velten (1943), Aoki (1970), and Rude (1985). Aoki (1994) is a dictionary. Additional studies of specific aspects of Nez Perce grammar are Aoki (1963a, 1968) and Rude (1982, 1986, 1986a, 1988, 1991, 1992a). In addition to Spalding's (1845) translations (fig. 4), Nez Perce is well represented by texts, as in Phinney (1934), Aoki (1978, 1979), and Aoki and Walker (1989)("Mythology," fig. 2, this vol.).

Pandosy (1862) began his work in Sahaptin in the 1850s, publishing a short grammar and dictionary in 1862, while St. Onge (1872) prepared a Yakima primer and catechism (fig. 5). The standard grammar of Sahaptin for many years was Jacobs (1931); there is a grammatical sketch in volume 17:666–692. Rude (1989, 1991a, 1992, 1994) studies grammar. Sahaptin is also richly represent-ed in published texts; see Jacobs (1929, 1934–1937), and Rigsby (1978) gives one Coyote story. V. Hymes (1987) is a more recent analysis of native texts. Beavert and Rigsby (1975) is a dictionary of Sahaptin. Hunn (1980) is a study of native classification of fish, and Hunn (1979) considers folk classification in Sahaptin more generally. Hunn (1990) includes a chapter on the Yakima language, and there is much Sahaptin vocabulary throughout the vol-ume, including an exhaustive list of names for Sahaptin

kinship terms, fauna, and flora in appendixes. Hunn (1991) examines place-names.

The early missionaries undertook linguistic work and reli-gious translation for the express purpose of converting the Indians more quickly and with better understanding to Christianity. Small numbers of Nez Perces and Yakimas learned the missionary alphabets and used them for person-al correspondence and lexicographic work, but writing the native language never became common in either communi-ty. Undoubtedly more people learned to read the several Bible translations and other religious materials, but their use too has become moribund, although they retain great sym-bolic value. Serious attempts by the White missionaries to use Sahaptin or Nez Perce in their endeavors dropped off considerably by 1900, by which time most Sahaptins and Nez Perces spoke English in all degrees of fluency and com-petency. Some Sahaptins and Nez Perces had earlier used the Chinook Jargon to communicate with the Whites, but it never achieved the same popularity in the Southern Plateau that it had in the Willamette Valley and along the Northwest Coast.

The number of people who regularly and competently spoke Sahaptin or Nez Perce decreased tremendously dur-ing World War II and the years following. The wholesale transfer of speech functions to English in many households and schooling only in English resulted in many Indian children acquiring little or no native language competence. In 1997 the number of people who could narrate the extensive repertoires of Coyote stories and other oral literature was fewer than 25 in either language. People who could converse in various topical domains numbered several hundreds, but with varying degrees of fluency. Fluent speakers under 40 years of age were exceptional. On the Nez Perce, Umatilla, Warm Springs, and Yakima reservations there have been efforts to revive and maintain the native languages through classroom instruction and the development of written materials.

Cayuse

The Cayuse Indians originally spoke a language that is now extinct, having been replaced mainly by a Lower Nez Perce dialect. The loss of the Cayuse language was apparently well advanced in the first half of the nineteenth century and was not occasioned by the arrival of the Whites. Lewis and Clark in 1806 regarded the Cayuses as one of the Nez Perce bands and did not remark upon Cayuse linguistic distinctiveness (Lewis 1961:688–689). Samuel Black (1829) collected a Cayuse vocabulary in the 1820s (vol. 17:41)(fig. 6). The missionary Marcus Whitman wrote in 1837 that the Cayuses had so intermarried with their Nez Perce neighbors that all spoke Nez Perce and that the younger Cayuses did not understand Cayuse at all (A.B. Hulbert and D.P. Hulbert 1936–1941, 6:279). H.W. Henshaw of the Bureau of Ethnology visited the Cayuses on the Umatilla Reservation in 1888 and found only six old men and women who spoke the Cayuse language (Henshaw 1888; Powell 1891:128), although he must have missed a few more. Melville Jacobs, Verne Ray, and Morris Swadesh (Jacobs, Ray, and Swadesh 1930) collected some Cayuse lexical items in the early 1930s, but were unable to work with the few remaining fluent speakers. In the 1960s older Indians on the Umatilla Reservation told Rigsby that some family groups had continued to use Cayuse into the 1920s and that the last fluent speakers died during the 1930s.

During the early nineteenth century, the Cayuse Indians lived in and controlled the following territories: the Butter Creek drainage system, the upper Umatilla system, the upper Walla Walla system, the Touchet system, the Tucannon system (less Pataha Creek), the upper Grande Ronde system, the Powder River system, and the Burnt River system (Confederated Tribes of the Umatilla Reservation 1959:13). It seems likely that Cayuse speech may have had a wider distribution in the past, but it had been extinguished from its western, northern, and eastern fronts by Sahaptin and Nez Perce. The lexical resemblances that Cayuse shared with Molala may reflect their prior contiguity.

Rigsby (1969) assembled the known Cayuse linguistic materials, which consist almost exclusively of lexical items and yield little information on grammatical structure. Their phonetic accuracy and reliability leaves much to be desired, so that it is not possible to reconstitute more than the broader outlines of Cayuse surface phonetics. The phonetic inventory includes a voiceless bilabial fricative and a velar nasal, whose phonemic statuses are not clear. Both features are

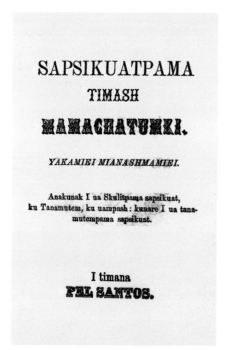

Eastern Wash. State Histl. Soc., Cheney Cowles Mus., Spokane.
Fig. 5. Yakima primer by St. Onge (1872), title p. and pp. 38 and 39, biblical passages. It included teaching materials, selections from the gospels, songs, and a catechism. Lesson 27 focuses on the sacred heart of Jesus, how he loves all people and how his blood flowed to cleanse hearts ('made to become white'). Lesson 28 centers on the heart of Mary and how the gospel delivers people from sin.

found in the neighboring Northern Paiute language and in Molala and the several Kalapuyan languages of the Cascades slopes-Willamette Valley area, but they do not occur in the surrounding Sahaptian languages.

Molala

Although the Molala Indians most likely occupied a single large tract from Oregon City south to Douglas County along the Cascade Mountains, they are frequently divided into two groups—the Northern Molala, who occupied the Molalla River drainage system and the southwestern tributaries of the Clackamas River (Frachtenberg 1910–1911), and the Southern Molala, who were found on the upper Rogue River and on the upper portions of the North and South forks of the Umpqua River (Spier 1927:360–361).

There are no linguistic materials available from the Southern Molala. Hale (1846), Gibbs (1851), and Gatschet (1877, 1877a, 1877b) collected word lists, texts, and structural materials in Northern Molala, but its major documentation is found in the field notes of Frachtenberg (1910–1911) and Jacobs (1927–1930). Frachtenberg's materials comprise texts, vocabulary, and extensive paradigms, but his transcriptions are often poor. Jacobs's materials are well transcribed but do not cover the same broad range of structure. Swadesh (1954) tape-recorded a word list from Fred Yelkes, the last known speaker of the Molala language, who died in 1958. Besides Hale's the only data published on Molala are a word list in Curtis (1907–1930, 8:195–198).

Little can yet be said of Molala deep phonology, but in surface phonetics, it exhibits moderate clustering of consonants, as compared to Sahaptian and Chinookan, and frequent geminate consonants. Like Chinookan and Sahaptian, it is synthetic to polysynthetic in morphological structure and mainly agglutinative in technique of composition, employing both prefixation and suffixation. Its syntax is nominative-accusative in type, with partially suppletive nominative and accusative independent pronoun sets. The independent possessive pronouns are built upon the accusative bases, which are also suffixed to nominals to mark possession. This pattern is similar to Klamath, but differs from Sahaptin and Nez Perce, which evidence a former identity of nominative and possessive case endings. Like Sahaptian and Chinookan, nominals are cross-referenced in the verb by affixes: object nominals (including the reflexive) are indexed by prefixes, subject nominals by suffixes, of which there are several series that also mark tense-aspect distinctions. However, there are no apparent historically significant formal or functional resemblances in these cross-reference systems. Berman (1996) explores the position of Molala in Plateau Penutian.

Earlier scholars generally grouped the Cayuse and Molala languages together in a family called Waiilatpuan. Rigsby (1965, 1966, 1969) surveyed the relevant materials and con-

Hudson's Bay Company Arch., Winnipeg, Man.: B. 146/e/2 fol.21 (N3218). Fig. 6. Comparative vocabulary of English, Walla Walla (Sahaptin), Nez Perce, and Cayuse collected by employees at Fort Nez Perces and submitted by Samuel Black in his report to the Hudson's Bay Company in 1829, folio 21 of 31 folios. Black was a Hudson's Bay Company chief trader or master at Fort Nez Perces, 1825–1830 (Stern 1993:87). These vocabularies are among the earliest language material collected in the Plateau.

cluded that there was no clear evidence for their genetic relationship or for the Waiilatpuan subgrouping that had been assumed since Hale (1846) grouped them under the name Waiilatpu.

Chinook

The Upper Chinook branch of the Chinookan family was a chain of languages that extended from the Northwest Coast area to the Plateau. On the Plateau it was represented by Kiksht, which was spoken in two villages, Wasco and Wishram, situated near The Dalles, Oregon, on the Columbia River at the western border of the Southern Plateau. Other dialects of Kiksht were farther downriver around the Cascade Rapids and on the lower Willamette and Clackamas rivers, and a second Upper Chinook language was spoken beyond these by the Cathlamet. The Chinookans appear to be fairly recent arrivals from downriver and their expansion to The Dalles area with its rich salmon fisheries was no doubt connected with their role as traders and middlemen (D.H. French 1961; Rigsby 1965:241–249).

Although Kiksht (like the other Chinookan languages) has a thoroughly nominative-ergative syntax with extensive appositional cross-referencing by pronominal prefixes or ergative, nominative, and dative nominals that are incorporated into the verb (Silverstein 1972:386–405), its easternmost Wasco-Wishram varieties have borrowed three case endings and a derivational suffix (Sapir 1911a:650–654, 1921b:206) from their Sahaptin neighbor, which displays a nominative-accusative syntax of quite different type. They include the possessive, instrumental, and locative case endings. Wasco-Wishram may also have borrowed the Molala allative suffix. Sapir (1911:638–645) described the Wishram consonantal ablaut system, which uses sound-symbolism to mark diminutives and augmentatives. Sound symbolism is discussed in Silverstein (1994). It is clear that Sahaptin has an almost identical system, lacking only the voiced-voiceless opposition. Silverstein (1974) discussed the development of complex tense categories in Kiksht and noted the presence of a similar recent versus remote past tense distinction in Nez Perce. Molala too distinguishes recent from remote past (Frachtenberg 1910–1911). Kiksht shares cislocative and translocative directional categories with Sahaptin, Nez Perce, and Columbian Salish (Rigsby 1971). Cayuse and Molala have the cislocative only, it appears. Dyk (1933) is a grammar of Kiksht; Dyk and Hymes (1956) and Silverstein (1977, 1978, 1984a) are studies of various grammatical issues in the language. Wasco and Wishram texts appear in Sapir (1909). Studies and presentations of several Upper Chinookan texts are to be found in Hymes (1981).

Kiksht had the reputation among the Sahaptins and Nez Perces, at least, of being a difficult language to learn and speak. Oriented toward trade and commerce, the Wasco-Wishram valued bilingualism and most also spoke a Sahaptin dialect. Few Sahaptins spoke or understood Kiksht well. In the 1990s there were a handful of Wasco-Wishram speakers on the Warm Springs and Yakima reservations. Most people of Wasco-Wishram descent there spoke Sahaptin, if they spoke an Indian language at all. There were no fluent speakers of Kiksht under 60 years of age in 1990.

Klamath

The Klamath language was spoken in two dialect groupings: Klamath proper and Modoc. The Klamath and the Modoc lived "on the high plateau of eastern Oregon, wherein lies the group of lakes that gives rise to the Klamath River. The southern half of this basin about lower Klamath and Tule lakes is Modoc territory, extending southward across the lava beds in the direction of Pit River. The northern half, which lies against the Cascade range, is the home of the Klamath"

(Spier 1930:8). The habitat of the Modoc, in northeastern California, was somewhat different from that of the Klamath, and the linguistic distinction probably reflects social separation resting in part on this factor.

Gatschet (1890) and de Angulo and Freeland (1931:2) described the Klamath and Modoc dialects as perhaps no more different than "English of New England and that of Virginia." M.A.R. Barker (1964:1) characterized the two dialects as "very close." However, Voegelin (1946:96–98) observed some lexical differences between Klamath and Modoc in semantic ranges and phonemic shapes. Voegelin considered that differences in inflectional paradigms, and more particularly, in derivational paradigms (verb theme composition) in the two dialects overshadowed the lexical differences. He also suggested that there had been local group dialects at a level lower than the traditional Klamath-Modoc split.

Gatschet (1890) published a massive two-volume work on the Klamath Indians that contained a grammar, texts, and a dictionary (fig. 7). It was one of the first treatments of a North American language to present the structure of that language in its own terms. M.A.R. Barker (1963, 1963a, 1964) published a collection of Klamath texts, a dictionary, and a grammar. His excellent works have provided the basis for a number of papers that treat aspects of Klamath phonology from the generative phonological point of view (for example Kean 1973; Kisseberth 1972, 1973, 1973a). See also Rude (1988a) for a syntactic study of Klamath and DeLancey (1987, 1988, 1991) for pronouns.

Barker (1964:1) mentioned 50–60 good speakers and 200–300 persons with some knowledge of the language, but by 1990 only four individuals remained who could speak Klamath and only one who knew the Modoc dialect. An effort to revive the language was pursued by tribal leaders ("Klamath and Modoc," fig. 14, this vol.).

Areal Features

There is no outstanding set of language traits that sets off the Plateau as a major linguistic diffusion area distinct from other regions; rather it is part of a larger area that includes the Northwest Coast culture area. Many of the features found in this larger Northwest region are rare elsewhere in the world, and the combination of a number of them marks this region as linguistically unique and unusual. However, clusters of features are distinctive to the Plateau, and it is possible to divide the Plateau into two subareas according to shared features. These two subareas correspond to the division between Kootenai and the Salishan languages on the one hand and the six languages sometimes included in the large Penutian phylum on the other. Features cut across language family or phylum boundaries less noticeably than on the Northwest Coast, although adjacent Salishan and Sahaptian languages do share a number of specific features (such as the use of affixes for translocative and cislocative direc-

ers have noted loanwords shared across family boundaries (Rigsby 1965, 1971, 1996; Aoki 1975) and shared grammatical categories and semantic structures (Silverstein 1974). The lack of adequate descriptions of some languages makes it more difficult to identify widespread morphological, syntactic, and semantic features; this is particularly true for Nicola, Cayuse, and Molala, and specific reference to these three languages must often be omitted from what follows.

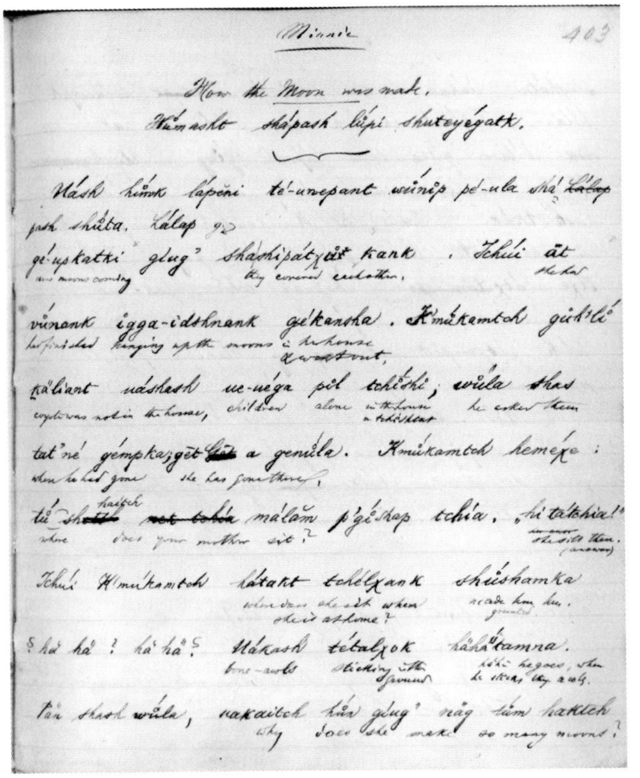

Generally speaking, Plateau languages have elaborate consonant systems, especially Salishan languages and the languages adjacent to them to the south, Sahaptin and Kiksht (table 6).

Kootenai, Nez Perce, Cayuse, Molala, and Klamath have one-third fewer stops and fricatives than Salishan languages; they lack the rounded velars and uvulars, and they have fewer lateral consonants (especially Kootenai, which has only the voiceless lateral *ł*, a sound absent on the Plateau only in Klamath). All the languages oppose a glottalized (ejective) series with an unglottalized series of stops and affricates. $λ$ is found only in Sahaptin, Kiksht, Cayuse, and Molala. Plateau Salishan languages uniformly lack voiced stops, except for Coeur d'Alene, which developed *d*, *ǰ*, and g^w from, respectively, **y*, **γ*, and **w*. A contrast between a *c* (alveolar) series and a *č* (palato-alveolar) series is found only in Kalispel, Coeur d'Alene, Sahaptin, and for sound symbolic purposes in Kiksht; the contrast between retracted and unretracted apicals is limited to Lillooet, Thompson, Shuswap, and Columbian. The bilabial fricative $φ$ occurred only in Cayuse and Molala and had apparently developed from a rounded velar fricative x^w. Glottalized resonants are not reported for Sahaptin, Kiksht, Cayuse, or Molala, and are limited to nasals in Kootenai. The velar nasal $η$ occurred only in Cayuse and Molala. The resonants *z*, *r*, *γ*, *ʕ*, and $ʕ^w$ are found only in one or another Salishan language; in spite of the symbols used to represent these sounds, they all function as resonants, and there is often a grammatical interchange of related sounds between these resonants and obstruents or vowels. Otherwise Plateau languages only have *m*, *n*, *l*, *y*, and *w* (and Kootenai lacks *l*). The consonant inventory of Klamath is most unlike those of other Plateau languages; it has a full series of voiced stops matching voiceless and glottalized stops, it has only two fricatives (*s*, *h*), and is unique

Smithsonian, NAA: ms. 1581:403.

Fig. 7. "How the Moon was made," a Klamath text dictated to Albert S. Gatschet by Minnie Froben in 1877. Froben was one of Gatschet's 2 most important informants for his Klamath-Modoc myths and ethnological texts and assisted him in editing all of them. P. 1 of the original manuscript recording, with changes, was published in Gatschet (1890, 2:105). In this myth, Coyote, *was*, a female diety, creates 24 moons rather than 12, so that winter can be twice as long. The primary deity, the god of all life, *gmokʼamč*, thinks Coyote is too greedy so he decides to punish her for prolonging winter for her own purposes. He visits Coyote's home, when he knows she is away, and from a daughter learns Coyote's sitting place, which he then booby-traps with an awl. He destroys half the moons and when Coyote returns and sits in her usual place, she is disemboweled by the awl (Janne Underriner, communication to editors 1996).

tion markers, the use of pronominal affixes for specifying direct objects that are the topic of discourse, the structure of native taxonomies of flora and fauna). Phonological features distinctive to a given area are easiest to recognize (Boas 1899, 1911, 1920, 1929; Jacobs 1954; Haas 1969; Rigsby 1996; Sherzer 1973, 1976; vol. 7:30–51; Velten 1943). Oth-

Table 6. Plateau Consonants

	Lab	Apic	Alve	Lat	Pal	Vel	Uvu	RdVl	RdU	Ph	Lar
Voiceless or fortis, often aspirated	*p*	*t* *ç*	*c*	*λ*	*č*	*k*	*q*	k^w	q^w		*ʔ*
Glottalized	*ṗ*	*ṫ*	*ċ*	*λ̇*	*č̇*	*k̇*	*q̇*	$k̇^w$	$q̇^w$		
Voiced or lenis	*b*	*d*			*ǰ*	*g*	*ġ*	g^w			
Fricatives	*φ*	*ṣ*	*s*	*ł*	*š*	*x*	*x̣*	x^w	x^w	*ḥ,ḥ^w*	*h*
Resonants	*m*	*n* *z*	*r*	*l* *ļ*	*y*	*γ* *η*		*w*		*ʕ, ʕ^w*	
Glottalized resonants	*ṁ*	*ṅ* *ż*	*ṙ*	*l̇* *ļ̇*	*ẏ*	*γ̇* *η̇*		*ẇ*		*ʕ̇, ʕ̇^w*	
Voiceless resonants	*M*	*N*		*L*	*Y*			*W*			

Table 7. Language Features Characterizing the Plateau as a Whole

	1	2	3	4	5	6	7	8	9	10	11	12	13	14	15	16	17	18
Kootenai	●	●		●	●	●		●				●	●				●	
Lillooet	●	●		●		●	●	●	●	●	●	●	●	●		●	●	
Thompson	●	●		●		●	●	●	●	●	●	●	●	●	●	●	●	
Shuswap	●	●				●	●	●	●	●	●	●	●	●	●	●		●
Okanagan	●	●				●	●	●	●	●	●	●	●	●	●	●	●	
Kalispel	●		●	●		●	●	●	●	●	●	●	●	●	●	●	●	
Coeur d'Alene			●	●	●	●	●	●	●	●	●	●	●	●	●	●	●	
Columbian	●	●		●		●	●	●	●	●	●	●	●	●	●	●	●	●
Sahaptin	●	●		●		●	●	●	●	●	●	●	●	●	●	●	●	●
Nez Perce	●	●		●	●	●	●	●	●	●	●	●	●	●		●	●	●
Cayuse	●			●	●		?	?	?	?	?	?	?	?		?	?	?
Molala	●			●	●		?	?	?		?	?	?	?		?	?	?
Kiksht			●	●									●					●
Klamath		●		●	●	●	●	●			●	●	●	?	●	?	●	●

Features

1. Two stop-affricate series (glottalized and voiceless) only.
2. A single alveolar or palatal affricate-spirant obstruent series (or both alternating nondistinctively).
3. Contrast between alveolar and palatal affricate-spirant positions; symbolic only in Kiksht.
4. Velar and uvular obstruent series contrast.
5. An ejective lateral affricate ($\grave{\lambda}$) is lacking.
6. Glottalized resonants contrast with plain resonants.
7. Clusters of four or more consonants are allowed word-medially and word-finally.
8. Vowels may be drawn out for emphasis, especially in narratives.
9. Numeral classifiers (for counting various types of objects) are present.
10. Three (or more) primary aspectual categories are distinguished.
11. At least some aspect markers are suffixed or postposed.
12. Marking of plurality is largely optional.
13. Different formations are used for distributive and collective plurals.
14. The language is at least partly ergative.
15. Predicates/verbs marked for plurality refer to a plural subject in intransitive forms, but a plural object in transitive forms.
16. Possessive constructions may be used as main predicates with at least a few roots (e.g., 'my liking ...').
17. 'Ripe' and 'cooked' are expressed by the same lexical item, or one is derived from the other; the same is sometimes true for 'unripe' and 'raw'.
18. Different roots are used for the singular and plural of various concepts (e.g., 'sit', 'stand', 'take'), although each member of such pairs is considered a distinct concept within the language, coded by a single stem; in Lillooet 'die' is the only such pair.

Table 8. Language Features Typical Primarily of Salish

	1	2	3	4	5	6
Kootenai			●			
Lillooet			●	●	●	
Thompson			●	●		
Shuswap	●		●	●	●	
Okanagan	●	●	●	●	●	●
Kalispel	●	●		?	b	●
Coeur d'Alene	●	●	●	●	●	●
Columbian	●	●	●	●		b
Cayuse	?	?	?		?	●
Kiksht	a	●				
Klamath			●	●	●	

^a Few instances of the feature; not systematic.
^b Partial presence of the feature.

Features

1. Clusters of four or more consonants are permitted word-initially.
2. Aspect is marked primarily by prefixes or proclitics.
3. Tense is not a basic grammatical category and is not obligatorily marked.
4. Two temporal categories are marked (although they are usually not obligatory).
5. Deictic particles resembling definite articles are used.
6. 'Blue' and 'green' are expressed by a single lexical item, opposed to 'yellow'.

on the Plateau in having a full series of voiceless resonants matching plain and glottalized series.

Vowel systems on the Plateau are much simpler than consonant systems. Only three or four vowel positions generally contrast. The only exception is Nez Perce, which has five contrasting vowels. On the other hand, vowel systems are augmented by adding a long set in Sahaptin, Nez Perce, Klamath, and, as far as can be determined, in Molala. Several Interior Salish languages increased an original four-vowel inventory by including a set of vowels produced by retracting the root and body of the tongue; the full set of retracted vowels is found in Thompson and Columbian. This retracted set merged fully or partially with nonretracted vowels in the other languages, thereby again decreasing the number of basic vowel contrasts. Kalispel and Okanagan also merged original *$\hat{\partial}$ with other vowels, so that now Kalispel has only five vowels and Okanagan only three. The origin of these retracted vowels is unclear, but it is likely that they resulted from the loss of pharyngeal resonants.

Plateau languages are predominantly polysynthetic, incorporating a number of concepts such as subject, object, tense, aspect, and mode into a single word. Morphophone-

Table 9. Language Features Found in Salish and Kootenai

	1	2	3	4	5	6	7	8	9	10	11	12
Kootenai				•			•			•		
Lillooet	•	•	•	•	•			•	•	•	•	•
Thompson	•	•	•	•	•			?	•	•	•	•
Shuswap	•	•	•	•	•	•	•	•	•	•	•	
Okanagan	•	•	•	•	•		•	•	•	•	•	•
Kalispel		•		•	•	•	•	•	•	•	•	•
Coeur d'Alene			•	•	•		•	?	•	•	•	
Columbian	•		•	•	•		•		•	•	•	

Features
1. A glottalized lateral affricate ƛ̓ occurs, but a matching nonglottalized λ does not.
2. There is one or more voiced velar spirant (γ).
3. There are pharyngeal consonants present.
4. Metathesis can be shown to have been a relatively common phenomenon historically; occurs in Kootenai at the phonetic level.
5. Lexical suffixes (expressing concrete notions, but phonologically unlike independent roots expressing the same notions) are common; possibly incipient in Nez Perce.
6. Two primary aspectual categories are distinguished.
7. 'Past' and 'future', when indicated, are marked by prefixes or proclitics; some are also in Lillooet.
8. Concepts of space and time occur within the same deictic particle.
9. A negative is often followed by a subordinate construction.
10. All words (except for particles) can be marked for use as the heart of clause predicates.
11. The most usual position of a main predicate is initial in a sentence.
12. 'Yellow' and 'green' are expressed by a single lexical item, opposed to 'blue'.

Table 10. Language Features Characteristic of Non-Salishan Plateau Languages

	1	2	3	4	5	6	7	8	9	10	11
Kootenai		•							•		
Sahaptin		•	•	•	•	•	•	•	•	•	
Nez Perce			•	•	•	5/6	•	?		?	?
Cayuse		•	?	?	?	?	?	?		?	?
Molala		•	•	?	?	4/5	•ᵃ			?	?
Kiksht	•			•	•				•	•	
Klamath	•	•	•				•	•	•	•	

ᵃ Partial presence of the feature.

Features
1. Three stop-affricate series (glottalized, fortis, and lenis); in part also in Coeur d'Alene.
2. Labialized velars are lacking.
3. A set of long vowels contrasts with the set of short vowels.
4. Consonant symbolism occurs (i.e., consonant changes may indicate diminutive, augmentative, etc.); as historical residue in Klamath.
5. Tense is a basic, obligatory grammatical category.
6. Three primary tense categories are distinguished.
7. Tense is marked by suffixes or postposed elements.
8. Aspect is not a basic grammatical category.
9. The pronominal system distinguishes hearer-included and hearer-excluded in nonsingular first-person forms; also Shuswap.
10. Nouns are marked for case distinctions.
11. The language has a copula (linking predicate/verb like English *be*).

mic adjustments—changes of sounds in combination with each other in the derivation and inflection of words and in juxtaposition of words in phrases—are often complex. Reduplication, often of several different kinds, is extensively used to signal grammatical and lexical distinctions, except that it is absent in Nicola Athapaskan and is not a productive process in Kiksht or Kootenai. Consonant symbolism—the changing of one consonant or class of consonants to another—is widespread in the Plateau, especially south of Salishan, and is most frequently used to indicate diminutive or affectionate categories. Among grammatical categories often expressed by inflection aspectual distinctions are basic and tense is secondary in Kootenai (where particles are used, rather than affixes), Salishan and Klamath (and presumably Nicola, since this is characteristic of all other Athapaskan languages), but tense is basic and aspect less important in Kiksht, Sahaptin, and Nez Perce.

Word order in Salishan languages and Kootenai is relatively fixed, with the main predicate (generally equivalent to a verb in English) first, followed usually by no more than a single nominal argument; this nominal will be subject if the predicate is intransitive, and object if it is transitive. Kiksht also favors initial position for the verb. Word order in Nez Perce, Sahaptin, and Klamath, on the other hand, is remarkably free.

The four accompanying tables show the distribution of some of the phonological, morphological, syntactic, and semantic features shared by languages on the Plateau. Many features show distribution widely throughout the Plateau (table 7). A smaller number of features (table 8) are most frequently found in Salishan languages, but also turn up in at least one language to the south. Salishan languages are characterized by a larger number of features (table 9), while 10 features occur widely in the Penutian languages of the southern Plateau (table 10), but not in Salishan. Kootenai shares features about equally with Salishan languages and Penutian languages, although from a more general perspective it is more like Salishan.

Prehistory

The immediate, family-level relationships among Plateau languages were recognized in nineteenth-century schemes of classification. Their more remote, suprafamily, relations have undergone different interpretations and remain in some cases a matter of uncertainty. The first definitive classification of all North American languages north of Mexico, that of Powell (1891), grouped the 15 Plateau languages into seven families. Three of these, Athapaskan, Salishan, and Sahaptian, had long been recognized as natural groupings, since at least the time of Hale (1846). Five of Powell's families comprised either two-language groupings (Chinookan, Sahaptian, "Waiilatpuan"), or isolates, single languages without clear or close external relationships (Kootenai, Klamath).

It has been observed (Elmendorf 1965a:95; Miller 1966:76) that the great majority of Powell's families comprised groupings in which the interrelationships of the included languages are clear and close. When a language did not show obvious relationship to others, Powell proceeded conservatively (Powell 1891:140) and assigned it to a single-member family, a "linguistic isolate" as denoted by Haas (1965:77). This method obviously did not preclude later assignment of Powell's family units to broader classificatory schemes in which relations would be relatively remote. Such assignment was provided in the drastically

consolidated classification of Sapir (1921, 1929). This reduced Powell's seven Plateau families to parts of three much more inclusive groupings, Na-Dene, Algonkin-Wakashan, and Penutian, sometimes designated superfamilies or superstocks. Of these, Na-Dene was represented in the Plateau only by Nicola Athapaskan. Sapir's large Algonkin-Wakashan superstock represented the intriguing picture of a broad belt of genetically related languages extending across North America from the British Columbia coast to the Atlantic. However, actual relationships among the Algonkin-Wakashan units remain dubious and undocumented.

The distribution of the native languages of the Plateau reflects what is known of their genetic affiliations. The seven Salishan languages form a continuous block along the breadth of the northern half of the Plateau, and the six languages to the south of them have been most commonly placed in a Plateau division of the proposed Penutian phylum. This designation is by no means a demonstrated genetic grouping, although additional similarities among these languages have been found. Kootenai and Nicola in the northern part of the Plateau stand out as distinctive from other Plateau languages, although Nicola belongs linguistically with the Athapaskan languages north of the Plateau, and Kootenai has no close relatives.

Even though very little of the Nicola language was ever recorded, its genetic affiliation with Athapaskan has never been in doubt. It is not surprising that it appears most similar to Chilcotin and Carrier, other Athapaskan languages spoken less than 200 miles to the north, and most likely represents a migrant group who broke off from them. Their location in the Nicola Valley left them isolated and surrounded by the Thompson, Shuswap, and Okanagan, all Salishan languages. These Salishan peoples were expanding into the Nicola Valley and had already largely absorbed the Nicolas by the nineteenth century when fur trappers from eastern Canada first began entering the area.

Kootenai has been more difficult to relate to other languages, and is generally classified as an isolate. Sapir (1929; echoed by Greenberg 1987) classified it as one of three branches of Algonkin-Wakashan, but later students of these languages have abandoned this stock entirely. Haas (1965) looks at possible Kootenai relationships with Algonquian and Salish, but is inconclusive. Morgan (1980) is a detailed study of lexical and grammatical similarities between Kootenai and Salish. Morgan, from a detailed knowledge of Kootenai, attempted to sort out similarities that are best attributed to borrowing or areal influences from those that might represent genetic correspondences. He presented 129 sets of words and morphemes that he considered as probable cognates. He concluded that Kootenai is "a single member language family which is coordinately related to the Salishan family" and suggested that it should be classified as "an isolate within the Kootenay-Salishan language stock." Morgan's study is the most detailed and rigorous yet to suggest a linguistic relative for Kootenai.

Interior Salish languages almost certainly expanded into the Plateau from the coast. Nevertheless, archeological work by Harlan I. Smith (1899, 1903, 1907) suggested that the Coast Salish originated in migrations from the Plateau interior, one of the important routes having been down the Fraser River. This view was followed by Boas (1902), Kroeber (1923), and Borden (1954, 1960). This thesis would hold that Salishan peoples have an original homeland in the Plateau and that the adaptations of Coast Salish to maritime environments are secondary, more recent, and less complete than those of more ancient coastal groups such as Chemakuans or Wakashans. Boas (1905) supplemented this archeological evidence with evidence from other disciplines and suggested that physical types, archeological evidence, and mythological motifs pointed to a Salishan migration to the coast from somewhere in the interior. Ray (1936) based his claim that the Interior Salish represent the oldest strata of Columbia Basin culture on cultural traits.

Studies by Suttles and Elmendorf (1963) and Suttles (1987) suggest a coastal origin for Salish on the basis of where the greatest differentiation within the language family occurs and where the deepest splits are found (vol. 7:30–51). Kinkade (1991a) provides specific lexical evidence for a coastal origin by showing that words for several plants and shellfish that occur only on the coast can be reconstructed for Proto-Salishan; he suggests a specific homeland (or point of dispersal) for Salishan languages between the Fraser and Skagit rivers and between the Cascade Range and the southern end of Georgia Strait. The Interior Salish split would represent one of the earliest divisions within Salishan; given a homeland along the lower Fraser River, the most likely expansion of Salishan into the Plateau would be along the Fraser and Thompson rivers, then down the Okanogan and Columbia into eastern Washington. The Skagit River may also have served as a secondary migration route, although connections between the Skagit Indians (Southern Coast Salish) and speakers of Columbian on the Plateau may represent later contacts. Archeological evidence supports this scenario; R.L. Carlson (1991) points to specific and distinctive types of tool assemblages that suggest groups of people in the plateau who were different from those living west of the Cascade Range, although his archeological dates extending back 11,500 years are far earlier than linguistic evidence can substantiate. Carlson suggests that the peoples of the Stemmed Point tradition found in the Plateau were the ancestors of speakers of Penutian languages, and the pebble tool assemblages of the coast were used by the ancestors of Salishan- and Wakashan-speaking peoples. No very specific date has been suggested for Salishan expansion into the Plateau, although the degree of diversity among the languages indicates that they began differentiating well over 1,500 years ago.

The lexicostatistic method for determining degrees of linguistic relationship was introduced by Swadesh (1950) in a study of Salishan. It rests on controlled comparison for two or more languages of basic vocabulary items in a standard test list and derives percentages of related words (cognates) for the languages compared. Degrees of relationship in this method are presumed to vary directly with the cognate percentage figures (Swadesh 1952, 1955; Gudschinsky 1956; Hymes 1960).

Glottochronology denotes a method of deriving dates of separation for related languages from lexicostatistic data. Glottochronological dates are hypothetically indicators of the beginning of linguistic divergence between related languages. Thus, such a date purports to indicate the time at which linguistic division began in a past speech community; this might denote social as well as linguistic division and thus have relevance for the history of peoples and cultures as well as languages.

The lexicostatistic work on Plateau languages was Swadesh's (1950) study of Salishan. This provided a classification of Salishan languages and subgoups that has remained in fairly good accord with later findings. In particular, Interior Salish was shown to be a markedly distinct subgroup.

Patterns in lexicostatistic data lend themselves to interpretations regarding the earlier history of the Interior Salish speech communities. Such interpretations were advanced by Suttles and Elmendorf (1963) and Elmendorf (1965), to the effect that Interior Salish languages had expanded southward and eastward from an original center in what is now the northwestern corner of their area, roughly, the southwestern edge of interior British Columbia. The chronology of these events rests on rather uncertain glottochronological figures. Swadesh has variously (1950, 1958:673) dated the depth of linguistic divergence within Proto-Salishan at over 55 and at 49 to 41 elapsed centuries. Internal divergence within Interior Salish was dated in the 1950 study at 45 centuries, a period that now seems much too long. However, these figures might give maximum possible dates for the beginning of Interior Salish expansion.

Once the Interior Salish reached the Plateau they may have expanded along the river valleys fairly rapidly, absorbing whatever people may have been there before. The broad regions occupied by Shuswap, Okanagan, and Kalispel speakers, and the shallow dialect diversity within these languages, all suggest a late spread of these languages, possibly within the past 500 years. What languages were replaced by Salishan intrusion cannot be determined, but it is not unlikely that some were additional Penutian languages, and if the Kootenai-Salishan connection is valid, languages intermediate between these. Specific suggestions of Kalispel expansion are made by Turney-High (1937:5), who speaks of peoples whom "the Kalispel and the Flathead claim to have inhabited the country before their arrival." To the north, Athapaskan languages appear to have undergone southward expansion within the past 1,000–1,500 years, and it is unlikely that they preceded Salishan in the eastern Plateau (cf. Hoijer 1956; Hymes 1957).

Nez Perce and Sahaptin are closely related, and the dialect divisions and the large area covered by Sahaptin suggests that that language has expanded its territory in the last 500–1,000 years. Teit (1928) suggests that, under pressure from expanding Numic peoples to the south, there was some possible "northward movement of Sahaptin-speaking peoples . . . from their postulated former habitat south of the Columbia river." Teit's evidence consisted largely of otherwise unsupported assertions of a Columbian Salish informant, and the existence of a number of Salish place-names in the Kittitas Valley, which was occupied by a Sahaptin-speaking group in historic times. The Kittitas Sahaptins were apparently friendly with, and intermarried with, the Columbian-speaking Wenatchee to the north; this is perhaps sufficient to explain the place-name situation without recourse to Teit's supposed northward mass movement of Sahaptins, which subsequent research workers in the area have considered highly dubious (Ray 1936:101; Jacobs 1937:68–71; cf. Rigsby 1965:221–228). Sahaptins have undoubtedly lived in the Plateau region for many centuries; their intermarriage with neighboring peoples, especially Salishan and Chinookan, was often extensive, and could, over time, shift a language boundary in one direction or the other, without effectively changing the population. Sahaptin-speaking peoples certainly expanded across the Cascade Range to the west. In a study of speech community shifts Jacobs (1937:72) showed that language replacement was going on in historic times in Sahaptin-Salish bilingual chains of intermarrying villages west of the southern Cascade Range in Washington, without invasion or migration. In this case the replacement involved westward drift of Sahaptin speech over the southern Cascade passes at the expense of Salish dialects on the upper Nisqually and Cowlitz rivers.

The Kiksht are the one Penutian group that may be intrusive into the Plateau. Because the greatest diversity in the Chinookan family is downriver on the Columbia, the group presumably began its dispersal and expansion there, perhaps from around the confluence of the Willamette. The Chinookans then moved early down the Columbia to the ocean, and later spread back up the Columbia as far as The Dalles; the greater diversity along the lower stretches of the river and "the apparent way the tense-aspect systems must have developed indicate this direction of expansion" (vol. 7:47; Silverstein 1974).

Further relationships among Sahaptian, Cayuse, Molala, Chinookan, and Klamath are much less certain. These languages share a number of typological similarities, but lexical comparisons have not yielded solid evidence of genetic relationship. The early ethnologist-linguists Gatschet, Hewitt, Curtis, and Frachtenberg believed that the Sahaptian, Waiilatpuan, and Klamath languages belonged to a single language family. Sapir (1929; cf. 1921a) assigned the six southern Plateau languages to his Penutian superstock, which included Tsimshian in British Columbia, and other languages in western Oregon, California, and southern Mexico. Penutian was first set up by Dixon and Kroeber (1913, 1919) as a consolidation of five Californian groups treated as separate families by Powell. Sapir's enlarged Penutian included the two Sahaptian languages with Cayuse, Molala, and Klamath as a Plateau subgroup, while treating Chinookan as another separate subgroup.

Jacobs (1931:93–95) extended the name Sahaptin to refer to this Plateau Penutian subgroup, although this terminology has not been generally adopted. Rigsby (1965, especially Chap. III) reviewed the history of Southern Plateau language classification and concluded that none of the earlier workers had definitively proved or established the Plateau Penutian subgrouping. Considerable suggestive evidence of a closer connection between Sahaptian and Klamath is presented in Aoki (1963), Rude (1987), DeLancey (1992), and DeLancey, Genetti, and Rude (1988). Data on Cayuse may be too sparse to permit definitive classification of this language and archival materials on Molala remained unstudied and unanalyzed before 1990, again precluding the possibility of an accurate classification of this language. However, Silverstein (1979:679–680) argues against a Plateau subgroup, claiming that each of these languages has closer connections elsewhere in Penutian than with each other, for examples Molala with western Oregon languages or Klamath with California Penutian (on which see also Shipley 1966 and DeLancey 1987, 1987a). Nevertheless, a number of research workers who have examined much of the data believe that all six Southern Plateau languages belong to the great Penutian stock (Aoki 1963; Hymes 1957a, 1964, 1964a; Sapir and Swadesh 1953; Shipley 1966; Silverstein 1965; Swadesh 1954, 1956, 1964). The Penutian affiliation of Sahaptian, Chinookan, and Klamath seems certain, while that of Cayuse and Molala is probable. The languages of the Plateau that are included in Penutian (other than Kiksht) have all presumably been on the Plateau for many millennia, and there are no legends or traditions that suggest that they originated elsewhere.

Language Contact

Contacts and mutual interinfluences among the languages and language families of the Plateau are of long standing. It is clear that the majority of them participated in a common linguistic area. Plateau ethnographic studies have demonstrated mechanisms of group interaction that, projected into the past, would have produced these linguistic results. In this area intermarriage, trade, and joint participation in economic and ritual activities set up social relationships that frequently crossed linguistic boundaries (Anastasio 1972; Walker 1967; Brunton 1968; cf. Jacobs 1937).

Bilingualism, produced and maintained in this context, was frequent in all Plateau speech communities. In general, areas of maximum bilingualism were those where different language communities abutted. The spread of sign language from the Plains to the Plateau also represents a kind of bilingualism between groups between whom there was limited

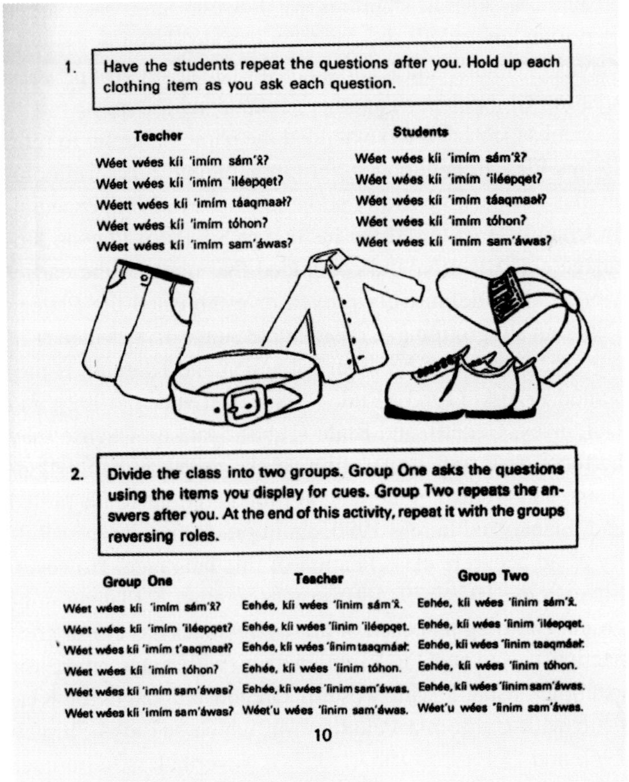

1. Have the students repeat the questions after you. Hold up each clothing item as you ask each question.

Teacher	Students
Wéet wées kíi 'imím sám'x̂?	Wéet wées kíi 'imím sám'x̂?
Wéet wées kíi 'imím 'iléepqet?	Wéet wées kíi 'imím 'iléepqet?
Wéett wées kíi 'imím táaqmaał?	Wéet wées kíi 'imím táaqmaał?
Wéet wées kíi 'imím tóhon?	Wéet wées kíi 'imím tóhon?
Wéet wées kíi 'imím sam'áwas?	Wéet wées kíi 'imím sam'áwas?

2. Divide the class into two groups. Group One asks the questions using the items you display for cues. Group Two repeats the answers after you. At the end of this activity, repeat it with the groups reversing roles.

Group One	Teacher	Group Two
Wéet wées kíi 'imím sám'x̂?	Eehée, kíi wées 'íinim sám'x̂.	Eehée, kíi wées 'íinim sám'x̂.
Wéet wées kíi 'imím 'iléepqet?	Eehée, kíi wées 'íinim 'iléepqet.	Eehée, kíi wées 'íinim 'iléepqet.
Wéet wées kíi 'imím t'aaqmaał?	Eehée, kíi wées 'íinim taaqmáał.	Eehée, kíi wées 'íinim taaqmáał.
Wéet wées kíi 'imím tóhon?	Eehée, kíi wées 'íinim tóhon.	Eehée, kíi wées 'íinim tóhon.
Wéet wées kíi 'imím sam'áwas?	Eehée, kíi wées 'íinim sam'áwas.	Eehée, kíi wées 'íinim sam'áwas.
Wéet wées kíi 'imím sam'áwas?	Wéet'u wées 'íinim sam'áwas.	Wéet'u wées 'íinim sam'áwas.

10

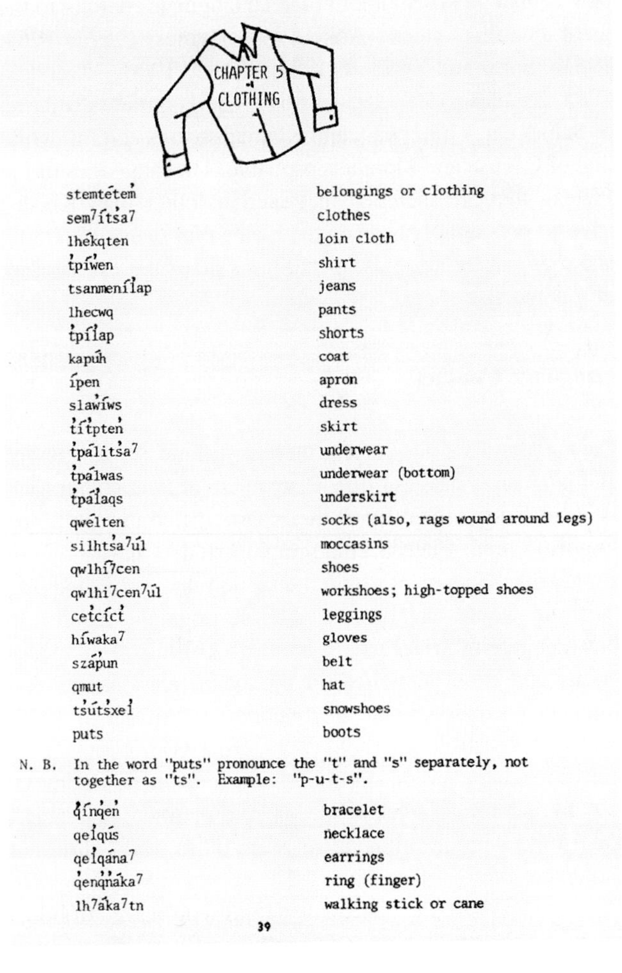

stemtétem	belongings or clothing
sem7ítsa7	clothes
lhékqten	loin cloth
tpíwen	shirt
tsanmeníl̓ap	jeans
lhecwq	pants
tpíl̓ap	shorts
kapúh	coat
ípen	apron
slawíws	dress
títpten	skirt
tpálitsa7	underwear
tpálwas	underwear (bottom)
tpál̓aqs	underskirt
qwélten	socks (also, rags wound around legs)
silhtsa7úl	moccasins
qwlhí7cen	shoes
qwlhi7cen7úl	workshoes; high-topped shoes
cetcíct	leggings
híwaka7	gloves
szápun	belt
qmut	hat
tsútsxel̓	snowshoes
puts	boots

N. B. In the word "puts" pronounce the "t" and "s" separately, not together as "ts". Example: "p-u-t-s".

qínqen	bracelet
qel̓qús	necklace
qel̓qána7	earrings
qenqnáka7	ring (finger)
lh7áka7tn	walking stick or cane

39

top, Natl. Bilingual Materials Development Center, U. of Alaska; bottom, Mount Currie Cultural Centre, B.C.

Fig. 8. Nez Perce and Lillooet language program materials. By the last 3 decades of the 20th century no language of the Plateau was being learned by children as a first language. In the face of this imminent loss, teaching programs were begun in community after community. They were provided both as part of the regular school curriculum and in extracurricular classes. top, P. from the 23-p. Nez Perce unit of study on clothing (Aoki and Pulu 1981:10), which also included information on who made the clothing, thus including kinship terms. bottom, Vocabulary on clothing in Lillooet (Lower Lillooet dialect) followed by exercises utilizing these words in an 88-p. intermediate study book (Williams 1979:39).

contact; Plateau people were using this sign language as late as the 1970s (vol. 17:276–277).

These patterns of bilingualism in certain parts of the region obscured linguistic boundaries, and at times led to language replacement. It is not possible, for example, to find a sharp break between Sahaptin and Interior Salish speech along the eastern slope of the Washington Cascades (Rigsby 1996). There, a gradient of Sahaptin-Columbian-Okanagan bilingualism extended along a social interaction chain from the Yakima north through the Kittitas, Wenatchee, Entiat, Chelan, Methow, and Southern Okanogan.

Methow is probably a case of language replacement, during the nineteenth century, through an intermediate stage of bilingualism. The primary language there at one time appears to have been a Columbian dialect, evidenced among other things in place-names, but later an Okanagan one (Kinkade 1967:197; Elmendorf 1949). Many other cases of replacement or incipient replacement occurred in the Southern Plateau, among Northeast Sahaptin, Umatilla Sahaptin, Cayuse, and Nez Perce speech communities. Cayuse eventually, between the 1850s and the 1930s, underwent total replacement by Sahaptin and Nez Perce.

The social and linguistic dynamics producing these patterns of bilingualism and language replacement were probably of long standing in the Plateau area. It seems certain that they antedate the earliest contacts of Plateau peoples with agents of Western civilization. Since the mid-nineteenth century, all native speech in the Plateau has been undergoing replacement by English at an accelerating rate.

Survival of Languages

Three of the Plateau languages (Nicola, Molala, and Cayuse) were extinct by the middle of the twentieth century, and the number of speakers of the others were severely reduced. By 1990, Klamath, Kiksht, Columbian, and Coeur d'Alene had fewer than 50 speakers each, and the others had only a few hundred. The Salishan languages in British Columbia were strongest (with 300 to 500 speakers each by 1990), but even these declined rapidly in the second half of the twentieth century. Because these remaining speakers were overwhelmingly adults, mostly middle-aged or older, prospects for survival of these languages appeared bleak.

alá? xast
i? kʷu
kʷliwt uł
xʷa?spínt
k kʷu
sxasts i l sc'íłntət, i l scxʷəlxʷáltət uł
i? sckʷlíwtət axá? i l təmxʷúla?xʷtət.
naqs sxəlxˤált t'i kʷm'ił ki? kʷu kícəc
i? t t'íxʷləm uł ixí? ?úməntəm t
sáma?. c'xilx itlí? ki? əct'íxʷxʷləm i?
sckʷlíwtət.

We lived here happily, and many years we were satisfied with our food, and our way of life in our land. One day all at once we were visited by different people, we called them sáma?. And that's how our way of life changed.

alá?	xast	i?	kʷu	kʷliwt	uł	xʷa?-spíntk	kʷu	s+xast+s	i	l
here	good	the	we	live	and	many-years	we	satisfied	the	in

sc'íłn-tət,	i	l	scxʷəlxʷál-tət	uł	íʔ	sckʷ·uw-tət	axa?	i	l
food-our	the	in	livelihood-our	and	the	live-our	this	the	on

təmxʷúla?xʷ-tət.	naqs	sxəlxʷált	t'i	kʷm'ił		ki?	kʷu	kícəc
land-our	one	day		at_once	that	we	were_reached

EN'OWKIN CENTRE   7   COPYRIGHT 1993

© Secwepemc Cultural Education Society
Language Department
355 Yellowhead Highway, Kamloops, B.C.

left, En'owkin Centre, Penticton, B.C.; right, Secwepemc Cultural Education Soc., Kamloops, B.C.
Fig. 9. Reading materials in Northern Okanagan and Shuswap. left, Paragraph about Indians first meeting with Euro-Americans in a 42-p. Northern Okanagan primer (Mattina 1993a:7). right, Western Shuswap dialect booklet of 31 pages adapted from a 1985 book on the Shuswap family (Secwepemc Cultural Education Society 1996) that describes cultural activities common to the Shuswap. Title p.; the Shuswap caption translates 'Our grandfather here shows us many things, and tells us many stories of our people.' Although Okanagan and Shuswap are neighboring Salishan languages, slightly different orthographies were adopted by the 2 communities (Shuswap ⟨c⟩ is equivalent to Okanagan ⟨x⟩ both representing the voiceless velar fricative x).

Few early attempts were made to use native languages for educational purposes. One remarkable exception was undertaken by Father Jean-Marie Le Jeune at the Saint Louis Mission in Kamloops, British Columbia. Adapting the French Duployé shorthand for writing native languages (as well as English and Latin), he printed numerous manuals, primers, vocabularies, and guides at the mission (Le Jeune 1896, 1897, 1897a, 1897b, 1925). Most of his publications were written in Chinook Jargon (vol. 17:127). There were elderly Shuswap people in the 1980s and 1990s who could read this material.

In the last quarter of the twentieth century, a resurgence of awareness of and pride in cultural heritage (including language) among the native people of the region led to attempts to establish language learning programs for children. A few language programs were begun after 1970, more extensively on reserves in British Columbia than in the United States; few have had more than limited success in teaching the languages to children, and numbers of speakers have continued to decline. Sahaptin has been taught in some of the schools on the Yakima and Warm Springs reservations (and briefly on the Umatilla Reservation), and short-lived efforts to teach Nez Perce (fig. 8

top), Colville, or Columbian have been made on the Colville Reservation. The most extensive programs were in British Columbia. At Mount Currie (Lillooet)(fig. 8 bottom), instructional books were prepared (van Eijk 1978a, 1981; van Eijk and Williams 1981; Joseph et al. 1979; Williams 1979), and Lillooet was taught there beginning in 1975. A program was begun at the Lillooet reserve about 1990, and the language has been taught in grades 1–12 since 1993; in addition, a partial immersion course was begun for grade seven. Shuswap, Thompson, and Okanagan (fig. 9) have been taught in band-run schools at both elementary and high school levels, and Shuswap has been taught in the Williams Lake school district. Between 1991 and 1995 Simon Fraser University, Burnaby, British Columbia, established four-year sequences of language courses leading to the Certificate of Language Instruction for Shuswap (in both Kamloops and Williams Lake), Lillooet (in both Lillooet and Mount Currie), and for Thompson (in Merritt). Kootenai has been taught with some success (fig. 10; "Ethnobiology and Subsistence," fig. 1, this vol.); the Kootenai language teachers are employed by the band itself. Language programs were also begun in both Kootenai and Flathead on the Flathead Reservation in Montana. Informal language instruction in Okanagan was begun at the En'owkin Centre in Penticton in the 1990s, and efforts in language instruction also began on the Colville and Spokane reservations. These programs all generally came too late to meet with more than a limited measure of success because one or more generations of speakers were lost to the suppression of native languages by schools, churches, and governments; these generations without native languages are the parents of the children in school in the last quarter of the twentieth century, and cannot give reinforcement at home to school programs.

In the 1960s and 1970s the British Columbia provincial government and the Union of British Columbia Indian Chiefs sponsored the development of writing systems for all languages of the province still spoken and encouraged the recording of traditional narratives and customs in an effort to maintain or revive tribal traditions and practices. Beginning in the 1960s researchers at the University of British Columbia, Vancouver; Simon Fraser University; and especially at the University of Victoria; the British Columbia Indian Language Project, Victoria; and the Royal British Columbia Museum, Victoria, worked with various Indian groups on the development of written notations of tribal traditions using these writing systems, and they also made tape recordings of traditional narratives. Similar independent programs involving the cooperation of Indians and university researchers were developed in Washington and Oregon on the major reservations.

Kootenai Culture Committee, Elmo, Mont.

Fig. 10. Trilingual coloring book. Flathead, Kootenai, and English are spoken on the Flathead Res., Mont. This unusual trilingual coloring book *Living in Harmony* (Salish Kootenai College 1987), showing various cultural activities, was developed for the use of both native language communities. P. 1 of 16-p. book with Kootenai at the lower left of each page, Flathead at the lower right, and English translation on top.

Prehistory: Introduction

JAMES C. CHATTERS AND DAVID L. POKOTYLO

The Plateau is set apart from the neighboring Plains, Great Basin, Subarctic, and Northwest Coast partially by mountain barriers, but largely by an aboriginal cultural adaptation to a unique set of resources and its inland maritime environment. For the past 4,000 years, most Plateau cultural adaptations have emphasized the mass harvest and long-term storage of three key resource groups: fish (usually anadromous salmonids), edible roots, and large ungulates. Although the importance of each resource varies regionally and diachronically, all three played some part in the subsistence of Plateau cultures. Settlement systems were also similar throughout, characterized by winter settlement in lowlands, and a series of resource harvesting forays throughout warmer seasons into the uplands or to prime fish intercept points along the rivers. Population densities varied with the abundance of anadromous fish, being concentrated in large villages in the valleys of the Fraser and Columbia rivers and their tributaries, and declining to scattered, mobile bands in the Rocky Mountains.

In the three chapters that follow, the Plateau is subdivided on the basis of environment, archeology, and to some extent the international boundary, into three subareas: Northern (or Canadian) Plateau, Southern (or Columbia) Plateau, and Eastern Plateau periphery. The characteristics of each subarea are described by individual authors, who make further geographic subdivisions. In general, the Northern Plateau encompasses the drainage basins of the Fraser River and the upper Columbia River beginning approximately 50 kilometers south of the Canadian border. This subarea is heavily forested, higher in latitude, and has higher relief than the Southern Plateau. The Southern Plateau includes the middle reaches of the Columbia River, the Columbia tributaries downstream of falls that impede upstream movement of anadromous fish, and the Snake River and its tributaries upstream to Hells Canyon. This is the Columbia Basin, a great, rolling plain, and its surrounding, forested highlands. The Eastern Plateau periphery includes the remainder of the area. Lands above natural barriers to salmon migrations comprise the Kootenai-Pend d'Oreille region of northern Idaho and northwestern Montana. The upper tributaries of the Snake River in central and southwestern Idaho, which have some anadromous fish, are the Salmon-Clearwater region.

There is minor overlap among the presentations of each subarea, particularly between the Southern Plateau and Eastern Plateau, both of which include discussions of camas harvesting sites in the Calispell Valley and mortuary practices of the Western Idaho Archaic Burial complex, although each emphasizes different aspects of these phenomena. Culture history is the main emphasis of all chapters, although subsistence, technology, resource intensification, settlement pattern, trade, sociopolitical organization, ethnicity, and culture change are examined where research permits.

Major Trends in Plateau Prehistory

The prehistory of the Plateau is divisible into three broad chronological units: Early, 9000 to 6000 B.C.; Middle, 6000 to 2000 B.C.; and Late, 2000 B.C. to A.D. 1720 periods, during which similar or complimentary trends can be seen in cultural development among all subareas. The Middle period is divided into Early (6000–3300 B.C.) and Late (3300 to 2000 B.C.) subperiods. The Late period includes three subperiods: Early (2000 to 500 B.C.), Middle (500 B.C. to A.D. 500–1000), and Late (A.D. 500–1000 to 1720). Similar chronological divisions are marked in each area, although the labels may differ because of longstanding local traditions or a paucity of information. This chapter summarizes current interpretations of adaptive strategies, housing, tool inventories, trade, mortuary practices, and social complexity. Details, examples, and more complete references are provided in the regional chapters. References presented here pertain to either specific facts or information not given in regional chapters. Paleoenvironmental changes, synopses of which begin the discussion of each period and subperiod, are presented in more detail in "Environment," this volume.

Early Period, 9000–6000 B.C.

The Plateau area had recently emerged from the effects of overlying or nearby glacial ice. Climates were initially more continental than they are today and were characterized by greater seasonal variation in temperature. Because of dry winters and hot summers, this is the most arid period in the Northern Plateau, and forests region-wide were at or near their minimum Holocene extents. Salmon already populated at least part of the Columbia River basin, occurring in apparently great numbers near The Dalles (Cressman et al. 1960), but the earliest indication of their presence in the Northern Plateau is 7100 B.C. This is the age of the Gore

Creek skeleton, which has a stable carbon isotope value indicative of a diet including some marine-derived protein (Chisholm and Nelson 1983). Terrestrial faunas consisted almost entirely of modern species, except for the occurrence of extinct *Bison antiquus* in the central Columbia Basin (Lyman and Livingston 1983).

In the Eastern Plateau and most of the Northern Plateau, human activity during the Early period is represented only by a scattering of projectile points of diverse styles. Finds are typically identified with lithic traditions and linked to the core regions of those traditions. Plano forms are taken as indicative of links with the northerly plains, early stemmed points with the Southern Plateau and the more distant western pluvial lakes tradition of the Great Basin, lanceolate forms with the Old Cordilleran culture of coastal Washington and British Columbia, and microblades with the early microblade complexes of the far north and northern Northwest Coast (Rousseau 1993). The relative rarity of these materials may be due more to the dynamic nature of mountain landscapes and regions stabilizing from deglaciation than from a lack of human activity.

The most complete data from this period come from the Lower Snake and Lower Columbia rivers, although well-dated single components with intact features and faunal remains have been found on the middle Columbia and south Thompson rivers. Settlements consist of numerous small, low-density scatters of debris representing short habitation events. Evidence exists on the middle Columbia of small, possibly tepeelike surface dwellings with floor areas 11 to 15 square meters (Chance and Chance 1985; Chatters 1986). Although limited in number, Early period sites in the Northern Plateau consistently have small assemblages of microblades and expedient flake tools. Tool kits in the Southern Plateau were simple, consisting largely of leaf-shaped and stemmed dart points, ovate bifaces (knives?), crescents, and end and side scrapers. Grinding implements, consisting of small milling stones, manos or hand stones, and the unique edge-ground cobble occur in most sites on the Southern Plateau. Much of the artifact inventory of later sites from this period consists of expedient tools, often flaked from river cobbles. In addition to simple, versatile lithics, Early period inhabitants of the Southern Plateau made use of a variety of composite implements, including weighted nets, composite and single-piece harpoons, and bolas. Delicate bone needles indicate tailored leather attire and possibly the manufacture of coiled basketry.

Mortuary practices are evident only from Marmes Rockshelter, where, around 9000 B.C., the dead were cremated repeatedly in the same corner of the shelter over what may have been decades or centuries (Rice 1969). Ocher and large implements were the only offerings. Additional, unburned interments with olivella shell beads and large bifaces resumed toward the end of the period.

Peoples of the Early period are identified as highly residentially mobile foragers (Binford 1980; Ames 1988; Chatters 1986; Rousseau 1993; Stryd and Rousseau 1996), living in small groups, and generalized in their subsistence to varying degrees, depending on the seasonal potentials of their territories. Emphasis to the north, and possibly the east, was on large game hunting; the south was more diversified, including more collecting and fishing as represented in both artifact inventories and faunal remains. Faunal remains present in Northern Plateau sites include: deer, elk, and fish (possibly salmon). Riverine resources, small mammals, and birds assumed a greater role in the Southern Plateau, where Early period assemblages frequently include extensive middens of river mussel shell and bones of fish. At some locations, such as the Roadcut site on Fivemile Rapids, salmon predominate (Cressman et al. 1960; Butler 1993), but elsewhere, suckers and minnows occur in equal or greater numbers (Chance and Chance 1982; Randolph and Dahlstrom 1977; Minor and Toepel 1986; Reid and Gallison 1993).

Middle Period, 6000–2000 B.C.

Climatic conditions continued warmer than in modern times. However, the climate became more maritime after 6000 B.C., allowing conifer forests to move downslope in the north and perhaps east, and shrub steppes to replace grasslands in the Columbia Basin. In general, the north is thought to have become somewhat cooler and moister, the south warmer and drier. This would have increased ungulate productivity in the north, and reduced overall productivity in the south. Maritime conditions would have promoted populations of root plants such as balsam root, biscuitroot, and camas.

The Fraser and Columbia rivers continued cutting through glacial drift, and the Columbia drained steppes; both conditions provided high sediment loads and, at least in the Columbia, warm temperatures. Conditions for salmon productivity were poor but began to improve in the Fraser system by around 3500 B.C. A sharp increase in regional moisture was evident by 3000 B.C., increasing the productivity of southern steppes and allowing forests to expand to nearly their present extent.

Early-Middle Subperiod, 6000 to 3300 B.C.

In many ways, cultures of the Early-Middle subperiod were a continuation and distillation of Early period patterns. Although it is only known from the Thompson and middle Fraser rivers, the Nesikep tradition is identified as an interior ungulate hunting culture with a foraging adaptive strategy (Stryd and Rousseau 1996). Except for projectile point style changes, the tool kit resembles what little is known from the Early period, including the continued use of microblades. In addition to deer and other ungulates, people subsisted on rabbits, beaver, waterfowl, muskrats, marmots, carnivores, salmon, freshwater fish, small birds, turtles, and plant resources. Freshwater mollusks were collected

Fig. 1. Excavation of a midden at the Lagoon site (450K424) near Brewster, Wash., dating to about 5700 B.C. The piles of mussel shell and scatter of artifacts are characteristic of sites dating to the Early and Early Middle phases of regional prehistory. Photograph by James Chatters, 1984.

still in use. Roots appear to have become increasingly important foodstuffs. A new food grinding technology, the hopper mortar and pestle, which is thought to have been used to pulverize the tough roots of the steppes (Reid 1991, 1991a) began to replace the millingstone and edge-ground cobble. In the Eastern Plateau periphery, the first direct evidence of root utilization appears by 4400 B.C. in the form of earth ovens, and camas was in regular use by 3500 B.C. (Thoms 1989).

Mortuary practices were elaborated in the southeastern Plateau during this time, but little is known elsewhere. Finds at Damoss (Green et al. 1986), and in the Boise Basin (Pavesic 1985) include secondary inhumations, some cremated, and caches of large, delicately flaked bifaces, projectile points, pipes and beads, often made from exotic materials. Manifestations of this practice, known as the Western Idaho Archaic Burial complex, may occur on the Lower Snake River at Marmes Rockshelter, where the tradition of inhumations continued (Rice 1969) and on the Middle Columbia River at Cox's Pond (Hartmann 1975). This phenomenon began as early as 4000 B.C. at Damoss and fluoresced between 2500 and 3700 B.C.

Late-Middle Subperiod, 3300–2000 B.C.

The Late-Middle subperiod is marked by a reduction in mobility, at least in the most favorable habitats, which was probably made possible by coincident increases in moisture and lowland terrestrial productivity. From southern British Columbia to southwestern Idaho, small hamlets of from one to three semisubterranean pit houses appeared at the newly established interface between steppe and forest. At localities such as Baker on the south Thompson (Wilson 1992), 450Kll and the Confluence complex on the upper middle Columbia (Lohse 1984; Chatters 1986), Hatwai on the lower Clearwater (Ames, Green, and Pfoertner 1981), and Givens Hot Springs (Green 1988) inhabitants had nearby access to resources of most or all seasons of the year and adopted a seasonally to fully sedentary lifeway. Houses were extremely variable in size and shape: 3–4.5 meter diameter ovals on the south Thompson, 3.5–12 meter diameter rectanguloids on the lower Okanogan and upper middle Columbia rivers, 7–9 meter subrectangles and circles on the Lower Snake River, and 4–6 meter circular structures in southwestern Idaho.

Technologies remained little changed from the preceding subperiod. Faunal assemblages from Late-Middle subperiod sites are the most diverse in regional prehistory, showing use of not only numerous species but also the relatively even use of many of them (Chatters 1995; Stryd and Rousseau 1996). Like their predecessors, sites show strong local resource emphases. On the upper middle Columbia, large game and mussels were heavily used; on the lower Snake and Clearwater rivers, deer and roots are thought to have been the key resources. At the Baker site, increased reliance on salmon is reflected by salmonid remains, probable food storage or

throughout the subperiod, but occur in larger amounts toward the end (fig. 1). A second cultural unit, the Lochnore phase, characterized by wide side-notched projectile points, is thought to represent the movement of Salishan-speaking peoples up the Fraser River from the coast near the end of this subperiod, following the developing salmon runs. However, there is no evidence for the intensive utilization and storage of anadromous salmon at this time.

In the south, adaptations remained little changed from the Early period, although the technology underwent notable deletions and additions (Bense 1972), and there are apparent stylistic and technological influences from both the Northern Plateau and Great Basin. The occurrence of microblades throughout much of the upper middle Columbia links the subarea to northern developments, and large side-notched dart points in the southeastern Plateau have been interpreted as Great Basin influence during this arid interval (Browman and Munsell 1969). In general, however, the technology became simpler. Composite tools and fine needles became rare or disappeared, and the technology took on an increasingly expedient character. Predation strategies focused on the highest ranking or most abundant resources of each season—deer in some cases, fish, mussels, or rabbits in others (Chatters 1995), evidence that a forager strategy (Binford 1980) of resource procurement was

refuse pits, and a possible fish smoking pit. Stable carbon isotope studies of individuals near the middle Fraser River valley that may date to this subperiod show that nearly 40 percent of the protein in the diet was marine based.

Salmon storage has been inferred as a component of the adaptation of Baker site occupants, and by extention to other Northern Plateau adaptations during this subperiod. Their inital presence as early as 3300 B.C. has been identified as the beginning of the Plateau Pit house tradition, thought to represent a logistically organized adaptive strategy (Stryd and Rousseau 1996) that continued to the historic period. However, evidence from a larger number of sites in the south has shown that storage was not critical. Most researchers in that subarea, working with data resembling that of the Baker site, consider the adaptation to have been that of infrequently mobile foragers, due to the broad spectrum of the diet and absence of field camps for food harvesting and processing (Chatters 1989, 1995; Lohse and Sammons-Lohse 1986; cf. Ames 1991; Ames and Marshall 1980).

Throughout the Plateau, activity continued to be oriented toward lowlands, although mid-altitude valleys in the Northern Plateau were utilized. Some increase in trade may have been associated with semisedentary settlement, as items such as marine shell and obsidian became more common at some sites (Chatters 1986; Stryd and Rousseau 1996). It is possible that trade in exotics and local manifestations of the Western Idaho Archaic Burial complex helped maintain sedentism or semisedentism in the relative absence of storage, the demand for exotics forming a conduit for evening out seasonal variations in local resource productivities. Whatever combination of environmental and cultural processes maintained it, the brief affair with sedentism ended or became extremely rare everywhere after 2500 B.C., and at least in the Southern Plateau, the human population crashed (Ames 1991; Chatters 1989, 1995). Evidence for semisubterranean dwellings is rare or absent for up to 500 years thereafter in both subareas.

Little activity is evident during this period on either side of the forest edge. Either the population coalesced in the optimal localities (Ames and Marshall 1980), the people in less favorable habitats continued the high mobility of their predecessors (Chatters 1989), or both. For the eastern and northern margins of the Plateau, little information is available for the Middle period as a whole. In the Eastern Plateau, continuity of the highly mobile hunting adaptation is assumed, although a greater diversity of habitats came into use. One example of this diversification is the first habitation of high-elevation sites around 2500 B.C. in what are thought to have been pine nut gathering camps (Munger 1993a).

Late Period, 2000 B.C. to A.D. 1720

Beginning around 2000 B.C., changes began that culminated in the ethnographic cultures of the region. During three

intervals of broad contemporaneity similar or complimentary changes occurred.

Early-Late Subperiod, 2000 to 500 B.C.

Around 2500 B.C., regional temperatures declined sharply, as reflected in glacial advances, downslope movement of subalpine conifers, and declines in Columbia River temperatures. This downslope movement may have meant expansion of alpine and subalpine parkland zones in the Northern Plateau and Rocky Mountains. Forests expanded over the Blue and Ochoco mountains. Precipitation continued the high levels of the Late-Middle subperiod. Closure of the watershed under dense forest and prolonged retention of snowpacks cleared and cooled Columbia River waters (Chatters et al. 1995) and probably had similar effects on the Fraser River system. Salmon productivity increased, and its seasonality probably became the most restrictive of the Holocene up to that point.

At 2000–1900 B.C., the shift in adaptations from non–storage-dependent, foragerlike strategies to storage-dependent collector strategies was well underway throughout the Plateau. The cooler, more seasonal environment probably influenced this change, along with declines in ungulate productivity and increases in salmon abundance brought on in part by forest closure (Chatters 1995; Kuijt 1989; Stryd and Rousseau 1996). In the Southern Plateau, small hamlets of semisubterranean houses (fig. 2) reappeared after several centuries of absence, this time definitely in association with an emphasis on storage and a complex logistical resource acquisition strategy. Throughout the Plateau, houses were larger and deeper where they formerly had been small and shallow in the Late-Middle subperiod, although in some cases the reverse trend occurred. Sites show signs of greater settlement permanence in increased artifact densities and reuse of house depressions. Field camps for fish, game, root, and mussel acquisition and processing appear in proximity to river valleys, particularly in the Southern Plateau. Storage pits and processing ovens often occur in house floors, or in some cases in older house depressions within a hamlet. Activity remained concentrated near the valley floors, particularly in the north, although there was some increase in the use of root grounds in the Columbia Basin later in this subperiod. The first evidence of root procurement and processing on the Northern Plateau occurs in this subperiod at approximately 1500 B.C. at the Parker site in Oregon Jack Creek valley near the Thompson River (Rousseau, Muir, and Alexander 1991a). Salmon was the focus of resource intensification efforts on the Columbia as well as the Fraser and Thompson rivers, as indicated by its dominance of faunal assemblages and isotopic indicators of more than 50 percent marine-derived protein in human skeletal material. It also increased in importance on the Lower Snake River. Net weights and composite harpoon parts became

Fig. 2. Exposed floor of the 3,000-year-old pit house at site 45D0189 near Grand Coulee Dam, Wash. The large flat stones are anvils and hopper-mortar bases. Photograph by Jerry R. Galm, 1986.

common constituents of tool inventories. Trade does not seem to have been as extensive as it was in the Late-Middle subperiod, although nephrite celts and steatite beads from the Fraser River make their first appearance along the middle and upper Columbia River (Nelson 1973; Campbell 1989). Researchers often comment on the poor quality of lithic materials used during this period, most of which appear to have been obtained locally. Projectile point styles also became more localized. Mortuary practices for this period are little known, except for a small number of graves in house floors on the Thompson River. Approximately contemporaneous manifestations of this pattern include the Kettlebrook, Shuswap, and Deer Park phases in the Northern Plateau and the Hudnut, Chiliwist, late Frenchman Springs, and late Tucannon phases of the Southern Plateau. Settlement densities were high in the Northern Plateau and upper middle Columbia, but lower in the southeastern Plateau. Little activity is seen in the southwest.

In the Eastern Plateau, where this is known as the Late Middle period, the first evidence of plant intensification and widespread use of river floodplains appear. Camas intensification is evident in the explosion of dated earth ovens between 1500 and 500 B.C. in the Calispell Valley. Notched pebble sinkers, which became common in floodplain sites at this time, may be evidence that fish had become a significant part of the diet. Despite these changes, much of the prehistoric record shows little change from the mobile hunting cultures of the past.

Middle-Late Subperiod, 500 B.C. to A.D. 500–1000

There is evidence for a warming and drying climate during at least the early half of this period. Forests opened somewhat in the Northern and Eastern plateaus and subalpine zones again moved upslope. The Columbia and Snake rivers underwent rapid floodplain formation, indicating more frequent flooding and/or the increased availability of sediment from less densely vegetated uplands. Alluvial fan formation at the mouths of small canyons in the Southern Plateau may be indicative of small-scale summer storms, which would be consistent with warmer conditions. Grasslands developed in the southeastern Columbia Basin, replacing shrub steppes.

This is a time of expansions and contractions. In the Northern and Southern plateaus, people extended the range of their food-harvesting activities into the uplands, in both cases primarily focusing on roots. Inhabitants of the Columbia and Snake rivers became active in the arid central Columbia Basin and the forested Blue and Ochoco mountains, Oregon. Many encampments contain hopper mortar bases for processing tough roots, or the remains of prey taken during hunting excursions. Bison, which appear to have undergone a fluorescence at this time in the Columbia Basin, may have been a major draw away from the rivers. The first and only mass bison kills found in that region date to this period (Schroedl 1973; Chatters et al. 1995a). In the Northern Plateau, large root-processing ovens (fig. 3) are common during this subperiod in highland valleys above the Thompson and Fraser rivers (Pokotylo and Froese 1983), but pestles and mortars are absent. Antler digging-stick handles make their first appearance in both the Columbia and Fraser systems. Despite the increased use of uplands, salmon remained a staple of Northern and most Southern Plateau subsistence systems.

Settlements contracted into large villages on the lower reaches of the great rivers, some with more than 100 houses (fig. 4). The houses themselves tend to be smaller than during the Early-Late subperiod, although toward the end of the Middle-Late, great disparities in size appear in single villages. Semisubterranean dwellings, and the associated salmon-focused collector strategy, having already begun extending their range downstream early in the period, reached the lower Middle Columbia by 500 B.C. Pit house settlements reached peak numbers in remote Hells Canyon on the Snake River (Reid 1991, 1991a, 1992). Activity at the important fishing site of Kettle Falls, Washington, intensified (Chance and Chance 1985), whereas village settlements largely disappeared from the Arrow Lakes-Slocan Valley area, British Columbia. At the same time, camas utilization in the Calispell Valley of the Eastern Plateau reached a minimum, possibly because of drought damage in the moist meadows. There is evidence that people began to manage upland ecosystems with fire during this period (C.S. Smith 1983).

Across the Plateau, there was increased diversity and quality of lithic materials during this period, which may be a consequence of greater mobility range taking people to new geologic formations and increasing encounters with neighbors at upland resource patches. The bow and arrow came into use throughout the Southern Plateau between 400 and 100 B.C. (Schalk 1983a; Chatters et al. 1995a), but not until approximately A.D. 500 in the Northern and Eastern regions (Richards and Rousseau 1987). Portable art and

Fig. 3. Rock pavement exposed in excavation of a large root-processing oven at site EeRj 55, Upper Hat Creek Valley, B.C. Photograph by David Pokotylo, 1977.

trade goods, including dentalium shells, shell disk beads, steatite pipes, stone and bone clubs, and elaborately carved implements and ornaments of stone, whalebone, and antler increased or made their first appearance along both the Fraser and Columbia river systems. These items are most common on the lower reaches of the major rivers, where the largest villages and greatest population densities had developed. Both raw materials and art styles show strong coastal influences. Certain settlements, which Hayden, Eldridge, and Eldridge (1985) term "gateway communities," were located at key points on trade routes and may have specialized in commerce. Wakemap Mound on the Columbia River near The Dalles and housepit village sites in the middle Fraser River valley near Lillooet appear to have been such communities.

There is also evidence of strife and social inequality. Rock art and large cemeteries began to appear in numbers, seemingly serving, at least in part, to identify band territories (Reid 1991). Fortified mesas in the root grounds of the central Columbia Basin (W.C. Smith 1977) and projectile points in human bone (Chatters 1988) are direct

Fig. 4. Housepits in the core area of the Middle Late period Keatley Creek site, near Lillooet, B.C. Photograph by Brian Hayden, 1995.

evidence that intergroup conflicts had begun to mount. Indirect indicators may be the appearance of numerous storage facilities in the caves and rockshelters of the Columbia and Snake river canyons (Reid 1991, 1991a; Swanson 1962), and the placement of large villages on islands (Schalk 1983; Osborne 1957), where both might be less easily reached by enemies. Disparities in house sizes and variations in the amount, quality, and exotic character of burial furniture on both the middle Fraser and middle Columbia reach their greatest extent late in this period and seemingly evince a growing social inequality (Hayden 1997; Hayden and Spafford 1993; Hayden, Eldridge, and Eldridge 1985; Pokotylo, Binkley, and Curtin 1987; Schulting 1994). This inequality probably created or amplified the demand for exotic goods and art objects.

Late-Late Subperiod, A.D. 500–1000 to 1720

Environmental change was relatively minor from approximately A.D. 1 on. Although the little climatic optimum of A.D. 900–1200 brought droughts and floods, and increased forest openings in the north and east, and the subsequent Little Ice Age depressed temperatures, major vegetation zones approximated their modern composition and extent for the last 2,000 years.

For the most part, this period is a continuity of the Middle-Late subperiod, with notable exceptions. Human populations appear to have declined in the Northern and southwestern Plateau after A.D. 1000, village sizes declined, and the inequalities in grave furniture seem to have largely disappeared. On the middle Fraser, this may have been the result of an ecological catastrophe when a landslide blocked salmon runs (Hayden and Ryder 1991). Upland usage also declined. On the lower middle Columbia, houses on at least the south side of the Columbia River became smaller and less permanent, and disparities in grave furniture all but disappeared. Despite these changes, mobile art continued to develop in both regions, reaching its fluorescence. Upstream, there were contrasting changes. Along the upper Columbia River and its tributaries, populations appear to have increased. Villages again appeared in the Arrow Lakes-Slocan Valley area and camas harvesting in the Calispell Valley underwent a second period of intensification after A.D. 500. In contrast, occupation of Hells Canyon on the Snake River declined shortly after the beginning of the subperiod (Reid 1991, 1991a). A small number of mass bison kills occurred in southwest Montana, perhaps made possible by Little Ice Age expansion of herds on the Northern Plains. Otherwise, particularly in the Kootenai River valley, there is little evidence of change in overall adaptive strategies from since the Early-Late period.

Movements of ethnic groups are a frequent subject of prehistoric research and discussion for this period. Changes in house form, projectile point styles, artifact inventories, and settlement patterns are thought to mark the arrival of Athapaskans in the Chilcotin Plateau no earlier than A.D. 1400 (Magne and Matson 1987). Great Basin projectile point styles and settlement patterns occur in the southern part of Hells Canyon and the nearby Blue Mountains after A.D. 1000 (Reid 1991, 1991a, 1992) and conflict with Numic speakers (Northern Paiute), which was common historically (Schalk 1980a), may have influenced changes in settlement permanence on the south side of the lower middle Columbia River. Farther downriver, the appearance of plank longhouses at Wakemap Mound has been seen as evidence for the upstream expansion of the Chinookan peoples into the territory they held historically.

Antiquity of the Ethnographic Pattern

Characteristics distinctive of most ethnographic groups on the Northern Plateau include a seminomadic-transhumant settlement pattern, group aggregation and dispersal at various stages in the annual cycle of activity, subsistence specialization centering on intensive harvesting and storage of salmon, ungulates, and roots; and winter housepit villages in major river valleys (see Palmer 1975a; Ray 1939; Teit 1900, 1909). Major archeological research efforts have asked when each of these features first appeared and when they began to occur together in prehistory.

No archeological study has yet covered the entire range of environments reportedly utilized within the ethnographic seasonal subsistence round, thus limiting truly regional perspectives of prehistoric subsistence-settlement patterns. However, in the Northern and Southern Plateau, a composite picture can be derived from studies that have separately examined sites in riverine and upland environments to provide a preliminary understanding of adaptive patterns.

Most components of the ethnographic pattern were in existence for millennia before they merged into a coherent adaptation. Salmon has been in use for at least 10,000 years in parts of the Southern Plateau and for more than 8,000 years on the Northern Plateau. However, its intensive exploitation began no earlier than 3300 B.C. and was not established areawide until as late as 500 B.C. Root gathering and processing, as indicated by ovens for reducing complex starches, began in parts of the Eastern Plateau by 4400 B.C. and in the Northern Plateau by 1500 B.C. If the hopper mortar and pestle were indeed root-processing implements, roots began to be important in the Southern Plateau as early as 5000 B.C. Semisubterranean dwellings made their first appearance around 3300 B.C. and were in continuous use after about 3900 B.C. Food storage is evident as a minor element of technologies in the southerly Plateau in the Early period, as indicated by a single grass-lined pit at Marmes Rockshelter, and at least since the later Lochnore phase (ca. 3300 B.C.) in the Northern Plateau. These four important components of ethnographic adaptations—intensive salmon fishing, root processing, semisubterranean settlements, and dependence on food storage—did not combine into a coherent adaptation until after 2000 B.C.

The final elements—high mobility and the use of uplands in the seasonal round of food harvesting—began only after 500 B.C. During the next 1,500 years, cultures became increasingly complex as populations grew, as evinced by indicators of social inequality in housing and mortuary treatment on middle and lower reaches of the major rivers. Trade and the influence from the Northwest Coast that was evident historically increased in significance. Stable carbon isotope studies of human bone show a maximum dependence on salmon at this time. Apparent declines in population density and cultural complexity after A.D. 1000 led to the more egalitarian societies observed at contact.

In summary, the various characteristics of ethnographic subsistence and settlement have different starting dates in prehistory. The evidence suggests that the subsistence-settlement components of regional cultures have been in place for at least 2,500 years but that after a period of greater population density and at least in some regions, complexity, sociopolitical patterns similar to those described for the ethnographic period were in existence for the last 700 to 1,000 years of prehistory. Certainly the introduction of the horse in the eighteenth century, and the introduction of diseases at or before that time led to disparities between prehistoric and ethnographic cultures that are not fully known.

Prehistory of the Northern Plateau

DAVID L. POKOTYLO AND DONALD MITCHELL

The Northern Plateau covers the intermountain zone of south-central British Columbia and north-central Washington State, an area inhabited at contact solely by groups speaking Interior Salish or Athapaskan languages. Kootenai-speaking peoples also dwell on the northern portion of the interior plateau but the prehistory of their area is discussed in "Prehistory of the Eastern Plateau," this volume.

The geographic limits of the Northern Plateau are marked by the Coast Range on the west, the Columbia Mountains on the east, a line about 65 kilometers below the United States-Canada border on the south, and roughly 52° 30´ north latitude (fig.1). The area consists of a series of gently rolling uplands of low relief (1,300–1,700 meters elevation), separated by deeply incised river and lake valleys, and intermittent highlands and mountain ranges rising to 2,500 meters (Holland 1964). Most of the area lies within the Fraser River drainage basin. The southern portion is drained by middle and upper reaches of the Columbia River system and the westernmost portion of the Chilcotin Plateau by several streams that flow through the Coast Range, directly to the sea.

The presence of alternating highlands and river valleys results in both marked altitudinal zonation of flora and fauna, and rich diversity of local habitats, ranging from semiarid to alpine. The entire area is in the rain shadow of the Coast Range, and has an average annual precipitation of 25–30 centimeters. Nine major "biogeoclimatic" zones, characterized by distinctive vegetation, soils, topography, and climate, occur within the area (MacKinnon, Meidinger, and Klinka 1992; Meidinger and Pojar 1991). The Ponderosa Pine–Bunchgrass Zone is restricted to hot, dry valley floors south of 51° 31´ north latitude. To the north, the Subboreal Pine–Spruce Zone and the Subboreal Spruce Zone predominate. Throughout the area, middle elevations to 1,450 meters support the Interior Douglas Fir Zone, while the Interior Cedar–Hemlock Zone is situated in moister eastern regions. Douglas Fir Zone and the Montane Spruce Zone occurs between the Engelmann Spruce–Subalpine Fir Zone. Alpine Tundra is present above treeline.

Northern Plateau groups at contact had a generally riverine focus, with a semisedentary winter pit house village settlement pattern and subsistence relying primarily on salmon, ungulates, and wild root crops. Their variable degrees of sedentism and population density seem related to proximity and access to salmon-bearing streams. Ethno-graphic models are probably applicable for the past 3,000–4,000 years.

The Fraser and Columbia River basins demarcate two subareas distinguished by environment and culture history. The most significant difference is in anadromous fish resources; salmon runs in the middle and upper Columbia drainage are considerably less than those in the Fraser River and its tributaries.

Nature of the Record

The archeological record of the Northern Plateau is primarily derived from excavations of housepit sites in the major river valley bottoms. This emphasis is due to the high visibility and accessibility of these surface features, and the abundant assemblages localized in the buried deposits. Although housepit sites provide valuable chronological, typological, and subsistence data, many researchers recognize that the research provides a distorted view of the past. Investigation of housepit sites at the expense of other site types has overemphasized the last 4,000 years in prehistoric cultural sequences and has stressed the winter subsistence and settlement aspects of the annual round. It has also been acknowledged that there are significant difficulties in interpreting housepit site deposits (Hayden, Alexander, and Kusmer 1986) as complexities of site formation and transformation processes can result in component mixing (Fladmark 1982:123; Von Krogh 1978; Wilmeth 1977a). Inventories and formal sample surveys of river valleys and uplands have identified regional-level patterns of site distribution and environmental relationships. Investigations have been conducted in most regions of southern interior British Columbia and northwestern interior Washington to document the presence of archeological material.

Fraser River Basin

The Early Period of Occupation

Although substantial areas of the Northern Plateau were ice-free and supporting grasslands by 9500 B.C. (Clague 1981; Hebda 1982; Mathewes 1985; Mathewes and Rouse 1975), well-dated evidence of human activity is not available until some 3,000 years later. Surface finds of fluted, stemmed,

81

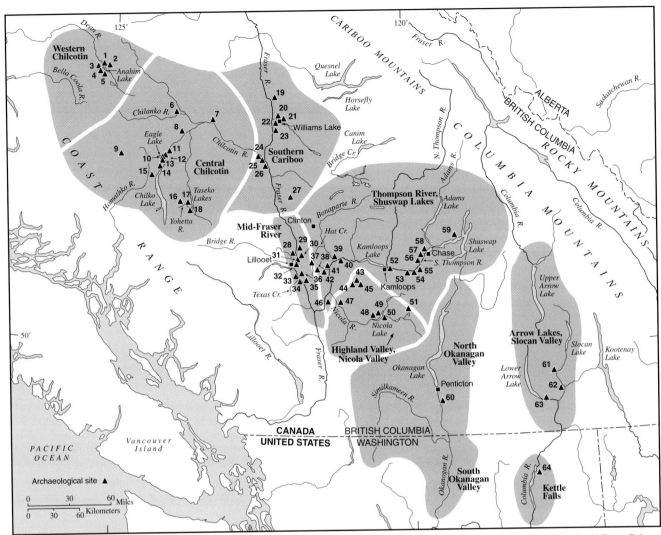

Fig. 1. Northern Plateau archeological sites and localities: 1, Danikto (FdSi 3); 2, Nakwantlun (FdSi 11); 3, Natsadalia Crossing (FdSi 2); 4, Goose Point (FeSi 1); 5, Potlatch (FeSi 2); 6, Poplar Grove (FaRx 1); 7, Alexis Creek locality; 8, Quiggley Holes (ElRw 4); 9, Horn Lake Southwest (EkSe 1); 10, Shields (EkSa 13); 11, Brittany Creek (EkSa 33); 12, Boyd (EkSa 32); 13, Bear Lake (EkSa 36); 14, Canoe Crossing (EkSa 5); 15, Potato Mountain locality; 16, EhRw 11; 17, EhRw 15; 18, EhRv 2; 19, Deep Creek (FbRn 13); 20, FaRm 23; 21, FaRm 8; 22, Stafford Ranch (FaRn 3); 23, ElRn 3; 24, EkRo 48; 25, EkRo 18; 26, EkRo 31; 27, EiRm 7; 28, Bridge River (EeRl 4); 29, Keatley Creek (EeRl 7); 30, Bell (EeRk 4); 31, Fountain (EeRl 19); 32, Terrace (EeRl 171); 33, Texas Creek (EdRk 1); 34, Nesikep Creek (EdRk 4); 35, Lochnore Creek (EdRk 7); 36, Lehman (EdRk 8); 37, Upper Hat Creek Valley locality; 38, Parker (EdRi 25); 39, Cache Creek (EeRh 1); 40, Rattlesnake Hill (EeRh 61); 41, Oregon Jack Creek (EdRi 6); 42, Landels (EdRi 11); 43, Valley Mine site (EcRg 1); 44, EdRg 2; 45, EcRg 1B; 46, Drynoch Slide (EcRi 1); 47, Honest Paul (EcRh 1); 48, Cottonwood (EaRd 2); 49, Monck Park (EbRd 3); 50, Guichon Slough (EbRc 6); 51, Chapperon Lake (EbRa 1); 52, Van Male (EeRb 10); 53, Baker site (EdQx 43); 54, EdQx 41; 55, EdQx 42; 56, Moulton Creek (EeQx 5); 57, Gore Creek (EeQw 48); 58, Chase (EeQw 1); 59, Fraser Bay (EfQt 1); 60, McCall (DhQv 48); 61, Vallican (DjQj 1); 62, Slocan Junction (DiQj 5); 63, Deer Park (DiQm 4); 64, Kettle Falls locality.

leaf-shaped, and Plano-like points have been reported in many parts of the Northern Plateau (Fladmark 1986:25; Grabert 1974:67; Rousseau 1993; Sanger 1970:119); but there is no consensus on the proper interpretation of these points. Their presence may reflect contemporary but independent regional variants of several widespread early cultural traditions defined for the Pacific Northwest: Plano, Early Stemmed Point, Old Cordilleran, and possibly Western Fluted point (Rousseau 1993; Stryd and Rousseau 1996).

Evidence of a Western Fluted Point tradition (Fladmark 1981; Fladmark, Driver, and Alexander 1988; Rousseau 1993), which could date as early as 8500 B.C., is equivocal.

Three specimens that might be attributed to the tradition are all derived from the Thompson River region (Fladmark 1982:126, 134; Stryd and Rousseau 1996). Evidence for the Early Stemmed Point tradition in British Columbia is also slight. Points from the mid-Fraser and Thompson River regions resembling Lind Coulee stemmed points and Windust phase stemmed points may have been introduced 8500–8000 B.C. by peoples affiliated with the Lind Coulee tradition or Windust phase (Rousseau 1993; Stryd and Rousseau 1996). Finely crafted lanceolate, stemmed, and foliate points surface collected from the Fraser-Thompson and Okanagan regions are highly similar to Plano tradition

POKOTYLO AND MITCHELL

types from the Northwestern Plains. Such point forms may represent a northward extension of early Plateau populations, shortly after deglaciation, that were influenced by Plains cultures and Plano point technology (Grabert 1974). Leaf-shaped points and pebble choppers in surface collections throughout the Northern Plateau may be derived from the Old Cordilleran tradition on the south and central coasts of British Columbia and the Columbia Plateau and may be early, but they are artifact types that persist for many millennia in interior British Columbia (see Eldridge 1974; Richards 1978; Rousseau 1993). It must be emphasized that none of the materials identified with these several early traditions has been found in a firmly dated cultural context, and their place in the cultural sequence is unknown.

After 6500 B.C. the regional sequence has a firmer chronological footing. Three sites have material radiocarbon dated to the 6500–5000 B.C. period: Landels (EdRi 11), Gore Creek (EeQw 48), and Drynoch Slide (EcRi 1).

The Landels site (fig. 2), located in Oregon Jack Creek Valley, a tributary of the Thompson River, has the earliest conclusive evidence for human occupation of the Northern Plateau. A "pre-Mazama" component with two brief occupation episodes dated at 6450 B.C. ± 90 and 5720 B.C. ± 80 (Rousseau, Muir, and Alexander 1991a) contains a small assemblage of microblades. Associated faunal remains indicate a subsistence focus on deer.

The Gore Creek "burial" site in the South Thompson River valley contained the postcranial remains of a young adult male accidentally killed and buried by a mudflow (Cybulski et al. 1981). The skeletal remains lay immediately beneath a layer of Mazama tephra and yielded a radiocarbon date of 6300 B.C. ± 115. No cultural material was associated with the remains, but stable carbon isotope analysis (Chisholm 1986; Chisholm and Nelson 1983) indicates that the individual's diet included around 8 percent marine origin protein, most likely salmon. If the Gore Creek individual's diet can be considered representative, human subsistence at this time focused on terrestrial rather than riverine resources, perhaps on land mammals (deer and elk) rather than salmon.

The Drynoch Slide site in the Thompson River valley yielded charcoal dated at 5580 B.C. ± 270 (Sanger 1967). Reported recoveries include a stemmed basalt point, three microblades, and unifacial and unretouched flake tools (Stryd and Rousseau 1996). A limited faunal assemblage includes deer, elk, and fish remains, tentatively identified as salmon. Stryd and Rousseau (1996) suggest the presence of microblades and use of fine-grained basalt may allow assignment of the site to the Early Nesikep tradition.

Nesikep Tradition, 5550/5050–4050 B.C.

The Nesikep Tradition is considered a distinctive interior ungulate-hunting culture that, from a mix of early regional cultures, possibly in response to increasingly cooler and wetter climatic conditions (Stryd and Rousseau 1996). The

Fig. 2. View of completed excavations at the Landels site (EdRi 11); wall profile to the right of the vertical scale shows Mazama tephra layer that overlies the "pre-Mazama" component. Photograph by Michael Rousseau, 1989.

tradition is subdivided into the Early Nesikep tradition and the Lehman phase.

The Nesikep tradition and Lochnore phase–Plateau Pit house tradition represent separate ethnic groups with different linguistic affiliations, the Nesikep tradition represents non-Salishan groups while the Lochnore phase and Plateau Pit house tradition are Salishan (Stryd and Rousseau 1996). The fishing-oriented, Lochnore phase people first coexisted with, and then absorbed, culturally and genetically, the indigenous, hunting-oriented, Lehman phase people, ending the Nesikep tradition and beginning the Plateau Pit house tradition.

• EARLY NESIKEP TRADITION, 5050–4050/3550 B.C.   The Early Nesikep tradition is represented at four excavated sites in the mid-Fraser and Thompson River valleys: Zone VII at the Nesikep Creek site (EdRk 4), Zone IIB from the Lehman site (EdRk 8) (see Arcas Associates 1985:84–86), Zone IV at the Rattlesnake Hill site (EeRh 61), and Component 3 at the Fountain site (EeRl 19). Only one radiocarbon date is reported for the tradition—3685 B.C. ± 190 for the Nesikep Creek site. An early Nesikep component may also be intermixed with a later occupation at the Landels site (Rousseau, Muir, and Alexander 1991a). The presence of early Nesikep material at the Landels site would indicate utilization of upland zones as well as river valley bottoms.

The Early Nesikep tradition is characterized by finely crafted lanceolate, corner-notched and barbed projectile points (fig. 3a–b); a high frequency of formed unifaces (scrapers) (fig. 3c–d); a microblade industry with wedge-shaped microblade cores, antler wedges, ground rodent incisors; bone points and needles, red ocher, and small oval formed unifaces, some with bilateral side notches (fig. 3e) (Arcas Associates 1985; Sanger 1970; Stryd 1973; Stryd and Rousseau 1996).

The projectile points are unique to southern interior British Columbia. They are characterized by V-shaped corner notches, straight or convex basal margins, basal thinning by removal of multiple flakes from both faces, and basal edge grinding. Many specimens were probably resharpened. Zone VII at the Nesikep Creek site contains several well made specimens that Sanger (1970) viewed as related to points of the Plano tradition. Fladmark (1982:126) notes that they are more similar to points from the Windust phase in the Lower Snake River region. Nevertheless, the Nesikep Zone VII points are quite distinct from forms characteristic of the following Lehman phase (Arcas Associates 1985, 1986).

Subsistence included large amounts of deer, as well as elk, salmon, steelhead trout, and bird. Freshwater mollusks, avoided by ethnographic groups in the region (Teit 1900, 1909), were also collected. No evidence of intensive utilization of salmon exists during this time.

• LEHMAN PHASE, 4050/3550–2450 B.C. The Lehman phase is recognized in the Fraser-Thompson valleys and in the mid-elevation Highland Valley. Sites with major Lehman phase components include: the Lehman site Zone IIA (Arcas Associates 1985); the Rattlesnake Hill site, Zones IIB and III (Arcas Associates 1985); the Oregon Jack Creek site (EdRi 6) (Rousseau and Richards 1988) and EdQx 42, Zone 1 (I.R. Wilson 1991). Radiocarbon dates are available for Oregon Jack Creek (2900 B.C. ± 100) and Rattlesnake Hill (2520 B.C. ± 110 and 2520 B.C. ± 400).

This phase is characterized by the Lehman obliquely notched point type—thin, pentagonal projectile points with obliquely oriented, V-shaped corner or side notches (fig. 4a); lanceolate knives with straight cortex-covered bases (fig. 4b–c); elliptical or leaf-shaped knives with prominent striking platforms at their bases; thin circular scrapers retouched around the entire margin (fig. 4f–g); horseshoe-shaped convex end scrapers (fig. 4d–e); a high occurrence of fine and medium grained basalts; and the absence of microblade technology. Only two artifact types—Lehman obliquely notched points and lanceolate knives with

a–b, after Sanger 1970:figs. 24c and 24 b; c–e, after Arcas Associates 1985:figs. 22d, 22e, and 19n.

Fig. 3. Early Nesikep tradition artifacts: a–b, lanceolate, corner-notched and barbed points from the Nesikep Creek site (EdRk 4); c–e, formed unifaces (c, d) and oval formed uniface with bilateral side notches (e) from the Rattlesnake Hill site (EeRh 61). Length of a, 9 cm; others to same scale.

straight, cortex-covered bases—are unique to the Lehman phase. Most other traits are shared with the Early Nesikep tradition, while some are found also in the succeeding Lochnore phase. Continuity in projectile point, scraper and knife styles, and in such technological traits as heavy point base grinding, suggest the Lehman phase developed out of Early Nesikep tradition cultures (Stryd and Rousseau 1996).

Subsistence focused on deer and elk hunting. Large amounts of freshwater mollusks were collected at the Rattlesnake Hill site, indicating intensive utilization of this resource in the river valleys. Lesser amounts of mussel shell were present at the Oregon Jack Creek site, which is interpreted as an elk-butchering station or camp (Rousseau and Richards 1988), and EdQx 42 at Monte Creek. Freshwater mollusks are absent at sites along the Fraser River, likely owing to a river current too rapid to support shellfish. Turtle remains are present in the faunal assemblage from EdQx 42 in the South Thompson valley. The main rivers were fished for salmon and other unidentified species, but there is no evidence for intensified use of salmon during this phase. Stable carbon isotope analysis of skeletal remains of two individuals buried near Clinton (site EiRm 7) and dated to 3000 B.C. ± 170 indicates food sources of marine origin (probably river-run salmon) supplied 37 percent ± 10 and 38 percent ± 10 of the dietary protein (Chisholm 1986). These values are slightly lower than the 40–60 percent range of marine-based protein reported for late prehistoric period groups (Chisholm 1986). However, it is uncertain whether the individuals should be assigned to the Lehman phase or the Lochnore phase. Other faunal remains at Lehman phase sites include: bird, rabbit, and small rodent. Existence of Lehman phase sites at upland lakes may indicate fishing and hunting of beaver and waterfowl. Fire-cracked rock at the Rattlesnake Hill and Oregon Jack Creek sites and a possible cooking pit reused as a refuse pit at Oregon Jack Creek may indicate the practice of food boiling or use of underground ovens, although earth oven features are not documented.

• LOCHNORE PHASE, 3550–2050/1550 B.C. The Lochnore phase is interpreted as a dry forest and river-oriented adaptive pattern that developed from the movement of Salishan-speaking peoples from the coast up the Fraser River system into the Northern Plateau approximately 3550 B.C. to exploit increasing salmon resources near the onset of cooler and wetter climatic conditions. Evidence of seasonal sedentism and salmon storage midway through the phase at approximately 2550 B.C. may mark the onset of the Plateau Pit house tradition, although that tradition may have begun much earlier in the phase (Stryd and Rousseau 1996). The Lochnore phase continues for a milleninum during the initial part of the Plateau Pit house tradition until it terminates at 1550 B.C. The initial part of the Lochnore phase overlaps with the Lehman phase of the Nesikep tradition for approximately 1,000 years, suggesting that two different lifeways were maintained in the region.

The Lochnore phase includes assemblages previously attributed to the Lochnore complex (Sanger 1970). The

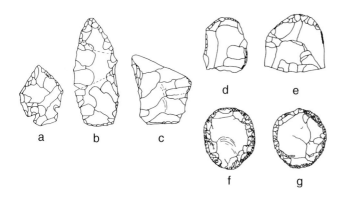

a–e, after Arcas Associates 1985:figs. 19m, 20c, 20e, 22b and 21c; f–g, after Rousseau and Richards 1988:figs. 7p and 7s.

Fig. 4. Lehman phase artifacts from the Rattlesnake Hill site (EeRh 61) (a–e) and the Oregon Jack Creek site (EdRi 6) (f, g): a, Lehman obliquely notched point; b–c, lanceolate knives with straight, cortex-covered bases; d–e, horseshoe-shaped convex end scrapers; f–g, circular scrapers. Length of b, 8 cm; others to same scale.

Lochnore complex—characterized by leaf-shaped points, macroblades, edge-battered pebbles, pebble choppers, concave-ended unifaces, and the absence of microblades—was initially considered to be an interior manifestation of the Old Cordilleran culture and typologically comparable to the Milliken and Mazama phases of the Fraser Canyon (Sanger 1969). It consisted of a collection of materials underlying a housepit floor at the Lochnore Creek site (EdRk 7) and some artifacts hand-sorted from the later housepit assemblage on the basis of carbonate and sand surface coatings, which were taken as indications of greater antiquity. Although the housepit floor was dated at 720 B.C. $\pm$ 130 and 1330 B.C. $\pm$ 125, Sanger (1970a:106) thought the underlying, undated Zone III containing the Lochnore complex to be much older.

Assemblages similar to the Lochnore complex were recovered at the Terrace site (EeRl 171) in the mid-Fraser valley, dated at 2195 B.C. $\pm$ 205 (Richards 1978), and at the Moulton Creek site (EeQx 5) along the South Thompson River (Eldridge 1974), beneath a layer of Mount Saint Helens "Y" tephra (about 2000 B.C.), indicating the complex is not contemporary with the Old Cordilleran tradition.

Lochnore phase sites are found on upper terraces of main river valley bottoms, lake shores, and mid-altitude valleys in the mid-Fraser and Thompson River regions. Major components are Lochnore Creek, Zone III; Rattlesnake Hill, Zone IIA; Valley Mine (EcRg 1), Component II; Moulton Creek, below-tephra component; Terrace, Component 2; EdQx 42, Zones 2 and 3 (Wilson 1991); Baker (EdQx 43), Zone 3 (Wilson 1992); and Landels, stratum II. Radiocarbon estimates are available for five sites: Terrace (2195 B.C. $\pm$ 100); two Highland Valley sites: EcRg 1B (1980 B.C. $\pm$ 100, 2800 B.C. $\pm$ 190, 3440 B.C. $\pm$ 90, and 3540 B.C. $\pm$ 190) and EdRg 2 (3560 B.C. $\pm$ 90); Baker (2290 B.C. $\pm$120, 2250 B.C. $\pm$ 90, 2400 B.C. $\pm$ 90, 2500 B.C. $\pm$ 100, 2000 B.C. $\pm$ 260, and 2310 B.C. $\pm$ 90); and Landels (1410 B.C. $\pm$ 70 and 1570 B.C. $\pm$ 70).

Characteristics diagnostic of the Lochnore phase are: Lochnore side-notched points (thick, leaf-shaped, lanceolate, unbarbed points with wide side notches, heavy basal edge grinding, and pointed or convex bases (fig. 5 a–b), concave-edged endscrapers on silicas, and a macroblade technology. Other traits include: leaf-shaped points often made from end-struck flakes, oval bifaces, round to oval scrapers on relatively thick flakes with almost continuous retouch (fig. 5 c–d), microblade technology (present at some sites), end and side scrapers on macroblades, unifacially retouched backed flake scrapers, flake scrapers with an obliquely oriented straight scraping edge, edge-battered pebbles, unifacial pebble choppers, notched pebbles, use of nonvitreous basalts, a sinuous/denticulate edge retouch, leaf-shaped elliptical knives with a prominent striking platform at the base. While I.R. Wilson (1991, 1992) argues the assemblages from EdQx 41, 42 and the Baker site represent a different cultural unit, Stryd and Rousseau (1996) consider these to be Lochnore components. They accordingly add several artifact classes (primarily bone) to the list of Lochnore phase characteristics.

Excavations at the Baker site revealed three dwellings radiocarbon dated between 2500 and 2000 B.C. (I.R. Wilson 1992). These structures predate other Northern Plateau dwellings by a millennium. All three house depressions are round to oval in shape, ranging from 3.0 to 4.5 meters diameter, and 35–50 centimeters pit depth. They have steep side walls, shallow saucer-shaped floors, central hearths, and interior storage pits. The framework, which has closest similarities to house forms on the Columbia Plateau during the Indian Dan and Kartar phases, is presumed to have been of light poles, possibly with a single central support. There also is evidence of a birchbark mat roof covering. Refuse in the interior storage pits includes remains of salmon. Outside the dwellings, a pit lined with charred wood and pine cones containing salmon and dog remains is inferred to be a smoking pit.

Rousseau, Muir, and Alexander (1991a) characterize the Lochnore phase as possessing a "forager" subsistence-settlement strategy, in the context of Binford's (1980) "forager-collector" continuum; and faunal remains support this interpretation. Subsistence was broad based and included deer, elk, beaver, snowshoe hare, turtle, duck, goose, salmon, and freshwater mussel. There is some evidence for salmon storage but the intensity of salmon fishing is still unknown. If the two skeletons from Clinton should instead be attributed to the Lochnore phase, then a reasonable part of the diet was based on food of marine origin.

Plateau Pit House Tradition

The Plateau Pit House tradition is thought to represent an at least 4,500-year-long cultural continuum culminating in the historic Interior Salish peoples of the region. Its beginnings are seen to lie at least as early as 2550 B.C. at the mid-point of

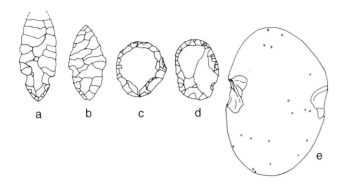

Royal B.C. Mus., Victoria: a, EeRh 61:7434; e, EeRh 61:7402; Simon Fraser U. Mus. of Archeol. and Ethnol., Burnaby, B.C.: b, EeRl 7:4312; c, EeRl 7:7419; d, EeRl 7:5093.

Fig. 5. Lochnore phase artifacts from the Rattlesnake Hill, site (a and e) and the Keatley Creek, site (b–d): a–b, Lochnore side- notched points; c–d, round-oval scrapers; e, notched pebble. Length of a, 5.5 cm; others to same scale.

the Lochnore phase. The Plateau Pit House tradition is characterized by changes in subsistence and settlement pattern and most notably by the construction of semisubterranean winter lodges (Stryd and Rousseau 1996). The earliest semisubterranean structures dating to 2500 B.C. have an architecture distinctive from later forms, and there is almost a 1,000-year gap separating these from the first evidence of widespread use. Various models have been proposed to account for these changes in houseform and settlement (Kuijt 1989; Rousseau 1990; Stryd and Rousseau 1996). The shift to a semisedentary earth-covered winter lodge settlement pattern may reflect adaptive responses to altered environmental conditions during the cool, moist climatic maximum, 2050–1350 B.C. Kuijt (1989) proposes that these changes in the environment resulted in reductions in the density and distribution of ungulates along with coincidental increase in availability of anadromous fish, which in turn led to major adaptive responses from human populations in the region.

Mid-Fraser Sequence

Stryd (1972, 1973, 1974, 1978, 1983a) conducted extensive surveys and excavations in the vicinity of Lillooet to refine the culture history for the mid-Fraser valley and to study differences between late prehistoric and ethnographic housepit village settlement patterns. Hayden carried out major excavations at the Keatley Creek site (EeRl 7)—a large pit house village with a wide range of housepit sizes—and investigated the development of cultural complexity (Hayden, Eldridge, and Eldridge 1985; Hayden, Alexander, and Kusmer 1986; Hayden, Breffitt, and Friele 1987; Hayden and Ryder 1991; Hayden and Spafford 1993).

Stryd (1973) divided the Nesikep tradition into a microlithic period 5000–800 B.C. and a nonmicrolithic period 800 B.C.–A.D. 1858. His original four phases for the later Nesikep tradition—a scheme intended to be of broad scope, including material from the Nicola Valley in its formula-

tion—were later regrouped and renamed as three phases of more local application (see Richards and Rousseau 1987:9; Stryd 1983a, personal communication 1991).

• KETTLEBROOK PHASE, 1650–450 B.C. This is a poorly defined unit, constructed mainly to describe an early stage of pit house occupation in the Lillooet area (Stryd 1983a). Patterned after the Shuswap phase assemblages of the Lower Thompson River and Shuswap Lake area, its principal characteristics include medium-sized corner-notched points with concave bases (fig. 6 a–c); key-shaped formed unifaces (fig. 6 d–e); "thumbnail" scrapers; convex-edged unifaces; split pebble tools; large numbers of expedient flake tools; and a diverse bone and antler industry. The temporal relationships of this phase are little understood and overlap with the Lillooet phase.

• LILLOOET PHASE, 850 B.C.–A.D. 750 The Lillooet phase is seen to include what was once separately identified as the Nicola phase (850 B.C.–A.D. 150) (Arnoud Stryd, personal communication 1991). It is distinguished by Lillooet corner-notched points (fig. 6 f–g); bilaterally barbed antler points; deer scapula scrapers; and possibly steatite pipes. Some attributes—dentalium beads, the rare ground slate knives, small barbed and corner-notched points, cairn burials, and steatite disk beads—overlap with the succeeding Fountain phase. Housepits during the phase exhibit the largest size range reported for any prehistoric period, attaining diameters up to 25 meters. The early part of the phase (roughly the span of the former Nicola phase) differs in that assemblages characteristically include relatively small round to oval pit houses, large to medium barbed corner-notched points (an inferred use of the atlatl rather than bow and arrow), and presence of possible boulder spall tools.

Stable carbon isotope analysis of human skeletal remains from the Lillooet area (radiocarbon dated A.D. 350–750) indicates that marine origin foods constituted an average of 60 percent of protein in the human diet (Chisholm 1986).

• FOUNTAIN PHASE, A.D. 950–1750 Characteristic traits of the Fountain phase include Kamloops side-notched points (fig. 6 i–k), a steatite and antler carving complex (fig. 6 l–n), zoomorphic hand mauls, pecten shells, tubular steatite pipes, bird-bone beads, flaked and drilled slate pendants, a possible weaving complex, small asymmetric leaf shaped points, notched flaked stone drills, spall tools, flaked stone spokeshaves, metapodial awls, mica-flakes, and some large pit houses.

Hayden departed from Stryd in defining a Classic Lillooet period (50 B.C.–A.D. 950) and a Late Prehistoric or Protohistoric period (Hayden and Ryder 1991) to distinguish an earlier time when large housepits were occupied by what are inferred to have been corporate residential groups.

Thompson River and Shuswap Lake Sequence

R.L. Wilson (1980) proposed a preliminary culture-historical sequence for the last 2,000 years in the Kamloops locality. This sequence was later revised and expanded by

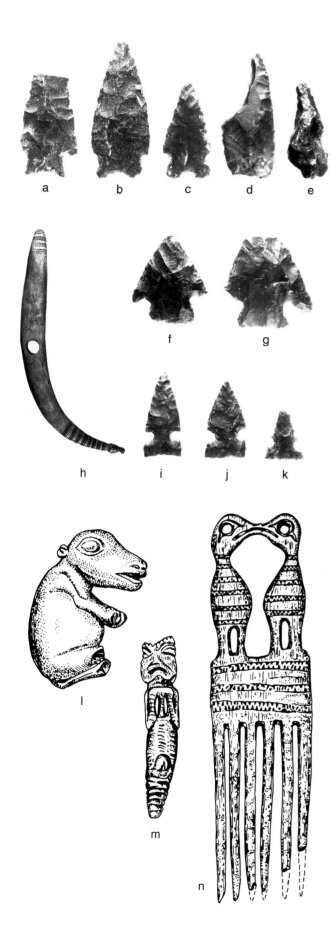

U. of B.C. Laboratory of Archaeol., Vancouver: a, EeRj 55:2812; b, EeQw 3:5; c, EfRl 9:299; d, EeRh 1:33; e, EeRj 63: 327; f, AC II:76; g, EeRj 55:657; h, EeQw 1:101; i, EeRh 1:6; j, EeRh 1:5; k, G31-I:77; l-m, after Stryd 1973:figs. 40m, 40f, and 38.

Fig. 6. Mid-Fraser and Thompson River artifacts: a–c, Kettlebrook or Shuswap phase medium-sized corner-notched points with concave bases; d–e, Kettlebrook or Shuswap phase key-shaped unifaces, f–g, Lillooet or Thompson phase barbed corner-notched points; h, Lillooet or Thompson phase antler digging stick handle; i–n, Fountain or Kamloops phase artifacts: i–k, Kamloops side-notched points; l, zoomorphic carved siltstone figurine; m, carved antler tine figurine; n, zoomorphic carved antler comb. Length of a, 4 cm; b–g and i–k to same scale; length of h, 30 cm; length of l, 6.5 cm; m–n to same scale.

Rousseau and Richards (1985) into a three-phase model covering the last 4,000 years, and its application extended a short distance into the North Thompson River valley and eastward up the South Thompson River into the Shuswap Lake region. Here the framework includes the main stem of the Thompson River, from its formation at Kamloops to a few kilometers above its junction with the Fraser River.

• SHUSWAP PHASE, 1550–450 B.C. The Shuswap phase marks the beginning of the Plateau Pit House tradition. It is characterized by the initial appearance of semipermanent winter pit house villages and intensive salmon utilization. Most reported Shuswap phase sites are situated close to lakes or rivers in large river valleys. There is only limited evidence of utilization of mid-altitude or upland areas. Housepits are relatively large, averaging 11 meters in diameter. The structures contain evidence of one to two occupations. Hearths, storage and cooking pits, and flexed burials in pits are present within housepit floors.

Subsistence was based on hunting of large and small mammals and birds, collection of freshwater mussels, and fishing salmon and other freshwater species. The most substantial excavated faunal assemblage is reported for the Van Male site (EeRb 10), a housepit village near Kamloops (Richards and Rousseau 1982; R.L. Wilson 1980). Identified species from this and other housepit sites include: elk, deer, mountain sheep, black bear, beaver, muskrat, striped skunk, porcupine, marmot, domestic dog, wolf, red fox, snowshoe hare, waterfowl, salmon, trout, and other freshwater fish species.

The Fraser Bay site (EfQt 1), on the shore of Shuswap Lake, is one of the few non-housepit, valley bottom, lakeshore sites investigated on the Northern Plateau. During the Shuswap phase, the site was repeatedly used as a seasonal residential base and salmon fishing camp (Rousseau, Muir, and Alexander 1991). The lithic assemblage contains few projectile points but abundant simple retouched flake tools and leaf-shaped bifacial knives, possibly reflecting expedient processing of fish. A notched discoidal pebble may indicate the use of fish nets. No other fishing gear is evident. A limited faunal assemblage primarily consists of highly fragmented medium-sized mammal remains.

The Parker site (EdRi 25) in Oregon Jack Creek Valley is the only excavated upland site dating from the period (Rousseau, Muir, and Alexander 1991a) and provides the earliest direct evidence of floral resource procurement and processing on the Northern Plateau. A small (1 m diameter) earth oven feature yielded a radiocarbon date of 1180 B.C. ± 100. Although only a single Oregon grape seed was recovered, the pit was likely used to cook roots such as bitterroot and balsam root.

Characteristics of Shuswap phase assemblages include a variety of distinctive point styles (fig. 6a–c); key-shaped formed unifaces (fig. 6 d–e); small "thumbnail" scrapers; convex-edged unifaces with straight proximally tapered lateral margins; split pebble tools; strong reliance on local lithic material of fair to good quality; relatively simple lithic technology; high frequencies of utilized and unifacially retouched flake tools; and a well-developed bone and antler industry.

• THOMPSON PHASE, 450 B.C.–A.D. 750   Thompson phase housepits are small (5.0–7.5 m diameter), but housepit villages are larger than those during the Shuswap phase, with up to 100 houses present at some sites (Mohs 1980; R.L. Wilson 1980). Many villages have storage pits within the village area or in close proximity. Thompson phase sites are frequently found in upland locations. A diversity of site types suggests a wider range of economic activities carried out by specific task groups in different locations.

Several characteristics distinguish the Thompson phase from the Shuswap phase. Projectile point size decreases throughout the phase. Barbed points with either corner or basal notches are the main types present (fig. 6 f–g). Basally notched point forms are more common 450–50 B.C., while corner-notched types, classified as Lillooet corner-notched points by Stryd (1973), predominate from 50 B.C. to A.D. 750. Leaf-shaped and stemmed points are present but rare. Convex-edged endscrapers and key-shaped formed unifaces become more common than in the Shuswap phase. Specialized artifact types, such as antler digging stick handles (fig. 6 h), first appear. Lithic assemblages often have high amounts of good quality material, relative to Shuswap assemblages. Vitreous basalt dominates, but exotic cherts and chalcedonies and occasionally obsidian constitute 20–30 percent of the assemblages. The bone and antler industry is much more substantial, but this increase may be due more to preservation than cultural factors. Multiple-barbed unilateral and bilateral harpoons and composite toggling harpoon valves appear along with tubular beads from sections of bird and small mammal longbones.

Intensive utilization of root resources is evident in the uplands (Pokotylo and Froese 1983; Rousseau, Muir, and Alexander 1991a) as a major change in subsistence. In Upper Hat Creek Valley, substantial numbers of circular to oval cultural depressions represent cooking pits or "earth ovens" (Pokotylo and Froese 1983). Excavations at 15 pit features yielded carbonized remains of root resources (*Allium* sp., Compositae, and Liliaceae). Faunal remains recovered indicate that meat from mule deer, elk, grouse, and unidentified fish were also cooked. Few lithic artifacts were recovered from the pit features. All excavated pits have rock-lined basins (fig. 7 top), and many have superimposed layers of fire-cracked rock (fig. 7 bottom) indicating re-use. The dimensions of many depressions are larger than reported for the ethnographic period. Repeated usage of capacious pits suggests that large task groups were necessary both to construct and maintain the facilities and to collect the substantial number of roots they could hold.

• KAMLOOPS PHASE, A.D. 750–1750   Salient attributes of this phase include large housepits, averaging seven meters in diameter, with prominent raised earth rims; and the small Kamloops side-notched triangular arrow point (fig. 6 i–k). Multi-notched variants of the Kamloops point occur during the last 400 years of the phase. Small corner- and basally notched, shouldered or barbed points are present in small numbers approximately A.D. 750–950. Various well-formed flaked stone tools are present, but not the key-shaped formed unifaces of preceding phases. There are examples of elaborate mobile art (fig. 6 l–m) and decoration of utilitarian items (fig. 6 n). These artistic traditions are poorly dated and may have their origins well before the Kamloops phase (Stryd 1983). Some of the soft stone sculpture of this tradition rivals if not exceeds the quality of coastal material.

Subsistence resources are similar to those reported for previous phases of the Plateau Pit House tradition. Lesser amounts of freshwater mussel occur closer to the historic period. Fewer upland sites reflect a reduced emphasis on mid to high altitude floral and faunal resources. In Upper Hat Creek Valley, excavated cooking pits dating to the Kamloops phase are smaller and show less evidence of re-use than those of greater age (Pokotylo and Froese 1983). There is evidence that bottomland plant resources were important (Rousseau and Howe 1987).

Subregional differences in the proportion of marine-based protein in the diet are evident. The average amount of marine protein decreases slightly with distance upriver in the Fraser River system (Chisholm 1986; Lovell et al. 1986), and this is apparent even within the tributary Thompson River drainage area. Stable carbon isotope analysis indicates that at this time groups from the Thompson River, the South Thompson River, and Adams River displayed marine protein values of 56, 48, and 41 percent, respectively (Richards and Rousseau 1987:47).

Numerous burial sites are attributable to the phase. The main form of inhumation is primary flexed burial in a shallow pit, although wood cyst burials marked with rock cairns, talus slope burials, and multiple tomb burials are noted (Hills 1971; Pokotylo, Binkley, and Curtin 1987; Skinner and Copp 1986; H.I. Smith 1900). Burials contain varying quantities and types of grave furniture. Select individuals at some major sites such as Cache Creek (EeRh 1; Pokotylo, Binkley, and Curtin 1987) and Chase (EeQw 1; Sanger 1969a) contain grave goods that may reflect ascribed status and socioeconomic inequality (Hayden, Eldridge, and Eldridge 1985; Pokotylo, Binkley, and Curtin 1987).

The late part of a local Plateau Pit House tradition sequence for the mid-altitude Highland Valley is divided into two phases (Arcas Associates 1986): Highland, 450 B.C.–A.D. 750, and Kamloops, A.D. 750–1750. Arcas Associates suggest that during these phases, and for the earlier Lehman and Lochnore, the valley was used only sporadically presumably by small nomadic groups of people from the nearby river valleys in search of specific resources such as elk and deer. The Highland phase assemblages do not significantly differ in age and form from those of the Thompson phase of the adjacent Thompson River region.

Paralleling the sequence just outlined is the Highland Valley's Quiltanton complex. It probably dates 150 B.C.–A.D. 950 but may extend from as early as 2550 B.C. to as late as the protohistoric period if two problematic dates are accepted as valid (Arcas Associates 1986). The complex has a well-developed microblade industry with wedge-shaped cores; poor quality basalts and other lithics used in stone tool manufacture; high frequencies of graving implements and multiple tools (often retouched or utilized flakes with gravers); small and large projectile points with broad shallow side notches, recurved bases, rounded shoulders, straight or slightly convex blade margins, and haft-element edge grinding; concave-based lanceolate points with slightly converging stems and basal grinding; and small leaf-shaped points. Although the microblade industry is technologically similar to that from Lochnore-Nesikep and Upper Hat Creek Valley, the dating may be different and the culture-historical relationships are not understood (Arcas Associates 1986:189). Some of the microblade assemblages with late prehistoric dates are mixed with Lochnore phase material and thus may ultimately be affiliated with the Lochnore phase (Stryd and Rousseau 1996).

As the Quiltanton complex is contemporary with the Highland and Kamloops and phases in the valley (and possibly also with the earlier Lehman and Lochnore), Arcas Associates (1986:190) speculate that this temporal overlap may reflect the coexistence of two different populations. They tentatively identify at least the Highland and Kamloops phase sites with Salish peoples who are thought to have only seasonally visited from the Thompson River valley, while Quiltanton complex sites may represent occasional presence of Athapaskan-speaking groups from the Nicola Valley.

Survey work and small-scale excavation at four sites (Wyatt 1971, 1972) and excavation at Monck Park (EbRd 3) (Archer 1971) provide only the sketchiest outline of a Nicola Valley sequence. The Monck Park site on Nicola Lake has two housepits: one of 14 meter diameter with an interior cachepit and evidence of roof support posts; and a small one with no apparent support posts. The housepits are associated with an assemblage that, in general, seems fairly typical of the Kamloops phase. Included are a number of small points of leaf-shaped or notched triangular form. Beneath that assemblage is one with larger side-notched and corner-notched points and a high proportion of microblades—characteristics that suggest attribution to the Lochnore phase. Site materials recovered have been equated to the Kamloops phase (Chapperon Lake site, EbRa 1), Thompson phase (Cottonwood site, EaRd 2), and Shuswap phase (Guichon Slough site, EbRc 6) (Wyatt 1972). A distinctive assemblage for the valley's historic Athapaskan occupants has not been distinguished, although the protohistoric Honest Paul site (EcRh 1) material (Wyatt 1972) would seem to be a likely candidate. It is a small settlement of three housepits and some 30 cachepits with a set of artifacts unusual for such a late period in its total absence of small side-notched triangular points.

Chilcotin Plateau–Southern Cariboo Sequence

It is difficult to make an appropriate assignment of this area where Plateau dryland and northern forest intermingle. Although the Chilcotin are included in the *Subarctic* volume of the *Handbook*, the "questionable affiliation" of that tribal group was noted by Ray (1939:149), who observed they might well be regarded a Plateau people. Many aspects of the environment and culture support that position, and archeological research has suggested the central and eastern portions of the Chilcotin plateau, at least, were home to Interior Salish groups prior to A.D. 1500. The position of the Southern Cariboo is not in question. This area lay within the territory of a Plateau group: the Shuswap. This review of Chilcotin and Southern Cariboo archeology augments the treatment in volume 6:107–129.

Research has been scanty, and the few sequences proposed are either very shallow or of quite uncertain time depth. Good temporal unit markers are limited to the last 1,000 years; however, informal cross-dating of general phase characteristics with better-known sequences of the Middle Fraser-Thompson River region, has permitted provisional extensions back to approximately 2,000 years ago. Helmer (1977) outlined a tentative three-period chronology for the whole north central interior of British Columbia, including the Chilcotin and Southern Cariboo regions. His periods were Early Prehistoric (2500 B.C. to A.D. 1), Middle Prehistoric (A.D. 1–1300), and Late Prehistoric (A.D. 1300–). Mitchell (1970) suggested that in the central and western portions of the Chilcotin Plateau there was evidence of at least three phases of occupation.

Western Chilcotin

Research in the western portion of the Chilcotin Plateau has focused on sites and areas in the vicinity of Anahim Lake. Survey of a small stratified random sample of 500 square meters quadrats from the 742 square kilometer upper Dean

Fig. 7. Rock-lined basins in Upper Hat Creek valley. top, Basin in excavated earth oven at site EeRj 101. bottom, Profile of superimposed rock-lined basins from multiple uses in excavated earth oven at site EeRj 55. Photographs by David Pokotylo, 1977.

River valley (extending north from Anahim Lake) disclosed few sites overall, but a significant concentration along river and lake shores (Eldridge and Eldridge 1980). Sites types included those with housepits or cachepits and lithic scatters. No large, clustered "Salish type" settlements (Lane 1953:274) were noted. Some sites, at up to one kilometer from the water's edge, consisted of but a single housepit. Mitchell (1970, 1970a) excavated Natsadalia Crossing (FdSi 2) at the outlet of the lake—a site at which there was no evidence of structures—and Wilmeth (1978, 1980) excavated four village sites on the lake or a short distance down the Dean River. Wilmeth (1980:3–4) recorded a calibrated date of 1948 B.C. ± 188 for the basal level of the Nakwantlun site (FdSi 11) and suggested a possible association with a "McKean type" point (stemmed, with ground basal edges), but the assemblage content remains unreported. He derived a series of provisional phases or "component clusters" to construct a local archeological sequence for the late prehistoric and early historic periods in the region.

Component Clusters I–III are relatively similar and span the period A.D. 1–1200. They are characterized by settlements of one to four shallow basin-shaped housepits with no interior benches or evidence of interior support posts. Microblades (fig. 8 a–d) are present in the first two but not the third, a very small assemblage. Projectile points are medium to large and of leaf-shaped or corner-notched form although there is also a characteristic small, parallel-stemmed point in the third. Bipolar cores are found in the first and third component cluster and a distinctive type of "eared" end scraper (fig. 8 i–j) in the second.

Component Clusters IV and V (dating from around A.D. 1700–1850) have strong similarities and almost certainly represent protohistoric and historic Chilcotin occupations. The winter dwellings of IV were markedly different from those found earlier. The pits had steeply sloping walls, a ground level bench, four posts to support the main roof timbers, a central hearth, and an interior cache pit excavated into the bench face. The style of the one house attributable to Component Cluster V may have been a unique introduction from the Bella Coola of the Northwest Coast. It was a rectangular structure whose walls, whether sloping or perpendicular, were anchored in shallow trenches. There were corner posts, a line of posts perhaps supporting a central ridge beam, and two hearths. Assemblages contain several distinctive artifact forms and increasing amounts of European trade goods. Characteristic artifacts of non-European manufacture include small projectile points with contracting stems (Kavik points, fig. 8 e–h), small side-notched points, tci-tho (cortex spall) scrapers (fig. 8 r–s), spurred end scrapers (fig. 8 n–q), and a variety of bone and antler implements. Natsadalia Crossing's artifacts most closely match these "Chilcotin" assemblages, but the site likely predates Component Cluster IV as no trade goods were encountered.

Central Chilcotin

Intimations of an early occupation of the central Chilcotin plateau are provided by the distinctive Poplar Grove (FaRx 1) assemblage on the banks of the Chilanko River (Mitchell 1970, 1970a). Its situation (on the shore of a since-vanished lake) and the character of its artifacts suggest considerable age, which, by cross-dating with Sanger's (1970) Lochnore-Nesikep Creek sequence, was put at perhaps 3000–1500 B.C. The assemblage includes leaf-shaped points, stemmed

Canadian Mus. Of Civilization, Hull, Que.: a, 200:123; b, 200:30; c, 3:132A; d, 3:113; e, 200:225; f, 201:214; i, 3:24; j, 3:20; k, 201:284; n, 200:169; o, 201:962; s, 201:716; U. of B.C. Laboratory of Arch., Vancouver: g, ELP:32, 1–188; h, CR 92:1007; l, ELP:32–1122; m, ELP:19 1–24; p, EkSa 13:1564; q, EkSa 13:5431; r, ELP:32 1–273.

Fig. 8. Chilcotin–South Cariboo area artifacts. a–b, Microblades from the Goose Point site (FcSi-1); c–d, microblades from the Danikto site (FdSi-3); e–h, Kavik contracting stem points from the Goose Point, Potlatch, Bear Lake, and Britany Creek sites; i–j, eared end scrapers from the Danikto site; k–m, Athapaskan-style Kamloops side-notched points from the Potlatch site and sites EkSa 36 and EkSa 27; n–q, spurred end scrapers from the Goose Point and Potlatch sites and site EkSa 13; r–s, tci-tho cortex spall scrapers from the Bear Lake and Potlatch sites. Length of a, 3.3 cm; others to same scale.

leaf-shaped points, medium-large corner-notched triangular points, split cobble tools, formed and unformed bifaces, and numerous flake unifaces. Over 60 percent of these artifacts display a medium-gray patina, a much greater incidence than has been reported for later, more firmly dated assemblages.

There is also evidence in the area of a "microblade occupation," comparable in assemblage content to Wilmeth's (1978) Component Clusters I–III and perhaps equivalent in age (A.D. 1–1200), although it should be noted that to the east and southeast on the Plateau microblades occur very much earlier. The only excavated components of this kind are at Horn Lake Southwest (EkSe 1) (Mitchell 1970, 1970a) on the Homathco River system and from two sites near the settlement of Alexis Creek (Bussey 1983). The Horn Lake Southwest assemblage included medium-sized leaf-shaped points, medium-sized corner-notched and side-notched triangular points, microblades, flake unifaces, and flake bifaces. The Alexis Creek artifact assemblages are very small and consist only of flaked stone items, including small side-notched points, microblades, formed unifaces, and cortical spall tools.

• EAGLE LAKE   Probabilistic sampling of an area around Eagle (Choelquoit) Lake, survey along the Chilko River, and test excavation of nine sites in the region have revealed a chronological sequence for the last 2,000 years that documents the migration of Athapaskan speakers into the area (Magne and Matson 1982, 1984, 1987; Matson 1982). The sequence is mainly based on excavations of three sites: Bear Lake (EkSa 36), Boyd (EkSa 32), and Shields (EkSa 13). The Bear Lake site contains historic and prehistoric components. Excavation of one of the two historic structures indicates a six by seven meter rectangular lodge with a shallow floor dug into the ground and a central hearth under two ridge poles. It has been dated by dendrochronology with cutting dates of A.D. 1877. The structures are attributed to a historic Chilcotin occupation, termed the Lulua phase, that commenced after A.D. 1850. The prehistoric component has a large roasting pit (placed by radiocarbon date at A.D. 1655 ± 75) and rectangular lodge of undetermined dimensions. This is interpreted as a prehistoric Athapaskan occupation identified as the Eagle Lake phase.

The Boyd and Shields sites have locational characteristics, artifact assemblages, and pit house features typical of the Kamloops phase identified in the Middle Fraser-Thompson River region to the southeast. Radiocarbon dates of A.D. 1445 ± 70 for the Boyd site and A.D. 1200 ± 90 for the Shields site place both well within the Kamloops phase interval of A.D. 800–1700.

Two undated sites with clusters of very large pit houses (A.D. 1–800) are assigned to the Lillooet phase reported for the mid-Fraser area north to the mouth of the Chilcotin River.

• POTATO MOUNTAINS   Located immediately south of Eagle Lake, the Potato Mountain Range is part of the northeastern flank of the Coast Range. Probability sampling was conducted in an area of alpine tundra and the subalpine-alpine tundra ecotone at the south end of the range, and brief reconnaissance of the north end was also carried out (Alexander and Matson 1987). The following pattern applies to the south area.

Archeological sites are concentrated in the subalpine parkland. Site density in this zone equals the values recorded for Eagle Lake and other probabilistic surveys of river and mid-elevation valleys in the Northern Plateau, while the density of pit features is greater. Radiocarbon dating of six roasting pits indicate use between A.D. 50 and 1850, while a carbon-14 date of 270 B.C. ± 80 for a buried cultural horizon at the Mountain Fan site extends use of mountain resources back even further. Medium-sized corner-notched projectile points suggest earlier occupations, 2050–450 B.C. The high density of sites and limited time range for use of the roasting pit features indicates that a relatively large number of people used the area at any one time.

The record is thought to reflect a Chilcotin-Athapaskan model of land use: alpine and parkland environments were intensely used in the summer (July to August) by a large number of people (100–200) from a number of different bands who gathered to dig, process, and store "mountain potatoes"—the corms of spring beauty (*Claytonia lanceolata*)—and hunt ungulates and marmots.

It is noteworthy that the archeological evidence is concentrated in the parkland, even though the main resource (*Claytonia*) exists mainly in alpine tundra. Most root procurement likely took place in the alpine zone, but campsites and roasting pits were situated in the parkland where wood and shelter existed. The distribution of sites appears to depend more on the firewood and water requirements of camping and root processing than the location of the major subsistence resources.

• TASEKO LAKES   Probabilistic survey sampling of an area in the Gunn and Yohetta Valleys of the Taseko Lakes region recorded 16 archeological sites in a relatively forested setting, although none was found in continuous subalpine forest (Magne 1984, 1985). Types reported include a large pit house village, small housepit sites, roasting pit sites that vary considerably in the number and size of pits present, and lithic scatter.

The settlement pattern of the region was one of winter residence near larger lakes and summer utilization of root crops. Limited test excavations were carried out at three sites. At EhRv 2, a large housepit village, two large (15 m diameter) housepits yielded radiocarbon dates of A.D. 290 ± 80 and A.D. 785 ± 70. A date of 25 B.C. ± 70 was obtained for a third housepit eroding from a cutbank exposure. All the dates fall within the expected time range of Lillooet phase dwellings. The location of this large Lillooet phase housepit village along a drainage system that presently does not support a sizable salmon run suggests that the fishery must have been much more substantial to support the group occupying the site. Although the specific cause of salmon decline in the Gunn Valley system is unknown, it may be related to the decline of large Lillooet phase villages elsewhere in the Northern Plateau after about A.D. 950. The small housepit sites in the area are thought to postdate EhRv 2.

Roasting pits at two sites (EhRw 11 and 15), having dates of A.D. 1895 ± 70 and A.D. 1940 ± 55, respectively, indicate a historic age. The roasting pits excavated are similar to others investigated at Eagle Lake and in the Potato Mountains. Excavations show that human occupation of the Taseko Lakes region extends back to at least 2,000 years ago with two main episodes of prehistoric settlement: the Lillooet phase occupation from A.D. 1–800 with considerable dependence on salmon resources of the Gunn Valley and Chilcotin occupation beginning at some unknown time, but from at least 200 years ago to the present, and focusing on roots and large game.

Southern Cariboo Area

• CHILCOTIN–FRASER CONFLUENCE A probabilistic survey of an area of benchland and adjacent forested slopes on the west bank of the Fraser River between McEwan Creek and the Chilcotin River was carried out to study archeological settlement patterns in the region and to determine their relationship to ethnographic semisedentary western Shuswap and sedentary Canyon Shuswap subsistence-settlement patterns (Ham 1976; Matson, Ham, and Bunyan 1984). The survey identified a variety of housepit and cachepit site classes, and a distinctive group of lithic surface scatters containing a predominance of chert artifacts and debitage. Sites in this class are situated on ridge tops and lack pit features of any kind, as well as the cortex spall tools and stone wedges associated with housepits.

Excavated assemblages from two housepit sites (EkRo 48 and 31) are characterized by the predominant use of vitreous basalt for flaked stone tool manufacture, small side-notched points, the absence of microblades, and a relative absence of formed scrapers, and have general similarity to the Kamloops phase identified for the mid-Fraser region. The assemblage from a third excavated housepit (EkRo 18) has similar characteristics but lacks points and is associated with very large housepits typical of the mid-Fraser Lillooet phase. The faunal assemblages from all three excavations are dominated by deer and salmon, although the variety of remains present suggests a broad-based subsistence pattern.

Radiocarbon dates for two of the excavated housepits range from A.D. 1080 ± 80 to A.D. 500 ± 75. Points from surface contexts include types characteristic of the Kamloops and Lillooet phases in the mid-Fraser region. The artifacts, features, and radiocarbon dates are considered similar enough to extend the Kamloops and Lillooet phases north to the Chilcotin River. The following sequence is proposed: Kamloops phase (A.D. 800–1850); Lillooet phase (A.D. 1–800); and the "Chert debitage" site components that predate the Lillooet phase. Survey and excavation data suggest that a semisedentary settlement pattern typical of the North-

ern Plateau was in place for the last 1,500 years, and that the Canyon Shuswap large sedentary villages at the mouth of the Chilcotin River may have begun as early as A.D. 1150.

• WILLIAMS LAKE LOCALITY Excavations of three pit house sites and mounds associated with a pit house (Kenny 1972; Whitlam 1976) and one lithic scatter site (Rousseau and Muir 1991) in the general vicinity of the town of Williams Lake provide data for this area. Radiocarbon dates for two excavated housepits at the Stafford Ranch site (FaRn 3) and site E1Rn 3 indicate occupation between A.D. 1 and 1000. Although cultural deposits in both sites are mixed, the radiocarbon dates suggest at least two distinct occupations at each housepit. At the undated site FaRm 8, two mounds associated with housepits were excavated, yielding an assemblage that is different from those at the two housepit sites. There is a preponderance of flaked stone artifacts and a virtual absence of faunal remains. The corner-notched, side-notched, small triangular points, pentagonal bifaces and the low incidence of formed unifaces, bifaces, microblades, cobble tools agrees with a Kamloops phase assignment (Whitlam 1976:43).

The Deep Creek site (FbRn 13) is a village of 12 to 13 housepits ranging in size from 6 to 16 meters in diameter and in shape from circular and oval to nearly rectangular (Kenny 1972:1). The larger pits fall well within the range of those found at Lillooet phase sites, but no structural features characteristic of plateau pit houses were noted. The artifacts, also, are different from what would be expected for a Lillooet phase assemblage. There are medium-sized contracting stem and leaf-shaped points, formed and unformed bifaces and unifaces, and gravers.

Site FaRm 23 is a small, single component deer-hide-processing site radiocarbon dated to 1470 ± 110 B.C. (Rousseau and Muir 1991). Two small (35–48 cm diameter), shallow (10–13 cm deep) pit features at the site were probably used as smudge-fires for hide processing and for meat cooking. Faunal remains of at least one mule deer are clustered around the two pit features. Most of the lithic assemblage consists of expedient flake tools, which are similarly clustered around the two shallow pits along with some formed endscrapers and unformed scrapers. The medial section of a single slightly stemmed lanceolate biface with a very small amount of basal grinding was also present. This lithic assemblage has characteristics similar to those of Shuswap horizon sites (1550–450 B.C.) to the south.

Columbia River Basin

Investigation of the Columbia River drainage portion of the Northern Plateau has been very limited. There is a comprehensive sequence for the Kettle Falls portion of the Columbia River (Chance and Chance 1977, 1982, 1985; Chance, Chance, and Fagan 1977), and there are partial sequences for the Arrow Lakes–Slocan Valley (Eldridge 1984; Mohs

1982; Rousseau 1982; Turnbull 1971, 1977) and the Okana-gan Valley (Copp 1979; Grabert 1968, 1971, 1974).

Okanagan Valley Sequence

After what may have been very similar beginnings, the northern and southern portions of the Okanagan Valley developed along somewhat different lines. In the end, the north was most similar to contemporaneous phases of the Thompson River and Shuswap regions, while the south continued a long period of close resemblance to the Middle Columbia sequences. The South Okanagan sequence, as outlined by Grabert (1974), consists of four phases. On the basis of work at the McCall site (DhQv 48), Copp (1979) has suggested subdivisions of the third phase.

• OKANAGAN PHASE   The Okanagan phase is poorly defined and provisional. Its characteristics are drawn from a number of small and apparently early assemblages from the Okanagan Valley that may include large leaf-shaped and stemmed points, large leaf-shaped "pre-forms," and a high proportion of flake tools. Basalt is the most common raw material. The only faunal remains are fragments of mussel shell. These sites are either stratigraphically early or situated on the higher river and lake terraces. The phase is guess-dated to the early post-Pleistocene to 4000 B.C. period.

• INDIAN DAN PHASE, 4000–1000 B.C. This phase is distinguished by large basal-notched stemmed points (some with distinct barbs), medium and large leaf-shaped points, milling stones, pestles, and numerous flake tools. Sites are in rockshelters or open locations, and earth ovens are sometimes present. Faunal remains include land mammal and fish bone and mussel shell.

• CHILIWIST PHASE, 1000 B.C. to A.D. 1100 As defined by Grabert (1974), Chiliwist provides the first evidence for pit houses in the South Okanagan: deep, steep-walled circular housepits clustered in small settlements. Other characteristics include large leaf-shaped points, medium sized barbed basal-notched stemmed points, microblades, ground stone celts, milling stones, and occasional bone artifacts. Raw materials other than basalt are prominent in the flaked stone industry. Fish remains (including salmon) and mussel shell are now reported as "abundant," and identified mammal bone consists of deer, elk, and mountain sheep.

Copp's (1979) refinement of the Chiliwist phase distinguished three subphases, of which the last, beginning about A.D. 100, is, in fact, a 900-year hiatus in the record. The earlier subphases (1000–400 B.C. and 400 B.C.–A.D. 1000) are separated by presence in the first of microblades and in the second of points similar to but smaller than those of the first subphase. Copp (1979:193) also interprets a late subphase II shift in dominance from wide-necked to narrow-necked points as indicating introduction of the bow and arrow and partial displacement of the atlatl.

• CASSIMER BAR PHASE, A.D. 1100-CONTACT The principal characteristics of the Cassimer Bar phase are: a variety of small projectile points—including corner-notched and side-notched forms—milling stones, carved steatite items, and bone composite toggling harpoon heads. Some bone and stone artifacts are decorated with geometric or zoomorphic designs. There are circular or ovoid, shallow, saucer-shaped housepits and rectangular matlodge depressions. Grabert (1974) reports the presence of wood cyst burials. Faunal remains are dominated by the bones of large ungulates but, compared with earlier phases, there is also increased abundance of fish bone and freshwater mussel shell.

The main differences between the northern and southern portions of the Okanagan Valley are the presence, in the north, of a long tradition of side-notched points and an apparent "richness" to northern assemblages in the number of ornamented items. Grabert (1974) views these and other long-lasting differences as evidence of northern "stability," which he attributes to less severe altithermal climatic variations than were experienced to the south.

Arrow Lakes-Slocan Valley Sequence

The first sequence for this region was developed by Turnbull (1977) from excavations on Lower Arrow Lake and at the stratified Slocan Junction site (DiQj 5). Mohs's work at the lower Slocan Valley's Vallican site (DjQj 1) was the basis for expansion and modification of the sequence by Eldridge (1984), Mohs (1982), and Rousseau (1982).

• DEER PARK PHASE, 1300–450 B.C. The phase is characterized by stemmed projectile points, some medium to large corner-notched points, large side-notched eared points, cone-shaped pestles, nephrite celts, utilized flakes, and housepits. Microblades are a rare but distinctive part of the assemblage. Resemblances between this phase and the contemporaneous Skitak period of Kettle Falls are few. Deer Park is represented as a phase of comparatively dense occupation by pit house dwellers while the other had few people and no housepits.

• VALLICAN PHASE, 450 B.C.–A.D. 650 The Vallican phase is coeval with the last two-thirds of the Takumakst period (Eldridge 1984: fig. 13). The main point forms are corner- or basally notched. Key-shaped or crescentic chalcedony scrapers or perforators and carefully fashioned end scrapers are also considered diagnostic. Many Deer Park phase categories, such as the simple flake tools, continue in use. The one housepit attributed to this phase is a rimless saucer-shaped depression of seven meters diameter. Faunal remains are rarely encountered but include mammal bones and the shells of freshwater mussels (Mohs 1982:95; Rousseau 1982:112–13).

Vallican differs from Takumakst in quality of stone-working, which is far from "clumsy," and in the presence of a substantial proportion of exotic lithics. However, its characteristic point, scraper, and perforator forms closely resemble those of Takumakst, the South Okanagan Valley Chiliwist phase, and, in general, the Thompson phase.

• SLOCAN PHASE, A.D. 650-CONTACT The Slocan phase is formed of two subphases divided about A.D. 1450 with the late subphase being distinguished by prevalence of small, thin, side-notched flaked stone point varieties (commonly of chert) and a noticeable increase in the amount of mussel shell (Mohs 1982:97).

For the phase as a whole, the principal characteristics (after Eldridge 1984 and Mohs 1982) include small side-notched points, occasional Columbia corner-notched points, and infrequent ground stone items. Purcell siliceous siltstone (argillite) dominates lithic detritus while gravers and scrapers are mainly of chalcedony. Various housepit styles are represented, including some with side entrances and shallow rectangular depressions that are probably remains of matlodges. Other features include hillside roasting platforms and, situated outside the dwellings, cache pits and hearths. Burials are flexed and in pit graves. Faunal remains now include bones of salmon and freshwater fish along with those of both small and large mammals. Mussel shells are especially plentiful.

Kettle Falls Sequence

• SHONITKWU PERIOD, 7600–6800 B.C. The earliest components fall in the Shonitkwu period, which is distinguished by the presence of medium to small leaf-shaped points, side- and corner-notched points, microblades and keeled cores, thick quartzite slab tools such as choppers, notched pebble sinkers, and numerous utilized flakes—including some of large size (fig. 9 a–d). There are also a roughly fashioned pestle or hand maul (fig. 9 w), some manos (handstones), and a drilled fragment of ground slate that may be part of a tubular pipe. Faunal remains reported include bones of waterfowl, grizzlies, and a large, now extinct, species of tortoise.

It is inferred that but a small number of people were then involved and that they were at the Falls to catch salmon. The plentiful crude chopping tools may have been used during the construction of fishing platforms and weirs (Chance and Chance 1977:154). Projectile point styles are seen as allying the occupants, culturally, with the Windust and Cascade phases to the south, while the microblades provide evidence of perhaps stronger ties to the north (Chance and Chance 1982:422).

• SLAWNTEHUS PERIOD The Slawntehus period, which lasted until at least 5300 B.C., represents a significant decline in local population and in use of the fishery. The assemblages include slightly shouldered leaf-shaped and side- and corner-notched points, pebble tools (fig. 9 e–j), and the occasional microblade. At a village site 32 kilometers upriver, and dating to about 5000 B.C., are the floor of a small hut, some sinkers, and many grinding stones (Chance 1986:15).

The decline in use during the poorly represented Slawntehus period and a succeeding long interval of only inter-

mittent occupation (5300–2800 B.C.) are thought to reflect drastic reduction in the number of salmon available, resulting from increased sediment in the glacier-fed Columbia River tributaries which, in turn, was the outcome of climatic warming (Chance and Chance 1982:423).

• KSUNKU PERIOD, 2800–1600 B.C. Ksunku period materials include leaf-shaped points, medium-sized points with shallow side-notches, contracting and square stemmed points, medium-sized "hawk-tail" side-notched points (Chance, Chance, and Fagan 1977:189), formed bifaces and uni-

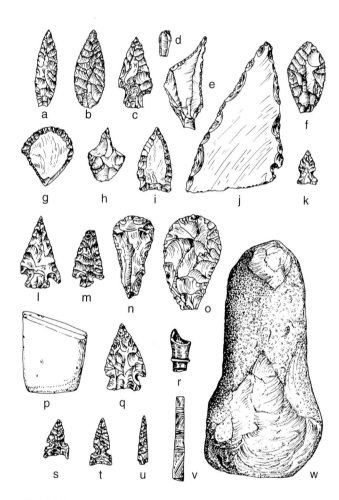

a–d, w, after Chance 1986:153; e, after Chance 1986:15; f, h, after Chance 1986:169; g, after Chance 1986:167; i, after Chance 1986:21; j, after Chance 1986:16; k, after Chance and Chance 1982:351; l–m, after Chance and Chance 1982:353; n–o, after Chance and Chance 1982:357; p–q, after Chance 1986:26; r, after Chance and Chance 1982:347; s–v, after Chance and Chance 1982:337.

Fig. 9. Kettle Falls sequence artifacts. a–b, Shonitkwu period leaf-shaped projectile points; c, Shonitkwu corner-notched projectile point; d, Shonitkwu microblade; e, Slawntehus period perforator; f, Ksunku period leaf-shaped projectile point; g, Ksunku formed uniface; h, Kunsu perforator; i, Skitak period projectile point; j, Slawntehus quartzite biface; k, Takumakst period side-notched projectile point; l–m, Takumakst corner-notched projectile point; n–o, Takumakst formed unifaces; p, Sinaikst period nephrite celt fragment; q, Sinaikst corner-notched projectile point; r, Sinaikst or Shwayip period fragment of tubular pipe; s–t, Shwayip side-notched projectile points; u, Shwayip leaf-shaped projectile point; v, Shawyip incised stone object; w, Shonitkwu pestle or hand maul. Length of a, 4.8 cm; others to same scale.

faces—including both convex and concave scrapers, and flaked stone perforators (fig. 9 f–h). Boiling stones are plentiful. Although there is no evidence of net technology (the assemblages have no sinkers), salmon bones are abundant and Kettle Falls was obviously once more an important fishery. Ksunku period beginnings appear to lie in the few, small assemblages found during the long 5300–2800 B.C. period. Its end at the Falls is abrupt, apparently coinciding with flooding (Chance 1986:19).

• SKITAK PERIOD, 1600–800 B.C. For 1,400 years following the Ksunku period and the beginning of the Skitak, there is little evidence of human occupation. When signs of human presence are once again common, in the Skitak period (Chance and Chance 1985:295), assemblages include medium to small leaf-shaped points, points with square and contracting stems (fig. 9 i), formed bifaces and unifaces, flaked stone perforators, and a few pebble-based cutting tools. A high proportion of these artifacts are made from cryptocrystalline materials.

• TAKUMAKST PERIOD, 800 B.C.–A.D. 300 Characteristics of the assemblages include small to medium contracting stem and side- and corner-notched points (some with distinct barbs), formed bifaces and unifaces, flaked stone perforators and drills (including some of keyshaped form), carved and polished steatite tubular pipes with thin flaring bowls, small choppers or cores, one to two-meter deep pit houses, storage pits (some with quartzite slab superstructures), and earth ovens (fig. 9 k–o). The preferred stone material is quartzite, and its working is described as "gross or clumsy" and exhibiting "the lowest level of skill in stone technology of any component at Kettle Falls" (Chance and Chance 1982:425).

The ethnographic pattern is probably first manifested in Takumakst period components and from this time on the sequence may be identified with Plateau Salish. The Takumakst is also seen as a time of stylistic uniformity (Chance and Chance 1982:425), a contrast with the succeeding Sinaikst period that may indicate ethnic homogeneity during the earlier period.

• SINAIKST PERIOD, A.D. 300–1400 Sinaikst projectile points are most commonly small and side-notched, but a very wide variety of other forms are represented as well (fig. 9 q). As this is accompanied by a significant increase in the number of exotic lithics (fig. 9 p–r), it is easy to conclude either greater contact with distant groups through an expanded trade network, seasonal assembly of an ethnically diverse population at the fishery, or, perhaps, a combination of these two.

Deep pit houses continued in favor and appear to have been occupied in summer "which is certainly at odds with the accepted wisdom about such houses in the Plateau" (Chance and Chance 1982:426). Construction of substantial pit houses and the size and number of contemporaneously occupied settlement suggest a considerable population was resident for much of the year.

• SHWAYIP PERIOD, A.D. 1400-CONTACT The Shwayip period is characterized by abundant small, ovate, quartzite knives (presumably used to prepare salmon for drying) and the overwhelming predominance among projectile points of the small, thin, side-notched form (fig. 9 s–t). Pit houses are no longer built at the Falls, the principal dwelling being the stilt house, the form described and depicted at early contact. Evidence of ethnic diversity, while still present, is much reduced, as are estimates of the number of people assembling at the fishery.

Conclusions

Integrating Regional Sequences

Several local and regional culture-historic schemes for the Northern Plateau have been proposed (Sanger 1967, 1969, 1970; Fladmark 1982:127–128; Arcas Associates 1985; Richards and Rousseau 1987:8–13; Stryd and Rousseau 1996). Fladmark (1982) challenged the worth of any Plateau-wide culture-historic units, noting that adaptive differences in each ecological zone may limit the utility of a broad classificatory scheme over the entire area—"a mosaic of related variant cultures separated by mountain ranges or drainage divides may be the only 'typical' long-standing regional pattern" (Fladmark 1982:124–125). His answer was simply to divide the prehistory of interior British Columbia into three periods: Early (pre-6000 B.C.), Middle (6000–1550/1050 B.C.), and Late (1550/1050 B.C.-historic), an approach followed also by Stryd and Rousseau (1996).

For the late prehistoric period (essentially the duration of the Plateau Pit House tradition), Richards and Rousseau (1987) have attempted a synthesis for the entire Northern Plateau. This relies heavily on data from the Thompson River-Shuswap Lake region and is largely an extension of the scheme developed for that area (Rousseau and Richards 1985). In their view, a shared Plateau Pit House tradition (marked by a pattern of pit house settlement and intensive utilization of salmon) cross-cuts other regional differences and unites the area. Change during the long span of this tradition is reflected in three pan-regional cultural horizons defined by direct comparison of components, rather than of regional or local phases: Shuswap (1550–550 B.C.), Plateau (550 B.C.–A.D. 750), and Kamloops (A.D. 750–1750). Although these horizons were not intended to replace local or regional phases, they have been used by many researchers as the main culture historic units for the late prehistoric period.

Investigation of the Columbia River drainage portion of the northern plateau has been very limited relative to the Fraser drainage subarea. Although there is a comprehensive sequence for the Kettle Falls portion of the Columbia River (Chance and Chance 1977, 1982; Chance, Chance, and Fagan 1977), and partial sequences exist for the Lower

96

Arrow Lakes–Slocan Valley (Eldridge 1984; Mohs 1982; Rousseau 1982; Turnbull 1977) and the Okanagan Valley (Copp 1979; Grabert 1968, 1974), they have not been integrated into larger areal units.

Microblades

Studies of microcores and blades in Northern Plateau assemblages have considered their significance in a variety of contexts. They have been viewed as chronological indicators of early cultures (Borden 1952; Sanger 1967), as ethnic group markers (Sanger 1967, 1968a, 1969, 1970, 1970a; Stryd and Lawhead 1983), and as a functionally specific technology and activity set (Pokotylo 1978; Fladmark 1986; Ludowicz 1983; Greaves 1991).

Sanger (1968a) regarded the microblades and cores from the Lochnore-Nesikep locality as sufficiently different from industries in neighboring regions to warrant a separate technological tradition. The resulting Plateau Microblade tradition, an important part of his initial culture historic model for southern interior British Columbia (Sanger 1967, 1969, 1970), was defined by several microcore attributes, including a wedge-shaped form, microblade removal from only one end of the core, an apparent absence of ridge flakes to prepare fluted surfaces, striking platforms on weathered surfaces, and single striking platforms resulting from a lack of core rotation (Sanger 1968a:114). The weathered striking platform characteristic is absent in Sanger's (1970a) description, and re-examination of the Lochnore-Nesikep materials used in the original definition does not reveal this attribute (Ludowicz 1983). Sanger considered the tradition to be at its maximum intensity between 5000 and 1500 B.C., with subsequent decline and virtual absence in the record by A.D. 1.

The Plateau Microblade tradition has generated considerable debate since its formulation, with the most pressing problem being its temporal span. Radiocarbon age estimates for microblade-bearing components at the Landels site indicate microblade technology is present in the Thompson River region by at least 6500 B.C. (Rousseau, Muir, and Alexander 1991a). However, the prevalence of the industry throughout the Northern Plateau after this time and its termination date remain uncertain.

Fladmark (1982) argues that microblades do not occur in any quantity prior to 4000 B.C., and that the demise of microblade technology may have started as early as 3000 B.C. He concludes that microblades were no longer in use by 2000 B.C., a termination date compatible with regions outside the Plateau. In a reformulation of the Nesikep tradition for the Fraser-Thompson region (Stryd and Rousseau 1996), microblades are seen as characteristic of the Early Nesikep tradition but are absent in the succeeding Lehman phase. However, they are present in the Lochnore phase. Stryd (1973) noted that microblades are absent in Lillooet housepit assemblages postdating 850

B.C. but has changed his interpretation (see Arcas Associates 1986:155), noting nonintrusive microblades and microblade cores in housepits with Shuswap horizon (1550–450 B.C.) components and situated on earthflows postdating 2750 B.C.

The evidence for microblade industries in the last 2,000 years is equivocal. There are sites with microblades that span the last two millennia in several regions, but they have acknowledged dating problems. These include the Quiltanton complex assemblages in the Highland Valley (Arcas Associates 1986), and microlithic assemblages in housepit deposits in the Anahim Lake area (Wilmeth 1978). The Quiltanton complex may ultimately be affiliated with the Lochnore phase (Stryd and Rousseau 1996). Wilmeth (1978) acknowledged that the presence of microblades in housepits in the Anahim locality may well result from post-depositional disturbance, although he included microblade technology in component clusters dating between A.D. 1–1700. Microblades are also present in the mixed components from two housepit sites near Williams Lake with radiocarbon dates spanning A.D. 1–1000 (Whitlam 1976).

Some researchers have suggested that microlithic technology on the Northern Plateau, particularly assemblages found in upland areas, may be affiliated with prehistoric Athapaskan groups. Arcas Associates (1985, 1986) propose that if the Quiltanton complex of the Highland Valley is indeed contemporaneous with the Valley's Kamloops and Highland phases, the simplest explanation is that it represents Athapaskans seasonally coexisting with Salishans. Microlithic industries are present in the nearby Nicola Valley, an area that has ethnohistoric evidence of Athapaskan occupation, but possibly only earlier than the Kamloops or Thompson phases (Archer 1971). It is also evident that, while microblades are an artifact class at least weakly associated with Athapaskan components in the Chilcotin Plateau (Magne and Matson 1987), the other characteristics used to identify Athapaskans are absent from the Quiltanton complex.

Although much research has focused on the temporal and ethnic affiliations of microlithic industries, relatively little work has considered the role and function of microblade assemblages in prehistoric Plateau subsistence and settlement systems. Proposed uses of microblades include hafted engraving tools (Sanger 1968a), cutting tools (Pokotylo 1978), and side-slotted barbs in composite projectile shafts (Fladmark 1986), but these inferences are largely speculative and not based on systematic research such as analysis of wear patterns. Pokotylo (1978) noted that sites in Upper Hat Creek Valley exhibited a mutually exclusive distribution of assemblages with microblades and those with formed unifaces, which suggest a dichotomy between cutting and scraping tool use. Residue analysis of a small sample of microblades from the Highland Valley indicated use in tasks involving plants and mammals (Loy 1986). Greaves's (1991) analysis of wear patterns on microblades from Upper Hat Creek and Highland Valleys indicated that blades were used in a variety of tasks relating more to food processing and tool manufacture than to food procurement. Almost half the microblades showing wear, were inferred to have been used in scraping of soft materials.

Ludowicz (1983) and Greaves (1991) have examined regional variability in assemblages with a microlithic technology. Ludowicz (1983) compared microlithic tools from riverine and upland areas, using material from the Lochnore-Nesikep locality and Upper Hat Creek Valley. Ludowicz reported that upland sites contained higher proportions of expedient tools and exhibited evidence of more microblade manufacture and microcore rejuvenation. She proposed that the presence of microcore technology at base camps reflected a "collector" subsistence strategy that was established prior to Richards and Rousseau's (1987) inferred shift from a foraging to a semisedentary collecting pattern. Greaves's (1991) study of assemblage variability in microlithic and nonmicrolithic sites in Upper Hat Creek Valley and Highland Valley concluded that the two types of assemblages do not reflect different activity sets within the subsistence settlement system, but microlithic technology had different roles in each area. Prepared microcores were brought into Upper Hat Creek Valley, while in Highland Valley they were prepared at residential camps, and microblades were removed at both residential camps and at field camps. Microblade use also varied somewhat between the two valleys, with microblades in Upper Hat Creek Valley being less versatile in the range of uses to which they were put. Although microcore technology was associated with high residential mobility in Upper Hat Creek Valley, it was associated with both high residential and logistical mobility in Highland Valley. The differences observed in these two studies may account in part for the varying temporal and geographic distribution of microlithic industries throughout the Northern Plateau. Microlithic technology probably had a variety of roles among subsistence-settlement systems in different environmental settings.

Migration of Athapaskan Speakers

Identification of prehistoric Athapaskan cultures and dating their entry into the Northern Plateau has been a longstanding research problem (see Ives 1900; Fladmark 1979; Helmer, Van Dyke, and Kense 1977). Although attempts to recognize the Nicola Valley Athapaskan occupation have been unsuccessful (Wyatt 1971, 1972), several studies (Wilmeth 1977, 1978; Magne and Matson 1982, 1984, 1987), have made progress toward defining a prehistoric Athapaskan presence on the Chilcotin Plateau. However, the timing of the migration remains elusive.

Using a direct historic approach, Wilmeth (1977, 1978:160, 171) isolated several traits considered diagnos-

tic of prehistoric ancestral Chilcotin in the Anahim Lake locality: small contracting-stemmed (Kavik) points, tcitho cortex spall scrapers, spurred end scrapers, and the shallow rectangular winter pit house. Additional distinguishing characteristics have been identified through comparison of Chilcotin Plateau material with assemblages from sites of almost certain Athapaskan or Salishan affinity (Magne and Matson 1982, 1987). Although Kavik points may be characteristic of Athapaskan sites in the Chilcotin Plateau and regions to the north, small side-notched (Kamloops) points common to the mid-Fraser and Thompson River region are also present in the Chilcotin assemblages. Multivariate statistical analysis of attribute variation among Kamloops points from seven localities shows that they can be differentiated into Salishan and Athapaskan groups (Magne and Matson 1982, 1987). Athapaskan style Kamloops points generally have indented bases, short spurs, and elongate blades, while Salishan forms are more equilaterally triangular and often have multiple notches. In addition to differences in point form, some of the variability in artifact assemblages from these same localities can be attributed to Athapaskan-Salishan ethnic differences. Multivariate analysis of flaked stone tool classes in 20 housepit and lodge assemblages revealed a number of classes useful in identifying Athapaskan components (Magne and Matson 1987), including the Kavik points and spurred scrapers previously suggested by Wilmeth (1978), as well as microblades, small formed bifaces, and unifacial retouch flakes. All these classes are most abundant in Athapaskan assemblages, while sinuous-edged unifaces have higher relative frequencies in Salishan assemblages. Although microblades are a significant artifact class, they tend to occur in mixed components and therefore are of dubious status (Magne and Matson 1987). Site location and architectural differences are also evident. Salishan pit house sites are located along shores of rivers and lakes in which salmon spawn, while Athapaskan sites, containing rectangular lodges with shallow excavated floors, are situated by small lakes (Magne and Matson 1984).

Although Wilmeth (1978:172) did not with certainty identify any prehistoric Athapaskan components in the Anahim Lake area, he proposed that ancestral Chilcotin established themselves in the area within the last 500–600 years (Wilmeth 1977:101). This estimate was based mainly on a discontinuity in his component cluster sequence and an assumption that the Yukon's White River ashfall (about A.D. 700) precipitated Athapaskan migration to southern regions. Component Clusters I to III (A.D. 1–1200) are more attributable to Salishan than Athapaskan speakers as little similarity exists between them and protohistoric-historic Chilcotin Clusters IV and V (A.D. 1700–1850). The postulated migration could have occurred at any time during the 500-year gap between these two groups.

Magne and Matson (1984) applied a "parallel direct historic approach" (Matson 1982) to establish the Chilcotin migration into the Eagle Lake region. They looked for divergences in historic to prehistoric sequences of the Eagle Lake and Chilcotin River mouth localities, which although sharing some environmental characteristics, were historically occupied by Athapaskan Chilcotin and Salish Shuswap, respectively. They argued that, given environmental similarity, sites in both regions should be comparable up to the time of the Athapaskan migration, but different afterward. Although the work seems to have successfully identified prehistoric Athapaskan components, the timing of the Athapaskan migration into the Eagle Lake locality continues to be uncertain. The prehistoric Athapaskan component identified at the Bear Lake site most likely dates A.D. 1700–1850, while the Boyd housepit site provides a maximum limiting date for the migration at A.D. 1400. Thus, the migration most likely occurred 200–500 years ago.

Causes of the Athapaskan migration also remain undetermined. Wilmeth (1977, 1978) accepted the hypothesis first proposed by Workman (1974, 1979) that Athapaskans in the southwest Yukon dispersed south after the catastrophic east lobe of the White River ashfall dated about A.D. 1250. Ives (1990) doubts the significance of this event and argues that the group-forming principles in Athapaskan social and economic systems are the important causal factor in explaining northern Athapaskan dispersal.

Complex Hunter-Gatherers

In some areas of the Northern Plateau the development of nonegalitarian societies in the late prehistoric period is suggested by pit houses of different size, some exceeding 20 meters in diameter, present in village sites located in the middle Fraser River valley and the Chilcotin River basin (Hayden, Eldridge, and Eldridge 1985), and by burials containing marked differences in grave goods in the Fraser and Thompson River valleys (Pokotylo, Binkley, and Curtin 1987). There may have been as many as eight such large villages in the Lillooet area but only three—Keatley Creek (EeRl 7), Bridge River (EeRl 4), and Bell (EeRk 4) sites—remain. Four similar large villages are reported in three areas of the Chilcotin drainage: EkRo 18 at the Chilcotin-Fraser River confluence, the Quiggley Holes (ElRw 4) and Canoe Crossing (EkSa 5) sites along the Chilko River; and EhRv 2 in Gunn Valley. The large pit houses in the Lillooet area were occupied predominantly during the Lillooet phase spanning the first millennium A.D. and appear to have been abandoned by about A.D. 950. A similar occupation span is inferred for the Chilcotin sites. Although relatively few burials have been excavated in the Northern Plateau, the Texas Creek (EdRk 1), Chase, and Cache Creek burial sites, and the Bell site provide some details on the kinds and distribution of grave goods associated with interred individuals. These sites span the Lillooet and Kamloops phases.

Extensive research has been carried out at two of the Lillooet area housepit village sites. Stryd's (1973) excavations at the Bell site indicated that large cultural depressions (greater than 15 m diameter) were residential structures, and he proposed that differences in pit house size probably reflected inequalities in the prehistoric community. Hayden and Spafford (1993; Spafford 1991) present a detailed analysis of the nature of social organization at large pit house villages, based on excavations at the Keatley Creek site. Keatley Creek is the largest pit house village site recorded on the Northern Plateau, containing over 115 residential-sized depressions, some up to 25 meters in diameter. Between 1986 and 1989, 21 pit house features and 13 smaller depressions representing storage pits, roasting pits, or very small structures were test excavated. In addition, excavation exposed most of the floor area of three differently sized housepits (9, 14, and 19 meters diameter), all last occupied just before site abandonment about A.D. 850 (i.e., early Kamloops phase). Hayden and Spafford (1993), using an estimated 2.5 square meter floor space per person, infer that population at the peak of site occupation during the first millennium must have been at least 500 and may have exceeded 1,000.

Analysis of the faunal remains, fire-cracked rock, lithic debitage and tools, and features in the floor deposits of the three extensively excavated housepits reveals distinct patterns of usage of different areas of the house floors. Some differences are attributed to gender specific activities, craft specialization, or status distinctions of the residents.

Few of the small pit houses show evidence of interior structural posts. It is inferred that 19 people, perhaps three nuclear families, lived in the smallest of the three extensively excavated housepits. The presence of a single set of activity areas on the floor suggests communal use of the house. There is no indication of any hierarchical organization or unusual wealth. However, excavations at other small housepits indicate considerable variability between households in the social, economic, and possibly ritual status of residents.

In the medium-sized housepit excavated, four major support posts divide the living floor into sectors: one central and four peripheral, suggesting separate domestic spaces. It is estimated that the structure housed 30 people, representing five to six moderately well-off nuclear families. Artifacts found in the floor deposits and inferred as wealth items were nephrite fragments, copper sheeting, soapstone pipes, graphite, decorated bone, obsidian, and hawk bones. Although wealth items are present, separate hierarchically organized families appear not to be very developed.

The large housepit excavated shows pronounced differences in the floor deposits from smaller-sized housepits. It contains much greater amounts of artifacts, botanical remains, and faunal remains; and a wide array of wealth items and exotic faunal remains. The structure is estimated to have housed at least 45 people, organized into as many as eight separate domestic units, each with its own hearth, abrading stones and anvil stones, cooking rocks (fire-cracked rocks), cluster of debitage and similar kinds of tools, bedding material (Douglas fir needles, pine needles, and grass) near the wall, and storage pit. Differences amongst the household units suggest the presence of a hierarchically organized corporate group. Such differences include large hearths and storage pits in the west half of the housepit in contrast to small hearths and the absence of storage pits in the eastern side—a pattern that likely involved some families with greater control over resources than others.

Hayden and Spafford (1993) infer that the Keatley Creek community was divided into poorer families that generally lived in small pit houses or that attached themselves to some of the "great houses" as common domestic tenants or even servants. Intermediate-size houses appear to have had modest economic advantages or rights to moderately productive resources. It was the large households that are thought to have developed into the most powerful economic and social forces in the community. The highest-ranking residents of these large houses appear to have been relatively wealthy and influential; others may have been individually and hierarchically arrayed.

To Hayden and Ryder (1991), the existence of both large and small housepit villages at the regional level suggests a two-tiered settlement hierarchy, characteristic of chiefdom-level complexity. Using this argument, a high degree of complexity would be evident at other locations on the Northern and Columbia plateaus, such as the Chilcotin Plateau, the Lower Slocan Valley, and The Dalles along the Columbia River.

After A.D. 950, all the large villages in the Lillooet region were apparently abandoned. The cause of this "cultural collapse" is attributed to a landslide downstream of the present town of Lillooet that dammed the Fraser River approximately 1,100 years ago (Hayden and Ryder 1991). Such a catastrophe would have blocked all or large parts of the salmon runs—a devastating event for all communities along the Fraser upstream of the slide. Migration out of the area may have followed, and possibly starvation for a large part of the population. Even if the Fraser River was able to cut through the dam relatively soon after the slide, regeneration of the salmon stocks must have been a long and gradual process with a long term effect on human resettlement of the region. The large pit house sites were never reoccupied.

Although the number of burials excavated is small, there is mounting evidence of ascribed status at sites in the mid-Fraser and Thompson River valleys. Many of the grave goods associated with children at these sites can be interpreted as items reflecting ascribed status (Hayden, Eldridge, and Eldridge 1985; Pokotylo, Binkley, and Curtin 1987). In the mid-Fraser region, Stryd (1973, 1983) excavated a child burial from one of the largest

housepits at the Bell site, accompanied by over 200 dentalium shells, plus elaborately carved bone and stone objects. Sanger (1968) also reports grave goods such as nephrite adzes, carved bone, scallop shells, a stone club, and elaborately carved stone and bone objects from the disturbed burials at the Texas Creek, which may be contemporaneous with the large Lillooet villages (Hayden and Ryder 1991). Along the Thompson River system, burial sites dating to the Kamloops phase are present at Chase and Cache Creek. These burial sites attest to considerable socioeconomic inequality and complexity that continued long after the "cultural collapse" suggested for the Lillooet region. Three of the five burials excavated at the Chase site (Sanger 1969a) are infants or children interred with grave goods including a dentalium shell necklace, decorated antler objects, pierced shell ornaments, miniature bone bows, and ocher. The two adult burials contained a much wider variety of materials including jade celts, crystal quartz and obsidian tools, and various bone and antler objects. At the Cache Creek site (Pokotylo, Binkley, and Curtin 1987), the burial goods associated with a child are much more elaborate than those interred with adults, and include a decorated wapiti incisor necklace inset with dentalium shell, and a decorated bird bone tube.

During the first millennium A.D., several lines of evidence suggest the development of complex, nonegalitarian hunting and gathering societies in parts of the Northern Plateau. Housepit data suggest the existence of corporate residental groups, and significant differences in the socioeconomic status of residents and households. Burials also indicate socioeconomic differences and the existence of ascribed rather than achieved status. Cultural collapse around A.D. 950 seems to be linked to catastrophic blockage of the Fraser River near Lillooet, with resultant decline of the salmon fishery, an event that seems not to have impacted Thompson River settlements. Available evidence suggests that during the last 2,000 years on the Northern Plateau there was a degree of socioeconomic inequality or stratification that is markedly different from the traditional model of egalitarian social organization.

Antiquity of the Subsistence-Settlement Pattern

Characteristics distinctive of ethnographic groups on the Northern Plateau include a seminomadic-transhumant settlement pattern of group aggregation and dispersal at various stages in the annual cycle of activity, subsistence specialization centering on intensive harvesting and storage of salmon, ungulates, and roots; and winter housepit villages in major river valleys (see Palmer 1975a; Ray 1939; Teit 1900, 1909). Major archeological research questions have been: when does of each of these features first appear and when do they occur together in prehistory?

For the Fraser-Thompson areas, a composite picture can be derived from a series of research projects that have examined sites in riverine and upland environments. In the major river valleys, sedentary winter settlements first appear during the Lochnore phase. The three semisubterranean mat lodges at the Baker site near Monte Creek, with dates ranging from 2500–2000 B.C. (I.R. Wilson 1992) are the earliest reported housepit dwellings on the Northern Plateau. However, these are distinct in architecture from the ethnographic earth-covered winter homes, which start to appear about 1,000 years later during the Kettlebrook and Shuswap phases in the Fraser River and Thompson River-Shuswap Lake areas. Although the size of most archeologically excavated housepits on the Northern Plateau approximates the dimensions reported for ethnographic structures (7–13 m diameter), there is marked variation in size during the first millennium A.D., with structures in some villages in the Lillooet and Chilcotin River system areas approaching 22 meters in diameter.

Use of upland zones apparently occurs very early. The earliest radiocarbon dated evidence is at the Landels site, placed at 6450 B.C. (Rousseau, Muir, and Alexander 1991a). However, a substantial time gap occurs between Landels and the next securely dated material, a cooking pit feature at the Parker site in Oregon Jack Creek Valley from 1180 B.C. (Rousseau, Muir, and Alexander 1991a). In the adjacent Upper Hat Creek Valley, similar root-processing facilities are dated between 350 B.C. and A.D. 1350 (Pokotylo and Froese 1983). The Hat Creek cooking pits dating prior to A.D. 800 have substantially larger dimensions than those reported in ethnographic records, suggesting that this was a period of relatively intense root gathering and processing for storage, presumably for consumption at riverine housepit villages.

The most direct evidence of salmon subsistence on the Plateau is provided by stable carbon isotope analysis, which monitors the proportion of marine-based protein, most likely salmon in this case, in an individual's diet. Although the data are minimal prior to A.D. 1, there is a trend toward increasing amounts of salmon in the prehistoric diet. The single individual from the Gore Creek site (6300 B.C.) suggests this early inhabitant of the Northern Plateau consumed relatively little salmon, perhaps less than 10 percent (Chisholm and Nelson 1983). Two individuals dating from over 3,000 years later indicate salmon may have supplied 34–42 percent of dietary protein by that time (Chisholm 1986). In the last two millennia, analysis of a sample of 44 individuals from the mid-Fraser River, Thompson River-Shuswap Lake, and the middle and upper Columbia River indicates that they obtained about one-half to two-thirds of their protein from salmon (Lovell et al. 1986).

Although salmonid remains may be present in archeological deposits as early as 5580 B.C. at the Drynoch Slide site, evidence of intensive use of salmon in the Fraser basin does not exist until 2500 B.C., with the presence of storage pits containing salmon remains at the Baker site. In the Columbia River drainage portion of the Northern Plateau, salmon remains first become abundant at the Kettle Falls locality during the Ksunku period of 2800–1600 B.C., although inferred use of the resource extends back to the Shonitkwu period. External and internal storage pits are common features at Northern Plateau housepit village sites during the last 3,000 years.

In summary, the various characteristics of ethnographic subsistence and settlement have different starting dates in the archeological record. The evidence suggests that salmon was a reasonably well-established part of the prehistoric diet around 3500 B.C., approximately 1,000 years before the first appearance of housepit settlements and food storage pits. Although plant resources are generally acknowledged to leave a negligible archeological record, by 1180 B.C. roots were being gathered at a scale requiring construction of facilities to process them. Although all attributes of the ethnographic pattern are certainly present in the record by approximately 3,000 years ago, during the first millennium A.D., many of them exceed the scale and dimensions reported ethnographically.

Analysis

Although unquestionably subject to further refinement, for most parts of the Northern Plateau, culture-historical frameworks covering the last 3,500 years appear reasonably well established. The most noticeable gaps are for the Chilcotin Plateau and Southern Cariboo areas, and for both the Nicola and Similkameen valleys. What clues are available hint that at least the central Chilcotin Plateau and the Southern Cariboo area will ultimately reveal a sequence very similar to that of the mid-Fraser, and that the Nicola Valley may prove much like that of the Thompson River-Shuswap Lakes area.

Prior to about 1500 B.C. the culture history is much less clear. Little or nothing is known about this early period for the Chilcotin Plateau, Southern Cariboo, Nicola Valley, Similkameen Valley, or the Arrow Lakes and Slocan Valley, and there are voids or significant periods of uncertainty in even the best of the remaining sequences. Research at Kettle Falls has provided glimpses of the early past and reasonably secure placement of the phases or "periods" in time. However, the 2,500 years between the Slawntehus and Ksunku periods and the end of that period and the beginning of the subsequent Skitak are poorly known. The archeological record that supports the Okanagan Valley sequence is meager. The beginnings of the Okanagan phase are acknowledged to be indefinite, but its end, and what, if anything, may lie between it and the Indian Dan phase are also unknown. Another problem is the confused picture that has emerged in the comparatively well investigated Middle-Fraser and Thompson

River system areas, where there is a supposition of lengthy coexistence of the Lehman phase and the early Nesikep and Sqlelten traditions.

In addition to problems with the culture-historical framework, there is limited understanding of regional variability. Syntheses based on integrating concepts such as horizons risk masking the knowledge of regional variation necessary to determine how Northern Plateau cultures interacted with specific environments. Chronological sequences and cultural reconstructions reflect primarily what is known about winter village sites. The addition of information from some upland root-processing and deer or elk hunting sites expands the comprehension of subsistence and settlement but has provided only a partial picture of Northern Plateau lifeways in each area and for each period in the past.

Prehistory of the Southern Plateau

KENNETH M. AMES, DON E. DUMOND, JERRY R. GALM, AND RICK MINOR

The Southern Plateau, as defined here, encompasses a vast region. Its northern boundary is the rugged Okanagon Highlands at the international border. On the east, the region is bounded by the Bitterroot mountain range. The crest of the Cascade Mountains in Washington and Oregon (to Crater Lake in the Oregon Cascades) forms the western boundary. In Oregon, the southern boundary runs along the uplands at the southern edge of the drainages of the Deschutes and John Day rivers. This boundary crosses the Snake River above Weiser, Idaho, at the southern end of Hells Canyon and follows the rugged mountains that form the southern rim of the Salmon River drainage east to the Bitterroot Range.

In terms of physiographic regions, the Southern Plateau corresponds to the Walla Walla Plateau, Blue Mountains section, and the northern quarter or so of the Payette section of the Columbia–Snake River Plateau (C.B. Hunt 1974). It also includes portions of the Northern Rocky Mountains in central and northern Idaho, and north-central and northeastern Washington. For the purposes of this chapter, the Southern Plateau is divided into three subregions—Southeast, South-central, and Southwest (fig. 1). This sub-division reflects the research history of the Southern Plateau as well as local and regional differences in its culture history.

Culture History

Period I, 11,500 years ago to 5000–4400 B.C.

• PERIOD IA (PALEO-INDIAN), 11,500–11,000 YEARS AGO The Richey-Roberts Clovis Cache is the only known site containing intact deposits of this age (Mehringer 1989). Other supporting evidence of these earliest occupations consists entirely of surface finds of Clovis points. Formed bone objects (spear shaft spacers and foreshafts), large bifaces and bifacial blades, fluted points, unifacial implements, and debitage are all part of the artifact assemblage recovered at Richey-Roberts. Richey-Roberts attests to the evolved ceremonial practices and socioreligious systems of these people. The context, size, and styles of artifacts recovered here are strongly suggestive of intentional burial associated with ceremonial activity, possibly a human interment.

Rare surface finds of Clovis points occur throughout the region (Galm et al. 1981; Hollenbeck 1987). The similarity of these finds to dated sites in other regions implies an early link to areas south and possibly east of the Plateau. Less evi-

dent is the nature of relationships between Clovis and succeeding phases of prehistory. There is little evidence of a cultural continuum from Clovis to later-dating cultural manifestations in this area, though Aikens (1984) describes what may be transitional artifact forms in Oregon. Thus, while a Clovis presence is documented, it is unknown whether this culture had any bearing on subsequent cultural development in the Plateau region.

• PERIOD IB, 11,000 YEARS AGO TO 5000/4400 B.C. Post-Clovis cultures of the region are characterized by: a "broad-spectrum" hunter-gatherer subsistence economy; high seasonal and annual mobility; low population densities; and a technology geared to maximum flexibility. In a broad-spectrum subsistence economy, a wide array of food resources is exploited during a year, though people may tend to focus on a narrow range of resources under particular circumstances. People appear to have moved frequently; there is no evidence of dwellings or structures of any kind during this period, as there is also no evidence of food storage. Hunter-gatherers under these conditions can be expected to have quite low population densities (Ames 1988).

Chronological placement of sites during this period depends primarily upon radiocarbon dates and temporally diagnostic artifacts. The presence of volcanic ash from Mount Mazama in the southern Oregon Cascade Mountains, whose eruption has been radiocarbon dated to 5682 B.C. (Bacon 1983), provides a major means of dating sites excavated before the development and widespread use of radiocarbon dating, or sites where datable carbon is not present.

Artifact assemblages typically contain projectile points, cobble tools, bifaces (some of which may be knives), utilized flakes, scrapers, gravers and burins, grooved stones interpreted as bolas, and cores. Assemblages sometimes also will include hafted bone points (sometimes with barbs); large and small eyed-needles; bone awls (pointed bone tools with no evidence of hafting); ocher; beads; edge-ground cobbles; hammerstones; and antler wedges. Occasionally assemblages will contain fishing tackle (harpoon parts and net weights), abraders, small milling stones and anvils; antler flakers (probably used to pressure flake stone tools) (Ames 1988); and some flakes and blades removed from cores prepared using the Levallois technique (Muto 1972).

These assemblages are characterized by a variety of projectile point forms; variation is both spatial and temporal. Assemblages before 7000 B.C. typically contain shouldered and stemmed, and unstemmed lanceolate points (some with

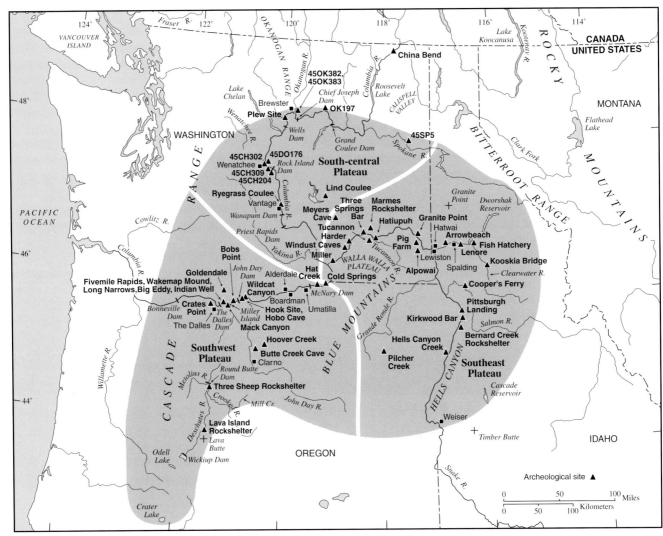

Fig. 1. Southern Plateau archeological sites and regions.

indented bases or with rather weakly differentiated stems, many of which may have an indented base) (fig. 2 top) (Rice 1972). While some of the formal variability displayed by these points can be attributed to resharpening and reworking during the useful life of the point, not all of it can be. After 7000 B.C. projectile point variability is more limited. Between 7000 and 5800 B.C. projectile points are commonly, though not exclusively, the laurel-leaf shaped form known regionally as Cascade points (fig. 2 bottom). These points are stemless, either bipointed or having one pointed end and one rounded end. This rounded end is thinner than the rest of the tool, often has ground edges, and probably was the haft. This description actually obscures a great deal of poorly understood (or described) variation. Most of these Period IB points are probably armed darts thrown from a throwing board or atlatl. After 5800 B.C., large side- and corner-notched (Northern Side Notched, Bitterroot) points are added to the repertoire.

Sites with faunal remains dating to this period are rare, and include Marmes Rockshelter, Lind Coulee, Bernard Creek Rockshelter, Kirkwood Bar, Deep Gully, and Granite Point in

the southeast Plateau, sites in the Wells Reservoir area in the south-central plateau, and the Fivemile Rapids (or Roadcut), Bobs Point, and Umatilla sites in the southwest plateau. Marmes Rockshelter and Lind Coulee are dominated by large terrestrial herbivores, including bison (*Bison bison*), elk or wapiti (*Cervus elaphus*), deer (*Odocoileus* spp.) and pronghorn (*Antilocapra americana*). Seals were taken at Fivemile Rapids. Birds and smaller mammals such as rabbits and large rodents occur at many sites (Atwell 1989). Fish remains are common. At Wells Reservoir sites and Bobs Point, salmon dominate, but minnows, sturgeon, and suckers are present. At Bernard Creek Rockshelter and Kirkwood Bar, both in Hells Canyon, suckers and minnows dominate, but salmon are present. At Fivemile Rapids, at least 150,000 salmon vertebrae were recovered. This collection is one of the largest faunal assemblages ever recovered from a single site on the southern Plateau. Some researchers (Schalk and Cleveland 1983) have suggested that the association of salmon bones and human artifacts at Fivemile Rapids was the coincidental result of natural processes, but V.L. Butler (1993) has shown that the bones were the result of human butchering of salmon. The

after Leonhardy and Rice 1970:figs. 2, 4.
Fig. 2. Early projectile point forms. top, Windust phase unstemmed (left) and indented base points; bottom, Cascade phase lanceolate and side-notched (right) points. Length of top left, 5 cm; others to same scale.

role of a salmon fishery at Fivemile Rapids in the subsistence economy of this period remains a matter of debate.

Southeast Plateau

The great majority of Period IB sites, particularly before 7000 B.C., are concentrated in the central and eastern portions of the region. Only one major site, Lind Coulee, is located in the Columbia Basin. Meyers Cave, a little-known site in the basin, may contain materials from this period (Bryan and Tuohy 1960). The major sites are along the Snake River and its tributaries. Sites are also documented in the surrounding plateaus and mountainous uplands, indicating that all regional environments were used (Butler 1962; Keeler 1973; Brauner 1985; McPherson et al. 1981).

Marmes Rockshelter (fig. 3) (Bense 1972; Fryxell and Daugherty 1962; Gustafson 1972; Rice 1969, 1972) is the major site for this period in the southeast plateau. Its large, diverse artifact assemblages, reported faunal assemblage, and lengthy series of radiocarbon dates (Rice 1972; Sheppard et al. 1987) have made it the basis for much of the published discussions of this period in the southeast Plateau. However, the site is unusual: it is one of the few excavated rockshelters dating to this period; its artifact assemblages are unusually diverse (containing artifacts such as very small bone needles, which seldom occur elsewhere); and it was used for burials throughout this period, which makes it unique.

Materials from this period are more commonly recovered from open sites with poor faunal preservation and few features. Early materials have also been recovered from the surfaces of deeply buried gravel bars at Hatwai (Ames, Green, and Pfoertner 1981), Granite Point (Leonhardy 1970), Lenore (Toups 1969), and Cooper's Ferry (Butler

Fig. 3. Excavations at Marmes Rockshelter on the Lower Snake River in southeast Wash. Photograph by Roy M. Chatters, 1964.

105

1966) along the Snake and its tributaries. Lind Coulee (Daugherty 1956a; Irwin and Moody 1978) is an important exception to this. It is an open site located north of the Snake River in the Columbia Basin. The site contains a significant faunal assemblage dominated by bison.

A number of upland sites have been excavated in the tributary basins of the Clearwater and Salmon rivers in Idaho, and in the Blue Mountains of northeast Oregon (Butler 1962; Keeler 1973; Corliss and Gallagher 1972; Hackenberger 1988; Hackenberger, Sisson, and Womack 1989; Wildesen 1982; Womack 1977; Reid 1988, 1991, 1991a; Reid, Draper, and Wigand 1989). Of these, Pilcher Creek (Brauner 1985) is particularly interesting. Quarrying soapstone and carving beads out of it were among the activities pursued at the site.

Leonhardy and Rice (1970) organized these materials into two cultural phases: Windust, 11,000 years ago–7000 B.C., and Cascade, 7000–5000 B.C. The Cascade phase was further subdivided into Early (7000–5800 B.C.) and Late (5800–5000 B.C.). The differences among these phases and subphases were originally based on projectile points: Windust is marked by the stemmed and unstemmed lanceolate points (Windust points), Early Cascade by laurel-leaf shaped points (Cascade points), and late Cascade by the presence of Northern Side Notched and Cold Springs points with Cascade points (Bense 1972). While some researchers have suggested no other differences exist among these periods (Bense 1972; Rice 1972) it seems evident that there were some shifts in settlement patterns (Ames 1988) and tool technologies around 7000 B.C., including the disappearance of bola stones.

South-central Plateau

While Period 1a assemblages have not been identified in the south-central Plateau, considerably more is known of the latest cultural occurrences of Period IB. Original definition of the Vantage phase in the middle-Columbia area (Swanson 1962; Nelson 1969; Galm et al. 1981) incorporates many of the characteristics of the Cascade phase defined for the Lower Snake River region (Leonhardy and Rice 1970; Bense 1972). The hallmark artifact of these phases, the lanceolate bipointed projectile, is ubiquitous throughout the region. Strong similarities in general artifact assemblage content also exist as edge ground cobbles, large bifacial knives, formed scrapers, and a wide variety of expedient flake and spall tools have been reported from throughout the area. Comparable assemblages in the Okanogan (Chatters 1986) and Kartar (Campbell 1985) phases defined for Wells and Chief Joseph reservoirs may include a slightly higher proportion of cobble and spall tool forms than found in the southern components. The presence of the Levallois-like Cascade Technique lithic technology (Muto 1976) is better represented in southern assemblages but is known to occur as far north as site 45CH309 in Rocky Island Reservoir (Stevens and Galm 1991). The relatively high percentage

use of fine-grained basalt recognized in southern assemblages is less well represented in the north. However, silicified mudstone and related metamorphic rocks are reported from Kartar phase assemblages at Chief Joseph Reservoir (Campbell 1985), although an association with this technology is uncertain. The presence of microblades in assemblages of this age is best represented at sites along Chief Joseph Reservoir (45DO282 and 45DO273; Campbell 1985) and Wells Reservoir (45OK49; Chatters 1986), and Ryegrass Coulee near Vantage (Munsell 1968). Despite descriptions of a microblade industry from southwestern Washington (Kelly 1982), microblades do not appear to be part of the assemblage documented for the Lower Snake River region (Bense 1972; Leonhardy and Rice 1970). Edge ground or "edged" cobbles are well represented in assemblages reported from Wells Reservoir (Chatters 1986) to Kettle Falls (Campbell 1985; Chance and Chance 1982, 1985). Large side-notched points, considered a hallmark of a late subphase of the Cascade phase (Leonhardy and Rice 1970) are very poorly represented on the Columbia River upstream of Rocky Island Reservoir (Galm and Masten 1988) north to Kettle Falls (Chance and Chance 1985).

Chatters (1986) reports two, possibly three, Period IB (Okanogan phase) dwellings from Wells Reservoir (fig. 4). Two Period IB dwellings from Wells are extremely small examples (<11 square meters) constructed on the natural ground surface. They consist of circles of stones with a trampled interior. Associated hearths are outside the structures, indicating their use as sleeping quarters only. At Kettle Falls, Washington, in the Northern Plateau, is a similar surface dwelling with an area less than 15 square meters dating to the Slawntehus period.

Southwest Plateau

In the southwest Plateau, the occupation sequence can confidently be extended back to about 8500 B.C. Evidence of occupation during this period was first encountered in Hat Creek and Cold Springs, both in McNary Reservoir (Shimer 1961). Other important sites include Indian Well (Butler 1959) and Goldendale (Warren, Bryan, and Tuohy 1963). Apparently the remains of a short-term camp, Goldendale was located on a camas flat. Without features, there were nevertheless numerous edge-ground cobbles; basalt slab milling stones with small handstones; ovoid knives; drills and gravers; two projectile points with weakly contracting stems and concave bases; and a small leaf-shaped point with serrated edges. The Goldendale site has an unusually high frequency of milling stones for this period, and so it is one of the best possibilities of a plant-processing locality dating to this period on the southern Plateau.

Fivemile Rapids, at the upstream end of the Columbia River Gorge, like Marmes Rockshelter, defined and shaped archeologists' understanding and research questions of this early period for many years. It was one of the first major

Fig. 4. Excavations at the Plew site (45DO387) on the Columbia River near Pateros, Wash. The circle of large stones in the left portion of the excavation marks the floor of a small structure. The site dates to about 5500 B.C. Photograph by James Chatters, 1984.

sites on the southern Plateau to have been dated using radio-carbon dates, an honor it shares with Lind Coulee. The presence of large numbers of salmon bones at Fivemile Rapids lead Cressman to conclude that intensive salmon fishing existed on the Plateau by 9,800 years ago.

Cressman (Cressman et al. 1960) assigned water-lain deposits below a volcanic ash to the Early stage of culture at that site. (The ash, although not identified at the time, appears almost certainly to have been from Mt. Mazama.) The Early stage was in turn divided into three substages (Cressman et al. 1960). Initial entry, from the lowest meter of the Fivemile excavation, comprised a limited inventory of stone-cutting implements. A composite date on this entire stratum of 9300 B.C. is the earliest from this site. Given the river-borne origin of the matrix, however, it seems possible that the composite date applies to elements of the redeposit-ed fill other than the limited cultural material.

The Paulina Lake site, in Newberry Crater in central Oregon, contains one of the Plateau's major early occupations (Connolly 1995). One feature produced a radiocarbon date of 11,000 B.C., which while quite early, is contemporary with the earliest radiocarbon dates from the Hatwai site in the Southeast Plateau (Ames, Green, and Pfoertner 1981). The site also produced a well-defined structure, either a wickiup or windbreak, with a series of radiocarbon dates

averaging to 9500 B.C. This is the earliest structure anywhere in the Plateau culture area. Artifacts associated with these features include the stemmed, lanceolate Windust points typical of the earliest assemblages on the Southern Plateau, as well as the somewhat younger Cascade points. The assemblage is distinctive for its large number of cobble and ground stone tools, including what may be abraders or grinding slabs.

The Full and Final Early stages saw the development of a rich bone and antler industry, and stone implements including burins and bolas stones. Composite charcoal from throughout 1.2 meters of the lower of two strata assigned to this substage yielded a radiocarbon age of 6524 B.C,. while a sample from a more restricted layer some 40 centimeters higher produced a date 200 years earlier. Although the deposit yielding the date of 6524 B.C. was not so obviously water-borne as the lowest cultural stratum, the numerous raptor birds in the faunal sample seem a strange component of the human diet and of a culturally constructed deposit. Fortunately, the date obtained is confirmed by that immediately above it, so that the cultural material must date before 5000 B.C.

Projectile points of the Early stages were largely unstemmed or with constricted stems, although illustrated points are not identified as to precise provenience (Cressman et al. 1960: fig. 41a). Milling stones are said to have been found from the beginning, although no distribution is given (Cressman et al. 1960:59, 62). With the end of the Early stages the bone and antler tools and faunal remains disappear, perhaps as the result of local preservational rather than cultural factors.

Bobs Point (Minor and Toepel 1986), located just upstream from Miller Island, has produced nondiagnostic flake tools, cobble tools including an edge-ground cobble, and thousands of pieces of debitage below Mazama pumice. Charcoal from a fire hearth exposed below the ash yielded a radiocarbon date of 6469 B.C. Use of the site resumed after the Mazama ash fall, with the later assemblage including one leaf-shaped and two side-notched points. Bobs Point is situated just upstream from Hells Gate Rapids, a highly productive fishery now inundated by the reservoir pool. A preponderance of fish remains in the pre-Mazama component at Bobs Point suggests that fishing was an important activity at sites other than Fivemile Rapids during the early portion of the cultural sequence.

At the Wildcat Canyon site in the John Day Reservoir, the Philippi phase is estimated to date from about 7000 to 5500 B.C. on the basis of one radiocarbon determination and the position of the materials beneath a primary deposit of tephra from the eruption of Mount Mazama. Materials from what were apparently open, ephemeral campsites included projectile points of lanceolate form, a large proportion of which contain indentations at the base, some with weakly set-off stems; broad, chipped knives; scrapers; gravers; some burins; and occasional milling stones. Fauna included the remains of artiodactyl, not further identified (Dumond and Minor 1983).

At Umatilla, evidence of early occupation was limited, consisting of three artifacts and 27 flakes from Stratigraphic Zone 7 assigned to Component D. Faunal remains were also scant but among the animals represented were salmonid and nonsalmonid fish, rabbits, hares, bison, sheep, and freshwater mussel (Schalk 1980). No radiocarbon dates are available, but the position of Zone 7 stratigraphically below a deposit of Mazama ash suggests that Component D relates to the Philippi phase downstream at Wildcat Canyon. This idea is supported by the recovery along the shoreline of the river of two lanceolate points of the type characteristic of this phase (Minor and Toepel 1986a).

What seems clear is that all the assemblages mentioned above bear considerable similarity of one another in stylistic terms and, where dated by absolute means, in temporal terms as well. They also appear to represent some differing facets of a broadly oriented hunting-gathering economic adaptation, an adaptation that included fishing, the hunting of fairly large land animals, the taking of birds and, to judge from the milling apparatus, the grinding of something that must include vegetal materials. What is not so clear is the relationship of stylistic variants within the universe of the finished projectile points.

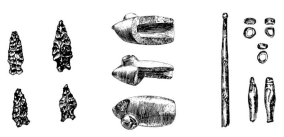

Fig. 5. House I and associated artifacts at Hatwai on the Clearwater River, near Lewiston, Idaho. top, House floor dating 3500 B.C. with hopper mortar bases and a scatter of artifacts and fire-cracked rock within the central 4 by 4 m pit of the house. The 2 m wide bench around the pit has been removed. The pit house was 8 m square. Photograph by James P. Green, 1978. bottom, Selected artifacts from House I and other Hatwai localities: left, 4 Hatwai-eared projectile points; center, 3 views of a carved stone pipe; right, bone ornaments including one elongated grooved and incised pin, a smaller grooved pendant, and 3 bone beads (2 views of each) recovered from deposits postdating A.D. 1500 in another part of the site. Drawings by Joy Stickney. Length of pipe, 9 cm; others to same scale.

Period II, 5000/4400–1900 B.C.

This period is difficult to characterize in some ways. In some parts of the southern Plateau, the evidence differs little from Period I. However, Period II is marked by important changes in settlement and subsistence patterns in some areas, and the disappearance of certain artifact types and technological traits characteristic of Period I. Semisubterranean pit houses appear in the region's archeological record for the first time; there is evidence for increased levels of exploitation of certain nutritious roots and of salmon; projectile points decline in frequency among artifact assemblages across the region relative to Period I; milling stones, which in Period I were small, are large, substantial stone slabs, sometimes associated with stone pestles; less investment was made in working chipped stone tools, which appears in some areas as a decline in quality. Edge ground cobbles and prepared cores are among the artifact types that become rare or disappear during this period.

Projectile point styles present at the end of Period I continue, including Cascade, Bitterroot, Northern Side Notched and Cold Springs points. Projectile point styles become more variable in space after about 3800 B.C., with some styles having wide distributions, others being more localized. The reasons for this variability are little understood.

Southeast Plateau

Period II incorporates the last portions of the Late Cascade subphase and part of the Tucannon phase. While a number of sites, such as Marmes Rockshelter (Rice 1968; Kennedy 1976), Granite Point (Leonhardy 1970; Kennedy 1976), and the Tucannon site (Nelson 1966; H.K. Kennedy 1976) are relevant to this period, the most crucial are Alpowa (Brauner 1976), Hatwai (Ames 1940), and Hatiuhpuh (Brauner and Stricker 1990; Chance et al. 1989). These three sites contain semisubterranean pit houses with radiocarbon dates having calibrated age ranges concentrated in the millennium between 3200 and 2400 B.C. Hatwai has at least one earlier structure, House 6, which has a charcoal-based radiocarbon date of 3825 B.C. House 1 at Hatwai (fig. 5) has one date as early as 4387 B.C. But the average date for three other charcoal dates from the same floor complex has an age range of 3133–2927 B.C. House 2 at Hatwai has a charcoal date of 2665 B.C. with an age range between 2940 and 2420 B.C. House 5 at Alpowa dates to approximately 2700 B.C. Houses 2 and 3 at Hatiuhpah span a period between 2900 and 1800 B.C.

These dwellings are seven to eight meters across, circular to rectangular in plan view, and one to two meters deep. Some have earthen annular benches approximately two meters wide around their interior circumference. The houses generally lack evidence of superstructures. Their contents are very similar to each other and include clusters of large hopper mortar bases and anvils resting on their floors (fig. 5 top). Hopper mortar bases are round, flat milling stones with evidence of grinding and pounding on one or both flat surfaces. This evidence is usually a circular depression at the center of the stone's surface. This depression is probably the result of a hopper—perhaps a basket—being placed on the stone base, filled with vegetal material or perhaps dried meat, and then this food pulverized into a flour or meal with a stone pestle. Anvils are essentially large flat stones that lack the evidence of pounding but are in contexts that suggest their use. Associated faunal remains include freshwater mussels and the bones of a diverse array of large and small mammals, including herbivores and carnivores. Elk, deer, and pronghorn were the principal game animals. Fish remains include those of small numbers of salmon and other, resident fish. There is a single net weight at Hatiuhpuh. There is some debate (Lyman 1980a) as to whether this period is marked by increased exploitation of mussels. The presence of large mortar bases, anvils, and pestles has lead some (Ames and Marshall 1980) to argue that plant foods, particularly certain roots, were of major importance in the

subsistence of this period, but this interpretation is a matter of debate (Lohse and Sammons-Lohse 1986; Thoms 1990).

The presence of semisubterranean pit houses is generally taken to represent a region-wide shift in settlement patterns to some form of semisedentism (Chatters 1989; Ames 1991). This shift is widespread, and apparently short-lived. There are few dated dwellings in the region 2000 to 1800 B.C. There is considerable controversy over the subsistence and economic changes that accompanied this preliminary shift to semisedentism (Ames 1991; Chatters 1989, 1995; Lohse and Sammons-Lohse 1986).

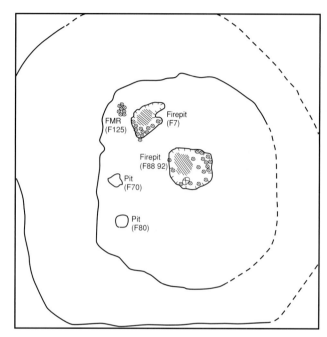

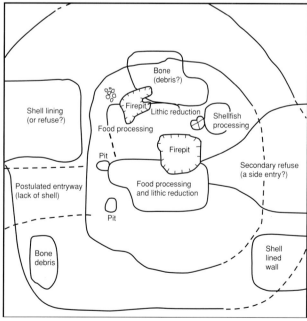

after Lohse 1984:figs. 6–13, 6–23.

Fig. 6. Late middle period Upper Housepit I at site 45OK11 at Chief Joseph Reservoir, Wash. top, Plan drawing of housepit showing associated features; bottom, postulated activity areas based on excavated remains.

Dominant projectile point styles include side- and corner-notched forms and a stemmed point. The side-notched points are notched low at the side; and they have very rounded shoulders, a deeply convex base, and thick cross-section. These have been termed Hatwai-eared (fig. 5). Corner-notched points have expanding stems and barbed shoulders and are sometimes called Snake River Corner-Notched (Leonhardy and Rice 1970). The stemmed points have a diamond- or lozenge-shape blade and contracting stems. These points have overlapping, but distinct spatial distributions (Ames 1990; Brauner 1976; H.K. Kennedy 1976).

While sites of this period are somewhat less common than those of the preceding or following periods, archeological materials of this time are found in all the major physiographic zones of the southeast Plateau (Ames 1990). There is no widely accepted explanation for this reduction in site numbers (Ames and Marshall 1980; Brauner 1976; Hammatt 1977).

South-central Plateau

The transition to Period II is marked by changes in material-cultural assemblages, including the disappearance of Cascade technique technology. Fewer sites of this period are known from the southern portion of the study area than from the northern. However, the entire region appears influenced by an expanding population base and significant changes in subsistence strategies. More efficient exploitation of root crops and salmon are at the center of interpretations of changes in Period II adaptive strategies. Nevertheless, assessments of how and why such changes occurred remain topics of considerable debate.

Throughout the region, post-3000 B.C. economic adaptations appear to have a stronger linkage to the exploitation of anadromous fish than in the preceding period. The seasonal reoccupation of sites is a phenomenon that commonly begins in Period II and continues into the late prehistory of this region. This trend toward increasing sedentism is part of an overall pattern of intensive exploitation of riverine environments for the procurement of foodstuffs, most likely focusing on the harvesting of salmonids (cf. Campbell 1985; Chatters 1986; Galm and Masten 1985).

The earliest-dating pit houses in the study area are reported from Chief Joseph Reservoir (Lohse 1985)(fig. 6), where the oldest excavated dwelling was identified at 45OK11 and dated to about 3200 B.C. Portions of perhaps as many as 11 separate pit houses were reported from this site. Of these, seven are dated by radiocarbon dates that span the period from 3200 to 2200 B.C. The largest in this group is circular in outline and approximately 12 meters in diameter. Pit house forms include both circular and oval outline plans, and most exhibit shallow depressions excavated into relatively soft sediments. Internal or external post or post-mold patterns occur infrequently in association with these dwellings. However, the size of these dwellings, in many cases, exceed the physical capabilities of a simple tepee-style external pole arrangement erected over an excavated depression. Pit houses measuring over approximately eight meters in diameter would have required an internal superstructure, usually taking the form of a two- or four-post structural support in the center of the dwelling.

Projectile point forms include a variety of laurel-leaf, or Cascade, forms (Lohse 1985) as well as Cold Springs Side Notched. In addition, Lohse (1985) reports a form he calls the Mahkin Shouldered. This point style has a blade with a variable outline and a broad stem. Artifact assemblages in general are similar to those described for the southeast Plateau.

The faunal remains are much more diverse (Lohse 1985) than those at Hatwai and Alpowa (Ames, Green, and Pfoertner 1981; Atwell 1989; Lyman 1976) and include much larger numbers of fish and freshwater mussels, suggesting a more diverse subsistence economy. The excavators believe the site was occupied year-round, representing a form of full sedentism.

Other dwelling sites, with smaller, shallow pit houses and similarly diverse faunal assemblages have been found in Wells Reservoir (45OK382, 45K383; Chatters 1986) and near Wenatchee (Cox's Pond; Hartmann 1975). These sites also contain evidence of trade, in the form of pipes of exotic material at Cox's Pond and marine shell at 45OK383. Nonpit-house sites include hunting camps, and open sites that in many ways resemble Period IB (Campbell 1985; Chatters 1986; Chatters and Zweifel 1987).

Southwest Plateau

This period is largely hypothetical in this subregion, since no clearly definable habitation or even coherent living floor can be definitely assigned it anywhere in the subregion. What is possibly the clearest evidence of occupation is from the middle strata of Hobo Cave (Musil 1984). Among these materials were more than 59 projectile points that included several varieties with contracting stems (see Shiner 1961: pl. 46), additional side-notched points, and a series of primarily broad-necked, corner-notched points; scrapers; pounders; bone awls; and some shell beads. A small amount of obviously intrusive historical material, largely derived from looters' disturbance, may cast doubt on the coherence of the remainder of the collection. Faunal debris includes remains of fish, deer, sheep, hare, and rabbit. The existence of numerous remains of young deer or sheep (not distinguished) suggests spring to have been the season of use.

At Wildcat Canyon, a similar but small assemblage can be derived from strata between that yielding remains of Period IB occupations and the overlying stratum in which were enclosed most of the constructed houses of the ensuing Late period (Dumond and Minor 1983, reference to strata F and Gh). However, this assemblage could easily be the result of physical mixture of underlying and overlying materials rather than a component in its own right. No living surfaces can be assigned to it.

The same may be the case at Fivemile Rapids, where artifacts from more than a half-meter of deposit above the levels yielding the radiocarbon date of about 4000 B.C. show no real change in type from the earlier period (which included a number of projectile points with contracting stem). Above this, the projectile point forms that occur are those particularly characteristic of the period after 500 B.C. so that there appears to have been a hiatus in occupation between 4000 and 1000 B.C. Essentially the same can be said for the nearby Big Eddy sites. Finally, although two radiocarbon assays from the base of occupation at the Hook site suggest a possible beginning at 2000 B.C., the nature of the materials that follow suggest them to date to at least a millennium later.

If there is a cultural manifestation represented during this interval, then, it is clearly transitional in its stylistic elements between the better represented Period IB, and the vastly better represented Period IIIA. Any such entity must also have continued the subsistence orientation of the earlier time and continued a pattern of living that involved ephemeral and shifting, rather than stable, settlements.

Period III, 1900 B.C.–A.D. 1720)

The beginning of this period is marked by the widespread reappearance of pit houses (Chatters 1989; Ames 1991), indisputable evidence of increasingly heavy reliance on fishing (Johnston 1987; Thomison 1987) and storage of salmon (Chatters 1988), intensive exploitation of camas (Thoms 1989), and evidence of land use patterns that persisted into the nineteenth century. These land use patterns include seasonal (usually winter–early spring) villages in the canyons and exploitation of uplands and mountains from special use camps during the summer and fall. The period ends with the appearance of the horse—the harbinger of the arrival of Europeans—on the Plateau.

By 500 B.C., pit houses are ubiquitous in the Southern Plateau. The house pits found in Period III tend to be highly variable in size, and evidence of superstructures ranges from little in the southeastern subarea to complex post structures in the south-central area. Large pit houses (diameters greater than 12 meters) became increasingly common after A.D. 1000. Very large concentration of houses—towns and villages—also appear in the record by A.D. 500. The best known of these is the Miller site on Strawberry Island near the confluence of the Snake River with the Columbia (Cleveland 1976; Schalk and Cleveland 1983; Schalk 1980).

At the same time, new house forms develop. Longhouses enter the record after A.D. 500. Though longhouses were sometimes erected over a pit as much as a meter deep (Rice 1987), their superstructure was a pole frame covered with bark and woven reed mats.

Like pit houses, net weights become ubiquitous. While nets may have been in use since the earliest occupation of the region, the evidence indicates that their use increased markedly after 2000 B.C. Net weights display increasing variation in size through time, and there are changes in how they were suspended from the nets, perhaps suggesting a greater variety of nets, and refinements in net making. Harpoons and barbed bone points continue to be present in the record.

There was very little direct evidence of storage in Periods I and II. Storage pits with salmon remains in them are present in the Wells Reservoir at the beginning of Period III. For the first time, generally contemporary assemblages of faunal remains from many parts of the plateau have large numbers of salmon bones in them. At the Wells Reservoir, faunal collections are completely dominated by salmon bones (Chatters 1986), and they form a significant proportion of the faunal remains in sites in the Chief Joseph Reservoir as well (Campbell 1985).

This is the only period in Plateau prehistory that is also represented by fiber and wood artifacts and other perishables. Storage pits in dry caves along the middle reaches of the Columbia and Lower Snake rivers typically contained cordage and matting, but basketry, fishing implements, bows, arrows, and even dried food have been found as well (Swanson 1966).

While Period II land-use patterns are not clear, those of Period III are clearer. The archeological record of this period is rich in residential sites, marked by the presence of pit houses. Sites with pit houses are found along the Columbia and its tributaries and their tributaries, for example, along the Salmon River in central Idaho (Knudson et al. 1982; Wildesen 1982; Hackenberger 1988; Hackenberger, Sisson, and Womack 1989). Clusters of house pits have been located on terraces of very small streams that flow into the larger rivers. House pits have also been found in totally unexpected places, at relatively high elevations (Reid and Gallison 1992) and out in the middle of the Columbia Basin itself (Osborne 1959). Archeologists have usually assumed that these house pit clusters are the remains of winter residences, or "winter villages" (Swanson 1962; Nelson 1973), but some may have been constructed at other times of year (Lohse 1985) and been "summer villages," for example. Sites and isolated artifacts from this period are distributed across all of the major landforms and ecological zones of the southern Plateau. It is thought that much of this material represents short-term encampments or special use sites.

Southeast Plateau

Period III corresponds to the last half of the Tucannon phase and includes all of the Harder, Piqúnin, and Numípu phases as originally defined. Some have suggested that the Harder and Piqúnin phases should be lumped (Yent 1976), but others prefer the split (Ames 1990; Brauner and Stricker 1990).

• SUBPERIOD IIIA, 1990–500 B.C. The beginning of this subperiod is clearly marked by an increased intensity of occupation, or even reoccupation, of certain major sites along the Snake and Clearwater rivers, such as Granite Point (Leonhardy 1970), Alpowa (Brauner 1976), and Hatwai (Ames, Green, and Pfoertner 1981), occupations that are continuous after this time. Houses appear to have been much smaller than during Period II (Ames 1991). Sites assigned to this subperiod are distributed across all of the major environmental zones of the southeast Plateau (Randolph and Dahlstrom 1977; H.K. Kennedy 1976; Leonhardy 1970; Mattson 1983; Keeler 1973; Gaarder 1967a; Brauner 1975, 1976) based upon projectile point styles.

Projectile point forms are similar to those at the end of Period II: Hatwai-eared, large Snake River side notched, and the unnamed style with a diamond shaped blade and contracting stem known downriver as Rabbit Island stemmed. Laurel-shaped points continue to be found in small numbers, as they were during Period II. These may be technologically different from the classic Cascade point. Artifact assemblages have low frequencies of projectile points and relatively high frequencies of cobble tools, fishing gear, and mortars and pestles.

The few faunal assemblages from this period are dominated by deer, though elk, pronghorn, fish, birds, and furbearers such as martin and beaver are present (Atwell 1989). The wide distribution of sites assignable to this period suggests a broader resource base than earlier. The sites with fauna, all found along the major rivers, may represent seasonal occupations. The increased frequency of net weights in the artifact assemblage may indicate an increased role of fishing in the economy (Ames 1990). Fish bones are the third most common bones in these faunal collections.

Because sites chosen for excavation were confined to those in the river bottom and also were those that promised to yield the most remains, there is a bias toward base camps and permanent villages in the archeological evidence, and knowledge of activities in places of more ephemeral use is underrepresented. Despite this shortcoming, and despite the inability in many cases to be absolutely certain of the season in which the base camps were inhabited, two things seem clear: that there were seasonal movements between base camps and more temporary habitation sites and that the base camps themselves evidence much more stability of settlement than had been the case in earlier periods.

• SUBPERIOD IIIB, 500 B.C.–A.D. 500/1000   Sites dating to this period are well represented on all the major drainages in the southeast Plateau. Crucial sites include Harder (Kenaston 1966), Tucannon (Nelson 1966), Three Springs Bar (Daugherty, Purdy, and Fryxell 1967), and Alpowa (Brauner 1975) on the Snake River; Arrowbeach, Lenore (Toups 1969), the Fish Hatchery (Sappington 1988), and Kooskia Bridge on the Clearwater; as well as Hells Canyon

Creek (Pavesic 1986) and Pittsburgh Landing in Hells Canyon (Reid 1991, 1991a). Materials from this period are widely dispersed in the uplands. It is also during this period that extensive utilization of the dry central Columbia Plateau begins (Chatters 1980; Greene 1975).

House pits become increasingly common during this subperiod. These pit houses are presumed to represent the semi-subterranean houses known elsewhere in the Plateau in historic times, roofed with a light framework covered with mats and earth. That any earth cover was light, however, is clear from the lack of heavy fill above the uppermost floor in most houses. The fill between superimposed floors in excavated houses, with many of them including three such floors, suggests that no roof inhibited the encroachment of the plentiful sand during periods of nonoccupation. The conclusion is that the roof was light and was removed at the end of each season of occupation.

Projectile points are the single most common artifacts in artifact assemblages, and their forms change somewhat. Early forms such as the Hatwai Eared, the stemmed form, and the laurel leaf points of the preceding subperiod disappear. The broad-necked Snake River Corner Notched continues to be present in assemblages, accompanied first by large, basal notched forms. These are subsequently replaced by smaller corner and basal notched forms that are probably arrow points, which appear between 350 and 150 B.C. (Brauner 1976; Schalk 1983).

While artifact assemblages during this subperiod are dominated by large numbers of projectile points, these assemblages are much more diverse and varied than during subperiod IIIA. Significant trends include increasing numbers of net weights, though hand-held fishing gear such as leisters and harpoons are still present. Grinding and pounding tools increase in absolute numbers, though their proportional representation declines (because projectile points are so common).

Faunal assemblages also diversify. Once again, the assemblages are dominated by deer. Interestingly, bison bones are the second most common bones in these assemblages, displacing elk. Fish continue to be the third most common animal in the assemblages. There has developed a question as to what this appearance of bison may represent (Schroedl 1973; Lyman 1985)—a shift in climate, a change in bison range, a sampling problem, or a change in subsistence? What is clear is that the resource base expanded during this subperiod to include more animal species. This parallels the trends in the artifact assemblages.

• SUBPERIOD IIIC, A.D. 500/1000–1720   The appearance of the horse on the Plateau ends this period at approximately 1720; the shift in domestic architecture from pit house to longhouses is among the changes that initiates this subperiod. Why this shift occurred is unknown. It did not occur everywhere at once; for a time the house forms were used side-by-side, but pit houses were not in use on the southeast plateau at contact. Chance (1978, 1978a; Chance and Chance 1985a) excavated the possible remains of a longhouse at Spalding, Idaho, in 1978. The structure postdates 1400 and may be the earliest excavated longhouse on the southeast Plateau. In general, this period is poorly known on the southeast Plateau.

There is evidence for the formation of very large pit house villages and towns at the confluence of the Snake and Columbia rivers at the beginning of this subperiod. The Miller site (Cleveland 1976; Schalk 1983) on Strawberry Island, in the Snake River, just above that confluence, contains several hundred pit houses that postdate 500. The pits vary in size from three meters across to 20 or more meters. These size differences may reflect some social differentiation among households, or functional differences, that is, the pits may not all represent pit houses. Some could represent storage features, for example (Thoms 1989).

Sites and materials from this period are ubiquitous through all environmental zones on the southeast Plateau. It is very likely that settlement patterns were similar to those of the nineteenth century, with winters spent in small villages in the canyon bottoms, and then groups dispersing into the uplands and mountains to hunt and collect plant foods. During the eighteenth and nineteenth centuries, very large groupings would form in late summer and early fall around major camas grounds. Other individuals would be in the canyons fishing. The data suggest that human populations were at their peak numbers during at least the early portion of this subperiod.

Artifact assemblages are generally similar to those of IIIB. There are changes in projectile point styles. These are dominated by small, delicate corner and basal notched forms. These small projectile points doubtless armed arrows. Reported faunal assemblages are dominated by deer, fish, and elk remains. Though bison bones are present, they occur in much lower frequencies than during Subperiod IIIB.

South-central Plateau

• SUBPERIOD IIIA, 1900 B.C.–A.D. 1 Some of the more significant changes characterizing the transition to Period IIIa settlement in the west-central Plateau can be summarized as follows: large populations relative to earlier periods, increased sedentism and associated changes in patterns of subsistence, large riverine villages and the appearance of communal dwellings, larger and more functionally diverse artifact assemblages, and a more vigorous trade in non-local commodities using the pre-existing trade network. Elements of these patterns can often be seen in Period II but do not reach their full expression until Subperiod IIIA. At the center of changes recognized in late prehistoric adaptations is an increasingly efficient exploitation of the natural environment with attendant shifts in the seasonality, timing, and duration of settlements. Improvements in storage technology (Schalk 1986) presumably facilitated more efficient use of foodstuffs, thereby reducing the time spent in subsistence

pursuits. An expansion in human populations is indicated by a larger number of sites in both riverine and off-river, upland environments and by the larger sizes of riverine villages.

Larger numbers of pit houses and a greater diversity in their form mark the transition to Subperiod IIIA. Nineteen Hudnut phase houses are reported from five sites at Chief Joseph Reservoir (Sammons-Lohse 1985), 10 from three sites at Wells Reservoir (Chatters 1986; Grabert 1968), and a possible occurrence at Rock Island Reservoir (Hartmann 1975). Subperiod IIIA houses also are thought to occur at sites along present-day Wanapum and Priest Rapids reservoirs (Greengo 1986, 1986a).

Circular, subrectangular to oval, and square floor plans all occur in this sample of pit houses. Dimensions vary from a low of four to five meters in diameter (Chief Joseph and Wells reservoir sites) to a high of 11 by 9 meters for Housepit 1 at 45OK250 (Sammons-Lohse 1985: table 14–4). The smaller structures in this range are likely to represent ancillary structures, such as menstrual houses and storage facilities, while the larger examples are capable of housing multiple family groups. The greater diversity in the physical styles of housing and the larger numbers of dwellings documented during Subperiod IIIA are thought to be reflective of an expanding regional population base. There is also some suggestion, particularly in the northern portion of this region, of movement of peoples into the area. Although there is no clear understanding if or when such movements of people occurred (cf. Chance and Chance 1985), the pit house style of dwelling was already present in the region.

At Chief Joseph Reservoir, Subperiod IIIA sites reveal increasing richness and densities of artifacts over those of Period II, a condition also common along the upper Columbia (Campbell 1985). Artifact assemblages throughout the period are dominated by expedient tools such as flake knives and scrapers, gravers, and spokeshaves. Local, cryptocrystalline silica raw materials predominate, and there is a marked reduction in the use of fine-grained basalt over the preceding period.

At sites ranging from the middle to the upper Columbia, salmon are a dominant component of faunal assemblages. Large mammals are also a principal source of food and the raw materials required for implement and clothing manufacture, judging from the faunal samples. Off-river hunting of game is part of a settlement pattern involving seasonal movements of people into upland areas for extended periods of time. In addition to hunting, root and vegetal food gathering and raw material extraction were among the prominent activities pursued from these upland camps.

Storage facilities have been found in both house floors and dry caves. Extensive collections of perishable artifacts made by Swanson (1962, 1962a, 1966) in the Priest Rapids and Wanapum reservoirs contained numerous varieties of wood and fiber artifacts. This period, which he called the Frenchman Springs phase, was distinguished from the next by its content of predominantly Z-twist cordage, which became nearly exclusive toward the end of the phase.

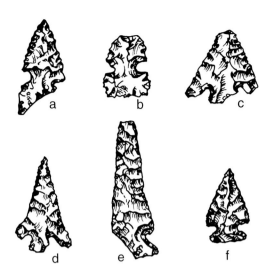

after Chatters 1984:figs. 14–16.
Fig. 7. Late prehistoric projectile points from site 45OK197, a hunting camp on the Columbia River near the Grand Coulee Dam, Wash. a–d, side-notched arrow points; e–f, corner-notched arrow points. Length of a, 3 cm; others to same scale.

• SUBPERIOD IIIB, A.D. 1–1720 In all sections of the subregion, north to south, Subperiod IIIb occupations bear the unmistakable stamp of the ethnographically defined "winter village pattern" (cf. Ray 1933; Ames and Marshall 1980). The seasonality and scheduling of Subperiod IIIB subsistence activities and attendant settlements follow a pattern first recognized, at least in southern sections of this subregion, during IIIA. By about 500 B.C.–A.D. 1, pit house villages are found along most salmon-bearing rivers and streams, and upland camps and use areas occur in expanded numbers. Upland sites (Chatters 1980; Chatters and Zweifel 1987; Gough 1990; Galm et al. 1981; Dancey 1974) typically exhibit artifact assemblages best suited for use in specialized activities. Hunting and hunting-related activities, plant gathering and processing, and lithic quarries and collection areas are among the most common of site occurrences in these areas.

Artifact assemblages reveal relatively few outright changes in the type categories represented but instead reflect the accretion of new forms along with changes in the frequencies of occurrence of specific styles. Large cobble chopping and cleaving tools, large flake and bifacial knife implements, formed scrapers ("keeled end" varieties), hammerstones, hopper mortar bases, and even some types of bone implements are very similar in style to examples present in the preceding period (Galm et al. 1981). Small basal notched-barbed, stemmed, and corner and side notched projectile points predominate in period assemblages (fig. 7). However, the late components at 45CH302 (Boreson and Galm 1997) and 45DO176 (Galm and Masten 1985) are typical of many in the region in that the frequencies of specific point types often vary widely between components of the same age. Small point forms mark the appearance of

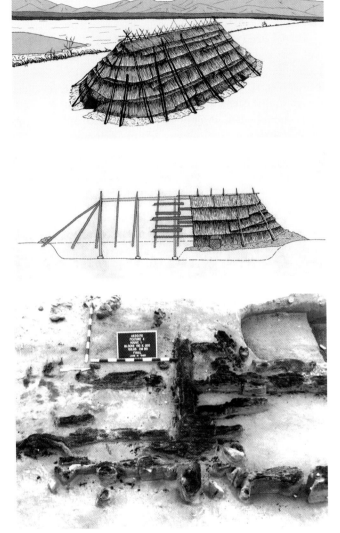

Fig. 8. Late late period longhouse at Avey's Orchard site in East Wenatchee, Wash. top, Artist's reconstruction of the longhouse. center, Partial cutaway view of the longhouse showing the principal construction elements including the central and side support beams, the cross-pieces, and the covering mats. This view also shows the depth of the house floor beneath the surrounding ground surface. Drawings by Pamela K. McKenney. bottom, Excavated burned beams from the longhouse. Photograph by Jerry R. Galm, 1983.

bow and arrow technology throughout this area at least by A.D. 1. Riverine villages contain the largest and most functionally diverse assemblages of any time period. Items of ornamentation, often manufactured from materials representing trade with areas outside the Plateau, proliferate and include dentalia and olivella marine shell beads, bone cylinder and cut disk bone and shell beads, incised steatite and soapstone pendants, and bone pins. Examples of incised beads, mainly dentalia and bone cylinder types, are not uncommon, with typical motifs consisting of continuous chevron, ladder, and simple hatch designs. So-called "wine glass" stem pipes manufactured primarily from steatite and soapstone also are common occurrences in larger site assemblages. Despite a general increase in the occurrence of formed objects, expedient tool forms continue to dominate combined implement categories at most sites. Swanson (1966) found a change from predominantly Z to predominantly S twist in cordage at the start of Subperiod IIIB.

The most dramatic changes in residential architecture are represented in the transition from Period II to Period III occupation of the subregion. The first documented examples of the ethnographic "long lodge" or longhouse appear in a slightly modified form during Subperiod IIIB. These are multifamily or communal structures that in the postcontact era are known to have held as many as several hundred residents (Smith 1983). During late prehistory, this style of dwelling is represented by a single, dated example from the Avey's Orchard site in East Wenatchee (fig. 8). This structure, dated to about A.D. 889, measured over 15 meters long and 11 meters wide (Falm and Masten 1985). Unlike historic longhouses, this prehistoric example was a semisubterranean structure, implying an evolution of the longhouse from a semisubterranean structure to a surface structure, a change most likely linked to the adoption of a equestrian lifeway over most of the region after 1720. Other examples of longhouses are reported farther south on the Columbia along the present-day Wanapum, Priest Rapids, and McNary reservoirs, but none is firmly dated.

Other large styles of dwellings appear during this period as well. These are also semisubterranean structures that, in the main, range from circular to subrectangular in plan view. Sizes generally range from 10 to 14 meters in diameter (or long dimension), although even larger examples are known to occur. Large communal houses are documented, including occurrences at Chief Joseph (Campbell 1985), Wells (Grabert 1968), and Rock Island (Galm and Masten 1985; Boreson and Galm 1997) reservoirs. From this evidence, changes involving the incorporation of communal residences in the composition of village structure and an apparent aggregation of riverine settlements are represented during the last half of Period III. Dates on these larger, communal houses indicate that this important change in settlement structure occurred between A.D. 500 and 1000 throughout this area. As Grabert (1968) observed during his work at Wells Reservoir, there is a tendency for earlier-dating pit house forms to exhibit a deeper depression than those forms representing the post-A.D. 1000 period. This trend applies most consistently to the approximate northern half of the study area and may be indicative of connections to cultural developments in the Northern Plateau.

Despite the above mentioned changes in housing, the circular, semisubterranean pit house or mat lodge remained the dominant form of housing for the entire span of Subperiod IIIB. Like the larger longhouse, the mat lodge was easily adapted to a surface structure with the introduction of the horse and the attendant increase in settlement mobility. Size range distributions are distinctly bimodal with clusters occur-

U. of Oreg., Oreg. State Mus. Of Anthr., Eugene: 1–110.
Fig. 9. Two views of a sculpted stone head resembling a mountain sheep. The features of this figure were pecked into a block of vesicular basalt using a tool of harder stone. Collected by Thomas Condon near the mouth of the Deshutes River, Oreg., before 1872. Height 23 cm.

ring around six- and eight-meter diameter intervals. The number and diversity of nondwelling structures likewise increases in sites of this period. Such structures most likely include sweatlodges, menstrual huts, framed brush arbors or ramadas, and covered storage facilities.

Southwest Plateau

• SUBPERIOD IIIA, 1000 B.C. TO A.D. 1000   The occupation of Wakemap Mound, a large, very important site on the Washington shore in the vicinity of The Dalles (Strong, Schenck, and Steward 1930; Caldwell 1956; Butler 1960), apparently began during this period, but the bulk of the occupation falls into Subperiod IIIB. The Big Eddy site on the Oregon side of the Long Narrows may have been occupied during this period, but it had been too heavily affected by construction to draw firm conclusions.

One house depression of this period was excavated at Mack Canyon on the lower Deschutes River not far from The Dalles (Cole 1967, 1969). More information derives from work in the John Day Reservoir, where more than 30 houses in nine sites were excavated in whole or in substantial part. Although a few of these do not pertain to Period IIIA, the majority of them do.

In original form these houses were apparently round to square or rectangular, three to eight meters across in two opposing dimensions, anywhere from about 30 centimeters to one meter deep, often with areas of charcoal or even stone-ringed fireplaces somewhere within them, sometimes with superimposed floors. In almost no cases were structural details apparent, although in one (at Wildcat Canyon) a portion of the sidewall was lined with rock, presumably to stabilize the sand (Dumond and Minor 1983), and at another (at Umatilla) a square floor was outlined by small posts (Cole 1966). Charcoal from the Umatilla house yielded a radiocarbon date of 559 B.C., which remains the earliest dated pit house feature along this section of the Columbia River.

Whether some of these features are actually datable to a time as early as 1000 B.C. is not entirely sure, although it seems clear that a number of the excavated examples date from as early as about 500 B.C. Throughout the same period, the presence of occupation floors that had apparently not been deeply excavated into the contemporary surface suggests the use of more immediately portable shelters, possibly the mat-covered tentlike lodge known in the region at the time of contact (Southard 1973; H. Rice 1985). The resulting picture, then, is one in which during certain seasons most or all of the population resided in semisubterranean houses, or at least in mat lodges or other tentlike habitations set well into the ground, and that in other seasons they resided in tentlike shelters set on the surface and less suggestive of permanence.

Contributing even more to the impression of stability and sedentism conveyed by the pit house villages, is the fact that near the habitation clusters in a number of cases were cemetery areas thick with inhumations. The most extensively excavated of these sites is at Umatilla, where 224 burials or other human remains were recorded in excavations that led to formal reinterment (D. Rice 1978). The majority of these inhumations can be assigned to Period IIIB on the basis of grave offerings of projectile points and other items. Contemporary with these burials, as indicated by a series of radiocarbon dates, were deeply excavated circular pit houses with benches around the periphery, hearths, and storage pits (D. Rice 1978; Schalk 1980; Minor and Toepel 1986a).

Features associated with house pits included earth ovens, those masses of fired rocks that are interpreted as having been used in the underground cooking of camas or other foodstuffs. Consistent with the occurrence of these features are the remains of pestles and their close formal relatives, shaped stone mauls. The increased importance of fish is indicated by the presence of notched pebble net sinkers and by the more common occurrence of fish among the faunal remains. Other fauna represented include many deer, some elk, bison, and sheep, animals that are indicative of seasonal hunting. At the Wildcat Canyon site there were also recorded a series of dog remains, apparently buried, although the purpose is, of course, unclear.

It is in this period, too, that the famous stone sculptures of The Dalles region began to appear (fig. 9) (Butler 1959; Strong 1961). Among the most plentiful of the portable artifacts are the projectile points, which appear frequently in corner- or basal-notched forms with expanding stems. Early in the period these were relatively broad—more than eight millimeters—across the neck (that point where the stem meets the body of the point), but as time progressed more and more small and narrow-necked examples of the same form appeared, presumably as the bow and arrow supplanted the atlatl and dart. This appearance becomes unmistakable before the beginning of the Christian era, and at about A.D. 1 the narrow-necked points begin to outnumber broad-necked ones. In The Dalles region and the lower area of the

John Day Reservoir the fashion began to shift again around A.D. 500 to one in which points began to be made with very narrow stems, straight-sided or even contracting, that have been called "pin stems" (Dumond and Minor 1983). Whether these reached the upriver areas around Umatilla and the McNary Reservoir at such an early date is not so clear. Excavations at Alderdale on the Washington side of the Columbia River produced no pin-stemmed points (Oetting 1986), and at Umatilla very few of them, although in other respects the assemblages appeared to be of times only shortly before contact.

• SUBPERIOD IIIB, A.D. 1000 TO CONTACT   Although relatively permanent sites were sought for excavation in projects such as that of the John Day Reservoir, their selection involved no strong preconceptions regarding artifactual indicators of relative date, so that late sites, at least, should be represented in proportion to their actual occurrence. But the remains actually explored are overweighted toward Subperiod IIIA: of 30 radiocarbon determinations from the inception of the subperiod in the John Day Reservoir, only six relate to time after A.D. 1000. On the one hand, the paucity of dates for the later subperiod may relate to the relative impermanence of habitations, compared with those of Subperiod IIIA (for the habitations were a major target of dating efforts). On the other hand, this dating situation may also relate to some shrinkage of population in the John Day Reservoir area.

So far as excavations reveal, habitations were most commonly in the form of above-ground lodges, possibly mat-covered. And around The Dalles and the lower John Day Reservoir area, projectile point styles changed so that pin-stemmed points were favored over those with slightly expanding stems. Upriver, even in the upper portions of that reservoir, this is not so clearly the case.

At Umatilla, the earlier substantial house pits were succeeded by shallow circular houses without benches and rarely containing storage pits. These were found in considerable number, and to judge by the quantity of relevant radiocarbon dates there was no shrinkage of population. Associated burials had little burial furniture, and projectile points were predominantly small and corner-notched rather than pin-stemmed (D. Rice 1971, 1978). That pin stems were not entirely unrepresented in prehistoric times in this upstream region of the John Day Reservoir is indicated by some material from Umatilla and by a site at Boardman, Oregon (35MW1), in which they are plentiful. In the McNary Reservoir they appear at least by early historic times, but with some small triangular side-notched forms that are virtually nonexistent in the John Day and The Dalles areas (Shiner 1961:pl. 46b). It has been suggested (Dumond and Minor 1983) that the appearance of the pin stem style is the result of interaction with peoples from the west along the lower reaches of the Columbia River, where a similar style seems to have been perceptible since about A.D. 1 or before (Pettigrew 1981). This projectile point style is not the only downriver trait to appear in the region treated here.

Whereas the mat-covered surface lodge appears to have been the favored habitation in the John Day Reservoir area, at Wakemap Mound, the lower village level dating from about A.D. 900 to 1400 apparently consisted entirely of mat lodge dwellings set into the ground (Butler 1960:27). The upper village level was indicated by a large number of pit house depressions exposed on the ground surface, which apparently were the remains of rectangular plank houses representative of the Chinook house style known downstream (Caldwell 1956; cf. Butler 1960:82–83). This is not surprising, inasmuch as the Wishram of the Washington shore of the Long Narrows were the easternmost Chinookan-speaking people. Whether their characteristic houses appeared also on what is now the Oregon side of the Narrows is not known, although it is by no means impossible. People of the lower end of the Narrows were reportedly the Chinookan Wasco. Those of the upper end, at what was to become the Fivemile Rapids archeological site, were apparently not Chinookan but rather the westernmost of the Sahaptin speakers of the John Day region (Rigsby 1965).

The earlier mortuary pattern involving primary interments in flexed or semiflexed positions continued to be practiced during this period, in association with pit, talus, and cairn burials (Strong, Schenk, and Steward 1930:16–25; Cole 1954:74–77; Caldwell 1956:268–286). The use of talus burials is particularly well illustrated at Crates Point just downstream from The Dallas where this practice persisted into protohistoric times (Minor and Hemphill 1990). Aside from this basic pattern, large cremation pits with the charred remains of many individuals are known from both The Dalles and the McNary Reservoir area. Although many of these cremations apparently date to early historic times, especially in the McNary area (Osborne 1957; Osborne, Bryan, and Crabtree 1961), at least some of them appear to have been prehistoric.

At The Dalles in historic times, as on the lower Columbia, the principal means of disposal of the dead was in charnel houses, usually located on islands in the river, as in some of those removed for reburial from the vicinity of Bonneville Dam (Phebus 1978), and others removed for the same purpose from islands near The Dalles Dam (Cole 1958). A similar means of disposal may have been used at Umatilla prehistorically, following the earlier period of inhumation burials (D. Rice 1978:31).

These changes from the preceding period notwithstanding, the overall subsistence practices of the people during Subperiod IIIB do not appear to have diverged from those of their predecessors. The same styles of net sinkers, pestles (fig. 10), and milling stones continue to be represented. Faunal remains continue to reveal fishing but include numerous deer, elk, mountain sheep, sometimes pronghorn, often some bison. Toward the very end of the period horse bones appear in some sites in the McNary region (e.g., site 45BN6 as described by Shiner 1961).

Smithsonian, Dept. of Anthr.: left, 333582; right, 333581.
Fig. 10. Late period polished stone pestles. left, Granitic stone pestle; right, greenstone pestle. Excavated by Herbert W. Krieger, Wahluke Ferry, Wash., before 1926. Length of left, 35 cm.

All in all, the impression is of great continuity with the preceding period, although with some shift in housing styles, and with the adoption of some artifact and burial styles from downriver.

Hinterland: The Southern Periphery

Early but limited work in the upper John Day River drainage produced rare evidence of mortuary practices in the interior Southern Plateau (Cressman 1950). At Butte Creek Cave a burial in the form of an extended inhumation was found in a grass-lined pit. Associated Catlow twine basketry produced a radiocarbon date of A.D. 1443. Nearby, a talus slope above Hoover Creek was found to contain a cremation pit, suggesting ties to the late prehistoric cremation complex along the Columbia River. Among the associated artifacts was a copper pendant, indicating that this feature dates to the early historic period.

Seasonal camps in the Clarno Basin involving apparently a variety of activities have been radiocarbon dated between 500 B.C. and A.D. 1517. The artifacts are said to reflect close ties with the Columbia River cultures to the north (Gannon 1976; Endzweig 1994).

Salvage excavations were conducted at sites along the confluence of the Metolius and Crooked rivers with the

Deschutes River in connection with the Round Butte Dam project (Ross 1963). At Three Sheep Rockshelter, a small assemblage including projectile points of general oval shape reminiscent of those of Period I of the Columbia River area was found below a heavy deposit of unidentified pumice. A radiocarbon date of 7047 B.C. was associated with these materials and, in view of the magnitude of this date, it seems likely that the pumice was from Mount Mazama. Two smaller rockshelters contained evidence of later occupation by hunting peoples who also made heavy use of river mussels, with use of 35JE1 radiocarbon dated at 868 B.C. and use of 35JE2 dated at 848 B.C. Although the artifact samples from individual rockshelters were relatively small, a number of the projectile points are strongly reminiscent of the broad-necked corner-notched points of Subperiod IIIA of the Columbia. The same is true of collections from two hunting camps along Mill Creek upstream in the Crooked River drainage (Pettigrew 1982), the earliest component of which was dated by radiocarbon at 1082 B.C., the latest at A.D. 337. At the same time, the closeness of these sites to the volcanic outcrops of the northern Great Basin is reflected in a far more frequent use of obsidian than by peoples residing along the shores of the Columbia River.

Early discoveries of artifacts beneath Mazama pumice were reported (Cressman 1937a, 1948) at Wikiup Dam and Odell Lake along the crest of the Cascades. Still farther to the southwest in the upper Deschutes River drainage, early surface surveys (Osborne 1950) were followed by work near Lava Butte (Ice 1962), where what was interpreted as chiefly a hunting camp also yielded hopper mortar bases. Although thought by the excavator to be a recent site, the styles of projectile points represented suggest that it was occupied over a span of several millennia (Davis and Scott 1991). Evidence of earlier occupation in this area has been reported at Lava Island Rockshelter (35DS86), where a cache of lanceolate projectile points was found (Minor and Toepel 1984). Although unsupported by radiocarbon dates, the lanceolate points were presumed to have respectable antiquity based on their stylistic similarity to specimens found below Mazama pumice at sites elsewhere in the Plateau and Great Basin. Later use of the rockshelter was found in the form of broad-necked corner-notched points, which are likely associated with radiocarbon dates of 241 B.C. and A.D. 596, while charcoal from a bark-lined storage pit associated with small narrow-necked arrow points produced a date of A.D. 1668.

Trade and Regional Connections

Of the commodities represented in trade and exchange systems of the west-central Plateau, none is more common in prehistory than glassy volcanics (i.e., obsidian, vitrophyre, ignimbrite) and marine shell. While the representation of trade materials in regional sites is undoubtedly biased by consideration of differential preservation factors, the exchange system identified by those materials encompasses a wide region of the Pacific Northwest and presumably a wide range of goods as well. The trade in glassy volcanic raw materials stems from the fact of a poor representation of sources in the Washington section of the Cascade Range. Low grade sources do occur in the Washington Cascades (McClure 1987, 1989; Schalk and Mierendorf 1983; Galm 1994), but the relatively small sizes of nodule supplies and the generally poor quality of these materials appear to have limited their use. The large number of sources known from central and south-central Oregon, southeastern and south-central Idaho, and the few sources from northern and central British Columbia all appear to be part of the exchange network that operated during prehistory.

The other primary commodity, marine shell, incorporates several varieties of shells, the most common of which are dentalium and olivella (fig. 11). While many other species are represented in the growing list of marine shell varieties from Plateau sites, most consist of a single reported occurrence or identifications labeled provisional. In addition to dentalium and olivella, the most common occurrences of marine shell include examples of *Haliotis kamtschatkana* (northern abalone), *Mytilus californianus* (sea mussel), and *Pecten caurinus* (weather-vane scallop), and *Tresus* species (horse clams). Beads, principally modified shell (i.e., spire-lopped olivella), cut section, and cut disk varieties, pendants, and occasional gorgets dominate marine shell assemblages throughout the prehistoric sequence (Galm 1994; Erickson 1983).

The earliest dated occurrences of glassy volcanic materials are from the southern section of the study area in association with Windust phase components (Rice 1972; Galm 1994). Sites along the Lower Snake River (Granite Point, Windust Cave, and Marmes) contained examples of obsidian in what remains the earliest dated contexts for these objects (Rice 1972). The recovery of obsidian from the Richey-Roberts Clovis Cache implies even earlier use of this material and establishes a pattern of usage that extends

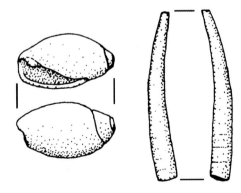

Fig. 11. Trade marine shells from site 45SP5 in Spokane Co., Wash. left, Olivella spire-lopped bead, 2 cm; right, dentalium shell, 4 cm. Drawings by Pamela K. McKenney.

through the entire chronological sequence. Obsidian is also reported from 45CH204 in the middle Columbia area. The available evidence indicates that glassy volcanic materials have made their way into all subareas of this region by 8000–6000 B.C. (Cressman et al. 1960; Rice 1972; Irwin and Moody 1978; Grabert 1974; Chance and Chance 1982; Borden 1960; Salo 1985). Occurrences increase during the late half of this period, although projectile points and flakes continue as the most common artifacts manufactured in this material.

Subperiod IB finds of olivella shell beads include the Pig Farm and Marmes on the Lower Snake River (Brauner 1976; Rice 1972). Mussel shell occurs (pendant or rattle) in at least one early component along the Fraser River in south-central British Columbia (EdRk:7), and a wider distribution to other areas along the Columbia River is not unexpectable (Sanger 1970). Olivella shell beads also are reported from slightly later contexts at the Tucannon site (Nelson 1966) and 45OK11 (Lohse 1984e) on Chief Joseph Reservoir. The association of olivella shell beads and obsidian with burials at Marmes has been suggested as a possible connection to the Western Idaho Archaic burial complex (Pavesic 1985; Galm 1994). While the distribution of this complex remains to be documented, there is some evidence to suggest a possible association of burial patterns over a wide area of the Plateau at least by 4500–4000 B.C. (Galm 1994).

The trade in glassy volcanics and marine shell expands considerably during Period II as is indicated by a greater representation at regional sites. However, virtually no change occurs in the proportional representation of these materials in specific assemblages. The obsidian trade continues to involve the exchange of "finished" biface or projectile point forms. Like the preceding Subperiod IB, most finds of this material consist of debitage. Possible associations of the trade in obsidian and burial practices linked to the Western Idaho Archaic burial complex are likely to continue into this period (Galm 1994).

The exchange in olivella shells is supplemented by the addition of haliotis, tresus, mytalis, and dentalium during Period II. Fewer associations of shell beads and burials are reflected in the sample of sites containing shell objects, and this is viewed as part of a trend involving representation of larger numbers of these items.

Period III trade and exchange patterns mirror those described for Periods I and II. Certainly, the numbers and diversity of items in the exchange network appear to have expanded, but in each instance, within the pattern established during earlier time periods. A greater variety of obsidian artifacts appears to correspond to the representation of a much larger number of source materials as well (cf. Sappington 1984; Hughes 1986).

Marine shell artifacts also exhibit expanded distributions in the region, but like obsidian, the groundwork for this expansion lies in patterns established during preceding periods. Numbers and diversity represented in the shell trade increase, although proportions of these items remain relatively low. The highest proportion of shell trade items occurs immediately prior to and following Euro-American contact. The role of the horse in the expansion of trade and exchange generally should be apparent and tends to skew analyses of sites in which chronology is poorly controlled.

Finally, the analysis of trade and identification of exchange networks implies very early-dating relationships to groups residing south and west of the west-central Plateau. Obsidian was obtained from northern Great Basin sources, including several in central and south-central Oregon and southeastern and south-central Idaho. Marine shells also may have been a part of this Great Basin network assuming that olivella was obtained in quantity from sources along the California coast. Coastal ties continue into Period III but extend to the north for sources of dentalia. Vast numbers of dentalia were obtained from sources along northern Vancouver Island, at least some of which must have worked its way inland through trade with groups residing along the Fraser River. The Fraser River corridor, like the lower Columbia, most likely served as a major commerce route throughout prehistory. Indeed, the trade in marine shells along the Fraser is likely to have incorporated the abundant supplies of nephrite, serpentine, steatite, and soapstone known to occur in the Lytton-Lillooet region of British Columbia. Occurrences of artifacts manufactured from these materials are far more common in Period III assemblages as are finds of dentalium shells. Sources of talc-based rocks used in ground stone industries are very rare in southern portions of this region, a fact no doubt well known to native traders of this period.

Prehistory of the Eastern Plateau

TOM E. ROLL AND STEVEN HACKENBERGER

The Eastern Plateau encompasses an area of substantial environmental diversity. Five rivers in the Eastern Plateau—the Kootenai, the Pend Oreille, the Spokane, the Clearwater, and the Salmon—contribute significantly to the Columbia drainage. The drainage basins of the three rivers that drain the north and east portions of the Eastern Plateau—the Kootenai, the Pend Oreille, and the Spokane—are called the Kootenai-Pend Oreille region. Together, the Clearwater and the Salmon rivers drain west-central Idaho, herein identified as a second region, the Salmon-Clearwater (fig. 1). This diverse mountainous terrain presented opportunities and challenges that resulted in substantial variation in human adaptations that reflect both physiographic situation and cultural relationships.

The presence or absence of migrating salmon and steelhead probably impacted the course of cultural development more than any other single factor. Bonnington Falls on the Kootenai River, Metaline Falls on the Pend Oreille River, and Spokane Falls on the Spokane River arrested spawning migrations of anadromous fish on the upstream courses of those rivers throughout the post-Pleistocene (Fulton 1968, 1970). The absence of anadromous fish from these rivers led to cultural strategies that contrast with those of the remainder of the Plateau. It was this phenomenon that led to the term "Barrier Falls subarea" (Roll and Singleton 1982:1.11–1.15) to refer to this large portion of the Columbia drainage system devoid of the resource often considered essential to the emergence of Plateau culture.

In comparison, anadromous fish figured prominently in the diet of native people who occupied territory drained by the Salmon and Clearwater rivers. On these drainages and their tributaries the cultural responses more nearly resemble those of the Plateau although flavored by the diversity of this mountainous habitat.

Anadromous fish represent the only significant food resource for which a presence/absence contrast exists between the two regions of the Eastern Plateau. Relative abundance/scarcity characterizes other kinds of resource variation. Within the western portions of the two districts the distribution of camas (*Camasia quamash*) and ease of transportation on lakes and low gradient streams dampens some disparities created by salmon distributions. Camas grounds assume an east-west gradient with greatest abundance to the west. Native peoples exploited extensive camas beds, such as those of the Calispell Valley downstream from Pend Oreille Lake and those of the Lower Coeur d'Alene,

St. Joe, and St. Maries rivers, clustered along the western periphery of the Kootenai-Pend Oreille region. Density and size of camas grounds decreases dramatically upstream from Lake Pend Oreille. Particularly well-known beds within the Clark Fork Basin include Camas Prairie near Hot Springs, Montana, and the Evaro camas grounds northwest of Missoula, Montana. The easternmost of the famous camas prairies lies in the Potomac Valley some 35 kilometers east of Missoula. In appropriate meadow situations small camas patches appear scattered over much of the Kootenai-Pend Oreille region. The significance of these infrequent patches to aboriginal camas procurement remains undetermined.

Camas meadow density in the lower reaches of the Salmon-Clearwater region probably exceeded that anywhere in the Kootenai-Pend Oreille by several orders of magnitude. Famous camas grounds such as Camas Prairie and Weippe Prairie near Kamiah, Idaho, stand out but numerous other documented and undocumented camas-gathering localities contributed to prehistoric larders (cf. Thoms 1989:127, 154, 167). Large portions of the territory drained by the Salmon River possess the conditions identified (Statham 1982) as optimum for camas. Statham observed numerous camas beds along the upper reaches of the main Salmon River and in the valleys of the Weiser, Payette, and Little Salmon. Despite spots of appropriate habitat along the Middle Fork of the Salmon, camas appears infrequently. Notably, Statham's survey failed to identify camas on the main Salmon between Stanley and Salmon, Idaho. Her habitat hypothesis accounts for the absence of camas in the Snake River Plain and the valleys of the Little Lost, Big Lost, Birch Creek, Pahsimeroi, and Lemhi rivers (Statham 1982:53).

Steep gradients, with frequent cataracts or rocky rapids, characterize most river systems of the Eastern Plateau. These steep gradients limited or precluded prehistoric human use of the rivers for upstream transportation corridors and reduced their utility for downstream use. Along the western margin of the Kootenai-Pend Oreille region the gradient of most rivers decreases sufficiently to produce near flatwater conditions on many streams. Downstream from Bonners Ferry, Idaho, about 60 kilometers of low gradient conditions permitted access to the normally calm waters of Kootenay Lake. Other flatwater sections include Priest Lake, Pend Oreille Lake, and Lake Coeur d'Alene. Low gradient conditions permitting two-way travel by aboriginal

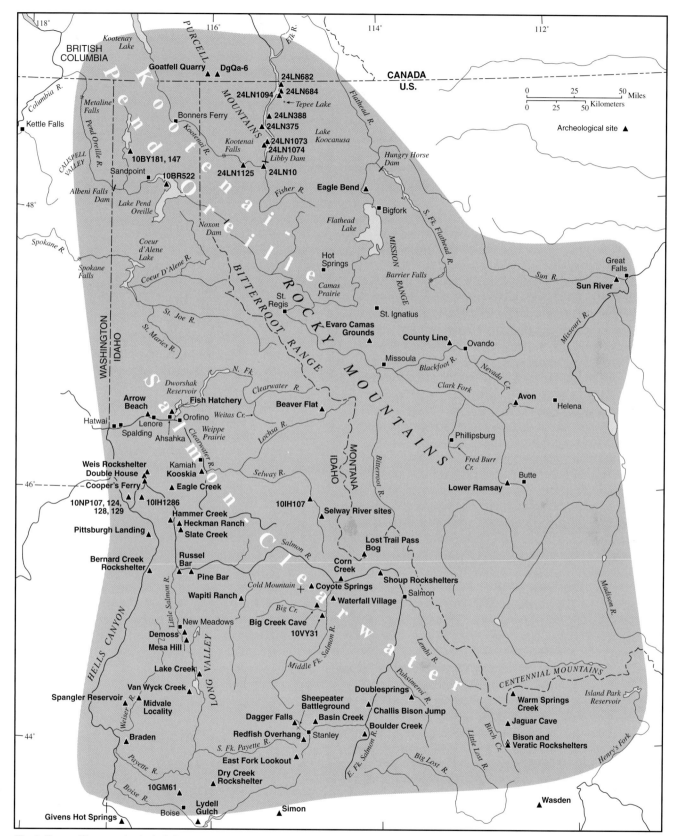

Fig. 1. Eastern Plateau archeological sites.

watercraft prevailed over substantial portions of the lower courses of the Coeur d'Alene, St. Joe, and St. Maries rivers, all sources for Lake Coeur d'Alene. Other waterways at least seasonally practical for aboriginal navigation included the lower reaches of the Clark Fork and parts of the Pend Oreille. Proximity to areas with high salmon productivity like Kettle Falls on the upper Columbia, abundant camas beds, and reasonable transportation of bulky products combined to provide people living on the western edge of the Kootenai-Pend Oreille region with means of intensifying their potential in ways not readily available to their upstream contemporaries.

Dams constructed along the lower Snake and on the Snake River above Hells Canyon make it impossible to compare accurately the productivity of salmon runs in the Clearwater and Salmon river basins. Probably the middle and upper reaches of the Salmon River represented a more important fishery than the upper Clearwater basin. Reid (1991) notes that an important division occurred between Nez Perce fishing bands on the lower Salmon and Snake rivers and hunting bands on the Snake River above the Salmon River confluence. Also, dugout canoes more readily navigated the Lower Snake and Clearwater rivers.

Cultural Chronologies

Chronologies developed by typological cross-dating from nearby regions shed light on substantial portions of the Eastern Plateau. Projectile point types provide the reference for most typological dates. Archeologists have generally failed to perceive chronologically sensitive artifact forms other than projectile points. To confound the issue, mountain environments introduce complex forces that muddy the chronological picture. Diverse forces participated in the process of site formation throughout the region. Alluvial forces planed and redeposited cultural materials laid down in sites on floodplains resulting in mixing of cultural deposits. On floodplains and elsewhere animals and plants contributed to bioturbation that mixed cultural remains. Prehistoric people frequently utilized the same landforms as their predecessors. As a result, few sites with stratigraphic separation or clear indication of single occupations exist. Many archeological excavations produce the equivalent of a surface collection composed of artifacts from two or more occupations of uncertain relationship, duration, or antiquity.

Archeologists have presented a number of synthetic schemes to account for Kootenai-Pend Oreille region culture history. Most of those have focused their attentions to the more intensively investigated Kootenai River valley (cf. Taylor 1973; Choquette and Holstine 1980; Choquette 1987; Roll 1982) with different levels of applicability to the region as a whole. Several have proposed regional schemes (Malouf 1956a; Flint 1982). None of the proposed culture histories has gained a substantial following. Thoms (1984; Thoms and Burtchard 1987) has returned to a three-period classification, frequently an adaptation of Mulloy's (1958) Northwestern Plains sequence.

Following systematic classification of phases on the lower Snake River by Leonhardy and Rice (1970), several investigators have defined local phases and complexes in the Clearwater and Salmon river basins (Pavesic 1971; Ames, Green, and Pfoertner 1981; Sappington 1994; Holmer and Ross 1985). Early attempts to define cultural phases in the

Fig. 2. Excavations at site 24LN10, a Late period camp site at the mouth of the Fisher River, Mont. Photograph by Ron Savage, 1979.

ROLL AND HACKENBERGER

eastern portion of the region typically emphasized broad-based comparisons that stressed cultural continuity; therefore, the Birch Creek chronology remains little modified (Swanson 1972).

The diversity and complexity of schemes developed to present the archeological interpretation of Eastern Plateau prehistory cries for the adoption of a simplified overarching chronology. The division into Early, Middle, and Late periods has substantial utility particularly with further subdivision of the Middle period into early and late segments (Reeves 1970).

Early Prehistoric Period, Before 8000–5000 B.C.

Despite long interest in questions regarding the earliest use of the area by peoples of Plateau and Plains origin, data from these investigations have remained unassembled in separate bodies of regional literature. The search for megafauna and the related interest in the ancient grasslands of the Snake River Plain and Columbia Plateau, combined with the tendency to view rivers as travel corridors, has obscured the probable importance of mountain tributaries as base territories of the earliest hunting, gathering, and fishing people.

Kootenai-Pend Oreille Region

Discussions of the Early Prehistoric period assemble sparse archeological remains with supporting paleoenvironmental data to demonstrate the potential for Paleo-Indian utilization of the area. Certainly, most of the area opened to human occupancy by the onset of the Holocene, about 10,000 B.C. Before that time, glacial lake Missoula had flushed its contents over the eastern Plateau for the last time (Atwater 1986), and the largest of the mountain glaciers had retreated to higher elevations. Reestablished vegetation of cold sagebrush-steppe types developed over much of the area with cold forest varieties developing in selected localities.

Large lanceolate and stemmed lanceolate projectile points of Paleo-Indian type characterize the Early period and generally predate 5000 B.C. The earlier and most distinctive of the traditionally recognized Plains Paleo-Indian projectile points such as the distinctive Clovis and Folsom fluted forms, or the classic lanceolate Agate Basin (cf. Frison 1991; Frison and Stanford 1982) occur infrequently if at all. Later, and perhaps less distinctive, forms frequently identified as Agate Basin-like, Plainview-like, or Plano appear rarely, but most frequently, in the more eastern valleys. Melton (1984) listed 18 sites from counties wholly or partially west of the continental divide that had yielded classifiable Paleo-Indian projectile points. Identified projectile point types included Plainview (2), Midland (1), and Agate Basin (8). Reports also list the presence of Cascade points more commonly associated with the post–Paleo-Indian

occupation of the Plateau proper. Melton's search failed to document the presence of any fluted points.

One of the more commonly acknowledged Paleo-Indian sites in the Eastern Plateau is the Avon site (24PW340) (cf. Flint 1982; McLeod and Melton 1986; Knight 1989). Excavations at the Avon site on the Blackfoot River apparently produced single examples of "Agate Basin" and "Fredrick" point types (Melton 1983). Samples from nearby sediments yielded radiocarbon dates of 7670 ± 330 B.C. (M–1973) and 7250 ± 300 B.C. (M–1974) (Davis 1982). Interpretations of the association between the early artifacts and the radiocarbon dates vary (cf. Melton 1983:154; Flint 1982:184). Four sites were identified as Early Prehistoric based on the presence of "Agate Basin" points (Cameron 1984:132). Cameron also identified Agate Basin, Frederick, and Lusk point types at the Avon site.

Artifacts traditionally considered diagnostic of later Paleo-Indian affiliation such as Hell Gap, Alberta, and Cody (Scottsbluff and Eden) appear mostly as rare surface finds on the Atlantic slope drainages that lead onto the Northwestern Plains. Wormington and Forbis (1965:23) identified an ongoing problem with the classification of "generic" lanceolate projectile points, some dating as much as 3,000 years later, as "Agate Basin" on the basis of form alone. For the west slopes of the Northern Rockies specimens so identified receive infrequent mention and many such identifications need authentication.

Miss and Hudson (1986) illustrate artifacts accumulated from 10 surface collections in the vicinity of Lake Pend Oreille. Their illustrations include a number of lanceolate and stemmed or shouldered lanceolate projectile point forms suggestive of considerable antiquity (fig. 3). Many show strong similarities to Plateau forms, particularly certain of the Windust phase varieties among which base treatment exhibits considerable range (Rice 1972).

Choquette (1984, 1987) identifies such projectile points as characteristic of the Goatfell complex (9000–5000 B.C.). Although most of these early points have appeared in surface collections from near Lake Pend Oreille, excavations have turned up single points from sites 10BY181 and 10BY147 in northern Idaho. A suggestion of affiliation with later materials from the Lower Snake River region comes from the identification of a Cascade look-alike point and other artifacts common in the Plateau from 10BY138 (Choquette et al. 1984:109, 116 fig. 42A; Choquette 1984:309). Choquette also attributes a component of the Goatfell complex to site DgQa-6 in southeastern British Columbia. He bases this on appropriately early geomorphic context for quantities of lithic debris that he identifies as composed almost exclusively of siltstone from the Goatfell quarry on the west slope of the Purcell Mountains in British Columbia (1987:91).

Choquette suggests that early occupation of the Kootenai region by Goatfell people emphasized the Purcell Trench and southwestern Purcell Mountains. He sees a gradual shift of emphasis toward the southeastern Purcells due to changes in ungulate range (1987:113). Thoms (1987:243) argues that the distribution of Goatfell materials may reflect vagaries of archeological survey on different landforms throughout the Kootenai region rather than a cultural shift.

Some differences may exist between the eastern and western portions of the Eastern Plateau during the Early period. Projectile point forms reminiscent of recognized Plains varieties seem to appear with greatest frequency along the upper reaches of the Clark Fork River and its tributaries. Downstream on the Lower Clark Fork, Pend Oreille, and the Lower Kootenai projectile points more consistent with early Plateau forms predominate (Melton 1984). Choquette (1987:96, 112) suggests the possibility of a Great Basin origin coeval with the lowering of the great pluvial lakes. These early components may exhibit differential raw material use with greater emphasis on metamorphic siltstones to the north and west and greater dependence on cryptocrystalline silicates to the south and east. Kelly and Todd (1988), whose geographic emphasis rests primarily east of the continental divide, note reliance on high quality cryptocrystalline silicates (often derived from distant sources) as characteristic of the earliest Paleo-Indian components.

Discussions of subsistence, settlement, and human population dynamics derive mostly from environmental assessments and archeological data outside the immediate region. The few surface finds and data from limited excavations provide little evidence directly applicable to such issues. Faunal remains from Early period components have not preserved or remain unreported. Remains of bighorn sheep, wapiti, deer (both mule deer and white-tailed deer) as well as extinct and contemporary forms of bison appear in noncultural fossil localities along the upper Clark Fork River in deposits of Late Pleistocene and Early Holocene age (Rasmussen 1974). The diverse faunal assemblages represented in early sites on the Plateau (cf. Rice 1972:157–160) and on the Rocky Mountain front (cf. Davis, Greiser, and Greiser 1987; Davis and Greiser 1992) contrast with the apparent homogeneous Plains Paleo-Indian focus on mammoth or bison (cf. Frison 1991). Presumably the inhabitants of the Eastern Plateau maintained adaptations as catholic as those of their neighbors in habitats that favored diversity over speciality. A dispersed human population that maintained itself with a forager strategy dependent on seasonal movement regulated by the behavior of resident big game and seasonal abundance of selected plant foods seems consistent with the available information. Regional variations consistent with proximity to other geographic areas probably figured into the subsistence equation.

No buried Paleo-Indian site with indication of reasonably intact deposits has come to light within the Kootenai-Pend Oreille region. Several possibilities offer explanations for this phenomenon. Lack of Paleo-Indian occupation seems an unlikely possibility. Probably an inadequate sample of landforms of sufficient antiquity has been examined. Most reconnaissance has emphasized floodplain and alluvial terrace settings where preserved sediments of appropriate age and context may occur infrequently if at all. Some notable exceptions to the riverine-oriented reconnaissance do exist (cf. Mallory 1961; Fredlund and Lacombe 1971; Hogan 1974; Choquette and Holstine 1980; Gough 1984; Choquette 1987:81; Munger 1993), but such efforts have recovered little definitive evidence of Paleo-Indian occupation. Unpublished radiocarbon dates of microparticulate charcoal found with obsidian flakes support Paleo-Indian associations (9230 B.C. $\pm$ 100, BETA-27973, ETH-4590; and 8340 B.C. $\pm$ 95, BETA-27974, ETH-4591) (Nancy Anderson, personal communication 1997). A third charcoal date from a bulk soil sample taken from a peaty deposit layered above the earliest culture-bearing strata helps confirm these dates (6290 B.C. $\pm$ 90).

Salmon-Clearwater Region

Surface finds, rockshelter excavations, and limited deep testing of open sites testify to the early occupation of the mountain tributaries of the middle Snake River. Reports indicate the presence of Folsom materials from Timmerman Hills on the Big Wood River (Meatte 1989), the upper Salmon, and the divide between the East Fork Salmon and the Big Lost River (Butler 1965b, 1972). Four sites tested on the Henry's Fork suggest possible Paleo-Indian associations (Swanson and Sneed 1971). Druss (1983) illustrates Paleo-Indian artifacts from the Doublesprings site (10CR29) in the high elevation Pahsimeroi Valley including an unspecifiable fluted point type, Haskett, and Humboldt-like forms. Butler (1962) identified Plains-like lanceolate points at Weis Rockshelter and Cooper's Ferry and suggested that the Clearwater Plateau may have become a refuge for early bison hunters.

Occupation of Redfish Overhang began by at least 8150 to 7910 $\pm$ 300 B.C. (Sargeant 1973:63). Excavation of six layers from a deposit only one meter deep revealed eight

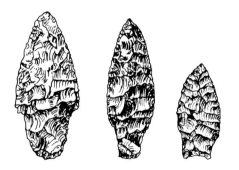

after Miss and Hudson 1987: fig. 13.

Fig. 3. Early Prehistoric period stemmed lanceolate projectile points from surface collections at site 10BR522 on Lake Pend Oreille, west of Sandpoint, Idaho. Length of left 7 cm; others to same scale.

strata. The lowest layers included a cache of Haskett lance-olate points and fire hearths (Butler 1978). A layer with a hearth dated to 6110 ± 285 B.C. contained a single large side-notched point (Bitterroot). Gallagher (personal communication 1982) sourced the Haskett point obsidian to the south-central Idaho Camas Prairie. An early component at the nearby Basin Creek site has yielded Plains Plano tradition points (Gallagher 1973; Towner 1986). Jaguar Cave, located just outside the tributary system reviewed here, also has early period occupation (vol. 11:127–134).

Several sites have yielded Lind Coulee and Windust type stemmed and shouldered points; these include Weis Rock-shelter (Butler 1969 and Ruebelmann 1978); and Bernard Creek Rockshelter (Randolph and Dahlstrom 1977). Test excavations of open sites along the Upper Clearwater River at Weitas Creek (Keeler 1973) and the Lochsa River at Beaver Flat (Sappington and Carley 1989) and Boulder Creek (Benson et al. 1979) have also disclosed the presence of Lind Coulee and Windust materials. The Shoup Rock-shelter (Alpha-10LH23 and Beta-10LH63) dates extend from 10,460 ± 115 B.C. (shell in alluvial deposit) to 3650 ± 230 B.C. (Swanson and Sneed 1966:44); however, the extent to which the deeper assemblages represent Early or Early Middle period occupations remains undetermined due to the failure to produce diagnostic point types.

Middle Prehistoric Period, 5000 B.C. to A.D. 500

Chatters ("Environment," this vol.) perceives the first of a set of progressive increases in effective precipitation for the Eastern Plateau as initiated in the interval from 6500–6000 B.C. Ponderosa pine and Douglas fir forests expanded at the expense of grasslands in the Flathead and Kootenai drainages while sagebrush steppe replaced grasses at lower elevations in the Columbia Basin. Chatters accounts for contradictory indicators such as forest expansion (suggestive of moister conditions) concomitant with increases in shrub steppe (symptomatic of generally warmer climate and occasional or frequent drought conditions) by arguing for a change of basic climatic pattern from continental to maritime at about this time.

The quantity and timing of precipitation and the amplitude of seasonal changes have promoted considerable debate. From the pollen record at Tepee Lake in the Middle Kootenai Mack, Rutter, and Valastro (1983:189) inferred that shortly before 5000 B.C. mean monthly temperatures had increased by 1–4 °C and annual precipitation reduced by one-half since the beginning of the pollen record at about 8600 B.C. Examination of the pollens from Lost Trail Pass Bog on the Idaho-Montana border lead to the opinion that at 5000 B.C., a climate "...warmer but not necessarily drier than the present" prevailed (Mehringer, Arno, and Petersen 1977:366). Thoms (1987:151) comments on the "importance of the open-canopy Douglas Fir/grass habitats as winter and

early spring range for big game, especially mule deer, elk, and mountain sheep."

In the Kootenai region the pollen record documents increases in larch and Douglas fir pollens and decreases in pollens from open terrain species (grasses and sagebrush). Mehringer, Arno, and Petersen (1977) and Mack, Rutter, and Valastro (1983) interpreted the pollen record between 5000 and 2000 B.C. as indicative of a more prominent forest community with Douglas fir and possibly larch as dominant. Mehringer, Arno, and Petersen (1977:366) also observed a 100 percent increase in the frequency of charcoal from this time, suggestive of increased forest fire frequency. Choquette (1987:98) postulates that during this time an increase in forest development reduced open terrain available for big game habitat in the southwestern Purcell Mountains and promoted a cultural shift in geographic focus to rainshadow-maintained grassy slopes on the east side of the Purcell-Cabinet divide.

While this paleoenvironmental data may seem clear-cut, more precise information about the seasonality of precipitation might change the interpretation of both the numbers and key species of big game available for human predation. For example, mule deer populations key closely to vegetation as predicted by seasonality of precipitation (Pac, Mackie, and Jorgensen 1991:269). If summer precipitation prevailed and maintained a longer pulse of green forage so the animals could build up substantial winter fat reserves, populations might increase dramatically beyond those observed today. On the other hand, cold wet winters and hot, dry summers would probably have an adverse impact on deer (and presumably other ungulate) populations.

The cultural developments of Early Middle Prehistoric period (5000 to 2500 B.C.) appear almost coevally with the inferred transition from a continental to a maritime climate. The inventory of the Early Middle period, composed largely of lithic implements, shows little if any increase in frequency over that of the Early Prehistoric period. Projectile points representative of the initial Early Middle period most commonly fit one of two basic patterns, triangular side-notched or lanceolate unnotched. Bitterroot side-notched, Salmon River side-notched, and related forms reresent the earliest frequently identified varieties. Swanson posited the Bitterroot and Salmon River side-notched varieties while working in the Birch Creek valley in eastern Idaho (Swanson, Butler, and Bonnichsen 1964; Swanson and Sneed 1966:26). He estimated an earliest appearance at about 6200 B.C., based on a depositional period bracketed by radiocarbon dates (Swanson 1972:110). The association of these point styles in a range of assemblages led Swanson to posit the Bitterroot culture pattern, which he saw as the archeological expression of the Northern Shoshone that began in the early altithermal and continued in the Birch Creek valley to 1450 B.C. (Swanson 1972:65). Implications of ethnicity and linguistic affiliation in the Bitterroot culture have caused archeologists working elsewhere to apply different terminology to archeological manifestations represented by similar or identical projectile point forms (cf. Reeves 1969 on the "Mummy Cave complex").

The lanceolate Cascade projectile point defined by Butler (1961:29) provides the hallmark artifact of the Cascade phase, dated from 6000 to 3000 B.C., in the Lower Snake River region of southeastern Washington (Leonhardy and Rice 1970). Archeologists frequently cite the presence of Cascade points in the eastern Plateau as indicators of temporally early human occupation. Choquette (1984:309) identifies points "morphologically and lithologically similar to Cascade points" from northern Idaho in association with Goatfell materials, which he extends into post-Mazama times. According to McLeod and Melton (1986:V–17), after Agate Basin, Cascade represents the "most frequently identified, possibly paleo-point types, in Montana." The problem of identification of the Cascade point type corresponds to that discussed in relation to the Agate Basin type. Because of the generalized lanceolate shape and substantial intra-type variation Cascade points intergrade with exhausted knives (Plateau pentagonal types) and small biface blanks or preforms. Without some form of corroborating evidence such as indisputable stratigraphic context, very large sample size, or reliable association with other uniquely Cascade phase artifacts, the identification of "Cascade" points must remain uncertain. This presents a particular problem for isolated surface finds or specimens from excavations with small sample sizes and dubious stratigraphic integrity.

Leonhardy and Rice (1970) identified a late subphase of the Cascade phase characterized by addition of the Cold Springs side-notched projectile point (Shiner 1961; Butler 1961) as a horizon marker. The subphase marked by the Cold Springs side-notched points invariably postdate the Mount Mazama ash fall (about 4700 B.C.). Traditionally, specialists in the Lower Snake River region have viewed Cold Springs side-notched as distinct from the eastern Idaho side-notched points (Bitterroot and Salmon River side-notched) although they overlap chronologically and exhibit substantial morphological similarity.

Kootenai-Pend Oreille

The Montana site records identify Bitterroot, Salmon River, Mummy Cave, and Mt. Albion (?) side-notched points from 10 sites in counties west of the continental divide (Melton 1984:table 3). The comparative rarity of artifacts attributed to the Early Middle period may result more from lack of consistent identification than from actual occurrence. Many initial site records identify site presence based on limited surface examination and contribute little in the way of artifactual information. Reports on more extensively investigated sites contain more frequent mention of large, dart-sized, side-notched projectile points. Thoms and Shalk (1984:fig. 12–1, d and e) identified specimens from 24LN1054 as "Bitterroot Side-Notched-like," and Draper (1987: B–27,

fig. B–5, I–k) classified similar specimens as "Large Side-Notched"; both assigned their materials to the Early Middle period.

A distinctive side-notched variant appears in the area near the end of the Early Middle period. A nearly square length-width ratio and broad open side-notches combined with a large, shallow basal concavity and rounded "ears" at the base of the haft element distinguish Oxbow or Oxbow-like points (fig. 4d) from earlier side-notched varieties. Originally identified on the Northwestern Plains (Nero and McCorquodale 1958), Oxbow remains appear commonly (Dyck 1976:8) throughout the late half of the Early Middle period and extend well into the Late Middle period. Dates from the Sun River site on the east slope of the Rockies near Great Falls, Montana, range from about 3300 to 1500 B.C. (Greiser, Greiser, and Vetter 1985:853). Melton (1984:table 4) found reports for 10 sites west of the continental divide that identified Oxbow projectile points in their artifact inventories.

Reconnaissance and excavations in the Middle Kootenai region have disclosed Oxbow in relatively substantial numbers. Choquette (1980:40) recognized "'eared' side notched concave base points resembling the Oxbow type" as elements of his Bristow complex (5500–2000 B.C.) in the Kootenai region. Roll (1982:5.10, figs. 5.1 and 5.2) identified single projectile points from three different sites in the Libby Additional Units and Pelton Reregulating Dam area immediately downstream from Libby Dam as consistent with the Oxbow type. More than 27 morphologically similar points from at least seven sites also appeared in Lake Koocanusa (Roll and Bailey 1979:fig. 8; Thoms 1984:509).

As postinundation studies, the efforts of Jermann and Aaberg (1976), Roll and Bailey (1979), Thoms (1984), and Thoms and Burtchard (1987) focused largely on landforms at substantial vertical distances above the natural floodplain of the Kootenai River. The results of these efforts contrast dramatically with results (cf. Roll and Smith 1982; Roll

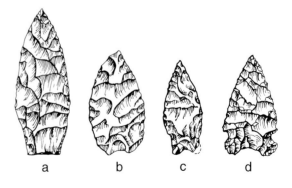

after Thoms 1984:figs. 12–1, 12–2 and Thoms and Burtchard 1987: fig. 11–6.
Fig. 4. Early Middle period projectile points from the Kootenai-Pend Oreille region. a-b, Indented base lanceolate points from sites 24LN682 and 24LN1074; c, lanceolate stemmed indented base point from site 24LN1094; d, oxbow-like eared point from site 24LN1054. Length of a, 6 cm; others to same scale.

1982) that dealt primarily with floodplain deposits for about 13 river miles immediately downstream from Libby Dam. The results from the high terraces along Lake Koocanusa disclosed substantial Middle period cultural materials with a strong Early Middle period expression. Downstream, studies focused on the floodplain found only sparse suggestion of Early Middle period remains. Intensity of floodplain occupation appeared to increase throughout the Late Middle period with relatively abundant terminal Middle period representation. This has lead some to the interpretation that Early Middle period occupations relied on higher terrace and mountain slope resources of the middle Kootenai (Thoms 1984; Choquette and Holstine 1980; Choquette 1987). The observed geographic distribution of chronologically different cultural deposits may result from sampling error or geomorphic processes rather than prehistoric land use patterns.

Lithic implements show substantial morphological similarities over large areas of North America at particular points in time. Artifacts of the Eastern Plateau share many morphological traits with specimens throughout parts of western North America, in particular the Great Basin and the Northwestern Plains. Throughout much of the west, lanceolate indented base points appear sometime around 3000 B.C. Immediately north of the Great Basin, Swanson (1972) identified a total of seven lanceolate indented base "Plainview-McKean" points as constituent elements of both the Birch Creek phase (9000 to 5200 B.C.) and the Bitterroot phase (5200 to 1450 B.C.). A range of problems plague the identification and dating of the similar Humboldt series, leading Thomas (1981) to issue the caution that a chronological span of at least 5,000 years in the Great Basin limits the value of the Humboldt series as a time marker. Clearly, Thomas's caution about the chronological value of the Humboldt series in the Great Basin applies to the lanceolate indented base points of the Birch Creek valley of Idaho.

Also in the Birch Creek valley of Idaho, Swanson excavated stemmed indented base points from strata attributed primarily to the Bitterroot phase and the Beaverhead phase (1450 to 950 B.C.). Thomas warns that analogous specimens radiocarbon dated from 3000 to 1300 B.C. from Gatecliff Shelter, Danger Cave, and Sudden Shelter in the Great Basin and perhaps Pinto Basin in California appear earlier.

On the Middle Kootenai, Thoms (1984:367) uses lanceolate indented base and stemmed indented base projectile points (fig. 4 a–c) as "period markers" for the advent of the Late Middle period. On the Northwestern Plains lanceolate indented base projectile points labeled McKean (Wheeler 1952) mark Reeves's (1969) McKean phase at about 2500–1500 B.C. while Reeves attributes stemmed indented base Duncan and Hanna points (Wheeler 1954) to the Hanna phase from 1500 to 1000 B.C. The recovery of McKean, Duncan, and Hanna types in apparent association have led many to treat them as part and parcel of the same manifestation, thus the McKean culture complex (Frison

1991:88–91; McLeod and Melton 1986). Frison (1991:24) assigns McKean and its variants to 3000 to 1000 B.C.

The similarity in form and temporal occurrence between Great Basin and Northwestern Plains specimens have led to substantial discussion about the relationship between the two areas during this time (Kehoe 1955; Husted and Mallory 1967:224; Swanson, Powers, and Bryan 1964). Less intense debate, but equally problematic, has accompanied the discovery of similar lanceolate indented base and stemmed indented base projectile points in the Eastern Plateau.

Montana site records for the 12 counties all or partly west of the continental divide contained reference to McKean, Duncan, or Hanna point types with comparatively high frequency (Melton 1984:table 5). Archeologists identified McKean points in 18 sites, Duncan in 11, and Hanna in 18. Four sites share two or more of the three varieties. Lanceolate indented base and stemmed indented base projectile points have also appeared in a number of excavated contexts across the Kootenai-Pend Oreille region.

Fuzzy type definitions and inadequate to nonexistent chronological controls have led to controversy over the identification of the McKean "complex" also. Reconnaissance along the Idaho-Montana border in the Bitterroot Range discovered materials referable to McKean and associated varieties in contexts interpreted as animal drives with associated hunting blinds (concealment features) at elevations approaching 2,200 meters (Fredlund 1970; Fredlund and Lacombe 1971; Hogan 1974). Fredlund and Fredlund (1971:32) note similar prospects for a high pass site near the continental divide at an elevation of 2,285 meters in the South Fork drainage of the Flathead River. Choquette and Holstine (1982:54) contend that no adequate reason exists to "assume either cultural affiliation or contemporaneity with the plains styles." They suggest that lanceolate and stemmed points with indented bases may represent nothing more than size reduction from earlier indigenous stemmed and lanceolate types and, as such, reflect localized change. An interesting addendum to this discussion comes again from the Great Basin where Thomas (1981:37) notes that the lanceolate concave base "Humboldt points are most commonly found on sites directly related to intercept hunting strategy sites."

Corner-notched and corner-removed projectile points (fig. 5) occur in abundance throughout the Kootenai-Pend Oreille region (Malouf 1956; Borden 1956; Taylor 1973; Choquette 1974). Deaver and Deaver (1986) examined the frequency of projectile point types, radiocarbon dates, and identified diagnostics from site report forms for western Montana, including materials from both sides of the continental divide. Their results indicate that terminal Late Middle period projectile point forms appear more frequently (36% of total) than any other single type and that radiocarbon assessments indicative of Late Middle Prehistoric period occupation occur at about the same rate as those of the Late Prehistoric period (25% each). The last 3,000 years as represented by Late Middle period corner-notched and Late period small side-notched points account for about 70 percent of all identified projectile points. Thoms and Schalk (1984:371) observed similar results in the Koocanusa Pool area where the frequency of Late Middle period components exceeded that of any other period. The relative abundance of large- to mid-sized corner-notched projectile points and Late Middle period sites is a commonly recognized but poorly understood phenomenon throughout the Kootenai-Pend Oreille region.

Within the Kootenai-Pend Oreille region corner-notched projectile points also appear frequently in excavated components. These types appeared in six sites and represent about 23 percent of all identifiable point types. Speaking to the river bottom setting Roll (1982:5.115) comments that "it appears that full-scale utilization of the area equivalent to that of later occupations had been achieved by this time." They also represent the dominant form in L.B. Fredlund's (1979) excavations at the Big Creek Lake site near the Bitterroot divide, elevation 1,780 meters. She identifies two corner-notched varieties, Big Creek Corner Notched and Serrated Pelican Lake–Elko corner notched (36% and 46% respectively of the site total of 85 specimens). Using Thomas's criteria (1981) the Big Creek Corner Notched (generally larger) would key out as Elko corner-notched in the western Great Basin. The smaller Serrated Pelican Lake-Elko fall on the border between Thomas's Elko corner-notched (probably atlatl dart points) and the chronologically later Rosegate series (probably arrow points). On the basis of neck width alone, most, if not all, of Fredlund's Serrated Pelican Lake-Elko corner notched fall in the upper range of arrow points (cf. Thomas 1978). Regardless of the identification of the Serrated Pelican Lake-Elko points, the site contains a strong representation of Late Middle period corner-notched specimens. Hogan (1974:63–64)) illustrates corner-notched points collected from the surface of the Dalton site interpreted as an intercept hunting strategy site at the crest of the Bitterroot divide (elevation 2,190 m) near Saint Regis, Montana.

In the Eastern Plateau, archeologists treat a wide range of large- to medium-sized corner-notched to corner-removed projectile points as markers of the terminal Late Middle period. The Elko series of the Great Basin, Pelican Lake on the Northwestern Plains, and variably named corner-notched varieties from southern Idaho and the Plateau all appear as approximate contemporaries. In reference to western North America, Foor (1981:182) concluded "wherever large corner notched points are found, the associated time period is about the same. Pelican Lake can be viewed as a regional expression of a widespread trend in projectile point technology in North America." Thomas (1981:32), however, concedes that in the Great Basin points morphologically consistent with Elko corner-notched and Elko Eared may date before 5000 B.C. Swanson (1972:114–121) observed similar corner-notched materials in equally early contexts in the Birch Creek valley. Excavators found a single corner-

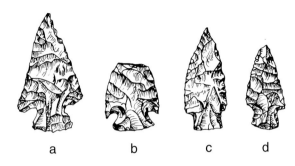

after Roll 1982: fig. 5.7 and Thoms 1984: fig. 12–2.
Fig. 5. Late Middle period projectile points from the Kootenai-Pend Oreille region. a–b, Corner-notched points from sites 24LN375 and 24LN1125; c, stemmed point from site 24LN388; d, corner-removed point from site 24LN1073. Length of a, 5 cm; others to same scale.

notched specimen in cultural layer 16 (5680 ± 170 B.C., I–1588) from the deeply stratified Mummy Cave site (Husted and Edgar 1970). Excavations on the east slopes of the Rocky Mountains in Montana have also resulted in identification of Early Middle period contexts that contain corner-notched specimens in apparent association with large side-notched projectile points (Leslie B. Davis, personal communication 1993). So far, in the Northern Rockies the ratio of corner-notched points associated with large side-notched has remained low with no more than one or two specimens in any site. Without corroborating evidence, corner-notched projectile points, particularly singly or in small numbers, probably provide a poor basis for assigning chronology or cultural affiliation.

Salmon-Clearwater Region

The Middle Prehistoric period of the mountain tributaries cannot be divorced from that of the Lower and Middle Snake river canyons. Warren, Sims, and Pavesic (1968) concluded that subsistence along the Middle Snake shifted from fishing (Squaw Creek II phase) to hunting (Big Bar phase) between 1000 and 500 B.C., and that winter ungulate hunting intensified settlement in the canyon. Settlement along the Lower Clearwater and Lower Salmon rivers intensified as early as the Tucannon phase, by about 2500 B.C. (Ames, Green, and Pfoertner 1981; cf. Butler 1978a); however, pit house occupations occur more commonly in these tributaries during the Harder phase, about 500 B.C.

The Midvale complex of the Weiser and Payette rivers and sites along the Boise River (Meatte 1989; Hackenberger and Meatte 1991) reflect increased settlement in tributaries and their upper valleys at about 2000 B.C. Between 1500 and 500 B.C. evidence for the first intensive, perhaps year-round occupation, of the Middle Salmon River canyon and seasonal use of the uplands of the Middle Fork Salmon River indicates continued population expansion or shifts to upland settlement. Larger camps and more frequent rock-shelter use in the upper Salmon River Basin and Birch Creek valley probably reflect increased activities of mountain sheep and bison hunting parties during moister periods between 1500 and 500 B.C. Shifts toward settlement in the Middle Fork Salmon and other higher tributary valleys results from decreased spring and fall salmon runs and dispersed ungulate populations caused by lower winter precipitation and spring river discharge (Hackenberger 1988). However, the possibility of absolute population growth and expansion deserves further consideration.

• WEISER, PAYETTE, AND BOISE RIVERS   The enigmatic early cemeteries of this area provide the only evidence of formalized burials, with the exception of the rare burials found in later rockshelter deposits and intrusive burials in housepits. The Braden site and affiliated sites led Pavesic (1985) to define the Western Idaho Archaic Burial complex, which may have persisted from about 4000 until 2000 B.C. The 30+ individuals from Middle period burials of this complex outnumber the total number of Late period burials known for the entire region of Snake River tributaries. The Braden site (3840 ± 120 B.C.) near the mouth of the Weiser River (Meatte 1989; cf. Pavesic 1979, 1985) contained a mass grave with the remains of at least four men, two women, and four children. Burned bone indicated at least two cremations. The site has divulged numerous grave goods, and one possible burial pit contained a cache of large "turkey-tailed" bifaces. The inventory of artifacts for the complex includes: turkey-tailed blades, large bifaces, large side-notched points, obsidian caches, olivella shell beads, pipes, shell and bone beads, and ground stone (Green et al. 1986). A trench excavated for spring development at the DeMoss site (10AM193) near New Meadows disclosed the presence of prehistoric human skeletal remains of at least 22 individuals of all ages. The nature of fragmentary bone indicates surface weathering prior to burial, and a bone date gives an estimated age of 4015 ± 60 B.C. (corrected). Large side-notched points and leaf-shaped bifaces suggest affinities with the Cascade phase (Green et al. 1986).

Salvage excavations at 10 sites at the Midvale locality on the Weiser River focused on a basalt quarry area and led to the definition of the Midvale complex first suggested to date between 2000 and 500 B.C. (Warren, Wilkinson, and Pavesic 1971; Bucy 1974; Dort 1964). Quarried basalt nodules used to manufacture leaf-shaped Cascade points and large side-notched, "Bitterroot" points, combined with a variety of cutting and scraping tools characterize this complex. Meatte (1989) interprets the prevalence of ground stone tools as suggestive of an emphasis on plant processing. Bowers's (1967) excavations at Spangler Reservoir documented assemblages similar to those from the Midvale locality. Plew (1977) tested three sites on the Payette River related to the Midvale complex. In Long Valley small sites in the vicinity of the Cascade Reservoir have numerous early Middle period Cascade-like points (Arnold 1984). Large lanceolate bifaces from test excavations at 10VY95, 96, 97, relate

to Midvale (Plew 1977, 1981; Wylie and Flynn 1977). Boreson (1979) tested a shallow prehistoric campsite on the nearby upper stretches of the South Fork (10VY165); there basalt bifaces similar to those from the Mesa Hill basalt quarry (distance 40 air miles) (Ruebelmann 1973) suggest association with the Midvale complex. A limited and uniform tool assemblage indicates seasonal fishing and hunting. Archeologists have little information on the relationships of these assemblages with those of the Cascade phase, or the Tucannon phase (Meatte 1989). The fact that Midvale materials have appeared with greatest frequency in southwestern Idaho and eastern Oregon adds confusion to the issue as does the possibility of links between the Midvale assemblages and the earlier Western Idaho Burial complex.

Tests of several sites in the upper Payette River Basin reveal the beginning of cultural material influences from the Great Basin. Artifact deposition rates show that occupations began as early as 3,000 years ago; however, repeated seasonal occupations (or occupations of longer duration) occurred mostly between 500 B.C. and A.D. 500 (Moore and Ames 1979; Ames 1980, 1982, 1982a; Plew, Ames, and Fuhrman 1984). A pit house feature at 10GM61 (5–6 m diameter) dates to approximately 1000 B.C. (Artz 1983). This buried feature stands as the only identified house in the Weiser, Payette, and Boise river basins. It may show affinities with Tucannon phase houses or equally early houses farther south on the Snake River such as those at Given's Hotsprings (Green et al. 1992). In the upper Boise River Basin components at Lydell Gulch (Sappington 1981) and at Dry Creek Rockshelter (Webster 1978) reflect two periods of intensified settlement—one, early Middle period (pre-2000 B.C.); the other, early Late period.

• CLEARWATER RIVER   Significant work on the Lower Clearwater above the Hatwai site ("Prehistory of the Southern Plateau," fig. 5, this vol.) includes test excavation at Arrow Beach and Lenore (Toups 1969), and at Spalding (Iverson 1975; Chance 1978a, 1979; Carley 1981; Chance and Chance 1985a). Tucannon and Harder phase pit house sites suggest initial population growth on the Lower Clearwater. Harder phase houses and campsites on the Upper Clearwater suggest population expansion from the Lower Clearwater into the Upper Clearwater and seasonal use of the Lochsa and Selway rivers (Sappington 1993). Residents hunted elk, deer, and bear; and the possibility exists that winter settlements occurred despite the absence of identified winter habitation features (Sappington and Carley 1989; Mattson 1984). Limited testing at seven sites on the Selway River and an analysis of a large private collection from 10IH107 suggest that regular seasonal occupations of the area began after 1000 B.C. (McLeod and Melton 1984, 1986).

• SALMON RIVER   Elsewhere within the Lower Salmon canyon test excavations at Heckman Ranch (Pavesic 1978) revealed occupations spanning the late Cascade, Tucannon, and Harder phases. Test excavations in surrounding uplands indicate extensive seasonal gathering and hunting. Hunting

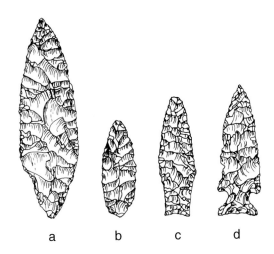

after Sappington 1994: figs. 5.5, 5.7.

Fig. 6. Early and Early Middle period projectile points from the Salmon-Clearwater region. a–b, Cascade lanceolate points from the Weitas Creek site on the North Fork of the Clearwater River near Orofino, Idaho; c–d, stemmed lanceolate point and side-notched point from the Boulder Creek South site on the Lochsa River east of Orofino, Idaho. Length of a, 9 cm; others to same scale.

and hide processing tools, as well as pestles and hopper mortar bases and hearth features that reflect camas processing characterize the Eagle Creek site during these phases (Thoms 1989; cf. Gaarder 1967).

Along the Middle Fork Salmon the Shoup Rockshelters (Alpha-10LH23 and Beta-10LH63) excavations penetrated to a depth of two to four meters, and excavators identified eight layers (Swanson and Sneed 1966:44). Five radiocarbon dates extend from 10,460 ± 115 B.C. (shell in alluvial deposit) to 3650 ± 230 B.C. Bitterroot side-notched points (77) made up about 50 percent of the point collection and 21 percent of the total tool collection. Elko and Pinto types also occur. Scrapers and fleshers constitute 26 percent of the total collection of artifacts. Chalcedony predominates in the collection of tools and lithic debitage. The collections contain a single bone harpoon point. Swanson and Sneed (1966:12) hypothesized that shellfish use increased from 5200 B.C. up until A.D. 1400 and concluded that rockshelter use declined after 1500 B.C. (thus Holmer and Ross's designated Shoup Phase) (Rossillon 1982; cf. Swanson and Sneed 1966:22).

Big Creek Cave (10VY67) extends to roughly one meter deep (dated 1950 ± 90 B.C.) (Wylie, Scott, and Gallagher 1981). Occupations began by at least 2000 B.C. with the most intense use indicated at 1200 B.C. (thus the Big Creek Cave phase). Initial occupation of the Corn Creek site took place at approximately 3000 B.C. (Holmer and Ross 1985). Occupations resume about 1300 B.C., but intensive occupation with house features began after about A.D. 750 (thus the Corn Creek phase). Layers dated to 1300 B.C. disclosed the great-

est frequency of deer elements and shellfish. Mountain sheep remains outnumber those of deer in all components and especially dominate later components.

Sporadic surveys of elevations higher than 1,675 meters have revealed sites with shallow buried deposits on the upper Middle Fork Salmon River tributaries (Bowers 1964; DeBloois 1977; Gallagher 1975; Holmer 1988; Knudson et al. 1982); in the Chamberlain Basin, Cold Mountain, and Big Horn Crags areas (Dahlstrom 1972; Kulesza 1982; Leonhardy and Johnston 1984); and the Bitterroot Range (Munger 1993). Site locations suggest upland hunting, root gathering, and white-bark pine nut procurement (Hackenberger 1984, 1988; Munger 1993a). Occupations at Coyote Springs on Cold Mountain began by at least 3000 to 2000 B.C. and include the McKean point type (Leonhardy 1987). Initial occupations began by 3000 B.C. at Sheepeater Battle Ground, and rates of artifact deposition, which more than double about 500 B.C., suggest increased use of the site during warm, dry periods after 500 B.C.

Dagger Falls (a salmon spearing station on the uppermost Middle Fork of the Salmon) revealed occupations dating 2000–1000 B.C. Excavations revealed an assemblage with high frequencies of Great Basin Elko points (Holmer 1988; Togler 1993). Analysis of pollen samples from several discrete radiocarbon dated features help confirm Hackenberger's (1988) model of climatic change. Holmer (1990) and Togler (1993) review evidence in support of a Numic expansion into the Salmon River Mountains by 1000 B.C. during an extended cool moist period. However, the most intensive site occupations fall in a period that includes the shift to warm, dry conditions between 1000 B.C. and A.D. 1, and pottery appears by the end of this period.

• UPPER SALMON BASIN AND BIRCH CREEK   Swanson (1972) speculated that the early Middle Period Bitterroot phase originated within high elevation uplands during the post glacial maximum. He hypothesized heavy use of upland rockshelters during two major periods marked by low effective moisture, when less hospitable conditions prevailed at lower elevation areas: first during the Beaverhead phase (1450 to 950 B.C.), and second during the Lemhi phase (A.D. 1250 to 1850). The Beaverhead phase occupation included high relative frequencies of chalcedony, and Swanson speculated that these occupations were associated with groups centered in the Salmon River Basin. Proxy climatic data indicate that both of Swanson's proposed periods of low moisture are in fact periods of greater moisture. Increased frequency of rockshelter use probably reflects increased activity by hunting parties, rather than human population trends or major settlement shifts (Hackenberger 1988). Hunting of mountain sheep and bison may have typified the moister period between 5500 and 1500 B.C.; bison hunting increased during the moister period after A.D. 1250.

Epperson's (1977) survey included the main stem of the Upper Salmon, the East Fork Salmon River, and substantial amounts of adjacent upland. The survey identified roughly 125 sites, 42 with stone structures such as talus pits or hunting blinds with Middle or Late period affiliations. They located lithic scatters at high elevation springs, or on knolls and saddles in areas above 2,700 meters above sea level. The nature and pattern of sites suggests the significance of mountain sheep hunting. Elko corner-notched points (n=17)(1500 to 500 B.C.) outnumbered other point types.

Test excavations have yielded evidence of relatively heavy use of quarry sites in the high elevation uplands of eastern tributaries of the Upper Salmon. Rossillion (1982) notes several quarries in the upper Salmon and Pahsimeroi river areas. Site 10CR60 (elevation 7,800 ft.) includes occupations dating to between 5800 and 1000 B.C. (Haskett, Pinto, and Elko points). Three charcoal samples date between 1700 and 2900 B.C. The site contained evidence suggestive of quarrying locally available lithics (multi-colored cherts) as well as hunting for marmot, bison, mountain sheep, deer, and antelope (Miss and Anderson 1984).

Butler's 1974 excavations at 10CR322, adjacent to the Late period Challis Bison Jump site, revealed three strata, each apparently with some evidence of bison hunting: Stratum 1, after 130 ± 70 B.C.; Stratum 2, 2220 ± 90 B.C.; Stratum 3, 3380 ± 90 B.C. (Epperson 1977). At Boulder Creek, occupations with Elko points may date as early as 2,000 years ago. However, radiocarbon dates begin at about A.D. 1, and later Rose Spring, and large Northern Side-notched point types also derive from the shallow camp desposits. A great variety of chert (62%) as well as rhyolite (27%), and some exotic obsidian (12%), vitrophyre, and basalt comprise the lithic materials identified. Most obsidian came from Timber Butte but Yellowstone Park's Obsidian Cliff provided lesser quantities. Highly fragmented mountain sheep remains indicate the processing of bone for grease or collagen.

Pippin and Davis (1980) reinventoried the Island Park Reservoir during low water levels and tested six sites where occupation begins after 4000 B.C. and large ovens indicate vegetable processing (pine nuts or root cooking?) by 3000 B.C. Use of the Centennial Mountains began by 6000 B.C. (J.A. McDonald 1982; Murray, Keyser, and Sharrock 1977; D.G. Roberts 1976; Sims 1979). Reconnaissance has identified hundreds of limited activity sites and base camps. The Warm Spring Creek (Kimball 1976) vicinity includes nine high-elevation ignimbrite quarry sites where biface blanks were being manufactured after 1000 B.C.

Adaptations

Throughout the Middle period the frequency of identifiable and presumably chronologically sensitive materials increases, and their distribution expands into more diverse habitats. Several factors may account for the perceived expansion. Thoms (1989:14–43) provides a summary of models used to explain the process of intensification; most tend to emphasize environmental attributes or population pressure. One useful perspective presumes initial low population densities

gradually increasing to the point of resource depletion for a particular subsistence strategy. (Environmental change could produce similar resource stress with no increase in population.) To sustain population some form of intensification must take place. Intensification may result from more efficient use of preferred resources, by extending the subsistence quest to include lower order resources, reducing competition for existing resources, incorporating previously unused habitats into the subsistence round, or some combination of all. A second explanation contends that a combination of differential preservation and exposure has led to the perception that later materials occur in greater quantities and in more diverse habitats.

From the beginning of the Early Middle period (5000 B.C.) the Eastern Plateau saw forests increase at the expense of grasslands. Between 3600 and 2400 B.C. lower summer temperatures may have led to an increase of alpine and subalpine vegetation at high elevations. Forest density in the Eastern Plateau achieved its maximum extent between 2400 and 2000 B.C. The interval 2000 to 500 B.C. saw game populations at a Holocene low because of complete forest closure and lowered fire frequency. Increased alpine habitats may have supported larger populations of well adapted species such as mountain sheep and mountain goats. If present, alpine caribou might have flourished but their presence remains conjectural. A single archeological attribution, from 24LN700 on Lake Koocanusa, consists of a right maxillary fragment "tentatively identified as *Rangifer*" (Olson 1984:229).

Expanded forest would diminish ungulate carrying capacity, forcing human populations to direct their attentions on those areas retaining high capacity, in particular, the reduced grasslands of the valley bottoms, the enlarged alpine-subalpine zones of the mountain crests, and the remaining south-facing open, grassy slopes. The perceived increase of Middle period occupations into different habitats through time may correlate with environmental changes. Munger (1993:48) explicitly comments that apparent use of the high-country of the Bitterroot Range, does not begin until about 2500 B.C. He attributes this "first systematic use of the timberline in western Montana" to the reestablishment of whitebark pine and its availability as a nut resource during the Late Middle period. Reduced grassland area would concentrate people in areas to which they and their prey were habituated, both in the valley bottoms and grassy mountainside clearings. Expanded alpine-subalpine habitat and increased populations of sheep, goats, or caribou would attract people to areas of previously low capacity. Having established utilization of these diverse habitats intensification of plant resources such as pine nuts, bitterroot, biscuitroot, and camas in appropriate settings might well provide for populations that would otherwise have exceeded the reduced capacity of their traditional territory.

The above scenario has little supporting data other than the observed distribution of presumably chronologically sensitive lithic cultural items. Limited physical evidence exists at this time that supports a widespread Middle period resource intensification focused on plant foods. Positive testimony comes from the Calispell Valley on the Pend Oreille River in eastern Washington. Using a radiocarbon database of 85 dates from features identified as camas ovens, or other features that yielded camas remains as a measure, Thoms (1989:444) indicates that a "regular use" interval of camas processing in the Calispell Valley began by 3500 B.C. with a period of "initial intensification" between 1500 and 500 B.C. His data show a marked decrease, an "intensification nadir," between 500 B.C. and A.D. 500 after which camas exploitation apparently increases to achieve a period of "final intensification" that lasts for nearly 1,500 years (Thoms 1989:445). Thoms (1989:247–276) addresses the problem of identifying camas exploitation from archeological data. He concludes "except for the actual remains of camas, few other cultural materials are likely to be diagnostic of camas exploitation."

Few would argue that the people of the Eastern Plateau did not utilize the large mammals of the area, but their remains occur in archeological contexts in relatively small numbers. Hunting practices, quarry, carcass size, and physiography all figure into the equation. Individual or small group hunts do not produce large kill middens. Solitary or small herd quarry also limit the amount of bone deposited at a kill. Small carcass size permits ready transport to desired localities for dismemberment and subsequent additional processing. Difficult terrain encourages transportation of small rather than larger packages to base camps. Extensive processing by smashing and stone boiling for acquisition of bone grease and collagen may reduce the bony parts to nearly unidenfitiable fragments. In addition to these factors, the regular churning of often shallow coniferous forest soils by both plants and animals as well as by geomorphic processes further contributes to questionable contextual integrity and degredation of bone remains. These represent only a few of the forces that obscure the faunal contribution to prehistoric diets.

Late Prehistoric Period, A.D. 500–1750

Kootenai–Pend Oreille Region

Everywhere in the Eastern Plateau the introduction of the bow and arrow, as indicated by distinctive small side-notched and corner-notched projectile points (fig. 7), marks the beginning of the Late Prehistoric period. Through at least the eastern two-thirds of the Kootenai-Pend Oreille region specimens consistent with the Avonlea type (fig. 7 c–d) on the Northern Plains appear sometime after A.D. 500. (Roll 1988). In either the side-notched or corner-notched Avonlea form the knapper first formed a thin flake blank into an isosceles triangle with excurvate isosceles margins and then placed very shallow hafting notches near the base

of the blade. While the Middle Kootenai valley has yielded the greatest concentration to date, other documented sites occur in Montana near the mouth of the Flathead River, on the Blackfoot River east of Missoula, on the Clark Fork near Saint Regis, Montana, and on the west slope of the Mission Range near Saint Ignatius. Projectile points from collections on Lake Pend Oreille appear to lie within the range of variation of Avonlea (Miss and Hudson 1986:25, fig. 7, 54–59). Most of these materials come from high diversity sites (probably occupation sites) on floodplain terraces. The Lower Ramsay site, a specialized bison kill a few kilometers west of Butte, Montana, contained a mixed assemblage of Avonlea and later small side-notched projectile points.

Sometime after A.D. 1000 bow-and-arrow hunters in the Kootnai-Pend Oreille region began to replace the small stylistically homogeneous Avonlea points with slightly larger side-notched and less frequent corner-notched points. Greater notch depth and, in the instance of side-notched forms, notches placed higher on the lateral edge, distinguish these from the earlier Avonlea forms. Analogs for the Late period side-notched varieties abound throughout the western United States and Canada. Both Forbis (1960) and Kehoe (1966) have proposed typologies for the small side-notched points of the Northern Plains. Neither scheme has received universal adoption and many regional archeologists simply lump the various forms into a loose "Old Women's" category after Reeves' (1970) Old Women's phase. Elsewhere archeologists label similar specimens found in the Great Basin Desert Side-notched (Thomas 1981) or in the Plateau, Plateau Side-notched (Lohse 1985).

Small, corner-notched projectile point forms appear in variable frequencies throughout the Eastern Plateau. Archeologists have identified similar specimens over much of the desert west. The Rosegate series occupies a time span from A.D. 700–1300 in the Great Basin (Thomas 1981). Within the Plateau there appears a variety of small, corner-notched types identified as Columbia Corner-notched (B) and Wallula Rectangular Stemmed. Columbia Stemmed (A, B, and C) subsumes similarly sized stemmed types. Generally the small Columbia Corner-notched and Stemmed points date about A.D. 1–1800 in the Rufus Woods Lake projectile point chronology (Lohse 1985). Some evidence seems to suggest presence of these forms in the Salmon-Clearwater somewhat earlier than elsewhere. The Basin Creek site obsidian hydration dates of 400 B.C. to A.D. 250 associate with small corner-notched points (Towner 1986). These dates correspond with hydration dates from the Middle Fork Salmon and support the suggestion that the Rose Spring (now Rosegate) small corner-notched points may date somewhat earlier than previously recognized (Webster 1978; Hackenberger 1988) An emerging frequency gradient seems to indicate greater abundance with location south or west and comparative rarity with distance north and east. Small corner-notched forms occur in approximately equal numbers with small side-notched throughout the Salmon-Clearwater (fig. 8). In the vicinity of Lake Coeur d'Alene and Lake

Pend Oreille the ratio of small corner-notched to small side-notched resembles that of the Salmon-Clearwater. The frequency of small corner-notched points decreases to the east until they represent a marginal percentage in the upper tributaries of the Clark Fork and Flathead rivers. Predictably, the upper Bitterroot, because of proximity to the headwaters of the Salmon-Clearwater, demonstrates an increase in the ratio of Late period corner-notched and side-notched point types.

In almost all contexts deer or deer-sized mammals dominate the Late Prehistoric period faunal inventories. During this same time interval the assemblages start to contain a bit more diversity. A few elements of bison figure in the faunal assemblages from several sites. The Eagle Bend site near Bigfork, Montana, and the County Line site on the Blackfoot River west of Ovando both contained elements attributed to bison. Bison was the most commonly identified species, but the total number remained low (Cameron 1984:147). The Lower Ramsay kill dated to A.D. 1260 ± 120 (RL-951) (Davis 1982). This sole unquestionable communal bison kill in the Kootenai-Pend Oreille region contained mixed Avonlea and other Late Prehistoric period assemblages. The absence of a cliff or drop, the concentrated nature of the deposits, and the excavators' discovery of several post molds suggest the use of a containing corral or pound (Jewell Werner, personal communication 1993). A small site on Fred Burr Creek south of Phillipsburg, Montana, contains a diverse Late Prehistoric period assemblage that includes Avonlea points and bison remains, but the association remains uncertain. Bison also appeared at this time or a bit earlier in the Kootenay and Elk River valleys in southern British Columbia. Butchered bison bone from DjPv-14 "1 km northeast of the confluence of the Wildhorse and Kootenay Rivers" contributed a radiocarbon date of A.D. 1390 ± 190 (RIDDL-245) (Choquette 1987:113–114). Clearly, bison roamed the grassy valleys throughout the upper Kootenai-Pend Oreille region.

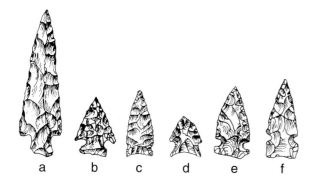

after Roll 1982: figs. 5.13, 5.14, 5.16, and 5.17 and Thoms 1984: fig. 12–2.
Fig. 7. Late period projectile points from the Kootenai–Pend Oreille region: a, corner-removed point from site 24LN1073; b, corner-notched point from site 24LN684; c–d, Avonlea-like points from sites 24LN1125 and 24LN10; e–f, side-notched points from sites 24LN110 and 24LN1125. Length of a, 6 cm; others to same scale.

Whether they ever figured prominently in the prehistoric subsistence quest of that region remains a significant question.

Salmon-Clearwater Region

• WEISER, PAYETTE, AND BOISE RIVERS Great Basin point types and Great Basin–derived pottery characterize the most intensive episode of site use in the Horseshoe Bend area. This interval of intensive use occurred between 500 B.C. and A.D. 1000 (Lewarch, Benson, and Miss 1988). Arnold (1984) also argues that the most intensive period of settlement in upper Long Valley occurs after A.D. 1. He draws attention to obsidian hydration dates from the Van Wyck Creek site component (200 B.C. and A.D. 650) where Great Basin Pinto-like stemmed points appear contemporaneous with small side- notched and corner-notched points. In the upper Boise River Basin the second of two periods of intensified settlement at Lydell Gulch (Sappington 1981) and the Dry Creek Rockshelter (Webster 1978) occurs between 500 B.C. and A.D. 500. Webster (1978) argues that small corner-notched points of the Rose Spring series characterize the period and that these points may represent one of the earliest occurrences of the type in the Great Basin.

• CLEARWATER RIVER Sappington (1990, 1991, 1994), and Sappington and Carley (1983, 1986) have reported on test excavations at the mouth of the North Fork at Ahsahka. The Fish Hatchery site (10CW4) contains multiple components that date from about 1000 B.C. to historic times (Sappington 1988; Brauner 1990). Artifacts include numerous cutting tools, cobble tools and anvils, and pestles; and most test units contained widely distributed fire-cracked rock. The majority of poorly preserved faunal remains exhibits evidence of burning. Brauner (1990) and Sappington (1994) identified house features. Sappington (1990a, 1991, 1991a, 1994) documented both Late Tucannon phase materials and Harder phase house occupations (500 B.C.–A.D. 100) at the Ahsahka Boat Ramp (10CW5) and Maggies Bend (101H-10009). A set of 30 radiocarbon dates includes several samples from house deposits that date to roughly 300 B.C. Deer remains dominate the faunal inventory, although meat weight estimates from six elk and five bison elements exceed the estimated weight of deer meat. Extensive areas of fire-cracked rock may represent refuse from stone boiling, or large smoking and drying hearths. Whitaker (1992) reviewed the radiocarbon database for most of the above occupations.

Occupations at the Kooskia Bridge site (10-IH-1395) date between 500 B.C. and A.D. 1300. A date from a house floor suggests occupation at about A.D. 1250 + 50. The most intensive occupation took place between A.D. 1300 and 1700. A historic component correlates with a Nez Perce village of 1891. Numerous tools include bifacially flaked tools, cobble and spall tools, and pestles. Deer dominate

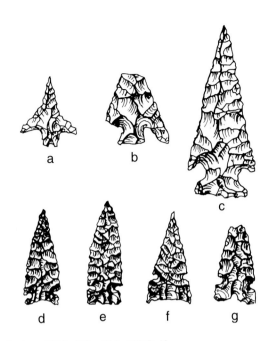

after Sappington 1994: fig. 7.15 and Butler 1971: fig. 16.

Fig. 8. Late period projectile points from the Salmon-Clearwater region. top, Corner-notched points from the Clearwater Fish Hatchery site; bottom, side-notched points from the Challis Bison Jump site. Length of top left, 2 cm; others to same scale.

faunal remains, which also include river mussel and salmonids. Excavations documented several fire-cracked rock features and one burial (Sappington and Carley 1987).

• SALMON RIVER   A long history of survey and site inventory activity (Harrison 1972; Swanson 1958, 1958a, 1958b, 1958c, 1958d, 1958e, 1959; Swanson, Tuhoy, and Bryan 1959; Sawnson, King, and Chatters 1969; Price 1982; Swisher 1973; Sisson 1980, 1983, 1984, 1985; Sisson and Conca 1988; Miss 1990) deserves credit for the majority of Late period sites recorded in the Salmon River basin. Surveys along the Middle Fork Salmon and Big Creek included those conducted by Swanson (1958, 1958e, 1959), Dahlstrom (1972), Pavesic (1978), Knudson et al. (1982), Kulesza (1982a), and Leonhardy and Johnston (1984).

Hackenberger, Sisson, and Womack (1989) compare prehistoric household and community sizes along the Middle Snake, Salmon, and Middle Fork Salmon rivers. The confluence of the South Fork Salmon and Salmon rivers appears as a major locus of house pit settlements with over 110 houses (Harrison 1972; Ranere 1971; Price 1982). The South Fork Salmon has received only limited inventory and testing (Ranere 1971; Wylie and Ketchum 1978; Rebillett 1981). Large houses (5–10 m diameter) in small clusters along the Middle Snake and Lower Salmon rivers may reflect extended families and multiseason or year residential bases of small groups of collectors (10 to 50 people). Small houses (4 m diameter) in small and large clusters along the Middle Salmon and Middle Fork Salmon suggest nuclear families and single-season or year residence of mobile groups (10 to 100 people). Total numbers of house features

(approximately 1,400) and estimates of short (1–2 years) house occupation length suggest average regional populations of less than 280 people per year during the last 1,000 years. Either house feature occupations lasted for as long as 100 to 200 years per feature, or local groups maintained populations at normally low densities. Swanson (1958) attributed the Middle Fork great significance due to the large numbers of Late period rock ring sites.

Archeologists have performed few excavations of house features and none of rock ring features on the Salmon or Middle Fork Salmon rivers. On the Double House site one small circular and one small oblong house feature date to between A.D. 1 and 1650, and a similar but larger pair of house features date as recent as 1750 or 1850 (Butler 1978a). The later houses include hopper mortar bases and small side-notched points. Cobble tools, ground stone, and antler wedges also appear in the artifact assemblages found in the houses, and deer and mussel shell dominate the faunal remains. Pine Bar (10IH396), Russel Bar (10IH57–58), and Hammer Creek (10IH60) appear to contain Harder phase occupations (post 500 B.C.) with flaked and ground stone tools, mussel shell, and bone (Boreson 1979; Sisson 1985).

Along the lower Salmon, Swisher (1973) recorded longhouses (30–35 ft.) for three sites, a plank house with four compartments (each about 12 by 12 ft.) and "Shoshone" pottery found with rock-ring features. Chalcedony corner-notched points outnumber obsidian side-notched points, and projectile point neck widths correspond with those suggested for Sahaptin affiliation (Corliss 1972). Warren and Fitzwater (1963) discovered burials, storage pits, and house depressions. Historic burials included trade items. Hill (1974) tested 10NP107 along the lower Salmon, where a collector discovered over 1,300 points and basket fragments from caches. One of two tested "house" depressions contained large quantities of animal bone and the other contained a hearth and associated tools. A house depression (6 by 7 m) at 10NP124 produced artifacts in association with ash lenses, hearths, and at least four floors. Historic artifacts characterize the most recent floor; the two lowest floors contained hearths. Sites 10NP128 and 129 consisted of shell and bone midden (20–30 cm deep) with cobble tools, net weights, and flaked tools. Oswald (1975) assigned similar occupations at Slate Creek (10IH94) a date of 1350. Assemblages on the Lower Salmon reveal diverse sources of stone (Markos et al. 1990).

Big Creek Cave deposits revealed 11 undecorated brown-gray pottery sherds in the top 20 centimeters of sediments estimated to date 500–1500 (Owl Creek and Corn Creek phases) (Wylie, Scott, and Gallagher 1981). Mountain sheep, deer, and elk dominate the faunal remains. Salmon vertebra indicate the presence of a chinook salmon and three other salmon ranging from 30 to 5 pounds (Manion 1981:2). At Waterfall Village (10SL267) an excavated house feature dated A.D. 1250 ± 70. Upper levels contained small side-notched points and high frequencies of obsidian; lower lev-

Fig. 9. Fire-cracked rock feature at site 24LN1125. These concentrations of discarded boiling stones are commonly found at Late Middle and Late period sites on the Eastern Plateau. Photograph by Tom E. Roll, 1979.

els (floor or subfloor) contained small corner-notched points and higher frequencies and cherts and quartzites (Wylie, Scott, and Gallagher 1981). Occupations of nearby 10VY31 began by A.D. 1; however, relatively intensive occupation with house features (fig. 10) occurred between 750 and 1650 (Leonhardy 1987), Late Owl Creek and Corn Creek phases. The floor of one burned house feature contained a complete tool kit of points, knives, scrapers, and worked flakes. Relatively intense occupation at Corn Creek with at least one human burial continued from 650 to at least 1450. The greatest frequencies of bone fragments associated with layers dated between 1100 and 1200. Mountain sheep dominate the faunal remains in all levels and features at Corn Creek (Holmer and Ross 1985) and 10VY31 (F. Thomas 1988).

Fourteen radiocarbon dates refer to house features from the Middle Salmon near the Middle Fork confluence; those along the Middle Fork and Big Creek date to two centuries before or after A.D. 1000. Prior to the availability of these

dates Swanson (1972) hypothesized that the house features belonged to the relatively early Bitterroot culture (possibly the Bitterroot phase?). Butler (1978a) conjectured that the house occupations related to protohistoric Nez Perce who abandoned the area following adoption of the horse. Hackenberger (1988) hypothesized two separate periods of intensified settlement, the second characterized by the use of small shallow houses. These periods are: 500 B.C. to A.D. 1 (identified by obsidian hydration dates of small corner-notched and side-notched points), and A.D. 1150 to 1350 (based on mean of radiocarbon-dated house features). Both periods may correspond with warm, dry periods during which increased ungulate availability would characterize forested valleys. Hackenberger (1988) also hypothesizes that ancestral Numic peoples occupied central Idaho by 500 B.C. and may have established the first regular year-round settlement of the Middle Fork Salmon River Basin (Butler 1979, 1981, 1981a, 1983, vol. 11:127–134). The Basin Creek site obsidian hydration dates of 400 B.C. to A.D. 250 associate with small corner-notched points (Towner 1986). These dates correspond with hydration dates from the Middle Fork Salmon and support the suggestion that the Rose Spring small corner-notched points may date to earlier periods than previously recognized (Webster 1978; Hackenberger 1988). Upland Mountain sites probably reflect mountain sheep hunting and white bark pine nut harvesting (Hackenberger 1988; Manger 1993).

Pictographs occur throughout the Snake and Salmon river basins ("Rock Art," figs. 6–7, this vol.). They commonly portray human and animal stick figures, and dots and dashes in red paint on smooth rock faces of overhangs and shelters (Boreson 1975, 1976, 1979; Leen 1988; Knudson et al. 1982; Kulesza 1982a). They depict elk, deer, mountain sheep, dogs, bows, and at least in one instance a mounted horseman with a possible rifle. The greatest concentration of pictographs outside the Snake River and Hells Canyon occurs on the Middle Fork. Between Big Creek and the Salmon River prehistoric people created numerous pictographs. Talus pits also appear frequently throughout the Snake and Salmon River basin and very commonly along the Middle Fork (especially between Pungo and Bernard creeks) and in the Upper Salmon River Basin. These may have served as hunting blinds or food caches.

• UPPER SALMON BASIN AND BIRCH CREEK   Swanson, King, and Chatters (1969) identified several sites with probable housepits between Challis and Salmon, Idaho. They suggested that the combined area of the Upper Salmon and the Big Lost River served as a principal winter occupation area and pathway between the Salmon and Snake rivers and that people used valleys to the east primarily for seasonal (spring and fall) hunting and gathering base camps (Swanson, King, and Chatters 1969:33). According to Swanson (1972) the Lemhi phase was distinguished by use of Yellowstone obsidian and increased procurement of bison. This suggested to them that occupants entered the valleys from the Upper Snake River and Yellowstone Plateau.

At the Challis Bison Jump site (10CR196) Butler (1972) identified five stratigraphic layers in a two-meter deep trench, but only Layer 1 contained cultural materials. The excavations found limited evidence for butchering implements and disclosed numerous (n=74) small side-notched points. Historic trade beads suggest the kill postdates 1840. Site 10CR197, a small cavity associated with the Challis Jump, yielded small corner-notched points, bison, and mountain sheep in Stratum 2 (A.D. 680 + 90).

Chatters (1982) infers that sites located in the upland steppe of the Pahsimeroi Valley reflect relatively large (average about 900 sq. m) summer or fall sites between 500 B.C. and A.D. 350, medium (average 700 sq. m) size sites between A.D. 350 and 1250, and small camps (average 240 sq. m) after 1250. Chatters based his site chronology on statistical refinements of the relative point chronology proposed by Swanson (1972). The earlier larger camps

may represent fall hunting camps during periods of more moderate fall and winter weather when larger ungulate populations may have used the high elevation valley. Shifts from communal hunting of mountain sheep and antelope before 1250 to summer hunting of bison by small task groups thereafter may explain decreases in site size through time. Chatters argues that bison populations increased due to climatically induced improvements in summer grass productivity at high elevations. Palynological evidence from Bisonweh Pond correlates with tree-ring records and documents improved grass productivity, while faunal remains from Buck Creek Cave suggest increased animal populations.

The unique high elevation East Fork Lookout site (10-CR-358) includes a rhyolite quarry, talus pits (hunting blinds or cache pits) and two possible house features. One of these features has a circular wall (2 m diameter) laid three courses high; the second more pitlike feature (3.3 m diameter) has fragments of Douglas fir "beams" protruding from its "wall." A wood fragment subjected to radiocarbon analysis dated to A.D. 1340 ± 70 (Butler 1978:73).

Fig. 10. Excavations at site 10VY31, a Late period housepit site on Big Creek, a tributary of the Salmon River, Idaho. top, River terrace on which the site is located; bottom, exposed remains of a pit dwelling showing burned beams arranged in a roughly circular shape. Photographs by Robbin Johnston, 1984.

Conclusion

Archeologists have argued that locally adapted mountain populations semi-independent from extraregional diffusions and migrations characterize the Middle and Late Prehistoric periods. Population growth and riverine settlement intensification continued throughout the Middle and Late Prehistoric periods. In the Early Middle Prehistoric period, cool, moist conditions that improved plant and ungulate resource availability in areas of upland steppe promoted seasonal, and in some areas year-round, upland settlement. However, whether upland steppe settlement in the mid-Late and early-Late period relates to increased upland resources due to cool, moist conditions, or reduced riverine resources caused by warm, dry conditions remains uncertain. Warm, dry periods in the mid-Late period probably reduced upland resource availability and promoted intensified settlement of lower river valleys accompanied by intensive utilization of reduced salmonid runs in the Salmon-Clearwater region. It is not yet clear if the population consolidation and intensified plant resource use is related to climatic changes, population growth, or technolog-ical innovations in root processing. Cool, moist temperatures at about 2000 B.C. may relate to increased plant productivity that permits storage for semipermanent winter house settlements. It is also possible that cool, moist temperatures may simply have required more substantial forms of winter housing. More frequent or longer spring and summer occupations in the uplands should coincide with more intensive utilization of plant resources during the early-middle period, regardless of the mitigating conditions.

It apears that population and settlement intensity continued to grow throughout the Middle and Late prehistoric periods on the Northern Plains as on the Plateau. An exception may exist in the case of the Late Middle period. Mulloy (1952, 1958) was among the first to suggest a trend toward broad-spectrum foraging in the Late Middle Prehistoric period on the Northern Plains and to suggest possible climatic correlates for this trend. Settlement intensification in the upper valleys of the Rocky Mountain edge appears between A.D. 200 and 700. These trends apparently manifested themselves among the Late Prehistoric inhabitants of the Kootenai-Pend Oreille region where strong similarities exist with the valley extensions of the Northern Plains.

137

History Until 1846

DEWARD E. WALKER, JR. AND RODERICK SPRAGUE

Protohistoric Period

The protohistoric is the period between the first introduction of nonaboriginal influences and the first recorded historic contact with non-Indian people. The dates have been set between about 1600 and 1750. Protohistoric developments stemming from the impact of the horse, epidemic disease, trade goods, and Christian missionaries had similar transformational effects throughout much of the Northern (Canadian) and Southern (United States) Plateau.

Trade goods were noted in 1805 by Meriwether Lewis and William Clark. They found Spanish coins, blue beads, copper kettles, knowledge of many other goods and practices, and perhaps most importantly, a knowledge of White men (Thwaites 1904–1905; Moulton 1983–). Some Plateau inhabitants claimed to have traded at the British posts in Alberta, at the Spanish settlements in New Mexico, and with seagoing traders along the Northwest Coast. Plateau inhabitants taken in slave raids sometimes were traded far from their homes and later returned, bringing knowledge of the Whites. Like Sacagawea, a Nez Perce woman was captured in a slave raid and traded farther east, eventually becoming the wife of a French fur trader. Returning to her people years later, she was named Watkuese (*wetxuwi·s*) 'returned one'.

The most dramatic new influence during the protohistoric period was the introduction of fatal epidemic diseases. The subsequent decimation of Plateau populations brought many changes as evidenced by altered burial practices, a heightened concern with death, and new religious practices. For example, protohistoric burials reveal a dramatic increase in the number and variety of grave goods. New burial practices included using canoes, cedar cists, fenced burials, and log enclosures. The burial position of the body was changed from a uniform flexed orientation to either a flexed or extended position, oriented to the east or west. Later in the historic period, the orientation was to the west for Christian converts, and east for nonconverts (Sprague 1967). The practice of sacrificing a horse at the grave of the deceased owner was introduced during the protohistoric period. There was an increased use of cremation, and often there were multiple burials consisting of infants and children, generally thought to reflect the toll of the epidemics that swept the Plateau during this period (Walker 1969).

The earliest date for the first epidemics is thought to be the late sixteenth century. Campbell (1989) argues for a sixteenth-century epidemic based on discontinuities in the archeological record at selected sites in the Northwest. The small size of the sample and the limited evidence makes her case stimulating, but not convincing.

Somewhat less certain are the sources of protohistoric epidemics. The first wave of smallpox probably came from the west via ships exploring for furs along the northern Pacific coast, rather than the well-documented epidemic up the Missouri River in the 1780s that swept across the Plains (Boyd 1985:81–90). From this time forward, the dates of epidemics are fairly well established. For example, smallpox swept throughout the Columbia Basin in 1801. Such epidemics eliminated whole groups in some cases, and generally reduced the population by as much as a half overall (Boyd 1985).

In their 1805 journals, Lewis and Clark describe old men with pockmarked faces among the Chinookans of the Lower Columbia River, where they were told that the disease had struck a generation before (Thwaites 1904–1905, 4:241; Boyd 1985:78–80, 91–92, 102–103). Asa Bowen Smith documented the impact of smallpox among the Nez Perce as early as the 1780s (Drury 1958:136). Smallpox epidemics throughout the Plateau occurred numerous times, striking as late as 1853 when one such epidemic was documented by the railroad survey party (McClellan 1855). The fatality rate of one epidemic of *Variola major* has been estimated at 30 percent in previously unexposed populations. With its intricate web of kin and intergroup relations and riverine settlement patterns (Anastasio 1972), the Plateau people were quickly infected with these epidemics. The horse also accelerated the spread of epidemic diseases, especially in the Southern Plateau. The relative geographical isolation of Northern Plateau groups, such as the Shuswap, may have limited the impact of the epidemics in that region.

First encounters with the horse by Plateau inhabitants have been recorded by several authorities (Teit 1930:350–352; Haines 1938a:434–436), and they are recounted in various oral traditions of the Plateau tribes. Haines (1938, 1938a) traced the spread of horses from the Spanish colonies in what is now New Mexico, especially after the Pueblo Revolt of 1680 (Spicer 1962), when many Spanish horses were set free. The Navajo, Apache, Kiowa, Comanche, Ute, and others quickly acquired these horses and traded them northward

138

along existing trade routes. The Northern Shoshone in southern Idaho had horses by the 1700s, as did the Southern Plateau tribes. It is likely that this process of acquiring horses from Spanish settlements in the south and trading them northward from California was repeated numerous times. During the historic period horses were acquired from the Mormon settlements.

Most Plateau bands, especially the Cayuse, Nez Perce, Palouse, and various Yakima groups, were quick to recognize the utility of the horse. Their territory contained some of the best horse country in the world, with lush grasses and excellent wintering areas producing what Lewis and Clark recorded as large herds of horses. These observations were repeated by historical observers such as Isaac I. Stevens, who estimated 20,000 horses in the Umatilla, Cayuse, and Walla Walla tribes around 1855. Influential families owned herds of more than 1,000 selectively bred horses (Osborne 1955). Large numbers of horses provided a ready source of wealth and were used by the leaders to attract large followings. Horses were also a source of spirit power in their own right.

Owning horses changed Plateau life in many ways. Greater mobility expanded the seasonal round, enabled people to travel greater distances, and provided transport for heavier loads (Stern 1993:33). Tribal gatherings on an unprecedented scale became common. The size of local groupings increased significantly as well (Ray 1960). Wealth differences among tribal members became evident, giving rise to an incipient social class system of rank that resembled that described for the tribes of the northern Great Basin (Stewart 1965). Horses also expanded tribal knowledge of regions well beyond the Plateau, with the greatest attraction being the rich bison resources of the western Plains. Even before the adoption of the horse, the Nez Perce and other tribes occasionally would journey over the Rocky Mountains to hunt bison in this favored region.

Following Ray (1939), Anastasio (1972) described the tribalization that occurred in the eastern Plateau due to the horse. Formerly autonomous villages and bands joined together becoming composite bands. Composite bands combined into larger, multitribal task groupings in order to counteract the power of the Blackfoot Confederacy on the Northwestern Plains and the Northern Shoshone–Bannock in the northern Great Basin. For example, the Flathead unified into a single group by the late eighteenth century. Then they began to forge even broader political alliances for mutual defense with neighboring groups, the Pend d'Oreille, Kootenai, and sometimes even the Northern Shoshone–Bannock. While the horse culture spread rapidly throughout the Southern Plateau during the protohistoric period, its influence was less significant in the Northern Plateau. Nevertheless, the horse brought major transformations for virtually all Plateau tribes during this period.

The horse provided an increased incentive to engage in warfare. Mounted war parties could strike enemies at greater distances and with greater force than ever before. A war party on horseback could easily defeat a much greater number of men on foot. Predictably, this new style of warfare was especially evident on the eastern and southern peripheries of the Plateau, as well as in the neighboring northeastern Great Basin. By 1800 the Northern Plains had become a scene of perpetual equestrian conflict as the mounted Shoshone left the Great Basin to pursue a life of raiding and buffalo hunting, ultimately going as far as Canada. The Blackfoot, with both firearms and horses, began their own campaign of expansion and drove the Shoshone to the south and west, thereby establishing their dominance in the Northwestern Plains by 1750–1800. In some cases, the Blackfoot nearly annihilated competing groups such as the Flathead and Kootenai. Portions of these groups had formerly resided on the western Plains, but they were driven west of the continental divide by 1800. The Blackfoot decimated other tribes by traveling in large groups under military discipline with superior armaments and by deploying a large number of remounts. Plateau groups ultimately retaliated with similar tactics and by allying with groups such as the Crow, who helped resist the Blackfoot Confederacy.

By the time of the Lewis and Clark expedition, the situation had become critical for certain Blackfoot enemies, especially for the easternmost Plateau groups. Also at this time, the Nez Perce and Cayuse were being challenged in their traditional hunting grounds in the Blue Mountains of Oregon, south of the Columbia River, by Northern Shoshone and Bannock raiding parties. Although Plateau warfare was mostly against external adversaries, groups like the Nez Perce and Cayuse occasionally raided tribes at The Dalles, as well as certain interior Salishan groups. However, this internal Plateau conflict was on a small scale.

Increased military activity by the Blackfoot against external adversaries during the protohistoric period had several important effects in the Plateau. To bring about safety, villages consolidated into bands, bands into composite bands, and composite bands into even larger regional task groups, especially along the eastern and southern edges of the Plateau. Military prowess quickly became an important factor in political leadership. War chiefs and warrior societies developed as the Blackfoot continued to raid deep into the eastern Plateau and northeastern Great Basin. These raids went on well into the historic period.

By the time of the protohistoric period most of the Plateau groups were also enmeshed in a widespread trade network connecting them with other groups throughout the west (Anastasio 1972; Stern 1993; Walker 1967). Trade centers such as The Dalles and Kettle Falls saw large intertribal gatherings during the protohistoric period with roots in the prehistoric period. Even though all Plateau groups relied on similar substantive resources, there were sufficient regional variations to make trade within the Plateau both desirable and necessary. Traditional trading partnerships were reinforced by systematic intermarriage, travel by horse, regular trade fairs, and regional economic specialization. This traditional system of trade formed the basis for the later fur trade, which enriched an already established system (Stern 1993). The Flathead, Nez Perce, Yakima, and other Plateau inhabitants participated in the Shoshone rendezvous held annually in southwestern Wyoming (vol. 11:504). They also participated at the trade centers along the Upper Missouri River and in the Boise Valley. Here they met people from tribes of the west, including Ute traders who offered knives, mules, saddles, and other goods from the Spanish settlements in New Mexico (vol. 11:512–513). Goods acquired from the Plains were exchanged throughout the Plateau, especially buffalo robes, pipestone, and sweetgrass. Some of these goods reached Northwest Coast groups by way of both Chinook traders from the Lower Columbia River and Yakima and Klikitat traders from across the Cascade Mountains.

The Walla Walla, Cayuse, and Yakima also opened a long-distance trade route with the Spaniards in California during the late eighteenth century. Horses, buffalo robes, parfleches, dried salmon, and dentalium shells were traded along the route that extended southward along the eastern edge of the Cascade Range into central California. These goods were bartered for slaves, bows, beads, and metal goods. Plateau tribes had reputations for raiding as well as trading on these California expeditions. Much of the human and material booty they brought back was exchanged at The Dalles with other Plateau tribes (Heizer 1942).

During the protohistoric period, there were several emigrations of Iroquois, Delawares and other easterly groups into the Plateau (vol. 15:544–546). Between 40 and 100 Iroquois emigrated to the Northwest in 1790, and there had been at least one other Iroquois emigration before that (Ewers 1948). The Iroquois were established in Saskatchewan and Alberta by 1802 and had brought Roman Catholicism with them. The Iroquois in the employment of Hudson's Bay Company were very religious, singing hymns more often than paddling songs (Ross 1855).

The continued transformation of the Plateau world was brought home forcefully in the summer of 1800 when the sky went dark all over the Plateau. A powerful volcano in the Cascade range erupted, cloaking the sun and showering the Plateau with ash for days. Ashes accumulated to several inches deep over most of the region (Miller 1985).

These and other protohistoric changes helped stimulate new religious practices among the Nez Perce, Spokane, Yakima, Colville, Northern Okanagan, Lillooet, Kootenai, Sanpoil, Nespelem, Coeur d'Alene, Flathead, Umatilla, Pend d'Oreille, Thompson, Shushwap, and other groups. These religious practices have been examined under the general heading of the Prophet Dance (Spier 1935). The idea of death and revival was widespread in the Northwest. It existed among founders of the Indian Shaker Church and later among Pentecostal groups (Walker 1985; Ruby and Brown 1989). Some individuals were thought to have died and later to have come back to life. After returning from death, these people would announce that they had journeyed to the land of the dead, received a vision, and learned a new dance and song that followers were to perform. These prophecies sometimes included predictions of the coming of the White people and other world-transforming events. The Prophet Dance had numerous Christian elements. It is very probable that epidemic disease influenced the development of the Prophet Dance (Walker 1969).

Various concepts of Christianity preceded missionaries in the Salishan tribes of the Northern Plateau (Duff 1964). Certain individuals were said to have gained knowledge through visions and by dying and returning to life after an instructive visit to the afterlife. These individuals traveled throughout the Northern Plateau haranguing their followers, instructing them, making the sign of the cross, observing the sabbath, worshiping a supreme being, and publicly confessing sins. Christian elements seem to have reached the Interior Salish from both the Pacific coast and the Southern Plateau and to have become integrated into their beliefs very quickly during the protohistoric period.

The Interior Salish Prophet Dance included the worship of a deity, an inspired leader or prophet, and public confession of sins. It also included a circular dance in which the entire community participated, plus a marriage dance. Its millennial purpose was to hasten the end of the world and the return of the dead to their living relatives (Suttles 1957).

In the Fraser Valley near Agassiz, British Columbia, a prophet appeared in the 1840s (Duff 1952). The prophet told of hunting in the mountains when he met three men who told him to kneel, make the sign of the cross, and pray. When he opened his eyes he saw a large church inside the mountain. It was lighted with very bright colors. The men taught him rules of conduct that would please God, while describing stoves, matches, and other marvels that White men would bring. They said that black-robed priests soon would arrive.

Exploration and the Fur Trade

Although Euro-American influences may have reached Plateau inhabitants from the Pacific coast explorations as early as the sixteenth century when the Russians and Spaniards visited the area, most authorities think of the eighteenth century as the time period when Euro-American influences first reached the Plateau. In the late eighteenth century, Britain, Russia, Spain, and the United States were competing for the Pacific Northwest (Meinig 1968; Wishart 1979). By the beginning of the nineteenth century, the United States and Britain had become the leading contenders for the region (Fuller 1931; Johansen and Gates 1967; Meinig 1968; Quimby 1948).

When Lewis and Clark reached the southern Plateau, numerous Spanish, Russian, British, and American trading vessels already were visiting the Pacific Northwest Coast (vol. 7:119–134) (Johansen and Gates 1967). British ships began annual visits to the Northwest Coast as early as 1774, and increased their visits to two per year between 1775 and 1779 (Quimby 1948).

American economic interests were first established in 1788 when Capt. Robert Gray began trade with the various coastal populations (Fuller 1931). European priests were among the Nootka as early as 1789 (Johansen and Gates 1967), and it is highly probable that certain of these Christian influences diffused eastward into the interior within short order, perhaps accompanied by epidemic disease and other Euro-American influences.

The period of initial exploration by Euro-Americans in the Plateau began with the arrival of the westbound Lewis and Clark expedition in late September 1805, culminating with the start of the fur trade in 1811–1812. Accompanied by a Lemhi Northern Shoshone guide, Sacagawea, the Lewis and Clark party encountered the Nez Perce at what is presently Weippe, Idaho. From there they followed Jim Ford Creek to the Clearwater River at a point just east of the present town of Orofino, Idaho. Opposite the mouth of the North Fork of the Clearwater River, the expedition camped for several weeks in September and early October of 1805. There they recovered from their ordeal in the Bitterroot Range and prepared canoes for the final phase of their journey to the Pacific. While camping near Orofino, parties investigated the surrounding area and made numerous, useful ethnographic observations concerning the Nez Perce (Sappington 1989; Ray 1971a). After entrusting their horses to the Nez Perce, the party moved down the lower Clearwater River to the lower Snake River where they passed through Palouse territory. They continued down the Columbia River through various Sahaptin-speaking groups including the Walla Walla, Cayuse, Wasco, Nez Perce, Klikitat, Umatilla, and Yakima (fig. 1).

Not only did Lewis and Clark describe the bands they contacted, but also they described other tribes of whom they had only indirect knowledge. The Chinookans demonstrated to Lewis and Clark their long familiarity with English and American traders by repeating many words of English. The Chinookan groups traded copper goods, iron knives, hatchets, files, blankets, clothes, wool and cotton cloth, and other items for Plateau dried salmon, beargrass, camas, and buffalo robes at The Dalles. Articles traded by Whites at the entrance of the Columbia River found their way up its tributaries, according to Lewis. The desire for Euro-American goods expanded the traditional trade between the Plateau and the Northwest Coast. The Lewis and Clark expedition was followed by several fur-trade explorations; the next scientific exploration, the United States Exploring Expedition, was conducted from 1838 to 1842 under Capt. Charles Wilkes (1845:464). The ethnographer for this expedition, Horatio Hale (1846:209–210), made many observations, including one concerning the Coeur d'Alene that, because they have no migratory fish and "seldom go to hunt the buffalo," their subsistence is based on "roots, game, and smaller kinds of fish."

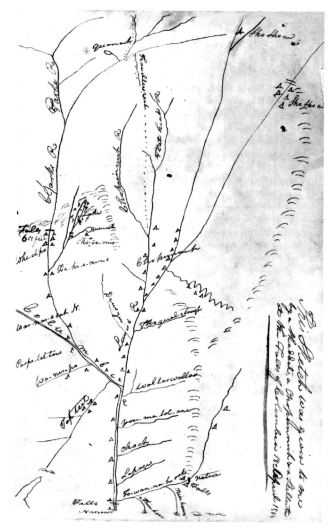

Mo. Histl. Soc., St. Louis: Voorhis #3.

Fig. 1. Confluence of Snake and Columbia rivers. Drawn by William Clark, April 1806, from information received from Nez Perce (Chopunnish), Klikitat (Skaddat), and Wasco (Skillute) informants. The triangular symbols are Indian villages.

Other valuable ethnographic observations were recorded by missionaries during the period of exploration. For example, in 1842 Father Pierre Jean de Smet traveled back and forth between the Flathead country and Fort Colville, often meeting with the Coeur d'Alene at the north end of Coeur d'Alene Lake. He also met with the Flatheads and populations resident at Kettle Falls, Washington, where the Jesuits built a mission in 1848. In 1842 Father Nicolas Point established a mission on the north bank of the St. Joe River. Based on his writings, Point had a rather low opinion of the Plateau tribes with whom he came in contact and he suggested, among other things, that one reason the Coeur d'Alene were so "lazy" was because they had plenty to eat and did not have to work (Donnelly 1967:50). In 1841 Point wrote, "the Coeur d'Alene had their great hunt, but their country, dotted with lakes and interlaced with rivers, abounds in fish no less than in game animals, so they also have their great fishing expeditions. Fishing like hunting is done almost the year around" (Donnelly 1967:174–175). Point mentioned that 180 deer were killed in one day by one group and, in turn, another group claimed that they killed 300 in six hours (Donnelly 1967:67).

After 1800 the number of visiting ships declined. Trade was conducted mainly by American ships until the Hudson's Bay Company became active on the Pacific coast. The Americans' normal process was to load their ships with trade goods such as iron, copper, brass, muskets, cloth, rum, and trinkets. Then they would sail around Cape Horn and up the Pacific coast, trade with the Indians for furs, and then sail directly to China trading the furs for a cargo of tea, spices, silk, ginger, and porcelain. Finally, they would sail for home. The motive was profit, not territorial expansion. After engaging in trade, the Americans went about their business, leaving the Indians mostly undisturbed on their land.

The first Euro-American contacts with peoples of the Northern Plateau probably came indirectly from these coastal visits and settlements at various times during the eighteenth century. Epidemics swept across the central and western parts of North America, and there is little doubt that their effects reached at least some of the tribes of the Canadian Plateau (Boyd 1985). In 1787 for example, a Captain Portlock described the effects of a smallpox attack that had occurred some years before among the Tlingit (Dixon 1789:271). In 1794 a captain recorded that there had been a severe epidemic some years before at Kaigani, and found the disease actively raging among Chief Shakes and his people at Kitkatla (Bishop 1795:105, 116). By 1835 epidemics, firearms, and alcohol had taken their toll on native traditions. Reports in early journals indicate that people in a number of areas in the Northern Plateau had suffered from smallpox epidemics, as had those of the Southern Plateau. It is difficult to judge whether the effects of the epidemics in any given instance were local or widespread.

In the Northern Plateau, a devastating smallpox epidemic occurred in 1862. It spread faster and farther than other epidemics, and within two years had reached most of British Columbia. According to some estimates, smallpox killed approximately one-third of the native inhabitants. Before this epidemic there were approximately 60,000 Indians in British Columbia, and within two to three years there were only 40,000. After 1835 the overall population trend in native populations in the Canadian and United States Plateau was one of rapid decline.

Studies of the Plateau fur trade (Chance 1973; Stern 1993) have added much to understanding this complex period involving exploration. In 1807 the first British traders of the North West Company, led by David Thompson, penetrated the Rocky Mountains and reached the Plateau. A number of trading posts were established by Thompson, who also made valuable scientific observations rivaling those of Lewis and Clark.

After a period of competition with the Pacific Fur Company from 1811–1813, the North West Company monopolized trade in the Columbia Basin until its merger with the Hudson's Bay Company in 1821. A joint occupancy agreement assured both Britain and the United States of open trapping and trading rights in the region. When the Hudson's Bay Company merged with the North West Company they inherited four Plateau trading posts. Three of these were: Flathead House, a supply depot on the Snake and Blackfoot rivers; Spokane House, abandoned in 1825 when Fort Colville was established; and Fort Nez Perces (fig. 2), a post at the confluence of the Walla Walla and Columbia (Ruby and Brown 1981; Simpson 1847).

In 1793 Alexander MacKenzie traveled up the Peace River by way of the Fraser and West Road rivers to the Pacific coast at the mouth of the Bella Coola River. He was the first White man to reach the coast overland from Canada. Other famous explorers for the North West Company were Simon Fraser who traveled down the Fraser River to the sea in 1808, and David Thompson who culminated his explorations of the Columbia River in 1811 by following it to its mouth, where he found Fort Astoria. Beginning in 1805 the North West Company founded trading posts in the northern interior, then known as New Caledonia. One of the earliest fur trading posts in the Northern Plateau was established by David Thompson and the North West Company in 1807 at Kootenai House among the Kootenai (Coues 1897, 1, 2; Tyrell 1916). The North West Company built a temporary depot at Kootenai Falls in 1808, and the following year the Company built Kullyspell House on Pend Oreille Lake and Saleesh House near Thompson Falls on the Clark Fork River (Coues 1897, 1, 2).

Donald McKenzie and Wilson P. Hunt moved through the Plateau on their overland trip to Fort Astoria, recording valuable observations about numerous tribes. In 1812 McKenzie established the only fur trading post to operate in Nez Perce country, at the confluence of the Snake and Clearwater rivers. McKenzie became discouraged by the reluctance of the Nez Perce to engage in trapping, but the Nez Perce country was not abundant in fur-bearing animals. The Nez Perce preferred hunting buffalo and engaging in war. They were described as an independent people as the horse allowed them to trade for guns and ammunition. After a year of failure, McKenzie returned to Fort Astoria.

By 1846 the fur harvest in the Columbia Basin was only a fraction of what it had been a decade before. To the north, in the Colville and New Caledonia districts of the northern Plateau, the fur trade remained profitable, but the number of furs was sharply reduced. By the 1840s, the end of the fur trade was in sight, and the Hudson's Bay Company had begun a slow exodus northward, abandoning their Columbia River holdings. A big drop in the price of beaver pelts on the world market forced the Hudson's Bay Company to enter new ventures such as production of grain, raising livestock and other agricultural goods, har-

top, Oreg. Histl Soc., Portland:4047; Smithsonian, Dept. of Anthr.: bottom left 419945, bottom right 419959.

Fig. 2. The fur trade. top, Hudson's Bay Company trading post at Walla Walla (Fort Nez Perces) with Archibald McKinlay, master, inspecting pelts displayed by Indian women. This site was chosen as a trading post because it was located near a traditional intertribal rendezvous and was near the heavily populated area around the Columbia River, which was seen as "the most hostile spot on the whole line of communication," and thus needing to be brought under control (Stern 1993:9–10). Colored pencil drawing by Joseph Drayton, 1841. bottom left, North West Company brass token imprinted with a profile of King George IV and the date of 1820 and on the other side the image of a beaver. Used as money, the token represented one beaver skin, about 50 cents. Sometimes called "skins" or "beavers," they were frequently perforated and used as ornaments (Sorensen 1974:219–222). bottom right, Phoenix buttons commonly found in archeological sites on the lower Columbia River, and infrequently on the middle Columbia River. Manufactured in England for uniforms of the regiments of King Christophe of Haiti, these buttons bear the image of a phoenix, a regiment number, and the inscription "Je renais de mes cendres" (I am born again from my ashes). After Christophe's death in 1820, the buttons and jackets they were made for were sold to traders. These buttons were probably brought to Oregon in 1832–1833 by Nathaniel Wyeth, who attempted to establish a salmon packing and trading venture on the Columbia River (Strong 1960). Collected by Herbert W. Krieger, Sullivans I., Wash., 1934. bottom left, 3 cm. bottom right, diameter of largest, 2.5 cm.

vesting timber, and especially fish for export to Russian Alaska, Britain, South America, the Far East, and elsewhere.

The impact on the aboriginal economy due to declining beaver populations, and the huge increase in demand on other furbearers has been widely examined. Jealously guarded family hunting territories were a result of the fur trade, as was growing hostility to the fur traders, which increased as fur supplies dwindled. By 1840 the tribes of the Thompson River District were said to be at war among

themselves, and Chief Factor Dr. John McLoughlin was concerned that the conflict would lead to a neglect of salmon fishing, on which the post was dependent. In 1841 Donald Manson reported that Shuswap groups between Kamloops and Alexandria, the southernmost post of New Caledonia, had repeatedly plundered, grossly insulted, and nearly murdered several of his people. Late in the autumn of 1841, chief trader Samuel Black was shot to death inside the trading post, revealing the deep tensions between the Shuswap and the fur traders.

When the Kamloops trading began, relations between traders and the Shuswap and Northern Okanagan were excellent. David Stuart and Alexander Ross, working out of the Astorian post in 1811 and 1812, described both groups as well-disposed and anxious to trade.

The fur trade had many unforeseen consequences. For example, traders were always enlisting men to assist in the trade. The traders offered rewards that enabled these men to more easily establish and maintain positions of influence in their communities. This tended to upset local political leaders. The fur trade also affected the demand and use of more advanced technology. Whereas spears had been used for killing beaver, within 10 years, at the start of the Kamloops trade, it was reported that guns and steel traps had been adopted and were the only implements in use. Guns, ammunition, iron blades for knives (fig. 3), and traps were among the most sought-after trade goods throughout the period. Other trade goods included tobacco, blankets, and brass kettles (vol. 4:340).

In 1823 American interests formed the Rocky Mountain Fur Company, but it had little effect on Plateau tribes until 1829 when Joseph Meek moved into the upper Snake River country and held a rendezvous in Pierre's Hole, on the boundary of Nez Perce country. He and other American traders drove down the prices of cargo so low that the tribes began to trade exclusively with them (Simpson 1847). American trappers and traders were soon followed by missionaries and military officers on various official survey parties. By the 1840s, small parties of American settlers were arriving via the Oregon Trail. The trickle became a flood by 1843. De Smet (1905) called the Oregon Trail the "Great Medicine Road of the Whites." With the withdrawal of the Hudson's Bay Company to Vancouver, British Columbia, major fur trading in United States Plateau country essentially came to an end. The Hudson's Bay Company was the longest enduring and most successful fur trading company in the Columbia Plateau before 1846 (Chance 1973; Fuller 1931). The Company had brought many changes to the Plateau tribes, such as metal cutting-blades replacing those of stone, bone, and shell. The gun replaced the bow and arrow, dagger, and club. Tailored clothes and blankets replaced garments and robes of bark, wool, and skin as well as the ancient techniques used in their manufacture. New forms of fishhooks and nets replaced the old, as did new paints and dyes, fire-making equipment, traps, jewelry. Even houses changed from large multifamily dwellings to smaller ones typical of Euro-Americans. Most important was the opening that the fur traders made for missionaries and later Euro-American settlers in the Plateau.

Missionaries

Throughout the Plateau, the Hudson's Bay Company promoted Christianity. They favored the Anglican Church while tolerating the Roman Catholics. In 1825, Gov. George Simpson, who was the head of the northern division of the Hudson's Bay Company, wrote to Alexander Ross, trader-in-charge of Spokane House, that he would like two Indian boys about eight years old to be sent to the school at Fort Garry on the Red River (now Winnipeg, Manitoba). The school was run by missionaries from the Church Missionary Society of the Church of England. Simpson's request was the result of an agreement with the pastor in charge of the mission, David T. Jones. He agreed to bring Jones approximately 30 Indian children from all over the continent (Raufer 1966; Burns 1966).

One of the boys was a Spokane, the son of the head of the Middle Spokanes; his English name was Spokane Garry (fig. 4; "Spokane," fig. 4, this vol.). The other boy was named Kutenai Pelly, after the governor of the Hudson's Bay Company. On the morning of April 12, 1825, they left for eastern Canada. At the Red River mission at Fort Garry they received an intensive education in the mysteries of the Christian faith, as well as the English language, reading, and writing. In 1829, after four years away from their people, they returned home, dressed as White men, wearing their hair short. They were devout Christians bringing with them knowledge of Euro-American ways, and the Church of England's Book of Common Prayer and the Bible. Their teachings spread far beyond their own tribes; the "Columbia Religion" spread to Fort Alexandria in northern British Columbia during 1834 or 1835 (Jessett 1960:34–36). Kutenai Pelly was injured in a fall from his horse, and the burden of preaching fell to Spokane Garry. He was able to persuade five other boys to go to the Red River mission school in the spring of 1830. They were in turn educated and returned as missionaries to the Plateau peoples.

In 1836, the first Roman Catholic church was built at Champoeg in the Oregon country west of the Cascades. The French Canadians of the area erected it in anticipation of the arrival of priests to the area despite previous requests for Catholic priests going unanswered because of the opposition from Protestants. Eventually, Father Francis N. Blanchet, Vicar General, and another priest, August

Fig. 3. Hand-made knife made from an iron blade and a wooden handle lashed with fiber cord. Metal blades and machine-made metal knives were one of the earliest items traded by European settlers and one of those most valued by native peoples. Collected by Joseph Simms in Wash. along the Columbia River, before 1921. Length 28 cm.

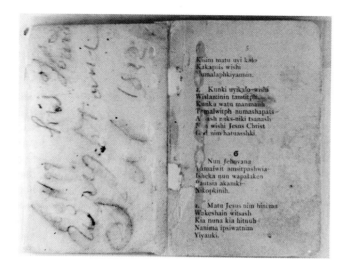

Eastern Wash. State Histl. Soc., Cheney Cowles Mus., Spokane: top, RAR 970.497 Sp65; bottom, 1334.

Fig. 4. Hymnal and pipe said to have belonged to Spokane Garry (b. 1811, d. 1892). Garry was one of 2 boys sent with Hudson's Bay Company Gov. George Simpson in 1825 to the Missionary Society School at Red River, Oregon Country (present-day B.C.). During his 5 years at the Red River school Garry learned to speak and write both French and English. When he returned to his people he established a church and a school. It was his knowledge that spurred the Nez Perce to send their delegation to St. Louis in 1831 to ask for Bibles and teachers, thus bringing Protestant missionaries to the Northwest. Garry aided one of these missionaries, Elkanah Walker, in writing *Etshiit*, a Spokane primer published at the Lapwai mission in Dec. 1842 (vol. 17:38; E. Walker and Eells 1842). Garry remained influential in Indian-White relations but, after 40 years of negotiation, was not able to maintain the Spokane's rights to their lands (W.S. Lewis 1917). top, Nez Perce hymnal *Talapusapaiain Wanipt Timas*, published at the Lapwai mission by Henry H. Spalding, 1842–1843. Shown is the first intact page, with the last part of the hymn "Who is without sin" and the first part of "We have disobeyed Jehovah." Collected by Clifford Drury in 1935 from Mrs. Joe Nozer, granddaughter of Spokane Garry. Handwritten inscription, of unknown significance, reads "[illegible name] Wright, his Hand and Seal 1842." bottom, Black stone pipe with lead inserts and wooden pipe stem. Length, 21.5 cm.

Demers, were sent to establish a mission in Oregon. Blanchet departed with the Hudson's Bay brigade on May 3, 1838, and was joined by Father Demers while enroute. In October of that year, while traveling to Oregon, Father Blanchet said the first mass in western Canada at the summit of the Rocky Mountains. The first mass in the northern Plateau was said by Father Demers in British Columbia, about 250 miles north of the present international boundary. By October 18, the party had reached Fort Walla Walla, where mass was also offered. After the service, the chiefs of the Cayuse and Walla Walla tribes came to Father Blanchet to consult with him. He performed three bap-

tisms, establishing a Roman Catholic influence. Father Blanchet and Father Demers traveled farther west to establish missions at Fort Vancouver and at Cowlitz. During this time, Father Blanchet devised a representation of Christian salvation history, which had a series of instructional pictures and dates in the form of a ladder on a wooden stick, called the sahale stick (Hanley 1993:16; Whitehead 1981:98–106). It became popular among the tribes and was printed as a large chart in 1843. It was then copied by Presbyterian missionary Eliza Spalding, who made a "Protestant ladder" (fig. 5) for use at Protestant missions (Drury 1958).

On September 8, 1839, a fourth delegation of Indians seeking "Blackrobes" left the Northwest for Saint Louis. Young Ignace, an Iroquois-Flathead (vol. 15:545), and another Indian named Pierre Gaucher traveled by canoe as far as Saint Joseph's mission in Council Bluffs, Iowa. There they met Father Pierre Jean de Smet, a Jesuit, who promised to come to their aid. Young Ignace went on to St. Louis with Father De Smet where arrangements were made to establish a mission in the Northwest. On March 27, 1840, Young Ignace and de Smet left Saint Louis traveling west via the Oregon Trail to Flathead country. At the Green River rendezvous they met 10 Flatheads who were waiting to escort them on the remainder of their journey. On July 26 mass was offered in the vicinity of Red Rock Lake on the Idaho-Montana border; 1,500 Indians were present. De Smet, observing the welcome given him, decided to return to the east for more help, and in April 1841 returned with four other Jesuits. Father Nicolas Point joined them enroute. On August 29 Saint Mary's mission (fig. 6) was established near Stevensville, Oregon Country, the first Jesuit mission in the Pacific Northwest.

In October 1841, de Smet traveled the 300 miles to Fort Colville and met many of the tribesmen of that area. During his stay, he baptized 190 Indians, many of whom were extremely old. He then returned to Flathead country with seeds for lettuce, carrots, beans, onions, potatoes, wheat, and oats for their first farm. He continued to travel extensively, reaching the Kootenai in northern Idaho and the Spokanes and Coeur d'Alenes in April 1842. From there he went back to the Kettle Falls Indians where, in a single day, Christian prayers were translated into the Flathead and Kalispel languages. On that occasion, 100 children and 11 adults were baptized.

In November 1842, Father Point left Saint Mary's for the Coeur d'Alenes, establishing a mission near the present town of Cataldo, Idaho. After consulting with the Indians, Point made his temporary residence on Lake Coeur d'Alene, close to the Indians' winter fish camp. In 1843, after meeting with a large number of Indians, Father Point built the first permanent Roman Catholic mission to serve the Coeur d'Alene tribe in Idaho on the banks of the Saint Joe River near present-day St. Maries. By October 1844, the Coeur d'Alene village contained 100 Christian families. The village and mission were both abandoned three years later due to flood-

Oreg. Histl. Soc., Portland: 87848.
Fig. 5. Eliza Spalding's Protestant chart or ladder based on the Roman Catholic ladder (see vol. 6:149). Ink, berry dyes, natural pigment on paper, about 1842. Size 172 cm by 55.5 cm.

ing. They relocated on the present site near Cataldo on the Coeur d'Alene River (vol. 4:495).

Protestant evangelism in the Southern Plateau came to a temporary ending in 1847 with the massacre of Dr. Marcus Whitman and others who resided at the mission (Drury 1958, 1973). The Cayuse identified Whitman with the epidemic diseases that were killing their people, and the growing White migration to the Oregon country. There was general disillusionment among the Cayuse with Christian missionization as well. Several missionaries were ready to abandon their mission station before the massacre occurred. Elkanah Walker and Myron Eells, as well as Henry H. and Eliza Spalding, had planned on leaving because of quarreling over the direction of evangelism among the missionaries in the field and the American Board of Commissioners for Foreign Missions. Within a few days of the massacre, which took place on November 18, 1847, the Walkers, Eells, and Spaldings departed for the Willamette Valley. There was very little missionary activity after their departure, although some Roman Catholic priests remained in the area. Henry Spalding returned in 1870 and successfully renewed the Presbyterian Lapwai mission (Walker 1985).

Catholic missionization in the Plateau was more successful than the Protestant effort (Johansen and Gates 1967:175–176) with the possible exception of the Nez Perce Presbyterian influence. The Jesuits, during the nineteenth and early twentieth centuries, had several advantages over their Protestant counterparts. The Jesuits, in the Columbia Plateau, worked primarily with isolated populations, and they limited their expectations to fit the capacity of the people, required no study of theology, and required their converts to provide a very limited expression of faith (Burns 1966; Johansen and Gates 1967). Their success was also influenced by their ability to travel freely without uprooting their families, and because of the appeal of daily, weekly, and seasonal Catholic rituals, especially extreme unction, which guaranteed everlasting life (Donnelly 1967). The colorful religious symbolism, which included pictures of Jesus and Mary, the Catholic Ladder, vestments, embellished chalices, crucifixes, and rosaries, also contributed to their success. Tribal members were impressed by the religious power they believed was inherent in the objects used in ceremonies. Catholic missionaries were also trained in classical languages and did not need to rely solely on interpreters, because they were better able to develop religious materials and Native American dictionaries than their Protestant counterparts (Burns 1966; Johansen and Gates 1967).

In the Northern Plateau, similar conversion efforts were evident. The first missionaries to reach the Northern Plateau were Catholic priests from Quebec and France.

top left and bottom left, Jesuit Mo. Prov. Arch., St. Louis; top right, Wash. State U. Lib., Histl. Photograph Coll., Pullman: 537–7–25; bottom right, Archives de la Compagnie de Jésus, Saint-Jérôme, Que.

Fig. 6. St. Mary's Mission among the Flathead. top left, Insula, also known as Red Feather and the Little Chief, baptized Michel. A devout Christian, he wears a large cross and rosary beads as well as a gun with decorated inlaid handle and fringed jacket decorated with beads. top right, Building the mission. top left and right, Graphite and ink on paper by Nicolas Point, about 1841–1842. bottom left, Catholic altar in a tule mat tepee. Watercolor on paper by Nicolas Point, 1841–1847. bottom right, First mass baptism of the Flatheads, Dec. 3, 1841. The Latin text above the chapel translates 'May all things be made new'; that beneath the gathered Indians reads: 'Thou shalt cleanse me and I shall be whiter than snow.' Oil or tempera painting by Nicolas Point.

Early in the 1840s Oblates of Mary Immaculate and Jesuit from eastern Canada reached the southern coast and interior and penetrated north into New Caledonia. The first priests to arrive were Father Blanchet and Father Demers.

Father Demers was installed as the first bishop of Vancouver Island in 1851, and priests were sent to the Coast Salish Indians and to the Fraser Valley. In 1859 Father Charles Pandosy was sent to establish a mission among the Northern Okanagan. Two years later another Saint Mary's Mission was established on the Fraser River above New Westminster, and soon became a center of activity, as well as the site of an industrial school. In 1869, Father Jean Lejacq began serving the vast area bounded by Hagwilget, Fort Connolly (Bear Lake), Fort McLeod, and Fort St. George until 1885. His successor was Father Morice. During the 1850s, Victoria, British Columbia, became an important center of Catholic missionary endeavors.

Catholic priests throughout the Plateau were convinced that it was necessary to change the secular as well as the spiritual lives of the Indian people. They often imposed new social and political structures on the Indian communities in which they worked.

Sechelt, a Coast Salish community, became a model of a system where the community was under the control of the local priest. At Sechelt, control was put into the hands of four chiefs who had a number of assistants reporting on the conduct of the people. They also had various disciplinarians to administer penance and punishment. A eucharist chief assisted the priest in looking after spiritual matters. In the name of temperance, Indians were required to abandon all dances,

Fig. 7. Wascopam Mission among the Wasco, Wishram, and Cascades Indians at The Dalles, Oreg. This Methodist mission was founded in 1838 by Henry Perkins and was active to 1847. Clergy preached in the Chinook Jargon, which was then interpreted into Sahaptin. The Nez Perce and Cayuse had winter camps in this area from before Christmas each year until mid-February (Boyd 1996:18, 63). Mat tepee in the foreground with Indian cooking on the left. Oil painting (cropped) by William Henry Tappan, 1849.

potlatching, shamanism, and gambling. Instead, they were required to participate in the religious forms and rituals of the church. The new order worked well for a time, but like other missionary experiments in the Plateau region, it too began to disintegrate by the late nineteenth century. Nevertheless, the Roman Catholic influence remained, and of the 40,000 Indians in British Columbia in 1997, more than half were Catholic. They include: Kootenai, Shuswap, Northern Okanagan, Lillooet (except for a few Anglicans at Bridge River), and the Thompson (except those from Lytton to Boston Bar who are Anglican). Catholic boarding schools are located at Kamloops, Williams Lake, Lejacq, and Cranbrook.

In 1845 over 3,000 United States immigrants traveled the Oregon Trail, passing through the Columbia Plateau (Ruby and Brown 1972). An additional 1,350 immigrants entered the Oregon Territory in the following year (Fuller 1931) with over 5,000 arriving in 1847 (Fuller 1931; Harper 1971; Johansen and Gates 1967; Ruby and Brown 1972, 1981).

Due to the constant flow of Americans to the Oregon Country, the United States and Great Britain finally resolved their dispute over the boundaries of that area in 1846. The Congress of the United States did not grant territorial status to the area until 1848, a move that was directly influenced by the massacre of the Whitmans.

History Since 1846

STEPHEN DOW BECKHAM

Issues of Sovereignty

Resolution of the long dispute over the international boundary between the United States and Canada in 1846 brought a rush of changes to the tribes of the Plateau. Armed with a militant attitude referred to as Manifest Destiny, citizens of the United States unleashed in the 1840s a strong, expansionist fervor. In western Canada, the tenure of the Hudson's Bay Company was secure. The Oregon Treaty fixed 49° north latitude as the northern boundary of the United States, extending the line from the crest of the Rockies to the Pacific Ocean. The treaty recognized the possessory rights of the Hudson's Bay Company, its subsidiary the Puget Sound Agricultural Company, and British citizens south of the boundary. The agreement ignored all tribal land claims, interests, and native involvement in the settlement discussions (Oregon Territorial Legislature 1854:19–21).

The Oregon Trail passed through the Nez Perce homeland and crossed the Plateau south of the Columbia River (fig. 1). More than 11,500 emigrants had passed over the Southern Plateau on the trail by 1850. These newcomers brought goods, diseases, and prejudices in far greater magnitude than introduced by nearly four decades of the fur trade. Land speculation and the prospect of securing claims in the lush valleys west of the Cascades spurred on the American pioneers (Unruh 1979:118–120).

In 1843 the Americans established an Oregon provisional government, elected a legislative assembly, and recorded their land claims. Their government was extralegal, neither approved by the Hudson's Bay Company nor endorsed by the United States. With the Indian attack on the Presbyterian mission of Dr. Marcus Whitman in November 1847 (vol. 4:696), George Abernethy, provisional governor, raised volunteer companies who invaded the Plateau to retaliate against the Cayuse, Walla Walla, and Umatilla. Destroying villages and capturing alleged perpetrators of the incident at the Waiilatpu Mission, they returned to the Willamette Valley to try five Cayuse prisoners, who were hanged in 1850 at Oregon City (Lansing 1993:95–98).

Establishing Indian Policies

Faced with a growing American population and the consequences of warfare between settlers and Indians, Congress in 1848 passed the Organic Act to establish Oregon Territo-

ry. The law was of singular significance for the course of Indian affairs in the intermontane Pacific Northwest. First, it explicitly affirmed the "rights of person or property" of the Indians "so long as such rights shall remain unextinguished by treaty." Second, it granted up to 640 acres per claim in Indian Country to sites occupied as mission stations at the time of its enactment. This addressed the mission claims of the Protestant American Board of Commissioners for Foreign Missions in Washington and Idaho and the Roman Catholics in Idaho and Montana. Third, it created the office of superintendent of Indian affairs, initially entrusting the responsibilities to the governor. Fourth, it extended the provisions of the Ordinance of 1787 to all of Oregon Territory, including the "utmost good faith clause" as a philosophical foundation for dealing with the Indian tribes. Fifth, it appropriated $10,000 for the purchase of presents to the tribes to secure the "peace and quietude of the country" (Oregon Territorial Legislature 1854:28–37).

The creation of Oregon Territory set the stage for the rapid extension of federal services. These included the operations of the Bureau of Indian Affairs, U.S. Army, and General Land Office. In 1849 the Army dispatched mounted riflemen overland on the Oregon Trail. That fall the soldiers established their headquarters and quartermaster's depot at Fort Vancouver. Over the next decade the military presence extended steadily into the Columbia Plateau. The new posts included Fort Dalles, 1850; Fort Cascades, 1853 and its adjacent blockhouses, Fort Rains and Fort Lugenbeel; Fort Simcoe, 1856; Fort Walla Walla, 1856; and Fort Klamath, 1863 (Guie 1977; Meinig 1968:163–64; Stone 1964). Collectively the U.S. Army posts at Walla Walla, The Dalles, and Simcoe in the Yakima country gave the military positions from which to maneuver against the highly mobile and armed tribes of the Southern Plateau (Minor and Beckham 1984:44–47).

From the outset of administration of Indian affairs the United States sought to break off trade and other connections between the native peoples living on either side of the border with Canada. Commissioner Luke Lea instructed Oregon Superintendent Anson Dart in 1850, when making presents to the tribes, "to impress on the Indians that it is the American Government and not the British that confers upon them these benefits." He further noted: "The Indians should also be prevented from crossing the line into the British possessions" (ARCIA 1850:118).

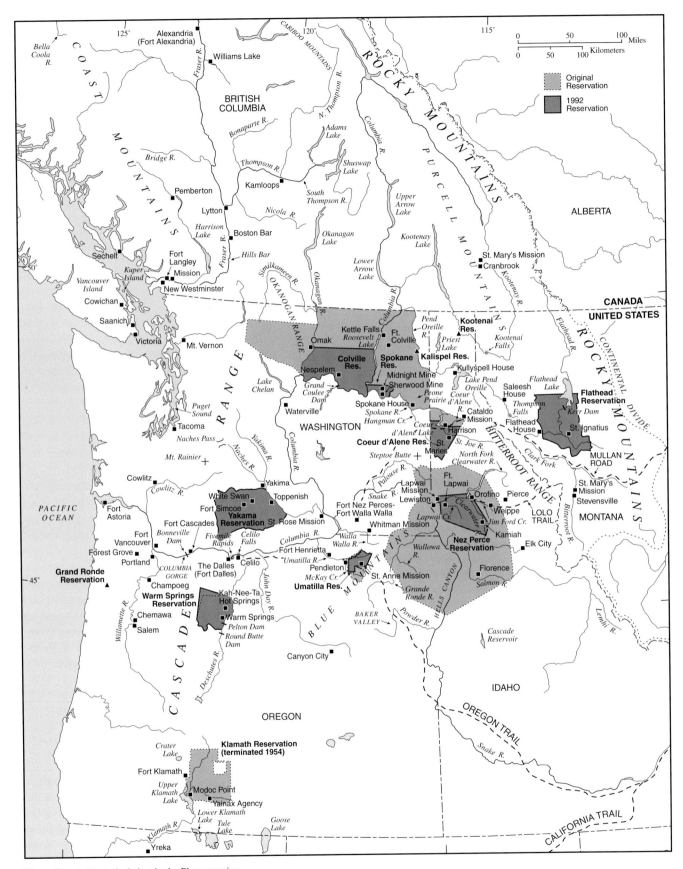

Fig. 1. Selected historical sites in the Plateau region.

Commissioner Lea in 1850 stressed the importance of maintaining peace and friendship with the tribes and reconciling differences where they existed between the tribal communities. "The best way to accomplish this, is by inducing bands, hostile to each other, to enter written treaties of peace and amity," he wrote, and "to refer all their misunderstandings and differences to the umpirage of the proper representatives of the United States government." The government sought to encourage agriculture and Christianity. In addition to the superintendent, the president appointed an agent for west of the Cascades and for east of the mountains, Henry H. Spalding, a former Presbyterian missionary serving at Lapwai among the Nez Perce (ARCIA 1850:118–119).

The Bureau of Indian Affairs had in 1850 only sketchy information about the native peoples in the interior of the Pacific Northwest. The Hudson's Bay Company held closely its assessments of native population, armaments, and culture, retaining extensive records in its archives at Beaver House in London. The first superintendents and agents were thus charged with expanding the cursory assessments made of the natives by the detachment of the U.S. Exploring Expedition, which in 1841 had traveled as far east as the fur trade post at the mouth of the Walla Walla River. Joseph Lane, Oregon territorial governor and ex-officio superintendent of Indian affairs, in 1850 estimated a population of 10,820 people (ARCIA 1850:128–129). His successor, Anson Dart, estimated in 1851 a population of 7,103 (ARCIA 1855:254).

In 1851 Superintendent Dart traveled across the Southern Plateau. He selected a site for Umatilla agency, visited the Hudson's Bay Company's Fort Walla Walla ("History Until 1846," fig. 2, this vol.) and the site of the Whitman mission, and met in council with the Cayuse. Dart later met with the Nez Perce. He found them prosperous with corn fields, apple orchards, packed camas roots, and large herds of horses. He met in council with the tribe near Lapwai, Idaho, where nearly 500 tribal members assembled. "They were all mounted on fine horses, which, as well as themselves, were decorated in the highest style of Indian art, and came riding into our camp with a great flourish of trumpets, beating drums, and firing their guns into the air" (ARCIA 1851:218–220).

Congress created Washington Territory in 1853 and entrusted responsibility of Indian affairs with its new governor, Isaac I. Stevens. Simultaneously Stevens was charged with mounting the Pacific Railroad Surveys. Capt. George B. McClellan headed the western division surveys and attached George Gibbs to his party as geologist and ethnologist. In August-October 1853, Gibbs traveled along the eastern flank of the Cascades, recording ethnographic and linguistic information, particularly in the watershed of the Yakima River (Gibbs 1855, 1955–1956; U.S. Congress. Senate 1855).

Commissioner George Manypenny charged Stevens with securing statistical information (table 1) (ARCIA 1854:184–249), regulating tribal trade, guarding against the influence of the Hudson's Bay Company over the Indians, developing budget estimates for staffing and facilities, and making conciliatory presents to the tribes (ARCIA 1853:213–216).

Stevens laid down his goals for Indian administration for Washington Territory. He hoped to secure treaties, reserve to the tribes a few tracts of good land, foster an agricultural program premised on farming, and encourage amalgamation of small bands under a few chiefs on the reservations. "It never could have been the intention of Congress that the Indians should be excluded from their ancient fisheries," he wrote. Stevens observed that the Donation Land Act of 1850 had fostered dispossession from the key fisheries locations (ARCIA 1854:247–248).

Tensions steadily mounted between the tribes and the westward rush of emigrants pouring over the Oregon Trail. Under the Donation Land Act of 1850 the claims included one at Lapwai Creek in Idaho, another on McKay Creek near Pendleton, a few in the Walla Walla valley, and a number along the banks of the Columbia River westward from The Dalles (Genealogical Forum of Portland, Oregon 1957:iii–viii). Of consequence to the people of the Plateau was that Congress had validated a process, prior to treaty ratification, for the wholesale taking of Indian lands. The law inspired even more Euro-American migration to the Pacific Northwest.

Trespass also increased. In 1853 overland emigrants opened a new route west from Fort Walla Walla via the Naches River and Naches Pass to Puget Sound. Although the trail never gained the volume of use of the Oregon Trail, it cut directly through the homelands of the Cayuse and

Table 1. Population of Tribes in Washington Territory, East of Cascades, 1853

Tribe	Population
Flathead	350
Kootenai	400
Pend d'Oreille	280
Kalispel	420
Coeur d'Alene	500
Spokanes	600
Nez Perce	1,700
Palouse	500
Cayuse	120
Walla Walla	300
Dalles Bands	200
Cascades	36
Klikitats	300
Yakima	600
Wenatchee and Southern Okanogan	550
Colville	500
Total	7,356

SOURCE: Schoolcraft 1851–1857, 5:705.

Yakima. A party of 175 crossed the route in its first year of use (Longmire 1917:26).

The Oregon territorial legislature in 1854 passed a law making the sale of firearms or ammunition to Indians illegal. The punishments ranged up to six months in jail or a $500 fine. The legislature prohibited the sale of "any spirituous liquor" to Indians with fines up to $500 and up to 15 days in jail for violators. The legislature also excluded Indians and persons of one-half or more Indian blood as competent to testify in court (Oregon Territorial Legislature 1854:111, 257–258). In 1866 the legislature prohibited Euro-American marriage with Indians, half-Indians, Hawaiians, Chinese, and Afro-Americans, a provision that remained law until 1955 (Hill 1887, 1:976; Oregon Legislature 1955).

Treaties

Governor Stevens launched his treaty program in December 1854 in western Washington. In June 1855 he moved east of the Cascades and joined Joel Palmer, Superintendent in Oregon Territory, to host the Walla Walla Treaty Council with the tribes of the Southern Plateau (fig. 2). The Stevens treaties captured his philosophy of dealing with the tribes: secure massive cession of lands, create reservations, provide for agricultural and educational programs, reserve fishing rights in common with Euro-Americans, and protect native hunting, grazing, and gathering rights on "unenclosed lands." Palmer picked up on those comprehensive provisions in a single treaty in Oregon, with the Confederated Tribes of Warm Springs (table 2). Otherwise the Oregon treaties remained mute on reserved rights of fishing, hunting, and gathering.

Three of the 11 treaties with Plateau tribes were negotiated by Governor Stevens and Superintendent Palmer acting jointly at Walla Walla. Each superintendent secured two additional treaties negotiating singly with tribal leaders. Superintendent J.W. Perit Huntington secured the Klamath treaty of 1864 and the highly disputed but ratified second treaty in 1865 with the Warm Springs tribes. By that agreement the tribes were persuaded (some say tricked) into ceding their off-reservation subsistence rights, an agreement never enforced though held over them for decades. Superintendent Calvin Hale secured the second Nez Perce Treaty in 1863, significantly reducing the size of the reservation and ceding the lands of Joseph's band in Oregon, not parties to the agreement, to the United States. Commissioner N.G. Taylor secured the third Nez Perce Treaty at Lapwai, Idaho, in 1868. Subsequent to the suspension of treaty ratification by the U.S. Senate, Chief Moses and his band agreed in 1883 to remove to the Colville Reservation, relinquishing the Columbia Reservation. Chief Sar-sarp-kin and his band requested to remain within the former reservation on allotments or to remove to Colville. Tonaskat and Lot of the Colville Reservation accepted the presence of additional people, provided the government erect a sawmill, grist mill, and a boarding school and send a doctor to live among their people. They entered this agreement with Secretary of the Interior Henry M. Teller and Commissioner Hiram Price, and in 1884 Congress ratified it (Kappler 1904–1941, 2).

The treaties were standard in provisions for ceding lands; creating reservations; mandating agriculture; providing for farmers, teachers, and doctors; calling for construction of mills, hospitals, blacksmith shops, and schools; and allowing for allotment of lands at the discretion of the president. Five of the treaties negotiated by Stevens and one by Palmer explicitly provided for fishing, hunting, and gathering rights. The Blackfoot treaty of 1855 created a jointly shared hunting ground in the Northern Rockies for 99 years, where all tribes and bands parties to the agreement from east and west of the Rockies could hunt, fish, gather, graze livestock, or cure meat. None was permitted to establish permanent settlements within the hunting area. The United States, however, secured the right within the reserved area to establish military posts, telegraph lines, wagon roads, missions, mills, stations, and agencies and to navigate all lakes and streams (Kappler 1904–1941, 2:736–740).

Warfare, 1855–1858

On the surface the treaty system appeared carefully constructed and, in light of land cessions west of the Cascades, remarkably generous; however, the treaties were incomplete. The entire northern Plateau in the United States as well as all of that portion in eastern British Columbia remained without formal agreements between tribes and the central government. Governor Stevens promised the Spokane, Southern Okanogan, Methow, Wenatchee, Moses Band and others that he would return from Puget Sound to negotiate with them. The outbreak of warfare deflected his intentions. Stevens ultimately left the territory and died early in the Civil War. No successor resumed the task of completing the treaty agenda.

"We are on the eve of an Indian war," wrote J. Cain on October 6, 1855, while acting as Indian superintendent during the absence of Governor Stevens at the Blackfoot Council. Conditions had deteriorated rapidly in the region. The passage of emigrants had introduced calamitous outbreaks of smallpox and measles. The distress surrounding these deaths contributed to the Cayuse attack in 1847 on the Whitman Mission. Each year the numbers of emigrants seemed to increase. Stevens was surveying and promoting the Pacific railroad and writing into the treaties rights-of-way and station locations even within the reserved Indian lands (ARCIA 1855:192–194).

The troubles deepened when in the fall of 1854 miners discovered placer deposits at the mouth of the Clark Fork 30 miles from Fort Colville. By 1855 miners from Oregon and Washington territories and British Columbia rushed to the diggings. "As is well known," wrote George Gibbs in 1858,

Smithsonian, NAA: top, 37,644–G; center, 45,738; bottom, Nez Perce Natl. Histl. Park, Spalding, Idaho: 2275.

Fig. 2. Flathead and Nez Perce negotiators. top, Treaty council of Flathead Indians in session with U.S. Commissioners, Gov. Isaac Stevens and Gen. Joel Palmer, July 1855. center, "Nez Perce Indians preparing the records of the Walla Walla Council, June 1855," which resulted in a treaty. These young men had been taught to read and write in their own language by Presbyterian missionaries (Ewers 1948:5). top and center, Pen and ink drawings by Gustavus Sohon, who served as official interpreter for some of the 1855 treaties. bottom, Delegation of Nez Perce from Ft. Lapwai to Washington, D.C., 1930. Continuing a tradition of negotiating with U.S. officials, this delegation went to the capital to discuss hunting and fishing rights, compensation for stone quarry leases, tribal timber reserve, extension of trust period for allotments, monies for higher education, and the introduction of a civil court on the reservation for dealing with Indian marriages and divorces. left to right, seated: Silas Whitman (b. 1871, d. 1935); Naw-min; and Harry Wheeler (b. 1884, d. 1963); standing Caleb Carter (b. 1885, d. 1971; interpreter, graduate of Carlisle Indian Institute, Pa.); unidentified; and Archie Phinney (b. 1903, d. 1949), a linguistic anthropologist who studied under Franz Boas at Columbia U. Photographed 1930.

"many of them were murdered by the Yakama and Isle de Pierre [Sinkayuse] Indians through whose country they passed, and an attempt was made on the part of the United States troops to capture the perpetrators, gave occasion for a long premeditated outbreak of these & some other tribes" (Gibbs 1858). While Gibbs may have erred on the numbers killed, tensions clearly gripped the Plateau as the tribes resisted the wholesale incursion unfolding in their country.

The murder of Andrew J. Bolon, agent to the Yakima, who had gone to investigate the alleged murders of miners, became the spark that ignited warfare. Learning of his death, Maj. Granville O. Haller crossed the Columbia with five officers and 102 enlisted men from Fort Dalles in October 1855. Haller's troops encountered strong resistance to their investigation. More than 300 men of the Yakima, Sinkayuse, Wenatchee, Spokane, Palouse, Walla Walla, and Cayuse tribes opposed them. The army forces retreated, suffering five casualties and a dozen wounded as well as loss of horses, supplies, and cannons (U.S. Congress. House 1856:80–89). Within days the region was engulfed in fear. The tribes of the Southern Plateau, rallied by Kamiakin, a Yakima chief, found common cause with the Coast Salish of Puget Sound. The stage was set for a major war on both sides of the Cascades (Stern 1996:324–326).

The Hudson's Bay Company abandoned Fort Nez Perces, a post held by fur traders for four decades. Governor Stevens was upset by this withdrawal, arguing that decisive action was needed to suppress the Indian uprising quickly and to restore order. The U.S. Army, however, moved toward a steady accumulation of supplies and massing of troops. "They can only be conquered or brought to terms," argued commander Gen. John Wool, "by occupying their country and such positions as would command their fisheries and valleys, where their cattle and horses must graze" (U.S. Congress. House 1856a:16; U.S. Congress. House 1856b:39–43). Wool's strategy was

Table 2. Treaties with Plateau Tribes, 1855-1883

Tribes	Negotiated	Ratified
Northern Molala, Kalapuya	Jan. 22, 1855	Mar. 3, 1855
Walla Walla, Cayuse, Umatilla	June 8, 1855	Mar. 8, 1859
Yakima	June 9, 1855	Mar. 8, 1859
Nez Perce	June 11, 1855	Mar. 8, 1859
Middle Oregon Tribes (Warm Springs)	June 25, 1855	Mar. 8, 1859
Flathead, Kootenai, and Upper Pend d'Oreille	July 16, 1855	Mar. 8, 1859
Blackfoot, Flathead, Pend d'Oreille, Kootenai, Nez Perce	Oct. 17, 1855	Apr. 15, 1856
Southern Molala	Dec. 21, 1855	Mar. 8, 1859
Nez Perce	June 9, 1863	Apr. 17, 1867
Klamath, Modoc, Yahooskin Band of Northern Paiute	Oct. 11, 1864	July 2, 1866
Middle Oregon Tribes (Warm Springs)	Nov. 15, 1865	Mar. 2, 1867
Nez Perce	Aug. 13, 1868	Feb. 16, 1869

SOURCE: Kappler 1904–1941, 2.

premised, in part, by the outbreak of hostilities in southwestern Oregon in the same month and the reality of considerable difficulty in maintaining and supplying field forces with the onset of winter. When the U.S. Army did not act, volunteer militias did. Forces from both Washington and Oregon territories moved toward the Walla Walla valley to erect Fort Henrietta at the former agency site on the Umatilla River and Fort Bennett, a few miles from the site of the former Whitman Mission at Waiilatpu. During the winter of 1855–1856 these men randomly attacked Indian villages. "It was precisely the kind of disorderly, indiscriminate killing and scavenging that disgusted the army officers" (Meinig 1968:162).

Col. George Wright, field commander, planned to secure the Walla Walla valley in spring 1856. He had only set out from Fort Dalles when he learned of the Indian attack and burning of the stockade, blockhouse, and garrison at Fort Cascades, gateway to the interior in the Columbia Gorge (Minor and Beckham 1984:18). Wright turned his forces back to try to subdue the Yakima and Klikitat. The U.S. Army moved into the Yakima, Kittitas, and Wenatchee homelands. Wright in July 1856 announced success in that area and laid plans in August for construction of Fort Simcoe to anchor the army presence on the main travel route along the eastern flank of the Cascades (Guie 1977:v).

Col. Edward J. Steptoe took four companies east in August to the Walla Walla country where militiamen from Puget Sound had tried to wrest control since early summer. On August 20, 1856, Steptoe announced plans to erect Fort Walla Walla and to close the area to settlement: "No emigrant or other white person, except the Hudson's Bay Co., or persons having ceded rights from the Indians, will be permitted to settle or remain in the Indian country, or on land not settled or not confirmed by the Senate and approved by the President of the United States." The only exception was made for miners in the Colville district. The militia departed in September, leaving the region wholly an Indian land except for 800 army personnel at the region's three forts: Simcoe, Walla Walla, and Dalles (Meinig 1968:164).

When reports circulated in spring 1858 that Indians had waylaid miners headed for the Colville district, Steptoe set out from Fort Walla Walla with four companies. He crossed the Snake and pushed through the Palouse homeland. The Indians withdrew, and Steptoe decided to invade the Spokane and Coeur d'Alene country. Reportedly 1,000 Indians met Steptoe's forces, demanded to know his intentions, and finally attacked. The tribes and soldiers fought all day on May 17 at Tehotomimme (Steptoe Butte). In the middle of the night the soldiers retreated south toward the Snake River. Among the dead were Victor, a Coeur d'Alene chief; James, a headman; and others (ARCIA 1858:272–274; Bancroft 1890:181). Steptoe's debacle led Colonel Wright to take 12 companies from Fort Dalles and move toward the Spokane. In September Indians and the U.S. Army fought repeatedly. Wright then initiated a scorched earth policy. His men swept through the Spokane Valley to Cataldo Mission. They burned grain fields, destroyed stored foodstuffs, and slaughtered over 900 head of horses. By the end of September Wright declared: "The war is closed. Peace is restored with the Spokanes, Coeur d'Alenes and Palouses" (Bancroft 1890:178–183, 188–91; Meinig 1968:167).

Wright's actions generated a cruel legacy of bitter memories. Not only did he encourage destruction of villages, vital food resources, and valued horse herds, but also he ordered the hanging of Indian men. These included Qualchin, the son of Yakima chief Owhi. Owhi was murdered when he

154

tried to escape a few days later. Kamiakin, another Yakima leader, fled to British Columbia. Wright hanged several Palouse men and then on October 9, 1858, held council with the Walla Walla. He asked those who had engaged in recent battles to stand. When 35 did, he picked four to be hanged. Without trial or any defense, Wright had ordered the execution of 16 Indians. The region east of the Cascades remained closed to Euro-American settlement until Gen. William S. Harney lifted the ban in 1859 following a meeting with a number of chiefs (fig. 3) (Victor 1894:497–499).

Reservations and Removals

The treaty programs in the Pacific Northwest were premised on the reduction of Indian land tenure, concentration of bands and tribes under the tutelage of the Bureau of Indian Affairs, confinement through the presence of military posts near the reservations, and transformation of the native peoples into the surrounding majority community. The reservation was the site where these changes were to be effected.

Although the tribes entered a majority of the treaties in 1855, Congress deferred for four years the ratification of the agreements. Finally in March and April 1859, the Senate approved 10 treaties from the Pacific Northwest (ARCIA 1860:395).

The hiatus between treaty agreements and ratification were the years of warfare. The delay also meant that not until 1860 did Congress authorize appropriations for pur-

chase of annuity goods, construction of agency buildings, or implementation of programs on the reservations. This period of deferral proved highly frustrating both for the tribes and the agents charged with keeping peace and encouraging the native peoples to remove to the newly designated reservations. The agent possessed little means to anchor the new communities where sedentary, agricultural pursuits were to transform the Plateau Indians into "civilized farmers." Even when the appropriations were made, the obstacles of shipping commodities to the reservations proved formidable. Milling burrs, circular saws, ploughs, harrows, shovels, bolts, and nails lay sometimes as much as 300 miles from supply points. For most of the 1860s construction of facilities lagged, in part because of the shipping problems.

The reservation experience unfolded in an atmosphere of tensions because of trespass incursions by miners, actions of territorial militias, the policies and actions of Colonel Wright, presence of military regulars, and the determination to force acculturation through Bureau of Indian Affairs programs. At the heart of the enterprise was the federal goal to transform the fishing, hunting, and gathering economies of the Plateau tribes into sedentary, agricultural lifeways. To accomplish this the agents promoted agriculture through crop raising, construction of mills, and manual labor training programs. The agents founded both day schools and, on larger reservations, boarding schools to facilitate the transformation (fig. 4). When students showed promise, they were dispatched after 1880 to regional training schools at Forest Grove and Salem (Chemawa) (vol. 7:174) in western Oregon, Cushman at Tacoma, Washington, or to distant schools at Lawrence, Kansas, and Carlisle, Pennsylvania.

The educational programs, rudimentary and engaging only a limited number of students in the 1860s, were defined narrowly. Edward R. Geary, Superintendent of Indian Affairs for the entire Pacific Northwest in 1859 when all jurisdictions were combined, articulated the philosophy for the reservation, industrial schools:

> The children educated at these institutions should, in most cases, be taken entirely from the control of their parents, and boarded under the care of a judicious matron, where habits of cleanliness, punctuality, and order should be carefully cultivated. The education of these schools should not only embrace letters, but the boys should be instructed in agriculture and trades; the girls in the use of the needle and the various branches of domestic economy. These schools should be governed and taught by persons of not only capacity, firmness, and amiability, but by those of decidedly religious character.

Geary saw the industrial boarding school as elevating the "savage" in "the presence of immoralities that always serve to degrade the civilized" (ARCIA 1860:755).

The school enrollment grew slowly; most drew 30–50 students a year during their first decade of operation. In 1864 at Yakima 20 boys and 10 girls met in a log building, half of which was a workshop for making shoes and harnesses. William Wright, the teacher, wrote: "The books used

Oreg. Histl. Soc., Portland: 624.

Fig. 3. Father Pierre Jean de Smet with chiefs of the Upper Columbia attending a meeting with Gen. William S. Harney to restore peace after the Plateau wars of 1858. seated left to right, Victor Alamiken or The Happy Man (Lower Kalispel), Alexander Temglagketzin or The Man Without a Horse (Pend d'Oreille), Adolphus Kwilkweschape or Red Feather (Flathead), Andrew Seltice (Coeur d'Alene); standing, Bonaventure (Coeur d'Alene), Dennis Tienemlietze (Colville chief from Kettle Falls), de Smet, and Francis Saya or The Iroquois (Flathead Chief). Photographed at Ft. Vancouver, 1859.

top, Wash. State U. Lib., Histl. Photograph Coll., Pullman:92–044; bottom, Okanogan County Histl. Soc., Okanogan, Wash.

Fig. 4. Indian schools. top, Colville and Spokane girls on Easter Sunday, at Ft. Spokane Boarding School, Wash., run by the federal government. This was the only Indian boarding school in the area not run by the Roman Catholic Church. Photograph by Frank Avery, 1901–1916. bottom, Track team at St. Mary's, Omak, Wash. (formerly Mission, Wash.), with coach W.E. Courtney. The team included Ernest Keogan, Basil Desautl, Eugene Wiles, L. Nicholson, John Cleveland, Pascal Sherman, Ed Ambrose, William Carden, Lee Kover, and William Edwards. Photograph by George B. Ladd, 1913.

in the school are Sanders's Primer, Sargent's Second and Third Readers, Sanders's Speller and Definer, Watson's First Reader, Cornell's Primary Geography, Davis's Primary Arithmetic, and the Holy Bible." He concluded: "They like to read the Bible." The students were engaged in virtual forced labor. They cut and hauled 15,000 feet of logs, cut and transported cordwood, hauled annuity goods 65 miles from the landing to Fort Simcoe, labored in the tannery, made furniture, and worked at ditching, plowing, sowing, planting, and harvesting. The girls washed, ironed, cooked, knitted, manufactured soap and candles, and sewed clothing (ARCIA 1864:73–74).

Highly important in bridging the transformation from aboriginal lifeways and languages to the acculturated condition was the presence of the Métis population on various reservations. These persons, often possessing multiple language proficiencies, created fascinating connections by marriage, kinship, occupation, and leadership roles. The Métis were far more than individuals of Indian and French heritage. Broadly perceived, the term embraced all of mixed ancestry and that included English, Scotch, French, Pacific Islander, Russian, Aleut, and Indians from east of the Rockies. These individuals, whose parents came from both native and fur trading communities, often served as interpreters, assisted Indian agents and traditional chiefs, and helped open the way for missionaries to teach, baptize, marry, and embrace the native community in their ministries (Van Kirk 1980).

The Métis were well documented in the Roman Catholic parish registers across the Plateau. For example, the missions of Saint Ann and Saint Rose of the Cayuse, founded in 1847, documented dozens of these people. Illustrative of the records was the following: "March 20, 1853, I the undersigned missionary priest, Oblate of Mary Immaculate, baptized Sophie Branchaut, aged about 7 months, legitimate daughter of Mr. Thomas Branchaut, Canadian by nation, and Angelique, his wife, of the Nez Perce tribe." This entry by Eugene Casamir Chirouse was but one of hundreds chronicling the flow of foreign surnames and other cultures into the native communities of the Plateau. Many of the reservation era spokesmen were of mixed backgrounds and multiple language skills. They helped link the native world and the new residents moving into the region (Munnick and Munnick 1989).

Charles S. Medary, agent at Flathead Reservation, wrote in 1876 about the seven or eight Métis families and their large numbers of children. "They have lived here unmolested for years," he noted, "but the citizens of Missoula County desire them removed in order to collect taxes on their property." He concluded: "I regard their presence beneficial to the Indians, and deem it unwise to compel them and their offspring to remove to a community where they would be looked upon and treated like Indians in every respect except paying taxes" (ARCIA 1876:89–90).

Trespass and Changing Policy

Although relatively isolated from Euro-Americans until the opening of the region east of the Cascades to settlement in 1859, the Indians of the Plateau were subjected to repeated trespass and carving up of their reserved lands. The portent of these events unfolded in 1853–1854 with the Pacific Railroad Surveys. Governor Stevens and a cadre of engineers, geologists, and naturalists combed the Northern Plateau from the Rockies to the Cascades to find a suitable railroad route. Their detailed maps and reports were published (Stevens 1855).

The discovery of gold on the Thompson River in New Caledonia in the fall of 1857 produced great excitement. In December, Gov. James Douglas issued a proclamation asserting that all gold deposits in the Thompson and Fraser watersheds were crown property and forbade prospecting and mining without permit. Douglas reported in April 1858 that mining was "almost exclusively by the native population, who had discovered the productive mines, and washed out all the gold, about eight hundred ounces" and wanted to exclude White miners. Control of the mines proved impossible. Douglas lacked the ability to enforce the permit procedure though he twice visited the mining districts in 1858 to attempt to quell the unfolding violence produced by the arrival of rowdies. Additional strikes only fueled the rush (Bancroft 1887:352–354, 390–391).

The influx of miners grew rapidly. Between May and July, an estimated 23,000 persons sailed from San Francisco for the mines of interior New Caledonia. Another 8,000 traveled overland. Douglas used provincial resources to open a new route via Harrison Lake to the diggings. In turn, gold seekers from Puget Sound cut trails across the Cascades to the Yakima watershed and then traveled north along the eastern base of the mountains 260 miles to the Thompson River district. The resident mining population dropped to 3,000 by 1859, but even this was a significant incursion into the Indian domain of the interior of British Columbia. Although the initial Fraser River rush was denounced as a humbug, miners remained and in the 1860s began extensive works in the Cariboo region between the headwaters of the Fraser and Thompson (Bancroft 1887:358, 365–366, 473–474; Gibbs 1858).

The gold rush into the Fraser-Thompson country was a turning point for the native peoples of the northern Plateau. For several decades they had adapted to the fur trade, responding to the economic opportunities it afforded and the slow acculturation. By 1858, however, the fur trade had largely ended, new diseases such as smallpox were spreading rapidly and with calamitous impacts, mining disrupted the salmon runs and drove Indians from their villages and fisheries along the rivers, settlers moved onto the arable lands, and the tribes lacked the population and strength to protect their interests. New residents clamored for Indian removal, alleging that the natives were responsible for crime, prostitution, and the thriving liquor trade (Fisher 1977:109–117).

The gold rush hit New Caledonia in transition. In January 1858 the Hudson's Bay Company began its surrender of jurisdiction to the Colonial Office. On August 2 parliament passed the act establishing direct rule over the new province of British Columbia. Douglas bridged the change, moving on August 14 from his post as head of company operations and governor of New Caledonia to governor of the province (Bancroft 1887:383–384). For the Indians of the southern interior of the province, these affairs of state were of little initial consequence. What was important was the rampant trespass they endured from those who exploited the natural resources of their homelands. The European newcomers wantonly killed their cattle and horses, destroyed their crops, murdered their people, and resisted their working in the mines. Tensions were particularly high at Hills Bar on the Fraser where an estimated 400–500 Indians worked the placer deposits in the midst of 60–70 hostile European and American miners (Fisher 1977:98–100).

South of the unsurveyed international border, the U.S. Army attempted to strengthen its position. In anticipation of the need for movement of troops and supplies, Lt. John Mullan, a veteran of the Stevens railroad studies, surveyed in 1854 a route to connect Fort Walla Walla with Fort Benton, terminus of navigable water on the upper Missouri. The goal was to build a wagon road as a prelude to railroad construction. Blocked by the Indian wars of 1855–1858, Mullan finally in 1859 put crews in the field. The opening of the Plateau to settlement, mineral discoveries, and flow of commerce from the shipping points at Fort Benton and Walla Walla generated considerable traffic over the Mullan Road. The route opened in 1862 and extended for 624 miles across the eastern Plateau and Coeur d'Alene Pass in the Rockies of Montana (Schwantes 1989:149).

In 1860 E.D. Pierce, a trader among the Indians, found gold on the Clearwater River in Idaho. That winter Pierce and 40 men eluded Army dragoons and holed up at the prospect on the Nez Perce Reservation. Unable to block the unfolding rush, Superintendent Geary met with Nez Perce leaders to promise military protection. The rush was on. Steamboats ascended the Snake to its junction with the Clearwater and there—on the reservation—emerged the boom town of Lewiston. By the summer of 1861 more than 5,000 miners had trespassed onto the reservation. They next discovered gold on the Salmon River. Rough towns—Oro Fino, Pierce City, Elk City, and Florence City—arose in the Nez Perce homeland (Bancroft 1890:239–249). In June 1863 the tribe was brought into treaty council and persuaded to accept a massive reduction of its reservation (Kappler 1904–1941, 2:843–848).

The discovery of gold on the upper John Day and Powder rivers in 1862 unleashed additional rushes of miners to the Blue Mountains of eastern Oregon. This flood of newcomers surged across the Umatilla and Warm Springs reservations. The miners established communities in the Baker and Grande Ronde valleys and at Canyon City on the John Day. Congress in 1863 recognized the impact of more than 35,000 new residents in the interior of the Pacific Northwest and on March 4 created Idaho Territory. In 1864, it created Montana Territory. Henceforth the administration of Indian affairs devolved upon the superintendents with the Pacific Northwest territories and the state of Oregon (Bancroft 1890:262, 642).

Euro-American entry into reservations unfolded in other ways subsequent to their creation. In the 1860s Congress authorized five military wagon roads. Buttressed by massive land grants—up to six square miles for each linear mile of road constructed—these projects inspired private companies to scramble for the right to build and operate the routes and to seek the transfer of title to the lands passed to the states. The Oregon Central Military Wagon Road developers turned south once they crossed the Cascade Range and carved a swath through the most fertile and watered portions of the Klamath Reservation. They secured 93,150 acres of prime Indian lands by their dubious ploy of constructing a wandering route into the river and lake lands of central and southeastern Oregon. The Indians of the Klamath Reservation were helpless to fend off this assault on their reserved lands (ARCIA 1874:75).

Railroad rights-of-way cut through other Plateau reservations. These included a Northern Pacific route through the Flathead (or Jocko) Reservation in 1882, a strip 200 feet wide plus land for depots, shops, and houses, a total of 1,430 acres, and through the Yakima Reservation in 1885, a strip of land 250 feet wide and containing about 1,000 acres (Kappler 1904–1941, 1:486–488; ARCIA 1882:103). Four railroad companies secured rights-of-way through the Colville Reservation between 1890 and 1898. The Oregon Railway & Navigation Company cut through the Umatilla Reservation ("Reservations and Reserves," fig. 2, this vol.), and the Missoula and Northern through the Flathead Reservation. Congress showed no compunction about opening arteries for transportation via both treaty and executive order reservations (Kappler 1904–1941, 1:349, 437, 486–489, 581, 643–644).

The assaults on tribally reserved lands also included congressional enactments to benefit non-Indian users. These special provisions included rights to drive sheep and cattle through reservations, permission to construct irrigation canals, and to carve out lands after the fact to buttress non-Indian title for the townsites of Pendleton, Oregon, and Harrison, Idaho (Kappler 1904–1941, 1:387–388, 457–460, 531–532, 600, 3:237, 524). Congress opened for mineral exploration and entry of claims the Colville Reservation in 1896 and the Spokane Reservation in 1902 (Kappler 1904–1941, 1:570, 754). It granted a general mineral opening on any reservation lands in the Pacific Northwest in 1919, at the discretion of the secretary of the interior. Allotments, administrative sites, springs and key water sources were generally exempted from such filing (Kappler 1904–1941, 4:223–224).

The advent of commercial salmon fishing and canning in the 1860s, patent and construction of fishwheels that harvested salmon and sturgeon by the flow of the current, and growing world markets for fish created further pressure on Plateau Indian subsistence resources. As early as 1859 the Thompson Indians near Lytton lost their salmon runs because of heavy fishing and mining on the Fraser. By 1877 the Indians of the Colville Reservation suffered from significant reductions in the fish catch because, it was believed, of the "large quantity caught near the mouth of the Columbia for canning and other purposes" (Fisher 1977:109; ARCIA 1877:187). In 1894 the chiefs and headmen of the Yakima Reservation were persuaded in a council to cede the Wenatchee fishery on the Pisquouse River, a tract six miles square, for $20,000 (Kappler 1904–1941, 1:529–530). The most notorious assault on the Indian fisheries in the nineteenth century occurred in the second treaty with the Tribes of Middle Oregon. Superintendent J.W. Perit Huntington on April 18, 1865, secured a treaty with the tribes of the Warm Springs Reservation supplemental to their agreement of April 8, 1855. By this new agreement the tribes relinquished all off-reservation rights—fishing, curing, hunting, grazing, and gathering. The treaty charged that the Indians who were often away from the reservation had abused their treaty rights. The government offered $3,500 in compensation. The Senate ratified this treaty on March 2, 1867 (Kappler 1904–1941, 2:908–909).

In British Columbia the tenure of the Northern Plateau tribes became increasingly problematic. Governor Douglas appointed gold commissioners to maintain order and to keep peace in the mining districts of the Fraser and Thompson. On the whole the Douglas policy worked, and vigilante action against the natives was dramatically less than in the United States. While the British government and that of British Columbia recognized Indian land title, after 1859 neither made any effort to compensate the tribes for the loss of their lands nor to enter into treaties to extinguish title. Douglas attempted to protect Indians at least in their places of residency by encouraging creation of reserves. In the early 1860s William Cox, one of the gold commissioners, staked reserves on the Okanagan, South Thompson, and Boneparte rivers. The reserve at Kamloops reached six miles up the North Thompson and 12 miles along the South Thompson. Douglas sought to create reserves within tribal homelands unlike the American programs of removal and concentration on regional reservations (Fisher 1977:153–154).

In 1864 Joseph William Trutch became chief commissioner for lands and works in British Columbia. The humanitarian influence of Douglas was gone; none of the

Fig. 5. Henry Thompson, Jôe Skahan, Louis Ike, and other Indians from Celilo present the Union Pacific Railroad engineer Tom Rumgay with a steelhead taken from the traditional fishing grounds of Celilo Falls, Oreg. Photograph by Everett Olmstead, 1940.

U. of Oreg. Lib., Special Coll., Eugene: M2529.
Fig. 6. Pendleton, Oreg., woolen mill. Opened in 1896, this mill became the best known maker of American Indian trade blankets and the only one to survive into the 1990s. The management of the mill chose to cater to the Indian market and sent out factory representatives to reservations throughout the western U.S. to learn the designs and colors most desired by the American Indian peoples. The Umatilla people were often enlisted to help in the marketing of the Pendleton blankets and modeled and posed for varous brochures and catalogues. The first catalogue of 1901 featured Chief Joseph arrayed in a Pendleton blanket (Kapoun 1992:121–151). Photograph by Lee Moorhouse, 1898–1912.

top, Smithsonian, NAA: 81–13422; center, Oreg. Histl. Soc.:CN 014910; bottom, U. of B.C., Mus. of Anthr., Vancouver:1.346.
Fig. 7. Economic readjustment. As native resources became scarcer, some Plateau Indians became migrant laborers. top, Yakima hop pickers. Photograph by Frank LaRoche, © 1903. center, Wasco-Wishram cherry pickers in camp. Photographed near The Dalles, Oreg., 1931. bottom, Lillooet laborers from the Pemberton, B.C., area in camp at the berry fields in Mt. Vernon, Wash. Photograph by Eric Broderick, 1947–1948.

successor governors had the conviction or strength to turn the tide of dispossession of the native peoples. Trutch, a former American surveyor and farmer, envisioned the province as founded in the advent of European civilization through agriculture. Reflecting on the Indians of Oregon Territory, where he lived for eight years, he said: "I think they are the ugliest & laziest creatures I ever saw, & we sho[ul]d as soon think of being afraid of our dogs as of them" (Fisher 1977:161). Trutch's assessment of the natives as subhuman, lawless and violent savages, led him to try to dispossess the tribes of as much land as possible. Trutch began the process of nibbling away at the reserves established by Douglas, particularly to wrest arable and pasture land in the southern interior. When he could, Trutch made "adjustments" that reduced Indian holdings and threw open the former reserves for pre-emption. Indians were barred in 1866 from pre-empting land claims (Fisher 1977:153–165).

In 1870 British Columbia joined the confederation with the other provinces of Canada. The Terms of Union contained no reference to the Indians. A motion to protect the Indians failed by a vote of 20 to one. A motion to extend Canadian policy and treaty making to the province was withdrawn. Ultimately officials in Ottawa added Clause Thirteen to the Terms of Union: "The charge of the Indians, and the trusteeship and management of the lands reserved for their use and benefit, shall be assumed by the Dominion Government, and a policy as liberal as that hitherto pursued by the British Columbia Government shall be continued by the Dominion Government after the union." The clause was specious and camouflaged the program of diminishing Indian reserves; it begrudgingly held Indians to tracts of 10 acres or less. "Clause thirteen . . . meant that some time was to elapse before the federal authorities realized just how illiberal the colony's treatment of them had been" (Fisher 1977:177).

The Indians of the Northern Plateau were subjected to other exclusions besides loss of land. As settler influence rose in the provincial government, no one held responsibility for Indian affairs except for the Indian reserve commissioner until the appointment in 1874 of James Lenihan as superintendent for the interior tribes. Lenihan, described as "weak of mind," was ineffective in office. In 1872 and 1875 parliament in Victoria prohibited Indians from voting. A provincial investigation in 1875 into the question of Indian lands and reserves led to publication of the Papers Concerned with the Indian Land Question, 1850–1875. The documents became an indictment of the reserve program but did little to change things. In 1876 Alexander C. Anderson, Archibald McKinlay, and Gilbert Sproat became commissioners to address the land questions. In 1877, as tensions mounted with news of the Nez Perce War and the possible exodus of Chief Joseph's people into Canada, the commissioners went to Kamloops to try to quell the Shuswap and Northern Okanagan ("Reservations and Reserves," fig. 10, this vol). The commissioners also visited Shuswap Lake, Okanagan Valley, and Similkameen. They managed to divide the native leadership, to defuse the tension, and to effect little resolution (Duff 1964:66–67; Fisher 1977:180–193).

Excluded from public life, the interior peoples from the Fraser, Thompson, Nicola Valley, and Similkameen gathered in 1879 for a pan-Indian conference at Lytton. Those present elected a council of 13 and selected a Lower Thompson Indian, Michael, to serve as chair. They adopted regulations to try to find improved medical facilities, schools, and subdivision of arable lands on their reserves. They abolished the potlatch and agreed to fines for drinking and gambling. Rather than viewing the conference, resolutions, and creation of the Indian council as productive, the settlers, mindful of the Nez Perce War south of the border, condemned the Indian confederation as a threat to their security (Fisher 1977:178–180).

Peace Policy

Momentarily the policy of control by military force of the U.S. Army gained the ascendancy in the administration of Plateau reservations. In 1869 military officers assumed the roles of agents. Bvt. Col. Samuel Ross, Washington Superintendent of Indian Affairs, lamented the lack of civil rights and the prejudicial treatment accorded the Indians. "This demoralizes and destroys his spirit of manhood," Ross noted. His solution was familiar—take all children between ages five and twelve away from their parents "either by compulsion or compensation" and place them in industrial schools. "I am satisfied that many of the Indians would really part with their children for a small compensation in blankets and presents," he wrote (ARCIA 1869:137).

The advent of the Peace Policy brought a significantly different philosophy to Oregon when Alfred Meacham became superintendent. In 1870, Meacham proposed that tribal leaders, not the Indian Bureau, determine the expenditure of annuity funds (ARCIA 1870:513). Meacham, an ardent champion of human rights, coped with U.S. Army officers at Umatilla, Warm Springs, and Klamath. In October 1871 he called a pan-Indian congress in Salem, Oregon, which drew three Indian delegates from each agency, except Klamath, which was deemed too distant. The delegates visited the state fair, listened to speeches, discussed Indian policy, and forwarded recommendations to the commissioner (ARCIA 1872:724). Meacham's humanitarian policies and practices proved too novel and threatening; he was dismissed in 1872 (Phinney 1963).

In 1870s the Ulysses Grant administration, bowing to considerable humanitarian pressure, embraced the Peace Policy, ignored the separation between church and state, and turned over the administration of Indian agencies to Christian denominations. Immediately there unfolded a scramble for "mission" opportunities and spoils in taking control of the reservations. When a denomination gained an agency, it could manage hiring, purchases, and teaching of sectarian doctrines in reservation schools. The stakes were both high and costly for the native communities. In the Plateau region within the United States the program led to dividing up the reservations. The Presbyterians, first in the field in 1836, secured Nez Perce Reservation ("Nez Perce," fig. 10, this vol.). Rev. Henry H. Spalding, the missionary who fled Lapwai, Idaho, in 1847, returned as agent under this program. The Methodists obtained Warm Springs, Yakima, and Klamath. The Roman Catholics, who had maintained an almost unbroken presence in the region, holding on through the disruptive wars of 1847 and 1855–1858, secured Colville, Umatilla, and Flathead (fig. 8) (Fritz 1963:76–79; ARCIA 1872:73).

The agents and their staffs in the 1870s and 1880s found the Plateau tribes impoverished yet wealthy. While many lived in what was deemed inadequate housing, they possessed disposable wealth, most of which they had no intention of selling. The Umatilla, for example, in 1870 had 10,000 horses, valued at $150,000, and 1,500 head of cattle, valued at $30,000 (ARCIA 1870:56). The agent at Yakima enumerated the assets of the residents of that reservation in 1878 as including 15,000 fenced acres, 5,000 cultivated acres, 16,000 head of horses, and 3,500 cattle (ARCIA 1878:140). The Nez Perce found ready

sale of cord wood, saw logs, and lumber to residents in Lewiston (ARCIA 1879:57, 1880:66, 1881:66). In 1896 the Indians of the Flathead Reservation shipped between 80 and 90 carloads of cattle to the Chicago market and sold another 500 head locally. Charles Allard, a reservation resident, specialized in raising buffalo and had a herd of 200 head (ARCIA 1893:185–186). The sales of

KSANKA KȻXAMAⱢIⱢ

KOOTENAI HYMNS AND PRAYERS

a

b

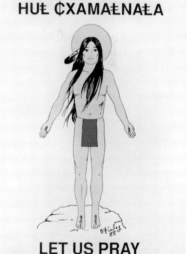

HUⱢ ȻXAMAⱢNAⱢA

LET US PRAY

top left, Spokane Public Lib., Teakle Coll., Wash.; top right, Eastern Wash. State Histl. Soc., Cheney Cowles Mus., Spokane; bottom left and right, Kootenai Culture Committee, Elmo, Mont.; a, Catholic News Service, Washington, D.C.; b, Amer. Mus. Of Nat. Hist., New York:16.1/584.

Fig. 8. Roman Catholic influence. top left, Masseslow, head of the Kalispel, with status symbols including a top hat, pipe, and crucifix. His brother Jim stands with him. Photographer and date not recorded. top right, Celebration of the Diamond Jubilee of Father Louis Taelman, St. Michael's Mission, Peone Prairie, Wash. left to right standing: Jerome Paschel, Spokane; Pete Valley, Jr., Spokane; Mary Michael, Coeur d'Alene; Mitch Michael, Spokane; Susan Michael, Spokane; Ellen Hubert, Colville; Agatha Isadore, Kalispel; unidentified man; William Hubert, Colville; Joe Seltice, Spokane and Coeur d'Alene; and Paschel George, Spokane. seated: Unidentified man; Joe Isadore, Flathead; Little Salmon, Flathead; Father Louis Taelman; Willie Andrews, Spokane; and Antoine Isadore, Kalispel. Photograph by Charles Libby, 1945. bottom left and bottom right, Cover and illustration on p. 50 from an 88-p. Kootenai hymn and prayer book (Kootenai Culture Committee 1989). a, Beaded buckskin cover of a "spiritual bouquet" made by the Kalispel people at St. Ignatius Catholic Mission on the Flathead Res., Mont., in 1954 for the mission centennial and delivered by Bishop Joseph M. Gilmore of the Helena diocese to Pope Pius XII. The buckskin, sewn over yellow and white silk, is adorned with the papal seal in beads. A spiritual bouquet is a list of devotions for a particular person (Nevins 1965:545). b, Thompson basket coffin, manufactured in the traditional fashion, using cedar-root coil construction and bark and beargrass imbricated ornamentation. Its European coffin shape and Christian design motifs reflect the influence of European ideas on Native culture Collected by F.M. Covert along the Thompson R., B.C., before 1910. Length 70 cm.

resources from the reservations provided important income to residents.

The tribes of the Eastern Plateau persisted in their annual buffalo hunts, traveling via mountain trails to the Northern Plains (ARCIA 1876:45, 1870:23). Almost all, in spite of growing wheat and vegetables, and planting orchards, remained actively engaged in fishing at their traditional grounds and stations. The Yakima and Nez Perce tested the suitability of their homelands for commercial fruit production. In 1878 the Nez Perce had over 3,000 fruit trees yielding apples, peaches, pears, and plums (ARCIA 1878:53). They also persisted in gathering activities. Lt. James M. Smith, Yakima agent, noted: "When the fishing season is over they betake themselves to the mountains gathering berries, part of which they also dispose of for cash" (ARCIA 1870:32).

The agents coped with the rising popularity of the teachings of Smohalla ("Religious Movements," this vol.) and concomitant Indian assertiveness among those who embraced the Washat religion. N.A. Cornoyer, Umatilla agent, estimated in 1872 that upward of 2,000 "renegade" Indians had gathered along the Columbia River under his tutelage. "These Indians are under no control whatever by the whites," he lamented (ARCIA 1872:747).

Modoc and Nez Perce Wars, 1873–1877

In spite of avowals of peace and a rapid shift from army personnel to Christian civilians in agency positions, the Plateau again became an arena for warfare in the 1870s. In both instances the advance of Euro-American settlement lay at the heart of the matter. Further, the ardent desire of the tribes or bands to remain in their homelands and their determination to try to do that in spite of mounting pressure to relocate on reservations increased the tension.

The Modoc War erupted in 1872. Settlers had passed through the Modoc homeland since the opening in 1846 of the Southern Emigrant Route. A branch of the Oregon-California Trail, this route annually brought travelers into Modoc country. Sporadic troubles, murders, and massacres both by Indians and by miners from Yreka, California, generated distrust and hostility. The Modocs were signatories to the Klamath Treaty of 1864 and, for a time, settled at Yainax Agency on the Klamath Reservation. Disenchanted with the drudgery of the farming programs, confinement under an agent, and most particularly the Bureau's anti-shaman campaign, Captain Jack and some 50 men and their families returned to their homes at Tule Lake, California. When the U.S. Army tried to force the Modocs back on the reservation, bloodshed ensued. Several Modocs attacked the Peace Commission on April 11, 1873, seriously wounding Alfred Meacham and killing Rev. Eleasar Thomas and Gen. E.R.S. Canby. The war then became a siege operation with the army and hired Indian scouts from Warm Springs and Klamath reservations surrounding the Modocs in the labyrinth of the lava beds (fig. 10). When the Modocs ultimately surrendered, the army tried the alleged murderers in a military tribunal at Fort Klamath. On October 3, 1873, the officers hanged four Modoc leaders. Two others were incarcerated at Alcatraz, and 153 Modocs were shipped by train to the Quapaw Agency in Oklahoma (Murray 1959:304–306).

The Modoc War catapulted Toby Riddle, or Winema as she was later called, onto the national platform ("Klamath and Modoc," fig. 11, this vol.). A bilingual Modoc and wife

Fig. 9. Economic life on the reservation. left, Flatheads farming on the Flathead Res. using a McCormick harvester. Probably photographed during the Flathead Indian Irrigation Project (Tom Smith, communication to editors 1997). Photographed at St. Ignatius, Mont., about 1910. right, Ranching, an important means of livelihood on the Colville Reservation. Ambrose, a cowboy from the Colville Res., Wash., is wearing chaps, beaded gauntlets, an holstered pistol and is riding an Indian horse, which is atypically shod. Photograph by Frank Matsura, 1903–1913.

Fig. 10. The Modoc War and Donald McKay. left, Toplash (left) and Winnishet, Warm Springs scouts, with Donald McKay. These men were instrumental in capturing Captain Jack and his Modoc followers ("Klamath and Modoc," fig. 11, this vol.). Photograph by Louis Heller, 1873. center, Loa-kum Ar-nuk, a Warm Springs scout in the lava beds at Tule Lake, Calif. He is wearing a strap across his shoulder that has a U.S. army buckle on it and a large sheathed knife at his waist, and he holds a Spencer carbine rifle. Photograph by Eadweard Muybridge, 1873. right, Reprint of the cover of book on McKay's life (T.A. Edwards 1884).

of Frank Riddle, Winema and her husband served as interpreters for the Peace Commission and the military tribunal. Following these events, the Riddles toured the United States with Alfred Meacham's lecture company. Meacham's books (1876, 1883) on the wars were influential in winning sympathy for Native Americans. Winema's son, Jeff C. Riddle (1914), wrote the history of the Modoc War and challenged other printed histories of the event.

Joseph's band of Nez Perce held fast to their homeland in the Wallowa valley of northeastern Oregon. Confirmed as part of the vast Nez Perce Reservation by the treaty of 1855, the band argued the homeland was theirs and not subject to the 1863 Nez Perce treaty ceding it to the United States, an agreement to which they were not party. In 1873 the Bureau of Indian Affairs proposed creating the Wallowa Reservation and President Grant did so on June 16. The tract was identified as a "reservation for the roaming Nez Perce Indians." Joseph's band had persisted in its seasonal round, including traveling the Lolo Trail for buffalo hunts on the northern plains. Settlers wanted the lush meadows of the Wallowa region and on June 10, 1875, Grant restored the region to the public domain (Kappler 1904–1941, 1:894–895).

Gen. Oliver O. Howard was ordered to compel Joseph's band to remove to the Nez Perce Reservation in Idaho. Joseph and his people ultimately complied but, as they prepared to move, hostilities erupted and became the Nez Perce War of 1877. Joseph, Looking Glass, and other leaders then began a remarkable retreat. Pursued by the army, which was outfitted with telegraphic communications and deep logistical support, the Nez Perce headed east over the Lolo Trail, engaged in several battles but escaped, passed through Yellowstone National Park, and were captured within a few miles of the Canadian bound-

ary in northern Montana. More than 500 men, women, and children had engaged in this epic journey. At their surrender, 431 surviving Nez Perces were removed to Kansas and Oklahoma; in 1885, reduced to but 280 people, they were moved to Nespelem on the Colville Reservation and to the Nez Perce Reservation in Idaho (Josephy 1965:618–624). Chief Joseph's (1879) assessment of the treatment of his people was so compelling that General Howard (1881) felt obliged to respond. This dramatic event in Nez Perce history continued to influence Indian people in the late twentieth century (fig. 11).

Warfare in the 1870s opened the opportunity for noncombatant Indian men to contract their services as scouts. One of the most enterprising was Donald McKay (fig. 10). Born to a Cayuse mother and a Scottish fur trapper father in 1836, McKay grew up in the Willamette Valley, participated in the California gold rush, and found employment by both the military and Bureau of Indian Affairs. In 1873 he enlisted a company of Warm Springs scouts, eventually 72 men, to work with the Army in its assault of the Modoc stronghold. McKay and a number of scouts then went on a national tour with the Warm Springs Indian troupe, visited Europe, and returned for the Centennial Exposition. In the 1880s McKay and his wife, Tuuepum, of Puyallup-Tenino heritage, were leading figures in the Oregon Indian Medicine Company. They promoted Nez Perce Catarrh Snuff, Wasco Cough Drops, Modoc Oil, and Warm Springs Consumption Cure. As part of its promotion the company published a biography of McKay (T.A. Edwards 1884). McKay's role as hired military assistant and participant in Indian medicine shows and traveling Indian troupes embraced several of the strategies nineteenth-century Indians used to leave the reservations and make a living (Clark and Clark 1971).

Fig. 11. *Grandfather Rock Series II*, depicting an episode in Chief Joseph's War. The rock is imagined to have witnessed Chief Joseph's last battle at Bear Paws, Mont., and tells the story through the artist's montage. The work includes 4 color snapshots of the landscape of the site representing the 4 sacred directions. Around them is a circle of photographs of standing, full-length Indian figures in ceremonial clothing. Bright, painted colors run through the circle of people, emphasizing their unity. At the center is a close-up of Grandfather Rock and below are photos of the rock being identified, measured, and weighed. The lower images are of the historical monuments marking the site of the battle. The beaded feathers and hanging blue strings recall both Plains Indian war shields and the sacred medicine wheel (Rabel 1993:12–17). At the lower left of the image, the artist writes: "Grandfather Rock remembers hearing the words of Chief Joseph, 'From where the sun now stands, I will fight no more forever.' (October 5, 1877)." Mixed media, 30 by 22 in., by Corwin Clairmont, member of the Confederated Salish and Kootenai Tribes, 1990.

Tightening Noose of Administration

Steadily the control of the federal government over the lives and destiny of the tribes mounted. Education, rudimentary and affecting only a small percent of the children on the reservations, became a primary focus for cultural transformation. In the 1870s and the 1880s this approach was driven by Roman Catholic missionaries through the schools at Saint Ignatius on the Flathead Reservation, boarding schools on the Colville and Coeur d'Alene reservations ("Coeur d'Alene," fig. 6, this vol.), and in the Christian-run

day and boarding schools on the other reservations. Rev. James Wilbur, long-term agent at Yakima, confirmed the approach when he wrote in 1878: "The Bible and the plow (which must never be divorced) have brought them up from the horrible pit, and put a new song into their mouths, and new hopes into their hearts. They are washed and clothed in their right minds." Wilbur hastened to observe: "There can be no lasting good accomplished with the children in school, without taking them to a boarding school, where they are taught to talk, read, and write the English language" (ARCIA 1878:141).

In 1880 Lt. M.C. Wilkinson founded the Indian Training School in Forest Grove, Oregon. This facility, located far from reservations, joined Carlisle and Hampton as national institutions designed to draw the finest students from the reservation schools into boarding programs where they would be trained as mechanics, agriculturalists, and domestics. During the summer the students were placed in the "outing system," apprenticed as laborers on farms about which the commissioner of Indian affairs noted: "Removed from the rules and restraints which make up the machinery of a large institution and render the life of its inmates more or less mechanical, they are thrown upon their own resources and responsibility" (ARCIA 1882:xxxii, xxxvi).

"The first rule here after cleanliness and obedience," wrote Wilkinson in his annual report of 1881, "is 'No Indian Talk'." He explained how he and staff carefully divided children "until all tribal association is broken up and lost." The English-only program and "their entire removal from family and reservation influences," he argued, "are the points of highest hope" (ARCIA 1881:199). The residents of Forest Grove resisted the presence of the school in their community. Thus, Wilkinson was compelled to relocate the institution at Chemawa, acreage purchased by the federal government four miles from Salem, Oregon. In 1884 the agent at Nez Perce dispatched 34 of the "brightest" students to this boarding facility (ARCIA 1883:57).

Agents also urged and aided the creation of Indian police force units on their reservations (fig. 12). At Flathead in 1877 the Indian police engaged in suppression of gambling and horse racing. They also erected a jail to hold violators. Agent Peter Ronan said: "This force is composed of the very best men of the tribes, who perform any duty required of them by their chief without any payment" (ARCIA 1877:136). The Bureau of Indian Affairs also encouraged tribal adoption of civil and criminal codes and establishment of the Court of Indian Offenses. These spread rapidly subsequent to 1884 and operated in conjunction with police force units. The goal was to eradicate nativism. The punishable "offenses" ranged from plurality of wives to gambling and obscenity. Common charges that resulted in trials and fines were gambling, drunkenness, theft, disorderly conduct, contempt of court, perjury, and assault (ARCIA 1884:67, 1885:71).

Charles Warner's approach at Nez Perce Reservation in the 1870s was to stress changes in personal appearance. "I

Fig. 12. Indian police. left, Colville Indian policemen. Photograph by Frank Avery, 1901–1916. right, Indian police badge, shield-shaped with bow and arrows. Indian police were authorized by the Dept. of the Interior in 1878 to enforce the agent's governance of the reservation. For a Cayuse Indian police badge see "Cayuse, Umatilla, Walla Walla," fig. 6, this vol. Length is 5.5 cm.

have induced many to cut their hair," he boasted (ARCIA 1879:57). The shift to log and frame houses, a transformation annually reported upon by the number of new units, was another measure whereby the Bureau officials calculated the success of their impact on eradicating old lifeways.

The tightening hold of the Bureau bore down steadily on Chief Charlo's band of 278 Flathead Indians. The 1855 treaty had provided a discretionary clause permitting residency in the Bitterroot Valley. In 1871 President Grant ordered the Flatheads removed to the Jocko Reservation; Congress in 1872 appropriated $50,000 to facilitate the removal and to compensate the families for the loss of their improvements. The Flatheads refused to move. A commission headed by James A. Garfield then secured a removal agreement and some tribal members under Chief Arlee moved to Jocko. In 1884 Chief Charlo went to Washington, D.C., to confer with the Interior Department; he insisted his people should remain in the Bitterroot Valley. Subsequently the Bureau offered 160-acre allotments, houses, tools, and other inducements; and 25 more families relocated (ARCIA 1891:278). For nearly four decades the government had pressed the Flatheads to leave their homeland and settle on the reservation. The Northwest Indian Commission of 1887 similarly sought to remove the Spokane and Pend d'Oreille to Jocko. The commissioners secured on April 27 the consent of both the removing tribes and the Indians of the Flathead Reservation to take them (ARCIA 1887:139–140).

In a subtle but calculated manner agents across the Plateau further drove the acculturation program by encour-

aging Fourth of July celebrations on the reservations. In time these became full-fledged patriotic events with a uniquely Native American character. George W. Norris, agent at Nez Perce Reservation, described the celebrations of 1888: "They were encamped near the agency for four days. The exercises consisted of camp-meeting, foot-races, and other games for the entertainment of the youth, a feast, horse-racing, and a war parade, in which about fifty Indians in paint, feathers, war dress, and undress paraded, singing their war song." Norris estimated more than 600 Indian men, women, and children marched four miles from Fort Lapwai to the banks of Clearwater as part of the celebration (ARCIA 1888:86–87). The Fourth of July events became a precursor to the pageantry associated with Indian participation in parades, rodeos, and round-ups across the Plateau in the twentieth century ("Flathead and Pend d'Oreille," fig. 8 right, this vol.).

The stress on patriotism became integral to day and boarding school programs. In 1889 Commissioner T.J. Morgan ordered: "National holidays—Washington's birthday, Decoration Day, Fourth of July, Thanksgiving, and Christmas—should be observed with appropriate exercises in all Indian schools." Morgan required display of the American flag and the teaching of reverence for it as a symbol of their nation's power and protection. The Bureau also called for reservation celebrations to observe the anniversary of the Dawes Severalty Act each February 8 and to "use that occasion to impress upon Indian youth the enlarged scope and opportunity given them by this law and the new obligations which it imposes" (ARCIA 1890:clxvii).

State governments also attempted to wrest resources from tribes. The State of Oregon asserted entitlement to swamplands and contested allotments on the Klamath Reservation. In Montana officials of Missoula and Flathead counties launched in 1897 an aggressive program to tax mixed-blood residents on the Flathead Reservation. "As nearly one-half the residents of this reservation are mixed bloods," wrote Agent W.H. Smead in 1899, "this question of taxation is a very important one to them, and they are anxious to have the courts pass on it" (ARCIA 1899:219).

Allotments

The Dawes Severalty Act of 1887 became the means for the most significant assault on tribal land tenure of any measure since the ratification of treaties and cession of aboriginal homelands in the 1850s and the 1860s. Allotment was another variant on the scheme of consolidating Indians, reducing their land base, and increasing government control and oversight over their activities. The guise of gaining citizenship at the termination of trust responsibility over their lands was not explained in terms of the tax responsibility that befell the holder of the fee-patented allotment.

The sixth article of the Treaty with the Omaha, March 16, 1854, was pivotal in defining the pressure on the Plateau for the allotment of lands. In the treaties negotiated with the Walla Walla, Cayuse, Umatilla, Nez Perce, Yakima, and Flathead tribes, Governor Stevens referred to the Omaha treaty clause and spelled out executive discretion for the survey and assignment of allotments. The treaty with the Tribes of Middle Oregon provided for 40-, 60-, 80-, and 120-acre allotments based on family size. The Klamath and Modoc treaty also provided a discretionary allotment program. The Molala treaty contained no such provision (Kappler 1904–1941, 2:740–742).

The lack of surveys rendered moot the possibility of allotments during the first two decades of reservation operation. On March 3, 1885, Congress passed an allotment act for the Umatilla Reservation. An allotment commission secured consent of the tribes but found insufficient agricultural lands within the reduced reservation to carry out the law. A second commission examined the needs and in 1888 Congress amended the 1885 act for allotments within a newly prescribed, but diminished reservation (Kappler 1904–1941, 1:891–894). Alice Fletcher, allotting agent, commenced the program at Nez Perce Reservation in 1890 (vol. 4:61). Many White men who had married Nez Perce women stepped forward immediately to select and lock up key parcels to the dismay of those on the reservation (ARCIA 1890:82). Within a year Fletcher had made over 1,000 allotments. The number by 1893 had reached, 1,905 (ARCIA 1893:138).

The progress of allotments only doubled the pressure to secure the cession of more lands from the tribes to the federal government for the opening of settlement. On May 1, 1893, the Nez Perce sold yet more of their alleged "surplus lands" to the United States ("Reservations and Reserves," fig. 4, this vol.). For the 542,064 acres, the tribe was to receive $1,626,222 of which one million was to go into a trust fund and the remainder distributed per capita (Kappler 1904–1941, 1:536–541). Congress in 1892 opened the northern half of the vast Colville Reservation and provided for allotments to those choosing to remain in that area but with the provision that at time of patent such lands were subject to state law and taxation (Kappler 1904–1941, 1:440–443). Allotment at Klamath did not commence until 1895 because of boundary disputes and claims of the Oregon Central Military Wagon Road Company's successor, the Oregon and California Land Company. The Klamaths secured a total of 775 allotments by 1897. Disputes by the State of Oregon over its entitlement to swamplands tied up 403 further allotments between 1903 and 1906 (Stern 1965:132–140).

The Indians of the Flathead Reservation staved off allotment as long as possible. Each time the agent raised the matter, they generally and vocally opposed it. On April 23, 1904, Congress authorized survey, allotment, and disposal of "surplus acreage" in the sprawling reservation. In 1909 President William Howard Taft opened the surplus lands to settlement (Kappler 1904–1941, 3:79–82, 655–657). On December 21, 1904, Congress recognized the survey error that had excluded 293,837 acres from the Yakima Reservation, authorized allotment, and provided the opening of surplus lands to settlement (Kappler 1904–1941, 3:110–113).

Each reservation had its own history of allotment. Acreages differed depending upon the enabling legislation or the agreements made between the tribes and the allotting commission. The entitlement of children and others subsequent to the initial round of allotments sometimes required new legislation to reopen the process. The allotment procedure created immense problems of checkerboard ownerships, fractional heirship interests, distribution of income from leased lands or revenues generated off of trust properties by timber harvest, farming, or grazing, and misuse of lands by non-Indian leaseholders. The program created the complex matrix of reservation lands: individual allotments, Indian fee land, non-Indian fee tracts, tribal trust lands, mission lands, and Bureau administrative sites. The legacy was unresolved throughout the twentieth century.

Some Indians obtained lands in trust in off-reservation settings. The fourth section of the allotment act provided that "any Indian not residing upon a reservation, or for whose tribe no reservation has been provided" could make an entry through the General Land Office. In 1890 Special Agent George Litchfield began assisting Indian homesteaders to secure lands under its provisions (Kappler 1904–1941, 1:33; ARCIA 1891:43).

In British Columbia the Joint Commission for the Settlement of Indian Reserves in the Province of British Columbia, appointed in 1876, was reduced to a single commissioner in 1877 but continued until 1908 when protests stopped the allotment program. The McKenna-McBride

Agreement of 1912 led to the creation of a five-member Royal Commission on Indian Affairs in 1913 to complete allotments and provide for reversion to the Dominion of Canada of unallotted reserve lands. The Commission worked throughout the province. It confirmed existing reserves, added some 87,000 acres to reserves, and cut off 47,000 acres. In 1916 it issued four volumes of reports. The province and Dominion ratified its work in 1924. The delay resulted from the petitions sent to Ottawa by the Allied Tribes of British Columbia, an intertribal organization of the Interior Salish, Nisgha, and Coast Salish tribes led by Peter Kelly and Andrew Paull. The Allied Tribes called for 160 acres per person on the reserves, $2,500,000 in cash settlement for lands, hunting and fishing rights, and educational and medical benefits (Duff 1964:68–69).

In 1926 the Special Joint Committee of the Senate and House of Commons agreed to hear the claims of the Allied Tribes. The committee heard Kelly and Paull but drew the conclusion that the Indians "have not established any claim to the lands of British Columbia based on aboriginal or other title." It decreed in 1927 the lands issue was closed, that the settlements had been at least as generous as under the Dominion's treaty policies, and recommended a grant of $100,000 a year for their benefit above normal administrative budgets. This effectively killed the Allied Tribes but did not put to rest the matter of the validity of the Indian land claims. The reserve lands were conveyed in 1938 to the Dominion by Order in Council No. 1036. By 1963 the 189 bands of Indians in British Columbia held 1,620 reserves or 843,479 acres (Duff 1964:68–70).

Searching for a Better Deal

In the first four decades of the twentieth century the Indians of the Plateau faced an uncertain future. Most resided on allotments. Prized allotment lands were the targets of would-be purchasers eager to work with the local agent to secure land under the easy patent provisions of the Burke Act of 1906. Such patents facilitated the transfer of ownership. Thousands of Indians either sold or lost their allotments for nonpayment of taxes during this period. Those who were able to hang on to their properties needed capital improvements to bring the land to higher levels of production, especially irrigation systems.

Technically the decision in *Winters* v. *United States*, handed down in 1908 by the Supreme Court, extended priority water rights to Indian users within the bounds of the original reservations. However, the entitlement meant little without the funds to construct diversion dams, canals, flumes, and siphons. The water right meant even less when non-Indian users, such as in the situation of the Umatilla River or the massive Lower Klamath Lake Reclamation project, appropriated the water. Unless the tribes could go to court by finding pro bono legal assistance or could persuade the Justice Department to protect their rights, they were

Colville Confederated Tribes Mus., Robert Eddy Coll., Cashmere, Wash.

Fig. 13. Wenatchee Indians of the Colville Confederated Tribes applying for homesteads under the Indian Homestead Act of 1884. This act allowed for a 160-acre homestead to each Indian family that settled on and improved a tract of land (Scheuerman 1982:116). left to right, Lucy K'see-humpt, sister of John Harmelt, Chief John Harmelt, Kami Sam, Felix, and unidentified Indian man. Photographed at Waterville, Wash., about 1884.

locked out from using water resources. Congress provided assistance to initiate reservation irrigation projects at Yakima, 1907–1914; Modoc Point on the Klamath Reservation, 1901–1920; and Flathead Reservation, 1909–1914 (Kappler 1904–1941, 3). Over the next several decades it made appropriations to fund repairs, build new canals, or purchase pumps (Kappler 1904–1941, 4). The Flathead project ultimately served 125,597 acres on the reservation, but by 1980 less than 12 percent of the irrigated lands were retained by tribal members. The Wapato Project at Yakima irrigated 90,000 acres of tribal lands (Ruby and Brown 1986:39, 62).

Some of the projects were charged against the tribe yet the beneficiaries were individual allottees whose lands lay adjacent to the canals and ditches. A number of the projects were far more complex and costly than envisioned, and years passed before Congress provided sufficient funds to make them operable. In 1914 Congress recognized that the Indians of the Yakima Reservation had been "unjustly deprived" of sufficient water from the Yakima River. Congress determined that they were to have 720 cubic feet per second but had been allowed only 147 (Kappler 1904–1941, 4:29–30).

Remaining tribal lands, though significantly diminished by openings for settlement, rights-of-way, and other reductions, retained bountiful timber and range resources. Hundreds of thousands of acres of ponderosa pine, tamarack, and Douglas fir beckoned loggers and lumbermen. The potential loomed large for further depletion of reservation resources by sale, theft, or destruction through fire. Regulatory legislation and programs were minimal. The Dawes Severalty Act permitted individual Indians to clear their allotments but prohibited sale of timber for profit. The Dead and Down Act of 1889 allowed harvesting only standing, dead trees. An initial appropriation of $100,000 in 1909 led to the creation of the forestry division within the Bureau of Indian Affairs (Kappler 1904–1941, 3:390). On June 25,

1910, Congress passed a law giving the secretary of the interior authority to regulate timber sales on both allotted and unallotted lands, provided the proceeds were used for the benefit of the interested Indians (Kappler 1904–1941, 3:478). In 1920 Congress implemented a fee to cover administrative costs on timber sales. The fee was to be funded either by the purchaser or from proceeds (Kappler 1904–1941, 4:242).

The advent of the Indian Forestry Service, its formulation of regulations, and the development of a professional staff to administer timber stands on reservations marked, in the 1910s, a new direction of treatment of reservation resources. The Bureau forestry officials oversaw scaling, fire protection, timber sale preparation, and timber management. Initially they worked under the philosophy of allowing clearcuts only when furthering agricultural goals and encouraged the preservation of permanent wood lots with selective thinning. Projected sales of timber in 1910 from the Flathead and Coeur d'Alene reservations were curtailed when fires swept through the national forests and flooded the market with burned logs. The fires, however, heightened the sense of need to build lookouts, construct fire trails, extend telephone lines, and markedly enhance the capability of protecting reservation forests (Newell, Clow, and Ellis 1986:2–26).

While World War I generated a brisk market for spruce and fir in airplane construction, the Plateau reservations lay distant from primary markets and were heavily stocked with pine. The downward turn in housing starts in the mid-1920s and the onset of the Depression did little to encourage Indian timber harvests in the Pacific Northwest. The Klamath Reservation was a clear exception. Rail connections, competing sawmills, and a market for box shook to pack California fruit led to a booming timber economy (Muck 1926:ii). Commissioner Charles Burke placed Indian forests under a sustained yield harvest. The rejection of the Indian Reorganization Act by Indians of the Colville, Klamath, and Yakima reservations removed clear provisions for conservation (Kinney 1973:74–75). A number of reservations, especially with the stimulus of market demands during and following World War II, moved into a level of harvest that threatened to liquidate the forests. In 1930 the Bureau of Indian Affairs merged its forestry and grazing operations, folding together 42 million acres of rangelands with seven million acres of forests (Newell, Clow, and Ellis 1986:3–8).

Only three of the nine reservations voting on the Indian Reorganization Act accepted the law and organized under its provisions. The Indians of the Flathead Reservation, first in the country to accept the law, adopted a government with representatives from the districts (and tribal groups) of the reservation, and formed a tribal corporation and constitution ("Reservations and Reserves," fig. 7, this vol.). Commissioner John Collier highlighted the Flathead as a showcase because allotments since 1910 had diminished the reserva-

tion by 750,000 acres, its timber revenues had been distributed per capita, and its people were "exhausted and ambitionless." The provisions of the act immediately restored 192,425 acres of "surplus land" to the reservation and made available the act's revolving loan fund to assist with tribal projects (ARCIA 1938:249).

There were problems at the Flathead Reservation. The Flathead and Kootenai who lived at the perimeter were primarily full-bloods. The residents of the central districts were mostly mixed-bloods, many less than half. Rivalries rooted in geography as well as ancestry made it increasingly difficult for the new council to proceed with its programs. Martin Charlo, a Kootenai chief, charged by 1940 that the council, of which he was an honorary member, was not communicating effectively with the districts. The difficulties at Flathead resulted in part from the effort to operate the reservation as a tribe when there were multiple tribes of different languages and interests on the same reservation (Taylor 1980:83–85).

The most important impact of the Indian Reorganization Act was curtailment of the allotment program and the extension of trust indefinitely over allotments yet held by individual Indians or their heirs. The New Deal also brought into action the Civilian Conservation Corps, Indian Division, which mounted projects of great importance to the timber-rich reservations. These included building truck trails, fire breaks, fire towers, stringing telephone lines, exterminating pests and forest infestations, constructing check-dams, reseeding range, making spring and water trough improvements, and fighting fires. The federal program had both direct benefits in terms of conservation and development of resources as well as generating jobs, modest incomes, and room and board for the young men enrolled (ARCIA 1938:228; Bureau of Indian Affairs 1938:42).

Claims and Termination

The specter of termination hung heavily over the tribes of the United States Plateau. Those who coveted the timber and range resources of the reservations were advocates of ending federal trust responsibilities. Those who championed efficiency and economy in government saw the end of Bureau of Indian Affairs dealings with the tribes as fundamental to their agenda of less bureaucracy and lower taxes. The Colville Confederated Tribes and the Klamath, both targeted for termination, were the focus of bills introduced in Congress.

The matter of outstanding Indian claims against the federal government was a long-festering issue with Plateau tribes. The invocation of sovereign immunity in 1869 by the United States from suits by Indian tribes necessitated that any complaint could proceed only with the consent of Congress. Securing a jurisdictional act was both difficult and expensive. Yet the Klamath were among the tribes who succeeded in litigation before the U.S. Court of Claims. They won an award of $5.3 million in 1938 for the taking of 87,000 acres from their reservation without adequate compensation (ARCIA 1935:215).

Creation of the Indian Claims Commission in 1946 and its lifting of immunity of the United States from tribal suit persuaded most Plateau tribes to file complaints. These cases had a mixed and convoluted history. The Confederated Tribes of Colville, for example, filed Docket 181 in 1947. Although parts of the case were settled, decades passed. The final resolution of part D, ownership of the ground beneath Grand Coulee Dam and Roosevelt Lake, was not resolved until 1994. By that date all plaintiffs were deceased. The victory, however, was substantial, for the Colville secured $53 million in a lump sum settlement and annual revenues of at least $15.25 million in the hydropower receipts from Grand Coulee Dam as long as the project functioned (Ulrich 1994).

Claims Commission cases, though persisting for decades, ultimately led to adjudicated settlements to approximately 70 percent of the lands in the United States Plateau. The complaints included the taking of lands without ratified treaty, unconscionable prices paid for lands, mismanagement by depletion of timber and range resources, and survey and accounting errors (Indian Claims Commission 1979). While many tribes viewed the funds as a legacy from the past, the awards were appropriated in an era when per capita distributions prevailed. Thus most tribes lost any opportunity to hold the claims award as a corporate asset and leverage it for economic development (Indian Claims Commission 1979).

While termination lurked as the next step to follow settlement of claims against the United States, only the Klamath felt the full impact of this disputed policy. In 1954 Congress passed the Klamath Termination Act. The law, effective in 1961, severed the tribe's federal relationship and set the stage for the disposal of 861,125 acres of reservation lands. When 75 percent of the tribe agreed to dispose of its timber, the federal government stepped in to avoid glutting the market. Termination was thus deferred from its initial target date of 1958, and the federal government created the Winema National Forest and acquired extensive wetlands in the Klamath Basin as part of the transition from trust status of the Indian properties (Newell, Clow, and Ellis 1986:4–42).

The devastating impacts of termination were soon evident. Some Klamaths spent the windfall assets of claims awards and sale of their lands, only to find themselves penniless and virtually homeless. Nearly 800 others placed their income in a bank-managed trust account to wait for 20 years before deciding what to do with their shares. The Bureau of Indian Affairs closed the agency, hospital, and schools. No longer were the Klamaths eligible for education or health programs. The scope of the disaster that befell the Klamath became evident in 1976 in hearings before the American Indian Policy Review Commission

(1976, 10:36–39). Slowly the Klamath regrouped, worked as a nonprofit corporation, and lobbied for restoration. Congress in 1986 overturned termination and renewed the federal relationship with the Klamath tribe (Buan and Lewis 1991:101).

Protection of Treaty Rights and Lands

Ten Pacific Northwest treaties were unequivocal in the assurances of their rights to fish, hunt, gather, graze livestock, and construct shelters for the preservation of foodstuffs. Assaults on these treaty-reserved rights commenced with Euro-American settlement and accelerated dramatically when competitors found commercial opportunities to exploit resources basic to Indian survival. The challenge to tribes was evident when as early as the 1870s the advent of seining, fish traps, fish wheels, and massive harvests on the lower Columbia River brought dramatic declines in the fish runs that once passed far into the Plateau to the streams cascading westward from the Rockies, Bitterroots, and Purcells.

Access to "usual and accustomed grounds and stations," the phrase used in the treaties, became an initial point of contention. In the 1880s, Frank Taylor, a homesteader on the Columbia River, built a fence to protect his crops. He blocked Yakima access to their fishery. The agent and tribe took the matter to District Court in 1887 where they received an adverse ruling. The Washington Supreme Court ordered Taylor to take down his fence because of the implied treaty guarantee of access to the fishery (Cohen 1986:54–55).

The next case, *United States* v. *Winans*, was filed in 1896. Winans operated a fish wheel at a "usual and accustomed" fishing station of the Yakima. Winans owned the land; his lawyers argued that his technology conferred on him a superior fishing right. The U.S. Supreme Court in 1905 found such distinction specious and rejected Winans's efforts to exclude Indian fishermen. Justice Joseph McKenna observed in the majority opinion that the Yakima had the right to cross the land, to fish at the site, and to erect temporary sheds for curing their catch. The case significantly held that the treaty of 1855 did not grant rights to the Indians but, instead, was a grant of rights from them, thus buttressing the "reserved rights" doctrine. The Court also observed that it did not "restrain the State unreasonably in the regulation of the right," a comment that proved of immense future trouble to tribes (Cohen 1986:55–56).

The question of where the reserved rights were located arose repeatedly, especially when the contest related to off-reservation fisheries. In *Seufert Bros. Company* v. *United States*, litigation between a major cannery and fish wheel operation on the western Plateau and Yakima fishermen, the Supreme Court ruled in 1919 that "usual and accustomed grounds and stations" may be either on or beyond the terri- *169* tory ceded to the United States by treaty (Strickland and Wilkinson 1982:450). The states sought to regulate the Indian fishery. As salmon became a scarcer and more valuable resource, the pressure mounted to regulate seasons, gear, who could fish, and where people could fish. Sampson Tulee, a Yakima, was arrested in 1939 for catching salmon with a dip net and selling without a state license. The county court and Washington State Supreme Court both ruled against Tulee. His case came before the U.S. Supreme Court in 1942 (Swindell 1942). In its decision the court ruled the state could not impose license fees on Indian fishermen (315 U.S. 681) (Strickland and Wilkinson 1982:450).

The taking of traditional fishing stations for construction of Grand Coulee and Bonneville dams in the 1930s caused great dislocation for tribes who secured subsistence and ceremonial fish from the Columbia. Grand Coulee Dam, constructed without fish passage, closed out the entire upper Columbia system to anadromous runs. Although the Bureau of Reclamation mounted two appraisals, Congress did not purchase allotments and tribal lands along the eastern margin of the Colville Reservation. Indian families were literally flooded out of their homes as the waters rose in 1940 behind Grand Coulee Dam. Their agent sent pleading telegrams to President Franklin Roosevelt urging action. Congress on June 29, 1940, approved the land acquisition program. It provided for the relocation of cemeteries; acknowledged tribal hunting, fishing, and boating on Roosevelt Lake; called

Oreg. Histl. Soc., Portland:44181.

Fig. 14. Confederated Tribes of the Warm Springs Res. signing an agreement for the compensation for Indian fishing sites that were to be lost at their Celilo Falls traditional fishing area. left to right, Nicholas Welter, Superintendent of Warm Springs Res.; Frank Suppah, tribal council member; Frank E. Nash, attorney for the Warm Springs Indians; Vernon Jackson (b. 1918, d. 1969), first college graduate of the tribe and secretary-treasurer of the tribe; Percy Othus, negotiator for the U.S. Army Corps of Engineers; and Avex D. Miller (b. 1905, d. 1978), tribal chairman. Photographed in Portland, Oreg., 1952.

for just and equitable compensation for lands inundated; and assured the Colville tribes that 25 percent of the reservoir was for the "paramount use of the Indians" (Beckham 1985; Kappler 1904–1979, 7:86–87).

In *Whitefoot* v. *United States*, an individual Indian claimed compensation for the loss of his fishery at Celilo Falls at the construction of The Dalles Dam. The Supreme Court found in 1962 that treaty rights were communal (fig. 14), not individual, and that Whitefoot's compensation was in the tribal settlement for the taking of its fishery (Strickland and Wilkinson 1982:451).

The issue of state regulation and types of gear used for fish harvest continued to generate tensions. In 1968 the arrest of David and Richard Sohappy for gill net fishing in the Columbia River above Bonneville Dam led 14 Yakima Indians to sue. In time the Yakima, Warm Springs, Umatilla, and Nez Perce as well as the federal government entered the matter and the cases—*Sohappy* v. *Smith* and *United States* v. *Oregon*—were consolidated for hearing in Portland. Judge Robert C. Belloni ruled in 1969 that tribes were entitled to a "fair and equitable share of all fish" that the state permitted to be taken from a run. Belloni ordered the State of Oregon to manage the fishery to insure that a "fair share" of fish actually reached the Indian fishing areas (Cohen 1986:78–79).

The judge encouraged the development of discussions where state, federal, tribal, sports fishing, and other interests could confront the issues surrounding the Columbia River fishery. In 1977 the Nez Perce, Yakama, Warm Springs, and Umatilla tribes founded the Columbia River Inter-Tribal Fish Commission. With a staff of more than 80 and a budget in excess of six million dollars per year, the Commission has worked on habitat protection, water quality, stock assessment research, fish passage, predator control, fishing access site issues, enforcement, public information, and other programs. This Indian organization has played a major role in raising public concern about the demise of salmon runs, hydropower generation policies, and the impacts of irrigation withdrawals and logging on fisheries (Columbia River Inter-Tribal Fish Commission 1992).

Questions arose about the hunting and fishing rights of the Klamath Indians within the bounds of the former Klamath Reservation. In *Kimball* v. *Callahan* in 1974 the U.S. 9th Circuit Court of Appeals held that the Klamath Termination Act of 1954 did not address reserved rights within the reservation. It held that the state could not regulate tribal members hunting, fishing, or trapping within the bounds of the former reservation, even when portions of it lay within national forests or private lands (Strickland and Wilkinson 1982:469).

In British Columbia a series of landmark court cases set the stage for the opening of treaty negotiations with the province's Indians. In 1973 the Supreme Court of Canada ruled in the Calder case on the contention of the Nisgha Tribal Council that its aboriginal title had never been extinguished in the Nass Valley. The court found that aboriginal title came from "long-time occupation, possession, and use" of traditional territories and existed at the time of contact with Europeans whether or not Europeans recognized it. Although the court split on the question of the continued existence of aboriginal title, it established the principle of aboriginal rights in Canadian law for the first time. As a consequence Canada agreed to begin negotiating treaties in the province to define aboriginal rights to lands and resources (Ministry of Aboriginal Affairs 1995).

In 1984 in the Guerin case, the Supreme Court of Canada ruled in the suit of the Musqueam Indian Band for breach of trust in the lease in the 1950s of 162 acres of its reserve to the Shaughnessy Golf Club. The court ruled the federal government had not leased the land on terms favorable to the band nor provided necessary information. The ruling proved highly significant because it recognized pre-existing aboriginal rights both on reserves and outside reserves and confirmed that the trust of the federal government was a fiduciary responsibility for Indian interests (Ministry of Aboriginal Affairs 1995).

In 1990 in the Sparrow decision the Supreme Court of Canada ruled on the appeal of a member of the Musqueam Indian Band who was arrested for using a drift net longer than permitted in the band's fishing license under the Fisheries Act. The attorneys argued the net length restriction was invalid because it was inconsistent with Section 35 of the Constitution Act, 1982, which recognized and affirmed aboriginal and treaty rights. The court interpreted the meaning of Section 35 by overturning Sparrow's conviction and ruling that the Constitution Act provided "a strong measure of protection" for aboriginal rights. It went further to lay out ground rules: (1) aboriginal and treaty rights are capable of evolving over time and must be interpreted in a generous and liberal manner, (2) governments may regulate existing aboriginal rights only for a compelling and substantial objective such as the conservation and management of resources, and (3) after conservation goals are met, aboriginal people must be given priority to fish for food over other user groups (Ministry of Aboriginal Affairs 1995).

The Delgamuukw decision, heard by the Supreme Court of British Columbia between 1984 and 1991, went to the provincial Court of Appeal. In this case—claims of ownership of 57,000 square kilometres of land near Hazleton by Gitksan and Bulkley River Carrier chiefs, the appeals court ruled the plaintiffs possessed "unextinguished non-exclusive aboriginal rights, other than a right of ownership" to much of their aboriginal territory and that the scope and content of the rights would best be resolved through negotiation rather than litigation (Ministry of Aboriginal Affairs 1995).

These and other court decisions set the stage for the British Columbia Claims Task Force in 1990 to enter treaty negotiations (Ministry of Aboriginal Affairs 1995a). During the course of the unfolding steps, the tribes (called First Nations) and province agreed to interim measures. These, like the process, were premised on negotiation rather than court battles. The agreements ranged from management and comanagement of lands and sources to protection of cultural sites in the midst of land or resource development (Ministry of Aboriginal Affairs 1995b).

The entire treaty process of the 1990s was subject to explicit "Treaty Negotiation and Openness Principles." These 18 understandings provided the context in which the tribes, province, and federal government operated. The principles included: equal application of the Criminal Code to all residents of British Columbia; phasing out of tax exemptions for aboriginal people; affordable agreements; equal application of the Canadian Constitution and Charter of Rights and Freedoms; continued access to hunting, fishing, and recreational activities; and the exemption of private property from the process. Important also among the several principles was "when the treaty process is complete, the total area of land held by First Nations will be proportional to their population" (Ministry of Aboriginal Affairs 1991).

Late Twentieth-Century Activities

The Confederated Tribes of Salish and Kootenai were among the first to realize the potentials for tourism on their lands. In 1946 they secured an appropriation of $550,000 for the design and construction of Flathead Hot Springs

Fig. 15. Kah-Nee-Ta Hot Springs resort. Facilities include a casino, mineral springs pool, and a European-style spa. top, Overview of lodge, which has 131 rooms; bottom, tepee accommodations. Photographs by John Rizzo, 1997.

Resort on the Flathead Reservation (Kappler 1904–1979, 6:308).

With the loss in 1953 of the great fishery at Celilo Falls and Fivemile Rapids on the Columbia, the Confederated Tribes of Warm Springs hired economists and planners to assist in finding ways to invest the funds secured in compensation to provide new opportunities for tribal members (Kappler 1904–1979, 6:583, 624, 702, 742, 788). The Tribes purchased a former allotment and developed the Kah-nee-ta Hot Springs resort in 1964 on their reservation (fig. 15). This complex eventually included swimming pools, cabins, a golf course, camping areas, a handsome lodge, and, in the 1990s, the Indian Head Gaming Center (MacNab 1972). The tribes' Warm Springs Forest Products Industries, a corporation founded in 1967, purchased a plywood plant, built a sawmill, and began harvesting tribal timberlands. The tribes leased sites to Portland General Electric for Pelton Reregulating and Round Butte dams. In 1979 the tribes secured a federal license—the first to a tribe in the United States—to operate a generator at Pelton Dam (Quill Point, Inc. 1984:53–59). The tribes' commitment to heritage tourism and preserving its own culture culminated in 1991 in construction of the museum at Warm Springs.

The lure of gaming dollars subsequent to the *Cabazon* decision in the U.S. Supreme Court and passage by Congress of the Indian Gaming Regulatory Act of 1988 led tribes to use their lands, resources, and partnerships with investors to construct and manage entertainment complexes. By 1997 these included the Colville's Okanogan Bingo and Casino, Coulee Dam Casino, and Mill Bay Casino; Spokane's Two Rivers Casino and Spokane Indian Bingo and Casino; Umatilla's Wild Horse Casino; and the Klamath Tribe's Kla-mo-wa Casino (Bear, Sterns, and Company 1997). Other tribes operated primarily bingo operations. The decades of Bureau of Indian Affairs efforts to suppress gambling on Plateau reservations had taken a new turn with the rush of non-Indians onto reservations to engage in gaming.

In 1965 the Nez Perce National Historic Park was created at Kamiah and at the mouth of Lapwai Creek, Idaho. The park, under the administration of the U.S. National Service, was founded to address native culture as well as Euro-American history (Kappler 1904–1979, 7:1041–1042).

Land remained central to the future of the tribes of the Plateau. The reservations contained a mix of tribal, individual, and token amounts of government-owned land.

Since the late 1940s tribes have studied options for use of their lands. Most, such as at Colville, Yakima, and Warm Springs, have engaged in tribally owned logging and sawmill operations. Others have secured important income through joint venture investments or leasing. The Spokane Tribe, for example, obtained a six-million-dollar irrigation system to bring 2,000 acres into cultivation subsequent to the building of Grand Coulee Dam. The Spokanes, like the Colvilles, engaged in logging, stock

top, Wash. State Histl. Soc., Tacoma:49632; bottom, Idaho State Histl. Soc., Boise.

Fig. 16. Indian organizations. top, First National Indian Congress representing the northwest tribes meeting in the Masonic Temple, Spokane, Wash., in response to the American Indian Citizenship Act of 1924, which declared all Indians born within the limits of the U.S. were citizens. The congress, sponsored by the Northern Pacific Railway and civic boosters, met Oct.-Nov., 1925. Attended by about 200, it stressed Native American cultural and social development and laid plans to raise money for a Northwest Indian museum. The congress, with its beauty pageant, judged contests, mock war games, races, and parades, made many of the Indian leaders feel they were on exhibit, rather than acting as policy makers (Fahey 1986:117–118). Photograph by Asahel Curtis. bottom, National Congress of American Indians gathering at which the newly confirmed commissioner of Indian affairs, Philleo Nash, was the concluding speaker. In his first official speech, Nash outlined the Kennedy administration's program, which focused on better development of tribal physical resources for the benefit of the Indians themselves; development of recreational resources for tourists; industrial development including vocational training and job placement for Indians; improved educational programs; expanded and improved housing on reservations; and development of arts and crafts skills. left to right, Sam Tilden, Nez Perce; Commissioner Nash; Josiah Red Wolf, Nez Perce; and Albert Moore, Nez Perce. All the Nez Perce were survivors of the War of 1877. Photograph by Howard W. Steward at Lewiston, Idaho, Sept. 1961.

raising, and farming. Uranium deposits led in the 1950s and 1960s to the opening of the Midnight and Sherwood mines from which the Spokanes received mining royalties (Ruby and Brown 1986:219). The Confederated Tribes of Salish and Kootenai of the Flathead Reservation leased the site of Kerr Dam to the Montana Power Company. They owned two resorts, Blue Bay on Flathead Lake and Flathead Hot Springs. The Confederated Tribes of the Yakama Reservation harvested timber, raised livestock, fished, invested in banking, and in 1980 opened a tribal cultural center at Toppenish. The complex included the Yakama Nation Museum, longhouse, library, theater, and restaurants (Ruby and Brown 1986:39, 62).

In the twentieth century the tribes of the Plateau forged numerous connections. These sometimes arose from the need for common action and led to regional Indian conferences or organizations (fig. 16). After World War II the Affiliated Tribes of Northwest Indians and tribal memberships in the National Congress of the American Indian became expressions of these commitments (fig. 16). Individual tribes scheduled a variety of cultural events. These included feasts and powwows to honor the salmon, tribal elders, root harvests, and treaty days. For many, the gatherings brought people from different tribes to the All-Indian Rodeo at White Swan, the Tygh Valley All-Indian Rodeo and Celebration, or the Pendleton Roundup at Pendleton, Oregon. Tribal involvement in the rodeo and Happy Canyon Pageant commenced in Pendleton in 1916. Annually the cavalry drove off a simulated Indian attack on the pioneer wagon train. In 1986 the Indians changed the story line in the Happy Canyon Pageant and attacked the cavalry and forced them into a surprised and angry retreat. Events at Colville Reservation range from the Circle Celebration with Indian stick games and dances to the Omak Stampede and its Suicide Race (fig. 17) (Nehl 1994; Ruby and Brown 1986:45, 54, 57, 62). Most of the riders are from the Colville Confederated Tribes, but other Plateau Indians participate in the gathering, which includes stick games, parades, dances, and ceremonies.

Fig. 17. Omak stampede. The Suicide Race is an organized event at the stampede and rodeo, which began in the 1930s. This type of racing was traditional among local Indian tribes. The race course, about 1,000 feet, starts below the crest of a hill (top) with a decent of 33 degrees, proceeds down the hill (center) and into the Okanogan River (bottom), crosses the river, and ends a short distance on the opposite side. Photographs by Sharon Eva Grainger, Omak, Wash., 1995.

Lillooet

DOROTHY KENNEDY AND RANDALL T. BOUCHARD

The Lillooet ('lílə‚wet) of southwestern British Columbia speak a language belonging to the northern branch of Interior Salish.* Two main dialects, known as Upper or Fraser River Lillooet and Lower or Mount Currie Lillooet, correspond to distinct geographical divisions.

There are pronounced cultural differences between the two main divisions of Lillooet. The Upper Lillooet are typical of Plateau cultures, and the Lower Lillooet are similar in many aspects to adjacent Northwest Coast societies.

Environment

Lower Lillooet territory falls within the Coastal western hemlock zone at lower elevations and within the Subalpine mountain hemlock zone at higher elevations. The Upper Lillooet region lies within the Interior Douglas fir zone at lower elevations. The dry area along the Fraser River is classified as the ponderosa pine–bunchgrass zone, whereas the montane areas of the Upper Lillooet lie within the Subalpine Engelmann spruce–subalpine fir zone. At the uppermost elevations throughout Lillooet territory there are alpine glaciers (Turner et al. 1987); a discussion of the ecosystems is in Matthews (1978). Descriptions of the geological history and major landforms can be found in Ryder (1978) and Holland (1964).

Territory

Lillooet territory in the early nineteenth century likely extended along the Fraser River from Leon Creek (fig. 1, no. 1) down to *šqiqáytn* (no. 47), and included the Bridge River drainage. The Seton Lake and Anderson Lake region was within this territory, as were the Birkenhead River and Green River drainages, and the entire Lillooet River drainage south to the head end of Harrison Lake, although

the Lower Lillooet hunted around the upper end of Harrison Lake for about 25 miles down.

The most significant change in Lillooet territory was along the Fraser River, particularly on the east side. Traditions recorded around 1900 indicate that prior to the nineteenth century the Lillooet lived only on the west side of the Fraser, with Shuswap territory extending almost as far south as the town of Lillooet, and Thompson territory extending almost as far north. Around 1900, there were more Shuswap than Lillooet both at Pavilion and Fountain, but by the mid-1900s this situation had reversed and the Lillooet predominated in both villages. Estimates of the southern extent of the Lillooet around the late 1800s range from *šqiqáytn* (no. 47), about 2.5 miles south from the town of Lillooet, to *naq̓áq̓tkʷaʔ* (no. 54), approximately 19 miles south. Lillooet and Thompson people in the 1970s recognized settlements in this area as bilingual. Villages as far south as *šəzázəl* (no. 51) were set aside as reserves (Dawson 1892:4, 5, 45; Hill-Tout 1900:500; Teit 1900:172, 1906:195–201, 253, 1908–1920, 1909:461, 463, 1910–1913; Bouchard 1968-1991; Kennedy and Bouchard 1978:22, 34, 35).

Teit's (1906:198, 1912:296–297) identification of the Green Lake area and the headwaters of the Lillooet and Squamish rivers as the original home of the Lillooet is not confirmed elsewhere. Powell's (1872) map indicates the area between Cheakamus Lake and Green Lake area as the boundary between the Lillooet and the Squamish. Teit (1908–1920, 1910–1913) states that Lillooet traditions point to the area around the head of Lillooet Lake and Pemberton as the earliest home of all the Lillooet.

Hill-Tout (1905:127–128) reported that the lower 12 miles of the Lillooet River was Halkomelem (Central Coast Salish) territory prior to the mid-1800s. Teit (1898–1910) specifically denied this, assigning to the Lillooet the entire area down to the mouth of the lower Lillooet River; this conforms to the Lillooet-Halkomelem boundary on the Powell (1872) map.

Territory was defined by the area of settlement and customary resource use. Where resources were not particularly valued or were very plentiful, the uninvited presence of non-Lillooet was tolerated. Where intertribal competition for productive hunting and fishing grounds was intense (as in the northernmost environs of Lillooet territory around Chilco Lake), Lillooet, Shuswap, and Chilcotin hunters were liable to attack one another (Teit 1909:554). In the

---

*The phonemes of the Lillooet are: (voiceless stops and affricates) p, t, č, k, kʷ, q, qʷ, ʔ; (glottalized stops and affricates) p̓, t̓, č̓, ƛ̓, k̓, k̓ʷ, q̓, q̓ʷ; (voiceless fricatives) š, ł, x, xʷ, x̣, x̣ʷ, h; (resonants) m, n, l, z, y, γ, w, ʕ (pharyngeal glide), ʕʷ; (glottalized resonants) m̓, n̓, l̓, z̓, y̓, γ̓, w̓, ʕ̓, ʕ̓ʷ; (vowels) i, a ([æ]~[a]), ə, ɔ, u ([u]~[o]); (stress) v́.

This inventory is adapted from Bouchard, Mitchell, and Edwards (1973), Bouchard, Mack, and Ritchie (1974a), and van Eijk (1985). Italicized Lillooet terms were transcribed in this orthography by Randall Bouchard. Additional information, in part reflecting a different analysis, is in "Languages," this vol.

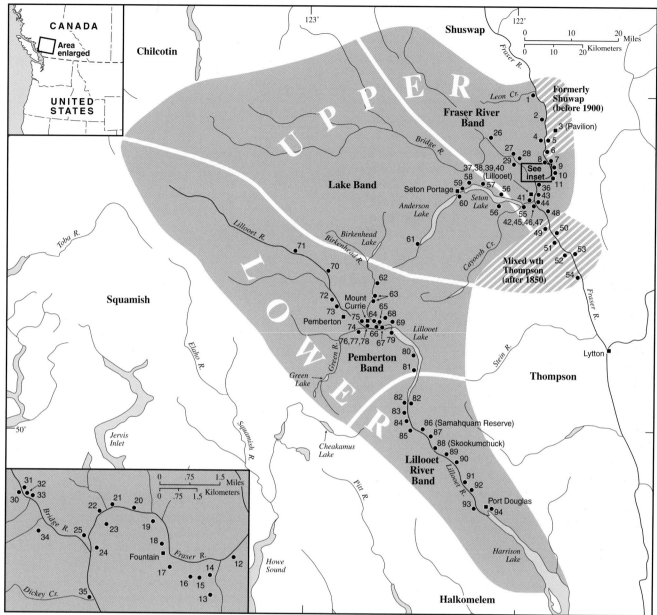

Fig. 1. Territory and villages of the Lillooet in the 19th century. 1, *čq̓ʷúq̓ʷšam* 'look upwards' (Shuswap); 2, *čx̣ayl*; 3, *čk̓ʷáylax̣ʷ* 'frosty ground' (Shuswap); 4, *šk̓əlpáq̓š* 'narrow point' (Shuswap); 5, *kʷlawt* 'many people living together' (?) (Shuswap); 6, *šq̓əwáql̓*; 7, *ƛ̓aƛ̓t*; 8, *š̓ʔax̣ʷ* 'slide area'; 9, *nq̓ʷašt*; 10, *ƛ̓iƛ̓q̓t* 'alkaline(?) earth'; 11, *q̓áq̓əz̓q̓n̓* 'small shelter top end'; 12, *laˢmím̓intn* 'place where something was dragged'; 13, *šx̣áx̣ələp*; 14, *štáx̣qa* 'foot of hill'; 15, *nhəlahílatn* 'place to dance and sing for spirit power'; 16, *tax̣ʷáx̣ʷwa* 'appears out of the bush' or *q̓ʷúq̓ʷu* 'spring of water'; 17, *šk̓ák̓ʷa* 'large boulders'; 18, *šx̣əliləm* 'false onion'(?); 19, *š̓ʔəq̓ʷəmq̓ʷəm* 'little hills'; 20, *šx̣ʷəlíʔk* 'protruding up out of the river'(?); 21, *nx̣əlúš* 'rock bluff'; 22, *x̣ələptáẃštn* 'short-cut over mountain'; 23, *k̓maq̓š* 'point of land'; 24, *šq̓áytəq̓ʷ* 'up on top'; 25, *nx̣ʷištn* 'place of foam'; 26, *múˢʷča?*; 27, *ntítxim* 'narrow place'; 28, *š̓ʔíʔštkn* 'little pit house'; 29, *nƛ̓uʔqímʔəm* 'water cuts into bank'; 30, *np̓sˢ́áˢ́nək* 'burned sidehill'; 31, *q̓ətx̣əlqnáz̓*; 32, *q̓ən̓q̓ánaz̓* black hawthorn bushes'; 33, *ləq̓əq̓íq̓*; 34, *q̓ələƛ̓x̣ən* 'little stockade'; 35, *šqaƛ̓* 'suspended'; 36, *čiẃt*; 37, *zaxq̓š* 'long point of land'; 38, *šaƛ̓*; 39, *ˢʷəča ˢʷáča* 'underground springs appear intermittently'; 40, *ƛ̓iƛ̓q̓t* 'alkaline(?) earth'; 41, *ƛ̓ix̣ʷt* 'gravel bar'; 42, *šək̓ʷəlwáš* 'split-open rock'; 43, *špəpx̣ʷtn̓* 'sand-drift'; 44, *npim*; 45, *ščamq* 'leftover food below'; 46, *nƛ̓əƛ̓k̓ʷ* 'small pond' (Thompson and Lillooet); 47, *šqiqáytn* 'place on top' (Thompson and Lillooet); 48, *q̓ʷix̣ʷxn* 'bridge at base' (Thompson and Lillooet); 49, *kələčx̣ʷúƛ* (likely Thompson); 50, *šx̣ópələq̓š* 'pierced nose' (Thompson and Lillooet); 51, *šəzəzəƛ* 'small circular gathering' (Thompson); 52, *nšak̓p* 'posterior cleft' (Thompson); 53, *np̓aˢčíčn̓* 'burned mouth' (Thompson); 54, *naq̓áq̓tkʷu* 'rotten water' (Thompson) or *naq̓áq̓tkʷa?* 'rotten water' (Lillooet); 55, *šk̓əmqín* 'head; top end'; 56, *kʷš̓áƛ̓qən*; 57, *čaláƛ* 'lake'; 58, *šk̓iƛ̓* 'pika'; 59, *štuʔúš* 'head of lake'; 60, *nqayt* 'on top'; 61, *nak̓ʷátkʷa?*; 62, *Qulpaútltɛn* 'portage' (Hill-Tout 1905:129) or *sûlpa´uɬtin* (Teit 1906:197); 63, *yax̣ʷəlá?*; 64, *(š)q̓ʷəx̣* 'oily'; 65, *ləqməč* 'hay mouth'; 66, *zəzəlkwa* 'eddying water'; 67, *nšəq̓* 'split'; 68, *x̣əƛ̓úlaʔx̣ʷ* '(also applies to the general area on the north side of the former mouth of the Birkenhead River); 69, *čəq̓číq̓əla* 'muddy' or (probably) *nk̓əm̓č* 'mouth of river' (Teit 1906:197); 70, *təƛ̓q̓ʷut* 'open rocky area'; 71, *šənáštam*; 72, *šúčmix̣ʷ*; 73, *nš̓ʔáq̓awəx̣*; 74, *tá?aq* 'foot of the mountain'; 75, *kʷóča* 'island' (?); 76, *qəq̓láluš* 'sore-eye'; 77, *k̓mámaq̓š* 'on the edge'; 78, *ƛ̓ƛ̓áləq̓* 'straight wood'; 79, *nk̓xín̓waš* 'island'; 80, *zaxq̓š* 'long point' (Hill-Tout 1905:129); 81, *q̓ʷix̣ʷlatn* 'sliding place'; 82, *nq̓íƛəq̓ʷ* 'head of the river'; 83, *p̓əq̓ʷpáq̓ʷuƛ* 'food storage caches'; 84, *(n)məšúš* 'narrow face'; 85, *q̓ələtkʷúʔəm* or *q̓əláx̣ən* 'fence; stockade'; 86, *šəmʔáq̓ʷam*; 87, *šəx̣čín* 'narrow straight' (Hill-Tout 1905:129) or 'serrated shore (?)' (Teit 1906:197); 88, *šqátin* 'waterfall'; 89, *skä´qictɛn* 'shallow water' (Hill-Tout 1905:128); 90, *(š)x̣ʷúmləq̓š* 'falling on nose'; 91, *smê´mits* 'little deer' (Teit 1906:196); 92, *lalá?x̣ən* 'fishing stage' (Halkomelem); 93, *tEkwä´tlōc* (Hill-Tout 1905:128); 94, *x̣áx̣ča* 'little lake' (Halkomelem) (Hill-Tout 1905:128; Teit 1906:196).

Upper Bridge River area, Shuswap and Thompson hunters joined the Lillooet without arousing any animosity (Teit 1906:225–226).

External Relations

Trade between the Lower and Upper Lillooet was said to have originated during the time of the mythological Transformers (Teit 1906:231, 1912a:296). The Lower and Lake Lillooet traveled frequently to the Northwest Coast to trade with the Squamish, Sechelt, and Klahoose. This trade was extensive; the route from Pemberton to Howe Sound was identified by Teit (1910–1913) as the most important interior-coastal trading route in southern British Columbia. From the coast tribes the Lower and Lake Lillooet obtained products to trade with the Upper Lillooet and with other tribes attracted to the trading center at the Lillooet River fishery. Products disposed of by the Lower Lillooet to Upper bands included dentalia, cedar bark, yew wood, mountain goat wool blankets, and sometimes slaves obtained from the coast. Included in the items received in exchange were dried salmon, Indian hemp, and dried soapberries and salalberries (Teit 1906:231–233).

Relations with the Chilcotin were generally hostile, and stories are common of their raiding the Lillooet for salmon and attacking isolated hunting parties and wandering children for slaves. One tradition describes an attack of the Lillooet on the Chilcotin. The Halkomelem on the Lower Fraser River, however, engaged in warfare with the Lower Lillooet over elk hunting in the Pitt and Harrison river areas, and hunters of both tribes were massacred. In the distant past, the Lillooet made war on the coastal people and took many slaves. Sometime earlier, the Shuswap waged war on the Lower Lillooet, driving them from their lands and fisheries between Anderson Lake and Birkenhead River, which they then occupied seasonally for as long as 15 years before being forced to retreat. The Lower Lillooet in the early 1800s were subjected to frequent raids by the Thompson. Allied forces of Thompson, Shuswap, and Okanagan attacked the Lake Lillooet but remained friendly with the Fraser River Band of Lillooet (Teit 1906:234–247; Nastich 1954; Bouchard and Kennedy 1977:40–41, 50–51, 1988).

Component Groups

Near Birkenhead Lake, a rock footprint said to be made by one of the Transformers marks the height of land and the major division between the Upper and the Lower Lillooet (A.C. Anderson 1846; Teit 1906:195–196, 1912a:296; Elliott 1931:168; Bouchard and Kennedy 1977:15).

The Upper Lillooet division consists of the Fraser River Lillooet, sometimes referred to as the šɬáɬimxʔúl ('real, original Upper Lillooet') and comprising the people living along the Fraser between Leon Creek and 25-Mile village, and the Lake Lillooet, known as the čaláɬmx or əxlíxmx who live around Seton Lake, Seton Portage, and Anderson Lake (Boas 1891:map; Teit 1906:197; Kennedy and Bouchard 1978:22–23). The Canadian government has classified the Upper Lillooet, from north to south, as the Pavilion, Fountain, Bridge River, Lillooet, and Cayoosh Creek Bands. The southernmost villages (nos. 52–54) are identified as part of the Lytton Band (Thompson Indians). The Lake Lillooet are classified as the Seton Lake and Anderson Lake Bands (Canada. Royal Commission on Indian Affairs 1916, 2:447–462).

The Lower Lillooet are comprised of the líɬwatʔúɬ, 'real original Lillooet', or Pemberton Band of the Pemberton, Mount Currie, and Lillooet Lake area, and the Lillooet River Band (líɬwat or nkʷúcin 'downstream') of the lower Lillooet River and Lake, Skookumchuck, and Port Douglas area (Teit 1906:196–197; Kennedy and Bouchard 1975b). Hill-Tout (1905:129) uses the term lilwatʔúl for the area around sites 77–79 (fig.1). The Department of Indian Affairs identified the Mount Currie people as the Pemberton Band, and the lower Lillooet River people as the Douglas Tribe consisting of the Samahquam, Skookumchuck, and Douglas Bands (Canada. Royal Commission on Indian Affairs 1916, 3:629–633).

Culture

Ethnographic sources available for the Lillooet date from around 1900 and reflect this culture as it was in the mid-nineteenth century. This sketch pertains to that time except where otherwise noted.

Subsistence

The availability of fish, game, and plant resources varied considerably throughout the Plateau; the Lillooet people of the Fraser River were more dependent on salmon than were their Interior Salish neighbors to the east or the Lillooet people of the Pemberton Valley and Lillooet Lake where the salmon were less fat and game was plentiful. Many resources were both temporarily and spatially restricted, requiring the Lillooet to plan their yearly moves accordingly. Apart from employing a seasonal strategy, Lillooet people engaged in exchange and raiding to compensate for specific resource shortfalls. The Lower Lillooet especially made arduous journeys across the coastal glaciers to fish and trade with Northwest Coast peoples.

• FISHING   All Lillooet people depended greatly upon salmon although the species available varied between the upper and lower divisions, as did the technology used to harvest these fish and to preserve them.

Salmon fishing began with the first run of chinooks in April on the Fraser River and in May on the Lillooet River system. It continued sporadically until October, with the concentration of the salmon harvest occurring in late summer. Steelhead were available to the Upper Lillooet from September through the spring; among the Lower Lillooet, this species was fished in April.

In the 1990s, Indian people continued to catch chinook, salmon, sockeye, and coho in the Fraser River near Lillooet by dipping them from the river using long handled, collapsible set (or bag) nets (fig. 2; "Fishing," fig. 16, this vol.). The fishermen, while using such nets, stand perched on rocky promontories or on scaffolds built out over the river. Differential access to these fishing sites has been described by Romanoff (1985:138–143, 1992a:241–247) and Kennedy and Bouchard (1992:305–316). Salmon are also taken in gill nets on the Fraser River. Among the Lower Lillooet in the 1990s, sockeye, chinook, coho, chum, and the occasional pink salmon were still caught in gill nets set in Lillooet Lake (Kennedy and Bouchard 1975b).

The Lower Lillooet traditionally also fished salmon with trawl nets suspended between two canoes, or harpooned the salmon from shore or from weirs constructed across rivers. Basketry traps of a conical, cylindrical, or flat-decked shape and made from split red cedar were set in smaller streams near the outlets of lakes or near mouths of creeks flowing into lakes. The Upper Lillooet constructed a box-shaped trap from split pieces of pine wood, and a cylindrical trap made of willow saplings. Basketry traps could also be used along the banks of rivers where the current was swift. The fish would pass out through the upper end of the trap and into a small corral made of sticks and brush, from which they were speared or scooped out with a small dip net. The use of both double and single weirs has been reported. Gaff hooks, leisters, and fishhooks completed the repertoire of fishing implements ("Fishing," fig. 14d, this vol.) (Teit 1906:227–228; Ray 1942:105–115; Bouchard and Kennedy 1977:64–69; Kennedy and Bouchard 1975b, 1978:39–40, 1992:280–290; Romanoff 1985:126–128, 1992a:229–230).

Prov. Arch. of B.C., Victoria: top left, 46505, top right, D-6014; Amer. Mus. of Nat. Hist., New York: bottom left, 43108, bottom right, 16/5952.

Fig. 2. Fishing. top left, Camp with salmon drying sheds at Birkenhead River, B.C. Photographed about 1930s. top right, Dipnet fishing on the Fraser River at Lillooet, B.C. Photographed about 1952. bottom left, Sockeye salmon drying at Skookumchuck, B.C. Photograph by Harlan I. Smith, 1899. bottom right, Fish spear head consisting of a single detachable barb with a metal tip and wooden setting. Collected by James A. Teit, 1899. Length of barb, 9 cm.

Fish could be boiled to obtain the oil (fig. 3) or preserved. Among the Upper Lillooet where traditional methods are still utilized in the 1990s, scored, fileted salmon was hung on shaded racks built along the riverbank (fig. 2). After about five days, the hot, dry winds blowing along the river have removed sufficient moisture from the filet for the cured salmon to be stored. Wind-dried salmon is eaten raw, boiled, or roasted over a fire. The dried backbones are kept for soup. Wind-dried salmon is supplemented with canned and frozen salmon, although wind-dried fish is preferred for its taste, and as an article for trade (Bouchard and Kennedy 1977:64–67; Kennedy and Bouchard 1992:290–298; Romanoff 1985:125–126, 131–134, 1992a:233–240).

In Lower Lillooet territory, where few locations are suitable for wind-drying fish, salmon filets are hung in an enclosed smokehouse and left to dry over a low fire of alder or cottonwood. Formerly, salmon caught late in the year could be hung whole on a rack or tree branch and "freeze-dried" (Kennedy and Bouchard 1975b, 1992:295; Bouchard and Kennedy 1977:68–69).

Salmon roe was sun-dried or smoke-dried, or fermented by placing the eggs in a birchbark basket that was buried for several months. Once fermented, the eggs were boiled with roots and eaten. The Upper Lillooet prepared powdered dried salmon using an elaborate process involving roasting, sun drying, and periodic pulverizing of the drying flesh. The resulting powdered meal when mixed with dried saskatoon-berries was a favorite food for hunters (Bouchard and Kennedy 1977:67; Kennedy and Bouchard 1992:296; Romanoff 1985:134–136, 1992a:237–238).

Freshwater species available to the Lillooet included rainbow trout, Kamloops trout, Dolly varden char, whitefish, squawfish, freshwater ling, sturgeon, and lamprey. These were taken with set-lines or with hemp lines fixed with baited sharp-angled hooks, or were speared with leisters, or impounded in fish traps. Pitch-torches were used at night to attract fish to the surface of lakes where they could be speared (Teit 1906:228; Ray 1942:105–115; Kennedy and Bouchard 1975b, 1992:278–280).

The Lower Lillooet marked the arrival of the sockeye salmon by holding a first salmon ceremony emphasizing the interdependence of salmon and humans. During this ceremony, the salmon was treated in a ritually prescribed manner, boiled, and then fed to all but the ritually impure (Hill-

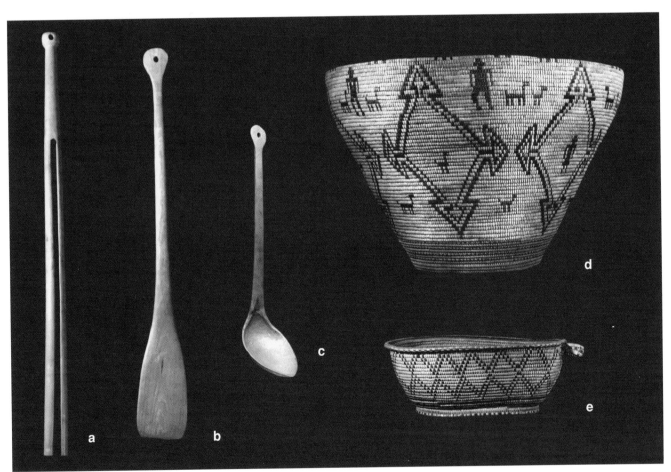

Amer. Mus. of Nat. Hist., New York: a, 16/6942; b, 16/6943; c, 16/6945; d, 16/6929; e, 16/6938.
Fig. 3. Implements for fish oil production. a, Tongs made of birch wood used for lifting hot stones in and out of boiling baskets; b, stirring stick made of birch wood; c, spoon used for skimming fish oil out of boiling baskets; d, fish-boiling basket with 4-pointed arrow design with figures of men, dogs, and ducks. e, Fish-oil basket with spout. After the fish were boiled, the oil was placed into this basket and then poured into skins or bladders. Collected by James A. Teit in 1899. Length of a, 78 cm; others to same scale.

Tout 1905:140; Teit 1906:280; Kennedy and Bouchard 1975b; Bouchard and Kennedy 1977:69).

• HUNTING Hunting was a specialized occupation for certain men known as *təwít* whose skill was enhanced by possession of an appropriate guardian-spirit power (Bouchard and Kennedy 1977:64, 70–71; Kennedy 1971–1991; Kennedy and Bouchard 1978:40). The rewards for such hunters could be substantial and included polygyny, labor, and gifts (Romanoff 1992:472,478–480).

Mule deer in Upper Lillooet territory, and blacktail deer in Lower Lillooet territory, were the most important land mammals. They were hunted using bow and arrows, snares, pitfall traps, spears and clubs. Trained hunting dogs were used to track deer by the Upper Lillooet, whereas specialized Lower Lillooet hunters did this themselves, chasing the animals to where a group of hunters would be waiting. Deer hunting was primarily a fall activity and lasted until the deer began to rut in November (Teit 1906:224–227; Kennedy and Bouchard 1977).

Mountain goat and black bear were hunted by both the Upper and Lower Lillooet. Like venison, goat and bear meat was prepared for winter use by drying it in the sun (in Upper Lillooet) or by smoking it (in Lower Lillooet). Upper Lillooet bear hunters sang to the animal as it was butchered (Teit 1906:279).

California bighorn sheep and Rocky Mountain elk were available only around the Fraser River area. Beaver, marmots, rabbits, pika, and snowshoe hare were hunted for their meat and fur by all Lillooet ("Ethnobiology and Subsistence," fig. 12, this vol.). In the nineteenth and twentieth centuries the Lower Lillooet people were active in trapping fur-bearing animals for sale to commercial furriers (Kennedy and Bouchard 1977). Teit (1906:223) reports that the Lillooet raised dogs for their flesh and skins. Horse meat was popular among the Upper Lillooet in the nineteenth century (Kennedy and Bouchard 1978:49).

Birds did not comprise a significant part of the diet, although approximately 100 species are distinguished in the Lillooet language (Kennedy 1976b).

• GATHERING Over 200 species of native plants were recognized by the Lillooet, most of which were used in the diet, as sources of materials in technology, and as medicines. The most commonly preserved berries were saskatoonberries. These were especially valued by the Upper Lillooet, who distinguished five sub-species. Huckleberries, blackcaps (fig. 4), and soapberries grow abundantly in the mountains of the Lower Lillooet territory. Large quantities of yellow avalanche lily and spring beauty corms were dug, as were skunk cabbage rhizomes. Large quantities of roots and berries were processed at high elevation intertribal harvesting grounds (Bouchard and Kennedy 1977:71–75; Kennedy and Bouchard 1978:41–42; Turner 1992; Turner et al. 1987; Alexander 1992).

Structures

The Lillooet occupied three basic types of settlements during their annual subsistence round: the winter village, the annually occupied seasonal site, and the camp.

Until the late nineteenth century the Lillooet maintained permanent winter settlements composed of clusters of semi-subterranean houses. These houses were generally situated alongside waterways, although numerous housepits were still visible on high terraces along the Fraser River in the 1990s. In the historic period, Lillooet settlements were situated along major waterways such as the Lillooet River and Lake, the Birkenhead River, Anderson and Seton Lakes, and the Fraser River. From these winter sites, small groups of people dispersed in the spring to camps used to obtain subsistence resources.

The depth of the excavation of Upper Lillooet houses was about four feet; those built by the Lower Lillooet were more shallow due to the higher water table. Upper Lillooet pit houses varied from 5 to 15 meters in diameter with a conical superstructure built over a square, round, or oval pit. Those in the Pemberton Valley had a square, pyramidlike superstructure covered with cedar bark and earth (fig. 5). Some large pit houses built by the Lake Lillooet had the wide opening on the top divided in half for the convenience of the numerous residents. The ladder used to provide access to the pit house was either carved or painted in red and white. Villages particularly vulnerable to attack were sometimes equipped with underground escape tunnels (Teit 1906:212–213, 236; Ray 1939:134; Bouchard and Kennedy 1977:62–64; Kennedy and Bouchard 1978:37).

Teit (1906:213) estimated that over half of the Lower Lillooet resided in gable-roofed cedar plank houses, square or oblong in shape, and large enough to accommodate as many as eight families. Permanently affixed furnishings included a bed platform, scaffolds for holding supplies, and sticks on which to dry clothes. Additionally, the southernmost Lower Lillooet villages had plank dwellings that were smaller but similar in construction to those used by the Halkomelem residing along the lower Fraser River. Hill-Tout (1905:134) reported that the Lillooet plank house differed from the neighboring style in that each family was segregated by permanent wooden partitions, although Teit (1898-1910) suggested that these partitions were used only on the sides of a family's compartment, leaving the front open to the central area of the house. Plank houses were used in both summer and winter. Figures associated with the resident family were carved on the interior support posts or on exterior walls or poles placed on the gable ends of houses (Hill-Tout 1905:154–155).

Some of the Upper Lillooet wintered in bark and earth-embanked lodges covered with a double layer of mats (Teit 1906:213). The Lower and Lake Lillooet sometimes used a winter house that was oblong in shape, strongly built of

top, Field Mus., Chicago: 115954.

Fig. 4. Berry picking. top, Coil-constructed cedar-root burden basket, partly imbricated with cherry bark and beargrass in a butterfly design. The strap is made of cedar bark. Collected by James A. Teit about 1917. Height 19 cm. bottom, Edith O'Donaghey with a coiled cedar-root berry basket full of blackcaps. Photograph by Nancy Turner, Lillooet, B.C., 1987.

poles supporting a double layer of bark, and covered entirely with earth (Teit 1908–1920).

Summer dwellings at resource sites consisted of two lodges, open in front and arranged so that the open sides faced each other. The gap between them served as a passageway and hearth site. Dwellings of this type that were constructed close to hunting or root-digging grounds had a base of logs placed horizontally, one on top of another to a height of several feet. The steeply pitched roof rested on long poles that were supported by shorter vertical braces. Similar dwellings constructed without the log base were used at fishing camps. Both divisions of the Lillooet also used willow-framed sweat lodges. Temporary shelters included the brush-covered lean-to, the hide-covered tepee, and mat lodges of the square, oblong, and conical Plateau style.

Girls at the onset of menses sat alone in a conical structure made of four small fir trees arranged in a square with their tops tied together. Menstrual huts were small, conical-shaped lodges made roughly of brush or cedar bark (Teit 1900:198, 1906:213–215; Ray 1939:137; Kennedy and Bouchard 1977).

Fortified villages have been reported among both the Lower and Upper Lillooet (Hill-Tout 1900:500; Teit 1906:235–236; Bouchard 1968–1991). One fortification observed by explorer Simon Fraser near Lillooet in June 1808 was said to measure 100 by 24 feet, surrounded with palisades 18 feet high that slanted inward. A shorter row of stakes inside the palisade supported bark-covered lodges (Lamb 1960:82).

Teit (1906:217) noted that carved human figures with masked faces resembling particular animals were erected outside Lower Lillooet houses.

Technology

Baskets, made by the women, were used for storage, carrying, stone-boiling, and serving food. Large baskets were used for bathing infants. Red cedar was the preferred basketry material, although Engelmann spruce was used also. Recognized and named designs were utilized in the imbrication of coiled baskets with wild cherry bark and bear grass (fig. 4; "Basketry," figs. 6, 10, this vol.). The bark from Englemann spruce, birch, white pine, and black cottonwood was also employed in basketry. As well, openwork baskets of cedar twigs were made. Only the Lower Lillooet wove baskets by using cedar splints for the warp and wrapping them with a woof of split cedar roots, a style common among the Northwest Coast tribes. The people of Lillooet River made water containers of bent cedar. Salmon oil was stored in vessels made from salmon skin.

Cattail and tule mats were used as lodge coverings, table mats, and bedding. The Lower Lillooet plaited mats and bags of inner red cedar bark. Dried elaeagnus bark and Indian hemp was spun and used in twining bags, mats, and wallets, as well as for fishing nets. Bowls were carved from maple. Douglas fir saplings were used as pole handles for harpoons, leisters, and gaffs, and as racks, scaffolds, and raised food caches. Western yew wood was used for bows,

180

Fig 5. Models of Lower Lillooet winter pit houses. left, Pit house covered with a conical structure of logs and earth, with a ladder near the entrance. Photographed near head of Lillooet Lake, B.C., around 1975. right, Charlie Mack's unfinished model of a semisubterranean dwelling showing exposed superstructure. Photograph by Dorothy Kennedy, Mt. Currie, B.C., 1977.

wedges, digging sticks, and snowshoe frames (Teit 1906:215–217; Turner et al. 1987).

Transport

According to Teit (1906:229), bark canoes were the common form of watercraft prior to the introduction of iron tools. The most common of these was the sturgeon-nose bark canoe although other bark canoes with rounded, high bow and stern, or long, flat projecting bow and stern were also made. Log rafts were used in still water. Single sheets of cottonwood, spruce, or red cedar (or, in the Bridge River area, paper birch) were used for manufacturing bark canoes. Dugout canoes carved from red cedar (fig. 6), cottonwood, or Sitka spruce were still in use among the Lower Lillooet in the 1970s. These watercraft were maneuvered up the rivers by use of canoe poles, and in Lillooet Lake by paddles (Bouchard and Kennedy 1977:77–78).

Eight styles of snowshoes (fig. 7) made from maple, yew, or occasionally, red cedar have been described (Teit 1906:230–231). Thus, travel was not restricted in the winter, and stories are told of the Lillooet walking great distances over glaciers on snowshoes (Bouchard 1968–1991).

Clothing and Adornment

Clothing, including socks, capes, aprons, pants, and shirts, could be made from plant fibers such as elaeagnus bark or black tree lichen, although animal skins, particularly buckskin, were preferred. Buckskin capes of wealthy men were sometimes painted with red, white, and yellow designs representing the owner's dreams. Goat wool robes, sometimes woven mixed with the hair of a small, white, curly-haired dog, were used mostly by the Lower Lillooet, while all Lillooet made robes of strips of rabbit, marmot, or dog skin.

People went barefoot except when hunting or in cold weather when socks, in addition to moccasins made of buckskin, and occasionally of elk, caribou, or outer deer skin were used. Salmon skin moccasins (fig. 8) and sandals were worn by the poor and by women. In winter, caps of bear, beaver, wolf, and marmot skin were worn. Some caps belonging to women were highly decorated with dentalium shells. Headbands were made from dyed cedar bark, buckskin, or skins of birds or animals (Teit 1906:210–211, 217–220; Turner et al. 1987).

Tattooing was common for both sexes, although not universal. During childhood, the ears of both girls and boys were pierced and decorated with shells. Most women and some men had a pierced septum in which they wore a bone nose ring, rods of bone or horn, shells, or porcupine quills (Teit 1906:220; Kennedy and Bouchard 1977, 1978:45).

Both sexes let their hair grow long, except for: slaves, whose hair was closely cropped; mourners, whose hair was cut straight across the back; and women who committed adultery, whose hair was cut short on one side (Teit 1906:221).

Kinship

Kinship was reckoned bilaterally. Kin terms make no distinction between relatives on mother's and father's side. In ego's generation the kinship terminology does not distinguish between siblings and first cousins but does differentiate with respect to sex and to the relative age of the speaker. Terms for ego's children denote their marital status (Kennedy and Bouchard 1977).

Social Organization

Lillooet villages consisted of lineagelike groups referred to by Teit (1906:252–253) as "clans" and by Hill-Tout

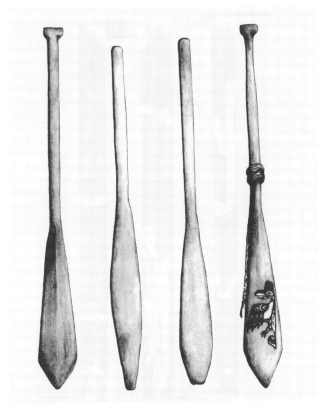

top, after photograph by Dorothy Kennedy, 1976.

Fig. 6. Water transportation. top, paddles made of broad-leaved maple (*Acer macrophyllum*) by Baptiste Ritchie of Mt. Currie, B.C. All are man's paddles except the second from left, which is a woman's paddle. center, Charlie Mack poling his newly made 18-foot dugout cedar canoe up the Birkenhead River, B.C. bottom, Mack inserting sticks between the gunwales of a red cedar canoe to spread the sides. Smoke-dried salmon heads, hot rocks, and water are in the bottom of the canoe. The oil in the salmon permeates the canoe to treat the wood. Once the sticks are in place, the canoe is covered with plywood and a tarpaulin and left to steam. Photographs by Dorothy Kennedy, Mt. Currie, B.C., 1975.

(1905:149) as "family groups." Each group was said to be descended from a common ancestor, such as a particular animal or mythical being. These groups did not regulate marriage; a person could claim membership in both parent's "clans" and marry a person of any group. Dances were performed with the members wearing masks representing their clan ancestor. The function of these groups remains unclear; Lillooet people in the 1970s recognized only a vague association between the residents of certain villages and particular animals (Kennedy and Bouchard 1978:41).

In early times each of these groups, originally a village, had a hereditary chief (*kʷúkʷpi*) whose family formed an aristocracy in name only. New villages formed by fission retained the same chief who continued to reside at the original home. Teit (1906:256) reported that the major berry patches harvested by a particular village were under the supervision of a "clan chief" who held a first-fruits ceremony and announced when the villagers and their neighbors could commence picking. The term *kʷúkʷpi* was also applied to a nobility of merit in which membership was acquired through wealth, wisdom, oratory, and liberality. The influence of these people in the community could be greater than that of the hereditary chief (Teit 1906:254–255, 282).

Among the Lower Lillooet, resource stewards known as *škələ?áwɬ* directed the use of specific hunting grounds and some fisheries. These were hereditary positions, at least in the historic period, but required special knowledge. Spiritual qualities were not requisite for this position, but such qualities were required for the specialized hunters known as *təwít* (Bouchard 1968–1991).

Teit's data, in addition to later data concerning Lillooet ownership of salmon fisheries and hunting territories, indicate that Lillooet society was stratified. While obligatory sharing may have formed the basic ethos of the society, there was not absolute economic egalitarianism. Privileged access to resource areas provided some individuals with more to eat than others. It also permitted them food to give away, thereby validating or securing status. Indiscriminate use of owned resources was monitored by requiring that those wishing to use a site asked permission. The data suggest, nevertheless, that the land and resources were the common property of the Lillooet, with certain groups having customary use of particular areas (Teit 1906:254–256;

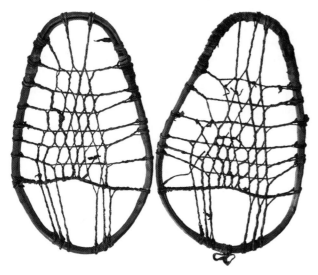

Canadian Mus. of Civilization, Que.: II-E-4 (neg. 75–7462).

Fig. 7. Snowshoes. The frames are made of bent wood spliced together and bound with strips of partially tanned skin. The webbing is made of twisted rawhide. Collected by Charles F. Newcombe, 1895–1901. Length 60 cm.

Field Mus., Chicago 111774.

Fig. 8. Salmon skin moccasins sewn and gathered with hide lacings. Collected by James A. Teit about 1911. Length 24 cm.

Bouchard 1968–1991; Romanoff 1985, 1988, 1992, 1992a; Hayden 1992; Kennedy and Bouchard 1992).

Decisions affecting the entire village were discussed at councils of men, although the advice of the elderly, particularly that of chiefs, was generally followed. Slaves had no say in village affairs (Teit 1906:257).

Life Cycle

During their first pregnancy, women (in addition to their husbands) were subject to restrictions on both diet and behavior, the observance of which was to benefit the unborn child. Birth was assisted by a midwife. Commonly, the pregnant woman lived alone in a brush birthing hut for up to several months after parturition, before returning to her home. For several nights after the birth the new father slept alone in the mountains, hunting often, but not carrying home any of his catch or touching fresh game. The baby was presented to the community at a feast hosted by the father at which time he distributed small presents to his child's first visitors (Hill-Tout 1905:139–140; Teit 1906:260; Ray 1942:193–195).

Twins were attributed to a grizzly bear's magical intervention. Four days after the birth the father received from the bears a song that he sung to his children whenever they cried. Parents of twins were isolated for up to four years, as contact with the village was potentially life-threatening to the twins. Ideally, a young man was hired to assist in raising the twins during this isolation period (Teit 1906:263; Kennedy and Bouchard 1978:45).

Responsibility for a child's upbringing rested mainly with the parents and grandparents, but instruction of children was an informal affair in which all members of the community participated. Upper Lillooet children were subjected to daily whipping by their father or family head as part of a training program to develop their physical and mental character. Each village also had an official flogger who visited each house and whipped those children said to be lazy (Teit 1906:262; Nastich 1954; Kennedy and Bouchard 1977).

Puberty rituals for girls included an isolation period of up to four years, although two years was common. During this time the girl remained secluded during the day. At night she roamed about while undergoing rituals to facilitate child-bearing, industriousness, and good health, and supplicating the "Day Dawn" and "Dusk of Evening." Some Lower Lillooet girls wore a headgear of goatskin, and all Lillooet girls donned special clothing, face paint, and hairstyle and carried a bone drinking tube and scratcher (Teit 1906:263–265; cf. Nastich 1954). Hill-Tout (1905:136) noted that a Lower Lillooet girl's seclusion ended with a purification ritual performed by a shaman.

The attainment of a boy's puberty was indicated by frequent dreaming. He then isolated himself in the mountains where he fasted, prayed, and sweatbathed for four days. Once he had returned to the village he spent his days associating mostly with other boys undergoing training. At night he went to some isolated area where he wandered about alone and practiced running, shooting, dancing, and praying. The ceremonies the boy performed depended upon his aspirations. At intervals over the subsequent years prior to his marriage, the young man returned to the hills for several days and passed his time sweatbathing, praying, and purging himself with medicines. A man wanting to obtain a guardian-spirit power continued training until he dreamed of some animal or bird that would be his lifetime protector and bestow upon him special knowledge and abilities. Both men and women could possess a guardian spirit. During puberty training, some boys and girls made a record or painted pictures of some part of the ceremonials. These pictographs were painted on rock bluffs, stones, or trees ("Rock Art," fig. 10, this vol.) (Hill-Tout 1905:143–147; Teit 1900:317–321, 1906:265–67; Nastich 1954; Bouchard 1968–1991).

The most honorable marriage customs were those described as the "placing down" and the "sitting" or betrothal marriage. The first was initiated by an intermediary acting on behalf of the groom; the second was initiated by the parents of the bride. The essential feature of both marriage types was the conducting ceremony that followed. This involved conducting the young couple first to the home of the bride's parents, where gifts of food and clothing provided by the groom's father were distributed to the bride's elderly relatives and friends, and then to the home of the groom's parents, where a similar distribution occurred. This concluded the marriage ceremony. Postmarital residence was bilocal with patrilocal preference (Teit 1900:322–323, 1906:266; Ray 1942:210; Nastich 1954). Among the Lower Lillooet at Mount Currie, the bride, together with the marriage gifts, was taken by her elders to the home of the groom on the second day of the ceremony. Her relatives did not remain for the feast that followed (Hill-Tout 1905:132).

A marriage among the Upper Lillooet not requiring the exchange of property occurred when a young man "touched" his desired spouse during a circle dance that was conducted specifically for this purpose. The woman's acceptance of the marriage was indicated by her permitting him to hold her sash while dancing and by her not shaking herself free when the chief announced that they were touching (Teit 1906:268; Ray 1942:210–211).

A more informal marriage was initiated by a young man lying beside a young woman after the other residents were asleep. If he was not rebuffed, he left before morning but was invited back by the girl's parents once they had been told of his visit. Occasionally, girls proposed to young men. Their marriage was announced after her parents were informed (Teit 1906:268; Nastich 1954). Commoners were also married by the groom simply going to the house of his father-in-law, once the union had been arranged between the parents (Hill-Tout 1905:132).

The girl's parents knew a marriage had been consummated when they found the buckskin undergarment that her husband had cut from their daughter's body placed on top of the woodpile, along with a new dressed buckskin. The neighbors were called to feast and receive a strip of the undergarment and buckskin (Teit 1906:268).

Polygyny was customary for wealthy men. When a couple separated, the woman took all her own property, including the food she had preserved (Teit 1906:269; Nastich 1954). Levirate and sororate were practiced (Hill-Tout 1905:133; Teit 1906:255–256).

Burial practices varied between the Upper and Lower Lillooet, although both divisions had specific sites where the dead would be disposed. Among the Upper Lillooet, a body was removed from the dwelling immediately after death and, in a flexed position, wrapped in skins or tule mats, and placed temporarily on a nearby scaffold to await burial one or two days later. The corpse was placed either on its left side with the head pointing west (Teit 1906:269), or in a sitting position with the head facing east (Ray 1942:217) in a grass, bark, or mat-lined grave. It was covered with grass and dirt and marked with a circle or pile of stones, or a mound of dirt. The possessions of the deceased were buried in the grave, burned, suspended on four poles erected above the grave, or left on the ground covering the grave. A man's dogs and slaves would be killed at the time of his death (or buried alive with him) (Teit 1906:269–270; Ray 1939:63, 1942:217; Kennedy and Bouchard 1978:47). Ray (1939:61, 1942:218) notes that the Lillooet practiced basket burials, but not cradle baskets, although Teit (1906:270) observed that infants would be buried in their cradle or, in later times, the cradle would be hung in a tree near the grave. Only the bodies of twins were deposited in trees away from human graves and habitations, as it was believed that the grizzly bears would reclaim their kin (Teit 1906:263). Tree burial, other than for twins, was a temporary method of disposal used only during the winter when inhumation was difficult (Ray 1939:61, 1942:218). The remains of people who died far from home were retrieved by their relatives, unless the distance was too great, in which case the body was burned at the time of death and the ashes taken home (Teit 1906:270). The earliest known burial practice among the Lower Lillooet was said to be placing the body in a sitting position, or on its side, on top of the ground, surrounding it with large boulders, then covering this with a heap of smaller rocks (Teit 1906:271–272). Shallow pit-burials and the use of scaffolds have also been recorded among the Lower Lillooet (Kennedy and Bouchard 1977). Funeral practices in the early 1950s are described in Nastich (1954).

Grave-boxes were used prior to the historic period, according to Teit (1906:272) who reported that the corner posts of these boxes were carved with the "totem of the clan." Graves were marked with carved and painted wooden figures representing the deceased (fig. 9). These figures were clad in the clothes of the deceased; and articles such as baskets, bows, or weapons that depicted the talents of the deceased were hung from the images (Teit 1906:273; Kennedy and Bouchard 1977).

Mythology

The Lillooet distinguish between *šptakʷl* 'myths, legends' and *šqʷə́qʷəl* 'historical tales, true stories' (Bouchard 1968–1991). Myths or legends tell of a time when the world was populated by beings with both animal and human characteristics, while historical tales or true stories record events that occurred in the Lillooet's own world. Coyote, the trickster, was sent to earth by the Chief or Old One to set the world in order for the people who are here now. This task

Teit 1906:fig. 96.

Fig. 9. Lower Lillooet grave monuments, placed in front of gravehouses, carved and painted wooden figures represented the deceased. Collected by Harlan I. Smith, 1899, near *lalá?xen*; height of left 86 cm; right, 120 cm.

was assisted by four Transformers who journeyed throughout Lillooet country killing extraordinary beings and leaving in their path transformed rocks as "proof" of their travels (see Teit 1912a; Elliott 1931; Bouchard and Kennedy 1977; van Eijk and Williams 1981).

Cosmology

Some Lillooet people conceived the earth as round (Teit 1906:274); others believed it to be flat (Kennedy and Bouchard 1978:48). The east was associated with light and life, and the west with darkness and death. The land of the souls, situated at the end of a long dusty trail leading from the west of the earth, was perceived as a pleasant place where everything was abundant. Old men positioned along the trail turned back the souls of people who were not ready to die. The Chief of the Dead sat on a stone wall separating the land of the souls from the trail of the dead. The souls inhabited a large four-room house; those who had not yet passed through the third room could be brought back to earth by shamans (Teit 1906:274–277; Kennedy and Bouchard 1978:48–49).

Ceremonies

The Upper Lillooet practiced religious circle dances initiated in the distant past when the Chief of the Dead sent word by returning souls that people should hold dances during which they were to paint their faces, fast, bathe, feast at noon, dance, and pray for protection from harm by ghosts and from evil and mysterious forces while harvesting food. During this dance the people asked for a long, healthy life. As instructed by the Chief of the Dead, Lillooet men smoked tobacco during the night of the ceremony. These dances were held irregularly, although in some areas they occurred most frequently in the winter, especially around the solstice (Teit 1906:284–285).

Dances at which the young men displayed the dance and song of their guardian-spirit power were held mostly for entertainment, and for the elders to evaluate the success of the boys' training. Sometimes all the men, in addition to those women who had powerful spirit helpers, participated. Among the Upper Lillooet, these dances were known as *ƛaƛ* 'imitate' (Teit 1906:286; Kennedy and Bouchard 1977).

Dances known as *šaq̓ʷúta* were held for entertainment among the Lower Lillooet. Included in these dances were demonstrations of power by shamans, as well as dances imitating certain animals. In the winter, the Lower Lillooet also held masked dances known as *mák̓ʷalmin* during which an eagle dancer and a kingfisher dancer performed for entertainment. A dance known as *miła*, which appears to have contained elements of the Coast Salish spirit dance, as well as the "biting" dance described by Teit (1906:286) and known to Lower Lillooet people in the 1970s, was used exclusively by the Skookumchuck Band (Kennedy and Bouchard 1977).

Occasions at which the people were called together to feast and receive gifts were known as *xǝlítxal*. Teit (1906:258) reported that such "potlatches" were given between individuals and between chiefs, although the chiefs represented their entire local group. Gifts were generally returned on future occasions. Masks depicting the groups's first ancestor were shown at large gatherings, although the host hired an elderly man to wear the mask and sing the associated song, as the wearing of masks was believed to invoke an early death. The public display of masks belonging to deceased mask-owners brought special distinction to the host.

The masked dancer carried a basketry rattle and wore a necklace consisting of the skin or claws of the animal being personified, or a feather headdress, if a bird was being represented. Those groups who did not dress in animal skins wore cedar-bark costumes. Masked dancers sang, accompanied by other members of their group, who occasionally assisted in a performance of the ancestor legend (Teit 1906:258).

Gatherings were also held for name-givings at which ancestral names were assumed and gifts were distributed to those witnessing the event. A special feast hosted by the community elders was held for the pubescent eldest son of a deceased chief, who reciprocated with a feast and distribution once his training was finished (Teit 1906:259).

Some gatherings were accompanied by a "scramble." By the nineteenth century, mountain goat wool blankets had been replaced with sticks imbedded with coins that were tossed into the house to be broken apart by the guests (Kennedy and Bouchard 1978:49). A "letting down" festival described by Teit (1906:259) for the Upper Lillooet consisted of bundles of small gifts being lowered on the end of a carved crooked stick down into the pit house. The visitors announced their arrival by throwing water into the house and extinguishing the fire. Once it had been relit, they joined the occupants for a meal and distributed their gifts, which consisted mostly of food, seldom more than they had consumed during the visit.

History

The first recorded contact between the Upper Lillooet and non-Indians was in 1808 when Simon Fraser of the North west Company descended the river subsequently named after him. Soon after the establishment of Fort Kamloops (Fort Thompson) in 1812, the Fraser River Lillooet became the major providers of dried salmon for the Europeans. Horseback convoys from Fort Kamloops regularly visited the rich fisheries at the confluence of the Bridge River with the Fraser to trade for salmon. The Indians seldom traveled to the fort themselves (McLeod 1822–1823; McDonald 1826–1827).

The first recorded contact between the Lower Lillooet and non-Indians was in 1827 (Rich 1947:31–32), the same year that Fort Langley was established by the Hudson's Bay Company. A detailed census was compiled at Fort Langley (Yale 1838–1839).

A.C. Anderson's May 1846 exploration of an alternate supply route for the Hudson's Bay Company brought him in contact with both divisions of the Lillooet. He traveled from Lillooet through Seton Lake and Anderson Lake, then down the Lillooet River and Harrison Lake to the Fraser River (A.C. Anderson 1846).

Significant contacts between the Lillooet and non-Indians occurred in the late 1850s, after the initial discovery of gold in the lower Thompson River area in summer 1856 (Douglas 1856). Thousands of miners flocked to the Fraser River area in 1858 to seek their fortune. The Lillooet were employed as boatmen, packers, and guides, but the influx of so many foreigners had a profound impact upon the aboriginal lifeway as introduced diseases, competition for resources, and encroachment on seasonally used sites resulted in changes in settlement patterns and the seasonal round.

One of the routes taken by the miners to reach the gold fields was by way of the lower Lillooet River, Lillooet Lake, Birkenhead River, and Anderson and Seton lakes. Trails

were built, and steamers were constructed to ply the lakes. Instant towns were established at Port Douglas near the end of Harrison Lake, at Port Pemberton near the mouth of the Birkenhead River, and at Cayoosh (Lillooet) on the Fraser River. But by the mid-1860s this travel route was largely abandoned.

Christianity first appeared among the Lower Lillooet in 1859, and among the Upper Lillooet in 1860, when Church of England missionaries visited the communities of Douglas and Lillooet to proselytize among the Lillooet and the miners (Bagshaw 1996:24–25). Bishop George Hills of the Church of England included Lillooet on his tour of the interior in 1860 and, impressed with the devotion of the Native people when he was warmly welcomed by the Fountain Chief Chilhovels, sent a resident missionary to the area the following year (Bagshaw 1996:180–181). The Upper Lillooet may have had already had some experience with religion at Fort Kamloops as the Fountain Chief crossed himself and repeated the Chinook Jargon term for God. Members of the Roman Catholic Order Oblates of Mary Immaculate maintained contact throughout the Lillooet-speaking area after 1860 when priests traveled periodically to the villages for offering baptism and some Catholic instruction. Catholic churches were ultimately established on most Lillooet reserves, together with a hierarchical system of watchmen and bell-ringers charged with regulating the morals and beliefs of the villagers.

The Establishment of Reserves

Serious land-based conflicts developed between the Native people and the newcomers along the Fraser River at the time of the gold rush in British Columbia. In response, James Douglas, appointed governor of the new colony of British Columbia in 1858, set about to protect Native village sites and cultivated fields by the establishment of Indian reserves that would promote stable, self-sufficient residency leading to Victorian ideals of civilization. In 1859, a local magistrate identified a new site for the Natives staying around Port Douglas, camped amidst the miners, and compelled them to relocate from the newly designated townsite (Nicol 1859). In 1860, after trouble between the races had escalated, Governor Douglas made a reconnaissance trip to the interior, stopping to meet miners and Natives along the way, including sojourns at Cayoosh, now called Lillooet, and at Port Douglas. Crowds of Natives assembled at Lillooet to speak with the governor, who promised protection for their village sites and agrarian pursuits by reserve creation (Douglas 1860). While in the area, Douglas confirmed at least one reserve near Pemberton. A few years later, other Lillooet villages were identified as Indian reserves, and by the end of the colonial period in 1871, when British Columbia joined the confederation of Canada, at least seven additional Lillooet villages had been designated Indian reserves.

In 1881, the Indian Reserve Commission visited Lillooet for the purpose of reserving other aboriginal villages. Some traditional sites had already been alienated by settlers. Reserve allotment in the Pemberton area remained incomplete until 1905 when the Department of Indian Affairs was able to purchase back land deemed sufficient for the Native people's needs (Vowell 1905). Indian reserves were reviewed and adjusted by a Royal Commission on Indian Affairs between 1912 and 1916. As part of its work, the Royal Commission visited the Indian reserves in the province, met with the Native people and obtained evidence of their current land needs. The Royal Commission confirmed 49 Indian reserves for the Lillooet. Additionally, 20 more parcels of land became reserved as a result of the Commission's review (Canada. Indian Reserve Commission 1881–1908:Books 4, 6–8, 22–23; Vowell 1905; Canada. Royal Commission on Indian Affairs 1916, 2:447–462, 3:629–633).

Political Activism

As early as 1910 the Lillooet declared their unity with other British Columbia Bands for the purpose of holding political meetings and seeking solutions to their land grievances. With legal counsel provided by A.E. O'Meara, a lawyer and minister, and J.M. Clark's Indian associations made appeals to the governments of Canada and British Columbia asking that aboriginal title be referred to the Judicial Committee of the Privy Council (Mitchell 1977).

In 1915, Indian chiefs from throughout British Columbia's interior, including the Lillooet, gathered to protest the work of the Royal Commission on Indian Affairs. Out of this meeting emerged an alliance of coast and interior Bands known as the Allied Tribes. Aided in their work by ethnographer James A. Teit until his death in 1922, the Allied Tribes participated in a review of the Royal Commission's reports, which they found unacceptable, and presented instead a comprehensive statement of their position and their claims (Mitchell 1977). The Lillooet chiefs submitted their independent petition to the government in 1922, requesting a restoration of alienated lands and a review of their land and water situation (Adolph et al. 1922). After government approval of the report of the Royal Commission, the Allied Tribes returned to their campaign for a determination of aboriginal title by the Judicial Committee of the British Privy Council. The organization failed in this attempt and dissolved in 1927 (Mitchell 1977).

Political activism among the Lillooet after 1927 was mostly issue-related and reserve-focused, until the formation of the Union of British Columbia Indian Chiefs in 1969. Beginning with the 1975 temporary blockade of a national railway track, the Lillooet took their land grievances before the public. Saul Terry, a Lillooet Indian from the Bridge River Band, had led the organization since 1983, although not all Lillooet-speaking Bands have chosen to participate in this provincial association (Tennant

1990:211). This organization's opposition to the treaty negotiation process begun in 1992 by the federal and provincial governments has set it apart from other Native organizations in British Columbia.

Since the early 1900s, Lillooet chiefs (fig. 10) have been elected and have administered Band affairs with the assistance of elected councilors. These Band governments, some of whom allied with other Bands to form tribal councils, are responsible for the administration of on-reserve social, economic, and educational affairs. Community policing in the environs of the town of Lillooet is assumed jointly by the Royal Canadian Mounted Police and the all-Native Stl'átl'imx Tribal Police.

From the time of the construction of the Cariboo Trail through to the interior in the late 1850s, some local people had been employed as wage laborers, not only at tasks in which they were already proficient such as fishing, trapping, and guiding, but also at new forms of employment such as logging, farming, and ranching. By the late 1800s, on reserves in the fertile Pemberton Valley, some Indian farmers had success growing abundant crops of potatoes, while increasingly productive harvests of potatoes, along with bushels of oat, wheat, and peas, as well as fruit, grew on Upper Lillooet lands situated on benches above the Fraser. Some Lillooet families worked seasonally picking berries in the Puget Sound area or hops in the Fraser Valley. Native foremen were hired by non-Indian farmers to assemble teams of pickers for the season and oversee their work and well-being. These gatherings, attended sometimes by several thousand people, were as important socially as they were in providing income. Alfalfa and, since the mid-1990s, Chinese ginseng, have been added to the roster of lucrative crops grown commercially by Upper Lillooet Bands. Stock raising developed early in the Upper Lillooet area and provided Band and individual income in the 1990s. Agriculture declined in importance among the Lower Lillooet until only a few subsistence crops supplemented income derived from logging and Band-sponsored initiatives in the 1990s. The Lower Lillooet reserves never provided adequate employment, and numerous people have these reserves to seek jobs in Fraser Valley towns and in Vancouver.

Beginning in the early 1860s, some Lillooet children attended Saint Mary's, the Oblate missionary school established in the Fraser Valley. A few attended public schools operating in the towns, but most received little schooling until Indian industrial schools in the Fraser Valley and at Kamloops opened in the 1890s. The educational policy of the schools was to encourage the development of vocational skills and domestic sciences, all taught in English, and with harsh punishment for those adhering to Native ways.

Since the 1970s, some Lillooet Bands have developed community-run schools and care facilities for children. Language programs (fig. 11) and traditional crafts have been incorporated into the curriculum, and Native elders participated in the instruction. With a greater emphasis placed on the value of education, increasing numbers of Lil-

top and bottom, Canadian Mus. of Civilization, Hull, Que.

Fig. 10. Headmen. top, Thomas Adolph (b. about 1865, d. 1938), Chief of Fountain Band, Upper Lillooet. bottom, Ignace Jacob (b. 1857, d. 1926), a traditionalist whose songs were recorded on wax cylinders by Barbeau (1957) and analyzed by George (1962). He was a chief of the Pemberton Band, Lower Lillooet. Photographs by Marius Barbeau, 1912.

looet young people pursued studies at community colleges and universities, particularly in the fields of teaching and law.

Population

Precontact population estimates for the Lillooet were calculated by Teit (1906:199) as around 4,000. Census figures provided by Department of Indian Affairs (1896:276, 297) reflect a total Lillooet population of slightly over 1,100. Population figures (table 1) for 1992 referring to people of Indian status indicate that the population may have reached precontact levels. Most Lillooet living off-reserve resided around Vancouver, Mission, and Kamloops.

Synonymy

The name Lillooet is from *lílwat*, the name of the Lower Lillooet.

The Lillooet have no all-encompassing term for themselves although the word *šƛáƛimxəč* designates all those who speak this language. This term is derived from *šƛáƛimx*, which is usually applied only to the Upper Lillooet (Dawson 1892:5, 45; Teit 1906:195; Kennedy and Bouchard 1978:22). However, Boas (1891:map), Hill-Tout (1905), and usage re-introduced in the late 1980s apply the term *šƛáƛimx* to all of the Lillooet.

Possibly the term *šƛáƛimx* is derived from *šaƛ* (Bouchard 1968–1991), the name of a former village site (no. 38) at the present town of Lillooet. Explorer Simon Fraser identified the Indian people he encountered at Lillooet in the summer of 1808 as the "Askettigh [*šƛáƛimx*?] Nation" (Lamb 1960:77–83, 120–121, 145, 153–154).

Transcriptions of *šƛáƛimx* include: stat-lam-chú (McLeod 1822–1823); Stla-Sli-muk (McKay 1858); sclaythamuk (Powell 1872); stlā´tliumQ (Boas 1891); stā´-tlum-ooh (Dawson 1892); stlatlumH (Hill-Tout 1905); sLā´Lemux (Teit 1906); STLA-tlei-mu-wh (Bouchard and Kennedy 1977; Kennedy and Bouchard 1985); and stl'átl'imx (Kennedy and Bouchard 1978, 1992).

Teit's (1906:292, 294) translation of *lílwat* as 'wild onions' is incorrect; it appears that *lílwat* is not analyzable (Bouchard 1968–1991; van Eijk 1985, 1990). Although some Lillooet-speaking consultants stated that *lílwat* was a Squamish word referring to the meeting of the Green, Lillooet, and Birkenhead rivers, this was denied by Squamish speakers (Bouchard 1968–1991, 1971–1981).

The term *lílwat* was first recorded in 1828, at which time it was transcribed as lillewaite (Rich 1947:31). Other transcriptions include: leilliuit (S. Black 1833); lilliwhit (Yale 1838–1839); lilooitt (A.C. Anderson 1846); lillooet (Powell 1872); li´luet (Teit 1906, 1912a); and LEEL-wat (Bouchard and Kennedy 1977).

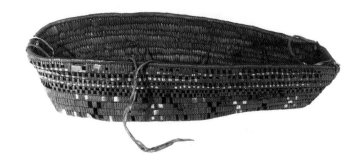

left and bottom right, Mt. Currie Cultural Centre, B.C.; top right, Canadian Mus. of Civilization. Hull, Que.: II-E-9 (neg. 71–4896).

Fig. 11. Traditional culture and the language programs. left, Cover of the advanced course book in the series *Cuystwí Malh Ucwalmícwts: Teach Yourself Lillooet* (van Eijk 1981). top right, Cradle basket constructed of split cedar-root coils whip-stitched with splints of the same material and decorated using the beaded technique with designs of black bark and yellow grass. Babies were sometimes carried in cradle baskets hung horizontally on the mother's back. Because the right side of a person is considered the lucky side, the child's head lay toward the right side of the mother, and the child's right side lay against the mother's back (Teit 1906:261). Collected by Harlan I. Smith, Kamloops, B.C., 1928. Length 60 cm. bottom right, Drawings showing method of rocking a cradle basket, from a bilingual reader in the same series (van Eijk and Williams 1981:85), where it illustrates a legend about a grandmother who always slept when asked to babysit. The family fooled her by taking the baby and putting a stick in its place, causing the grandmother anguish and regret about her lack of attention to the child. Drawings by Marie Joseph Abraham, about 1981.

Terms for the Lake Lillooet, *čaláɫmx* and *ləxlíxmx*, translate as 'lake people' and 'clear-water people' respectively (Bouchard 1968–1991). These appear in Teit (1906:197) as tcalê´ɫamux and lxalê´xamux.

By the 1970s–1980s, the Pemberton people were better known as the Mount Currie Band although they preferred to be called the *líɫwat*. The term *nkʷúčin* was seldom used to refer to the lower Lillooet River Indians; the terms Samahquam, Skookumchuck, and Douglas continued to be used to refer to these people (Bouchard 1968–1991). In the early 1990s, the term "In-SHUCK-ch" (taken from the name of a distinctive mountain near the southeast end of Lillooet Lake) began to be used as the name of the group representing these southernmost Lillooet-speaking people in treaty negotiations with the federal and provincial governments (In-SHUCK-ch 1993).

Sources

Ethnographic sketches of the Lillooet appear first in Simon Fraser's 1808 journal (Lamb 1960). For the 1820s–1840s, the primary sources are Hudson's Bay Company records (McLeod 1822–1823; McDonald 1826–1827; Yale 1838–1839; A.C. Anderson 1846). Additional brief descrip-tions are contained in the exploring journals of Downie (1858), McKay (1858), Begbie (1861), Palmer (1861), and Mayne (1862).

Journals and correspondence of missionaries of the Church of England (Bagshaw 1996) and the Oblates of Mary Immaculate order begin in the 1860s and include documentation of the Lillooet.

From the 1870s onward, the voluminous records of the Department of Indian Affairs (identified as RG 10 in the National Archives of Canada) chronicle all aspects of Lillooet life. These include documents relating to the establishment of Indian reserves.

Secondary sources describing aspects of Lillooet culture include local histories (Phair 1959; Decker, Fougberg, and Ronayne 1977; Harris 1977; Edwards 1978). Along with Drake-Terry's (1989) compilation of ethnographic and historical materials purporting to provide a Lillooet perspective, these have been produced without benefit of scholarly review.

The major source on Lillooet culture is the work of James Teit (1898–1910, 1906, 1908–1920, 1910–1913). His 1906 publication was subject to Boas's editing and reflects the editor's biases in organization and content. Dawson's (1892, 1895) publications include some Lillooet notes. Lower Lillooet ethnography, language, and mythology were discussed

Table 1. Lillooet Population, 1992

Reserve	On-Reserve	Off-Reserve	Total
Anderson Lake	82	132	214
Mount Currie (Pemberton)	1,019	442	1,461
Douglas	52	116	168
Skookum Chuck	25	278	303
Samahquam	12	208	220
Bridge River	111	190	301
Cayoosh Creek	85	61	146
Fountain	485	215	700
Lillooet	178	96	274
Pavilion	253	127	380
Seton Lake	226	277	503
Total	2,528	2,142	4,670

SOURCE: Indian and Northern Affairs Canada 1992.

by Hill-Tout (1905). This work was criticized by Teit (1906:292–300). Ray (1939, 1942) included the Lillooet in his Plateau survey. Fieldwork by Nastich (1954) among the Lake Lillooet provides some of the few data available on this area. Ames (1956) investigated economic change among the Upper Lillooet, focusing on the village of Fountain.

Beginning in the late 1960s, ethnographic and linguistic research among the Lillooet was undertaken by Bouchard and Kennedy (Bouchard 1968–1991; Kennedy 1971–1991; Bouchard and Kennedy 1977; Kennedy and Bouchard 1975b, 1977, 1978, 1992). Romanoff (1971, 1985, 1988, 1992, 1992a) studied fishing, hunting, and potlatching among the Upper Lillooet. Lillooet ethnobotany has been the subject of investigations by Turner (1974, 1987, 1988, 1988a, 1992; Turner et al. 1987). Alexander (1992) and Tyhurst (1992) did ethnoarcheological work in Upper Lillooet territory, in conjunction with archeological excavations by Hayden (1992) and his examination of social stratification in this area.

Topical studies include Cannon (1992) on warfare, Teit (1898, 1912), Hill-Tout (1905:177–205), Elliott (1931), Bouchard and Kennedy (1977), and van Eijk and Williams (1981) on mythology, and George (1962) on music.

Linguistic research among the Lillooet, including the compilation of word lists, texts, grammars and pedagogical materials, has been undertaken by Tolmie and Dawson (1884:62b–73b), Hill-Tout (1905:177–205), Bouchard (1968–1991; Bouchard, Mitchell, and Edwards 1973; Bouchard, Mack, and Ritchie 1974, 1974a; Bouchard and Mitchell 1975), Swoboda (1971), and van Eijk (1978, 1978a, 1985, 1990; van Eijk and Williams 1981).

Recordings of Lillooet songs collected in 1912 by Marius Barbeau and in 1912 and 1918 by James Teit are held by the Canadian Museum of Civilization, Ottawa. Significant collections of Lillooet material culture are held by: the American Museum of Natural History, New York; the Field Museum of Natural History, Chicago; and the Canadian Museum of Civilization, Ottawa.

Thompson

DAVID WYATT

The Thompson ('tämpsən) are Interior Salish speakers* who occupy portions of the territory drained by the Fraser, Thompson, and Nicola rivers in British Columbia. They have also been called Ntlakyapamuk (*nɬeʔképmx*) (Hodge 1907–1910, 2:88).

Environment

Upper Thompson valleys are the driest parts of the province, and at higher elevations their rolling grasslands and scattered groves of ponderosa pine give way to thicker stands of fir and aspen and to subalpine parklands. Lower Thompson territory—the steep-sided and wetter Fraser Canyon—is more heavily forested with cedar, fir, and hemlock. Salmon are more plentiful there, and Lower Thompson life was traditionally more settled than that upriver. The Upper Thompson were surrounded by other Interior Salish groups (and the Nicola Athapaskans)—groups culturally much like themselves. The Lower Thompson were in contact with Northwest Coast groups, and this, as well as adaptation to different natural environments, accounts for the cultural differences between the two divisions.

Territory

Teit lists 47 Upper and 19 Lower Thompson villages, noting that "many of the villages . . . are very small, consisting of two or three families; while others are large and contain about a hundred or more inhabitants . . . A list of villages thirty-five to fifty years ago [1850–1865] would be very different" (Teit 1900:174–175). Among the Upper Thompson these communities made up four bands: Lytton Band (*nɬeʔkèpmxʔúy*), Upper Fraser Band (*sɬexéyxʷ*), Spences Bridge Band (*nkʼəmcínmx*), and Nicola Band (*scwʼéxmx*) (fig. 1). Thompson territory was well defined along the rivers, for families passed on rights to salmon fishing spots and others needed permission to use them. Upland territory was shared more freely with other Thompson groups and

other tribes, although deer fences were inherited and hunters from one band could not build them in the hunting territory of another.

The daily organization of life was local, but the Thompson were a people because they shared a common identity. They spoke a common language, used a common name, recalled their common origin (Teit 1914:306), and had ties of custom and kinship.

Origins

The Thompson have a variety of accounts of their origins and the time when the world was new (Teit 1898, 1912, 1917).

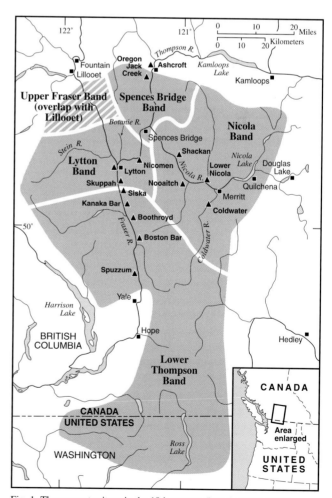

Fig. 1. Thompson territory in the 19th century (based on Teit 1900).

---

*The phonemes of Thompson are: (voiceless stops and affricates) *p, t, ç, c, k, kʷ, q, qʷ, ʔ*; (glottalized stops and affricates) *ṗ, (ƚ̇), ċ, λ̓, k̓, k̓ʷ, q̓, q̓ʷ*; (voiceless continuants) *ṣ, s, ɬ, x, xʷ, x̣, x̣ʷ, h*; (resonants) *m, n, l, z, y, γ, w, ʕ, ʕʷ*; (glottalized resonants) *m̓, n̓, l̓, z̓, y̓, γ̓, w̓, ʕ̓, ʕ̓ʷ*; (primary vowels) *i, u, e, ə*; (retracted vowels) *i̧, o, a, ə̧*; stress v́ (low), v́ (high), v̀ (secondary). Information on Thompson phonology is from Thompson and Thompson (1992). Words have been respelled by Dale Kinkade.

During this time their ancestors lacked many resources and skills, and it took the work of the Old-One, Old Coyote, and other powerful Transformers to create today's world and give the people the knowledge they needed to live in it. Some of the first people were changed into birds, fishes, animals, and trees; others, into stones (Hanna and Henry 1995:21–101). Because of wars among the animal people, sturgeon live in the Fraser River, the chum salmon mostly below Yale, sockeye salmon in the Fraser and Thompson rivers, pink there and in the Nicola. Old Coyote's son, tired of carrying his heavy lunch-bundle of roots, threw some to the four directions but dropped most of these "roots from the sky" in the Botanie valley, which became a famous gathering spot.

Thompson traditions tell of an original homeland near a large lake to the south or southeast, of a migration north, and of a time when their ancestors all lived in four houses at Lytton. The name *nɬeʔképmx* comes from that of the people there, and "there appears to be some evidence . . . that the Ntlakyapamuk language spread from around Lytton up and down the neighbouring river valleys" (Teit 1914:292).

Linguistic evidence ("Languages," this vol.; Suttles 1987) indicates an ancient coastal or lower Fraser River Salishan homeland and an early expansion upriver into the interior. Archeology suggests the move happened around 1500 B.C., that it was to take advantage of "improving salmon resources," and that salmon fishing, augmented by other fishing, hunting, and gathering, was the economic base of the entire Sqlelten tradition, which can be equated with the Interior Salish (Stryd and Rousseau 1996). Pit houses occur from 4,000 years ago on (Richards and Rousseau 1987), and the Kamloops phase, a part of the Sqlelten tradition that began around A.D. 800 and is typified by small side-notched arrowpoints, represents the immediate prehistory of the Upper Thompson and Shuswap (Sanger 1969a).

Culture

Traditional life was described most fully by Teit (1900), who studied the Upper Thompson. Unless otherwise noted this sketch describes the period 1800–1858.

Structures

The Thompson year began in November, when deer and bighorn sheep rut and ground hogs go into their winter dens; in the next month ('going-in time') or the third ('the last going in'), the people moved into their winter semisubterranean pit houses. Villages of one to four (occasionally more) homes, each built to house as many as 30 people, were located in low wind-sheltered spots near water, firewood, and possibly winter fishing.

Most pit houses (Laforet and York 1981) were 20–50 feet in diameter (fig. 2). Four houseposts were placed in a three- to five-foot-deep circular excavation; these in turn supported hip rafters and a framework of poles, chinked with "willow branches and honey-suckle fibre woven together;" more poles were layed vertically on this frame and were covered with birch or cottonwood bark (Lower Thompson: cedar bark) and then with the dirt previously excavated. People climbed into and out of the house on a notched log extending through a central hole in the roof; a large rock protected it from the cooking and heating fire. Some homes had side entrances. The earthern house walls were covered by birch or cedar bark slabs, and the floor by fir boughs. Several nuclear families might share a house, and sewn rush mats set off a corner for each. During the winter season fresh food was scarce and the Thompson ate mostly food they had stored. It was a time for entertaining guests or visiting others. During the rest of the year, when parties traveled to hunt, fish, and gather, they needed shelter they could dismantle and carry. Their homes then were pole-frame lodges, covered with sewn rush mats or bark (fig. 2).

Subsistence

• FISHING During the fourth ('spring winds time') and fifth months ('coming-forth time'), fishermen might come to the Thompson River near Spences Bridge to spear steelhead attracted by pitch-lamps hanging out from canoes (fig. 3). Suckers, peamouth, and trout, caught in uplands lakes, were often the first fresh food after a hard winter; trout fish-

Fig. 2. Habitations. left, Semisubterranean house in Nicola Valley, near Merritt, B.C. Photograph by Harlan I. Smith, 1899. center, A mat tepee near Thompson River, B.C. right, Women unfastening and taking mats off a tepee near Spences Bridge, B.C. center and right, Photographs by James A. Teit, 1914.

Fig. 3. Albert (Poncho) Wilson, Percy Minnabarriet, and Bruce Sampson pitch-lamp fishing on the Thompson River near Spences Bridge, B.C. Photograph by Gordon Mohs, 1984.

ing continued into the fall, using a variety of hooks, gorges, nets, and traps. Sturgeon were hooked in the Fraser River at and below Lytton.

Salmon were an important food for most Thompson. The name of the tenth month, 'nose,' referred to their arrival as they struggled upriver to spawn, and the next moon was called 'they reach the source'. Dip-netting platforms were erected along the Fraser and Thompson rivers at places where the salmon hug the riverbank to avoid the current ("Fishing," fig. 16, this vol.) Salmon were also speared ("Fishing," fig. 14, this vol.) from the banks, sometimes at night by torchlight; in shallow water they were netted or speared behind weirs. The fish were split and hung to wind-dry or boiled in pits to extract their oil.

• GATHERING Spring and summer were a time for gathering roots, bulbs, berries, bark, lichen, and mushrooms. The eighth moon was called 'they are a little ripe'; and when the sun is at its highest, during the ninth or 'middle' month, berries fully ripen.

Balsamroot, wild onion, mariposa lily, and bitteroot were dug in March. Wild greens, such as cow parsnip, fireweed, blackcap and thimbleberry shoots, were harvested in spring; and the edible inner bark of ponderosa and lodgepole pines was gathered. The roots of yellow avalanche lily (vol. 17:610) and spring beauty were sought, as root digging carried on throughout the summer and into the fall.

Wild strawberries, salmonberries (in the Lower Thompson area), squaw currants, and some varieties of saskatoon (vol. 17:613), were harvested, followed closely by red huckleberries, soapberries, wild blackberries, wild gooseberries and blueberries. Hazelnuts, balsamroot "seeds" (achenes) and Douglas fir sugar were harvested during the summer. By late summer and early autumn chokecherries, blue elder-

berries, mountain-ash fruits, and highbush cranberries were ripe, and black tree lichen, seeds of the white-bark pine, and mushrooms were ready to gather (Turner et al. 1990:25–26).

Women gathered plant foods (and looked after the household). They used digging sticks, pointed pieces of hardwood about 80 centimeters long with transverse horn or wood handles, to pry up roots, which were cooked in underground earth ovens, often for several days. Roots were also strung up to dry; berries were dried spread on mats and baked in cakes.

Turner et al. (1990) recorded 120 plant species used as foods, flavorings, or beverages. Plants were also important as materials for containers and as dyes, stains, preservatives, scents, and cleansing agents (more than 115 species recorded); others were used as medicine (200+ species) and in ritual purification and protective customs (35 species), including sweatbathing.

• HUNTING The Thompson used wooden bows, strengthened with a sinew backing. Nocked and feathered arrows had chipped basalt points, or, for small game, notched or detachable antler or bone heads: when the head came off, the dragging shaft caught the animal in underbrush. Deer and elk were run down by dogs, shot in the water at river crossings and at salt licks by moonlight, forced into snares placed in the openings of pole and tree limb fences, chased into gulches or over cliffs, or run down on snowshoes in deep snow. The Spences Bridge and Nicola Bands caught deer in large nets set between clumps of bushes.

> Hares, squirrels, and grouse of several varieties, were either snared in their haunts or shot with arrows.... Bears were generally hunted with bow and arrow, but sometimes with dogs. They were also trapped by means of dead falls. Mountain-goat and big-horn sheep were hunted with bow and arrows. Beaver were also occasionally hunted with dogs. They were killed with a spear with a bone point [except among the Lower Thompson]. Coyotes and foxes were often caught by digging or smoking them out of their holes (Teit 1900:249).

Hunters shared game with the others in their party and, if they had been very sucessful, with relatives, friends or poor hunters at home.

Technology

Men made implements of stone, bone, and wood, while women prepared skins, matting, and basketry (Teit 1900:182). Knives, scrapers, drills, and engraving tools were chipped from basalt, using percussion (hammerstones) and pressure (antler flaking tools). Nephrite adzes and axes were made by grinding down blanks split from between parallel grooves ground in the side of a boulder. They made up part of the woodworking tool kit, along with hammerstones and mauls, antler wedges, stone knives and drills, and beavertooth crooked knives (fig. 4). Bone and antler were cut and ground into awls, harpoons, and wedges.

The Thompson made more baskets than any other Salish people (Haeberlin, Teit, and Roberts 1928:142). They were fashioned from cedar root coils, and since cedar trees were most abundant in the Fraser Canyon, the Lower Thompson made the most baskets, the Spences Bridge and Nicola Bands the least. The roots were scraped, peeled, and split. A coil was made by whipping a bundle of small square cross-section pieces with a wide thin strip and lengthened by adding more pieces to the bundle from time to time. Baskets were built up by joining coil to coil: a hole was pierced in one coil and the cover strip of the next threaded through it. They were decorated by imbrication, a technique in which strands of decorating materials (red cherry bark, dyed black cherry bark, white rushes) were hooked in with the whip stitches so that the designs, usually geometric, showed only on the outside of the basket ("Basketry," fig. 9, this vol.). Basketmakers freely shared and adapted designs and handed them on to daughters or granddaughters.

Baskets were used for carrying, as kettles and bowls (a tightly woven basket was watertight and could be used for stone-boiling), and for storage. Bags of various shapes were made by openwork weaving of skins, furs, or the fibers of Indian hemp ("Ethnobiology and Subsistence," fig. 7, this vol.), which was also used to sew together tule or bulrush mats.

Clothing and Adornment

Upper Thompson clothing was tailored almost entirely of deer, elk, or small mammal skins (skins were also used for bedding and bags). Men wore shirts, belts, breechclouts, long leggings, and moccasins (fig. 5). Their headdresses were made of buckskin, birdskins, and fur; and those of hunters and warriors were the most elaborate. Women dressed much like men, although their leggings were sometimes shorter (reaching from ankle to knee), and they wore buckskin bodices, sometimes dresses and skirts, and headbands or skin caps (fig. 6). Both sexes wore skin robes, ponchos, and cloaks, and decorated their clothes with buckskin

Amer. Mus. Of Nat. Hist., New York: 16/8134.

Fig. 4. Beavertooth knife used for cutting, carving, or incising wood and stone. Collected by James A. Teit before 1900. Length 13 cm.

fringes, painted designs (especially in red and black), and dentalium shell and bone beads.

Cloaks, capes, and ponchos were best suited to the rainier Fraser Canyon, although Upper Thompsons might wear them as well, especially in the heat of summer (Tepper (1994:44–45); they were woven of Indian hemp, silverberry willow, the bark of western red cedar, sagebrush, mountain-goat wool (especially among the Lower Thompson), and the skins of mountain goat, rabbit, and marmot.

They wore a variety of ornaments or jewelry: beaded ear ornaments; necklaces of shells, seeds, claws, teeth; beadwork or snakeskin chokers; shell or bone nose ornaments (women only). Both men and women were tattooed and painted their faces each day (Teit 1930a).

Social and Political Organization

Every Thompson individual was a member of a family, local community, and either the Upper Thompson or Lower Thompson band, but ruled by none, for each man had a voice in the informal councils where hunting, war, and other matters were discussed. Leadership came from the wise and experienced, and there might be different leaders on different occasions; women spoke and led in their own areas of expertise (Wickwire 1992). Band chiefs and war chiefs might inherit their positions, but this was not automatic.

There were no classes among the Thompson, and ranking was informal, based on an individual's perceived wealth, knowledge, and family origin. Both Upper and Lower Thompsons purchased and captured slaves. The child of a slave woman and an Upper Thompson man became a full tribal member, as did his mother; among the Lower Thompson both would remain slaves.

There were no Thompson lineages, clans, or secret societies. Marriage was forbidden between first cousins and ridiculed between second cousins; blood and marriage ties were traced widely on both sides of the family. This made each person part of a large and loose network of kin to live, work, share, and trade with—an "ego-oriented kindred" (Jorgensen 1969:134). At naming ceremonies invited guests witnessed the passing on of inherited names; new ones came from personal experiences or features (Struck-on-the-head, Hairy-face), from dreams, from spirit quests, and (more commonly among the Lower Thompson) from animals.

The harmony in Thompson communities was maintained by the force of tradition and honor and the more subtle persuasion of small talk and humor, although disagreements could lead to longstanding feuds. At "Indian court," a suspected lawbreaker knelt before a chief and a fire, and the ordeal produced the truth (Hanna and Henry 1995:136). In very serious matters, like repeated adultery, those offended might kill the offender. The social and political flexibility that facilitated moving and sharing also made it easier to organize raids, for if a man experi-

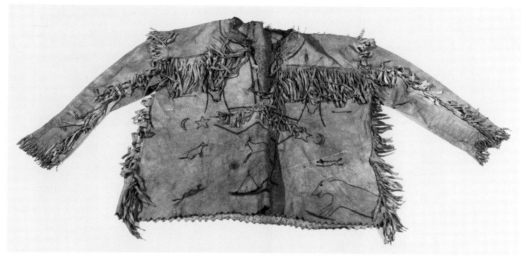

top left, Amer. Mus. Of Nat. Hist., New York: 16/9176; Canadian Mus. Of Civilization, Que.: top right, II-C-588 (neg. 73–2885); bottom left, 23129; bottom center, 26997; bottom right, 23204.

Fig. 5. Men's clothing. top left, Bear skin cap decorated with porcupine quills, feathers, and the head of a woodpecker. Length 74 cm. Collected by James A. Teit from the Upper Thompson before 1903. top right, Man's buckskin shirt decorated with the record of a hunting trip painted in red, green, and black. Width 45 cm. Collected by James A. Teit before 1925. bottom left, Alexander Kwikweitésket wearing a fringed shirt with painted designs, beaded leggings, and an eagle and hawk feather bonnet with rabbit and weasel trim. He holds a spear with antler tip. bottom center, John Tetlenitsa and Ewełemákst. He wears a painted buckskin shirt decorated with beads, a breechcloth of painted red cloth, beaded cuffs, and a headdress of eagle feathers and ermine. She wears a fringed buckskin dress decorated with beads and deer teeth. Her leggings and moccasins are beaded as is her belt and cap. She holds a woman's rattle in her hand. bottom right, Kałitāa from Spences Bridge, B.C. wearing a birdskin hat and buckskin cloak with painted designs and fringes. bottom, Photographs by James A. Teit, bottom left and bottom right, 1913; bottom center 1914.

enced in war (or public speaking) could raise a following, he could be a war chief. There are many stories of battles with the Central Coast Salish, the Shuswap, and the Lillooet (Bouchard and Kennedy 1977:40–42), which were fought with bows and arrows, clubs, spears, daggers, shields, and armor.

Trade and Travel

Thompsons traded with each other and with surrounding tribes: Lytton Band middlemen might pass on cedar roots for baskets from the Fraser Canyon, dentalium shells traded from the coast upriver and then south through the Chilcotin and Shuswap, buffalo hides from the Okanagan and the prairies (see A.H. Smith 1988:192–199 for a summary of trails and trade). Trade, early spring lake fishing, root gathering in the Botanie Valley, salmon fishing, and winter visits brought Thompson (and those from other tribes) together.

Thompsons traveled on foot and in dugout cedar canoes made by the Lower Thompson and traded upriver (where bark canoes were sometimes made).

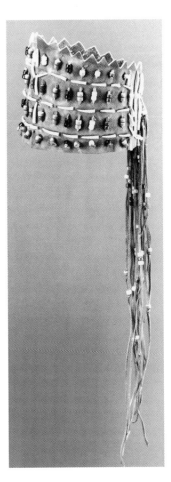

Canadian Mus. of Civilization, Que.: left, 23212; center, II-C-626 (neg. 72–4539); right, II-C-519 (neg. 94–90).

Fig. 6. Women's clothing. left, Christine Tsekenéłxemux in buckskin clothing consisting of a fringed skirt, leggings, and a sleeveless painted and quilled shirt with a pointed front. Her cape is trimmed with fur and painted in red realistic designs. Her hat is decorated with feathers and painted animal designs. She wears beaded moccasins (Tepper 1987:98). Photograph by James A. Teit, 1913. center, Woman's buckskin dress, back view. Many Thompson garments have a triangular or circular bib that is created by folding down the neck portion of the skin or adding a separate piece of buckskin (Tepper 1994:60–62). The back bib on this dress is decorated with painted figures representing dentalia, the moon, and stars. Length 101 cm. Collected by James A. Teit before 1915. right, Woman's caribou-skin headband decorated with dentalia, beads, and paint. Height without fringe 18 cm. Collected by James A. Teit before 1915.

Life Cycle

Pregnancy and childbirth, especially the first, were surrounded by many customs (Teit 1900:300–305). Before the birth of their first child, the parents had to bathe often in cold water, sweatbathe, and "pray much to the Dawn of the Day" (Teit 1900:303). The expectant mother bound her hair in the style of adolescent girls and was not allowed to touch salmon, eat salmon heads, or scratch herself. Parents observed many protective taboos: they did not hunt or eat bears, for example, for fear the baby would disappear from the womb or be stillborn.

A woman giving birth might be assisted by a midwife or by her husband, who celebrated the birth by firing arrows into the air. She sat up immediately and worked after one or two days, but for four days she avoided the cooking fire, and she remained secluded for two to four months. The newborn, bathed in warm water and anointed with fat mixtures, was nursed as soon as possible. Lower Thompsons rubbed

babies' feet with chipmunks' feet to make them swift, and sometimes they bound and shaped their heads. Babies were placed in birchbark or basketry cradles or on cradleboards with buckskin sacks (fig. 7).

Childhood was relatively free. "Only two restrictions were laid on them: they were made to rise early, and wash frequently in cold water, and were not permitted to play after sunset or make too much noise" (Teit 1900:308). A winter custom called "whipping the children" taught proper and courageous behavior, but in it children were more often chastened than actually whipped.

At puberty, both boys and girls went off alone for four months or more to prepare for their later lives. "Boys practised shooting with bows and arrows; purged themselves with medicine; sweatbathed and performed gymnastics" (M'Gonigle and Wickwire 1988:42).

During her first menstrual period a girl was secluded in a conical hut of fir branches; she wore a headdress of fir boughs and a heavy robe for the first four days (fig. 8). At night she ran about the hills to build strength, dug trenches to prepare for root digging, and learned discipline "in a number of arbitrary, time-consuming activities which have no practical purpose," including pulling the needles one by one from fir boughs (Ray 1939:56–57). She might paint a record of her travels and training on a boulder (Teit 1896) ("Rock Art," fig. 10, this vol.). In another rite, a shaman carried a dish carved out of steatite, in which he mixed herbs and water. He sprinkled a girl with herbal water, praying at the same time for her to have children (Boas 1890:90).

Seated human figure bowls are known from Vancouver Island to Lillooet and Kamloops, but "the style seems to have reached its high point in a number of small and complex bowls from the vicinity of Lytton" (Duff 1975:50). Those with rattlesnakes for backbones or brows might be ancient upriver symbols of the power and danger of birth: a 1,200+ year-old antler figurine with a human face (possibly masked) and vulva and a rattlesnake body was discovered in an infant burial at the Bell site near Lillooet (Stryd 1976:171).

Before a marriage the girl's family approached the boy or his family, or a go-between approached the girl's family for the boy. Gifts showed that intentions were serious. If the families agreed, the time was set for a wedding feast and exchange of gifts at the boy's home, although a few couples eloped. Newlyweds could live where they pleased. Polygamy was common, and divorce was frequent and informal. Either spouse could leave, but the children generally remained with their mother.

Upper Thompsons were buried in soft ground or at the bottom of a talus slope, their bodies flexed, their weapons, tools, and personal ornaments around them, their guardian-spirit bags with them or hung in a tree nearby. "Over most graves were erected conical huts made of poles covered with bark or with fir-branches" (Teit 1900:329), or canoes might be overturned on them. The Lower Thompson placed their dead in elevated cedar boxes or small houses, or on platforms in trees. They erected anthropomorphic grave figures nearby, and the Upper Thompson borrowed this custom in the early twentieth century (fig. 9). The deceased's summer mat lodge was burned, his winter house purified with tobacco water or juniper water. Wealthy persons opened a relative's grave a year or two after her death, wiped clean her bones, and placed them in a new skin or blanket.

Religion

Like the rest of Thompson life, religion was personal, informal, and tied to nature. While the Transformers had shaped the world, a more important belief was that all living things were given life by having a soul or spirit, and the religion was more one of respecting creation than worshiping the creator. Special regard was shown the sun, rain, some lakes, and the sweatlodge. "Every morning one of the oldest members of each household went out of the house at the break of day, and prayed to the Dawn" (Teit 1900:345). Women digging roots or picking berries near certain mountains painted their faces red and offered some of the first berries to the

left, Harvard U., Peabody Mus., Cambridge: 33649; right, Amer. Mus. Of Nat. Hist., New York: 16/9634.

Fig. 7. Cradleboards. left, Helen Jackson (Lekelus) holding a baby in a wooden board carrier with a buckskin sack. A beaded navel string pouch is attached to the hoop. A pack line was fastened through the holes on either side of the upper end of the board, and the board was hung down the mother's back or, when riding, on the pommel of a saddle. Photograph by James A. Teit, 1914. right, Moosehide cradle. Carriers of moosehide and older types made of bearskin were used by parties in the mountains when materials for other types of carriers were unavailable. These were carried horizontally across the mother's back. The right side of this cradle is painted red with ocher, and the left side is painted green with fireweed leaves. Collected by James A. Teit from the Upper Thompson before 1904. Length 74 cm.

Canadian Mus. Of Civilization, Que.: top left, 27099; top center, 27073; d, II-C-330 (neg. 94–55); bottom left, 23170; Amer. Mus. Of Nat. Hist., New York: a, 16/8680; b, 16/4572; c, 16/1324; bottom right, Royal B.C. Mus., Victoria: 999.

Fig. 8. Ritual structures and paraphernalia. top left, Pubescent girl covered with fir branches and a blanket tied at the waist. top center, Pubescent girl's tepee of fir brush supported by 2 guide ropes. Photographs by James A. Teit, near Spences Bridge, B.C., 1914. a–b, Skin scratchers used by young women during their puberty training. a, Bone scratcher with incised strokes possibly representing the number of days the owner had menstruated or the number beyond which she did not wish to menstruate. Collected by James A. Teit before 1901. b, Bone scratcher carved with an eye or butterfly pattern and decorated with hide thongs strung with dentalium shells. Collected by James A. Teit from the Upper Thompson before 1898. Length of b, 52 cm; a to same scale. c, Goose-bone drinking tube on hide thong used during the first days of their sequestered period of training following the onset of puberty when young women fasted and refrained from washing (Teit 1900:313). Collected by James A. Teit, Thompson River, before 1897. Length of c, 46 cm. d, Pubescent girl's cape woven of cedar bark. The neck and front opening are lined with groundhog skin and ties with hide thongs. Length 91 cm. Collected by James A. Teit in Lytton, B.C., before 1925. bottom left, Sweathouse covered with blankets weighted down with stones. Stones are being heated on a fire in the background. Photograph by James A. Teit, 1912. bottom right, Earth-covered sweathouse with a fir bough entrance. Photograph by Charles F. Newcombe, Nicola Valley, B.C., 1903.

spirits. Hunters sweatbathed and sang to their spirits before the hunt; they took special care to please those of the animals they killed. Although Teit (1900:348), says the Upper Thompson had no First-Salmon ceremony, Hill-Tout (1978:46), describes a feast where hosts and invited guests prayed and ate together, and Ray (1942:115–116) mentions the ceremony among the Lower Thompson.

Puberty training was a rite of passage not only to the adult world but also to the world of the spirits. The mountain running, dancing, singing, praying, fasting, and sweatbathing (fig. 8) prepared a young man or woman for a vision or dream in which a guardian spirit, appearing in human form, gave instructions about "the choice of a career, the selection of a name, of body paint and paraphernalia, [and] certain taboos"

(Barbeau 1914). The guardian also gave a song and in so doing left a share in its magical power: grizzly bear, thunder, and the sun made a man a better warrior than a crow or fox; a fisherman's skill might come from a duck or a canoe paddle; women shared in the power of mountain goat, grizzly bear, porcupine, huckleberries, basket, root digger.

The Stein River valley, with its powerful rapids, worn hollows, high ledges, and hidden caves, was a special place for spirit quests, and the rock paintings there record the private visions of spirit questors (M'Gonigle and Wickwire 1988:42–50). Many carried bags made from or containing the skin of their guardian-spirit animal, tied the skin into their hair, or wore it around the neck (Tepper 1994:106–107). In the Thompson guardian-spirit dance, men sang their guardian-spirit songs and painted their faces to represent their guardians (Teit 1930a:427–428). In 1877 George M. Dawson, camped in the Nicola Valley (Cole and Lockner 1989, 2:401), saw "men dancing to imitate different animals, as rabbit, Coyote &c. all to drumming & Singing" (although Indians were "collected here, from different parts of the country," and it is not certain the dancers were Thompson).

A shaman or "Indian doctor" was one whose spirit quest was especially long or intense, and who was blessed with greater spirit power (especially from otter, wolf, eagle, rattlesnake, badger, chicken-hawk, grizzly bear, coyote, owl). Broken bones and infections caused illness, but it could also come from spirit sickness—from a lost soul, from a foreign object in the body, from a broken taboo. The shaman smoked his pipe to communicate with the spirit world, called upon her spirit power, sang and danced his spirit song, passed her hands over and blew on the patient, searched for and returned the missing soul, sucked out the troubling object, and soothed the troubled spirit.

History

1700–1969

The Thompson began to see the possibilities and perils of new ways even before European settlers arrived. Thompson prophets revealed their visions at public gatherings where concentric circles of unmarried men, unmarried women, and married couples danced in unison (and where mates could be chosen with a touch). Some foresaw epidemics and the end of the Thompson. In one postcontact myth "A'tam and Im" mistake a horse, created by the devil, for God, who must transform it to make it useful (Teit 1912:399).

Horses allowed Thompsons to travel farther to hunt, gather, fish, trap, and trade. They had reached the Okanagan early in the eighteenth century, and Simon Fraser, the first White to visit the Thompson, saw horsemen with European trade goods (from east of the Rocky Mountains) at Lytton in 1808 (Lamb 1960:84–86). A Hudson's Bay Company post was built at Kamloops in 1812, but trading salmon soon

became more important than trapping furs. Warfare became more common, and chiefs who owned many horses and were great warriors and traders, like Cexpentlem (*səxpíntəm*) and Nkwala (*nkʷəlé*, for whom the Nicola Valley is named), became quite powerful and famous (and this may have made the position of band chief a more important and formal one). Hunting bands may have driven the upper Nicola elk to extermination (Teit 1930:268–269).

Thompson territory grew. Before 1800 it did not extend much beyond the mouth of the Nicola River, although Thompsons fished and hunted in the valley, occasionally wintering with the Nicola Athapaskans ("Nicola," this vol.). But the Nicola were few, one of their bands had been wiped out in a Shuswap raid shortly after 1800, and they often married Thompsons or Okanagans (Teit 1930:214). By 1835 the Thompson had spread 17 miles up the Nicola, and when Cexpentlem met Whites in 1858, he told them "the centre of my house is here at Lytton. . . . The doors of my house are at Spuzzum [in the Lower Fraser Canyon], at Łaha´hoa [Fountain], at StlE.z [near Ashcroft], at stcē´kus [near Quilchena, more than 50 miles up the Nicola valley], and at Tcutcuwī´xa [near Hedley]" (Teit 1917:50).

The Thompsons traveled and prospered despite epidemics that "carried off from one-fourth to one-third of the tribe" (Teit 1900:176), but changes leading to a more settled life had also begun. Some Thompsons were growing potatoes, corn, and grain as early as 1830–1840. In 1858, gold mining disrupted Indian fishing and farming in the Fraser Canyon, and that winter many Natives starved; many Lower Thompsons then moved "over the hill" into the Coldwater River and Nicola country, joining Thompsons who had earlier begun grazing their horses or running small farms there. White settlers followed and often preempted Native grazing and farming land. Indian reserves began to be laid out in the late 1860s, putting bounds on Thompson traveling ways.

Gradually, Thompson life became westernized. Anglican and Roman Catholic missionaries taught the settled life along with Christianity. More Natives became farmers, ranchers, loggers, miners, railroad workers, casual laborers. By 1910 cabins had replaced pit houses and mat lodges, store-bought food had replaced most wild plant food (but the Indians continued to fish and hunt), and cloth was replacing buckskin. Those in residential schools learned English and vocational skills, not Thompson language and traditions. Fifteen Department of Indian Affairs–defined bands (fig. 1), each with its elected chief and council, took the place of traditional communities and informal decision making. Indian agents saw to Native "protection and advancement."

Some Thompsons welcomed new ways: at an 1879 Lytton meeting, a "tribal council" planned for individual land ownership and an end to potlatching (Bouchard and Kennedy 1988:138). But from the time of the gold rush there had also been resistance, especially to the loss of Indian land. Only Cexpentlem's peacemaking prevented war with miners in the Fraser Canyon (Teit 1912:412). Nicola valley Natives resisted the setting out of reserves (British

Glenbow-Alberta Inst., Calgary, Alta.: 674–16.
Fig. 9. Chief's grave near Lytton, B.C. Possibly the grave of Chief Cexpentlem, it was embellished with horse skins "for eternal life" (Hanna and Henry 1995:112), 5 wooden figures, and a copper pail with a hole in it to prevent theft. Photograph by Frederick Dally, 1868–1869.

Columbia 1875:51, 86–90); and in the 1870s, fearing their claim to land would be compromised, they refused the farm equipment the government offered them. Interior chiefs made protests and sent a delegation to London, led by Chief John Chillihitza of Douglas Lake, Nkwala's great-nephew. Their 1915 meeting at Spences Bridge was the precursor to the Allied Tribes of British Columbia, which fought for aboriginal title and against shrinking reserve land (Tennant 1990:96–113). In 1927 a special government committee considered the Allied Tribes' case, but it misled their representatives, denied aboriginal title and the need for treaties existed, and finally made it illegal to collect money to fight for Indian claims.

1969–1997

Many British Columbia Native people saw 1969 as the time of a new beginning, the end of the era of residential schools and Indian agents. They united in rejecting the Canadian federal government's proposed White Paper and in supporting the Nisgha court claim to their traditional land. When the Union of British Columbia Indian Chiefs was formed to coordinate and pursue land claims, Thompsons were important in its founding.

The period from 1970 to 1997 saw increasing Thompson control of their own affairs. In the early 1970s the Nicola Valley Indian Administration began managing social programs for the valley bands (four Thompson, one Okanagan). Social assistance remained in 1992 the biggest item in band budgets, and the aim of local economic development was to reduce it by creating more opportunities for Indian workers

and entrepreneurs: the Lytton Band's Kumsheen Enterprises, for example, owned coop and hardware stores, a hotel, and shares in a logging company.

Thompson education was increasingly Native controlled, with a kindergarten to grade twelve school run by the Coldwater Band. Elders like Mabel Joe (vol. 17:612), Mamie Henry, Mary Anderson, Mary Coutlee (vol. 17:612), and Louis Phillips taught language and culture there and in public schools. The Nicola Valley Institute of Technology, Merritt, was British Columbia's first Native-run college. Founded in 1985, it offered adult basic education, university transfer, fine arts, and career programs. In 1996 it had students from 195 Native bands.

The Thompson claimed aboriginal title to their traditional territory, and other important events of 1970–1990 centered on the land. In 1976, the British Columbia government announced plans to open the Stein Valley for logging, and Lytton and Lillooet residents from both ends of the valley—Native and non-Native—joined in opposition. In 1987 the Lytton band affirmed its authority in the Stein Declaration, and in 1995 the provincial government designated the lower and middle valley as the Stein Valley Nlaka´pamux Heritage Park. In 1983, the Canadian National Railway proposed expansion of the tracks along the Fraser and Thompson rivers; Upriver Halkomelem–Thompson–Shuswap alliance fought it and took the matter to court. Reaction to Stein logging and track expansion increased public awareness of Thompson land and sacred sites (M'Gonigle and Wickwire 1988; Mohs 1987).

By 1997, other things were also strengthening the Thompson. Some were traditional: Native people were increasingly calling themselves Nlaka´pamux, not Thompson; hand drummers were again singing the old songs; a few couples had been married in traditional ceremonies; the Cook's Ferry band had resurrected the Sun Dance (Hanna and Henry 1995:131–134, 202–203); there was talk of new spirit quests and naming ceremonies. Some introduced other Native ways: big drums and medicine wheel teachings from the Plains complemented local dance and sweatlodge traditions, and Thompson students invited Sioux elders from Montana to conduct *yuwípi*. Some showed increased political autonomy: the 11 Lytton-area and Fraser Canyon bands formed the Nlaka´pamux Nation Tribal Council (table 1), while the Nicola Valley Tribal Council brought together the four Thompson bands there and the Okanagan Upper Nicola band; as Indians across Canada were declaring themselves citizens of First Nations with inherent rights, the Thompson Indian bands became the Nlaka´pamux Nation. Some served Natives without government status or living away from home: United Native Nations locals in Lytton and Merritt; the Merritt Indian Friendship Centre (Wyatt 1992). Some used White customs as the basis for Native events or groups: rodeo, ball teams, bingo. Thompson life was both traditional and changing.

200

Table 1. Thompson Band Population, 1997

	On Reserve	In Another Band	Off Reserve	Total
Nlaka'Pamux Nation Tribal Council				
Ashcroft	58	13	152	223
Boothroyd	83	25	150	258
Boston Bar	64	5	132	201
Cook's Ferry	71	34	177	282
Kanaka Bar	57	9	104	170
Lytton	623	143	814	1,580
Nicomen	61	2	34	97
Oregon Jack Creek	12	0	33	45
Siska	89	40	136	265
Skuppah	48	5	16	69
Spuzzum	31	1	144	176
Nicola Valley Tribal Council				
Coldwater	278	11	372	661
Lower Nicola	476	30	361	867
Nooaitch	127	4	42	173
Shackan	64	8	41	113
Totals	2,142	330	2,708	5,180

SOURCE: Canada. Department of Indian Affairs and Northern Development 1997.

Synonymy[†]

The earliest record of the use of the name Thompson is in field notes by Boas (1890a). This name derives from the Thompson River, which flows into the Fraser River within their territory. Because of this association, they have also been called Thompson River Indians (Dawson 1892:6).

Their most common name for themselves is *nɬeʔképmx*, and many native people prefer this both as a self-designation and as the name by which others should refer to them. However, the name properly "designates the people of the central part of the territory," and there is "no native term that properly covers the speech community as a whole, although *nɬeʔképmx* is sometimes extended for that purpose" (Thompson and Thompson 1992:1). Also, "many speakers from outside the central area object to that extension to refer to their form of speech" (ibid.). The analysis of the form is clear, but not the meaning of its root; it includes a prefix *n-* 'localizer' and a suffix *-mx* 'people', but the rest is obscure. The earliest use of this name is corrupted as Neklakussamuk (British Columbia 1872), and has been used in many spellings: Neetlakapamuch (Bancroft 1874–1876, 1:311), Neklakapamuk (Good 1878, 1878a, 1879), Neklapamuk (Canada. Superintendent of Indian Affairs 1879), Nitlakapamuk (Good 1880, 1880a), Netlakapamuk (Good reported by Pilling 1893:30), Klackarpun (U.S. Hydrographic Office 1882), Ntlakápamaq (Tylor et al. 1889:234), Ntlakya'pamuQ (Boas 1890:806), Ntlakapamoh

[†]This synonymy was written by Dale Kinkade.

(Le Jeune 1890), N-hla-kapm-uh (MacKay [1891], quoted in Dawson 1892:6), N-tla-kā-pe-mooh (Dawson 1892:6), Ntlakyā'pamuQ (Boas 1891:632), NtlakyapamuQ (Boas 1891:693), Mtlakapmah (Le Jeune 1892), N'tlaka'pamuQ (Hill-Tout 1900:500), NLak·a'pamux (Teit 1900:167, noting that it is their own name, but sometimes given to the Lytton band alone), Ntlakyapamuk (Teit 1905; Hodge 1907–1910, 2:88; Freeman 1966:265 referring to Teit fieldnotes from 1896–1918), N'tla-ka-pa-moh, N'tla-kap-moh (Freeman 1966:265), and Ntlakyapmuk (Landar 1973:1411).

One of the two earliest references to the Thompson Indians is Mayne (1862). He called them the Nicoutameens or Nicoutamuch (1862:296), and a version of this name was used alongside variants of *nɬeʔképmx* until around 1900. Its origin and analysis is unclear; it is possibly a name given to the Thompson by neighboring groups, inasmuch as it was not possible to reelicit the form from Thompson speakers in the last half of the twentieth century. Teit (1900:167) cited the form as Lükatimü'x in Okanagan and as Nko'tamux in Shuswap. Kinkade elicited a form *nək^wtmíx^w* in Columbian to the south, where it was identified only as "a Canadian tribe," although it is clearly the same word. Kuipers (1974:192) obtained a variant *sxnək^wʔetk^wmx* 'North Thompson people' in Shuswap; this variant has been expanded with extra prefixes and a suffix meaning 'water, river'. The root is apparently *nək^w-* 'one, other', and the suffix *-mix^w* is 'people' (this suffix has apparently been lost from Thompson—another reason to think this may be a name applied to the Thompson by neighboring groups). Other variants that have been used are Nicute-much (A.C. Anderson 1863:76), Nikutemukh (Gibbs 1873), Nkutĕmíχu (Gatschet, reported by Hodge 1907–1910, 2:89 as their Okanagan name), N-ku-tam-euh (MacKay in Dawson 1892:5), Nicoutamuch (Powell 1891:180), and Nikutamuk (Landar 1973:1411).

Another early name that was applied to the Thompson Indians was Couteaux (A.S. Taylor 1862), and this was occasionally translated into English as the Knives (A.C. Anderson 1863:76) or Knife Indians (Teit 1900:167). Teit indicated that this is the name applied to them by the Hudson's Bay Company.

The name reported as used by Halkomelem speakers downriver from the Thompson is Saw-meena (said to be used by the Tait band; A.C. Anderson 1863:71). This was written as Samena in Gibbs (1873) and Somena by MacKay (in Dawson 1892:5), who said it means 'inland hunters'. MacKay identified this as their Cowichan name, but here Cowichan is apparently used as designating the entire Halkomelem language, not just the Cowichan dialect on Vancouver Island. This name is from Halkomelem *sʔámənə* 'inland'. Teit (1900:167) says that the Halkomelem of the "Fraser delta" called them the SEmā'mila; this is the plural form of *sʔámənə*.

Very few other designations are found. Teit (1900:167), reports a Lillooet name Cê'qtamux and says it is from their name for the Thompson River. He (1900:167) also gives

Sa´lic as their Okanagan name, but this seems unlikely. This is the Spokane-Kalispel-Flathead self-designation *séliš*; it also appears in Okanagan as *siləx* as a self-designation. MacKay (in Dawson 1892:5) reports Ske-yuh as the Thompson's name for themselves, and says it means 'the people'; it is actually *sqáyx*ʷ 'man'. Bancroft (1874–1876, 1:311) uses Clunsus; the source of this form is unknown. Murdock (1972:126) includes the designation Snare Indians and attributes this designation to Jenness (1939). However, Jenness actually concludes that the band of Indians called the Snare Indians would have been Shuswaps. The confusion arises because they were said to be on the upper Thompson River (which would be in Shuswap territory), and because Jenness describes them as "a portion of the North Thompson branch of the Salish" (Jenness 1939:105), but Jenness is using "Thompson branch" here to refer to the three northern Interior Salishan languages as a group.

Sources

Teit (1900) lived among the Upper Thompson at Spences Bridge and studied them most. He described them along with other Salish people (1914, 1930) and gave accounts of their mythology (1898, 1912, 1917), rock painting (1896), and tattooing and face and body painting (1930a). Works on basketry (Haeberlin, Teit, and Roberts 1928) and ethnobotany (Steedman 1930) were done jointly or based on Teit's field notes.

Hudson's Bay Company records and the accounts of Simon Fraser (Lamb 1960), George M. Dawson (Cole and Lockner 1989), and other early travelers (Mayne 1862; Good 1878) and missionaries (Crosby 1907) add little to Teit's work. Hill-Tout's (1978) ethnography is shorter and probably less reliable than Teit's, and Ray's (1942) list of Lower Thompson culture elements came from a few days' work with one informant.

McDonnel (1965) investigated Upper Thompson land tenure during the 1960s. Laforet and York (1981) described the traditional winter dwelling, Turner et al. (1990) brought ethnobotanical studies up to date, Tepper (1984, 1994) studied painted clothing in museum collections and collected ethnographic photographs (Tepper 1987). York, Daly, and Arnett (1993) described the rock paintings in the Stein valley, and Hanna and Henry (1995) collected creation and other stories. Construction projects of the 1980s resulted in salvage ethnography (Bouchard and Kennedy 1988; Smith 1988).

Shuswap

MARIANNE BOELSCHER IGNACE

Language and Territory

The Shuswap ('shoō͝,swäp) are speakers of an Interior Salish language.* There are two major dialects, Western Shuswap and Eastern Shuswap, which differ phonetically and morphologically (Kuipers 1974, 1989:17–20; "Languages," this vol.). Eastern Shuswap is spoken east of Kamloops, and Western Shuswap in the rest of Shuswap territory. In addition, there are lexical and intonational differences within Western Shuswap between the speech of the Fraser River Shuswap and that of the Kamloops area, and within Eastern Shuswap there are lexical and phonetic differences distinguishing the speech of the Shuswap Lakes people from that of Spallumcheen.

In the 1980s and 1900s the name Secwepemc came increasingly into local use for the Shuswap, the equivalent of their Shuswap name $sex^w épemx$ in the practical orthography.

The aboriginal territory encompasses some 180,000 square kilometers in British Columbia (Dawson 1892; Teit 1909; Palmer 1975a; M. Ignace 1992). Their homeland is traversed by the Fraser and Thompson rivers. Most Shuswap communities are and were along the valleys of these rivers and their main tributaries (fig. 1).

Component Groups

There were seven Shuswap divisions, each consisting of a number of aboriginal bands, communities occupying distinct portions of resource-producing territory and seasonal as well as winter settlememts (Teit 1909:452). Teit (1909:457–462) enumerated 25 aboriginal bands existing prior to the 1860s, along with a "principal village or headquarters" for each. Following the smallpox epidemic of the early 1860s, the population of several of these bands dwindled to very few, with the remaining members moving to neighboring communities. The 17 remaining bands that became Indian Bands as defined by the Canadian Indian Act during the late nineteenth century continued to exist as Indian Bands throughout the twentieth century.

In the Shuswap language, there are no general terms for divisions, bands or communities; rather, the suffix -emx designates the people of a locality or geographic region in a wide or narrow sense. The divisions and aboriginal bands, which by and large continue to be conceived of as regional, cultural, and social units, and their communities are the following.

In the Fraser River Division ($s\dot{\lambda}emx^wúlex^wemx$) there were 10 aboriginal bands. The northernmost was Soda Creek, with principal village at $\chi a\check{c}út$, now the Soda Creek Band ("Reservations and Reserves," fig. 11, this vol.). Next came the Buckskin Creek Band ($cexkex^wénk$; extinct); Williams Lake or Sugarcane Band (suk^wek^win), with principal village at $\dot{\lambda}e\chi elx$ (Teit's $pe\dot{t}ceq^wcícen$), now the Williams Lake Band; Alkali Lake ($es\check{k}et$), now the Alkali Lake Band; and Dog Creek ($x^\varsigma á\dot{\lambda}te\dot{m}$) and Canoe Creek ($cwexemx$). The last two have formed one administrative unit called the Canoe Creek Band since the early twentieth century. Also in this division was the Empire Valley Band ($cex^wépkemx$), most of whose members perished in the smallpox epidemic. Its few survivors merged with the Dog Creek people. Farther south were the High Bar Band at $ten\dot{t}ené\acute{y}ten$, the Clinton Band at $pe\dot{t}té\dot{q}t$ near the modern town of Clinton, and the Big Bar Band, referred to as people of $s\dot{\lambda}eqé\dot{w}s$ ('little hanging bridge') by Teit (1909:458). The survivors among the Big Bar people merged with the Clinton Band after the smallpox epidemic. The Clinton Band itself was relocated to the east bank of the North Thompson River during the early 1970s and has since been known as the Whispering Pines Band. Teit (1909) noted that the southern Fraser River Division, including the people of Dog Creek–Canoe Creek, High Bar, Big Bar, and Clinton, formed a subdivision somewhat distinct from the northernmost bands.

The Canyon Division ($sé\dot{\lambda}emx$) comprised the Riske Creek Band, the North Canyon Band, the South Canyon Band, and the Chilcotin Mouth Band, all of whom disappeared following the 1862 smallpox epidemic. The sur-

*The phonemes of Shuswap are: (voiceless stops and affricate) p, t, c ([c] ~ [č]), $k, k^w, q, q^w, ?$; (glottalized stops and affricate) $\dot{p}, \dot{\lambda}, \dot{c}$ ([ċ] ~ [č]), $\check{k}, \check{k}^w, \dot{q}, \dot{q}^w$; (voiceless fricatives) s ([s] ~ [š]), $\dot{t}, x, x^w, \chi, \chi^w, h$; (resonants) m, n, l, w, y, γ (velar approximant), ς (uvular approximant), ς^w; (glottalized resonants) $\dot{m}, \dot{n}, \dot{l}, \dot{w}, \dot{y}, \dot{\gamma}, \dot{\varsigma}, \dot{\varsigma}^w$; (vowels) i ([i] ~ [ɛ]), e ([ɛ] ~ [æ]), a, o ([ɔ]), u ([u] ~ [o]); (stress) $\acute{v}$. The short, unstressed vowel [ə] is treated as an allophone of e; a and o are retracted ("darkened"). The rare retracted consonants $\c{c}, \c{s}$, and perhaps $\c{l}$ are not distinguished from their nonretracted counterparts in the available sources (Kuipers 1989:11; M. Dale Kinkade, communication to editors 1997). Eastern Shuswap also has $\dot{t}$, the retroflex approximant r and its glottalized counterpart $\dot{r}$, and a phonemic distinction between e and ∂.

Forms cited in this chapter are in Western Shuswap (Kuipers 1974) unless otherwise indicated.

In the Shuswap practical orthography (Dixon and Kuipers 1974) the phonemes are written as follows: p, t, ts, k, kw, q, qw, 7; p', t', ts', k', k'w, q', q'w; s, ll, c, cw, x, xw, h; m, n, l, w, y, r, g, gw; m', n', l', w', y', r', g', g'w; i, e, a, o, u. In Eastern Shuswap, a is written ⟨ah⟩, and stressed e is written ⟨a⟩.

203

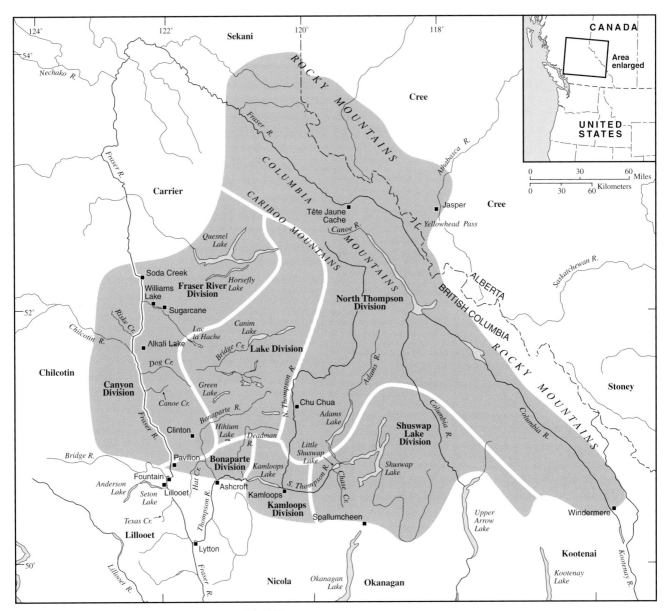

Fig. 1. Shuswap territory in the 19th century (based on Teit 1909).

vivors of this division joined the Alkali Lake Band during the 1860s (Teit 1909).

The Lake Division was called *styétemx* 'interior people'. They consisted of the Lac la Hache people (*txeⱡiínten*), the Green Timber Band (*peⱡceq̓ʷmúsemx*), and the Canim Lake people (*cq̓ésxenemx*). Only the last survived the diseases of the 1800s, absorbing the surviving members of the Green Timber Band. The few survivors of the Lac La Hache people merged with the Williams Lake Band.

In the North Thompson Division (*tqéqeltkemx*) the principal band (the *simpxwemx*) had its village formerly at *ciq̓ʷceq̓ʷéⱡq̓ʷ* 'red willow' and later at Chu Chua (*ⱡexʷⱡexʷcwex*). Since the early twentieth century, these people have been known as the North Thompson Band. The North Thompson Division also included the "People of the Upper Reaches" who lived near the sources of the Fraser,

North Thompson, and Canoe rivers and even a short distance east of the Yellowhead Pass toward Jasper, Alberta. They were a small band severely decimated early in the nineteenth century, even prior to contact with Whites (Teit 1909; MacGregor 1974). Some of its few survivors joined the Kinbasket people during the nineteenth century; others merged with the North Thompson Band during the early twentieth century, when they were relocated to live among the Band—after being refused a proposed separate reserve. The Kinbaskets (*kenpésq̓t*), in turn, are an offshoot of the Upper North Thompson people and the Shuswap Lake people who in the early 1900s migrated along the valleys of the Columbia and Canoe rivers to the area of Windermere (Teit 1909:467; Dehart 1985) and there settled in close vicinity of the Kootenai people. They are now called the Shuswap Band.

204

Teit (1909:455) referred to the people of the Shuswap Lake Division as the *sxstélenemx*, although this term more narrowly stands for the Adams Lake people (Ignace 1984–1992). The Shuswap Lake division is comprised of the people now known as the Neskonlith Band, who mainly wintered at *xeléwt* and *sk̓acin*, those of *xstélen* (the present Adams Lake Band), the people of the Little Shuswap Band, one of whose main villages was at *q̓ʷ ʔewt*, and the people of Spallumcheen Eastern dialect (*spalacin*) near the head of Okanagan Lake.

The Kamloops Division (*stk̓emlúpsemx*) contained *tk̓emlúpsemx* 'people of the confluence' (of North and South Thompson rivers), at and near the present city of Kamloops. Also reckoned as part of this division were the *sk̓emqínemx* ('people of the head [of Kamloops Lake]') with principal village at *skícesten* ('arriving place'), in anglicized spelling known as the Skeetchestn or Deadman's Creek Band. Until the mid-nineteenth century the people of this division also occupied a large number of winter village sites along both sides of Kamloops Lake.

The Bonaparte Division (*sexcínemx*) include the following: the *sƛextéwsemx*, or people of the Bonaparte and Hat Creek river valleys known as the Bonaparte Band; the *snekʷaʔétkwemx*, people of the main Thompson River above Ashcroft, who became extinct during the late nineteenth century, its survivors joining the Skeetchestn and Bonaparte Bands; and finally the people of *ck̓ʷáyƚexʷ* or Pavilion Band between Marble Canyon and the Fraser River. The last named have become Lillooet-ized through intermarriage. As Kennedy and Bouchard (1978) noted, the entire area along the Fraser River from Texas Creek to Pavilion, including Fountain village, was Shuswap until perhaps the eighteenth or nineteenth century; it became increasingly Lillooet-speaking through intermarriage after that time.

External Relations

Peaceful relations with the neighboring people were maintained through marital alliance. Typically, settlements at the edges of Shuswap territory (e.g., Spallumcheen, Windermere, upper North Thompson, Soda Creek and Sugarcane, Pavilion, Ashcroft) had a high rate of intermarriage, resulting in many members of these bands being bicultural and bilingual. Through recurrent intermarriage, the people of the Ashcroft and Pavilion areas eventually even became absorbed into the Thompson and Lillooet nations. Moreover, marital alliances were contracted to consolidate peace treaties with more distant groups or to sanction political alliances (see Teit 1930). Slavery followed the same general patterns of neighboring interior Salish groups (for a comparative discussion see L. Donald 1996).

Prior to the arrival of Europeans, a trade network linked the Shuswap to their immediate neighbors and to their more distant neighbors on the Northwest Coast, on the Columbia Plateau, and across the Rockies. The main trade routes to the coast were via the Lillooet and Chilcotin. Shuswap from each region would sell surplus foods from their region or foods that were scarce or nonexistent among their neighbors.

Teit (1930:535) notes that the people of the Canyon Division at the Fraser River were particularly adept traders, acting as middlemen in trade between other Shuswaps and the Chilcotin. While they sold salmon and salmon oil to the Chilcotin, they received dentalium shells, woven goat's hair blankets, rabbitskins and marmot skins, some of which they resold for a profit to Shuswap from other divisions. The northern bands of Shuswap traded salmon and salmon products to the Carrier in exchange for moose hides; the North Thompson division people also traded salmon to the Cree people. On the other hand, the Bonaparte, Kamloops, and Fraser River bands received dried salmon from the Upper Lillooet and Thompson people, who had particularly abundant salmon fishing grounds. The Shuswap also bought certain types of plants that were rare in portions of their own country, such as Indian hemp, bitterroot, and yew-wood, from the Okanagan and Thompson; they sold items such as hazelnuts, which were unique to the North Thompson people, and red cedar root. From the Kootenai people were traded buffalo skins. During the nineteenth century some Shuswaps traded with the Iroquois and Métis near Yellowhead Pass (Teit 1909:452, 468).

Teit (1909:540) noted that "the Shuswap were formerly noted as a warlike people; but this only held true of the Fraser River, Bonaparte and Kamloops Divisions. The others seldom engaged in war, and acted only on the defensive." Wars and feuds between Shuswap and neighboring tribes were mainly carried out over resources—fishing and hunting grounds—or to revenge insults and assaults against prominent individuals. Such intertribal wars or feuds were carried out until about 1860, and oral histories recorded from elders during the 1980s report armed conflicts dating back to approximately the same period (Ignace 1984–1992).

The Fraser River Shuswap frequently fought against the Upper and Lower Lillooet (Teit 1930), and occasional feuds occurred between the Shuswap and the Thompson Indians (Teit 1930:542; Ignace 1984–1992). During the eighteenth and nineteenth century the Kamloops Division repeatedly attacked and fought with the Okanagan as far south as Penticton. These feuds were eventually terminated by a formal peace treaty between the Kamloops chief Kwolila and the Okanagan chief Pelkamulox, which re-established the Shuswap–Okanagan boundaries (Teit 1930:265–266). During the early nineteenth century, following the death of Pelkamulox during an altercation with a Lillooet chief from Seton Lake, the Shuswap of K'emlups joined the Okanagan and Thompson people in an attack on the Lillooet from that area, killing more than 300 (Teit 1900; Dawson 1892:27–28; McLeod 1823).

Feuds or large-scale conflicts over the control of fishing and hunting grounds or provisions frequently occurred   *205* between the Fraser River Division and the Chilcotin, Carrier, and Sekani (Teit 1909), as well as between the North Thompson Shuswap and the Sekani, Cree, and Blackfoot. On some occasions, parties of Chilcotin and Cree penetrated deep into Shuswap country, but were expelled, with numerous bands usually joining forces against them (Ignace 1984–1992; Teit 1909:550).

Environment

Shuswap country includes at least nine major biogeoclimatic zones (Krajina 1970). They include diverse habitats such as the interior Douglas fir zone, bunchgrass–ponderosa pine, alpine tundra, subalpine fir, and Cariboo aspen–lodgepole pine zones.

The climate varies from the dry and warm climate of the interior dry belt in the Kamloops region to the wet and cold regions of the Columbia Mountains. In the Kamloops region annual precipitation is less than 30 centimeters, and mean annual temperatures range from 20°C in summer to -5°C in winter. Annual precipitation in the Cariboo region is only slightly higher than that in the Kamloops region but ranges from 100 to 250 centimeters in the Columbia Mountains (Farley 1979:43–45).

Culture

Subsistence

During their annual seasonal round, most bands maintained a nomadic lifestyle, traveling among fishing grounds, lakes, berry picking, cambium collecting, and root digging locations and hunting grounds in the river valleys and trout lakes at higher elevations, hunting on the forest edges and in the subalpine, and spending the coldest season in their semi-subterranean winter homes in the river valleys. While most bands spent at least two-thirds of the year camping and traveling, often covering hundreds of miles of territory in pursuit of food, a few bands, especially those near the prolific fishing grounds of the Fraser-Chilcotin Canyon, were almost sedentary (Teit 1909; Ignace 1984–1992).

• FISHING   Chinook salmon, which in precontact and early contact times apparently were the largest salmon resource (Bouchard and Kennedy 1992; Romanoff 1992a; Ware 1983), were fished between high water time in spring and early fall. They run in the Fraser River system as far as Tête Jaune Cache, as well as in the Thompson, North Thompson, and South Thompson rivers and their major tributaries, and used to be abundant in the Columbia River system.

With the decline of chinook stocks since the early twentieth century (Ware 1983; Ignace 1984–1992), sockeye salmon, have become the most important fish resource. The prolific lower Adams and the once-prolific upper Adams

River salmon, known for their pronounced four-year cycles, were caught in large quantities in the clear waters of the Thompson and South Thompson rivers with leisters, gaffs, and gill nets, either from shore or at night from canoes in which pitch fires to attract the fish had been lit (Bouchard and Kennedy 1975). Sockeye of the Chilko Lake, Horsefly, and Quesnel runs, which travel the muddy waters of the Fraser River, were caught with dipnets, gill nets, and set nets from platforms erected on rocks above back eddies. Much of the fishing there was carried out at night. Many Shuswaps from the southwestern Bands annually participated in the huge Lillooet salmon fishery at Six-Mile near Bridge River (Romanoff 1992a).

Coho salmon, which run in late fall, were caught with gaffs and nets, or in weirs and traps before approaching their spawning grounds. Pink salmon, the smallest of the Pacific salmon species, who return in alternating years, were the least desirable species, as their flesh softens considerably by the time they arrive in Shuswap country. They were caught and eaten only in years when shortages existed (Ignace 1984–1992).

Formerly, fishing nets were made of Indian hemp (*Apocynum cannabinum*) or cedar bark (Teit 1909), with stones used as sinkers. During the twentieth century, commercial fiber and eventually nylon netting and metal pullies with lead sinkers and cork floats replaced the indigenous netting materials. Harpoon spears formerly had hooks made from splinters of animal bone, although metal tips forged from metal implements replaced the bone tips during the twentieth century. Leisters or three-pronged creek spears were made of firwood with barbs of deer antler and attached to lodgepole pine poles 5–15 feet in length (fig. 2 bottom; "Fishing," fig. 14c, this vol.). Since the early twentieth century, the Shuswap reforged pitchforks into the required shape. Gaff hooks, which were "not much used before the advent of iron" (Teit 1909:530), became widely used during the twentieth century to catch sockeye at the mouths of many tributaries to the the Main and North Thompson. As with harpoon spears and leisters, the poles of gaff hooks were partially blackened to prevent the fish from seeing them. In many places, platforms were built into the river for gaffing, spearing, or dip-netting.

Until the early twentieth century, when the Canadian Department of Fisheries curtailed and disrupted traditional Indian fishing, the use of weirs and traps was widespread. The weirs consisted of a framework of poles, sticks, and brush, which were built across a creek like a fence. As they gathered in front of these fences, salmon were speared or dip-netted by the fishermen. Another form of weir consisted of two fences, the first one of which was built in such a way as to be penetrable by the salmon ascending the river, but preventing their return. The fish thus remained between the two fences until they were removed with spears (Teit 1909:530; Dawson 1892:16).

Next to the salmon fishery, the spring trout fishery was an important source of food. Large quantities of cutthroat and

Fig. 2. Thompson and Fraser river system and fishing therein. top, Fraser River, near Alkali Lake, B.C., showing the aridity of the general area. center, Dip-net fishing at Soda Creek, B.C. The fisherman rakes his net against the flow of the back current, which the salmon follow to migrate upriver. top and center, Photographs by Raymond Fogelson, 1965. bottom, Ron Ignace, Terry Deneault, and Robert Swite spear fishing at x̣k̓emčin, on the Thompson River, Skeetchestn Indian Res., B.C. Photograph by Marianne B. Ignace, 1987.

rainbow trout were caught with scoop nets at the outlets of many lakes in the plateau between the Fraser and North Thompson rivers. This lake fishery, carried out from the time the first lakes were ice free in late March and continuing until late May, provided the first large harvests of fresh fish after the winter. Families from many bands congregat-

ed at camping grounds near the creeks at the outlet of these lakes, where the salmon were caught in traps or bag nets. The trout fisheries at Hihium Lake (Xixyum) and at Green Lake were well known.

Other fish were caught throughout the year for immediate consumption as well as winter use. These included suckers and graylings, kokanee, ling cod, and sturgeon.

• HUNTING   As a dietary source, meat was nearly as important as fish; in fact, for the North Thompson and Lake divisions, it was the most important. Moreover, hunting was more prestigious and ritually significant than fishing.

The main sources of meat were mule deer; elk, which became rare after the nineteenth century; caribou, which also became rare in the early twentieth century; and moose, whose habitat expanded southward throughout Shuswap country during the early twentieth century. Mountain sheep, mountain goat, and black bear were hunted as well. In addition to large game, a variety of species of small animals provided meat for daily subsistence or in times of scarcity, including gophers, groundhogs, marmots, rabbits, porcupine, grouse, and waterfowl.

Until the availability of firearms during the nineteenth century, bows and arrows were the principal weapons used for hunting. Bows were made of yew-wood, available only to the North Thompson Division and Eastern Shuswap or of juniper wood, and were elaborately fashioned and decorated (Dawson 1892; Teit 1900:240ff, 1909:518). Bow strings were made of twisted sinew. Arrows were made of rosewood or saskatoonberry wood, with feathers attached to the shaft. The indigenous basalt arrowheads were eventually replaced by iron heads. The arrows often had grooves running along the length of the shaft, allowing the blood of a wounded animal to escape, and thereby facilitating its tracking (Teit 1909:519).

Dogs, sometimes cross-bred with coyotes or wolves, were widely used to track deer (Teit 1909). Hunting took place during all seasons, although it was during the fall rutting season when the quality of meat was best that large amounts of meat for winter storage were procured.

Hunting was carried out in task groups of several men, who in turn set up base camps with their families at the foot of mountains that were hunting grounds, where the meat was processed. In some cases, men partially dried the kill to facilitate packing it to base camp. Often, deer were ambushed at salt licks or driven into rivers or lakes to be killed. Deer or caribou fences and corrals near lakes or cliffs were also used (Teit 1900:248ff, 1909:521; Ignace 1984–1992).

• GATHERING   Even during the late twentieth century, more than 200 indigenous named species of plants were known to the Shuswap, and presumably more were known in earlier times. Of these, about 50 were utilized as food plants. Various plants, such as cactus, balsamroot, bitterroot, and hazelnuts, were limited in availability. Some of the most prolific and valued plants were yellow avalanche lilies and spring beauties, known as "wild potatoes," and balsamroot, which were harvested in great quantities in late spring with parts of the harvest dried and stored for use in later seasons. Other plants, such as wild nodding onion, tiger lily, and bitterroot offered a variety of tastes and condiments. Cambium, especially the inner bark of jack pine, provided a sweet delicacy in mid to late spring (fig. 3). From late June to the end of August, soopolalie, known as *xusem*, numerous species of blueberries, huckleberries, wild strawberries, and saskatoonberries provided daily food and were also dried or turned into fruit leather or cakes and preserved for use in winter. By making use of different growing seasons at different altitudes, the Shuswap had fresh plant foods available between April and September.

A large variety of plant species was used for medicinal purposes, many of them as preventative tonics and purgatives. Others were used as cures for specific diseases. While the detailed knowledge of such medicinal plants was left to specialists, several plant remedies and tonics were widely known, including balsam bark for respiratory diseases and influenza, soopolalie sticks as a purgative, and fir pitch as an external remedy for curing infections and extracting slivers (Turner 1974; Palmer 1975; Turner, Ignace, and Compton 1991–1992).

• OWNERSHIP OF RESOURCES   While each band had its commonly and habitually used hunting, fishing, gathering, and trapping areas, proprietary rights over the resource-producing territory were apparently held by all Shuswap in common (Boas 1891:638; Teit 1909:572). A strong ethic of egalitarianism and of sharing food resources prevailed (Ray 1939:21). At the fishing grounds, the entire catch procured by participating fishermen was equally distributed, and further fish were distributed to elders and others unable to fish for themselves. Meat was likewise distributed to all participants of a hunting party and to others in need. "Stinginess" in this respect caused harm to the hunter or fisherman's reputation and invited bad luck for the future harvesting of game, fish, or plant species (Ignace 1984–1992). Natural resources management was carried out through a variety of ways, including the burning of old plant growth to enhance new growth, the pruning of berry bushes, and the selective harvesting of plant and animal species in the sense of never taking more than

was needed to feed one's people. Most of all, resource management was carried out through a value system that enforced the use of all parts of killed animals and sanctioned individuals who were wasteful.

Fig. 4. Structures. top, Lodge made of bark with raised cache for storage of mats and other items. center, Earth-covered sweathouse. top and center, Photographs by Harlan I. Smith, Kamloops, B.C., 1898. bottom, Tepee covered with cloth. Photographed at Tête Jaune Cache, B.C.

Fig. 3. Tools for harvesting bark and sap. top, Double ended sap scraper made of caribou bone; bottom, bone bark peeler for stripping the bark off yellow pines. Collected by James A. Teit, Kamloops, B.C., before 1903. Length of top, 21 cm; bottom to same scale.

Structures

Dwellings included semisubterranean homes that were occupied from November until March, and tentlike lodges at different hunting, fishing, and gathering camps throughout the rest of the year. The underground homes were single dwellings, or clusters of three or four (Teit 1900:192), although prehistoric sites with several dozen pits exist. The underground homes, termed *xʔistkten* 'winter home' by the Shuswap and known as *keekwillies* in Chinook Jargon, were inhabited by groups of interrelated families, with each housing 15 to 30 people. They consisted of a pit four feet deep and 10 to 30 feet in diameter. Four posts erected in a rectangle supported the round roof of small poles covered with bark and sod (Boas 1891:633ff; Dawson 1892:7; Teit 1900:192ff, 1909:492). According to Teit (1909:492), the winter home was divided into four rooms. Many winter homes had separate entrances through the top for men and through the side for women.

Summer lodges consisted of a circular or rectangular framework of poles covered with tule mats, rushes, bark of coniferous trees (fig. 4 top), or bunchgrass. In addition to the family lodges, large double lodges were constructed at fishing camps to accommodate people at feasts and giveaways (Teit 1900:195; Ignace 1984–1992). Other shelters and structures included lodges or shelters for girls during their seclusion period at first menses, and women's menstruation huts or miniscule winter homes. In the immediate vicinity of their winter homes, and at resource-producing locations, the Shuswap built circular cache pits with a roof of small poles, in which provisions were stored wrapped in birchbark. Box caches on trees and scaffold caches were also utilized (Teit 1909:495). Sweatlodges were built along creeks in secluded places. They consisted of a round structure of red willow wands bent over and both ends stuck into the ground. Inside, near the door was a hole for hot stones. The frame was covered with birchbark and blankets when in use, although some sweathouses were permanently covered with sod (fig. 4 center). When in use, the ground inside the sweathouse was covered with fir boughs, juniper, and sage.

Technology

Arrowpoints, spear points, knife points, and scrapers were made from basalt, and occasionally from jade, chert, or obsidian (Teit 1909:473). Manufactures from stone included mortars and pestles for grinding paint and tobacco, pipes, whetstones, and files. These items were replaced by iron implements during the fur trade of the early nineteenth century. Other tools, such as root-diggers ("Ethnobiology and Subsistence," figs. 1, 14, this vol.), shovels, and the handles of various implements, were made of wood or antler. Bone supplied the raw material for needles, awls, and occasionally scrapers, adzes, and knives (Teit 1909:473ff; Dawson 1892:18ff).

All carrying, cooking, and storage containers were made of plant fiber (fig. 5). Square birchbark baskets, sewn with split spruce or cedar roots, were the predominant type of container. Coiled basketry was rare. The Shuswap wove mats out of tule, reeds or grass.

Virtually all clothing was manufactured from animal hides, often with the hair left on. Buckskin, the most widely used kind of hide, was softened by being soaked in a solution of deer brains before being stretched on a frame (fig. 6). The predominant articles of clothing were pants, leggings, breechcloths, shirts, coats, moccasins, pouches and bags, gloves, and caps (figs. 7–8). (Lamb 1960; Teit 1909:502ff, 1900:206ff; Ignace 1984–1992).

Division of Labor

In general, men were in charge of hunting, fishing, trapping, making tools and weapons, fighting, and the training of male children, whereas women were in charge of plant food gathering and domestic chores, including making lodges and bedding, cooking and storage containers, as well as processing meat and fish, fetching water, making clothes, including the tanning of buckskin, washing, cooking, and caring for young children.

Aside from these norms, the actual division of labor was more flexible. Some women had a reputation as expert hunters of large game (Ignace 1984–1992); moreover, at hunting camps, women invariably snared or shot small game to feed their families as their husbands procured large game. Men assisted in berry picking, the processing of fish and game, made their own clothing, and cooked. Some men assisted their wives in tanning buckskin.

Transport

On the rivers and lakes, the main means of transport were bark canoes or cottonwood dugouts. The dugouts became more widespread with the availability of iron tools during the nineteenth century. Bark canoes were made of spruce bark or white pine bark (Dawson 1892:14; Teit 1909:531ff). Smaller canoes were made of birchbark. Rafts were used for transporting fish, meat, and household gear (Ignace 1984–1992).

Aside from water transport, all travel in the old days was carried out on foot, and all goods and provisions were packed on the backs of men, women, children, and occasionally dogs.

The Shuswap were renowned for their finely made snowshoes, which were universally used for travel in winter. Horses were introduced by the late eighteenth century (Teit 1909:533; Lamb 1960), although with some of the more remote bands, they did not become prevalent until the mid-nineteenth century. Horses revolutionized travel and hunting, and the Shuswap fashioned their own pack saddles made of cottonwood, saddle blankets made of goat and deer skin, as well as carrying bags attached to saddles, and other pieces of tack (Teit 1909:534).

Social Organization

While kinship reckoning was generally bilateral (cf. Boas 1891; Teit 1909; Ray 1939), the preference for virilocal or patrilocal residence meant that most individuals developed a sense of primary "belonging" to or affiliation through birth and socialization with their fathers' people or aboriginal bands (Boas 1890:637; Ignace 1984–1992). These aboriginal bands were loosely knit networks of extended families and households centered around the habitual use and occupation of camping grounds, winter village sites, and hunting, fishing, and gathering grounds. Before the establishment of reserves during the late nineteenth century, settlements were dispersed, and the sense of reckoning membership in one band or another was rather flexible (Teit

top left, Smithsonian, NAA: 96–10675; Amer. Mus. of Nat. Hist., New York: top right, 16/8360; center right, 16/9301 and 16/9302; bottom left, 16/9279.

Fig. 5. Shuswap containers and the tools for making them. top left, Woman digging roots with a birchbark basket at her waist and a large coiled burden basket loaded with plants and suspended from her head by a tumpline. Photographer and date not recorded. top right, Birchbark basket. Painted designs on one side depict a man and a dog, a woman chasing a chicken, a tree, and a man shooting a bear. On the opposite side are arrowhead and net designs. The spruce root stitching around the rim is decorated with yellow and blue dyed horse hair. Collected by James A. Teit before 1901. center right, Bone awl and metal awl with wooden handle used for manufacturing baskets and sewing skins. Collected by James A. Teit, Kamloops, B.C., before 1903. Length of bone awl, 21 cm; metal awl to same scale. bottom left, Coil-constructed basket of spruce root. Collected by James A. Teit, Canoe Creek, B.C., before 1903. Height of top right, 20 cm; height of bottom left, 20 cm. bottom right, Mary Thomas with a cradle that she made of birchbark and sewed with strips of western red-cedar root. Photograph by Nancy Turner, Enderby, B.C., 1994.

Fig. 6. Hide preparation. left, Hide stretched on a frame being scraped with a stone or metal scraper affixed to a long wooden handle. Photograph by Harlan I. Smith, Kamloops, B.C., 1898. right, Nellie Taylor lacing buckskin onto her frame for tanning. Photograph by Marianne B. Ignace, Skeetchestn Res., B.C., 1987.

1909:457). The residential and economically productive units were extended households, centered around senior males and their wives, their children, grandchildren, nieces and nephews, but sometimes the wife's relatives. These people gathered, fished, and hunted together and processed their foods together, and eventually shared it. Households, through their members' consanguineal and affinal ties with other households in the same village or other villages, engaged in continuous cycles of reciprocal obligations. This involved the exchange and sharing of food, goods, labor, and mutual consultation. The blood relatives of a person's household were his *k̓ʷséltkten?uẃi* 'real relatives'; all other consanguines were classed as *k̓ʷséltkten* 'family, relatives', and included any individual with whom a person could trace genealogical ties. Depending on context, even affines (*sexʷnemt*) were occasionally classed as *k̓ʷséltkten*.

Kinship terminology was bilateral; however, some terms for parents' collaterals in the first ascending generation were distinguished according to the sex of the speaker, and different terms signifying different roles were used for father's sister (*tík̓ʷe?*) as opposed to mother's sister (*tetum*, w. sp.; *k̓uẏe*, m.sp.), and for mother's brother (*sise?*) as opposed to father's brother (*meqse?*, w. sp., *leẃe*, m. sp.). All kinship terms were used in a classificatory sense, with anyone who had a traceable genealogical connection as a relative being incorporated into a person's consanguineal terminology.

The terminological equation of cousins with siblings resulted in a taboo on cousin marriage (Teit 1909:591). In practice, however, the prohibition seems to have covered any persons who could be identified as blood relatives by a living elder (Ignace 1984–1992), with marriages between distant cousins sometimes being tolerated but rarely condoned.

During the late eighteenth or early nineteenth century, the Canyon Division and the northern Fraser River Division adopted a crest group and ranking system sanctioned by potlatching from the Northwest Coast via the Squamish Coast Salish, Lillooet, Carrier, and Chilcotin (Teit 1909:575ff). Membership in these crest groups, which, like the coastal crests, were largely derived from animals, was based on patrilineal descent and a brief initiation ritual. A division of nobles, including hereditary chiefs and "original" families of certain locations, established itself, and some of the northern bands were trying to establish individual control over land and resources. They had to abandon their attempts when the remaining Shuswap kept enforcing the notion of shared land ownership (Teit 1909:572).

Political Organization

Besides war chiefs, hunting chiefs, and chiefs of dances, who were task group leaders for specific occasions based on seniority and expertise, the Shuswap had political chiefship in the form of chiefs, called *kuk̓ʷpi?*, an office that was hereditary to a certain degree. The successor must always be deemed fit for chiefly office through personal skills and achievements. Such chieftainship existed at the level of the aboriginal band or community. No paramount chieftainship at the tribal level existed; however, the chiefs of certain bands, based on their oratorical and negotiating skills, were selected to represent the Shuswap to outsiders (Oblate Missions of British Columbia 1971; Ignace 1984–1992).

The chief had an informal body of advisors, *k̓ʷen?iple?ten*, composed of elders and representatives of all extended families of an aboriginal community (Teit 1909:569; Boas 1891:637; Ignace 1984–1992). Chiefly succession was patrilineal. However, if a chief had more than one son, the male relatives of the deceased, presumably with the advice of their *k̓ʷen?iple?ten*, selected and appointed the successor, based on

211

Fig. 7. Shuswap chiefs visiting at St. Mary's Mission, New Westminster, B.C., then the provincial capital. left to right, standing: Ta o'task, Canoe Creek; William, Williams Lake; sitting: Nan nah, Dog Creek; Quib quarlse, Alkali Lake; Seaskut, Shuswap; Timpt khan, Babine Lake, Silko salish, Lillooet; Kam eo saltze, Soda Creek; and Sosastumpt, Bridge Creek. They wear fringed skin jackets, which at this time were a symbol of high status (Tepper 1994:66–67). Photograph by Frederick Dally, 1867.

criteria of fitness for office. If no son was available, then a grandson, nephew, or brother of the deceased was selected. The case histories of chiefly succession in particular bands for the nineteenth century confirm the norm of patrilinear succession; however, probably due to the population loss at this time, more distant patrilineal relatives, in some cases even male affines, were appointed as successors to chiefs. In these cases, their personal skills were what had them appointed, with genealogical connections to previous chiefs further legitimating their position. Oral histories of succession during the nineteenth century also show that fitness for office was a major criterion; in fact, in numerous instances, sons were bypassed in favor of more distant male heirs who were deemed to have the requisite qualifications (Ignace 1984–1992).

The chiefs mainly functioned as mediators within the band, and as representatives of their people's interest to the outside, regulating food supply where necessary, "admonishing the lazy and quarrelsome" (Teit 1909:570), giving advice, and setting a good example for all others, without having any material or other privileges. The chiefs' role was to maintain consensus within the band and among families, rather than dictating the course of action (Ignace 1984–1992).

Social control was exercised through a variety of informal and formal ways. Shame, gossip, and ridicule played an important role, as did paying restitution and ostracizing in serious cases. Public arenas for dealing with deviants were

Fig. 8. Moccasins made of tanned hide, trimmed with wool, cotton, and velvet cloth and decorated with glass beads. Collected by James A. Teit before 1903. Length of moccasins, 24 cm.

212

"Indian courts," where, through the mediation of the chief, evidence was heard as to deviant acts, and the guilty party was publicly shamed and made to pay restitution (Ignace 1984–1992). During the mid-nineteenth century, the Oblates of Mary Immaculate missionaries observed these Indian courts and mistook them for acts of indigenous confession and penance (Dionne 1947).

Religion

Shuswap spiritual beliefs support an individual's respect for all living creatures and for nature in general. The focus is on obtaining and preserving communication with forces in nature through training and vision.

All living things, even rocks, fire, water and other natural phenomena were believed to have a soul, since, according to tradition they had been people, or had been connected to people, originally (Teit 1900:357, 1909). Upon a person's death, the soul was believed to separate from the body and start its journey to the land of spirits. If a person's life on earth included unfinished business, his soul would wander around trying to find peace of mind and visit the living, often as a ghost. In order to obtain guardian-spirit power, adolescents would spend intermittent periods of time in seclusion to practice or train, *ecxem*. The purpose of this training was to acquire a spirit helper (*sumex*), but in this process, also to become self-sufficient, rather than dependent and therefore a "nuisance" to one's community. A person who became "powerful" or "smart" (*xexe?*) through training established his power in the double sense of being able to communicate with the supernatural, and being practically self-reliant and able to provide for himself. Once a guardian spirit was acquired through fasting, praying, sweating, and dreaming while in seclusion, it would appear to the individual in his dreams and advise him. Guardian-spirit helpers were typically animals, but in some cases also involved culturally significant plants or implements, such as tobacco, pipe, blood, weapons, as well as natural phenomena, such as clouds, thunder, rain, water, or fire. The guardian spirit gave advice that ensured success in life, especially in hunting and gambling (Teit 1909:605ff).

Shamans (*λekwilx*) were religious specialists who showed a propensity toward particularly powerful guardian spirits during or after their initial training. Beyond practical knowledge over herbal remedies, shamans cured people though the help of their guardian spirits by drawing disease out of them. Disease was believed to be caused by invading substances or forces sent by others, or loss of soul. Most shamans were men.

Mythology

Old One, *ckewelx*, the creator, who was said to be magically omnipotent, brought order to the territory and introduced many of the plant and animal species to it or modified them so they would be useful to humans. He taught the people respect for nature and cultural skills, such as procuring fish, plants and game, basketmaking and other crafts, and sweat-bathing. However, to finish his work, Old One sent Coyote (*skelep*) to earth. Unlike Old One, Coyote was a trickster, being selfish, cunning and therefore often foolish as well as lazy. His trickery left landmarks throughout Shuswap territory, changing the character and features of plant and animal species. Most notably, he caused the salmon to ascend the mid-Fraser and Thompson rivers. Shuswap oral traditions cover Coyote's adventures, some of them carried out with his "brother," fox (Dawson 1892:28ff; Teit 1909: 621ff; Kuipers 1974, 1989; Bouchard and Kennedy 1979; Ignace 1984–1992). Other transformers who changed the character of Shuswap country were *q^weq^wel?i?lt* and *tli?sa* and his brothers, who, in battling man-eating monsters throughout the country, made the land and its resources accessible to the people. Other stories (*scpetek^wle*) about animals explain their physical and behavioral characteristics (Teit 1909:621ff).

Life Cycle

• BIRTH   After a child was born, his umbilical cord (*qu?*) was ritually buried on the ancestral land of his people, symbolically attaching him to the land (Ignace 1984–1992). Babies were wrapped tightly and kept in birchbark cradles, or occasionally in cradleboards that were hung in trees or thrown away after the infant outgrew them. Twins, considered especially lucky and powerful, were thought to have a spiritual connection with bears. From an early age on, children were trained by bathing in cold water and by sweat-bathing.

As soon as a child could walk, or sometimes earlier, he or she received a name during a public feast. Most names were hereditary names typically ending in -*esqt* 'day' or -*elst* 'rock' for males, and -*etk^we* 'water' or -*inek* 'bow' for females. Occasionally, dream names or nicknames were used, which subsequently became hereditary names. Children took the names of deceased ancestors of either parents in order to "keep alive the memory" of the deceased person (Teit 1909:570; Ignace 1984–1992). Because of this interest in keeping names and the memory of their former bearers alive, it was the donor of the name, rather than its recipient, who gave a feast when such a name was passed on outside of the donor's immediate family (Teit 1909).

• PUBERTY   At puberty, both girls and boys underwent ritual and practical training to prepare them for adulthood. Girls were secluded during their first menses. Supervised by an elder female relative, they rose early and bathed in cold water, practicing female crafts and skills by making miniature clothing and implements and looking after themselves and their lodgings as they would have to when ready for marriage. Thereafter, women went through seclusion with each menses, when they were considered as polluting to hunters.

Boys began their training when their voice changed, "or when they commenced to dream of women, arrows and canoes" (Teit 1909:588). Throughout their adolescence they spent periods of four days to several weeks to obtain their guardian spirit or *sumex*, continuing anywhere from one to 10 years until this was accomplished. The purpose of their training was also to acquire the practical knowledge and spiritual power for hunting, gambling, or warfare. They also purged themselves by sweatbathing and taking medicinal plants, which brought about dreams and hallucinations connecting them with animals and their spiritual essence.

• MARRIAGE   Upon completing their training, boys and girls were considered marriageable. Most marriages were contracted by betrothal arranged by the relatives of the groom and bride. Some marriages were contracted by the suitor "touching" the bride he desired during dances and public ceremony (Teit 1909:591). The betrothal was consolidated by a gift-exchange between the bride's and groom's family, where the bride was ritually "appointed to sit down" beside her husband (Ignace 1984–1992). Residence was usually virilocal, although for a time after marriage, newlyweds resided among the wife's people as a form of bride service. Both levirate and sororate were common, although the replacement spouse often was a member of the deceased's kindred rather than an actual sibling. According to oral histories, some chiefs were reputed to have had several wives as a result of political alliances with other nations and communities; however, the vast majority of marriages were monogamous (Teit 1909; Ignace 1984–1992).

• DEATH   Following the death of an individual, his or her soul departed from the body through a process lasting four days. During this time, a wake was held. A fire was kept to communicate with the departed soul, and food and tobacco were burned to nourish the deceased along his journey (Ignace 1984–1992). The body was then interred, although people who died during warfare were cremated. Personal possessions of the deceased were buried along with him. Following the interment, the grave was swept with rosebush branches to wipe away the tracks of the deceased. On the morning following the burial, the relatives would visit the grave to check for "tracks" or omens the deceased had left on his journey. The burial was followed by a communally provided feast to thank those who consoled and helped the mourners and to lighten their spirits. During this feast, the guests would play bone games with the stakes provided by the family of the deceased, and often consisting of some of the deceased's valuables (Ignace 1984–1992).

Ceremonies

As taught to them by Old One, the Shuswap consider sweatbathing (*sqilye*) to be one of their essential ceremonies. Sweatbathing involves cleansing, both from a physical and mental point of view. In providing physical cleanliness, it was also seen as drawing sickness from people's bodies,

healing wounds, relieving pain, and providing longevity. Beyond this, the physical cleanliness derived from sweating and the scents of the forest derived from using fir boughs, juniper, sage, and herbs, ensured success in hunting or warfare, and aided communication with the spiritual and natural worlds. Women and men sweated separately.

Teit (1909:574) noted that "the Shuswap were great smokers." Smoking of tobacco was carried out mainly for ceremonial purposes, as a sign of friendship and good will. It was carried out before political negotiations or business transactions, and before public meetings, any event requiring advice or seeking consensus. It was also a ritual offering to the forces of nature and to the dead and accompanied prayers to spiritual helpers and Old One. According to the Shuswap origin of the world, tobacco at one time was a bush that ate people. It was turned into the tobacco tree by Coyote and then became beneficial to humankind. Before contact with Whites, the Shuswap grew patches of an indigenous tobacco, *Nicotiana attenuata*. With the fur trade, commercial tobacco came to be smoked, and trading relationships with the Hudson's Bay Company incorporated the ritual exchange of tobacco. In addition, other plants such as sumac, lovage, red willow, or kinnikinnick mixed with bear grease were smoked (Dawson 1892:23; Teit 1909; Palmer 1975; Turner, Ignace, and Compton 1991–1992).

While gift exchange as a means of putting events on record and fulfilling obligations was part of traditional culture, formal potlatches were unknown to the Shuswap before the mid-nineteenth century. Then for a brief period they spread from the Fraser River to other bands and then declined quickly (Teit 1909:574). However, "giveaways," to show respect to one's guests at feasts, seem to have been a feature of traditional culture (Ignace 1984–1992).

During social gatherings, sports contests and gambling games were favored activities. The game variously known as the bone or stick game (Shuswap *steḱmeẃs*), was widespread ("The Stick Game," fig. 6 center, this vol.). It involved two teams facing each other, with the members of one team having to guess which of four "bones" in their opposites' hands were marked and which were unmarked. The game was accompanied by hand gestures, verbal discourse, and the pounding of boards in rhythm with songs to distract the opponents. Good luck in gambling demonstrated the strength of the spirit power of the contestants.

The Shuswap had a range of songs, accompanying various activities, such as berry-picking or hunting songs, lullabies, lyric or "lonely-songs," dancing songs, and songs derived from encounters with animals, including "mystery songs" obtained from the guardian spirit (Teit 1909; Laforet 1981; Boelscher 1986).

Some animal or guardian-spirit songs were impersonated by dancing to them. Ceremonial dances were carried out at the midsummer and midwinter solstices to communicate with the dead and to ensure their happy life in the afterworld (Teit 1909:604). In addition, there were dances for social occasions (Ignace 1984–1992).

History

The first European to encounter the Shuswap was Alexander MacKenzie, who briefly stayed among the Soda Creek Band en route to the Chilcotin and the Pacific. In 1808, Simon Fraser met members of some western Shuswap communities as he explored the river that was to be named after him. Three years later, Alexander Ross and David Stuart, traveling under the auspices of the Pacific Fur Company, arrived in Kamloops, and Stuart spent the winter with the Kamloops Division. From the early 1820s until the 1860s, as the Hudson's Bay Company assumed the monopoly of the fur trade, relations between the Shuswap and Whites were dominated by the natives' trade of furs and dried salmon for western commodities. Native people were in the overwhelming majority and little social and economic change was yet introduced (Fisher 1977). The Shuswap called these first Whites, who were largely fur traders of French Canadian background, the *seme?uẃi* or "real Whites," and thought of them as guests in their country (Shuswap Nation Tribal Council 1989).

Drastic and devastating change occurred after the late 1850s, when the Fraser River gold rush brought a flood of White immigrants into the area. The smallpox epidemic of the early 1860s, which reduced the Shuswap population by two-thirds (Teit 1909), was a result of the gold rush. As the mainland of British Columbia became a British colony in 1858, the colonial government laid out large reserves of land "as severally pointed out by the Indians themselves" in the interior among the Kamloops and Shuswap Lakes divisions. However, in the final years of the colony and after British Columbia became a province of Canada, the Native groups saw the curtailment of their reserve lands and the increasing preemption of land by settlers. Following threats by the Shuswap and Okanagan to take up arms against the Whites (Fisher 1977:191; Oblate Missions of British Columbia 1971), a Joint Commission for the settlement of Indian Reserves in the Province of British Columbia established by the Canadian federal and British Columbia provincial governments laid out reserves totaling some 100,000 acres for the 17 remaining Shuswap bands. These reserves and their residents were subsequently administered by the federal Department of Indian Affairs through Indian Agencies in Kamloops, Williams Lake, and Lytton.

The period of missionization began during the late 1850s, when the Oblates of Mary Immaculate, a French Catholic order, established a mission to serve the Okanagan and surrounding tribes on Okanagan Lake. In 1866 and 1867, Oblate missions were established in Kamloops and Williams Lake. Within the next two decades, virtually the entire Shuswap population became Roman Catholic through baptism. However, since missionaries visited each community only once or twice a year, and since the liturgy was celebrated in the native language, aboriginal beliefs continued to co-exist with Christianity during this period (Ignace

1986–1992). During the 1920s the Canadian government worked hand in hand with missionaries, enforcing attendance at residential schools. There the speaking of aboriginal languages by pupils was prohibited, and young children were isolated from the socialization of their native communities and families (Haig-Brown 1988).

Following the establishment of reserves during the 1870s, Shuswap leaders continued to lobby for a permanent resolution of the land and aboriginal rights question by way of treaty making. Various delegations of chiefs, headed by Chief Louis of Kamloops and Chief Basil Dick of Bonaparte, traveled to Ottawa and London during the first decade of the twentieth century, petitioning the Crown to acknowledge their rights and title to their homeland. In 1910, a memorial was handed to Canadian Prime Minister Sir Wilfred Laurier during his visit to Kamloops. This memorial, which lays out the Interior Salish peoples' version of their history with Whites; and addresses the issues of sovereignty, land title, and jurisdiction; and proposes solutions to these issues, continued to serve as the ideological basis for the Shuswap aboriginal rights struggle during the late twentieth century (Shuswap Nation Tribal Council 1989).

In 1913, the Royal Commission on Indian Affairs for the Province of British Columbia was struck. However, rather than addressing the fundamental questions of treaties, land title, and jurisdiction, it narrowly focused on reserve lands being "used" for agricultural purposes by native people and therefore disallowed or "cut off" tens of thousands of acres of Indian land throughout Shuswap territory (R. Ignace 1980). During the 1920s, the Shuswap joined the Allied Tribes of British Columbia, continuing to lobby for a solution of the land question. These efforts came to an end with amendment of Section 141 of the Indian Act, which prohibited the raising of funds by Indian groups for purposes of advancing land claims, filing court cases, or retaining lawyers for these purposes.

Throughout this period and up to World War II, social and cultural change continued to affect the Shuswap confined to small reserves within their homeland. During the early twentieth century, while continuing to hunt, fish, and gather plants, throughout the still unsettled parts of their territory, most Shuswap made a temporarily successful transition to ranching (fig. 9), farming, and gardening for subsistence and for cash crops within the confines of reserve life. Extended-family based ranches formed the units of social and economic life. In addition, many Indians sought seasonal employment as fruit pickers in Canada and the United States or worked as farmhands, guides, and packers (Knight 1978; Burrows 1986; Ignace 1984–1992). Despite the wardship policy of the Indian Act, the more isolated reserves continued to remain relatively autonomous in terms of internal social and political affairs.

Fostered by the legacy of the Indian residential schools and changes in provincial and federal Indian policy, the post-World War II period saw the breakdown of the traditional social fabric within the reserve communities. Welfare dependence, alcoholism, and family separation became pervasive (Furniss 1987; York 1989; Johnson 1986). The Shuswap Bands continued to be administered out of Indian Agencies in Kamloops, Williams Lake, Lillooet, Okanagan, the Kootenays, and Lytton.

Chief George Manuel from Neskonlith became a key player on the Canadian aboriginal political scene as leader of the North American Indian Brotherhood and eventually, the National Indian Brotherhood. In 1975, the native bands of the area forced the closure of the Kamloops District (Agency) Office and demanded greater fiscal and political autonomy. In 1981, the Shuswap Nation Tribal Council was formed by 10 bands as the political voice of the Shuswap nation, to offer economic and social advisory services to increase self-sufficiency at the local and national level. The northern Bands aligned themselves through the Cariboo Tribal Council. Pavilion is part of the Lillooet Tribal Council, and the Shuswap Band is part of the Ktunaxa/Kinbasket Tribal Council. In 1982, all 17 Shuswap Bands signed the Shuswap Cultural Declaration, aimed at preserving and perpetuating the Shuswap language, culture, and history, and leading to the formation of the Secwepemc Cultural Education Society in 1983. This movement led efforts to provide public education and curriculum for the perpetuation of the Secwepemc language ("Languages," fig. 9, this vol.) and culture (fig. 10), including a Secwepemc Museum, and a Native postsecondary education institute in Kamloops. It also re-established the annual Shuswap gatherings, which had traditionally been held at Green Lake (Teit 1909:536). Throughout the 1980s and 1990s, the employment and housing standards improved, gradually recovering from the economic and social disarray and dependency of the 1950s to 1970s.

The Shuswap language had barely survived the legacy of the residential schools. During the 1990s, less than 10 percent of all Shuswap were fluent speakers of their language, and these were largely individuals at least 50 years old.

Language classes at the preschool to adult education level sought to remedy this situation.

During the 1980s and early 1990s, various Shuswap bands were involved in litigation with the Canadian federal and provincial governments regarding the exercise of aboriginal fishing and hunting rights, as well as the negotiation of specific and comprehensive land claims.

Population

In the absence of any reliable census data for the precontact or early contact period, it is difficult to assess the precontact population. Teit (1909) estimated that the population about 1850 was 7,200, and it should be noted that by this time, smallpox (see Lamb 1960) and typhoid fever had already reduced the population for several decades. Palmer (1975a) estimated the precontact population at up to 9,000, based on the "carrying capacity" of the territory. He based his "carrying capacity" on the exploitation of the species deer, elk, and sockeye salmon only, neglecting other species of fish, game, and plant food; and his population estimate is very likely conservative.

During the 1860s until the early twentieth century, the population suffered devastating losses. Nearly two-thirds of the Shuswap population perished in the smallpox epidemic of the early 1860s. In the subsequent years other epidemics of introduced diseases, such as measles, diphtheria, influenza, scarlet fever, whooping cough, and tuberculosis took a further toll. By 1900 the population was barely 2,000 (Teit 1909) and the 1918–1919 influenza epidemic killed up to one-third of the remaining population on some reserves, most of them elders and young children (Ignace 1984–1992). After the 1920s, the population began to recover gradually, as living conditions and health care facilities, which had been poor since the establishment of reserves and forced assimilation, began to improve. In 1989–1990, 6,058 status Indians were registered as members of the 17 Bands (Coffey et al. 1990). This figure does not include nonstatus natives of Shuswap ancestry, whose numbers are difficult to estimate. Of the status Indians, approximately 50–60 percent lived on their reserves.

Synonymy

The name Shuswap is an adaptation of the Shuswap self-designation *sexʷépemx*. While Alexander MacKenzie, and Simon Fraser, who approached the Shuswap from Carrier country, learned to call them by the Carrier term Atnah 'foreigner' (MacKenzie 1801), the earliest version on record of the term Shuswap derives from David Stuart and Alexander Ross, who called them She Whaps (Ross [1849] 1969:151). In 1823, John McLeod, chief trader at the Kamloops post operated by the Hudson's Bay Company, referred to the Indians in the vicinity of Kamloops and Shuswap Lake as

Fig. 9. Native cowboy at Canoe Creek, B.C. Photograph by Raymond Fogelson, 1965.

Fig. 10. Cultural persistence. left, Evelyn Camille and Mona Jules, preparing food for pit-cooking at Kamloops Res., B.C., now a special event rather than daily activity. right, Pauline Baptiste and Ida William singing traditional songs during an anniversary celebration of the North Thompson Band Church, Chu Chua, B.C. Photographs by Marianne B. Ignace, left 1993, right 1987.

the Shew-shapps. McDonald (1827; Rich 1947) used the spellings Shewshapes or She Whaps in referring to the people of the Kamloops and Shuswap Lake divisions, who have competed for the name *sexʷepemxʔuẃi* 'real Shuswap' (cf. Teit 1909:455). Boas (1891:632) spelled the tribal name Shushwap, but noted Su´quapmuq or Sequapmuq as the "proper" name for the tribe; Dawson rendered their name as Shoo-whaʹ-pa-mooh, but used Shuswap to refer to all Interior Salish people in British Columbia. Since Teit (1909), the most commonly used anglicized spelling has been Shuswap. With the spreading of the practical orthography (Kuipers and Dixon 1974), most Shuswap prefer the spelling Secwepemc according to the practical orthography.

The origin and etymology of the root *secwep* is somewhat uncertain. Kuipers (1974:187) suggested three alternatives: a derivative of *suxʷ-* 'to recognize'; a derivative from Kalispel *sixʷ*, "a root of terms of relation"; a derivative from *xʷep* 'to unfold, to spread'. The last would mean that *sexʷepemx* can be analysed as *s-* (nominalizing prefix) + *xʷep* 'spread, unfold' + *-emx* 'people'. This etymology was corroborated by some elderly speakers of Lillooet, who use the same name for their eastern neighbors. Another etymology suggested by elderly speakers has it derived from *sixʷ-* 'to spill' + *-ep* 'to arrive into a state', hence 'spilled people' (Ignace 1984–1992).

Since the early nineteenth century, the names for some of the principal subdivisions, bands, and villages have also been rendered in various attempts at phonetic spelling by explorers, traders, missionaries, and ethnographers. In addition, place-names have some variation, because plural and consonant reduplication and some prefixes are optional. D. Thompson (1813–1814) referred to the Fraser River Division as Sklim hoo lim oo, spelled by Teit (1909:453) Slemxuʹlexamux. The earliest rendition of the term

stḱemlups, anglicized as Kamloops, goes back to Ross and Stuart, who, upon reaching the "She Whaps on Thompson's River . . . there encamped at a place called by the Indians Cumcloups" (Ross [1849] 1969). Teit (1909:455) used the diminuitive reduplicated form Stkamluʹleps, and Dawson used the alternate form Kamaloo'la-pa (*ḱemlulpeʔ*, diminuitive of *ḱemlupeʔ* 'confluence of tributary'). The name for the Skeetchestn Band was rendered as Ski-shis-tin by Dawson (1892:44), as Stskitcestn by Teit (1909:461), and as Skijistin by the Oblate missionaries. By the fur traders, these people were commonly designated as "Lower Lake" people, or people of the outlet of Kamloops Lake, hence their alternate self-designation, *sḱemqínemx*. They were also commonly called by the English designation Deadman's Creek people, after the English name for the main creek or river that traverses their country.

The name for the Bonaparte division, *seẋcínmex* 'downstream people' (cf. Kuipers 1989:178) was rendered as Satchimenas by McDonald (1827), and as Zaxtci´nemux by Teit (1909:456). The *sɬuẋtéwsemx*, 'people of the Bonaparte valley' (Ignace 1984–1992; Kuipers 1974) were spelled Sloxtáʹus (Teit 1909:461). The name of the Pavilion Band, *cḱʷéylexʷ* 'hoar-frost land' was rendered as Skwai-luh by Dawson (1891), as Skwaʹilâx by Teit (1909:461) and has been Lillooet-ized as Ts'kw'aylaxw in the Band's self-designation.

The name of the North Thompson Band, *simpxʷemx* (Ignace 1984–1992), also known in English to traders and missionaries as people of the North Fork of Thompson River, was spelled Chin-poo by McLeod (1823) and McDonald (1827), Shinpoo by the Oblate Missionaries (Oblate Missions of British Columbia 1971), and Nsi´mpxemux by Teit (1909:454). Their former main vil-

Fig. 11. Percy Casper in powwow dance regalia. He is wearing a traditional form of clothing made in modern materials including a breechcloth made of wool with fringe and metal studs; a bandolier decorated with mirror pins; a paisley shirt; a feather bustle; a hairpipe breastplate; and a feather headdress. He holds a feather fan and short staff with a bird's foot and feathers on its end. Photograph by Ben Marra, 1991.

lage, *ciqʷceqʷélqʷ* 'red willows' (*Cornus stolonifera*) (Ignace 1984–1992; Kuipers 1974) was referred to as Tsuk-tsuk-kwalk, erroneously translated as 'red pine' by Dawson (1892:44) and as Tcoqtceqwa´llk by Teit (1909:460). The reserve name Chu Chua is not derived from this but is an anglicization of *ɬexʷcwex* 'creek running through the bush'.

Similarly, a variety of terms and spellings have existed for the Eastern Shuswap Bands. In general they are referred to as *s(e)xqeltkemx* 'people of above or Upper Lake' (Ignace 1984–1992; Kuipers 1974; cf. Bouchard and Kennedy 1975), although specifically *sxqeltkem* designates the settlement and reserve at the outlet of Little Shuswap Lake entered on maps as the "Sahaltkum" Reserve of the Adams Lake Band. An alternate term is *sxstélenemx*, rendered as Sxstê´llnEmuᶍ (Teit 1909:455), which represents another Adams Lake reserve, anglicized as "Hustalen" on maps. The band whose principal village was *ᶍeléwt*, spelled Halá´ut by Teit (1909:461), and Halaut by the Royal Commission on Indian Affairs (1916) has become known as the Neskonlith Band after their nineteenth-century chief Neskainlith or Niskahnilth (*nesqenel*) (Joint Reserve Commission 1875). Finally, the village of

qʷʔewt on Little Shuswap Lake was spelled Kwout (Dawson 1892:44), Kwā´ut (Teit 1909:462), and Quaaout (Royal Commission on Indian Affairs 1916). Another term for this area is Squilax (Eastern dialect *sqʷleqs* 'black bear'), although the name is not an indigenous place-name, but the Shuswap rendering of the name for a railway siding in the area. During the late twentieth century, the people of this area were generally referred to as members of the Little Shuswap Band.

Sources

Early ethnohistoric accounts of the Shuswap can be gleaned from the published accounts of fur traders and explorers, including MacKenzie (1801), Fraser (Lamb 1960), Stuart and Ross (Ross [1849] 1969; Spaulding [1855] 1956), A. McDonald (1827; Cole 1979; Rich 1947), Simpson (1931; Rich 1947), Kane (in Harper 1974), Milton and Cheadle (1865), Wade (1931), and the published records (Rich 1947) and unpublished journals of the Kamloops (Fort Thompson) Hudson's Bay Company post, the Alexandria Post and Jasper House Post. These are housed at the Manitoba Public Archives, Winnipeg, and the Kamloops Museum and Archives. The fur trade also produced the first, albeit partial maps of Shuswap territory by McDonald (1827), D. Thompson (1813–1814), and A.C. Anderson (1876).

For the second half of the nineteenth century, a wealth of ethnohistorical information can be extracted from the missionary records of the Oblates of Mary Immaculate, some of them published and analyzed (Whitehead 1981:19; see also Dionne 1947). Further unpublished correspondence and accounts are housed in the Oblates of Mary Immaculate Archives in Ottawa and Vancouver. The unpublished sessional papers, correspondence, and other documents by the Department of Indian Affairs housed in the National Archives of Canada, Ottawa, for the 1870s to 1910s give further information on the changed economic and social life for this period.

The ethnographic works begin with Boas's (1890, 1891) short essays on Interior Salish kinship terms and on Shuswap ethnography, followed by Dawson's (1892) article with appended map and list of aboriginal place-names. Teit's (1909) monograph is by far the most detailed and accurate portrait of traditional culture. It should be read in conjunction with his work on the Thompson (Teit 1900). Teit (1930) includes some information on the Shuswap and on their relationship with the Okanagan. Some ethnographic data are included in Harlan I. Smith's (1900) archeological report of the Thompson River region. Ray (1939) includes material on the Soda Creek Band.

Palmer discusses Shuswap cultural ecology (1975a) and ethnobotany (1975); Turner (1974, 1979) and Ignace (1984–1992) refer to plant use. Bouchard and Kennedy (1979) have provided an edition of Shuswap Stories as well as some ethnographic notes on Lillooet-Shuswap relations (Kennedy and Bouchard 1978) and some unpublished manuscripts and reports (Kennedy and Bouchard 1975; Bouchard and Kennedy 1985). Texts and myths in transcription and interlinear translations have been published by Kuipers (1974, 1989). MacLaury (1987) has examined Shuswap color categories.

Brief works on history from the Shuswap point of view include Coffey et al. (1990) and a booklet by the Shuswap Nation Tribal Council (1989). Perspectives of contemporary social problems in Alkali Lake, a community well known for its struggle with alcohol addiction, are dealt with in F. Johnson (1986), Furniss (1987), and York (1989). Some aspects of Shuswap social and economic history are explored in Burrows (1986) and R. Ignace (1980, 1985). Haig-Brown (1988) wrote about the impact of the Kamloops Indian residential school.

Unpublished manuscript materials are in the archives of the Secwepemc Cultural Education Society in Kamloops, at the Kamloops Museum and Archives in Kamloops; British Columbia; and with the British Columbia Indian Language Project, Victoria.

Nicola

DAVID WYATT

The Nicola (nǐ'kōlu), an Athapaskan group who lived in the midst of Interior Salish in the Nicola and Similkameen valleys of interior British Columbia (fig. 1), are the mystery people of the Northern Plateau. Dawson (1892:25), who first reported their existence to the scientific community, recorded only a few words* from a Nicola Valley man who claimed "that he, with seven other men and some women and children belonging to them were now [in 1888] the only remaining true natives of the Nicola region."

The ethnographic and linguistic work that followed tells little about the Nicola, for it came too late. As early as 1845 the Nicola residents of the Similkameen and Nicola valleys "looked upon themselves as Thompson" (Teit 1900–1921), and Teit found that the last person who could speak the language properly had died about 1890. Anthropological work has provided only speculations about Nicola origins and specks of their culture.

Origin

According to the story Dawson (1892) reported, from J.W. MacKay, Indian agent at Kamloops, the Nicola were originally a Chicotin war party that one spring set out to attack a Shuswap village west of Kamloops. They calculated that most villagers would be away fishing and resistance slight, but the previous winter had been so severe that all the Shuswaps had gone fishing. The Chilcotins continued past the vacant village to the mouth of the Nicola, and from there were forced up the Nicola valley by Thompsons. They "obliged their pursuers to desist from molesting them," settled, and intermarried with the Thompson and Okanagan (Dawson 1892:24). Allison's (1892:305) story of a Chilcotin war party arriving in the Similkameen valley about 1740 could be regarded as independent verification of Dawson's account, were it not that she knew MacKay and said, "he was such a well-informed man . . ., and what he said was always reliable" (Allison 1970:21). Teit's informants disagreed with the Chilcotin war-party theory and were "quite indignant" at

* There are insufficient data available on the Nicola language to deduce a phonemic inventory with any certainty. Given the probability that the Nicola were an offshoot of the Chilcotin, its phonemic inventory was probably very much like that found in Chilcotin (vol. 6:402). Since the names cited in this chapter are actually in either the Thompson or Okanagan language, the orthography used for them is the same as that found in the chapters for those groups.

the suggestion; Teit concluded the Nicola had a long local history (Boas 1895).

Teit (1912–1921) did, however, decide that the Nicola language was "somewhat closely related to that of the Chilcotin tribe," a conclusion supported by Boas (1899) and Harrington (1943). Other linguists have been more guarded in their judgments: Davis (1975) could neither support nor deny a Chilcotin-Nicola connection; Krauss (1979:869) concluded that "the pathetic data are not adequate so far to substantiate this."

Krauss and Golla (in vol. 6:68) believe pre-A.D. 500 expansion from a Proto-Athapaskan homeland in northern British Columbia, the Yukon, interior Alaska produced central British Columbia and Pacific Coast Athapaskan; Workman (1979) believes the expansion was triggered by volcanic ashfall about A.D. 700. But is Nicola a remnant of the tail of a Pacific Coast Athapaskan comet? Is it a later offshoot from central British Columbia Athapaskan? Does the war-party story reflect some connection to Chilcotin, but no actual war party? Linguistics reveals almost nothing about these questions.

Archeology doesn't say much more. Microblades have long been thought to accompany the spread of Athapaskans, but how the simple trail heading south from central Alaska around 10,000 years ago (Borden 1962; Carlson 1996:217) leads to the Plateau Microblade tradition (Copp 1996:74–78) after 5000 B.C. is unclear. Microblades have been found in Nicola and Similkameen valley sites, and a Nicola-microblade-uplands connection has been suggested (Arcas Associates 1986). Magne and Matson (1987) were able to define an "Athapaskan style" side-notched arrowpoint through a statistical analysis of points from central British Columbia sites of the last 1,200 years. However, Nicola and Similkameen collections have not been analyzed in this way, nor were spurred side scrapers and Kavik stemmed points, artifacts of about the same age that Wilmeth (1979) believes link central British Columbia Athapaskan sites to those farther north, found in Nicola territory.

Culture

Teit (1900–1921) and Allison (1892) give a little information about nineteenth-century Nicola culture, which was much like that of the Thompson and Okanagan.

The upper Nicola country has few salmon, high and Similkameen country none. The Nicola relied on hunting and lake fishing more than the Thompson and Okanagan. In this respect they were like the Chilcotin, who did less salmon fish-

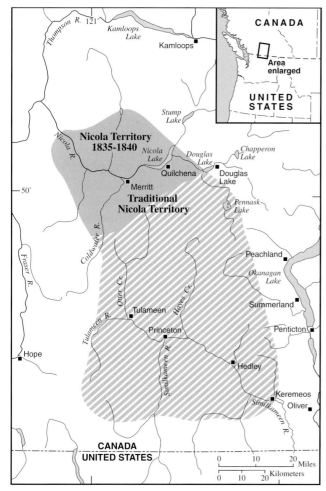

Fig. 1. Traditional Nicola territory, including reduced area inhabited from 1835 to 1840 (after Teit 1900–1921).

Girls' puberty rites were like those of the Thompson; according to Allison, girls painted their faces with red ocher at this time. Marriage was by purchase, a price being paid the girl's father or guardian. "It was thought wicked for a man to marry any of their mother's relations, but they might marry their father's" (Allison 1892:315). Polygamy was common. Adultery was punished by cutting a woman's nose or ears.

Evil spirits caused sickness, and a shaman lured the spirit or wrestled it away. An owl's cry or dog's or coyote's howl foretold death. The deceased was laid out in new clothes with tools and weapons, and a feast was held in which a portion of the food reserved for him was burned along with other offerings. A carved figure might decorate the grave. Relatives moved after a death and cut their hair, and a spouse was forbidden to eat meat for a month. If the deceased's spirit troubled the living, it was appeased when his bones were dug up, placed in a new blanket or clothes, and reburied.

History

The Nicola had "a tradition that at one time their tribe was numerous" (Boas 1895:552). They had winter villages at Nicola Lake—one at Guichon's (just northeast of what is now Quilchena), the second at the lake's outlet (Teit 1930:214)—and others downriver along the Nicola. The total Nicola valley population could have been as many as 400 (Teit 1898–1910), while the Similkameen numbers are unknown.

Sometime before 1700 the Nicola occupied not only the Nicola valley and Canadian Similkameen but an adjoining bit of Washington State, with the southern boundary of their territory stretching approximately from Loomis to Oroville. Bouchard and Kennedy (1984:17–20) recorded Nicola placenames "almost as far as Tonasket," another dozen or so miles farther south and noted that one Okanagan informant suggested their eastern boundary had stretched from Oliver to Penticton (Lerman 1952–1954).

Although the Nicola had retreated north and east during the seventeenth century, and Shuswaps wiped out the band at Guichon's around 1800 (Teit 1930:214, 257), it was the horse, arriving in the early eighteenth century, that sealed their "extinction"—their decline in population and territory and their intermarriage with others.

The horse brought more outsiders into Nicola territory. They crisscrossed the Nicola uplands instead of following the river courses; they came from farther away for early spring lake fishing and to hunt elk (which their drives helped exterminate); they grazed their horses in the grasslands and stayed to ranch and farm. Warfare became more intense and common and the Nicola always acted defensively. Thompson Indians had long come to the Nicola valley to hunt and fish, occasionally wintering with the Nicola. Nicola had traded with and married Thompsons and Okanagans. But the increased attractiveness and accessibility of Nicola land meant the difference between a small but

ing (and more lake fishing and hunting) than either the Carrier or nearby Interior Salish groups (Lane 1953:42–43).

"The people had a spring hunt, a fall hunt, and two winter hunts, first after deer about the middle of winter, [the] second after [mountain] sheep," which were formerly plentiful and killed in drives (Teit 1900–1921). Women often hunted with their husbands, both driving and killing game. Dogs were used in the hunt and also eaten, as were coyote and lynx. The Nicola dug roots in the spring and collected berries in summer and fall. Nearly every autumn, parties from the Similkameen went to Hope to buy salmon and oil.

The Nicola built semisubterranean houses, but a great many lived in mat lodges all winter. Birchbark baskets were commonly made, but cedar root baskets were not and had to be traded from the Thompson. A notched flaked stone was used to straighten arrowshafts, not the abrasive shaft smoothers used elsewhere (Teit 1930:218). A common snowshoe had a distinctive Nicola-type sole (Teit 1900:fig. 241).

A woman preparing for the birth of her first child could eat only the flesh of birds and fish, and she could not smell "anything bad" (Teit 1900–1921). She prayed to the dawn, washed often, and took sweatbaths, as did her husband.

relatively stable Nicola population and a decreasing one, between an "everyman's land," Nicola by default, and a land coveted and settled by Thompsons and Okanagans.

By 1858, when the gold rush brought White settlement, the Thompson had moved up the Nicola River and the Okanagan across the Nicola uplands to the edge of Nicola Lake. About 1830 "30 to 35 people in the whole Nicola talked Tinneh [Nicola], but a great number on the Similkameen talked that language at that time." About 1850 "very few remained in Nicola who could talk that language but probably 50 or more still used it at that time on the Similkameen" (Teit 1900a). By the time anthropologists came to study them, the Nicola were virtually gone.

Synonymy†

Very few names for the Nicola are attested, and it is not clear that any of them was a self-designation. The English name is from the Nicola River and Nicola valley, which in turn were named after a prominent Okanagan leader. The other names are either of Salishan origin, or have been adapted to one of the neighboring Salishan languages by adding a suffix -mxʷ meaning 'people' and (presumably) a general nominalizing prefix s-. The suffix is not the expected one, although it is attested in some of the neighboring languages; the usual suffix with this meaning in these languages is -míx or -mx.

The best-attested name would be something like stwíxmxʷ, phonetically [stəwíxəmᵊxʷ]. Removing the Salishan affixes from this form leaves a root twíx-, and this might have been the Nicola self-designation. Alternatively, it may be a Thompson form tˢʷ-íyx 'run, run around', a stem used in a place-name in Merritt (on the Nicola River) tˢʷíyxcín, a site where watercress was gathered (Thompson and Thompson 1996:364). Teit (1907–1910) recorded Shuswap tcawáxamux̱ and Lillooet .stcowaxɛm; these have clearly been subjected to folk etymology to match a root cwéx- 'lake'. The root for 'lake' cannot have been the source of twíx-, because Teit recorded several versions of the name, all with initial t; the vowel would also be the wrong one for all the neighboring languages except Okanagan, but this is not attested as the Okanagan name for the Nicola at all. The earliest record of this name for the Nicola is Stā-wih-a-muh (MacKay 1895, cited in Wyatt 1972:179). Nearly all the rest derive directly or indirectly from James Teit, in a variety of transcriptions: Stûwī´Hamuǫ (Boas 1895:552, based on information obtained from Teit), stuwí´xamux (Teit 1900:257, fig. 241), stawī´xɛmux̱, stɛwī´x̱ɛmux̱, stɛwixtcī´n (Teit 1904), Stawíx·ɛmux, stɛ´wī´x̱ɛmux̱, Stɛ´wī´x̱ᵘ̱ɛmuxʷ (Teit 1907–1910), StuwíxEmux̱ (Teit 1912–1921:10), Stɛwī´x̱ɛmux (Teit 1930:203), and Stuwixmux (Harrington 1943:204). Teit also gives a second Shuswap variant of the name, tɛwíx̱tcī´n (Teit 1907–1910), this time based on twíx-, but with a suffix -cin meaning 'language'. The Nicola valley itself was called stwíx, and this is the base

of all the other forms. Records of this name are Stûwi´H (Boas 1895:553, again from Teit), Stûwi´x· (Teit 1900:178), stuwī´x (Teit 1910), Ste'wī´x (Teit 1907–1910, cited in Wyatt 1972:182), Stuwī´x̱ (Teit 1930:203), Stuwix (Harrington 1943), and stewíx (Bouchard and Kennedy 1984a:13).

Another name was apparently applied only to the Nicola band found on the Similkameen River, and it appears to be specifically a designation by the Okanagan, who occupied the lower reaches of this river. The name is something like smlə́q(a)mxʷ, phonetically [smələ́q(a)mᵊxʷ]. The root of the form is √mlə́q- or √məlq-, although the meaning of this is uncertain; some Okanagan speakers associate the word with məlqnúps 'golden eagle'. All variants of this name are directly or indirectly from Teit: Smîlê´kamuǫ (Boas 1895:553, based on information obtained from Teit), smɛlêkamux (Teit 1898–1910, cited in Bouchard and Kennedy 1984a), smɛla´kamux̱, smelekɛmux̱ (Teit 1904), and Smɛlê´qɛmux̱ᵘ (Teit 1907–1910). Other apparent variations of this name refer to an Okanagan band, rather than to the Nicola (these are variant spellings of smlqmíx): schimilicameachs (McDonald 1827, cited in Bouchard and Kennedy 1984a), Sa-milk-a-nuigh (Ross 1849:289), smɛlkamīx (Teit 1907–1910), and smlḵamíx (Bouchard and Kennedy 1984a:13).

Teit also recorded Sɛi´lɛqamuǫ (Boas 1895:553, based on information obtained from Teit) and siī´lêxamux̱ (Teit 1904) as a Thompson name for the Nicola. This is presumably sʔílxamxʷ, phonetically [sʔílxamᵊxʷ]; the root is not attested for Thompson, but note the Columbian root ʔílx- 'upstream', a meaning that would be appropriate for the location of the Nicola. If this root existed in Okanagan or Thompson it would have this same form.

Teit (1907–1910) also gives a Shuswap name for the Nicola as ʟoʟowákamux̱. This is presumably łułwákamxʷ, phonetically [łu łʊwákamᵊxʷ], although a root łwák- is not identified for Shuswap or any other neighboring language.

Sources

Dawson (1892) noted some vocabulary and an origin story collected by J.W. MacKay (1895). Allison (1892) described Nicola origins and their culture of the previous 150 years. In 1895 a few more Nicola words were published in the *Kamloops Wawa*; and Franz Boas sent James Teit, who was to become the premier ethnographer of Interior Salish peoples, to investigate the group for the British Association for the Advancement of Science. Teit recorded little of Nicola culture but did collect about 20 words from Nicola valley natives (Boas 1895). Harrington (1943) collected a vocabulary list from eight Nicola valley informants. Wyatt (1972) conducted archeological investigations in the Nicola valley, and archeologists and ethnographers assessed the impact on heritage of construction in Nicola territory (Bouchard and Kennedy 1984a, 1985a; Arcas Associates 1986; Copp 1996).

† This synonymy was written by M. Dale Kinkade.

Kootenai

BILL B. BRUNTON

Language

The classification of Kootenai (kōōtǝnē) is uncertain. Sapir (1929) included Kootenai in his highly speculative Algonkin-Wakashan grouping, thus positing a possible genetic affinity to the neighboring Algonquian and Interior Salishan languages. This opinion was echoed by Haas (1965) when she suggested that there is evidence of probable relationship between Kootenai and Algonquian and Salishan. However, the weight of scholarly opinion, early and contemporary, seems to rest with the position that Kootenai represents a language isolate (see Powell 1891; Boas 1911; C.F. Voegelin and F.M. Voegelin 1966).

Kootenai embraces two dialects, an Upper (upriver) dialect and Lower (downriver) dialect, differing mainly in lexicon (Garvin 1948).[*]

Territory and Environment

The Kootenai territory was defined in terms of the course of the Kootenay River (fig. 1). The Kootenais' orientation to the river was basic to their culture (Schaeffer 1940:45; Turney-High 1941:25). The river and its environs provided the Kootenai with most of their subsistence needs. It was the means of both summer canoe (fig. 2) and winter snowshoe travel and transportation. It was also the location of their more permanent camp and village sites. Finally, its seasonal fluctuations "represented time indicators for the abandonment of certain activities and the onset of others" (Schaeffer 1940:45).

From the Kootenai point of view, the Kootenay River defined but two seasons, winter and summer. The winter season was marked by heavy snowfall and freezing of the river. It was the season of winter village occupancy, hunting and fishing at upriver locations, and bison hunting on snow-

shoes in the forest-sheltered valleys east of the Rocky Mountains. The summer season was marked by the melting of ice and snow, accompanied by flooding of the river. Canoe transportation and travel became the mode, swamps filled near the river, and fishing intensified. The people occupied downriver temporary camps. They participated in communal deer drives on islands, gathered plant foods (fig. 3), and netted waterfowl (Schaeffer 1940:44–45). During this time they also broke down into family groups (Schaeffer 1936:81).

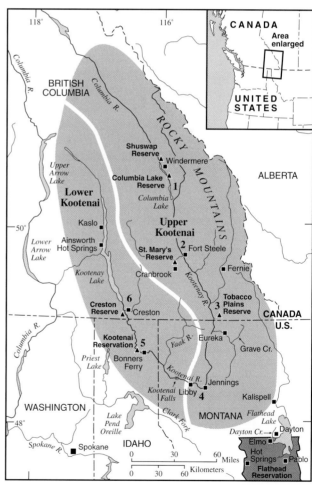

Fig. 1. Kootenai territory at contact in 1792, with modern reservations and reserves. Bands: 1, Columbia Lake band; 2, St. Mary's band; 3, Tobacco Plains band; 4, Libby-Jennings band; 5, Bonners Ferry band; 6, Lower Kootenay band.

*The phonemes of Kootenai are: (voiceless stops and affricate) p, t, c, k, q, ʔ; (glottalized stops and affricate) p̓, t̓, c̓, k̓, q̓; (voiceless fricatives) s, ł, x, h; (nasals) m, n; (glottalized nasals) m̓, n̓; (semivowels) w, y; (glottalized semivowels) w̓, y̓; (short vowels) i, a, u; (long vowels) i·, a·, u·. In loanwords l and č are also found. Stress falls predictably on the penultimate syllable of the word.

Information on Kootenai phonology and the transcription of Kootenai words appearing in italics was obtained from sources who prefer to remain anonymous (communications to editors 1997). The transcription of Garvin (1948) differs mainly in writing the glottalized (ejective) consonants as clusters with glottal stop, and in writing i· and u· as e· and o·, respectively.

223

Origins

Although the Kootenai exhibited a close adaptation to their Plateau habitat, which may indicate a long-term residence there, Schaeffer (1940:44–57) argues that their deepest roots link them to the circumboreal region to the north. Chief among the evidence for this is the Kootenai seasonal shift from summer fishing to winter hunting on snowshoes. According to this view, it is likely that they moved southward out of their circumboreal habitat following large game animals such as caribou, mountain goat, or even bison. One very likely route for this movement is the easily traversed Rocky Mountain trench (which forms the Kootenay River valley farther south). Having established themselves at a point along the Kootenay River (perhaps Tobacco Plains), they then began expanding along the

top, Laurie C. Duff, Calgary, Alta.; bottom left, Canadian Mus. of Civilization, Que.: J6495; bottom right, II-A-82a–b (neg. 72–4974).

Fig. 2. Transportation by canoes. top, Bark canoe anchored to the shore by tree branches held down by rocks. Photographed at Ainsworth Hot Springs, Kootenay Lake, B.C., about 1900. bottom left, Mr. and Mrs. Frank Basil of Creston, B.C., constructing a flat-bow bark canoe for the Canadian Mus. of Civilization (cat. no. II-A-170). Photograph probably by Harold Pfeifer, 1959. bottom right, Bailers. Each is made of a single sheet of folded birchbark stitched with bark splints and cotton string. The rims are reinforced with wood, and tanned hide loops are knotted under the rim. The containers are joined by strips of cotton. Collected by John L. Retallack, Kaslo, B.C., before 1957. Height 19 cm.

Amer. Mus. of Nat. Hist., New York: top, 50/1359; bottom, 50/1360.

Fig. 3. Berry-picking implements. Berries ripened in the late summer and were gathered by small family groups. top, Berry picker made of wood and sinew used for gathering small berries. bottom, Berry-collecting basket with leather ties for carrying or affixing it to the wearer's waist. Collected by Alfred L. Kroeber before 1900. Length of picker, 18 cm; basket, height 10 cm.

course of the river. The predominant direction of this secondary expansion was downriver. In one origin myth the Kootenai are described as entering the world by paddling down the river (Schaeffer 1935).

There is a legend that asserts that the Kootenai of the Plateau derive from a group known by the name *ktunaxa* (the Kootenai name for themselves), which was permanently resident on the Plains (Coues 1897:703–705; Chamberlain 1907:740; Jenness 1932:358). The cause for these Kootenai abandoning the Plains is usually given as depredation by the Blackfoot. Teit (1930:306–318, 1930b:625–628) presents a much more elaborate account of the Plains Kootenai but places no primacy on them as the ancestral band. Instead, he asserts that they were but contemporaries of Kootenai living west of the Rockies. He attributes their removal from the Plains to a combination of smallpox and attacks by the Blackfoot. Turney-High (1941:18–19) echoes the legend. Curtis (1907–1930, 7:117–119) and Schaeffer (1964) agree that the Kootenai were never permanent residents of the Plains but did make annual excursions for bison hunting. The legend of the Plains Kootenai involved a small band of Kootenai who were decimated by smallpox about 1730, while on the Plains, their survivors moving to the west.

External Relations

Kootenai relations with non-Kootenai were predominantly distant to hostile (Brunton 1969). Enemies included the neighboring Salish and the Blackfoot, particularly the Piegan. Although relations may have always been bad with the Blackfoot, hostilities were certainly intensified by the introduction of the horse, which facilitated deeper, more frequent, and larger-scale incursions into the Plains by the Kootenai. This brought them into direct competition with the Blackfoot for Plains resources, particularly the bison. It also became the focus for horse-raiding by both groups. Later, with the coming of the fur trade to the western Plains, Blackfoot conflict with peoples west of the Rockies, including the Kootenai, increased in intensity. This was in part due to jealous guarding of middleman trade prerogatives by the Blackfoot (MacGregor 1966:74). Both these factors forced at least a seasonal reduction of hostilities between the Kootenai and their Plateau neighbors. All these eastern Plateau peoples began to cooperate in joint bison hunting expeditions, which helped to reduce the Blackfoot advantage in having larger numbers and more firearms secured in the fur trade (Anastasio 1972).

Throughout the prereservation period, stable friendly relations shown by cooperation and visitation were predominantly between Kootenai bands. The only non-Kootenai group with which friendly relations were relatively continuous was the Plains Cree. The Kootenai gambled with groups with whom they were friendly. As they extended their "friendly frontier" in postcontact and particularly in reservation times, they included more and more groups within their sphere of gambling relations (Brunton 1974).

Divisions

The Upper and Lower dialects of the Kootenai language correspond to the two major social divisions as determined by position along the course of the Kootenay River. The Upper Kootenai occupied the river valley and its environs upriver from approximately the location of the present Montana communities of Libby and Jennings to the Columbia Lakes region, and even some of the upper Columbia River valley, British Columbia. The Lower Kootenai occupied the Kootenay River valley and surrounding country downriver from these communities to Kootenay Lake (fig. 1).

The major differences between the Upper and Lower Kootenai seem to derive from differences in habitat. The Upper Kootenai were principally hunters while the Lower Kootenai were more involved with fishing. The Upper Kootenai habitat, running along the western flanks of the Rockies, yielded a greater abundance of big game animals such as deer, elk, and mountain sheep and goat. The proximity of this country to the Plains added bison to the list of regularly exploited game animals. A few Lower Kootenai accompanied the Upper Kootenai on their yearly bison-hunting expeditions during the prehorse period (Boas 1890:818).

The introduction of the horse, sometime before 1792 (MacGregor 1966:76), intensified bison exploitation and differences between the Upper and Lower Kootenai. The result was more contact with Plains peoples and the adoption of a veneer of Plains culture traits, particularly by the Upper Kootenai (Schaeffer 1940:48, 56).

Bands

In expanding along the course of their river, the Kootenai established several bands. The order of establishing these bands is not certain, except for historically documented cases of migration.

Bands were the units of primary social and cultural significance. The usual practice was that each band was identified by name with a winter village site on the Kootenay River and its adjoining territory. These villages were composed of 150 to 200 people divided among some 10 lodges (Schaeffer 1935). During the summer, these villages or bands tended to break down into their constituent families or, at times, into small groups of families. Band territory was not rigidly defined, nor was membership exclusive. Bands mutually cross-utilized resources (see Walker 1967), and their social boundaries were open enough to permit individuals and families to shift residence from band to band (Schaeffer 1935). However, no matter where a person resided, his or her primary identification was with the band of birth (Lindburg 1962:200).

At contact, beginning about 1800, the Kootenai were divided into six bands (Schaeffer 1935). The Upper Kootenai comprised four of them:

The Columbia Lake band at Windermere, ʔa·kisq̓nuk̓nik̓ 'people of the two lakes'; the Saint Mary's or Fort Steele band (near Cranbrook), ʔa·q̓amnik̓ 'people of Saint Mary's River'; the Tobacco Plains band, ʔa·kanuxunik̓ 'people of the current', at Grasmere; and the Libby-Jennings band, ʔa·kiyinik̓, the parent band of the Dayton-Elmo Kootenai who moved to the western shore of Flathead Lake at Dayton Creek under the impact of the United States reservation system. There they form one component of the Confederated Salish and Kootenai Tribes of the Flathead Reservation.

The Lower Kootenai were the ʔa·k̓aq̓lahaɫxu 'meadow people'. The name derives from the swampy nature of the lower Kootenai (Kootenay) valley where these Kootenai reside. They included the Bonners Ferry band (known as the Kootenai Tribe of Idaho) and the Lower Kootenay band at Creston, British Columbia.

In addition to these bands that existed at contact, several had become extinct by that time. The survivors of such bands usually joined another, their distinctiveness being lost in a few generations (Schaeffer 1935). Of the extinct bands, the Michel Prairie band is of most interest since this band is the one identified as being the focus of the Plains Kootenai legend (Schaeffer 1964).

Culture

The description of Kootenai culture here applies primarily to the mid-nineteenth century.

Subsistence[†]

The Kootenai would go to their fishing grounds from early in the spring until May. Salmon, sturgeon, suckers, whitefish, and trout, the most important fish, were caught in basket traps and wicker weirs. When the fishing season ended women gathered roots, first the bitterroot and then camas. In mid-June the Upper Kootenai hunted bison. The Coeur d'Alene and Spokane often joined them (Turney-High 1941:54). From a separate bison hunt in the summer, which lasted about four weeks, the average man brought back two to three packhorse loads of buffalo meat in parfleches.

Hunting was of major importance to the Kootenai (Curtis 1907–1930, 7:167). Deer, elk, antelope, caribou, moose, as well as bison were first brought down with bow and arrows and later with guns. Beaver, muskrats, mountain goats, gopher, bear, lynx, wolf, and other furbearers were used not only for occasional food but also for their skins, which were used in making clothes (Phillips 1974:240). Bird hunting was important to the Upper Kootenai but essential to the Lower Kootenai (Turney-High 1941:41–44). Cranes, ducks, sea gulls, fool hens, and geese were consumed. Eagles were captured for their feathers, and young eagles were often eaten.

In late summer women would lay in berries, such as chokecherries, red currants, gooseberries, Oregon grapes, raspberries, and huckleberries. Vegetables such as onion were collected as were pinenuts and tree lichen. Mullein, willow bark, and other plants were used to treat illnesses (Phillips 1974:240).

In the autumn the Lower Kootenai bands gathered for communal deer drives, while the Upper bands again moved east to hunt bison. In the winter they hunted bison again but this time on foot, using snowshoes. The Kootenai considered their lands rich and bountiful; scarcity and famine were so unusual that they were believed to be of supernatural origin (Turney-High 1941:55).

Social Organization

• THE HOUSEHOLD   The basic residential unit in Kootenai society was the household. This group consisted of a man and woman of the grandparental generation, their unmarried children, their married daughters and their husbands and children, and an occasional married son, his wife and their children. These people shared a single lodge and fire and cooperated economically. The oldest, most experienced man was the recognized leader of the household group. This residential pattern was the

[†]The subsistence section was written by Joanna Cohan Scherer.

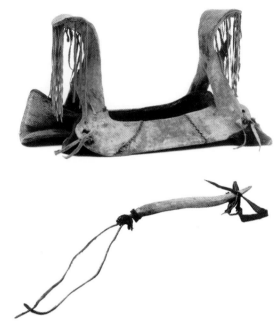

Fig. 4. Transportation by horse. left, Chief Francois holding coup stick and pipe. His valued horse has been decorated with feathers on his forehead and a feathered pendant hanging from his bridle. Photograph by Sumner W. Matteson, Pablo's Ranch, Flathead Res., Mont., 1904. top right, Saddle. The wooden frame is covered with rawhide, and the pommel and cantle are decorated with fringed leather. The attached pad is of commercial leather. bottom right, Antler quirt. Collected by C.E. Schaeffer, Tobacco Plains, Mont., 1935. Length of saddle, 57 cm; length of quirt with leather thongs 75 cm.

result of bride service whereby a young man lived with and hunted for his parents-in-law for a time after his marriage to their daughter. The service lasted at least until the young couple had accumulated enough property to be on their own. The households of the bride's parents and groom's parents tended to locate near each other after the marriage (Schaeffer 1936:116).

The division of labor prescribed that men hunted and cared for horses (fig 4). Women were responsible for domestic tasks such as preparation of food and hides ("Ethnobiology and Subsistence," fig. 12, this vol.), and the manufacture of clothing and household implements. They also were responsible for gathering vegetal food and caring for children (fig. 5). They had very little leisure time compared to the men who spent theirs in gambling and in ceremonial activities (Schaeffer 1936:113).

No full-time specialization existed. However, some individuals, because of acquired supernatural power, served as part-time specialists.

Societies

The exact number of societies possessed by the Kootenai is not known. Turney-High (1941:155) describes three while Schaeffer (1935) mentions four. Both indicate that the principal society was the Crazy Dogs. It was composed of men who received power from dog. The "dogs" had a leader and a second-in-command. The former gave orders to the "dogs" and the latter "drove" the "dogs" before him as they carried out the orders. The "dogs" functioned as a police

unit while on the bison hunt, maintaining order within the moving band. They also served as a group of especially brave, relentless warriors in battle who would not swerve from the enemy unless told to do so by their leaders. Their other function involved the Sun Dance ceremony. Here, they collected covers for the Sun Dance lodge. Their wives were called "she dogs." They served their husbands by carrying their quiver or war equipment and acquired prestige for their bravery. Unlike their husbands, they did not have power from dog. It appears that the Crazy Dog Society represents a borrowing from the Plains, adapted to Kootenai cultural patterns (Schaeffer 1936:120).

The Crazy Owl Society was a female association, the function of which was to ward off epidemics. Its form was very similar to that of the Crazy Dog Society and was based on shared supernatural experiences (Turney-High 1941:157).

There were associations for Conjuring (Blanket shamans), Sun Dance leaders, Grizzly Bear ceremony leaders, and healing shamans. Shamans would pool their power in joint healing sessions for particularly difficult cases. The other shamans' societies were likewise based on cooperation in ceremonial activities (Schaeffer 1935; Turney-High 1941:157–158).

Kinship

Descriptive accounts of Kootenai kinship abound (Chamberlain 1893; Sapir 1918; Boas 1919; Turney-High 1941; Lindburg 1962); however, these accounts differ from one another to the extent that it is difficult to know what the aboriginal system was like.

left, Oreg. Histl. Soc., Portland: 39320; right, Glenbow-Alberta Inst., Calgary, Alta.: NA–1897–5.

Fig. 5. Women transporting children. left, Child in horse travois at David Thompson's memorial pageant. David Thompson (b. 1770, d. 1857) was a fur trader, explorer, and surveyor who worked for the Hudson's Bay Company and then the North West Company. He was instrumental in building a trading post near Lake Windermere, B.C., which was of great benefit to the Kootenai. Photographed before 1923. right, Cecile Gravelle with her twin girls Elizabeth and Mary in beaded cradleboards. Photographed in 1922.

Generation, sex, and reciprocity are strongly evident in contemporary Kootenai kin terminology (Brunton 1974). Sex of relative is marked throughout the system, while sex of speaker is sometimes marked. This attribute is consistent with the rather clear-cut differences between male and female behavior found throughout the culture.

The first ascending and descending generations exhibit an authority-nurturance/subordination-dependence relationship vis à vis one another. For example, fathers and uncles serve as authority figures for sons and nephews (who are terminologically related to sons). They play an important role in the acquisition of important skills (Lindburg 1962:65, 69–71).

The second and third ascending and descending generations exhibit a close, affectively warm, relaxed relationship (Brunton 1970; Lindburg 1962:71–75). These kin categories are reciprocals (using the same term for each other). Grandparents were and are important agents of socialization, but without the context of an authority relationship. They advise and teach. They are the storytellers who recount the myths and thus instill within their grandchildren important cultural truths. They care for their grandchildren and often oversee their vision quests. A grandparent might even give his or her power to their grandchild, an act of supreme sacrifice, since such loss of power is thought to result in death (Brunton 1970).

A person's own generation is marked by distinctions in terminology based on relative age. The behavioral counterpart of this is that an authority-subordination relationship exists between older and younger same sex "siblings." For example, older brothers help to instruct their younger counterparts in the proper Kootenai ways and are owed respect in return. The same applies to older and younger sisters. There is a merging of siblings and first cousins.

The Kootenai blood kinship terminology is bilateral (tracing descent equally through males and females) and thus generates no lineages or clans. Each person has a set of close blood relatives (each with a specific term) and a set of distant blood relatives (classed together under a single term meaning 'my relatives'). They also have a set of close marriage relatives (each with a specific term) and a set of distant marriage relatives (classed together with the distant blood relatives).

Reciprocity is strongly represented in the marriage kinship terminology where it sets the expectation for and reinforces close, affectively warm and cooperative relations (Lindburg 1962:72–73). For example, in the typical aboriginal Kootenai household, the father-in-law and son-in-law (reciprocals) had to cooperate economically. The son-in-law was a provider and was seen as a "helper" of his father-in-law.

Friendship

A very special type of relationship used to exist between males. The two people involved used the reciprocal term, *ka swu* 'my friend or comrade'. This relationship was often established in childhood and normally endured throughout life. The relationship was most similar to brotherhood. In some ways it was an even stronger relationship. Two comrades often acquired the same tutelary spirit, played together while young, and hunted and fought side by side as adults (Schaeffer 1935). If a man were wounded his friend was obligated to remain with him, even at risk to his own life (Lindburg 1962:75). Adult comrades looked out for the economic well-being of one another, traveled together, and were gambling partners (Brunton 1974:65). They jointly owned property and often lived together (Schaeffer 1935).

Like brothers, comrades often married sisters. The relationship between each comrade and his friend's wife was marked by brother-in-law and sister-in-law terminology. Although no sexual license was practiced, each comrade was obligated to protect his friend's wife in his absence. The kind of relationship between a man and his comrade's wife was shown by her making moccasins for him, a practice that marked a close relationship in Kootenai social relations. A man could marry his deceased comrade's widow (Schaeffer 1935). The rare dissolution of comradeship derived from one of two sources (Lindburg 1962:75): either the marriage by one comrade to a woman of whom the other disapproved, or the violation of the rule against gambling between comrades.

Joking and Avoidance Relations

Brothers-in-law and sisters-in-law participated in a joking relationship (Lindburg 1962:74). They enjoyed a close relationship typified by sexual humor.

An avoidance relationship existed at least between a man and his mother-in-law (Lindburg 1962:72–73; Turney-High 1941:144). A uniform avoidance pattern between persons and their parents-in-law involved their not looking directly at or talking directly to each other (Schaeffer 1936:112, 134). They either spoke to each other through the spouse-child or used the third-person form of speech (Lindburg 1962:72–73).

A similar form of avoidance for mature individuals using brother and sister terms for each other occurred. The form of address used was the third person (Schaeffer 1936:127; Lindburg 1962:67).

Marriage

Marriage was a fairly informal affair. Sometimes parents would try to influence their son or daughter to marry someone they regarded as appropriate. If they succeeded, their son or daughter would go to the home of their prospective spouse and announce their interest. If the other person accepted, the couple was considered married. Young people also selected their own partners to whom they proposed. Acceptance again was considered marriage. Finally, a young man might sneak into the home and bed of his sweetheart, with or without her prior knowledge. If he were accepted—if she did not wake her parents—marriage might result by agreement. This form was socially scorned only if the couple were caught. If this happened, they were disgraced but not punished. Regardless of which approach to marriage was used, there was no special ceremony. Gifts were made to the new couple by both families (Schaeffer 1935). Marriage of a man to more than one woman (often sisters) was practiced as was the sororate and levirate.

Political Organization

It is very difficult to discern the nature of leadership for the aboriginal Kootenai. This may be due in part to the state of change this system was in during and immediately before White contact. Brunton (1970) and Schaeffer (1935) indicate three categories of leadership for the Kootenai. According to Schaeffer (1940:115; 1935), when the Kootenai bands were in their winter villages, each was under the nominal and relatively informal leadership of a respected man. This person had great supernatural power that helped him be successful in hunting, gambling, and warfare. He was known for his generosity. He coordinated day-to-day band activities, used his prestige-derived influence to maintain order, and met with the council of respected men in his lodge for the purpose of making band decisions. This village leader (nasuʔkin) used a functionary, a "camp crier" (kkiɬpaɬnikimik), for apprising his fellow villagers of all decisions and important news (Schaeffer 1935).

Another duty of the village leader was to appoint temporary leaders for special band activities. One such leader was the 'travel leader' ([yakásin]), chosen because of his extensive knowledge of trails and campsites (Schaeffer 1936:115). He was in charge of the band as it moved from one campsite to another and occasionally led war parties. There were two travel leaders chosen per year in each band, one for summer and one for winter. The travel leader announced the location of the next campsite to the rest of the band and then set out a few hundred yards ahead of the rest, leading and scouting at the same time. If he should encounter enemies, he gave a signal and the warriors advanced to meet them (Schaeffer 1935).

When the locale for a specific kind of activity was reached, another special type of leader would assume direction and responsibility for the band. There were fishing leaders, fowling leaders, and hunting leaders. Each of these had supernatural power for his activity. He led ritual to insure success in the venture, a first-fruits ceremony, and directed all phases of the activity (Schaeffer 1935).

The three kinds of leaders are of but two types, general and specific. The village leader was a general purpose leader whose "term of office" was relatively continuous, while the travel and economic leaders were special purpose and served intermittently for short spans of time.

The different types of leadership described for the Kootenai seem to reflect social change. According to a Bonners Ferry band informant (Schaeffer 1935), the status of village leader did not exist before the coming of the

Whites. The highest-ranking travel leader is said to have been made village leader at that time. In support of this, the Kootenai term for travel leader [yakásin] is often used to denote both the general band leaders and the various economic specialty leaders. The term is also used generically to denote 'leader' of all types. The historical priority of the travel leader was gradually supplanted in prestige and authority by that of the war chief, whose preeminence is rooted in the adoption of the horse and its attendant increase in raiding (Lindburg 1962:12–14, 23). This shift affected the Lower Kootenai much less than it did the Upper Kootenai (Schaeffer 1936).

The general overall social equality of the Kootenai was cut into four "social ranks" (Schaeffer 1935): *nasuʔkin* 'band or village leader', *kwanaqnamik* 'warriors', *knupqaqaqa* 'those with power from a vision', and [ʔumácini] 'those without power'. 'Those without power' were regarded as extremely unfortunate people without much social merit. The bulk of the people were included in the 'those with power' category, people with abilities acquired from the spirits that made them successful and valuable to others. The various kinds of shamans and those with supernatural sanction to lead in economic activities such as hunting, fishing, and bird netting belonged to this class. These individuals enjoyed high prestige, but apparently no other privileges of rank. The warriors included only those few males with the greatest power and greatest war deeds to their credit. This category is very likely a late, Plains-influenced addition to an earlier three-class system. The 'band or village leader' category included only the one, general purpose leader of the band or village. This person was thought to have very great power and was apparently always male. Recruitment to this category was nominally hereditary, usually passing from a man to his eldest son, who often received supernatural power from the same source as his father. If the situation justified it, the village council could select another outstanding man as village or band leader (Boas 1890:836).

Mythology

Kootenai myths (Boas 1918; Linderman 1926; Schaeffer 1935; Kootenai Culture Committee 1984) depict a time before the arrival of humans during which the spirits in human form inhabited the world, preparing it for human occupation and setting forth behavioral precedents in the course of their everyday activities. The spirits all have power, which gives them special abilities. They possess the world until humans enter it, at which point they begin to grant their powers to humans who seek this in the vision quest.

A principal figure is Coyote who plays the role of trickster-transformer. Owl is a kind of bogeyman who keeps captured children in her nest. There is a water monster who is responsible for a great flood. A common theme involves the

spirits in athletic and other contests on which wagers are made. Monsters are eliminated before humans enter the world.

Boas (1918:281–284) argues that Kootenai myths are closely related to those of their Salish neighbors and to the Blackfoot. In typifying Kootenai myths he points out that they systematically develop a society among the spirits and that the individual tales are tied together into groups of related stories.

Religion

According to Kootenai cosmology (Schaeffer 1935), the "world" or nature is composed of three parts—Earth, Water, and Sky. The Earth is seen as an island surrounded by Water, these two being covered by the dome or hemisphere of the Sky. Day and night, the two polar conditions of the Sky are thought to "hold down the Earth." Each of these natural realms serves as a medium for the activities of "actors." Earth-realm actors include humans, land plants, land animals, natural objects such as rocks, and human-made objects. Those of the Water include aquatic life forms. Avifauna, such natural phenomena as thunder, and celestial bodies such as the sun are the actors of the Sky.

All actors were and are viewed as having both a physical and spiritual aspect or quality. The spiritual aspect of humans is the soul. All other actors' spiritual qualities are known by the term, *nupika* (Lower Kootenai *nipika*), meaning 'spirit'. These spirits are the characters of myth who, after the arrival of humans, became the generic tutelary spirits and offered their power to those who would seek it through a vision quest (Brunton 1974).

The vision quest is undertaken at night. The first quest can begin at about the age of seven and continued through adolescence, after which time a person loses the ritual quality thought to be necessary to attract a spirit as a tutelary (Brunton 1974). Although both sexes are involved in vision questing, boys always have been involved with greater regularity and usually have received greater powers than girls (Schaeffer 1935).

Once the decision is made to send a child out, he or she undergoes ritual purification. First, the child is instructed to disrobe completely. This is done because the spirits are "wild" and want things completely natural. They will not approach if anything, even a ring, is worn (Brunton 1970). The child is then purified in the sacred smudge made by crumbling dried juniper needles over glowing embers. This is rubbed over the body as if it were a liquid. The spirits are drawn to this sacred juniper smoke and thus to the individual. The child is then sent to a designated place with the additional instructions to refrain from food and water and to sit quietly and await a spirit. Sometimes, specific activities are engaged in while keeping the vigil.

Although the Kootenai generally maintain that people have very little control over which spirit comes to a child, which kind of power is given, or in what amount, there is some attempt to influence the outcome. One such means is for the visionary to take a token from a relative's spirit bundle along on the quest to attract the desired spirit. Activities engaged in while on the quest are used to attract a particular spirit or to influence the type of power granted. Spirits can each give a range of types and amounts of power (Brunton 1974; Schaeffer 1935). However, each is known for giving a certain kind of power in the greatest amount (Brunton 1974).

When the visionary returns, the person who sent him or her out knows whether or not the quest has been successful. If it has not, they enter the sweatlodge together for further purification and instructions from Sweatlodge (wisiyał) regarding future quests. The child is usually sent out again the following night (Brunton 1974).

The spirit, Sweatlodge, is available to all, regardless of whether or not they have tutelary spirit power. Dreams are another avenue (through power from a dream) for some assistance from the spirits.

The tutelary spirit relationship is for life. To lose one's spirit is to die. Shortly before death, a person's tutelary announces the impending event. It then leaves their body and they die (Brunton 1974; Schaeffer 1935).

At death a person's soul departs. In one version, the soul wends its way to the west, to return from the east at the end of the world (Curtis 1907–1930, 7:127; Schaeffer 1935). In another version, the disembodied soul hovers about the village, waiting for a baby to be born, which it then inhabits to enjoy another life (Brunton 1970).

Ceremonies

A principal ceremony, held until the middle of the twentieth century, was the Conjuring or Blanket ceremony (Brunton 1974; Schaeffer 1935). It is also called "putting-up-the-blanket," or the Blanket Dance and is similar to the Shaking Tent of the Blackfoot and other Algonquians. It was essentially a ceremonial meeting with various spirits in order to seek assistance from them. The ceremony began in the evening and was under the direction of two or three "blanket" shamans. It was ideally held in a tepee but could be held in a frame house.

A "blanket" (actually two blankets skewered together) was suspended opposite the doorway, which always faced east. The participants entered, the lodge was darkened, and a juniper smudge was made. The smoke was supposed to fill the lodge. Spirit songs were then sung to summon spirits, one after another, behind the blanket. The spirits were offered tobacco and were asked questions. The spirits "screamed" their answers, which one of the shamans interpreted for the people. This continued until all participants had asked for aid.

In an older form of the ceremony (probably dating from the nineteenth century) a third shaman, who was the principal, went behind the blanket and was either tied up or untied (if he previously had been tied) by the spirits. He then returned behind the blanket and was carried away by the owl spirits while the ceremony went on as described (for a more detailed account see Brunton 1974; Schaeffer 1952).

Another major ceremony and one perhaps introduced from the Plains, was the Sun Dance (fig. 6). It was held annually in the spring and brought the whole Kootenai people together (Schaeffer 1935). It has not been conducted since the middle of the twentieth century. A number of other ceremonies, such as the Grizzly Bear ceremony, game calling ceremonies, and the scalp dance are also no longer held.

The Sweatlodge ceremony remains quite important. This ceremony is a communion with the spirit, Sweatlodge. It is accomplished by building and using a sweatlodge. Participants, both male and female, enter the small hemispherical lodge to sweat and pray in the evening. They will do this three or seven days in a row. During one session, when inside, they put water on red-hot rocks three or seven times while they sing three or seven spirit songs. Between each of the three or seven times in the lodge, a cold water plunge is taken in a nearby lake or stream. Sweatlodge gives auditory or visual messages and ritual purity. By following the message, Sweatlodge's power is added to any possessed by the participants. Sweatlodge is used primarily for ritual purification, healing, and gambling (Brunton 1974).

The Bluejay Dance is a traditional ceremony of the Kootenai that is similar to the midwinter Spirit Dances of the Salish. It is a nighttime ceremony with power demonstrations, prediction of the future, and spiritual healing as its centerpieces (Brunton 1974).

The Jump Dance is a ceremony that is unusual in that outsiders are allowed to attend. It is a New Year's observance that consists of dancing and singing for three nights. Each person prays for good fortune for the coming year. Naming is often done at this event (Brunton 1988).

The ceremony called the Medicine Doings, or MDs, seems to have replaced the Blanket Dance. It is a night ceremony that is under the direction of shamans. Spirit songs are sung to call the nupiḱa, who are asked to help people in various ways. Healing, divining the future, and solving other problems are typical tasks for the Medicine Doings (Brunton 1988).

Finally, first-fruits ceremonies were still conducted in the 1990s by Kootenai women to honor the first of seasonal traditional foods. A small amount of bitterroot is gathered, prepared, and eaten in a ritual setting directed by a women with power for this. After this "feast," the food can be gathered in whatever quantity is desired.

Curing

Two categories of illness were recognized in the aboriginal period; those resulting from natural causes and those resulting from supernatural ones. The former were treated by an herbalist, the latter by a healing shaman.

Smithsonian, NAA:52550.

Fig. 6. Sun Dance. Raising the Sun Dance poles at Hot Springs, Mont. It was put on by the Elmo, Mont., Kootenai as a demonstration and may have been sponsored by the photographer. The Sun Dance leader was Chief George Hat, who is said to have fallen from the center pole during its erection. Photograph by Frederick E. Pesso, 1908–1914.

Supernaturally caused illness was the result of an intrusive object, sent by a malevolent person, lodged in the body of the victim. The shaman used his or her power to first locate and then suck out the object, which assumed a tangible form upon removal. It was then placed in juniper smoke to "kill" it. It could be sent back to its source, if desired.

Twentieth-century Kootenais still followed this two-fold classification of illness and healing, substituting a medical doctor for the herbalist. Ceremonies were used to increase the power of the shamans for the purpose of healing. Healing ritual was also conducted by calling a shaman for that purpose.

Structures

The aboriginal household group occupied a conical lodge (Schaeffer 1936:98–99). During summer, temporary conical lodges covered by spruce or fir boughs or bark were used. The winter conical lodge was of several layers of closely set poles with half-round poles set in the gaps between the whole poles. After adopting the horse, with the attendant increase in bison hunting, the skin-covered tepee replaced these less mobile types (fig. 7). Lower Kootenai are reported to have used a long, mat-covered lodge similar to those of the surrounding Salish (Schaeffer 1935).

Technology

Kootenai manufactures included hide- and bark-covered canoes (fig. 2); skin clothing of the Plains type (fig. 8); stone pipes; several types of bows including a compound-

curved, sinew-backed type; flight nets for trapping water fowl; funnel traps and weirs for fishing, leister, and detachable-point fish spears ("Fishing," figs. 10–12, this vol.); coiled spruce-root baskets; fired and unfired clay vessels; stone knives and other cutting and scraping implements; and snowshoes. Cooking was accomplished by both the stone-boiling and earth oven methods. Clay pots were set directly on the fire when used for cooking (Schaeffer 1940).

Gambling

Gambling, long an important part of Kootenai culture, surfaces repeatedly in their mythology (Boas 1918). This involvement continued unabated in the 1990s.

Gambling was and is a dimension of virtually all sports. There were also several gambling games—the men's hoop and pole game, the women's dice game, and the stick game ("The Stick Game," this vol.).

The Kootenai form of the stick game in the 1960s had a sizable spiritual component. For example, some individuals were known to have power for gambling, the physical accoutrements of the game had spiritual counterparts, and the major axis of the game on the ground was along an east-west line for maximal luck. Further, the spirits were consulted in a Blanket ceremony or Sweatlodge for messages concerning forthcoming gambling events (Brunton 1974). In the 1990s supernaturalism was somewhat less a part of the game, at least for younger players.

History

The Kootenai first encountered Euro-Americans in 1792, when Peter Fidler met a small party east of the Rocky Mountains (MacGregor 1966).

European diseases had a substantial impact on the Kootenai. Beginning at least by the early decades of the eighteenth century, the Kootenai were ravaged by smallpox and diphtheria. The rapid population decline had major social consequences. Later the impact of these diseases increased Kootenai mistrust of Whites. For example, in 1855 and again in 1901, smallpox killed many Kootenai. For the first, a physician was not available. By the second the Kootenai no longer trusted White ways, including physicians (Schaeffer 1936:61).

The beginning of the nineteenth century marked the start of the fur trade period for the Kootenai and their neighbors. David Thompson crossed the Rockies in 1807 and built trading posts there two years later, thus bringing the Kootenai directly into the Euro-American market economy. This also intensified hostilities with the Blackfoot. The better-armed Plateau tribes could travel to the western Plains together in large groups and effectively compete with the Blackfoot in raiding and exploiting the bison (see Anastasio 1972). The traders also brought the Kootenai other cultural change such as exposing them to Christian ideas and

Fig. 7. Seasonal camp. Skin- and brush-covered summer tepees with large fish trap in the foreground. Photographed on the North American Boundary Commission Survey, 1860–1861.

encouraging them to adopt European values that would facilitate their involvement in trade on a predictable basis. They even brought in some Roman Catholic Iroquois to live among the Flathead and Kootenai and teach them by example how to trap and trade. As a result of the Christian influence, particularly of the Christian Iroquois, delegations went to Saint Louis in the 1830s to request that missionaries be sent to work among them (vol. 15:546). Also during the early 1830s, the Flathead and their neighbors were practicing religious forms associated with Prophet Dance movements to the west (Schaeffer 1936:25–36).

The period of missionary influence began in 1840 with the arrival of Father Pierre Jean de Smet, a Jesuit. The first mission, Saint Mary's, was built among the Flathead. Its influence on the Kootenai was limited. It was abandoned in 1850. In 1854 priests returned and established the Saint Ignatius Mission among the Pend d'Oreille and Kootenai. This had a greater impact on the Kootenai. The priests were interested in making fundamental changes throughout the culture.

The reservation period began in 1855 with the signing of a treaty negotiated by Gov. Isaac I. Stevens. In addition to establishing the Flathead Reservation, the treaty formally ended hostilities between the Plateau people and the Blackfoot.

The Kootenai were somewhat insulated from cultural change due to their isolation. For example, they were able to keep their community intact, persist longer in their subsistence economy, and keep their religion to a greater extent than the Flathead.

During the 1860s a road was built into the intermontane area and gold was discovered. This led to a large-scale incursion into the area by Whites. In 1864 a boarding school was established at Saint Ignatius. The agency sponsored programs that were intended to break cultural transmission in families. By the late 1860s the native economy of the southern reservation had been disrupted, and White-inspired farming was not working either. White settlements provided destructive influences such as liquor and alternatives to native authority. The disintegration and threat of disintegration of the native culture led to an ebb in morale and attendant periodic epidemic diseases.

Throughout the 1880s the Kootenai subsistence economy remained functional. By 1885 the Kootenai had 200 acres of land under cultivation as a communal garden. However, the Indian agent encouraged them to establish a scattered settlement pattern more like Euro-American farmers, at Dayton Creek, Montana.

By the end of the 1880s the Jesuits sought to eradicate gambling and aboriginal religion. In 1897 the Jesuits

233

forced a destruction of medicine bundles and gambling equipment. The religion went underground as a result, as the bundles destroyed were fake (Brunton 1988). Gambling did also.

Intermarriage with Whites created a new class of people, mixed bloods, who settled the more fertile lands. By 1899 nearly half the reservation was of mixed descent. This led to factionalism. The mixed bloods had little loyalty to the tribes and were wealthier than the full-bloods.

Allotment of the reservation began in 1904 and continued until 1920. By 1912 the community at Dayton Creek had been broken and the residents scattered on individual allotments. Surplus lands after allotment were opened to White settlers in 1909. After this, Indians became a minority on the Flathead Reservation. Many took their allotments on marginal land and many lost them. As a result, by 1938 one-half of the Indians on the Flathead Reservation had no land and one-third had too little land to use effectively or too marginal land for productive use.

In 1935 the the tribal council system was established on the reservation under the Indian Reorganization Act. It had little true power. By 1939 intermarriage had progressed to the point that out of 3,208 enrolled members of the reservation, only 343 were full-bloods. In 1954 the reservation was considered for termination. The action failed, but the issue reappeared from time to time (Brockmann 1968; Schaeffer 1936).

In addition to the Flathead Reservation in Montana, the Kootenai of the 1990s were found on a small reservation near Bonners Ferry, Idaho, and on small reserves in British Columbia. They are also found scattered in communities throughout the Pacific Northwest. The principal settlements on the Flathead Reservation are Dayton and Elmo,

Montana. Elmo is the tribal headquarters. The principal settlements in British Columbia are Creston, Cranbrook, Tobacco Plains, and Windermere.

There are essentially two kinds of residents on the reservation; the "traditional" and the "progressive." The traditional residents are very poor, they participate in a subsistence economy that emphasizes sharing, they live in substandard housing, their households tend to be headed by women, their marriages are not very stable, they are likely to speak a native language, they are likely to have a seasonal job (if any), and they are more likely to adhere to a native religion than are their progressive counterparts.

The progressives are uniformly wealthier than the traditional group. They aim at individual achievement and are less involved in reciprocity. They live in standard frame houses that are indistinguishable from their Euro-American neighbors. The progressives tend to have more stable marriages and are, in general, more acculturated than are the traditionals.

The Kootenai on the Flathead Reservation tend to belong to the less acculturated, traditional group. They have a higher degree of Indian blood, more speak their native language, and are more involved with their native religion than are the other ethnic groups on the reservation (Brockmann 1968). In the 1990s they were still somewhat isolated on the northern end of the Flathead Reservation.

A proposal to build a hydroelectric dam on the Kootenai River in 1981, which would have flooded Kootenai Falls, galvanized the United States and Canadian Kootenai groups into action. Spirited public meetings, retaining legal representation, hiring anthropologists as consultants, and a demonstration of Kootenai ethnic identity were the results.

Smithsonian, NAA: left, 96–10679; right, 95–10414.

Fig. 8. Clothing. left, Man on left wearing a fringed buckskin jacket; other men wearing leggings and capotes made of Hudson's Bay Company blankets. Their hairstyle includes cut bangs and hair decorations made of shell or bone. They all hold horse quirts. The man on the right also has a medal hung from a cord around his neck. Photographed on the North American Boundary Commission Survey, 1860–1861. This is the earliest known photograph of the Kootenai. right, Flathead and Kootenai women wearing cloth and velveteen wing dresses decorated with buttons and cowrie shells or elk teeth. They have painted their faces in a variety of designs as was customary for the War Dance. Madeline Couture and her mother Josephine, Kootenai, are fifth and sixth from right. Photograph by James R. White, Kalispell, Mont., © 1907.

top, Prov. Arch. of B.C., Victoria: C-782; bottom, Eastern Wash. State Histl. Soc., Cheney Cowles Mus., Spokane.

Fig. 9. Headmen. top, Chief Isadore, center standing, wearing what appears to be an amulet. left to right, Sebastian Joe; on horseback: Phillip Beaver Tail, Alpine Gus, Joe Nana, Skookum Joe, and Joseph Kootenay Pete; front row, kneeling: William Paul, Louie Storiken, a constable on the Shuswap Res., Athlmere; and Kapulo or Capilo. Photographed at Ft. Steele, B.C. bottom, Conference at Bonners Ferry, Idaho, with Capt. John McWebster, U.S. Indian Agent (stands back row to right), and A.J. Kent, a real estate agent, who acted on behalf of the Kootenais. At this conference Chief Isadore agreed to have his group of Kootenai enrolled under the Colville Agency so that his band could have a school built for them. Included in this group are: Chief Isadore Chiquiet (front row seated far left), Saul Chiquiet, Osay Joseph, John David, Simon David, Tamia Abraham, Moyse or Moses Paul, Terry Isadore, Kalili Baptiste, Osnay Ironpaddle, Sophie David, Alice David, Charlotte Alexander, Baptiste Cutsack, Rosalie Alexander, Takla Adams, Charlie David, Michelle Temo, Stanislaus David, Phillip Cutsack, Abel Alexander, Alexander Kanaka, Moise or Moses Chiquiet, Pierre Neo Alexander, Mary David, Ann Temo, Atha David, Simon Francis, Narcisse Isadore, Pierre Adams, Terry Chiquiet, Pierre Chiquiet, and Stanislaus Pierrson. Photographed May 31, 1911.

In 1974 the Bonners Ferry Kootenai declared war on the United States in order to "reclaim their aboriginal land rights lost during 1855" (Pembroke 1976). The 1855 treaty had ignored the Lower Kootenai in favor of the upriver people, so the "war" focused attention on their problem. The strategy did get the attention of the state of Idaho (fig. 10) and the federal government and resulted in the transfer of 12.5 acres to them for a reservation.

Along the major highway through the reservation are signs of an active tourist industry with many types of small businesses such as restaurants, tax-free cigarette concessions, and campgrounds. Since the 1980s the Kootenai Culture Committee has hosted interreservation gatherings and published on tribal culture (Kootenai Culture Committee 1984). The Salish Kootenai College in Pablo, Montana (fig. 11), also published language materials ("Ethnobiology and Subsistence," fig. 1, this vol.).

The Kootenai of the 1990s maintained their culture in many ways. The language was still spoken. The religion was remarkably tenacious considering the history of Roman Catholicism. Kinship functioned in important ways in day to day social relations. Gambling remained a centerpiece of their recreational and social lives.

Population

Figures for the postcontact Kootenai have been reported (Chamberlain 1893, 1907; Coues 1897; Boas 1890; Powell 1891; Turney-High 1941; Tax et al. 1960; Schaeffer 1935). The Kootenai were fairly evenly divided between the United States reservations (Kootenai and Flathead) and Canadian reserves (Columbia Lake or Windermere, Creston, Fort Steele or Saint Mary's, and Tobacco Plains (table 1). The aboriginal population may have been as much as four times as great as the postcontact figure.

When part of the Libby-Jennings band moved to the Flathead Reservation, they were absorbed into the Flathead Salish and no separate population data are kept on them.

235

Boise State U. Lib., Idaho.
Fig. 10. Demonstration to give visibility to Bonners Ferry Kootenai land claims. Photographed by William Hargrove, Sept. 1974.

Fig. 11. Entrance to Salish Kootenai College, Pablo, Mont., a tribal college offering bachelor of arts and science degrees as well as certification and apprenticeship programs. Tribal colleges are required to maintain a student body of 51% federally recognized enrolled tribal members; thus, priority is given to enrolled tribal members who have completed high school. A Native American Studies program at the college includes courses in drumming and singing, hide tanning, beading, Coyote stories, Flathead Res. Indian arts and history, Native American images in film, as well as courses in the Flathead language (Salish Kootenai College 1995–1997). Photograph by Michael Crummett, Flathead Res., Mont., 1985.

Coues (1897:550) reported 425 Kootenai on the Flathead Reservation "based on a recent census." Tax et al. (1960) reported 99 Kootenais in 1950 at Bonners Ferry. An estimate for the 1980s is around 800 for the Flathead Reservation (Brunton 1988).

Synonymy

In 1800 Thompson used the spelling Kootanaes (Dempsey 1965:7), while Chamberlain (1893) used Kootenay, which became the preferred spelling in Canada. Kootenai may be (Turney-High 1941:11) an anglicized form of Blackfoot kutunáiua (Uhlenbeck and van Gulik 1934). Or it may be an anglicized form of an old Kootenai word transcribed by Boas (1890:806) as [kutona´qa], a rendering of their self-designation *ktunaxa*. This name has no clear derivation; explanations referring it to a Kootenai verb [kulnáki] 'to pull a hide legging over the nose of a canoe'(Schaeffer 1935), or to verbs meaning 'to go out into the open' or 'to eat lean meat' are folk-etymologies (Morgan 1991). The name *ktunaxa* is especially used by the Canadian Kootenai and appears in English as Ktunaxa.

The Kootenai in Montana use the term *ksanka* 'standing arrow' for themselves and for all Kootenais (Brunton 1970;

Curtis 1907–1930, 7; Schaeffer 1935; Turney-High 1941; vol. 17:784). Probably related to this is the sign language symbol for the Kootenai, which is made by thrusting the arm forward and down with the index finger extended while sliding the other hand along the extending arm until the shoulder is reached. It is possible that *ksanka* originally applied only to the Lower Kootenai while *ktunaxa* applied to the Upper Kootenai.

The Dayton-Elmo band is called *ʔaˑkicqaniḱ* 'people of the fish weir' (Schaeffer 1935; Turney-High 1941:16), referring to the weir that was built by these Kootenai across the mouth of Dayton Creek where it turns into Flathead Lake at Dayton, Montana.

In Flathead the Kootenai are *sqĺsé* and the Lower Kootenai *slqʷolá* (Sarah G. Thomason, communication to editors 1996).

Sources

Although the bibliography on the Kootenai (Murdock and O'Leary 1975, 3:231–235) is rather extensive, the sources tend to be restricted in scope or to suffer from other limits.

Aboriginal culture is covered by Chamberlain (1893), Schaeffer (1935), Turney-High (1941), and Brunton (1974). Chamberlain's material is early and is valuable for that alone. The ethnographic coverage is quite thin. It has a section containing anthropometric measurements of Kootenai persons and a section on language. Schaeffer's field notes contain interinformant contradiction, uncorroboratable data, and other confusing characteristics. Turney-High's monograph is best considered a starting point.

Boas (1918) published myths transcribed in Kootenai and given English literal translation. Kootenai Culture Committee (1984) contains English translations of 49 myths along with illustrations.

Schaeffer (1936) and Brockmann (1968) review the history of Kootenai-White contact and its consequences. Brockmann describes the socioeconomic situation on the Flathead Reservation, Montana. Brunton (1968) looks at the ties among reservations through ceremonial means. Pembroke (1976) describes a social movement among the Lower Kootenai in order to gain reservation status.

The Glenbow-Alberta Institute in Calgary, Alberta, has a collection of Kootenai materials, including early photographs. The American Museum of Natural History, New York, holds the Schaeffer manuscripts and artifacts in three collections. The Museum of the Plains Indian in Browning, Montana, has a few cradleboards. The University of Montana, Missoula, has early twentieth-century photographs and artifacts.

Table 1. Population of Canadian Kootenai by Band

	Columbia Lake	Creston	Ft. Steele	Tobacco Plains	Total
1887	65	160	235	30	490
1891	106	159	312	78	696
1904	80	172	216	61	553
1950	101	82	182	62	427

SOURCES: Chamberlain 1893:551, 1907:742; Tax et al. 1960.

Northern Okanagan, Lakes, and Colville

DOROTHY KENNEDY AND RANDALL T. BOUCHARD

Northern Okanagan (‚ōkə'nägən), Lakes, and Colville ('käl‚vĭl) are the northerly components of an Interior Salish grouping that also comprises the Methow, Southern Okanogan, Nespelem, and Sanpoil. There is no commonly accepted name for this larger comprehensive grouping, but for convenience it may be termed Okanagan-Colville. Its four southerly components are treated in the chapter "Middle Columbia River Salishans," this volume. Within the Northern Okanagan, the Similkameen Okanagan may be distinguished from the Northern Okanagan proper.

The Northern Okanagan villages (in the narrow sense) are along Okanagan Lake and in the Okanagan River drainage in Canada. The Similkameen Okanagan have been, since at least the early eighteenth century, along the Similkameen River and tributaries. The Lakes territory is along the Arrow Lakes and Slocan Lake and the Columbia River from Revelstoke to as far south as Northport, Washington. The Colville were traditionally along the Columbia below the Lakes and above the Sanpoil and Spokane and along the lower Kettle River. Earlier writers placed the boundary between the Lakes and the Colville farther south, just above Kettle Falls (Mooney 1896:pl. 88, 732; Work 1830; Ray 1936 b:118, 122, 140 141; Bouchard and Kennedy 1984: 45–53, 1985:25–26).

Language

The Okanagan-Colville groups all speak a single language, called for convenience simply Okanagan.* In Okanagan this language is called *nsilxcín* 'people's speech'.

Each of the component groups has a separate dialect: Northern Okanagan (Northern Okanagan and Similkameen Okanagan), Lakes, and Colville, plus the four dialects of the southerly tier of Okanagan-Colville. The greatest dialectal difference separates a westerly Okanagan dialect continuum (Northern Okanagan, Southern Okanogan, and Methow) from an easterly Colville dialect continuum (Lakes, Colville, and Sanpoil-Nespelem).

*The phonemes of Okanagan are: (voiceless stops and affricates) *p, t, c, k, kʷ, q, qʷ,* ʔ; (glottalized stops and affricates) *ṗ, ṫ, ċ, ƛ̓, k̓, k̓ʷ, q̓, q̓ʷ*; (voiceless fricatives) *s, ł, x, xʷ, x̣, x̣ʷ, h*; (resonants) *m, n, l, r, y, ɣ, w,* ˤ (pharyngeal glide), ˤʷ, *h*; (glottalized resonants) *m̓, n̓, l̓, r̓, y̓, ɣ̓, w̓, ˤ̓, ˤ̓ʷ*; (vowels) *i, a* ([æ] ~ [a]), *ə, u* ([u] ~ [o]); (stress) v́.

This inventory is adapted from Bouchard and Pierre (1973). Italicized Okanagan terms were transcribed in this orthography by Randall Bouchard.

In Canada, speakers of the Okanagan dialect belong to seven British Columbia Bands living on Indian reserves as far north as Douglas Lake, which has a mixed Okanagan and Thompson population. In the United States, the Southern Okanogan, Methow, Nespelem, Sanpoil, Colville, and Lakes comprise five of the 12 "tribes" (sometimes called "bands") identified collectively as the Colville Confederated Tribes who reside on the Colville Reservation in Washington.

Territory

The distinction of a northern and southern division of Okanagan was introduced by Spier (1938:85–86, 73). It is probable that such a distinction did not exist aboriginally (Teit 1930:204). Okanagan-Colville people in the 1950s (Lerman 1952–1954) and in the 1980s (Bouchard and Kennedy 1984a:25) did not distinguish between Northern Okanagan and Southern Okanogan.

In the 1700s, apparently, the head of Okanagan Lake marked the northernmost boundary of Northern Okanagan territory. There were Okanagan villages along this lake and the people used the hills contiguous to the lake for hunting. But they did not range more than a few miles farther back; Shuswap hunters roamed the interior hills almost as far south as Penticton (Teit 1930:213; Lerman 1952–1954). Later in the eighteenth century, Northern Okanagans began to use the upper Nicola Valley, displacing the Shuswap Indians who had hunted this upland area since the early 1700s (fig. 1). Eventually, the Douglas Lake area was ceded to the Okanagan who used this country on a seasonal basis before establishing a permanent settlement there in the mid-1800s (Teit 1930:213). The Shuswap-speaking Spallumcheen Band around Enderby became largely intermarried with Okanagan; one ethnographer (Hill-Tout 1911:130) included the Spallumcheen in a list of 10 Northern Okanagan winter settlements.

The Nicola Valley, the Similkameen River Valley, and an area along the Okanagan River almost as far south as Tonasket were originally occupied by the Nicola-Similkameen, an Athapaskan group, prior to an Okanagan expansion that began around 1700. A second encroachment from the north by Thompson Indians left the Nicola-Similkameen occupying a small area around Keremeos in the mid-1700s, but soon they were absorbed by Okanagans. The new residents of the valley became known as the Similkameen, derived from the name of a site at the mouth of the Similkameen River. The locations of about 12 Similkameen

Okanagan winter villages have been recorded (Teit 1930:205–206, 214; Bouchard 1966–1991; Bouchard and Kennedy 1984a:17).

In the eighteenth century, the core territory of the Lakes extended from as far north as the vicinity of Revelstoke to as far south as Northport on the Columbia River (Bouchard and Kennedy 1985). How much more extensive it may have been at one time is uncertain. Some writers (Teit 1930:210; Ray 1936:118–121, 1977:10) have extended the southern Lakes boundary as far downstream as the vicinity of Kettle Falls, although historical evidence supports the Colville occupation of this lower area.

After the Hudson's Bay Company established Fort Colville near Kettle Falls in 1825, the Lakes Indians began wintering near the fort. By 1870 the Lakes had expanded southward, displacing the Colville from the banks of the Columbia north of Kettle Falls, and from the Colville valley in the vicinity of Addy (Work 1830; Winans 1871). This expansion led Elmendorf (1935–1936) to propose a southern lobe of Lakes territory (Ray 1936:121, 1954) that was rejected by the United States Indian Claims Commission.

As many as four subgroups, comprising almost 30 winter settlements situated along the Columbia River, have been identified. Homes in the Colville Valley and on the east side of the Columbia River were abandoned a decade after the Colville people had been assigned to the Colville Reservation (Ray 1936:140–141; Bouchard and Kennedy 1984).

Environment

The Northern Okanagan-Lakes-Colville territory is distinguished by a high level of vegetational diversity resulting from great variation in topography and climate. In the southeast, the area known as the Columbia Basin has an annual precipitation of only 10–12 inches, much of it in the form of winter snowfall. The summers are dry and hot and the winters severe. To the north, the territory of the Lakes is dominated by the Columbia Mountains where a number of peaks rise to over 9,000 feet, and the annual precipitation ranges from 20 to 67 inches. The temperatures in the valleys are generally cooler than those of the Okanagan Highlands to the west, an area characterized by rounded mountains and gentle upland slopes averaging about 4,000 feet, but with a few scattered peaks of higher elevation (Franklin and Dyrness 1973; Krajina 1970; Turner, Bouchard, and Kennedy 1980:2–5).

Most of the traditional villages were situated in the valley bottoms and along the major waterways. The upland areas were visited periodically for hunting, root digging, and berry picking.

External Relations

The Northern Okanagan-Lakes-Colville intermarried with adjacent peoples, regardless of differences in speech, although this varied among the divisions. The Colville negotiated marriages with all neighboring Salishan-speaking groups and had extensive intercourse with Sahaptin speakers as well. The Lakes intermarried mostly with the Colville but came into contact and negotiated a few marriages with the Shuswap, Kootenai, and Northern Okanagan. With the introduction of the fur trade, Colville and Lakes marriages with French Canadians and Iroquois were common. The Northern Okanagan married with other Okanagan-Colville speakers and with Shuswap, Thompson and, to a lesser degree, Nicola-Similkameen Athapaskans (Teit 1930:215; Miller 1990:146).

Traditions exist of conflict between the Lakes and the Kootenai, who were assisted by Shuswap warriors (Teit 1930:258); between the Lakes and the Shuswap (British Columbia 1866:28); between the Lakes and the Sanpoil (Ray 1933:115); between the Northern Okanagan and the Nicola-Similkameen, who were assisted by the Thompson and Shuswap (Boas 1895:31); between the Northern Okanagan and the Shuswap (Spier 1938:82); between the southern groups of Okanagan and the Nez Perce (Raufer 1966:21–22); between the Colville and the Shuswap (Bouchard 1966–1991); and between the Colville and the Blackfoot (Bouchard 1966–1991; Miller 1990:146). A more ritualized form of face-to-face combat observed at Kettle Falls has also been noted (Chance 1973:16). One such incident ended with an exchange of presents and a feast (D. Douglas 1914:206–207).

Traditions record how the Colville enslaved female captives taken during raids on Blackfoot and Umatilla villages, or purchased from the south, although Ray (1977:24) portrays slavery as "an unaccountable and indefensible practice of foreigners." The Northern Okanagan purchased Lillooet and Northwest Coast slaves from the Thompson, and from southern slavers. While the Lakes kept few slaves, they were victimized by Shuswap and Kootenai slave raiders. Descendants did not inherit slave status, although their tainted ancestry might be raised during quarrels (Teit 1930:254, 277; Elmendorf 1935–1936; Ray 1939:31; Kennedy 1971–1991).

Culture

The cultural summary that follows is based primarily on ethnographic accounts compiled between the early 1900s and 1991, supplemented by historical observations from the 1800s. These data describe culture as it was in the early nineteenth century.

Subsistence

Culturally, the Lakes Indians differed in several respects from the Colville and the Northern Okanagan. The Lakes were far more mobile, were canoe oriented rather than horse or foot oriented, and placed a greater emphasis on hunting

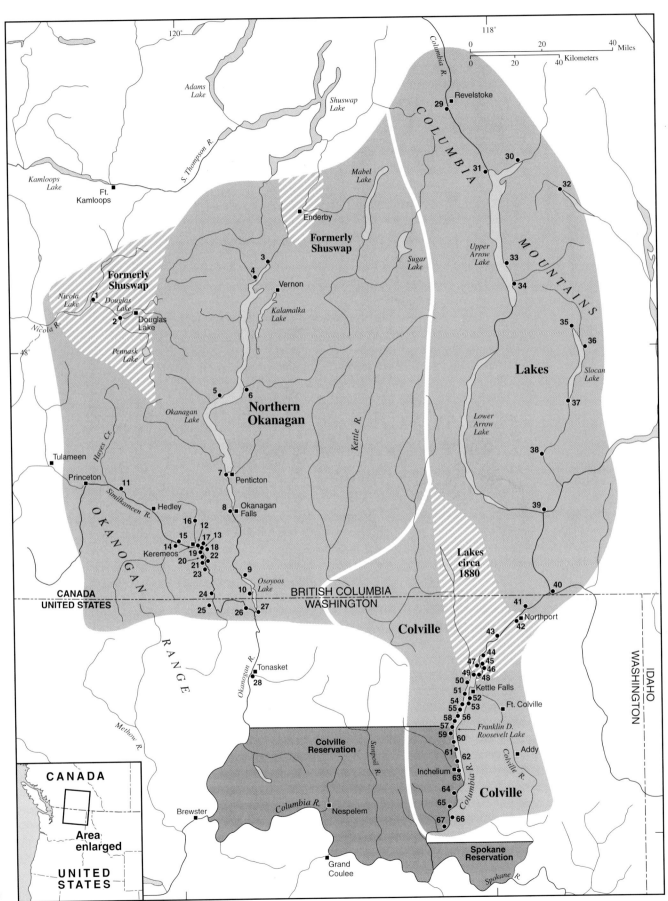

Adams
Lake

Shuswap
Lake

120°

118°

COLUMBIA

Columbia R.

40   Miles

20

0

0   20   40   Kilometers

Revelstoke

29

30

31

32

S. Thompson R.

Kamloops
Lake

Ft.
Kamloops

Mabel
Lake

Formerly
Shuswap

Enderby

33

Upper
Arrow
Lake

34

M
O
U
N
T
A
I
N
S

Sugar
Lake

3

4

Vernon

Kalamalka
Lake

35

36

Lakes

Slocan
Lake

37

Formerly
Shuswap

Nicola
Lake

1

Douglas
Lake

Nicola R.

2   Douglas
Lake

48°

Pennask
Lake

Kettle R.

Lower
Arrow
Lake

38

5   6

Northern
Okanagan

Okanagan
Lake

39

Hayes Cr.

Tulameen

Princeton

11

Similkameen R.

Hedley

16   12

15   17 13

14   19 18

Keremeos   22

20

21   23

7   Penticton

8   Okanagan
Falls

9

Osoyoos
Lake

10

Lakes
circa
1880

40

O
K
A
N
O
G
A
N

CANADA
UNITED STATES

24

25

26 27

BRITISH COLUMBIA
WASHINGTON

Colville

41

Northport

42

43

44

45

47   46

49   48

50

Kettle Falls

51   52

54   53

55   56

Ft. Colville

58

57

59   60

61   62

63

Inchelium

64

65   66

67

IDAHO
WASHINGTON

Okanagan R.

Tonasket

28

R
A
N
G
E

Methow R.

Colville
Reservation

Sanpoil R.

Franklin D.
Roosevelt Lake

Addy

Columbia R.

Colville R.

Colville

CANADA

Area
enlarged

UNITED
STATES

Brewster

Columbia R.

Nespelem

Grand
Coulee

Spokane
Reservation

Spokane R.

240

Fig. 1. Northern Okanagan, Lakes, and Colville territory, late 19th and 20th centuries. Villages are: 1, *nɬq̓ítməɬx* 'bushy area'; 2, *spaxmn* 'shaving; paring' (referring to the open rolling country devoid of trees); 3, *nk̓mápələqs* 'head end of lake'; 4, *nⱡx̌ʷəx̌ʷtán* 'killing place'; 5, *stqaʔtqʷtńíẃt* 'lake on side'; 6, *nx̌ʷáqʷaʔstn* 'arrow-scraper'; 7, *snpintktn;* 8, *sx̌ʷəx̌ʷnítkʷ* 'little waterfall'; 9, *nk̓mip* 'end of lake'; 10, *sʔúyuʔs* 'gathered together; meeting'; 11, *aʔkłqix̌ʷlx* 'having suckerfish'; 12, *aʔkłqiʔísxnm* 'having marked rock'; 13, *cəcəwíxaʔx* 'a bunch of creeks'; 14, *asnúlaʔx̌*; 15, *ɣipxⱡút* 'standing rock'; 16, *q̓iq̓iʔísxn* 'lots of marked rocks (pictographs)'; 17, *sntamt̓ktn* 'eight-tie-top lodge'; 18, *nk̓ʷərʔúlaʔx̌ʷ* 'having yellow on ground'; 19, *kłk̓ərmíẃs* 'cut along the flat'; 20, *kłk̓ək̓ərmiwaʔs* 'little cut in flat area'; 21, *snⱡx̌ʷəx̌ʷtán* 'killing place'; 22, *sk̓mqin* 'head end'; 23, *aʔcsmⱡáˊla ʔx̌ʷ* 'clay land'; 24, *sk̓nnúsəstn;* 25, *nʔaʔsəlítaʔk̓ʷ* 'having 2 small creeks'; 26, *stəx̌ʷta ʔx̌ʷíⱡxtn* 'where fish jump'; 27, *saˊtitx̌ʷ* 'piled-up rock dwelling'; 28, *k̓ʷax̌ʷlús* 'creek runs into river'; 29, *skxikńtn;* 30, *nk̓mápələqs* 'head end of lake'; 31, *qʷəspíca ʔ* 'buffalo robe'; 32, *snpəⱡmíp;* 33, *k̓ʷusxənáqs* 'point of land sticking out; long point'; 34, *nk̓ʷusp* 'come together'; 35, *snk̓míp* 'end of lake'; 36, *tqelˊáytckst (?)* 'trout ascend' (?); 37, *six̌ʷílx (?);* 38, nk̓ʷeioˊxɛn (?); 39, *k̓piⱡəls;* 40, *nk̓ˊlilaʔ* 'burned area' (?); 41, *yumcn;* 42, *ncəċərism* 'having kingfishers'; 43, *nʔiʔsitkʷ* 'disappears-from-sight water'; 44, *kłtətqˊús* 'just touching the edge'; 45, *sk̓łˊállqˊa ʔ* 'reach the river'; 46, *kłkiẃs* 'brush in middle'; 47, *nqʷəqʷúlqʷtəlaʔx̌ʷ* 'dusty ground'; 48, *npəpqʷ ĺickʷm* 'having lingfish'; 49, *ksunkw* 'island'; 50, *sməcnúlaʔx̌ʷ* 'desert parsley ground'; 51, *ncmútaʔstm* 'a lot of deep snow' (?); 52, *scáˊycup* 'small springs of water along the bank' (?); 53, *sⱡqiym* 'stuck out'; 54, *nʔilˊilmiń* 'zigzag flow of water'; 55, *npaʔalcínm* 'having a flat area at the mouth'; 56, *kmúmaɬxḿ* 'having a small amount of cottonwoood'; 57, *ncəcqəqíńk* 'hit against sidehill'; 58, *k̓ʷəluʔsásq̓t* 'singed sky'; 59, *qəqəlápiyaʔ* (diminutive form of *qəlápiyaʔ*); 60, *kłəkłák* 'brushy place'; 61, *nqʷaʔsíʔm* 'bay'; 62, *ncaʔliʔm* 'water hitting against something'; 63, *nlk̓ʷutm* 'go-around area'; 64, *sk̓ʷíʔikstn* 'bite-hand place'; 65, *ntək̓laʔx̌ʷcin* 'dirt in mouth of stream; delta'; 66, *pəx̌ʷpx̌ʷəx̌ʷíⱡx* 'splashing'; 67, *tk̓ʷək̓árk̓ərxnm* 'yellowish-green plant growth'.

than fishing or plant gathering. The Similkameen Okanagan were also hunters. The Colville subsisted mostly on fish, while the Northern Okanagan depended equally on resources obtained by fishing, hunting, and gathering. Teit (1930:247) reported that the Okanagan-Colville had four great hunts: in spring for deer and sheep; in late fall for deer, sheep, elk, and bear; in midwinter for deer; and in late winter for sheep.

Communal deer hunting throughout the region was organized by a headman or leader known as *xaʔtús* (derived from *xʔit* 'first; best; most') selected by common consent for his skill and knowledge of the hunting grounds. After personal preparation involving cleansing in a sweathouse, sexual abstinence, drinking herbal decoctions, and fastening a deer's musk gland to their leggings, a group of men chased the deer toward secluded hunters armed with bows and arrows. Sometimes the deer would be herded toward the water where the hunters would be waiting in canoes. Lakes and Colville hunters also drove the deer down a narrow runway, formed by men or brush, toward the edge of a bluff where they closed in on the animals and forced them over the cliff.

In addition to the double-curved bow used by the Northern Okanagan and Colville, the Lakes possessed a flat bow. Deer were also caught by trapping them in snares and pitfalls; by chasing them onto thin ice; by waiting for them at salt licks; by attracting them with deer whistles; and by stalking them on snowshoes and breaking their neck, stabbing them, or clubbing them. Specially trained hunting dogs were employed to chase the deer toward a waiting hunter. The use of boleros among the Colville has been reported (Teit 1930:241–242; Elmendorf 1935–1936; Ray 1975, 2:137, 139; Kennedy 1971–1991).

Caribou and the occasional elk and moose were stalked by individual Lakes hunters. Both black bears and grizzlies were dragged from their hibernation dens or caught in pitfalls. Lakes and Similkameen people hunted mountain goat and mountain sheep, the sheep killed by driving them off high cliffs. The Colville hunted antelope south of the Columbia River. Throughout the area, marmots, beaver, rabbit, marten, and porcupine were eaten, while wolf, coyote, fox, lynx, otter, mink, fisher, and weasel were hunted for their fur. At least in the early nineteenth century, some

Lakes and Colville hunters participated in annual excursions to hunt bison east of the Rocky Mountains. The use of dogs for food has been reported for the Similkameen (Gibbs 1855:413; Teit 1930:242–245; Ray 1975, 2:140; Lerman 1952–1954; Kennedy 1971–1991).

Bear ceremonialism involving the singing of special songs while skinning, streaking the bear's head with charcoal and propping it up in a tree, returning the paws and the gristle found under the bear's tongue to the woods, and ritual feasting, has been reported among the Lakes (Moberly 1885:47) and the Colville and Northern Okanagan (Teit 1930:291; Kennedy 1971–1991). Care had to be taken with the bones, spleen and head of a deer. Prohibitions based on age and gender restricted the eating of certain parts, including fetuses, which were reserved for older people (Miller 1990:117; Kennedy 1971–1991).

Of the approximately 95 birds identified by the Okanagan-Colville, 16 were used for food, killed in snares or shot with a bow and arrow. Parts of birds were utilized also in witchcraft, such as love charms (Kennedy 1971–1991).

The catching of salmon and the manufacturing and care of fishing equipment was usually the job of men, while women were responsible for butchering the fish and preparing it for winter storage by means of sun-drying and smoke-drying. In 1866, a government official among the Colville estimated that five-eighths of their diet was comprised of salmon (Paige 1866), most of which was caught at Kettle Falls. People from throughout Northern Okanagan-Lakes-Colville territory, in addition to Spokane, Flathead, Kootenai, Nez Perce, and Coeur d'Alene, camped at the Kettle Falls fishery in July and August to fish chinook, coho, and sockeye salmon, and to trade, engage in competitions, and socialize (de Smet 1905, 2:481; Wilkes 1845, 4:474). Salmon were caught there in large J-shaped basketry traps suspended over the falls, sketched first by artist-explorer Paul Kane in 1847 ("Fishing," fig. 9, this vol.), and by individual fishermen wielding dip nets and harpoons (Kane 1859:219; C.W. Wilson 1970:114; Teit 1930:246; Kennedy and Bouchard 1975a).

Weirs were used by the Lakes Indians to catch salmon on the Slocan and Kootenay rivers, and the Lakes have been observed picking up spawned-out salmon from the shores of the Arrow Lakes (Kittson 1826; Dawson 1890:19b; Ross 1855:165). At Okanagan Falls on the Okanagan River, and along the lowermost Similkameen River, the June run of chinook salmon was followed by sockeye salmon, the main species fished by the Indian people who gathered here (Bouchard and Kennedy 1984a:30).

The Northern Okanagan distinguish at least three species of kokanee, a landlocked sockeye salmon caught in large numbers and dried for winter use, and plentiful in several lakes throughout Northern Okanagan and Lakes territories. Fish of economic importance throughout the Okanagan-Colville area included six species of suckerfish, two species of whitefish, ling, lamprey, Dolly Varden char, sturgeon, steelhead, rainbow, and cutthroat trout. Freshwater mussels (*Margaritifera falcata*) were collected from the riverbeds when other foods were scarce (Kennedy 1971–1991; Kennedy and Bouchard 1975a; Bouchard and Kennedy 1984).

Fishing devices used throughout the territory included weirs, several styles of basketry traps, leisters, harpoons, hook and line, dip nets, and seine nets (C.W. Wilson 1970:118; Bouchard and Kennedy 1984a:30; Lerman 1952–1954; Teit 1930:246). An infusion made from the roots of *Lomatium dissectum* was used as a fish poison in creeks by the Colville (Turner, Bouchard, and Kennedy 1980:66), while the Northern Okanagan used pitch torches at night to attract fish to the surface of lakes and rivers where they could be speared (Teit 1930:247; Kennedy 1971–1991).

Salmon fishing at communal sites such as Kettle Falls and Okanagan Falls was under the direction of a salmon chief, called *xaʔtús* (the same term used to refer to the leader of a hunting party). This person controlled the construction of the fishing equipment and the catching and distribution of the salmon, at least for the first month (Kane 1859:218–219). The salmon chief performed a ceremony to mark the catch of the first salmon, a ritual that symbolized the people's dependence on the annual salmon harvest. Ray (1975, 2:133) reported that the salmon chief performed the ceremony privately, although the feast that followed was served to all present. It was the custom among the Lakes (Elmendorf 1935–1936) that only men were permitted to eat the first catch. Colville people in the 1970s described the salmon chief officiating at a public ceremony followed by a feast shared by all assembled. Bones and viscera left from the meal were wrapped in Douglas fir boughs and thrown into the river in the belief that they would return again as salmon. The role of salmon chief continued at Kettle Falls until the late 1930s when construction of the Grand Coulee Dam prevented the salmon from ascending the river (Kennedy and Bouchard 1975a). In the 1980s, a First Salmon ceremony was reintroduced at Kettle Falls.

Among the prohibitions observed by the Colville to ensure a constant supply of salmon were the exclusion of children, widows, and widowers near the fish traps; restrictions on smoking, swimming, and drawing water above the traps; and disallowance of fresh salmon to menstruating women and parents of newborns (Kennedy and Bouchard 1975a). The consequence of not observing such taboos was commented on by fur trader David Thompson in 1811 when one of his men thoughtlessly tossed a horse bone into the river at Kettle Falls. Despite the bone being retrieved rapidly by an Indian diving after it, the salmon disappeared for the remainder of the day (Thompson 1962:335–337).

First-fruits and first-roots ceremonies were held in the spring for saskatoon berries, bitterroot, and other plants to thank the spirits of these plants for the return of the crop (Turner, Bouchard, and Kennedy 1980:152; Hill-Tout 1911:132). Dancing and feasting were central components of these rituals. Among the Lakes, women were served certain foods that had been prepared by the men, after which the men burned all leftovers and the sticks on which the food had been roasted, in the belief that not doing so would cause the plant foods to wither (Elmendorf 1935–1936). Such ceremonies continued to be held on the Colville Reservation in the early 1990s.

Plant foods included black tree lichen, mushrooms, green shoots, tree cambium (fig. 2), roots and other underground parts, seeds, nuts and berries. In Lakes country, huckleberries replaced saskatoon berries in importance. Among the Northern Okanagan and Similkameen, saskatoon berries were so important that at least eight varieties were distinguished in the 1990s. Sometimes entire families participated in harvesting plant foods, although it was generally the task of women ("Ethnobiology and Subsistence," fig. 3, this vol.). The digging grounds and berry-picking patches were not considered either village or group property; and although the women worked together, each kept her own harvest. Many plant foods were stored for winter consumption: fruits, such as berries, were mashed and dried into cakes; roots were dried (fig. 3), either raw or after being pit-cooked; bitterroot and avalanche lily corms were sun-dried, as were mushrooms (Turner, Bouchard, and Kennedy 1980:146–148; Joe 1981).

Structures

In the early nineteenth century, semisubterranean pit houses that housed one or at most two families were used as winter dwellings by the Lakes; larger ones were used by the Northern Okanagan and Similkameen. The floors were excavated to a depth of two to six feet. Their use among the northernmost Okanagan peoples extended into the late 1800s, whereas the Lakes discontinued their use a generation earlier. Some reports deny Colville use of pit houses (Teit 1930:226–227; Miller 1990:147), while others state that pit houses were used by the Colville prior to about 1800 (Ray 1939:133; Bouchard and Kennedy 1984).

More commonly known were mat lodges, both conical (fig. 4) and oblong, that were used by all the Northern Okanagan-

Fig. 2. Louie Pichette, Colville, harvesting tree cambium from the outer bark of a ponderosa pine. A sharpened sapling stick on the ground behind Pichette was used to pry the outer bark from the tree. He is scraping off the cambium with a pocket knife. Photograph by Dorothy Kennedy, Colville Res., Wash., 1979.

Lakes-Colville. An early Hudson's Bay Company report described a Lakes settlement consisting of two lodges, one a tule mat-covered conical lodge, and the other a square-topped lodge (Work 1823), as described by Teit (1930:227-228) and utilized to some extent among all these groups.

For winter, the square-topped lodge was covered with a layer of poles, brush, and large sheets of cedar bark, similar to the covering of a pit house. Elmendorf (1935–1936) reported

that these mat (or bark) lodges were sometimes excavated to a depth of two feet and had separate entrances and sections of the house for men and women. Colville people seldom used bark-covered lodges, according to Teit (1930:228), although an oblong lodge covered with several layers of tule mats, fir boughs, and bark, and ranging 20 to 60 feet long, has been reported (Miller 1990:147). A tule mat-covered winter dance lodge, approximately 40 feet long and 15 feet wide, was used as recently as about 1920 by Colville people in the vicinity of Inchelium (Bouchard and Kennedy 1984).

The Lakes Indians also used mat-covered lean-tos. Occasionally two such structures would be built face-to-face with a fire between them (Teit 1930:227; Elmendorf 1935–1936). A rectangular lodge with a pole framework, raised flooring, and mat-covered walls was observed at the Kettle Falls fishery in 1811 by David Thompson (1962:335) and depicted in a painting by Paul Kane in 1847 ("Fishing," fig. 9, this vol.). Thompson's description of these cedar-plank and mat-covered houses indicates that they measured approximately 20 feet in width to as much as 60 feet in length. Salmon were hung to dry from the poles comprising the raised flooring (Kane 1859:216).

Other structures included a separate lodge where children were born, women stayed during menstruation, unmarried girls were secluded, and elderly women stayed to chaperon young people. Men and women had separate sweathouses (Elmendorf 1935–1936; Ray 1939:133). Skin-covered lodges were adopted by the Colville, and to a limited extent by the Okanagan, after hunting parties began making excursions to bison grounds on the Plains. In the early 1900s, the

left, Smithsonian, NAA:56,803; center, Glenbow Alberta Inst., Calgary, Alta.: NA-2244–35.

Fig. 3. Women. left, Colville woman with baby. She wears a single strand bead necklace and Hudson's Bay Company blanket. Her use of cloth for the headband, leggings, and baby wrapping are representative of the period before the adoption of Plains-style clothing made of hide and beadwork. This is the earliest known photograph of a Colville Indian. Photographed on the North American Boundary Commission Survey, 1860–1861. center, Louise Lezard, Northern Okanagan, drying bitterroot in her kitchen for winter use. Photograph by Eric D. Sismey, Penticton Indian Res., B.C., 1960s. right, Celeste Jeanette Desautel and her son Dylan Roberty Wesley Burris, Lakes. The cradleboard, which is the same for either a boy or a girl, is being used for the third generation. Photograph by Sharon Eva Grainger, Colville Res., Inchelium, Wash., 1994.

Plains-style tepee, covered with canvas and other fabrics, was adopted for summer use among the Colville (Teit 1930:229; Ray 1977:39).

Technology

Women made baskets from birchbark and from coiled cedar and spruce roots. Some baskets were used as watertight containers, and others for carrying or storage purposes ("Basketry," fig. 8, this vol.). The construction of Lakes baskets differed from that of the other groups; the Lakes manufactured a greater number of styles and sizes. Large storage casks, especially for underground caches, were made from cottonwood bark. Woven bags used for storage were made in varying sizes from several plant fibers including Indian hemp and inner cedar bark. Deer and buffalo hide was used to make rawhide bags and parfleches, seldom painted by the Lakes and Similkameen, unlike those made by the Northern Okanagan and Colville. Animal intestines were inflated using an elderberry stem tube and then used for storing grease, pulverized dried meat or fish, crushed nuts, berries, or camas. Other household items included pillows of dressed skins stuffed with down feathers (Teit 1930:220–229; Elmendorf 1935–1936; Turner, Bouchard, and Kennedy 1980:149–150).

Transport

The Okanagan-Colville constructed several styles of canoes, although the Colville procured most of their canoes from the Lakes. The distinctive sturgeon-nosed canoe made from the bark of white pine (*Pinus monticola*) and large enough to carry two people, was the usual mode of travel for the Lakes Indians. Dugout canoes were sometimes made, using ponderosa pine, cedar, cottonwood, or grand fir. Pole and tule rafts were used on mountain lakes. Paddles were commonly about four feet long with a long, broad blade and rounded end (Teit 1930:248; Elmendorf 1935–1936; Turner, Bouchard, and Kennedy 1980:149).

Only the Similkameen Okanagan are said to have used dogs for hauling purposes. In the early eighteenth century, horses were first obtained by the Colville from Indians to the east. Their use spread quickly to the Northern and Similkameen Okanagan, who had grazing land available for these introduced herds, but the Lakes environment never permitted horses to be kept until the people began wintering

Fig. 4. Dwellings typical of Northern Okanagan, Colville, and Lakes habitation. Both the canvas tepee and conical mat lodge have mat entrance doors. A woman is working a skin between them. Photograph by Anders B. Wilse, 1897–1900.

along the Columbia. A detailed account of the changes that took place in trading patterns after the acquisition of horses is provided in Teit (1930:249, 252–254).

Teit (1900:256–257, 1930:249) described a shortened, up-turned form of the "magpie-sole" style snowshoe utilized by the Lakes and adapted to walking up steep, snow-covered hillsides. The Similkameen Okanagan made long, narrow snowshoes, known as the "Nicola-Similkameen style" (fig. 5) by the Thompson Indians.

Clothing and Adornment

Clothing included moccasins, leggings, belt, breechclout or apron, shirt or vest, and cap or headband for the men (fig. 6), and moccasins, short leggings, long dress, belt, and cap or headband for women. In warm weather, men and children occasionally went nude, or wore a robe or blanket draped around the waist; women remained modest in all temperatures. The Colville and Northern Okanagan replaced the goat-skin robes and breechclouts worn by the Lakes with hides of deer, elk, and antelope, although poor people among the Similkameen Okanagan made clothing from the inner fibers of big sagebrush (*Artemisia tridentata*) (fig. 7). Additional hide outer clothing, fur robes, and mittens were added during the winter (fig. 5). Bison skins became common throughout the Okanagan-Colville area. Only the Similkameen wore robes of dressed dogskin. Buckskin garments were painted and embroidered for special occasions, and capes and sashes were sometimes ornamented with feathers, fringes, puncturing, tufts of hair or skins, or quills, seeds, hoofs, shells, or teeth.

People often went barefoot, or wore buckskin moccasins, sometimes lined with bunchgrass, goat hair, or down feathers for warmth. Men's headwear was made of dressed skin and all types of animal fur, animals' head-skins, and bird skins. Headdresses of eagles, hawks, and owls were also common (fig. 6). Caps worn by women were made mostly from dressed skin, although Colville women wove Nez Perce–style grass caps, and Similkameen Okanagan women wove caps of willow bark (Teit 1930:231–236; Elmendorf 1935–1936; Lerman 1952–1954; Turner, Bouchard, and Kennedy 1980:78, 136).

Okanagan-Colville men usually wore their hair long and styled in various forms of braiding: plaited on either side of the head with the hair on the back of the head braided, tied, or allowed to hang loose; plaited in two braids; plaited on one side with the opposite side either hung loose or tied with a string; or parted in the center and worn in a ponytail, either

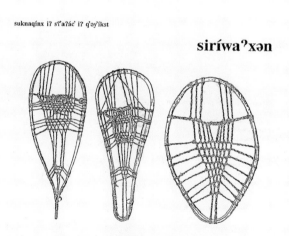

suknaqínx iʔ sƛ'aʔác iʔ q'əy'íkst

siríwaʔxən

siríwaʔxən əck'ʷúl'mstəm k'əl wist ƛaʔ cxʷʔit iʔ smík'ʷət.

We use snowshoes in the mountains where there is a lot of snow.
əck'ʷúl'əmstəm 'what we use.' What does əck'ʷúl'əmstip mean? Right, 'you pl. regularly use them.' ƛaʔ cxʷʔit iʔ smík'ʷət 'when there is lots of snow.' You already know ƛaʔ, and c- is also something you have seen. xʷʔit iʔ sɪwɬk'ʷ 'snow.' sɪwɬk'ʷ 'water.' What does ƛaʔ cxʷʔit iʔ sɪwɬk'ʷ mean? snɪw't means 'wind,' but it wouldn't be right to use xʷʔit with it; one would say something like ƛaʔ ck'ʷəkʷʔáct iʔ snɪw't 'when there is strong wind.' scək'ck'ám means 'thunder,' and one would say ƛaʔ ck'ʷʷəck'ʷʷáct iʔ scək'ck'ám 'when the thunder is strong.' k'əl wist 'on / in the mountains, up high.' So you can have k'əl sɪlxʷaʔ iʔ sɪwɬk'ʷ 'to the ocean (lit. the big water),' k'əl t'k'ʷʷət 'to the lake,' k'əl cəcwɪxaʔ 'to the creek.'

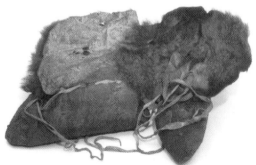

left, En'owkin Centre, Penticton, B.C.; Amer. Mus. of Nat. Hist., New York: top right, 16/9553; bottom right, 16/9556.

Fig. 5. Northern Okanagan winter clothing and equipment. left, Snowshoe entry in a coloring book used to maintain language viability. The snowshoe drawings, based on Teit (1900:figs. 240–242), show the Nicola-Similkameen styles left and center; at right is a rounded type best adapted for travel on steep mountains. top right, Robe of squirrel skins sewn with deer sinew. Collected by James A. Teit, Douglas Lake, B.C., 1904. bottom right, Winter moccasins made of hoary marmot skin. Collected by James A. Teit, Similkameen, B.C., 1904. Length of robe, 114 cm; length of moccasins, 25 cm.

top left, U. of Wash. Lib., Special Coll., Seattle: 1040; top right, Ind. U., William Hammond Mathers Mus., Bloomington; bottom left, Okanogan County Histl. Soc., Okanogan, Wash.; bottom center, Eastern Wash. State Hist. Soc., Cheney Cowles Mus., Spokane, Wash.: 1.90 a–b (neg. 95.24); 1780.558 (neg. 95.27).

Fig. 6. Clothing. top left, Culculaweela, Northern Okanagan, wearing a Plains-style feather bonnet and jacket with fur strips hanging from the shoulder. Photograph by Edward Latham, Box Canyon, Wash., 1890–1910. top right, Chief James Bernard, Lakes, wearing a beaded vest and leggings and a feather bonnet. Photograph by Joseph K. Dixon, Davenport, Colville Res., Wash., 1913. bottom left, Unidentified woman in transitional clothing. She wears a Euro-American dress with necklaces of hairpipe, dentalium, and beads and holds a beaded flat bag. Photograph by Frank Matsura, 1903–1913. bottom center, Colville buckskin gauntlets beaded in a floral design of red, green, and blue beads on a tan background. Collected by W.M. Manning before 1916. Colville flat bag beaded in a stylized floral motif in green, yellow, white, dark blue, and burgundy on a light blue background. Probably manufactured 1880–1910. Length of gauntlets 34 cm; length of bag, 33 cm. bottom right, Larry and Lorretta Finley, Lakes, wearing items of clothing inherited from their families. He wears a feather bustle, beaded gauntlets, hairpipe necklace, feather headdress, and holds a feather fan. She is wearing a cloth dress decorated with beads and cowrie shells and holds a beaded flat bag. Photograph by Sharon Eva Grainger, 1995.

246

braided or loose. Another style parted the hair front to back and pulled the front hair forward and knotted it above the brow, while a similar knot was made at the nape of the neck. Bangs were sometimes cut straight across the brow above the eyebrows and worn with the remaining hair hung loose (Teit 1900:224–227, 1930:236).

Women generally wore their hair parted and braided on either side of the head and tied together at the back, although some wore their hair loose or tied at the back (Teit 1900:225).

Special hairstyles were worn by warriors, young women, and girls and boys undergoing puberty rites. The practice of widows, widowers, and other mourners cutting their hair continued in the 1990s. Hair was often decorated with strands of beads, animals' tails or pieces of animal skin, hair ribbons, or long buckskin tongs to which were fastened pairs of feathers (Teit 1900:226–227, 1930:236). It was common among some Okanagan-Colville men in the early 1990s to wear their hair in long braids decorated with such hair ornaments.

Social Organization

Individual villages or clusters of villages, comprised of autonomous households linked to each other by kinship, exchange, association and geographical proximity, formed named communities or "bands" under the direction of a "chief" (known as *ilmíxʷm*). Village membership was highly flexible, and at the will of the individual, so some individuals could winter with one village and spend the summer with another, before choosing whether to return to their own winter camp. As individuals were permitted to sever ties when disagreements arose and gain full membership in another village, village composition constantly changed (Ray 1977:31). Those people who did not conform were ostracized; this was a common theme in Okanagan-Colville mythology.

The kinship system has been described as bilateral without lineages (Walters 1938; Anastasio 1972), but Ackerman (1994) suggests the existence of nonunilinear descent groups.

Within the Lakes area, Teit (1930:209–210) and Ray (1936:124–128) recorded at least 20 sites that were utilized as winter settlements. One early observer of a Lakes winter camp noted that the size of such villages ranged from one to six lodges, each containing two or more families (Work 1829). Lakes summer camps witnessed in the early 1800s were generally smaller, with a solitary family or the residents of two lodges traveling and harvesting resources together (Bouchard and Kennedy 1985).

Political Organization

The fluidity of village composition did not undermine a chief's authority in the community. His position was dependant upon the support of the villagers, but his function was to guide, arbitrate, and judge, roles that required influence and respect rather than absolute rule. A highly esteemed and generous chief attracted a large following, which increased the economic and political strength of a village.

Amer. Mus. of Nat. Hist., New York: top, 16/9670; center, 16/9561; bottom, 16/9562.
Fig. 7. Okanagan bark clothing. top, Poncho made of white clematis bark (*Clematis ligusticifolia*). Length 94 cm. center, Leggings made of sagebrush bark (*Artemisia tridentata*). Length 72 cm. bottom, Shoes or socks made of sagebrush bark. Length 31 cm. Collected by James A. Teit, Similkameen, B.C., 1904.

The chief was an inherited position with succession based generally on patrilineal descent, but the people were permitted to select any person of their choice if the qualifications of the deceased chief's son, brother, nephew, or even son-in-law were considered unworthy. Daughters and sisters were considered suitable candidates among the Lakes and Colville, both of whom have traditions of great women chiefs (Ray 1975, 2:143; Elmendorf 1935–1936; Ackerman 1982; Kennedy 1971–1991).

The chief regularly called councils, known as *səxʷkɬpaxám* ('those who think') to discuss major issues (Kennedy 1971–1991). Among the Lakes, these councils were comprised of a selected group identified by Elmendorf (1935–1936) as subchiefs, each appointed by their local group, and by Ray (1975, 2:147) as a group chosen by the chief himself, who met with him every evening during the winter. Present at these meetings among the Lakes was their totemic symbol—a pole with a mountain goat's head fastened on top (Elmendorf 1935–1936). No such formal council existed among the Colville, whose councils were open to all villagers, although a description of these councils among the Colville in the late 1880s suggests that it was predominantly men who attended (Miller 1990:107). With reference to the Northern Okanagan, D. Hudson (1990:71) noted that a council of elders was drawn from the community at large. Transgressions of individuals were brought before the chief at such meetings. Punishment was administered by an official "whipper" who, like the chief's speaker, acted on behalf of the headman. Parents would also call upon this whipper to discipline their children. This practice may not antedate the arrival of the fur traders and the priests (Teit 1930:282; Chance 1973:96–97; Miller 1990:107).

Carstens (1987) noted that the Northern Okanagan authority system involved an elaborate division of both labor and power. As Teit (1930:262) first proposed, the native classification appears to distinguish leadership that tended to be hereditary from that which was task-specific and open to all. The second category included leaders known as *xaʔtús*, identified commonly as "chiefs" (salmon chief, hunting chief) whose position was based on skill, knowledge, oratory, and often an appropriate guardian-spirit power. The term *xaʔtús* also referred to the head of a household who represented his family in village affairs (Kennedy 1971–1991).

Beginning in the 1830s, the political autonomy of the headmen and leaders was undermined, sometimes unwittingly, by the presence of fur traders, priests, and government officials, many of whom influenced the selection of chiefs or appointed their own. Fur trade managers at Fort Colville took on roles ordinarily deemed the authority of chiefs, including providing goods to indigents, receiving the first-caught salmon, and adjudicating disputes. At least by 1848, managers at Fort Colville were addressed as *ilmíxʷm* ('chief') (Chance 1973:95–96).

Differentiation in status distinguished the families of chiefs and other generous, morally upright individuals from those whose undisciplined habits and lack of spiritual aid and prestige resulted in their economically disadvantaged position. D. Hudson (1990:72) described families of low status as having "lost their history," suggesting that property included privately held knowledge, although this has not been confirmed elsewhere.

Kinship

Kinship was reckoned bilaterally, with males and females using different terms of address for mother, father, and grandparents, and assuming different forms of behavior toward them. In ego's generation the kinship terminology does not distinguish between siblings and cousins but does differentiate with respect to sex and to the relative age of the speaker. Marriage with cousins, including second cousins, was proscribed. Residence was usually patrilocal. Polygyny occurred among those who could afford it, with cowives generally occupying separate houses. Sororate and levirate marriages, along with marriages by betrothal, placing down of gifts, touching, and elopements were practiced (Teit 1930:287–288; Elmendorf 1935–1936; Bouchard, Pierre, and Louie 1973; D. Hudson 1986:454, 1990:75–78; Mattina 1987; Miller 1990:49–59; Carstens 1991:10–12). An extensive list of Okanagan-Colville kin terms is published in Mattina and Jack (1990:163–165).

Life Cycle

During and after pregnancy, the expectant woman observed restrictions regarding diet and behavior, whereas the father modified his activities for only the first 10 days after the birth. Avoidance of unpleasant sights, such as a human corpse, was especially important. For the last month of pregnancy the woman stayed in a birth hut where parturition was attended by midwives, and by a female shaman if the mother experienced difficulty.

The newborn child was bathed in cool water, wrapped in buckskin and for the first day fed only warm water. The afterbirth was burned or buried immediately. The baby's face was massaged daily to shape the nose and palate. For the first few months, a child spent most hours fastened to a cradleboard (fig. 3) (Teit 1930:278; Kennedy 1971–1991; Miller 1990:70–78).

After the mother and child had remained secluded in the birth hut for a month, they returned home and a feast was given at which the child received his first name, decided upon by the elderly relatives. Among the Northern Okanagan, a female baby was called "blanket" and presented with this gift, and a male baby was called by the name of the particular object he was given. These nicknames were retained until the child was about nine years old, at which time an ancestral name was bestowed upon the child at a feast accompanied with a giveaway of gifts (Kennedy 1971–1991). Sometimes Northern Okanagan girls received names of plants, and boys of animals (D. Hudson 1990:79). Colville babies were given ancestral names as infants and later in life took names referring to a war honor, spiritual power, or special feat (Miller 1990:74). Among the Lakes, young children were given nicknames or ancestral names and later named for some trait they exhibited (Elmendorf 1935–1936).

In former times, abortion was practiced, and herbal birth controls ensured that children were spaced well apart. Infanticide was practiced, although it was believed that bears raised abandoned children (Kennedy 1971–1991).

Prepubescent boys and girls were sent away from the village to a secluded site where they would train for guardian-spirit power *(sumíx),* which would appear in a vision. Training involved physical activity, a daily regime of sweathouse and bathing using special herbal rubs, and observation of the natural world. Each day the trainee marked his or her face with red paint or charcoal, and supplicated the dawn and sunset, asking for good luck. At night, they wandered to lonely parts of the hills where they danced and implored spirits to protect them. Eventually an animal, bird, or other creature appeared in a dream or vision and offered its protection and a song to the pubescent child. In connection with puberty training, some adolescents painted pictographs of their visions on boulders or rock faces, cut the images into the bark of trees, or burned them into the wood. The menarche for adolescent girls was observed by a seclusion in a menstrual hut during which time she used scratchers and drinking tubes. Her diet, activities, and association with males were severely restricted after this (Teit 1930:282–287; Kennedy 1971–1991; C.W. Wilson 1866:295; D. Hudson 1990:80; Miller 1990:78; Corner 1968).

Marriage was accompanied by an exchange of gifts between the parents of the young couple, but there was little ceremony. C.W. Wilson (1866:296) described how the wedding day was marked by a gathering of friends and relatives who smoked and wished the couple joy. A ritual last seen among the Colville in the early 1900s involved the young couple walking abreast under an arch of saplings while wishing for unity in their marriage (Kennedy 1971–1991).

At death, bodies were flexed, wrapped in mats or robes, and interred on their side in sandy places or talus slopes (fig. 8), which were then marked with a pile or circle of stones. A single long stick, or three if the deceased was a shaman, was erected at the head of the grave. In the early 1900s, canoes and effigies marked graves in the Similkameen area (Teit 1930:288; Bouchard 1966–1991; R.N. Atkinson 1952:5–12).

Ceremonies

Teit (1930:292) identified four main dances among the Northern Okanagan–Lakes–Colville: the guardian-spirit dance, the war dance, the scalp dance, and the religious dance. The first of these continued to be practiced in the early

1990s by about a dozen families. The guardian-spirit power that each Okanagan-Colville person acquired before puberty manifested itself and was announced publicly once the person was an adult. At that time the spirit helper again sang the power song and instructed its protege to hold a winter dance (also called a Chinook Dance or medicine dance) known as *snix^wám* 'take sickness and drop it down'. Sometimes the person experienced an illness diagnosed by a shaman as "spirit-sickness," for which the cure was to give a dance, sing the newly acquired spirit song, and distribute gifts.

Winter dances were held around January and continued until the snow half-disappeared from the mountains. The purpose of the dance was to cure illness, to express thanks for a successful year, and to ask the guardian spirits for protection and luck in the coming year. The singing of guardian-spirit songs was a central component of the ceremony. At one time a winter dance could last as much as two weeks; in the 1990s it consisted of a weekend. Dancing occurs from sunset until sunrise.

Shamans sponsored dances, or acted as masters of ceremony, assisted by the interpreter, the doorkeeper, and the host. These roles (Spier 1938:146–153) are essentially the same throughout the area. The focal point of the dance room is a partly peeled fir pole erected in the center of the room and said to symbolize the connection being made by the singers and shamans between the human and nonhuman worlds. Only these people touched the pole. Singers carried dance sticks and a symbol of their spirit helper. Once the house was ritually purified by sweeping, dancing and singing by those present was initiated after a singer grabbed hold of the pole and began to sing his spirit song and to dance. Other activities occurring at a winter dance included doctoring the sick, power contests between competing shamans, gambling, feasting, and distributing gifts said to be given by the guardian-spirit power (Spier 1938:141–157; Ray 1939:103; Lerman 1954; Pierre 1970).

Prior to the 1930s, Colville men who possessed a bird *sumíx* held three-day dances in late winter that were known as *sk^wca?núx^wəm* 'calling for south wind'. The purpose of these Chinook Dances was to bring rain and melt the snow (Kennedy 1971–1991; Spier 1938:146).

A few Colville men who had Bluejay power were said to transform into this bird at winter dances. Then naked, with his face painted black, the Bluejay would disappear from the dance house and "fly" about the country looking for lost objects. On his return, the people and the Bluejay spoke to one another "backward," using only terms having a reverse meaning (Spier 1938:162; Ray 1937:596–597).

The power seance called *sk̓tu?scút* 'cut oneself in two', during which a man who had ling fish for his guardian-spirit power "cut himself in two" by a cord around the waist, was performed by the Colville and Lakes. The ceremony took place at a winter dance and was used to forecast the outcome of raiding expeditions or other events, to locate lost people and articles, and to cure illness (Spier 1938:152; Miller 1990:130–135; Kennedy 1971–1991).

Fig. 8. Reburial. Charley Quintasket, Lakes Indian from the Colville Res., Wash., brushing out a grave with wild rose branches during a reburial ceremony. Skeletal remains were exposed by the water of Franklin D. Roosevelt Lake. Photograph by Dorothy Kennedy, Inchelium, Wash., 1978.

simply by touching the selected person was held in conjunction with the prayer dance.

Dances known as *sƛáyəm* were performed at Northern Okanagan social festivals. The dances and songs of the individual performers imitated the sounds of animals and birds. The dance was followed by a giveaway (Teit 1930:293; Kennedy 1971–1991).

In the 1990s, it was still common among the Northern Okanagan–Lakes–Colville to hold a giveaway of a deceased person's possessions immediately after a funeral, and to have subsequent giveaways if the family continued to be bothered by ghosts (Kennedy 1971–1991).

Illness and Witchcraft

These people classified illness by etiology; illnesses were caused either naturally or unnaturally. Natural or secular illnesses included headaches, colds, cuts, injuries from accidents and the like. Unnaturally induced ailments included: injuries inflicted by animate beings other than human; diffuse internal illnesses; afflictions of the mind caused by shamanistic action; spirit-illness; magical poisoning or sorcery. When therapy did not produce immediate results, an illness could be designated unnatural and a shaman was consulted for a diagnosis. Among the Northern Okanagan–Lakes–Colville in the 1980s, the greatest number of unnatural or prolonged illnesses were still considered to be caused by magical poisoning, called *pƚaχ*, practiced by women of postmenopausal age. The power of *pƚaχ* can be used to alter events for both good and evil ends. *pƚaχ* includes love medicine, good luck charms, and spells and curses that cause people to have bad luck or die (Spier 1938:162–165; Kennedy 1984).

History

Fur traders in 1811 representing the North West Company and the Pacific Fur Company (who amalgamated the following year) established depots among the Colville and Lakes. Fort Okanogan was established at the mouth of that river and exploration of the Okanagan drainage was undertaken, during which the traders encountered Northern Okanagan Indians. These same Natives occasionally visited Fort Kamloops, founded in 1812, to the northeast.

In a verbal agreement with the Kettle Falls chief and some of his followers, the Hudson's Bay Company acquired land at Kettle Falls and established Fort Colville in 1825 (Merk 1968:139). Indian people provided food, labor, and wives for the traders; the traders provided the Indians with iron tools, guns, clothes, and tobacco (Chance 1973).

Although the Indian people received some religious instruction from the fur traders, Christianity brought by missionaries began with the visit of two French-Canadian Roman Catholic priests in 1838 (R.H. Fleming 1940:xxviii). By

Preparatory to raiding enemy villages, warriors held dances in which they challenged one another to enlist. As special songs were sung, a blanket was taken around the camp and those who wished to go along grabbed hold of the blanket and joined in the singing. Later, fully armed and attired for fighting, the men performed a mock battle. The Northern Okanagan women performed their own war dance, while the men were away. On the return of the warriors, a Scalp Dance ("Music and Dance," fig. 7, this vol.) was held consisting of a procession and singing, followed by a dance similar to the war dance during which the men recounted their exploits. A feast often followed (Teit 1930:293; Ray 1939:48; Kennedy 1971–1991).

Teit (1900:352–353, 1930:292–293) described a "prayer dance" directed by one or two chiefs during which the assembled people danced in a circle and offered prayers to the "Chief Above." These dances were held to strengthen the bond between the living and the dead and to hasten the return of the souls of the departed (Teit 1909:604). A distribution of food followed this dance. The touching or marriage dance by which young people could choose a spouse

1845, a log chapel had been constructed at Kettle Falls and a Jesuit priest, Pierre Jean de Smet, conducted services among the Indians assembled at the fishery (de Smet 1905, 1:480–481). In 1859 French missionaries from the Oblates of Mary Immaculate settled among the Northern Okanagan (Thomson 1990:118–141).

After the Treaty of Washington in 1846 divided Okanagan territory, Indian people on both sides of the boundary experienced increasing White settlement upon their lands. Meetings to cede Indian land by treaty were interrupted by the tensions created by the steady influx of settlers and gold seekers. Although government representatives were appointed to teach farming and to supervise the activities of the Colville and Lakes, the Colville Reservation was not established until 1872. By 1880, fewer than half of the Indians assigned to the reservation had moved within its borders. Sahaptin- and Columbian-speaking peoples were also moved onto the reservation, and long-held animosities among these peoples surfaced. In an attempt to diffuse hostilities, a judicial council comprised of an Indian leader from each group was created in 1889. The north half of the reservation was ceded in 1891 and opened to settlement. In the early 1900s, people residing on the Colville Reservation were assigned individual allotments where they established farms. Many Colville men worked as loggers and wage laborers ("Reservations and Reserves," fig. 9, this vol.) (Bouchard and Kennedy 1984).

On the British side of the boundary, Indian reserves in Northern Okanagan territory marked out by the colonial government in 1861 were later diminished despite protestations from the Indians. Armed rebellion was seriously considered (Thomson 1978). In 1877–1878, Indian reserves with different boundaries were set aside for the Northern Okanagan and Similkameen Okanagan Indians. The process by which Northern Okanagan territory was lost to settlement, ranching, and mining has been discussed by Thomson (1985).

The Lakes were included among those assigned to the Colville Reservation, which was defined by executive order in 1872. However, some of the Lakes people continued to travel throughout the Arrow Lakes on a seasonal basis. At least one Lakes family continued to winter at the confluence of the Kootenay River with the Columbia, on a site that had been posted as an Indian reserve in 1861. Around 1920 this site was abandoned (W.G. Cox 1861; Teit 1912; Bouchard and Kennedy 1985).

In 1902, an Indian reserve near Oatscott on the west side of the Arrow Lakes was set aside by the Canadian government for a small, previously scattered group comprised mostly of Lakes people and known as the Arrow Lakes Band. Besides the settlement at the Kootenay River mouth, Oatscott was the only other Lakes community in British Columbia at this time. Yet few people resided at Oatscott; by the mid-1930s only one woman remained on the membership roll. When this woman died, Department of Indian Affairs officials concluded that the Arrow Lakes Band had become extinct. The Oatscott reserve in 1953 reverted to the province of British Columbia, becoming the first Indian reserve in British Columbia to revert to the Provincial Crown due to the "extinction" of an Indian Band. At this time, there were 257 people registered as Lakes Indians who were living on the Colville Indian Reservation in the United States (Bouchard and Kennedy 1985). Attempts to reclaim the Lakes ancestral homeland were initiated in the late 1980s by Native Americans and Canadians of Lakes descent.

Synonymy

The Northern Okanagan have no name to distinguish themselves from others living along the Okanagan River drainage. The term *ukʷnaqínx* refers to all those Indian people living along the Okanagan River drainage from Vernon in the north to Brewster in the south, an area encompassing Northern Okanagan and Southern Okanogan. The term *ukʷnaqín* (anglicized as "Okanagan") identifies the ancestral home site, although there is little agreement on its location (cf. Dawson 1892:6; Teit 1930:198–199, 264; Spier 1938:73; Curtis 1907–1930, 7:65).

The term *sxʷəyíʔɬp*, taken from the name of the Indians who formerly lived in the vicinity of Kettle Falls, is used to identify the Colville. *sxʷəyíʔɬp* first appears in the 1804–1806 journals of the Lewis and Clark expedition where it is transcribed as Whe-el-po (Thwaites 1904–1905, 6:119). Variant historical spellings include Ilthkoyape, Quiarlpi, Isnihoyelps, Shuyelpi, Chualpays, Schwoyelpi, Swi-el-pree, Squeer-yer-pe, Skoyelpi, Sweielpa, Suj-el-pa, Sgoielpi, Skuyelpi, Sohhweihlp, Sxoēʹlpix, Sxuiēʹylpix, Sxweiʹlpᴱx, and Sxoieʹlpᵘ. The *sxʷəyíʔɬp* were also identified historically by the French term, Les Chaudières, because of the presence of kettlelike depressions in the rocks at Kettle Falls.

The name of the *snꞓayckstx* ('Dolly Varden char people') or Lakes Indians appears historically as Sinachicks, Snaichksti, Sinuitskistux, Sen-i-jex-tee, Senijextee, Sínūaʹitsktŭk, Snaiʹtcᴱkst, Snraiʹtcᴱkstᴱx, Snāiʹ.tcᴱkstᴱx, Snaiʹtckstkᵘ, and Sinaitsks15ˣ. Early historical sources also refer to them as the Columbia Lake Indians.

The term *ukʷnaqín* (Okanagan or Okanogan) appears first in 1811 as Oakinacken (Ross 1849:289). Subsequent spellings from various sources include Teek-a-nog-gan, Okanăkans, Ookanawgan, Okiakanes, Okinakanes, Okinagenes, Okanāʹqēn and WEkanaqaʹn.

The term *smlqamíx* (Similkameen) was first transcribed in 1811 by Ross (1849:289) as Sa-milk-a-nuigh. Variant transcriptions include Schimilicameachs, Shmel-a-ko-mikh, Schimilacameachs, Si-mi-lacamichs, Milkᴱmaxiʹtᵘk, Milakitekwa, and Smᴇlêk̲amux̲.

Sources

In addition to the journals that record non-Indians' first encounters with the Northern Okanagan–Lakes–Colville, *251* beginning in 1811 (Thompson 1962; Cox 1831; Ross 1855), detailed information from the 1820s onward appears in the records of the Hudson's Bay Company (Work 1829, 1830; Merk 1968). Dating from the mid-1800s are accounts by Kane (1859), whose sketches (in Harper 1971) of the Colville and Lakes are particularly valuable (MacLaren 1989). Wilkes (1845, 4), Gibbs (1855), and C.W. Wilson (1866, 1970) describe Indian culture and provide census data from the 1840s–1850s. Descriptions of Lakes and Northern Okanagan Indians are found in several exploring journals of the mid-1860s (British Columbia 1866, 1869).

Ethnohistorical studies have been undertaken by Chance (1973, 1986), Turnbull (1977), and Bouchard and Kennedy (1984, 1985, 1985b) on the Colville and Lakes, and by Thomson (1978, 1985, 1990), and Dolby (1973) on the Northern Okanagan. Carstens (1991) and Christie and de Pfyffer (1990) document the social history of the Northern Okanagan.

Teit (1910–1913, 1930) provides the most comprehensive ethnographic source on Okanagan-Colville although his work focuses on the western divisions and often describes Okanagan culture in relation to that of the Thompson. Several of the papers edited by Spier (1938) contain data pertaining to Colville and Northern Okanagan. Brief descriptions of the Okanagan-Colville are contained in Curtis (1907–1930, 7) and Hill-Tout (1911). Overviews of Northern Okanagan compiled by D. Hudson (1986, 1990) are based mostly on earlier ethnographies but do contain some data he elicited around 1980. Popular accounts of the Colville have been published by Yanan (1971) and Chance (1986). Lerman's work among the Okanagan, apart from a report on the winter dance (1954), remains in his field notes (1952–1954). Data pertaining to the Similkameen Okanagan can be found in Allison (1892, 1900). Ray's (1931–1944, 1933, 1936, 1936a, 1937, 1939, 1954, 1975, 1977) extensive research, beginning in the late 1920s, included Colville and Lakes, in addition to his better-known Sanpoil-Nespelem work. The most complete studies on the Lakes (Elmendorf 1935–1936; Ray 1931–1944; Bouchard and Kennedy 1985) remain unpublished, although a popular account of the Lakes (Wynecoop and Clark 1985) is in print.

Hines (1976) and Miller (1990) have edited the work of a Colville writer, Mourning Dove (Christine Quintasket).

Collections of Okanagan-Colville mythology, some of which include Native language texts, have been compiled (Hill-Tout 1911; Teit 1917; Gould 1917; Mourning Dove 1933; Ray 1933a; Shuttleworth 1936–1938; Yanan 1971; Bouchard 1966–1991, 1978; Mattina 1985; Robinson and Wickwire 1989). Flynn (1976) and Jilek and Jilek-Aall (1974:143–149) have analyzed unpublished Okanagan-Colville mythology in English translation, as compiled by Bouchard (1966–1970).

Topical studies include: Ackerman (1982) and Carstens (1987) on leadership; Turner, Bouchard, and Kennedy (1980) and Gabriel (1954) on ethnobotany; Bouchard and Kennedy (1984, 1984a, 1985, 1985b) on place-names and land use and occupancy; Kennedy (1984) and Watkins (1970) on witchcraft and Indian health care; Kennedy and Bouchard (1975a) on Colville fishing; Wickwire (1978, 1982) on music; Schultz (1968, 1971) and Schultz and Walker (1967) on religion; R.N. Atkinson (1952) on burials; Verma (1954) on Northern Okanagan economics and land use; J.A. Ross (1968), Hirabayashi (1954), and Lahren and Schultz (1973) on factionalism; and May (1969) on termination of the Colville Reservation.

Linguistic research among the Okanagan-Colville, including the compiling of word lists, texts, dictionaries, grammars, and pedagogical materials has been undertaken (Gibbs 1877:248–264; Gatschet 1885; Boas 1900; Le Jeune 1897a; Teit 1908; Watkins 1971, 1971a; Bouchard 1966–1991; Bouchard and Pierre 1973; Bouchard, Pierre, and Louie 1973; Mattina 1973, 1985, 1987; Mattina and Jack 1990; Somday 1980; Doak 1983).

Historical data concerning the Northern Okanagan and Lakes can be found in the records of the Department of Indian Affairs (Record Group 10) held by the National Archives of Canada, Ottawa. Data on the Colville and Lakes is found in Bureau of Indian Affairs records (RG 75) and documents compiled during the Indian Claims Commission (RG 297), held by the National Archives of the United States, Washington, D.C., and Seattle.

Middle Columbia River Salishans

JAY MILLER

The Middle Columbia River Salishans (ˈsālĭshənz) lived traditionally along the middle Columbia River in northwestern Washington. Their population has been concentrated on the Colville Reservation since the nineteenth century. The component peoples of this regional grouping are the Sinkayuse (ˈsĭŋkuˌyo͞os), Wenatchee (wəˈnăchē), Entiat (ˈăntēˌăt), Chelan (shəˈlăn), Methow (ˈmetˌhäw), Southern Okanogan (ˌōkəˈnägən), Nespelem (nesˈpēləm, nezˈpēləm), and Sanpoil (ˌsănpōˈĭl).

These groups were settled along the Columbia River (fig. 1) and, except for the Sinkayuse, also along its western or northern tributaries, which drain the eastern slopes of the Cascades and the area north of the Big Bend. The Sinkayuse (or Columbias) were east and south of the Big Bend. Their main village was at the mouth of Rock Island Creek, and their resource domain was transected by Grand Coulee, Moses Coulee, Moses Lake, and the Potholes region. There were distinct subgroups at Quilomene Bar on the southwest, where a separate subdialect was spoken (the Quilomene band, *sn̓q̓ʷəlq̓ʷəlmínəxʷ*), and at Creston in the northeast. The central location of their territory and the siting of their winter villages along its borders put them in contact with all the other Middle Columbia River Salishans.

The Southern Okanogan in the United States (or River Okanogan) and the Northern Okanagan in Canada (the Lake Okanagan) constitute a single people that was divided by the international boundary (Spier 1938).

The Sinkayuse came to be known as the Moses-Columbias after their famous nineteenth-century chief. After settlement on the Colville Reservation the name Moses-Columbian or Moses came to be used for the Wenatchee and Entiat as well.

Languages

Two closely related Interior Salish languages are spoken, in several dialects, by the Middle Columbia River Salishans. Columbian* (*nxaʔamxcín* 'the language of the people here') is the language of the downriver bands, the Sinkayuse, Wenatchee, Entiat, and Chelan (Kinkade 1981). Okanagan (Okanagan-Colville; *nsilәxcín*) is spoken upriver by the Methow, Southern Okanogan, Nespelem, and Sanpoil (Mattina 1973, 1987). Okanagan is also the language of the peoples immediately to the north, who are treated in the chapter "Northern Okanagan, Lakes, and Colville."

Territory and Identity

Downriver Middle Columbia River groups have not often been distinguished. Curtis (1907–1930, 7), for example, separated only the Moses-Columbia and Peskwaws (Wenatchee), which included Entiat and Chelan. Ray (1936, 1939) noted Columbia, Peskwaws, and Chelan but not Entiat until later (Ray 1974; A.H. Smith 1983).

Methow occupied an intermediate status between these two chains, but historically was becoming more like those upriver. Some Methows insist that their language was once much more distinct from either chain.

The boundary between Nespelem and Sanpoil was Swawilla Basin and the highlands that included Buffalo Lake. During the unsettling times after 1800, many Sinkayuse, including members of the Split Sun family, moved and married into the remote Sanpoil valley for their own safety.

External Relations

Because the Sinkayuse network was so extensive, they had access eastward and involvement with Flathead and Sahaptians. After acquiring horses, they led bison hunts onto the Plains, which encouraged the development of a confederacy of Middle Columbia tribes under the leadership of the family of Split Sun (*sə̀q̓tatk̓ʷúsm*, also known as Half Sun and Shooktalkoosum) (Curtis 1907–1930, 7:67; Ray 1960; Ruby and Brown 1965). Salishans living along the rivers draining the western Cascades developed trade and marriage networks with Coast Salish, such as between the Skagit (Southern Coast Salish) and the Chelan. Their hunting of mountain goats and other alpine mammals was important for the regional trade. The Wenatchee traded through formal partners with Kittitas and Snoqualmie

*The phonemes of Columbian are: (voiceless stops and affricates) *p, t, c, c̣, k, kʷ, q, qʷ, ʔ*; (glottalized stops and affricates) *p̓, t̓, c̓, ƛ̓, k̓, k̓ʷ, q̓, q̓ʷ*; (voiceless fricatives) *s, ṣ, ł, x, xʷ, x̣, x̣ʷ, ḥ, ḥʷ, h*; (resonants) *m, n, r* (tap), *y, l, ḷ, w, ʕ* (pharyngeal glide), *ʕʷ*; (glottalized resonants) *m̓, n̓, r̓, y̓, l̓, ḷ̓, w̓, ʕ̓, ʕ̓ʷ*; (plain vowels) *i, a, ə, u*; (retracted vowels) *ị, ạ, ə̣, ụ*; (stress) v́.

This orthography is the one used by Kinkade (1981, 1991). Columbian names and words cited in italics have been spelled in this orthography by M. Dale Kinkade (communications to editors 1996, 1997). Okanagan names are from Kinkade and Anthony Mattina (communications to editors 1997).

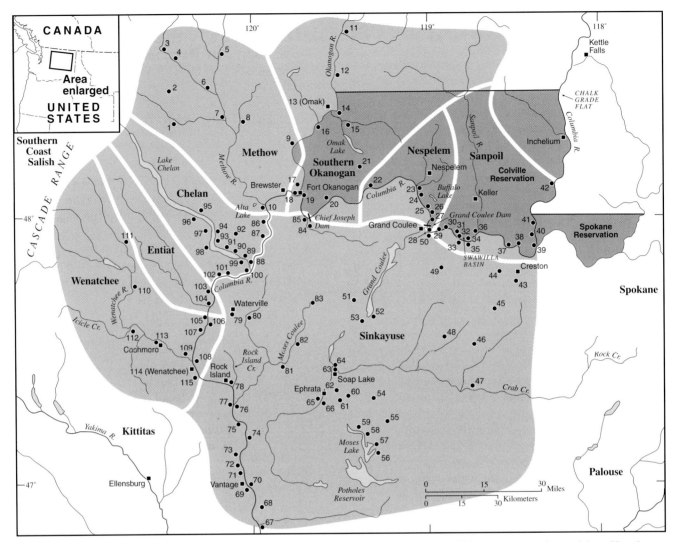

Fig. 1. Territory and settlements of the Middle Columbia River Salishan peoples in the 19th century, with 20th-century reservations and dams. Nespelem and Sanpoil data are from Ray (1936), with phonemic transcriptions from Anthony Mattina (personal communication 1997). The data from other groups were compiled with the assistance of M. Dale Kinkade (personal communication 1997; communication to editors 1997), incorporating information from Spier (1938) and Ray (1975), with phonemic transcriptions by Kinkade. Transcriptions from Ray that could not be phonemicized are in roman, slightly normalized; translations that could not be confirmed by analysis are queried.

Okanagan-speaking groups. Methow: 1, *ntqʷláks*; 2, *k̓aʔsálqn* 'two peaks'; 3, *nkʷaʔttánk* 'water on cliff' (?); 4, *nᶾəᶾəqʷús* 'brush next to bank'; 5, *cwáx* 'creek'; 6, *stx̣ʷiyyáp*; 7, *tx̣ʷə́čp*; 8, *łčəpčəpús*; 9, *sləxʷíʔst(m)* 'bluff with holes'; 10, *nx̣ə́ncin* 'bluff at the mouth of the river'. Southern Okanogan: 11, *q̓ʷax̣ʷlús* 'smoke across the face'; 12, *qəqčús*; 13, *tuʔtána*; 14, *nstpičaʔ(m)* 'bison robes'; 15, *skʷə́nt* 'falls'; 16, *q̓ʷúnq̓ʷuntp*; 17, *scəx̣ʷčixʷátxʷ* 'osprey house'; 18, *tk̓ʷráʔtm* 'yellow rock'; 19, *nx̣x̣áʔx̣aʔm* (?) 'flower smell'; 20, *qəlácmn* 'big rapids'; 21, *katár̓* 'rows on it'. Nespelem: 22, *nəkuktʼsíptin*; 23, *nspílm* 'prairie'; 24, *x̣aˤmísxn* 'brow of the hill'; 25, *səlx̣ʷaʔxwił* 'big trail'; 26, *sk̓x̣ʷítxʷ*; 27, *m̓əsm̓əsálimxw*; 28, *k̓əłʔamcin* 'opposite the coulee'. Sanpoil: 29, *ntx̣ʷítk* 'deep spring'; 30, *wəlʼwəláskin* 'solid rocks'; 31, *sék̓čiksxən̓* 'rough rock'; 32, *n̓ʔák̓ʷ* 'across the creek' (?); 33, *x̣əx̣súlaʔx̣ʷ* 'level ground'; 34, *kłp̓əsp̓ústən* 'ryegrass place'; 35, *səẏámtk* 'the wind roars against the cliff'; 36, *snpᶜʷílx* 'gray as far as one can see'; 37, *x̣láʌst* 'mountains at the edge of the river'; 38, *nx̣ʷúx̣ʷəˤʷus* 'deep eyes'; 39, *snqílt* 'above the rapids'; 40, *xʷaʔłćám* 'many bones'; 41, *npúx̣ʷsiẏaʔm* 'water splashing on the grass'; 42 *tkʷk̓ʷar̓k̓ʷr̓xnm*.

Columbian-speaking groups. Sinkayuse: 43, *tk̓ʷəliʌxtn̓* 'place where elk lie to dry their horns'; 44, swá'xwanikáłpu; 45, t'sitso'yiq̓ǎn; 46, katskatskúlu 'red land'; 47, skwkwəlátuku; 48, kenwáqi 'traveling afoot'; 49, ntomataíqu; 50, *n̓q̓aʔq̓aʔáẃs* 'middle one' (Sanpoil name for Sinkayuse site); 51, name not recorded; 52, *sx̣astátkʷaʔqn* 'pepper-grass place'; 53, name not recorded; 54, qasiáiyatpám 'serviceberry flat'; 55, qatqowáus 'dip in the ground' (?); 56, ta'aɣasik 'turtle place'; 57, nqiẏx̣ʷátkʷ 'stinking water'; 58, siálilaqən 'spring' (?); 59, squɣátqu 'narrow channel' (?); 60, *nipałníwt* 'rock on the hillside'; 61, kláx̣áwas 'rocks in a pile'; 62, name not recorded; 63, name not recorded; 64, *kłk̓áxʷaʔst*; 65, *ntx̣tx̣áẏłpm* 'cottonwood place'; 66, name not recorded; 67, loqástən; 68, nímuqwást; 69, qátqat; 70, qǎmuqwátu 'muskrat den that never washes away' (?); 71, npaqnít; 72, qwílqwinátku; 73, *sn̓q̓ʷələq̓ʷəlmín* 'place of roasting spits'; 74, nxəlʼkúxlʼku 'cove in the hills' (?); 75, *tapísqn*; 76, nłǎ́qʼlaus; 77, *n̓q̓ʷuláqaʔəm* 'raven place'; 78, *kwáxcən* 'river edge'; 79, *səlẏaʔ* 'round top'; 80, qwǎtstǎ́ʔp; 81, skiǎk̓ǎmapást 'cliff bottom' (?); 82, *cqəmapáʔst*; 83, name not recorded; 84, name not recorded; 85, *spək̓ʷpək̓ʷmín* 'water over the rocks'. Chelan: 86, nayárp; 87, *kałók* 'brush on the flat'; 88, *sx̣átkʷ* 'water pouring out' (?); 89, *scúpaʔst* 'shale rock'; 90, *k̓łćə́m̓* 'narrow land'; 91, piʔpiʔkúʌəxʷ 'sunflowerlike-plant land'; 92, *naq̓ʷáṣt* 'deep water'; 93, qatqʼát 'long narrow flat' (?); 94, *k̓ʷəx̣ʷcín* 'pine tree'; 95, *ləq̓ʷcín* (?) 'broken nose of mountain'; 96, *sq̓ʷətn̓ałʔítxʷ* 'big creek' (?); 97, *nləq̓ʷpánk* 'rock wall breaks off'; 98, name not recorded; 99, name not recorded (village of chief *yənmusíčaʔ* 'lightning robe'); 100, *nax̣ólq̓*; 101, *niʔyáłqn̓* 'basin where creek meanders'; 102, *q̓ʷíyq̓ʷiyt* 'greener place'. Entiat: 103, *swahəmà(ł)x̣x̣əʌcín̓tn* 'barking dog'; 104, *nᶾiyátk* 'grassy water'. Wenatchee: 105, swaxčiłtǎ́ʼn 'horse haven'; 106, xaxátqw; 107, *p̓əʌknúʌəxʷ*; 108, stóxpas; 109, *nk̓əmcin* 'place at the mouth'; 110, *cwáx* 'creek'; 111, ccẃáxaʔ 'small creek'; 112, *scə́m̓áẃs* 'narrow in the middle'; 113, *nᶾəẃáck̓m*; 114, *niʔsk̓ʷiʔk̓ʷiẏáʔst* 'rocks scattered all over'; 115, *skʷəʌtakʷcín* 'warm shore'.

254

MILLER

(Southern Coast Salish). Raiding for horses and hostilities with Plains tribes like the Blackfoot encouraged a warrior ethic among these tribes, although pacifism was a strong ethic among Plateau Salishans. Gender equality also remained important (Ray 1933:25, 115; Ackerman 1996; Klein and Ackerman 1995).

In addition to fishing their own rivers, Plateau people gathered at major fisheries in season, each drainage under the control of a salmon priest. Huge numbers gathered at Kettle Falls, the prime Salishan emporium, managed by the resident Colvilles before it was flooded behind Grand Coulee Dam in 1940. Sinkayuse, Nez Perce, and Palouse fished, traded, and dug roots in Spokane territory, while Nespelem and Sanpoil dug across the Columbia River in the Big Bend. The Wenatchee had a major fishery at the junction of Icicle Creek and the Wenatchee River, where thousands gathered. Members of the downriver chain also went to the prime Sahaptian fishery at The Dalles and Celilo Falls.

When travel became more extensive after the introduction of horses (Ray 1933:117), features of equestrian Plains culture were adopted: new leather clothing styles, pack and riding saddles, horsehair bridles, stirrups, the tepee, and travois. Skin bags replaced coiled baskets.

Trade centers for the region were located at Soap Lake, Waterville, the mouths of the Wenatchee River and Icicle Creek during the June salmon run, and The Dalles (Ray 1933:116), along with Kettle Falls and modern Brewster (mouth of the Okanogan River). Shells from the coast were traded through the Chelan, with the inland tribes trading tanned buckskins, dried roots, and, in particular, furs.

The Wenatchee formal trading partnerships (*sc̓úq̓ʷiʔ*) were passed on to family members in every generation. A man could only trade with his partner, and thus scheduled his visit during large gatherings when he could be sure the partner would be there (Spier 1938:75). In October, Wenatchees went to the mouth of the Okanogan to fish and trade with local friends.

Once the Wenatchee had horses, the earlier trade in pipes, tobacco, hemp, dressed skins, and bows also included more bulky items such as ground root cakes, dried berries, and buffalo robes (Teit 1928:121).

Culture

Subsistence

Access to the Cascade Mountains made mountain goat hunting an important specialty of the Wenatchee, Entiat, and Chelan. The wool, along with dried goat meat, was traded as pelts or woven into blankets (Teit 1928:113). Strips of white fur were used to lure the goats close to the hunter. The slain goat was treated with great respect. The head was sprinkled with bird down and roasted (Ray 1942:element 1236).

As the various root crops were ready for harvest, family groups left the village, giving the winter village leader the location where they would set up camp. Staple plant foods were camas bulbs and bitterroots (also called rock rose). A first food rite was held whenever a fresh species of plant or animal was ready to harvest (Ray 1933:97, 99).

Throughout the year, other plant foods included parts of balsam, avalanche lily corms, prickly pear fruits, sunflower seeds, sweet coltsfoot petioles, pine nuts, hazel nuts, mints, and pine lichen (locally called moss), which was roasted in a pit with wild onions and camas (fig. 2) (Ray 1933:103). Fall foods included serviceberries, huckleberries, blackberries, elderberries, and chokecherries (Ray 1933:101), which were used to make a pemmican mixed with salmon flour.

At the root grounds, each woman daily dug up over half an acre for roots. A senior woman led each group, planning and coordinating their overall movements. In the evening, the roots were skinned, cleaned, and sorted. Meanwhile, men visited, scouted, and hunted to supply meat, while also preparing for the fishing season. At the end of the harvest, the bags of dried roots were taken to winter camps for storage before most people moved on to fishing camps.

May through August was and is the fishing season. While sturgeon and some small fish were always available, it was the runs of anadramous salmon and trout that provided the Plateau staple (Ray 1933:28). As an indication of the importance of this food, the first salmon rite lasted five days.

Five salmon species appeared in this region during May to November runs. In the Columbia these were chinook, averaging 32 pounds with a few of 100 pounds, during a run of May through July; coho; pink; and chum. Sockeye, which spawn in lakes, ran in the Wenatchee and Okanogan rivers. Steelhead trout, weighing 10 to 15 pounds, ran from March to July. The fall runs of both coho and chum, from September to November, provided a less productive last harvest. Both species weighed about 6 pounds (Ray 1933:57). Fall water levels were low so cohos were speared or seined from canoes. Lake Chelan had a small landlocked coho salmon. Pinks were obtained mostly in trade since this species was more common on the coast.

Fishing technology utilized weirs ("Fishing," fig. 6, this vol.), funnel traps, basket traps, and elevated traps ("Fishing," fig. 8, this vol.) (Ray 1933:61). If the trap had few fish, the "salmon tyee" (salmon priest, Okanagan *xaʔtús* 'task leader') in charge of the fishing wrapped himself in a robe and prayed at the trap all night. Men caught and hauled all the fish, while women prepared each one for sun drying. At the end of the season, people visited upriver to collect the last spawning fish. Menstruating women stayed well away from the water and salmon because of a belief that menstruation odors repelled the fish.

Aside from traps, men used spears and nets, particularly at Columbia River rapids where fish had to move through a narrow passage. In some places, artificial channels were made, generally as three parallel trenches along the shore to allow for the rise and fall of water level. Children collected

Fig. 2. Collecting and preparing black tree lichen (*Bryoria fremontii*). top left, Cecelia Pichette, Sanpoil, harvesting the lichen from ponderosa and lodgepole pine trees in the late summer, using a long stick with a forked end. top center, Nettie Francis, Sanpoil, arranging hot rocks in a pit. top right, Women tending a small fire that has burned all night on top of the covered pit while the food cooks. center left, Francis shoveling away the remains of the fire and uncovering the pit while Pichette watches. center right, Women removing the damp, pungent ryegrass from the pit after the cooking has been completed. bottom left, Exposing the cotton cloth covering the sacks of lichen. bottom right, Uncovering the cooked lichen, which now resembles black jelly, to cool it. Photographs by Dorothy Kennedy, Colville Res., Wash., 1979.

white rocks to line the trench bottoms to aid visibility. Salmon were taken with a spear from a triangular scaffold supported by pole tripods built at either end of the trench and braced against the shore. Along some riverbanks, more elaborate fish platforms were built, owned by the whole fishing camp, but used by only one man at a time.

Nets were only used in murky or rough water, unless the nettle fibers could be dyed to match water conditions. Seines were used for chum and coho, while dip nets, for salmon and suckers, had a small mesh spread between handles. For eels and small fish, willow dip nets were made two feet wide and one foot deep. While Ray (1933:69) suggested that seining technology was borrowed from the Pacific coast, Sinkayuse believe that it was given to humans by supernatural Spider people who lived near modern Vantage, Washington. Indeed, Columbian ʔáxʷin means both web and seine.

Other significant water resources were sturgeon, suckers, eels, trouts, and roe. One technique for taking sturgeon involved killing a mountain goat on the cliffs above the Columbia River, letting it fall into the shallows, and spearing the fish that came to feed.

In late summer, some people moved from the river fisheries into the mountains for fall hunting, berrying, and the digging of late roots. A few families might stay in the hills for the winter, tending a trap line, but most other families moved to winter locations near firewood, water, and shelter against deep snow or brisk winds.

Hunting occupied the fall and winter. Deer were taken from November to March, along with some elk. Communal hunts were the most productive. Prior to leaving, hunters entered the sweatlodge morning and evening for 10 days to remove body odors offensive to deer. They sang and prayed for success. They also practiced ritual sexual continence, particularly the hunt leader.

During the day, weapons and gear were prepared or repaired. Each hunter carried clothes, snowshoes, and packs with mats for a hut, robes for bedding, and only a snack because hunters expected to eat freshly killed game. For longer hunts, women went along to keep camp, sleeping separately from men in the same huts.

The leader coordinated all activities and assigned all tasks, appointing drivers to chase game toward the hunters waiting at the end of a canyon or draw. The Sanpoil and perhaps the Sinkayuse conducted communal antelope drives.

Deer were also driven into the Columbia River by trained dogs and killed. Such dogs were guided by their owner using special gestures and calls. Individual deer were taken at a watering spot or a salt lick, using a blind, or along a game trail (Ray 1933:82).

A slain deer was carried into the house through the back and placed on a special bed of fir boughs to be welcomed by family and friends (Miller 1990:114–122). The animal was then ritually butchered in a precise way (Ray 1933:91), as a special prayer of thanks was said as each cut was made. The meat was divided evenly among everyone in camp, but the hide belonged to the hunter who made the kill. Women, as always, dressed and tanned the hides of deer, elk, antelope, and buffalo.

Along with Spokane, Flathead, and others, Sinkayuse went to hunt bison on the northern Plains under the leadership of Split Sun.

When everyone returned to the winter village, a special feast was held for the elderly, with the young excluded, consisting of stewed hoofs, lower leg muscles, head, and lungs (Ray 1933:92).

Black and grizzly bears were hunted for their hides, but the meat had a strong taste and was eaten only as a matter of personal preference. Bear and deer meat was sometimes baked in an earth oven. Wenatchee used special poisoned arrows to hunt grizzlies.

In addition to spears or bows and arrows, hunters also used traps, deadfalls, and snares set over game trails (Ray 1933:85) for mink, fisher, marten, badger, otter, fox, lynx, wildcat, cougar, coyote, and wolf. Shellfish was used as bait for otters, beavers, and muskrats. Snares were set for grouse, coyote, lynx, wildcat, and some deer (Ray 1933:86).

People did not eat coyote, mink, wolf, land otter, buzzard, raven, crow, eagle, snakes, gopher, mouse, wood rat, frogs, dog, insects, the heart of a fool hen, or deer eyes (Ray 1942: elements 1350–1375). Women were specifically forbidden to eat deer kidneys and deer blood (Ray 1933:90), presumably to avoid excessively bloody discharges during menstruation. Famine foods included rose hips, hides, and tree-cached fish and game bones previously left as offerings (Ray 1933:107).

A strong ethic of sharing applied to all fish and meat (Ray 1933:26) produced by men and by women according to their mutual division of labor (Ray 1933:33).

Technology

Considerable time was spent in the production of hemp cordage (Ray 1933:44), which had a great variety of uses, including weaving into tumplines (Ray 1933:120). Tule rushes (Ray 1933:38) were sewn into mats for bedding, corpse shroud, housing, table runners, and berry drying. A willow shoot mat was made for drying salmon. Cedar roots, often traded from the Methow, were formed into coiled baskets, decorated in simple bands and triangles. Baskets served as containers for water, berries, and other foods ("Basketry," fig. 8, this vol.), as cups, and as cooking vessels. Flat twined storage bags of bast, tule, or cattails were decorated by weaving in colored fibers dyed yellow from the inner bark of Oregon grape or blue from huckleberries, along with natural browns and blacks. Berry and root baskets were also made from the bark of birch (fig. 3), cottonwood, or pine (Ray 1933:37). Tightly twisted sagebrush bark served as a slow match for transporting fire. Rushes and bark were used for torches during night fishing.

257

Basalt or granite were pecked and ground into pestles and hammers; flint was chipped into knives, points, drills, gravers (Ray 1933:35). Arrowpoints might be further baked, hung in a sweatlodge, or soaked in rose branch water to increase their efficacy. Pipes were made from polished soapstone (Ray 1933:40). Dense rocks were used as sweatlodge stones, and flat lap stones provided a handy work surface (Ray 1933:90). Granite schist, particularly from Kettle Falls, made excellent hide scrapers (Ray 1933:95).

Log mortars with a rawhide lining were used with hardwood or stone pestles to make flour of salmon, venison, and sunflowers. Carved sticks served as handles and were bound together as fan-shaped combs (fig. 4) (Ray 1933:54). Dishes, spoons, forks, and firepokers were made from wood. Individual spoons were used at feasts, but at home meals a family shared a single one. Log mauls were cut with a handy branch to serve as the handle. A fire drill of pine was rotated over a base hearth of jack pine. Tinder was dried grass or antelope brush. Driftwood provided firewood, although a dense root was used to keep the banked fire going overnight. Long mat needles were carved from sticks, as were fire and cooking tongs (Ray 1933:44). The largest wooden artifacts were canoes (fig. 4) (Ray 1933:122) or rafts. Snowshoes (Ray 1933:120) were made by men from maple, and dibbles (digging sticks) by women, who pointed and smoothed a slightly curved hardwood stick and added a wood or horn handle. Three types of bows—sinew-backed, stave, and elk-rib—were used (Ray 1933:87). Salmon skin or deer-hoof glue was used to attach the deer leg sinews (Ray 1933:88). Bowstrings were made of hemp or deer back sinews. Arrow shafts were straightened and smoothed

before three feather vanes were added. Wooden blocks served as net spacers or gauges (Ray 1942:327).

Pelts, hides, and skins served for bedding, clothing, and robes (Ray 1933:35). An eight-foot packstrap or tumpline was made entirely of buckskin or had a bearskin center piece. Quivers were made of coyote or buck deer pelts (Ray 1933:89). Parfleches, borrowed from the Plains, were made from buffalo or deer hides (Ray 1933:44). Mountain goat wool was woven into blankets (Ray 1942: element 3032).

Pointed bones served as awls. Spoons were steamed and shaped from buffalo, mountain goat, and antelope horns. Elk horn and bone provided wedges and dibble handles. Smaller deer bones became needles and hooks, while deer ribs served as scrapers (Ray 1933:95). Mountain sheep horn was steamed and molded into a bow.

Freshwater clamshells served as spoons, and colored shells were used as counters in games. Abalone and other large shells were traded from the coast.

Structures

Ancient semisubterranean pit houses were replaced in historic times by mat houses, used both winter and summer, because less labor was required among the decimated population. Menstrual lodges, sweatlodges, and camping huts of mats or skin tepees were also built (Ray 1933:31).

Distinctive of the Wenatchee, their towns included a special weaving house, built over a pit two feet deep and entered through a roof hatchway, where women spent the day making coiled baskets and goat wool textiles (Spier

Fig. 3. Camp and household equipment. left, Methow family of Chilliwhist Jim at their camp. Metal buckets and pans have replaced tule and bark containers. Photograph possibly by Paul Standar, about 1920s. top right, Southern Okanogan tule round bag made by Lucy Joe. bottom right, Southern Okanogan birchbark container with rawhide and rope handles. Both collected by Leslie Spier, Colville Res., Wash., 1930. Height of top 34 cm; bottom, 53 cm.

1938:124). These specialized weavings were important trade items.

The pit house, a circular pit about 10 to 16 feet wide and four to six feet deep, had either a flat roof or a conical one with a center post and pole stringers set two feet apart along the edge. The roof was covered, in turn, by layers of driftwood planks, if available, or by willow mats, a six-inch layer of grass or brush, and an outer covering of dirt removed from the pit excavation, sometimes plastered with clay as waterproofing. Entry was by a hatchway, which also served as smokehole. A log ladder rested near the central fire. During storms, the roof hole was covered with a mat.

Wenatchees built a pit house over a square pit, a supplementary form shared with the Southern Okanogan and the Kittitas.

The best-known winter dwelling has been the gabled, communal longhouse (fig. 5). The frame was a peaked or inverted V with rounded ends, about 16 feet wide by 20–60 feet long, capable of holding two to eight families. The framework consisted of crossed poles, tied at the top, with parallel side poles tied three feet apart along the sides. The ends were formed by leaning poles against the frame, like a half tepee held in place by horizontally tied willow poles (Ray 1933:32). The lower walls were covered with grass and dirt; the upper walls with tule mats, later canvas, tied to the uprights. An open gap, a foot wide, along the roof ridge allowed for the passage of smoke and light. At the ends were double doors, an outer one between the curved poles and an inner door between end mats hung over the square end of the main frame.

Set up at the fisheries, summer mat houses were rectangular, with a flat roof, and nine feet wide because inside there was only a single row of beds and a passageway. Side poles were forked to hold roof cross-beams. The upriver half of the house was used for drying fish because prevailing winds blew odors away. Small fires burned outside. Mats enclosed the back, sides, and roof, while the open front faced the river (Ray 1933:34).

A sweatlodge consisted of a six- to eight-foot dome made of bent willow saplings covered by dry grass and six inches of dirt (Ray 1933:55). In the 1990s blankets and canvas provided the covering. Rocks were heated in an outside fire and carried to an inside basin where water was sprinkled to create steam. Menstrual huts were built like mat homes.

Only in special cases, at vision quest sites, would stone walls be built of talus basalt rocks to mark sacred precincts along the Columbia River or on mountain peaks. Hollowed-out boulders were and are regarded as petrified sweatlodges associated with Coyote and the Spirit Age. Shamans of great power painted pictographs on rock faces to memorialize their power and to provide a place where friends could petition it for help (Spier 1938:143–144).

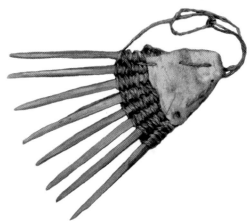

top, Wash. State U. Lib., Histl. Photograph Coll., Pullman: 91–116; bottom, U. of Wash. Thomas Burke Memorial Mus., Seattle: 2–270.
Fig. 4. Objects of wood. top, Dugout canoe on the Okanogan River, Wash. Photograph by Bart Robinson, 1890s. bottom, Southern Okanogan hair comb made of wood bound with Indian hemp and wrapped with leather. Made by Cecile Brooks and collected by Leslie Spier on the Colville Res., Wash., 1930. Length 8.5 cm.

Transport

In addition to packstraps (Ray 1933:122), people relied on rafts, canoes (fig. 4), snowshoes, and improvised toboggans of deer and bear hides (Ray 1933:118, 120, 122) before horses were introduced.

Clothing and Adornment

Aboriginally, clothing materials varied with the seasons. Animal skins were used in winter, woven plant fibers for summer. Tailored deerskin styles were adapted from Plains

259

top, U. of Oreg. Lib., Special Coll., Eugene: M–4005; bottom left, Wash. State U. Lib., Histl. Photograph Coll., Pullman: 91–083. bottom right, Wash. State Histl. Soc., Tacoma:34678.

Fig. 5. Structures. top, Colville Indian village at Nespelem, Wash. with tepees and ceremonial longhouse. Photograph by Lee Moorhouse, 1898–1912. bottom left, Tepee, tent, and reservation house of Stimatwua, Colville Res., Nespelem, Wash. A planted field is in the foreground. Photograph by Frank Avery, about 1915. bottom right, Fishing camp in the Sanpoil Valley. Fish are drying on racks. Photograph by Asahel Curtis and Walter P. Miller, Colville Res., Wash., 1916.

tribes (Ray 1933:45). In summer, men often went nude among themselves; otherwise they wore a sagebark pubic sheath or leather breechclout. Women wore a belted poncho, with a diamond-shaped head space, and aprons woven with a bark and deerhair warp and a hemp weft.

Sandals, worn by men and women, were woven from sagebark or fresh rose branches left to dry. Leather moccasins were made of a rectangular skin, folded and sewn up the heel and along a pointed toe to an instep insert, which flared the shape to fit a foot. Narrow ankle flaps were added. A tab, made by shaping the heel, was decorated with a cutout pattern. Winter moccasins were more roomy so grass or fur insulation could be padded around the foot. Ceremonial moccasins had simple geometric designs in feather or porcupine quills arranged over the front.

In heavy brush or cold weather, women wore wrap-around skirts and hemp leggings, while men wore leggings of an entire inside-out hide of a badger, beaver, coyote, or small bear. Men wore their leggings above the knee, tied at the top and bottom, while women wore theirs below the knee and wrapped only at the top.

In winter, men also wore an overrobe of bear or deer hide or a tunic of double coyote skins sewn together at their shoulders. Woven willow or sage bark or a trimmed hide served for breechclouts for men and women.

Fur caps were worn in winter. Male caps had front and back visors (fig. 6), but women's caps had no visors. The cap was made from a green skin stretched and shaped by gently pounding it over a round rock, then flexed to keep it soft, except at the ends which stiffened to be trimmed into the visors.

The feathered headdress typical of the Plains was introduced as chiefly attire by Split Sun, as an aspect of his increased leadership during bison hunts and war expeditions into Montana.

Mittens were made of coyote and other skins, except rabbit, which was too thin. For safety, mittens were tied to a cord around the neck on long trips. Robes and blankets used deer, bear, coyote, and rabbit hides. Some woven rabbit fur robes were also made, and rabbit skins were preferred for baby clothes.

Particular ornamentation depended on instructions from a guardian spirit. Caps were made from the pelt of the same species as a spirit ally. Powerful shamans wore feathers (fig. 7) and porcupine quill decorations because only they dared to call attention to themselves. Random perforations in a shirt indicated immunity from weapon wounds, a warrior power like that of the Nez Perce.

Men and women wore headbands, and some women donned basketry hats, like neighboring Sahaptians. Eyebrows were plucked and painted (Ray 1933:52). Face painting was used for protection from sun and wind; at public gatherings, it invoked guardian spirits (Ray 1933:51).

260

Girls dressed their own hair, while mothers, then wives, did this for men. Women wore bangs, sometimes with three braids (at the sides and back). Men plucked their own facial hair with tweezers made of wood or small animal ribs (Ray 1933:56). Men's hair was worn in two braids, sometimes wrapped with fur (Ray 1933:52). Women often painted, daubed, or treated their hair to indicate characteristics of age, activity, and status. Both men and women rubbed their hair with salmon oil or used a perfume made from deer marrow mixed with crushed hemlock needles. Men rubbed their hair and body with a leather pouch impregnated with beaver testes oil as a cologne. During mourning, hair was cut short.

Baby bedding and diapers were made from birchbark or buckskin. Children went unclothed in summer until puberty.

Wealth

Wealth items, though not abundant, included clamshell beads, locally called wampum, and dentalium tusk shells (Ray 1933:50) traded from the coast. Only shamans remained wealthy, being able to retain what they were paid for curing (Ray 1933:26). Chiefs and other leaders were expected to be generous and so could not retain wealth while holding a position of responsibility.

Life Cycle

After conception, a woman was careful to lay on her side to prevent twins from forming. Eating eggs would result in a caul. If the fetus faced the mother's back, it would be left-handed; if it faced her front, it would be righthanded (Spier 1938:121).

Thus, pregnancy imposed strict taboos on the mother and father concerned with the well-being of their baby. Often, the pregnant woman returned to the home of her mother until the birth. She undertook a regular regime of exercise by walking, running, swimming, and eating sparingly.

When labor began, the woman and an elder female retired to a birthing hut or a screened-off section of the house. For delivery, the woman knelt against two stakes and held on to the tops. The baby emerged onto a mat. The elder woman tied off the umbilical cord with deer sinew, bit through it, and buried the placenta. When the umbilical cord fell off, it was saved and tied to the babyboard. Later it was carefully buried by the father to insure good health for his child.

The newborn was washed and massaged to shape features and limbs (Ray 1933:125). In difficult deliveries, shamans were summoned to assist by using their spirit power to ease out the baby. If the fetus was born dead, it was buried immediately.

Herbal tea was drunk by the mother to reduce bleeding. The father beat a dog or horse or ran a horse or himself into a lather so that the child would not cry excessively or convulse. At no other time was an animal deliberately injured.

Close relatives of the father made the new cradleboard (fig. 8) once a healthy baby was born. Often a man made the wooden frame and a woman made the leather sack attached

left, North Central Wash. Mus., Wenatchee, Wash.; center, Eastern Wash. State Histl. Soc., Cheney Cowles Mus., Spokane: Dungan 1976.43; right, Ind. U., William Hammond Mathers Mus., Bloomington.

Fig. 6. Men's clothing. left, John Harmelt (b. 1845, d. 1937), Wenatchee headman who fought to remain in the Wenatchi Valley and who sought redress for the wrongful sale of the traditional Wenatchee fishery. He is wearing beaded vest, pants, gauntlets, and a hat decorated with feathers. Photograph by Alfred G. Simmer, © 1931. center, Sanpoil beaded vest depicting brown and white bears, eagles, and red fawns on a blue background. The back is tanned hide. Made by Icot Francis before 1940. Length 50.8 cm. right, Jim Homas, Sinkayuse, and Weyes Weit, Colville Res., Wash. Homas wears a beaded vest and gauntlet, multiple-shell necklace, and a fur cap with visor. Weit wears a cloth coat decorated with beaded strips and fur, beaded leggings and moccasins, and a Plains-style headdress. Photograph by Joseph K. Dixon, 1913.

Fig. 7. Chilliwhist Jim, a Methow shaman. He wears beaded leggings, moccasins, and belt; his cloth shirt is decorated with fur strips. His feather headdress was a sign of his spiritual power. Photograph by Frank Matsura, 1903–1913.

to it. Slight differences marked male or female cradleboards and bindings, in addition to the kinds of dangles hung from the protecting head loop. For a boy, the penis was exposed, while a girl had a buckskin fold between her legs (Ray 1933:130) to allow urine to run off. A baby's buckskin diapers were always emptied into the same hole as protection from sorcery, and, similarly, the umbilical stub was buried in the hills.

The mother rested for a week and relaxed for a month, drinking a fortifying herb tonic twice a day. At the end of confinement, she bathed and held a small feast for the baby, being forbidden to cook while she was losing blood. Children born out of wedlock were usually permanently adopted by relatives. Important families might betroth their infants to forge a permanent bond. If the mother died, the baby was adopted by another nursing mother for about two years, the two nursing babies becoming "milk kin" to each other.

Throughout infancy, the mother massaged the baby to make it grow tall and slim, with a fine nose and chin. Thick hair was especially prized, made shiny by using a sunflower root shampoo (Ray 1933:54). Leading families named their babies soon after birth as a mark of status. Older children had their ears pierced. Baby teeth were given to a dog with a prayer for new strong teeth (Miller 1990:209). Parents

threatened children, but actual whipping was done by an elderly man, sometimes disguised, in return for gifts from the parents.

Children were urged to help adults wherever possible. Grandparents nurtured and protected their grandchildren, developing a close bond between them. During family meals, children were given pieces of meat or fish that included the killing wound to make them strong (Ray 1933:132).

Children never ate their first food efforts. When a boy killed his first game, he give it away to an old man or served a feast for old men to teach himself the value of sharing. When a girl gathered her first roots or berries, a feast was held for the old women (Ray 1933:26, 133). The Wenatchee held a ceremony the first time that a child smoked a pipe (Spier 1938:193).

By puberty, boys and some girls should have acquired a guardian spirit by questing in the hills after dark or, in some families, diving into deep pools. At first menstruation, a girl was secluded for days in a menstrual hut, wearing her oldest clothes and her braids in coils (Ray 1933:134). At the end, she was given new adult clothes and sent forth as a woman. Boys engaged in strenuous exercise during puberty, but there was no special ritual observance. After a successful hunt or other good deed, he was pronounced a young man in public.

Women returned to the menstrual hut during each successive occurrence and were careful to avoid men's hunting and religious gear. If a weapon were contaminated, it was rubbed with coyote mint leaves to restore it (Ray 1933:135). Girls from better families were chaperoned. Boys courted them with flutes and songs. For second marriages, love medicine was used to compel the spouse (Ray 1933:136; Miller 1990:79–90). Parents arranged marriages, and, as in-laws, exchanged gifts periodically for the duration of a marriage. The couple often lived with relatives of the husband.

To thwart parental objections, a couple might elope or allow themselves to be discovered in bed together. Successful hunters, gamblers, shamans, and leaders had more than a single wife, sometimes in separate camps. Levirate and sororate were practiced at the death of a spouse. Adultery and incest were offenses punishable by lashing, cutting off ears, or, in extreme cases, death. Jilted spouses might commit suicide.

Following courtship and betrothal, the time and place were set for the wedding. The bride-to-be moved to a mat house built a distance from the village. Her family provided her with food and comforts, but she was to spend her time quietly deciding on her future goals. After several days, two other lodges were built near her. One camp was that of the groom and family, and the other was that of her family. She remained in seclusion in her own shelter until the wedding.

The groom's family carried a feast to the other family, and gave them gifts appropriate to women, such as baskets, woven bags filled with dried food, robes, blankets, and yardage. Prayers were said to bless the marriage and to ask

left, U. of Wash. Lib., Special Coll., Seattle NA1310; center, Pat Albers Coll., Salt Lake City, Utah; right, Ind. U., William Hammond Mathers Mus., Bloomington.

Fig. 8. Women's clothing and children in cradleboards. left, Methow woman with child in cradleboard. Photograph by Edward W. Latham, 1890–1910. center, Group dressed up for the photographer. Man on left has a beaded octopus bag, 2 of the girls have necklaces or collars decorated with fur strips, the woman in center wears a velveteen wing dress with beaded belt, and the woman at right holds an infant in a beaded cradleboard. Postcard photograph by N.A. Delaney, before Aug. 1920. right, Cecile Charlie, Sanpoil, wearing dress decorated with cowrie shells and beads. Her hair is wrapped in fur, and she has a beaded bag at her waist. Photograph by Joseph K. Dixon, Colville Res., Wash., 1913.

for long life and many healthy children. In private, the bride was given a special eagle feather to wear as a married woman.

The next day the bride's family carried a feast to the groom's camp and gave male-related gifts, such as meat, tools, and weapons. Great care was taken to see that the exchange of gifts was equal and that neither family outdid the other. For a life based on sharing together, both families had to start equivalent. The groom received his marriage braid.

On the third day, the couple married. Both families prepared a new home, supplying it with all necessities for the newlyweds. The bride was dressed in fine garments and her eagle feather. Standing together outside, leaders asked the Creator to bless the union and proclaimed them married. Sometimes, elite families used a wedding robe to wrap around the couple during these prayers.

When near death, a person might call for one or more old men to act as confessor to keep his or her soul from wandering, tormented by past wrongs. At death, the extended body was wrapped in a rush mat or deerskin. If a shaman died inside a lodge, the mats were removed and the structure burned. As soon as possible after dawn, a grave was dug and the body carried there, followed by mourners. After the eulogy, a shaman swept out the grave with wild rose branches and the body was placed inside fully extended. Important possessions, such as keepsakes and talismans, were also placed in the grave, but no clothes or food, which were burned or buried separately.

Closely related mourners set up huts in the woods, sweating, bathing, fasting, and drinking a rosebush decoction morning and night for a year. Fir bough bedding protected hunting luck while a man mourned his wife. A male mourner wore his hair loose, but a woman had hers cut off at shoulder length. Leather bands, providing a protective circle, were worn around the wrists, until they fell off.

At death, the soul, located near the heart, departed for the afterworld at the end of the Milky Way, or, if unabsolved, became an anguished ghost wandering the earth (Ray 1933:171). The guardian spirit, as a spirit-ghost, hovered nearby waiting for another relative or a shaman to reestablish rapport with the living (Ray 1939:99).

Kinship

Like other Plateau communities, these Salishans had a bilateral system pairing the duties of men and women within kindreds, assuming extensive genealogical information to keep track of relatives by descent or marriage throughout the Plateau and beyond.

Interior Salish kinship terms stress generation, gender, and collaterality (Elmendorf 1961). Parents and own children are distinguished from uncles, aunts, and niblings (nephews, nieces); yet all cousins are called siblings. At the death of a linking relative, special "decedence terms" (Miller 1985) are introduced among surviving collaterals to move their relationships closer together, much as the levi-

MIDDLE COLUMBIA RIVER SALISHANS

rate and sororate reaffirmed family alliances by marrying a surviving sibling to the widow or widower.

Polygyny, great mobility, and scattered resources contributed to the overall flexibility of this system so that kindreds were not localized and relationships remained as broad as possible. Faint memory of what seem to have been cognatic corporate groups or totemic kindreds suggests there was more formality to prehistoric patterns.

Social and Political Organization

Throughout the Plateau, the winter village was the most basic and effective political unit. Each village had a leader, who was advised by an assembly of married adults, regardless of their own origins or length of residence. People moved with the seasons or by personal choice among these villages and affiliated camps, especially to berry, hunting, and fishing sites.

Communities intensely identified with their locales. Until the 1980s, well-informed Colville elders recalled animal emblems, sometimes vaguely called "clans," for various native districts, such as Frog for those at Chalk Grade, Eagle for those in Grand Coulee, Mourning Dove for those at the mouth of the Methow, and Bear for those at Ellensburg. In each case, this animal emblem can be traced to an epic involving a spirit family named for that species living at that locale prior to the change in the world brought on by Coyote or the Creator just prior to human arrival.

Leadership was hereditary among males, with the most able candidate receiving assembly approval from men and women. Women of leading families also held high rank and, as the wives and daughters of chiefs, undertook task leadership roles during female and domestic activities.

Once selected, a chief held office until he died or left the village. Qualities sought were honesty, sound judgment, even temperament, and arbitration skills. Larger villages included multiple chiefs and subchiefs, who advised the main chief in his roles of judge, arbitrator, and manager. While the chief (Columbian yalmíxʷəm) had overall responsibilities for management and coordination, each public task had its own leader who was an expert in that activity. A speaker, noted for his loud voice, repeated or reinforced the words of a leader. Message runners called people to an assembly or coordinated the seasonal movements of related groups.

For the duration of salmon runs, the salmon tyee of each river had overall charge of that fishery and all, whether local or visitor, involved in it. In this regard, inhabitants of each river functioned as a tribe during the summer.

As judge, the chief held open court, calling on witnesses, evaluating evidence, and hearing from the accused. Crimes included murder, stealing, perjury, assault, sexual indiscretions, abortion, sorcery, or revenge. Under pressures from missionaries and federal agents, punishment often involved a three-foot lash braided of deer neck sinews (Ray 1933:113). Murder was compensated for with goods, never executions. Other punishments might exclude someone from participating in a ceremony, impose social ostracism for a set time, or demand specific acts such as providing food to the family of the victim.

As the adoption of the horse increased mobility, loose confederacies formed for mutual defense, led by the Split Sun family for the downriver Middle Columbians (Ray 1960). As his sons succeeded to the title and position, they arranged dynastic marriages with other leading families to extend their influence. As upheld by Moses, a younger son who inherited the Split Sun title, this Sinkayuse leadership grew out of the locations of their winter villages at tribal borders, with access across the Big Bend through intersecting coulees.

Games

In the spring, shinny was played by teams from 10 to 30 boys, men, or women, using a wooden ball covered with buckskin and sticks made from tree branches crooked at the end. The goals were robes set 200 feet apart on a level field.

Men challenged each other to contests of swimming, wrestling, jumping, weight lifting with stones, and tug of war, when two men sat with their soles touching, grasped the same stick, and pulled until one of them was lifted up. In winter, men tried to swim across the Columbia, accompanied by canoes for safety (Ray 1933:166). Men and women had different swimming areas and separate contests.

Women played dice games with four decorated beaver teeth or deer ribs that had been steamed, straightened, polished, decorated, and pointed at the ends (Ray 1933:159, 1942: element 4034). One side of each piece had four dotted circles, the other side had stripes. These dice were shaken in cupped hands and thrown onto a skin. Each woman threw until all pieces fell with the circles-side down. About 50 counters were involved, and all had to be won before a single player could win by getting them all. Score was made by getting all four circles-side up for two counters, three circle-sides up for one counter, one side up to lose a counter, and no circles up to lose two counters. Women made their own dice.

During winter, two teams of women stared at each other until one woman smiled. Sometimes, two women's teams squatted on their heels and sang before hopping and clapping in place. The last one upright won, but most players laughed and fell over (Ray 1933:160). Other teams of women held their breath while touching, every half inch, a yard long spiral traced in the sand. The woman won who held her breath longest and touched more of the spiral.

Both men and women played ball and pin (Ray 1933:161). The tule ball was held in the mouth to keep it moist, then dropped toward a thorn in the right hand. Every successful thrust was named for a month "to shorten the year." In summer, men played hoop and pole, using a pottery or wood disk and a bone-tipped hardwood staff decorated with bands of buckskin, along a runway dug six feet wide, 16 feet long, and nine inches deep. The six-inch hoop was wrapped in buckskin, with crossed inner thongs hung with colored shells. Two players or teams took turns rolling or throwing the hoop underhand. Score was kept with stick counters, and computed by the touching of particular pole bands and ring shells. A heavier ring was made of clay covered with buckskin, or of polished and pierced stone.

Another throwing game used a hoop twisted from a limb and a four-foot willow pole (Ray 1933:164). Men stood and threw at the hoop target set about 30 feet away. Slings of buckskin and hemp cord or of shaved willow string were used in contests. A more quiet game was cat's cradle to create string figures.

Running was another sport, with marathons for small teams covering 15 miles (Ray 1933:165). Men might race each other to a mountain top. Race courses were laid out to a tree and back, with heavy betting on the winner.

Children had playgrounds on sandbars or sandy beaches where they played house. Girls used stick dolls, with an added head and clothes. Boys had tops of wood, started with a string, or a bark disk, twirled with the hand. Favorite diversions were hide and seek, seesaw with crossed logs, willow whistles, snowball fights, and hide toboggans. Children played with shuttlecocks made from duck feathers, and used, at the request of elders, bull-roarers made of wood or deer ribs to influence the weather (Ray 1942: elements 4064, 4094).

The most popular pastime was and is the stick game ("Music and Dance," fig. 5), with bets matched by both sides before play (Ray 1933:155). Poker, monte, and other card games were modern introductions.

Mythology

On Naming Day, at the end of Spirit Age, just prior to human arrival, the spirit leader, who created the world before becoming Sweatlodge, gave names to all creatures at a dawn assembly. Coyote stayed up all night intending to be first in line to receive the name of Salmon, Bear, or Eagle. Instead, he fell asleep and was the last to appear. Because he had thought for himself, however, the Creator put Coyote in charge of making the world ready for humans. The chief himself gave up his head and limbs, providing the sweatlodge now available to humans in need.

One of Coyote's greatest adventures was to steal Salmon from the trap of Bird Women at the mouth of the Columbia and bring them upriver. Every village at the mouth of a stream or tributary was visited, and Coyote left salmon there according to the beauty and industry of the woman he "married" there (Boas 1917; Ray 1933a; Spier 1938; Miller 1992:93–98).

Coyote also issued "commandments" about how the world was to be organized. In some places, he left a spirit emblem or rock picture to indicate these resources and rules. At other times, he changed the landscape, petrifying monsters and scattering foods. A council of spirits decided that the unnatural sons of Mole, Coyote's wife, would become Sun and Moon.

The world was also populated with various dwarfs, dangers, and monsters. Various lakes and water obstructions had resident spirits, such as a nude woman with long flowing hair and exposed breasts and hairy, long horned beings in Omak and Alta lakes.

Cosmology

The earth was a sky dome over an earth disk, with the Columbia River through the middle and the Cascade Mountains and Plains along the edge surrounded by ocean.

Fundamental to everything, spirit powers (Columbian *sumáx*, Okanagan *sumíx*) included both animate and inanimate forms, such as driftwood and fish traps. Among the most powerful were and are Grizzly, Wolf, Badger, Skunk, Flying Squirrel, Pack Rat, Spider, Hawk, and Eagle. More dangerous powers were and are Grizzly, Bear, Wolf, Cougar, Badger, Summer Weasel, and Rattlesnake. Rabbit and Magpie were weak powers.

During successful questing, spirits appeared as humans to confer power before changing into their species form just as they departed. Good looks and a strong body were particularly attractive to spirits (Ray 1933:173), who went away as one became old, feeble, or sickly. When a human partner died, the spirit became a spirit-ghost in quest of another human, preferably from the same family unless it was lured away by a powerful shaman. When a spirit-ghost was itself killed, a shoulder blade was found at the spot.

While a child received a spirit at 8 to 10 years of age, the encounter was forgotten until the spirit returned, some 15–20 years later, and the person became sick with a feeling of loneliness and despondency. A shaman was called to treat the patient, fixing the spirit inside him or her by allowing the singing of the song signaling the bond. When winter came, the patient sang his or her song in public during a winter dance.

Though some spirits conferred the ability to cure particular ailments, only shamans received power to heal persistent and supernatural illnesses (Ray 1933:202), including wounds from animal attack, fevers, mental upset, spirit return or loss, and magical poisoning by a jealous woman.

Ceremonies

The First Salmon ceremony was conducted by two shamans when the first chinook was caught at a communal weir. Prior rites of thanksgiving were held for the trees cut to make the weir, for the dried poles carried to the stream banks, and for the completed weir. The salmon tyee spent five nights at the trap praying and singing to consecrate its use (Adeline Fredin, personal communication 1996).

As men built the trap, women put sunflower leaves on the roof of an open-sided sunshade and over the ground inside and nearby. When the women finished, they took the children and withdrew from the river for five days. Men removed all their clothes and went naked during this time. All the work, cooking, and feasting was then done only by men. The first four days, only salmon flanks were eaten, boiled the first two days and roasted the last two, with the men using a special triangular spoon made from a bent willow twig.

Salmon heads, tails, fins, backbones, and roe were dried upon a woven willow platform until the fifth day, when they were mixed into a soup with serviceberries, bitterroot, camas, and water. This was the most holy meal of the rite since it included virtually every food. A man was expected to eat as much as possible so these foods would be bountiful.

After the fifth day, women rejoined the camp and began the large-scale processing of fish. Women resumed cooking all meals and prepared all fish (Ray 1933:71).

The harvesting of any other resource was also begun with a public feast to consume that new food. After the berry feasts, married couples were expected to increase fertility to bolster the harvest (Spier 1938:32).

The Winter Dance acted as a world renewal and all-purpose thanksgiving, hosted in rotation among tribal communities during January and February. Traditionally, a large mat house was cleared, poles suspended along its sides to hold gifts, and a tree with only top branches, decorated with wrappings and dangles, was set up in the middle. Led off by the host, each visionary grasped the pole in turn and sang his or her song provided by a encounter with a spirit. Participants and audience fasted during these recitations, but a feast ended the service. Later in the season, dances were dedicated to bringing the Chinook or warm winds of spring.

In the 1990s the dance was held in a large public room specially built into the homes of hosting families. Within the house, men sat on the right and women on the left. The host was and is usually a powerful shaman since displays of spirit powers often led to attempted thefts of the spirits by unscrupulous shamans. A speaker announces for the host and others, stating intermissions and times to drink water and smoke.

In public, a novice proclaimed his renewed ties with his or her spirit by dancing, protected by a sponsoring shaman since he or she was particularly vulnerable while the power was new (Ray 1933:192). After this initiation, the visionary would briefly describe the circumstance of the vision during a later intermission, or, alternatively, ask for guesses about what his song and motions had been evoking. On the last morning, gifts were distributed by the host to other performers, then to the audience as quantity allowed.

Witchcraft

Malevolent sorcery caused a victim to have a scared look in the eyes, be jumpy and twitchy, and became delirious, often identifying with and naming the shaman who caused the condition at the moment of death. Only a more powerful shaman could effect a cure. If the victim died, a family member might kill the malicious shaman by magic or with a physical weapon, assured of acquittal by the consensus of the community.

History[†]

Routes for trade and the transmission of information, used for centuries between the coast and interior, carried word of Spanish and Russian explorations during the 1600s, followed by the first European goods. News of the horse preceded its arrival by the 1740s, with a shift to settlements near good pastures and long-distance bison hunts onto the northern Plains.

The greater mobility provided by the horse fostered the Salishan confederacy under the family of Split Sun to coordinate bison hunts by Sinkayuse, Wenatchee, Entiat, Chelan, and others onto Blackfoot lands in Montana. With the murder of the father, the name passed on to his sons in the order of their births, the most famous being Moses.

Epidemics decimated whole regions, destroying communities during the 1770s, 1830s, and 1850s. In the next decade, the fur trade encouraged men to spend more time hunting. Iroquois and other Northeast natives, long immersed in the trade, came West in the 1790s, bringing word of the Roman Catholic Mass and Euro-American avarice.

During 1806, while Meriwether Lewis and William Clark did not travel through Salishan territory, rumors of their presence reached upriver tribes. David Thompson of the North West Company came down the Columbia in 1811, the same year David Stuart built Fort Okanogan for the Astor company.

Intrigued by Flathead and Nez Perce pleas for missions, Protestants—Congregationalists and later Methodists—arrived in the 1830s, soon followed by Jesuits and other Roman Catholic clergy. A mission near Cashmere served the Wenatchee after 1872. In 1898 the Jesuit boarding school at Saint Mary's Mission near Omak was built (Raufer 1966) (fig. 9; "Music and Dance," fig. 6, this vol.).

After the separation of Washington Territory in 1853, Isaac I. Stevens, simultaneously governor of Washington Territory, Indian commissioner, and head of the Northern Pacific Railroad Survey, forced treaties in 1855. That of June 9 at Walla Walla ceded lands that included those of Salishan tribes of the downriver chain along the Big Bend

---

[†] John Bower and Gary Palmer contributed to this section.

of the Columbia. Intermittently over the next decades, in response to American oppression, warfare erupted, particularly the war of 1856–1858.

For upper Columbia River Salishans, the Colville Reservation was set aside by executive order of 1872, but within a month its boundaries were redrawn so the fertile Colville valley was lost. In 1885, Chief Joseph and those survivors of his Wallawa Nez Perce band who were under indictment in Idaho joined the Colville Reservation.

For several months during 1879, the army maintained a post at Lake Chelan before establishing a post at the mouth of the Spokane River (Ruby and Brown 1965:173). In 1881, to protect its national border, the United States unilaterally claimed a 15-mile strip along the northern border of the Colville Reservation. Silver mines and claim in this zone were also a factor in this decision.

The downriver Middle Columbians, led by Chief Moses (fig. 10), received, in 1879, the Columbia Reservation west of the Colvilles, mostly on Methow and Southern Okanogan lands, which was expanded in 1880 to include Lake Chelan. In 1883 chiefs Moses, Lot, and Sarsarpkin relinquished the reservation in favor of a move to the Colville Reservation. Native families, however, were allowed to take individual allotments within the former Moses Reservation. Many Entiats and Methows relocated to Colville lands, but Chelans, who were moved at gun point, later returned with the Entiat Wapato family to take allotments on the lake. Long Jim, the Chelan leader (fig. 10), with his wife and children, including Jesse Jim, a famous beauty, were allotted near the mouth of the Okanogan River where Chief Joseph Dam was built in 1958.

Wenatchee long remained in their homeland, suffering the loss of their treaty-protected fishery in 1894, with the money going to the Yakima Reservation by misunderstanding of the treaty. Indeed, the Bureau of Indian Affairs mismanaged the Wenatchee fishery. Those Wenatchee homesteads and allotments not lost through demands for taxes or outright fraud remained part of the Colville Reservation. Many Wenatchees did not live at Colville until 1910, while their chief, John Harmelt (fig. 6), never moved (Scheuerman 1982).

During the 1890s, gold was found on the Colville Reservation, resulting in the loss of the north half in 1892 and the allotment of the south half after the 1905 McLaughlin Agreement.

Since the 1930s, reservations suffered the consequences of the dams along the Columbia River, beginning, in 1936, with that at Grand Coulee. In 1938, after defeated votes on an Indian Reorganization Act constitution, the tribes on the Colville Reservation confederated and elected a business council to govern their affairs. Four voting districts (identified with Inchelium, Keller, Nespelem, and Omak) were established to elect councilors, who serve two-year terms.

After a bitter fight over termination, the Colville business council embarked on a policy of successful economic development (Gidley 1985; Schultz 1971; Reichwein 1990).

In the 1990s Colvilles identified themselves as Roman Catholics, Methodists, Pentecostals, Bahai, Shakers, Seven Drums, Shamans, Peyote (Native American Church), and Ecumenical. Local Jesuits were tolerant of native traditions, encouraging much interfaith cooperation, now as in the past.

Recast traditions included pit baking recipes done by slow cooking in an oven, continued first foods rites, and tribal feasts and name givings. While many significant sites and resources have been inundated by waters behind dams along the Columbia, family memory of them continued, with the hope for their eventual return.

Population

Estimates by Anastasio (1972:202) suggest 2,500 Middle Columbian River Salishans in 1805, including 1,600 Nespelem-Sanpoil and 800 Southern Okanogan, decreasing to 1,300 by 1835, while Curtis (1907–1930, 7:68) reported 1,000 in 1870. By 1853, only 350 Southern Okanogan are listed. While only 139 Columbia "attached to the agency" were reported for 1888, Agent H.J. Cole (in ARCIA 1892:487) noted 390 Moses-Columbia, including 139 males above 18 years, 150 females above 14 years, 9 children 6 to 16 years old, and 32 others. In 1898, Agent Anderson listed 311 members of the "Moses Band." In the 1990s membership in the Colville Confederated Tribes numbered about 8,000, about half of whom lived on the reservation. Reservation lands included allotments and homesteads on the former north half, Moses Reservation,

Okanogan County Histl. Soc., Okanogan, Wash.

Fig. 9. St. Mary's Mission, Omak, Wash., baseball team of 1914. The uniforms were gifts from the Philadelphia Athletics team. left to right, top row, R. Newell Ustal, M. McLean, Paschal Sherman; middle row, Eugene Wiley, Louis Nicholson, William George, Edward Ambrose, McKenzie; bottom row, unidentified, Francis Abraham, William Horrell, and Louie Smitkin. Photograph by George B. Ladd.

Wash. State U. Lib., Histl. Photograph Coll., Pullman: top left, 91–123 and top right: 92–071; bottom left, Okanogan County Histl. Soc., Okanogan, Wash.; bottom right, Eastern Wash. State Histl. Soc., Cheney Cowles Mus., Spokane.

Fig. 10. Tribal leaders. top left (left to right), Chief Moses (d. 1899), Sinkayuse; Jim Chil-lah-leet-sah, nephew of Chief Moses; Peo-peo-mox- mox, Umatilla; and Kah-lees-quat-qua-lat, Umatilla or Cayuse. Photograph by Joseph Buchtel, 1879. top right, Billy Curlew (b. 1871, d. 1961; Sinkayuse); Harry Nanamkin (b. 1887, d. 1961; Sanpoil); and Cleveland Kamiakin (b. 1863, d. 1959; Palouse) in the Grant County Title Abstract Company office in Ephrata, Wash. Photographer possibly Cull White, about 1957. bottom left (seated), Johnny Louie or Wapato John, a Colville who acted as the interpreter, and Chief Smitkin (d. 1919), Sinkayuse; (standing) Long Jim (b. 1859, d. 1931), Sinkayuse; Charley Swimptkin (d. 1918; Southern Okanogan); and Louie Timentwa (b. 1863, Southern Okanogan). In an effort to prevent liquor from being sold to their people, these headmen met in Omak, Wash., in 1908 with Judge Edmond K. Pendergast, who went to Washington, D.C., on their behalf. On his return the judge arranged for "dry squads" to patrol the saloons (Raufer 1963:240). Photograph by Frank Matsura, probably 1908. bottom right, George Friedlander (b. 1904, d. 1977), Sinkayuse (left), wearing the outfit that he inherited from Chief Moses, and Joe Moses (b. 1862; Sinkayuse). Photographed about 1930s.

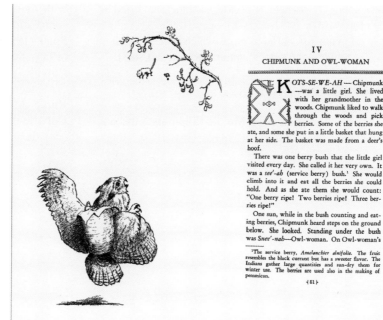

Fig. 11. Christine Quintasket (*haṁishaṁis* 'mourning dove'; b. about 1885, d. 1936), Southern Okanogan. The foremost native woman author of the Plateau, she published a novel in 1927 titled *Co-Ge-We-A, the Half Blood* under the pen name of Mourning Dove. She was also active in reservation politics and a public speaker (Miller 1990). left, Portrait in traditional clothing. Photographed before 1934. right, Two pages from her book *Coyote Stories* (1933).

Wenatchee fishery, and Palouse River (Gary Palmer, personal communication 1996).

Synonymy‡

Sinkayuse. The name Sinkayuse was spelled Sinkiuse by Hodge (1907–1910, 2:576), who lists variants. It is from Columbia *snq̓aʔáẃs*; the Okanagan form is *snk̓eʔíẃsx*. Another term for the Moses Band is *skwáxcnəxʷ* 'people of *skwáxcn*', a place-name meaning '(where people) live against the shore' used for Rock Island and the lower part of Moses Coulee. Another name for them was Isle de Pierre (Mooney 1896:743).

Wenatchee. Wenatchee is from the Sahaptin name for this group, which in the Yakima dialect is *winátšapam* (Beavert and Rigsby 1975). The Columbian name is *snṗəsqʷáẃsəxʷ*, meaning 'the people of the Wenatchee River' (*nṗsqʷáẃs*). Hodge (1907–1910, 2:263, 932) lists synonyms in separate entries for Pisquows and Wenatchi, being uncertain of the synonymy of these terms.

Entiat. Entiat is the name of a settlement, *nt̓iyátkʷ* 'grassy water'; the band was called *snt̓iyátkʷəxʷ* 'people of Entiat village'. These are the Inti-etook of Alexander Ross (Hodge 1907–1910, 1:611) and the Entiatook of Mooney (1896:734).

Chelan. The name Chelan is that of Lake Chelan, called *cəl̓án*. The band is called *scəl̓ámx* or *scəl̓ámxəxʷ* 'people of Lake Chelan'. These are the Tsill-ane of Ross (Hodge 1907–1910, 2:826).

Methow. The name Methow is from the name of the Methow Valley, *mítxaw*; the Methow River may be called this or, explicitly, *nmitxawátkʷ*. The Methow people are called *sṗaƛ̓múl̓əxʷəxʷ* 'people of Methow Valley', based on an alternative name *sṗaƛ̓múl̓əxʷ* 'bitterroot country'. Mooney (1896:734), who used the spelling Mitaui, included the Chelan and Entiat under this name. Ross spells their names Meat-who and Battle-le-mule-emauch (Hodge 1907–1910, 1:850).

Southern Okanagan. In Okanagan the Okanagans are called *uknaqínx* 'people of *uknaqín*', their traditional place of origin, said to be at or near Okanagan Falls (Teit 1930:198; Anthony Mattina, communication to editors 1996; M. Dale Kinkade, communication to editors 1997). Hodge (1907–1910, 2:114–115), who used the spelling Okinagan, gives spelling variants and synonyms. Mooney (1896:734) used Okanagan. The Southern Okanogan have also been called Sinkaietk (Ray 1936:122; Spier 1936:10), a name based on that of the Okanogan River, *nqʕítkʷ* (Columbian *nqḥátkʷ*).

Nespelem. The name for the Nespelem in Okanagan is *nspílm* (Mattina 1987:133). Hodge (1907–1910, 2:57), who used the spelling Nespelim, gives variants.

Sanpoil. The Okanagan name for the Sanpoil is *snpʕʷílxx* 'people of *snpʕʷílx*', the name of the Sanpoil River and valley.

‡ This synonymy was written by Ives Goddard incorporating Columbian and Okanagan linguistic information furnished by M. Dale Kinkade (communication to editors 1997). The names of each band are in the language spoken by that band.

Variant spellings N'pochele, N'pockle, and others are listed by Hodge (1907–1910, 2:451–452). Mooney (1896:733) reported their Yakima name as Hai-ai´nĭma, which is the Hi-high-e-nim-mo of Lewis and Clark (Moulton 1983–, 6:480, 488).

Sources

Primary published sources on Middle Columbia Salishans are the classic works by Ray (1933, 1936a, 1939, 1942), with more limited work by Teit (1928). Ethnohistorical sources include Chalfant (1974), Ray (1936, 1960, 1974), Spier (1936), Ruby and Brown (1965, 1989), and Smith (1983). Voluminous government documents relating to the Colvilles are cited in Palmer (1991).

Meager museum collections can be found at the Thomas Burke Memorial Washington State Museum, Seattle; Colville tribal museum, Coulee Dam; and local historical societies in nearby counties and in Spokane.

Spokane

JOHN ALAN ROSS

Language, Territory, and Environment

The Spokane (ˌspōˈkăn) of northeastern Washington spoke an Interior Salishan language* shared, in different dialects, with the Kalispel, Pend d'Oreille, and Flathead.

Aboriginally the Spokane comprised three bands: Lower Spokane with a principal settlement near Little Falls, Middle Spokane on Hangman or Latah Creek, and Upper Spokane on the Little Spokane River and upriver from the junction with Hangman Creek (fig. 1). The principal Middle Spokane village was a year-round encampment (*ntuʔtʔulmétkʷ*) where Hangman Creek joins the Spokane River (Elmendorf 1935–1936).

The Middle and Upper Spokane considered themselves "all one people" (Elmendorf 1935–1936) in distinction to the Lower Spokane. This formulation of Spokane band divisions agrees essentially with that of Teit (1930) but differs from Ray (1936), who would make the "Lower" Spokane an Okanagan-speaking group at the mouth of the Spokane River.

The Spokane language was probably a lingua franca in the northeastern Plateau (A. Kennedy 1823; Work 1829), and many Spokane men who traded along the Columbia River also spoke Chinook Jargon (Teit 1930:373).

The Spokane area is a predominantly semiarid basalt plateau reflecting the leeward rainshadow position of the region to the Cascade Mountains (Quinn 1984). Vegetation is dominated by drought-tolerant shrubs, sagebrush-bunchgrass, and mixed montane conifer transitional woodlands, which the Spokane modified annually with controlled burning (Ross 1981).

External Relations

Interaction of the Spokane and other Interior Salish groups was influenced by north-south and east-west trade routes tra-

*The phonemes of the Spokane dialect of Kalispel (Spokane-Kalispel-Flathead) are: (voiceless stops and affricates) *p, t, c, č, k, kʷ, q, qʷ, ʔ*; (glottalized stops and affricates) *ṗ, t̓, c̓, č̓, ƛ̓, k̓, k̓ʷ, q̓, q̓ʷ*; (voiceless fricatives) *s, š, ł, x, xʷ, x̣, x̣ʷ, h*; (resonants) *m, n, l, r, w, y, ʕ* (pharyngeal glide); *ʕʷ*; (glottalized resonants) *m̓, n̓, l̓, r̓, w̓, y̓, ʕ̓, ʕ̓ʷ*; (vowels) *i, e, a, o, u*; (stress) *v́*.

Flathead and Kalispel have slightly reduced inventories in comparison. Both lack *r* and *r̓*. Flathead also lacks *k̓* and *x*, and Kalispel also lacks *k, k̓, x*, and all four pharyngeals. Kalispel has *ƛ*, but only as the deglottalized form of *ƛ̓*.

The Spokane inventory is from Carlson and Flett (1989:iv), the Kalispel from Vogt (1940:11–14), and the Flathead from Sarah G. Thomason (communication to editors 1997).

versing the Plateau, especially the Columbia and Spokane river systems (Griswold 1970:42). The Spokane area possessed focal sites for fishing and trading (Anastasio 1972:155) that facilitated trade between the Plains and the Upper Chinook and Western Columbia River Sahaptin area (Teit 1930:356). In late summer, the Spokane went onto the Plains (Stevens 1855, 12:134; Elmendorf 1935–1936) with the Pend d'Oreille, Columbia, Kootenai, and Nez Perce to form task groups for hunting bison (Teit 1930; Anastasio 1955:6) and for trading (Elmendorf 1935–1936; Walker 1967:16). Some Spokanes traveled annually to The Dalles for salmon and to trade horses (Teit 1930:355–359). However, prior to acquiring the horse, the Spokane had conflict mostly with the

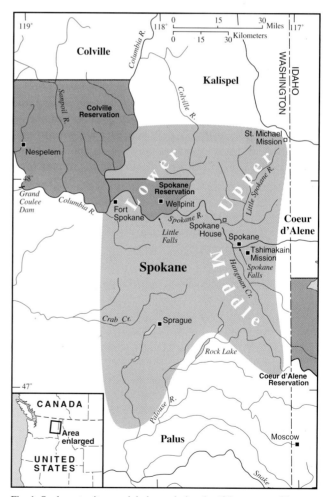

Fig. 1. Spokane territory and drainage during the 19th century, with modern towns.

Yakima and groups westward along the Columbia (Teit 1930:360; Walker and Lahren 1977:40) and on occasion with the Coeur d'Alene and Nez Perce (Cox l957).

Intergroup hostility was reduced through pacification efforts of fur traders (Chance 1973). The Spokane traditionally had peaceful relations with the Sanpoil, Nespelem, Flathead, Kootenai, and Okanagan (Curtis 1907–1930, 7:45; Teit 1930:360), though L.V.W. Walters (1938:79–80) states they fought with the Okanagan.

Culture

Settlement Pattern

The Spokane utilized three types of settlements: permanent winter villages located along the Spokane River, temporary summer fishing villages, and summer camps for hunting, plant gathering, and mineral and lithic exploitation. Winter village territories included hunting grounds, certain resource areas, burials, and sacred sites. Access to resources was along lines of kin affiliation and fictive associations based on joking relationships and trading associations. Summer fishing villages supported relatively large polyglot populations that came together to share technologies and mutually exploit anadromous fish (Walker and Lahren 1977:14), and to horserace, gamble, trade, court, and play games of endurance (Elmendorf 1935–1936).

Temporary summer and fall camps, comprised of numerous extended families, were located for root digging, collecting berries, hunting, and gathering tules, grasses, and medicines. Some major root fields, located south of the Spokane River, were visited in early June, before shifting to major fishing villages (A. Kennedy 1823), which were adjacent to less productive root areas. In mid-July, before going to berry areas, the Spokane traveled to the area of the Kalispel to exploit camas fields (Thoms 1989:219).

Subsistence

• HUNTING   The most important game animals were the whitetail and mule deer, despite an early report that deer were relatively scarce in the Spokane area (A. Kennedy 1823). During winter months, deer were sought to supplement depleted stored foods and to acquire animal by-products, particularly hides, horn, and bone marrow. Methods of hunting were determined by the particular animals sought, size of the hunting party, area and distance to be traversed, and other logistical arrangements. Individual hunting was most effective in winter using snowshoes (fig. 2) and tracking to facilitate stalking with bow and arrow. Traps, snares, and deadfalls were utilized in areas near camps or villages where it was easy for the hunter to check these devices, as other animals could destroy the dead or immobilized game (Ross 1964–1991).

Eastern Wash. State Histl. Soc., Cheney Cowles Mus., Spokane Wash.: 2.1a, b (neg. 95.42).
Fig. 2. Snowshoes. The frames are made of tree branches with the bark left on, bent into teardrop shapes, and fastened with metal wire. The webbing is made of thin branches that have been soaked, pounded, and split so that they can be bent. Collected before 1917. Length of left, 84 cm.

Group hunting of elk, antelope, and deer, using animal drives, surrounds, and jumps, required considerable coordination of the participants as well as preparation of the area to be hunted. An individual, possessing deer power, who dreamed of a successful hunt would announce his intention to hunting partners who, at dawn of the hunt day, assisted him in strategically placing burnt moccasins and bird feathers around the designated area in a funnel-shaped fashion. These devices aided the hunters when the deer attempted to avoid the burnt scent, and the feathers aided the arrows to their mark (Ross 1964–1991). Another variation of the surround was when 30–40 men encircled an area, slowly reducing their enclosure while shouting, waving their arms, and pushing the deer to a high point where they were dispatched with bow and arrow (Ross 1964–1991). Some of the hunters would have already located themselves in shallow excavated pits on the upper reaches of talus slopes from which they easily shot their quarry. The day prior to this type of hunting, men possessing deer power would enter the area and place tree moss on low shrubs as a food to entice deer to the area (Ross 1981).

In the fall, upon returning to winter riverine villages, large numbers of men would drive deer over precipices (Diomedi 1978) at the end of runs channeled by cairns, or into narrow canyons where permanently constructed low stone walls were strategically located. Another method of hunting was to erect permanent channel walls that effectively controlled the direction of deer driven onto loose basalt talus fields and served to cripple and immobilize the fleeing animals (Ross 1964–1991). Tree stands for fall deer hunting were often controlled by extended families who, upon request, gave permission for nonkin use (Ross 1982).

Land mammals were never stalked or taken at springs as this was disrespectful and, if violated, was believed to be the main reason for game leaving an area (Ross 1964–1991). The hunt preparations with sweating, cleansing weapons, and procedures of strategy as well as distribution of game were conducted by a hunt leader, an individual possessing a tutelary spirit for deer hunting, who probably was the recipient of the dream that instigated the particular hunt. This leader supervised all sacred field preparations and even the placing of bound slain deer legs in tree crutches, and the sweeping of human footprints from the areas of deer jumps (Ross 1964–1991). Though hunting was male-oriented, it was not unusual for women to accompany kinsmen on distant collective expeditions to assist in cooking, shelter construction, skinning and preliminary preparation of hides, drying meat, and to assist in transporting the game.

The techniques of deer hunting were employed for elk and antelope. However, antelope was the only large land mammal that was decoyed or enticed within bow and arrow range by smoke or moving hide or feather wands (Ross 1968). Mountain lion, wolf, and fox were usually hunted by individuals. Grizzly bear was sought by a person possessing specific power, who, after dreaming of success, would observe a three-day period of intense sweating, sexual abstinance, and strict adherence to numerous food taboos that recognized the diet of the bear. After a hibernating bear was forced from its den by smoke, and dispatched with bow and arrow or spear, the successful hunter sang the bear's death song, observing three days of strict behavioral and dietary taboos to avoid dreaming of the bear or being burned later by fire or struck by lightning (Ross 1968). Bear hides were highly prized, and the fat was used for burn medicine and a variety of soaps and utensil lubricants. Black bear meat made excellent jerky, though black bears were seldom hunted in late May when their diet was skunk cabbage, or in late July when bears ravage red ant nests, thereby tainting the taste of the meat (Ross 1964–1991).

Spokane hunting parties in late summer or early fall traveled to the region around Helena or to the Flathead country near the Bitterroot Mountains in search of bison (Elmendorf 1935–1936). Little evidence exists that suggests the Spokane ventured onto the Plains for bison in the early nineteenth century (L. Hudson et al. 1981; Chance 1981). In all probability the Spokane and the Colville formed bison hunting parties in the mid-1800s (McDonald 1927), leaving for the Plains in fall and returning in early spring. Spokane and Colville groups would take dried salmon and camas, which were traded for bison hides and meat (L. Hudson et al. 1981; Chance 1981).

Many smaller animals were hunted in winter and prized for fur and used to supplement stored food, particularly muskrat, marten, bobcat, porcupine, and snowshoe hare. Throughout the year, grouse, ground squirrel, and beaver were taken; and in the autumn turtles and turtle eggs were collected by women while gathering tules. Some animals were not used as food—frogs, reptiles, birds of prey, or grizzly bear (Ross 1964–1991). Bald eagles were hunted, and golden eagles for feathers and power bundles. Blue heron were prized for the legbones, which were used as flageolets and sucking tubes in curing rituals (Ross 1964–1991). Different types of grouse and the spruce partridge were easily taken and utilized for their meat and feathers.

• TRAPPING   Small game, such as mink, marmots, otter, badger, fisher, and porcupine were taken with traps and snares; pitfalls and deadfalls were used for wolf, cougar, coyote, fox, lynx, and wildcat. These devices were located along game trails, but never at springs or salt licks. Yarrow was rubbed on cordage and trap parts to conceal human odors (Ross 1964–1991). Land mammal traps and snares had no special powers though a hunter might sing over a device to encourage its success.

• GATHERING   The most important gathering technology was the woman's digging stick, made usually of fire-hardened yew wood with a section of deer antler or hard wood affixed as a handle at one end. A rite of passage recognized a young girl when first receiving her "digger," and on her death it was used to mark her grave. The first camas dug by a girl was ritually cleaned and saved in a hide bag, one she would always wear around her neck when digging roots (Ross 1964–1991).

Though approximately 130 plants were gathered, constituting about 40–50 percent of total annual caloric intake, the major food plants gathered were camas, bitterroot, and numerous species of *Lomatium*. Gathering of plant food was done by women in varying degrees of participation from early April until late November or an early killing frost. Camas was dug when the flower had left the plant. The several species of this plant constituted a great portion of the vegetal intake and was an important stored winter food. Despite the importance of summer fishing activities, and the often comparatively low yields of root fields, older women would sometimes remain in these areas gathering and sun-drying their harvest, often until late July when the second phase of gathering began with moving to higher elevations to collect berries while the men hunted deer (Thoms 1989).

The introduction of agriculture actually destroyed numerous root fields. Cattle may have been introduced to the general area as early as 1841, and were, according to Merk (1931), immediately destructive to many traditional root fields. Several older Spokanes recall plowing large camas fields in the early 1900s when camas became a cash crop, but after realizing the deleterious effects of plowing, they reinstated traditional methods (Ross 1964–1991).

Spokane women collected chokecherry, serviceberry, many varieties of currants, kinnikinnick, and Oregon grape   *273* in late summer and early autumn, sun-dried them on tule mats, and then transported them to winter villages for storage. The major berry crop was huckleberry, which was collected, depending on elevation, in August, in great quantities for winter consumption. The importance of this berry is seen in various sacred rituals and associated taboos as the first berries collected were blessed and sung over. A sick person was forbidden to eat huckleberries, and it is one of the few berry crops that a male berdache might have had a specific power to locate. Balsamroot, sunflower, and coltsfoot were collected at the same time as hazelnuts and pine nuts (Ross 1964–1991).

Certain stems and barks were collected for immediate consumption or storage. Many barks were adscititious to the Spokane pharmacopoeia and often collected and later administered by a person possessing a particular curing power and skill. Western larch, ponderosa pine, white fir, and subalpine fir provided chewing gum, and sap from paper birch was considered a delicacy, whereas the sap and bark of aspen was a basis for medical infusions. Many barks, such as scouler willow, river alder, dogwood, and wild cherry, were important as medicines. Two species of mushrooms were eaten raw (Ross 1964–1991).

Nuts, seeds, gums, and sap, collected by both sexes during late autumn, stored well, sometimes in their shells, or, if processed, in salmon skins. Limited amounts of nuts and seeds were extracted from squirrel caches. Similarly, stored wapato were taken from muskrat dens during times of starvation. The greater yield of nuts was provided by hazelnut trees and pine trees; sunflower was the main ground plant exploited. The cambium layer from ponderosa pine, white fir, and subalpine fir was gathered and eaten in early spring or as a winter survival food.

Leaves from numerous plants were collected primarily for producing beverages or medicines, particularly plants such as mint, liverberry, and trillium. Other plants collected by the Spokane were bracken, needles from the Douglas fir, and buttercup, which was consumed after the poisonous principal protanaemonin was removed (Kirk 1975:23). Also, greens, gathered at lower elevations, primarily many stream and pond hydraphytes, were important as foods, dyes, and medicines. Mushrooms known to be poisonous were effective in sorcery and the killing of wild dogs (Ross 1964–1991).

Several types of lichens, epiphytes, and mosses were gathered and utilized as foods, medicines, and dyes. Pine moss was highly valued as a food and gathered during the summer from tamarack, which is not so bitter as other tree mosses. This moss was also used for diapers and as a lining in cradleboards (Ross 1964–1991).

Prescribed burning altered the understory to encourage animal browsing, increase huckleberry yields, prevent crown fires, propagate certain seed crops, and reduce insects (Ross 1981; Daubenmire 1968).

• FISHING   The importance of fishing was apparent from summer village locations, specialized fishing technology,

and from myth, ritual, and other aspects of the culture (Elmendorf 1935–1936). Salmon, the mainstay of Spokane economy, was a highly nutritious food, one that stored well, and was important as a traded commodity. Four species of salmon—coho, chinook, pink, and chum—were taken in great numbers (Cox 1831:230-231; Gibbs 1855, 1:415; C. Hunt 1936) Other fish taken were different species of trout, whitefish, lamprey, chub fish, sturgeon, and suckers. Some fish were eaten immediately, but most were dried on racks and stored in tule bags, placed high in low-limbed ponderosa trees, on prominant rock islands, or in sealed talus pits for winter consumption. Fish eyes were a delicacy, and roe was stored in salmon skins.

Fishing commenced in May at several major fisheries along the Spokane River with a First Salmon ceremony and continued intermittently, according to species, until early autumn. The methods of procurement were set nets, traps, leisters, harpoons, hooks, gaffs, dip nets, and even by hand. After the arrival of the horse, men occasionally fished from horseback using spears and lariats. Night fishing was done by torchlight from rafts or the banks of narrow streams (Ross 1964–1991). Crushed granite lined sections of narrow stream beds to afford better visibility for the spearman, and some sunshades on narrow streams were erected for the same purpose (Walker 1967). A salmon chief presided over communal fishing stations, supervising the repair of traps and weirs, propitiatory ritual, observance of taboos, and the distribution of the catch.

Technology

The principal tools of hunting and primary weapons of warfare were the bow and arrow, and no protective armament was used. The Spokane had three types of bows: the sinew-backed bow, a straight bow, and an elk-rib bow used in heavy brush areas. Favored woods for construction were syringa and ocean spray as well as mountain mahogany that was traded from the south for arrowshafts. Sinew-backed bows had numerous layers of deer sinew glued with an adhesive of boiled deer hoofs and sturgeon skin; they were often named and never loaned to other hunters.

Arrows were made of alder and dogwood, with either a foreshaft designed to remain implanted, or a single shaft, and vaned with three radial redtail hawk feathers. Projectile points of basalt, obsidian, chert, and flint were made by percussion and pressure flaking. Blunt arrows were used in hunting small game, birds, and suckers. Arrow straighteners were commonly of paired sand stones with a transverse groove.

The principal basket was a coiled basket of spruce or cedar root that served for storage, drinking cups, burden loads, and water containers. Baskets were round for ease of construction and strength, and rectangular baskets of the same materials were for berry collecting. Baskets of young cottonwood, pine, and cedar were made by debarking sections, then soaking and bending them into shape with internal and external willow hoops secured with willow bark thread. A round basket had either a bark disk bottom or sides folded to form a concave crescent bottom with long hemp cord or buckskin straps attached as a tumpline. Ornamentation was not common but there was occasional imbrication with beargrass; and vegetable or mineral dyes provided yellows, blues, and a reddish brown (Ross 1964–1991). Flat, flexible bags for storing food were made by twining and twilling hemp, sagebrush, inner bark of scouler willow, and bark from antelope brush, or from flattened tule, and cattail stalks, and sewn with hemp cord (Flett 1974).

In early fall, quantities of thinly split lengths of spruce, cedar, and pine roots for making baskets were coiled and carefully stored in protected tree caches. The most complex technology of the women was making tule mats for dwellings, floors, bedding, and baskets. After a killing frost, a woman with power directed the collecting, bundling, and distribution of gathered tules, and before departing the area it was burned over to ensure a successful harvest the following fall (Ross 1981).

There was no pottery though clay was used for cleaning buckskin garments and occasionally for medicinal purposes (Ross 1964–1991) or in making toys (Ray 1933). Lithic technology provided knives, hide scrapers, arrow points, mauls, arrow straighteners, mortars, pestles, net sinkers, weir weights, charms, and elbow and tube pipes. Manufacture was by flaking, grinding, and pecking of local materials; obsidian was obtained from the south by trade.

Structures

The Spokane utilized three types of dwellings: a permanent winter village type that was a conical semisubterranean pit house constructed of poles covered with layers of tule mats; a permanent double-apsidal lodge with inverted V pole construction covered with tule mats; and a smaller temporary tule mat summer structure. In early March, tule mats were rolled and carefully stored in trees. Some mats were carried to spring and summer fishing and root-digging fields to cover temporary structures. Each extended family had a sweatlodge and menstrual house.

Transport

The principal mode of water travel was by canoe, which prior to the Spokane acquiring iron tools (Teit 1930:340) were "poorly made dugouts" (Teit 1930:288). Some sturgeon-nosed bark canoes were acquired from the Lakes, and crude fire-hollowed craft from the Okanagan (Ross 1989). Canoes and rafts were used primarily to gain access and transport great quantities of roots from root fields south of the Spokane River. Wood and bundled tule rafts, anchored

with large weir weights, were used by men when diving for freshwater mussels (Ross 1964–1991).

The snowshoe (fig. 2), toboggan, and frozen animal hides were used in winter to transport heavy loads. Besides the hand load, the commonest method of transport was with head or shoulder tumpline utilized mainly by women. Small shoulder travois skids were pulled by men for transporting game and equipment after a hunt. After acquiring the horse, the socioeconomic patterns changed considerably as the Spokane were then capable of traveling longer distances and transporting heavier loads.

Clothing and Adornment

Clothing was made from brain-tanned, smoked deerhide or woven bask materials. Women's dress was a loose, full-length garment, sometimes with an attached shoulder cape and long sleeves (Elmendorf 1935–1936). Premenstrual girls wore woven cedar bask pubic aprons over their dresses. Men wore minimal clothing, but some exceptional hunters wore full costumes with leggings tied to a belt and a buckskin shirt that covered the hips (figs. 3–4) (Elmendorf 1935–1936). In the winter both sexes wore hide leggings, with the fur on the inside, and moccasins (Wilkes 1845:447) with short tongues.

Clothing was enhanced with painting, stone and shell beads, elk teeth, bear claws, burnt work, feathers (Teit 1930:337; Wilkes 1845:447; A.B. Lewis 1906:187), and dentalium shell traded from the coast. Red ocher was not used to decorate women's clothing, except on the bottom of menstrual dresses (Ross 1964–1991). The Spokane used no facial painting (Elmendorf 1935–1936); however, red ocher was applied to the face and arms of an elderly woman during a late winter ceremony when she occupied a small tepee and conducted rituals to encourage the arrival of spring (Ross 1964–1991). Charcoal was used as facial painting by Bluejay men during the Midwinter ceremony (Elmendorf 1935-1936; Ross 1964–1991).

The Spokane wore their hair long and hanging loose unless tied back for certain activities or ceremonies when it was parted and plaited into two braids, often with feathers or small pelt tails. In the morning and before retiring, a woman would comb her husband's hair. Men removed facial hair using split hardwood tweezers or joined mussel shells.

Social Organization

Kinship was reckoned bilaterally (Elmendorf 1961; Roy 1961; Jorgensen 1969) with patripotestal authority, and recognized sororal polygyny, which was practiced by men of high status: chiefs, exceptional hunters, shamans, and successful gamblers. The levirate and sororate existed but were not obligatory. The major social unit of economic production was the extended family, which recognized a high divi-

S'pokan Chief Spokan River

top, Stark Mus. of Art, Orange, Tex.: 31.78/43, WWC43; bottom, Eastern Wash. State Histl. Soc., Cheyney Cowles Mus., Spokane, Wash.: 1780.947a & b (neg. 95.21).

Fig. 3. Men's clothing. top, Tum-se-ne-ho, also known as The Man Without Blood, wearing buckskin moccasins, fringed leggings, and a perforated shirt. Perforations indicate that the wearer possessed a power that gave him protection from harm caused by arrows and bullets (Ray 1933:49). He has a quiver full of arrows and another bow. His hairstyle includes cut bangs and a decoration on a side braid. Watercolor by Paul Kane, 1847. bottom, Leggings. The beadwork shows Plains influence. This item belonged to Chief Willie Andrews and was manufactured 1920–1940. Length of legging 72.4 cm.

sion of labor by age and sex. Spokane bands were ethnocentric composites of kin-related resource groups comprised of 150–250 or more persons who shared a living area and mutually exploited resource sites.

Political Organization

The basic unit of social control was the autonomous winter village, headed by a chief who retained his office through consensus, generosity, skillful decisions, oratory skills, and the possession of power. Each band had two or three petty chiefs (Gibbs 1855; Manring 1912). During times of mutual resource exploitation, a leader was an individual who possessed the power necessary for exploiting a particular resource. War leaders were self-designated, who after experiencing a dream of the pending event, organized and supervised war or horse-stealing parties. Councils met on important matters confronting the group, often in lengthy sessions to achieve consensus. Both male and female adults enjoyed the right to participate and present their opinions. Chiefs treated one another with respect while maintaining autonomy, and chieftainship was essentially hereditary, but a capable individual could assume leadership.

A chief's main obligation and concern was to maintain village tranquility by resolving differences of opinion, and making final judgment in cases of arbitration. The chief was essentially a counselor and a leader who was generous with his time and concern for village welfare; he invariably possessed powers that were of benefit to the group and was renowned for his oratorical skills.

Life Cycle

• BIRTH Pregnant women observed strict dietary and behavioral taboos and were expected to work industriously to ensure an easy delivery, the child's well-being, and to strengthen themselves for the pending ordeal. Congenital defects and psychological or behavioral problems were always related to the parents' transgressions while the woman was pregnant (Ross 1988).

After birth, the baby was immediately plunged into cold water for stimulation and rubbed vigorously with soft hides

276

Fig. 4. Spokane Garry and his followers. left, Chief Garry, an important headman. right, Some of his young followers. All wear moccasins. The 2 men on the left wear buckskin leggings and necklaces of feathers and bear claws. The man on the right wears a fabric breechcloth and has feather hair decorations. The bow and arrow being held and tomahawk (left foreground) were purchased for the British Museum. The gun was said to have belonged to Angus McDonald, the chief trader, who lent it for the picture (Monroe 1982:16–17). These are the earliest known photographs of Spokane Indians. Photographed on the North American Boundary Commission Survey, 1860–1861.

by an attendant who tied the umbilical cord with deer sinew, and severed the cord by biting. The placenta was buried. The navel cord was placed in a buckskin bag and attached to the cradleboard (Ross 1988), though in some instances the cord was contained in a bark pouch and placed in a tree (Elmendorf 1935–1936).

With complicated deliveries, such as a breech birth, an older woman or midwife would attend the child's delivery. A wet nurse was enlisted if the flow of breast milk was restricted, or if the mother died in childbirth; as an adult, the child was forbidden to marry any offspring of the wet nurse (Ross 1964–1991). Adoption was a prerogative of grandparents or the deceased mother's married sister, and with permission, an orphan could be adopted by a childless married couple (Ross 1964–1991). Parents felt particularly blessed with twins (Elmendorf 1935–1936). After the death of a firstborn, the next child born possessed the same soul, but parents recognized the child as different (Elmendorf 1935–1936). A child was never given the name of a deceased sibling as eventually the child might also die prematurely (Ross 1964–1991).

After several weeks, the baby was placed in a cradleboard (fig. 5) with attached prophylactic devices, such as a small section of buckskin dipped in menstrual blood, or miniature moccasins with perforated soles so the baby could say to a malicious spirit that it was unable to make a spirit journey as its feet would hurt. The Spokane considered infanticide and abortion moral transgressions; nevertheless, unwanted pregnancies were sometimes terminated by drinking an infusion that created severe peristalsis, and with advanced pregnancies the amniotic sac was pierced with a sharpened stick (Ross 1964–1991).

• PUBERTY   The girl's menarche initiated her monthly confinement to a menstrual hut where she received instruction on prohibited foods and other taboos and adult expectations. When confined she wore her oldest dress, could not comb or braid her hair, and could only scratch herself with a special sharpened stick. Until a woman was married she was never permitted to be alone, and she was chaperoned by an older woman when in public.

A boy's puberty ceremony was marked by a strict and rigorous program of running and swimming to condition him for the anticipated vision quest, when the novitiate fasted in seclusion for three days, waiting for a tutelary spirit to appear. If successful, he received a power bundle, a song, and a specific power from an animal that ensured him of later success, usually one characteristic of that particular animal for hunting, fishing, gambling, love, or curing. A man's status as a berdache may be determined at this time (Ross 1984).

Both sexes used the sweatlodge daily, which served for spiritual and physical cleansing, curing, enculturation,

Fig. 5. Cradleboards. left, Woman with baby on a plain board. She has a wooden box behind her in which she will put the apples she picks. Photograph by Frank Palmer, about 1906. center, Cradleboard, beaded in yellow and pink floral motif on a light blue background. The laced pouch is made of tanned hide, and the hood is red wool. Collected in 1887. Length 102 cm. right, Woman with her infant in cradleboard attached to her horse. Photograph by Harry J. Allyn, © 1899.

social control, prophetic visions, socializing, and physical conditioning. The sweathouse of each extended family represented a major deity and was considered sacred.

• MARRIAGE Marriage was arranged by a couple's family and performed when the man was about 18 years of age, and the woman between puberty and 20 years of age. Reciprocal feasting preceded the ritual when the groom's kinsmen gave the bride's family dried salmon, camas, and other root products and items such as baskets and buckskins. In-law avoidance was not formalized by taboo, but a man was respectful and helpful to his wife's mother (Elmendorf 1935–1936).

• DEATH Immediately upon death, the body was removed from the dwelling, flexed, wrapped in deerhide, and buried (Elmendorf 1935–1936). Since a major concern was the soul's transition and incorporation in an afterworld, the deceased's ghost should not be offended (Ross 1964–1991). After burial, a person's possessions were distributed among his kinsmen (Elmendorf 1935–1936), though there was sometimes theft (Wilkes 1845, 4:448). During a one- to two-year period of mourning, a widow or widower never mentioned the deceased's name, to prevent dreaming; however, occasionally a widow's husband's spirit could appear in a dream to warn her of impending danger (Ross 1964–1991). A widow never renewed her bereavement clothing and was properly addressed as "widow." The mourning was terminated with a ceremonial feast hosted by the family of the deceased (fig. 6).

Games

Games and gambling were a favorite amusement of the Spokane and invariably involved hand-eye coordination skills and feats of strength and endurance. At large gatherings, the most important gambling game was the stick game (fig. 7), played with two pairs of bones and 20 counter sticks in which two sides would bet against each other for horses, clothing, weapons, and other goods. Women played a variety of dice games in which the losing individual, or group, surrendered goods to the winner.

Both children and adults participated in games of endurance that involved stone-lifting and putting, tugging, jumping, swimming, running, and even holding one's breath (Ross 1988). Games of dexterity such as ring and pin, hoop and stick, and cat's cradle were popular, and during the winter storytelling by elders was a favorite pastime.

Religion

The main figure of Spokane animistic belief was the Sweatlodge deity, a benevolent force who created the order of the universe as well as humans, animals, plants, and spirits. The Spokane supernatural had five distinct categories of supernatural entities: the soul; a life spirit; a guardian spirit or tutelary; ghosts; and a general category of monsters, dwarfs, weird beings, and ogres. A major creative figure

ROSS

Eastern Wash. State Histl. Soc., Cheney Cowles Mus., Spokane.

Fig. 6. Death feast of Willie Andrews (d. 1946), Wellpinit, Spokane Res., Wash. top, Gathering. The covering extended from the house is a tepee painted with a buffalo, half-length human figure, lines and circles, among other paintings. bottom left, Participants at ceremonial feast. left to right, Lizzie Ford, Spokane; Mattie Boyd, Spokane; Agatha Isidore, Kalispel; Catherine Fry, Kalispel; Ellen Hays, Kalispel. Framed photographs show, left to right, Willie Andrews (2 left photos and far right photo); Ellen Andrews, his mother; and Owiyawaxen. bottom right, Funeral feast. Identified people are, from front of table to rear, right side only: Henry Covington, Colville; Jerome Paschel, Spokane; Mary Adrian, Spokane; Martha Joshuah, also known as Semtet, Spokane; and Tom Blossom, from Wellpinit, tribe not known. Photographs by Richard T. Lewis, about 1947.

was Coyote, a trickster whose frantic and lascivious behavior modified most animals and many land forms.

The major religious ceremonies were a spring Sun Dance, and the Bluejay ceremony held in conjunction with the Midwinter ceremony, a rite of intensification concerned primarily with world renewal and resource availability (Elmendorf 1935–1936). Bluejays were men of extraordinary prophetic power who served as sentinels and control agents during the Midwinter ceremony, who blackened their faces as bluejays and made similar sounds when they leapt with ease to the ridge pole of the ceremonial lodge. Prior to the cere-

mony they slept in a special lodge and ran naked in the snow looking for lost items (Ross 1982).

Illness and Curing

The principal explanations for physical maladies were spirit illnesses: moral transgressions, soul loss, object and spirit intrusion, spirit possession, or poisoning through sorcery. Beyond familial treatment, practitioners were male or female shamans who conducted group medical inquests to reveal etiology, prognosis, and required treatment (Ross

1989). Curing procedures involved manipulation, massage, sweating, sucking at the site of illness, blowing smoke or atomizing water over the patient, dancing, and singing—often supplemented with an extensive materia medica collected and prepared by specialists.

Curing shamans enjoyed high status and their prestige accumulated with age and successful curing. Curing rituals were psychodramas in which practitioners employed ventriloquism, hypnotism, legerdemain, and demonstrated their power through glossalalia, various dramatic and even painful proofs of ordeal, or by transformation. A shaman conferred directly with his spirit helper who took possession of the practitioner, making potent various prophetic devices for establishing a disease etiology or responsible sorcerer. If unsuccessful, an attending shaman could be accused of being the sorcerer.

Knowledge

The Spokane named the lunar months, nine for the presence of certain resource plants and animals. The solstices were named and recognized as delineating the seasons. The time of day was judged by the position of the sun, and times of the month by lunar phase. Distance was quantified by a trip's duration and the location of geonomically designated topographical features. Wind direction correlated with named cardinal directions, and approximately 14 colors were recognized.

History

Although the year 1805 is generally used to indicate the first Euro-American contact of southern Plateau groups by Meriwether Lewis and William Clark, in the late 1700s, communicable disease, certain trade items, and horses had already wrought considerable change in Spokane culture. David Thompson (Fuller 1931) surveyed the Spokane region from 1808 to 1811 for the North West Company. In 1810, the North West Company established, in the vicinity of the Middle Spokane, the fur trading post Spokane House (Drury 1949). By 1812 The Pacific Fur Company had established a trading post adjacent to Spokane House, but the following year it was purchased by the North West Company. In 1824 the Hudson's Bay Company purchased this company and assumed complete control over the area. In 1826 Spokane House was abandoned.

Due to severe population decline and concomitant alteration of demographics and socioeconomic patterns, the Spokane and contiguous groups were influenced by religious nativistic movements, particularly the Prophet Dance (Walker 1968) and the Dreamer cult (J.A. Simms in ARCIA 1875, 1876; Raufer 1966). By 1831 some Spokanes joined a small group of Flatheads who ventured to Saint Louis to request missionaries (Ruby and Brown 1970). As early as 1824, George Simpson, governor of the Hudson's Bay Company, was responsible for the establish-

Fig. 7. Stick game. Young people sitting outside the stick game tents have their own game during the annual Labor Day powwow. Photograph by Sharon Eva Grainger, Wellpinit, Spokane Res., Wash., 1994.

ment of a mission station at Spokane House, stating that conversion to Christianity would encourage trade and raise the standard of living of the Spokane (Merk 1931). After Samuel Parker's 1835 survey of the Spokane area for the American Board of Commissioners for Foreign Missions, Presbyterian missionaries Cushing Eells and Elkanah Walker and their wives established the Tshimakain Mission on the edge of what is now the Spokane Reservation. Father Joseph Cataldo contacted the Spokane in 1866, later establishing the mission Saint Michael. Christian missionaries introduced and maintained religious pluralism, which became the basis for inter- and intragroup political conflict (Ross 1968).

Relations between Euro-Americans and the Spokane and contiguous groups deteriorated with the 1847 massacre of Whites by Cayuses at Dr. Marcus Whitman's mission and the abandonment of the Tshimakain Mission. The 1850 Donation Land Act, passed by Congress, served to increase White encroachment and open conflict by miners and other settlers upon the Spokane, which led to warfare with the U.S. Army, and the 1858 military defeat of the Spokane at the Battle of Four Lakes, when troops destroyed Spokane livestock, horses, crops, and farms. The Army maintained Fort Spokane at the mouth of the Spokane River from 1880 until 1898, when the War Department turned it over to the Interior Department for an Indian boarding school. Colville and Spokane children were enrolled there until its closure in 1906. Major smallpox epidemics occurred in 1846 and 1852–1853, which Mooney (1928) estimated destroyed one-third to one-half of the area inhabitants (Drury 1940:152).

The Spokane Reservation was established in 1881 in a greatly reduced area, with the Spokane River as the southern boundary. A waterpower dam was built in 1911 at Little Falls, essentially destroying the upstream salmon fishing site at Spokane Falls. The 1940 completion of Grand Coulee Dam prevented salmon from entering the Spokane River, denying the Spokane a major source of food. In 1970 the

Bureau of Indian Affairs gave full agency status to the Spokane with the establishment of the agency and tribal headquarters in Wellpinit.

In the 1990s a few older people still made baskets, collected roots, and practiced some Spokane customs, but only a few spoke the language or used the sweathouse. Many participated in occasional pan-Indian celebrations. The reservation is organized around an elected tribal council, with headquarters, community center, and tribal store. Roman Catholic and Protestant churches are on the reservation. Factions are formed basically along lines of religious affiliation and between political and geographical groups. Issues of high unemployment, gaming, litigation over loss of fishing sites and resources, and control of cultural resource management were dominant in the 1990s. Approximately 50 percent of the 2,128 enrolled Spokanes lived on the reservation in 1990 (table 1).

Synonymy

The name Spokane is mentioned by David Thompson (1916:53), whose writings establish the Spokane ethnographically as early as 1810. Alexander Henry (Coues 1897:711) contended that the Spokane lived along the Spokane River and belonged to the Flathead. Work (1829:20) called the Lower Spokane, Scaitseeuthinsh; the Middle Spokane, Sinhomenish; and the Upper Spokane,

Sintotoluh. Gibbs (1855:20) used the term Spokehnish for the Spokane, and Curtis (1907–1930, 7:54) designated the native appellation of the Lower Spokane as Sinhomene, the Middle Spokane, Tskaisfshihlni, and the Upper Spokane, Sintutuuli. Teit (1930:298) designated the Spokane as Spōqiénic, calling the Lower Spokane, Stsêkjasti, Stkastsī'ln, or Stkastsī'łenic, the Middle Spokane, Sntutuū'li, or Sntutu'ū´, and the Upper Spokane, Snxo'mē´, Sɛnxomê, Sɛnxomê´nic. As a tribal group, the three Spokane bands were called *spoqíni* 'round-head' (Elmendorf 1935–1936) or *spoqín* (Carlson and Flett 1989:61). Elmendorf (1935–1936) designated the Lower Spokane as *scqescíłni?* ('fishery'), the Middle Spokane as *sntu?t?úlixʷ* (cf. *ntu?t?ulmétkʷ* 'cloudy-water creek'), and the Upper Spokane as *snxʷméne?* from *snxʷméne?m* (Little Spokane River, literally 'steelhead place').

The spelling Spokan has also been used.

The Middle Spokane have also been called South Spokan (Spier 1936:9). Ray's (1936:116) Lower and Middle Spokane make up the *Handbook*'s Lower Spokane, and his Upper Spokane comprises the *Handbook*'s Upper and Middle Spokane.

Sources

Though there is a paucity of reliable ethnographic material on the Spokane, the primary ethnographic sources are

Table 1. Population

Year	Population	Source	Comment
1780	1,400	Mooney 1928	
1805	600	Thwaites 1904–1905, 6:119	30 lodges
1829	704	Work 1829	222 men, 241 women, 111 boys, 130 girls
1841	405	Wilkes 1845	including Colville, probably adult men only
1853	450	Gibbs 1855	
1859	600	ARCIA 1859:417	
1867	750	ARCIA 1867:56	
1871	725	ARCIA 1871:294	
1880	685	ARCIA 1880:153	
1896	900–1,000	Mooney 1896:733	Coeur d'Alene and Spokane Res.
1908	634	Hodge 1907–1910, 2:625	301 Lower, 238 Upper in Wash.; 95 on Coeur d'Alene Res.
1916	611	Bureau of Indian Affairs 1916	
1925	700	Bureau of Indian Affairs 1925	
1950	979	Bureau of Indian Affairs 1950	
1960	1,357	Bureau of Indian Affairs 1960	
1970	1,672	Bureau of Indian Affairs 1970	
1980	1,907	Bureau of Indian Affairs 1980	
1990	2,128	Ross 1964–1991	
1994	2,025	Bureau of Indian Affairs 1994	

Teit (1930), Curtis (1907–1930, 7), and Elmendorf's (1935–1936) field notes on kinship, linguistics, and general ethnography collected from native speakers born prior to the reservation system. Ray's (1933) data on the contiguous Sanpoil and Nespelem is significant. Wynecoop (1969), a native scholar, wrote a brief tribal history, and ethnohistorical studies were conducted by Burns (1966), Ruby and Brown (1970), Chalfant (1974), Anastasio (1972), and Chance (1981; L. Hudson et al. 1981). Roy (1961) studied the consequences of Euro-American contact. Ross (1964–1991) conducted ethnographic fieldwork, and L.B. Carlson and P. Flett (1989) have compiled important linguistic and ethnographic data.

Collections of material culture are dispersed and incomplete, and known collections are generally devoid of ethnographic data, an exception being Flett (1974), a native scholar, who described basketry in the Cheney Cowles Memorial Museum, Spokane.

282

Kalispel

SYLVESTER L. LAHREN, JR.

Territory

The Kalispel ('kălĭ,spĕl) spoke an Interior Salish language.*
Two divisions, the Upper and Lower Kalispel, each had a
name, a specific geographical area, and a separate political
structure. Neither was considered a tribe in terms of
sociopolitical organization (Alan H. Smith, personal communication 1985).

The Lower Kalispel occupied the territory along the Pend
Oreille River below Lake Pend Oreille in Idaho to the con-
fluence of the Salmon River in British Columbia (fig. 1).
For specific camp sites see Ray (1936:128–129) and A.H.
Smith (1950:30–56). It appears that the Upper Kalispel
occupied the area around Lake Pend Oreille and up the Pend
Oreille River to the confluence of the Clark Fork and Flathead rivers near Plains, Montana (A.H. Smith 1950:12–29).
After the introduction of the horse, there is no question that
their territorial limits were extended eastward to the Mission
Valley and Flathead Lake in Montana and south to include
the Bitterroot Valley (Malouf 1974:162, 1982:17; Chalfant
1974b:59–60).

Environment

The riverine orientation of the Kalispel followed the Clark
Fork River northwest into Idaho to Lake Pend Oreille west
to Sand Point, Idaho, and then west to Newport, Washington, where the river turns north at Usk, Washington, and
across the Canadian boundary to the mouth of the Salmo
River. The river course length of their prehorse territory is
approximately 230 miles.

The elevation at Plains is 2,500 feet, 2,080 at Sandpoint,
2,050 at Newport, and 1,722 at the Canadian border. The
entire region is mountainous, and as a result the area is characterized by a dendritic trellis geomorphological pattern
with the Pend Oreille River being the stem of the trellis. It
is bisected with lateral streams and rivers flowing into the
Pend Oreille River.

The area is heavily forested with interspersed meadows
and abundant water. Precipitation averages 15.5 inches per
year at Plains, Montana; 22.5 inches at Thompson Falls,
Montana; 31 inches at Sandpoint; and 28 inches at Newport.

*For the phonemes of Kalispel see the orthographic footnote in
"Spokane," this vol.

This comes in the form of both snow and rain. Due to the
low elevation of the main river its winter temperatures are
very mild. The mean temperatures at Thompson Falls,
Sandpoint, and Newport are 47.5, 47, and 45°F. respectively. Thompson Falls consistently reports the warmest temperatures in this mountainous area of Montana.

External Relations

Kalispel interaction with other groups was predicated on the
co-utilization of economic resources, on trade, and on bison
hunting. It is well known that they shared their camas fields
near Cusick, Washington, with neighboring groups. They
went to Spokane country to fish and collect flora not found
in their area and to Kettle Falls to fish and trade (Diomedi
1879; A.H. Smith 1950; Ray 1942).

The Kalispel were located along an important east-west
trade route, the Pend Oreille River, "which was the easiest
and the most important gateway through the mountains
toward the Columbia River region" (Teit 1930:355–356).
The Colvilles at Kettle Falls controlled one of the most
important trade centers in the Plateau, where Lakes, Okanagan, Sanpoil, Spokane, Coeur d'Alene, Nespelem, Methow,
Chelan, and Kalispel met (Ray 1933:115–116; Teit
1930:356).

At the Spokane trade center the Kalispel encountered, in
addition, Columbia, Nez Perce, and Palouse (Anastasio
1972:154–157). These trading relationships were intensified
with the appearance of the horse in the Plateau. By 1810 the
horse was "abundant" (Anastasio 1972:128–130). Nez
Perces, Coeur d'Alenes, Spokanes, southern Kootenais, and
Flatheads congregated with Kalispels (Josephy 1965:27) in
the Flathead Valley area of Montana. They joined into a
larger group for protection against their mutual enemy the
Blackfoot in order to hunt bison on the Plains. Most of the
groups used the Clark Fork River valley trail to reach the
Plains.

Intermarriage was most common with the contiguous Salish groups such as the Flathead, Coeur d'Alene, Spokane,
and Colville and occasionally with the Sahaptin-speaking
Nez Perce. These intermarriages solidified co-utilization of
economic resources, promoted trading relations, and facilitated mutual protection for bison hunting. Only the Blackfoot, enemy of the Kalispel and other Plateau groups, were

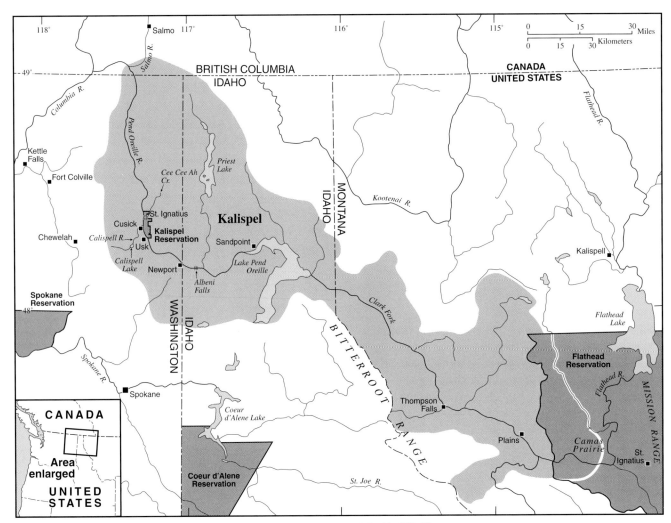

Fig. 1. Aboriginal Kalispel territory with modern towns and reservations (from A.H. Smith 1950:13).

repulsed from their valley (Anastasio 1972:128–130; Ray 1942:224–228).

Warfare was almost nonexistent prior to the arrival of the horse. Prehorse warfare could be caused by infringement on economic rights, murder or injury, itinerant raiders, or by insulting a chief. War associated with economic infringements could be avoided by compensation.

Circle war dances were associated with warfare. They required the presence of a shaman, and could last all day or night. Kalispels had war chiefs, war dreams, sought neighbors as allies, had scouts and guards, painted their faces, wore feathers in their hair, and took scalps. Fighting occurred in open fields and they conducted early morning and night surprise attacks. They used bird or animal calls, whistles, and smoke signals to communicate when conducting warfare. In earlier times they took prisoners, but later on they took fewer prisoners and always killed all the Blackfoot (fig. 2). Victory ceremonies lasted one day or night and consisted of victory dances, singing, drumming, and arrangement of marriages. Scalps were carried about on poles (Ray 1942:224–228).

Very brief hostilities occurred with the Coeur d'Alene and Kootenai prior to the horse. With the arrival of the horse warfare took on a new dimension. Kalispels allied themselves with the Flathead, Spokane, Coeur d'Alene, Columbia, Kootenai, Nez Perce, Bannock, Northern and Eastern Shoshone, and Ute for mutual protection. Their primary enemy was the Piegan Blackfoot, but they also had considerable warfare with the Crow. On occasion they did encounter the Cheyenne, Assiniboine, and Sioux. When the Spokane and Coeur d'Alene fought U.S. troops under Lt. Col. Edward Steptoe in 1858, about 20 Kalispels, related to the Spokane through descent and marriage, joined in this engagement (Teit 1930:360–373).

Culture

The following cultural description is primarily derived from ethnographic fieldwork conducted early in the 1900s and again during the 1930s and 1940s. It is intended to describe the culture as of the mid-nineteenth century.

284

Fig. 2. Quilix or Red Shirt, a woman warrior. Drawing depicting her exploits against the Blackfoot in which 30 of the enemy were killed. Ink on paper by Father Nicolas Point, 1841–1847.

Subsistence

When the snows disappeared the winter camps located along Pend Oreille River would break up and one or more families would begin moving to specific areas for hunting and fishing (A.H. Smith 1950:60–62). They would remain in these localities until camas became ripe in June at which time they would congregate at camas fields, the most important of which were located in the vicinity of the present-day Kalispel Reservation.

After camas harvest, completed in July, they would engage in fishing, hunting, and gathering activities until late fall (Diomedi 1879:2–3, 21). In late July and August certain families would go to fish for salmon. Those who did not go to catch salmon went to favorite hunting and berrying grounds along the rivers and in the mountains (A.H. Smith 1950:60–62).

From about the end of August until late fall they separated into smaller groups and concentrated on hunting. As the snows began to fall, families or in some cases bands migrated to their winter camps located along Pend Oreille River where the snowfall would be lighter and temperatures milder (A.H. Smith 1950:60–62).

Property rights were held by the tribe and the individual. Tribal grounds could be used by alien groups with permission of the chief or if they were in the company of the Kalispel. Village territorial rights extended to hunting and fishing sites and large weir sites where there was communal distribution of fish. Individual rights extended to fish traps, small weirs, spearing platforms, snares, and deadfalls. Other Kalispels were welcome to use these individual sites when they were not being used by the owner. Title to all fishing sites was held on the basis of use with the exception of large weir sites (Ray 1942:231).

The arrival of the horse altered the subsistence cycle. Those Kalispel who had horses began to hunt bison on the Plains with the entire family. They left for the summer hunt about mid-July, and after their arrival on the Plains they would hunt for 3–4 weeks and return home. In November other Lower Kalispel families would leave for the Plains. These families would winter at Saint Ignatius on their return trip because the snow was too deep for them to return to their winter camps along the lower Pend Oreille River. The bison was only taken on horseback with the bow (A.H. Smith 1950:203–213).

Fishing was of greater importance to the Kalispel before the horse, but it continued as a subsistence activity up through the nineteenth century (Teit 1930:348–349; Chalfant 1974a:223).

Historical records indicate that food supply in this area went through cyclical patterns of abundance and scarcity. During the first two years among the Lower Kalispel the missionaries found it difficult to live because their main food items were camas and dried berries, which contained very little nourishment (de Smet 1859:282). Father Anthony Ravalli, one of the missionaries, said that even though they were "surrounded by water, they often had difficulty getting fish even for Friday dinner" (Evans 1981:56). At another time, Father Pierre Jean de Smet recorded that the deer in the territory of the Lower Kalispel were in plentiful supply. During the winter of 1853–1854 there was a great scarcity of food among the Kalispels (de Smet 1905:466–467, 1231). The area appears to have been chronically short of food, and early fur traders were required to eat horses and dogs. This food shortage seems to have lasted until the late 1820s (Chance 1973:102).

• FISHING   Fish caught were char, chub, shiners, squawfish, suckers, trout, whitefish, and "goldfish." Salmon were found only in the northeast part of the territory, and fishing for them occurred on the lower Salmo River and lower Clark Fork River. Occasionally, they would fish for salmon on the Little Spokane River with the Spokane, but mostly they would go to Kettle Falls in Colville territory (A.H. Smith 1950:253–399).

Fish were eaten fresh, stone boiled, dried, and smoke dried. They were taken by the use of weirs, basket traps, spears, spear and torchlight, harpoons, hook and set line, hook, line and pole, hemp nets, seines, dip nets, conical falls traps, dams and impoundments, standing platforms and stranding traps for salmon. Once in a while they were shot with a bow and caught with a noose. Live fish were clubbed or killed by breaking their necks or biting them.

Weirs accounted for about two-thirds of all fish caught. Two types of weirs were used. One was a barrier trap made of fir balsam boughs and erected primarily in sloughs for taking "common fish" such as suckers, squawfish, and chub. The second type was a stick weir used in the faster-flowing streams and rivers and designed for trapping mainly whitefish. Control of a specific weir, by either the family or the larger "tribal" group, was determined by its productivity. Any site that produced a catch beyond the needs of a family was tribal property. These larger weirs were constructed by the group, and there was at least one and sometimes two headmen who possessed more spirit power that the rest and supervised its construction and operation (A.H. Smith 1950:253–399).

A hook and line was used throughout the year and mostly for catching fresh fish. Men, women, and children fished the year around with a pole, line, and hook from the bank; a canoe; and through the ice in winter. Several types of hooks were made from wood and bone, baited with meat (e.g., fish, entrails of fish, particularly the gizzard of the trout, grubs, grasshoppers) and sunk with stone sinkers. The line's usual length was 30–40 feet and consisted of hemp and later

horsetail hair. Set lines and hooks were also used to catch larger fish (A.H. Smith 1950:253–399).

• HUNTING   Kalispel hunting was principally done with deadfalls and bow and arrow. The common arrow with a sharpened shaft and the stone-tipped arrow were the two types of arrows used. The stone-tipped arrow was never used in rocks (e.g., marmot hunting) or areas where the tip might be broken because they were hard to replace. Bows were accurate only up to 50 yards. In the river valleys the prevailing winds came down the stream in the evening and up stream in the morning. To face these winds while hunting gave them an advantage so they hunted upstream in the evening and downstream in the morning (A.H. Smith 1950:63–251).

Deadfalls were used to take marten, fisher, mink, weasel, ermine, fox, wolverine, mountain lion, lynx, black bear, mice, and all other small furbearing animals. Fresh deer meat, dried fish, and slightly burned deer hooves were used as bait as well as the blood from previously trapped animals.

Birds eaten by adults were swans, ducks, geese, grouse, partridge, prairie chicken (pintail grouse), fool hen, sandhill crane, and chicken hawks. Young boys ate chickadees and robins. Large birds that were snared or shot with a bow were grouse, partridge, fool hen, and prairie chicken. Waterfowl were netted. Boys took small birds with a bow for sport, but they were not allowed to kill young songbirds. Birds taken only with a bow were sandhill cranes, ducks, geese, and swans. Sandhill crane feathers were used for veining arrows. Eggs of waterfowl, particularly goose, mudhens, and ducks, were purposely sought and eaten in large numbers. The eggs of other birds were eaten if they were happened upon. Eggs were cooked or eaten raw (A.H. Smith 1950:63–251).

Bald and golden eagles were sought for their feathers. The young golden eagle feather was most prized because of its black tip. The tail feathers were secured from the eaglets before they left the nest. In certain locations eagles were shot with the bow.

Black bears were shot with the bow in bear drives, along trails, in berry patches, and when hibernating. They were also captured in deadfalls. A hibernating bear would be coaxed to appear at the den entrance where it was shot with a bow. If the hunters were not able to bring the bear to the entrance, a hunter would enter the den with his two-foot bow and shoot the bear. Bear meat was equally divided among all families. Bears were called by imitating a cub (A.H. Smith 1950:63–251).

Grizzlies were not specifically hunted by the Kalispel. They would take one if they encountered it while hunting, but they did not like grizzly meat and killed it only for prestige.

Mule and white-tailed deer were the most important game animals to the Kalispel. They were hunted throughout the year, but most were killed in the winter. Deer were hunted all winter long on snowshoes and with bows. They herded deer in the winter, and sometimes they used dogs to help with herding. Once in a while they would run deer down on snowshoes and break their necks. Spears were periodically used during the winter hunt and only at that time (A.H. Smith 1950:63–251).

At other times of the year deer were driven into the water with dogs or by fire. Once in the water they were lanced with a steel knife that was attached to a pole, drowned by hand, or roped and pulled ashore and killed. At other times they were caught swimming and were shot with bows from canoes. Fire was also used to drive deer on land. Once in a while they were driven over cliffs, helped by the women. Deer were snared and killed at licks. Kalispel hunters would call does by imitating fawns and call bucks during the mating season. Deer meat was dried, smoked, or eaten raw (A.H. Smith 1950:63–251).

Caribou, more plentiful in the Lower Kalispel country than in Upper Kalispel, were stalked or driven by fire, and there were winter drives. Elk were more abundant in Upper Kalispel country. They were taken with the bow and sometimes a spear in winter. A calf elk call was used to lure them within bow range. Moose were rare in Kalispel country but were killed. Mountain sheep and goats were only found in the country of the Upper Kalispel. Sheep were stalked and hunted from blinds. Mountain sheep robes were considered very important. Goat meat was not well liked, but they did use goat skin for clothing (A.H. Smith 1950:63–251). Blood, carried in tripe, was used raw, boiled, and dried and stored. Marrow was extracted for orphan babies and used for hair oil and as a cosmetic (Ray 1942:136).

Otter skins were used to make quivers. Rabbits were taken with deadfalls, bow, clubs, and snares for food and bait. Muskrats were dug out of their holes and clubbed to death or shot with a bow for eating and for their fur. Skunks were shot with a bow or clubbed for food and their skin was used for robes. Squirrels were primarily taken by boys for food. Marmots were eaten and the skins were used. Beavers were taken for food, and their skins were used for blankets. Bobcats were scarce, but they were eaten, and the hide was used for clothes (A.H. Smith 1950:63–251).

Certain animals were not purposely hunted but would be taken if encountered. These were the wolverine, badger, wolf, mountain lion, and coyote. Wolverines were taken for food and the fur was used for quivers. The Kalispel deliberately tried to exterminate this animal because it would destroy their deadfalls and eat the bait or captured animal. Periodically, a wolf or mountain lion was shot for food and fur. Badger was also eaten once in a while. Coyotes were primarily taken for their fur (A.H. Smith 1950:63–251).

• GATHERING   Camas was probably the most important of the vegetable foods (A.H. Smith 1950:407), and Kalispel territory was rich in camas areas (Teit 1930:341).

Other food items gathered were the Indian potato, moss (from the tamarack), cattail roots (eaten raw), pine vambium layer, wild garlic, wild celery, wild carrot, Easter lily, black pine sap (small amounts), and bitterroot. Plants not found in Kalispel country and taken in Spokane country on an occasional basis were the wild onion, white camas, and wild parsnip (A.H. Smith 1950:400–477).

Berries were abundant, and they were eaten fresh and dried. Gathering berries was the exclusive domain of the women, and berry patches could be harvested by anyone. Berries taken were red willow, goose, kinnikinnick, thimble, elder, huckle, service, foam, straw, black, rasp, dew, currants, thorn, chokecherries, and Oregon grapes.

Hazel and pine were the only nuts harvested. The hazel nut was more important but neither was very significant to the diet. Seeds and mushrooms of any type were not eaten. Cherry and hackberry leaves were used for tea. Gathered foods were stone boiled, steamed, dried, and eaten raw (A.H. Smith 1950:400–477; Ray 1942:132).

Technology

Fishing technology consisted of cattail or tule creels, awls, weirs, basket traps, spears, spear and torchlight, harpoons, hook and set line, sinkers, hook, line and pole, nets, seines, dip nets, conical falls traps, fish dams and impoundments, standing platforms, stranding traps for salmon, bow, and nooses (A.H. Smith 1950:253–399; Ray 1942:135, 214).

Kalispel hunting was principally done with deadfalls and bow and arrow. The sinew-backed recurved, self, and compound bows with sinew or fiber strings were used with the common and stone- and bone-tipped arrows. Other technology associated with hunting were stone knives and spear points, bone and stone hide scrapers, snares, ropes, waterfowl nets, and snowshoes (Ray 1942:148–151; A.H. Smith 1950:63–251).

Items associated with gathering were side baskets, checker-woven cedar baskets, cedar bark bags, hip baskets, unwoven bark baskets, mortar and pestle, wooden shovel, and digging sticks. Baskets were both of the coiled and twined type. Watertight coiled baskets and rawhide containers were used for stone boiling and carrying water (A.H. Smith 1950:400–477; Ray 1942:136, 159–161).

Other items were parfleches; cradleboards (fig. 3); horn, bark and wooden spoons; wooden bowls; earth ovens; stone mauls; elk horn hammers; hafted hammers with grooved heads; stone pile drivers; horn chisels; wood and stone pipes; beaver tooth engravers; horn and wooden wedges; wood, horn, and bone awls; pack straps; both simple and bow fire drills; wooden tongs; bone and wood needles; thorn and fish bone needles for tattooing; bone and wood tweezers; bone and beaver teeth dice; wooden combs; wood scratcher; matting from cedar, tule, and cattail; woven wallets; and clubs (Ray 1942:104–189).

Structures

Conical mat lodges (fig. 4) were used in the summer and winter, and a lean-to was used only in the summer. The

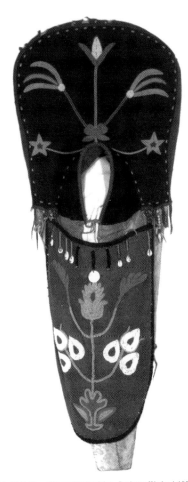

Fig. 3. Cradleboard. This board was covered first with buckskin to form a pouch for the child. Dark woolen cloth was then laid over the headboard, forming a hood for the child's head and hung across the front of the buckskin pouch. The floral design was worked in blue, yellow, white, orange, and green beads. Collected by W.M. Manning before 1916. Length 96.5 cm.

Plateau type house was used as the winter lodge. Its floor was excavated about one foot and was covered with bark or mats. These excavated structures were elongated lodges 20 to 60 feet long, housing 3 to 12 families or about 100 people in the longer lodges. They averaged 50 people per lodge. A second housing type was the round tepee, 15 to 20 feet in diameter and housing 3 families or about 20 people. Encampments varied in size from a few families to 900 people (A.H. Smith 1950). The skin tepee replaced the mat tent and was used by some Kalispel when they were home (Teit 1930:331–333; Ray 1939:174–176, 179; A.H. Smith 1950:33–34).

Sweatlodges (fig. 4) consisted of a bent willow frame covered with mats and earth. Floors were excavated about one foot, and they were always located near fresh water. Other structures were menstrual huts; dance houses, which were simply large living houses that were set up at the opening of a ceremony; and elevated storage platforms (Ray 1942:180–182, 193, 249).

Transport

Prior to the horse, transportation was overland by pedestrian means with packs or by water. Water transportation consisted of the dugout and bark canoes with a shovel-nose, sharp-nose or sturgeon-nose (fig. 5). Kalispels used rafts, paddles, poling rods, and stone anchors. Occasionally they would attach tule mats to bark canoes to keep them afloat (Ray 1939:140–144, 1942:154–158). One of their canoes differed from all others in that the ends were squared off and sewn together.

Clothing and Adornment

Men wore breechcloths, buckskin shirts with fringes, fur or bird-skin caps, and aprons. Women wore buckskin gowns (fig. 6) and basketry hats. Other items were the skin cape, hooded cape or coat, rabbit and raccoon skin robes, fur headbands, buckskin leggings and moccasins, and skin pipe bags. Mountain sheep and skunk skins were used for robes, and the sheep robe was considered very important. Goat and bobcat were used for clothing, and beaver and buffalo skins were used for blankets. Quivers were made from wolverine, otter, raccoon, beaver, and fisher skins. Elk skin vests or ponchos and twined rod jackets were used for armor with rawhide shields. Clothing was decorated by burning, painting, dying, pinking, puncturing, and fringing and with elk teeth, deer hoof pendants, quills, shells, and beads (Ray 1942:151, 153, 164–168, 173; Teit 1930:326–327, 334–339; A.H. Smith 1950:199, 202, 238, 241).

Body adornments were dentalium necklaces, shell string and bent bone wrist bracelets, elk teeth ear pendants, large shell ear pendants, trade beads, tattooing of limb joints, and face and body painting. Red and yellow were the most frequently used colors. Men plucked their beards with tweezers. Kalispels braided and oiled their hair, pierced their ears, and used tallow, marrow, and mud for cosmetics (Ray 1942:169–173).

Political Organization

The tribe as a political entity does not exist in a great part of the Columbia Basin. The political unit was the village (Ray 1936:111–112).

The term band in the Plateau can be used in two different ways. One use refers to a grouping of villages and the other is a small migratory group. The village grouping is "merely the embryonic tribe developing under indirect influence from the Plains" and has been observed among the Kalispel (Ray 1939:14). The village and band were the basic social units in the Plateau, and tribal development was a postcontact phenomenon (Anastasio 1972:180, 182, 191).

Upper and Lower Kalispel each had its own male head chief and subchiefs. Even though they were separated polit-

top, Smithsonian, NAA: 83–14081; center left and center right, Eastern Wash. State Histl. Soc., Cheney Cowles Mus., Spokane; bottom left, Pat Albers Coll., Salt Lake City, Utah; bottom right, U. of Okla. Lib., Western Hist. Coll., Norman:1199.

Fig. 4. Structures. top, The Indian village of Cusick, Wash. The majority of the habitations at this time were still tepees, but Euro-American structures are present. Photograph by Edward S. Curtis, © 1910. center left, Village where the majority of structures are built with lumber. Photographed about 1950s. center right, Sweathouse at Cusick. Photograph by Dick Lewis, 1930s–1940s. bottom left, Lucy Peuse in front of a structure made from tule reeds, bark, and earth. Formerly such structures were used as homes, but by this period, it was used as a work area, especially for drying and smoking foods. Photographed about 1900. bottom right, Mat tepee with stove pipe extending from the top. left to right, Annie Nick and Moses Nick. Photographer and date not recorded.

289

Fig. 5. Fishing from a canoe. Sturgeon-nose canoe made of bark in the Cee Cee Ah Creek, Pend Oreille River, Wash. Photograph by Frank Palmer, about 1908.

ically, one division did not claim any specific territory as its own. Both groups could jointly occupy and use the same area. They felt that their entire aboriginal territory belonged to all of them and that any Kalispel could use these lands. Chiefs and subchiefs were not regarded as leaders of a specific group of people because the people could migrate throughout the entire region and when they changed areas they would fall under the leadership of the chief in that area (A.H. Smith 1957:8–10). "There is no direct evidence to substantiate any claim for a single chieftainship over the whole tribe" (Chalfant 1974a:214–215).

Chieftainship was not hereditary, and chiefs led by persuasion rather than authority. Chiefs were recognized by title, insignia, and the presence of a spokesman. Women were included in the assembly, and there was a strong emphasis on equality among members (Ray 1939:26, 1942:229–230; Teit 1930:374).

The development of chieftainship among Indians of western Montana has also been attributed to the marauding Blackfoot. Centralized leadership would have allowed these groups to protect themselves against their warring neighbors (Malouf 1974:176).

The terms Upper and Lower Kalispel were references to geographical focuses rather than political or tribal units. The nature of Kalispel village settlement along the Pend Oreille River as well as the flow of people among these villages militates against the use of the term tribe when referring to the Kalispel. Designation of Kalispel "tribe" and "chiefs" refers to postcontact times.

Life Cycle

At the time of birth women were secluded in a hut with an older related midwife who had guardian-spirit power. The woman reclined, held on to a ceiling cord, gave birth on a mat, and drank some kind of liquid concoction. After birth the woman's abdomen was bound, and her breasts were steamed or warmed with heated pine needles or ashes from the fire in the hut. After four days she bathed and began to work. The afterbirth was hidden in the woods on a tree by the shaman midwife. Men were excluded until the umbilical cord was cut, and a new mother abstained from sex for at least six months and sometimes longer.

The newborn was bathed in a basket with warm water. The baby was then put in a cradle bag, blanket, or on rawhide padded with skin. It was nursed immediately if possible. After 10 days it was "baptized" in the river by its mother. Occasionally, there would be a feast where relatives gave presents of bedding. The navel string was tied to the cradleboard.

At puberty, girls were isolated in a menstrual hut with a closely related old woman proctor. A fire was kept burning during the isolation period. Special dishes were used and destroyed afterward. The young girl could drink cold water and she could only leave the hut in the early morning. She could make baskets for others, run uphill before sunrise to insure strength, rub against old stumps and pray for old age and prick her head with pine needles to insure against lice. A wood scratcher was used for the head, a conical hat was worn both inside and outside of the hut, her hair was rolled at the side of her head by her mother, and her face was painted with white clay. She was isolated for more than five days before the 1930s. At the end of the period of isolation she would bathe in a river or lake before dawn and then her mother would chaperon her return.

During subsequent menstruation she would be isolated in a menstrual hut for the duration, required to fast, and could not be seen by others. Her husband could hunt; she would make baskets and be purified by bathing. Boys would engage in vision seeking during puberty.

In marital matters the boy's or girl's intentions were not taken seriously. The parents of the boy's family would initiate the ceremony. The date of the ceremony was set by the parents of the girl usually one to two days later. There was a circle marriage dance around the girls by the boys, and selection would occur by touching the girl. There was a return visit after the marriage, which was considered part of the marriage ceremony. A feast was held with the bride and groom present, and return gifts of food were given. The couple's was patrilocal first residence and their later pattern alternated between matrilocal and patrilocal.

Elopement occurred, and both the male and female were lashed for not observing chastity. Adultery caused feuds, and the lover could be killed by the husband's brother. Divorce could be initiated by the husband or wife for maltreatment or incompatibility. Husbands were criticized for desertion if children were involved. Remarriage was possible and followed the same ceremony as the first time. The levirate was observed after the mourning period and was obligational to the man. Sometimes the claim could be relin-

top left, Eastern Wash. State Histl. Soc., Cheney Cowles Mus., Spokane; Smithsonian, top right, NAA:83–14078; bottom left, 96–10678; a, Smithsonian, Natl. Mus. of the Amer. Ind.: 10/7903; Eastern Wash. State Histl. Soc., Cheney Cowles Mus., Spokane, Wash.: b, 1.96 (neg. 95.17); c, 1.87 (neg. 95.46).

Fig. 6. Clothing. top left, Group in front of a tepee and house with bark roof. left to right, Aneas Conko, Flathead; unidentified child; Annie Nick, Kalispel; unidentified woman and 2 men; and Meshell Ignace, Kalispel. The women wear cloth wing dresses decorated with cowrie shells. The men wear reservation hats, beaded belt and vest, and multiple-shell necklaces. All have commercially made blankets. Photograph by Frank Palmer, 1908–1915. top right, Touch Her Dress, wearing a cloth wing dress decorated with cowrie shells and beads, a shell choker, and earrings. Photograph by Edward S. Curtis, © 1910. bottom left, Couple. The woman is wearing a buckskin fringed dress decorated with beads and multiple bead necklaces. The man wears what appears to be a capote made of a Hudson's Bay blanket decorated with appliqué and beads and moccasins. He holds a quirt. This is the earliest known photograph of the Kalispel. Photographed on the North American Boundary Commission Survey, 1860–1861. a, Breast ornament made of pipe bones strung on hide with brass and blue and red glass beads. A medicine pouch hangs from the upper left corner. Collected by T.T. Waterman in Cusick, Wash., before 1921. Length without neck ties 44 cm. b, Black leather belt decorated in geometric designs with brass rivets and light and dark blue, red green, and yellow seed beads. Collected by W.M. Manning before 1916. Length 99 cm. c, Beaded moccasins with a floral pattern over the toe and geometric patterns around the sides and heels in blue, yellow, green, black, red, and white seed beads. The laces are made of hide and there is a strip of pink silk where the flap joins the body of the moccasin. Collected by W.M. Manning before 1916. Length 25 cm.

quished and the woman could remarry with the permission of the husband's family. The sororate was also observed after mourning, and it was optional to the male. Polygyny was practiced only among men of prominence or wealth, and the first wife was the head of the household.

Upon death the body was removed immediately from the house. Preliminary mourning consisted of weeping and singing of weeping songs. The body was given new clothing and tightly bound in a flexed position in a new tule mat, parfleche, or deer hide. Burial occurred in the early morning, one day after death. The body was taken out through the door, and a relative presided over the ceremony. Gravediggers were friends and relatives. Adult relatives and friends went to the grave site. Interment occurred in talus slopes, rockshelters, on riverbanks and islands near the village or camp. Graves were exorcised by a shaman with rose branches, and valuables were buried with the corpse. A split erect stick or post was used as a marker. Everyone was buried in the same manner. After the funeral keepsakes were kept by relatives, valueless property was destroyed, good clothing was given to the children, and the rest was burned; the deceased's sweathouse was destroyed. The only purification rite that occurred occasionally was the burning of a temporary house and the mats. Mourning lasted slightly beyond one day. A surviving wife would singe her hair or cut it to ear length and would not comb it. It was taboo to sing, and the name of the deceased was not mentioned for over a year. Reburial occurred only after temporary burial in the ground (Ray 1942:191–224).

Mythology

Teit's (1930) work contains some information on mythology, but it is difficult to isolate specific Kalispel mythology. Vogt (1940) recorded 19 Lower Kalispel myths.

Religion

Kalispels believe adults, children, and fetuses all have a soul, which is responsible for animating the body. It is visible only to a shaman, and temporary absence will cause unconsciousness. Ghosts are disembodied anthropomorphic souls that are white skinned. They linger at grave sites, travel on trails, throw rocks at humans, are identified with owls, and are feared. A ghost's proper place is in the land of the dead, and they are tormented while on earth. They are held on earth by secrets carried to the grave and can only be released by confessing to a relative in a dream. The land of the dead is similar to life on earth but less pleasant (Ray 1942:232–233).

Guardian spirits could come from any animal, insect, bird, inanimate objects, natural phenomena (chinook wind, whirlwind, thunder, clouds, fire and snow), heavenly bodies, fabricated objects, and mythological characters (dwarfs and dangerous beings). Sometimes certain spirits were more powerful, and they had generic spirits. Any spirit could convey any power. Weather control was nonshamanistic. Most boys participated in the spirit quest at the time of puberty. Boys were sent alone by their fathers to named sites and were given symbols to carry. Instructions were given before departure and bathing was required. Old men could bestow their power on the youth. There were one-night quests that could be repeated and extended quests that may last 7–20 days. Spirit sites consisted of bodies of water, mountains, an isolated sweathouse, or the prairie. During the vigil the boys are to keep alert, sweat, build rock piles with or without fires on mountain peaks, play stick games with the spirits, and eat food gathered. The spirit appears in a vision or sometimes a dream as an animal or human. If it appears as a human, it takes on its animal form while disappearing. It gives the individual a symbol, song, and sometimes an animal cry. The symbol is wrapped and kept secret and retained for life. Early revelation of the power may cause the spirit to depart or the death of the individual, but it will be made obvious at the winter dance. However, the father knows if a spirit has been received. Unsought spirits are common when an individual is alone, and they must be accepted. A guardian spirit dies with the owner and becomes a spirit ghost. It seeks reacceptance by anyone and can cause serious illness if not accepted. Many individuals may have the same generic spirits. Spirits may become malignant through malignant use, and spirits do confer among themselves about the welfare of humans (Ray 1942:234–240).

Shamanism was a specific power, and the shaman was the only one who had clairvoyant power. He acquired his power in the same manner as others, but he usually had more spirits. A categorical and functional distinction is made between shamans and others.

Initiation preceded practice, and shamans did not practice until they were very mature. Shamans could become evil for purposes of revenge, and at other times they would just become evil. Their powers may be specialized, and a layman may cure disease related to his own spirit power. Duties are performed without pay and gifts were optional. They selected healthful camp sites, supervised certain construction activities, and frequently sponsored winter dances. Malignant shamans had to treat their own victims, and they could be killed spiritually by other shamans with recourse.

Diagnosis was essential for treatment, and the patient offered no information. The shaman placed his hands on the patient's body, sang, and predicted success or failure of treatment. Therapy might involve singing by the shaman, singing by the audience, and rubbing or massaging (Ray 1942:240–248).

The most common method used for intrusive objects or spirits was a drawing out process. An intrusive spirit may come from a lost spirit or one sent by a malignant shaman. In the case of an intrusive spirit it may be removed by the sender or stronger shaman and it is kept by the shaman for his own use.

Removal of either an object or spirit consists of passing the hands over and on the body from the feet to the head and head to feet repeated times and blowing. Sickness can be removed through the head or feet and may come out in parts. It is hard to control, and the assistant holds on to the shaman's hand. Once in hand it is carried to water and immersed. The shaman is smudged after removal. A sucking process near the heart is used for accidental illness or wounds (Ray 1942:240–248).

Personal spirit illness may occur due to wandering loss, because of mistreatment, or from theft by an evil shaman. In the former cases the spirit will return at maturity. It can also cause illness if its directions are not followed. Natural illness consists of wounds, and these are treated by a shaman. Several shamans may work on one individual and they may work separately or together. If one fails, he may name a successor (Ray 1942:240–248).

Sweatlodges were used by one person or groups of up to 12. The Sweatlodge was considered a deity, called grandfather, and prayed to. Special songs were sung during its use. Kalispels preferred to sweat before eating and sometimes before hunting and gambling. The sweatlodge was also used for curing. Sweating was always followed by a fresh water plunge. Lodges were communally used, ownership was held by the camp, and women used men's sweat houses (Ray 1942:180–182).

Ceremonies

First-products rites consisted of speeches and prayers. The ritual food was taboo until after the ceremony whereupon they would feast solely on it. A first food gathering rite was conducted for the first animal killed by a boy. It was taboo for the boy to eat the killed animal; only old people could eat it (Ray 1942:133–134).

Winter Spirit Dances began with the winter solstice. Dances could be sponsored by a shaman and his assistant, a layman at the request of a spirit, or initiates. Individual dances lasted for eight days and were held in the dance house. Initiation consisted of the novice taking his place near the center pole while the audience sang. This ceremony was followed by spirit dancing. Each person with a spirit danced and sang their song, and sometimes guardian-spirit impersonations were manifested through cries and actions.

The Bluejay Dance represented a ceremonial transformation of the individual rather than simple identification with a spirit. This occurred when a dancer would identify with mythological beings and only those with bluejay spirit could make the transformation. Faces and sometimes the body were blackened. Dancers perched in the rafters, exercised clairvoyant and curing powers, and traveled from one dance to another. Retransformation was forceful and resisted at the end of the dance. The individual would be captured

by other dancers, ritual death would occur, and revivification was performed by a shaman (Ray 1942:252).

The Weather Dance, also called Chinook Dance, was to bring milder weather. It was the same as a guardian-spirit dance and was performed by those with weather power. Eating was prohibited during the dance, but they did ritual drinking of water.

Some gift-giving was practiced at the dances. Gifts contributed by gamblers were distributed at the end of a dance, by a shaman's assistant, to young people and the best dancers. This gift-giving was secondary to other ceremonial objectives (Ray 1942:231, 252–253).

Knowledge

A lunar calendar was used, and Kalispels recognized that a new month begins with a new moon. Solstices were observed, a few constellations were named, and their position would indicate direction. The four cardinal directions were recognized. A knotted string was used as a mnemonic device (Ray 1942:189–190).

Games and Music

Games engaged in by the Kalispel were shinny, wrestling, hoop and arrow, hoop and pole, a lance thrown at opponent's lance, dice, cat's cradle, laughing, kicking, and hide and seek; women also gambled. They also had tops, a buzzer toy, and a bull-roarer. Canoe, foot, horse, and swimming races were popular. Some of these activities were played with other villages.

Musical instruments consisted of the skin drum and drum stick, a log drum on the floor, rawhide rattle with pebbles, deer hoof rattle, deer hoof pendants on clothing, willow whistles with reed, leaf whistles, and a nine-hole courting flute (Ray 1942:182–187).

History

The first major acculturational pressures among the Kalispel were associated with the appearance of the horse. The horse facilitated Plains bison hunting and intensified trading among the Kalispel, which resulted in an abandonment and concomitant restructuring of certain aboriginal cultural patterns.

The first Whites to encounter the Kalispel were Meriwether Lewis and William Clark in 1805 (Moulton 1983–, 5:188–189, 6:481, 488). David Thompson, working for the North West Company, was the first fur trader to enter the area. He established two trading posts in the Clark Fork valley. In 1809 he built Kullyspel House on the east end of Lake Pend Oreille and Saleesh House near Thompson Falls, Montana. Several other trading posts established adjacent to the valley had a direct influence on the Indians—Kootenae

House, Fort Spokane, Fort Okanogan, and Fort Colville. The North West Company concentrated its main effort in the valleys of the Clark Fork and Snake rivers where furs were more plentiful (Swanton 1952:400; M.C. White 1942:251–252; Spritzer 1979:3).

The fur traders introduced an entirely new concept of trade, based on furs and the use of barter and money (Malouf 1974:175). Prostitution, drunkenness, and increased gambling activities were negative impacts that occurred during this period (J.A. Ross 1967:29–36). "Basically, the fur trade led to severe economic exploitation, and a dependency on Euroamerican material culture. In both cases, the results were deleterious to the Indian" (Schultz 1971:26).

Father Adrian Hoecken established the first Roman Catholic mission among the Lower Kalispel near Albeni Falls on the Pend Oreille River in 1844. In 1845, Father Pierre Jean de Smet selected a new site for the mission near the cavern of New Manresa in the vicinity of the present-day Cusick, Washington, and named it Saint Ignatius. In 1854 this mission was abandoned, and a new Saint Ignatius mission was built in the Flathead Valley near the old mission of Saint Mary (de Smet 1905, 2:466–474, 1859:299). Initially the Upper Kalispel and most of the Lower Kalispel moved to the new Saint Ignatius in 1854. A year later Victor and his band returned to their home on the Lower Pend Oreille River (Chalfant 1974a:230–231).

The Roman Catholic missionaries sought to bring not only Christianity to the Kalispel but also the adoption of agriculture. Agriculture among the Kalispel would eliminate the traditional seasonal round and result in the abandonment of their "wandering life" (de Smet 1843:130).

When miners and homesteaders arrived, they had as their goal the removal of the Indians from their aboriginal territory. The motivating factors were resource exploitation and territorial acquisition. Establishment of reservations by the United States government can be viewed as a direct response to the opening of the west for permanent habitation by White miners and homesteaders. After Indians were removed from aboriginal lands and relocated on reservations, then payment was made for these lands. Agriculture was introduced and eventually the American economy was dominant.

On July 16, 1855, Gov. Isaac Stevens concluded a treaty in the Bitterroot valley with the Flathead, Kootenai, and Pend d'Oreille. Victor of the Kalispel did not attend this council. Alexander Temglagketzin signed for the Pend d'Oreille, but Stevens would not let him speak for the Kalispel (Ewers 1948:47).

This treaty, known as the Hell Gate Treaty of 1855, was for the cession of 12,806,000 acres and the creation of the Flathead Reservation (also called Jocko Reservation) in Mission Valley, Montana. In 1904 a law was passed to allot the reservation, and in 1910 it was opened to settlement under the homestead laws (Fahey 1974:301–307). In 1936, the members ratified a constitution and the reservation became known as the Confederated Tribes of Salish and Kootenai of the Flathead Reservation.

The original reservation consisted of 1,243,969 acres. As of 1989, 611,353 acres were held in tribal trust and 43,835 were in individual Indian trust. This is 53 percent of the land set aside for them in the 1855 treaty. Trust land is mostly forested and grazing lands along the edges of the reservation. The interior of the reservation is farming land and most of it is owned by non-Indians.

In 1887 the United States wanted the remaining Lower Kalispel to cede their lands and move to the Flathead Reservation. If certain families desired, they could move to the Colville or Coeur d'Alene reservations. At this time the Lower Kalispel consisted of two major bands. One was under Victor and his son Marcella, and the other under Michael. Michael signed the agreement and moved his band to the Flathead Reservation. Marcella did not sign the agreement and remained in the Pend Oreille valley. His descendants lived on the Kalispel Reservation in the 1990s (United States Congress. House 1887:41–43; Chalfant 1974a:203–204, 230–231).

President Woodrow Wilson issued an executive order in 1914 to create the Kalispel Reservation. It consisted of 4,629 acres. In 1924 it was allotted, but the allotments were only for 40 acres in contrast to the 160-acre allotments on other reservations. Sixty acres are held in tribal trust and only one 40-acre allotment has been lost to non-Indian ownership. They ratified a constitution in 1938.

The first church on the Kalispel Reservation was built in 1914 by Father Edward M. Griva, a Jesuit missionary. A year later 41 Indians and 6 Whites were confirmed. Superintendent Morton D. Colgrove of the Coeur d'Alene Agency was instrumental in establishing the first school on the reservation in 1915. He estimated that there were 24 children in accessible distance. He recorded 114 adults of which there were 54 men and 60 women. The Indian school on the reservation was closed in 1948, and the students were sent to the non-Indian school in Cusick (Fahey 1986:99–100,102, 155).

In the 1920s there was some part-time work for White ranchers and lumber companies, but the Kalispels mostly supported themselves with hunting and fishing. During this period they adopted many Euro-American material cultural items but maintained much of their aboriginal way of life (Fahey 1986:103–104).

It was not until 1925 that the first set of allotments was allocated, and the second set was completed in 1933. The first timber sale occurred in 1928, but timber sales did not bring the economic prosperity that they had thought (Fahey 1986:124–126).

In 1938 the Kalispel Reservation residents ratified a constitution under the Indian Reorganization Act. This administrative reorganization, without chiefs, represented a marked change for the Kalispels. The Kalispel held onto the idea of beef cattle as a means of economic development for 30 years but it never materialized (Fahey 1986:98, 134–135).

The Kalispel tribe only made three decisions during the 20 years after their reorganization. They sued the United States, moved the mission to higher ground in 1948, and granted Pend Oreille County Public Utility District an overflow easement in 1954. From 1938 to 1960 the Kalispel had not improved their living conditions. Their income was far below the average rural income for the state. They were the lowest of any Washington tribe and poverty was the norm. In 1960 there were 145 enrolled members. Land allotments were so split that leasing land was impossible (Fahey 1986:157–158).

In 1963 the Kalispels were awarded $3 million by the Indian Claims Commission. There were 67 eligible Kalispel voters, and the 35 present voted to accept the award. However, before the monies could be awarded, a plan for spending the money was to be developed. Half the money was to be put in a trust, and when received, the tribe should be terminated. In June 1963 the Kalispels had a plan that included monies for youth development, community building, housing, and industrial development. Acceptance of the plan was stalled by Congress until the Kalispels came up with a plan for termination. In 1964 a bill was passed to release funds but the threat of termination still hung over the Kalispels. No matter how hard they tried, they could not change the senators' position on trusts or termination. When the Senate committee approved $1,232,000 of the plan, family plan funds allowed Kalispels on and off the reservation to build or buy new homes. Thirty-eight houses were erected on the reservation in 1966, and a community hall was built a year later (fig. 7) (Fahey 1986:161, 163, 166–167, 169–173).

With federal authorization of $100,000 the Kalispel began to acquire allotments. By 1971 they had spent approximately $156,000 to acquire 34 allotments. An additional $50,000 was approved in 1971 to continue this process. They took possession of 1,260 acres that could have been lost (Fahey 1986:175).

The first economic enterprise that the Kalispel became involved with was the Aluminum Box Manufacturing Company. It was constructed in 1974 on the reservation and was renamed Kalispel Metal Products (fig. 7). While it did not make a lot of money, it did generate jobs and was the biggest business in Cusick. It produced aluminum gun cases, steel marine structures, and metal fabrication to close tolerances (Fahey 1986:177–181).

The termination threat eventually disappeared, and Congress allocated the remainder of the Kalispel funds, which mostly went into certificates of deposit and a trust fund (Fahey 1986:182–183). The tribe acquired a bison herd for the sale of meat (Fahey 1986:185–186).

Population

The Kalispel may have numbered 1,200 in 1780. In 1805 Lewis and Clark estimated a population of 1,600. In 1905

top and center, Eastern Wash. State Histl. Soc., Cheney Cowles Mus., Spokane.
Fig. 7. 20th-century life on the Kalispel Res., Wash. top, Modern home, with tepee at left. center, Kalispel Metal Products. top and center, Photographs by John Fahey, left, 1985, right, 1984. bottom, Dedication of the community center on the reservation. left to right, N.H. Locher, contractor, county sheriff, and county commissioner; Louis Andrews, Tribal Chairman 1964–1970; Congressman Tom Foley at the lectern; Robert Dellwo, tribal attorney; Bureau of Indian Affairs assistant superintendent from the Lapwai Agency; and Rose Eli, tribal program chair. Photographed in 1967.

there were 640 Upper and 197 Lower Pend d'Oreilles under the Flathead Agency (Jocko Reservation) and 98 under the Colville Agency. The 1910 census reported 386 Kalispels in Montana, 157 in Washington, 15 in Idaho, and 6 elsewhere. The United States Office of Indian Affairs reported 97 in 1937 (Swanton 1952:400).

In 1915 there were 138 and in 1960 there were 145 enrolled members (Fahey 1986:102, 158).

The Kalispel Reservation faces a demographic issue. With only a total of 246 enrolled members in 1989 even minor outmarriage will erode the membership (Fahey 1986:190).

Synonymy†

The name Kalispel is from the Spokane-Kalispel-Flathead designation *qlispél* (younger variant *qlispé*). An earlier or dialectal variant is Kalispelm, Kalispelum, Kullespelm; compare Okanagan kälespilum (Hodge 1907–1910, 1:647). The form of this name in the Colville dialect of Okanagan is *qlspílx*. The etymology of this term is uncertain.

Another term for the Kalispel used in the Flathead dialect is *snxʷmé*. The Spokane term corresponding to this, *nxʷméneʔ*, refers to the Little Spokane division, and the corresponding term in Colville, *snxʷmínaʔx*, applies to all speakers of the Spokane-Kalispel-Flathead language.

The Kalispel were first referred to in the records of the Lewis and Clark expedition in 1806 under the name Coospel-lar's Nation (Moulton 1983–, 6:488). This name resembles a Sahaptin name kúshpĕlu recorded for them by Mooney (1896:731) in Yakima or Palouse. The Nez Perce name for them is *qeṁéˑspeĺuˑ*, literally 'camas people' (Aoki 1994:577), an allusion to their camas digging at Calispell Lake, Washington (Teit 1930:296–300).

The names Kalispel and Pend d'Oreille have both been used for a single group comprising both peoples, sometimes one or the other and sometimes both interchangeably (de Smet 1843:335–337, 1905:470–474, 764–765, 995–996; Hodge 1907–1910, 1:646–647; Ruby and Brown 1970:37, 118, 1986:86; Chance 1973:10; Malouf 1974:120, 1982:13, 17; Fahey 1974:81, 113). The ethnic unity of these peoples has been stressed by ethnographers (Turney-High 1937:5; Ewers 1948:44). David Thompson referred to the "Kullyspell or Earbob Indians" (Coues 1897:708–709), 'earbob' being a translation of French *pend'oreilles* 'ear-drop'. When these groups were distinguished in this terminology, the Kalispel were referred to as the Lower Pend d'Oreille (Isaac Stevens in de Smet 1859:282; John Owens in Dunbar 1927, 1:183–184, 2:208–210); and the Pend d'Oreille of the area of Flathead Lake were called the Upper Pend d'Oreille (Stevens

1901:79). The terms Lower Kalispel and Upper Kalispel have also been used the same way (Swanton 1952:399–400), but these names are used in the *Handbook* for the two divisions of the Kalispel in the narrow sense. The name Kalispel was sometimes used to comprise the Flathead as well (Adrian Hoecken in de Smet 1859:299) and has been used as a linguistic term for the language that comprises the Spokane, Kalispel, and Flathead dialects (Giorda et al. 1877–1879; vol. 17:6). In contrast, a distinction between the Kalispel and the Pend d'Oreille was made by Diomedi (1879:2–3). The practical differentiation of the two segments of the original larger group was ultimately made concrete by their settlement separately on the Kalispel Reservation in Washington and the Flathead Reservation in Montana, corresponding to their terminological differentiation as the Kalispel and Pend d'Oreille, respectively (see "Flathead and Pend d'Oreille," this vol.).

In the Plains Indian Sign Language the Kalispel–Pend d'Oreille were referred to by a sign meaning 'paddlers', a reference to their use of bark canoes (Teit 1930:300). The same allusion is found in the Crow name *akbinnaxxuˑwé*, literally 'one who makes waves' (Hodge 1907–1910, 1:646; Medicine Horse 1987:15).

Sources

The best early historical source of information on the Kalispel is de Smet's (1843, 1859, 1905) records. Diomedi (1879) also made specific but limited observations on the Kalispel. Coues (1897), Stevens (1901), Josephy (1965), Ronan (1890), Chance (1973), and United States Government (1887) contain good historical information on the general area with some references to the Kalispel. White (1942), Spritzer (1979), Ruby and Brown (1970, 1986), Smally (1885), Fahey (1974), Dunbar (1927), and Evans (1981) contain limited historical facts. Fahey's (1986) history of the Kalispel presents an overview, but it was written for a popular audience.

Mooney (1896), Hodge (1907–1910, 1), and Curtis (1907–1930, 7) are the earliest anthropological documents that specifically mention the Kalispel, but their factual base is very limited. The first and most detailed ethnographic work is that of Teit (1930). A.H. Smith (1950) conducted fieldwork among the Kalispel in 1937, and his field notes represent the most comprehensive ethnographic treatment of the Kalispel. Ray (1942) also conducted fieldwork among them in 1937 and is the next best comprehensive ethnographic source. Malouf (1974) and Chalfant (1974a, 1974b) also worked for the Indian Claims Commission and are excellent ethnohistorical sources. Other anthropological works of limited use are Ray (1933, 1936, 1939), Spier (1936), Ewers (1948), Turney-High (1937), Swanton (1952), A.H. Smith (1957, personal communication 1985), Anastasio (1972), and Malouf (1982).

† This synonymy was written by Ives Goddard on the basis of data compiled by Sylvester L. Lahren, Jr.; the phonemic forms in Flathead and Colville were provided by Sarah G. Thomason.

Flathead and Pend d'Oreille

CARLING I. MALOUF

The Flathead ('flăt‚hed) and the Pend d'Oreille ('pändə‚rā) are two groups of Salishan-speaking people with dialects mutually understood by each other.[*] They had separate but somewhat overlapping geographic locations.

Territory

Aboriginally, the Flathead occupied an area north of Yellowstone National Park extending to where the Missouri River emerges from the northern Rocky Mountains (Chalfant 1974b). They ranged east to Billings, Montana, and the Pryor Mountains, and west to the continental divide. The Pend d'Oreille described here were also known as the Upper Pend d'Oreille, in contrast to the Lower Pend d'Oreille, or Kalispel. Their domain was mostly west of the continental divide, west of the Flathead domain, and extended down a tributary of the Columbia River, the Clark Fork River in Montana (fig. 1). The boundary between the Pend d'Oreille and the Kalispel, since they were aboriginally actually one cultural entity, was and is still somewhat hard to define. Their descendants are on two reservations, one in Washington and the other in western Montana.

The Pend d'Oreille had an important center of activity around Flathead Lake, where many archeological sites are found. Other Pend d'Oreilles lived around Missoula, in the Bitterroot Valley south of Missoula Valley, along the Clark Fork River as far up as the continental divide near Butte, Montana. They also occupied the Camas Prairie, west of Flathead Lake. These areas are all drained by the Clark Fork River and the Flathead River, the two converging near Paradise, Montana, where the Kalispel began to predominate. The Sematuse band of Pend d'Oreille (Teit's SEmtē´use) was located on the upper Clark Fork River between Missoula and Butte (Teit 1930:307).

There was another band of Salishan speakers located just east of the Pend d'Oreille, in the Sun River valley on the Plains east of the mountains. These were the Plains Salish, referred to by Teit (1930:297, 303, 314–316) as the Salish-Tunā´xe. They merged with the Pend d'Oreille around Flathead Lake, having moved into western Montana very early in the historic period, or during very late prehistoric

times, and lost their identity. Their language was not understood by either the Flathead or the Pend d'Oreille.

Environment

It is important to view the environment of both the Flathead and Pend d'Oreille as being astride the continental divide, in the Rocky Mountains and the adjoining Plains.

The Pend d'Oreille placed greater emphasis on hunting and gathering than did the Kalispel, who, like others in the Plateau, relied more on fishing than did their eastern neighbors. Part of the cause was that fish were more scarce in the higher elevations near the Rocky Mountain crest, but game animals were relatively more plentiful in the mountains than they were in the Columbia Plateau. The range of the bison on the Plains extended into the northern Rocky Mountain valleys, even to some extent west of the divide.

Culture

Subsistence

The Flathead and Pend d'Oreille who were living east of the divide, and into the adjoining Plains in prehorse days, used an elaborate system of buffalo drive lanes, jumps over cliffs, and compounds or corrals, the remains of which are commonly found in the headwaters of the Missouri River system in this area. Smaller drive systems were also employed sometimes in the mountains and mountain valleys to hunt deer or antelope. Through communal efforts bison herds were lured into the fenced lanes where they were driven over cliffs or into corrals.

Communal drives required considerable organizational and managerial abilities. Besides repairing the drive lanes, which often extended for miles, the operation required religious preparations to ensure its success. Thus a shaman was regarded as necessary to lead the drive or at least to give advice to the chiefs in its planning. Part of the religious exercises, which often also included divination in order to locate the herds, involved charming the souls of the animals, and enticing them to move toward the drive lanes. After the drive was successfully completed there was a system for dividing the meat and other parts of the carcasses.

[*]For the phonemes of Flathead, see the orthographic footnote in "Spokane," this vol.

297

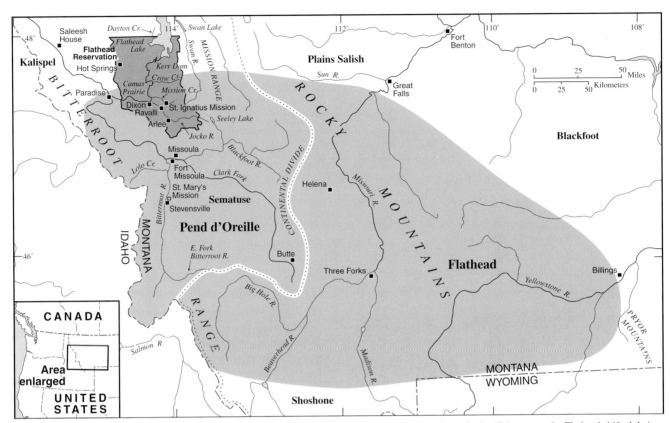

Fig. 1. Precontact 18th-century Flathead and Pend d'Oreille territory, with modern towns and reservations. In the 19th century the Flathead shifted their range to the west, extending into the Bitterroot Valley.

When horses were introduced to the Flathead and Pend d'Oreille, around 1730 (Haines 1938a:429–437), these elaborate preparations in repairing lanes and corrals were no longer necessary, although many of the religious aspects were retained. By the time trappers and other travelers entered the territory the horses had become an integral part of the native culture, and communal drives over cliffs had already become obsolete. One of the best-known communal hunting shamans was Grizzly-Bear-Tracks (Ewers 1948:40–41). With horses the Indians could travel farther and faster to the herds, and new methods of approaching and shooting the animals were devised.

In the mountains deer were communally hunted, it was more often that the animals were sought by individual hunters, or by small groups of hunters stalking, ambushing, or trapping them. Deer were fairly evenly distributed throughout the mountain valleys, but moose were concentrated in places where adequate plants, including aquatic plants, were plentiful. In some sections of Pend d'Oreille country caribou were present, and occasionally they were seen as late as the 1880s near Missoula. In the plains and valleys antelope were hunted, and in the mountains goats and bears were sought. Coyotes and wolves were usually ignored due to religious and mythological reasons. Smaller game animals included rabbits, ground hogs, and large waterfowl such as ducks and geese. Duck eggs were also gathered and consumed.

Game was obtained with deadfalls, nets, and snares and bows and arrows. Small birds were not sought unless there was a famine condition existing, the reason being that considerable effort was required for the small amount of meat and other materials they provided. When flocks of small birds appeared, particularly the waxwings on their fall migration from Canada to the southern United States, they were caught by enveloping them in trees and bushes with a large net system.

Fish were of importance to the Pend d'Oreille. Canoes, rafts, weirs, nets, and hooks were usually employed. People fishing by canoe, for example, floated down the Clark Fork River, or other large streams, casting lines with fishhooks made of bone, wood, and sinew. Weirs and catching baskets were often employed at the mouths of side streams. The Flathead placed much less importance on fishing than the Pend d'Oreille. They still did some fishing, but the activity was of less importance in their subsistence than it was to Salishans farther west. One reason was the very plentiful supply of large game animals, such as bison, and another was the greater lack of fish resources available in the upper reaches of the Missouri River system, although species such as graylings and trout were available and even sought. There is no evidence, as a result, that the Flathead ever made or used canoes, but the Pend d'Oreille sometimes made dugout canoes or used rafts.

298

Of considerable importance to both the Flathead and Pend d'Oreille were the numerous plant foods and materials usually obtainable in their domains. Plant foods offered a welcome variety in their diet, many were storable for future use, and people confined to camps for various reasons could seek them nearby when hunting required vigorous activity away from camps. Thus, old people, women, and even children helped in obtaining these resources. Plants also were valuable for making shelters, some kinds of tools and implements, containers, weapons, medicines, dyes, and even playthings for the children. The collection of plant foods was not always just the chore of women. The plant harvest began early, usually in March or April, when the bitterroot plant first emerged from the ground. A short communal ceremony ushered in the collecting season when the first day's harvest was placed in a pile in front of a woman who had been selected by the chiefs and shamans to conduct it (fig. 2). During precontact times the people all gathered around the pile of these first plants of the season, which had been dug by the band. They faced the sun, and a prayer was offered. After the Jesuits arrived in 1841, Christian elements were added to the ceremony. Following the prayers a feast was held, with the cooked bitterroot being consumed first.

bottom, Eastern Wash. State Histl. Soc., Cheney Cowles Mus., Spokane.
Fig. 2. Bitterroots. top, Saying a prayer over a pile of collected roots. Later they were taken to the house of Suzette Hemestoo (Pend d'Oreille, last leader of the Bitterroot ceremony) for the feast. Photograph by Carling Malouf, Camas Prairie, Flathead Res., Mont., 1962. bottom, Washing the bitterroots. Photograph by June Moncure, Missoula, Mont., 1940s.

When other plant foods and materials reached maturity, ceremonies as extensive as that used for the bitterroot were not necessary, but gatherers often uttered individual prayers at the time of collection. For example, when digging camas, some women placed a bead or other offering in the hole left in the ground after the bulb was extracted, and a short prayer followed. Over 60 different plants were collected and eaten, although some could only be consumed in season.

Bushels of bitterroots and other plants were harvested and dried for future use. The roots, including camas, provided a major source of carbohydrates in the diet. Berries were important and often were added to bitterroot and other foodstuffs. Some also served as dyes for weaving materials or skins. Berries included serviceberries, elderberries, chokecherries, and the very popular huckleberries. Berries were dried in the sun while still on their stems or branches or pounded with a pestle on a smooth, flat rock, and dried in cakes. Unlike some of the Plains tribes the Salishans did not pound meat and berries together, and each was pounded and dried separately with conical pestles. During late prehistoric times the use of the grooved maul had diffused from the Plains to the tribes of the Northern Rockies, and it was used for pounding meat before drying it.

The inner bark of many kinds of trees, especially among the evergreens, provided a delicacy during the early spring when the sap was running from the roots to the upper part of the plant. The bark was only edible for a few weeks during this season, and it could not be stored for more than a few days. The inner bark, or cambium layer, was eaten.

Some plant foods were cooked in pits dug in the ground for this purpose. After the pit was dug hot stones were set in the bottom, or a hot fire was ignited. Then the coals were covered with grass or leaves for moisture during the cooking process. On top of these were placed other plant foods, particularly camas, and then the mass was covered with earth and allowed to cook for about 24 hours. Then the earth was removed. For ordinary family cooking stone boiling techniques were used in baskets or bags.

Structures

Shelters were usually conical-shaped tepees, or conical lodges with a similar framework, but covered with branches and more poles, or grass mats. The pole and branch structures were more common in the field and were useful to hunters or war parties. Caves and rockshelters also provided cover, when needed by travelers or family groups on a food gathering quest. Lodge poles for the tepees and the brush-covered lodge were plentiful in the forests. Most of the time the poles were merely leaned against a tree to be used the next time they passed through the area, or they could be used by someone else who happened to come by. Skin or later canvas tepee covers had to accompany the travelers (fig. 3).

Clothing and Adornment

Deerskin was preferred for making clothing for men and women since its thickness was the most comfortable to wear. Elk hides were regarded as too thick, although they could be used for some other objects. Bison hides were also a little thick for clothing, but they made very good robes, especially for winter covering, and for bedding or other uses.

Women's clothing usually consisted of a decorated buckskin dress (fig. 4), while the men wore leggings and a loose shirt (fig. 5). Both wore one-piece moccasins, and in winter fur pieces could be added inside to keep their feet warmer. Hats were made of fur for winter use, and gloves were made of skins. Rabbit furs were used as diapers for babies placed in cradleboards as they were highly absorbent.

Clothing was decorated with dyed porcupine quillwork, and shells or animal teeth such as those from elks. Dyes for the quills came from dried berries, certain clays, or from iron oxides. Sometimes designs were painted on shirts or leggings.

Trade

Abalone and olivella shells from California and dentalia from the Pacific Northwest reached the Flathead and Pend d'Oreille through trade channels up the Columbia and Fraser rivers. The shells were usually sewed onto shirts or dresses, or they became part of a necklace or other forms of decoration for the body. In exchange, the Flathead traded porcupine quills and hides.

Wealth

Generally families among the Flathead and Pend d'Oreille were about equal in their level of wealth and possessions. There were, of course, some differences, but social practices tended to shift wealth from those who had more goods to the poor, or to those who through some accident or loss to an enemy had lost many of their belongings. The aged, widows, and infirm also were given whatever care could be offered them. Some men were better hunters than others, for example, and some other people had better skills in making material goods such as baskets, weapons, tools, or implements. But they also looked with favor on persons who had a better than average reputation for bravery, and for generosity, or if they had special spiritual powers useful to the community as well as to the individual. These were some of the qualities desired of a person who wanted to be a chief, so there were incentives to acquire these reputations.

Technology

Containers were useful for carrying belongings, foodstuffs, and medicines; for storage; and for cooking. The range of uses was considerable, and the sizes, too, varied. Some bags and containers were decorated with painted designs using both unilinear and curvilinear motifs. Materials were usually organic in origin, made with skins or parts of plants.

Babies were carried in cradleboards that resembled those of the nearby Plains tribes. That is, these were not woven, but had a hard backboard covered with tanned skins and decorated with quillwork, or beads. Curvilinear designs, such as floral motifs, have been and continue to be very popular (fig. 6).

Projectile points consisted of arrowheads and similar but larger spearpoints. The Flathead and Pend d'Oreille both used the common, or self-bow, but they also used the compound bow. Another weapon they used was the pogamoggan, which was much like modern blackjacks with a stone inside a small bag attached to a staff about an arm's length long.

Other stone tools and implements consisted of knives, scrapers, and conical-shaped pestles about 8–10 inches in length. No mortar or bowl was used with the pestle, and a simple flat smooth rock served as a base upon which berries (fig. 6) and meat were pounded and ground with the pestle.

left, Mont. State U., Mus. of the Rockies, Bozeman; right, Smithsonian, NAA:96–10683.

Fig. 3. Tepees. left, Camp of canvas tepees near Missoula, Mont., 1880–1895. right, Home of an Indian farmer with both canvas tepee and frame house; an older log cabin is behind the house. Photograph by George or Flora Seymour, Mission Valley, Mont., 1923.

MALOUF

Fig. 4. Women's clothing. left, Angelic LaMoose, daughter of Joe LaMoose, wearing a buckskin dress decorated with glass beads of various sizes. The dress was made by Angelic and her mother. Photograph by Harry T. Cory, 1913. right, Women in transitional clothing at the celebration of the 75th anniversary of the founding of St. Ignatius Catholic Mission, Flathead Res., Mont. left to right: Adele Chalwain; others unidentified. Their cloth wing dresses are decorated with beads, thimbles, cowrie shells, and ribbonwork. They hold beaded purses, the one on the left dated 1915. Postcard photograph by Al Gusdorf, 1938.

During the nineteenth century stone pipes began to appear in Flathead culture. Ethnologists have not been able to find cases where a shaman used a pipe in curing or hunting rituals. However, sometimes pipes were used in some group ceremonies such as the Winter Spirit Dance, but these were late additions to such rituals.

Long bones and antlers were made into a wide variety of tools and implements, and even into musical instruments. They included needles, awls, punches, stone chipping tools, and scrapers. Antlers made good punches to open holes in skins through which sinew can be used to sew pieces together, or they can be used to facilitate the weaving of baskets. Hollow long bones, such as some that can be obtained from eagles, were made into whistles and even flutes. Ribs of large animals, like bison, can be made into scrapers to remove hair from hides ("Ethnobiology and Subsistence," fig. 12, this vol.).

Plants were used for making bags and baskets. Bags made of strips of bark were easily made and were disposable since they were not decorated.

Besides hides, meat, and bones there were other parts of some animals that were useful. For example, some organs made good containers, while another one made a good rattle when prepared properly, and a short stick was added as a handle. Deer hooves attached to a long stick also made a good rattle. Wood and hide together became drums, and equipment for a number of games such as those utilizing sticks from willows, and sinew from animals to make hoops.

Life Cycle

Among the Flathead and Pend d'Oreille, when a woman became pregnant she was not expected to be able to work as hard as she did before, but she was urged to keep busy. There were some taboos and food restrictions placed on her, and sometimes she was given special spiritual attention. At the time of birth, a woman who was a midwife, usually a relative, was called to assist. In some cases, if the process was difficult, a shaman was called. After the birth the mother usually spent about three days resting, and then she resumed her duties.

Besides the mother and the father, the grandparents and older siblings played important roles in the raising of young children. While they were growing up they were seldom spanked, but they were scolded and admonished when misbehaving.

Marriage required the consent of the girl's parents. Polygamous unions were sometimes arranged, but monogamy was the usual form of marriage. Descent was bilateral; that is, kinship was recognized about equally on both sides of the family. The new husband and wife formed an important economic team as well as a family group. For example, the husband provided necessary raw materials, usually after hard work out in the countryside, which was processed into finished goods such as foodstuffs, clothing, containers, and even shelters from the large game animals brought in by the father and older sons in the family. He also sometimes helped the wife in the gathering of plants.

Fig. 5. Men's clothing. top left, Headdress decorated with eagle and hawk feathers, brass bells and beads, glass beads, and ermine fur. Collected from Pierre Big Hawk by William Wildschut on the Jocko Res., Mont., in 1925. Length from edge of headband to tip of center feather, 39 cm. bottom left, Buckskin shirt decorated with beaded bands and weasel tails wrapped with red flannel. In the traditional Plateau fashion it is made from two deer hides. The hind legs hang down in front and back, and the forelegs are attached as sleeves. This shirt was reportedly manufactured in the late 19th century. Collected by C.E. Schaeffer in Arlee, Mont., in 1934. Length from top to bottom, 76 cm. right, Jim Sapiel Pierre, also known as Bitterroot Jim, wearing beaded leggings, moccasins and buckskin shirt. He carries a shield on his back and wears a horned headdress. His horse wears a decorated, horned face mask. He is participating in the 75th anniversary of the founding of St. Ignatius Catholic Mission, Flathead Res., Mont.; the mission church is behind him. Postcard photograph by Al Gusdorf, 1938.

When a person died, and after proper prayers and other funeral procedures were performed, the body was buried nearby amongst talus rocks, or along river terraces, and similar places, part of the location depending on the season. When the ground was frozen, for example, it was less difficult to make the burial in rock deposits, such as in talus slopes. At other times corpses were placed in holes dug in soils. There were no graveyards since the people were usually traveling about their domain in their quest for materials, foods, and other items. After the burial a feast was held, and belongings of the deceased were distributed among relatives and friends.

Political Organization

During late prehistoric and protohistoric times, or up to about the mid 1600s, the Flathead were numerous enough to justify having bands, possibly six (Teit 1930:303–304). Severe smallpox epidemics during the 1600s, and some other factors, particularly the heavy incursions of Blackfoot from the north, and to some extent, Shoshoneans from the south, further reduced their numbers to one band, which centered for a while in the Big Hole Valley. Then, about 1700, they crossed the divide west into the Bitterroot Valley. Chiefs were heads of bands, and subbands, and earlier there apparently was a chief and council that served some

duties in intertribal matters or between bands. The bands varied in numbers seasonally since many of their activities were performed more efficiently when the group broke up into smaller units.

Less is known about the bands of the Pend d'Oreille except that their structure, including chieftanships, was similar to that of the Flathead. Like the Flathead, their bands centered at least part time in a main valley of their domain. Besides a political chief there were war chiefs who took charge when they were engaged in military operations. Other men were available to serve as councilmen and to provide spiritual help when needed. Chiefs had some powers to punish those who misbehaved, and sometimes they even used whips.

Neither the Flathead nor the Pend d'Oreille had formal societies or sodalities, such as the war societies of the Plains Indians. Among the members of such societies were men referred to as Dog Soldiers. The Flathead and some Pend d'Oreille bands did have Dog Soldiers (fig. 7), but they were not organized into formal societies.

Games

The types of games played by the Flathead and Pend d'Oreille were identical or similar to those played by most of the other tribes in the Plateau and even in the Great Basin

Fig. 6. Processing berries. left, Dried huckleberries being sorted. The stone pounder for crushing the berries is hanging above the boy. An empty beaded cradleboard is in the background. Photograph by Sumner W. Matteson, St. Ignatius Mission, Flathead Res., Mont., 1905. top right, Stone pounder with a wooden handle encased in hide. Pounders were used for pulverizing meat or berries. Collected by C.E. Schaeffer in Arlee, Mont., in 1934. bottom right, Berry bag made of buffalo rawhide and painted in geometric designs. Collected by William Wildschut on the Jocko Res., Mont., in 1925. Length of pounder, 29 cm.; bag to same scale.

areas. The most common games played were shinny, hoop and dart games, a moccasin race, and stick games ("The Stick Game," fig. 5 top right, this vol.). All were often played against teams or with individuals from other tribes, and gambling and bets were almost a regular part of it. The stick game remained a favorite of these tribes at powwows in the 1990s.

Mythology

The Rocky Mountain Salishans have a considerable body of myths that involve animals, birds, and humans in their area. Approximately 50 percent of their stories involve the character of Coyote and his escapades (L. McDermott 1901, 1904; Teit 1917:114–118; H. Miller and Harrison 1974). Myths were usually told to children in the wintertime by their grandparents, and they served to teach them many of the ways and moral values of their people.

Religion

Through myths and legends children were also taught many aspects of their religion, such as the search for spiritual power through vision quests. Ideas of what might be included in medicine bundles, equipment and paraphernalia, the kinds of powers that can be given to a person, and even the forms of songs provided by the spirit were sometimes included in the stories.

Spirits could appear to an individual in a human form, or as an animal, bird, insect, and even inanimate items such as

a rock or a stick. They could appear unsought such as when a person (usually as a youth) was alone and away from camp on some adventure or activity, or the individual could seek such a contact. In that case they made some preparations with rituals before leaving camp, and often they went to a selected place such as a cave, a pictograph panel on a cliff where others had also received their spirits, or to hill tops and mountain tops, usually lying there for days (Dusenberry 1959). The number of days was not set at four as is so common among among Plains tribes.

When the spirit appeared to the person it conveyed to him the kind of spirit power (*suméš*) he was receiving, its strengths and limitations (if any), the paraphernalia to be used, songs, prayers, actions, and other matters involved. A partial list of such powers received includes: curing, hunting, war, fishing, gambling, and love. Some of the rarer powers were clairvoyance, rain producing (very rare), and finding lost objects or persons. Such powers gave the individual that little extra gift (a term often used by elderly Flathead when describing the experience) that made them a success in life, and to many others in the community as well.

Some individuals had more than one power, each awarded at a different time, but rarely was it more than three or four. With every power there were also restrictions on their lives, such as rituals, and other matters that could encumber them if they had too many of them.

Among some tribes in the Great Basin and Plateau specific spirits, say for example, a bear, gave a specific power, but among the Flathead and Pend d'Oreille spirits such as bear, deer, and antelope might have given one power to one person, and another to someone else.

In spite of their proximity to Plains tribes, especially during historic times, the Flathead and Pend d'Oreille did not adopt the more elaborate ceremonials of their eastern neighbors. They did, however, share some of the ceremonials characteristic of the Plateau area, such as Winter Spirit ceremonies. The Flathead themselves referred to it, though, as Jumping Dance, thus named because they used a short hop while dancing in place.

The Winter Spirit ceremonies were held locally for small groups. The leaders of these ceremonies obtained their authority through a spirit visitor, so that each, thereby, had a slightly different ritual, songs, and other features connected with it. Similarly, the first bitterroot ceremony was held for groups smaller than bands.

Shamans

Sorcery was in relatively little use among these people, but it was present. Often, it was regarded as negative in nature, and the powers could "bounce back" to the sorcerers. Shamanistic powers were more potent and powerful if there was a contest between a shaman and a magician, so magic was employed mostly when the shamanistic sources were not available to an individual. For example, a man without specific love powers discovered his wife was being lured away from him by magical forces being used by another man to entice her. He was unable to solve his problem except through recourse to magic. So, he sought the advice of the elders of his band, and learned of a potion that could be used to counter the spell he suspected had been cast by his rival.

Denver Public Lib., Western Hist. Dept., Colo.:B128.

Fig. 7. Dog Soldier honoring ceremony *(esnqʷq̓ʷosmíni)* for Bitterroot Jim, who is on the horse. On the left is Iplaha (Abraham Isaac) and on the right is An, wife of Pasi. The Dog Soldier would ride through the camp, singing special songs and using his rattle. People in the camp would tie all kinds of food onto the horse in the trappings, the tail, and the mane. Gifts included a pack of cards, food, and pieces of cloth. The Dogs, special scouts and warriors of great value to the tribe, had to be spoken to in particular ways. The spiritual aspects of the Dogs, considered sensitive information by the Flathead in the 1990s, are not openly discussed (Tony Incashola, communication to editors 1997). Photograph by Edward H. Boos, 1899–1910. The background of this photograph was digitally reproduced from a photograph taken at the same place and time.

A council of shamans, some of whom were also chiefs, could cast a spell on a person who was found to be guilty of breaches in morals, or other rules of behavior in the group. For example, during the 1940s a group of Flathead and Pend d'Oreille shamans cast a spell on a man who was discovered to be guilty of incest with his daughter. He fell ill and became partially crippled (the medical doctors at a hospital diagnosed it as muscular dystrophy).

Divination was utilized by some shamans. Grizzly-Bear-Tracks utilized it, when asked by the chiefs to locate bison or other animals when a hunting party was having difficulty in finding the location of the herds. He built a fire, and when it died down he was said to have been able to locate the animals by examining the positions of the live coals and embers.

Curing

Most adults had some knowledge and skills in minor injuries and maladies and could use well-known herbs, and other medicines, and could even set some broken bones and treat infections. In more severe and complex cases, specialists had to be called. These were persons, men or women, who had special skills, much of it derived from supernatural forces through spiritual help. Their treatments often used medicines such as herbs, but they also relied on their spiritual powers for successes in treatment, employing rituals, paraphernalia, and songs that had been given to them through these supernatural processes.

History†

The first non-Indians to make their way into Flathead and Pend d'Oreille territory, and to record their journey, were members of the Meriwether Lewis and William Clark expedition in 1805. They encountered an encampment of 33 lodges—about 400 people and 500 horses—at a place on the East Fork of the Bitterroot River, in southwestern Montana (Moulton 1983–, 5:187; E.E. Clark 1966:143). Lewis and Clark were preceded in western Montana by three products of Euro-American culture, all of which had wrought enormous changes among the Flathead and Pend d'Oreille by 1800—epidemic disease, horses, and firearms.

The earliest epidemics were the waves of smallpox that struck from the west in the 1770s and from the upper Missouri in 1781–1782 (Ewers 1958:28–29; Campbell 1989:22–25; Boyd 1985; Thompson 1916:336–338; Burns 1966:13). The Flathead and Pend d'Oreille population decline is estimated at 45 percent between 1770 and the arrival of Lewis and Clark in 1805 (Boyd 1985:72, 93–94). The Plains Salish, who became associated with the Pend d'Oreille, were eliminated (Salish Culture Committee 1977:tape 98; Teit 1930:314–316).

†The History section was written by Thompson R. Smith.

Teit estimated that the predisease Flathead and Pend d'Oreille population was about 15,000. By the time of Lewis and Clark, this was probably reduced to somewhere between 2,700 and 5,500 (table 1). Successive waves of disease would continue to ravage the Flathead and Pend d'Oreille throughout the fur trade period, including in 1801 (smallpox), 1807–1808 (distemper), 1831–1837 (respiratory diseases and smallpox), 1846–1848 (smallpox and measles), and 1853–1855 (cholera, fever, and smallpox) (Boyd 1985:chart 13; Ewers 1958:65–66; Richards 1979:228; Burns 1966:1; Teit 1930:316; Scott 1928).

Numerous historians and anthropologists, relying almost entirely on scanty non-Indian written sources, have traced the arrival of the horse among the Flathead and Pend d'Oreille to around 1730 (Haines 1938a; Ewers 1955:3, 17, 18). An account in the Pend d'Oreille oral tradition of the first acquisition of the horse, or of the donkey, was assigned a similar date (Turney-High 1935:183).

For the Flathead and the Pend d'Oreille, the horse brought a complex mix of changes. It expanded their range, enabling more efficient travel and more effective hunting, particularly of buffalo. But the consequent erosion of tribal boundaries, along with the horse's cultural status as a highly mobile unit of wealth and prestige, also contributed to an intensification of conflicts with enemy tribes, primarily the Blackfoot, but also the Cree, Crow, Sioux, and Cheyenne. Rising mortality from warfare, and more difficult access to hunting grounds and other resources, became a much greater problem once the Blackfoot began securing firearms through the Hudson's Bay Company following the establishment of Buckingham House on the Saskatchewan River in 1780 (Ewers 1958:28, 30). The Flathead and Pend d'Oreille suffered heavy losses until they too began to secure appreciable numbers of guns and ammunition through the North West Company about 1811, and from American fur traders beginning about 1820. By then, the Blackfoot had already dramatically expanded their range to the south and the west, pushing Flathead and Pend d'Oreille

Table 1. Population, 1800-1908

Date	Bitterroot Salish or Charlot's band	Pend d'Oreille	Source
Aboriginal	1,200	600	Mooney 1928
1800	996	2,250	Boyd 1985
1840	800		de Smet 1873:33
1855	350		Stevens 1855b:150
1867	558		ARCIA 1867:396
1872	460	1,000	ARCIA 1872:48, 280–282, 393
1887	278		ARCIA 1887:356
1902	150		ARCIA 1902: 230–231, 636
1908		670	Teit 1930:315

winter camps west of the mountains (Ferris 1940:91–92). The tribes were still heavily utilizing the plains to hunt bison, using traditional areas such as Three Forks, Helena, and the Sun River on a more seasonal basis. By this time, the Pend d'Oreille had also abandoned some major camps along the west shore of Flathead Lake, including Dayton Creek, called *liłixʷ* ('something woven', probably referring to fish weirs) (Salish Culture Committee 1996:82), and joined bands to the south at places including *sk̓ʷłɫʔóʔlq̓ʷeʔ* ('coming to the water'; near Ravalli, Montana) (Salish Culture Committee 1996:60–61; Salish Culture Committee 1979:tape 211; Sarah G. Thomason, communication to editors 1997). The Libby-Jennings band of the Kootenai, who had used the Flathead Lake area seasonally, established themselves more permanently near Dayton Creek.

Some traders may have come into the Flathead and Pend d'Oreille country, or at least its fringes, before Lewis and Clark. David Thompson dispatched two traders to winter among the Kootenai people about 1801, and Joseph Whitehouse, of the Lewis and Clark expedition, reported the Flathead as saying they had already seen bearded men who came from a river six days to the north (Schaeffer 1966a; Whitehouse in Thwaites 1904–1905, 7:146–155). But it was not until after Lewis and Clark that the fur trade really became established in the area. Except for the brief presence of John McClellan in 1807 (Majors 1981:555–556), the trade west of the mountains was dominated by Hudson's Bay and the North West Company. In 1809, North West's David Thompson established Saleesh House on the Clark Fork River. But the Flathead and Pend d'Oreille never showed much interest in the fur trade. They engaged in trapping only sporadically, as their own limited needs demanded (A. Ross [1849] 1923:235–236).

Sometime around 1820, a group of Iroquois, apparently from Caughnawaga, settled among the Flathead in the Bitterroot Valley (Ewers 1963:8; Weisel 1955:28, 30, 36, 63). The Iroquois, who had become familiar with the area through their involvement with the fur trade, introduced the Flathead to Roman Catholicism (vol. 15: 545–546).

A man named Shining Shirt received a prophetic vision of strange men in black robes who would teach the people a new way of prayer (Salish Culture Committee 1975: tape 30; E.E. Clark 1966:139–141; Woodcock 1996:8–9; Peterson 1993:14, 17). The Flathead began sending out parties in search of the "Blackrobes," whose power they sought to combat loss from disease and raids (E.L. White 1990:46–55). Between 1831 and 1839, the Flathead and the Iroquois Catholics sent four delegations toward Saint Louis, which they knew about from American fur traders. An Iroquois served as the guide for Pierre Jean de Smet, the Belgian Jesuit who met the Flathead at the last of the fur trade rendezvous, held at Pierre's Hole, Idaho, in 1840 (White 1990:56–60; Lamar 1979:425–426; Ewers 1963:7). De Smet helped establish, in 1841, Saint Mary's Mission ("History Until 1846," fig. 6, this vol.) near present-day

Stevensville in the Bitterroot Valley (Salish Culture Committee 1996:188).

Saint Mary's operated initially for eight years among the Flathead. From the start, a fundamental tension permeated the Flathead relationship with the Jesuits: the Flathead sought to expand their existing spiritual pantheon with Christianity and to gain power in their struggle against the Blackfoot, while the missionaries were intent on complete conversion and the expunging of tribal traditions, which they characterized as "the work of the devil" (Peterson 1993:115). It was probably a heightening of the priests' campaign against Flathead spiritual practices, and their establishment of a mission among the Blackfoot, that led to the Flathead apostasy in 1849. The Flathead abandoned the church and no longer shielded the priests against Blackfoot raiders. The Jesuits relocated among the lower Kalispels in eastern Washington and sold the mission in 1850 to John Owen, who converted it into a trading post. In 1854, Jesuits established Saint Ignatius Mission in the heart of Pend d'Oreille territory, some 60 miles north of Saint Mary's (Partoll 1939:399–415), near a major Pend d'Oreille encampment now called Crow Creek (Salish Culture Committee 1996:36–37).

In 1855, Isaac Stevens, the governor and superintendent of Indian affairs for Washington Territory, convened treaty negotiations in a place known by fur trappers as the Hell Gate Ronde, near present-day Missoula ("History Since 1846," fig. 2, this vol.). As in his other treaty meetings with tribes throughout the Northwest, Stevens primarily aimed to concentrate Indian people of several tribes on a single reservation, thus opening the rest of the land to Whites. Stevens wanted the Flathead, Pend d'Oreille, and one band of Kootenai to take as their reservation the area surrounding the Saint Ignatius Mission and Fort Connah. Chief Victor (fig. 8) refused Stevens's demand that the Flathead relinquish control of the Bitterroot Valley. Stevens then inserted complicated language in the treaty that required the president to direct a survey of the valley, which would determine which place was better suited to the "wants of the Flathead Tribe." A Jesuit observer of the negotiations remarked that due to poor translation, "not a tenth" of the negotiations were "actually understood by either party" (Partoll 1938; Bigart and Woodcock 1996). Stevens followed up the Hell Gate Treaty with the Judith River Treaty in October 1855, which established tribal buffalo hunting territories on the plains east of the mountains. Stevens sought to reduce intertribal warfare, an impediment to the establishment of markets and regular non-Indian transportation across the region (Partoll 1937:199–207).

The Hell Gate Treaty's establishment of a "conditional Bitterroot Reservation" set up a long, bitter, but largely non-violent struggle between the Flathead and Whites who coveted the fine grazing lands, soils, and timber of their valley. This conflict began to intensify following the construction in 1859 of the Mullan Road, a rough military track running from Fort Benton to Fort Walla Walla, and further increased

Fig. 8. Headmen. left, Chief Victor, xʷetx̣Àcín or Plenty Horses (b. about 1800, d. 1870) wearing the military coat and yellow sash given to him at the Hell Gate Treaty. He was the headman that Governor Stevens selected as head chief (an invented office of the governor) of the Confederated Tribes of Flathead, Kootenai, and Pend d'Oreille during those treaty negotiations. Victor refused to move to the Flathead Res. and to leave the tribe's traditional home in the Bitterroot valley. Carte de visite made in 1864. This photograph has been digitally retouched. right, Chief Charlo, also known as sɫmx̣é q̓ʷox̣qéys or Claw of the Small Grizzly Bear (b. about 1830, d. 1910) participating in a Fourth of July parade. He wears the military coat and sash given to Chief Victor by Governor Stevens at the Hell Gate Treaty of 1855. Photograph July 4, 1907.

with the first gold rushes in Montana in 1864. Farms, gardens, and grazing paddocks sprang up in the Bitterroot to supply the military parties and mining camps. The Flathead felt that the treaty prohibited any White settlement south of Lolo Creek, but Montana officials rejected the suggestions of some Indian agents that troops be used to keep out or even evict the squatters. Although Chief Victor had repeatedly pledged to never wage war against the Whites, the newcomers began to issue demands for the permanent removal of the Flathead. Following the death of Victor in 1870, settlers and U.S. officials hoped his son and successor as chief, Charlo (fig. 8), would agree to leave (Flathead Culture Committee 1983). Although the official survey of the valley was never conducted, President Ulysses S. Grant in 1871 issued an executive order declaring that the Flathead Reservation was "better adapted to the wants of the Flathead tribe," and ordered them to be "removed" to the reservation (Fahey 1974:161). An official delegation led by future President James Garfield was sent to the Bitterroot in 1872, but Charlo also refused to move, and most of the Flathead stayed with him. Garfield recommended the government proceed as if the chief had signed (ARCIA 1872:115), and Charlo's X mark was forged onto the copy of the agreement that was sent to the U.S. Senate for ratification. The "Garfield agreement" unleashed a sudden influx of settlers. Charlo was reviled in the press as a treaty breaker until the counterfeit signature was exposed by Sen. G.G. Vest in 1883 (Fahey 1974:166, 233). Missoula County, which claimed jurisdiction over the Bitterroot Valley, used the agreement as

a pretext for various efforts to force the Indians out, including an attempt in 1876 to tax their property.

Two subchiefs, Arlee and Ninepipes, did sign the Garfield agreement, and moved to the reservation in 1873, accompanied by a few families. The U.S. treated Arlee as head chief, giving him a house and a small stipend, which only deepened Charlo's anger and distrust. The government required the remaining Flathead to take individual allotments of land, many of which were then encroached upon or altogether taken by non-Indian settlers. Whites then appealed to the government for military protection, and in 1877 Fort Missoula was established with a threadbare crew of poorly equipped soldiers (Rothermich 1936; Blades and Wike 1949). Nevertheless, when Chief Joseph's band of Nez Perce came through the valley later that year, the Flathead refused to join their long-time friends and relations, and their warriors instead defended the settlements. But neither officials nor the majority of settlers focused on distinctions between tribes, and pressures for removal of the Flathead only increased. Charlo and most of the Indians stayed anyway, and although they now supplemented their food supply with some limited agriculture, they continued to live largely by their traditional ways, including trips east of the mountains to hunt the dwindling herds of bison.

Wild bison were almost eliminated by 1883, when workers completed the last leg of the Northern Pacific Railroad, linking Montana to national and international markets. Mining exploded in Butte, and agriculture boomed both east and west of the mountains. The heavily timbered, relatively flat western valleys were logged intensively, profoundly altering the ecology of the Bitterroot Valley, the Blackfoot Valley, and the Seeley-Swan valleys, and with it the way of life of the Flathead and Pend d'Oreille people. Within the Flathead Reservation, tribal leaders largely anticipated the effects of the railroad, bluntly telling U.S. officials in 1882 that they did not want it because it would lead to further incursions on their land by Whites (Arthur 1883). But the following year, the railroad was built through 52 miles of reservation land.

Five years later, the Missoula & Bitter Root Valley Railroad was built, partly through Flathead allotments. In November 1889, faced with worsening conditions for his people, Charlo finally agreed to move, having secured guarantees of housing and other material help for the people once they relocated to the reservation (Bureau of Indian Affairs 1889). The Flathead, expecting to move in the spring of 1890, planted no crops. But Congress failed to appropriate funds for the removal. The same thing happened the next year. Finally, in October 1891, General Carrington and a contingent of troops from Fort Missoula uprooted the people from the Stevensville area (fig. 9), and marched them north to the reservation (Bureau of Indian Affairs 1891; Salish Culture Committee 1975). Belying popular notions that the Bitterroot lands were desperately needed by settlers, it took the government about 25 years to sell off the Flathead lands. Officials repeatedly reappraised the lands and lowered the prices in order to attract buyers (Bureau of Indian Affairs 1897, 1904).

Indian Agent Peter Ronan executed government policies with considerable energy from 1877 to his death in 1893. Utilizing newly formed Indian courts and an Indian police force, Ronan implemented policies that banned dances, spiritual ceremonies, feasts, and other traditional public gatherings. He worked closely with the Jesuit priests to enforce adherence to church law, including imprisonment for adultery or for marriage outside the church. He cut off resistant people from receiving supplies, including agricultural equipment, and rations, on which the tribes were increasingly dependent as traditional food sources declined (Bureau of Indian Affairs 1887). In the 1880s, when the Jesuits built boarding schools at the Saint Ignatius Mission, Ronan used these same tools of coercion to compel parents to send their children, as young as age five, into the institutions, where they were corporally punished for infractions such as speaking their own languages. Ronan also supported the priests in their ongoing effort to discredit, isolate, and disempower non-Christian spiritual leaders and healers (McDermott 1904). His policies drove the practice of ceremonies underground (Salish Culture Committee 1975: tapes 9, 42, 43). In general, it appears that Ronan protected the boundaries of the reservation and laws against non-Indian intruders, and he passionately forwarded the concerns of tribal leaders to officials in Washington (Bureau of Indian Affairs 1888).

In 1898, William Smead, a state legislator dedicated to the opening of reservations to White settlement, was appointed Flathead agent. From 1895 to 1901, Charlo and other tribal leaders rejected the efforts of a congressional commission seeking further cessions of reservation lands. "You all know that I won't sell a foot of land," Charlo told the Crow, Flathead etc. Commission; chief Isaac of the Kootenai concurred: "You had better hunt some people who want money more than we do" (Crow, Flathead etc. Commission 1901).

Despite the losses of the nineteenth century, by 1900 the Flathead and Pend d'Oreille community within the reservation was, in comparison with other tribes in Montana, relatively prosperous and healthy. Many had by this time established successful family farming and cattle operations, most for subsistence and as a supplement to hunting, fishing, and gathering. Traditional culture was not only surviving but also showing the vitality of innovation; in the late 1890s, celebrations or "powwows" were introduced to the reservation by Sam Resurrection, a Flathead man who had discovered them on a visit to the Northern Cheyenne Reservation (Salish Culture Committee 1975:tapes 13, 35). The overwhelming majority of tribal people were still fluent speakers of Flathead or Kootenai. The native communities of the reservation had become more numerous and diverse as Flathead, Pend d'Oreille, and Kootenai leaders agreed to allow the removal to the Flathead Reservation of about 60 lower Kalispels (1887), 60 Idaho Kootenais (1892), and over 100 Spokanes (1893) (ARCIA 1887, 1892, 1893; Bureau of Indian Affairs 1894, 1887a).

But this hard-won stability was dealt a devastating blow by the Flathead Allotment Act, ushered through Congress in 1904 by Rep. Joseph Dixon, a Missoula Republican. The bill called for the allotment of individual tracts of lands to Indians on the Flathead Reservation, and then the opening of any "surplus" lands to White homesteaders. From 1904 to 1907, Charlo fought the allotment and opening of the reservation through letters and visits to Washington. After 1907, Charlo appears to have become dispirited, and other men, including Sam Resurrection, picked up the mantle of resistance, though it was to no avail (B.M. Smith 1979; Bureau of Indian Affairs 1907, 1908, 1909, 1910).

In 1910 homesteaders poured into the Jocko and Mission valleys, where they quickly outnumbered tribal people and assumed a dominating social and economic position on the reservation. They were aided by former Agent Smead, who had been dismissed under a cloud of corruption in 1904, and promptly established the Flathead Land and Information Agency in Missoula, where he promised used the knowledge gained in his years as agent to the benefit of settlers seeking the best agricultural tracts on the reservation (Smead 1905). Whites were further attracted to reservation lands by passage of the Flathead Irrigation Act in 1908, which called for the construction of a massive canal and reservoir system to serve over 150,000 acres of dry lands on the reservation. Much of the system was built using tribal

top, U. of Pa. Mus., Philadelphia; center, Mont. State U., Mus. of the Rockies, Bozeman; bottom, Salish Culture Committee, St. Ignatius, Mont.

Fig. 9. Bitterroot Valley removal and struggles to return. top, The removal of Oct. 15, 1891. Individuals identified are Paul Vanderburg, Katrine Pielle, Paul Lumpry, John Tenore, Chief Charlo, Mary Lumpry, Gen. Henry Carrington, Katrine Tiboo, John Charley, Charlo's wife Isabel, and Charlo's daughter Ann Felix. Saint Mary's Mission church, Stevensville, Mont., is behind the group. center, Pilgrimage of the Flathead back to the Bitterroot Valley in 1911. Many visited the graves of their ancestors and St. Mary's Mission. Individuals identified are Mrs. Joe LaMoose, Catherine Lassaw, Ellen Big Sam, Frances Vanderburg, Sophie Moiese, Francis Lassaw, Mary Louise Barnaby, Katherine Barnaby, Louie Pierre, Enos Broken Leg (Kiser), Mrs. Stanley, Mrs. Louie Lassaw, Louie Lassaw, Susette Charlo, Louie Vanderburg, Nellie Kiser, Cecil Big Knife, Charley Coop, Pierre Lamoose, Joe Lamoose, Antoine Ninepipe, Antoine Moiese, Stiella Charley, Mrs. Natale Delaware, Chief Martin Charlo, Father Carr, Pierre Vanderburg, Bitterroot Jim, Pierre Big Hawk, Paul Charley, Adolph Barnaby, and Alex Matt. Photograph by John G. Showell. bottom, Depositions for Indian claims case. left to right, Unidentified clerk; Paul Charlo holding sash, coat, and medal given to his great grandfather Chief Victor; Bob Adams; and Pete Pierre. Photographed at the Missoula County Courthouse, Oct. 1952.

patented, with nearly all eventually transferred to non-Indian control. Over half a million acres—the majority of the most productive and valuable land of the Flathead Reservation— were lost from tribal ownership. The bulk of this was transferred to non-Indians between 1910 and 1915 (Matt 1997; Trosper 1974). Lands served by the Flathead Indian Irrigation Project were especially sought after by Whites; and by the 1920s, over the objections of the agency, White water users, in the majority, were forming their own water districts and beginning to exercise control of the project.

In 1920, the government, attempting to ameliorate the impact on the tribes of the opening of the reservation, made a second allotment of lands to those children born after the 1908 allotments. These new allotments were located in mountainous, forested, inaccessible land on the edge of the reservation (Matt 1997). Many of these parcels were in later decades bought back from the allottees by the tribal government.

In 1909, just prior to the opening of the reservation, the government effectively expropriated 18,000 acres of land for the establishment of the National Bison Range. The Pend d'Oreille themselves had saved the bison. In the 1870s, the tribe herded some bison calves back with them from the plains to the reservation (Salish Culture Committee 1979:tape 95; Zontek 1993). The herd grew until it reached about 1,000 animals in 1906, when the U.S. Indian agent compelled the remaining owner, Michel Pablo, to sell the herd off in preparation for allotment of the reservation and the enclosing of unfenced lands. Most were sold to the Canadian government, but a few years later, prompted by outcries from the newly formed American Bison Society, the United States government bought many of them back.

At the same time that the reservation was being opened to White settlement, an incident in the Swan Valley, an

funds and proceeds from the sale of Indian land (Commission 1914:21–40).

Between 1910 and 1929, 409,710 acres of the best agricultural land on the reservation were opened to homesteaders (Fenton 1968). In addition, many Indian allotments were allowed or forced by the Indian agent to be patented and then sold to non-Indians. Between 1910 and 1935, when the Dawes Severalty Act of 1887 was canceled by the Indian Reorganization Act, 131,239 acres of allotments were

Fig. 10. Dancers. left, Eneas Conko preparing his dance outfit. His leggings are made of Hudson's Bay Company blanket material; feathers and bells, possibly for his dance bustle, are placed around him. He wears wide metal bracelets and a beaded choker. A feather hair roach is at his knees. Conko, on the tribal council in the late 1930s and 1940s, was active in political and cultural activities. Photograph by Edward Boos, about 1908. right, War Dance. left to right, foreground, John Delaware and Felix Fisher. Photograph by Barbara Merriam, Victory Field, Missoula, Mont., 1950.

ancestral hunting ground adjacent to the reservation, demonstrated to tribal people the determination of the state of Montana to suppress, if necessary with violence, their treaty rights to hunt off the reservation. For decades, Flathead and Pend d'Oreille hunting parties had been harassed, taken to court, and occasionally attacked (Salish Culture Committee 1975:tapes 16, 28, 38; Bureau of Indian Affairs 1889a, 1894a, 1896). But beginning in the 1890s, this became more systematic, as the newly established state of Montana began implementing game laws and deploying game wardens in the western valleys, intent on the elimination of traditional Indian hunting practices. In 1908, an overzealous warden burst into a Pend d'Oreille camp and killed two middle-aged men, an elderly man, and a 14-year-old boy. Three women and a small girl escaped, but the message was not lost on tribal members (Salish Culture Committee 1977:tape 145; Bureau of Indian Affairs 1908a).

The tribes of the Flathead Reservation, known officially as the Confederated Salish and Kootenai Tribes, were the first in the U.S. to be reconstituted under the Indian Reorganization Act of 1934 ("Reservations and Reserves," fig. 7, this vol.). They would be governed by a tribal council of 10 persons, representing various districts but elected by the membership as a whole. The council then would select officers, including a chair, from among its members. From this point on, the tribes gradually began reasserting their sovereignty, often to the consternation of Whites who had become accustomed to considering the Flathead a "former reservation."

For traditional people, there were serious problems with the Act. Two of the chiefs living in 1935—Martin Charlo of the Flathead, and Kustahtah of the Kootenai—were given permanent seats on the new tribal council. But upon their deaths, they would not be replaced, and the position of chief would be officially abolished. Many "full bloods" felt that the new system only gave more entrenched power to a group of "mixed bloods" who were more conversant in White power structures and more able to use the system for their own benefit (Poston 1950:165–183). The Pend d'Oreilles noted that even though they constituted the largest tribal group on the reservation, they were excluded in both the new official name of the government and in chiefly representation on the new council.

The general exclusion of traditional people from policy questions was illustrated by the case of Kerr Dam ("Fishing," fig. 17 top left), completed in 1938 by the Montana Power Company on the lower Flathead River, near the center of the reservation. When the idea first arose in the 1920s, the government proposed to build the dam and split the revenues between the Flathead Irrigation Project, the Bureau of Indian Affairs, and the White water users' districts. Much of the income would be used to retire the enormous debt that the Irrigation Project had accumulated during its construction. This ignited a fierce debate that spread to the national level, where John Collier's American Indian Defense Association (1923–1936) championed the cause to secure substantial income from the dam for the Tribes. This was eventually accomplished, and the dam has played a key role since 1938 in the Tribes' economic and political fortunes. Missing from the debate, however, and largely from the historical record, were those traditional people who for spiritual reasons opposed construction of the dam at the falls of the Flathead River (Bigcrane and Smith 1991). Out of 10 people killed in the dam's construction, nine were tribal members.

The 1930s also saw the establishment of a large Civilian Conservation Corps program on the Flathead Reservation.

Until it was closed down during World War II, the CCC employed hundreds of people, giving many their first extended experience with wage labor, building trails and roads (fig. 11 top) throughout the forested hills and mountains on the reservation's boundaries.

Although a number of tribal members had served in World War I, the second war involved many more people, men and women, both in the services and in wartime industries in western cities, especially Portland and Seattle. Traditional families on the reservation found that it was much harder to maintain their cultural ways after the war (Bigcrane and Smith 1991). Many of the collective activities involving the gathering of traditional foods dwindled to a few families, mainly comprised of elderly people. Fluency in the Flathead language dropped off precipitously among children born after 1940. A number of tribal members left the reservation in the late 1950s and early 1960s under the federal policy of relocation, which subsidized the moving of Indian people to large cities to train and work in a variety of skilled labor programs.

In 1953, tribal leaders feared the reservation might cease to exist altogether, for when the House of Representatives, in Concurrent Resolution 108, adopted the policy of "terminating" the federal relationship with reservations, the Flathead Reservation was at the top of the list (Malouf 1954). After concerted lobbying by the council and others, this action was narrowly averted.

In the late 1960s and early 1970s, as the American Indian Movement swept across many reservations, a growing number of young people on the Flathead Reservation took a renewed interest in learning and perpetuating their traditional culture and languages. In 1974–1975, the Tribes established the Flathead (now Salish) and Kootenai Culture Committees, which since that time have grown into departments of the tribal government. Their mission has been the preservation and revitalization of the traditional cultures and languages, but in being directed by Elders Councils, they have also served to reintegrate traditional culture into the decision-making structure of tribal government. Nevertheless, the effort at cultural revival faced enormous obstacles; by 1997, the number of completely fluent Salish speakers had probably declined to 1–3 percent of the tribal membership (Bilingual Education Program, Salish Kootenai College). During the 1980s, the Tribes established Cultural Resource Protection programs, designed to safeguard cultural sites both on and off the reservation, within each of the Culture Committees. These programs grew into a central Tribal Preservation Office.

The governing structure of the confederated Salish and Kootenai Tribes is among the largest in the nation. Employing over 850 people in 1997, their programs included an extensive Natural Resources Department, and a Legal Department that had won repeated victories for the Tribes (fig. 11 bottom), including at the Supreme Court level. These capacities helped ensure that when the relicensing of Kerr Dam arose in 1984, the Tribes secured a far more

top, Natl. Arch.: 75–RAFB–27D; center, Salish Culture Committee, St. Ignatius, Mont.
Fig. 11. Reservation life. top, Lumber being sawed during the construction of the Mill Creek Trust Trail. This was a project of the Indian Emergency Conservation Works, Flathead Indian Agency, Dixon, Mont., a New Deal program initiated by John Collier (Philp 1977:243). Photograph April 1935. center, Ground breaking ceremony for the camas bath house, Hot Springs, Mont. Photograph about 1947; the building was dedicated June 1948. bottom, Confederated Salish and Kootenai Tribes legal department. left to right, Dan Belcourt, Ronald McDonald, Marion Yoder, Dan Decker, Rhonda Whiting Lankford, John Carter, and Karen Atkinson. Photograph by Michael Crummett, Flathead Res., Mont., 1994.

lucrative settlement. When the first deal was struck in 1930, the Tribes received an annual payment from the Montana Power Company of $140,000. In 1997, this figure stood at over $13 million. The Tribes also earn income from timber production, leasing of agricultural lands, and business operations, including a resort hotel on Flathead Lake, where gambling operations began in 1997.

Environmental protection remained a strong commitment of the Tribes, who in the 1970s became the first in the nation to establish a Tribal Wilderness Area, extending protection to over 90,000 acres of the Mission Mountains. This has increased to over 100,000 acres and is supplemented by protected lands along the Lower Flathead River, where the council has twice rejected proposals to build more hydroelectric dams. The Tribes are heavily involved in efforts to protect and restore a number of endangered and threatened species on the reservation, including grizzly bears, gray wolves, peregrine falcons, bull trout, and trumpeter swans.

In the 1990s, the Tribes maintained a program to repurchase reservation lands, with an annual fund of one million dollars. In education, Salish Kootenai College ranked in 1997 among the top tribally controlled community colleges in the nation. In the 1990s, it established a four-year program in environmental sciences and offered fully accredited nursing and dental hygienist programs.

In 1990, the population of the Flathead Reservation was 21,259, of whom only 5,130 were Indians; and about 4,000 were members of the Confederated Salish and Kootenai Tribes (U.S. Bureau of the Census 1991a). In 1997 tribal membership was 6,859, with 4,132 living on the reservation and 2,727 elsewhere.

Synonymy‡

The Flathead were referred to as "Flat head Ind[ian]s" and "Flat heads" by Lewis and Clark, who learned of them from French traders on the Upper Missouri during the winter of 1804–1805 (Moulton 1983–, 3:368, 444–445). The name is a translation of French *Têtes-Plates*, which in turn renders the meaning of the names used in several Indian languages: Hidatsa *ahtu·tsuhká²iš* (Douglas R. Parks, communication to editors 1975), Arikara *paxiníwiš* (Douglas R. Parks, communication to editors 1975), Mandan *papšíre nų́mąkaki* 'flat-head people' or *papápi nų́mąkaki* 'thin-head people' (Robert C. Hollow, communication to editors 1975), Blackfoot *apaksísttohkihkiní·tsitapi·koana* (Frantz and Russell 1989:14), Cheyenne *kAhkoestséataneo²o* (Glenmore and Leman 1984:201), and Arapaho *ko·kée²eit* (Salzmann 1983:96, phonemicized). Earlier names from some of these

languages are given in Hodge (1907–1910, 2:416). The reason for the name is a matter of debate, since the Flathead did not practice head deformation. The sign for the Flathead in Plains Indian Sign Language suggests flattening or shaving of the sides of the head (Moulton 1983–, 5:188).

The name Flathead (or its French equivalent) has also been applied to a number of other tribes, including the Catawba, Lower Chinook, Choctaw, Nez Perce, Spokane, Waxhaw, and a band of the Mandan (Hodge 1907–1910, 2:1054).

In the Flathead-Spokane language the Flathead proper, the people who were in the Bitterroot Valley in the nineteenth century, are called *séliš* (Sarah G. Thomason, communication to editors 1996). From this comes English Selish and more commonly Salish (Hale 1846:205, 569), the preferred designation used by many (Hodge 1907–1910, 2:415–416). In the 1990s the name Bitterroot Salish was used locally, and the language was sometimes called Montana Salish. These names have not been used in the *Handbook* to avoid confusion with the widespread use of Salish for the whole Salishan family, and because different groups have been in the Bitterroot Valley during the period covered. A borrowing from the Flathead name is Nez Perce *sé·lix* (Aoki 1994:631).

In Okanagan (Colville dialect) the name *snxʷmína²x* 'steelhead people' is applied collectively to the Spokane, Kalispel, and Flathead. Flathead *tayáqn* and Colville *ppílya²qn* are also used for the Flathead, but these terms, literally meaning 'flat-head (people)', appear to be literal translations of the English name (Sarah G. Thomason, communication to editors 1996).

Lewis and Clark generally referred to the Flatheads as Tushepaw or Tushepau; their first spelling of this term was ⟨Tut-see-was⟩ (Moulton 1983–, 3:444). This has been most plausibly interpreted as a Shoshone term *tatasiba* 'people with shaved heads' (Sven Liljeblad in Moulton 1983–, 5:188). It may have originally had a general reference to the tribes north of the Shoshone (Hodge 1907–1910, 2:853). Another name Lewis and Clark learned for the Flathead was Ootlashoot, variously spelled (Hodge 1907–1910, 2:137; Moulton 1983–, 6:474, 480, 482, 488); its origin is unknown.

For the name Pend d'Oreille, see the synonymy in "Kalispel," this volume.

Sources

Bigart et al. (1981) compiled an annotated bibliography on the history and culture of the Flathead and Kootenai tribes.

‡This synonymy was written by Ives Goddard.

Coeur d'Alene

GARY PALMER

Language

Coeur d'Alene ('kərdə,lān) is one of seven mutually unintelligible languages* of Interior Salish. Fifty-five percent of Coeur d'Alene vocabulary is shared in cognate words with its nearest linguistic and territorial neighbor, the Kalispel (including the Spokane, Chewelah, Kalispel, Pend d'Oreille, and Flathead dialects). Before it was flanked on the north and east by dialects of Kalispel, Coeur d'Alene may have occupied the eastern frontier of the Interior Salish languages, having branched off and differentiated from them sometime between 2500 B.C. and A.D. 1 (Elmendorf 1965; Suttles and Elmendorf 1963).

In 1962 the language was spoken by about 100 people (Aoki 1968); in 1997, by less than 20. It was taught in the tribal grade school (Nicodemus 1975, 1975a).

Territory

The aboriginal Coeur d'Alene territory extended over the drainage and headwaters of the Spokane River. Before 1700 three clusters of permanent winter villages constituted three major territorial divisions of the Coeur d'Alene tribe: the Spokane River–Coeur d'Alene Lake division (17 villages), the Coeur d'Alene River division (12 villages) and the Saint Joe River division (9 villages). Names are listed for 38 of 40 habitation sites (Teit 1930; Ray 1936), some of which were winter villages and some summer camps (fig. 1). There may have been a fourth division at Chatcolet on the southwest corner of Lake Coeur d'Alene (Chalfant 1974c).

Villages and some nearby resource sites were no doubt held by individual bands, but places between tribal centers, such as the Rathdrum Prairies, the camas prairie on Hangman Creek, and portions of the Clearwater and Clark Fork may have been regarded by more than one tribe as lying within their territories. Such places were utilized mutually.

Environment

Coeur d'Alene territory contained rolling palouse prairie, foothills, mountains, and valleys, all drained by streams tributary to the Spokane, Coeur d'Alene, Saint Joe, Palouse, and Clearwater rivers. The conformation of these features, which vary in altitude from sea level to 2,100 meters, creates an environment of exceptional diversity.

Annual rainfall over the territory varies from 460 millimeters in the west to 1,260 millimeters along the mountain crest. The moderately cold winter temperatures of their territory range from -5.5 to 1.5°C, while the warm summers range from 18.5 to 24.5°C. Winter rains and snows provide most of the effective moisture, which is realized in a surge of growth in May and June. Most of the hundreds of small streams dry up only in late summer.

In aboriginal times, the eastern palouse prairie was dominated by Idaho fescue and by blue bunch wheatgrass, which provided good habitat for sharp-tailed grouse. Chokecherry thickets surrounded by thickets of snowberry and wild rose provided cover and forage for white-tailed deer. Coyotes preyed upon mice, which lived in the thickets. The steppe vegetation of the fescue–snowberry zone maintains one-third of its maximum growth throughout the winter. Some of this growth would have occurred in roots and forbs utilized by the Indians in spring and early summer.

On the edge of the prairie, open stands of ponderosa pine provide patches of grazing land for blacktailed deer. In the foothills, the valleys of the Coeur d'Alene, Saint Joe, Saint Maries, Benewah, and Palouse send tongues of grassy camas meadows up to the foot of the Rockies themselves. These small meadows were favorite camping and root-digging grounds for parties on their way to hunt and fish in the mountains. Along creeks and rivers grow cottonwoods, chokecherries, hawthorns, nodding onions, and cow parsnips.

The Coeur d'Alene lakes and streams teemed with fish, both landlocked and anadromous. West slope cutthroat trout, sometimes called salmon trout, spawned in the Spokane, Coeur d'Alene, and Saint Joe rivers from the last week in March to the first week in April. Spent spawners returned to the lake, making a second run in early June.

*The phonemes of Coeur d'Alene are: (voiceless stops and affricates) p, t, c, č, kʷ, q, qʷ, ʔ; (glottalized stops and affricates) ṗ, ƚ̓, c̓, č̓, k̓ʷ, q̓, q̓ʷ; (voiced stops and affricate) b, d, gʷ, j; (voiceless continuants) s, ƚ, š, xʷ, x̣, x̣ʷ, h; (resonants) m, n, l, r, w, y, ʕ, ʕʷ; (glottalized resonants) m̓, n̓, l̓, r̓, w̓, y̓, ʕ̓, ʕ̓ʷ; (vowels) i, e ([ɛ]), a, u, o, ə.

In the practical orthography used by the Language Preservation Project of the Coeur d'Alene Tribe, the phonemes are written: p, t, ts, ch, k, kw, q, qw, '; p', t', ts', ch', k'w, q', q'w, b, d, gw, j; s, ł, sh, khw, qh, qhw, h; m, n, l, r, w, y, (, (w; 'm, 'n, 'l, 'r, 'w, 'y, '(, '(w; i, e, a, u, o'; ə is not written (Nicodemus 1975, 1). This orthography also uses the right parenthesis (⟨)⟩) for a lenis allophone of ʕ.

313

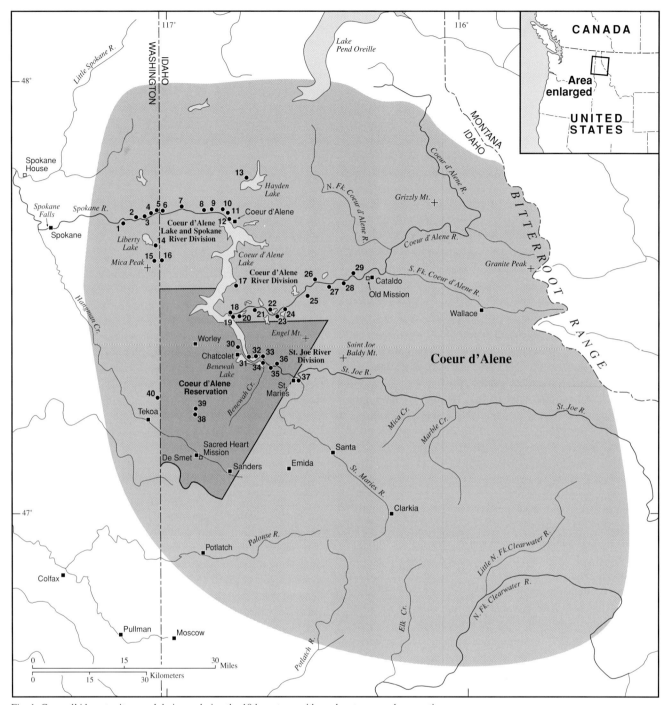

Fig. 1. Coeur d'Alene territory and drainage during the 19th century, with modern towns and reservation.

Spokane River–Coeur d'Alene Lake Division: 1, *čatənwáx̣iʔłpəm* 'flat by dogwoods'; 2, neslíx̣um; 3, nesx̌ʷáx̌ʷe; 4, ntsetsak̓ʷolsák̓ʷo (?); 5, neʔəwáshalqs; 6, *hənċaq̓íłpenč* 'fir on the mountainside'; 7, *q̓emílən* 'throat, gorge'; 8, *sčétk̓ʷeʔ* 'flat water'; 9, *hənšárəpt* 'upstream'; 10, *tpuʔníłpəm* 'bubbling plant'; 11, smələlína; 12, *hənčəmqínk̓ʷeʔ* 'surface at the head of the water' (Coeur d'Alene, Idaho); 13, *hənłáq̓ən* 'Hayden Lake, Idaho'; 14, *múlš* 'cottonwood'; 15, *čnák̓ʷaʔqən* 'one on the head'; 16, family camp, name unknown; 17, cheléchəlichəmən.

Coeur d'Alene River Division: 18, chłáchalx̌ʷ; 19, *ałk̓ʷáriʔt* 'source of gold'; 20, neʔatsx̣áx̣stəm; 21, déʔłtəlpʷ 'a large clump of cottonwoods' (?); 22, nestʔáq̓ʷast; 23, qoqolételps 'black pines'; 24, *smáq̓ʷqən* 'things lying on the mount'; 25, camp, name unknown; 26, *hənsélut* 'whirlpool'; 27, sənshél*ə*mənts; 28, nalstqíłx̌ʷən; 29, *sq̓ʷłú* (Old Sacred Heart Mission).

Saint Joe River Division: 30, *ċəmíẇəs* 'waist, narrow peninsula between lake and river'; 31, stíq̓ʷtakəshən (?); 32, chetíshtashəshən; 33, *słúčteẇəs* (Mission Point); 34, schishátət; 35, schləlidshiketən; 36, *čatʔuẇášalqs* 'little dwelling on the spur'; 37, *hənčémcən* 'confluence, inner mouth' (St. Maries, Idaho); 38, táx̌ʔolks (?). Summer camps not associated with divisions: 39, *niʔlox̌ʷálq̓ʷ* 'hole in the woods'; 40, nłpótsəntsən.

SOURCES: Palmer, Nicodemus, and Felsman (1987); Ray (1936:130–133); Teit (1930:38–39). Names given only by Ray or Teit, or both, are in a slightly normalized transcription in roman.

Whitefish run in the Saint Joe in late October and early November (William Goodnight, personal communication 1978). The Coeur d'Alene also had access to the steelhead trout and chinook salmon runs in the Spokane and Clearwater rivers. Steelhead have a "summer" run from May to October and a "winter" run from November to April (Fulton 1970).

Culture

Subsistence

The Coeur d'Alene relied upon hunting, fishing, and gathering of plant foods for their subsistence. There is scattered evidence that they maximized the productivity and reliability of their food sources by basic techniques of management, such as burning and pruning, and perhaps also by loosening the soil during root digging as suggested by a Nez Perce (Ames and Marshall 1980).

Leaders of bands, divisions, and camps were much involved in the management of resources. They regulated access to resource locations, they timed root and berry harvests, and they distributed game and fish. Band and division territories were recognized but were open to all for exploitation by appeal to the appropriate leader. Spokanes fished with Coeur d'Alenes at the outlet of Lake Coeur d'Alene and in the 1850s were pasturing their horses in the prairie near the Cataldo Mission (David Chance, personal communication 1978). Spokanes, Kalispels, Nez Perces, Palouses, and Cayuses shared the Coeur d'Alene camas prairie. However, Teit (1930:162) reported that "parts of the country in proximity to villages of bands were seldom used by outsiders, for they depended on this territory for the gathering of roots and berries, and for everyday fishing and hunting." Thus each band and division maintained a sphere of influence in which it regulated use by its own members and by parties from other tribes, divisions, and bands (JP 47).

While sizable groups formed for winter guardian spirit ceremonies, the populations of most neighborhoods were not so great as the groupings that formed for the early spring cutthroat trout fishing at the mouths of the Saint Joe and Coeur d'Alene rivers and the outlet of the Spokane River. However, the trappers of spawning trout could not have been too numerous, as some families were already gathering by April at Hangman Creek prairie. By early June, camas digging attracted what may have been the largest Coeur d'Alene annual assembly. There they were joined in root digging, gambling, and horse races by Spokanes, Kalispels, Nez Perces, Palouses, and Cayuses (Burns 1966; Coeur d'Alene Teepee 1939). Smaller groups of Coeur d'Alenes spent the late summer in the upstream meadows of the Coeur d'Alene, Saint Joe, and Palouse river drainages, where they dug late camas and went out in even smaller parties for berries. Berry picking, especially for huckleberries, continued into the early fall as the groups from the camas meadows broke up to depart in still smaller groups of two or three related families for hunting and fishing in the uplands. After the fall hunt, they reassembled in their villages in the lowlands for hunting, fish trapping, and ice fishing in the late fall and early winter. On the Saint Joe River, whitefish could have been trapped during their spawning runs in late October and early November. Point (1967) observed trapping of fish at the outlet of the Spokane River from Lake Coeur d'Alene in November. Many Coeur d'Alenes no doubt departed from this pattern by gathering at the outlet of Lake Coeur d'Alene for spring fishing, and then moving down the river toward Spokane Falls for summer salmon fishing and trading. Perhaps those with Spokane relatives went still farther west in May to the neighborhood of Davenport to gather bitterroots.

After they acquired the practice of buffalo hunting, most families were absent from early fall to late spring. After their return from across the mountains, buffalo hunting parties probably rode almost directly to Spokane Falls or to the summer camas grounds. The gatherings for fishing and root digging may have expanded after the horse increased the ease of communications and transport. The short distance and easy communications between the major salmon fishery at Spokane Falls and the camas grounds at Hangman Creek may have shifted most of the Coeur d'Alene population to the western side of its territory during late prehistoric and early historic summers, so that the annual round became one of crisscrossing the territory, with the traditional villages providing midpoints where people rested, pastured weary horses, put up food, and prepared for the next foray.

Prior to 1700 the primary game hunted were deer and elk. After the Coeur d'Alene obtained horses, they began to focus more of their hunting efforts on buffalo. The Coeur d'Alene developed bow and arrow making to a fine craft, relying upon an unusually wide, flat bow about one meter in length, backed with 30 strands of sinew from the leg of a deer. The sinew was attached with glue made from the skins of salmon. The newly glued bow was wrapped with twine made from the bark of bitter cherry. From the wood of serviceberry they made many different kinds of arrows, some with grooves to bleed the game.

Deer were driven upwind toward a line of scorched hides set up on sticks to confuse them and render them easily shot with arrows. The same method was used to keep the deer within a circle. At other times, hunters with dogs drove the deer along the side of a ridge that terminated in a bluff over a lake. Others, waiting out of sight in canoes behind the bluff, took them easily from the water (JP 47; Teit 1930).

Another method brought the deer to the hunters without the necessity of a drive and in fact appears to be a means of herd management. In 1860 Coeur d'Alenes were observed burning extensive areas of forest to eliminate the lichen (*Bryoria tremonti*) that hangs from trees (Mullan 1863). During the winter this caused a scarcity of forage, which forced the deer to descend to the low country where they could be easily taken in deep snow, as they were in the winter of 1842–1843 (Point 1967). The burning of lichens probably also encouraged the growth of shrubs and grasses needed for browsing and grazing during the subsequent spring and summer, thereby improving the physical condition of the herds.

An individual hunter would climb a tree and tie himself to a branch to await the deer through the night. Deer were also taken in nets, pitfalls, corrals, and nooses. Bear were taken in deadfalls. According to Teit (1930), the Coeur d'Alene did not receive guns until at least 1850. Trapping fell into disuse after 1800 because so few capable men remained home from the buffalo hunts. Buffalo were taken from horseback or driven over cliffs.

There were winter deer drives, possibly conducted by division headmen, on the shores of Lake Coeur d'Alene, the Coeur d'Alene River, and the Saint Joe River (Chalfant 1974c). The Coeur d'Alene also hunted along the Little North Fork of the Clearwater, on Goat Mountain, on Grizzly Mountain, along the upper Coeur d'Alene River, and the Spokane River. Muskrat, beaver, and otter were trapped along the Coeur d'Alene River and no doubt along the other streams as well, for the Coeur d'Alene provided significant numbers of pelts of water mammals to the fur trade at Spokane House (David Chance, personal communication 1978).

The Coeur d'Alene were skillful fishermen who used a great variety of techniques for angling, gaffing, spearing, and netting trout, whitefish, and salmon in both long nets and bag nets. Several varieties of fish traps were used, including screens, cylindrical traps, trap doors, large salmon traps, and weirs. Fish could be directed into a trap by ritual pipe smoking (Antelope 1938a). Fish traps were constructed at the outlet of the Spokane River from Lake Coeur d'Alene, on the Saint Joe River near the old mission, and on Hangman Creek near Tekoa. The trap at the outlet of Lake Coeur d'Alene was "a barrier made of wicker screens attached to a line of tripods, solidly jointed together by traverse poles" (Point 1967). For salmon, many Coeur d'Alenes went to Spokane Falls and other parts of the Spokane River while others bought dried salmon from the Spokane Indians. Some fished for salmon on the main Clearwater and on its northern tributaries. Salmon were also taken on the Graywater and beyond Smeda.

Plant collecting, the subsistence task that required a very extensive knowledge of species and their growing characteristics, paradoxically required only a few simple digging, scraping, and carrying instruments for its practice. More elaborate instruments and constructions were necessary for the preparation, storage, and transportation of plant foods after they had been collected. The Coeur d'Alenes gathered berries, roots, nuts, seeds, tree sap, and tree cambium. For scraping the cambium of ponderosa pine, special tools were made from rib bones, most probably those of deer and elk. For stripping "blackpine" (possibly lodgepole pine), scrapers were made from shoulder blades. Roots were dug with diggers modified in various ways to suit diverse soil condi-

tions—square in cross-section to provide a better grip in the ground, wide and curved for soft ground, rounded and almost straight for hard ground. Huckleberries were gathered by breaking off the branches and using twigs to strip berries from the broken branches onto a blanket or, in former times, a mat placed on a slight incline. This pruning technique of gathering may have promoted a better harvest the following season. The growing stalks of cow parsnip, and balsamroot were plucked, peeled, and eaten raw. Dwarf huckleberries were collected by combing them from their tiny bushes into a basket.

Most plant foods required extensive processing. Roots were steamed and baked in earth ovens or boiled in baskets with hot stones. Camas, lichens referred to by Teit (1930) as "Black moss," and wild onions were baked in pit ovens. A foul-smelling root, called *másmas*, probably edible valerian (but Teit 1930 thought wild carrot) was steamed in a specially constructed pit oven. Peace root, dogtooth violet, camas, couse, and an unidentified root called *taʔqemxʷ* were boiled (Teit 1930:92).

After baking, camas and couse were mashed and kneaded into flat cakes. Camas and black lichen were sometimes cooked to a paste, cooled, and cut into cakes, which were dried on frames of slats woven with bark or thongs. Such cakes could later be boiled for soup. Berries were also mashed or boiled and made into cakes by being poured over thick layers of grass. By 1909 sugar was being added to fresh mashed berries (Teit 1930).

In addition to the preservation provided by drying the cakes of roots and berries, methods of storage were available. Roots were spread to dry and hung in sacks of open weave, or they were hung on strings to dry and store. Meat and salmon were dried in the sun or over a fire. Dried meat and salmon were ground and sealed in sacks as pemmican. Dried fish, meat, and roots were stored in circular pits. Such pits were used into the twentieth century for storing potatoes and water potatoes called *sqíg*ʷ*əc*. Foods were kept out of the way of animals by means of platform caches and suspension from tree limbs.

Roots were available in meadows. Perhaps the most productive grounds for camas and wild onions were in the prairie near the modern town of DeSmet (Mullan 1863:97). Camas and wild onions were also dug in the neighboring localities of Tekoa, Sawmill, Sheep Creek, Sanders, Emida, Potlatch, and, with Spokanes, on the west side of Water Lily Lake. Some families journeyed west to the drier Big Bend of the Columbia, in Spokane country, to dig bitterroots. Berries were gathered at Mica Peak near Worley, at White Mountain near Clarkia, on the upper Coeur d'Alene River, on Smoke Mountain near DeSmet, on Engel Mountain (formerly Round Top), near Santa, north of the Saint Joe River, north of the Clark Fork River, and in the neighborhood of Spokane. The territory along the North Fork of the Saint Joe eight and one-quarter miles above the fork, probably on the slopes of the Saint Joe Baldy Mountain, was considered good berrying grounds in the 1860s (Mullan 1863:105–106).

Technology

Tools, instruments, and artifacts were made of stone, wood, bone, antler, and plant fiber (Teit 1930). Many items were wrapped or bound with rawhide, sinew, or plant fiber (Ray 1942).

Bags, wallets, and parfleches were made from fiber or from hides. In historic times, cloth and corn husks were used (fig. 2). Pliable containers were ornamented with quills, embroidery, and paint in geometric designs, usually of blue and red on a yellow background. In woven baskets cedar served as the warp and hemp as the woof. Such baskets were used for berries, water, and, if lidded, for storage. Large wide-mouthed coiled baskets were employed for boiling water. Bags and coiled funnel baskets were used for crushing berries. Winnowing baskets were also coiled.

Clothing was made primarily of skins ("Kinship, Family, and Gender Roles," fig. 5, this vol.), which were smoked by

top, Mus. of North Idaho, Coeur d'Alene: NA–1–83; bottom, Eastern Wash. State Histl. Soc., Cheney Cowles Mus., Spokane: 1013.7 (neg. 95.28).

Fig. 2. Women's clothing. top (left to right), Unidentified woman wearing a velveteen dress decorated with beads and shells; Mary Theresa Joseph (b. 1863, d. 1938) wearing a cloth wing dress decorated with beads and cowrie shells; unidentified woman wearing a cloth wing dress decorated with cloth appliqué on the sleeve and collar and a wide beaded belt; unidentified young woman with a fringed wing dress decorated with ribbon appliqué and cowrie shells; Agatha Michele Joseph wearing an elaborately decorated yoke dress. Photograph by Mary Gimble, about 1910. bottom (back and front), Purse of twined cord decorated with yarn and cornhusks. The leather fringes on the bottom are strung with glass beads, and tiny colored beads are sewn at the edge of the leather binding around the top. Collected by Sister Providencia on the Coeur d'Alene Res. near DeSmet, Idaho, 1937–1939; probably manufactured in the early 20th century. Height with fringe 19 cm.

stretching them either flat or in a tepee shape over a fire. Some skins were treated with brains and salmon oil.

Structures

The Coeur d'Alenes apparently made no semisubterranean earth lodges. The most common dwelling was the mat lodge of tule, which took three forms: the conical family house used in summer or winter, the communal single or double lean-to lodge for summer gatherings, and the permanent lean-to long lodge used for gatherings and training quarters for young men. Double lean-to lodges contained one central fire for each pair of families. Where good cedar bark was available, a short, oblong bark lodge was made to accommodate one to four families at all seasons. In these, the bark was laid on poles in a vertical position against the support poles, either overlapping on the sides or placed together at the edges with an additional piece laid over the seam. Single lean-to bark lodges were used by summer parties. Ray (1942) recorded a flat top temporary dwelling with four supporting poles. Temporary brush lodges were made of fir and balsam. Women and adolescent girls spent their isolation periods in small conical lodges. Sweathouses were dome-shaped willow frames supporting a covering of brush, grass, and earth.

The Coeur d'Alenes apparently had reason to fear raids by the Blackfoot or by other tribes of the Plateau. Some Coeur d'Alene villages centered on stockades up to three meters high constructed either of rows of vertical posts set deeply in the earth or of stacked horizontal poles. Entry was possible only through zigzag passages that closed with wooden bars. Underground escape passages led to the edges of banks or to outcroppings of rocks or thickets.

Transport

Prior to the use of horses, much transportation must have followed the waterways, using double-ended, sharp-pointed "sturgeon nose" cedar bark canoes. The Coeur d'Alenes also made tule rafts that were pointed at both ends like the canoes.

Religion

Aboriginal Coeur d'Alenes recognized a preeminent deity called *amótqn*, literally 'he who sits at the head'. Conceived of as living on the highest mountains from where he could survey the earth, he was offered the first berries and roots of the season by the band chief. Hunters thanked him for game. Apparently next in importance came the Sun, from whom the Coeur d'Alenes sought health and luck in the Sun Dance and hunting success in the Horse Dance. The Sun Dance of the Coeur d'Alenes resembled that of the Plains Indians in its pattern of dance motions toward the sun and in its motives. However, it could be performed at any time of the year and it required no self-torture.

Sought and obtained by both men and women, guardian spirits could assume many forms, including animal (fig. 4), bird, celestial body, and probably inanimate ones such as

Mus. of North Idaho, Coeur d'Alene: left, NA-6-67 and right, NA-7-2.

Fig. 3. Horse transportation. left, Annie Ike Coyote with horse sporting a feather headdress. Photograph by Mary Gimble, about 1910. right, Pete Barsaw on a small native horse. Photographed at Benewah Lake, south end of Coeur d'Alene Lake, Idaho, 1884.

Fig. 4. Chief Ignace acquiring his hunting medicine. Drawing depicting the chief going into the mountains to fast, sweat, and pray for a guardian-animal spirit who then would give him hunting prowess. His spirit, a male deer, is in the center of the painting. Ink on paper by Father Nicolas Point, about 1842.

mountain, stone, and plant. Some known guardians were wolf, bear, wolverine, deer, and the "calumet bird," perhaps a heron (Point 1967:181). There is some evidence that guardians were grouped according to similar habitats, and probably according to similar qualities. For example, warriors obtained power from the Sun, a particularly powerful spirit, and from Thunder, Eagle, and certain kinds of hawks and owls, all spirits to be found in the sky.

Songs and actions of guardian spirits were enacted in the Guardian Spirit Dance, which was held "several times a year, but chiefly in winter, by each band independently" (Teit 1930:187). Persons with bluejay power underwent transformation for winter dances and acted out their patron's role, blackening the face and body, perching in the rafters, finding lost objects, and undergoing capture, ceremonial death, and revival (Ray 1942).

Mythology

It was a spirit that provided the original substance of the Coeur d'Alenes and neighboring tribes when Coyote cut out his heart. The version reported by Reichard (1947) derives the Coeur d'Alene people from the heart of the "Gobbler monster," a motif that combines the Coeur d'Alene idea of being mean, or perhaps fierce, with their concept of the heart as the seat of the emotions. Diomedi (1978) identified the creator water spirit as *amótqn*, who was stationed at the head of the Coeur d'Alene River and ruled over the waters.

This was the same spirit who required a payment when one passed a certain quiet spot in the river. The Coeur d'Alene story of creation by dismemberment is discussed by Palmer (1989).

While life on earth came to the Coeur d'Alenes through the agencies of Coyote and a water spirit, death came about through a contest between twins. One twin wanted life, the other death. Because they could not agree, humans have neither total life nor total death, but always some living people and some dead, some being born and some dying (Teit 1917). After death, a person's spirit survived to become a ghost that remained near the grave, wandered its accustomed places, and tried to visit people it had known.

In American Indian myths, nonhumans, such as animals, plants, and inanimate objects, often display humanlike personalities. All kinds of mythological persons, human and nonhuman, may transform themselves. In an important Coeur d'Alene tale, Chief Child of the Root, *yəlmíxʷum asp̓uxʷeníčelt*, performed several types of transformations. He changed Pestle Boy and man-eating awls, combs, bladders, and cords into their present inanimate forms. In an apparent human-to-bird transformation, he modified the outer forms of Kingfisher and Fishhawk. He transformed himself into a salmon and then into the moon. At the same time, Helldiver's child became the sun. Chief Child of the Root was also an instructor who taught Fisher not to be foolish by killing and reviving him; he told Foolhen to eat moss raw instead of falling into the fire to cook it; and he showed

top, Eastern Wash. State Histl. Soc., Cheney Cowles Mus., Spokane; center, Mus. of North Idaho, Coeur d'Alene: NA-1-64.

Fig. 5. Dancers. top, Group in dance costume including beaded vests and leggings with bell decorations. left to right, unidentified Coeur d'Alene and Spokane man holding a pipe tomahawk; Yal-il-mee', Kalispel; Ishpoo-ah', Coeur d'Alene holding a coup stick; Louis, Coeur d'Alene; Etz-kow-tae', Kalispel and Coeur d'Alene; Tzeh-tzo, Kalispel; unidentified Kalispel and Spokane man wearing a horned headdress. Photograph by Frank Palmer, 1908–1916. center, War Dance participants. Harriet Meshell (d. 1951) (sixth from left) wears a war bonnet. Alec Abraham (b. 1897, d. 1961) (third from left) wears a shirt decorated with animal fur strips. Bill Meshell is fifth from left. Photograph by Mary Gimble, about 1910. bottom, Chatcolet culture camp participating in a War Dance. left to right, Judy Wilson, Coeur d'Alene; Sam Moses, Spokane; Roger Moses, Spokane; unidentified child; Lawrence Aripa, Coeur d'Alene. Participants in the drum group right background are unidentified. Photograph by Gary Palmer, Chatcolet, Idaho, 1982.

and a blunderer. He commits every kind of transgression and indulges every lust. He is vain, imitative, and ungrateful, but he is not all bad. Coyote transformed the earth for the benefit of the Indians, taught them the use of fire and other arts, destroyed or transformed monsters, and released the salmon.

In addition to the origin myths and the Coyote stories, there are stories of Lynx and the Dog Husband, both of whom received scorn at first but gained respect through their powers or through transformations. There are stories of girls who became stars but did not have star husbands, of Woodticks who were the keepers of the deer, of Catbird who wished things into existence, of Skunk and Fisher who fought over the girls Chipmunk and Squirrel, of bones that turned into dentalium, and of a hunter who sought his wife in the Thunder's lair. Water monsters and man eaters provided the recurrent villains. Man eaters took diverse forms including Gobbler, mosquitoes, water monsters, and four sisters who became terns. Water Monster Woman appeared in the tale of a boy who poked out the eyes of children and animals. As the monster tried to drown the boy and his family, they were saved by the plant-persons Tangled Bush, Braided Bush, Serviceberry, and Thornberry. Other characters in the tales are dwarfs who live in trees, always descending head first; men who turn into trees; giants who smell like burning horn, dress in bearskins, and eat fish; and monsters combining human-animal or human-fish forms.

Political and Social Organization

Coeur d'Alene social organization prior to White contact can be reconstructed, but contradictory statements abound in ethnographic descriptions, often within the same source. Many changes in organization are ascribed to the use of the horse for buffalo hunts across the Bitterroot Mountains, but equally fundamental changes must have followed the smallpox epidemics that decimated Coeur d'Alene populations shortly after their acquisition of horses.

Each village or small cluster of villages was the winter residence of bands of no more than 300 persons. Families

Splinter Leg how to make a spearhead from elkhorn instead of from his own leg bone (Reichard 1947). This tale and others like it present a creation in which the animate, inanimate, and cultural realms are shaped at the same time and by the same magical processes in no apparent sequence.

Coyote appears as a major character in about half the recorded tales. Often aided by three or four powers, he is alternately a culture-giver, a trickster, a transformer, a hero,

and individuals tended to return to natal locations, but no formal restrictions prevented visiting and residence with kinsmen in other bands or divisions. By Teit's (1930) account each division recognized a chief who was also the elected leader of either the largest band or of a band that supplied the division chief by tradition.

In addition to the permanent peace chiefs, transitory enterprises called for the recognition of war chiefs and hunting chiefs. As successful war chiefs maintained their authority for subsequent expeditions, the same probably held true for hunting chiefs. Such warfare as may have occurred during this period was chiefly with the Kalispel, Nez Perce, and Kootenai. It is unlikely that conflicts ever involved a larger number of warriors than those supplied by a single division. Most, if not all, probably occurred on the level of the band or family. To avoid warfare and strengthen their military position, chiefs attempted to form and maintain alliances by exchanging their daughters in marriage.

When the Coeur d'Alenes acquired horses, it became possible for them to reach the plains east of the Rockies, where they encountered hostile bands of Blackfoot, Crow, and Sioux Indians. For protection they traveled in groups made up of members from more than one band or division. Intertribal hunting parties with Flatheads, Spokanes, Kalispels, and even Nez Perces became common.

As smallpox reduced Coeur d'Alene populations, joining together into composite bands or tribal hunting parties must have become critical for survival. The survivors could regain some of their lost productive capacity and perhaps rebuild some sense of community by pooling their skills in the new composite band made up of remnants of the entire tribe. Tribal coordination and intertribal cooperation were accomplished by political centralization that vested authority, still consensual, in the new offices of tribal chief and tribal council. At the same time, the position of band or village chief may have declined in importance or disappeared. In 1820, there were three recognized division chiefs, one of whom was the tribal chief. These were Stellam (Spokane síəláṁ 'thunder'), the tribal chief from Coeur d'Alene City and Hayden Lake; xʷist he sčəníceʔ 'Walking Robe', from Cataldo; and Gabriel Shilshilccho (šəlšəlčásq̓ət) 'Revolving Sky', from the Saint Joe division.

The tribal hunting band comprised women, children, and several men's groups, each group with a captain. Called "companies" by Teit (1930:156), the men's groups included the chief's messengers, who were youth; the horse guards, who were also young; the warriors, who were middle aged; and the elderly men who helped to make camp. There were groups that had particular duties in connection with buffalo hunting, war, or defense (Teit 1930:156–157). While age sorting is evident, there is no indication that these groups had become formally named, age-graded societies with supernatural patrons and membership payments, such as developed among the tribes of the Plains.

The flexible band organization, the lack of merging of kin terms on the parental generation, and the use of identical terms for siblings and cousins of the same sex suggest that aboriginal kinship organization was essentially bilateral. The levirate, residence with the husband's family at marriage, and (weakly developed) succession to the office of chief through males appear to be patrilineal characteristics.

Life Cycle

• PUBERTY Proper behavior and self-control were stressed in the training of boys and girls, who sought guardian spirits by suppression of emotions and by concentration in hopes of receiving a vision and a song. They sweated and bathed daily in cold water, and they received tattoos of vision designs pertaining to their guardian spirits. At the time of puberty, a girl underwent seclusion during which she practiced working as she would be expected to work in her adult life. She avoided touching herself other than with a scratcher or a comb, apparently an expression of the idea of female power that becomes more manifest during life crises and menses. A boy underwent a longer training, which included scarification and ordeal by burning the skin with live coals or dry lighted tule stalks. Some received several guardians and songs.

• MARRIAGE Marriage was polygamous (Point 1967:70), and the Coeur d'Alenes practiced the levirate (Teit 1930:171). Even though a woman might refuse to live with the brother of her deceased husband, her children of sufficient age continued to live with the family of their father. Such arrangements may have created the setting in which arose the special Coeur d'Alene kin term for grandparents of either sex who take over the responsibilities of child-raising for a deceased parent.

This custom of the levirate, examples in legends, and modern instances suggest that it was traditional for Coeur d'Alene wives to live with the families of their husbands. A strict taboo was followed forbidding a man to speak to his mother-in-law. In some families a woman was forbidden to speak to her father-in-law.

Marriages could be initiated by the family of the man, the family of the woman, or by the man and woman themselves. Gifts were normally given by the man's family, but if the man had high wealth or prestige, the woman's family might initiate the marriage and give gifts.

• DEATH The Coeur d'Alenes buried their dead in the earth or, more commonly, in rock slides in the nearest suitable place, under a campfire if necessary to conceal the body, which was "tied up with cords, knees to chin and wrapped in a robe" (Teit 1930:173). The body was placed on its side or in a sitting position facing in no particular directions. Earth graves were circular, three feet in depth above the corpse, and protected with heaps of rocks. With the deceased were buried his guardian spirit objects, such as small stone carvings of guardians. One to three poles, peeled and painted red, were erected at the grave. From these were suspended property of the deceased and funeral presents. On the grave were placed offerings: roots and berries for women; horse skins, horse hooves, and canoes for men. The lodge of an adult was sometimes burned or moved to another location.

History

From 1780 the Indians of the Plateau began experiencing the physical and psychological horrors of smallpox epidemics and the social disorganization that accompanies radical reductions in population size (table 1). Some tribes looked to native prophets for interpretations of their misfortunes and for rituals to stabilize their lives. The Coeur d'Alene also received a prophecy, but rather than developing an indigenous movement of cultural revitalization, they embraced the Roman Catholicism brought to them by Jesuit missionaries.

In the Coeur d'Alene prophecy, Chief Circling Raven had a dream in which he foresaw men sent by the "Great Chief who dwells in the sky" to teach the Coeur d'Alenes (Tolan 1980). The prophecy was pursued by his son Stellam, who encountered the Jesuit priest Pierre Jean de Smet at Post Falls in 1842. Impressed by the eagerness of the Coeur d'Alenes for religious instruction, de Smet sent Father Nicolas Point in November of that year. The first Sacred Heart Mission was on the Saint Joe River, but by 1846 annual flooding forced Joseph Joset, who had replaced Point, to move to the Coeur d'Alene River site now known as the Old Mission at Cataldo. The mission building was constructed by Father Anthony Ravalli and the Coeur d'Alene Indians in 1850. From 1846 to 1876, some 40–50 Coeur d'Alenes lived at the mission (vol. 4:495). The missionaries boarded youth whom they trained in agriculture and animal husbandry.

In May 1858, in spite of remonstrations by Chief Vincent, the Coeur d'Alenes joined the Indian wars by putting up a brief resistance to the U.S. Army in a successful skirmish against Lt. Col. Edward Steptoe. Their resistance was suppressed in August 1858. Thereafter Andrew Seltice, a participant in the battle, replaced Vincent as tribal chief (Burns 1966).

In 1873 an appointed commission recommended a reservation of 600,000 acres with title conferred on the tribe and a settlement of $150,000 for 2,200,000 acres to be ceded. President Ulysses Grant established a reservation by executive order, which failed to confer title to the land or to pay compensation for ceded lands. The Coeur d'Alenes at first refused to move to the reservation, but settlement was encroaching. The Mullan Road from Fort Walla Walla in Washington Territory to Fort Benton on the Missouri River passed through the Coeur d'Alene valley and close by the mission. Beginning in 1865, gold strikes in the Coeur d'Alene mountains had brought thousands of miners to the area, causing the missionaries and the Indians to fear even

Table 1. Population, 1780–1994

Year	Population	Source
1780	3,000–4,000	
1853	320	JP 47
1890	520	U.S. Congress 1890:32
1905	494	
1973	900[a]	
1981	1,111[a]	
1989	1,213[b]	Coeur d'Alene Tribe, personal communication 1989
1994	1,216	Bureau of Indian Affairs 1994

SOURCE: Palmer 1981.
[a] Includes ethnic Spokanes enrolled on the Coeur d'Alene Res.
[b] 383 on-reservation.

greater loss of land, especially the fine camas prairies at Hangman Creek.

Having learned farming skills at the mission, the Coeur d'Alene young adults were eager to move to the fertile prairies and turn them to agriculture. After the reluctant elders had been won over, the tribe moved in November 1877. The new Sacred Heart Misssion was at DeSmet (fig. 6). The Coeur d'Alenes settled near the mission along Hangman Creek and ceased hunting buffalo. They plowed land, raised wheat, and built roads, fences, and two-story farm houses. Several families developed large prosperous farms. Most obtained a portion of their subsistence from gardening and from traditional pursuits of root digging in summer, with berrying, deer hunting, and trout fishing in the mountains in late summer and fall. Shortly after the move to DeSmet, the Sisters of Charity of Providence of Montreal were petitioned to send teachers, and a school was built. This developed into separate boarding schools for boys and girls.

In the 1870s, under continuing pressure from non-Indians seeking timber, mineral rights, and homesteads, Chief Seltice renewed his petitions for title to the reservation. A second agreement reached in 1877 also failed to obtain congressional approval. During the years 1887 through 1889 the Coeur d'Alenes negotiated an agreement for a reservation of 598,000 acres, ceding "3,000,000 acres more or less" of land for $650,000, or approximately 22 cents per acre (U.S. Congress 1890). As part of the settlement, about 100 Spokanes were permitted to settle in the northern sector of the reservation and become enrolled members of the Coeur d'Alene tribe. The government constructed homes for them and plowed 10 acres for each (Dozier 1962; U.S. Congress 1890). The Coeur d'Alenes received their compensation in two disbursements, $500,000, which was paid on a per capita basis, about $960 for each of the 520 Coeur d'Alenes, and $150,000 which was paid in installments, $30,000 the first year and thereafter in 15 annual installments. There were additional appropriations of $20,000 for payment of the salaries of "a competent physician, medicines, a blacksmith,

top, Sacred Heart Mission, DeSmet, Idaho; Eastern Wash. State Histl. Soc., Cheney Cowles Mus., Spokane: bottom left and bottom right: 1013.4(neg. 95.39).

Fig. 6. Sacred Heart Mission, DeSmet, Idaho. top, Indian village with mission buildings on the hill (left to right): Mary Immaculate School, run by the Sisters of Providence, 1883–1908, when it burned down; church, 1882–1939, when it burned down; priests' house; priests' and boys' dining hall; and boys' boarding school, 1883–1945. Photograph by Grayson or Joseph Maxwell, 1885. bottom left, 4th through 8th grades at the mission school. Photograph 1936–1937. bottom right, Cedar bark basket constructed of alternating rows of plaited and twined cedar strips. The top edge is finished in braid, and leather thongs are attached beneath the rim. Collected by Sister Providencia on the Coeur d'Alene Res., near DeSmet, Idaho, 1937–1939. Height 23 cm.

and carpenters" and $5,000 for marking boundaries (U.S. Congress 1890:32).

In 1951 the Coeur d'Alene Tribe of Indians filed a petition before the Indian Claims Commission alleging that the compensation of $150,000 was "grossly inadequate and unconscionable" (C.M. Miller 1956:2). The appraiser for the commission determined the value of the land in 1891 to be $3,500,000, or approximately $1.35 per acre (it is not clear why the $500,000 in per capita payments was not mentioned by the appraiser for the Claims Commission).

Long opposed by Chief Peter Moctelme of the Coeur d'Alene, the Dawes Severalty Act of 1877 was finally applied to the reservation in 1909. Each tribal member, man, woman, and child, was required to take an allotment of 160 acres and to give up any other claims on reservation land. The numbers allotted were 541 Coeur d'Alenes and 97 Spokanes. For the most part, the Coeur d'Alene allot-

ments were located on good farming land in the original settlement area of Hangman Creek and along the Washington border. The Spokane allotments, in the north, were on partially timbered land that required cleaning before cultivation. The tribe should have received $428,732 (less than two dollars per acre) for the land sold by the government in 1909, but there has never been an exact accounting for these funds (Cotroneo and Dozier 1974). Although the act originally specified that allotted lands would remain in trust for 25 years, this stipulation was removed in 1906. The first patents were issued to Coeur d'Alenes in 1913. "In spite of high wheat prices and good markets which prevailed from 1900 to 1919, the loss of land through sales and fee titles began immediately after allotment and resulted in the present checkerboard pattern of land ownership in the west third of the Reservation" (Delwo 1975:23). Most allottees began to rent their lands to non-Indians for a portion of the crop, an

center, Mus. of North Idaho, Coeur d'Alene; right, Ind. U., William Hammond Mathers Mus., Bloomington.

Fig. 7. Headmen. left, Joe Seltice. Photographed about 1950. center, Chief Peter Wildshoe and his son Philip Wildshoe. The son is wearing a buckskin shirt with painted floral designs on the collar, cuffs, and bib. He holds a pipe and beaded pipebag. Photograph by Mary Gimble, about 1910. right, Peter Moctelme. Photograph by Joseph K. Dixon, Tekoa, Wash., 1913.

arrangement that dominated agricultural production on Indian leases in the 1990s.

Teit (1930) and T.R. Cox (1979) have stated that after the consolidation of 1877, the Coeur d'Alene retained only a chief and one subchief. However, in addition to Chief Seltice ("Reservations and Reserves," fig. 8, this vol.), three subchiefs signed the agreement of 1889. These were Peter Wildshoe (fig. 7), Vincent, and Moctelme. When Seltice died in 1902, he was succeeded by Wildshoe (d. 1907), who was succeeded by Peter Chi'yarpásqEt, and then by his brother Peter Moctelme, sons of a former chief of the Saint Joe division (cf. Teit 1930:154; T.R. Cox 1979). Under the influence of Moctelme, the Coeur d'Alene at first rejected the Indian Reorganization Act of 1934. Moctelme was succeeded by Joe Seltice (fig. 7), the last traditional chief before the Coeur d'Alene accepted the Act in the 1950s as well as the first chairman of the tribal council (T.R. Cox 1979).

Ind. U., William Hammond Mathers Mus., Bloomington.

Fig. 8. Preparing a meal outside a typical reservation house. Photograph by Joseph K. Dixon, Tekoa, Wash., 1913.

In 1997 the tribe had six council members, elected for terms of three years. By the constitution, enrolled members include all whose names appear on the official census roll of the tribe as of July 1, 1940, with subsequent correction, and all children of enrolled members, provided they have "one-fourth or more Indian blood" (Coeur d'Alene Tribe 1961).

The tribal government has evolved to combine executive, judicial, legislative, and corporate economic functions in a bureaucracy employing both Indian and non-Indian managers. Begun in 1971, the Tribal Development Enterprise operates the Tribal Farm with a capitalization of three million dollars, the Utility Service Enterprise for general contracting, the Timber Enterprise, and a service station. In addition, the tribe operates the Department of Law and Order, the tribal school, and the Community Services Agency, which has health and nutritional functions.

In 1958 the Indian Claims Commission awarded the tribe approximately four million dollars for the lands ceded in 1891. Of this the tribe budgeted one and one-half million for land purchases, which have amounted to over 5,000 acres of agricultural lands for the Tribal Farm. Under the chairmanships of Joe Garry and Ozzie George, the tribal farm was organized. The farm leases about 40 percent of its wheat land from tribal members who hold allotments. The tribe also owns 2,600 acres of mixed timber and grazing land on highly erodible soils. Half of this land is harvested as timber and half is kept in sustained yield timber (Charles Finan, personal communication 1978). The tribal timber operations received technical and managerial assistance from the Bureau of Indian Affairs and from the Center for Native American Development and College of Forestry of the University of Idaho, Moscow.

Synonymy

Meaning 'heart of (like) an awl' in French, the name Coeur d'Alene has inspired several unsubstantiated derivations, both plausible and implausible. Observing that the name was also translated 'Pointed Hearts', Joset (JP 47) speculated that it was applied to the tribe by trappers who found them hardhearted. Hodge (1907–1910, 2:594) stated that the name "was originally a nickname used by some chief of the tribe to express the size of a trader's heart." Another writer with equal imagination proposed that some travelers experienced hunger until "their hearts were pierced with sorrow as with an awl" (quoted in Garraghan 1938:316).

There is a more reasoned, but still highly speculative theory. The first recorded instance of the name 'Pointed Heart' is found in David Thompson's journal of 1809. A historian has suggested that the French members of Thompson's party were using the name Coeur d'Alene and that Pointed Heart was an attempt to translate it into English (Thompson 1978). Since no fur traders had been established in the region previously, he advanced the clever alternative idea that the Coeur d'Alene were called "thin hearts" by their enemies to the East of the Rockies and that Thompson may have learned of the name from Roman Catholic French-speaking Iroquois living among the Flathead Indians. From the original Indian language, whichever it may have been, the Iroquois may have translated "thin heart" into French as Coeur d'Alene. An ethnographer who worked closely with the Coeur d'Alene offered the explanation that Coeur d'Alene refers to bravery. She wrote, "The name was given to them by the early French settlers from an origin tale which depicts these Indians as superior because they are 'mean,' that is brave" (Reichard 1943:96). In the tale, Coyote told the newly created Coeur d'Alenes, "You'll be mean." The actual Coeur d'Alene expression is *čeƚkʷučést* from *čést*, which is commonly glossed 'bad' (Reichard 1947:71). Another word for brave means to lack fear. While the intent behind the name is plausible, the original naming could not have taken place as suggested because they received the name Pointed Hearts before French settlers entered the Columbia Basin. Not an explanation, but perhaps the most important interpretation is that of modern Coeur d'Alenes, one of whom has said, "Our modern name of Coeur d'Alene should be translated 'Pointed Hearts,' to represent a forceful, strong, perceptive people" (Tolan 1980:45).

The traditional Coeur d'Alene name for themselves, *sčícuʔumš*, in the practical orthography Schitsu'umsh, was given as Schizue, formerly the name of a single band or camp "on the southern bank of the little lake which empties into the St. Joe at the Lewistown trail" (JP 47). A modern Coeur d'Alene speaker has translated the name as 'the discovered people' from *čic-* 'find' and *-umš* 'people' (Nicodemus 1975). From this stem derives the term for the Coeur d'Alene language, *snčícuʔumšcn*. Other historical spellings of the tribal name are Skeetsomish, Skitswish, Skeetshoo, Skeetshues, Sketsui, Sketch Hue, Sketch Hughe, Skitsuish, Schizuumsh, Skee-cha-way, Skeelsomish, Skeetsonish, Sketsomish, Skit-mish, Skitsaih, Skitsaish, Skitsǎmǔq, Skítsui, Skítwish, Skitawish, Stchitsui, Stiel Shoi, Stietshoi (Hodge 1907–1910, 2:594; Rust 1912; A.W. Thompson 1978).

Sources

Anthropology owes its published knowledge of Coeur d'Alene ethnography and linguistics almost entirely to two closely related families, those of Louis Antelope (M. Antelope 1938) and Croutous Nicodemus, one of the signers of the petitions leading to the treaty agreement of 1889. Teit stayed with Croutous for several weeks in 1904, obtaining from him most of the material in the ethnography (Teit 1930; Reichard 1947; Lawrence Nicodemus, personal communication 1978). Containing information on material culture, cooking and food preservation, subsistence techniques, religion, and social organization, this work by Teit and Croutous remains the best ethnography of the Coeur d'Alene. Dorothy, the widow of Croutous, was one of Reichard's (1947) two main sources for an important collection of 48 stories, including origin myths and Coyote stories. The other source was Tom Miyal. Teit (1917) published abstracts of tales.

Reichard's (1938) grammar was based on the speech of Julia Antelope and Lawrence Nicodemus. The grammar, a comparative study (Reichard 1958–1960), and a list of verb stems and nouns (Reichard 1945) continue to be used as primary sources for language comparisons. For example, Shapard (1980) discussed Coeur d'Alene transitive suffixes. Mattina (1980) described imperatives. Newman (1979) demonstrated the relationship of Coeur d'Alene pronouns to those of other Salish languages. In these three studies and one by Vogt (1940a) the data are drawn entirely from Reichard's publications.

Sloat (1966, 1968, 1971, 1972, 1980) clarified several aspects of Coeur d'Alene phonology. R.E. Johnson (1975) covered much the same territory. His primary source was Lawrence Nicodemus (1975, 1975a), who directed the publication of a dictionary and grammar.

Ray published a list of Coeur d'Alene villages and a great deal of ethnographic information in tabular and summary form (Ray 1936, 1939, 1942), and he testified on behalf of the Coeur d'Alene before the Indian Claims Commission (Ray 1975b).

The Coeur d'Alene versions of the texts that appeared in English in Reichard (1947) have been microfilmed by the American Philosophical Society, Philadelphia, along with Teit's vocabulary (APS Film 372 Reel 18). Reichard's letters to Franz Boas during the summer of 1927 appear on microfilm (APS Film 1263 Reel 7). A manuscript of Reichard's collection of Coeur d'Alene texts, numbers 1–27 only, and several of her notebooks, consisting almost entirely of word lists, are in the possession of the Archives of the Languages of the World, Indiana University (Reichard 1946). The earliest known Coeur d'Alene vocabulary list is that of Roehrig (1870). Much good primary information, including myths, subsistence techniques, and historical texts, has been republished by the Coeur d'Alene tribe in a bound version of the tribal newsletter, *The Coeur d'Alene Teepee*, first published in 1937 to 1939.

Coeur d'Alene stories, ethnography, and history are available in popular form in several sources. Connolly (1990) is a historical reader for the fourth grade. Connolly and Palmer (1983) present a summary of Coeur d'Alene history and land use values. Palmer (1981b) is a biography of the Coeur d'Alene farmer Louis Mchtor (Victor), whose life spanned the transition from hunting-gathering and mission farming to commercial farming in the twentieth. Ewing and Grossen (1978) edited four tales from Reichard (1947) for use as a reader in elementary school classrooms. Walker (1973) summarized Coeur d'Alene ethnography and edited tales for use in Idaho public schools. Pelticr (1975) is a popular, but not scholarly, description of the Coeur d'Alene. Crowell and Aleson (1980) published several interesting stories from the Aripa family of the Saint Joe River. McGeorge (1939) is a bad romantic novel of the Indian princess variety, full of racist aspersions and lacking the slightest ethnographic content.

In 1894 the Tribe organized the Coeur d'Alene Language Preservation Project. The Project employed two native speakers to teach language classes in the primary school and it commissioned the production of four textbooks. It also collected video and audio tapes dealing with tribal history. The Language Preservation Project and some of its products are described in Palmer (1988, 1992). Among them are a pair of workbooks in phonology, vocabulary, and elementary syntax (Palmer, Nicodemus, and Felsman 1985), a workbook in Coeur d'Alene geography (Palmer, Nicodemus, and Felsman 1987), and a dictionary of Coeur d'Alene personal names (Palmer, Nicodemus, and Connolly 1987). Both the geography and the dictionary of personal names contain cultural, linguistic, and historical information not published elsewhere. Lutz and Barlow (1981) compared the functioning of the school boards of three schools serving Coeur d'Alene Indian children on the reservation, including the tribal school board, which operates a contract school.

Historical sources with extensive bibliography include Cotroneo and Dozier (1974), Dozier (1961, 1962), Burns (1947, 1966), T.R. Cox (1979), and Palmer (1981, 1981a). Burns (1966) has an annotated list of archives. Landar (1980) has a bibliography of Reichard's published work on Coeur d'Alene. Kowrach and Connolly (1990) is an important oral history dictated by Chief Andrew Seltice to his son. De Smet (1895) contains writings on the Coeur d'Alene woman Louise Sighouin.

Other manuscript materials are in the Sacred Heart Mission Papers, Oregon Province Archives of the Crosby Library at Gonzaga University in Spokane, Washington, and in the National Archives in Washington, D.C., and Sand Point, Washington. Photographs and drawings are in the tribal archives; the Smithsonian Institution; the Missouri Province Archives of the Society of Jesus, Saint Louis University, Pius XII Library, in Saint Louis, Missouri; and the DeSmet Project, Washington State University, Spokane, Washington. Coeur d'Alene artifacts are in possession of the Coeur d'Alene Tribe and the Cheney-Cowles Museum in Spokane, Washington.

Yakima and Neighboring Groups

HELEN H. SCHUSTER

The Yakima ('yăkīmu), Kittitas ('kītītăs), Klikitat ('klīkītăt), Taitnapam ('tītnəpəm), and Wanapam ('wänəpəm) were closely related but independent bands and villages of families, who once occupied contiguous territories in the south-central part of the state of Washington (fig. 1).

The Yakima and the other groups in aboriginal times did not have the formal political unity under a permanent central authority that is characteristic of tribes. Rather, they were small, politically autonomous groups, joined together by bonds of territorial contiguity, linguistic affinity, a common culture, and a high level of recurring social interaction. While language or dialect differences existed between peoples in this part of the Plateau, they followed an essentially similar way of life in customs, beliefs, and traditions. Shared cultural characteristics contributed to a feeling of unity, reinforced by a network of intervillage kinship ties, intermarriage, co-utilization and sharing of subsistence resources, trade relationships, and a recurring round of visiting and other social activities. It was not until the treaty of 1855 that a true tribal polity was formed: The Consolidated Tribes and Bands of the Yakima Nation.

Language*

The groups covered in this chapter all spoke Sahaptin (sə'hăptīn). The Yakima, Klikitat, Kittitas, and Taitnapam spoke dialects of the Northwest Sahaptin dialect cluster (Rigsby 1965; vol. 17:666–667); Wanapam was in the Northeast Sahaptin dialect cluster, along with the Palouse, Lower Snake, and Walla Walla. A fifth dialect of Northwest Sahaptin was spoken by the Mishalpam in the upper Puyallup and Nisqually valleys, who were also (or became) speakers of Lushootseed and are also known as the Meshal

*The phonemes of Sahaptin are: (voiceless stops and affricate) p, t, c, λ, č, k, k^w, q, q^w, $?$; (glottalized stops and affricate) $\dot{p}$, $\dot{t}$, $\dot{c}$, $\dot{\lambda}$, $\check{c}$, $\dot{k}$, $\dot{k}^w$, $\dot{q}$, $\dot{q}^w$; (voiceless fricatives) $s, \dot{t}, \check{s}, x, x^w, \chi, \chi^w, h$; (resonants) m, n, w, y, l; (short vowels) $i, a, u, \dot{i}$; (long vowels) ii, aa, uu; (stress) $\acute{v}$. In initial position $?$ is not written before a vowel and $?i$ is not written before m, n, or l plus a consonant. The unitary phonemes $c, \check{c}, \lambda$, and k^w contrast with the phoneme sequences $ts, t\check{s}, t\dot{t}$, and kw, respectively. Information on Sahaptian phonology is from volume 17:666–672, which also covers details of pronunciation and dialect variants. Words that could not be phonemicized, including village names from Ray (1936), are given in roman in a normalized orthography.

In the Yakima practical alphabet the phonemes are: p, t, ts, tł, ch, k, kw, k̲, k̲w, '; p', t', ts', tł' (tl'), ch', k', kw', k̲', k̲w'; s, ł, sh, x, xw, x̲, x̲w, h; m, n, w, y, l; i, a, u, i̲; ii, aa, uu; stress: acute accent (') over vowel (over first vowel of a double vowel).

band of Southern Coast Salish (vol. 7:486–488, vol. 17:667). The Northwest, Northeast, and Columbia River dialect clusters were the three components of Sahaptin, which with Nez Perce forms the Sahaptian language family. The Yakima dialect is referred to in Sahaptin as the language of the Mamachat band (*mámačatpam*), as in the expression *mamačatimki* 'in the Yakima language' appearing as ⟨mamachatumki⟩ on the title page of St. Onge (1872).

While dialectal differences in pronunciation were apparent between and within the territorial boundaries of each of the above tribal groups, communication in the 1980s apparently remained relatively effortless among all the people. Many elders and other adults in the 1980s retained their Indian language, and one or another of the Sahaptin dialects was used in the 1990s as the ceremonial language in longhouses throughout the area.

Territory

During the middle of the nineteenth century, Yakima territory was divided roughly along Wenas Creek into two closely connected principal bands: the Upper and Lower Yakima (Gibbs 1855; Robie in ARCIA 1857:350). Each one was made up of a number of smaller, locally autonomous bands or villages, under the authority of one or more chiefs. The Lower Yakima (Yakima) recognized three principal chiefs: Kamiakin ("Palouse," fig. 6, this vol.) and his brothers Skloom and Shawaway; the Upper Yakima (Kittitas), their uncles Teias and Owhi (fig. 2) (Gibbs 1855:407).

Between 60 and 70 independent villages, seasonal camps, or local bands have been identified in Yakima country (fig. 1) (Ray 1936:119–151; Spier 1936:16–20; Gibbs 1855; Robie in ARCIA 1857:350; Desmond 1952; Mooney 1896:737; Schuster 1965–1985).

Kittitas

The largest settlement in this region was *kłáła*, a village of around 500 people, located one mile above the present town of Thorp. Four miles below Thorp was a village of around 400 people, called yumísh. Another of equal size, *náanim*, was located seven miles northeast of present-day Ellensburg. Two miles below Ellensburg on the west side of the Yakima River was Kittitas (*k̓títaas*), a popular vil-

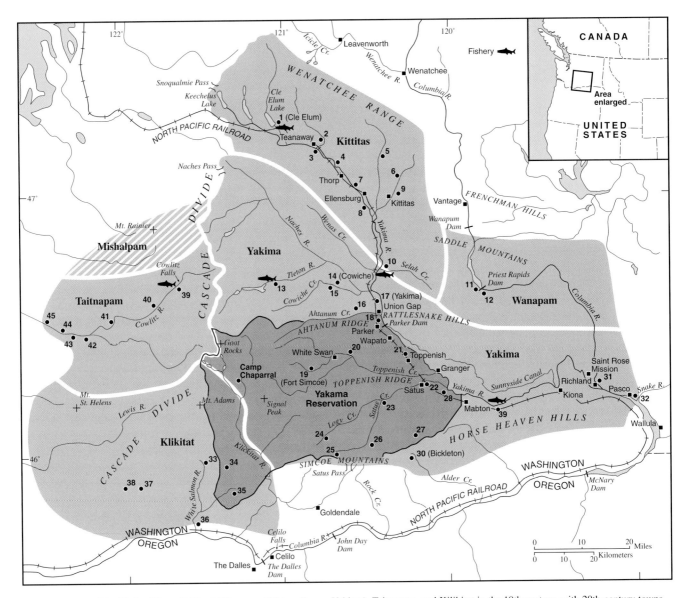

Fig. 1. Territory of the Kittias (Upper Yakima), Wanapam, Yakima (Lower Yakima), Taitnapam, and Kilikitat in the 19th century, with 20th-century towns, drainage, and reservation boundaries. The Mishalpam are shown in their approximate location before being absorbed into the Southern Coast Salish. Native settlements. Kittitas: 1, *ƛ̓iyálɨm*; 2, tiánawĩns; 3, tátxanĩxsha; 4, k̓ɫáɫa; 5, *náanim*; 6, ntsämtsá′mchĩn; 7, yumĩ′sh; 8, *k̓títaas*; 9, ch'ĩláxän; 10, síla. Wanapam: 11, sháp′tĩlĩk; 12, *p̓ná*. Lower Yakima: 13, miyáwax̣; 14, wápatuxs; 15, táytän; 16, *átanam*; 17, tsikik; 18, *páx̣utaktyuut (p̓ákyuut)*; 19, múlmul; 20, nikás; 21, si′; 22, x̣úkyimkt; 23, páwankyuut; 24, latáma; 25, wáx̣shäm; 26, tamanchätäni; 27, patkwáyp; 28, išĩčt; 29, táptät; 30, *tápašnaq̓it*; 31, *tanáx̣alu*; 32; *k̓ʷsis*. Klikitat: 33, *šax̣šax̣ʷinmí*; 34, pásx; 35, kawáwkay; 36, láwli pamí; 37, ch'ikwásh; 38, *kalamát*.

lage in summer, where Yakima families in the 1980s remembered stopping to camp when they journeyed from the reservation to Ellensburg. *ƛ̓iyálĩm* was an important summer camp situated at the south end of Cle Elum Lake, where as many as 1,000 persons fished for salmon during June and July. Hundreds of people gathered in May and June at the camas meadows and council grounds near the villages of ch'iláxan and n'tsamtsámchin, near the present town of Kittitas, for trading, feasting, sports, and gam-

bling, as well as for root digging. In June 1814, Alexander Ross, clerk of the North West Company, sought to barter for horses at the encampment, which he described as "covering more than six miles in every direction" with "not . . . less than 3,000 men, exclusive of women and children, and treble that number of horses" (Ross 1855:22). Splawn (1917) and Desmond (1952) presented descriptions of intervillage horse racing, which had become a highlight of seasonal gatherings at this site by the 1860s. A second

Fig. 2. Chief Owhi, principal chief of the Kittitas. Watercolor by Johnson K. Duncan, on the Northern Pacific Railroad Survey, 1853.

large encampment was held the beginning of August at camas grounds near present-day Teanaway (Desmond 1952:44). People came to dig roots, visit, trade, gamble, compete in sports, and hunted for game in the area in fall.

Yakima

In this territory, one of the main villages was called *pákyuut* or *páxutakyuut* 'where two mountains almost join'. Although the village extended for a mile or two along the river, it had only one headman. Upstream about a mile was the largest Lower Yakima village, called *tsíkik* 'spring', which was regularly occupied by about 2,000 people. Another village, named wápatuxs and situated at present-day Cowiche, was where headmen and chiefs held council meetings. Twenty miles to the west was an important encampment area for hunting, fishing, and berry gathering, located at the east end of Rimrock Lake on the Tieton River.

Many other villages were scattered along what is now the eastern boundary of the Yakima Reservation, between Union Gap and Mabton. The largest of these was *išíčt* 'nest', at the mouth of Satus Creek, a center for festivities where several chiefs or headmen resided. About six miles above the mouth of Satus Creek was *xúkyimkt* 'burial grounds', site of both a permanent village and cemetery. Winter religious ceremonies or "dances" were held regularly at *páwankyuut* 'meeting place', a populous village on Satus Creek near the mouth of Logy Creek, which was also presided over by more than one headman or chief. Numerous Rock Creek, Celilo, and Skin visitors came from villages to the south through Satus Pass in the Simcoe Mountains to attend these ceremonials.

A permanent village and scout camp, *tápašnaqit*, was located in the Horse Heaven Hills at present-day Bickleton, jointly occupied by Yakima, Umatilla, and Celilo, where horse racing was the popular event. At the Sunnyside Canal intake area was *awátam* 'deep water', a natural fishery where, in the 1960s, Indians could still dip-net for steelhead in the early spring and salmon during the early summer and fall runs. A large village and noted fishing site, *tanáxalu*, was located east of the Columbia opposite the mouth of the Yakima River (Ray 1936:119–151). About 16 kilometers downstream was kʷsís 'two rivers meet', an important trading center and fishing site at the junction of the Snake and Columbia rivers, where "annual trade fairs" attracted Sahaptian-speaking tribes "by the thousands" (Griswold 1970:25–26). Walula Walla Walla, Umatilla, and Yakima peoples resided there together.

Wanapam

On the west side of the Columbia was the principal Wanapam village of *pná* . Two miles farther upstream was *sháptilik*, present location of the Priest Rapids Dam, occupied in the 1990s by 8–10 Wanapam families and location of the Priest Rapids Longhouse since the 1950s. Ray (1936) listed three other villages in Wanapam territory.

Klikitat

Klikitat territory was also the scene of large gatherings. Ray (1936:148–150) located 17 villages, camps, and gathering places in their territory. The Klikitat were a scattered, roving tribe, and Gibbs (1855) located them as far west as Mount Saint Helens, among the Taitnapam. Spier and Sapir (1930:167) placed the Klikitat among Upper Chinookan groups along the Columbia from the White Salmon to The Dalles. Between 1835 and 1855, aided by mobility with the acquisition of horses, the Klikitat also ranged far to the south on trading and gambling expeditions, traveling down the Willamette Valley and along the Pacific coast to the Umqua and Rogue rivers. When ordered out of the Willamette Valley in 1854 by Joel Palmer, Oregon superintendent of Indian affairs, they returned to their lands in Washington Territory.

Taitnapam (Upper Cowlitz)

Taitnapam (*táytnapam*) villages and seasonal camps were located throughout the headwaters of the Lewis and Cowlitz rivers, west of the Cascade divide (Jacobs 1934–1937, 1:228–237; Jermann and Mason 1976:82–84). The most popular fishery was located at Cowlitz Falls, where "a great many people used to stay and obtain fish" (Jacobs 1934–1937, 1:230). Other seasonal camps supported mountain goat and deer hunting, root digging, and berry picking.

External Relations

In the first half of the nineteenth century, both The Dalles and Celilo Falls were important trading centers for coastal Salish peoples as well as interior Plateau tribes, and a great rendezvous where people, including the Yakima and Klikitat, came from "hundreds of miles round" for war dances, gambling games, and other social activities in summer (Ross [1849] in Thwaites 1904–1907, 7:130). Although goods were commonly exchanged, such as roots for dried salmon, or horses and hides for eulachon oil or dried clams, the medium of exchange was dentalium shell (Chinook Jargon *haiqua)*, also known as tusk-shell money, harvested from ocean beds off the west coast of Vancouver Island. Other popular trade items included furs, dressed skins, oil, pemmican, robes, clothing, baskets, canoes, feathers, furs, shells, beads, Hudson's Bay Company blankets, slaves, and horses (Teit 1928:121–122). When horses were introduced into the Plateau about 1730, they superseded shells as a standard of exchange.

Kittitas territory was the scene of larger summer gatherings and encampments, while Yakima villages and bands were more populous and hosted interband and intertribal meetings as well as winter social activities more frequently. The encampments in Klikitat territory as well as those along the middle Columbia were the center of major trading activities as well as horse racing, gaming, gambling, and other social activities.

Most relations with other bands and tribes were of a friendly, peaceful nature. The Salish-speaking Wenatchee shared the fishery in their territory with the Kittitas (Ray 1936:142). Intermarriage between them was so common that some Wenatchee adopted the Sahaptin dialect, and some moved to the Yakima Reservation in 1859. The Taitnapam intermarried with the Klikitat.

Information on hostilities, war, and raiding for the Yakima and related tribes is meager until the period of the Yakima wars that followed the treaty of 1855, probably because the Walla Walla, Umatilla, and Nez Perce served as a buffer zone between the Yakima and the traditional enemy of these Sahaptin-speaking groups, the Northern Shoshone to the south. There is some evidence of raids against the Northern Shoshone by an alliance of Yakima, Nez Perce, and Walla Walla in the late eighteenth and early nineteenth centuries (Cox 1831:259). Other hostilities appeared to have been directed against various Salish groups to the east. The Middle Columbia River Salishans carried on horse-stealing raids against the Yakima around 1780 (Teit 1928:123). A Yakima-Umatilla alliance was formed against the Spokane, Kalispel, and Coeur d'Alene, who were raiding for slaves and horses (Anastasio 1955:40). In 1847 there were hostilities between the Yakima and Cayuse (Splawn 1917:17). Alliances appeared to have been of a shifting nature and involved local bands rather than large tribal groups.

Environment

The people lived along the western border of the Great Columbia Plateau, from the glaciated summits and forested slopes of the Cascade Mountains on the west to the semiarid sagebrush deserts and basalt canyons along the Columbia River to the east (fig. 1). The floor of the plateau, formed by an ancient lava flow, sloped gently from 1,500 to 900 meters in elevation. Mount Adams, a dormant volcano and sacred mountain, dominated the ridgeline of the Cascades in this area at 3,801 meters. A series of long narrow ridges known as the Yakima Folds extended eastward from the mountains, intruding into the sagebrush plains.

Many natural features on the land held sacred or mythological significance, such as a distinctive high point on Toppenish Ridge near Signal Peak. The Cascades held many other sacred places, repositories of spiritual resources.

The major watercourse was the Yakima River with its tributaries. The Columbia River loosely defined the eastern and southern perimeter of the territory. The waters of all the rivers abounded in fish, especially salmon and steelhead; eel and shellfish were also important subsistence resources.

The climate ranged from temperatures of −5° F in winter to 100° F in summer. There was relatively low humidity and precipitation. Rainfall averaged from 6.71 to 8.24 inches per year (YIRRA 1962:C-1).

This part of the plateau was a semiarid valley of open windswept country, rolling prairie, and flat volcanic plains. Land supported a thin cover of sagebrush, juniper, greasewood, bunchgrass and cheatgrass. Willows, cottonwoods, and tall grasses grew in the vicinity of perennial streams and rivers. Small animals such as coyotes, jackrabbits, and various small rodents as well as sage hens, sharp-tailed grouse, and pheasant could be found on the plains. Rattlesnakes found a natural haven in the canyons, coulees, and rocky banks of the rivers. In spring, migratory birds nested in ponds and along streams.

While seemingly barren and unproductive because of low moisture, the soil was rich. Extensive areas of edible roots were once found throughout the region, a major source of subsistence for the people.

In contrast to the plateau, on the eastern slopes of the mountains were rich forests: stands of Garry oak, Douglas fir, and ponderosa pine at lower elevations; western hemlock, red cedar, western larch, white pine, fir and Englemann spruce farther up the slopes; and lodgepole pine and spruce at higher elevations. When the Yakima Reservation was defined, the western one-third contained these mountain slopes. In the 1980s and 1990s, the harvesting of timber provided a major source of income for the Yakima Nation.

The forest was also rich with other resources. At timberline, huckleberry bushes grew extensively in forest "burns" and in second-growth timber; and at lower elevations, nutritious roots such as bitterroot, camas, wild carrots, and

Indian potatoes were once plentiful. The forests abounded in wildlife, including mule deer, black- and white-tailed deer, elk, black bear, mountain sheep, and smaller animals such as beaver, whistling marmot, raccoon, muskrat, river otter, bobcat, martin, cougar, and snowshoe hare. While roots were no longer plentiful in the mountains by the 1960s, traditional Indian families still gathered huckleberries in late summer, and the hunting of wild game remained a popular pursuit.

Culture

This section draws on written accounts and records of nineteenth-century explorers, fur traders, missionaries, military personnel, and early settlers as well as ethnographic work from the late nineteenth century to the 1930s. The major portion is derived from the Yakima people in the 1960s to 1980s (Schuster 1965–1985, 1975).

Subsistence

Although each village or band held authority over a recognized territory, the right to use the hunting or gathering grounds within these territories was shared as part of reciprocal agreements with other autonomous villages or local bands. Access to fishing stations differed somewhat, as apparently the major fishing sites were owned by individuals or families and passed on by inheritance. However, families readily gave permission for use of their fishing sites, even providing gear and scaffolding on which to dry the fish if necessary.

• ANNUAL ROUND   The seasonal round of subsistence activities began when the snows melted in February or March. Before leaving the winter villages, the people gathered together for a "first foods feast" in the community longhouse, focused on "first celery" (*Lomatium grayi*), the stalk of the first of the numerous wild plants to be gathered.

The first salmon usually reached the interior Plateau in late February or March. Fishermen waited until the headman gave permission to fish. A salmon feast was held in mid-spring; and the people then left their villages to gather at their fishing stations on the Columbia, the Yakima River and its tributaries, or along the Klikitat, White Salmon, and Cowlitz rivers. As the fish runs diminished toward the end of April, families once again dispersed to popular root-digging grounds, where women prepared roots for storage while men went off to hunt for game. In June, families gathered at various fishing stations to intercept the second, and largest, run of salmon.

In July, as the summer heat reached the valley, families moved into the higher elevations of the mountains, where men hunted and women continued to gather wild plant foods. At the beginning of August, people convened at the large camas grounds in Kittitas country, and then dispersed

to meet again at the extensive root-digging grounds in Klikitat territory, where trout fishing, berry picking, trading, and horse racing also took place. During the middle of August, when the huckleberries became ripe in the high mountains, another first-foods feast was held before families moved up to the forest burns to gather berries and nuts.

In fall, people returned to the river valleys for the fish runs and to travel to the trading centers on the Columbia. Families visited friends and relatives in other villages, gathered up their cached food supplies, and men hunted for deer and elk in the mountains. About the middle of November, families returned to their winter villages along the various rivers and streams, bringing their supplies of roots, salmon, berries, venison, and other foods they had accumulated and preserved. Hunting and fishing continued in winter as needed.

• FISHING   Fishing, in particular for salmon (*núsux* 'anadromous fish'), provided one of the principal food resources. Several varieties of salmon (chinook, coho, sockeye, and chum) made annual spawning runs up the Columbia and its tributaries. In addition, steelhead trout, sturgeon, trout, sucker, and lamprey were caught. Salmon were caught by a variety of methods, including spears, two-pronged toggling harpoons, leisters, gaffs, seines, fish weirs and traps, gill nets, and dip nets from platforms. Weirs were fashioned from willow branches. Dip nets were made of reeds and grasses, such as Indian hemp. Fishing platforms were constructed by securing horizontal planks on a series of tripod supports jutting out into the water. Fishermen fastened themselves to the platforms with safety belts or ropes for protection from the swift rapids. Yakima in the 1970s–1990s relied on these methods at Sunnyside Diversion Dam on the Yakima River ("Fishing," fig. 17, this vol.) and at Parker Dam near Union Gap. Freshwater mussels were also gathered (Gibbs 1855:408).

While men fished in relays day and night, women cut up the fish, dried it on scaffolds in the sun and wind, and packed what was not eaten for storage. The dried salmon was first pounded in a tall oak mortar with a stone pestle until finely pulverized, then pressed down as hard as possible, in layers separated by rye grass to prevent spoilage, into a basket lined with dried salmon skin to eliminate air, covered with the skin of a fish and secured by a cord. Salmon preserved this way would keep for a long time without spoiling. Twelve baskets were wrapped together in mats, each bundle containing 90–100 pounds of dried, powdered fish, a delicacy and popular trade item. During the height of the fishing season, as many as 3,000 people might gather at the main fishing camps (Ross [1849] in Thwaites 1904–1907, 7:129; Ray 1936:142; Simpson 1931:94).

• HUNTING   Deer was the most important animal hunted as it provided clothing, shelter, and household utensils in addition to venison. Elk, bear, mountain sheep and mountain goats, wolves, and foxes were also hunted. The meat was eaten fresh or preserved for the winter by drying. Hides of deer and elk were fleshed, scraped, and tanned for use as

331

top left, Smithsonian, NAA: 96–10693; top right, U. of Mont., K. Ross Toole Arch., Missoula: 91–236; center left, Wash. State U. Lib., Histl. Photograph Coll., Pullman: 70–0429; bottom left, U.S. Forest Service, Rosslyn, Va.: 435968; bottom right, Yakama Nation Mus., Topppenish, Wash.: YIN–994–01.1 (neg. 3822–18).

Fig. 3. Food gathering and preparation. top left, Drying bitterroot. Photograph by Edward S. Curtis, 1909. top right, Elvina Stahi and children Leroy and Marthella gathering huckleberries in the Columbia Natl. Forest, Wash., using Klikitat-style baskets. Photograph by Kenneth Swan, 1933. center left, Grinding roots, probably for root loaf, using mortar and pestle. Photographer and date not recorderd. center right, Warner Jim putting the finishing knots in the rim strip on this berry basket made of folded cedar bark. Photograph by William T. Schlick, 1983. bottom left, Drying huckleberries by the reflected heat from a wood fire built in a trench. Photograph by Ray M. Filloon, Gifford Pinchot Natl. Forest, Wash., 1937. bottom right, Coil-constructed cedar-root berry basket. The decorations on this basket are different from those on typical Klikitat baskets, which are fully imbricated. These decorations combine an imbricated stepped zigzag design with beaded strips of undyed beargrass. The dark blue color of the dyed beargrass was obtained from huckleberries, a dye not used by traditional Klikitat basketmakers. Made by Nancy Yettona Washsise about 1900. Height 32 cm.

clothing, including moccasins, and to dress the dead for burial. Envelope-folded bags of rawhide, some painted with geometric designs, were used for storage and for packing. Squirrels provided fur hats and soft baby clothes. Bone and antler were used for tools or the handles of implements, such as root digging sticks, or large needles for sewing mats. The horns of mountain sheep and goats were used for making spoons, ladles, and other utensils. Deer hooves were dried to be made into ceremonial rattles.

In the distant past, buffalo could be found along the Columbia, and after acquisition of horses in the 1730s, the Yakima occasionally joined some of the eastern Plateau groups to hunt for buffalo on the Plains east of the Rocky Mountains. Buffalo hide robes were highly valued, as well as the meat. Meat from game animals was preserved by smoking and drying it over a smoldering fire for at least a day. Before guns were obtained in trade from Euro-Americans, the people hunted with bows and arrows. In contrast to fishing activities, hunting was an individual or small group venture.

Game birds included duck, quail, pheasant, sage hen, grouse chuckers, and geese. Because of the special power represented by eagles, they were hunted for their feathers, captured but never killed, and released after the desired feathers had been plucked.

• GATHERING   The quantity and variety of wild plant foods provided significant food resources: over 20 kinds of roots and 18 varieties of berries, as well as other fruits and nuts, and a nutritious and flavorful moss that hung from pine trees. A favorite root was bitterroot (*Lewisia rediviva*), which could be found in the hills in April, preserved by peeling and drying in the sun (fig. 3 top left), then boiled and mixed with fish. *panḱú (Tauschia hooveri)*, a round button-like root, was dug in early spring and eaten raw. There were also wild carrots (*Perideridia gairdneri*), which were boiled, pounded with a grinder, and dried into flat cakes or biscuits, to reboil in winter. Camas bulbs were dug in May and June, roasted in a covered pit for several days until turning black, then dug up, pounded and formed into cakes, which were baked and preserved for storage. There were Indian onions (Allium spp.), Indian potatoes (*Claytonia lanceolata*), and breadroot (*Lomatium canbyi*), all dug in Kittitas Valley in April or May and eaten raw or cooked. Wild plant products provided the people with medicines as well as foods.

Roots were dug with a hardwood stick about 30 inches long, curved and pointed, with a short crosswise handle of horn or antler. Root diggers in the 1990s were made of steel.

Most shoots or greens, such as "first celery," were eaten raw, as were fruits and berries. Berries abounded throughout the area: chokecherries, huckleberries, serviceberries, Indian cranberries, currant berries, blueberries, and others. A great favorite was huckleberries, the focus of the first berry feast held the end of summer. Huckleberries were picked at timberline in the mountains, where they were dried before a smoldering log so that they could be stored for the winter (fig. 3 bottom left).

In the 1990s, 15 different roots were dug in quantities sufficient for some daily use as well as for feasts and to give away or trade. It has been estimated that, in the past, one-half or more of the Plateau food supply was composed of roots and bulbs. At least one-third of the diet consisted of fish, in particular salmon; the remainder of foods came from hunting and from plant products (Anastasio 1955:18–19).

Technology

Most foods were stored in woven baskets, a specialized art form for which Plateau people were famous. Materials for making baskets were usually gathered in fall when families went up to the mountains to gather huckleberries. Cedar and spruce roots; elk and rye grass; strips of the bark of willow, cedar, alder ("Ethnobiology and Subsistence," fig. 6, this vol.), or bearberry; Indian hemp; and other plant fibers were used for making and decorating baskets, as well as rope, netting, twine, and cordage.

"Sally bags" for roots were soft, twined, round-bottomed cylindrical bags, often decorated with human or animal figures. Large, flat "cornhusk" bags for root storage were also twined and decorated with false embroidery of dyed fiber. In the late nineteenth century women began to decorate these bags with colored yarns. There were large, hard, coiled imbricated "Klikitat" baskets that could hold from two to five gallons of fruits and berries, made out of cedar roots, with rye grass from the mountains dyed various colors for imbricated designs. Watertight coiled baskets were used for cooking, woven with tapered bottoms for wedging in an upright position. Food could quickly be brought to a boil by dropping heated stones into water in a cooking vessel. Smaller coiled baskets of about one quart were used by girls for picking berries. The inventory of containers included a   *333*

334

Fig. 4. Structures. top left, Mat-covered lodge of Weaselskin, holding a coup stick and bow and arrows, Yakima Res., Wash. Photograph by Lucullus V. McWhorter, 1915. top right, Summer camp, Yakima Res., Wash. with canvas tepees and rectangular brush sun shades. Photograph by Heister Dean Guie, 1954. center and bottom, Gilbert and Flora Onepennee setting up a tepee. Photographs by John W. Thompson, 1955.

folded and sewn cedar-bark container in which huckleberries could be stored without spoiling (fig. 3 center right) (Gogol 1979, 1979a, 1980, 1985; Kuneki, Thomas, and Slokish 1982; Schlick 1979, 1980, 1994; Lobb 1978; Teit 1979).

Large mats, from three to six feet wide and up to 20 feet in length, were constructed of tule bulrush or cattail reeds, sewn together with Indian hemp. Mats were layered on the sides of lodges (fig. 4 top left) and used for household items such as wall linings, insulation, partitions, floor coverings, bedding, and plates and platters.

Settlement Pattern

Residential patterns shifted from a population concentrated in villages in winter to smaller, dispersed camps during the rest of the year; but even the seasonally occupied camps had an air of permanancy as people returned annually to the same rich root-digging meadows, huckleberry fields, or popular fishing areas.

Permanent villages were clustered in the river valleys, often within 10 miles of the nearest neighbor. The river valleys were preferred, not particularly for water transportation or for aquatic food, but primarily because they afforded protection against winter weather and provided good pasturage for horses. For almost a century before contact with Whites, the Yakima people had depended on the horse for traveling.

Structures

The average Yakima village probably held from 5 to 15 multi-family lodges, later called longhouses, built to accommodate related conjugal families. A few smaller conical-shaped lodges may have been occupied by nuclear families. There were also a few sweatlodges (fig. 5). Religious dances or other ceremonials were commonly held in the multifamily lodge of the headman or of the shaman. It was not until the late nineteenth century that a community ceremonial longhouse began to make its appearance.

Before the acquisition of horses, people wintered in semi-subterranean circular pit dwellings excavated three to four feet and roofed over with a dome-shaped or conical radiating frame of light poles covered with mats and grass, and banked on the outside with up to three feet of earth. Their size varied from 12 to 30 feet in diameter, depending upon the number of persons living in the lodge. A notched log ladder led up to the entranceway, which was also the smoke hole in the center of the roof.

The later rectangular lodge was built as an elongated A-frame structure of poles covered with several layers of stitched tule mats, with additional poles laid on top of the mats to hold them in place. The walls were banked with earth if further protection was needed from the wind and cold. This type of dwelling could be readily dismantled in spring and was well adapted to the mobility that the horse made possible. This multifamily dwelling was called *káatnam*, the same term used for community longhouses in 1992. A typical mat lodge was rectangular with rounded ends, 40–60 feet long, 12–15 feet wide, and around 10 feet high at the ridge, which was left open so that smoke could escape. Fires were built down the center of the longhouse, six to eight feet apart. Generally each family had its own fire. An entrance was usually found at each end, framed by pliable willow branches. A large section at the rear was reserved for racks on which fish were hung to dry (Kane 1859).

Fig. 5. Sweatlodges. left, Temporary lodge on the Columbia River. Photograph by Lucullus V. McWhorter, 1918. right, Permanent earth-covered lodge, Gifford Pinchot Natl. Forest, Wash. Photograph by Ray M. Filloon, 1937.

The popular summer shelter was a portable, mat-covered conical lodge, easily carried on pack horses and set up at fishing or gathering sites. On short hunting trips to the mountains, a mat lean-to or temporary shelter of brush was used. When people began hunting for bison on the Plains, the skin-covered tepee was adopted, followed by the canvas tepee. The Yakima used a three-pole foundation for their tepees (fig. 4).

Political Organization

The basic political unit for all groups was the village; and except for rare alliances in times of warfare, a multivillage band was the largest political grouping. Men held the position of headman because of their qualities of wisdom, personal character, and leadership. Being an orator with the ability to persuade others was also noted as a necessary quality. Headmen were expected to provide for those in need. The rare position of chief tended to be hereditary, but these men, too, had to possess the requisite admired qualities of leadership. Chiefs were generally associated with larger band or tribal organizations, such as came about in times of warfare, and principally dealt with relationships with other bands and tribes.

The headmen were assisted by an informal village council made up of respected men, and sometimes women, of the village. When requested to do so, they heard cases and tried to settle internal disputes; and they maintained informal control over village activities.

Leadership roles in special activities were given to men and women who were skilled specialists. There were important positions for the shaman or medicine doctor, the sweatbath leader, heads of hunting or fishing parties, a woman leader of ritual root digging before first food feasts, a longhouse ritual leader, or a war chief. There were also admired statuses that carried considerable prestige: master of ceremonies; one "rich in horses," especially race horses; or one who sponsors "giveaways" and feasts.

Among the most valued cultural ideals for behavior were cooperation and sharing, closely associated with expectations of reciprocity and responsibility for the welfare of others. These ideals were informally taught within the extended family, demonstrated in subsistence activities, and reinforced during community ceremonies.

Kinship

Descent was reckoned according to bilateral kinship. Within a multifamily lodge, a bilateral extended family was the basic residential unit, usually with close kinship ties to neighboring lodges.

Kinship terms distinguished different categories of relatives, depending on whether a relative came from mother's side or father's side, whether brothers or sisters were older or younger than ego, whether ego was a female or male, and

so forth. One knew who was an older relative and should be shown respect. Blood relatives were also distinguished from affinal relatives; one knew whom to tease and whom one treated more formally.

The relationship between grandparents and grandchildren was characterized by warmth and affection. Grandparents were the principal caretakers of grandchildren, while parents and younger adults left to participate in subsistence activities. It was also the grandparents who taught the children about values and correct behavior, who taught respect for this traditional way of life, and who imparted knowledge and understanding about the mythological past, the mythic heros, and the ancestors.

An unusual custom of kin term–sharing was found between grandparents and grandchildren. Each grandparent was called by a different name, depending upon whether they were father's parents or mother's parents, and they, in turn, called each grandchild by this distinctive name. Every grandchild, then, had four names, depending upon which grandparent was speaking to him; these were usually the first terms learned by a child. These were the four most commonly used terms in the 1990s in the Northwest Sahaptin dialect, popular even among Indians who did not speak the language.

Affinal ties between families were formally validated by a series of ritual "trades" or exchanges between individual in-laws, which began with a "wedding trade" and continued with the birth of children and with the death of either spouse. Even if the married couple divorced, the families of in-laws continued to maintain their ties with one another, keeping the social network intact. This system of ritual exchanges between families of in-laws has been maintained by traditional families.

Life Cycle

• BIRTH The birth of an infant took place in a small, conical-shaped mat lodge erected some distance behind the main lodge, assisted by several older women in the family. After five days of isolation, mother and child were brought back to the family lodge, where the infant was laced into its cradleboard, admired, and a special feast was held. The child slept in a cradleboard until two or three years of age; as one was outgrown, a larger one was made (fig. 6).

• CHILDHOOD Most learning was informal and imitative. Boys were taught to hunt, to fish, and to catch and break wild horses. Girls were given small berry baskets and encouraged to imitate their mothers and grandmothers in gathering activities. A special community feast was given to honor a boy when he shot his first deer or brought in his first significant catch of fish and when a girl gathered her first basket of roots or berries. "First products" ceremonies were accompanied by giveaways of gifts by the family to guests at the ceremony. Giveaways were also held the first time a child danced in public, or when a new dance outfit or an

336

inherited outfit was worn, or when the child received an ancestral name, linking the child to the deceased, who would serve as a model for the child. The guests received the gifts, not the person being honored. In return, the presence of the guests served to validate the accomplishment and bestow honor on the recognized individual.

Childhood was the principal time to obtain a supernatural guardian spirit, by means of a vision quest. A spiritual helper assured one of unusual skills and abilities. Some people possessed power to bring rain, to prophesy, to find missing objects, to assist in childbirth, to hunt or fish successfully, to win at gambling, to be a salmon chief, or to cure illness derived from supernatural causes.

Guardian-spirit power could be sought on a vision quest or it could be inherited, conferred on a person without being sought. In all cases, it was the spirit that gave the power; it could not be bought or obtained unless the spirit was willing. While an individual had no choice of the kind of power he or she might obtain, there was a tendency for the same kind of power to be found in the same family.

To seek guardian-spirit power, a child was instructed to go to some remote place, usually in the mountains and at night, a spot known to be frequented by spirits. The child was sent alone with a token to be left at the place of vigil as a sign that the child had been there. The child usually stayed just

overnight, but he might remain for several days. If a spirit came, it would talk to the child, give instructions on how to use the power it conveyed, what special taboos to observe, how to dress or paint one's face, and how to express the power in song and dance.

• PUBERTY Compared with childhood, puberty was relatively uneventful for boys and girls. When a young man began to do men's work at about 13, he was called *íwinš* 'a man'. At first menses, girls were isolated in a menstrual hut and placed under restrictions that prevented endangering themselves and others, after which a brief ceremony was held with a distribution of gifts. A girl then became known as *tmáy* 'a girl who is ready for marriage'.

It was at this time that a young woman usually began her ⟨Ai Ya To Mat⟩ 'counting the days ball' or 'time ball', which was like a diary (fig. 7). For each significant event in her life, a young woman tied a knot in a piece of hemp string, sometimes adding a shell or bead, gradually winding it into a ball. This hemp string ball became a record of her life from the time she first became *tmáy*, her first courtship, her marriage, the birth of her children, and so forth, until she died, when the counting ball was buried with her (Leechman 1921).

• MARRIAGE Marriages were usually arranged, but with the agreement of the young couple involved. The couple

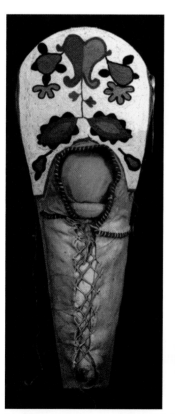  

left, High Desert Mus., Doris Swayze Bounds Coll., Bend, Oreg: 9.10.4; center, U.S. Forest Service, Rosslyn, Va.:435967; right, Smithsonian, Natl. Mus. of the Amer. Ind.:23/1167.

Fig. 6. Cradleboards. left, Yakima cradleboard. The headboard is contour-beaded with a floral design in yellow, lavender, green, and blue on a white background. The lower portion is canvas with tiny blue beads around the hood. Made by Mary Teneche-Shuh-Pum in the mid-late 19th century and used by 3 generations. center, Child in an undecorated cradleboard. Photograph by Ray M. Filloon, Gifford Pinchot Natl. Forest, Wash., 1937. right, Klikitat cradleboard with beaded buckskin. The designs depict human figures, horses, eagles, and fish. Brass bells hang from the hoop. Collected 1880–1900. Length of left, 90 cm; length of right, 78 cm.

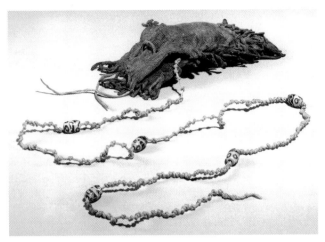

Fig. 7. Yakima woman's time ball. Important events and the passage of time are marked on this cord by the placement of knots and beads. Formerly owned by the Wesley family, a prominent Yakima group; manufactured in the mid-19th century. Total length 315 cm.

lived with either one of their families, usually the girl's. Some time later when it was apparent that the young couple were compatible and fruitful, with the birth of a child, a formal wedding trade (*pápšx̣wít*), also known as an "Indian custom wedding," was held. Wedding trades gave notice and publicly validated a marriage by means of a ritualized exchange of gifts and feasting between members of the two extended families ("Kinship, Family, and Gender Roles," fig. 1, this vol.). The wedding trade was initiated by the man's side, who traveled to the woman's side for an exchange of gifts and a feast. Sometime later, when families had had time to accumulate more gifts, a return exchange and feast was held.

The man's side gave gifts known as *šaptákay* goods, named for the parfleches in which most of the goods were carried. These included blankets, dress material, shawls, buckskin suits, saddles, tanned hides, and for a large, prestigious trade, horses and cattle. The woman's side gave *pšátani* goods, decorated cornhusk bags filled with dried roots (*x̣nít*) and berries, beaded bags, soft twined baskets, glass and bone or shell strings of beads, imbricated Klikitat baskets, beaded buckskin dresses, and so forth, all wrapped in tule mats. Before being given away, the goods were laid out on tule mats for display. A trading partner from one side exchanged goods with a partner from the other side until the ritual exchange had been completed. Then the host extended family served the guest families a feast, with salmon, roots, berries, and other traditional foods, after which the plates, cooking pots, and even the mats on which the food had been served were gathered up and taken home by the guests.

Since 1956, couples have obtained marriage licenses. However, the custom of wedding trades continued to be held by traditional Indian families.

• DEATH Death was a time, more than any other, when the entire kindred of related families came together for funeral rites, the most complex and lengthy of the longhouse community rituals. Traditionally the services lasted for five days and nights. Kinfolk and friends, accompanied by the sacred drums, circled the body as they sang and danced the deceased "along the way." The deceased, dressed in plain buckskins and wrapped in blankets and tule mats, was taken to one of the ancient burial grounds, where the body was interred with head toward the east. The funeral procession then returned to the longhouse for mourning rites. An heirloom costume and, later, pictures of the departed were displayed before being put away until a memorial ceremony was held. Possessions of the dead person, including household items, were distributed as keepsakes to close relatives and friends, and other gifts were given to mourners and to those who had brought food and had helped prepare and serve it. In the past, when families lived in tule mat lodges, it was also customary to burn down the lodge.

Three types of burials were customary in the Yakima area: rockslide burials in talus slopes; cremation circles; and burials in domes of volcanic ash. Some burial sites were marked by grave poles decorated with items such as eagle feathers, or strings of shell, and later glass, beads (Smith 1910; Ross [1849] in Thwaites 1904–1907, 7; Gibbs 1855).

Death brought not only grief but also danger. To remove the contamination of death, close members of the family bathed in the sweatlodge or washed in water in which the branch of a wild rose bush had been soaked. Mourners might also carry a small twig from a wild rose to ward off any danger from ghosts.

The death of a husband or wife was another occasion for ritual exchanges of goods between the affinal families. The childhood family of the dead spouse brought mourning clothing for the surviving spouse, his or her hair was cut short, and two kerchiefs were tied around the head, one to the back and one under the chin, to be worn as a symbol of widowhood during the mourning period, traditionally until the hair had grown back to its customary length. The family of the dead spouse also brought blankets, shawls, linens, and other household items to replace those given away. This was followed by a traditional exchange between the man's side and the woman's side, dinner served to the visitors, followed by prayers and a eulogy for the deceased. When the mourning period was over, another trade was initiated by the family of the dead spouse. In the past the in-laws provided a brother or sister (or fictive kin) as a replacement for the dead spouse.

After a funeral, it was customary to avoid speaking the name of the deceased until about a year later, when the name was revived at a memorial ceremony, usually held along with some other community celebration. A memorial parade was held and dinner was served by the deceased's family for all those attending. People who had inherited heirloom dance outfits and other accessories wore them for the first time as they solemnly danced before those in attendance. Gifts were distributed in honor of the dead by those who had inherited from the deceased. The family was then

Fig. 8. Hide preparation and decoration. left, Woman removing hair from a deer hide using a large scraper. Photograph by Ray M. Filloon, Columbia Natl. Forest, Wash., 1937. right, Klikitat deerskin moccasins beaded in a floral design in light and dark blue, red, white, and gold. Collected by Roxie S. Shackleford, Yakima Res., Wash., 1900. Length 23 cm.

"released from mourning" and once again could participate in ceremonial and other community events.

Division of Labor

A clear-cut division of labor existed for subsistence activities for adult men and women. Men hunted, fished, participated in offensive and defensive raiding, and prepared meats for special occasions, such as when a boy shot his first deer or when special visitors came to the lodge. Women gathered plant foods and preserved all types of foods, including fish and meat, for storage, took care of children, dressed skins (fig. 8), furs, and processed plant fibers for clothing, robes, lodges, mats and baskets for household use and for gift giving, carried wood and water, and cooked.

There was also close cooperation for many tasks. Men caught horses and broke them; women packed them for travel. Men tied the three-pole foundation for tepees; women set them up and took them down. Men erected the pole scaffolding for longhouses and set the layers of tule mat siding; women made all the matting used for the lodges and inside the household for bedding, floor coverings, partitions, and for wrapping baskets of food for storage.

Clothing and Adornment

In prehistoric times, sagebrush or shredded cedar and willow bark were woven into clothing materials. After contacts with Indians of the Plains increased, buckskin garments became popular, worn throughout the year (fig. 9). War bonnets of eagle feathers were also introduced. Men's clothing consisted of a breechclout and belt, long leggings, moccasins, a shirt (fringed and beaded for ceremonial occasions), a headband (sometimes decorated with an eagle tail feather) or fur cap (set with deer antlers or buffalo horns for a leader).

Robes were made of bear, goat, bison, elk, and large deerskins. Men's hair was traditionally worn long and loose. After extensive White contact, men with long hair began to braid it to each side, twisting strips of otter fur into the braids for special occasions. Wool blankets replaced animal skins.

Women's clothing consisted of a two-piece buckskin dress reaching to the calf or ankle, high one-piece soft moccasins, short leggings, a wide decorated belt, and a robe, blanket, or shawl. Dresses were sometimes decorated with painted dots across the yoke and near the bottom hem or embroidered with dyed porcupine quills, shells, or prized elk teeth or dentalia. Later, when trade beads were introduced, beaded decorations became popular. Women also wore long strings of beads made from bone, or dentalium shells (fig. 10), or cut and drilled "wampum shells." A distinctive conical basketry hat was woven and worn by women, twined of mountain rye grass and decorated with dyed designs. These were 8–10 inches high and tapered like a cone but truncated at the top. These became heirlooms and were worn only for ceremonial occasions, such as first food feasts.

In the twentieth century, traditional Indian women began to wear a cloth dress cut much the same way as the buckskin dress, known as a *ƛ́píip* 'wing dress' (fig. 10). A colorful scarf or bandana was tied over their hair, except at longhouse ceremonies when heads were left bare. Women's hair was worn long, with braids at each side. Women wrapped themselves in shawls and wore soft moccasins and cloth or decorated buckskin dresses for ritual occasions or for powwows.

Religion and Ceremonialism

Traditional Indian beliefs and practices generally fell into two distinctive spheres of religious activities: the older

top left, Lib. of Congress: Prints and Photographs Div.: LC–USZ62–92917; top right, U. of Wash., Thomas Burke Memorial Wash. State Mus., Seattle: 2–482 (slide 01.41222) and 2–374 (slide 01.03782); bottom left, Douglas Co. Mus., Roseburg, Oreg.: N7838; bottom center, Mus. of Hist. and Industry, Seattle: CO–063.

Fig. 9. Men's clothing. top left, Chief Frank Seelatse and Chief Jimmy Noah Saluskin wearing beaded buckskin leggings and multiple shell necklaces and holding a beaver fur strip, a feather fan, and a beaded bag. Their braided hair is wrapped in fur. They were delegates of their tribe in Washington, D.C., to address several issues, including relocating the agency to Ft. Simcoe, Wash., from Toppenish, Wash., and opposing the building of a tuberculosis sanitorium at Ft. Simcoe. Photographed in 1927. top right, Beaded vest and gauntlets. By 1900 the manufacture of traditional buckskin clothing was being replaced by the construction of garments made of European materials and fashioned after European styles. This vest is made of cotton trade cloth, trimmed in black velvet, and decorated in floral design beadwork. The floral beaded gauntlets are machine sewn leather trimmed with velvet. Collected by Levi J. Goodrich, Yakima Res., Wash., 1904. Length of vest, 59 cm; gauntlets to the same scale. bottom left, Klikitat man wearing a Plains-style hair roach, hairpipe breastplate, and dance bustle. Photograph by Benjamin A. Clifford, The Dalles, Oreg., © 1899. bottom center, Unidentified man holding a flute amd wearing a cloth shirt, a vest and hat decorated with metal studs, and a wool blanket. Photograph by E.J. Hamacher, about 1890s. bottom right, Win-wey-titt or Gerrod Goudy wearing Plains-influenced clothing and dance bustle, which he made for powwow dancing. Photograph by Ben Marra, Seattle, Wash., 1991.

guardian-spirit complex, which included the vision quest, the sweatlodge, and winter sings and curing; and Washat, the traditional Indian longhouse religion, which included first foods' feasts, funerals, and family and community celebrations.

• THE GUARDIAN-SPIRIT COMPLEX   The vision quest, as well as the sweatlodge, "medicine sings" or Winter Spirit

Dances were a part of this complex, as were the powers of a "medicine doctor" (shaman) to diagnose and cure supernaturally caused illnesses. Medicine doctoring and Winter Spirit Dances were traditionally held in an extended family lodge and, later, in family homes on the reservation.

One of the most powerful guardian spirits was *x^{w}yátš* 'sweatlodge', which protected one and restored one to spir-

340

Fig. 10. Women's clothing and accessories. top left, Wife and daughter of Shutamone. The young woman wears a buckskin dress with a heavily beaded yolk, a wide beaded belt, and a typical basketry hat. Her face has been covered with powder. The older woman wears a cloth wing dress, a wool blanket shawl, and a cloth head-scarf. Photograph by Thomas Rutter, © 1900. top center, Klikitat beaded bag with red wool backing depicting an elk, birds, and stylized floral designs, all popular patterns in Plateau beadwork. The background beadwork is full contoured, following the outlines of the design figures. This technique suggests that the bag was manufactured in the late 19th century. Collected in Wash. before 1925. Height 42 cm. top right, Yakima beaded hat fashioned after older twined basketry hats. On this hat, the star motif and fringe are innovative, but the 3-part V design and feather tassel are similar to decorations on basketry hats. Probably manufactured in the early 20th century. Height 17 cm. bottom, Klikitat dance dresses. Plateau dresses were typically constructed of 2 hides sewn up the sides and across the top with a folded yoke. Deer tails were often retained on this yoke as part of the ornamentation. bottom left, Buckskin dress beaded in striped design in black, white, green, and red pony beads. At the neck where a deer tail is frequently affixed is a small beaded design in red and yellow. bottom right, Deer-tail dress beaded in black and white pony beads. Large red and white glass beads and brass bells adorn the fringe below the beaded design. Dresses collected by Roxie S. Shackleford on the Yakima Res., Wash., 1900. Length of left without fringe, 124 cm; right to same scale.

itual and physical purity. It cured disease and imparted strength, skill, and good fortune to fishing, hunting, gambling, courting, and other activities. In the sweatlodge the bather was renewed and cleansed not only of body dirt but also of illness and contamination by death or other dangerous conditions. The most potent of medicine doctors received their powers from xʷyátš.

Both men and women used sweatlodges, a small dome-shaped structure made of arched willows, covered with mats and earth, built by a stream (fig. 5) for purification of body and spirit. Inside the ground was covered by green fir or cedar boughs. A fire was built outside, stones were heated and raked into a shallow pit just inside the entrance, and water was sprinkled on stones to furnish the steam. The bather chanted as he or she sweated, then rushed out to plunge into the cold stream, repeating the procedure several times.

Guardian-spirit visitations leading to spirit sickness most frequently took place during the winter season. A specialized doctor *(twáti)*, one skilled in knowledge of guardian-spirit power, was called in by a family. This type of Indian doctor was considered the most powerful of the medicine doctors. To aid the patient, the *twáti* helped the patient to bring out the power he or she had received. The patient was then ready to honor and express this power during a 'medicine sing' or winter spirit sing: this was referred to as *wánpša* 'he or she is singing spirit power songs' and lasted five nights.

Spirit power sings were held in private lodges from December to mid-March. A Winter Spirit Dance was sponsored by a medicine doctor or by families of persons who had been troubled with spirit sickness.

• CURING Because a medicine doctor had the potential to help or to cause harm, a great deal of ambivalence surrounded this role. The actions of a *twáti* were kept under some measure of control, as a medicine doctor who lost a patient and who was judged as careless or inept in his curing could be killed by the patient's family as a justified action (Alvord 1884). In addition to curing, some medicine doctors had powers to change the weather (Splawn 1917), to foresee the future, or to impart unusual powers to an inanimate object (Schuster 1965–1985). Traditional Indian medicine doctors were becoming rare in the 1980s.

In addition to spirit sickness, other kinds of supernatural agents or events could cause illness: contact with or breaking a taboo of a powerful sacred object; moral transgressions; soul or spirit power loss; and the practice of sorcery by means of evil thoughts or harmful spirit powers.

The usual insignia of office of a medicine doctor were a bear claw necklace, a coyote or wolf headdress, and a rattle made from the dewclaws of a deer. During a curing rite, the medicine doctor sat by the patient, singing his power songs in sets of five (the power number) and working up his power, accompanied by drummers beating on long planks. Sometimes the doctor cured by sucking out the offending disease; or giving the patient medicine to drink; or passing his hands over the patient, pressing and massaging to remove the source of illness and plunging it into water to make it harmless before throwing it away.

For some curing, Yakimas relied on their extensive knowledge of plants that could be used for home treatment of sores, infections, colds, bruises, boils, burns, and even toothaches. Women medicine doctors in particular were skilled in using medicinal plants and herbs for poultices, healing broths, emetics, and so forth. A small dried yellow flower of a cactus affectively treated toothaches; a poultice from spider webs stopped external bleeding; the steam from a branch of boiling sagebrush relieved nasal congestion; tea made from Indian rose bush or chokecherry peelings or dried sagebrush helped a bad cold; and the leaves of a certain red sumac bush were boiled and applied to stop hemorrhaging (Schuster 1965–1985).

Two curing cults existed: the Indian Shakers, a messianic curing religion, which was founded on Puget Sound in 1882 and introduced to the Yakima in 1890 (vol. 7:633–639), and the Feather cult, begun by a Klikitat, Jake Hunt, from the White Salmon area near the Columbia about 1904 (Du Bois 1938). The Indian Shaker religion, which combined Roman Catholic, fundamental Christian, and Indian doctor characteristics, maintained three churches on the Yakima Reservation ("Religious Movements," figs. 7–8, this vol.). Members with the "shake," or power to cure, performed curing rituals in private homes, accompanied by bell ringing and foot stomping. Members of the Feather cult also performed their curing rites in homes, concentrating mainly on curing people with drinking problems.

• WASHAT RELIGION Washat *(wáašat* 'dance') was popularly called the Seven Drum or Longhouse religion, the "Indian religion," the "longhair religion," or the "Sunday Dance" when referring to regular services, which were held in a community longhouse on Sundays. A member of the religion was called *wáašhani* 'dancer'. Washat prayers were sung accompanied by small drums ("Religious Movements," fig.1, this vol.) before public celebrations and before and after meals in the longhouse and in traditional private homes.

The Washat religion was probably derived from an older revivalist religious development known as the Prophet Dance, a millennarian movement with both Indian and Christian religious elements (Spier 1935; Schuster 1975). Although Washat has incorporated some Christian elements within its services, the majority of its features remained Indian. Of more significance, it was perceived as indigenous, not only by the Indians who followed it, but also by the Yakima Reservation population as a whole.

The oldest rituals within this religious system were probably first foods feasts (fig. 11; "Music and Dance," fig. 8, this vol.). Common longhouse religious activities included funeral rites, memorial ceremonies held before annual tribal celebrations, and the Sunday Dance. In the twentieth century, it became customary to celebrate rites of passage in a community longhouse, such as namings, first dancing, first products of young people, or departure for the armed services or return of a veteran. In the 1960s, a marriage rite (different from a wedding trade) became part of ceremonies held in the longhouse ("Religious Movements," fig. 2, this vol.).

History

The Yakima acquired horses in the 1730s, probably from Northern Shoshonean bands, through trading or raiding for them. The horses enabled increased mobility, expanded gatherings, and increased contacts with Plains tribes. Items of Plains material culture were adopted, and buffalo hunting on the Plains was undertaken.

342

U. of Wash., Thomas Burke Memorial Wash. State Mus., Seattle: top, 13594; bottom 13593.
Fig. 11. Root Feast activities at the ceremonial longhouse, Rock Creek, Wash. top, The large tent at the conclusion of the day's activities. Oscar Billy, chief of the feast, stands near the exit (center), where first the men then the women leave the tent, march completely around it and assemble in front awaiting the dismissal of the chief from that day's activities. As soon as the floor of the tent is cleared of the remains of the feast, dancing commences and continues until late hours. bottom, Women preparing the fish for the feast. Photographs by John W. Thompson, 1953–1955.

Epidemics of smallpox invaded the Plateau from both east and west in the 1770s and 1780s. Population estimates vary for the early period (table 1).

On October 17, 1805, Meriwether Lewis and William Clark reached the confluence of the Yakima and Columbia rivers, the first Whites to enter the area. They noted previous European influence in the presence of trade goods and evidence of smallpox (Thwaites 1904–1905). In 1811, the first traders traversed the Yakima area: David Thompson of the North West Company and Alexander Ross of the Pacific Fur Company. They described Wenatchee and Wanapam camps on the Columbia River (Glover 1962; Ross 1855). In 1814 Ross visited a Yakima camp in Kittitas Valley to buy horses. For a few years, Yakimas had sporadic contact with Whites. When the Hudson's Bay Company established Fort Vancouver in 1825, Yakimas began to trade there, particularly with horses. After 1833, Kittitas and Yakimas traded at

Fort Nisqually. From 1829 to 1832, epidemics of malaria spread through the area (Anastasio 1972).

Around 1840 the Yakima leader Kamiakin traded horses for cattle at Fort Vancouver, bringing the first cattle to the Yakima valley. Shortly thereafter, Kittitas chief Owhi traded for cattle at Fort Nisqually. Herds of livestock became established, as well as the cultivation of gardens.

In 1841 part of the United States Exploring Expedition under Charles Wilkes met with Kittitas chief Teias and Kamiakin near present-day Ellensburg (Wilkes 1845; G. Wilkes 1845). In 1847 Oblate Fathers Pascal Richard and Eugene Casimir Chirouse established Saint Rose, the first Christian mission in Yakima territory. They had been invited by Kamiakin, but the mission was abandoned the same year during the Cayuse War. The next year a mission was established in the Kittitas valley by Chirouse, G. Blanchet, and Charles-Marie Pandosy. In 1849 Oblate Fathers Pandosy and L. d'Herbomez founded Saint Joseph's Mission near Kamiakin's camp.

In 1853 the first White settlers arrived in Klikitat country, and wagon trains of others, headed for the coast, passed through. A traveler passed through Owhi's and Kamiakin's camps (Winthrop 1862:173–180). In 1854 Capt. George B. McClellan conducted a survey for building a wagon road through Yakima country over Naches Pass. George Gibbs, who accompanied the party, recommended to Gov. Isaac Stevens that there be no land cessions and no reservation, that Indians should retain their lands. Stevens rejected the recommendation (Gibbs 1855; McClellan 1853, 1855). Kamiakin called a council of Plateau tribes, meeting in the Grand Ronde valley of Oregon, to form a confederacy for mutual protection and to resist occupation of their lands. But on May 28, 1855, Governor Stevens convened the treaty council at Fort Walla Walla to negotiate for land cessions and removal to reservations. The tribes included Umatilla, Cayuse, Walla Walla, Nez Perce, Yakima, and related bands (Doty 1855, 1855–1856; Stevens 1855). On June 9, the Yakima treaty was signed, ceding almost 11 million acres (Gates 1840; Kappler 1904–1941, 2:698–702; Pace 1977). A new political entity was established, comprised of 14 independent "tribes and bands," speaking three languages, who had occupied this territory. It was known as the Confederated Tribes and Bands of the Yakima Nation. The reservation, also known as the Simcoe Reservation, consisted of 1,200,000 acres of the ceded lands (fig. 1). The treaty stipulated that no Whites, except employees of the government, could live on the reservation without permission of the Yakima, their agent, and the Indian superintendent. The government was to provide two schools, a hospital and doctor, a farmer, sawmill and flour mill, and craftsmen to teach the Indians their trades. The Indians received an annuity.

That summer, gold was discovered east of the Cascades in northeastern Washington. Prospectors crossed Yakima country to reach the gold fields. When hostilities erupted, some miners were killed by Indians. Indian Agent Andrew J. Bolon, investigating the murders, was himself killed

Table 1. Population, 1780–1992

Year	Population	Source
1780	3,000 Lower Yakima	Swanton 1952:451
pre–1805	7,000	Anastasio 1955:16
1805	3,500	Anastasio 1955:16
1806	1,200	Swanton 1952:451
1814	3,000 men	R. Stuart in Spaulding 1953:22
1835	3,000	Anastasio 1955:107
1845	2,500	Anastasio 1955:107
1847	1,500	Schoolcraft 1851–1857, 1:521
1851	1,000 Lower Yakimas	Gibbs 1855:418
1853	600 Lower Yakima	Gibbs 1855:418
	300 Klikitat	
1853	2,000	Anastasio 1955:107
1855	2,000–2,500	Indian Claims Commission 1974:645–647
1862	2,629	ARCIA 1862:504
	633 Klikitat	
	471 Wishram	
	808 Columbia River	
	667 Yakima	
	50 Waratka	
1865	3,000	ARCIA 1865:578
1871	4,000	de Smet 1905, 4:1302–1303
1874	3,500	Ewers 1955:22
1881	2,938	ARCIA 1881:174
1895	2,000	ARCIA 1895:624
1910	2,679	Curtis 1907–1930, 7:159
1923	2,939	Swanton 1952:451
1939	2,972	ARCIA 1939:2–3
1945	2,367	Bureau of Indian Affairs 1945
1955	4,316	*Yakima Nation Review,* Jan. 26, 1990:3
1962	5,110 enrolled	*Yakima Nation Review,* Jan. 26, 1990:3
1975	6,239 enrolled	*Yakima Nation Review,* Jan. 26, 1990:3
1980	6,646 enrolled	*Yakima Nation Review,* Oct. 31, 1980
1992	8,315 enrolled	*Yakima Nation Review,* Aug. 28, 1992

NOTE: Figures after 1946 include not only Yakima and Kittitas bands but also most Klikitat, Wanapam, and Taitnapam who are enrolled tribal members. In 1960, about 59% were full bloods. Over 50% of reservation enrollees had 3/4 or more Yakima blood.

(McWhorter 1937). In October 1855 Maj. Granville O. Haller was dispatched to Yakima country to Fort Dalles to avenge Bolon's death and suppress any uprising. Haller was attacked by an Indian force led by Kamiakin. Haller exonerated the Indians' action, pointing to illegal conduct by Governor Stevens and others in opening the interior Plateau before the treaty was ratified as the cause of the hostilities. Other Plateau tribes joined the Yakimas to drive the Whites from their country, and the Yakima Wars began (Haller l855–1856, 1855–1856a). U.S. Army troops pursued the Indians, and looted and burned Saint Joseph's Mission, claiming falsely that the Oblate fathers were providing the Indians with arms and ammunition (Bischoff 1949, 1950; W.C. Brown 1961). In spring 1856 Indians, including

Yakima and Klikitat, attacked an army post at the Cascades. The army crushed the Indian resistance and declared peace (Wright 1857, 1859; J. Ross Browne 1858).

Fort Simcoe was constructed in autumn 1856 to control the Yakima valley and to keep White settlers out (Guie 1956). However, when gold prospectors again traversed the Plateau, warfare broke out in 1858. Yakima and their allies (Coeur d'Alene, Spokane, Palouse, and Nez Perce) were finally defeated by Col. George Wright's forces at the Battle of Four Lakes. Owhi's son, Qualchan, was captured and hanged; Owhi was killed while trying to escape. Kamiakin escaped to Canada then returned to settle among relatives in Palouse country (Manring 1912; Peltier and Payette 1972; Wright 1859; Keyes 1884).

The Yakima treaty was ratified by the Senate in March 1859. Fort Simcoe was turned over to the Indian Department to serve as the Yakima Indian Agency and boarding school for Indian children on the reservation. Kamiakin refused to return as chief; Agent Richard Landsdale appointed a Klikitat, Spencer.

Starting in 1860, permanent White settlers arrived in the Yakima valley. The Rev. James H. Wilbur, a Methodist, who came to teach at Fort Simcoe in 1860, became Indian agent in 1865. His first school had 15 boys and 3 girls. In 1863 most Taitnapam moved to the Yakima Reservation, when their lands were appropriated by the U.S. government.

In 1867 Saint Joseph's Mission was rebuilt. White settlers became so numerous that a stagecoach road was opened through the reservation. In 1868 Joe Stwire (White Swan), a Klikitat, became the first elected head chief of the Yakima.

Under the Peace Policy, President Ulysses Grant in 1871 assigned the spiritual welfare of the Yakima Reservation to the Methodist church, to be guided by Reverend Wilbur. Wilbur tried to enforce haircutting, and he denied annuities to those who followed the Indian religion. Although Indian children were required to attend the agency boarding school, many traditional Indian families refused to comply. By 1876, Wilbur reported that the Yakima had 5,682 acres under cultivation, raising wheat, corn, oats, and vegetables. They owned 3,000 head of cattle and 16,000 horses (ARCIA 1876:549).

In 1885, to avoid Agent Robert H. Milroy's authority, Kotiahkan, a son of Shawaway, moved his longhouse just off the reservation below Union Gap, where he continued as the leader for the Washat religion. Another center of Washat was at Priest Rapids, where Smohalla, a Wanapam, led services (MacMurray 1887; ARCIA 1885:200–201; Relander 1956).

Education for Yakima children was available at Saint Joseph's Academy in North Yakima, founded in 1875 by the Jesuits, and at the Chemawa Training School for Youth, a boarding school opened north of Salem, Oregon, in 1885 by the federal government (vol. 7:173, 174).

In the 1880s White settlement on lands adjacent to the reservation, and the Northern Pacific Railroad, operating through the reservation, led to disputes over water and fishing rights (MacMurray 1884, 1887:241–242). Agent Milroy, an advocate of allotment, opposed the homesteading by some Klikitat and others near their original village locations, but around 100 homesteads had been taken up by Indians in Klickitat County by 1891. After the passage of the Dawes Severalty Act in 1887, the reservation community became split over acceptance of allotments. However, government agents undertook the allotment of reservation lands.

Some Indian rights were upheld by state government decisions. In the earliest Northwest Indian fishing rights case, *Taylor* v. *Yakima* Tribe in 1886, a settler's fence blocked access to a Yakima fishery. The judges ruled in favor of the Indians' treaty right to fish (ARCIA 1886:129–131; Cohen 1986). Moreover, the Washington constitution of 1889 declared that the state would have no authority over Indian tribes and lands.

In 1902 Young Chief Kotiahkan (son of Kotiahkan) led a delegation to Washington, D.C., to oppose the sale of unallotted reservation lands (fig. 12). He was successful, and the unallotted lands remained in trust as tribal property. Many of the allotted lands were sold to White settlers.

The reservation towns of Wapato, Toppenish, and Parker were founded, 1905–1911, on allotted lands that had been granted special patents so that they could be sold. By 1913, practically all the agriculturally productive land on the reservation was occupied by Whites, through leases or sale of allotments (McWhorter 1913). The presence of settlers made it difficult for Yakimas to reach their customary fishing stations, and litigation ensued. In 1905, in *United States* v. *Winans*, the Supreme Court upheld the Indians' right to their "accustomed" fisheries (ARCIA 1905:149–152; vol. 7:175). In 1913, two Yakima chiefs, George Meninock and Jim Wallahee, were parties in *United States* v. *State of Washington*, in which Yakima treaty fishing rights were again affirmed (ARCIA 1913).

By 1914, when allotment rolls were closed, 4,506 individuals had been allotted about 440,000 acres. About

Smithsonian, NAA: 2879-B.

Fig. 12. Delegation, left to right, Bill Owhie, Kittitas; Scannowa or Thomas; Young Chief Kotiahkan or Alex Shawaway; and Yumtobe Kamiakin, all 3 Lower Yakima. Photograph by De Lancey Gill, Washington, D.C., 1902.

780,000 acres remained tribally owned (Relander 1962). Families dispersed after allotment, and material culture changed, but social ties for ceremonies remained strong.

In 1922 the agency headquarters was moved near Toppenish, and the reservation school was closed. Yakima children began to attend public schools or off-reservation boarding schools.

In 1933 a Yakima tribal council of 14 elected headmen was established for the first time. Two members were elected from each of seven districts on the reservation. Members, who served for life, reached decision by consensus. In 1946, the council established a minimum of "one-fourth or more of the blood of one of the original 14 tribes or bands" to become a member of the Yakima Nation.

The Celilo Falls fisheries, one of the areas secured to Yakimas by treaty, was flooded by the Dalles Dam in 1956. The federal government paid over $15 million in compensation to the Yakima. This money was both disbursed to enrolled adults and held in trust for education. However, the loss of this fishery caused Yakima unemployment. Other dams such as Wanapum Dam (fig. 13) on the Columbia River also added to the loss of fishing resources.

In the 1960s Headstart and the Job Corps operated on the reservation, and a new health center opened.

The 1980s and 1990s

The Yakima Reservation extended to almost 1,400,000 acres in the 1990s. In the late 1970s, the grazing areas held about 12,000 head of cattle and 14,000 sheep. A total of 154,000 acres were under cultivation. Principal crops were sugar beets, hops, mint, apples, cherries, and wheat. Of the Indian-owned irrigated lands, 81 percent were leased by non-Indians for cultivation in the 1970s. Non-Indians also leased Indian lands for grazing and other purposes.

Yakima cultural and language studies were part of the regular school curricula. The state school system was contracted to run grade schools on the reservation (Yakima Indian Nation. Education Division 1978, 1979; Beavert and

U.S. Dept. of Interior, Bureau of Reclamation, Ephrata, Wash.

Fig. 13. Wanapams at the dedication of the Wanapum Dam, Wash. left to right, Rex Buck, Louie Dick, Sr., Harry Wyena, Frank Buck, and a boy, possibly Grant Wyena. Photograph by Ron York, 1966.

Rigsby 1975). A tribally run school for grades 7–12 was in Toppenish.

Camp Chaparral, a summer educational facility located on five acres of semiforested land in the foothills of Mount Adams, was maintained by the Yakima Nation. Yakima language and culture were taught, as well as classes in various grade school subjects to improve basic skills.

A private, accredited four-year liberal arts college, the Heritage College, was opened on the reservation in 1980. In the 1990s, about 30 percent of the enrollment was American Indians.

In the 1990s, Yakima Reservation Indians utilized many different medical services, depending on the nature of the illness. Some illnesses were recognized as White diseases, such as chickenpox, influenza, measles, and diabetes. For these diseases they went to the modern medical facilities at the reservation agency and to hospitals in the area. For alcoholism, they were encouraged to enroll in the tribe's alcohol treatment program. In addition to Western medicines, some Indians also relied on native medicines. For illnesses that didn't seem to respond to a regular doctor's treatment, traditional people sometimes attended an Indian Shaker curing rite, or a Feather cult rite, or called on an Indian doctor.

The tribal police force and tribal courts had their own code of laws and law enforcement programs. The tribal police patrolled the reservation, supervised encampments during celebrations, and enforced fish and game laws ("Reservations and Reserves," fig. 3, this vol.). The tribal courts heard cases involving civil and criminal offenses committed by Indians and some civil suits between Indians and non-Indians. In 1977, a federal court in San Francisco ruled that the Yakima Indian Nation, not the state, should have jurisdiction over criminal and many civil matters on non-Indian lands within the Yakima Reservation.

The *Yakima Nation Review*, a tribally sponsored newspaper, founded in May 1970, was published biweekly.

The Cultural Heritage Center of the Yakima Nation, opened in June 1980, includes a modern version of a traditional longhouse, towering 76 feet above the plains, used as a community hall (fig. 14 bottom). Another highlight of the Cultural Heritage Center is the Yakima Nation Museum. The Kamiakin Research Institute's historical photograph files of elders and leaders were housed at the museum, as well as videos and tape recordings.

The calendar of annual community events included powwows with dance contests, drum group competitions, Indian food booths, craft exhibitions, and Indian games; all-Indian rodeos; and arts and crafts fairs. Since 1955, the Yakima Nation has sponsored an annual All-Indian National Basketball Tournament in March. The Toppenish Creek Indian Encampment and Powwow, a 10-day encampment held each July near White Swan, was one of the largest intertribal gatherings, attracting as many as 3,000 Indian people from the Northwest, Canada, and the Plains. Celebrations were scheduled at Toppenish Creek and the

Toppenish community centers, as well as the Wapato Longhouse in February; the Speelyi-Mi Arts and Crafts Fair at the Cultural Heritage Center in March; the Satus Longhouse Powwow in April; the Weaseltail Powwow in May; Tinowit International Powwow at the Sun Dome in Yakima City in June, as well as the Treaty Days Celebration and the Indian Rodeo at White Swan; a Toppenish Powwow, Rodeo, and Pioneer Fair in July; an Indian encampment at the Labor Day Rodeo in Ellensburg; Indian Days Powwow in September; an Indian summer celebration at White Swan in October; National Indian Days, and Veterans' Day Powwow and Celebration in November, a Christmas Powwow at longhouses at Wapato and at Toppenish Creek in December; and a New Year's Celebration, Memorial and Veterans' Dinner at Toppenish Creek.

In the 1990s, there were four active longhouses on the Yakima Reservation: the Toppenish Creek Longhouse south of White Swan, the Wapato Longhouse just outside the town, the Satus Longhouse east of Highway 22 on Satus Creek, and a longhouse built in Toppenish in 1992. For the reservation as a whole and for closely related communities, the longhouse itself, more than any other tribal institution, represented Yakima Indian identity, the place where the Sahaptin language, foods, dress, customs, values, and beliefs were maintained and perpetuated. Washat prayers were a part of invocations at public events at all the tribal centers, intoned in Sahaptin.

Many different Christian denominations were represented in Yakima Reservation churches: Roman Catholic, Methodist, Presbyterian, Lutheran, Baptist, Union Gospel, and Disciples of Christ. Fundamentalist congregations included the Indian Full Gospel Assembly, Yakima Indian Christian Mission, Pentecostals, and Assembly of God. Three Indian Shaker churches were active in 1990 (Fitzpatrick 1968; Harmon 1971; Ruby and Brown 1996). Christianity was embraced simultaneously with Indian religious beliefs and practices. Christian faith was not perceived as a contradiction but rather an addition to the Indian religion.

The largest industry within the reservation was logging. Ninety percent of the tribe's annual income was derived from timber on the slopes of the Cascades, the largest stand of commercial timber on any Indian reservation in the United States. Other tribal income was derived from selling hunting and fishing permits to outsiders, or leasing tribally owned farming and grazing lands.

A 114-acre industrial park was established in the Wapato-Parker area for light manufacturing industries. One of the primary tenants in the 1990s was the Mount Adams Furniture Factory, which began operation in 1973 and was the largest tribally owned and operated business there. The factory produced furniture that was marketed throughout the country. Most workers were of Indian descent. Northwest Hardwoods, Inc., a private industry, manufactured wood components for furniture, moldings, and cabinets. The canning of fruits and vegetables grown in the Yakima Valley,

canning of salmon, processing of sugar beets, meat packing, and agricultural service industries were other privately owned industries at the industrial park. Hiring Indian workers was a priority. A tribal tobacco warehouse on the reservation served licensed Indian retailers. Profits were used for various social programs.

Fig. 14. Late 20th-century visual markers. top, Entrance sign to Yakima Res., Wash., showing a drawing of sacred Mt. Adams in the Cascades, and mention of the treaty of 1855 in which the Confederated Tribes and Bands of the Yakima Nation was formed. center, Flag folding at close of ceremony to honor Indian veterans on Veterans Day. left to right, Willard Hart (Yakima), unidentified Umatilla, James Selam (John Day River Indian), unidentified Umatilla, and Lewis Spino (Yakima). Photograph by Eugene Hunn, Toppenish Community longhouse, Wash., 1986. bottom, Cultural Heritage Center, near Toppenish, Wash., during events held to celebrate the anniversary of the signing of the Yakima Treaty, June 9, 1855. top and bottom, Photographs by Helen Schuster, 1988.

Employment on the reservation varied. Families worked in agriculture, livestock, logging, and construction. About 600 Yakimas were employed at the Yakima Agency.

Competition for jobs on or near the reservation increased in the 1960s when Hispanic migrant farm workers settled in towns in the Yakima Valley. The census of 1990 indicated that the Hispanic populations had grown to over 50 percent of two reservation towns, Wapato and Toppenish, and two off-reservation towns on the eastern border, Granger and Sunnyside.

On the reservation, low income and unemployment, which usually varied between 40 and 60 percent, remained a problem. In 1980, the median Yakima family income was $11,324, only 30 percent were unemployed, yet 39 percent lived at the poverty level. In 1988, due to a depressed lumber industry, unemployment was 61 percent, and only 21 percent of workers made over $7,000 (*Yakima Nation Review* 2/3/1989:1). In order to augment their low incomes, many people continued to rely on natural resources, by hunting for venison or elk, fishing for steelhead and salmon, digging for roots, and gathering berries.

In order to exercise the right to take fish from off-reservation fisheries, granted in the Yakima treaty of 1855, and to stop unlawful state regulation of treaty fishing, the Yakima, along with four Columbia River tribes and the federal government, brought suit in federal courts against the states of Washington and Oregon. In 1969, in *Sohappy v. Smith*, Judge Robert C. Belloni held that states were limited in their power to regulate Indian fisheries and might do so only when necessary for conservation. Indians were also entitled to a "fair and equitable" share. In 1974, Judge George Boldt mandated that a "fair and equitable" share was 50 percent of the harvestable fish swimming to "usual and accustomed" tribal fishing grounds and stations. After several appeals, the U.S. Supreme Court upheld the Boldt decision. The federal courts have also ruled that this was a tribal right, not an individual right, meaning that authority to regulate tribal fishing on and off reservations was reserved for tribes.

By 1975, 19 hydroelectric dams had been built on the Columbia and Snake rivers, severely impairing the natural salmon migrations. In 1977, to overcome continuing declining fish runs, the Yakima, Warm Springs, Umatilla, and Nez Perce tribes established the Columbia River Inter-Tribal Fish Commission (CRITFC) to coordinate common fishing concerns and provide a fisheries technical service. This consortium of Plateau Indian tribes has been influential in protecting treaty rights and tribal jurisdiction over off-reservation treaty fishing instead of the states. In addition, from 1979 to 1982, the tribes sued the Department of Commerce over its deficient ocean fishing regulations, which involved a large number of Columbia River fish. The consortium influenced Congress to legislate a conservation program to help restore upriver fish runs by promoting controls of ocean harvests of Columbia River salmon, and by placing water restrictions on hydroelectric power dams during spawning runs (CRITFC 1988; *Yakima Nation Review*, 11/17/1986:5).

A fisheries management and enhancement program, the Yakima-Klickitat Production Project, took a major role in the 1990s in rebuilding the fish runs of chinook, sockeye, and coho salmon and steelhead trout in the Yakima and Klickitat River basins. Where formerly from 500,000 to 900,000 salmon and steelhead used to return annually to the Yakima River, by 1990 only 10,000 fish returned. The project was a joint effort by the Yakima Nation and Washington State's Fish and Wildlife Departments, funded by the Bonneville Power Administration.

Synonymy

The etymology of the term Yakima is by no means clear. According to McWhorter (1937), the name Yakima was not a local term but was borrowed from the Spokane designation *yiʔáqmeʔ* (Carlson and Flett 1989:123), which he translated 'a growing family' or 'tribe expansion'. Ray (1936:123) employed a more direct translation, 'pregnant ones', which would be Sahaptin *iyakíma* (Bruce J. Rigsby, communication to editors 1996). Other translations have been made, such as 'black bear' (*yákama* 'black bears'; Bruce J. Rigsby, communication to editors 1996) or 'runaway' (Mooney 1896:737). Ross ([1849] in Thwaites 1904–1907, 7) first recorded the term in 1811 for the name of a river entering the Columbia from the west as the Eyakima. Ross (1855, 1:185) referred to Indians in the Kittitas Valley in 1814 as E'yack-im-ah, later simplified to Eyakema. Cox (1831, 2:14) recorded the name Yackamans in 1814 for Indians along a considerable stretch of the Columbia River north of its junction with the Snake and past the mouth of the Yakima River. Parker (1838:318) wrote of Yookoomans in 1835–1836, and Hale (1846:213, 569) referred to Iaákema, Jaakema and Yakemas. De Smet (1905) wrote about Yacomans. Lane recorded the names of Yacamaws, Yackaws, and Yacaaws (in Schoolcraft 1851–1857, 3:632, 1:521). In the same volume, Dart used Yackimas. Although Gibbs noted Yakima in 1854 (1855:407), and McClellan (1855:194) used Yakima for the river and the tribe, Stevens (1855:231) wrote about Yakamas, and the name was inscribed as Yakama in the treaty of 1855. Keyes (1884) recorded Yackimas. The Yakima tribal council adopted the spelling Yakama in 1994, but the *Handbook* has retained Yakima for the historic band.

In the journals of Lewis and Clark of 1805, Indians in the area were designated as Cutsáhnim (Lewis and Clark 1817, 2:475), Cuts-sâhnem (Thwaites 1904–1905, 3:128), Cuts-sâh-nim (Thwaites 1904–1905, 6:119), and Cut-sa-nim (ARCIA 1854:252). Based on the Sahaptin name of the Yakima River, Tapteal (also spelled Tapteel and Tapteil) or Tapteet, said to mean 'narrow' (Lewis and Clark in Thwaites 1904–1905, 3:123–125); the Indians were called Tap-teíl-min, or by a more common cognate Wap-taíl-mĭm, their own name for 'narrow river people' (Mooney 1896:737; Swanton 1952), referring to the narrows in the Yakima River at Union Gap. According to Ray (1936:145), Tap-teil-min has also been used to designate Indians living along the Yakima River from the mouth of Satus Creek to present Kiona, and probably refers to *táptat*, an important village once situated at Prosser, Washington. Lyman (1919) suggested that Tapteel or Tapteet was the original name and that 'Yakima' was of fairly recent origin, though in use when the first Whites arrived in the Yakima Valley. Mooney (1896:737) used the term Pa´´kiut-'lĕ'ma 'people of the gap', representing *pakyuutłáma.*

The Klikitat were *x̣ʷáłx̣ʷaypam,* sometimes interpreted as 'prairie people' (referring to Camass Prairie) but actually derived from *x̣ʷašx̣ʷay* 'Steller's jay' (Bruce J. Rigsby, communication to editors 1996). Keyes (1884) wrote Clicitat. The name is Chinookan, Lower Chinook *łáqatat* and Kiksht *iłgádatukš* (Michael Silverstein, communication to editors 1997).

In 1811, Thompson ([1916] in Glover 1962) referred to natives in the vicinity of the juncture of the Yakima and Columbia rivers as Skaemena, and also Shawpatins. In a footnote by T.C. Elliott (Glover 1962), the Indians are identified as the Sokulks, who entertained Lewis and Clark in 1805 at a large camp one mile below Pasco, Washington. Elliott first identified the Skaemena as Eyakema River Indians (in Thompson 1916), but later (in Glover 1962:376) identified the Sokulks as "really Nez Perces." In view of what is known about tribal territories, these people were more probably Palouse or Walula (Walla Walla), or a mixed gathering, including Yakima. The term Sokulk has also been used to refer to Wanapam Indians from the Priest Rapids area (Guie 1937). In 1824–1825, Simpson (1931:168–169) recorded the following names for peoples living along the banks of the Columbia in the vicinity of the Yakima River: Eya Kimu on the north side of Small River (unidentified); Naputsemacks, Ispipichimacks, and Scam-namnacks, all situated on the north side of the Eyakima River.

While camped among the Kittitas people in 1853, McClellan (1855:193) referred to Ketetas. In 1848, Pandosy recorded Ki-tatash in his baptismal records (Glauert and Kunz 1976:95). Various meanings have been assigned to Kittitas: "land of plenty, hard place or 'something hard, grey gravel bank, and clay gravel valley. . . . a bank of white chalk, for 'Kittit' meaning 'white chalk', and tash 'place of existance'. . . . Such a bank of chalk is found at the Menastash Ford on the Yakima River below Ellensburg" (Glauert and Kunz 1976:95). Instead of Kittitas, Tolmie (quoted by Lord 1866, 3:245) wrote of the Pishwanwapum 'river rock people' (for *pšwánwapam*) in the Yakimaw or Eyakema Valley; Lewis and Clark (1817, 2:595) mentioned the Shan-wap-poms; and Keane (1878:531) said they have also been referred to as Pshawanwappam.

Wanapam (*wánapam* 'river people') Indians were referred to by Thompson (1916) as people of the Shawpatin or Sararpatin nation (in Glover 1962). In 1811, Ross wrote of camping on the Columbia River at a place with strong, rocky rapids, which his fur party named Priest's Rapid after a "priest" who led ceremonies there. He called the Indians Ska-moy-num-acks (Ross [1849] in Thwaites 1904–1907, 7:143–144).

Discrepant and multiple names were probably a reflection of the shifting, ambiguous nature of local groupings along the Columbia River and its tributaries, as well as lack of familiarity with local dialects. Names may or may not have referred to indigenous Yakima bands.

Sources

An evaluation of almost 300 general and specific references on the Yakima Indians can be found in Schuster (1982). Schuster (1990) presents an overview of the ethnohistory and culture of the modern Yakima Nation through the 1980s. Daugherty (1973) summarizes the archeology, ethnography, history, and modern reservation life of the Yakima. Hunn (1990) is an invaluable resource of the ethnobiology and ecology of the middle Columbia River region, as well as a summary of the history, language, and ethnography of the people who lived along the river, most of whom are enrolled in the Yakima Nation. A detailed ecological, prehistoric, historic, and ethnographic overview of the Taitnapam and Klikitat is included in Jermann and Mason (1976). Uebelacker (1984) studied the environment of traditional Yakima lands and their significance for the Yakima people. Pace (1977) contains illustrations and the treaty of 1855. An annotated historical bibliography covers the Yakima and other eastern Sahaptian tribes (Trafzer 1992a).

Changes with the introduction of horses to the Plateau are discussed by Haines (1955), Roe (1955), Ewers (1955), and Guie (1937). Borrowing of Plains material items (Gunther 1950; Griswold 1970; Anastasio 1972) and trade goods from the East and Pacific coasts were documented (Thwaites 1904–1907, 3, 7).

Evidence of severe population losses by epidemics is found in Thwaites (1904–1907, 3), Du Bois (1938), Mooney (1928), C. Wilkes (1845), Gibbs (1855), Splawn (1917), and Robie (1858). Cook (1955) summarizes the information for epidemics in 1830–1833. Population declines due to epidemics before 1853 are discussed in Anastasio (1972).

The earliest firsthand accounts of contact between Whites and Indians in Yakima country are found in the Lewis and Clark journals (Thwaites 1904–1907, 3 and 4). Journals kept by employees of fur trading companies are important early records (Thompson 1916; Ross [1849] in Thwaites 1904–1907, 7; Gibbs 1855; Cox 1831; Franchère 1854; Simpson 1931; Work 1920; McLoughlin 1948; McDonald 1917). The artist Paul Kane (1859) accompanied Hudson's Bay Company parties in the 1840s.

Other early works with important evaluations of Indian-White relationships as well as descriptions of the area were written by Wyeth (1853, 1899), Townsend (1839), David and James Longmire (1917, 1932), George Wilkes (1845), and Charles Wilkes (1845). Hale (1846) recorded philology and mapped tribal boundaries. The introduction of cattle and gardens was noted by the McClellan exploratory party of 1853 (Gibbs 1855) and in early settler reports (Splawn 1917; Guie 1937). Meinig (1968) is an invaluable historical geography that evaluates some of the early factors for change.

Early missionary accounts are found in Parker (1838) and Glauert and Kunz (1976). For early Roman Catholic missions see Bischoff (1945), Nelson (1928), Winthrop (1862), and Garrand (l977).

McClellan's journal and reports (1853, 1855, 1855a; Overmeyer 1941) are in the Library of Congress. The reports of George Gibbs on Indian attitudes toward land cessions and reservations are important resources (Gibbs 1855), as well as his letter criticizing Governor Stevens (Gibbs 1857). Stevens (1855–1860, 1) includes Gustav Sohon's sketches of the treaty council of 1855. Records of the Washington Superintendency of Indian Affairs for 1854–1856, which contain Agent Bolon's report for 1854 are located in the National Archives (1854–1856). The text of the Yakima treaty is found in Kappler (1904–1941, 2:698–702), and land cessions are documented in Royce (1899). Kip's (1855) journal and Lansdale's diary ([1855] in Pambrum 1979) are sources on the treaty council (Garrand 1977; Richards 1979).

An invaluable firsthand account of events of the Yakima war years of 1855–1856 appears in the manuscripts of Haller (1855–1856, 1855–1856a). Bischoff (1950) is the principal investigation of the war. Background documents are collated by Furste (1857). Other resources include Wright (1857), J. Ross Browne (1858), and Cram (1859). Approaches representing the Indian position are found in W.C. Brown (1961), Splawn (1917), and McWhorter (1937). A good account of Fort Simcoe history is Guie (1956).

The principal resource on the hostilities of l858 is Wright (1859). Keyes (1884) covers the deaths of Qualchan and Owhi. The best overviews of the war of 1858 are Manring (1912) and Dryden (1968). Burns (1947) contributes a reassessment of some pioneer accounts.

The ARCIA reports, 1865–1883, are crucial for population estimates, and the development of farming and other reservation resources. Brunot's (1871) report also contains critical information.

Accounts of reservation life are presented by the Yakima Tribal Council (1955), Relander (1962), Masterson (1946), Desmond (1952), and MacMurray (1884). A fine evaluation of the Peace Policy has been written by Whitner (1959). The legal position of Indians during the unrest of 1878–1879 is reviewed by Ekland (1969). MacMurray (1884) provides some of the best analysis of events on the Yakima Reservation and among the Wanapam.

Problems of the allotment period and legal battles to retain tribal lands and prevent land sales to non-Indians are reviewed in McWhorter (1913, 1916), Relander (1962), E.E. White (1965), and Yakima Tribal Council (1955). Concerns over irrigation, water, and fishing rights are the topics of McWhorter (1913, 1916, 1920), and fishing rights are argued by Garrecht (1928). The findings of the Indian Claims Commission (1974) contain the records of Yakima land claims and land returns. The socioeconomic status of the modern Yakima reservation has been studied by Roy (1961) and Fitch (1974), and tribal investment programs are described in Pace (1977). Reservation alcohol use was studied by Krause (1969), and a study of children's drawings and "Indianness" was completed by Schuster (1978). Willard (1990) presents pictorial essays on powwows and life on the reservation.

Glauert and Kunz have reproduced a sampling of well-known articles, books, or journals relating to the history of the Yakima (1972) and Kittitas (1976). Helland (1975) has assembled vignettes that cover over 150 years of Yakima Valley history.

W.C. Brown (1961) and Splawn (1917) have written extensive accounts about Kamiakin. Relander (1956), MacMurray (1887), and Splawn (1917) have examined Smohalla. The Smohalla "cult" and its doctrine are detailed in Mooney (1896), Sharkey (1984), and Ruby and Brown (l989). Sheller's (1965) biography of Nathan Olney concerns the founder of the large Olney family on the reservation.

Specific ethnographic resources on the traditional culture of the Yakima and related peoples are not so readily available as historic ones. Curtis's (1907–1930, 7) photographs of the Yakima and Klikitat are excellent representations of early twentieth-century life. An early, well researched account of the traditional cultures of tribes of the Columbia valley is written by Lewis (1906). Kuykendall (1889) presents the ethnographic data he collected while serving as Yakima agency physician from 1872 to 1882. Some of this material is included in Lockley (1928). Maddock (1895) writes about the Klikitat near Celilo Falls. Daugherty (1973) contains sections on ethnographic materials along with other topics.

The legend of tribal unification in the 1700s is related by Splawn (1917). The network of alliances on the Plateau is described in Ray (1939) and Anastasio (1972), and Brunton (1968) joins relationships to ceremonial patterns. Aboriginal patterns of Plateau trade with the northern Plains are the focus of Griswold's (1970) study. Gibbs (1855) notes trading activities with the Pacific coast.

The Lewis and Clark journals (Thwaites 1904–1905, 3) contain an excellent, detailed description of salmon preparation for storage. Early reports on fishing activities (and some hunting) can be found in Ross (1849), Simpson (1931), Thompson (1916), C. Wilkes (1845), Kane (1859), Gibbs (1855), and Hale (1846). Some information on subsistence activities is also in Ray (1936, 1939), Curtis

(1907–1930, 7), Desmond (1952), Anastasio (1972), and Filloon (1952).

Study of the basketry of the Yakima, Klikitat, and Taitnapam is found in Haeberlin, Teit, and Roberts (1928) and Teit (1979:14–17). Gogol (1979, 1980, 1985) studies Klikitat textiles. Schlick (1980) covers flat twined cornhusk bags of the Yakima. Kuneki, Thomas, and Slockish (1982) have produced a classic on coiled Klikitat baskets. Schlick (1994) covers Columbia River basketry.

Accounts of ear piercing, naming, marriage, and canoe burials are found in Curtis (1907–1930, 7), of burial customs in Thompson (1916) and Splawn (1917), of sweathouses in Filloon (1952). Leechman (1921) and Harrington (1921) have both written about calendar strings.

Traditional Yakima religious beliefs and curing are presented by Splawn (1917), Helland (1975), and Alvord (1884). Washat religion ceremonies are described by MacMurray (1884, 1887), Spier (1935), Du Bois (1938), and Schuster (1975). The Feather religion is presented by Du Bois (1938) and Beach (l985). The Shaker church is discussed by Barnett (1957), Ruby (1966), Fitzpatrick (1968), Harmon (1971), and Ruby and Brown (1996).

George Gibbs (in Clark 1955–1956) assembled one of the earliest collections of mythology from the Yakima area, followed by Kuykendall (1889). Boas (1917) and Farrand (1917) edited a memoir of Sahaptin folktales. The first extensive group of myths and legends from the Klikitat, Taitnapam, and Kittitas regions was collected by Jacobs (1929, 1934–1937). Several modern versions of Klikitat folktales are found in Bunnell (1933) and Clark (1953). The Yakima Nation oral history project has produced an outstanding book of myths and legends (Beavert 1974).

Hale (1846) produced the first linguistic material on the Yakima. Pandosy (1862) published the first grammar and dictionary of the Yakima language; St. Onge (1872) produced an alphabet and a catechism of Roman Catholic prayers. Jacobs's grammar and lexicon (1931) and kinship terms (1932) are in the Klikitat and Taitnapam dialects. Aoki (1962) compared Nez Perce and Northern Sahaptin. Rigsby (1965a) produced a definitive study of linguistic relations in the Southern Plateau, as well as a study of Sahaptin vowel systems (1965).

Artistic traditions in carving are discussed in E. Strong (1959), Butler (1957), Seaman (1967), and Warren (1968). Pictographs and petroglyphs are featured by Strong and Schenk (1925), Cain (1950), Butler (1957), and Keyser (1992).

Valuable materials are located in the National Archives and Records Center, Seattle, which houses the Wilbur Collection, and the Federal Archives and Records Center, Washington, D.C. Important unpublished manuscripts are in the Bancroft Library, University of California, Berkeley; the Suzzallo Library, University of Washington, Seattle; the Holland Library, Washington State University, Pullman; Whitman College Reference Library, Walla Walla, Washington; the Hargreaves Library, Eastern Washington State University, Cheney; the Washington State Historical Society, Tacoma, and the Oregon Historical Society, Portland.

Larger museum collections for Yakima and Klikitat materials are found in the Yakama Indian Nation Museum, Toppenish, Washington, and the Burke Museum at the University of Washington, Seattle. Smaller collections are located in the Fort Simcoe Museum, White Swan, Washington; the Smithsonian Institution; and the Portland Art Museum, Oregon.

Palouse

RODERICK SPRAGUE

Language

The linguistic position of the Palouse (pə'lo͞os) was early defined, and the literature has changed that position little since. Hale (1846:542) recognized that the Sahaptian family (his Sahaptin) was divided into the Nez Perce language and the Sahaptin language (his Walawala) with Palouse as one of the dialects within Sahaptin (Gallatin 1848:14). Scouler (1848:237), Latham (1850:323), and Gibbs (1862:iii) all failed to make the same dialect distinction, putting Palouse on an equal basis with Nez Perce. Jacobs (1931:93) gave Walla Walla–Palouse (his walu'la-palu's) as one of the four divisions of Sahaptin (his Northern Sahaptin) and contrasted this larger group with Nez Perce as a second division of the unnamed northerly component of Plateau Penutian (his Sahaptin).

Rigsby (1965, 1965a:306; vol. 17:667; communication to editors 1996) classifies the dialects of Sahaptin into three clusters, putting the Palouse dialect (spoken historically at Palus Village) in the Northeast Sahaptin dialect cluster* together with the Lower Snake dialect of the *naxiyamłáma* band at Chamna and Wauyukma (*wawyukmá*) villages (spoken on the lower Yakima and on the Snake up to the mouth of the Palouse), Wanapam (spoken from Pasco to the head of Priest Rapids), and Walla Walla (*walúula*). Relying on linguistic and native testimony Rigsby separated the *naxiyamłáma* of Wauyukma village from the Palouse, as did Jacobs (1931:94). This conclusion is not supported by the ethnohistorical and ethnographic evidence, which indicates that the Palouse territory extended to the mouth of the Snake River (Lord 1866, 2:244; Mooney 1896:735).

Territory

At the time of contact the Palouse were found from near the confluence of the Snake and Clearwater rivers to the confluence of the Snake and Columbia rivers (figs. 1–2). The center of their range was at Palus with dominance through the Fishhook Bend or Page area to the mouth of the Snake River where they shared territory with the Wanapam. Upriver they were apparently dom-

---

* The phonemes of Sahaptin are given in the orthographic footnote in "Yakima and Neighboring Groups," this vol. The Palouse dialect differs from the others in having four additional vowels: (short vowels) *e, o*; (long vowels) *ee, oo.* These additional vowels correspond to the matching vowels of Nez Perce, in which Palouse speakers were bilingual (Rigsby and Silverstein 1969:48, 50).

inant at Almota and shared territory with the Nez Perce in the historic villages of Penawawa, Wawaiwai, and to a lesser extent Alpowa. They ranged over much of the Plateau for root digging and berry picking, joined forces for hunting bison in the Plains, and visited all of the important fishing centers, including The Dalles, Kettle Falls, and Spokane Falls.

From archeological evidence it is clear that there were other villages occupied at various times within Palouse territory (Ray 1960a:738). As with other groups in the Plateau, there was a major population loss due to Euro-American communicable diseases in the protohistoric and again several times after contact. Thus the four named villages are most likely the results of population loss and coalescence of the remaining population into a few villages.

The villages listed by Mooney (1896:735) are, in the Palouse dialect, *alamótun, pelúus, tásiwiks, and kʷsís* (Bruce J. Rigsby, communication to editors 1996) (Almota, Palus, Page, and Ainsworth). Mooney (1896:745) includes the Soyennom Band on the north side of the upper Clearwater River in Idaho as Palouse.

External Relations

The Palouse participated in both the Walla Walla and Yakima task groups for fishing, root gathering, and war dances.

Fig. 1. Palouse territory during the 19th century, with modern towns and drainage.

Fig. 2. Communal mat house near present-day Ainsworth, Wash. The extended family consisted of Palouses, Wanapams, and Yakimas. Photograph by Lee Moorhouse, 1898–1912.

These groups also included the Umatilla, Cayuse, Nez Perce, and sometimes the Spokane and Coeur d'Alene (Anastasio 1972:158). They joined the Nez Perce and others to hunt bison on the Plains (Anastasio 1972:164).

The southern warfare task group included the Nez Perce, Walla Walla, and Umatilla (Anastasio 1972:159).

In terms of material culture, the Palouse are closely related to the Nez Perce. In terms of language, they seem to be aligned more closely with the Walla Walla and other downriver groups.

Culture

Subsistence

The ethnohistorical record for the Palouse is rich in statements concerning their hunting, fishing, gathering (Stevens 1860:199), horticulture (Doty 1860:563), and stock raising, largely horses (Grover 1855:499). Meriwether Lewis and William Clark in 1803 noticed "a large fishing establishment, where there are the scaffolds and timbers of several houses piled up against each other, and the meadow adjoining contains a number of holes, which seem to have been used as places of deposit for fish for a great length of time" (Allen 1814, 2:5–6). They also reported the hunting of antelope, ducks, and geese (Thwaites 1904–1905, 3:109, 113).

In August 1811 Ross Cox (1832:85–86) visited a village of 40 "mat-covered tents" where the "inhabitants were busily employed in catching and drying salmon for their winter and spring stock." In 1838 the missionaries Elkanah Walker and Myron Eells bought salmon and potatoes from the Palouse (Drury 1976:69). The next year, when the Presbyterian missionary Henry H. Spalding was considering the mouth of the Palouse River as a mission site, he reported,

Fig. 3. Chief Slo-ce-ac-cum. He wears a Euro-American jacket, probably decorated with beadwork, and holds a flute. The artist noted that the chief "wore his hair divided in long masses, stuck together with grease" (Kane 1859:191). Watercolor and pencil sketch by Paul Kane, 1847.

"not favorable for a location. No land, no fish" (Drury 1958:257). This is a surprisingly early mention of no fish being available and may have represented a seasonal variation.

In 1846 Pierre Jean de Smet (1905, 2:561) encountered Palouses at a village of 12 lodges. The Indians traded fresh salmon to his party in return for powder and lead. "Small patches of land under cultivation" were reported at the mouth of the Palouse River the next year (Lowe 1847:1–2). In 1849 Newell (1959:150) noted the Palouse "have horses and cattle and subsist on Fish, Roots, and some small game." Five years later another observer noted, "They lived in comfortable mat houses, were rich in horses and raised corn, wheat and potatoes" (Grover 1855:499).

Between the mouth of the Tucannon and Alpowa were two Palouse villages. In 1860 these Indians planted crops on islands and irrigated from tributary creeks (P.M. Engle 1861:137–138). Twenty years later the Indians had allotted lands, and used "good teams, harness, wagons, plows and other agricultural implements" to "raise wheat, oats, barley, potatoes and other vegetables" (Hunter 1887:378).

In 1871 Indian Superintendent William C. McKay (1871) reported that the Palouse along with the Spokane and Nez

Perce went as far as Mount Adams to pick berries. In 1903 Palouse went to Moses Lake to gather couse as well as gamble and race horses with the Middle Columbia River Salishans and Umatilla (Anonymous 1903). They shared grounds for digging camas roots near Moscow, Idaho, with the Nez Perce and Coeur d'Alene (Spinden 1908:173; Anonymous 1937).

In 1896 the Palouse Indians at the mouth of the Palouse River had about 10 acres of land under cultivation. They were no longer catching sufficient salmon to support the group because of the use of fish wheels and nets on the Columbia River below the mouth of the Snake (ARCIA 1897:299).

Structures

Ray (1960a:739–740) lists three types of architecture occupied by the Palouse—the plank house, the mat lodge (fig. 2), and the semisubterranean pit house.

Although Ray (1960a:734–735) contends that the Palouse were the only people using plank houses east of The Dalles, based largely on the journals of Lewis and Clark, there is no other strong evidence of this trait among the Palouse. Some very late structures shown in photographs from after the construction of the railroad trestle about 1906 (Relander 1956:192; Sprague 1967:56) appear to be made of milled lumber (fig. 4) rather than split planks and thus probably represent adoptions from the Euro-American structures in the construction camp.

Another source of confusion might be the trait of the Palouse and other Plateau tribes of storing planks for fishing platforms, when not in use, on frames to keep them off the ground to prevent rotting, animal damage, or burning in grass fires. A classic example of this practice is seen in the illustration of the mouth of the Palouse River from the Stevens railroad report (Stanley 1862:151; Sprague 1967:22).

U. of Idaho, Arch. of Pacific Northwest Anthr., Moscow.
Fig. 4. Residence of Chief Bones, Lyons Ferry, Wash. A communal lodge, tepees, and sawed lumber house made up this last identified village of the Palouse. Photograph by R.A. Fife, 1914.

Religion

There is very little direct evidence of the religious practices of the Palouse. They were often separated from the Nez Perce in that Nez Perce were considered largely Christian and the Palouse of native religion. The village of Alpowa, the last village in Nez Perce territory to have any sizable Palouse population, was dominated by Timothy, an early Nez Perce convert to Christianity.

The Washat religion, a nativistic movement led by the prophet Smohalla, a Wanapam, had a very strong influence upon the Palouse.

The archeological record shows clearly that precontact burials were in a flexed position and orientation was to the west. After contact, especially with shovels replacing digging sticks, the position became universally extended. However, a dichotomy in orientation developed where Christian burials continued to be oriented west but then in imitation of the Judeo-Christian practice rather than due to precontact beliefs. On the other hand, native religion burial orientation reversed and became east. This reversal is attributed to the general Plateau nativistic practice of performing ceremonial actions such as walking or turning in an anti-Christian direction or manner. This dichotomy has been shown to have an extremely high reliability in the southern Plateau, if not the whole of the Plateau. Within the Palouse territory virtually all the historic period burials were extended and oriented easterly while the prehistoric ones were oriented westerly. This strongly suggests, along with historical data, that the Washat religion was the dominant practice among the Palouse during the historic period. The last resident of Palus Village, Sam Fisher (fig. 5), was known to have practiced this religion. If the modern Seven Drum religion is descended from the Washat of Smohalla, then the descendents of the Fishhook area are still practicing this religion on the Yakama Reservation.

At Palus Village Kip (1859:116) reported passing "the grave of some distinguished Indian chief. It was large, covered with stones, and surrounded with wooden palings. On a long stick, just within the paling, was a tin cup, and underneath was hanging the tail of a horse. It is a common custom among these Indians when a chief dies, to kill his favorite horse and bury him near him." Also at Palus Village, Leighton (1884:59) in 1866 saw: "graves of chiefs; the bodies carefully laid in east and west lines, and the opening of the lodge built over them was toward the sunrise. On a frame near the lodge were stretched the hides of their horses, sacrificed to accompany them to another world." It is important that in this unusual case the lodge was built over the burial.

Social Organization

The earliest pattern of social organization was to have several extended families living in one large mat lodge, which

U. of Idaho, Arch. of Pacific Northwest Anthr., Moscow.
Fig. 5. Sam Fisher and his first wife. Photograph of a tintype, 1870–1880.

was still observed at the mouth of the Snake River about 1900 (Sprague 1967:55). But Taggart (1905) described a series of smaller structures built close together with only one extended family per unit.

History

Lewis and Clark visited Palus Village in 1805. They presented a silver peace medal to Kepowhan, a band chief (ARCIA 1854:432; Sprague 1965:8, 52–55).

In 1811, David Thompson encountered a village of 50 men, who "danced til they were fairly tired and the Chiefs had bawled themselves hoarse. They forced a present of 8 horses on me, with a war garment" (Thompson 1914:121, 1916:527, 1917:261–262). One of Thompson's factors, John Clarke, was among the Palouse in 1812 when a silver goblet was stolen from him. As punishment for the theft, Clarke hanged the thief (Cox 1832:202–206; Ross 1849:210).

In 1853 Washington Territory was established with Isaac I. Stevens as governor. Stevens, in his dual capacity of governor and superintendent of Indian tribes, embarked upon a campaign of placing all Indians in the territory under treaties. The Palouse were listed as participants in the Yaki-

ma Treaty of 1855 with Kamiakin and Kohlotus as signers (Kappler 1904–1941, 2:698, 702).

Obtaining signatures on the treaty, especially that of Kamiakin, was less than voluntary and involved a great deal of pressure and questionable negotiations. For a detailed review of the contorted happenings of these few days, especially from the point of view of the Native American participants, see the works of Splawn (1917), Ray (1960a), and Brown (1961).

The Yakima War following the 1855 treaty did not involve the Palouse as much as some writers have indicated. But they did participate in resistance to settlers in 1858.

Apparently two Palouses murdered two miners going to the Colville area gold fields. In response, Col. Edward J. Steptoe left military Fort Walla Walla with 150 men. They crossed the Snake River then moved north into Spokane country where they were attacked by the combined forces of the Palouse, Spokane, Coeur d'Alene, and others. Badly outnumbered and strangely short of ammunition, Steptoe fought a retreat to a small prominence near the present city of Rosalia, Washington. With the coming of night, the troops were surrounded on the west by the Palouse, on the north by the Spokane, and on the east and south by the Coeur d'Alenes. With the help of Nez Perce guides and, according to some, through the treachery of the Coeur d'Alenes to the other bands, Steptoe and his men were able to beat a retreat to the Snake River at Alpowa and eventually back to Fort Walla Walla (Steptoe 1858; Kip 1859; Keyes 1884:266–282; Dunn 1886:284–309; Manring 1912).

As part of the continued military activity against these "northern tribes," Fort Taylor was established in August 1858 at the mouth of the Tucannon River, a few miles upriver and on the opposite bank of the Snake River from the mouth of the Palouse. In early September, Col. George Wright and his forces moved in retaliation against the northern tribes crossing the Snake River and moving north. In two days of battle in the area south of Spokane, Wright scattered the forces of the northern tribes, destroyed all the available horses, and burned stores and supplies. It is claimed by some that the majority of the 500 or more horses destroyed near Spokane belonged to the Palouse chief Tilcoax.

Wright then embarked upon a campaign through the Coeur d'Alene country and back down the Palouse River, hanging various individuals arbitrarily and without benefit of any trial. On 30 September Wright was back in Palus Village and from there returned to Fort Walla Walla (Kip 1859a; Wright 1859a; Keyes 1884:266–282; Dunn 1886:284–309; Manring 1912; Beall 1917; Burns 1947).

In 1859 Army Lt. John Mullan arrived at the mouth of the Palouse River to build a military road from Fort Walla Walla to Fort Benton (Anonymous 1859). He was using the mouth of the Palouse as a shipping point between Walla Walla and the Coeur d'Alene Mission (Mullan 1861:550) and established a ferry there. The number of troops using the ferry and steamboat landing and thus moving through Palus Village must have had a tremendous impact on the local population. In 1860 the Palouse were reported to be reduced in numbers from war, disease, and starvation; to be poor, having few horses and cattle; and to be reliant upon fish and gardens for subsistence (ARCIA 1860:208).

Beginning in 1884 there were several commissions sent out to determine the condition of the Palouse and to make recommendations on their future. In 1897 Indian Agent L.T. Erwin (ARCIA 1897) reported that he visited Palus Village and found 50–100 "who live in tepees at this place. There is not a house of any kind there and only about an acre and a half of land fenced and under cultivation." Later he mentioned another plot of 35–40 acres, of which 10 were cultivated.

The Northern Pacific Railroad track on the north side of the Snake River was laid through the Palus Village area shortly after 1900. The high trestle crossing the Snake River below Palus Village was started by the North Coast Railroad about the same time and was completed by the Union Pacif-

ic Railroad in 1912. A temporary city situated very near the site and occupied by the workers on this high bridge was less than a mile from Palus Village (Wegars and Sprague 1981).

From the turn of the century on there is very little recorded about the Palouse as a group. Most of the evidence is contained in descriptions of individuals rather than the band. Probably the best-known Palouse was Kamiakin, who traced his ancestry to a Spokane-Nez Perce or Spokane-Palouse named T'si-yi-ak (b. about 1778), who controlled territory on the Little Spokane River, the south end of Rock Lake, and near Sprague, Washington. This father of Kamiakin was powerful among both the Spokane and Palouse (Brown 1961:70–71). One of his wives, a Yakima named Kah Mash Ni (Relander 1955:17), had three sons, the second of whom was Kamiakin (q̇amáyaʔqin) (b. about 1800, d. 1877) (Splawn 1917:12; W.C. Brown 1961:398). Acknowledged as being a Yakima chief, Kamiakin exerted strong influence over certain sections of the Palouse band.

left, Wash. State U. Lib., Histl. Photograph Coll., Pullman:91–108; right, Smithsonian, NAA:79–4310.

Fig. 6. Kamiakin and son. left, Tintype identified as Chief Kamiakin or one of his sons. Chief Kamiakin died in 1878, so this could be the Chief Kamiakin who was the signer of the Treaty of 1855 (Kappler 1904–1941, 2:698–702). He wears a fringed shirt probably made of cloth; around his neck is a breast piece decorated with beads and fur tassels. His hair is decorated with upright feathers and strips of fur. He holds a large tomahawk and a quirt. Photographed about 1864. right, Tesh Palouse Kamiakin, son of Chief Kamiakin. He wears Plains-style clothing of the period: a beaded vest, wool blanket breechclout, beaded moccasins, looped necklaces, abalone shell earrings, and feather bonnet. Photograph by Andrew Jackson Splawn, © 1908.

It is interesting that Kamiakin, a signer of the Yakima Treaty of 1855 and one who spent most of his earlier life on what was to be the Yakima Reservation, did not return to the new reservation or even live at Palouse where several of his sons lived (fig. 6). After the Yakima War he left for his own safety, went to Canada for a brief period, and then lived out his life either on a small tributary of the Palouse River or in a camp at the lower end of Rock Lake near Sprague, Washington. Kamiakin could see what happened to other leaders following defeat by the U.S. Army and he was not about to let that happen to him. With his close followers and relatives, he was well provided for without the need for support from the Indian Service or the military. He did continue to have influence among other leaders and on events at the Yakima Agency.

The other Palouse signer of the Yakima Treaty of 1855 was Kohlotus (*qalató·s*, Kappler 1904–1941, 2:702), also spelled Quillatose (Stevens 1860:199) and Kahlatoose (Relander 1955:14).

Another important chief claiming Palouse ancestry was Tilcoax (*toqli·ks* 'fish trap'), a chief of the village at Fishhook Bend. He died on the Umatilla Reservation in 1914 (W.C. Brown 1961:309, 393). His son Tilcoax the Younger, or Peter Wolf, was also rich in horses and continued to live at Fishhook. Another reference to the Fishhook Bend area concerns Big Sunday, who is listed as a "chief" in 1911 (Anonymous 1911). In 1854 Slow-we-archy was second chief of Palus Village below Wattai-wattai-how-lis (ARCIA 1854:432) or Wi-to-my-hoy-she (H. Stevens 1900, 1:402).

An agreement (Wilkinson 1877:8) signed at Spokane Falls in 1877 by two Palouse individuals, O. Yellse and Tah-ne-na-tin, states, "We hereby agree as Chiefs and head men of the Palus tribe of Indians to go upon either the Coeur d'Alene or Spokane Reservation by 1st November 1877." Nothing more is known of this agreement of these men, but it does indicate that attempts were being made from several directions to force the Palouse onto reservations.

In the 1880s the chief of Palus Village was recorded as Big Thunder (Hunter 1887:36; Reimers 1947:60), reported to have died of "consumption" in 1886 (Hunter 1887:377). A Palouse known to the local population as Five-Sack, Fire-Star, or George Lucas is known from a popular and clearly embellished booklet about him (Reimers 1987).

The last permanent resident at Palus Village was known as Sam Fisher (Sam Fisherman or yosyóstuleké̇tsin 'something blue laid on') (Sprague 1967:59). Sam was the great-grandson of Husis-husis or Naked head, the grandson of a man by this same name, and the son of yosyóstuleké̇tsin, which was Sam's name. His first wife was apparently Palouse (fig. 5). Fisher and his second wife, Helen, a Nez Perce, lived at the mouth of the Palouse River from probably the late 1920s and definitely from 1936 until her death in 1945. She was buried in the cemetery at the mouth of the Palouse River while Sam was buried at Nespelem.

A onetime resident of Palus Village was Old Bones or Charlie Bones (d. 1916), who was the son of a Cayuse man by the name of O-quo-sky (Reimers 1947:61).

Sam Fisher contended that Charlie Bones was neither a chief nor a Palouse (McWhorter 1939). Bones, whose native name was Tee-wa-tee-na-set (tiwésinú·set), lived with a Cayuse wife named Me-a-tat (mi·yá·tat). Other members of the Bones family are interred in the Southside Cemetery on the Spokane Reservation. Pete Bones (coos-el-i-can) (d. 1952), apparently the grandson of Charlie Bones, was an occasional visitor to Palus Village after the death of Sam Fisher but did not live there. Additional Palouse names may be found in W.C. Brown (1961:389, 393).

Members of the Sohappy family, Palouse descendents on the Yakima Reservation, observed the excavation of the Palus Burial site, necessitated by the raising of the reservoir behind Lower Monumental Dam. The fight for the repatriation of the Palus burials removed prior to the flooding of Ice Harbor, Little Goose, and Lower Monumental dam reservoirs on the Snake River was led by Mary Jim, a direct descendant of Fishhook Jim of Fishhook Village, and her daughter Carrie, residents on the Yakima Reservation.

The inhabitants of Palus Village dwindled down to Sam Fisher, Helen Fisher, Charlie Bones, Susie Bones, Pete Bones, Moses Kentuck, and some part-time residents. Fishhook Bend was largely limited to the Jim family. With the death of Sam Fisher in the mid-1940s and the removal of the Jim family due to the flooding of the Ice Harbor Dam reservoir in the 1960s, the Palouse ceased to exist on the Snake River.

In the Indian Claims Commission hearings, the Palouse claim was originally part of the Yakima claim but due to a counterclaim from the Colville Reservation, the settlement eventually was split between the two modern reservations. This had the additional effect of the Colville claiming, by virtue of the Claims Commission findings, specific rights limited to the Yakima and Nez Perce. These claims have generally been rejected by the courts.

The number of Palouse moving to the Colville Reservation is considerably less than suggested by Ray (1971). In 1954 the tribal rolls of the Colville showed 30 people claiming Palouse ancestry. In 1966 the tribal rolls of the Yakima listed 250 claiming Palouse ancestry (Sprague 1991).

Descendants of the Palouse in the 1990s were scattered, residing on the Yakima, Nez Perce, Umatilla, Coeur d'Alene, Colville, Spokane, and Warm Springs reservations. They retained their Palouse heritage regardless of where they resided.

Population

Lewis and Clark in their list of bands and populations for the Chopunnish on the Snake River below the Clearwater listed 30 houses and 10 lodges with a population of 2,300 (Thwaites 1904–1905, 6:115), which included both Palouse

Fig. 7. 20th-century skin preparation and use. left, Sophie Williams or Wakwak (d. 1953) smoking deerhide, Toppenish, Wash., 1949. She used pieces of mountain wood and green willow on this skin; different wood would give the buckskin different color tones (Relander 1949). Yakima and Palouse, she was the granddaughter of Chief Kamiakin. right, Gift exchange with the Yakimas from Priest Rapids, Wash., in connection with Justin Pinkham's wedding, 1950. left to right, Ida Pinkham, Sophie Wakwak, Nancy Wakwak Goudy, and Alice Wynookie with parfleches. Photographs by Click Relander.

and lower Nez Perce. Samuel Parker (1837:349) estimated the Palouse in 1835 at 240. In 1847 Paul Kane (1859:191) said, "The tribe do not number more than seventy or eighty warriors." The next year Newell ([1848] 1959:150) gave the population as 200. Joseph Lane (in ARCIA 1850:159) gave the population as 300. In 1851 another report listed 60 men, 62 women, and 59 children for a total of 181 (ARCIA 1851:216). The report for 1854 set the number at 100 lodges and about 500 people in three villages: 40 lodges at the mouth of the Palouse, 12 lodges on the north bank 30 miles downstream, and 50 lodges at the mouth of the Snake River (ARCIA 1854:430–431). De Smet (1905, 3:991) stated in 1858 that "There are scarce 300 of them." In a report to the secretary of war for 1859–1860 (U.S. War Department 1860:139) the population of the Palouse as part of the Yakima nation was listed as 600.

The census of 1890 listed the Palouse as residing on the Yakima Reservation without any estimates of population (U.S. Bureau of the Census 1894:604). ARCIA (1897:299) listed only the group at the mouth of the Palouse River, who at this time numbered about 75. The 1910 census put the number at 82, 75 in Washington and 7 in Oregon (U.S. Bureau of Census 1915:95). After 1910 no accurate records are available, and information from local informants would indicate that there were only a very few families residing at the mouth of the Palouse River.

The varied population estimates listed are not as divergent as they might appear at first glance. The estimates are often for Palus Village plus one, two, or three of the other villages. A contact figure of 75 for Almota, 200 for Palus Village, 75 for Fishhook, and 150 (plus 150 Wanapam) for Ainsworth for a total of 500 would not seem unreasonable given the ethnohistorical evidence.

Synonymy

The spelling Palouse follows the generally accepted spelling for the river, the physiographic region, and the town, all in eastern Washington; and the creek in Coos County, Oregon. It has also been used in the historical and ethnolinguistic literature for the Palouse tribe or band. Palus has been the more widely used spelling in ethnographic writings, corresponding to that used for the village at the mouth of the Palouse River. The suggestion by the Bureau of American Ethnology that the preferred form be Paloos (Kappler 1904–1941, 1:1021) has not found widespread acceptance. For a full review of the derivation of the word Palouse and other names for the area, see Sprague (1968) and A.W. Thompson (1971). The village name comes directly from Sahaptin *palúus* (Palouse dialect *pelúus*, literally 'what is standing up in the water'). The people are *palúuspam*. The name appears to be a reference to a large rock in the center of the Snake River just upriver from the mouth of the Palouse River. In Nez Perce the village is called by the cognate name *ʔipelúˑtpe*, literally 'the place of something sticking out of the water' (Aoki 1994:408). Nez Perce also has the loanword *pelúˑc* 'Palouse River and area', and from this *pelúˑcpuˑ* 'Palouse people' (Aoki 1994:526). The standing rock is variously identified, but most often as Coyote's canoe (Sprague 1968:23).

358

The spelling of Palouse includes a multitude of variations: Pal-lace 1806 (Lewis and Clark in Thwaites 1904–1905, 8:map 40); Paw-luch 1813 (Ross 1855, 1:185); Palooche 1813 (Ross 1855, 2:6); Palooshis 1825 (Work 1914:92); Pelusbpa 1826 (Douglas 1959:200); Pelushes 1826 (Work 1915:31); Palouches 1835 (Gairdner 1841:252); Polonches 1835 (Gairdner 1841:252); Polanches 1836 (Gallatin 1848); Paloose 1837 (Parker 1840:284); Paluses 1838 (Drury 1958:92); Pelus 1842 (Hale 1846:143); Palooses 1845 (de Smet 1905, 2:455); Pelouses 1847 (Stanley 1862:67); Peloose 1848 (Scouler 1848:236); Pa-toas 1849 (Newell 1959:150); Palvas 1850 (Lane in ARCIA 1850:171); Ploluse 1851 (Phillips 1962:118); Pieuse 1854 (Grover 1855:499); Peluses 1855 (Stevens 1860:200); Palouse 1855 (Kappler 1904–1941, 2:698); Palouses 1856 (Craig in ARCIA 1856:191); Opelouses 1857 (Gilbert 1882:214); Palosse 1858 (Browne 1858:66); Palus 1858 (Hamilton 1900:41); Pälus 1896 (Mooney 1896:735); Páus 1900 (Culin 1901:156); Paloos (Pä-lus) 1910 (Farrand in Hodge 1907–1910, 2:195); and Palous 1928 (Teit 1928:98).

The use of Palloats by Todd (1933:192) for the Palouse is derived from the Palloats Pallah of Lewis and Clark and did not originally refer to the Palouse but rather to a village on the Clearwater (Sprague 1968). For a list of variant spellings of Pelloat Pallah see Sprague (1967:36).

Another exception not in this list is Ross (1849:210) who speaks of the people found at the mouth of the Palouse River in 1811 as Calatouches. Also a map by Ross (1821:map) lists Calatouches Indians on the opposite side of the Snake River from the mouth of the Palouse. This name should most likely be equated with the name of the village (Sprague 1967:30) found at the mouth of the Tucannon River, *toqá·latoyno* (Schwede 1966:39). A.W. Thompson (1971:72) suggests that it comes from the name of a chief located in the area (Sprague 1967:57).

Another synonym is *Pavillon* from the French for flag (perhaps meaning waterfall) used by Paul Kane (1856:418) in 1847 to refer to the Palouse River. The term *flag* was actually used on occasion to refer to the river. For a list of this and other variations in the spellings of Pavillon, or the English Pavilion for which 'flag' is one archaic meaning, see Sprague (1967:31).

The conception that Palouse comes from French *pelouse* 'lawn' or 'greensward' has been thoroughly discredited (Sprague 1968; A.W. Thompson 1971:1974). The name of the popular spotted horse breed Appaloosa is also derived from the band name.

Sources

The linguistic analysis of the position of the Palouse within the Sahaptian language family is best described by Rigsby (1965) who owes much to the earlier work of Jacobs (1931).

Mooney (1896) wrote the most detailed study of the Ghost Dance and the associated forms such as the Washat religion. The Palus Village, very likely Fishhook Village, and probably the other Palus villages were practitioners of Washat.

The most complete ethnographic work on the Palouse, by Ray, is found only in claims case (1960a) and other legal documents (1971). An ethnography was compiled by Chalfant (1974c). The first detailed summary of Palus Village and the first historical and ethnographic description of the Palouse band not oriented to a specific claims case position was that of Sprague (1967).

Historical works on the Palouse include those found in government correspondence and reports, such as those of Indian Agents L.T. Erwin (1897) and S.L. Taggart (1905).

Kip's (1859) good description of the Steptoe disaster and the Wright campaign as they affected the Palouse served as the basis for the work by Keyes (1884). Also of value is the work by Manring (1912). The official reports by the military leaders in each case are of value in understanding those opposing the Palouse (Steptoe 1858; Wright 1859a).

Splawn (1917) is the most complete work on Kamiakin. Another view is by Hunter (1887). W.C. Brown (1961) includes Kamiakin and other Palouse individuals and presents data on the Palouse in general.

Modern histories are highly variable. Relander (1956) is largely based on a study of the Wanapam and Smohalla but also includes an excellent summary of primary data. Trafzer and Scheuerman's (1986) popular work includes an extensive set of references, but this is offset by a lack of differentiation among fact, inference, and speculation or opinion combined with an uncritical use of secondary sources. It suffers from a decided anti-White bias yet also presents the Palouse in a negative light. Trafzer (1992a) is an annotated historical bibliography.

Sprague (1967, 1968) gives synonyms for the name Palouse. A.W. Thompson (1971) and Sprague (1967) give the origins of names for the Palouse River.

Wasco, Wishram, and Cascades

DAVID H. FRENCH AND KATHRINE S. FRENCH

The Wasco ('wäskō) and Wishram ('wĭshrəm) Indians are the Chinookan peoples who have spoken Upper Chinook dialects and have lived just east of the Cascade Mountains in Oregon and Washington. They wintered close to the Columbia River, as did White Salmon, Hood River, and Cascades (kăs'kādz) villagers, who lived where the river cuts through the mountains and somewhat to the west. All other Chinookans are described in *Northwest Coast* (vol. 7:533–546).

Wascos and Wishrams are typically enrolled on different reservations—Warm Springs and Yakima, respectively. The terms Wasco and Wishram denote social and geographic differences. The hyphenated form Wasco-Wishram refers to the dialect of Upper Chinook that they share.

Language

The Chinookan family of languages is customarily assigned to the Penutian phylum or stock (Sapir 1929; cf. Silverstein 1979). The family is divided into Lower Chinook and Upper Chinook; Upper Chinook is a chain of languages and dialects formerly scattered for nearly 200 miles east of (modern) Astoria on both sides of the Columbia River and in a nearby section of the lower Willamette and Clackamas rivers. (Chinook Jargon, often called "Chinook," is a pidgin, sometimes creolized; it should not be confused with Chinookan itself or any of its subdivisions.)

The Upper Chinook–speaking peoples described in this chapter refer to their language as Kiksht (kĭkšt).* (The term includes the extinct Clackamas dialect, covered in vol. 7; see also vol. 7:41 for a general discussion of Chinookan.)

There are negligible differences between Wasco and Wishram speech, and only a slightly greater difference between the Cascades dialect and the Wasco-Wishram dialect. The variations are principally in details of vocabulary and in the exact ways in which certain prefixes and suffixes are used. White Salmon and Hood River villages were intermediate in location between Wasco and Wishram sites to the east and the Cascades to the west. Evidently, White

Salmon–Hood River speech was also "intermediate," though close enough to Wasco-Wishram to be easily assimilated to it. The people themselves in time became identified as Wishrams or Wascos.

Multilingualism has long been characteristic of these peoples, largely because they functioned in the region as traders and as hosts to visitors. In the nineteenth century, Sahaptin, Nez Perce, Chinook Jargon, and English were widely known and spoken. A few Chinookans also knew Plains sign language. By 1993, Wasco-Wishram was the only remaining dialect of Chinookan; a few Wascos, Wishrams, and linguists could speak it, with varying degrees of competence. Wasco language courses were well established on the Warm Springs Reservation by 1993 in response to strong local interest.

Group Identities

None of the peoples in the entire region had a truly tribal form of political organization. The larger geographic and cultural (including linguistic) distinctions and identities were more like those that differentiate ethnic groups and subgroups. There is no simple, unequivocal term referring to the Wasco, Wishram, intermediate, and Cascades populations collectively and exclusively. Here, they will sometimes be called "easterly Chinookans."

After the treaties that established reservations were negotiated in 1855, the Wishram villagers, and perhaps a few Cascades, became legally associated—enrolled at— Yakima, to the north in Washington, but many of them continued to live in their traditional locations. Most of the others were assigned to the Warm Springs Reservation in central Oregon; a few Cascades, after the signing of the Dayton Treaty, went to the Grand Ronde Reservation. Like the Wishrams, many Cascades, some of the intermediate peoples, and some Wascos also lived part of the year near the river. There is ambiguity about the White Salmon Indians. Mooney implied (1896:741) that they were included in no treaty; evidently, they were defined later as parts of other, enrolled populations.

On and off the reservations—under the new conditions— broader ethnic groups emerged from the mingling (and differentiating) of populations and the subsequent social interactions. Among Kiksht speakers, Wascos became the most like an ethnic unit. Not surprisingly, reservation enroll-

*The phonemes of Wasco-Wishram and Cascades dialects of Kiksht are as follows: (voiceless stops and affricates) $p, t, \lambda, c, č, k, k^w, q, q^w, ʔ;$ (voiced stops and affricates) $b, d, g, g^w, ġ, ġ^w;$ (glottalized stops and affricates) $ṗ, ṭ, ƛ̓, ċ, č̓, k̓, k̓^w, q̇, q̇^w;$ (voiceless continuants) $ł, s, š, x, x^w, x̣, x̣^w, h;$ (voiced continuants) $l, m, n, w, y;$ (vowels) $a, i, u;$ stress (ˇ), also on syllabic resonants.

ment itself provided new points of reference and identity. A question about "tribal" membership could then evoke the answer, "I'm a Warm Springs [Reservation] Indian." Depending on the level of understanding of the listener, "I'm a Wasco," could be added, and—in the right context—"My grandparents were downriver Wascos from Hood River." Specifying the name of an ancestral village became much less likely. Wishrams living on the Yakima Reservation have been in an analogous situation. They became potential variants of "Yakima Indians." All of these considerations were made more complicated by the traditional, and continuing, high frequency of intermarriage between Indians of various ancestries, as well as the growing incidence of marriage with non-Indians. Consequently, it became truly difficult to specify the ancestral group identities of many persons. Linguistic distinctions had once served as major social-boundary-defining mechanisms, but these decreased in importance as the use of English grew. Hood River or White Salmon affinities were rarely mentioned by 1993, but the three identities reflected in the title of this chapter were still significant (cf. D.H. French 1961:373–374, 398–405, 416–424).

Environment

Markedly contrasting kinds of terrain, flora, and fauna were in this area (Franklin and Dyrness 1973; Daubenmire 1969; D.H. French 1961:337–338). Simplified, they were: the semiarid Plateau region, cut by rivers, east of the Cascade Mountains; the mountains themselves, with their foothills; and the Columbia Gorge. The Wascos and Wishrams lived at the western edge of the Plateau, a region that yielded enormous quantities of edible roots, fish, and other wild foods. The Cascades Indians had easy access to the resources of the Columbia Gorge, as well as to parts of the present Portland–Oregon City area; however, they could not so easily reach the best Plateau root-digging locales. The mountains provided berries—and some roots, nuts, game, basketry materials, and medicines—for all the groups.

The Chinookans tended to stay much closer to the Columbia River than did most of their Sahaptin neighbors. The river was a source of food (especially salmon), a means of defense against enemies, and—by canoe—an easy way to travel. These Kiksht speakers did not live continuously or randomly along the river. Most were concentrated at a series of rapids, falls, mouths of tributary streams, or restricted flow areas—mainly whitewater localities where salmon could not easily elude nets. These were: Celilo Falls and Tenmile Rapids, both used, but not occupied, by Chinookans; Fivemile Rapids or The Dalles, Threemile Rapids, not far above the present city of The Dalles; and the Cascades (fig. 1). The first three of these were obliterated in 1957 by the filling of The Dalles Dam reservoir; the last two had succumbed in 1938 to the Bonneville Dam.

Territory

Conceptions of space and boundaries differed from those of typical horticultural or agricultural peoples and were related to the fishing, gathering, and hunting economy of these Chinookans. Land was "owned" neither by groups nor by persons, with fishing sites being apparent exceptions; the right to fish at a locality (usufruct) was owned by families (cf. Spier and Sapir 1930:175). Stretches of territory were traversed by water or by trails; the land was a series of points (or small areas) linked by lines, such as the trails and the Columbia River. Strangers could pass through the territory (cf. Suphan 1974:35–37), though there came to be expectations that Whites, especially, would acknowledge the presence of the Chinookans and make suitable economic arrangements if goods or services such as portaging were involved (D.H. French 1961:349–355; B. Adams 1958:26–29, 36–73). Some kinds of terrain, such as the highest parts of the volcanoes (Mt. Hood and Mt. Adams) were rarely visited by anyone. Some areas, such as those used for hunting and gathering, were shared with Sahaptins (cf. Murdock 1965:203) and later with Whites. Few instances in which any Chinookans resisted the actual settlement of outsiders within their "territory" were reported. As for visiting the hinterlands away from the villages, during a given period of time there was simply a higher probability that one group rather than another (Chinookan or otherwise) would be in a given area. In short, the Euro-American model of tribal boundaries, circumscribing a territory that had various inviolate characteristics, did not fit the earlier thinking of these Indians. Later, when farming and logging became important to them, ideas about territory changed.

Easterly Chinookans thought about—and talked about—much of the land they utilized in terms of the Columbia River. Keeping this in mind, one could place northern and southern "tribal" boundaries at the headwaters (watersheds, really) of the streams that join the river. The mapping for this chapter, however, shows arbitrary, more restricted boundaries.

The southern shore of the Columbia River has a well-attested "boundary" between Wascos and Sahaptins near the head of Fivemile Rapids. On the northern shore, the demarcation was at Tenmile Rapids. Spier and Sapir (1930:164) list a place there called aɬaɬátia (or adaɬátia) ičaǵítxuq (or ičaǵítquq) 'underground oven of ogress' as if it were a village, but evidently it was significant only in mythology and as a fishing site.

Whether or not Salish speakers lived in the Wasco-Wishram area in past centuries has been debated. The case for a "tribe" named nkutɛméxu or Nɛkɛtɛméux having lived there was made by Teit (1928:89, 96–98, *et passim*). Ross ([1855] 1956:126) had used similar names for a local "tribe"; in Hodge (1907–1910, 2:50) the spelling is "Necootimeigh." Spier and Sapir (1930:160, 161–164), *361*

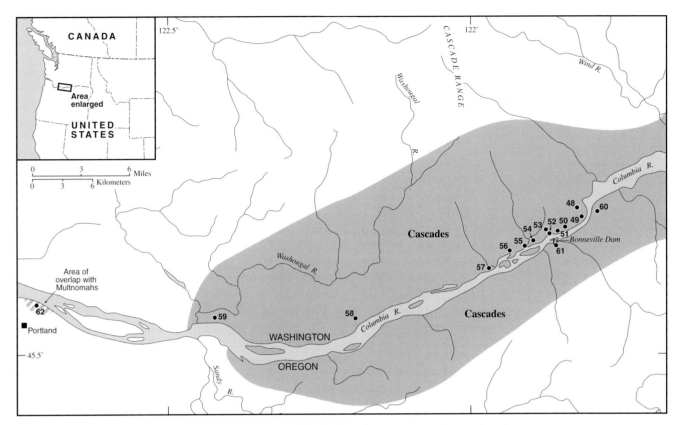

Fig. 1. Easterly Chinookan groups and villages in the 19th century. Not all village sites were occupied at any given time.

Wasco. 1, *ɫgaxáč'a* 'her grease'; 2, *iɡi ́sqis* 'bluejay(?)'; 3, *wasq̓ú* 'bowl (in stony place)'; 4, *nuƛáik*; 5, *waɡúpan* '(natural) rocky pavement'; 6, *wi q́atx*; 7, *wacáqʷs* 'one ("lone"), small pine'; 8, *wi ́nkwat* 'indentation in (river) bank'; 9, *wi ʔlukɫ* Mill Creek mouth, with Wascos living nearby; 10, *ɫilwáiɫxdix* (?) '(pines) heading toward river place' (approximate location); 11, *ɫiápqənun* or *ɫiápq̓nun* 'its foam(?)'; 12, *aɫaxačak wimaɫ* 'they are not finished, river'; 13, *gayaxsi ́tix* '(shaped like) small canoe' (approximate location); 14, *ɫi ʔlxʷdix* 'whirlpools' (probably a village); 15, *gaɫónλíčx* 'it is put on or lowered down'.

Wishram. 16, *ɡawidašɡánik*; 17, *wáyagwa* (*mankšaxlix* 'a little above'; 18, *wáq̓map* 'mound'; 19, *nixlúidix* 'coming-together place'; 20, *siq́ɫdapdix* 'torn out place'; 21, *šabánčkš* (later called Cyclone); 22, *isḱúksxat* 'lamprey mouth'; 23, *wasnániks*; 24, *wapánm*; 25, *niúxtaš* "Big Eddy (village)" [*nuxtaš* "Big Eddy (itself)"]; 26, *ɫiluslcɫix* 'the place where it (water) keeps running down (or in)'; 27, *ɡáwišila*, [referring to the village and to Three Mile Rapids]; 28, *čaláitglit* 'her willow grove'; 29, *kwálasinc*; 30, *kawaqánučq* 'badger (?) story'; 31, *ɡáwilapčk* 'great place for cast up objects (e.g., driftwood)'; 32, *nayaqáčix* 'place with teeth (sharp rocks)'; 33, *capxadidlit* (or *ča-*) 'her alder grove'; 34, *sq̓wánana* '(two) sitting on lap', Squally Bar or S. Hook (shared with Klikitats); 35, *škáɡč* (phonetically [*šɡágɪtš*]) 'nose(s)' (shared with Klikitats); 36, *ɫádaxat* (Wishram name for *ɫátaxat*, a Klikitat village with resident Chinookans); 37, *šɡwáliks*, Wishram name for a Klikitat village, evidently shared with Wishrams, who later applied the name to Lyle, Wash.; 38, *waɡínxaq* (or *ɡáwamuitk* 'mud place').

White Salmon. 39, *ɫgasɡúču* 'her (or their) bones' (shared with Klikitats); 40, *ɫmiyaqsáq* (many variants); 41, *it-ḱilak* or *iɫ-* 'pulverized dry salmon' (shared with Klikitats), later called White Salmon Landing; 42, *námnit* [possible Klikitat loanword] refers to the White Salmon River and to a Chinookan village at its mouth; *nánšuit* is evidently a synonym for the village site, which acquired the name Underwood; 43, *skaɫxɫmax* 'eating place' and *sq̓ɫdalpɫ* 'it keeps tearing out' (both names refer to the locale later called Cook).

Hood River. 44, *ɡawilamaixn* 'well-known for cottonwood, balm trees'; 45, *iɫgakáwa* 'her (the place's) badgers'; 46, *ninúɫdidix*; 47, *wi-*, or *wa-maɫn ɡáxitk* 'water's edge island' (later Wells I.).

Cascades. 48, no name recorded, possibly the actual site of 49; 49, *waɫála* 'small lake'; 50, *sḱmániak* 'obstructed' (*skmania* in Wishram speech), not at site of modern Skamania; 51, *qixayagílxam* 'middle village'; 52, *wimaɫɡikšat*; 53, winter village of site 52 people?; 54, *gayačáqɫq̓ʷtix* (?) (name based on 'manzanita' and 'place'?); 55, *kamigwáixat* 'upper road'; 56, *-ɫxawwálukɫ* 'they are running by her continually' (approximate location); 57, *nimišxáya* (west of Beacon Rock); 58, *waxix* 'daylight', or possibly 'face place' (cf. 60); 59, *wašúxwal* (or *wašúxal*); 60, *-wáyaxix* 'his face place' (Oreg. side) (cf. 58); 61, *swapapáni*; 62, Cascades village, name not recorded; Ne-er-che-ki-oo and nitciáptcEn have been given as the village name, though probably the first was based on *nitxɫayu* 'they went back home' (Michael Silverstein, personal communication 1974). Sources: Thwaites 1904–1905; Lee and Frost 1844; Mooney 1896; Sapir 1905; Hodge 1907–1910; Curtis 1907–1930, 8:180; Sapir 1909; Spier and Sapir 1930; Strong, Schenck, and Steward 1930; Dyk 1930–1933; Spier 1936; D.H. French and K.S. French 1950–1993; Hymes 1951–1990; Strong 1959; Silverstein 1966–1974.

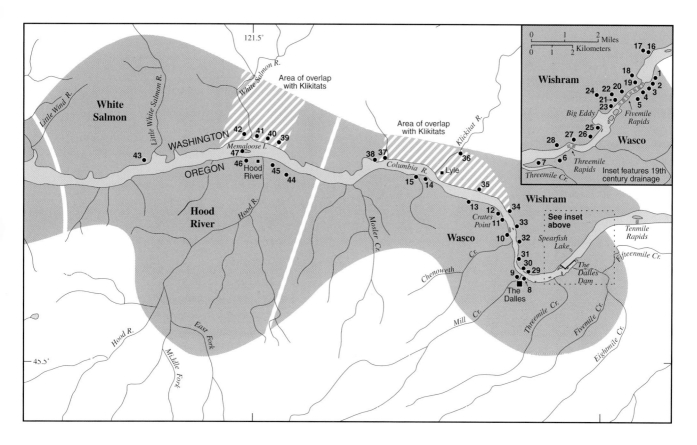

Spier (1936:20), and Berreman (1937:20, 41, 58) treated Teit's reconstruction seriously. Ray et al. (1938:384, 393–395, 400–402) were among those who were skeptical, while postulating other regional population shifts, for example, by Sahaptins. A cautious view is that there were indeed non-Chinookans in the area, but that seasonal visitors and intermarried outsiders were mistakenly seen as members of a Salish community or "tribe."

There was no single, firm boundary in the westerly area where the transition from the Cascades dialect to the Multnomah dialect occurred. Cascades village (fig. 1, no. 62), fully occupied while wapato tubers were being gathered, was to the west of the most easterly Multnomah village (vol. 7:534, fig. 1, no. 58).

External Relations

Before the reservation period, the Chinookans, especially the Wishram and Wasco, were heavily involved with Indian outsiders. Their situation was similar to that of the Sahaptin speakers at Celilo Falls and to the Salish speakers at Kettle Falls (Murdock 1965:202–203; Anastasio 1972:139). All were fishing and trading communities.

Lower Chinookans figured significantly in trade and marriage, as did the nearest Sahaptins: Klikitat, Tenino, Wayampam, and Tygh. Next in frequency of interactions were: Yakima, John Day, Umatilla, Nez Perce, and Cayuse. Among peoples with whom relations were intermittent were Klamath, Walla Walla, Middle Columbia River Salishans, Molala, and Kalapuyans (A.B. Lewis 1906:193; Spier and Sapir 1930:224–228; D.H. French 1961:343–349, 376–379). For the Cascades, the Klikitat (plus Upper Cowlitz people?) and to some extent the Yakima, were the important Sahaptins; Lower Chinookans and other westerly peoples were also known. In general, the Cascades did not experience as much visiting by distant people intending to trade as did the Wasco and Wishram.

Raiding by the Nez Perce or others occurred (D.H. French 1961:348; Anastasio 1972:145). Feuds between a group at the Cascades and some fellow Chinookans to the west have been reported. Klikitats were twice hired to aid in vengeance raids by those from the east (Curtis 1907–1930, 7:38). Northern Paiutes were feared because they sometimes attacked the Columbia River villages and later the Warm Springs Reservation settlements. They were traditional, but not inveterate, enemies: at times, they traded with Chinookans; later certain Paiutes settled on the Warm Springs Reservation.

Various peoples to the south of the Columbia were sources of slaves through capture: Northern Paiutes, perhaps rarely Klamaths and Modocs, western Oregon Indians, Shastas, and especially Achumawi and Atsugewi. The Wasco and Wishram more often obtained slaves in trade than by mounting or joining raiding parties (Spier and Sapir 1930:231; D.H. French 1961:363–364). In fact, except to visit each other by canoe, the Chinookans did not travel as widely as did others in the area, before or after the introduction of horses.

On the whole, there was an evenhanded quality to relations with outsiders (except with some of those to the south). Although the Chinookans were proud and could be arrogant, they were not xenophobic. They had special relationships with some individuals, for example, trading partners, but treated most visitors more or less alike.

Culture

Wishram culture has been moderately well described (Spier and Sapir 1930, Curtis 1907–1930, 8:85–154, 172–181, 185–191, 198–205). Wasco and new Wishram data, as well as historical records, have been evaluated (D.H. French 1961), and fieldwork (D.H. French and K.S. French 1950–1993) has provided additional information. These sources as well as the research of Dell H. Hymes, Robert E. Moore, and Michael Silverstein have informed this description of easterly Chinookan culture. The culture is described for the decades around 1850 except as otherwise indicated. Wishram data are almost entirely applicable to Wascos, and only slightly less so to downriver populations.

Subsistence

Most of the Chinookan techniques for acquiring food differed from those of neighboring peoples east of the Cascades only in the intensity or frequency of use. While in many parts of the Plateau there was a rough balance among gathering, hunting, and fishing, the Chinookans were fishermen first, gatherers second, and hunters least of all.

• FISHING   Several types of Pacific salmon, notably chinook salmon, were available in enormous quantities, and these were supplemented by steelhead (*Oncorhynchus mykiss*). Such fish ascended the Columbia in a series of "runs" from spring through fall. Other fish included sturgeon, suckers, trout, "chub," "whitefish," and "smelt" (or "eulachon"); lampreys ("eels") were also eaten. Sea lions, and especially seals, were available in the Columbia and were eaten by the Cascades people.

Fishing terminology and technology were elaborate; netting (figs. 2–3), spearing, harpooning, hooking, and trapping were part of the total array (Spier and Sapir 1930:174–179; Lord 1866, 1:64–70, 180–183; see Rostlund

1952 for interpretations). Cascades techniques, including food preparation, sometimes differed slightly from the others.

In due course, it became possible to sell fresh fish in quantities to Whites, and some Chinookans became commercial fishermen. Traditional fishing techniques were supplemented with new ones; preservation with salt was added to air-drying and (incidental) smoking. The building of dams on the Columbia markedly decreased the opportunities to obtain fish for subsistence, ceremonial dinners, and commerce.

• GATHERING   Because of the emphasis on hunting or fishing in anthropological writings, it is easy to overlook the importance of plants in the diets of peoples like the Chinookans. Wild root foods were so abundantly available in season that they can be thought of as if they were crops ready to be harvested (fig. 4). (For general perspectives on plant food in the region, see D.H. French 1965; for Wishrams and Wascos, see Spier and Sapir 1930:182–185; D.H. French 1961:356; cf. D.H. French 1957, 1957a; D.H. French and K.S. French 1989).

The "roots," that is, various tubers and bulbs, were the major source of starch and, in the case of onions, a source of sugar. The most important for the Wasco and Wishram were members of the genus *Lomatium*, couse and the parsley or carrot family (Hunn and French 1981). Some of these were fashioned into cakes of standard sizes (hence the nickname biscuitroot); often, they were simply cooked fresh or dried for future use. Other roots of importance were wild carrot (*Perideridia gairdneri*) and bitterroot (*Lewisia rediviva*), some members of the sunflower family, and, for the Cascades, wapato. Various amaryllids and lilies were also eaten, but camas was not of the importance that it was elsewhere in the region.

Fresh leaves and stalks from species of *Lomatium* provided greens. Teas were prepared from plants of the mint family; such beverages were not consumed regularly, and they were also seen as medicinal.

Hazelnuts grew in the westerly areas; they were thus available mainly to the Cascades and traded elsewhere. Acorns, pinenuts, and a few smaller seeds were prepared and eaten.

Berries, especially huckleberries and blueberries, were relished; they were eaten fresh and dried for winter food. Other fruits included gooseberries and currants, chokecherries, haws (*Crataegus* spp.), service or saskatoon berries (*Amelanchier*), strawberries near the Cascades, and blackberries and their kin. A black lichen (*Bryoria* syn. *Alectoria*) and a few fungi were also eaten.

Wild tobacco was smoked. Chinookans also planted and harvested another type of tobacco (Curtis 1907–1930; 8:173). Aspects of easterly Chinookan culture and organization resembled those of horticultural peoples in that the adequacy and dependability of the "harvest" of wild plant food and of fish was crucial in permitting village life, with its complexities and amenities. Village life, in turn, facilitated

Fig. 2. Fifteenmile Creek, east of The Dalles, Oreg. left, Fishing camp built as protection from the strong west winds that blow in the Columbia River gorge. Photograph by Arthur Seufert, about 1900. right, Fishing from platforms with long dip nets. Photographer and date not recorded.

tobacco growing and the early adoption of the same garden crops grown by the missionaries, such as corn and potatoes (D.H. French 1957).

• HUNTING Spier and Sapir's (1930) description of hunting does not make clear that it could take place when women as well as men were on trips away from the river.

Depending on the season, the women gathered roots (spring) or berries (summer and fall), while the men hunted deer, elk, mountain goats, mountain sheep, bear, or smaller game. Carnivores were hunted mainly for their skins. In general, animal products were among the items received in exchange for fish.

Fig. 3. Fish net technology. Twine held on a wooden shuttle was wrapped and knotted around flat rectangular gauges to produce nets with uniform mesh size. Different gauges were used to make different size meshes according to the type of fish to be caught. top left, Jasper Tufti, Wasco and Molala, making a fish net. The shuttle, which in this case is also used as a gauge, is in his right hand. Photograph by David and Kathrine French, Hehe Butte, Warm Springs Res., Oreg., 1952. a, Wishram elk antler net gauge decorated with 2 birds, perhaps eagles, one of which is holding a fish in its talons. Collected at Spearfish, Wash., across from The Dalles, Oreg., and probably manufactured in the late 19th century. b, Wishram bone net gauges. Collected by T.T. Waterman in Wash. opposite The Dalles, Oreg., before 1921. c, Wasco wooden shuttle. Collected at Celilo Falls, Oreg., before 1928. Height of a 12 cm; height of b left 5 cm; b right to same scale; length of c, 24 cm.

365

Technology and Art

Tools and other manufactured articles were appropriate not only for subsistence, shelter, and war, but also for commercial activities. Baskets and bags (fig. 4) had domestic uses, but some types customarily were packed with items for trade. Basketry was also an occasion for distinctive, nonutilitarian decoration (fig. 5).

In addition to baskets, bags, and mats, there were cooking utensils, bowls, pestles and mortars (fig. 6), spoons (fig. 7), ladles, cutting and piercing tools, weapons, skin dressing, blankets, parfleches, packstraps, hats, other clothing and ornamentation, and musical instruments, as well as canoes ("Columbia River Trade Network," fig. 5, this vol.), and housing (Spier and Sapir 1930:185–208).

Smithsonian, Dept. of Anthr.: a-c, 374093, 374094, and 374092 (neg. 95–20810); d, 9041 (neg. MNH–1773).

Fig. 4. Gathering. top left, Viola Kalama, Wasco, digging roots. a-c, Wishram root diggers. Sharpened iron rods with carved wooden handles replaced earlier root diggers made of antler or wood. a, Iron root digger sharpened on both ends. b, Iron digger with curved wooden handle. c, Iron root digger with carved antler handle. Collected by H.W. Kreiger in Spedis, Wash., 1934. d, Wasco-style twined round bag used primarily for carrying and holding roots but also for medicines, household goods, and other foods, such as nuts and dried salmon. The bag is made of hemp and decorated with stylized eyes and geometric designs twined in dyed grass. Collected by James F. Ghiselin at the Cascades of the Columbia R. before 1869. Length of a, 70 cm. Height of d, 22 cm. bottom right, Root Feast, Warm Springs Agency longhouse. left to right, Silas Williams, bell ringer; Prosanna Williams, Robinson Mitchell, Anthony Mitchell, and Rodney Mitchell (crouching), all Wasco. top left and bottom right photographs by Cynthia D. Stowell, Warm Springs Res., Oreg.: top left, 1978; bottom right, 1980.

Fig. 5. Baskets used in food preparation. Before metal pots and kettles were available, Plateau native peoples used coiled cedar-root baskets for cooking and storing food and water. They were particularly well suited for storing fragile household goods and foods, such as berries. left, Wishram coiled basket used for holding water. Photograph by Edward S. Curtis, 1909. center, Wishram coiled cedar-root basket with imbricated geometric design. Collected by H.W. Krieger, Spedis, Wash., 1934. right, Eva Winishut, Wasco, picking huckleberries and placing them into baskets tied around her waist. Huckleberries, which grow abundantly in the Cascade Mts. of Oreg. and Wash., were and still are an important food for Plateau native peoples. Photograph by David and Kathrine French, Kinzel Lake, Wolf Camp area, south of Mt. Hood, Oreg., 1951.

The decoration on twined baskets could be described as semi-realistic or conventionalized naturalistic; similar styles were used with stone and wood sculpture (Wingert 1952; E.M. Strong 1959; Feder 1971).

Petroglyphs and pictographs are especially common near The Dalles (Strong and Schenck 1925; Smith 1946); their aesthetic as well as supernatural functions should be considered. In the arts, a relationship with death has received particular notice (W.D. Strong 1945).

In the arts and technology one finds characteristics shared not only with Northwest Coast (vol. 7:606, 622, 627) and Plateau peoples, but also with the Plains and even the Great Basin. Among the distinctive skills was the use of fire planes, which is possibly unreported from elsewhere in the Americas as a whole. In addition to the usual fire drills, fire planes of two types were used at the Cascades and near The Dalles (Mohr and Sample 1983).

Red cedar (*Thuja*) was used for canoes, house boards, and smaller items. The wood or bark needed to be transported to the more easterly Chinookan areas but was of importance even there. Canoes varied in shape, size, and function; most were obtained from coastal Chinookans or indirectly from Salish speakers (Curtis 1907-1930, 8:173).

Fig. 6. Preparing plant food. left, Wasco woman pounding roots. Photographer and date not recorded. right, Wishram wooden bowl or mortar. This bowl was carved from a large hardwood tree root, oak or maple. The handles are carved with human figures and perforated for suspension. Collected by H.W. Krieger, Spedis, Wash., 1934. Height 22 cm.

Smithsonian, Dept. of Anthr.: top, 379264 (neg. 74–2767); middle, 374077; bottom, 374076 (neg. 31972–G).

Fig. 7. Wishram carved implements. top, Horn bowl. The peoples who lived on the Columbia River in the vicinity of The Dalles were particularly skilled at crafting bowls and ladles from the horns of mountain sheep and goats. The horn was steamed or boiled, shaped into the desired form, and then carved with geometric designs. These bowls were commonly used as trade items. Collected in Wash. from Hood River Indians about 1870. middle, Wishram carved wooden spoon with deep elliptical bowl and straight handle terminating in a representation of 2 interlocked figures, possibly a man and a dog. bottom, Wooden spoon with rounded bowl and curved handle with head of a birdlike animal. Collected by H.W. Krieger, Spedis, Wash., 1934. Height of top, 13 cm; length of middle, 6.3 cm; bottom to same scale.

Structures

Winter houses were semisubterranean, as among most Plateau Indians, but had walls of vertical planks, as among coastal peoples. Houses varied in size; those at the Cascades

were larger than those upriver. Strips or slabs of bark were also used, especially for roofs; log houses, reported from the Cascades, may actually have been made of bark or may have had an outer layer of bark slabs. Summer houses were above ground and covered with tule (*Scirpus*) mats (fig. 8). Fish were dried in the same or similar structures. Small, domed sweathouses were also built.

The Euro-American pattern of living on scattered homesteads was not fully adopted by many post-treaty Chinookans. For example, the Wasco farmers on the Warm Springs Reservation tended to live near each other or in the agency area; Yakima Reservation Wishrams clustered near White Swan, Washington. Also, the persistence of village life along the Columbia was another version of their continuing urban or semi-urban life.

Clothing and Adornment

Clothing was always largely of prepared skins, but it was scantier before strong Plains influence reached the area. Furs provided warmth in winter; dressed skins were summer wear. Porcupine quills were once used as buckskin decoration, replaced by beads and beadwork during the nineteenth century (fig. 9). Shell beads, obtained in trade, especially dentalia, were valued. Horn and bone ornaments on clothing were supplemented by conical metal ones.

Hair was worn long in two braids (some men cut the front hair and wore it as a pompadour or wore one braid down the back). Pendants were worn in the ears, and facial painting was practiced (fig. 10).

In due course, European-style dress became commonplace; exceptions in the twentieth century are buckskin garments, decorated primarily with beadwork, worn on special ceremonial occasions. Older women in the 1990s wore their hair long more often than older men; young people followed the fashions of their generation in the general western U.S. population.

Trade and Wealth

Dentalia and other shells were traded and accumulated, but there was no single kind of money. Wealth had diverse manifestations: tradable goods, slaves, and (later) horses being examples. The flow of goods and services influenced the social and economic positions of individuals and families.

Villages, or groups of people, were known for certain specialties: items they made customarily or trade goods they could supply. The importance of trade in earlier times can hardly be overstated. The Dalles was one of the most important trade centers in aboriginal America (Murdock 1965:202). Chinookans produced a surplus of fish, which they traded for other food products; in addition, other owned or manufactured items were traded. Many things were individually owned, people had a strong sense of the worth of goods either because of the labor invested or a price paid (Kelly 1955:44–46), and it seems clear that the manipula-

Fig. 8. Wishrams making rope probably from Indian hemp or horse hair. The woman sitting next to the mat summer house, a kind constructed at fishing sites on the Columbia River, is rolling the rope on her thigh; new strands were fed in at one end to create length; thin twisted strands were twisted together to make heavier cordage. The woman on the left is cutting the rope, while the men are brushing and rolling it. Photograph by Lee Moorhouse, probably near The Dalles, Oreg., 1898–1912.

tion of wealth was a process valued in its own right. Exchanges of goods took place as economic transactions between persons and families, as socially significant exchanges between in-laws, and in connection with multiple kinds of gambling (Thwaites 1904–1907, 7:129–131, where the host people are mistakenly called "Wyampam," local Sahaptins). Traditional trading partners, who in effect extended credit, facilitated the movement of goods over considerable distance.

Euro-American goods and trading provided a stimulus to activities at The Dalles even before any Europeans arrived in the area. Misunderstandings between Whites and Indians did arise regarding particular trades or in some payments for portaging (B. Adams 1958). Later, the Hudson's Bay Company helped to maintain orderly patterns of business.

Social and Political Organization

Villages, rather than the linguistic and ethnic categories discussed above, were the largest groupings with any significant political unity or structure. Both villages and households were corporate social units, controlling certain resources regardless of personnel. With the exception of aspects of the class system, there were no groups with well-defined boundaries constituting parts of easterly Chinookan "society" (D.H. French 1961:421). There were no clubs, societies, or other sodalities (cf. Spier and Sapir 1930:236). It has been made clear that there were no overt, maximal, political groupings easily identified as "tribes." This did not mean that collections of compatible individuals did not join in tasks, or that leaders lacked legitimate authority.

Armed conflicts between villages and groups of villages occurred in the Plateau. Although Chinookans fought offensively as well as defensively, and participated in raiding for slaves, peace was a significant norm (cf. Murdock 1965:203).

The upsurge in the number of Whites around the middle of the nineteenth century disturbed the previous relationships in the area. Chinookans did not fight against the Whites during the Yakima War, except for some individual Cascades (Williams 1980:108–115). Individuals, again, joined White soldiers in the 1850s and 1860s in campaigns against other Indians, especially in central and southeast Oregon (K. Clark and D. Clark 1978:129–130; Sapir 1909:204–227). Northern Paiutes were the targets in the

Fig. 9. Men's clothing. left, Oscar (Mark) or Little Vessel, Wasco. He is wearing a buckskin perforated shirt, leggings decorated with beadwork and a wide bandolier sash. His visor is decorated with shell and fur. He holds a pipe-tomahawk. Photograph by Charles M. Bell, about 1876. right, Martin Spedis, Wishram. A leader at Yakima in the 1930s and 1940s, he wears a blanket decorated with a fur strip, buttons, and feathers, all finery worn on important occasions. His fur hat is decorated with feathers and beads and is distinctively Chinookan. Photograph by Lee Moorhouse, 1898–1912.

1860s and Modocs in 1873 for the U.S. Army and Wasco and Sahaptin volunteers (Shane 1950).

Wascos joined the fighting against the Modocs out of proportion to their numbers on the reservation. Of 72 Warm Springs Scouts, 32 were Wascos (Murray 1959:200); Wascos at about this time numbered one-third of the reservation population (Huntington 1867:62). They were closer to the center of reservation life, living near the agency and accessible to the Indian agent, who did some of the recruiting.

• SOCIAL STRATIFICATION   Aside from language, the characteristic that most sharply distinguished the easterly Chinookans from their Sahaptin neighbors was the strength of the system of caste and class. The slaves, largely originating in California or southern and coastal Oregon, were obtained typically through trades. They and their children were a separate caste; they worked hard, were usually well treated, but (as property) could be killed, especially when a chief died (Spier and Sapir 1930:221–224). At the top of the hierarchy were chiefly families. Wealth, prestige, and (sometimes) political influence separated upper-class, nonchiefly fami-

lies from the lower-class people (D.H. French 1961:388–389).

• KINSHIP   There were no clans, lineages, or similar descent groups. "Kindreds"—extended bilateral groups of kin related to a bride and to a groom—functioned in particular situations: they exchanged goods in connection with a marriage and provided the basis for later exchanges and claims related to that marriage. The system of kin terms was bilateral in most respects. Terms for relatives distinguished clearly between affinal and consanguineal kin. There are 16 consanguineal word-stems. Certain stems were used reciprocally. Cross- and parallel cousins were called by sibling terms (a Hawaiian-type system). Various distinctions were made on the basis of age (in relation to siblings), sex (both of speaker and person spoken to), connecting relative (father, mother, son, daughter), and generation. There were fewer terms for relatives by marriage (only six, including "spouse"), which distinguished variously between speaker's generation and those above and below, sex of relative, and sex of speaker. Sapir (1913, 1916a) found Wishram data useful in discussing general problems of kinship.

left, Royal Ont. Mus., Toronto: 946.15.195; Stark Mus. of Art, Orange, Tex.: right: 31.78/55, WWC 55.

Fig. 10. Cascade men. left, Chief Tamakoun (d. 1848), who met members of the Wilkes Expedition in 1841, when his son was sketched (fig. 12). He was an early convert to Christian teaching, and his infant daughter and wives were baptized. right, Man wearing striped facial paint, sketched about 40 miles above Ft. Vancouver, B.C. Watercolor drawings by Paul Kane, left, 1846; right, 1847.

Life Cycle

• BIRTH Pregnancy placed some constraints on the behavior of expectant parents, particularly that of the mother. To ensure a normal baby and an easy delivery, a pregnant woman was warned to avoid any contact with death, not to stand in doorways, and to avoid fatty foods; a father was advised not to hunt, because he would have no luck, and it might harm (disfigure) the child. The birth of a child led to unusual weather; it might be very hot or very cold, or a rainbow might appear (a double rainbow was an indication that twins had been born). Birth was aided by a woman specialist. A new mother remained inactive for five days after giving birth; she was then given a different set of clothes and expected to resume her normal routines. At about the same time, a cradleboard was made (or refurbished) for the child by an old person, preferably of the same sex as the child. It was appropriate that the cradleboard maker have Dog or Coyote as spirit powers, as these beings were thought to be able to communicate with babies in a special language (Sample and Mohr 1980; Spier and Sapir 1930:255–256; D.H. French and K.S. French 1950–1993).

Infants were kept on cradleboards for a year or more (fig. 11). In the early nineteenth century and before, it was cus-

tomary to flatten the heads of individuals (male and female) by placing a stiff pad on the head just above the eyes and tying it tightly to the cradleboard. A few months of carefully calculated pressure thus applied resulted in a permanently flattened, backward-sloping forehead (fig. 12) (cf. Moulton 1983–, 5:350, 369, 373). As a result, Chinookans once had an appearance that distinguished them from slaves and from many of their visitors. The practice disappeared sometime during the 1840s (Robert T. Boyd, personal communication 1997).

• CHILDHOOD Children were first named at the age of six to eight months. The name of a deceased relative was chosen, and the name-giving ceremony was an occasion for a display of wealth in the form of a feast and the distribution of valuables to relatives and friends. Names were themselves valued keepsakes (Silverstein 1984:3–6); they were ranked on the basis of wealth, social position, and the reputation of former holders. A person frequently held a series of names; ideally, names were acquired in ascending order of rank and importance over a lifetime. Each assumption of a new name (and the passing on or discarding of the old) was accompanied by the largest possible distribution of food and property to those who were witnesses, and these events were among the most important experiences that an individual had. In addition, nicknaming was common; nicknames were given informally, they offered a means to avoid the constraints on casual use of formal names, and they provided opportunities to express affective relationships, both positive and negative.

The ears of boys and girls were pierced to hold ornaments when they were a few years old; the greater the number of holes, the greater the prestige. The accompanying ceremony was similar to that in which a name was given, but usually considerably less elaborate (Sapir 1909:177). Nasal septa were also pierced (Boyd 1996:98).

Distributions of food and property accompanied those many events that signaled changes in the relationship of a person to his family and his community. The elaborateness of these celebrations depended upon the nature of the event celebrated, the size of the participating extended family, and the class position and wealth of that family.

Children learned from adults, and from other children, by observation and by participation in the routines of life, and they were taught self-discipline, endurance, and strength of body and character. They were sent on excursions away from home involving tasks of increasing difficulty (Sapir 1909:187–191). When they reached the age of 10–12, they were instructed and encouraged in the acquisition of spirit power; trips into the mountains or elsewhere became opportunities for such experiences. Meanwhile, their more domestic accomplishments were celebrated by distributions

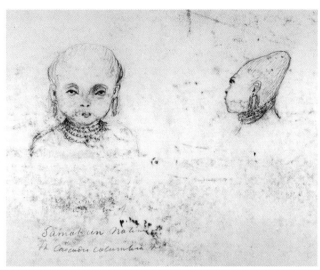

Fig. 12. Tamakoun's son after the process of head flattening was completed. Detail of sketch by Joseph Drayton at the Cascades, Columbia R., 1841. An engraving after this sketch misidentified this drawing as "Niculuita" (Wishram) instead of Cascades (Wilkes 1845, 4:415).

of what they had produced, plus other food and property. For example, the products of a girl's first picking of huckleberries and digging of roots and a boy's first catch of fish and the product of his first successful hunt were given to elders at a celebratory meal. When a girl reached puberty, she was secluded (the only time in her adult life) for five days in a shelter separate from the family house. During this period, people were asked to dance for her and food was provided for them (Spier and Sapir 1930).

• MARRIAGE   Marriage was between persons defined as nonrelatives and was arranged at the initiative of the groom's family (sometimes when the bride was very young). Ideally, and usually, marriages were between members of the same social class, establishing useful economic and political connections between extended families; this was one reason that spouses were frequently from different villages, including speakers of differing languages. Intermarriage was usually with Chinookans from other communities and with Sahaptins; such marriages were frequent in the 1990s, occurring with members of many other Indian groups and with non-Indians. Village exogamy was most common among upper-class people as were plural wives (who were frequently sisters). The levirate and sororate were customary.

In contrast to the distributions of gifts to guests (witnesses) on certain occasions, marriages were validated by a series of exchanges of valuable property between the families. Each family presented gifts to the other; the groom's relatives gave first and probably gave the largest amount (Sapir 1909:174–175). Situations that involved the affinal ties between families (such as the birth of children to a couple, the death of a spouse) required comparable exchanges of wealth (K.S. French 1955).

Fig. 11. Ida Palmer or Wallulatum, Wasco, with baby in cradleboard decorated with beadwork. Photograph by Joseph K. Dixon, Warm Springs Res., Oreg., 1913.

After marriage, a couple often lived with the wife's family for a time, but residence was usually (sooner or later) patrilocal. Households were composed of a few extended families, possibly with some immediate relatives, visitors, and slaves as well (D.H. French 1961:364); the make-up of houses and households fluctuated, influenced by access to economic resources or the congeniality of women who formed task-oriented work groups. Families or households lived near others at traditional sites. Residence varied from season to season, and even from year to year, so that one could describe the residence at a given time as a village, a hamlet, a cluster, or a camp. Often a site was unoccupied; however, important villages would have at least a few people in residence at all times.

• DEATH   When a person died, family members and friends mourned officially for a period of days, after which the body, dressed in finery and wrapped in a skin robe, was taken with some personal belongings to a family (or customary) sepulcher, a structure on a bluff or on one of various islands in the Columbia River. The deaths of leaders and other important people received wider attention, drawing mourners from other villages and groups. For a period after the death, widows, widowers, and close family members observed various restrictions of behavior and dress, such as wearing their hair cut short and avoiding contact with fresh foods.

Religion

The possession of personal guardian-spirit powers was a crucial aspect of supernaturalism and crucial for success in life. Children of both sexes were sent to distant or traditional places, where a spirit might appear to them. Repeated vigils might be needed. Some people had multiple guardian spirits; a few persons had none. Spirits were mainly animals, including birds and fish; Thunder and a water being were among the others (Spier and Sapir 1930:236–248; D.H. French 1961:366–367). Shamans ("Indian doctors") were employed to control new powers, as well as to cure illnesses. The spirit powers of shamans were not wholly distinct from those of other people, but shamans typically were linked with especially powerful spirits—and more of them. Those persons hoping to become shamans needed special assistance from existing practitioners; aspirants also needed to show the public, through performances, that they had powers. Winter singing and dancing sessions were important, as elsewhere in the region. Shamans could be leaders but were not priests; they worked for those who hired them, not for a community or congregation.

One could cure oneself, as well as others, with powers; they could also be used to injure or kill one's enemies. (There was sorcery, but no people inherently disposed to witchcraft.) Certain guardian spirits provided invulnerability; some protected one from spiritual dangers while preparing bodies for funer-

als; others gave success in activities such as hunting. In the 1990s, there were a few Wascos and Wishrams with power. Some curing occurred, and one Wasco with power held winter power "sings."

The world, or universe, to the Chinookans has been significantly one of animate beings (cf. Jacobs 1955), including animals, plants, places, and heavenly bodies. Also, there were extinct myth-age beings, cannibal women frightening to children, and living land and water monsters (cf. D.H. French 1957; Spier and Sapir 1930:236–238). Despite invocations addressed, for example, to the sun and to sweathouses, theistic interpretations are inappropriate.

The importance of salmon was indicated by ceremonial recognition of the first fish caught in the spring (Spier and Sapir 1930:248–249). Reservation life led to a shift in emphasis to annual ceremonial attention to the first roots dug and the first berries picked. Some people from Warm Springs attended First Salmon ceremonies held on or near the Columbia River.

Chinookans have been participants (D.H. French 1961:367–368, 392–395) in a tradition of religious revelation that is old and widespread (Spier 1935). Those receiving the revelations—songs, dances, certain moral injunctions—have been called prophets. Along with subsequent leaders in the religions, they could have priestlike functions; however, ritual was sometimes quite informal, and the "congregations" were variable in nature. Some Wishrams (also Wascos, Cascades?) became followers of Smohalla, a nativistic prophet (Mooney 1896:708–731; Spier and Sapir 1930:251–254). The Feather cult (Du Bois 1938) also had Chinookan converts. Very few Wascos or Wishrams have been leaders in the Washat religion (cf. D.H. French 1961:414). Of special importance to Chinookans has been the Indian Shaker Church ("Religious Movements," fig. 9, this vol.) (Mooney 1896:746–763; Gunther 1949; Pope 1953; Barnett 1957; D.H. French 1961:394–395, 414; Harmon 1971).

These revealed religions, some of which include curing, share with shamanism the assumption that there is an active supernatural world that can affect the current affairs of humans (D.H. French 1961:367–368). The above religions, and Christianity, are not defined as necessarily mutually exclusive; some people participate in more than one of them. Syncretism occurs, for example, in the combining of Christianity with aboriginal curing patterns.

Mythology

The oral literature and other narratives of the Wasco, Wishram, and Cascades peoples are understandably similar to those of the Northwest Coast and other western inland valley peoples (Sapir 1907a; Miller 1989a; vol. 7:593–601). A notable feature of the mythology of the easterly Chinookans is the Coyote cycle, a series of narratives in which Coyote travels up the Columbia River as trickster, transformer, and announcer of changes. There   *373*

Fig. 13. Installation of chiefs of the Confederated Tribes of the Warm Springs Res. According to the constitution of the Confederated Tribes each of the 3 ethnic groups—Warm Springs Sahaptin, Wasco, and Northern Paiute—is represented on the tribal council by a chief. left to right, Joe McCorkle, Wasco and Warm Springs Sahaptin, the newly selected Wasco chief, and Alfred Smith, Wasco. McCorkle speaks during a break in the songs performed at the ceremony. Photograph by David and Kathrine French, Agency longhouse, Warm Springs Res., Oreg., 1953.

are also other myths and historical accounts. Easterly Chinookan narrations were first collected in the late nineteenth century, and publication of English and Kiksht versions and summaries followed (e.g., Curtin 1909 [1885]:[237]–314; Kuykendall 1889; Boas 1909 [1892]:232–233; Sapir 1907a, 1909; Curtis 1907–1930, 8:106–154; Spier and Sapir 1930:273–281; Hymes 1953, 1975; Ramsey 1972; Moore 1986a; Hines 1991). E.E. Clark (1953), and others, have published expurgated versions of Chinookan narratives, selected for their appeal to non-Indians. Various myth recordings are unpublished (Dyk 1933:145–156; D.H. French and K.S. French 1950–1993; Hymes 1951–1990; Cosminsky 1964; Silverstein 1966–1974; Moore 1983–1993, 1986a). Some of these are in Kiksht and English, others in English only.

The mythology of the easterly Chinookans has been discussed in diverse ways. Hymes is well-known for writing myth texts as verse (1981). He also addresses other myth topics, as do Phillips (1955), D.H. French (1958), Jacobs (1962), Cosminsky (1964), Lévi-Strauss (1964–1971, especially 1971:IV, cf. 1985:177–185), Ramsey (1983), and Moore (1993).

History

From the mid-nineteenth century, there was participation and membership in Methodist, Presbyterian, Pentecostal, and other churches. There have been few Roman Catholics. Incidentally, in furtherance of Christianity, Indian agents, some of whom were also missionaries, actively worked to suppress other revealed religions as well as shamanism.

Population

The prehistoric population probably numbered about 10,000; White-derived diseases from the east and from the west, carried by Indians, caused a decline to an estimated 6,000 by 1806. Other pre–1850 epidemics caused further declines: soon after the Yakima and Warm Springs reservations were settled, the total number of Chinookans reported was 850–1,200. By 1930 there were 233 Chinookans. Subsequently tabulations by tribe were discontinued, as intermarriage with other Indians and with Whites made such categories meaningless.

Synonymy

The name Wasco is the broadest of the tribal designations, sometimes being used by Indians to include Wishrams, Cascades, and others. Usually, it means the easterly Chinookans who traditionally lived in Oregon near The Dalles. It was derived from *wašq́ú* village (fig. 1, no. 3). This name, in turn, was based on the word *wašq́ú* referring to traditional bowl-shaped dippers or spoons; *wašq́ú* was also the place-name for a bowlike rock formation—into which spring water flowed—and (diminutivized) was the name of the village nearby. The *wa-* is an (archaic) feminine singular prefix; the stem is /-sq́u/ (pronounced [-sq́o]) 'small dipper'. The Chinookan name for the residents is *gałásq́u* or *gałásq́ú* 'those of Wasco' or 'those of the dipper' (cf. Sapir in Hodge 1907–1910, 2:917; Sapir 1909:240; Spier and Sapir 1930:168, 172); *gała-* (g-a-ł+a-) is one set of prefixes that relate people to a place (cf. Silverstein in vol. 7:533).

Based on *gałásq́u* are a number of names for Wascos to be found in early publications: Caclasco, Cathlas, Cathlascans, Cathlasco, Cathlascons, Cathlaskos, Cathlassis, Cathlatscos, Catlascon, Guithlasko (a Clackamas version), and Kaclasko (see Hodge 1907–1910, 2:918 for sources).

Many versions of the Sahaptin name *wasq́úpam* (D.H. French and K.S. French 1949–1993) have been published: Was-co-pam, Wascoparns, Wascopaw, Wascopens, Wascopum(s), Waskopam, Wiss-co-pam, and Woscopom (Hodge 1907–1910, 2:918).

Other synonyms for Wasco(s) include: Afúlakin and Awásko ammim (Kalapuya names); Ámpχänkni (ʔampġeʼnkniˑ), explained as 'where the water is' (Klamath name); also, Uncoes, Wacoes, Wasko, Waskosin, and Waskows (Hodge 1907–1910, 2:918); Dalles Indians, with Wishrams sometimes included (Mooney 1896:741; Farrand in Hodge 1907–1910, 1:380–381). Gatschet (cited by Hodge 1907–1910, 2:918) listed "Sáχlatks" as the Molala name, but this is a loan from Chinookan; Jacobs (1958–1959, 1:275) gave *šáχlát* as Clackamas Chinook for 'upriver Wishram-Wasco' people; cf. "Shahala" under Cascade synonyms, below.

The name Wishram is not based on a Chinookan name for these peoples. Rather, it is an anglicization of *wíšχam*, the

Yakima and other Sahaptin name for the most important village (*nixlúidix*, no. 19) and for the people as a whole (Sapir 1909:240; Spier and Sapir 1930:159). (Nevertheless, it was suggested by Philip Kahclamat, a knowledgeable Wishram, that these Sahaptin forms were themselves originally borrowed from Upper Chinook *wilxam* 'village, community, country'.)

Probably the first reference in the literature to Wishram was the publication (in French) in 1821 of Hunt's 1812 diary notation regarding Ouichram village (Stuart and Hunt 1935:305). Some of the later names based on Sahaptin *wíšxam* were: Nishram, Wesh-ham, Wícxam, Wisham, Wishham, Wish-ram, Wishrans, Wissams, Wisswhams, and Wushuum (see Hodge 1907–1910, 2:762 for most of the sources). Mooney (1896:740) wrote Wŭshqŭmă-pŭm, translated as 'Wŭshqŭm people', and listed other synonyms.

Some Wishrams have called their group *iłáxluit*; -*xluit* can be regarded as a stem from which various names have been derived. For example, Sapir (1909:38; Spier and Sapir 1930:159, 164) suggested that the first-person singular form *ičxluit* 'I am an *iłáxluit*' is probably the "Echelute" of Lewis and Clark (cf. Moulton 1983, 5:336, fn. 2). Another related form is "Tlakluit," the name for the Wishram "tribe" used by Farrand and Sapir (in Hodge 1907–1910, 2) but since used perhaps only by Swanton (1952:449). Mooney (1896:740) had written "Tlaqluit"; it is not clear on what basis he said that this and Wŭshqŭm "refer to a species of louse or flea abounding in that neighborhood." In a lengthy discussion of the meaning of the village name *nixlúidix*, Spier and Sapir (1930:164–166) related it to *iłáxluit* and discuss Wishram folk etymologies in which the stem would mean 'come together' or 'head for [the village]'. 'A smooth, level place' was a translation offered to Curtis (1907–1930, 8:180).

Among the other names related to *iłáxluit* in the older publications are: Echebool(s), E-chee-lute, E-che-loot, E-che-lute, Ehelutes, Eloot, E-lute, E-ske-lute, Eskeloot, Hellwits, Helwit, Niculuita, Nihaloitih, Tchelouits, Tchilouit(s), Telhuemit, Tilhalluvit, Tilhiellewit, Tilhilooit, Tilhualwits, and Tilhulhwit (Mooney 1896:740; Hodge 1907–1910, 2:762 lists sources).

White Salmon Indians, as an ethnic grouping, may not have had a standard Chinookan name. Sapir (1909:30) published what was possibly a consultant's coinage, perhaps influenced by Sahaptin and English-type names: *itq̇áwanbam idĺxam* (phonemicized) 'White Salmon [i.e., 'mature chinook salmon'] people'; this was repeated (with an erroneous translation) in Spier and Sapir (1930:167). Lewis and Clark had tried to elicit a name but instead evidently recorded a word that was a description of their own elicitation process (the act of pointing); one spelling of their recording was Chilluckit-te-quaw. Hodge (1907–1910, 1:268) accepted this as the "tribal name" and cited 14 published versions. In Curtis (1907–1930, 8:180), it is suggested that the word recorded by Lewis and Clark was chilktígwax 'to point at one' or 'he pointed at me'. Philip Kahclamat reconstituted it as *ičilqdigwaix* 'he who pointed at the

place', but he did not suggest a valid ethnic name (D.H. French and K.S. French 1950–1993).

The Hood River Indians were scarcely included in Hodge (1907–1910, 2:922).

Dog River, an early name for Hood River, may be a translation from Chinookan, and Dog River Indians and Dog River Wascos were early names for the people there (cf. Mooney 1896:741).

Mooney (1896:741) uses the term Kwikwû´lĭt (followed by diverse "synonyms") to refer to both Hood River and Cascades people. This is *gigwálat* 'downward' and can be used as that with affixes *iłgigwálatkš* to mean 'downriver people', that is, 'Hood River Indians' (and sometimes also, or instead, 'Cascades Indians').

The name Cascade or Cascades is based on the series of three rapids that once occurred where a stretch of the river passed through the heart of the Columbia Gorge and thus through the Cascade Mountains; the range itself may have been named after the rapids. In the course of the nineteenth century, Indians joined Whites in referring to the rapids and the associated Indians as "Cascade(s)," and the name became a loanword in Chinookan (*ayaxáskit*) with customary affixes. It is remotely possible that a "tribal" name reported from the area, Cathlakaheckit (Hodge 1907–1910, 1:216), is derived from the preceding.

A local Chinookan name or description for 'Cascade people' is *gałáxišačk*, based on *ikíšačk* ('rapids, cascades'). Curtis (1907–1930, 8:181) used the term as a collective name for the villages on the north (only) bank of the river. The fact that Boas (1894:276, 277) recorded a similar form, *giλáx̣išačk* 'Cascade(s) (people)', from a Lower Chinook attests to its widespread use.

Farrand (in Hodge 1907–1910, 2:922) used Watlala as the main entry for the Cascade peoples. He also confusingly subsumed the Hood (Dog) River Indians under this name, and this has contributed to the problem of determining synonyms. Watlala was, narrowly speaking, the important Cascade village *watála* (no. 49) 'small lake (place)'; it is the diminutive form for *witála* 'lake'. Other prefixes may precede -*tała*, such as *gała-* ("Cathla-," etc.) 'people of' or 'people'. The same translations will serve for *iła-*. Thus, *gałatála* and *iłatála* were 'small lake (village) people', but the names were sometimes extended from the people of this village to all or many of the Cascade Indians. In the literature, the following names of groups and communities were based on -*tała*: Cath-lath-la-la(s), Cathlathlaly, Cathlathlas, Clahclellah, Wahclellah, Wah-lal-la, Wah-ral-lah, and Watlalla. (See Hodge 1907–1910, 2:922, 1:217, 302 for the sources of these names.) Spier and Sapir (1930:167) gave *watálidĺxam* as one name for the Cascade people, but this may have been coined by one of their Wishram consultants; later Indians had never heard it. Spier subsequently (1936:21) added *iłatála* 'lake people' as a synonym.

Amidst the synonyms for Hood River was -*gigwálat*- 'downward' and (with affixes) 'downriver people'. Upriver people (e.g., Wascos) also included the Cascades people under the term. Ironically, Chinookans downriver from the Cascades were referring to the same Cascades people as -šaxlat- 'upward' (referring to such upriver people). Lewis and Clark (Moulton 1983–, 7:57, *et passim*; cf. Farrand in Hodge 1907–1910, 2:519) rendered this as Shahala. To them, it was a "nation," comprising these "tribes" (the spelling varied): Yehhuh(s) (*wáyaxix*, Cascade village no. 60), Wahclellah(s) (*watála*, no. 49), Clahclellah(s) (*łatála* or *gatatála*, also no. 49), and Neerchekioo(s) (perhaps *nitxkłayu*, no. 62) (cf. Sapir in Spier 1936:24).

Another starting point for synonyms was *wáyaxix* village on the Oregon bank; Curtis regarded *gatawáyaxix* 'people of *wáyaxix*' as a "tribe" that occupied the south side of the river. For the village or the people, the literature has included: Cathlayackty, Wahe (Lee and Frost 1844:176), Weeyarkeek (D. Thompson 1916:498), Weyeh-hoo (Spier and Sapir 1930:173), Yehah, and Yehuh (the initial "Y" was probably intended to be pronounced /wáy/ in English). Although Ross (in Thwaites 1904–1907, 7:121–124, 254–261) was most concerned with the north bank, his "Cath-le-yach-e-yach" (three villages with 250–300 people) was possibly *gatawáyaxix* and other peoples. For more sources, see various Cascade entries in Hodge (1907–1910, 2:996).

A further name proposed as a synonym is Katlagakya (Farrand in Hodge 1907–1910, 2:519, 922). Possibly it can be reconstituted (respelled) as *ʔgataxiqaya(k)* 'middle people', with the name being related to *qixayagílxam* 'middle village', no. 51.

Gass (1958:238) evidently heard the word "Al-e-is" and believed it referred to a "nation" of (Cascade) Indians. Probably it was not a proper name; a tentative reconstitution is *ʔi-lx-i(x)* 'the land', with the terminal "s" being the English plural or the -x of -ix (locative), often omitted by Chinookan speakers from the Cascades westward.

Certain Cascade Indians who went to Warm Springs under the 1855 treaty signed at The Dalles were known as the "Ki-gal-twal-la band of the Wascoes," the term "Wascoes" thus being extended downstream. Farrand (in Hodge 1907–1910, 2:922) related this "band" to Watlala, but neither *watála* nor *gigwálat* is necessarily the Kiksht source for Ki-gal-twa-la, even though both have been used to refer to all or some Cascades Indians. A tentative linguistic reconstitution is *gaygltxʷila(l)* 'standing away from'. Avex Miller, a Wasco, called it a "tribe," without specifying its locale (D.H. French and K.S. French 1950–1993). It is related to a place-name, *gaygltxʷili*, also *gayagltxʷilalix* 'it was standing out from there', the name of prominent rocks at Multnomah Falls. Although the Multnomah Falls area may not itself have had a resident population, the people present at the treaty-signing may have regarded the name as suitable to symbolize the diverse Cascades populations covered by the treaty.

Sources

Summaries of archeology (and also of history and other topics relevant to easterly Chinookans) are included in Toepel, Willingham, and Minor (1980). Strong, Schenck, and Steward (1930) did pioneer research near The Dalles, and Caldwell (1956) based his dissertation on Wakemap (*wáq̓map*, Wishram village no. 18) excavations. An Idaho State University journal, *Tebiwa*, includes relevant articles by Butler and others. Amateurs have been active (e.g., E.M. Strong 1959); the Oregon Archaeological Society (1959) has published a small monograph on Wakemap mound; its newsletter, *Screenings*, has included original data. Cressman and collaborators (1960) integrated their research not only with the prehistory of other regions in the West but also with Upper Chinookan ethnography and linguistics. Cascades data are incomplete and scattered, but Phebus (1978) and University of Oregon archeologists improved the situation (see Toepel, Willingham, and Minor 1983:105).

The accounts of Meriwether Lewis and William Clark are fundamental sources; the many editions (e.g., Coues 1893) based on N. Biddle's version of 1814 are satisfactory for most purposes, but for thorough study the original journals (Thwaites 1904–1905, or, preferably, Moulton 1983–) are also needed. Jackson (1978) is one of the useful supplements; others include the journals of Lewis and Clark's companions (e.g., Gass 1958). Accounts of fur traders, such as Ross (1849, 1956), can be valuable; Irving's *Astoria* (1951) contains some data not found elsewhere, but it should be used with caution. Other useful accounts are by missionaries (e.g., Lee and Frost 1844; Boyd 1996) and explorers, such as Wilkes (1845). The mid-nineteenth-century settlers made passing references to Indians in their diaries, many of which have been published by state and local historical societies. A history of the Warm Springs Reservation to 1900 was written by Cliff (1942).

Chinookan ethnographic data are included in Zucker, Hummel, and Høgfoss (1983) and Stowell (1987). Hines (1996) is a collection of Wasco myths and legends. As of the 1990s, Yakima and Warm Springs residents' own offices were collecting video, audio, and written data. Indians themselves published newspapers, pamphlets, and books (Quill Point, Inc. 1984); author Chuck Williams (1980) is a Cascade Indian.

Vocabulary lists overshadowed texts or grammar in nineteenth-century writings (Lee 1840; Lee and Frost 1844; Hale 1846; Gallatin 1848; Gatschet 1877); see Pilling (1893) for data on sources. Boas collected samples of Wasco linguistic material (1892a, 1909); he encouraged Sapir to undertake the study of Wishram (Sapir 1905, 1907a, 1909, 1926; see also Boas [with Sapir] 1911a:625–626, 627, 638–645, 650–654, 673–677); Hymes (1973a) described unpublished Sapir material.

Curtis (1907–1930, 8:198–205) published some Wishram vocabulary. Dyk (1930–1933, 1931, 1933; Dyk and Hymes 1956), continued the Wishram work. Since 1950, linguistic research and writing has been done by: D.H. French and K.S. French (1950–1993, 1989); D.H. French (1957, 1958, 1985); Hymes (1951–1990, 1958, 1961, 1966, 1972, 1975, 1975a, 1976, 1980, 1980a, 1981, 1984); Kahclamat and Hymes (1977); Silverstein (1966–1974, 1972, 1974, 1976, 1977, 1978, 1979, 1981, 1984, 1984a, 1993); Moore (1980, 1983–1993, 1986, 1986a, 1988, 1993); Fowler (1982); and Millstein (1979–1993), who has been preparing and using Wasco-Wishram and other language course materials on the Warm Springs Reservation (see also Hymes 1973). A Wasco-Wishram dictionary is being prepared (Silverstein, D.H. French, K.S. French, and Moore 1976–1996).

Western Columbia River Sahaptins

EUGENE S. HUNN AND DAVID H. FRENCH

The Sahaptin (sə'hǎptĭn) peoples treated here are more frequently, if inexactly known as Tenino or Warm Springs Indians. Tenino refers properly to the westernmost Sahaptin-speaking village of the Columbia River Sahaptin dialect group, not to any larger "tribal" confederation. The term Warm Springs Indians suggests a focus on the Confederated Tribes of the Warm Springs Reservation of Oregon. However, the Warm Springs Tribes include not only Sahaptins but also Chinookans ("Wasco, Wishram, and Cascades," this vol.), and Northern Paiutes (vol. 11: 435–465). Furthermore, the Sahaptin-speaking groups on the Warm Springs Reservation were separated by the treaties from their close kin: those who lived on the north bank of the Columbia River were assigned to the Yakima, while those living upriver came to be designated Umatillas.

Territory and Language

Western Columbia River Saphaptins identify themselves as members of village communities located on the Columbia River or its tributaries from just above The Dalles, Oregon, to above Alder Creek (fig. 1). Together with the Umatilla, these villages are grouped as the Columbia River dialect group of the Sahaptin language. The Columbia River dialects* are rather sharply distinguished by certain lexical features from dialects of the Northeast (Walla Walla, Lower Snake, Palouse, and Wanapam) and Northwest (Yakima, Kittitas or Pshwanwapam, Upper Cowlitz or Taitnapam, and Klikitat) clusters (Rigsby 1965:36–37; vol. 17:666-667). Descendants of Western Columbia River Sahaptin peoples are enrolled as Warm Springs, Yakima, and Umatilla tribal members since the treaty boundaries arbitrarily divided traditional social networks. Both the Warm Springs Reservation and the Southern Yakima Reservation were probably within range of traditional foraging, socializing, and trading activities.

These Sahaptin villages were politically autonomous units each associated with an extensive hinterland systematically utilized to harvest subsistence resources. Residents of several villages met at particularly productive resource sites. Such gatherings might also include members of other dialect or language groups, as at the Indian Heaven berrying grounds southwest of Mount Adams, Washington. Thus, it

is inappropriate to draw a sharp line around a contiguous "territory" belonging to the Western Columbia River Sahaptin peoples.

Component Groups

The following long-term residential sites were occupied by Western Columbia River Sahaptin groups: Tenino, Skin, Celilo (Wayam), Tygh Valley, Maryhill, John Day, Rock Creek, Arlington, Roosevelt, Pine Creek, and Alderdale (fig. 1). The villages of Paterson and *tamalám* were part of the social network of Columbia River Sahaptins but are treated in "Cayuse, Umatilla, and Walla Walla," this volume. The Pishquitpah, encountered by Meriwether Lewis and William Clark near Paterson, Washington, in April 1806 (Moulton 1983–, 7:165), may have been Yakima (Moulton 1983–, 6:474-475) or Columbia River Sahaptin.

External Relations

Sahaptin villages and camps were located for the most part on islands in the Columbia River or on the north shore. Lewis and Clark believed that the reason was the Indians' fear of the Northern Shoshone and Bannock to the south (Moulton 1983–, 5:318). Such hostilities most likely postdate the introduction of horses in the 1700s (vol. 11: 517–524).

Slave raids against northern California groups, such as the Shasta and Achumawi, and perhaps against certain southern Oregon groups as well, such as the Modoc and Northern Paiute, were regularly mounted by Sahaptin and Chinookan parties based at Celilo and The Dalles in the 1830s (Perkins 1843; vol. 11: 519–521). Most of these slaves were kept by Upper Chinookan chiefly families or traded toward the coast.

The hypothesis of protohistorical displacement of Salishan speakers from the Columbia River between The Dalles and Priest Rapids by Sahaptin speakers driven north by hostile Numic-speaking groups (Teit 1928) has been thoroughly discredited (Ray 1938; Murdock 1938a; Rigsby 1965). Linguistic evidence, such as patterns of dialect diversity (Rigsby 1965), place-names, and environmental vocabulary (Hunn 1990, 1991a), clearly supports the conclusion that Sahaptian speakers have continuously occupied this stretch

*Sahaptin forms in this chapter are in the orthography described in the footnote in "Yakima and Neighboring Groups," this vol.

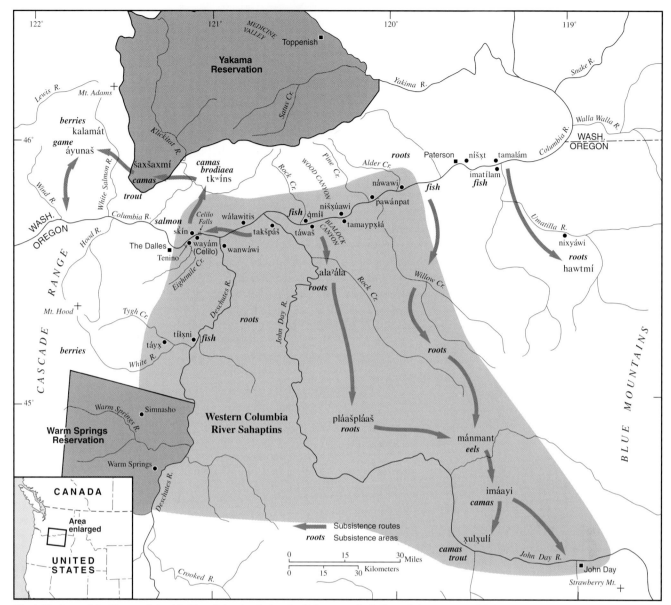

Fig. 1. Territory of the Western Columbia River Sahaptins during the 19th century, including subsistence routes. Modern reservations are shown. Settlements located approximately are indicated by name alone.

of the Columbia and at least the lower reaches of its tributaries for many centuries, if not millennia. The hypothesized displacement of Molala peoples by the Tygh in protohistoric times (Murdock 1938a) is also doubtful, given the documented peaceful joint utilization of resource sites in this area by Sahaptin, Northern Paiute, Cayuse, and Nez Perce groups (D.H. French 1961; Rigsby 1965:57–62, 1969:80–82; Suphan 1974).

The historic linguistic and cultural boundary between Sahaptin and Upper Chinookan speech 10 kilometers below Celilo Falls was apparent to Lewis and Clark, whose Nez Perce guides explained that "(*They could no longer understand the language of those below the falls ...*) and ... [they] would Certainly kill them; perticularly as They had been at war with each other;" (Moulton 1983–, 5:329).

The Sahaptin communities at and below Celilo Falls maintained civil relations with their Upper Chinookan

neighbors, as was evident at the time of the Lewis and Clark expedition and later during the operation of the Methodist mission at The Dalles (Perkins 1843). Upper Chinookans often were bilingual in Sahaptin, though the reverse was rare (Rigsby 1965:63), and joined with their Sahaptin neighbors in common task groups, such as slave-raiding parties to the south (Perkins 1843; Anastasio 1972).

Western Columbia River Sahaptins frequently camped and socialized with other Sahaptin speakers as well as with Nez Perce and Cayuse Indians. The vast majority of named resource sites documented in 1940 in the Blue and Wallowa mountains of northeastern Oregon were reported to have been jointly utilized by groups of Umatilla, Warm Springs, Columbia River, Cayuse, and Nez Perce Indians, at least during the early twentieth century (Suphan 1974). The berrying grounds southwest of Mount Adams brought Western Columbia River Sahaptins from as far east as Pine

379

Creek into regular and intimate contact with Yakimas and Klikitats (Norton, Boyd, and Hunn 1983; Schuster 1975). Parties from different regions camped in this area separately at traditional locations (James Selam, personal communication 1983) but joined in horse racing at the site of *kalamát* southwest of Mount Adams. Berrying grounds south of Mount Hood, Oregon, were jointly exploited by Tygh Valley, Northern Paiute, and Molala (Suphan 1974:50–64).

Well-traveled Indian trails linked The Dalles with Tygh Valley and points south, Celilo Falls with Fort Simcoe to the north and the Klikitat country to the northwest, Maryhill with Satus Creek, and Paterson with Taptat (Prosser) and Horn Rapids on the lower Yakima River and Priest Rapids upriver on the Columbia (Murdock 1980:133, map 1). Yakimas traveled regularly to Celilo Falls to trade surplus roots, berries, and skins for dried salmon, while Klamath came from the south. Nez Perce and Cayuse parties frequently visited Celilo (Walker 1967), establishing early winter camps there (Perkins 1843). Their arrival was impressive: mounted parties circled the hosts in mock military display before dismounting. The hosts greeted them and presented them with gifts. This dramatic ritual entrance may have misled early White observers (Farnham 1843; Perkins 1843) and subsequent commentators (Haines 1955; Garth 1964; Ruby and Brown 1972) to conclude that the Nez Perce and Cayuse "dominated" and "extracted tribute" from the Western Columbia River Sahaptins. No such tradition of subordination has been recorded from the Columbia River Sahaptins themselves.

In sum, Western Columbia River Sahaptins participated in a network of peaceful trade relations reinforced by intermarriage that encompassed all Columbia River basin Indians, whether speakers of Sahaptin, Nez Perce, Cayuse, or Upper Chinookan. Chronic hostile relations were restricted to distant peoples to the south accessible only after a journey of several to many days.

Environment

The Western Columbia River Sahaptin peoples occupy a semi-arid basin in the rainshadow of the Cascade Mountains fringed by montane coniferous forests. The land ranges from near sea level on the major rivers to 3,000 meters on Mounts Adams, Hood, and Jefferson. Lower timberline varies from about 800 meters on the Cascade east slopes to about 1,200 meters in the foothills of the Blue Mountains. Upper timberline is reached at about 2,000 meters in the Cascades. Celilo Falls, the greatest Indian fishery of the Plateau, provided access to several major salmon runs from late April through October. Other importnat fisheries were located on the Columbia near the mouth of the John Day River and at Sherar Bridge on the Deschutes.

Culture

Subsistence

Winter villages and major summer and fall fisheries were situated at low elevation on or adjacent to the major rivers. Spring root harvests drew people away from the river to lithosol and meadow habitats at progressively higher elevations as summer approached. Root-digging parties returned burdened with their stockpiles of dried roots, arriving at the summer fisheries in early July after the Columbia flood had receded. The majority of families ascended to the high huckleberry fields in August, some remaining to hunt and gather until the first snows of October, others returning for the September salmon runs (Hunn 1990). In late winter hunting parties ranged widely from the winter villages far up the major tributaries and into the mountains seeking deer and elk.

In comparison with their downstream neighbors, the Wasco and Wishram, the Western Columbia River Sahaptins traveled greater distances inland from the Columbia River, harvested a greater variety of plant foods, and consequently depended less on the exchange of surplus dried fish for their economic support. In contrast to the Umatilla, Walla Walla, Cayuse, and Yakima, their upstream neighbors, they relied less on hunting and more on fishing.

Western Columbia River Sahaptin village communities were not sedentary in the sense that the bulk of the village population remained at or within a short walk of the village for most or all of the year. Nor were they nomadic, that is, wandering in search of food with no recognized and stable home base and range. The people of each village ranged in extended family parties systematically over a large and topographically diverse area, allowing the harvest of a diversity of species and types of resources according to season. Within this general strategy there was scope for choice. A family might choose to spend the early summer fishing along the Columbia for sockeye salmon or steelhead, while their kin might prefer to remain in the mountains harvesting "wild" carrots (*Perideridia gairdneri*) and spring beauty (Indian potatoes) (*Claytonia lanceolata*). Those who found the rigors of travel too difficult might remain all year on the river, moving only between the winter village and nearby summer fishing camps. With the introduction of the horse, bison east of the Rocky Mountains could be pursued by intertribal "task groupings" (Anastasio 1972).

• GATHERING Western Columbia River Sahaptins derived an estimated 60 percent or more of their food energy from gathering (Hunn 1981). Roots, berries, and several species of "Indian celeries" contributed key minerals and vitamins to the diet (Hunn and French 1981; Benson et al. 1973). Root staples and important supplementary foods included bitterroot, several "desert parsleys" or lomatiums, and yellowbell (*Fritillaria pudica*). Camas, false onion, Indian carrot, Indian potato, and edible valer-

Oreg. Histl. Soc., Portland: top, 67628; bottom left, 7248; bottom right, 60409.

Fig. 2. The importance of fishing. top, Celilo Falls on the Columbia River, Oreg., one of the most important fishing sites to the Western Columbia River Sahaptins (vol. 17:187). Drying sheds and temporary dwellings parallel the river. Photograph by Heinrichsen before 1957. bottom left, Catherine Cushinway roasting salmon at a festival in honor of Chief Tommy Thompson. Photograph by Mel Junghans, 1956. bottom right, Edna David and Stella Mckinley, members of the Confederated Tribes of Warm Springs Res., drying salmon at Celilo, Oreg. Photographed about 1950s.

ian (*Valeriana edulis*) were sought in meadow habitats, mostly at mid-elevations. The mariposa lily was a winter emergency ration that could be harvested near the winter villages. Altogether more than 25 species were harvested for their edible underground parts. Large quantities of several species were sun-dried whole or as cakes for later consumption (Hunn 1990).

Berries and other fruits, including a very few species of seeds and nuts, were harvested between June and October. Most favored were chokecherries and the black huckleberry. The first fruits to ripen, golden currants (*Ribes aureum*) and red-osier dogwood berries, may be harvested as early as June. Ripening somewhat later are the chokecherries, serviceberries, hawthorn berries, and blue elderberries. Next

381

black huckleberries, grouseberries, low mountain blueberries, strawberries, blackberries, blackcaps, and other species were harvested. Black huckleberries were dried over a slow fire and packed home to add to the winter stores (Filloon 1952). "Black moss," tree lichen, was collected in mountain forests and baked underground to make a much-enjoyed confection (Turner 1977). Altogether some 28 species of fruits were consumed, plus acorns, hazel nuts, white-bark pine nuts, and at Warm Springs, at least, the seeds of large balsamroot species.

For a few months in late winter and early spring the sprouts, stems, leaves, and inner bark of various species were important. Still favored in the 1990s were the sprouts of Gray's lomatium and the petioles and scapes of bare-stemmed lomatium. The scapes of large balsamroots are also peeled and eaten raw when still in bud. Later, at higher elevations, the stems of cow parsnip were peeled and eaten.

• FISHING   Western Columbia River Sahaptin peoples are well known as expert fishermen, harvesting salmon by spearing, gaffing, dip and set netting, gill and seine netting, by hook and line, in weirs and traps, and even by means of a plant poison extracted from the root of chocolate tips (Meilleur, Hunn, and Cox 1991). Five species of Pacific salmon were of outstanding importance, as were two species of suckers (*Catostomus columbianus, C. macrocheilus*), the lamprey (*Entosphenus tridentatus*), and resident trout (*Onchorhynchus mykiss, O. clarkii*). Mountain whitefish were caught in winter through the ice. Also eaten were several resident cyprinids including the Northern squawfish, chiselmouth, peamouth, and red-sided shiner. Curiously, Western Columbia River Sahaptins disdained the mighty white sturgeon (cf. Moulton 1983–, 7: 130–131), though their neighbors considered it edible. They also avoided Dolly Varden trout.

Large quantities of salmon were dried for later consumption (fig. 2) or for trade. Notable is the practice of preparing dehydrated salmon flour by pounding dried salmon flesh. This flour was then packed in bags of cattail leaves lined with salmon skin, each about 30 by 70 centimeters and weighing about 40 kilograms (Moulton 1983–, 5: 323–325).

The completion of Bonneville Dam in 1938, The Dalles Dam in 1957, and other dams and diversions on the Deschutes, Umatilla, and streams upriver have contributed to an 80 percent reduction in Columbia River salmon stocks (Zucker, Hummel, and Høgfoss 1983:167) and destruction of a key element of Western Columbia River Sahaptin Indian identity.

• HUNTING   Mule deer of both interior and black-tailed varieties were the most sought after big-game species ("Kinship, Family, and Gender Roles," fig. 3, this vol.). A single mule deer provided 25–110 kilograms of dressed meat and supplied in addition a skin transformed by women into soft, durable, tailored, and artfully decorated garments and accoutrements.

Elk (wapiti) were less often encountered, being of more limited distribution, but yielded 130–260 kilograms of

top, Oreg. Histl. Soc., Portland: 7246; bottom, Smithsonian, Natl. Mus. of the Amer. Ind.: 10/7628.

Fig. 3. Hemp fishnets. top, Jimmy George, a Wayampam fisherman, and Charley Quittoken holding fishnets made by Quittoken. Photograph by Archie W. McKeown, 1957. bottom, Stone net sinker. Collected by T.T. Waterman, Warm Springs, Oreg., before 1921. Length 11 cm.

dressed meat and a thick hide used for robes, blankets, and war armor and shields. Other large mammals hunted include white-tailed deer, big-horn sheep, and pronghorn. Family heirloom buffalo robes were brought back from east of the Rocky Mountains or from the upper Snake River plains by hunting parties (which may have occasionally included Western Columbia River Indians) (Anastasio

top left, Wilkes 1845, 4:410; top right, Oreg. Histl. Soc., Portland: 37343; bottom left, Smithsonian, Natl. Mus. of the Amer. Ind.: 10/7697; bottom right, Nez Perce Natl. Histl. Park, Spalding, Idaho: 331.

Fig. 4. Tule mats. top left, Fishing houses at The Dalles, Oreg., made of tule mats, poles, and cedar bark. The structures, about 20 by 12 ft., were considered temporary dwellings during the fishing season (Wilkes 1845, 4:410). Engraving after original drawing by Joseph Drayton, 1841. top right, Mat shelter at Celilo Falls, Oreg., with fish wheel in background. Photographed about 1900. bottom left, Eating mat sewn with fiber string and needle made of bone. Collected by T.T. Waterman, Warm Springs, Oreg., before 1921. Length of needle, 44 cm; mat to same scale. bottom right, Mat tepee at Celilo Falls. Photographed 1894.

1972), then widely traded within the Columbia basin. Black bear were regularly hunted; the meat was cooked underground; the skins were made into robes.

Smaller mammals regularly hunted for their meat included cottontail rabbits, jackrabbits, yellow-bellied marmots, ground squirrels, western gray squirrels, and porcupines. Mammals hunted or trapped for their skins included beaver, muskrat, grizzly bear, gray wolf, coyote, gray fox, red fox, mountain lion, bobcat, lynx, otter, long-tailed weasel, in summer and winter pelage, and raccoon (Hunn 1990; Murdock 1980:137).

Grouse and waterfowl were also hunted. Sage grouse and sharp-tailed grouse were once abundant in shrub-steppe and bunchgrass habitat below the tree line. Blue grouse and ruffed grouse were widespread in forested areas. Canada geese nested on islands in the Columbia River where their eggs were collected. In winter, ducks, geese, and swans were hunted with bow and arrow or trapped in nets. Painted turtles might also be collected and eaten.

Several species of freshwater mussels (e.g., *Margaritifera falcata, Gonoidea angulata, Anodonta* spp.) were harvested. These occurred at certain places in the river and were most often harvested as a winter famine food (cf. Thompson in Glover 1962:372). Deep shell middens found along the Deschutes River indicate a more substantial dietary role for shellfish at certain periods of prehistory than is attested ethnographically (Lyman 1984). Saltwater clams (*Clinocardium*

nuttallii, Saxidomus giganteus, Tresus spp.) were obtained in trade from Puget Sound Indians via Klikitat and Yakima intermediaries (see "Ethnobiology and Subsistence," this vol.).

Technology

Stone was worked by flaking (using an elk antler tool and a piece of elk hide for protection while working), pecking, and grinding. Flint and obsidian were fashioned into arrow points and knife blades. Basalt and granitic river cobbles were selected for use as "heat exchangers" in the sweat lodge, mud bath, underground oven, and for boiling food in baskets. Basalt was most often pecked and ground to fashion pestles, ax and club heads, stone adzes for scraping hides, and weights for gill and seine nets. Basalt talus was stacked to form low fences on ridge crests as hunting blinds or shelters, and river cobbles were arranged to form stone weirs for diverting fish into basket traps.

Wood was essential for fuel. Drift logs, predominantly of ponderosa pine or Douglas fir, were a primary fuelwood source along the Columbia; where available willow, alder, cottonwood, maple, oak, aspen, even big sagebrush (Moulton 1983–, 7:176) were used. The scarcity of firewood here has been exaggerated, as tributary canyons are heavily wooded with alder, willow, and maple. Alder was preferred for baking and smoking salmon, enhancing the flavor of the meat.

Douglas fir saplings were used for net poles; peach-leaf willow for lodgepoles; vine and Douglas maples for net hoops; ocean spray or some other "iron wood" such as mock-orange for cross-braces and the sticks used to bake fish over an open fire; garry oak burl or root for mortars and garry oak branches for bows and digging stick shafts; sandbar willow withes for sweatlodge frames, basket traps, rough-and-ready bindings, and whips. Serviceberry branches were preferred for arrow shafts; greasewood twigs for needles to sew tule mats; hollow elderberry canes served as "straws" to vent the earth oven or used to make a whistle to attract deer (Murdock 1980:137); western juniper logs were fashioned into drum frames.

Rose wood was incorporated into cradleboards for its power to deter ghosts. Sprays of wild rose are hung on the walls of houses to protect the occupants from haunting, are burned in a house as a fumigant after a death, and used to purify a grave site prior to burial.

Other plant products include two of paramount importance: Indian hemp and bulrush or "tule." Indian hemp was the primary and preferred source of fibers used for binding and twined weaving. The thin reddish inner bark was stripped from the pithy stems after the plant had dried. The bast fibers were separated by beating and the shredded fibers then twisted together by rolling a bunch of fibers on the leg ("Wasco, Wishram, and Cascades," fig. 8, this vol.). Women devoted many hours to this task during the long winters, and a ball of hemp twine was highly valued in trade. Hemp twine was knotted to make fishing nets (fig. 3) and nets for catching rabbits, the size of the mesh fixed using a wooden net guage. "Seine nets" made of Indian hemp near the mouth of the John Day River in 1811 were 2.6 meters wide by "50 fathoms" (100 m) long (Glover 1962:353). Hemp string was also used to twine root-collecting bags and the characteristic Plateau woman's hat in the shape of a truncated cone ("Basketry," fig. 2, this vol.). Such twined "baskets" were decorated with beargrass leaves and later with cornhusk imbrication (Schlick 1994). Hemp was also essential for binding hoops and points to shafts, and rope of various weights could be made by braiding the twine.

Tule stalks were cut in late summer while still green, then spread on the ground to dry in a house or shed. They were cut and sewn to form the mats used to cover winter lodges and summer tepees (fig. 4) and to cover walls and floors within the lodges. The cellulose matrix of the stalks provided excellent insulation. They were also used as table mats or food-drying platforms. A corpse was clothed in buckskin, then wrapped in a tule mat shroud for burial.

Cattail leaves, flat and flexible, were used to weave rough-and-ready bags, which were lined with salmon skin for storing salmon meal. If a more rigid, open-work mat were required, for example as a support for draining freshly cleaned salmon, the stalks of common reed were preferred. Stalks of giant wild rye grass were placed between salmon

fillets to absorb the blood and oils, as it imparted no unpleasant taste to the fish, and served as a layer separating food stuffs from the soil used to cover the earth oven. Dye plants and colorants include the bark of alder and Oregon grape, wolf lichen, Indian paint fungus (*Echinodontium tinctorium*), and the rhizomes of sand dock.

Deer and elk were as important for their hides as for their meat, if not more so. Mule deer hides were first pegged-out for initial drying, then stored until ready for softening. Women took charge of this process. The hides were soaked overnight in a fatty solution of deer brains in water, sometimes with sturgeon heads added. They were then wrung out and draped over a curved tree branch for scraping. The hide was dehaired and cleaned of flesh with a two-handled metal-bladed scraper, aboriginally with an elk rib (Murdock 1980:136). The scraped skin was then stretched on a vertical wooden frame ("Yakima and Neighboring Groups," fig. 8, this vol.) for final scraping and softening with a hafted polished stone ax blade. Skins might then be smoked (fig. 5) or bleached, using the root of chocolate tips.

Dressed hides were cut to pattern for moccasins, leggings, shirts, and wing dresses. The thicker elk hides were used for moccasin soles, robes, armor, and drum heads. Rabbit skins dried with the fur intact were sewn to make winter socks and mittens. Twisted rabbitskin blankets are reported in the early 1800s in lieu of deerskin clothing or for their superior warmth (Suphan 1974). River otter and weasel skins were cut in strips and braided into the hair for decoration.

Other animal products used in technology include deer sinew (taken from the backbone) used for bowstrings and as backing for the wooden bow; rawhide strips for bindings; deer hooves for dance rattles; elk antler for flaking stone or for gaff hooks; and deer bone for fish spear points, hooks, and chokers (Murdock 1980; Hunn 1976–1993). Bighorn sheep horn was used to make spoons and bowls; porcupine quills were cut, dyed, and sewn to clothing for ornamentation; beaver musk sacks were prized by men as love charms; horse hair was employed to "lasso" small fish and as a horse's bit and bridle (Moulton 1983–, 7:167). The hollow wing bones of geese and eagles were fashioned into whistles; Northern flicker feathers were used for personal adornment; tail and flight feathers of bald and golden eagles were considered sacred regalia and were buried with the deceased.

Shell ornaments were obtained in trade from coastal Indians; the antiquity of this trade is attested by large quantities of abalone, olivella, and tusk shell found in the Marmes Rockshelter on the lower Snake River dating back 9,000 or more years (Browman and Munsell 1969; Kirk and Daugherty 1978:68).

Structures

Two types of winter dwellings are known. Most familiar is the A-frame tule-mat-covered lodge or longhouse. James

Fig. 5. Deer hide preparation and products. left, Mary Hote Tom smoking a skin, which helped to preserve and color it. The slow-burning fire is in the metal container in front of her. Photograph by David and Kathrine French, Warm Springs Res., Oreg., 1953. center, Flat case with long side fringes used to store ceremonial materials. Collected by E.T. Houtz, Warm Springs Res., Oreg., 1899. right, Tenino parfleche with diamond and triangular design in orange, brown, yellow, and green. Parfleches were used for the storage and transport of dried foods and household goods. Collected by R.E. Stewart, 1905. Width of center without fringe, 31 cm; height of right, 152 cm.

Selam, a John Day River elder, was raised in such a house in the 1920s. About 20 meters long by nine wide, it housed nine families (personal communication 1989). Such lodges were built parallel to the river shore, if the lay of the land allowed, with the door or doors in the side facing the winter sun but away from the prevailing winter winds.

The floors of the lodges were excavated 60–90 centimeters, the lateral lodge poles set down in the excavation and braced against the sides, leaning steeply against a rectangular roof frame supported by vertical house posts set in the center of the floor. Additional poles were leaned against the ends of the roof frame to form the semicircular end walls. Willow branch stringers tied the frame together horizontally and provided a surface on which to tie the tule mats. Up to three overlapping layers of mats might be used for maximal protection from the cold. On the outside the bases of the mats were banked up 60–90 centimeters with dirt over a layer of giant wild rye grass. The doorway could be double—a sort of airlock to keep out the weather—covered at either end with mats. A sloping walkway led down to the level of the sunken floor.

Hearths were placed along the center line, allowing smoke to escape through the open roof frame. Most lodges accommodated three or more related nuclear families. Two brothers' families often shared a single hearth. A household head was recognized; his family occupied the western end of the lodge. Though food might be prepared on more than one hearth, it was shared by all occupants of the lodge, who considered one another *náymu* 'family'. These lodges were

dismantled in spring and the mats transported for use with tepee poles stored at overnight camp sites.

A second type of winter dwelling was circular and excavated to a depth of about 2.5 meters. Poles were leaned from the ground surface against a roof frame supported by vertical poles set in the center of the floor. One entered by means of steps or a ladder through a doorway on one side or through the central smoke hole by means of a ladder (Ray 1942). Archeological evidence for such houses in the form of roughly circular depressions is widespread, suggesting the possibility that the A-frame lodge replaced the earlier circular semisubterranean house in protohistoric times.

Summer housing was either a circular mat-covered tepee, typical of camps in the mountains, or a rectangular, open-walled ramada serving also as a fish-drying shelter (Perkins 1843). Sweatlodges were typically dome-shaped structures approximately two meters in diameter and 1.2 meters high. They were constructed of a willow branch framework tied together with willow bark, covered with a rug, blanket, or robe, or aboriginally with earth over layers of giant wild rye grass. A rectangular doorway was framed facing the fire where the stones were heated (fig. 6) and the river where the bathers rinsed after each stint in the lodge. The heated stones were placed in a hearth just to the left inside the entrance. The floor was covered with branches of fir, favored for its healing scent. This daily ritual was performed by men and women separately. If a hunt was planned it was essential, as decreed by Coyote (cf. Jacobs 1929:200).

385

Fig. 6. James Selam, John Day River, fanning flames of an open fire to heat sweatlodge rocks. Photograph by Brien Meilleur, near Toppenish, Yakima Res., Wash., 1977.

A menstrual seclusion hut is reported (Ray 1942). Food storage cellars were pits lined with giant wild rye grass and tule mats and sealed with dirt. They were constructed near the winter lodge. Most food was stored in such cellars rather than in the lodge, in contrast to what has been reported for their Upper Chinookan neighbors (Moulton 1983–, 5:331, 335).

Lean-to structures were constructed as charnel houses on islands in the Columbia. Lewis and Clark describe one about 18 meters long by four meters wide located in the Columbia River a short distance above Alder Creek (Moulton 1983–, 5:311–312).

Transportation

Travel and transport was by foot, canoe, and, since before 1750, horseback. Large burden baskets were carried on the back supported from a rawhide tumpline across the forehead (women) or the shoulders (men). Canoes were dugouts, carved from drift logs of cedar or pine.

Social Organization

• KINSHIP A web of kinship relationships constituted the fundamental organizational basis for Western Columbia Sahaptin society, a web extending well beyond the borders of the territory covered in this chapter. Dyadic relations rather than sociocentric corporate groups were the most important filaments in this web. Unilineal descent groups were entirely lacking.

Kinship is reckoned bilaterally with very few exceptions. The cousin terminology has been classified as Hawaiian, while first-ascending generation referential kinship terminology is bifurcate collateral, that is, "uncles" and "aunts" are distinguished from parents as well as by maternal or paternal side. Sibling terms differentiate elder and younger siblings by sex of alter and, among younger siblings, by sex of ego as well. All six sibling terms are generalized to same

generation collateral kin beyond first cousins without specific limit.

Terms for first-ascending-generation collateral kin are likewise "extended" to more distant collateral, parent-generation relations; that is, father's "brother" is not distinguished from father's "male cousin," just as one's own "brother" is equated with one's own same-generation male cousins. These parental-generation collateral "extensions" hold two key distinctions constant: sex of alter and sex of linking parent. As a consequence of these naming conventions, each person has a very large number of "aunts," "uncles," and "siblings," all of whom are expected to treat one with the special consideration due one's kinfolk in Plateau society.

The principle of nomenclatural reciprocity is pervasive. It is best illustrated by the referential terms for second-ascending-generation kin. Four terms are used that distinguish father's father, mother's mother, father's mother, and mother's father. However, since these terms are each self-reciprocal, the term for paternal "grandfather" is also used by a senior male to refer to his son's children, in other words, his "grandsons" and "granddaughters" via his son. These same four terms are extended to the siblings (and cousins) of one's "grandparents" as well as to one's great-grandparents and their siblings (and cousins). In each instance, two key criteria remain constant: the sex of the senior party to the relationship and the sex of the parent of the junior party. This system, which is described for the John Day and supported by Hunn's (1976–1993) consultants, contradicts Murdock (1958).

The first-ascending-generation collateral terms are not in general self-reciprocal but exhibit a complex (and variable) pattern. Father's brother and a man's brother's child are separately named. The terms for father's brother and his reciprocal are "extended" to father's male same-generation cousins, to mother's sister's husband, and to step-fathers and their reciprocal relations. Mother's sister and father's sister are likewise distinguished from their reciprocals, but these are in turn distinguished by sex. Each is then extended to parents' cousins and their respective male and female junior-generation reciprocals. Mother's sister is equated with father's brother's wife and stepmother, while father's sister and mother's brother's wife are equated, as are their respective reciprocals. Finally, by contrast, mother's brother and a man's sister's child are *not* distinguished from one another but are labeled self-reciprocally, with the term "extended" as usual to mother's male same-generation cousins, etc (cf. Murdock 1958).

Sibling-in-law terms (likewise extended to same-generation cousins of spouses and spouses of cousins) single out the opposite sex relationships. These are labeled by a single self-reciprocal term, *pnúk*, which is changed to *awít* at the death of the linking spouse/sibling (cousin). This is a simple expression of the importance of the levirate and sororate in Western Columbia River Sahaptin society.

The three parent-in-law/child-in-law terms are also self-reciprocal, the husband but not the wife distinguishing his mother-in-law from his father-in-law. A single term is used self-reciprocally by coparents. Spouses of siblings-in-law are labeled by an alternate set of three sibling/friend terms that distinguish, as do the sibling-in-law terms, male-male, female-female, and cross-sex linkages. Cowives in premodern polygynous marriages referred to each other by the female-female sibling/friend term in cases of sororal polygyny (Hunn 1990:205).

• SOCIAL GROUPS   The dyadic relations among kin described above coalesced to constitute distinct social groups at four levels: the nuclear family, the hearth group, the winter lodge household, and the village (sometimes including satellite settlements). The nuclear family shared a common hearth and sleeping area within the winter lodge and traveled together throughout the seasonal round (though groups of men might travel on hunting, fishing, or raiding excursions, while groups of women might travel to root-digging camps). In the case of sororal polygyny, such nuclear family units were extended to include the two wives and their offspring. In other polygynous marriages the husband divided his allegiance between the two families, which typically lived in different villages (cf. Murdock 1958:306). Relations between cowives in such cases were strained, as is indicated by the use of the term ƛáwi 'rival' (Hunn 1990:205).

Hearth units paired closely related nuclear families, often those of "brothers." The casual intimacy expected between cross-sex siblings-in-law facilitated the close cooperation of such joint families. The winter lodge was occupied by an extended family unit under the recognized leadership of a household head, a senior man. Little specific information exists as to the precise composition of winter lodges other than the repeated assertion that all occupants were of one 'family' (náymu) and that all coresident families freely shared all food consumed within the house. Membership in such winter lodge groups varied from year to year, with nuclear families or hearth units free to realign themselves with kin who were resident in other lodges or in other villages. The size of such lodge groups varied from a few nuclear families to perhaps as many as 40, numbering several hundred individuals (cf. Glover 1962:353).

One to a dozen or more such lodges erected in close proximity constituted a winter village (nišáykt). One or more outstanding men in each such village were recognized as 'chiefs' (miyúux). Chiefs (more accurately, 'village headmen') were expected to exhort their people to hard work and proper conduct, yet to do so in an appropriately dignified, quiet manner. To this end, each chief was assisted by a spokesman (sínwiłá) who repeated the chief's exhortations in a commanding voice. The village chief's authority was based on proven talents and abilities, ideally combining generosity, eloquence, self-discipline, and devotion to the welfare of his people. The position of 'chief' was not strictly speaking hereditary, but there was a recognized "hierarchy of right" by which the chieftainship would normally

pass from a father to his sons, in order of seniority, then to a brother (or male cousin) (cf. Murdock 1980:144). However, many eligible individuals declined or were passed over for lack of the motivation or talent judged necessary to fill the role. It is not clear whether women in certain unusual circumstances might be recognized as chiefs.

Since the early twentieth century a "salmon chief" has been recognized at Celilo Falls. His authority included declaring fishing seasons open and closed and ordering that fishing stop for purposes of escapement or when ritual required (e.g., for funerals). The antiquity of this role is not clearly attested. Other specialized roles include one or more senior men designated as 'whippers' (pawawyałá), who were called upon by parents to administer discipline to unruly children. Paternal grandfathers also whipped their grandchildren with sandbar willow withes to instill values of self-discipline and hardiness (Murdock 1958:311). A role of 'disciplinarian' (iyánča) may also have been recognized (Hunn 1990:253).

• DIVISION OF LABOR   Other than by sex and age there was no division of productive labor. Women normally gathered roots, berries, and other vegetable foods. They also had

Fig. 7. Chief Queahpama's monument. Photograph by Francis Seufert, Indian cemetery at Simnasho, Warm Springs Res., Oreg., date not recorded.

charge of cleaning, drying, and cooking those foods as well as the fish and game caught by the men. Men assisted in these tasks, for example, by hauling wood and heating stones and excavating for the underground oven. Men and women cooperated in certain hunting activities, such as rabbit drives. Men also helped collect plant material that the women used to make mats and twined bags.

Women spun the hemp cord, but men knotted it into fish nets. Making clothing and beadwork has changed in the twentieth century (fig. 8).

Life Cycle

At puberty boys were sent on vision quests and were expected to learn adult skills appropriate to their gender; these achievements are ritually marked. Puberty per se was not marked by special rituals for boys, but girls were secluded in a menstrual hut where they were attended by older women.

Marriages were usually arranged at the instance of the young man but occasionally by his parents, whose permission was always required. Males typically married at about 20 years of age, females at between 15 and 18. Weddings involved an elaborate exchange of presents between the families of the bride and the groom. The gifts made by the groom's relatives consisted of items associated with the male role, and the bride's kinsmen contributed products of feminine industry (Murdock 1980: 140–141).

Religion

Fundamental concepts of Western Columbia River Sahaptin religion include *waq̓áyšwit* 'life', an animating principle or "soul" possessed by people as well as animals, plants, and forces of nature. The presence of 'life' implies intelligence, will, and consciousness. This is the basis for a pervasive animistic morality, in which all living beings should respect one another and are involved with one another in relations of generalized reciprocity. One's 'life' might weaken but could also be strengthened, particularly at critical seasonal transitions, by consuming certain tonic medicines, for example, an infusion of lodgepole pine foliage.

For even average success in life a person required the assistance of spirit powers, which are called *súkat* or *táaχ* locally. One obtained this assistance most often through a vision quest (Murdock 1980:145).

"Indian doctors" (*twátima*), male and female, were shamans, individuals recognized as possessed of extraordinary spiritual powers by virtue of numerous and particularly powerful spirit allies (Murdock 1965a:167) gained through a charismatic calling and repeated vision questing. Shamans were called upon to cure diseases attributed to soul loss or the intentional or unintended intrusion of spirit powers. Shamans prepared patients and their kin for a cure by demonstrating their extraordinary powers by drinking boiling water or handling hot coals. They were assisted by family members of the patient designated as 'beaters' (*wapašałá*), who kept up an intense rhythmic accompaniment throughout the shaman's performance by beating sticks against a resonant log.

Shamans conducted rituals of community-wide significance, such as the First Salmon ceremony at Celilo Falls (Perkins 1843, 1:7). They also hosted Winter Spirit Dances and helped neophytes express their spirit powers in dance and song. Certain shamans were known to have used their powers to kill, spirit power itself being morally neutral. They were called *wałayłam* 'sorcerers'.

center, Smithsonian, Dept. of Anthr.: 204234 (neg. 95–20812); right, High Desert Mus., Doris Swayze Bounds Coll., Bend, Oreg.: 2.6.177.

Fig. 8. Beadwork. left, Eva Polk beading the front of a buckskin vest, while Blanche Tohet works on another piece of the garment. In the 1950s beadwork was done by women, but in the 1980s men began to take it up both as a pastime and as a source of income. Photograph by David and Kathrine French, Warm Springs, Oreg., 1952. center, Beaded red stroud cloth bag. The shape and stylized tripartite floral design of this bag and the absence of background beading suggest that this bag may have been manufactured in the mid-19th century (Gogol 1985:5). Collected by E.T. Houtz, Warm Springs, Oreg., 1899. right, Beaded bag. While deer had been a popular subject of beaded bags since the late 19th century, some 20th-century Plateau artists began to portray deer and other animals in detailed depictions of their natural settings. Made by Ellen Heath in the 1930s. Height of center, 20 cm; height of right, 37 cm.

HUNN AND FRENCH

Fig. 9. Charles Spedis at prayers during a Celilo Festival, Celilo Park, Oreg. Photograph by Gladys Seufert, 1966.

A native concept fundamental to traditional social and moral conduct is *tamánwit* 'the law' or 'creation': patterns of conduct considered natural and necessary, as decreed by the Creator (*tamanwiłá*), a figure distinct from but sometimes conflated with the myth-hero Coyote (*spilyáy*), who declares the "law" in preparation for the imminent coming of Indian people at the conclusion of the myth age. This law is, of course, unwritten, but is embodied in the collectivity of Western Columbia River Sahaptin mythology. There are at least 60 distinct stories or episodes, in most of which Coyote figures as the central character. Western Columbia River Sahaptin myths are reproduced in English translation in Ramsey (1977) and in Sahaptin with interlinear translation by Rigsby (1978). Recorded Klikitat and Upper Cowlitz myths (Jacobs 1929, 1934–1937) are familiar to local Indian elders, differing only in minor details (James Selam, personal communication 1977).

•WASHAT RELIGION The institutional focus of contemporary Sahaptin religious practice is Washat *(wáashat* '(a) dance', from *wáasha-* 'to dance, especially a worship dance'), whose adherents are *waasaní* 'dancers'. Four Washat congregations were active as of 1990 in the Western Columbia River Sahaptin area, at Rock Creek, Washington, and at Celilo, Simnasho, and Warm Springs, Oregon. Each selected a spiritual leader who conducted Sunday services as principal bell ringer, and whose responsibilities included regular exhortations to the congregation, as well as assuring the proper conduct of life cycle rituals, the most important of which were funerals.

The basic forms of worship for the Washat have been faithfully maintained at least since the late nineteenth cen-

tury ("Religious Movements," this vol.). Many details of Washat ritual conduct and ideology derive from the dream-inspired messages of the nineteenth-century prophet Smohalla, who died but was returned to his body with instructions for the proper conduct of one's life and worship. A contemporary prophet was *šxmáya*, resident at Skin. Many features of Washat worship attributed to Smohalla, such as a sacred flag and the oriole as symbol of life, were also part of *šxmáya*'s teaching, suggesting a more diffuse and perhaps aboriginal origin to many elements of this practice. The central importance of the worship dance, including details of its form, are clearly aboriginal (Glover 1962:353; cf. Spier 1935).

Essential to contemporary Washat ritual are the thanksgiving feasts for the first appearance of traditional foods (fig. 10). The Rock Creek congregation honors *latítlatit* (Indian celery) and suckers in late February, for example.

Washat congregations are not exclusive. Individuals with complementary allegiances to a Christian denomination, to the Indian Shaker church, and to the Feather cult are welcome to participate fully in Washat services. The last stronghold of the Feather cult in 1993 was on the Warm Springs Reservation (Stowell 1987:52, 171).

History

Sometime after 1730 horses obtained from Spaniards were introduced via the Cayuse, Nez Perce, and Umatilla. About 1780 a pandemic smallpox spread either from Northwest Coast or Plains contacts. A second epidemic is dated in 1801 and affected those born since the first; cumulative mortality is estimated at 45 percent. During 1805–1806 the Lewis and Clark expedition passed through the area along the Columbia River. In 1811 David Thompson of the North West Company traversed the region accompanied by Astorians seeking to establish upriver fur trading stations. The Hudson's Bay Company established a post at the mouth of the Walla Walla River in 1818, a key point of contact through 1855 (Stern 1993, 1996). From 1825 to 1831 Hudson's Bay Company fur brigades traversed the John Day River basin. During 1838 to 1847 there was a Methodist mission at The Dalles (Perkins 1838–1844). In 1847, 4,000 immigrants passed through The Dalles; by 1852 the settler stream had become a flood, with 12,000 traversing Western Columbia River Sahaptin lands en route to coastal valleys.

In 1855 Joel Palmer negotiated a treaty with the tribes of middle Oregon. In that treaty the tribes ceded 10 million acres to the United States and the United States established Warm Springs Reservation, about 640,000 acres. In 1865 a second treaty restricted off-reservation travel and subsistence rights; this treaty was ruled invalid in 1969. In 1874 the first on-reservation boarding school was built; the Agency boarding school, *389*

Fig. 10. Root feasts. top, Rock Creek Longhouse, Wash., where root feast and other tribal celebrations of both the Warm Springs Res., Oreg., and Yakima Res., Wash. are held. Photograph by Helen Willard, 1980. bottom left, Root gatherers led in prayer by Elsie Pistolhead (third from left) on a ridge above Medicine Valley, Yakima Res. These prayers were in preparation for a "first foods" celebration to be held at Rock Creek Longhouse. Photograph by Eugene Hunn, 1977. bottom right, Annual first-foods ceremony, at the beginning of root-digging season. Religious songs are being sung, and the women are keeping time to the singing with their right hands. Photograph by David and Kathrine French, Warm Springs Res., Oreg., 1951.

established in 1897, did not close until 1967. About 1900 Jake Hunt (*tiičam-nášat* 'Earth Thunder') established the Feather cult.

In 1937 the Warm Springs Tribes adopted a tribal constitution and by-laws under provisions of the Indian Reorganization Act. In 1953 the Warm Springs Tribes were exempted from Public Law 83–280, which transferred civil and criminal jurisdiction over reservations to local authorities. When The Dalles Dam was completed in 1957 (fig. 12), flooding Celilo Falls, the Warm Springs

Tribes received a four million dollar settlement for loss of a share of those fisheries. Pelton Reregulation Dam was completed on the Deschutes River in 1959; the John Day Dam was completed in 1962; and Round Butte Dam in 1964.

In continuing litigation, in 1969 *United States* v. *Oregon* established a treaty right to "a fair and equitable share" of anadromous fish runs (vol. 7:175–176). In 1975 the fishing rights decision was extended to the Columbia River tribes, and a Comprehensive Fisheries Management Plan

Fig. 11. Mancemuckt, chief of the Skin. He was wearing a fox skin cap and leather deerskin shirt (Harper 1971:112). Watercolor by Paul Kane, 1847.

was adopted. In 1980 the Sherar's Bridge fishery was purchased by the Warm Springs Tribes.

Warm Springs Reservation

The Confederated Tribes of the Warm Springs Reservation included three tribal groups (Zucker, Hummel, and Høgfoss 1983; Confederated Tribes of the Warm Springs Reservation of Oregon 1984; Stowell 1987). The four Sahaptin-speaking groups represented at the treaty council—Tenino, Wyampam (Celilo), Ta-ih (Tygh Valley), and Dock-spus (John Day), known collectively as Warm Springs Indians—were concentrated in the vicinity of Simnasho. Three groups speaking Kiksht (Upper Chinook) represented at the treaty council were in 1997 known as Wascos. They were concentrated in the central portion of the reservation near the agency. The third tribe, the Northern Paiutes, settled on the reservation after 1879 and were concentrated on the southern portion of the reservation. Each tribal division is represented on the tribal council by a chief, who serves a term for life; the eight other council members are elected by district and serve three-year terms. Tribal council decisions are subject to review by a general council of all adult tribal members. Membership requires one-quarter or more blood of the Confederated Tribes and birth to a tribal member residing on the reservation. Tribal enrollment was 3,410 in 1993.

A general manager appointed by the tribal council oversees the operation of the tribal corporation. The Warm Springs Tribes invested the bulk of the settlement for the destruction of the Celilo Falls fishery in tribal commercial enterprises. The most successful of these include the Warm Springs Forest Products Industries mill and plywood plant established in 1967. This enterprise allows the tribes to retain the financial benefits derived from the sustained-yield harvest of reservation timber and to employ 300 tribal members. Forest products accounted for over two-thirds of tribal income in the early 1980s (Confederated Tribes of the Warm Springs Reservation of Oregon 1984:54). Other tribal commercial enterprises include the Warm Springs Power Industries, which sells electric power from the tribally owned Pelton Reregulation Dam and the Kah-Nee-Ta resort complex.

Warm Springs Sahaptin survived as the predominant native language in the 1990s on the reservation. Sahaptin speakers are prominent among the leadership of the Washat religion. A small off-reservation community persisted at Celilo Village on trust land at the site of Celilo Falls. Many Western Columbia River Sahaptin descendants gathered there for the spring salmon and root feast at the Celilo Longhouse, home to a Washat congregation. In 1993 Howard Jim, originally of the Pine Creek community, served as Celilo chief. Joining him on the informal Council of Columbia River Indian Chiefs were Frederick Ike, Rock Creek chief; Johnny Jackson, Cascades chief; and Wilbur Slokish, Klikitat chief. Key concerns of this council were the federal government's unmet promise of in lieu fishing sites to replace those flooded by Bonneville Dam and the continued recognition of a Columbia River Indian identity and interest distinct from that of the established treaty tribes.

Population

Lewis and Clark (Moulton 1983–, 5:309–336) provide a detailed count of lodges seen along their route down the Columbia. From the mouth of the Umatilla River to the first Upper Chinookan village they tallied 174 lodges, though their population summary lists only 145 (Moulton 1983–, 6:474–475). While some parties were absent hunting, it seems that the bulk of the population was present on the river and that the count of lodges provides a reasonably accurate basis for approximating the local population.

It is possible to assign the lodges counted to contemporary village groupings roughly as in table 1. The 1805 population for the Western Columbia River Sahaptins is estimated at 4,156. This figure departs from Lewis and Clark's population estimates for their "E-ne-shur" division, extrapolating from the large number of lodges reported in the narrative and adding an estimate of the upper Deschutes River population of which Lewis and Clark were unaware. David Thompson's estimates yield a similar result (Glover 1962:347–354, 370–375). Combining his estimates, made while descending and ascending the Columbia in 1811 and using his estimated value of seven persons per family (Glover 1962:378) results in 162 families and 1,134 people

Fig. 12. Chief Tommy Thompson, head of Celilo Village, Oreg. left, Chief Thompson and his wife Flora dressed in buckskin clothing heavily influenced by Plains style. Photographer and date not recorded. right, Ceremonial fan constructed of beaded buckskin and 10 hawk feathers with beaded quills. It was made by Henry Thompson for his father Chief Thompson, who carried it at the dedication of The Dalles Dam in 1957. Length of handle, 9 cm.

in the Alder Creek to Rock Creek interval, 155 families and 1,085 people between Rock Creek and the Deschutes River, and 150 families and 1,190 people in the Celilo Falls vicinity for a total of 467 families and 3,409 people.

Synonymy

Tenino (*tináynu*) was a small fishing village located opposite the Upper Chinookan village of Spearfish (*wíšxam*; *nixlúidix* in Upper Chinookan; home of the "Wish-ham" of the Yakima treaty) at the head of Five-Mile Rapids. Residents were known as *tinaynułáma* 'people of *tináynu*' (Rigsby 1965:54–57). They are the "Tenino band of Walla-Wallas" of the Treaty of Middle Oregon. According to Murdock (1958:299), this summer village was linked to a winter village site (*tíqáxtíqax*) eight kilometers south on Eightmile Creek.

The term Tenino has been inappropriately generalized to refer to an arbitrary set of Columbia River Sahaptin-speaking village groups extending west from the Umatilla to the village of Tenino (Mooney 1896:742; Hodge 1907; Ray 1938 following Murdock 1938a; Murdock 1958, 1965a, 1980).

Skin (*skín*) was a large permanent village located at the foot of Celilo Falls on the Washington shore. People associated with this village are known as *skínłáma* (or *skínpa* in Northwest Sahaptin dialects, cf. the "Skin-pah" of the Yakima treaty). The village is named for a prominent rock at the lip of the falls shaped like a cradleboard, called *skín* (Mooney 1896:740), specifically Coyote's cradleboard as related in the myth of the Swallow Sisters' dam (Beavert 1974:34–37). The peoples about Celilo Falls are the E-ne-shur of Lewis and Clark (Moulton 1983–, 7:149), including the villages *skín*, *wayám*, and most likely *wápaykt*.

Celilo or Wayam (*wayám* 'above'), a large summer fishing village, was permanently occupied in the twentieth century. The people of this side of the falls are known as *wayamłáma* (cf. Mooney's ⟨waiäm-'lĕma⟩ 1896:741). They are the "Wyam band of Walla-Wallas" of the Treaty of Middle Oregon. Skin and Celilo were distinct, politically autonomous communities recognizing no common chief though closely intermarried (James Selam, personal communication 1992). Murdock (1958:300) states that the people of Wayam wintered at *wanwáwi*, a village "on the left bank of the Deschutes River just above its junction with the Columbia." Rigsby (1965:54) cites an associated winter village "/tqux/, at the mouth of the Deschutes River." Hunn's consultants locate a site called *tku* 'bulrush' on Miller Island opposite the mouth of the Deschutes, which may be the same site as that noted by Rigsby. Mooney (1896:740) located the

Ind. U., William Hammond Mathers Mus., Bloomington.

Fig. 13. Charlie Hellon (b. about 1867). Photograph by Joseph K. Dixon, Warm Springs Res., Oreg., 1913.

Table 1. Lewis and Clark Population Estimates

Village	Lodges	1805[a]	1775[a]
tamalám (imatílam)	44	1,364	2,482
níšx	24[b]	744	1,354
náwawi (kkáasuwi)	4[b]	124	226
Total	72	2,232	4,062
Pish-quit-pah	71	2,600[c]	4,732
pawánpat	8	248	451
q̓miłtáwaš	11	341	621
takšpáš	10	310	564
wálawitsis	5	155	282
Total	34	1,054	1,918
Wah-how-pum	33	700	1,274
wayám, wanwáwi, tku	45	1,395	2,539
sk̓in, wapáykt	22	682	1,241
tináynu	5	155	282
Total	72	2,232	4,062
E-ne-chur	41	1,200	2,184
Tygh Valley	20	620	1,128
Total	130	4,030	7,334
Total Sahaptins	198	6,138	11,170
Total Lewis and Clark count	145	4,500	8,190

[a]The 1805 population estimates are based on an average lodge population of 31, which is derived from Lewis and Clark's lodge and population totals for the Columbia River Sahaptins, 4,500 people in 145 lodges. The 1775 figures are 1.82 times as large to accommodate the 45% mortality from the 1780 and 1801 smallpox epidemics (Boyd 1985). The discrepancy in house counts for the E-ne-chur and the lodge counts cannot be reconciled.

[b]The Western Columbia River Sahaptin total includes the *náwawi-łáma* of Lewis and Clark's Pish-quit-pah subgroup, all the Wah-how-pum and E-ne-chur groups, plus an estimate for the Tygh Valley *(tayx)*.

[c]The total was reduced to 1,600 (Moulton 1983–, 6:477).

"Ochechotes" of the Yakima Treaty here, rendering the name "Uchichol," from "the name of a rock on the north side of the Columbia, opposite the upper end of the island [Miller Island], at the mouth of the Des Chutes." He also located a tribe he called the ⟨Tapänä´sh⟩ at this point, which he equated with Lewis and Clark's Eneshur (Mooney 1896:740).

Tygh Valley (*táyx*) was a village near the junction of Tygh Creek and the White River. The residents of this village were known as *tayxłáma*. They are the "Ta-ih or Upper Deschutes band of Walla-Wallas" of the Treaty of Middle Oregon; Mooney's ⟨Tai´-ăq⟩ (1896:742). Murdock (1958:300) asserts that Sherar's Bridge (*tiłxni*) was the summer fishing village of the people who wintered at *tayx*; however, Rigsby's (1965:57) consultants described the *tiłxniłáma* as distinct from the *tayxłáma*. Mooney (1896:742) also distinguishes them as ⟨Tĭ´lqûni⟩. Rigsby's consultants also recognized a group known as *mlitáma* 'people of the Hot Springs', resident at Simnasho. Mooney (1896:742–743) equates the ⟨Mĕli´-´lĕma⟩ with the Tenino, a term he uses to refer to the entire Columbia River Sahaptin population.

Maryhill (*wálawitis*) village was on the Washington shore. People associated with this village are known as *walawitisłáma*.

The John Day (*takšpáš*) village was located at a rapids on the John Day River. Its people are *takšpašłáma*. These are

the "Dock-spus band of Walla-Wallas" of the Treaty of Middle Oregon (cf. Mooney 1896:743). Murdock (1958: 300) states that "tekcpe´c" was "the principal winter village" of the John Day and located it "three miles above ... junction with the Columbia." He locates a second, smaller John Day winter village, "[name: maxa´xpa], a mile or two downstream on the left bank." He describes "ta´wac" [*táwaš*] as "the principal summer village... [of the John Day River people] located on the south bank of the Columbia River." Rigsby located *maxáx* above *takšpáš* on the John Day and placed *táwaš* near present-day Quinton. James Selam (personal communication 1976) was raised at *táwaš*, which he locates at the mouth of Blalock Canyon on the Oregon shore. He confirms that the people of *táwaš* are *takšpášłáma* but describes *táwaš* as a subsidiary winter village rather than as the summer retreat of the John Day people.

Rock Creek (*q̓mit*) is a permanent village located near the mouth of Rock Creek, Washington. The people associated with this village are known as *q̓miłtáma*. Murdock (1958:300) relegates "q'e´mel" to the status of "an offshoot of 'ta´wac,'" but Rigsby's and Hunn's consultants describe *q̓mił* as a politically autonomous community. Mooney (1896:736) misplaces this group, which he renders "Qamīl-'lĕma," locating them "about Saddle Mountain, on the east side of the Columbia, above Priest Rapids." Rather, they are the "Kah-milt-pah" of the Yakima treaty and most likely also Lewis and Clark's "Wah-how-pum" (Moulton 1983–, 7:161–162; cf. Mooney's ⟨Hāhau´pûm⟩ 1896:739), a term that has been incorrectly interpreted as a transcriptional variant of *x̣ʷátx̣way-pam* 'Klikitat' (Ray 1938:389).

Arlington (*tamaypx̣tá*) village may have been considered part of the John Day community (Rigsby 1965:53) or have been more closely associated with the Roosevelt and Pine Creek communities. Lewis and Clark identify a "band" in this vicinity they call the Met-cow-wes (Moulton 1983–, 7:164).

Roosevelt (*nišx̣úawi*) village was located just below the mouth of Wood Canyon on the Washington shore opposite *tamaypx̣tá*. Roosevelt people sometimes wintered at Pine Creek or Alderdale.

Pine Creek (*pawánpat*) village was located at the mouth of Pine Creek on the Washington shore. Its people, known as *pawanpatłáma*, consider themselves "one people" with those at Alderdale (Howard Jim, personal communication 1991).

Alderdale (*náwawi*) village was located at the mouth of Alder Creek on the Washington shore. Its people are known as *nawawiłáma*. Rigsby (1965:48) groups Alderdale people with his Umatilla dialect group. However, *náwawi* consultants recognize no such association and have their strongest social contacts with other Western Columbia River Sahaptins (Hunn 1976–1993). Mooney's (1896:739) k̓ásāwi-'lĕma [*kkaasuwiłáma*, from *kkáasu* 'serviceberry' (Kowwassayee of the Yakima Treaty) may be an alternative designation for Indians along this stretch of the Columbia, as a site with this name has been identified just above the mouth of Alder Creek on the north bank of the Columbia (Suphan 1974:159).

Sources

The most valuable ethnohistorical sources include the journals of Lewis and Clark (Moulton 1983–, 5, 7) and of David Thompson (Glover 1962). Both traveled down and then up the Columbia River throughout the length of Western Columbia River Sahaptin territory. Evidence for land use patterns and seasonal movements away from the Columbia is limited, coming mostly from the journals of John Work (1923) and Peter Skene Ogden (Elliott 1909–1910) of the Hudson's Bay Company, who explored the John Day River in the 1820s and early 1830s, and those of Nathaniel Wyeth (1899) and John Charles Frémont (1845). Wyeth explored the Deschutes River during the winter of 1834–1835, while Frémont traversed that area in 1843–1844. Hale (1846) and Wilkes (1845) report on the United States Exploring Expedition, in the area during 1841. The diaries and letters of missionaries stationed at the Methodists' Wascopam mission at The Dalles contain much relevant ethnographic information (Lee and Frost 1844; Perkins 1843). Kane (1925) left a pictorial record of the Indians at Celilo Falls in 1846. Doty (1855) and Palmer (1855) describe the context of treaty negotiations. Abbot (1855) reported the findings of a railroad survey up the Deschutes River. Western Columbia River Sahaptin word lists recorded by Meriwether Lewis and Henry K.W. Perkins have been lost.

Ethnographic summaries date to the 1930s. Spier and Sapir's (1930) Wishram ethnography includes some information specific to neighboring Western Columbia River Sahaptin speakers. Murdock spent the summers of 1934 and 1935 in the field at the Warm Springs Reservation (1938a, 1958, 1965a, 1980). V. Ray (1942) interviewed one local informant for the Culture Element Distribution project, Moses Hellon, identified as Wayampam. Spier (1935) and C. Du Bois (1938) interviewed Western Columbia River Sahaptin individuals during their investigations of Plateau religious movements. Suphan's (1974) testimony before the Indian Claims Commission provides a valuable ethnohistoric summary, while E.G. Swindell (1942) and Schoning (with Merrell and Johnson 1951) describe the Celilo Indian fishery in the decades prior to the construction of The Dalles dam.

D.H. French has investigated Western Columbia River Sahaptin ethnobotany since the early 1950s (1957, 1957a, 1965). His ethnographic summary of the Wasco (1961) has much valuable information on neighboring Sahaptin peoples. K.S. French (1955) has studied ceremonial practice on the Warm Springs Reservation. B. Rigsby (1965, 1969) recorded Sahaptin word lists and ancillary ethnographic information at Rock Creek, Celilo, and Warm Springs in 1965 and reviewed evidence for Sahaptin-Molala relationships. V. Hymes (1976) has studied the Warm Springs Sahaptin language and oral literature. S. Philips (1983) studied sociolinguistic aspects of education on the Warm Springs Reservation. E. Hunn has worked with Western Columbia River Sahaptins enrolled at Yakima since 1976, emphasizing ethnobiology and cultural ecology (1976–1993, 1980, 1980a, 1981, 1990, 1991a). Hunn and D.H. French (1981) collaborated in their ethnobiological work. Rude (1991b) initiated linguistic work at Warm Springs.

Cayuse, Umatilla, and Walla Walla

THEODORE STERN

Language

The Cayuse, Umatilla, and Walla Walla are peoples who long associated and in 1855 agreed by treaty to dwell together on the Umatilla Reservation. Linguistically, the Walla Walla and Umatilla speak dialects of Sahaptin, and the Cayuse traditionally spoke a distinct language of their own with uncertain affinities, perhaps within the Penutian superfamily (C.F. Voegelin and F.M. Voegelin 1966; Rigsby 1965, 1966, 1969). Sahaptin and Nez Perce are the two members of the Sahaptian subfamily of Plateau Penutian. Walla Walla, together with Palouse, Lower Snake, and Wanapam, belongs to the Northeast Sahaptin dialect cluster, and Umatilla is in the Columbia River cluster (vol. 17:666).

In historic times, intermarriage among the three peoples and with the Nez Perce was accompanied by bilingualism, in which Nez Perce came to be the favored language. The Cayuse spoke their own tongue among themselves and did not favor others learning it (S. Black 1829). By 1837 their youths no longer comprehended it, and all Cayuses commonly spoke the Lower Nez Perce dialect* (Hulbert and Hulbert 1936–1941, 1:279). In 1991 there remained perhaps six fluent speakers each of Walla Walla and Umatilla on the reservation, and Nez Perce had become the most commonly spoken Indian tongue, with English the near-universal language.

In intertribal discourse, two other forms of communication came into play. In trading at The Dalles, and in forays into western Oregon, Chinook Jargon proved useful, while in travels to the Plains the Plains Indian sign language was employed. In 1991 sign was still used occasionally by elderly men to accompany anecdotes.

Environment

In historic times, the Umatilla and Walla Walla occupied riverine tracts along the Columbia and the lower courses of tributary streams, including Willow Creek and Umatilla River for the former and the Walla Walla and Snake rivers for the latter. Although warm in winter and favored with salmon and sturgeon, it was otherwise unattractive, an arid plain of sand and gravel with a cover of sagebrush, shadscale, and greasewood, with jackrabbits the largest mammals. Windborne debris caused the loss of an eye for one Indian in 10 (F.G. Young 1899:183). Behind the river on both shores grew luxuriant bunch-grass, prime grazing for tribal herds: the Horse Heaven Hills that lie between the Umatilla and the Yakima to the north are felicitously named. On the south shore of the Columbia, beyond the Deschutes-Umatilla Plateau, the Blue Mountains rise to peaks ranging from 3,500 to over 6,000 feet, abundantly forested, and with extensive large fauna. Umatilla hunted here, and just east of them lay the Cayuse homeland, extending along the upper courses of the Umatilla and Walla Walla rivers, as well as that of the Grande Ronde, a tributary to the Snake River that takes its name from the large oval prairie in which it lies. To the north and east, the Cayuse extended in the interior behind the Walla Walla along the Touchet and Tucannon.

Territory

Size and complexity of organization are reflected in Ross's ([1855] 1924:176) characterization of the Cayuse and Walla Walla as tribes, while numbering the Umatilla among bands.

Nine Cayuse bands may be enumerated (fig. 1), designated by the site of their winter settlements (Ray 1936; Suphan 1974; Stern 1953–1968): *kimílehišpu·* 'tamarack people', on Butter Creek; *witú·npu·* '[Birch] Creek people,' on Birch Creek (Pilot Rock); *háwtmipu·* '[McKay] Creek people', on McKay Creek; *niχyá·wipu·* 'aspen springs people', on the Umatilla between Mission and Cayuse; *imeqícimenikenpu·* 'large confluence people', on the Umatilla between Thornhollow and Gibbon; *qapqapí·čpu·* 'cottonwood grove people', on Cottonwood Creek, a tributary of the Walla Walla; *imčé·me·pu·* 'mortar stone creek people,' on the upper Walla Walla, near Milton-Freewater; *pásχapu·* 'sunflower people,' on the middle Walla Walla and Mill Creek; and *e·ʔhétimepu·*, on Willow Creek, near Heppner. The last-named are said to have been driven out, perhaps by Northern Paiute raids, early in the nineteenth century, resettling in the foothills of the Cascade Mountains, possibly with the Molala.

The reservation Walla Walla spring from three proximate Sahaptin groups: the Walula (Sahaptin *walúulapam*), named after their settlement at the mouth of the Walla Walla River,

---

* Italicized forms cited in the text are Lower Nez Perce (Cayuse Nez Perce), unless otherwise labeled; these are based on the author's transcriptions. The phonemes of Nez Perce are given in the orthographic footnote in "Nez Perce," this vol.

Sahaptin forms are in the orthography described in the orthographic footnote in "Yakima and Neighboring Groups," this vol.

Forms from the old Cayuse language are cited in phonetic transcription or are phonemicized as if Nez Perce.

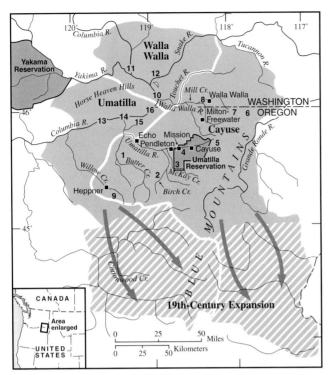

Fig. 1. Cayuse, Umatilla, and Walla Walla territory and expansion in the 19th century with modern town and reservation locations.

Culture

In protohistoric times, the riverine Umatilla and Walla Walla, and to a lesser extent the Cayuse, had become subject to Northwest Coast influences via the Upper Chinook at The Dalles (Osborne 1957; see also Shiner 1961; Osborne, Bryan, and Crabtree 1961; and Garth 1952, 1964), and more diffusely via the Northwest Sahaptins and Salish. From about the middle of the eighteenth century (Haines 1938; McKay 1839–1892; Painter 1946), their culture had been transformed by the introduction of horse pastoralism from the Northern Shoshone. The Cayuse joined with those Nez Perce who, adopting an equestrian mode of life, seasonally traveled with the Flathead and others in "going to buffalo" on the Plains. Some Umatillas and Walla Wallas also took part in those expeditions, while others maintained a riverine orientation, supplemented by the use of the horse in seasonal hunts. The changes arising from exposure to Plains influence (Ray 1939) were transmitted in turn to western neighbors: as Kroeber (1939:56) observes, it was only at The Dalles that Northwest Coast and Plains cultures met directly. The ethnographic information here deals with the first half of the nineteenth century.

Annual Round

Winter found the Umatilla and Walla Walla sheltered along the Columbia; some Umatillas also spent the season in the Yakima drainage (Thwaites 1904–1905, 6:115). The Cayuse were sometimes in composite villages together with visiting Nez Perces (Thwaites 1904–1905, 4:328; Irving 1895, 2:75). Dwellings consisted of mat lodges (fig. 2), some 60 feet in length, set over shallow depressions, and with up to 10 fires, and as many households, within each. Adjacent were pit houses, which served to store dried fish and roots and as a seclusion for young girls undergoing instruction, together with their aged teachers, and widows (S. Black 1829; Irving 1895, 2:82; Kane 1859:272). Sometimes, instead, seclusion was in another lodge. Adjacent were mud baths and sweathouses, used separately by the sexes. In the headman's lodge the villagers held their Winter Spirit Dances and witnessed shamanistic exhibitions. In the riverine villages, men caught steelhead and jacklighted from canoes for whitefish, suckers, and sturgeon. They and the Cayuse also sent out mounted hunting parties into the Blues and Cascades to surround deer and elk in the snow. In February, the Umatilla held the *wawínam* feast to greet the return of the wild celery (*Lomatium grayi*). With supplies dwindling, they looked forward to spring; if famine threatened, they would strip and eat the cambium of the ponderosa.

By April, the month of *gegít* roots (*Lomatium canbyi*), and soon of the couse (*Lomatium cous*) as well, bands of Indian women and their children went out to dig them along

and extending along both banks of the Columbia; a segment of the *naxiyamłáma* (Wauyukma Village), on the lower Snake; and the Chamnapam, named from their principal settlement, *čamná*, in the lower valley of the Yakima River, near present-day Richland. Although neighbors of the Yakima and participating in joint war parties with them under their own war chief (Cox 1957:199), the Chamnapam spoke the Lower Snake dialect ("Languages," this vol.) and are said to have been culturally close to the Walula (Verne F. Ray, personal communication 1956). As the influence of Walla Walla leaders grew, part of this body came to recognize them and chose to come onto the reservation.

The Umatilla dwelt on both sides of the Columbia as well as on islands lying within it. The name itself stems from *ímatilam*, a winter settlement of 500–600 persons at the mouth of the Umatilla (Ray 1936:150; cf. Suphan 1974: [36] 124).

The pervasive intermarriage characteristic of the Plateau gave rise to villages with composite populations, for example, one with Yakimas, Umatillas, and Walla Wallas and another with Yakimas, Umatillas, and Western Columbia River Sahaptins (Ray 1936:144, 148; cf. Ray et al. 1938:385; Ray 1959). These conditions are expressive of the permeable character of ethnic boundaries, as also are the "task groups" from different peoples engaged in a common venture (Anastasio 1972). If in what follows those peoples are sometimes termed tribes, the term must not be taken to connote a political centralization, since that condition did not emerge until nearly the middle of the nineteenth century and under White pressure.

396

top, Smithsonian, NAA: 96–11096; center, Nez Perce Natl. Histl. Park, Special Coll., Spalding, Idaho; bottom, Oreg. State Lib., Salem.

Fig. 2. Umatilla structures. top, Mat lodge of multiple households headed by Chief Homlai. Mrs. Peo is standing in front. Photograph by Lee Moorhouse, Umatilla Res., Oreg., 1898–1912. center, Women taking down a communal lodge and packing materials in wagons and on horseback. The traditional short and stocky Indian horses in the foreground have decorated parfleche bags loaded on them. Photographed about 1900. bottom, Single-family mat lodge with women working in sun shade in the foreground. A child in a cradleboard leans against a front pole of the sun shade. Photographed on the Umatilla Res., Oreg., 1890s.

the streams that flow from the Blues. The menfolk worked nearby, repairing their fish weirs and keeping an eye out for Northern Shoshone or Bannock raiders. In the settlements along the Columbia and on islands within it, men moored canoes to the shore and used them as platforms from which to take spring chinook with bident harpoon, gaff hooks, and dip net. Here there sprang up large composite settlements comprising villages side by side. One such community on the north shore of the Columbia and on midriver islands encountered by Meriwether Lewis and William Clark comprised 5 villages of 51 mat lodges, 44 of them longhouses, with an estimated population of 700 persons. Some of the augmentation may have been Yakimas (Boyd 1985:367), while others were hunters returned from the plains (Thwaites 1904–1905, 4:328). As the season advanced, lodges were dismantled and families built and moved into flat-roofed salmon-drying sheds. Elderly men made and repaired the equipment of active fishermen, and women cleaned and air-dried (S. Black 1829), sun-dried, or smoke-dried the catch (Stern 1953–1968). These activities required minimal clothing—a robe and perhaps a breechclout for men and both articles for women. A good day's catch in this reach of the Columbia was about 100 salmon per fisherman (Ross [1849] 1923:140), three of which sufficed to feed a family (F.G. Young 1899:60). Many Columbia natives fished through the year, often from dugout canoes, using seines or leisters. The Umatilla hollowed out their canoes from driftwood logs; the Walla Walla reputedly bought theirs from the Spokane (Gibbs 1855:403). On tributary rivers, weirs and stone barriers set with pens or fall traps were the major taking devices, joint projects sometimes directed by a man with spiritual power for such enterprises. Weirs were opened to permit escapement upriver, after enough fish had been caught (Thwaites 1904–1905, 4:335, 337). A thanksgiving feast celebrating the return of salmon and roots was held each April.

Some Cayuse and Walla Walla, together with Nez Perce, had spent the winter with the Wayampam at The Dalles (Perkins 1843:4 Dec.; Lee and Frost 1844:163; Drury 1958:135). On occasion, some groups traveled to the Yakima valley, where they dug roots, fished, and held council together. Once such encampment, of over 3,000 men and their families, spread out over six miles of country (Ross 1855:5–7).

In late June most of the Cayuse, along with many of their allies, crossed the Blues into the Grande Ronde. This may have been arduous in the days when dogs packed loads and hauled travoix but was simpler in the 1830s, when a Cayuse was thought poor who had no more than 15–20 head of horses, and the wealthy might own over 2,000 (fig. 3) (Farnham 1843:82). Others moved to a rendezvous in Nez Perce country, or traveled south to cross the Snake near Weiser, thereafter heading east into bison country. Few bison had crossed westward into Oregon (Kingston 1932), and the passage to reach the herds through hostile country entailed intertribal parties of Salish and Sahaptins numbering up to

397

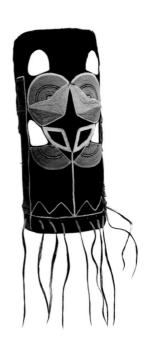

Fig. 3. Horses and horse trappings on the Umatilla Res., where horses were important as transportation and as markers of status and wealth. top, Men in full dress regalia in Pendleton, Oreg. Photograph by Walter Scot Bowman, 1890–1910. center left, Horse mask made of dark blue wool decorated with red satin ribbons, red wool-wrapped hair tassels, and beaded geometric designs in yellow, white, royal blue, and light blue. This mask was worn on the light-colored horse in the middle of the photograph, top. Probably made in the late 19th century. center middle, Cayuse bandoleer bag horse collar made of buckskin and red wool. The beaded geometric design in yellow, blue, pink, and red with white borders is typical of the Eastern Plateau beadwork (Loeb 1991:198–200). This collar belonged to the Showaway family. The pouch and strap were likely made in the late 19th century; the buckskin fringe was added later. center right, Cayuse saddle blanket of elkhide with red and navy blue wool border. The corners are beaded in a stylized floral design, and the edges are trimmed with tin tinklers. Collected on the Umatilla Res. and probably manufactured in the late 19th century. bottom, Umatillas passing through a town with horse travois. Photograph by Otto M. Jones, 1912–1918. Height of center left without fringe, 56 cm; width of center middle, 42 cm; length of center right, 140 cm.

2,000 persons (Anastasio 1972:163). In 1842 Pierre Jean de Smet (1905, 1:393) encountered 250 lodges on a tributary of the Yellowstone, including Flatheads, Kalispels, Nez Perces, Cayuses, and Snakes. Exposure to Plains tribes and cultures seems to have been a fascinating experience: those who "went to buffalo" referred to it by an oblique form of speech (Stern 1993:55) and in special month names; and the passion for sign language, for Plains articles and dress, for the tepee and the camp circle, spread even to the stay-at-homes. Plains-type clothing, decorated with quillwork and, later, beadwork, become the fashion, the men in shirt, breechclout, leggings, and moccasins, women in gown and the women's version of the other garments (fig. 4). These styles were caught up: the wealthy had several changes of garments, while the poor had but one, and that briefer and more ragged (S. Black 1829). The poorest of all were those who, lacking horses, had remained behind in the riverine settlements. Hunting there was limited to communal drives of prairie chickens, sage hens, or jackrabbits into net enclosures, where they were dispatched with clubs. Those who

Fig. 4. Cayuse women's buckskin clothing. left, Edna Kashkash wearing a deer-tail dress decorated on the yoke with small seed beads. Larger pony beads were strung on the fringes. Deer-tail dresses were constructed from 2 uncut deer hides joined at the sides and across the top, with the undressed deer tails folded down to form the neck and yoke. They were most popular from the middle to the late 19th century. Kashkash also wears a twined basketry hat. Photograph by Lee Moorhouse, Umatilla Res., Oreg., © 1900. right, Cayuse dress. The yoke of this buckskin dress is decorated with an abalone medallion, blue and white pony beads, and elk teeth. The fringe is strung with brass and multicolored glass beads. On the centermost fringes are strung deer dewclaws. The original owner of this dress was Charlotte Kanine (d. about 1930), who used this dress as her "digging dress" to be worn while digging roots. The dress was given away at her funeral. Length 118 cm.

dwelt in the Walla Walla villages reputedly were often clad only in rabbitskin clothing, with robes of twisted rabbitskin warps woven together by twined wefts.

Those tribesmen who summered in the Grande Ronde dwelt in villages of perhaps a dozen lodges or drying sheds (Gairdner 1841:253) near fisheries that seemed to be band usufructs (Hulbert and Hulbert 1936–1941, 2:231, 243, 246). Elsewhere on the streams, individuals fished with gaff hook, sometimes from horseback; or a line of fishermen wading in a line upriver drove the fish before them, spearing as they went. As at the weirs, and as in group hunts as well, the take was divided among participants, with shares to widows and the elderly. Meanwhile, the women were gathering camas roots: with her crutch-handled hardwood digging stick a dexterous woman could gather two sacks full, totaling 90 pounds, in half a day (Gairdner 1841:253). The digging party baked their roots together in a stone-lined earth oven along with an edible black lichen. Like couse, camas was formed into a bread, sometimes flavored with wild onions or berries, or into small biscuits; both were also cooked as mush by stone-boiling in baskets. Other roots were also gathered, including Indian carrot and bitterroot (see Hunn 1990).

Late summer was the time for intertribal gatherings at Walula, where Cayuses and Nez Perces joined the Walla Wallas (Ross [1849] 1923:137). It was also the time to send out composite war parties against Northern Paiute, Bannock, and Northern Shoshone. Such bodies were often sizable: one in 1818 under a Walla Walla numbered 480 men (Ross [1855] 1924:168).

In the fall, the parties in the Grande Ronde moved into the Blue Mountains for intensive hunting. Where individuals had formerly stalked deer with deer-head decoy and lured elk within bowshot with a flageolet, teams burned the underbrush, driving deer or antelope to hunters posted at stands, or mounted, surrounded and rode them down. Bears, often caught in the drive, were more often smoked out of winter hibernation.

In the hunting camps, the women butchered game and dried the meat, packing it into parfleches for storage. A family required 20–30 deer per year, or one-third that number of elk; and when they had enough, the hunter slew no more. Women tanned the skins. Through the seasons they and the children picked serviceberries, raspberries, gooseberries, huckleberries, wild currants, and chokecherries. Huckleberries were spread on mats to dry in the sun or before a slow-burning fire.

Intermittently through summer and fall, Cayuses and their associates visited the Wayampam and the band of their fellows who had wintered there, to fish, gamble, race horses, and trade with peoples who came from all directions for the same purposes to gather at the villages of the Wishram, Wasco, and their Sahaptin neighbors. Finally, with snows in the air, they made their way back from distant places to the winter settlements. Some of those beyond the Rockies chose to remain away for a year. The others returned to reerect their mat lodges and pit houses, to lay away their accumu-

lated stores, and to make themselves secure. Fishing and hunting parties still went forth, and hunters brought out their bearpaw snowshoes; but this was the time for reunion and, soon, for the sacred season of the Winter Spirit Dances and shamanistic displays.

Social Organization

Within the winter village, the 30 or so occupants of a mat dwelling were themselves called a lodge. Even the advent of the tepee did not end these units, since several tepees could be formed into a single longhouse. Within, each fireplace was the hearth of a family unit or of two related families; and the family heads of the lodge were commonly linked by either kinship or friendship. An influential man among the family heads served as spokesman for the lodge; his example, backed by the opinion of lodge mates, was usually effective to control the lazy and infractious. When hunting camps were formed, the men likewise chose a headman and the women a headwoman to coordinate their activities.

Villages with some hundred or more inhabitants were largely autonomous, with smaller hamlets on the same stream or, in the Columbia, on adjacent islands, loosely associated with them. One early census of Cayuse and Nez Perce bands found them to number from 10 to 150 persons, with one exceptional unit of 235 individuals (Drury 1958:134). Local groups such as this owned winter settlement sites and held usufruct rights to fishing sites, root grounds, berry patches, and hunting grounds, through it was customary to extend the courtesy of use to allied peoples. The Cayuse chief, Tawatoy, whose home lay on the Umatilla, also camped on the Walla Walla where "by his wife, he had a right to the land" of the Cayuse chief there (Brouillet 1858:34). The community constituted a moral order, dominated by primary relationships, and characterized by sharing of fish and game, particularly among kinsmen and within lodges. Work groups reflected the division of labor. Men, the hunters, fishers, and warriors, were also the woodworkers and toolmakers. Women, whose primary food-getting activities related to gathering, butchering and preserving the catch and other foods, also cooked, cared for the children, pitched tepees, and wrangled the horses when moving camp. They made cordage, wove coiled and twined baskets and bags, and sewed mats; and they tanned skins and sewed and decorated clothing (fig. 5). Cayuse women pecked out their own stone mortars and pestles. While superior skills were recognized—for example, the Umatilla had expert canoe makers—there were no full-time specialists.

Kinship, important within the village, provided the individual a bilateral network of kindred beyond the village, extending at times to fourth cousins. The kinship systems of modern Cayuse (that is, in Nez Perce) and Umatilla are of the normal Hawaiian subtype (Murdock 1949:229). Paternal and maternal lines were distinguished through the grandparents. Boys tended to receive formal names descending

top and bottom left, U. of Oreg. Lib., Special Coll., Eugene; bottom right, Smithsonian, NAA:3073–C–5.

Fig. 5. Cayuse women's activities. top, Uinmi bringing in a load of firewood on her horse. bottom left, Woman monitoring the smoking of elkskin or deerskin, the last step before cutting it into moccasins or clothing. Smoking prevented the wet skin from stiffening when it dried. bottom right, Woman weaving a flatbag. Photographs by Lee Moorhouse, Umatilla Res., Oreg., about 1900.

CAYUSE, UMATILLA, AND WALLA WALLA

from the paternal, girls in either parental, line. Kin terms reflect the linked practices of sororal polygyny, of the preferential remarriage of a widowed person to the sibling of his deceased spouse, and the fosterage of the children of a deceased sibling. The flexibility of such a bilateral system in practice was notable. It was furthered by the practice of addressing valued kinsmen by a more intimate term than their formal position warranted, and by the extension of terms to nonkin, such as trading partners. Travelers sought out the lodges of kinsmen or friends first, although courtesy dictated that the host offer food even to strangers who entered.

Within and among villages people recognized a social scale reflecting the wealth and respectability of family. Wealthy people had at least 100 head of horses, Plains clothing, parfleches, tepees, and other articles, and plenty of food. The wives of a rich man made a substantial contribution to his wealth; even the surplus roots they dug could be traded at The Dalles. Received opinion had it that rich men accumulated their wealth through industry, other than hunting and fishing. Samuel Black (1829) found them "indolent ... independent Gentlemen, Gaming Horse Racing ... dressing, lounging, Smoking, Chatting, &c." The poor, it was said, though sometimes simply unfortunate, owed their lot to laziness and lack of drive. Slaves, women or children captured in raids, were sometimes bought secondhand at The Dalles, where one boy is said to have cost 10 mares.

A ceremonial expression of precedence was exhibited in greeting Whites. Cayuse, for example, shook hands in the order of chiefs and principal men, commoners, women according to their rank—wives of chiefs, old women, and young women—and their children in order of age (Parker 1844:135).

Political Organization

It was from among the influential men of the village that the lodge spokesmen, forming a council, selected a headman. They sought a qualified person first among the sons of the former headman, then among close kinsmen. They desired the qualities of probity, good judgment, patience, and public concern, in a man of sufficient means, backed by a strong and devoted local kindred. The headman needed the means, for during the two or three days of a council or ceremony he had to provide for the visitors in attendance. Headmen have occasionally gained collateral note and followers as shaman, prophet, or warrior, but their duties were those of peace and the village: a headman of ordinary fighting prowess went to war as a common warrior. In everyday life he wore no distinctive dress, but morning and evening lectured the people upon proper behavior. In session with the council, with other responsible men in attendance, he coordinated village activities. For example, he set the time for moving camp and appointed a man to oversee the operation and he arbitrated disputes between villagers. The headman

also represented his village in regional affairs. The virtual autonomy of the riverine settlements is shown by the fact that, when the assembly of village headmen among the Umatilla had reached a decision, those headmen who dissented could not be compelled to follow it.

Among the Cayuse, headmen recognized as preeminent among the village leaders within a region comprised band chiefs, designated by much the same term as the headmen and differing from them only in scale. Early chiefs, like headmen, had to rely upon their powers of persuasion, rather than direct command. The Walla Walla chief, Yellepit, greeting Lewis and Clark on their return eastward, exhorted his covillagers to provide them with provisions and fuel, setting the example himself; but they brought only fuel, and the explorers were forced to buy dogs to cook (Thwaites 1904–1905, 4:328).

Like headmen, chiefs in their councils were assisted by heralds: Cayuse chiefs spoke in council in their own tongue, which the herald repeated in Nez Perce. Chiefs sometimes had an assistant, in later times a successor undergoing training, as well as a body of young warriors. A chief, sitting with council as court, heard and tried accusations of theft. In a case of deliberate murder he sought to reconcile the parties and secure a payment of horses to the family of the victim, but kinsmen sometimes exacted vengeance against the murderer on the sly. There were some murderers so dreaded that they were beyond retribution (S. Black 1829). Family disputes were private matters. In the 1830s, when the Hudson's Bay Company began to recognize paramount chiefs, they sometimes suggested laws for them to institute, as well as the penalties of flogging—the whipper for children is a distinct office—and of hanging (Irving 1868:372; Drury 1973, 1:276). Courts then judged matters of public morality. The example of the Hudson's Bay Company, which instructed the master of each post to conduct Christian services for their men and client Indians, may have led to the development of a form of Indian worship incorporating Christian elements (Spier 1935), in "Sunday" services led by chiefs and headmen.

By 1847, centralization among the Cayuse was so far from complete that one saw them "divided into three camps, entirely distinct from each other, each camp having its own chief, who governs his young men as he pleases; each one of the chiefs is independent of the others; and those three camps form, as it were, three independent states of a small federal republic, each of them administering their own private affairs as they please without interference from the others" (Brouillet 1858:52). They were the band-clusters of the brothers, Tawatoy and Five Ravens, on the middle Umatilla, of Qematspelu upriver from them, and that of Teloukaikt on the middle Walla Walla. Both Tawatoy amd Qematspelu were linked through marriage with Teloukaikt.

Among allies, the Nez Perce and Cayuse, as the most powerful and warlike peoples of the southern Plateau, were said to "regulate all the movements of the others in peace and war" (Ross [1855] 1924:176). Within the region of their residence, they dominated an asymmetrical multitribal order, in which wealth, in the form of horses and a Plains lifeway, formed one pole and the riverine orientation of those too poor or conservative to change formed the other. The differences were sometimes phrased in simple tribal terms: the Walla Walla were characterized by Nez Perce as descendants of their slaves (Parker 1844:251), as a poor people oppressed by the Cayuse (Hulbert and Hulbert 1936–1941, 2:268), and as a people whose women the Cayuse deemed it degrading to marry, though Walla Walla men might marry Cayuse women (Gairdner 1841:256). This assumption seems explicable in terms of Cayuse needs to replenish losses in manpower by permitting others to marry in. Thus, after the Cayuse war, Alvord (1857:11) wrote that about half the Cayuse warriors were then "slaves" of Shasta and Walla Walla origin. In fact, intermarriage among wealthy leaders provided important intertribal ties. For example, the Cayuse chief Wilewmutkin, born in the eighteenth century, through a Nez Perce union fathered Twitekis (Old Joseph), who became leader of the Wallowa band of Nez Perce. By a Cayuse wife he had three sons who succeeded him: a namesake, who died in 1831; Tawatoy; and Five Ravens. A daughter married the Walla Walla chief Piupiumaksmaks (fig. 6). Strengthening Cayuse influence among the Western Columbia River Sahaptins were a number of intermarriages; and one Cayuse, Wailaptulikt, even became war leader among the Tygh band of Sahaptins (Hines 1881:23; Hulbert and Hulbert 1936–1941, 3:87; Johansen 1959:132, 136).

In their external relationships, elements of the Cayuse and their associates combined with other Sahaptins and sometimes Salish in intertribal "task groups" (Anastasio 1972). At large intertribal gatherings there seems to have been an informal ranking of leaders (Ross [1849] 1923: 136). Any of these friendly gatherings was likely to be marked by trading, horse racing, and gambling. Individuals often had trading partners in other tribes; on the other hand, betting on horse racing and the stick game were frequent expressions of tribal solidarity. In interregional meetings, at The Dalles, on the Plains, and in intermittently peaceful transactions with the Northern Shoshone in the Grande Ronde, such competition might at any time give way to bluff, or to fighting and raids, whereby property might more readily be acquired.

This was particularly true at The Dalles, where the Wishram and Wasco served as middlemen in "the great mart of all this country," where dentalia, salmon pemmican, slaves, and other products of the lower country were exchanged for horses, dried roots, buffalo robes, and Plains clothing and accoutrements (Thwaites 1904–1905, 4:289). Their early attempts to monopolize the upriver movement of knives, axes, and later firearms was contested by the Cayuse and Nez Perce, for whom such articles were essential for withstanding the Blackfoot and their allies. About 1814 the two Plateau peoples had warred on the tribes at the Falls, slaying some, enslaving others, and driving the survivors into the woods (Coues 1897, 2:799); the Cayuse later

claimed to have been the original owners of the fisheries there (Lee and Frost 1844:177).

It is not always clear whether the objects of Cayuse and Nez Perce actions at The Dalles were the Western Columbia River Sahaptins or the Chinookans (or both), and whether marital or trading relations were also involved: White observers often saw their acts as simply coercive. The influence of the Cayuses and Nez Perces wintering or visiting at Celilo was undoubted (Douglas 1904–1905:328; Hulbert and Hulbert 1936–1941, 3:230, 243–244), and there were several acts of outright bullying (for example, Lee and Frost 1844:177; Oregon Pioneer Association 1893:141–143, 1885:34). Farnham (1843:81) asserts that the group of guests at Celilo held court over the Chinookans, flogging those found guilty, and characterizes the Cayuse as "the imperial tribe of Oregon." Garth (1964:55), elaborating on this statement, finds the Nez Perce and Cayuse presiding over the riverine fishers, Sahaptin and Chinookan alike, in "a semi-state with laws enforced by [them] and with the council and the whip as devices to achieve social control." This presumes (cf. Garth 1964:53) a division between riverine and equestrian peoples that is too absolute and a unity and political centralization among the latter that they were to realize only under government intervention. To judge by a Yakima myth that pits the Chinook brothers against the Walla Walla brothers (Splawn 1944:417), the domineering by members of the equestrian tribes was only the latest phrasing of an interregional friction; and indeed, the Walla Walla chief Piupiumaksmaks is recorded as being presented with a sturgeon from a Chinook while traveling past their settlements (Minto 1901:248).

It was that Walla Walla leader, also, who was the principal spirit in expeditions into northern California, where as a boy he had accompanied his father Tamatappam on horse raids (Splawn 1944:366). Together with Tawatoy, he led joint parties there to trade horses and other articles for slaves and furs with the Shasta (Wilkes 1845, 4:397; cf. Stern 1953–1968) and later to Fort Sutter, to trade for cattle (Hulbert and Hulbert 1936–1941, 3:129; ARCIA 1846:632–636; Kane 1859:281–284; Splawn 1944:365; Heizer 1942).

Warfare

Warfare was most common against the Northern Paiute, Bannock, and Northern Shoshone to the south and southeast and the Blackfoot and their allies on the Plains. In the early nineteenth century, the threat of raids from the southern foe had led to the siting of many Sahaptian villages on the north shore of the Columbia and Snake (Thwaites 1904–1905, 3:145); in 1811 a leader, welcoming David Thompson's proposal to trade with them, asked for weapons to enable his people to dislodge the "Straw Tent Tribe" of Snakes (Northern Shoshone, Bannock, or Northern Paiute) who had lately forced his people to abandon the southern part of their country (Glover 1962:352). Subsequent to the opening of a trad-

Fig. 6. Tribal leaders. top left, Piupiumaksmaks, Walla Walla, an important chief from the 1830s on. He attended the treaty councils of 1855 made with Gov. Isaac I. Stevens (vol. 4:200). Oil on canvas by Paul Kane, 1847. top right, Cap'n Sumkin, Cayuse-Nez Perce, an Indian scout for the army. He became the first captain of Indian police on the Umatilla Res., Oreg., and then a member of the Court of Indian Offenses (Stern, Schmitt, and Halfmoon 1980:342–343.) Photograph by Lee Moorhouse, Umatilla Res., Oreg., before 1906. bottom left, Jim Kanine, headman of the Walla Walla (b. 1872, d. 1952), wearing Plains-style war bonnet. He was a leader of the traditional community at the Umatilla Res. Photograph by Lee D. Drake, at Pendleton roundup, Oreg., date not recorded. bottom right, Heyoomhapima (Umapine) or Grizzly Bear In The Center, Cayuse (b. about 1845). A participant in the Bannock and Paiute War of 1878, he became a leader on the Umatilla Res. Photograph by De Lancey Gill, Washington, D.C., 1905.

ing post, one segment of the Cayuse, under the younger Wilewmutkin, became middlemen in trading with the "Snakes," while another segment maintained their traditional hostility (Stern 1993). From the north, the Salishan Spokane, Coeur d'Alene, and Kalispel occasionally raided the Umatilla (Anastasio 1972:145; Teit 1930:158).

Horse-raiding parties of five or six persons went out from the Cayuse and their allies in the summer or fall (fig. 7). The details reflect Plains practices: the preliminary sweatbath; the hide-beating farewell serenade; prescient warning of death; travel often afoot; cutting out favorite animals tethered within the camp circle; rendezvous of the raiders; triumphal return; claim of horse by brave women; horse marked with symbol of the raid; and recounting the deed, accompanied by the gift of a horse (Stern, Schmitt, and Halfmoon 1980).

Large war parties, sometimes several hundred strong, were raised by decision of the chiefs and headmen in council. Some were intertribal; on the other hand, an entire people never fought as a unit. In the Cayuse War of 1848–1850, though the Cayuse were few in number, and those directly involved were fewer (many on the Umatilla River remained neutral) over 400 warriors—Cayuse, Palouse, Umatilla, Nez Perce, and Walla Walla—fought a volunteer army at Sand Hollow (Victor 1894; Ruby and Brown 1972:127, 138). The Yakima War of 1855–1856 saw a similar coalition.

In warfare, warriors went mounted or fought from canoes (Cox 1957:194), with bow and arrow or gun, with spear, knife, and war club; they bore a shield and formerly had worn elkhide armor. From the early part of the nineteenth century ceremonial dress also included Plains war bonnets (fig. 6). There is no recollection of soldier soci-

eties, present among the Nez Perce (Walker 1973:107). Enemy villages were attacked in early morning, women and children being enslaved. There was a modified counting of coup and the striking and sparing of a live enemy warrior; the fallen foe was sometimes scalped (for a Nez Perce instance, see Stern, Schmitt, and Halfmoon 1980:373–375). The slayer sometimes ate the heart of a notable foe: in the nineteenth century a Umatilla chief thus treated a "Snake" whom he had slain, thereby gaining the war name *imcahapix* 'raw meat eater'. Captive warriors were tortured by severing in succession their fingers, wrists, and limbs, while the victim recounted his past tortures of Cayuses, until at length he expired (McWhorter 1952:28). On return from war, a successful party held a scalp dance, after which all warriors who had taken part had to undergo purification (Ray 1942:277).

Peace was concluded when major leaders on both sides met to smoke the pipe together.

Life Cycle

• BIRTH   An expectant mother swam to keep her baby small, used vomiting sticks to rid herself of "bile," and refrained from eating meat. She avoided ugly sights that might mark the child and, to ensure easy delivery, passed through doorways without hesitation. Her husband refrained from snaring game, did not hunt for five days after the birth, and remained continent for a month. Delivery took place in a separate hut under the supervision of a midwife. In a difficult delivery a shaman was summoned, who might employ herbs and manipulate the child within the womb in a breech delivery. Both specialists received payment. The mother remained in seclusion 10 days, during which she bathed herself and the child and "shaped" its body and features (Ray 1942:196). After 10 days, the parents sweated and bathed, and the mother discarded the dishes and clothes she had used in confinement.

Some 20 days after birth, the child was laced into the cradleboard, upon which the girl's head was frontally compressed, a custom that lapsed soon after Whites first recorded it (Hulbert and Hulbert 1936–1941, 1:268; Oregon Pioneer Association 1893:100). After six months the child was transferred to a larger board until he was a year old. Up to the age of two, it was breastfed, and if the mother was unable to nurse, a wet-nurse had to be found, usually among kinswomen. In the early days, many children died for lack of milk supply, for no adequate substitute was available (Oregon Pioneer Association 1893:100). Orphans, fostered by kinsmen, often occupied a subordinate status (S. Black 1829). The teething child was given dried meat to work on, and at about the age of two was weaned and fed mush and boiled foods.

• CHILDHOOD   The toddler was placed under the care of older siblings. When he began talking, between one and two years, parents first spoke baby talk to him. A child that

U. of Oreg. Lib., Special Coll., Eugene.

Fig. 7. Horse stealing. Horses were one of the most valuable possessions of a Plateau man, and horse stealing was an honored male pursuit. This drawing depicts a Plateau raiding party of 3 men in a hostile camp. A favorite horse has been tethered within a lodge. One raider, dressed in a capote, has cut away the lodge cover (the knife is depicted) and is leading the prized horse away. Dashes represent the man's route through the camp, and the semilunar marks are the horse's hoofprints. Drawing in plain and colored pencil from a book found in a house formerly belonging to Cap' Sumkin, Cayuse-Nez Perce, on the Umatilla Res., Pendleton Oreg. (Stern, Schmitt, and Halfmoon 1980). Artist unknown, probably about 1904.

could talk could understand, it was believed, and parents then began to teach him about his kinsmen. His mother also began to teach him bowel control, to give him a switching if he lapsed, and to punish him for disobedience. Independence training was likewise early. In a Cayuse family (Farnham 1843:79), two sons, aged seven and three, riding their horses behind their parents, lost the trail. The parents waited in camp until the two lads found their own way in and received them with quiet pride.

Children played with tops, stilts, buzzers, bull-roarers, and popguns, and made cat's cradles in figures such as "elk" and "porcupine." There were tug-of-war and hide-and-seek. Under the tutelage of older boys and men, boys learned to use the bow and arrow, shooting at a rolling hoop or straw ball, and to spear fish. Girls played with dolls, riding them on forked willow "horses," making little tepees and moving camp. By the age of 10 they were under persistent moulding, the boys being roused in early morning by an uncle to plunge into the water, then to run along the bank. On winter nights they were a rapt audience for elders reciting myths; daily they heard the headman's exhortations and on special occasions the war stories of men who had been invited to recount their deeds. From their parents and grandparents, as well as those brought in to speak of their lives, they heard praised the virtues of obedience, of honesty, and of charity to the unfortunate. For the unruly, there was the whipper, named by council and headman. When boys squabbled, the whipper was summoned and a blanket, his payment, was spread upon the ground upon which the boys, guilty and innocent alike, lay down in turn for a switching. Brave boys liked to go first; for if the willow whip broke, the punishment was at an end. The whipper ended with a lecture. An obstreperous child might also be sent out to seek power and to find in the loneliness of the quest a better perspective on life.

Children, who had formerly been addressed by a kin or age term, or by a nickname, might receive a formal name. The most noted names were vision names that had been won by an ancestor. Names were conferred by parents as an adjunct to a public ceremony, property being distributed by kinsmen and friends.

By the time they were 10, children were given direct training in work. Girls helped mother, aunt, or grandmother in household chores, while men took sons and nephews to observe and help in hunting and fishing. (However, until their early teens, boys were not permitted to take a full role in hunting, since it was considered derogatory to the prey.) For the boy's first kill, his first fish, his first deer, and for the girl her first roots and berries, there was a family ceremony, at which elders were feasted on the food thus taken, and spokesman later thanked the child and admonished him always to care for the old and needy.

It was at about this time in life that a child—usually a boy, but also some girls—would be sent out on the vision quest. Some parents reportedly declined to expose their children to the rigors of the quest and to the danger that unscrupulous persons of power might later covet a guardian power thus gained. Others, exasperated by an unruly child, might shout, "Go out and seek a power!" This was done in the expectation that the child, alone at the questing site, far from home and fellows, would come to a proper frame of mind, one that the powers might find appealing.

Girls from 12 to 16 were secluded together in a pithouse or lodge (Umatilla, Walla Walla: *wílči*), returning each day, except during menstruation, for household chores. Watched by matrons, they were taught to sew coiled willow baskets and to twine baskets and bags, to sew and decorate buckskin clothing, and (Cayuse) to peck out stone mortars and pestles. A woman of moral character also instructed them in feminine hygiene. If a girl's first menstruation occurred while in the hunting camp, she remained for five days in a secluded hut, after which she bathed, donned fresh clothing, and reentered normal life without ceremony.

It was at this time that boys began courting, though the girls were heavily chaperoned. A lover sought to meet the girl when she was fetching fuel or water; he serenaded her from the shadows with song or flageolet. Kinsmen were vigilant, for premarital sex was condemned. So also was love magic, the resort of older persons.

• MARRIAGE A boy about 16 and a girl of about the same age, were deemed ready for marriage. Although some families betrothed young children, it was usually when a boy was considered of age that his parents sent a respected relative to speak to the girl's parents. They considered the interest and views of their daughter, and if the suit was granted, reached an agreement on the bridewealth in horses the boy's parents were to pay. A young couple, barred by family opposition, might elope, returning, if their parents relented, after a month or so. Few in the end went unwed. Berdaches, though present in the early days among the Cayuse (Maloney 1945:4, 73; Stern 1993), were so infrequent, or passed so quickly from the scene, as to be denied by modern informants.

The marriage was confirmed in a public exchange of goods known as "trading." Primarily an affair of women, it comprised alternate feasting between the groom's relatives and those of the bride, accompanied by gifts brought by each of the visitors for one or more trading partners on the other side. The gifts reflected the contributions of the groom (e.g., meats, fish, and buckskin) and those of the bride (e.g., baskets, bags, and roots). The exchange had competitive overtones, as reflecting the status of the traders.

Women, who took satisfaction in their craft skills and their competence in providing for their families, did not fit Cox's (1957:266) early characterization of the Plateau woman as "condemned to drudgery" and "[possessing] little or no influence." They were keepers of the family records and, particularly when they had become elderly, were repositories of tribal tradition. The camp was woman's domain, and the gangs of boys soon learned to give it a clear berth during the daytime, to avoid the exactions and scoldings of the older women.

Initially, the married couple resided with his parents, the bride making periodic visits to her parents. Divorce was frequent in the first years, the children going with the parent of the same sex. In S. Black's time (1829), there were many divorced women who could not remarry because their former husband withheld permission, perhaps because the bridewealth could not be returned; and Davenport (1907:118) reports a camp of such cast-offs. Although husbands treated their wives with forbearance, they were likely to wound or slay an unfaithful wife (S. Black 1829). Wives had no redress against an adulterous husband.

With time, the couple established a separate household; and a prosperous husband, particularly when the union had been childless, took a second wife, often a sister of his first one. Compatible cowives dwelt together; otherwise they lived apart, and the husband divided his time between them. Chiefs, for whom polygyny reinforced political alliances, often had several wives in separate villages. The elderly who still desired independence were furnished a grandchild to help them and keep them company; others preferred to join the household of a son or daughter.

• DEATH Death came sometimes at one's own hand. S. Black (1829) found suicide and attempted suicide common with both sexes and all ages, often from wounded feelings. In a noted instance in 1825 a Walla Walla leader, perhaps Yellepit, at the burial of his last surviving son, asked to be interred with him. After assigning his property, he was buried in the grave (Ogden 1933:22–27; Kane 1859:285–289; Wheeler 1904, 2:256).

When death came, a shaman was summoned who directed friends and neighbors in washing and dressing the corpse in special white buckskin garb, after which it was carried to another lodge. The shaman then fumigated the dwelling and household members with rosebushes. Through the night, the family held a wake over the corpse, visited by friends and relatives, while children were kept away. Next day, the community and visitors, who had come at the news, bore the corpse to the cemetery where, wrapped in buckskin and tule mats, it was interred on its back heading west, surrounded by cherished possessions and farewell gifts. As late as the 1950s a horse was slain and propped on the grave of its master. The riverine tribes often interred their dead in burial vaults on islands in the Columbia (Thwaites 1904–1905, 3:139). Suicides were buried only by immediate kinsmen. All who had come in contact with the dead sweated to purify themselves.

Five days later a memorial feast was held (fig. 8), at which the virtues of the deceased were extolled and his name mentioned for the last time, upon which kinswomen keened their grief. His property—save major items, such as horses and tepees, which had been assigned to heirs—was then distributed by a speaker under the direction of the closest consanguineal kinsmen of the deceased. The mementos went to friends and relatives; and the surviving mate, who received a keepsake, might himself contribute property. Afterward, those wishing to "bring out" names of those long dead took this occasion to do so.

Immediate kinsmen went into mourning. If the deceased had been married, his mother or sister cut the widow's braids and gave her drab clothing. For a year the widow maintained seclusion, being given food by relatives, but observing no food taboos. At this time, ghosts of kinsmen visited one woman, seeking to draw her along with them. At the end of a year, the family of the deceased brought his spouse out of seclusion, clad her in "bright" clothing, and offered her an unmarried brother or cousin of her late husband as a spouse. The choice was hers: she might choose another, while some persons preferred to continue mourning for years. If the mate was accepted, a new exchange of gifts was sometimes initiated.

After the mourning period, at the time of a general ceremony, a person was chosen to dance a memorial dance in the clothing of the deceased. Then the garments were given away, together with property donated by kinsmen and friends. Only thereafter, on another occasion, could the name be "brought out" once more.

Knowledge, Art, and Music

Both the original Cayuse (Rigsby 1969:136) and the Sahaptin lexicons reflect a numeral system that is quinary for integers and decimal above 10. The ritual number was five. Elapsed time was measured in the rising and setting of the sun, and by moons. The year consisted of 12 moons, bearing names reflecting the succession of natural events and the appearance of important foodstuffs.

Riverine Sahaptins formerly marked the beginning of the year at the winter solstice with a gathering, *paiča'sa*, at which people danced and worshiped, praying to God. (This may in fact have been one of the early prophetic movements.) There was reportedly a corresponding ceremony at the summer solstice. Women maintained mnemonic thong or cord records, in a system that reflects White influence, employing a seven-day week, with a knot to mark each day and a trade bead for Sunday (see also Chance 1973:83). Distance was measured by encampments along the route and orientation from the sun and from natural landmarks. Astral lore recognized heavenly bodies such as the rainbow and various constellations. In one tale Frog, clinging to the face of Moon, dims his radiance. The Big Dipper is called "Grizzly Bear digging roots"; the handle stars are birds stalking her. The Milky Way is known as "Ghosts' Road" (Stern 1993:69).

Women's crafts in particular gave opportunity for aesthetic expression, in the adornment of skin clothing with quillwork and later with beadwork (fig. 9), in geometric decorations in twined overlay on bags and imbrication of coiled baskets, as well as in the painted designs on parfleches. Such designs were principally nonrepresentational. By contrast, men depicted their war exploits on elkskin robes; they painted a symbol, sometimes a life form, upon their shield; *407*

Fig. 8. Walla Walla Chief Homlai's memorial feast. top, Participants included: 1, Young Chief, Cayuse; 2, Chief Peo, Umatilla; 3, Narcisse Lavadour, Walla Walla; 4, Watis Temene, Cayuse; 5, Yatinawits, Cayuse; 6, Philip Minthorn, Cayuse; and 7, Narcisse Cornoyer, Walla Walla. Parfleches, satchels, and a trunk contain effects to be distributed following the feast. Photograph by Walter Scot Bowman, Umatilla Res., Oreg., 1891. See bottom drawing for identifications.

High Desert Mus., Doris Swayze Bounds Coll., Bend, Oreg.: top left, 6.3.1; top center, 2.6.185; top right, 2.6.146; bottom left, 6.15.46; bottom right, 6.22.4.

Fig. 9. Beadwork from the Umatilla Res. Artists of the early 20th century expanded upon the traditional beaded design repertoire by depicting new subjects, including human figures and patriotic designs. top left, Umatilla breechcloth constructed of red wool cloth with a beaded panel. The beadwork designs are dark blue, white, green, gold, and pink on a light blue background. Collected about 1920. top center, Cayuse beaded bag with patriotic motif depicting an eagle on a shield with American flags. Made by Emma Jones Burke, 1920–1940. top right, Umatilla bag depicting a woman wearing a twined hat. Belonged to Liza Bill; probably made 1920–1930. bottom left, Umatilla woman's buckskin moccasins. The side seam construction of these moccasins is typical of many Plateau moccasins. Collected in 1920. bottom right, Umatilla man's vest. The floral beadwork design on this buckskin vest was executed in large faceted beads that were popular around 1900. Made by Mis-Na-Kla (b. 1879, d. 1920), a Umatilla-Yakima woman. Width of top left, 30.5 cm; height of top center, 29 cm; height of top right without fringe, 30 cm; length of bottom left, 25 cm; length of bottom right, 58.5 cm.

and adorned their shirts and war horses with tallies of war prowess. Face paint was sometimes applied in symbolic representations, as when the director of social events painted a buffalo design upon his face.

Oral skills were manifested by men in oratory and by both sexes in the narration of myths and tales. Of musical instruments, the flageolet was employed solo in playing love songs, while whistles served as signals in war. The drum dates at least from the time of Frémont (1845:175). Stick-beating accompanied the stick game and shamanistic performances. General dances, which greeted early explorers, were often executed in one or more concentric circles, participants facing inward, with principal dancers in the inmost circle. Dancers sang as they performed, jumping in place or moving sidewards (Thwaites 1904–1905, 4:334; S. Black 1829).

Religion

S. Black (1829) reported that the Indians "had very little knowledge of a Supreme Being before the Whites came amongst them." They believed that an Old Chief, of great powers, who dwelt about the ocean, had established the succession of the seasons, in spring making roots sprout, in summer the salmon to run, and in winter providing snows to reveal the tracks of game. He was good, though invisible, and asked nothing from men; though they sought him, they offered him neither sacrifice nor ceremony.

The mythic beings who had preceded men, some in animal form, had included one who resembles the modern figure of Coyote in his role as destroyer of evil creatures; upon his departure, he had instructed them to remain on Earth, probably in transformed condition. Signs left behind by the mythic beings include drops of their blood (red pyrites) within stones and designs (pictographs?) like those the Indians themselves painted on their parfleches and shields. The founding myths of the Root Feast have elements in common with this view, for one connects the feast with the transforming role of Coyote along the Columbia, in the course of which he placed white clay, roots, and berries, and other foods for the people to come. Within the present world, beings of preternatural form and power still reside. They include mountain elves who formerly led mortals astray, and giants downriver who carried them off; dogs and horses dwelt in lakes and ocean. People have married giants and animals, and some have returned to establish ceremonies they learned this way.

There were powers even within man, which must be governed. Each person had vitality (*hé·šin*), likened to breath, produced by the food he ate, and pervading his body. The evil thoughts of another—a sorcerer, an ill-tempered waiter at the Root Feast, even a young girl grudgingly offering food to a guest—corrupted that vitality as he ate, causing him to sicken. At death, this quality dissipated. Distinct from it was the ghost-soul, *čé·wčew*, though modern thought (including that of the Washat religion) restricts the meaning to 'ghost' and distinguishes the soul, *waqí·šwit*, as a distinct entity. After death, the ghost-soul seems to have journeyed to an afterworld, though some remained on earth. The nature of that afterworld in historic times has probably been shaped by Roman Catholic Algonquian and Iroquois beliefs: the soul after death travels the Milky Way, the 'ghosts' road', which forks, a broad path to the left leading to hell, a faint track to the right to heaven (cf. Finley [1840] quoted in Berkhofer 1965:116). Those with unconfessed sins must return to earth. The unclean cannot advance along the road: fixed in place, they await the Day of Judgment.

For the living, soul loss led to madness and even death. Ghosts of the recently dead craved the company of kinsmen and sought to abduct them. Accordingly, children, who lacked tutelary spirits, were kept away from funerals; and they were spared excessive whipping, lest pitying kinsmen return from the dead to claim them. A person passing the scene of a past event might see or hear its reenactment; only if he dwelt upon it might he sicken. The elderly, with their minds in the past, found their souls slipping away to join the dead they recalled too keenly.

Though most souls in the afterworld lived as in life, there were those—some say, those of the unclean dead—that remained on earth as ghosts, normally invisible, signaling each other and mortals by whistling, and playing pranks on humans. At times, say Umatilla and Walla Walla, a ghost became a tutelary spirit.

No person could hope to succeed in life without the aid of one or more tutelary powers, supernatural beings that appeared as birds, animals, fish, flora, heavenly bodies, ghosts, and human artifacts, and also as humans. Some Cayuse have taken over a classification of tutelaries found also among the Nez Perce (Curtis 1907–1930, 8:51). Both the spirit and the power it imparted are termed *wé·yekin* (Umatilla *tá·x*); as a preparation for life, the quest is lexically likened to schooling.

A mentor directed the power-seeking child to a questing spot carrying an object to leave behind as evidence that he had been there, which the mentor would later retrieve. The quester remained on the spot, fasting and piling rocks until he had a vision, or until five days or more had passed. When his mood had become receptive, a power, pitying him, might appear, often in a dream at dawn, as either a visual or an auditory visitation. In the former, the power first appeared in symbolic human form, announced the quality conferred, then, reverting to "natural" form, vanished. Sometimes, soon afterward, the quester heard his song; some also were instructed to make an amulet. On his return, the successful quester fell unconscious near the village, was revived by a shaman, and for the next two weeks was isolated, purifying himself by sweating. Only after a latency of many years, when he was perhaps 20, did his tutelary spirit again manifest itself. Then, at the Winter Spirit Dance (*wé·yekwe·cet*), held in the long lodge of a headman, those with guardian powers danced and sang their songs; and the youth, hearing a song of his tutelary, fell unconscious and, as a shaman revived him, rose to sing and dance. His kinsmen hastily brought together and distributed gifts appropriate to the tutelary.

The qualities conferred were specialized; a tutelary might have two or more endowments to impart to different individuals, and several tutelaries might give the same power. Men were given fighting prowess, invulnerability, fleetness of foot, the capacity to amass wealth, to attract women, and to win at gambling; women, the ability to dig roots, and to find roots, berries, and medicines. Both were granted powers to cure wounds, colds, or other afflictions. Although the morality with which the endowment was exercised was not dictated by the tutelary, Rattlesnake and Spider gave power to kill others that was often used in sorcery, while Coyote might masquerade as another power. A person approached by an undesirable power had a shaman exorcise it. By providing the quester with an amulet of his own tutelary to take on his quest, a mentor might seek to direct that tutelary to the neophyte. A parent in his old age might teach his song to a child, then dance with him upon his back, to transmit his power. Usually, however, there was no control over which spirit might descend upon the quester. One with a power must show respect for his tutelary, though usually this did not include a prohibition on killing or eating its mundane counterparts. Shamans, *tiwé·t* (masculine, sing.), were recognized practitioners with powers of curing, attracting game, divining, and weather control, as well as the power to cause illness and death. Some among the Cayuse acquired from the tutelary spirit a property called *táʔaχtoyχ*, manifested as a shiny, elastic rod; it sometimes entered into sorcery.

Whatever the nature of his tutelaries, the novice waited some five years before demonstrating his powers in public. At this annual event, *weʔnípt* 'song', held in association with the Winter Spirit Dances, all novices in rotation sang their songs and performed gratis upon those in attendance, after which their relatives distributed goods to the spectators. At this time, shamans of several categories judged the novices and competed in demonstrating their own cures.

Shamans

Among the most feared of shamans were the *isχíˑpin*, whose powers derived from the tutelary of a dead shaman or, among the Umatilla, from his ghost itself. Its acquisition was attended by an illness that was sometimes fatal. In Cayuse thought, this tutelary then sought to gather in other masterless guardian spirits of the dead. Aged and few in number, the *isχíˑpin* were feared. The very *hé·šin*, radiating from their body ahead and behind them, endangered children; and their auxiliary spirits attacked those who aroused their anger. Through their powers of divining, the *isχíˑpin* located lost objects and foretold future or distant events. They spoke a secret language among themselves. Some had gained additional powers enabling them to cure. (For an early probable example, see Thwaites 1904–1905, 4:334).

A second class of shamans were the *wáptipasin*, who combined the powers of hunting—and perhaps fishing (Treide 1965; Chance 1973:15; Stern 1993:66)—shaman with that of curing. In an event in the early nineteenth century, one such Umatilla shaman relieved a winter famine by having his spirit wolves drive in elk for the people to eat. At the shamanistic exhibitions, the *wáptipasin* sported about the central fires of the lodge, vying with one another in handling hot rocks and exhibiting their ability to withstand heat.

Various other shamanistic powers existed. One Cayuse shaman asserted that his songs helped roots and berries grow. Others controlled the weather: one brought the snow, another melted it with a Chinook wind. Yet other cured certain diseases. Some persons made love magic; others, love sorcery that could turn a rejecting woman into a wanton.

Individuals resorted to a ritual regimen to condition themselves for a longer life, purging themselves with the willow vomiting sticks—by which a modern Walla Walla woman reportedly cured herself of diabetes—soaking in the mud bath, sweating in "Grandfather" sweathouse and sitting immersed in the frigid waters of a stream. When a person fell ill and could not cure himself, relatives summoned a shaman; he had already dreamed of the call. On his arrival, the kinsmen named the fee they would offer, and the shaman appointed an elder as his speaker, others to sing responses to his songs and to accompany them. Washing hands and face, he recounted how he had acquired his shamanistic tutelaries. With eyes closed, guided by his tutelary helpers, he began the diagnosis, singing his songs.

If the illness, *wáytat*, required only the application of herbal remedies, a shaman so endowed, often a woman, according to her diagnosis administered an infusion to be drunk, applied a poultice, or burned herbs on the fire so that the smoke bathed the afflicted part; and she sang her songs. If the ghost-soul had strayed, the appropriate shaman—one with ghost power—sent his guardian spirit to retrieve it. Should illness come from the abduction of the guardian spirit by that of a more powerful person, as often happened to the elderly, death was judged to be inevitable. Often, illness was diagnosed as the sickening of the *hé·šin* through another's malevolent wishes or through the shamanistic projection of *táʔaχtoyχ* into the patient. Sorcerers, it is said, preferred to work through malevolent wishes to sending their *táʔaχtoyχ*, since they might thus affect many at once and did not imperil themselves. If the curing shaman was treating an infected *hé·šin*, he stroked the body to keep it in and blew on it to cool it. He then removed and treated the *hé·šin*, after which he restored it to the unconscious patient. If it was a case of intrusion, the *táʔaχtoyχ* was extracted by hand or (Umatilla) by biting, then, while it fought the effort, the shaman plunged it into a bowl of water. Showing the gray, wormlike object around, the shaman consulted the spectators as to its disposal. If he threw it to the distant mountains, the sorcerer would have to search long for it; if he cast it into the fire, the sorcerer, wherever he was, would do likewise, and perish. As an intrinsic part of his cure, whatever the nature of the illness, the shaman recounted the manner in which the patient had contracted it.

If the patient showed no signs of improvement, the upright, prudent shaman returned the fee, and another shaman was called. A lingering illness brought suspicion upon the shaman himself, and death often brought revenge from enraged kinsmen: S. Black (1829) estimated that two or three shamans were slain every year among the tribes about Fort Walla Walla. The permeability of tribal boundaries is evinced by patronage and by sorcery accusations alike: for shamans were called in from allied tribes as well as that of the patient, and charges of sorcery were often leveled across, as well as within, tribal and, less likely, community levels, though not usually within kindreds.

As a class, shamans wore no distinguishing insignia, other than their amulets. They were not full-time practitioners, and a gradation ran from the gifted novice putting newly won powers to the test to the seasoned shaman on frequent call. Shamans married, sometimes indeed with other shamans, so long as their tutelaries were compatible. At the winter shamanistic exhibitions, shamans "played" together competitively, demonstrating their powers and consulted on the performances of novices, but otherwise they acted largely as individuals. There were no shaman societies, such as Walker (1973:105) reports for the Nez Perce; nor do consultants report the large array of tutelaries described for the Western Columbia River Sahaptin shaman (Murdock 1965a). When qualified a shaman might be chosen as headman. Chiefs and headmen, on the other hand, did not employ shamans to coerce recalcitrant followers, as was done, for example, among the Klamath (Stern 1965). Although prior to the departure of a war party a shaman divined the enemy's plans, shamans were otherwise rarely prominent as such in war. Gray Eagle, who rode in the forefront of battle with Five Ravens in the major engagement of the Cayuse War, claimed to be vested with powers of invulnerability (Clarke 1905, 2:592), an endowment suitable for a warrior.

History

In the early decades of the eighteenth century, the Cayuse must have resembled their riverine associates more closely than at later times, for they seem to have had canoes (Rigsby 1969:95), and they have long continued fishing pursuits adapted to their upstream locations. Although it was only within the first half of the eighteenth century that they acquired horses and began to master pastoral nomadism, by the end of the century they were well adapted to an equestrian life. By that time, they had already experienced new diseases, if they had already been upon the Plains with the Nez Perce, and heard indirect reports about the Whites. Such reports may have been responsible for the reception that the Umatilla or peoples just downriver from them accorded Lewis and Clark and David Thompson on first receiving them: it was behavior suggestive of the prophetic cults they were soon to evince (Spier 1935; Du Bois 1938; Stern 1960; Walker 1969). Expansion into the buffalo country was made possible, not only by the horse, but by the fur trade, which brought firearms and iron arrowheads to counter the armaments of the Blackfoot and their allies. From about 1811 to 1855, fur companies, their rivalries, and their economic dominion were major factors in Indian life. The mission of Dr. Marcus Whitman was a major presence 1836–1847. By that time, the Indians, whose lands were crossed by the Oregon Trail, had been exposed to both American settlers and to agents of the American government. The fate of the mission brought both these elements swiftly upon them, first in the Cayuse War of reprisal, 1848–1850, next in treaties pressed upon the Indians of the Northwest (locally, in 1855), and immediately thereafter in a general war in which the Indians sought by arms to oust the Whites, 1855–1858. In 1860, with ratification of their treaty, the Cayuse and their allies were removed to the Umatilla Reservation, in Cayuse territory.

The Fur Trade

When the Astorian overland party reached them in 1812, the Cayuse were already in possession of trade objects (Irving 1895, 2:34). Six years later, the North West Company, based in Montreal, erected Fort Walla Walla (or Nez Perces) near the mouth of the river of the same name. When, in 1821, the Nor'westers entered into a coalition with their former rivals, the British Hudson's Bay Company, the post became part of a powerful mercantile administration (Rich 1958–1960, 1), a remount center for the purchase of horses for the Snake Country brigades 'trapping' the beaver in competition with American rivals. The Cayuse interposed themselves as middlemen between the trading company and the Northern Paiute, Bannock, and Northern Shoshone, as well as extending their domains into Northern Paiute country. They sought for themselves the trade goods offered, and in particular the ammunition and guns essential to maintain themselves against their foes. For its part, the Company sought to conclude peace among its various Indian clients and to establish stable relationships with the native leaders. To this end, through gifts and honors, they enhanced the prestige of favored leaders, such as the Cayuse, Wilewmutkin, and Piupiumaksmaks of the Walla Walla; sought to regulate chiefly succession; undercut leaders who went against the Company; and bolstered the rule of those they favored by advocating systems of laws and penalties, such as flogging and hanging. In this way, the Company sought to foster tribal governments that would be responsive to Company needs.

Although the fort was manned by less than a dozen, and usually no more than eight or nine employees, it was powerful as a link along the chain of posts regulated by an organization with a virtual monopoly of essential trade goods. Moreover, it was a multiracial establishment, numbering Indians and Métis (the offspring of interracial unions) among employees and the wives of employees, and ready to hire some local Indians and to encompass marital alliances with the daughters of influential local leaders. About the fort there grew up a satellite settlement of the Home Guard, comprising the families of lesser employees and Indian laborers, together with hangers-on that included riverine Walla Wallas who were at home there. Often indigent, the Home Guard were a contrast to "the industrious and enterprising men of this tribe ... away trading salmon, kamas

Fig. 10. Cayuse women's reservation-style dress. Wool cloth T-shaped dresses, sometimes called "wing" dresses, became popular as cloth became more available on the reservations in the late 19th century. left (left to right), Mrs. Small Hawk, Cayuse; Tias, Cayuse; and Elisabeth Lindsley Shillal, also known as Petelshapinawit, Walla Walla, Cayuse, and Nez Perce. The 2 dresses on the left are decorated with dentalium shells, and the one on the right is decorated with elk teeth. Photograph by Lee Moorhouse, Umatilla Res., Oreg., about 1900. right, Dress of blue wool cloth decorated with 8 rows of dentalium shells alternating with rows of green, red, blue, and gold beads. Below the yoke is a fringe of gold tubular glass beads and small gold pendants used for jewelry in the Middle East. This dress, which originally belonged to Welahilakin (b. 1832, d. 1898), was handed down to daughters in 3 succeeding generations. Length 115 cm.

root, &c. to the mountain companies" (Townsend 1839:155–156). The first to be exposed to farming, if they gave a bad name to acculturation among their tribesmen and set a poor figure of the Indian for some traders, the Home Guard were essential intermediaries in culture change.

Company policy reached out primarily to the nomadic tribesmen, who were permitted to store roots in the fort, who held intertribal dances in its vicinity, and whose leaders frequented it for trade, news, and gifts. To train future leaders, the Company sent boys from leading families for schooling in the Red River settlements; one, Cayuse Halkett, son of the younger Wilewmutkin, returned for a visit in 1833, preaching to his fellows along the Umatilla; he died four years later while back at school. Out of such influences, as well as the religious instruction imparted by Company employees and others, there sprang up in the 1830s christianized forms of worship led by chiefs, which Spier (1935:30) has designated the Prophet Dance. (Indeed, the world view reported in 1829 by S. Black suggests the outlines of a native movement immediately antecedent to the christianized form.) The Company provided medicine during epidemic diseases and food, at least for the Home Guard, when the run of salmon failed (Chance 1973; Stern 1993).

Missionaries

During the time the Company ruled in the Oregon Territory—a region under the joint authority of Great Britain and the United States until settlement of the international boundary in 1846—it was receptive to missionary enterprises, and thus to the establishment in 1836 of mission stations by the American Board of Commissioners for Foreign Missions among the Cayuse, Nez Perce, and Spokane. The mission led by the Presbyterian missionary Dr. Marcus Whitman in the middle Walla Walla valley coupled Christian evangelism with programs of guided culture change, including schooling for the Indians. Friction soon arose, as the mission began to arouse invidious comparisons with the more openhanded, if calculated, policy of the Company. Culture shock on both sides was compounded by Cayuse fears that Whitman was prepared to establish his own small polity within Cayuse territory, with Walla Walla servants, probably from the Home Guard, as retainers. Whitman's preaching rivaled chiefly exhortations, while his medical practice placed him in competition with powerful shamans.

When the overland caravans began to roll in 1842, they passed through Cayuse territory; and the Indians soon became appalled by the numbers of immigrants. Whitman himself guided a large caravan to the mission (Oregon Pioneer Association 1894:64; Merk 1963:33). Moreover, the Presbyterian missionaries' teachings contrasted with Roman Catholicism. In 1843 Tawatoy, a Roman Catholic, declined election as head chief of the Cayuse in favor of his brother, Five Ravens, the sole Cayuse convert to the Protestant faith. The killing of his nephew, the Methodist-schooled son of Piupiumaksmaks, by an American settler during a trading expedition to Sutter's Fort, embittered Tawatoy. Probably acting as spokesman for his brother, the head chief, in 1845 Tawatoy urged Whitman to depart. The missionaries refused to go. During a devastating measles epidemic in 1847, Indian rumor had it that the medical missionary had brought it through sorcery, a charge that led Cayuses in the immediate vicinity, the band of Teloukaikt, to rise against the mission, killing the Whites there.

The Company acted promptly to ransom the survivors, while the territorial government raised a volunteer army and mounted a military campaign. It found the Cayuses disunited: the Umatilla River bands, led by Tawatoy and Qematspelu, repudiated the slaying of the Whitmans, as did the Walla Walla, Piupiumaksmaks; and they abstained. Five Ravens, who had forcibly taken a captive as a wife, joined the hostiles, as did segments of allied tribes. They were indecisively beaten by the Oregon volunteers; and it was only by threatening war upon the neutral Cayuses that the territorial government brought them into the field against their fellow tribesmen to capture the principal offenders, who were taken to Oregon City, tried, and hanged in 1850.

Government

The federal government first entered the scene in 1843, when Indian Subagent Elijah White had secured a tribal election among the Cayuse, at which they selected a head chief (Tawatoy, then Five Ravens) and subordinate chiefs and accepted a table of laws earlier adopted by the Nez Perce. The Walla Walla also accepted the new order, continuing under Piupiumaksmaks. In the midst of the Cayuse War Oregon gained territorial status, and afterward the superintendent of Indian affairs established the "Utilla" agency on the Lower Crossing of the Umatilla River, near present Echo, to handle local Indian issues. In 1855, as part of a series of treaties to settle Indian title in Oregon and Washington territories, the Cayuse, Walla Walla, and Umatilla agreed to accept a reservation in the Cayuse segment of the Umatilla valley. However, the sweeping changes

Fig. 11. Delegation to Washington, D.C. left to right, front row: Peo, Umatilla; Homlai, Walla Walla; Young Chief, Cayuse. back row, John McBain, Métis, interpreter; Showaway, Cayuse; Wolf, Palouse; and Agent Lee Moorhouse. Photograph by Charles M. Bell, 1889.

Fig. 12. Presbyterian Church at Tutuilla, Umatilla Res., Oreg. Photograph by Lee Moorhouse, 1897–1912.

Fig. 13. Otis Halfmoon and Amy Wildmoon fastening tepee cover to the pole. Photograph by Theodore Stern, Umatilla Res., Joseph, Oreg., 1957.

envisaged in those treaties, which entailed largely abandoning native life for that of an American farmer, together with anger aroused among the Indians by the pressures exerted by the treaty commissioners, led tribesmen to repudiate them soon after they had been signed. A gold rush in Washington Territory led to incursions of goldseekers before the treaties had been ratified; and step by step the country was plunged into war. The Indians had held intertribal councils and developed alliances anticipating conflict, which included coastal Salish and Sahaptins intermarried with them, with segments of each remaining neutral. In the so-called Yakima War, the Sahaptin tribes and Cayuse (the Nez Perces remaining largely neutral) were defeated by 1856, though invasion of the lands of the interior Salish tribes by the regular army renewed the conflict for two more years.

Following the conclusion of the war, the treaties were ratified; and in 1860, as the "Confederated tribes of the Umatilla Indian Reservation," the Cayuse, Walla Walla, and Umatilla were removed to their reservation. However, restless under the rule of the first Indian agents, large segments of the Walla Walla under Homlai (fig. 11), a nephew of the fallen Piupiumaksmaks, and the Umatilla, remained along the Columbia, moving seasonally into the Grande Ronde. Over the two decades during which treaty annuities and amenities were provided, they drifted on and off the reservation, largely spurning those offerings and following prophets of the Washat faith (Du Bois 1938) that had arisen out of the older movements in the aftermath of the war, including the Walula-Wanapam, Smohalla (Relander 1956; Ruby and Brown 1972), and the Umatilla, Luls (Stern 1960, 1989). Finally, during the Nez Perce War of 1877 and Bannock and Northern Paiute war of 1878, the absentee tribesmen were swept back upon the reservation or dispersed among the Sinkayuse to the north.

Upon the reservation, the agent somewhat strengthened the hand of the three salaried head chiefs, subject always to his own authority, striving to bring them to recognize a responsibility toward indigent tribesmen who were not linked to them as kinsmen or followers. He sought, through them, to encourage the general practice of farming and stockraising. As immigrants and miners traveled along the Oregon Trail down the Umatilla valley, and establishments sprang up on the borders of the reservation to serve them,

frictions developed. In what was to become Pendleton, one of those border communities, settlers discovered that some reservation lands were prime farmlands and urged that the Indians be moved elsewhere; but on two occasions (1871, 1878) the Indians refused to leave, and were upheld by the federal government. The major Christian presence on the reservation, responsible as well for the school, was a Roman Catholic order, although a handful of Indians retained Presbyterian leanings derived from Whitman (fig. 12). A large number, under Homlai, and the Cayuse, Young Chief, adhered firmly to the Washat faith.

Following the Bannock and Paiute War of 1878 and the end of the annuity period two years later, administrative changes were introduced, with an Indian police and a code of laws they were to uphold (1881), followed by a Court of Indian Offenses (1885). With these moves, Indian judges came to supersede the chiefs in authority. Meanwhile, the Slater Act of 1885 introduced allotment, which the men of the reservation voted to accept. Allotment undermined the freedom of chiefs and headmen to graze their livestock, their principal source of wealth, on the open reservation. A party of them, therefore, moved to the Flathead reservation, where they remained with their herds until in turn it was allotted. From 1881, a Protestant faction, initially led by the Umatilla chief, Winampsnut, and the reservation doctor, *415*

Fig. 14. Tribal government program. Cecilia Sheoships and Wenix Red Elk, members of the Umatilla Salmon Corps, a youth community service group, work to re-establish plant communities, especially wetland habitat. Here willows are being planted along a creek as part of a stream rehabilitation project. Photograph by Debra Croswell, 1995.

William C. McKay, challenged the power of the Roman Catholics and gained freedom for Indians to send their children to a government Indian school at Forest Grove. With allotment, a Métis contingent, largely sprung from former Hudson's Bay employees and their Indian wives, returned from Frenchtown, in the Walla Walla valley, were admitted to tribal membership, and took up lands in the upper Umatilla valley. Some of these acculturated descendants of the Home Guard were leaders in introducing farming innovations on the reservation, although many subsequently sold their allotments and moved away. Although reservation Indians had taken well to farming in the early days, some winning prizes at the Oregon State Fair of 1868 (Meacham 1875:182), with allotment, many, unable to muster the capital to farm their lands and pay taxes, turned to leasing them. Conservative tribesmen, refusing to be reduced to "little White men," took the same course. Ambitious Indian farmers, overextended during the First World War, were wiped out. A resumption of Indian farming, largely spurred by veterans of the Second World War, also met discouragement (Stern and Boggs 1971).

416

The proximity of Pendleton, together with the small size of the reservation (which in 1969 embraced only 86,262 acres), had acculturative consequences, as Indians found employment in town or moved. In 1968, fewer than one-quarter of the enrolled membership dwelt on the reservation, which was checkerboarded with the farms of Whites. No special Indian schools were maintained: Indians taught and studied in the public schools and at Blue Mountain Community College, Pendleton, Oregon.

Since the 1960s, the Confederated Tribes of the Umatilla Indian Reservation have launched vigorous programs to better conditions, to consolidate tribal lands on the reservation, to improve ecological conditions (fig. 14), and to develop economic resources ("Fishing," fig. 17, this vol.). It has secured a medical clinic and low income housing. In conjunction with the Yakima, Warm Springs, and Nez Perce tribal governments, it has, as a member of the Columbia River Inter-Tribal Fish Commission, entered into defense of treaty fishing rights. They have established a casino, dedicating 55 percent of the profits to meeting tribal needs.

With the assertion of Indian identity, the Washat faith, which in the 1950s was a clandestine presence on the reservation, emerged to a prominence in which its longhouse occupied a central position within the Celebrations Grounds. There, in the annual Root Feast, members offer thanksgiving for first fruits, and they participate in similar ceremonies on other reservations. Celebrations of births, marriages, and deaths, which attract kinsmen from far and wide, draw upon tradition to infuse life with rich meaning.

Population

Estimates of aboriginal population vary, in part because the term Walla Walla is sometimes restricted to the Walula proper and other times may be extended to include the Sahaptins on the Columbia from the Walula down to The Dalles. Ray (1959:11) estimates a total population for the three peoples of 5,000 before contact (table 1).

Hunn (1990:135), drawing upon population figures given by Boyd (1985), and setting forth population densities by linguistic subdivision, finds Cayuse density 0.10 persons per square mile. For the riverine peoples, densities are far higher, 0.55 for the Columbia River Sahaptin, which includes the Umatilla, and above 0.79 for the Northeast Sahaptin, among whom fall the Walla Walla. The warlike reputation of the Cayuse, despite their small historic population, together with a density far below that of associated peoples living a similar lifeway, suggest that when first encountered by Whites they had recently suffered great losses, possibly in the smallpox epidemic of 1780.

Synonymy

Cayuse is a term of uncertain derivation and many variants: Cailloux (Cayoux), Cayuse (Caiuse, Cayouse, Cayuce,

Confederated Tribes of the Umatilla Res., Pendleton, Oreg.

Fig. 15. Groundbreaking ceremony for the Tamustalik Cultural Institute, a facility of the Confederated Tribes of the Umatilla Res., where the history and culture of the Cayuse, Walla Walla, and Umatilla people will be featured. left, Elders drumming. around the circle from left: Alex Johnson, unidentified man, Ham Patrick, Louie Dick, Raymond Pop Corn Burke, and Marvin Wish Patrick. On horseback are Toni Minthorn, Levi Johnson, Jesse-Umapine Jones, Robinson Minthorn; 2 boys are unidentified. right, Brittany Cline (center) with other tribal preschoolers. Photographs by Debra Croswell, June 1995.

Cyuse, Kioose, Kaijous, Keyuse), Kayouiks, Kyemuse, Caäguas, Skiuse (Iskayouse); additional spellings are listed by Hodge (1907–1910, 1:224–225). Mooney (1896:744) was evidently told by Sahaptins that the name was from Nez Perce, but this origin is unsupported by later fieldwork. The trader Samuel Black (1829: query 25) stated that it was "a Name given them by the People from their living amongst the Stones or Rocks," assuming a derivation from French also implied by Hale's (1846:214) spelling ⟨Cailloux⟩. In Columbian Salish the name is *qayús*, also found with the redundant nominalizer prefix *s-* as *sqayús* (Teit 1930:202; M. Dale Kinkade, communication to editors 1996). Teit's (1930:300–301) claim that the name was originally Salishan and cognate with the Columbian Salish subgroup name Sinkayuse is refuted when the correct forms of the two names are compared, which clearly have nothing to do with each other: Columbian *qayús* 'Cayuse' and *snq̓aʔáẃs* 'Sinkayuse' (M. Dale Kinkade, communication to editors 1996). Teit (1928:92) reported that Columbian *(s)qayús* was from the "name of Umatilla valley or a place there," but it is evidently a borrowed word, comparable to the Columbian names for the Walla Walla, Umatilla, and other Sahaptin groups, which were borrowed in parallel fashion (Teit 1928:92). Against a derivation from French is the fact that French *cailloux* 'pebbles, gravel' is pronounced /kayu/, which does not account for the final *-s* of the name or for the back-velar /q/ attested by the Columbian form, which points to an Indian rather than a European source. It may be added that the Cayuse traffic in horses led to the extension of the tribal name to Indian ponies in general; some Indians con-

jecture that the name was originally applied to the animal, only later being extended to the ethnic group.

The term for the Cayuse in the Cayuse language is ⟨lík-si-yu⟩ (probably [líksiwʔ]), designating either the people as a whole or a local group (Rigsby 1969:133).

weyí·letpu· (Waiilatpu, Wailetpu, Waylette, Wy-eilat, Ye-let-po) is the Nez Perce term by which the modern Cayuse refer to themselves, whence the Sahaptin name for them, *wáylatpam*. Applied by Marcus Whitman to the site of his mission in the Walla Walla valley, it is glossed by him 'place of the rye grass'. Modern Cayuse deny that meaning, and Rigsby (1969:133) reports the folk-etymology 'people of the shady place'.

In Sahaptin the Cayuse and Nez Perce were known as *šíwaniš* 'strangers' (Mooney 1896:744; synonymy in "Nez Perce," this vol.). The Molala called the Cayuse and Nez Perce *háyłunci* 'upriver people' (Gatschet 1877a; Rigsby 1969:141). The Klamath designated the Cayuse, Nez Perce, and allied Sahaptin-speaking equestrians by the generic term *ya·makni·* 'northerners'. The Numic-speaking Bannock and Northern Paiute applied to the Cayuse, Nez Perce, Sahaptin, and others the name *saiduka* 'dwellers in tule-mat houses, enemy' (synonymy in "Nez Perce," this vol.). Variants are Saidökadö (Stewart 1939:140, 144) and Saidúikadú (Kelly 1932:70), a term applied by the Surprise Valley Paiute to the Nez Perce and to the Klamath, among others, and by the Humboldt River Paiute to predecessors of Numic speech (Hopkins 1883; Heizer 1970). Spellings in early writings include Scietoga, Scyatoga, Shyatogo.

Table 1. Population

	Cayuse	Walla Walla	Umatilla	Total	Sources
Aboriginal (1780)	500	1,500[a,b]		2,000[a]	Mooney 1928:18; Kroeber 1939:138
	1,000[a]	1,500[a]	2,500[a]	5,000	Ray 1959:11
	2,500	2,000	2,500	7,000	Walker and Leonhardy 1967
1805–1806	250	1,600	2,600	4,450	Thwaites 1904–1905, 6:115; Anastasio 1972: 202; Boyd 1985:384
1811			1,100		Glover 1962:353, 374
1812	250	550			Spaulding 1953:66, 75; Gunkel 1978:28
1829	340[a]	1,640[a]		1,980[a]	S. Black 1829: query 25
1835	320[a]	200			Gairdner 1841:257
1837	400	400			Hulbert and Hulbert 1936–1941, 1:122; Parker 1844:314, 315; Boyd 1985:375; de Smet 1905, 3:990
	2,000	500			
1841			1,100		Wilkes 1845, 5:140
	500				Wilkes 1845, 6:214
1849	160[a]		3,000[a]		Newell 1959:150–151
1851	126	130			Dart 1851:478
1853	120		300[b]		Doty 1855
1854	600	[200]			ARCIA 1854
1861	384	209[c]	340[c]	933	ARCIA 1861:165
1865	370	160	229	759	ARCIA 1865:485
1870	334	201[d]	302[d]	837	ARCIA 1870:55
1878	383	290	200	873[e]	ARCIA 1878:122
1888	401	406[f]	171[f]	978	ARCIA 1888:212
1899	369	529	188	1,086	ARCIA 1899, 1:320
1906	405	579	207	1,191	ARCIA 1906:483
1912				1,114	ARCIA 1912:83
1960				1,201	Wright, Mitchell, and Schmidt 1960
1987				1,610[g]	Bureau of Indian Affairs 1987:21
1991				1,691[g]	Bureau of Indian Affairs 1991:table 3
1996				1,500[h]	Tiller 1996:546

[a] Calculated by Stern from source figures. When figures are recorded for "men" only, the number is multiplied by 4 to yield total population.

[b] Walla Walla and Umatilla combined.

[c] Reservation numbers. Off-reservation is 120 Walla Walla, 35 Umatilla.

[d] Reservation numbers. Off-reservation is 404 Walla Walla, 153 Umatilla.

[e] Including 150 Columbia River Indians who went onto the reservation after the Nez Perce and Bannock wars.

[f] Including 216 Walla Walla and 16 Umatilla "mixed-bloods."

[g] Reservation residents.

[h] Tribal enrollment.

Walla Walla (*Walawála*) 'little rivers' is the reduplicated diminutive of Sahaptin *wána* 'river'. The name was applied to the river that runs westward into the Columbia on the Oregon-Washington boundary and by extension to the people who dwelt in part on its lower course. From their principal settlement, *walúula*, they were known in Sahaptin as *walúulapam*, a term alternating with *walawálapam* (cf. Relander 1956:62). The borrowed term in Columbia Salish is ·swalawálaox (Teit 1928:92). In various spellings (e.g., Wallow Wallow, Willa Walla), the tribal designation was extended by Whites to other riverine Sahaptins, including the Umatilla. In this usage, for example, the treaty of 1855 with the tribes of middle Oregon recognized the Tygh as the "Upper DesChutes band of Walla-wallas," and the Dock-Spus, or 'John Day's River band of Walla-Wallas' (Kappler 1904–1941, 2:536).

On the Plains, the Crow are said to have applied the term póxolokáti to the Nez Perce and Walla Walla; they may also have thus designated the Cayuse and Umatilla.

Umatilla (Yowmalolam, Umatallow, Umatalla, Emitilly, and in shortened form, Ottilah, Utalle, Utalah, Utilla, etc.), is derived from *ímatilam* 'lots of rocks, rocky bottom', a winter village at the mouth of the Umatilla River that was one of their two principal settlements (vol. 17:666; cf. Suphan 1974:124, 130). The Columbia Salish render the name ·samatélamux (Teit 1928:92). The Nez Perce call them *hiyówatalampo·* (Aoki 1994:171).

From an old Cayuse place-name, *nixyá·wi* 'aspen spring', designating a spot in the Umatilla valley, modern Umatilla sometimes designate themselves as *nixyé·wiła*, as dwellers on the lower end of the reservation; and by modern Nez Perce the place-name has come to be used for the entire Umatilla Reservation.

Northern Paiutes designate the Umatilla and other Columbia Sahaptins by the term *ayáyci* 'salmon (people)', seemingly in contradistinction to the term *saiduka* applied to the Cayuse and other equestrian peoples (thus Akaichies—Irving 1895, 2:81).

Columbia Sahaptins from the Walla Walla down to The Dalles were called in Cayuse [lúsmiwʔ] 'people of the big [Columbia] river' (Rigsby 1969:133) and in Nez Perce *pikúnma*, with the same meaning. In this term the Umatilla and perhaps the Walla Walla were included. To the Umatilla they were collectively *wanałáma*, from which is derived the loanblend *wánapum* used in Cayuse Nez Perce.

Sources

The prehistory of the area aboriginally occupied by the Cayuse, Umatilla, and Walla Walla has been treated directly by Shiner (1961), Osborne, Bryan, and Crabtree (1961), Osborne (1957), Garth (1952, 1964), and Toepel, Willingham, and Minor (1980). Little save survey work (Cole 1973) has been done within Cayuse country. The physical anthropology of the living populations has not been systematically studied.

Linguistic studies include the collections and classification of Hale (1846), which contains both Sahaptin and Cayuse materials. Umatilla and Walla Walla data are covered by Jacobs (1931) and Cayuse by Rigsby (1965, 1969). Because of the acculturation of the Cayuse to the Nez Perce at an early period of their existence, and because of changes that tribal cultures underwent through time, ethnohistorical data are of particular importance. Of special interest are the responses made in 1829 by Samuel Black, chief trader at Fort Walla Walla and a man long acquainted with Indians, to an ethnographic questionnaire circulated by the Hudson's Bay Company. The data cited and quoted from this document are published by permission of the Hudson's Bay Company. Black's observations are often general but seem to pertain in particular to the Cayuse and Walla Walla dwelling close to the post. The correspondence of the Whitmans, while it contains valuable vignettes of Indian life, is rarely given to systematic description. Ruby and Brown (1972) treats Cayuse history: the valuable research that has gone into it has not been matched in analysis and interpretation. The ethnohistorical period through 1855 has been reexamined (Stern 1993, 1996).

Among treatments of ethnography, the studies of Ray (1936, 1939, 1942, 1959; Ray et al. 1938) are preeminent. Stern's (1953–1968) fieldwork is a source for this chapter. Anastasio (1972) has provided a general socioecological analysis of the Southern Plateau that the Cayuse data support. Garth (1964, 1965) advances a provocative reformulation of Plateau relationships.

Spier (1935), Du Bois (1938), Stern (1960), and Walker (1969) treat religious movements among the Cayuse and their allies, to which Relander (1956) offers additional data. For the modern reservation, several studies concerning socioeconomic conditions were conducted in 1968, of which one, dealing with farming (Stern and Boggs 1971), has been published. A moving picture of the reservation, *Umatilla '68*, was made by Nancy Owens.

Nez Perce

DEWARD E. WALKER, JR.

Language

Nez Perce (ˌnezˈpərs)* is closely related to Sahaptin (Rigsby 1965; Aoki 1963) in the Sahaptian language grouping that dominates the southern Plateau. Neither historical linguistics nor archeological research (Leonhardy and Rice 1970) has produced evidence that the Sahaptians have ever resided outside the Columbia Basin. Existing research shows only that they are ancient dwellers of the Columbia Basin with possible external connections to the Penutian superfamily (Swadesh 1956).

Territory

Nez Perce territory centered on the middle Snake and Clearwater rivers and the northern portion of the Salmon River basin in central Idaho and adjacent Oregon and Washington (fig. 1). In 1800 there were over 70 permanent villages ranging from 30 to 200 individuals, depending on the season and type of social grouping (Walker 1958–1964). About 300 total sites have been identified, including both camps and villages (Schwede 1970).

The Nez Perce have been divided into Upper and Lower divisions, primarily on dialect grounds. The Upper Nez Perce were oriented more toward a Plains lifeway. The Nez Perce are also very closely related linguistically, culturally, and socially to the Sahaptin speakers of Oregon and Washington, including the Palouse, Walla Walla, Yakima, Umatilla, and Wayampam, and with them form an intertribal ceremonial congregation (Anastasio 1972).

Their territory was marked by a diverse flora and fauna, as well as by temperature and precipitation patterns reflecting sharp variations in elevation. The deep canyons cut by the

*The phonemes of Nez Perce are: (voiceless stops and affricate) p, t, c, k, q, ʔ; (glottalized stops and affricate) ṗ, ṫ, ċ, ḱ, q̇; (voiceless fricatives) ł, s, x, x̣, h; (resonants) m, n, w, y, l; (glottalized resonants) ṁ, ṅ, ẇ, ẏ, l̇; (short vowels) i, e, a, o, u; (long vowels) iˑ, eˑ, aˑ, oˑ, uˑ; (stress) v́. The plain stops and affricate are unaspirated before vowels, moderately aspirated before consonants, and strongly aspirated word-finally. The dental consonants (t, ł, n, l) are palatalized before u, and the alveolar consonants (s, c) are palatalized before i. In some varieties s and c are pronounced [š] and [č]. Information on Nez Perce phonology is from Aoki (1970:10–11) and reflects specifically the Upper or Upriver dialect.

The Lower or Downriver dialect of Nez Perce (also called Cayuse Nez Perce) has five additional phonemes: (voiceless stops) kʷ, qʷ; (glottalized stops) ḱʷ, q̇ʷ; (voiceless fricative) š. It also appears to lack the contrast between u and o (Aoki 1994:ix, xii).

Clearwater, Salmon, and Snake rivers encouraged seasonal subsistence migrations, a pattern typical of other Plateau tribes (Marshall 1977; Walker 1987).

Culture

Annual Cycle

Large game animals taken by the Nez Perce included elk, deer, moose, mountain sheep, and goat, as well as black and grizzly bear. After obtaining the horse (after 1700), the Nez Perce made annual trips to Montana to secure bison and to engage in trade and various other forms of exchange. Smaller game animals were taken as needed, including rabbit, squirrel, badger, and marmot. Birds taken included ducks, geese, grouse, sage hens, and birds of prey for ceremonial reasons. The Nez Perce were fortunate in having numerous anadromous fish and many streams well suited for fishing. With their complex fishing technology, they took the chinook, coho, chum, and sockeye, varieties of salmon; dolly varden, cutthroat, lake, and steelhead varieties of trout; several kinds of suckers; whitefish; sturgeon, lampreys; and squawfish. Their average per capita consumption of fish is estimated at over 500 pounds per annum (Walker 1967).

In the early spring when the cache pits had been emptied of stored food, the Nez Perce began their communal drives in the river valleys, with snowshoe hunting in deep snow and trips by canoe (fig. 2) down the Snake and Columbia rivers to intercept the early salmon runs. Although hunting was fundamental and continuous, it was of lesser importance during the seasons of salmon runs when all able-bodied adults turned to fishing where many thousands of pounds were customarily caught and processed (Walker 1967). As the spring progressed, salmon began arriving in Nez Perce territory, and the early root crops were taken at lower elevations.

Men were the principal fishermen, but women assisted in splitting, drying, and storing the fish. Hook and line, spears, harpoons, dip nets, traps, and weirs were all used in various ways ("Fishing," fig. 12, this vol.) (Walker 1967). Large traps and weirs were usually constructed communally by villages and regulated by a fishing specialist who regulated the fishing and divided the catch. Weirs and traps, constructed close to winter villages, often were located on smaller lateral streams. Salmon were also speared and netted from canoes and dipping platforms on the major tributaries. Fish were

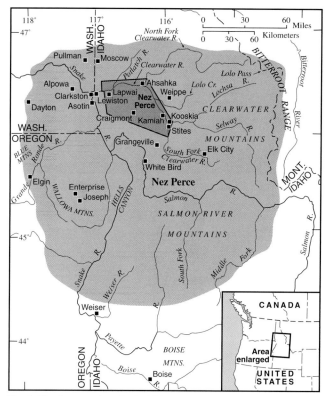

Fig. 1. Nez Perce territory in the 19th century with modern town and reservation locations.

mostly sun-dried and smoked for winter storage, while the more succulent parts were consumed immediately.

Roots in higher areas such as Weippe did not often ripen until mid-August (Harbinger 1964). The basic root staple was camas ("Ethnobiology and Subsistence," fig. 2, this vol.), but bitterroot, couse, wild carrot, and wild onion were also important. Fruits gathered included serviceberries, gooseberries, hawthorn berries, thornberries, huckleberries, currants, and chokecherries. Pine nuts, sunflower seeds, and black moss added to the abundant vegetable and fruit inventory of gathered foods.

By midsummer the Nez Perce would typically leave their villages in the lower river valleys and move into the highlands where later-growing crops were harvested, highland streams fished, and hunting intensified. The fall salmon runs, fall hunting, and gathering of late root and berry crops provided winter food stores, and brief bison hunting trips into Montana over the Lolo and other passes augmented winter supplies of meat. Hunting forays into Montana usually included members of neighboring tribes such as the Umatilla, Cayuse, and Yakima and were led by warriors (Anastasio 1972). Some Nez Perce groups would stay in the Plains for several years at a time, and few winters passed that did not see some Nez Perce wintering with the neighboring Flathead. By November most travel ceased, and the Nez Perce settled into their winter villages until the cycle began again in the early spring (Walker 1973:56).

Deer and elk were taken communally by encirclement methods similar to those used by many other tribes. Decoys

and scarecrows were used to entice them into areas where they could be easily dispatched. Fire and horses were employed in driving deer and elk into traps. A variant of the lake entrapment used by other tribes consisted of driving deer and elk into larger rivers where they could be easily dispatched from canoes and from horseback. The ambush was a popular hunting method, especially in prehorse days when it was used for bison by pedestrian Nez Perce hunters in Montana. Deadfalls were popular for larger game as were snares for birds and smaller game. There is some evidence for use of rattlesnake poison on arrow tips in certain types of hunting (Walker 1973:56).

Women dug roots with crutch-handled digging sticks (fig. 3). Some wooden containers were made, but coiled basketry was the major form of container. Food was stored in baskets in bark and grass-lined cache pits located on well-drained hillsides and in parfleche bags (fig. 4). Some horn spoons and drinking cups were made, but most spoons and bowls were of wood. Distinctive stone pestles were used with both basketry (with a stone base) and wooden mortars, primarily to grind meat and roots. Splitting wedges were made of antler. Club and ax heads were of stone hafted with a combination of antler, wood, and rawhide. Bows were made of syringa and yew, frequently backed with sinew.

Roots and meats were boiled in baskets by stone-boiling and baked in large earthen ovens. Generally, meat was broiled by attaching it to a wooden frame or to sticks inserted in the ground around an open fire. Roots were crushed and formed into loaves and biscuits for storage and later eaten in soups and stews.

Life Cycle

An expectant mother's older female relatives instructed her in the proper ways of guarding her health and that of her baby. Vigorous exercise was encouraged with both hot and

Fig. 2. Canoe made out of a hollow log. Photograph by Edward S. Curtis, Clearwater R., Idaho © 1910.

Fig. 3. Food preparation. left, Ahyahtoetuhnmy (Lizzie Pablo), collecting camas roots, probably near Kooskia, on the eastern part of the Nez Perce Res., Idaho, where she lived. She places the roots in the woven bag tied around her waist; a full cornhusk bag is in the foreground. She also holds her digging stick. Photographed about 1910. right, Woman grinding dried biscuitroot, from cloth bags around her, in a basket mortar with a stone pestle. A stone mortar is in the foreground. The man on the far right is holding a fishnet scoop, and the man in the center holds a pipebag and wears a buffalo robe, an item of prestige. Photograph by Merton L. Miller, 1901.

cold bathing, and numerous medicinal herbs were known and used freely. It was thought that touching, viewing, or ridiculing deformed animals or human beings could cause the expected baby to suffer similar misfortune. Likewise, the expectant mother did not tie knots or do other things symbolic of birth obstructions. Instead, she concentrated on activities and rituals that would ensure a safe delivery and a healthy baby (Walker 1973:107).

Nez Perce mothers usually delivered their babies in small, separate houses with the aid of a midwife and female relatives, but a male shaman was called if severe problems developed. The young mother was attended by her own mother whenever possible. Certain shamans were thought to possess special powers in obstetrics, and their methods typically combined herbs, physical manipulation, and special rituals, which they obtained from their tutelary spirits. They shaped the baby's head and feet immediately after delivery and took precautions to ensure that it breathed properly. The umbilical cord was retained in a small hide container and attached to the cradleboard, and it was believed that it would bring bad luck to destroy such an intimate part of the baby. Relatives gave gifts and held feasts for the mother and baby, particularly in the case of a firstborn (Walker 1973:107–108).

Babies were soon placed in cradleboards, where they stayed until they were ready to walk. Nursing usually continued for several years, and a mother was assisted in this task by close female relatives whenever necessary. When the baby was weaned, he was fed with softened meats and

vegetables as well as tough gristles to chew for teething. A system of adoption operated if a mother died, the child being taken either by the mother's relatives or by another wife of her husband.

Typically, grandparents cared for the children of a household after they were weaned, and very close ties developed between them. Children tended to be very formal and respectful with their parents but joked and teased with their grandparents, whom they regarded as equals; grandparents and grandchildren used the same kinship term to address one another (Lundsgaarde 1967).

Grandchildren learned many of the basic lessons of life from their grandparents. A boy's first hunting, fishing, sweatbathing, and horse riding were usually directed by his grandfather and older male relatives who were careful to see that he was properly instructed. Grandmothers and older female relatives had a similar influence over their granddaughters. Grandparents also spent many hours recounting myths, a primary means of educating the young. Uncles, aunts, cousins, and older siblings all took an active part in training the child. Children were rarely disciplined as infants but when older, they were routinely whipped in groups by special whippers.

Nez Perce spent much of their time with siblings and cousins, whom they generally treated as brothers or sisters. Older and younger siblings were called by different terms and respect was given accordingly (Lundsgaarde 1967; Ackerman 1971). Typically children were awakened each morning before daybreak during all seasons of the year and

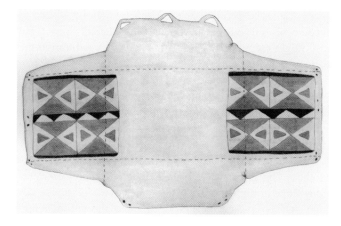

Smithsonian, Natl. Mus. of the Amer. Ind.: 23/2054 (neg 30733).

Fig. 4. Parfleche. Folded envelopes of rawhide were used to store and transport dried foods, clothing, and household goods. This parfleche is painted in red, yellow, and green with blue and black outlines. Manufactured about 1925. Length 63.5 cm.

taken to a bathing area, where their uncles or aunts supervised their essential training. Proper exercise and bathing in cold and hot baths were practices thought to make the child strong. Light switching of the child's body after bathing was administered by uncles or aunts with stern lectures on proper behavior.

Nez Perce children were given names of important family ancestors, because it was believed that this could favorably influence a child's development. Nicknames were common, and a formal naming ceremony with gift giving was held at adolescence. Nevertheless, names might be changed at any time during the life of the individual, primarily as a result of significant accomplishments. In general, names could be inherited, reflected important accomplishments, were given after spirit visions, highlighted outstanding personal characteristics, and were regarded as personal and family property.

At about age three, boys and girls began to assist in the various subsistence activities of the family. They were tied in the saddle and taken on horseback to the various hunting, fishing, root digging, and berry-gathering areas, where they assisted with toy bows, digging sticks, and other implements designed for children. By age six, girls and boys were making substantial contributions to family subsistence, and ceremonies were held at this time to celebrate the child's first game kill or first root digging. It was believed that if a renowned hunter or fisherman ate the boy's first game, the boy would become a good provider. Likewise, girls would become good providers if their first roots and berries were eaten by experts. A related, important event for the child at this time was a formal, private lecture from an outstanding elder. Although the elder said little the child had not already heard concerning proper morals and behavior, the dignity and formality observed on this occasion was impressive.

Shortly before, and for some time after, adolescence, Nez Perce youths were sent out to seek visions from tutelary spirits. If successful, this major event in the maturation of both boys and girls meant that they would be successful adults. Conversely, they could expect only mediocre lives if unsuccessful in securing a vision. Many went out numerous times in order to receive a vision.

The Nez Perce girl underwent an elaborate ceremony when she reached puberty. At menarche, she was isolated from the community in a special house where she was attended by older female relatives and her mother. Friends and relatives were quickly notified that the girl was making this transition into adulthood. During her isolation at this time she was urged to keep busy and to think good thoughts, as it was believed that anything she did during this period would influence her later life. She came outside only after dark and then for only short periods, and her meals were cooked on a separate fire. She could scratch her body only with an elaborately carved scratcher made especially for the occasion. Her isolation was ritually ended after about one week, and she was welcomed back into the community as a young woman ready for marriage. Friends and relatives gave her gifts and new clothes. Generally, well-to-do families took greater care with their daughters during this period of transition (Walker 1973:109).

Marriage among the Nez Perce was arranged by family heads, and childhood betrothals were known. Among the most important considerations was the relative prestige of each family. Rather sharp differences of wealth and social prestige separated some Nez Perce families. Slaves captured in war or obtained through trade occupied the lowest level of Nez Perce society and typically performed menial domestic tasks with little voice in family or village affairs. Exceptions are known; several male slaves rose to positions of some influence. Children of slaves were not regarded as slaves, and in general, slaves were treated similarly to other relatives. Female slaves were often taken as second wives.

When a young man expressed interest in a particular girl, his family met and decided if she came from a socially acceptable family. If she did, their genealogies were checked to see if they were related in any way, as marriage was forbidden between relatives, even distant cousins. If one son had already married into the family, the marriage was more favored, and in some instances families were linked by marriages between several sons and daughters. Sororal polygyny was common; transvestites were occasionally seen but not typically taken as second wives (Lundsgaarde 1967).

In other cases when a girl was desired as a wife, an older female relative of the boy began negotiations. If the girl's family reacted favorably, the female go-between moved into the home to observe the girl for a period of time to see if she were acceptable as a wife. During this time the boy and girl would be visiting one another, and their families would be meeting for occasional feasts. If the girl proved acceptable and the families were compatible, the couple then began living together. If they seemed compatible and well-matched after a sufficient time had lapsed, the necessary ceremony and exchange of gifts were performed, with the groom's relatives giving gifts first; the bride's family reciprocated.

In one type of gift exchange, a number of relatives from each family faced one another across a central area and began to trade item for item. Occasionally, a rich relative would trade with two, rather than one member of the opposite family. An element of competition existed in these exchanges, and no one was sure beforehand who would gain the most from the exchange. Relatives of the groom gave primarily male-related gifts such as horses, hunting and fishing implements, and buckskin, whereas relatives of the bride gave root bags, baskets, beads, digging sticks, and beaded bags. In marriages between important families, many people participated in such exchanges. In the exchange sponsored by the groom's family the food provided was primarily meat, but in the second exchange sponsored by the bride's family, roots of many kinds were the main dish. It is important to note that the exchange between the two families did not favor either side. Nor were there any obvious attempts to shame the other family by giving more, emphasizing the fact that the marriage was an agreement between equals (Lundsgaarde 1967).

After the second exchange the couple was regarded as married. While divorces could be obtained easily, there were few, since as time passed and cooperative ties developed between the two families, both families would discourage divorce. Couples could live with either set of parents, but more often they resided with the groom's parents. Although there was no formal mother-in-law avoidance, the son-in-law observed formal respect when in her presence and was similarly careful not to laugh or joke around his brothers-in-law. In contrast, he joked with his wife's sisters in an intimate manner relating to the fact that one of them might marry him if his wife died, or if he decided to take an additional wife. Conversely, the bride showed respect for her mother-in-law and sisters-in-law but joked freely with her brothers-in-law. Similarly, this relates to the operation of the levirate, wherein the wife would usually marry the eldest of her husband's brothers should he die; the sororate was also employed.

Age brought wealth and power with older males commanding respect widely and occupying the most important leadership positions. The death of such high-ranking persons disrupted the normal functioning of social life and was followed by elaborate funerals. If a person thought he was ready to die, he normally made known whom he wished to receive his surviving property and his tutelary spirits. He also might recommend that certain sons succeed him in the offices he held.

As soon as death occurred, it was announced by a herald or crier. Close female relatives immediately began the customary wailing, and a group of relatives and friends congregated around the corpse to mourn until it was washed, dressed, and buried the next day. The corpse was ritually bathed, combed, and decorated with red face paint and new clothes. The grave was normally dug by volunteers on a talus slope or high geological eminence overlooking the village. It was marked by a wooden stake and subsequently avoided. When prepared for burial, the corpse was wrapped in a robe, usually taken to the grave on a horse-drawn travois, and then interred with a number of the deceased's favorite valuables. Occasionally, after the grave was covered a favorite horse was killed and left in the vicinity. The ceremony ended with rituals by the shaman to prevent the ghost of the deceased from returning to haunt the living, especially the close relatives.

After the interment a feast was given by the deceased's relatives who conducted the distribution of the deceased's remaining personal wealth. Horses, robes, necklaces, and implements of hunting, fishing, and warfare were among the items distributed for males; beaded bags, robes, and cooking implements were given to females. Relatives might also contribute numerous additional gifts to the assembled friends and relatives. The deceased's wishes were closely followed in these distributions so that everyone attending received an appropriate gift.

Relatives entered mourning immediately after the death. Those who had attended the corpse ritually purified themselves, and spouses cut their hair short, wore old clothing, rarely laughed or appeared happy in public, and were barred from remarriage for at least one year. When a man had several wives this was not a great inconvenience, but for men with only one wife or for women, it was a period of substantial personal deprivation. Typically the surviving spouse and relatives attempted to minimize memories of the deceased. For example, the deceased's name was not mentioned, and houses were sometimes abandoned or destroyed. New household furnishings were acquired, and the deceased's sweathouse was usually destroyed. At the end of one year, the deceased's spouse's relatives formally released the surviving spouse from the obligatory mourning by providing a new set of clothes and a new spouse, if an unmarried brother, sister, or close cousin were available. If none existed, the survivor was encouraged to seek a new spouse from another family, related if possible (Walker 1973:112).

Political Organization

The Nez Perce lived primarily in villages along the many streams traversing their territory, a linear pattern of settlement

(Anastasio 1972). Individual villages were generally identified with small, lateral feeder streams that emptied into major tributaries such as the South or Middle Fork of the Clearwater River. Villages emptying into such a tributary were usually unified into bands and identified with the tributary system. Bands in turn were politically unified into composite bands; for example, the several bands on the upper Clearwater River made up the largest Nez Perce composite band centered on the present town of Kamiah in the Kamiah Valley. Three other Nez Perce composite bands centered on the present town of Lapwai, the confluence of the Grande Ronde and Snake rivers, and the Alpoway region below Lewiston and Clarkston on the Snake River. The question of whether the Nez Perce possessed tribal political unification before Euro-American contact remains controversial. They clearly did become a tribe with a head chief after their unification in response to historical forces, after 1830.

Nez Perce villages were usually composed of several extended families and led by a headman. Generally this individual was the eldest able man in the group but was usually assisted by prominent younger men. Shamans were headmen in some villages, but in all cases the powers of shamans were sharply limited by the village councils who elected them. In many cases the role of headman was hereditary, but councils occasionally substituted a more effective man for the ineffectual son of a former headman. The headman's duties consisted of demonstrating exemplary behavior, acting as spokesman for the village, mediating in intravillage disputes, and attending to the general welfare of village members. While influential, headmen did not overrule the wishes of the councils, which included the family heads of the village.

The band leader was normally the leader of the largest village in a locality and was generally assisted by prominent warriors. Although bands held ceremonies jointly and cooperated in certain economic activities, the more significant common undertakings for bands were associated with defense. Band councils elected leaders in much the same way as did village councils, and although succession to leadership positions was semihereditary, this pattern could also be overridden by the councils.

Composite band councils were made up of band leaders and prominent warriors. Clearly there had been extensive cooperation under powerful leaders during forays into the Plains during precontact times, such ventures requiring extensive coordination for strategy. Large war parties into southern Idaho also required similar leadership, but the Nez Perce rarely accorded permanent power to their leaders, preferring local temporary leadership.

It may be argued that Nez Perce political leaders were of two major types, a peace chief (primarily an administrator) and a war chief (an outstanding warrior). Political leaders could rise to eminence by developing a following through generosity, by taking scalps or counting coup in war, or a combination of these. Criers sometimes proclaimed their statements. Nevertheless, a candidate had a better chance if he came from a long line of leaders and a well-to-do family. Shamans exercised considerable political influence and sometimes became leaders because of their power to prophesy, heal, outwit rivals, and overcome enemies. Most Nez Perce leaders were expected to behave in a morally exemplary manner, to make sound decisions, and to be generous with their supporters. Their reward was prestige rather than economic gain. Serious crimes were handled primarily by groups of relatives and not by political leaders or councils, but councils could and did sometimes exile incorrigibles (Walker 1973, 1985).

Sodalities

The Nez Perce grouped themselves into various sodalities. For example, most shamans were associated for mutual support, meeting periodically to perform vital rituals, conduct initiations, and other activities. They also had a strong voice in selecting leaders at all levels and were often affluent. Established warriors led a sodality of established and budding warriors in each of the composite bands and in some of the larger bands. They performed rituals, conducted initiations, and directed military activities. Their emphasis on bravery in warfare is reminiscent of the Crazy Dog sodalities of the Plains by which they were influenced. They took a "no retreat" pledge. Members carried a special staff in combat that they planted at a chosen spot on the battlefield, not moving from the spot until relieved or until the battle was over. Warriors elected the leaders of their war parties, and their voice in all military matters was decisive. Several sodalities for women functioned among the Nez Perce, but little is known of them.

The Nez Perce were the most influential group in intertribal affairs in the Plateau. They roamed freely across present Oregon, Washington, western Montana, and Idaho; and together with their close allies, the Cayuse, were the main Plateau opponents of the Blackfoot who dominated the western Plains and raided into the Plateau (Anastasio 1972). Typically Nez Perce and Cayuse warriors were in charge of the large, intertribal bison hunting and raiding parties that went to the Plains with more than 1,000 individuals at times. They were also closely allied with the Flathead during such ventures; the Nez Perce together with the Cayuse were the major defending force against occasional Northern Shoshone–Bannock raiding parties who ventured out of the Great Basin from time to time. Indicative of their influence in the Plateau is the fact that Nez Perce was rapidly becoming the language of trade and diplomacy throughout the region when Euro-Americans arrived shortly after 1800. At that time the Cayuse language was already being lost in favor of Nez Perce.

Religion

Nez Perce society was characterized by a general rivalry for limited rewards in the forms of prestige, economic wealth, and religious power. This pattern of constant interpersonal and small group conflict has survived into the twentieth century. Superordinate means of social control imposed on the Nez Perce in the course of acculturation have clearly failed to replace earlier coordinate devices (Walker 1985, 1989).

The Nez Perce religious system and its underlying notion of the primacy of supernatural power gained in visions and dreams involved competitive social coordination. The root of an individual's capacity to thrive in any arena was the particular kind of supernatural power inherited from ancestors or obtained during the vision quest. Power was essential for anything beyond a mediocre life and was normally sought in visions at special places known as accesses to the sacred (Walker 1985).

Acquisition of power normally required assistance from shamans. The *tiwé·t*, shaman, was the most important religious specialist among the Nez Perce. Attribution of the term *tiwé·t* was somewhat arbitrary, since it was never certain exactly who might deserve the title. Generally, anyone who could cure an illness was thought to be a shaman and warranted the title, but there were also persons who operated in a surreptitious manner, using their power for sorcery. Such were often termed hidden shamans. There were also "near shamans," sometimes referred to as shamans and at other times merely as possessors of tutelary spirit power. Some informants have been unwilling to attribute the shaman title to the game shaman or fish shaman, preferring to regard them simply as supernaturally powerful.

The most important type of shaman undoubtedly was the *ʔisíx̣i·p* shaman (Walker 1967a). No satisfactory translation of the term has been obtained, largely because the role involves so many complex attributes. This shaman was temperamental, much opposed to disorder, and very desirous of property. If an *ʔisíx̣i·p* shaman commented on the attractiveness of an object belonging to another, it was advisable that it be given up immediately. Otherwise, he would become offended and sick, sometimes going into a tantrum in which he might lose control, cutting himself and cursing the object's possessor (Thwaites 1904–1905, 7:168–169).

The single most important aspect of tutelary spirit power was possession of the song imparted during the quest and later relearned when the individual had his power "straightened out" as an adult. Although there was a great deal of individual variation in the song inventory, there was a series of rather coherent complexes. The relationships among the various songs were known, at least in part, by most individuals, and if one song were being sung at the Spirit Dance when a bystander went into a trance or began dancing, the source of that individual's power was immediately limited to a few possibilities. The wáptipas complex is an example and was composed of tutelary spirits such as elk, deer, wolf, and cougar. Persons possessing these powers were known for their ability in handling fire, which they frequently demonstrated, especially during Winter Spirit Dances, and for their ability in locating and attracting game. Theoretically, any song in this complex of tutelary spirits and powers was capable of producing the legitimizing trance in individuals who had received their power from any other member of the complex (Walker 1967a, 1985).

The *ʔipé·tes*, package of sacred objects, possessed by each person with tutelary spirit power, was an essential ingredient of power. It had a power all its own, and great care had to be taken with it. Several anecdotes illustrate the dire consequences of failing to observe proper procedures in its care and use. Informants have stated that an individual would know what his *ʔipé·tes* should contain soon after undergoing the spirit-dance validation of his tutelary spirit. Not only did the shaman provide him with clues, but also he was thought to obtain information about it when in the trance (Walker 1985:22).

An important factor affecting the outcome of vision quests was the neophyte's general personality and the specific attitudes he held when on the quest. If a child were hostile, jealous, or customarily irascible, it was thought that he would be visited by an undesirable spirit, which might lead him to sorcery or other undesirable behavior. Any power could be used for moral as well as for immoral purposes. In fact, supernatural power among the Nez Perce must be regarded as morally neutral in most respects, but there were some powers that inclined to evil such as rattlesnake.

Tutelary spirits have been recorded for the following sources: sun, moon, and stars; clouds, lightning, spring floods, ice, mountains, trees, and rivers; a large number of land mammals, birds, reptiles, fish, and insects; day ghosts, night ghosts, and an illusory object called wéwtet wéwtet. One person might obtain self-curative power from Wounded Buffalo, and another receive bravery power from Charging Buffalo. On the other hand, a person might obtain only a small part of the total power conferrable by a spirit such as Grizzly Bear, whereas another would get all of Grizzly's power. Individual differences in ability were often thus explained.

The quest for supernatural power dominated much of traditional Nez Perce ritual activity, especially in the winter tutelary spirit dance. This annual set of rituals provided an opportunity for both public legitimizing of power newly acquired by neophytes and for establishing and confirming the power hierarchy among shamans. Loss of power was a constant threat when under the care of a shaman, and it encouraged great caution in selection of shamans. Shamans were never fully trustworthy and might begin killing people at any moment to satisfy their own ends. In general, more powerful shamans were the more suspect, since they were thought to easily protect themselves from possible retaliation.

Another technique widely employed for increasing power involved the transference of power from one person to another at the winter tutelary spirit dance. Power transfers required that a more powerful person help a supernaturally weaker individual, for which he was sometimes economically compensated. The stronger person carried the weaker

426

around the central dancing area until the weaker person entered a trance. During the trance the weaker receives additional power, often becoming ill and requiring the close attention of a shaman. As noted earlier, increases or decreases of power for any reason were risky, because they could involve fatal illness.

The use of power for immoral purposes among the Nez Perce took several forms, some essentially mechanical, others psychic (Walker 1989). Curtis (1907–1930, 8:68) noted that some sorcerers killed or wounded persons by obtaining a rag soaked in menstrual discharge from a female shaman and placing it in the victim's bed. He also described a Nez Perce belief that certain sorcerers had in their bodies a removable, bloody item that gave them power for evil. Herbal hate magic is a generic term referring to another mechanically implemented type of sorcery (Harbinger 1964:73).

Sorcery was an important component of the machinery of Nez Perce social control. It was interrelated closely with the tutelary spirit system and shamanism. All individuals were thought capable of causing sickness and disasters by wishing that such things would happen, but this could also occur quite involuntarily as a result of momentary pique. Generally, sorcery events tended to cluster around in-law relationships, illnesses, accidents, and death, although it also could occur in the most trivial situations as well as on an intertribal basis. Frequent motives were revenge for some damage or slight, for attempts to steal one's spouse, for lack of requisite generosity, for failure to observe kinship obligations, and for failure to give proper respect to elderly persons.

Removing a curse was a complex activity but resembled other healing rituals. It began with the shaman singing his song and dramatizing his tutelary spirit in some way. Sometimes the illness was gathered into one spot by gathering movements of the arms and hands, but powerful shamans rarely touched the body of the patient and were thought capable of concentrating and removing the curse without physical contact with the patient's body. Removal usually was accompanied by a group of assistants and spectators who sang and beat sticks rhythmically on an outstretched log placed close to the shaman and patient. Actual extraction of the curse might occur in several ways. The sucking shamans usually used a small leaf funnel or a bone whistle as a sucking instrument. Shamans with power from Woodpecker merely extended their index finger and placed it on the spot under which the curse was thought to have been concentrated. The curse was then symbolically withdrawn from the victim's body much as a woodpecker withdraws a worm from a tree. The constant dramatization of the shaman's tutelary spirit during such rituals was thought to be an essential ritual requirement in obtaining the requisite supernatural assistance (Walker 1967a).

Other duties of shamans centered on prophecy and weather control. For example, certain shamans were known for their ability to prophesy the outcome of war parties and other serious ventures, others were known for their ability to cause thunderstorms or dust storms, and yet others assisted in locating lost and stolen goods. Their major task, however, was maintaining the series of seasonal, religious ceremonials. One primary, seasonal ritual was the tutelary spirit dance, an annual affair, usually given in late winter. This was directed by a shaman or group of shamans and usually sponsored by a prominent headman or other leader. This sponsor would provide the material requirements necessary for the ceremony, particularly those required for the feasts and the mass giveaway occurring at the end of what was usually a 5–10 day affair. The sponsoring social unit was usually a band. It provided opportunities for validation of the tutelary spirit power of young persons as well as for shamanic power demonstrations and competitions.

Horses

The Nez Perce were the most renowned horsemen of the Plateau and used their horses in most activities. Men, women, and children were all mounted on their annual and seasonal movements among various resource areas. Relative wealth in horses helped create an incipient upper and lower class in which well-known leaders and their families commonly had large herds, some families owning hundreds and even thousands.

The Nez Perce manufactured elaborate horse trappings of rawhide, horse hair, bone, and antler and decorated them with dyes, porcupine quills, and beads (fig. 5). Saddles of differing styles were made for men, for women, and for packing. The travois was used widely to transport heavy equipment, and some informants have been able to describe the more ancient dog travois (the dog and horse have similar names in Nez Perce). The Nez Perce also practiced selective horse breeding, primarily for strength and endurance. They did not breed for particular colors such as the so-called Appaloosa, which Nez Perce say was acquired from the Mormons in trade. Horses were exchanged as gifts, sold, and occasionally acquired through raids.

Structures

The principal Nez Perce house was the mat-covered, double lean-to, longhouse found widely in the Plateau. It could measure well over 100 feet in length. Normally, such large structures were temporary and used on ceremonial occasions. Mat-covered, conical tents were employed on the trail and when hunting, fishing, or root digging in temporary locations. Bison skin-covered structures (fig. 6) became popular as the Nez Perce became more involved with Plains culture during the late eighteenth and early nineteenth centuries. Shallow semisubterranean men's and women's dormitories were sometimes used in conjunction with the longhouse. The typical, hemispherical, Plateau sweathouse was found in all permanent Nez Perce settlements, as were the menstrual hut and submerged hot bath. A few plank and log homes were found among the Nez Perce in the early historic

Fig. 5. Horse decorations and trappings. top left, Beaded wool horse collar constructed of red and blue wool cloth affixed to a canvas backing. White pony beads outline the dark blue appliquéd pieces, and brass tacks and bells add further decoration. The red wool cross-piece appears to be of later manufacture and is decorated with white and green seed beads. top center, Bandoleer bag horse collar. The geometric design beadwork of this piece is typical of the Eastern Plateau (Loeb 1991:198–200). The diamond designs on the pouch are in dark and light blue on a yellow background outlined in black. The rectangles on the straps are light blue with red, white, and black details. The elongated diamond stripes are unbeaded appliquéd areas of the red wool separated by white beaded hourglass shapes. Both collars collected in Idaho by John B. Monteith before 1876. top right, Fringed hide saddlebag decorated with wool cloth and beads. Collected by James Terry in Idaho, 1883. bottom left, Woman identified as Allicott's wife beading a saddle blanket. Photograph by Sumner Matteson, Pend d'Oreille R., Flathead Res., Mont., 1905–1906. bottom right, Looking Glass, one of the greatest 19th-century chiefs, holding a bow and arrows. His short, stocky horse, a Cayuse (white horses were favored by war leaders), is painted on both the rump and chest. Photograph by William H. Jackson, 1871. Length of top left, 95 cm; top center to same scale; width of top right, 29 cm.

WALKER

period (Walker 1958–1964). The tule mat-covered long-house survived and was seen in the Plateau well into the twentieth century. Canvas-covered structures dominated after the introduction of this fabric through trade.

Clothing

Nez Perce clothing was of the northern Plains type with long, fringed buckskin shirts, leggings, belts, breechclouts, gloves, gauntlets, and several types of moccasins (figs. 7–8). Feathered bonnets modeled on the Plains type were popular (fig. 8 top right) and Nez Perce men also wore robes of several kinds, particularly bison skin robes, although most buckskin clothing was made from deer and elk hides. Women wore long, belted, buckskin dresses, basketry caps, and knee-length moccasins.

Both sexes used face painting for various purposes, and women often embellished their wing dresses with numerous elk teeth and with sea shells obtained in trade. Clothing decorations were also made from vegetable and mineral dyes, porcupine quills, and many kinds of shell and bone beads. Furs were worn by women and men in their braids and sometimes fringed on their clothes. In general, clothing signified gender, age, and social status. Well-to-do families not only possessed striking clothing but also decorated their horses in expensive finery (fig. 5).

Diversions

Traditional Nez Perce diversions included a number of different types of dances with complex singing and drumming accompaniment ("Music and Dance," figs. 2–3, this vol.). Various forms of communal dancing accompanied religious ceremonies, but purely social dances such as the shawl dance and rabbit dance, were very popular. Gambling occupied an important place in Nez Perce culture, especially the hand or bone game in which there was team gambling that sometimes pitted members of one tribe against another ("The Stick Game," fig. 5, this vol.). Major amounts of property were wagered in this type of gambling. Both foot racing and horse racing were common and frequently involved gambling on the outcomes.

Artistic expression took many forms in Nez Perce culture. Perhaps most well known are the cornhusk bags ("Basketry," fig. 5, this vol.) and distinctive beading style of the Nez Perce. Such objects were eagerly sought by other tribes in Nez Perce giveaways and the formalized gift exchanges that accompanied certain ceremonies and other social events.

History

The Prophet Dance

The Prophet Dance involved a dance, usually circular, and an inspired leader who made prophecies obtained in visions.

Whole settlements participated in the ceremony, and great emphasis was placed on a creator spirit or god who reigned above the other spirits. In some cases confession of sins was stressed, and a world-renewal message or prophecy was a virtually universal feature of the cult (Spier 1935; Walker 1969). Protohistoric burial patterns (Sprague 1967) and tool assemblages (Nelson 1973) suggest that the Prophet Dance had origins in protohistoric times.

The Prophet Dance has been linked with protohistoric events in the Plateau, such as trade, the advent of the horse, and the presence of nonindigenous religious beliefs, practices, and native prophets seen by early explorers (Walker 1969). In fact, the protohistoric and early historic neighbors of the Nez Perce saw a continuing stream of prophetic figures who claimed inspiration after recovering from personal crises, especially from death. Generally, each prophet announced coming cultural transformations and introduced ritual innovations into syncretic cults.

Fur Trade

In 1805 the Nez Perce were the largest tribal grouping on the Plateau, with a population of about 6,000 (table 1). Trappers were living in Nez Perce villages as early as 1811, and traders attempted to establish a post among them in 1812 (Josephy 1965:45–47). By 1813, the Nez Perce were firmly engaged in trading with the North West Company post on the Upper Columbia, which led to substantial cultural changes. For example, the company urged "the men to take more wives, and so become a chief—the more wives, the more workers there would be to prepare the pelts, and the more business of buying and selling" (Fletcher 1891a:2–3). The furs in the Plateau were rapidly exhausted, especially the beaver. Trapping then extended into the northern Great Basin, and by 1846 there were few beaver left anywhere in the Columbia Basin.

A period of relative prosperity for the Nez Perce prevailed during the first half of the nineteenth century, supported by not only the fur trade but also an extensive trade in horseflesh and other commodities with fur traders and early immigrants to the Oregon Territory. Epidemics during this period eroded the population (Walker 1969), which declined to about 1,800 by the beginning of the twentieth century (table 1). The Nez Perce quickly became middlemen in a vast trade network extending from the plains of Montana and beyond to the Dalles-Celilo Falls trade center and the Northwest Coast (Stern 1993; Anastasio 1972; Walker 1967, 1996).

Missionaries

Nez Perce informants have emphasized that the coming of the Whites was predicted long before their arrival. This as well as the prediction that the Whites would bring great

430

Fig. 6. Structures. top left, Indian encampment called Yellow Dog Boom next to the Nez Perce Agency, Old Lapwai (Spalding), Idaho, along the Clearwater R. top right, Chief Mallicim standing in front of a new log cabin and tepees near Culdesac, Idaho. top left and right, Photographs by E. Jane Gay; left, 1892, right, 1889. center left, Winter hunting camp with canvas tepee at Cradle Lake, Wash. Photograph by Frank Palmer, about 1910. center right, Skin tepees with war shields on tripods in front of the tepees. Photograph by William H. Jackson, on Yellowstone R. near the Shields R., Mont., 1871. bottom, Chief Joseph's extended family's winter lodge of tule matting and cloth covering. Drying sheds are next to it and Euro-American frame structures are nearby. Photograph by Edward H. Latham, Colville Res., Wash., about 1901.

Fig. 7. Men's traditional clothing and adornment. top left, Man wearing a perforated buckskin shirt. He has face paint, a dentalium nose ornament, and a traditional hairstyle with cut bangs. Oil painting by Paul Kane based on sketch made in 1847. top right, Buckskin shirt decorated with beadwork and horsehair tassles wrapped with quills and red wool cloth. This shirt is cut from two hides in traditional Plateau fashion, with the hind legs hanging from the bottom and the forelegs used for the sleeves. bottom left, Leggings made of buckskin and decorated with black and white pony beads. Shirt and leggings collected in Idaho before 1883. bottom right, Yellow Bull (b.1828) wearing an upright feather and ermine headdress with beaded hoops, a dentalium shell necklace, and a buckskin shirt with bead and ermine decorations. His braids are wrapped with fur, and he holds a wolf skin cape. Yellow Bull was one of the principal leaders to survive the Nez Perce War and carry on tribal traditions. Photograph by De Lancey Gill, Washington, D.C., 1912. Length of shirt (neck to bottom), 94 cm; length of left legging 82 cm.

top left, Nez Perce Natl. Histl. Park, Spalding, Idaho; top center and right, Amer. Mus. of Nat. Hist., New York: 1/2068 and 1/2711; bottom left, U. of Wash. Lib., Special Coll., Seattle: 13600.

Fig. 8. Men's clothing. top left, Martin Seth wearing beaded arm bands (*kahṁáyn* or *kehṁáyn*), vest (*tukepilpeʔí*), leggings (*q̇alawníˑn tóhon*), belt pouch (*cúˑyesitkeʔs*), and moccasins (*waliˑṁlapqat*) (Aoki 1994:pl. 4). He wears a cloth shirt and breechclout and holds an elk whistle. Photograph by J.W. Webster, about 1910. top center, War club. The stone head is attached with hide onto a wooden handle ornamented with fur and feathers. Collected before 1883. top right, Plains-style headdress of eagle feathers affixed to cloth and hide backing, decorated with fur, glass beads, and brass bells. Collected in Idaho before 1883. bottom left, Joe Red Thunder and his sons Keith Soy and Kenneth dressed for a war dance on the Colville Res. Red Thunder wears a hairpipe breastplate and porcupine hair necklace. His sons wear beaded ties, collars, headbands, belts, and cuffs. Red Thunder was instrumental in getting land claims settled in the 1940s–1950s. Photograph by John W. Thompson, 1955. bottom right, Leroy Seth wearing feather dance bustle and headdress and holding a feather fan. His dance costume is a traditional style for powwows. He probably made the small shield he holds. Photograph by Ben Marra, 1991.

WALKER

Fig. 9. Otterskin bowcase. This bowcase was probably attached to a matching quiver, and a carrying strap or bandoleer may have then been fastened to both. In its most elaborate form, the 2-piece otterskin bowcase-quiver with strap required 3 otterskins and 6 beaded surfaces: 2 triangular flaps suspended from the openings of the case and quiver (as shown), 2 cylindrical pieces that fit around the bowcase and quiver, and 2 tubular pieces affixed to the strap (Holm 1981). The geometric beaded design on this bowcase uses many colors, including light and dark blue, red, white, pink, yellow, and green. Collected by Emile Granier before 1899. Length with fringe 107 cm.

changes may be a way of demonstrating the power of traditional Nez Perce prophets.

Roman Catholic and Protestant missionaries alike found the Nez Perce ready for conversion (Drury 1936, 1958; Haines 1937; Walker 1985). For example, Rev. Asa Bowen Smith confirmed an earlier interest in Christianity. In 1831 a Nez Perce–Flathead delegation arrived in Saint Louis to request Christian missionaries. They were desirous of having a copy of the "book" that their neighbors to the north had obtained through Spokane Garry and other youths trained in Christian teaching by the fur traders (Drury 1958:106–107).

Although Roman Catholic influence had been present in the area sometime before their arrival (and a sizable Nez Perce Catholic community was to develop later), the first permanent missionaries to the Nez Perce were Presbyterian. Rev. Samuel Parker went through their territory in 1832 and was well received but continued down the Snake and Columbia on a tour of exploration. The first phase of Presbyterian missionizing began in 1836 and lasted until 1847. During this time, Presbyterian missionaries were in permanent residence among the Nez Perce. Catholic influence was minimal and limited to the baptism of a few Nez Perces who happened to be visiting neighboring Salishan peoples where Catholic influence was stronger.

Establishment of the Nez Perce Presbyterian mission by Henry H. Spalding and Asa Bowen Smith followed Presbyterian work by Marcus and Narcissa Whitman among the neighboring Cayuse. In 1847, when the Whitmans were massacred by the Cayuse (Drury 1937), Presbyterian work was halted among the Nez Perce, not to be resumed until the 1870s, when Spalding returned.

Missionary activity during this period was concentrated along the Clearwater River at Lapwai and Kamiah. This area seems to have been the most densely populated at the time of contact (cf. Schwede 1966) and was also an artery for trade and travel. Some additional missionary activity was conducted among the *qemúynu·* and *walwá·ma* bands on the upper Snake and Salmon rivers, and west of Lapwai down the Snake River some 20 miles. This outlying work was undertaken largely by the native chiefs and headmen.

Table 1. Population, 1780–1994

Date	Population		Source
1780	4,000		Mooney 1928:16
1805	7,850[a]		Thwaites 1904–1905, 6:114–115
1841	2,000[b]		Gibbs 1855:417
1851	1,880[b]		ARCIA 1851:216
1860	4,000		ARCIA 1860:211
1870	3,200		ARCIA 1870:181
1878	1,156[c]		ARCIA 1878:53
	Colville Res.	*Nez Perce Res.*	
1886	120[d]	1,460[e]	ARCIA 1886:232, 396, 406
1900	127	1,634	ARCIA 1900:393, 222
1910	97	1,433[f]	ARCIA 1910:65, 62
1920	—[g]	1,462	ARCIA 1920:143
1950	—[g]	1,530	U.S. Congress. House. Committee on Interior and Insular Affairs 1953:877
1960	—[g]	1,152	Bureau of Indian Affairs 1961:17
1983	—[g]	1,968	Bureau of Indian Affairs 1983:18
1994	—[g]	3,250[h]	Bureau of Indian Affairs 1994:5

[a] Under the name Chopunnish; includes 1,600 Palouse and 250 Cayuse (see Hodge 1907–1910, 2:66).

[b] Washington Territory only.

[c] At Nez Perce Agency, Lapwai, Idaho; does not include about 500 Nez Perce living outside the reservation, nor 391 members of Chief Joseph's band exiled to Indian Territory (Kansas) after the 1877 war (ARCIA 1878:67), and less than 200 followers of White Bird who escaped to Canada in Oct. 1877 (Gidley 1981:31).

[d] Chief Joseph and his remnant band; the other former exiles settled on the Nez Perce Res., Idaho.

[e] Estimated (ARCIA 1886:113).

[f] Additional 200 Nez Perce listed as "not under an agent" (ARCIA 1910:62).

[g] No separate Nez Perce count available; the total figure for the Colville Res., Wash., refers to the Confederated Tribes.

[h] Total tribal enrollment; the same source placed the reservation residents at 2,455.

These individuals were the first to accept Christianity. They used it and their association with the missionaries to augment their prestige in the society (Drury 1958:151, 106). In the Kamiah and Lapwai areas permanent mission stations were constructed with the policy of developing small, self-sufficient, theocratically oriented communities.

The following customs were proscribed by missionaries: polygyny; gambling; shamanism; tutelary spirit seeking; warfare; stealing; most ceremonials with their attendant drumming, dancing, singing, and costumes, especially the cults, which were regarded as devil inspired; and sex outside monogamous marriage. In their place the missionaries taught the tenets of Protestant theology, Christian marriage, attendance during religious instruction and on holy days, adoption of horticulture, sedentary living, literacy, and

top, Idaho State Histl. Soc., Boise; bottom, Smithsonian, NAA:2969–b.

Fig. 10. Presbyterian missionaries. top, First Missionary Society in Idaho at the McBeths' cabin. Kate C. McBeth (d. 1915), sister and colleague of Susan L. McBeth (d. 1893), stands in the back row second from right. The Nez Perces include Fannie, Jeanette, and Emmey Allen with Mark Allen in the cradleboard at left. Photograph by E. Jane Gay, Spalding, Idaho, 1891. bottom, Missionary teachers. seated, left to right, Archie B. Lawyer, a Nez Perce lay preacher of the Presbytery of Oregon; Mark Williams, who became a career missionary to other Indian tribes; and James Reuben, a nephew of Chief Joseph and a scout for Gen. Oliver O. Howard (Lavender 1992:340–341), who taught in a boarding school at Lapwai. All were students of Susan McBeth, who was a government teacher, as well as a trainer of young Nez Perces for the Presbyterian ministry (vol. 4:661–662). Standing is Indian Agent John B. Monteith, appointed jointly by the Presbyterian Church and the Bureau of Indian Affairs for 1871–1878 (Haines 1955:156). Photographed about 1878.

Bible reading. Religious instruction was given by Indian leaders wherever possible.

The missionaries engaged in several important cultural innovations. They introduced medical practices, and they established gardens and mills to settle the Nez Perce around the mission settlements. A printing press and instruction in reading and writing were introduced in accordance with the Protestant pattern of placing biblical materials in the hands of native people. Native lay leaders were trained (fig. 10). An extensive array of Nez Perce–oriented worship forms was introduced, which involved prayers, hymns, and instructional materials, all in the Nez Perce language. Finally, there were a number of innovations surrounding the formation of a permanent government. A head chief and 12 subchiefs, each with five police assistants, were appointed, and a legal code with stipulated punishments was drawn up (Haines 1955:88–89).

Several important features of the initial christianization of the Nez Perce should be emphasized. First, there were few

converts. The reasons for this failure seem to lie principally in the varying functions of religion in Euro-American and Nez Perce cultures. In Nez Perce culture, religion was at the basis of secular success, and the various cults had probably created extremely high expectations of new and wondrous items of material culture. For the missionaries the functions of religion were moral and spiritual, and they failed to satisfy the complex mixture of religious and economic needs apparently responsible for early Nez Perce interest in Christianity (Drury 1958:107, 151). Second, the chiefs and headmen who quickly accepted Christianity were men desirous of further power and were the same people who dominated the government-supported head chief–subchief system introduced at the request of the missionaries in 1842 (Haines 1955:87–89). The leadership disputes stemming from competition for these new positions became a perennial feature of Nez Perce acculturation. Finally, it is clear that the Dream cult as well as most traditional religious beliefs persisted despite the best efforts of the missionaries to eradicate them. Differential retention of such beliefs came to play a significant role in the factional disputes that have marked Nez Perce history.

Until the 1940s the Presbyterian mission remained a dominant religious and political force on the Nez Perce Reservation (Drury 1936, 1937, 1958, 1963–1966, 1973). Roman Catholic Nez Perces attended the Slickpoo mission, which was administered by the Jesuits (Burns 1966; Morrill and Morrill 1978). Like the Methodists and Pentecostals they have been a minority among the Christian Nez Perce.

Treaties and Reservation Life

The most fundamental developments of the second half of the nineteenth century were the treaties of 1855, 1863, and 1868; establishment of the Nez Perce Reservation; and political dominance of the reservation by Presbyterian Nez Perces (Walker 1985). With the treaty of 1855 negotiated by Gov. Isaac I. Stevens at Walla Walla ("History Since 1846," fig. 2, this vol.). the Nez Perce were secured in their ownership of a large reservation with guarantees of continued off-reservation rights of hunting, fishing, gathering, and travel (Stevens 1855; Doty 1855, 1978). In 1863 the reservation was reduced, and there was continued pressure to sell Nez Perce lands. Off-reservation groups created by the 1863 reduction ultimately pitted Christian Nez Perces against non-Christian Nez Perces (Walker 1985). This division and opposition continued to function as part of the tribe's political life.

The year 1877 saw the unfolding of the historic drama known as the Nez Perce War or Chief Joseph's War. In May, following repeated encroachments by White settlers in the Wallowa Valley and other lands still belonging to the nontreaty Nez Perces, Gen. Oliver O. Howard held a parley with the nontreaty chiefs at Fort Lapwai to persuade them to remove to the reservation. To their refusal, Howard answered with a 30-day ultimatum demanding the Indians' prompt "voluntary" removal to the Lapwai reservation or they would be taken there by military force. While Joseph (fig. 11), White Bird, Looking Glass (fig. 5), and other non-treaty chiefs began making preparations to comply, a handful of young warriors attacked and killed some White ranchers. The raids prompted General Howard to pursue the "hostiles" with an initial contingent of about 500 soldiers and civilian volunteers. Thus began the three-month, 1,300-mile-long flight of the Nez Perce, who fought a skillful, defensive war against superior forces.

Battles between the fleeing Nez Perce and the pursuing soldiers, irregulars, and their Indian scouts (among whom figured some treaty Nez Perces) were fought in Idaho at White Bird Canyon (June 17); on the Middle Fork of the Clearwater River (July 1), with Looking Glass, who had not yet joined Chief Joseph; near the mouth of Cottonwood Creek on the South Fork of the Clearwater River (July 11–12), where Nez Perces numbered about 750, about one-third of whom were warriors. Following the Lolo Trail, in late July the Nez Perce crossed the Bitterroot Mountains into Montana; they found their way north blocked by the Flathead who, although traditionally friendly to them, did not want any part in this war. The Nez Perce thus headed south and camped at Big Hole, where a major battle ensued on August 9–10 with heavy casualties on both sides (vol. 4:182). With General Howard still in pursuit, the fleeing Indians continued south and re-entered Idaho through Bannock Pass before finally turning eastward hoping to involve their old allies the Crow in their struggle. On August 20 some 200 Nez Perce warriors under Looking Glass, Ollokot (Joseph's brother), and Toohoolhoolzote attacked General Howard's camp at Camas Meadows and once again outdistanced him. Following a northeasterly course, the Nez Perce moved then through Yellowstone National Park in Wyoming, and in early September they crossed into Montana along Clarks Fork.

The refusal of the Crows to join their fight—the former allies even provided scouts to the U.S. Cavalry to track down the hostiles—convinced the disillusioned Nez Perce that their only hope was to go north to join Hunkpapa Sioux Chief Sitting Bull, who a few months earlier had escaped to Canada (Manzione 1991). Shortly after crossing the Yellowstone River, on September 13 at Canyon Creek the Nez Perces repulsed an attack by troops of the reconstituted 7th Cavalry under Col. Samuel D. Sturgis and again managed to escape. Ten days later and 75 miles north, the hungry Nez Perce attacked a small army depot at the Cow Island crossing on the Missouri River, resupplied themselves with food, and pushed on.

On September 30 at Bear Paw Mountain about 40 miles from the Canadian border, the Nez Perce were intercepted by Col. Nelson Miles; a bitter battle ensued and the Indian camp was placed under siege. To save the wounded, women, and children, on October 5, 1877, Chief Joseph, who had assumed full leadership after the death of Looking Glass, formally surrendered with over 400 Nez Perces to General Howard and Colonel Miles. Only Chief White Bird and an undetermined number of his followers (estimated at 14–100) managed to escape to Canada, where they found refuge in Sitting Bull's camp.

The war took a toll in lives, property, and suffering. "Some 123 soldiers and 55 civilians . . . died with nearly an equal number wounded. Total Nez Perce casualties are less certain, but probably at least 155 died (perhaps as many as 200 if high estimates of those who lost their lives fleeing to Canada are included) and some 90 wounded" (Hampton 1994:310). There is a vast literature on the Nez Perce War, its antecedents and sorrowful outcome, including biographies of the Indian protagonists (ARCIA 1877, 1878, 1885; O.O. Howard 1881; Kirkwood 1928; Fee 1936; Haines 1939; McWhorter 1940, 1952; H.A. Howard 1952; Chalmers 1962; Beal 1962; Josephy 1965; M.H. Brown 1967; Tchakmakian 1976; Gidley 1981; H. Lane 1982; Wilfong 1990; Lavender 1992; Hampton 1994; Moeller and Moeller 1995).

Most survivors of the Nez Perce War of 1877 who were sent to Oklahoma after their defeat at the Battle of Bear Paw returned to the northwest in 1885 to reside on the Colville Reservation in Washington, with Chief Joseph, who died there in 1904. A few who accepted Christianity returned to Idaho. With the military defeat of the off-reservation, non-Christian portion of the tribe by 1878, the Christian Nez Perce came to dominate reservation life, and their descendants continued to do so in the twentieth century (Walker 1985). They adopted various intensive programs of economic development, formal education, and many features of Euro-American culture. These programs were designed and administered by federal agents of the Bureau of Indian Affairs, missionaries of the Presbyterian church, and by a number of educated Presbyterian tribal leaders.

By 1895 the Dawes Severalty Act led to allotment of the reservation and its opening to non-Indian settlement ("Reservation and Reserves," fig. 4, this vol.). This process, supported by the Bureau of Indian Affairs and Presbyterian missionaries, was overseen by anthropologist Alice Fletcher (vol. 4:61; "History of Research," fig. 6, this vol.) (Gray 1981; Mark 1988; Sappington and Carley 1995). It resulted in a loss of a majority of the remaining land that the Christian Nez Perce had saved in the treaty of 1863. Federally sponsored, forced fee patenting of allotments and other land losses due to taxation reduced the land in Nez Perce hands even more. An original tribal land base of about 13 million acres in 1800 reached a point of less than 80,000 acres by 1975. Since 1980, a tribal land acquisition program has resulted in Nez Perce ownership of about 110,000 acres.

Based on provisions of the treaty of 1855, the Nez Perce have preserved their off-reservation rights to hunt, fish, and gather as far west as the mid-Columbia River, south into the Upper Salmon River basin, and east to the Montana border. The tribe participates as comanagers of water, timber, and mineral resources of the lands ceded in 1855 and 1863.

Fig. 11. Chief Joseph (*hinmató·wyalahtq̓it*) (b. ca. 1840, d. 1904). After Chief Joseph's attempt to find refuge in Canada and his removal to Indian Terr., he and his followers were relocated to the Colville Res., Wash. In his attempt to have his people returned to their homeland, Chief Joseph traveled and spoke to numerous audiences. top left, Earliest known photograph of Joseph and his family. left to right: Heyoom-yo-yikt, Joseph's wife; Springtime, another wife; nephew of Joseph; Joseph; another nephew; and Heyoom-yo-yikt's sister, one of Chief Looking Glass's widows, whom Joseph married while in exile on the Colville Res. (C. James 1996:85). Photograph by F.M. Sargent of Anthony, Kans., probably after 1878. top right, Guncase, surrendered with rifle to Gen. Oliver O. Howard at Bear Paw Mountain, Mont. Terr., Oct. 1877. Length of guncase without fringe 114 cm. center left, Joseph; his friend Edmund S. Meany, whom Joseph called Three Knives; and Red Thunder, Joseph's nephew. Photograph by Edward S. Curtis, Seattle, Wash., 1903. center right, Announcement of and invitation to the Chief Joseph lecture at the Seattle Theatre, Nov. 20, 1903 (Gidley 1981:55–61). Photograph on the announcement by Edward H. Latham, © 1903. bottom, Six-cent Chief Joseph stamp issued Nov. 4, 1968, honoring his perseverance in the face of overwhelming odds. The stamp is based on an 1878 oil painting by Cyrenius Hall, in the Natl. Portrait Gallery, Washington, D.C. left to right, Ellen Grant, Joseph's great-granddaughter; Josephine Black Eagle Grant, Joseph's granddaughter; Ida Black Eagle, Joseph's daughter; and Norma Jean Collins, great-granddaughter. Photograph by Harry Newfield, Washington, D.C., 1968.

Tribal government is based on the constitution of 1948. The Nez Perce rejected the Indian Reorganization Act proposals in the 1930s. The constitution of 1948 established a council of all adult tribal members, but most of the power rests with the Nez Perce Tribal Executive Committee (NPTEC), which oversees a large array of programs. Tribally administered programs include the natural resource projects (especially fish and water resources), education, health, economic development, law and order, legal affairs, and housing. With a 1994 population of more than 3,000 (table1), approximately half of them residing on the reservation, NPTEC has major responsibilities for a youthful population with a high birth rate. Tribal politics continued to revolve around ancient differences concerning religion and acculturation (Riley 1961; Weil 1965; Walker 1985).

By the 1930s Presbyterian influence on the reservation had begun to wane and a reassertion of non-Christian influence was underway. By World War II the non-Christian element had reintroduced the winter tutelary spirit dances and powwows that had been prohibited by reservation authorities for more than 50 years.

Since the 1960s the Nez Perce have pursued a policy of cultural and economic recovery and expansion through legislative and legal means. Revival of traditional culture has paralleled this recovery.

Synonymy†

The name Nez Perce is from French *nez percé* (pronounced /ne pɛrse/), literally 'pierced nose', a reference to an early custom of piercing the nasal septum (fig. 7) for dentalium-shell ornaments (Aoki 1970:2). Because this practice was discontinued in the early nineteenth century the relevance of the name has been unclear to later observers and commentators and its historical appropriateness sometimes denied by tribal members and others. The first documented use of the name is in David Thompson's journal for 1810 (Aoki 1970). Early spellings like Nepercy (Hodge 1907–1910, 2:67) reflect three-syllable pronunciations derived orally from French. The English spelling Nez Percé continued in use as a hypercorrect form long after the spelling pronunci-

ation as two syllables (ˌnez'pərs) had become established as the norm. Variants such as Nez-percés are also found (Hale 1846:212). Before first encountering the Nez Perce in 1805, Meriwether Lewis referred to them descriptively as "the persed nosed Indians" and "Pierced nosed indians" (Moulton 1983–, 5:89, 90).

William Clark reported that the Nez Perce "call themselves *Cho pun-nish* or *Pierced noses*" (Moulton 1983–, 5:222), and subsequently Lewis and Clark regularly referred to them as Chopunnish; spelling variants are given in Hodge (1907–1910, 2:67). Chopunnish (ˈchōpənĭsh) is a borrowing and adaptation of the Nez Perce self-designation *cú·pn̓itpelu·* 'the Nez Perce people', formed from *cú·pn̓it* 'piercing (with a pointed object)' and *-pelu·* 'people' (Aoki 1967, 1970:2–3, 1994:542); this, or its first component, was recorded by A.S. Gatschet as ⟨Tchútpelit⟩ and appears also as ⟨Tsútpĕli⟩ (Hodge 1907–1910, 2:68, 66).

The more common self-designation used by the Nez Perce is *ni·mí·pu·* (Aoki 1994:489), also given as *nimí·pu·* (Aoki 1970:1). In the Downriver dialect this name is *nu·mí·pu·*. The name for the Wallawa band, *qemúynu·*, has been cited in the form ⟨kamū´inu⟩ as another self-designation (Hodge 1907–1910, 2:67; Aoki 1970:2).

The name Sahaptin was used by Hale (1846:212) for the Nez Perce; variants of this include Sahapotins, on Gallatin's (1836) map, and others in other mid-nineteenth-century sources (Hodge 1907–1910, 2:67). This name is a borrowing of a form in a southern Interior Salish language, for example Columbian *sḥáptnəxʷ* [sḥáptənəxʷ] 'Nez Perce' (Dale Kinkade, communication to editors 1996), Flathead and Spokane *saʕáptni* (in Flathead also *saʕá*), Colville *sʕáptnx* (Sarah G. Thomason, communication to editors 1996). Hale also used this name for the language family that includes both Nez Perce and the dialects of Sahaptin, and its use was later narrowed to apply only to Sahaptin.

The name for the Nez Perce in a number of other languages refers to nose piercing, including Crow *apupé* (Medicine Horse 1987:15), Hidatsa *apahoˀpáˀiš* (Douglas Parks, communication to editors 1975), Dakota *pʰóɣexdoke* (Riggs 1890:423, phonemicized), Lakhota *pʰóɣexloka* (Buechel 1970:733, phonemicized), and Arikara *sinitčiškataríwiš*, literally 'bone across the nose' (Douglas Parks, communication to editors 1975).

† This synonymy was written by Ives Goddard.

Another set of names refers to a men's hairstyle (fig.7): Kiowa ɔ́lk̄ɔ́tôygɔ̀ (Laurel Watkins and Parker McKenzie, communication to editors 1979), explained as 'people with hair cut across the forehead' (Mooney 1896:744); Osage *hpekásące,* literally 'plaited (hair over the) forehead', and Kansa *ppegáząʒe* (J.O. Dorsey in Hodge 1907–1910, 2:67, phonemicized; Robert L. Rankin, communication to editors 1996). Pawnee *cu·hárukac,* literally 'cut bangs', was recorded by A.S. Gatschet as the name for the Nez Perce (Hodge 1907–1910, 2:67, phonemicized), but in the twentieth century this term is used for the Pueblo Indians (Douglas Parks, communication to editors 1996). An apparent reference to the color of face paint is found in the early traders' name Blue Mud Indians (Moulton 1983–, 3:435) or Blue Earth Indians (in Hodge 1907–1910, 2:67; Aoki 1967, 1970:3). This also appears to be the allusion of the Blackfoot name *komonóítapiikoana,* formed from *komono-* 'dark green, dark blue' + *-itapi* 'person' + *-ikoan-* 'group member' (Frantz and Russell 1989:134; Allan R. Taylor in Aoki 1970:2; Uhlenbeck and van Gulik 1934:207); a form of this name without the suffix *-ikoan-* is also widely attested. The shorter form of the Blackfoot name is glossed 'Blue Mud Indians' on Peter Fidler's copy of the Blackfoot chief Ackomokki's map of 1801 (Moodie and Kaye 1977:8), and Hayden (1862:264) glosses the Blackfoot name as 'Green Paint Indians'. Another early traders' name, Green Wood Indians (Hodge 1907–1910, 2:67), may go with this set.

In the Bannock dialect of Northern Paiute the Nez Perce are called *cugadikaʔa,* 'couse (*Lomatium cous*) eater', and in Shoshone they are the *coikaʔa* 'couse people'. In Oregon and Bannock Northern Paiute they are included under the term *saiduka* (*saidukaʔa*) 'dwellers in tule-mat houses', literally 'under tule (*Scirpus*)', which is used generally for 'enemy' and may include also the Klamath-Modoc, Sahaptin, Cayuse, and others (Sven Liljeblad in Aoki 1970:1; Gatschet 1890, 1:xxxiii–xxxiv; Catherine S. Fowler, communication to editors 1996; vol. 11:464). The Sahaptin name *šíwaniš* 'stranger' (Bruce Rigsby in Aoki 1970:1), was borrowed into Chinookan in the identical form (Walter Dyk in Aoki 1970:1). An older Sahaptin term is *šukʷíšukʷi* 'dark brown', explained as a reference to skin color (Bruce Rigsby in Aoki 1970:1). Other names for the Nez Perce include: Kalapuya ⟨anípörspi⟩, Quapaw ⟨i´-na-cpĕ⟩, and Caddo ⟨tchaχsúkush⟩ (Hodge 1907–1910, 2:67). The term Flathead and its French equivalent *tête plate* were some-times used in a broad sense that included the Nez Perce (Aoki 1970:3–4; Moulton 1983–, 6:433, 10:140).

Sources

The earliest recorded description of the Nez Perce is contained in the journals of the Lewis and Clark expedition of 1804–1806 (Moulton 1983–, 5, 6; Sappington 1989). Following are various mentions of them in the fur trade documents but especially in missionary reports, diaries, and journals. Federal documents associated with treaty negotiations and reservation administration run to many thousands of pages, many of which are housed in archives such as the Library of Congress; Gonzaga University Archives, Spokane, Washington; Regional Federal Depository in Seattle; Whitman College Library Archives, Walla Walla, Washington; Washington State University Library Archives, Pullman, Washington; University of Idaho Library Archives and the Pacific Northwest Anthropological Archives (Laboratory of Anthropology, University of Idaho), Moscow; and the state historical society archives in Idaho, Oregon, Washington, and Montana.

The first serious ethnographic writing is by Spinden (1908, 1917) and Curtis (1907–1930, 8). Ray (1954, 1974, 1975a; Ray et al. 1938) provides broad ethnographic surveys of the Plateau, which include the Nez Perce, as well as ethnohistorical research on various land claims. Fully 90 percent of all published writing about the Nez Perce concerns the Joseph saga of 1877, this highly symbolic event of the expanding western frontier of the nineteenth century. The primary sources concerning this formative conflict are the two books by McWhorter (1940, 1952). Josephy (1965) provides an extensive historical treatment of Nez Perce and Euro-American contact and conflict.

The most important publications by anthropologists include the linguistic research of Rigsby (1965), Aoki (1962, 1963, 1994), Aoki and Walker (1989), the archeological research of Leonhardy and Rice (1970), and the ethnographic research by Walker.

Of considerable interest are the publishing projects directed by the Nez Perce tribe (Slickpoo and Walker 1972, 1973). The Nez Perce publications consisting of reports about land, water, fish, timber, nuclear waste, health, education, legal briefs, economic factors, law and order, and other topics are available from the tribe, state, and federal agencies.

Molala

HENRY B. ZENK AND BRUCE RIGSBY

Language

The name Molala (mō'lälu, 'mōlälu) refers both to an isolated language and to the people who spoke it, who in the early nineteenth century occupied the greater part of the Cascade Range in west-central Oregon. Frachtenberg (1910–1911) suggests that there were at least two distinct dialects (or perhaps, closely related languages) of Molala, referred to here as Northern Molala and Southern Molala. However, only the northern area of Molala occupation is represented by significant linguistic and ethnographic documentation.[*]

For over a century, ethnologists believed that Molala was closely related to the poorly attested Cayuse language of northeastern Oregon and that the corresponding ethnolinguistic groups shared a recent common historical origin. Some (Spalding 1851:71; Clarke 1905:133–135; Curtis 1907–1930, 8:80) said that the separation of the two groups resulted from the westward migration of the Molalas, while others spoke of the eastward movement of the Cayuses (Boas 1890:1; Garth 1964:45). However, Rigsby (1965, 1966, 1969) examined and discussed the evidence for close Cayuse-Molala genetic relationship—the so-called Waiilatpuan language family—and found it lacking. Likewise, there is no solid evidence for the migration of either people, although a number of shared words may indicate contact, if not their proximity in an earlier period.

Territory and Environment

Some sources distinguish only two Molala subgroups, Northern and Southern, assigning them noncontiguous territories. R.L. Benson (1973; in Farmer et al. 1973:14)

and Rigsby have independently considered the historical and ethnographic sources and concluded that Molala territory and range were continuous from north to south along the western and eastern slopes of the Cascades (fig. 1). Benson noted a discrepancy between documents accompanying the ratified treaties of 1855 (Belden 1855)—source of the earlier view—and the unratified treaty of 1851 (Oregon Superintendency of Indian Affairs 1851–1856:73–97), which clearly registers a Molala claim to the upper Santiam, McKenzie, and Middle Fork watersheds (claimed by the Upper Santiam subgroup). Other sources provide evidence of early historical Molala presence in the central areas (Applegate 1907:3–4; Boas 1890b:1; Carrothers 1959; Gatschet 1877:363; Menefee and Tiller 1977:55; Newell [1849] 1959:149; Palmer 1855).

Molala territory and range were nearly coterminous with the Western Cascades and High Cascades physiographic provinces of western Oregon (Franklin and Dryness 1969:4). The Western Cascades is an area of ridges and deeply cut river valleys, meeting Oregon's interior valleys along a gently sloping western perimeter, it becomes ruggedly mountainous to the east, where it abuts the High Cascades, an elevated lava plateau intersected by glaciated valleys and high volcanic peaks. Most of the region is densely forested, the Western Cascades being especially noteworthy for its ancient stands of Douglas fir, western hemlock, and western red cedar. At higher elevations, open areas provide browse for elk and deer, as well as a seasonal abundance of mountain huckleberries (*Vaccinium membranaceum*). The native groups of the region periodically burned over such sites to keep them clear of trees. Other open areas included prairie lands on the west and alpine meadows in the High Cascades.

External Relations

Most sources agree in locating the principal areas of Molala winter settlement to the west of the Cascades summit. In the north, Molalas were in close contact with Upper Chinookans, with whom they enjoyed cordial relations characterized by intermarriage and exchanges of foods and valuables (Jacobs 1929–1930; Drucker 1934). A number of Kalapuyan-Molala marriages have been reported. Reports of Molala-Klamath intermarriage,

---

[*]The phonemes of (Northern) Molala in the analysis used in the transcriptions of words in the *Handbook* are: (voiceless stops and affricates) *p, t, c, k, q* ; (glottalized stops and affricates) *ṗ, ṫ, c̓, k̓, q̓;* (voiceless fricatives) *f, s, ł;* (sonorants) *m, n, l, ŋ;* (glides) *w, y, ʔ, h;* (short vowels) *a, ([a]), æ, e, i, u;* (long vowels) *aˑ, æˑ, eˑ, iˑ, uˑ.* Primary stress is phonemic.

The phonemic analysis and the transcriptions used follow Rigsby (1964, 1965) and Howard Berman (personal communication 1991). They are based on materials collected by Frachtenberg (1910–1911), Jacobs (1928–1935), and Swadesh (1954). It is not certain that there is a phonemic distinction between the two low-vowel qualities (Berman 1996:4); from sound recordings of the last speaker Rigsby concludes that there was only a single phonemic low-vowel quality (*a, aˑ*). There is also the possibility of an aspirated series of stops (*p^h, t^h, k^h, q^h*) and additional phonemes *λ* and *x* (Berman 1996:3).

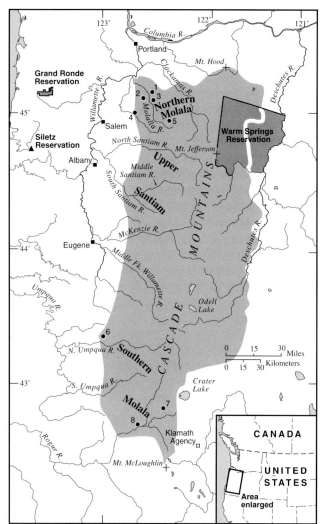

Fig. 1. Molala territory and range about 1848 (R.L. Benson in Farmer et al. 1973:14; Rigsby 1965:57–62) with selected winter settlements and other sites: 1, *hǽsnitælc*; 2, *hǽŋifiŋi*; 3, *muḱǽnti*; 4, Abiqua Creek settlement and Battle of the Abiqua (Down 1926:47–58, 246); 5, *fáwtæhaʔ* (Table Rock), a ceremonial site; 6, North Umpqua settlement (Applegate 1907:4); 7, *ʔiwamǵeˑni* 'huckleberry place' (Klamath name of Huckleberry Mountain), summer camp where Molalas met Klamaths (Spier 1930:9); 8, *bŭḳstubŭḳs* (Spier 1930:4; cf. Gatschet 1890, 1:xxxvi).

coresidence, and cooperation suggest contact between these two groups throughout the entire area of Molala occupation. Gatschet (1890, 1:xxxvi, 2:426), while observing that Klamaths and Southern Molalas were not always on good terms, adds that the Southern Molalas had acquired the Klamath language. A tangible indication of Molala contacts both with Klamaths and Chinookans is provided by the custom of frontal-occipital flattening, which Klamaths and Molalas—in contrast to other southern Oregon groups—considered a concomitant, though not an invariable one, of free birth (Spier 1930:59). Frachtenberg's (1911) information that Northern Molalas pressed the heads of all female, but not all male, infants suggests that they valued marriage alliances with lower

Columbia people, most of whom strongly associated flat-headedness with free birth and high social standing.

Some problems of documentation and interpretation complicate the description of Molala contacts on the east, especially in the Warm Springs region. According to Murdock (1938:397–398), aggressive Tenino Sahaptins attacked resident Molalas in this area sometime around 1810–1820, dispossessing them of a fishing site on the Deschutes River and an associated winter village site. However, Warm Springs Reservation informants interviewed by Rigsby and David French (see Rigsby 1969:81–82) could recall no tradition of Sahaptin-Molala conflict, although they did believe that Molalas used the area during early historical times. French considered the Murdock account inconsistent with regional norms characterizing territorial relations.

Dugout canoes, including small domestically made models, as well as large Chinook-type canoes obtained from Chinookans, facilitated Northern Molala visits to riverine groups. Horses, obtained by the 1820s–1830s from northeastern and central Oregon peoples (Drucker 1934a), were useful elsewhere. In the interior, a far-flung network of mountain trails linked Molalas to each other as well as to their Klamath friends and relatives.

Culture

The following sketch is based upon Frachtenberg's (1910–1911) and Drucker's (1934a) fieldwork with two Northern Molala informants of the reservation era, supplemented by Boas (1890b), Gatschet (1877a), Jacobs (1929–1930), and Spier (1930). Spier's few items on the Southern Molala comprise virtually the entire ethnographic record of that group.

Subsistence

Ethnographic sources and historical observations agree that large game constituted the single most important resource exploited by Molalas. Deer and elk were economically the most important game, providing hides for clothing as well as meat. Also hunted were a variety of small mammals and birds, including coyotes, bobcats, and eagles, taken for fur or feathers rather than for food.

Most large-game hunting was by bow and arrow. Snares, deadfalls, and pitfalls were also in use, as well as deer-head disguises for stalking. The training of dogs to track and drive deer appears to have been a Molala specialty: Klamaths used hunting dogs, but not to the same extent as neighboring Molalas (Spier 1930). The dogs used were large, with pointed ears; they were individually named (Drucker 1934a).

Among seasonally more restricted resources were: salmon and steelhead, taken by harpoon and in stationary basketry traps used with wiers; camas, dug on moist prairies

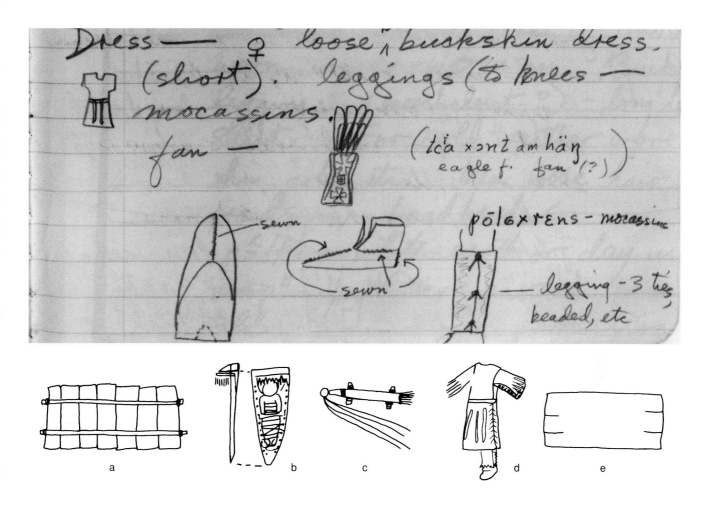

top, Smithsonian, NAA:ms. 4516(78), vol. I; bottom, after Drucker 1934a.

Fig. 2. Sketches of Northern Molala material culture from Philip Drucker's (1934a:100) fieldnotes. top, Drawings depict: a short, loose, belted buckskin dress, feather fan, moccasin and legging. bottom, Drawings after Drucker: a, Pattern of bark slabs lashed with hazel-stick ties to form a house wall (roof panels had 3 rows of binders); b, cradleboard, the same for male or female; both were sometimes decorated with beads and elk teeth although the female board might be fancier; c, weasel-skin ornament, fastened to hair or garments; d, woman's buckskin dance outfit tied or sewn on both sides with the sleeves long to the elbow; e, cedar-bark used as vessel for berries and other foods.

notably in the west; tarweed seeds and hazelnuts, gathered during the summer and fall on dry prairies and savannas in the west; and mountain huckleberries, harvested during late summer at high elevations. Molalas used tobacco, but so far as later informants knew did not cultivate it.

Meat and fish were dried and cached until needed. Camas was baked in pit ovens, dried, and mixed with hazelnuts in woven storage bags. Huckleberries were dried on wooden frames, then stored in sacks, or pounded into cakes after boiling, drying, and remoistening.

Technology

Drucker has provided some detail on manufactures (fig. 2). Women wove mats, made both coiled and twined baskets, and fashioned clothing from haired and dehaired tanned hides (fig. 3). Items associated with male pursuits included: sinew-backed yew-wood bows, otter or cougar skin quivers, and snowshoes.

Settlements

The local unit of Molala society was the winter settlement, consisting of one or more extended-family households at a sheltered low-elevation site. At other times of the year, individuals and family task groups dispersed to a variety of harvest locations, ranging from low-elevation prairies in the west to summer berrying and hunting grounds in the High Cascades.

Structures

Northern Molalas built rectangular, semiexcavated winter houses like those described for other interior western Oregon peoples. Planklike slabs of hemlock and cedar bark, peeled at full thickness during the spring and then weighted down to dry flat, comprised the basic building material. A single log ridgepole, positioned in the nocks presented by two upright forked center posts, supported a gabled framework of poles, to which overlapping bark slabs were

left, Oreg. Histl. Soc., Portland: 65285; U. of Wash., Thomas Burke Memorial Wash. State Mus., Seattle: top right, 1–10589 (slide 01.05017); bottom right, 1–10590 (slide 01.03948).

Fig. 3. Women's clothing. left, Kate Chantèle (*múswi*), consultant of both Philip Drucker and Melville Jacobs during the late 1920s and early 1930s. She wears a belted, open-sleeved dress of skin (fig. 2d), a beaded yoke with 3 trade coins, bead necklaces (the longer with glass beads and the shorter possibly clamshell beads), and a headband adorned with dentalium shells. In one hand she holds a feather fan (fig. 2, top), in the other is a beaded flat bag. She has painted her cheeks. Photographed about 1930. top right, Basketry flat bag depicting a deer, a man, and birds. The strap and fringe are trimmed with black and white beads. bottom right, Moccasins decorated with red, blue, white, and black beads. Collected by Melville Jacobs before 1929. Height of bag, 15 cm; width of moccasins, 10 cm.

lashed vertically as walls and roof. Inside, mats and hides covered walls and floor, and there was a central square pit holding one to several hearths. Smokeholes with moveable bark covers were located on either side of the roof peak. Dirt was banked around the walls outside. Doors were of mat or bark; according to Frachtenberg (1910–1911), each house had two, leading into the moderately excavated interior via dirt ramps.

Bark or thatched-rush structures resembling winter houses, but unexcavated, served as summer houses; mat or bough shelters made do at camps. Round-floored sweathouses, constructed of bark and dirt and heated by steam, varied considerably in size and substantiality: from a small dome built over a bent-stick framework; to a substantial structure supported by a center post with shorter framework uprights, and holding about 20 people. According to both

442

Fig. 4. Henry Yelkes, son of the treaty chief *yélqas*, a signer of the 1851 Champoeg and 1855 Dayton treaties, and father of Melville Jacobs's informant Fred Yelkes, the last known speaker of Molala. He wears decorated fringed fabric trousers, a beaded sash, a beaded bag hanging over one shoulder, and what appears to be a feathered headdress (Fred Yelkes, Jr., personal communication 1996). Photograph by Drake Brothers Studio, Silverton, Oreg.,1912.

Frachtenberg (1910–1911) and Drucker (1934a), sweathouses were used exclusively or primarily by men.

Society

Social organization is not well described. Evidently, local organization was minimal, and leadership primarily task oriented.

The kinship system presents some indications of paternal bias: residence was virilocal, and according to Drucker (1934a), at least initially patrilocal. With respect to terminology and classification, it is bilateral: sex of speaker and of relative or connecting relative, as well as relative age, were two of the princples used in classifying kin; grandparent and grandchild terms were identical; cousins were classified with siblings (Yvonne Hajda, personal communication 1991).

The marriage prohibition extended to all degrees of kinship, with the consequence that eligible spouses were available ordinarily only from outside the local group. Wealthy men preferred to be polygynous, often seeking their spouses from non-Molala neighbors. A marriage was contracted by the exchange of a bride price and a dowry, the dowry delivered during a ritualized surrender of the bride by her family to the groom's family. Subsequent visits and mutual exchanges reinforced the bond between the families, while the levirate and sororate ensured its continuance beyond the death of either spouse.

As elsewhere in western Oregon, a 'chief' (*yaʔqánt*) was just the wealthiest man of a local group. Tribal leaders emerged probably only during the historical period, although to be sure, the ability of a wealthy *yaʔqánt* to aid and hence to obligate his kinfolk could lend him considerable local influence. Wealth consisted of articles such as hides, ceremonial regalia, horses, blankets, and bead and dentalium-shell strings. The bead and shell comprised a standard valued according to length of string.

Control of slaves (*yáʿqi* 'slave') was presumably also a factor in establishing the prestige and power of a *yaʔqánt*. Most slaves were accustomed to their status from childhood and lived much as poor relations in their masters' households. Like other people, they could marry. However, they were also property, and as such the most valued form of wealth. According to Frachtenberg (1910–1911), a favorite slave might be killed on the grave of his or her master, in accordance with the master's wish. Some instances of marriage between free men and slave women, with removal of the woman's slave status, are also on record.

Although Frachtenberg denies that Molalas captured slaves, Jacobs (1945:41) indicates that Molalas had a reputation as slave raiders, preying on Central Kalapuyans in particular. It may be conjectured that Molala involvement in the slave trade reflected their close ties to Klamaths, who played a major role in supplying slaves to the regional trading and holding centers on the lower Columbia and lower Willamette rivers. Slave raiders usually tried to kill or rout the men of a victim group, seizing children and young women to be exchanged later for valuables presented by a client group. Molalas were victimized in turn by mounted raiders they called *haylúnci*, literally 'upstreamers', a term usually translated 'Cayuse' but referring also to Nez Perces and other Plains-influenced tribes.

Ceremonies

Ceremonies involving general participation were shamans' initiation dances, girls' coming of age dances, and summer "fun dances."

The summer dances provided an opportunity for people from different local groups to socialize. Both men and women, dressed in beaded and feathered regalia and holding bone-splint rattles and deer dew-claw rattle drums, made a circle around a central post. A "dance boss" led songs and called selected dancers out to the center of the circle. Costumed male dancers, pantomiming animals, provided special entertainment. In conformity with the Northern Molala pattern number, dances lasted for five days.

The initiation of a shaman (*twǽni* 'shaman') was accompanied by a five-night dance evidently resembling that of neighboring Upper Chinookans and Kalapuyans. The new shaman danced and sang, assisted by a hired older shaman and supporting dancers, who likewise were paid. Such little additional information as there is on Northern Molala shamanism suggests other parallels with their western neighbors. Young people, especially boys, were sent to the mountains to encounter guardian spirits, a number of which were believed to confer shamanistic ability. Disease was caused by small intruding objects, which shamans could detect and extract. Shamanistic regalia included feathered headdresses and shirts and carved hand-held figurines.

Northern Molalas accorded considerable ceremonial recognition to a girl's coming of age, greeting the event with a five- or 10- night dance. The girl, elaborately decked out, ran and danced along a path, while several other participants sang, shaking dewclaw strings hung from long poles. Others might also sing and dance. During the day, the girl slept outside or in a small shelter; she packed firewood and was subject to numerous restrictions. She was considered marriageable at the conclusion of the ceremony.

Simpler ceremonies marked other transitions in the lives of individuals. Feasts, with presents for those attending, marked a birth, as well as the formal bestowal of an ancestor's name upon a child. Less formal observances were held when individuals subsequently adopted additional names. According to Drucker (1934a), the dead were buried, the deceased's personal belongings and house being burned. Before the coming of the Whites, according to Frachtenberg (1910–1911), Molalas cremated their dead, leaving the bones to be buried in family coffins of hide.

Other occasions bringing Molalas together included games of strength and skill, which often involved betting. Games played exclusively for gambling included a beaver-tooth dice game and a four-stick guessing game identical to one played by Klamaths.

Mythology

In a myth fragment recorded by Boas (1890b), the world-sea receded to reveal first Mount Hood, then the lower Willamette Valley. The stage thereby was set for the travels of the trickster-transformer Coyote (*tǽlæpaˑs*), many of whose adventures are related in a rich collection dictated to Frachtenberg (1910–1911). In another fragment recorded by Gatschet (1877a), the character of the Molalas themselves is explained: after tricking Grizzly into killing himself in a contest, Coyote dismembered and scattered his body; Molalas would be hunters, because their country received the heart of Grizzly.

History

Molalas may have been among Meriwether Lewis and William Clark's (Thwaites 1904–1905, 6:118) 3,000 "Shoshones" (presumably, people of inland cultural type), reported to winter on the Willamette River, but to move east for summer fishing notably at the falls of the Towarnehiooks (Deschutes) River. Molalas are definitely identified in 1841 (Hale 1846:214), by which time they reportedly had suffered much from introduced diseases.

Fig. 5. Esther LaBonte (b.1895, d.1987), daughter of Douglas Jones, a well known Molala resident of Grand Ronde Reservation, Oreg. By tradition, tribal identity in the western Oregon region followed that imputed to one's father; however, LaBonte often presented herself as a Klikitat, preferring the greater public recognition accompanying her mother's identity. She also referred to herself and other members of her community as "Grand Ronde Indians" (Henry Zenk, communication to the editors 1996). Photograph by Henry Zenk, Springfield, Oreg., 1983.

Molalas came into occasional conflict with American settlers, who began filling the Willamette Valley during the 1840s. Stern (1956:233–239) has assembled scattered references to perhaps the most serious clash, which he terms the Molala War. According to one account of this obscure episode (Vernon 1934), the instigator was the Northern Molala leader Crooked Finger, who raised a multitribal, predominantly Molala-Klamath force against Willamette Valley settlements then weakened by the absence of men diverted to the Cayuse War in northeastern Oregon. According to a Molala point of view (expressed by Mrs. Joseph Hudson, daughter of *kúˑcta*, the principal Molala chief involved; Clarke 1885), Klamaths were in the area only to visit their Molala relatives, not as part of an invasion force. Either claim is consistent with Down's (1926:47–58) reconstruction, in which the settlers, alarmed by a large number of Molalas and Klamaths gathered at the Molala settlement on Abiqua Creek, decided to reduce the problem by expelling the Klamaths. The settlers attacked at the Battle of the Abiqua, March 5–6, 1848. According to some accounts, they massacred Indian women and children. According to others, there was no massacre, although one or more Indian women were killed or wounded while fighting alongside their men.

At the unratified Champoeg treaty of 1851 (Oregon Superintendency of Indian Affairs 1851–1856:73–97), there reportedly survived 121 Molalas, excluding Southern Molalas. The ratified Dayton and Molala treaties of 1855 (Kappler 1904–1941, 2:665–669, 740–742) provided for the removal of all Molalas to Grand Ronde Reservation, northwestern Oregon. A number, presumably Southern Molalas for the most part, found their way to Klamath Reservation instead, where U.S. census records showed 55 Molalas in 1881 (Gatschet 1890, l:xxvi). A few other Molalas took up residence on Siletz Reservation, while an undetermined number of others established themselves apart from any reservation. By the early twentieth century, tribal identity retained but minimal significance on the tribally and linguistically heterogeneous Grand Ronde Reservation (fig. 5). In this setting, tribal languages, including Molala, fell largely into desuetude in favor of Chinook Jargon and English (Zenk 1988).

Synonymy

The name Molala is given as mo·lális in Boas (1890b:1), where it is said to be of Clackamas (Chinookan) origin. Variations on the same form are regionally widely attested, usually as general designations of Molala speakers: Clackamas Upper Chinook muláliš (Jacobs 1958–1959, 2:551); Kalapuyan (Tualatin and Santiam) mule·lis, mulé·lis (Jacobs 1928–1936); Wasco Upper Chinook and Columbia River Sahaptin [mólališ] (Rigsby 1969:80–81). Historical spellings include Molala (Hodge 1907–1910, 1:930), Mólale (Gatschet 1877:372), Molále (Powell 1891:127), Molalis (Applegate 1907:3–4), Molalla (Dayton Treaty, 1855; also used locally on the Grand Ronde Reservation), Moolalle (Champoeg Treaty, 1851), Moléle (Hale 1846:561), Mollala (Belden 1855), Mollalla (Palmer 1855). Other synonyms include Columbia River Sahaptin łáytilpam, táytilpam (Rigsby 1969:80–81) and Klamath kúikni (Gatschet 1890, 2:157).

Subgroups

There were no groups that meaningfully may be termed "tribal." Berreman's (1937:57) Northern Molalla subgroup appears to include the Upper Santiam and Northern Molalla. Gatschet (1890, 2:157, 426) distinguished Southern Molalas from all other Molalas, whom he termed Straight Mólale.

Northern Molala. Roughly, these were the people signing the 1851 Champoeg treaty as the Principal Band of the Moo-lal-le Tribe, and the 1855 Dayton treaty as the Molalla band of Molallas. Northern Molala speakers used the self-designation lá·ti-, appearing in lá·ti·wi 'Molala person, Molala people', lá·ti?áyfq 'the Molala people', and lá·tilæŋs 'Molala country'. muk̓ǽnti, synonymous with Hodge's (1907–1910, 1:955) Mukanti, appears both as a place-name for the Molalla River area and as the name of a Northern Molala winter settlement.

Upper Santiam. The name is R.L. Benson's (Farmer et al. 1973:14) modification of Santiam Band of [the] Moolalle Tribe (Champoeg treaty, 1851), coined to distinguish the Molala subgroup from the neighboring Santiam Kalapuyans. cá?aył, appearing as an unidentified tribe name in Jacobs (1928) and as a name for Santiam River people in Drucker (1934a), is a possible Northern Molala synonym. čimbú·ihe, given by Boas (1890b:4) as the name of an unidentified group or place "below" Albany, Oregon, appears in Gatschet (1877:363) for a Molala settlement at the head of Santiam River—hence, Hodge's (1907–1910, 1:270) Chimbuiha.

Southern Molala. These were the people signing the 1855 Molala treaty as the Mo-lal-la-las or Molel tribe. tulǽnyaŋsi 'far-off people' appears in Frachtenberg (1910–1911) as the Northern Molala name for people of Douglas County, Oregon, who spoke Molala differently. In English, Northern Molalas often referred to Southern Molalas as the Eugene Molala. Variants of Klamath čakǵe·nkni· 'serviceberry-area-people' have been recorded with the following referents: Molalas and Rogue River people (Barker 1963a:70); Molalas resident on upper Rogue River (Gatschet 1890, 2:157, 426—hence, Hodge's, 1907–1910, 1:231, Chakankni); a Molala settlement at the head of Umpqua River (Gatschet 1877:363); Klamaths resident in Douglas County, Oregon (Frachtenberg 1910–1911). R.L. Benson (in Farmer et al. 1973:14) adopted the name Mace Mountain for the North Umpqua River area, omitted evidently in error by Belden (1855), but restored by Royce (1899: map 51).

Sources

Except for Spier (1930), all the sources cited in the culture sketch exist only in manuscript form. Besides Frachtenberg's (1910–1911) text collection, which includes historical and ethnographic texts as well as 23 traditional narratives, significant linguistic data are from Jacobs (1928, 1928a, 1928–1935) and Swadesh (see Swadesh 1954). Additional linguistic sources are Hale (1846:569–629), Gatschet (1877, 1877a, 1877b), Boas (1890b), Curtis (1907–1930, 8:195–198), and Marr (1941). Additional Molala traditional narratives, told in Clackamas Upper Chinook and Chinook Jargon by a Clackamas-Molala former resident of Grand Ronde Reservation, are in Jacobs (1936:1–12, 1958–1959, 2:431–451, 469–473). A body of oral history interviews and other local sources bearing upon Northern Molalas of southeastern Clackamas County is summarized in Baars (1982).

Some historical artifacts of identified Molala provenance are preserved at the Thomas Burke Museum, University of Washington, Seattle; and at the Museum of Mankind, The Ethnography Department of the British Museum, London, England.

Klamath and Modoc

THEODORE STERN

Language

The Klamath ('klăməθ) and Modoc ('mōdäk) are two peoples closely related in language, if somewhat divergent in culture, in aboriginal times dwelling adjacent within the Klamath Basin, east of the Cascades, in southern Oregon and northern California. The two peoples speak dialects of a single language, a member of the Plateau Penutian family (Hale 1846; Sapir 1929; Rigsby 1965; Hymes 1964; DeLancey, Genetti, and Rude 1988; C.F. Voegelin 1946).[*]

Cultural Position

The archeological record (Cressman 1956; Sampson 1985) shows that the country has been occupied by humans from at least 5000 B.C., with cultural links to its historic inhabitants. It has been postulated that a lifestyle that developed about the pluvial lakes of the Great Basin extended to the Klamath Basin, and when, during the altithermal period, those lakes contracted, the freshwater lakes and marshes of the Klamath Basin continued to be attractive. Indeed, there is evidence that even in protohistoric times Klamath-Modoc culture extended farther to the east than it did in historic times (Sampson 1985:42; Kelly 1932:70, 186; cf. Stewart 1939:140).

Positioned as they are near the juncture of the cultural provinces of the Plateau, the Great Basin, and California, which Kroeber (1939) sees as emergent segments of his Intermediate-Intermontane Area, it is understandable that they have been seen as intermediate in their cultural position. Kroeber has variously placed them as California (1925:334) or of the Great Basin (1939:51). Hofmeister (1968), treating statistically the comparative data of E.W. Voegelin (1942), which do not cover the Basin, found that the Klamath and Modoc, with closest affinities to each other and somewhat isolated culturally from the other peoples considered, manifested far stronger ties with California neighbors, the eastern Shasta, Achumawi, and Mountain Maidu, than they did with the somewhat remote tribes of the Columbian Plateau. Thus, although here considered within a Plateau volume, these are peoples who as Kroeber (1939:51) once said, were to be included (with the Achumawi-Atsugewi) in a bloc that could be assigned "with equal justice in the California and the Great Basin cultures."

If they share a basic culture, the Klamath and Modoc have diverged somewhat. Spier (1930:233) saw Klamath material culture as of Plateau character, although with Basin features, and with Northwest Coast social and religious institutions, while he saw the Modoc as somewhat more inclined toward California. When, in historic times, the Klamath came increasingly to trade northward with Chinookan and Sahaptian peoples along the Columbia, they reinforced their Northwest Coast and Plateau features and took on as well Plains influences. The Modoc, who received Plains features from their Northern Paiute neighbors to the east, also took on California elements that did not reach the Klamath. Indeed, Ray (1963:xii–xiv), who, like Stern, assigns both peoples culturally to California, on the basis of cultural features that he regards as diagnostic—religion, cremation, and slavery, for example—contends that the Modoc stood closer culturally to the Achumawi than they did to the Klamath. The statistical data of E.W. Voegelin and Hofmeister stand at odds with that finding.

Environment

The Klamath Basin lies within an elevated plateau on the east flank of the Cascade Mountains, which extends eastward some 70 miles to the escarpment above Silver and Summer lakes and ranges southward from the headwaters of the Deschutes River about 150–180 miles to the headwaters of the Pit and McCloud rivers. The scene of repeated volcanism, in many places the land bears a mantle of pumice. The Basin, the product of geological faulting, cradles the Klamath Lakes and tributary streams fed by extensive marshes; in turn the lakes are drained by the Klamath River, which plunges into a deep-cut canyon to run westward to the Pacific. Rainfall, which averages 15 inches per year, is heaviest along the Cascades, dropping rapidly toward the east. The land is clothed with conifer forests dominated by ponderosa pine in the west, with a mixed

---

[*]The phonemes of Klamath (Klamath-Modoc) are: (voiceless aspirated stops and affricate) *t, č, k, q, ʔ;* (lenis stops and affricate) *b, d, ǯ, g, ġ;* (glottalized stops and affricate) *ṗ, ṭ, č̣, k̓, q̓;* (voiceless fricatives) *s, ł, h;* (voiced lateral) *l;* (voiced resonants) *m, n, w, y;* (voiceless resonants) *M, N, W, Y;* (glottalized resonants) *ṁ, ṅ, ẁ, ẏ;* (short vowels) *i, e ([ɛ]), a, o;* (long vowels) *iˑ, eˑ ([ǽˑ]), aˑ, oˑ.* The lenis consonants are voiceless in initial syllables before a vowel but tend to be voiced by younger speakers. The glottalized (ejective) consonants contrast with sequences of consonant plus *ʔ.* For a fuller description of Klamath phonetics see Barker (1964:19–41), summarized in Barker (1963a:12–14).

446

vegetation characterized by mountain mahogany, and with aspen along watercourses. Marshes and lake shallows are thick with tules, cattails, and cane, and in season bear yellow water lilies. Eastward, vegetation gives way successively to manzanita, sagebrush, then bunchgrass prairie, and finally to juniper.

Klamath territory included lands surrounding Agency and Upper Klamath lakes (fig. 1), fed from the north and east from Klamath and Sycan marshes respectively by the Williamson and Sprague rivers. Their eastern border was sharply delimited by the escarpment of Winter Rim, although beyond, Chewaukan Marsh, in Northern Paiute country, bears a Klamath name. Modoc country (fig. 1) included Lower Klamath Lake, a variable body dependent on overflow from Upper Klamath Lake, as well as the Tule--Lost River–Clear Lake system to the east. That eastern section is continuous in character with the Great Basin ecology about Goose Lake.

Rich in vegetable foods, in mollusks, waterfowl, and larger fauna, the Klamath Basin was well endowed to support a foraging population; but its elevation, above 4,000 feet, also ensured long winters with heavy snowfall, bringing with them the perennial threat of freezing and starvation.

Territory

Major divisions of the Klamath and Modoc related to the winter settlements, at once a source and an expression of cohesiveness. Although not as a whole marked by subcultural differences, they constituted semiautonomous political entities.

Among the Klamath, the Klamath Marsh people (*ʔewksikniˑ*) comprised by far the largest group, as large as the others taken together. Their settlements, some 34 in number, of varying sizes (Spier 1930; Stern 1954; Barker 1963a), were clustered on the eastern shore of Klamath Marsh and of Agency Lake, as well as the middle course of the Williamson and lower Sprague rivers. To this group probably belonged the next division, the Agency Lake people, *ġoWasdikniˑ*, comprising but a settlement and a hamlet. The Uplanders, *blaykniˑ*, on the Upper Sprague and Sycan rivers, with some four or five settlements, sometimes considered a part of the Klamath Marsh division, seem to have been distinct and to have intermarried to some extent with both Modoc and Northern Paiute.

Linked by intermarriage and sometimes at odds with the Klamath Marsh division were two other bodies. The Lower Williamson people, *dokwakniˑ*, numbered about seven settlements at the mouth of the river on Upper Klamath Lake, while the Pelican Bay division, *gombatkniˑ*, extending from the northwestern shore of Upper Klamath Lake to the western shore of Agency Lake, counted some eight communities. Finally, largely independent of them was the southernmost Klamath division, the Klamath Falls group, *ʔiWłałłonkniˑ*, occupying both shores of the southern half of Upper Klamath Lake, with a total of about 14 villages.

The major Modoc divisions were three (Ray 1963). The Lower Klamath Lake people, at the southern tip of that body and along the initial course of the Klamath River, and extending eastward to the shore of Tule Lake, bore the name, *gombatwaˑs*, which, like that of the Pelican Bay division of the Klamath, refers to the rocky character of the land. They numbered some eight winter villages, of which those on Lower Klamath Lake were sometimes held to be distinct. On Lost River near its mouth on Tule Lake were five winter settlements of the *pasganwaˑs*, termed here the Lower Lost River division. To the east ranged a dozen winter villages of the Eastern division, who took their name, *ġoġewaˑs*, from Lost River, and were located on the eastern shore of Tule Lake, on the upper Lost River, on Clear Lake, and extended to the west shore of Goose Lake.

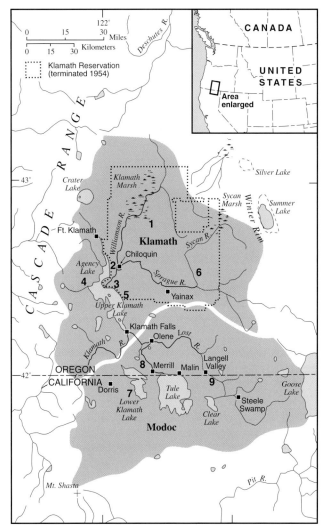

Fig. 1. Klamath and Modoc territories and subgroups in the 19th century (Stern 1965:280; Ray 1963) with modern town locations: 1, Klamath Marsh; 2, Agency Lake; 3, Lower Williamson River; 4, Pelican Bay; 5, Klamath Falls; 6, Upland; 7, Lower Klamath Lake; 8, Lower Lost River; 9, Eastern.

Culture

Annual Round

Life for the Klamath and Modoc was attuned to the seasonal runs of fish, the flight of waterfowl, the maturing of plant species, and the movement of game. Between the two peoples there were differences, as each, in its environmental setting, came to emphasize different aspects of their earlier shared culture. For the Klamath, there was more dependence on fish. Their country was somewhat richer in that resource: salmon ran up the Klamath River but did not reach Modoc waters; and Klamath fishing gear showed a somewhat larger inventory. They practiced greater emphasis on fish drives than did those of the Modoc. The Modoc relied to a greater extent upon hunting, and Ray (1963) asserts that they also placed greater reliance upon the gathering of wild seeds than did the Klamath.

Relief from the bonds of winter began for both peoples in March, when large suckers began to run, first in Upper Klamath Lake, then in Lost River. The Modoc were first to leave, drawing up shovel-nosed dugouts from the shallows where they had been submerged to prevent their splitting, loading aboard their family and household gear, and paddling off for the fisheries. Behind them at the winter settlements they left their semisubterranean winter lodges dismantled for a seasonal airing, along with the aged and infirm in their huts, with an occasional child to help out. From time to time, they sent back youths with provisions for those they had left behind.

Fishing for the Klamath was in fact a year-round activity, their winter villages being situated upon waters that remained open during the winters. For the Modoc, it was seasonal. Primarily, it was a masculine pursuit, although a woman might paddle the canoe or catch small fish by hand or with a pack basket. Men fished variously, according to water conditions and species. Fishing from the bank or a canoe, an individual fisherman plied a long-handled dip net (fig. 2 center) sometimes jumping into swift waters to secure his prey, then jumping back. He speared large suckers, trout, and salmon with a bident harpoon, often wielded from a blind. In shallow waters, he pinned down a bottom fish with a multipronged spear, then retrieved it with a barbed one. There was also team fishing. Two men drew a triangular net on an A-frame, or a purse net, through the water, while others drove fish toward them. Upon deeper, quiet waters, a fisherman plied the A-frame net at the bow of one canoe or tule raft, while the crews of other craft served as drivers. Similarly, gill nets might be drawn between two canoes or set out in the shallows. Angling was a minor pursuit, with a baited gorge or composite bone hook on a milkweed string leader and a line of nettle bark. Fishing for trout and salmon, the Klamath might set out 20 poles at a time overnight, each with 30 feet of line. In swift waters, they set

448

top, Klamath Co. Mus., Klamath Falls, Oreg.: 66–1697; center, Milwaukee Public Mus., Wis.: 421140.

Fig. 2. Fishing activities. top, Klamath camp on Lost River, Oreg., where suckers are being dried for winter storage. Photograph by Maud Baldwin, about 1898. center, Modoc man fishing on Klamath Lake using a big triangular dip net from a dugout canoe about 16–18 feet in length. The net is attached to a pair of poles held apart by a crossbar near the vertex of the angle formed by them (Spier 1930:150). Photographed before 1938. bottom, Blessing by tribal elder at the Klamath First Sucker ceremony. left to right, Don Gentry; Gordon Bettles, culture and heritage specialist (holding microphone); Neva Eggsman, Klamath elder; and Marvin Garcia. In this revival of the ceremony, the fish—endangered species—are returned live. Photograph by Taylor R. Tupper, Chiloquin Dam, Oreg., 1993.

out cylindrical fish traps for trout, the pressure of the waters alone preventing their escape.

On some streams, there were stone barriers providing backwaters where fish could more easily be taken. They were said to have been built in mythic times by the trickster-transformer, Gmukamps (*gmok'amč*). At a place on the lower Sprague where he is said to have dwelt, the Klamath, led by an elder, celebrated a first-sucker rite (fig. 2), two of the first fish to be taken in the spring being cast into the fire to foretell the fishing luck for the season, while those gathered there feasted ritually on the rest of that first catch, returning the entrails to the waters.

The abundance of the runs during early spring sometimes brought several peoples together. Both Klamath and Modoc gathered at a fishery near Olene, on Lost River, while another, on the upper Sprague, drew Northern Paiutes as well. During the sucker runs, all were kept busy, the women splitting the fish as they came in and hanging them to sun-dry (fig. 2 top), on the branches of pine saplings, which the Modoc sometimes transplanted for the purpose. The Klamath pounded part of their dried fish into a meal, storing it in sacks holding 50–70 pounds apiece, in imitation of the salmon pemmican they traded from The Dalles (Gatschet 1890, 2:116).

As the first run of suckers slackened, Modoc women made trips out in search of desert parsley (*Lomatium canbyi*), less sought by Klamaths, for the first taste of fresh roots. Soon thereafter, among both peoples parties of women fanned out to dig ipos roots (*Carum oregonum*), while the men kept them supplied with fish. This was a time when waterfowl eggs were gathered, and the tender cambium layers of young ponderosa pines added variety to the diet. By June, camas bulbs were ripe for the gathering in the meadows, while men took waterfowl and small game. In Modoc country, the poisonous white camas extended the root season, although the bulbs required soaking to render them edible (Ray 1963:199). Camas was often baked in earth ovens, then sun-dried for storage.

By July the yellow pond lily (*Nuphar polysepalum*) and its seeds, called wokas (Klamath *wokas*), became ripe in Modoc country, and a month later was ready for harvest in the north. Among both peoples, the harvest was preceded by a first-fruits rite, presided over among the Klamath by a shaman (E.W. Voegelin 1942:element 316 and note; Gatschet 1890, 1:76). According to Spier (1930:13) all the local divisions of the Klamath congregated on Klamath Marsh to gather wokas; and they may accordingly have participated together in this ceremony. Punting canoes of light draught in the shallows, women, children, and old men scooped the lily pods into tule bags and, returning to their wokas camps, dumped them into pits to decompose. By a somewhat complex set of procedures (Coville 1904), they separated the seeds, parched them, then lightly hulled them on the metate with a distinctive horned (handled) milling stone; later they winnowed and sacked them for storage ("Ethnobiology and Subsistence," fig. 5, this vol.). Each Klamath family gathered 5–15 bushels of this staple (Stern 1965:66). As other seeds became mature, women went out with woven beater and basket to gather them. The rootstocks of cattail were dried and ground into a meal.

Meanwhile, the men were off hunting in the east and south. Here the greater Modoc reliance upon this activity is reflected in the enhanced ritual with which they surrounded their preparations (E.W. Voegelin 1942:elements 278, 143–168b) and the greater range of game taken. Before going out, the hunter purified himself in the sweathouse, praying to earth, mountain, and rocks to "Give me your lice!" (Ray 1963:183). For both peoples, the hunting of waterfowl had been important since prehistoric times (Cressman 1956:450; Sampson 1985). They were taken by methods in part used also to take fish: they were decoyed into setnets, shot from canoes, or jacklighted in winter. As for larger game, Klamaths hunted deer and, to a minor degree, elk in the Cascades, while the Modoc found their best hunting between Tule and Goose lakes. A single hunter in deerhead disguise might stalk an animal; but it was much more popular for both peoples to chase deer with dogs, shooting their prey with bow and arrow. On occasion, men chased the animals into the lake where women in canoes dispatched them. Modocs stalked antelope and, in the lava beds to the south, sought mountain sheep. Both peoples practiced the fire drive, surrounding a small knoll and advancing uphill behind the flames to take the game that had fled to the top. Both also used a surround, of Great Basin style. Klamaths in the Klamath Marsh–Williamson River area enclosed an area with a net fence surmounted by brush, then with fire stampeded the antelope or deer within the area, so that hunters could shoot them and women capture them barehanded (E.W. Voegelin 1942:element 44 and note). In the wintertime, Modoc hunters, after a shaman had charmed the antelope, drove the herd between wings of individual fires tended by women, and into a pound consisting only of a rope held and shaken by shouting women. Hunters followed and dispatched the animals with clubs (Ray 1963:185–187). Modoc set spring snares or nooses hanging from limbs along deer trails. Both peoples also caught and ate a variety of small mammals. The flesh of larger animals was cut into strips and sun-dried for storage.

By early fall, which was counted as the beginning of the year, both peoples were gathering black cherries and prunes, as well as pine nuts and lowland blackberries and gooseberries. The Klamath were dipnetting whitefish, and a second run of suckers had drawn the Modoc back to the Lost River fisheries once again. As huckleberries ripened in the high country, some Modocs moved into the uplands east of Tule Lake, others to the base of Mount Shasta, the men hunting while the women picked berries. Klamaths, on their part, moved westward to the slopes of Mount Pitt and other peaks of the Cascades, in the process encountering the Southern Molala, similarly engaged from the western slopes. While the Klamath women gathered berries and dried them before a fire for storage, the men hunted deer and elk and set deadfalls for furbearers.

By October, both peoples had returned to their permanent settlements, there to rebuild their winter lodges. For the Klamath, the return was celebrated by a dance in one of the earth lodges used for communal ceremonies and inauguration of the rebuilt lodges, by a feast (Gatschet 1890, 1:75). Their supplies were placed in storage pits to which Klamaths added an odorous root to repel animals. Klamath storage pits were communal, but those of the Modoc were private for each household and carefully concealed from outsiders.

As winter set in and the snow fell in deep drifts, fishing and hunting became more restricted, particularly for the Klamath. In favored sites—and winter settlements were situated with this in mind—fish could still be caught. Even on frozen lakes, men stationed in blinds harpooned fish through holes cut in the ice. Where the waters were still open, Klamaths jacklighted waterfowl from canoes. Wearing bearpaw snowshoes, hunters pursued deer across the deep snow. It was at this time that the Modocs drove antelope into their pounds. Parties of hunters sought out the dens of hibernating bears, pulling the beast out by twisting crossed poles into its hide, then dispatching it with arrows.

The winter solstice came as heavy rains began to replace the snow. It was celebrated by the Klamath by a ceremonial gathering led by several shamans, with exhibitions of the performances of novice shamans. These performances, which drew members from an entire local division (E.W. Voegelin 1942:elements 4437, 4886, and notes), must have strengthened local ties. Winter evenings were also a favorite occasion for recounting tales of the myth times, when Gmukamps and Gopher, in rivalry, were bringing the world into its present form, when Mink and his brother, Weasel, slew monsters, and vain Skunk and trickster Coyote displayed a fallibility that was all too human.

As winter wore on and supplies dwindled, villagers withdrew more to themselves, and householders eked out their food sparingly. As hospitality and generosity were curtailed, all looked forward to the signs of winter's end. Children played the ball and pin game to "split the moon" and thus shorten winter, while those shamans who controlled the weather tried to summon their tulelary powers to bring on warming rains or a chinook wind to melt the snows. In straitened times, people fell back on famine foods—tree lichen and the cambium layer of the lodgepole pine—and sometimes were reduced to eating their leather moccasins. Even then, however, dogs were not eaten, nor is cannibalism recorded. At long last, as the weather turned once more to spring, the people eagerly began their preparations for the movement to the fisheries.

Structures

The Klamath and Modoc distinguished three main house forms. They were the semisubterranean earth lodge, called the "winter lodge;" a mat lodge erected over a shallow excavation, used in both winter and summer; and the small wickiup, also mat-covered (fig. 3). The earth lodge was built in a pit ranging in diameter from 12 to over 35 feet, with a depth of one to four feet. Against a central four-post frame and the stringers connecting

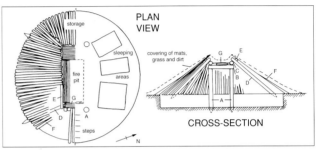

top, Klamath Co. Mus., Klamath Falls, Oreg.: 66–1684; center, after Spier 1930:54, 199.
Fig. 3. Klamath structures. top, Summer camp with 2 wickiups, one mat-covered and one cloth-covered. Photograph by Maud Baldwin, 1905–1910. center, Schematic drawings of an earthlodge in cross-section and plan view. The cross-section shows the principal construction elements, including the central upright posts (A), the crossbeams or stringers (B and C), the rafters (D and E), and the poles or planks (F) laid against the upper rafters. Over this structure would be placed layers of mats, grass, and dirt. The left side of the plan view shows the construction of the hatchway (G). The right side of this view shows how the interior space was divided among the fire pit, steps, storage space, and sleeping areas. bottom, Lulu Lang outside her summer lodge made of wooden planks with side entrance. Photograph by Theodore Stern, Upper Klamath Lake, Klamath Res., Oreg., 1956.

them, men set rough planks or poles that extended to the ground beyond the excavation.

Women laid on mats horizontally, starting from the bottom, shingle fashion, then covered the matting with earth. Such a lodge might take a month for the householders to build. Entrance was gained by ascending stairs built usually into the east flank of the house, then climbing down a ladder through the roof hatchway that served both as entrance and smokehole.

The other two structures, when used as winter homes, might be built for warmth over a shallow pit, and a bit of dirt might be thrown up over the matting to keep out the cold. What is here termed the mat lodge in construction resembled the earth lodge, save that it had a side entrance. It was a common dwelling in the spring fishing camps. The wickiup, built on a frame of bowed willows, sometimes reached a diameter of 10 feet when used as a dwelling but normally was smaller. Its portability (only the mats need be carried along) made it a popular dwelling during the warmer months.

The earth lodge, the dwelling of the wealthier leaders, usually sheltered several families, with the owner's family along the north wall and the others across from them. The house was conceived as facing toward the east. Within, firewood was stacked on the eastern side, while the western side served for storage of gear. Twice a day, the women of the household brought in cooked food from the kitchen wickiup, and the household ate together. At night, they slept with feet toward the fire, with their heads in any direction but west, where lay the afterworld. They slept on fine tule mats spread on grass. Their valuables were stored by their heads, on the shelf formed by the juncture of roof and ground.

The winter settlements of Klamath and Modoc varied widely in size, from the virtually continuous occupation in favored places that Spier (1930:11) terms "towns," such as those on lower Klamath Marsh, the middle Williamson, or the mouth of Lost River, down to isolated hamlets comprising a couple of houses. The typical community might comprise a score of dwellings, including a couple of earth lodges, which served also for public assemblies, the mat lodges of the common folk, and the wickiups clustered on their flanks. In the wickiups dwelt the aged who could no longer cope with the ladders of the earth lodge. In other

wickiups women from the larger houses cooked and wove baskets; during menstruation and childbirth they retreated to still others. Storage pits were dug into the ground nearby in Klamath villages; summertime shades stood nearby; there were semisubterranean sweathouses for common use; and, if this was a large village, there was a cremation ground nearby. A village of this sort might house upward of 100 persons.

Clothing and Adornment

Both men and women among the Klamath wore a fringed skirt of vegetable fibers or buckskin thongs; among the Modoc, women were similarly clad, while men wore a frontal apron. As Spier (1930:207) suggests, the terms for such garments suggest the two-piece apron of California–Great Basin style. On the head, women wore a decorated cap of twined tules (fig. 4), men a plain visored basketry cap (fig. 5). Poor people wore no more; and this remained the ceremonial costume. In cold weather, those who could, added robes of deer or coyote skin; Modocs used robes woven of rabbitskin, of featherstrips, or of birdskins (fig. 6). The wealthy among both peoples wore elkskin, puma, or bobcat robes, along with a fur cap. For summer travel, they donned buckskin moccasins, while in the winter they substituted woven tule moccasins lined with shredded sagebrush bark, together with leggings of twined tules or fur (fig. 7).

In the late nineteenth century, trading expeditions to The Dalles brought back to the Klamath buckskin clothing of Plains style, including a woman's gown and the man's shirt, to which sleeves and porcupine quill decora-

left, Oreg. Histl. Soc., Portland: 61962; center, Smithsonian, Dept. of Anthr.: 24075 (neg. 95–20790); right, Smithsonian, NAA: 91–13025.
Fig. 4. Women's hats. left, Grandma Reuben, Klamath, wearing a decorated tule hat. She has typical chin tattooing. Photograph by O.D. Springer, 1939. center, Klamath woman's work hat of twined split tule with feather tassel. While similar to the twined hats worn by women along the Columbia River, the hats made by Modoc and Klamath women tended to be shorter in height and wider on top. Decorative motifs were also distinct, and the parallelograms on this hat were a popular design not found among more northern Plateau groups. Collected by L.S. Dyar at the Klamath Agency, Oreg., before 1876. Height 11.5 cm. right, Klamath wife of Modoc Henry wearing a cloth cap decorated with beads and olivella shells. Photograph by Edward S. Curtis, Klamath Res., Oreg., 1916–1917.

left, Smithsonian, NAA: 79–4309; right, Smithsonian, Dept. of Anthr.: 24095 (neg. 95–20789).

Fig. 5. Klamath warriors' hats. left, Bennett Weeks wearing a tule headdress decorated with feathers. Photograph by Edward S. Curtis, Klamath Res., Oreg., 1916–1917. right, Klamath war hat constructed of a wide elkskin band painted with black and red figures and ornamented with 2 trimmed eagle feathers. Collected by L.S. Dyar, at the Klamath Agency, Oreg., before 1876. Height of elkskin band, 17 cm.

tion were later added, along with breechclout and leggings and moccasins of a new "Warm Springs" cut. Feather bonnets were the latest addition (fig. 8). The Modoc assert that they acquired the new style from the Northern Paiute (Ray 1963:165). These garments became the new costume of the wealthy.

Both sexes wore the hair loose or braided, one braid for women, two for men. The hair was combed with porcupine tail or grass comb and dressed with grease; shamans painted the part red. In cold weather they dressed their body with grease to prevent chapping and applied charcoal around the eyes to prevent snowblindness. Face paint was used on occasion, red in general, white at dances, and black for mourning (Spier 1930:216).

Some families, following customs seen on the Columbia, flattened the heads of their infants on the cradleboard. Tattooing was a practice said to have come from the south (E.W. Voegelin 1942:element 1621, notes). Men tattooed their arms and chests, cutting the flesh and rubbing in charcoal. Women tattooed two or three vertical lines on the chin (fig. 4 left). Through the nasal septum men wore a nosepin of bone or dentalium, or pine nuts. Men tweaked out facial hair with fingers dipped in ashes.

Technology

In the crafts, the conventional division of labor was flexible. Commonly, men did the woodworking and made tools of wood, bone, and obsidian, as well as the stone mortars, metates, pestles, and manos. On occasion, a woman, driven by necessity, might make her own dugout canoe (Spier 1930:171). Women wove baskets, made cordage of nettle fiber and Indian hemp, tanned hides, and made clothing. Men made nets from the cordage twisted by women. There were no craft specialists, only persons with different levels of skill.

Woodworking was less highly developed among the Klamath and Modoc than among the peoples of the lower Klamath River drainage. With fire and with elkhorn picks or wedges driven by knot-headed mauls, men hollowed out from ponderosa pine shovel-nosed canoes of relatively thin walls, but with a hull that retained the external contour of the original log. With similar means they split out rough planks for the earth lodge. Juniper, or by preference, yew, was sought for bows, broad of limb and recurved, plain for ordinary use but sinew-backed for war, with twisted sinew

Fig. 6. Duckskin blanket constructed of strips of duckskin with feathers twined together with hemp cord. Collected by L.S. Dyar at the Klamath Agency, Oreg., before 1876. Length 117 cm.

string. Mountain mahogany was the wood preferred for articles such as the foreshafts of reed arrowshafts, for spears and digging sticks.

The flexible twined basketry of the Klamath and Modoc was distinctive in having a warp of twisted tule, with a weft of either tule or cattail (figs. 9–10). Designs were worked in with weft elements of cattail (white), dyed tule (black), and porcupine quills (yellow), as well as other materials and colors. Household containers—winnowing trays, bowls, caps, as well as tule sandals and leggings—were made in close twine. Larger containers were twined in willow: burden baskets, sitting cradles, and seed beaters. Some coiled basketry was made in reservation times, apparently under Northern Paiute influence (Spier 1930:190).

Weaving was otherwise represented only by the twined rabbitskin, feather, and birdskin robes of the Modoc.

Skins were in greater use for clothing among the Modoc, who practiced hunting to a greater degree than did the Klamath. Both sexes (Ray 1963:190) took part in dressing hides, which they first soaked, then tied to an inclined post and dehaired with a bone spokeshave. After washing the hide, the operator dried it, then dressed it with brains. After some days, she then pounded and stretched it, grained it, and finally smoked it. Women made the finished leather into garments, cutting it to form and sewing it with awl and sinew thread.

Fire was produced by either sex, using a drill of ponderosa pine, sage-brush, or willow, and cedar—commonly a paddle blade—as hearth. A fuse of sagebrush bark was used to carry fire from one camp to the next (Spier 1930:172).

Social and Political Organization

Community life found its richest expression in the winter settlements, in which collective life was given character by those who through industry, foresight, and strength of character had amassed wealth and gathered about them households of kinsmen and followers. They were commonly men: the same term, *laǵi*, denotes a rich person, a leader, and the adult male of a species (Gatschet 1890, 2:178ff.). Eminence might rest in part upon inherited position, but a man who lacked the personal qualifications forfeited standing. Success was counted not merely in hunting but in the competition of games and gambling, and, for some, in warfare as

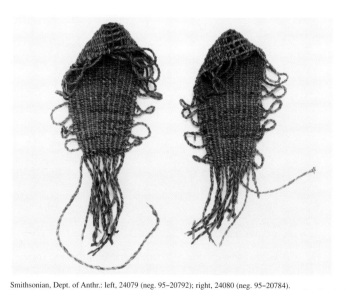

Fig. 7. Klamath tule legwear and footwear. left, Moccasins of plain twined tule for winter. right, Leggings of twined tule, worn with tule moccasins. Both collected by L.S. Dyar at the Klamath Agency, Oreg., before 1876. Length of moccasins, 29 cm; length of leggings, 38 cm.

Fig. 8. Men's 20th-century clothing influenced from Plains styles. Chief Sky, Klamath, wearing a fringed buckskin shirt decorated with beads, feathers, and shell. He is smoking a European long-stemmed pipe probably made of wood with a wind cap. Photographed 1929.

they were not standardized. The Modoc took apart their strings of clamshell beads to wear them as personal adornment (Ray 1963:178).

Influential men presided at the head of extended families that counted ties on both sides. Such a man was head of a household, often comprising several immediate (nuclear) families, including perhaps that of a recently married daughter or so, together with those of married kinsmen of either himself or his wife, or that of a friend of either, and perhaps aged parents. Thus, Spier (1930:53) details the household of a Klamath shaman, containing elements of five nuclear families totaling 20 persons.

Leading families in particular sought through the marriage of their children an alliance with families of equivalent standing, preferably beyond the village but within the regional division. There were, to be sure, unions that extended beyond the tribe itself. Both the Upland Klamath and the Lower Klamath Lake Modoc contained intertribal families: Modoc, Klamath, and Northern Paiute in the former and Modoc, Klamath, and Pit River in the latter. There were also Klamath–Molala unions.

Leaders counted upon a large household and following for support, for although they earned their own livelihood they received foodstuffs from their kinsmen that they redistributed to visitors and the needy. The Klamath treaty chief, Liliks, had a total of 10 wives at various times (Gatschet 1890, 2:186), nine drawn from different regional divisions of the Klamath and one Modoc (Spier 1930:44ff.). Quite apart from the importance of the alliances thus formed, those wives are said to have constituted a workforce capable of amassing foodstuffs to further the hospitality of the house. From among followers, leaders found messengers when needed or strong arms to take up their cause in feud. In

well. Those whose judgment and wisdom were reflected in their prosperity needed as well the oratorical skill to persuade their fellows. Since success was often attributed to the aid of supernatural allies, shamans often achieved prominence as leaders (Spier 1930:35), among them a few women. Shamans, indeed, dominated communal gatherings, in the midwinter shamanistic performances, in the first-fruit rites for wokas, and, among the Modoc, in the communal memorial services (E.W. Voegelin 1942: elements 4354 ff.).

It was the village that collectively owned productive areas, such as fishing stations or, among the Modoc, seed tracts, and on that basis expelled poachers (E.W. Voegelin 1942:elements 550, 556; see also Spier 1930:149). For the individual, possessions were counted in houses, canoes, and implements, as well as personal effects, wealth being phrased, not in terms of a class of treasures, but of mundane possessions of better quality and in more abundance, in plenty of foodstuffs, and in the possession of slaves and, later, horses (Spier 1930:43). Beads were a partial exception; but though dentalium shells were calculated in strings,

Fig. 9. Klamaths gathering tules and cattails for making baskets. These materials were gathered in October, before winter set in. In the traditional shovel-nosed dugouts, left to right, are Mrs. Lang with a small child, Millard Lang, Mrs. Mose, and Ike Mose (Gogol 1983:8–11). Woven mats of tule are in the canoes. Photographed about 1900.

Smithsonian, Dept. of Anthr.: top, 24104 (neg. 95–20791); center, 24106 (neg. 95–20787); bottom, 24105 (neg. 95–20793).

Fig. 10. Klamath baskets. top, Burden basket reinforced with sticks. center, Basket tray made from tightly twined narrow strips of the outer surface of tule stems. These baskets, also known as wokas shakers, were commonly used for winnowing wokas seeds from their shells and pods. Prior to the use of metal cooking implements, wokas were also roasted in such baskets by being tossed with live coals (Coville 1904:731–733). Finally, ordinary wokas shakers and later more elaborately decorated versions were also used in a stick game played by two persons. One player manipulated 4 marked sticks under the basket, while the other guessed the relative positions of the sticks (Gogol 1983:14; Culin 1907:329–331). bottom, Seed beater made of loosely woven twigs and used in harvesting seeds of grasses and other flowering plants (Barrett 1910:257). Basketry spoonlike implements resembling this beater but smaller in size were also used for scooping the floating seeds that burst from overripe wokas pods (*sbokẃas*). All collected by L.S. Dyar at the Klamath Agency, Oreg., before 1876. Diameter of top, 59 cm; diameter of middle, 60 cm; length of bottom, 59.5 cm.

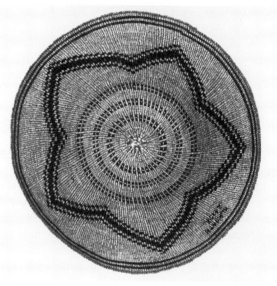

addition, alliance with a shaman, sometimes a kinsman, provided a supernatural dimension of support.

The influential men of a community acted together in informal council to reach decisions on the timing of eco-

nomic activities involving the entire village; and they sought as well to arbitrate internal disputes. From those leading families that set the style for the community, the society of both Klamath and Modoc ranged downward to the poor and the ne'er-do-wells. Slaves, captured women and children from other tribes, were often adopted or taken to wife and were thereafter treated much like members of the family, though the reputation lingered. However, those destined by the Klamath for the developing trade along the Columbia were roughly treated (Spencer 1952; E.W. Voegelin 1942:elements 4156, 4161).

Somewhat outside the pale of respectable Klamath society (Modocs deny having had them at all) was the berdache (*twini·qs*) of either sex. Berdaches usually took the role after puberty, wearing women's garb, taking a spouse, and performing work appropriate to the opposite sex. They were sometimes shamans, though their condition was not prerequisite to that office. Nor was their state immutable: the male berdache Liliks, after a vision, took on men's ways and became a noted chief (Spier 1930:51–53; E.W. Voegelin 1942:elements 3999–4018).

Controls within the community were weak. Leaders in the morning and evening, and at all public gatherings, exhorted the villagers to avoid quarrels and respect one another. Likewise, elders harangued their children upon the good life, urging them to do right, follow the advice of the old people, stay away from evil associates, refrain from stealing, and be kind to the poor and the blind, so that they might gain respect. Such counsel, says Spencer (1956:81), was the only formal educational process among the Klamath.

Enforcement of those standards required a marshaling of public opinion: the informal council of leaders could exert little more than moral suasion. If two men quarreled, or a powerful man abducted the wife of another, or slew him, the leaders urged the two parties involved to come to an agreement and the offender to pay compensation. Meanwhile, the aggrieved party might await redress, as they advised him; but he might recruit the assistance of kinsmen to take bloody revenge, or himself ambush his oppressor, or secretly destroy his property. Much depended upon the relative status of the two parties. A person of high standing, finding that an enemy had secretly smashed his canoe and fishing gear, might disdain to stoop to a quarrel himself. If he found that the aggressor was a relative, he might even spare him and gain a reputation for forbearance (Spencer 1956:84ff.). Otherwise, he might hire an assassin or shaman to act for him.

By the first quarter of the nineteenth century, the advent of the horse and of the fur trade, with its quickening of the trading network, altered the political scene. Within a few years, Klamaths were traveling the Klamath Trail northward to the Kalapuya and Clackamas settlements about Willamette Falls and to the Tygh band of Sahaptins, whence they visited the trading center at The Dalles. Particularly sought there were slaves, offering incentive for an enlargement of warfare and the emergence of a class of leaders whose wealth stemmed from the raid-and-trade cycle, while it added to society that category of chattel slaves destined to be traded to the north.

These events gave impetus to a consolidation of office as village headman and regional chief. Because the Klamath were more directly involved in the trading network, the leadership that emerged among them placed somewhat greater emphasis upon individual achievement than that among the Modoc, who tended to retain a hereditary principle in the selection of their leaders (E.W. Voegelin 1942:elements 2623–2633).

Until the emergence of the raid-and-trade leaders, the regional division cannot have exercised significant control over member villages. Such sense of unity as was entertained sprang largely from proximity, from frequent intermarriage, and through joint participation in certain ceremonies. As chiefs became important, those divisions achieved a greater internal unity and a virtual autonomy, qualities that led Spier (1930) to term them "tribelets." As such, they sometimes warred on each other, though they did not sell the captives into slavery. In one such conflict, extending over a decade, the Lower Williamson division, under the war leader, Kokdinks, attacked villages of other Klamath divisions, including the Pelican Bay group, to which they considered themselves related. The hostilities were only brought to an end when the Upland leader, Monchnkasgitk, a relative of Kokdinks, first joined his forces, then slew him (Spier 1930:28; Curtis 1907–1930, 13:163). By the middle of the nineteenth century, those divisions had been subordinated to a single leader, Liliks, recognized as the responsible chief by Whites. Indeed, in raids, Klamath and Modoc sometimes served under a single war leader, though they continued to consider themselves distinct.

Warfare

War was conducted against other peoples to repulse raids, to avenge past losses, or as ventures to secure booty. Experienced leaders recruited fighters from among the villagers and within neighboring communities. A village leader,

lacking special prowess, might go as a common warrior. Shamans often accompanied the party, divining the success of the enterprise, supernaturally poisoning the enemy, fighting during the engagement, and tending the wounded. Women might accompany their husbands, helping to round up women and children and slaying the aged (Spier 1930:31; Ray 1963:135ff.). Before leaving, warriors practiced dodging arrows, then joined in a dance of enticement. The major offensive weapons were obsidian-headed arrows dressed with a poison and driven by the sinew-backed bow (Coville 1897:101; E.W. Voegelin 1942:elements 1014–1019; cf. Spier 1930:32). The wealthy Klamath warrior carried several quivers of arrows. Clubs, obsidian daggers, and sometimes spears were also in use. For defense, leading warriors wore a cuirass of serviceberry rods or a tubular tunic and helmet of elkhide (fig. 5 right). Some carried elkhide bucklers. Combatants painted their face white before going into battle. In a feud, the parties lined up facing each other, ready to fight. In a meeting engagement, Modoc fighters operated in groups of two or three, one to serve as lookout while the others discharged their arrows (Ray 1963:141; see Gatschet 1890, 1:21–25 for a graphic Klamath account of one such engagement). When a village was to be attacked, it was encircled; then at dawn a signal was given and all rushed in. Houses were set afire and the inhabitants seized or slain as they emerged. Men and the aged were dispatched, women and children captured. The scalps of the slain were entrusted to a special custodian for the return march; the Klamath also cut off hands and perhaps heads as trophies and might eat the heart of a notorious foe. On its return, the war party held a victory dance, after which the scalps were sometimes given to the kin of persons who had thus been avenged.

To sue for peace, particularly when warfare had taken place within the tribe, the defeated party sent envoys to the victors. It was the peacetime leaders, not the war chiefs, that concluded peace, each side making payment in beads and women for those it had slain, according to the wealth of the victim. Recompense for a woman went to her husband, for a man to his family (E.W. Voegelin 1942: elements 2958–2990). There was no payment for those captured.

In the rising and routinized warfare of the mid-nineteenth century, when the Klamath and Modoc were engaged in the arms race for guns and horses, warfare was waged not merely with traditional foes, such as the Shasta and Takelma to the west, but increasingly with Northern Paiute to the east, and occasionally by Sahaptian raiders from the north. Drawn in were the inoffensive Achumawi and their kin, the Atsugewi, and the Kalapuya, who were a source of slaves and booty. The Achumawi normally did not dare retaliate. As one member of the Hewisedawi band of Achumawi recalled, "After the Lutuami had destroyed our dwellings and carried off our women and children, we made a great hunt lasting several weeks. We passed clear around

Goose Lake, killing much meat, feasted, and danced. When we arrived home we had forgotten (sic) our sorrows and were happy again" (Kniffen 1928:308).

Life Cycle

• BIRTH An expectant couple sought magically to protect the child, prevent the event of twins, and—if it was a first birth—ensure a son. Delivery took place in a wickiup, with midwife supervising, concerned women present, and, if he desired, the husband as well. While the mother kneeled on bedding, the midwife lifted her, massaged her, and "shook out" the child. In a difficult delivery, a shaman with the appropriate power was called. The afterbirth was buried, the umbilical cord saved, and the stump bound. The baby, washed after birth, was given a steam bath next day, massaged to "shape" his features and torso, and placed in an improvised tule cradle made by the mother's mother. For up to five days, mother and child were isolated in the hut, the mother for the first two days lying on a warm bed of sand spread over heated rocks. During the entire period she underwent dietary taboos, used a head scratcher, and refrained from bathing. Meanwhile the father either remained home under restrictions, using the scratching stick, or he went to the mountains, running, piling stones, and seeking power. Afterward, a Modoc father, on resuming hunting, gave away his first kill, as he had when a boy. When the mother was released from her ritual confinement, she and her husband took a sweatbath, swam, and changed to fresh clothes.

The baby nursed from the first day and was not weaned for two years or more. If the mother's milk failed, a relative served as wet nurse. The mother continued to "shape" the child, and some, emulating Chinookan fashion, bound pads to the head to produce a frontal flattening. After the first month, the mother replaced the tule cradle with a sitting cradle twined of willow. As the child grew larger, the Klamath father (and sometimes his Modoc counterpart) supplied a wooden cradleboard of northern style, in which the child was borne for the first year. Released from the board for bathing or to stretch his limbs, the infant was encouraged to move about. At about six months he sat up and at about a year was helped to stand and walk. From infancy the mother had begun that counsel for good conduct that the child would hear from elders throughout his life. Until the child had been weaned, the parents did not resume intercourse. At the age of one the child received a name, often that of an animal or a personal characteristic. Later in life, other nicknames might supplant that first name (see Barker 1963:528 for a sampling). As he began to speak, at first in baby talk, the child was taught the kinship terms for his relatives. Only gradually, when he had attained responsiveness, was the child trained in bowel control.

• CHILDHOOD Boys and girls played together until about six years of age. There were competitive games—contests of endurance and footraces—swimming, tops, and cat's-cradles, target shooting for boys, and dolls for girls. As boys grew older, they hunted together; and one Modoc woman recalled that as a tomboy she had had her own bow and hunted with them. At night, particularly in the winter, they listened to their elders telling myths and recounting narratives. Owl, who in the myths stole a baby, plucked out the eyes of sleepers who had offended him, and who foretold the death of mortals, was invoked as a hobgoblin against naughty children. Their parents, on occasion, scolded and even whipped the unruly. Frequently, children heard counsel on etiquette and proper deportment. Before sunrise each morning an elder man of the household aroused all the children for a swim and a run along the bank. Older children were assigned younger siblings to watch over, and they began by stages to help their parents in the food quest. When a youth slew his first large game, his mother gave it away to nonkinsmen (Pearsall 1950:350; E.W. Voegelin 1942:elements 137, 179), who thanked and praised him for his generosity.

• PUBERTY The pubertal girl was considered dangerous to men's enterprises and to herself. At the onset of her first menstruation, she was isolated for five days in a wickiup, attended by her grandmother. She sat or lay on a bed on pine needles, wearing a basket cap and old clothing, and sagebrush bark anklets and wristlets. She remained there during the daytime, eating sparingly, denied flesh or fish, grease, berries, or cold water, and using a scratching stick. Each night, she danced by a fire, supported by a girl or two, while women singers beat cadence with deerhoof rattle staves and a crowd looked on and sang the mocking songs called "love songs" (Gatschet 1890, 1:182–191). Thus, it was said, she was prevented from dreaming of Thunder, which might prove fatal. At the end of the fifth day, the girl sweated, bathed, and donned new clothing. The anklets and wristlets were burned. Ordinarily, within a year she was married. As adults, women continued to observe menstrual taboos, though some assert that only those who were members of shaman's households had to do so. Nonetheless, during their period they avoided hunters and the sick and stayed away from dances.

For some Klamath and Modoc boys about the age of puberty there was a power quest.

• MARRIAGE Children might be betrothed by their families; a Modoc who placed a gift on the funeral pyre of a friend might later seek the hand of a daughter in recompense. While there was room for personal inclination on the part of a young couple, parents sought to guide it. A girl's chastity was carefully guarded prior to marriage. A proper union was publicly registered by a ceremonial exchange of visits between the two families, who gave each other valuable gifts, which in turn were redistributed among kinsmen. A poor Modoc groom was still expected to make some payment, although he might also have to perform bride service. Those who simply took up housekeeping together were scorned as "living like slaves." Residence was with the bride's family until several children had been born, after which the couple were usually sufficiently well established to build their own lodge, commonly near that of the husband's parents.

First marriages often went awry, although families sought to stabilize them. Her parents might discipline the indiscreet wife, the husband slay her lover unless he paid recompense; and feuds often arose out of abductions without such payment. Even if the couple had divorced, her new husband must repay his predecessor before the union was recognized. A man of substance often took more than one wife, frequently a sister of his first wife. Unless relations grew strained between them the wives dwelt in the same household. Affiliation between families extended beyond the death of either mate: his immediate kinsmen had the right to offer a new spouse.

The newly wedded couple lived as junior members of the husband's parents' household, moving, when a child was expected, to that of the wife's parents, where they remained until one or more children had been born. By that time, they were sufficiently well established to set up their own lodge, usually near that of his parents.

● DEATH   When a tribesman died away from home, the body was sometimes interred among rocks; otherwise it was cremated and, if possible, the bones brought back to be added to the cremation pile. Each regional division among the Klamath and Modoc had at least one cremation ground. As for the semisubterranean mourners' sweathouses, the Klamath had but three, said to have been built by Gmukamps, plus a hot springs that served as one (Spier 1930:73ff.), while the Modoc built a sweathouse for the occasion (Ray 1963:121).

If an epidemic took an entire family, the house and their bodies were burned together. For an individual dying at home, the body was prepared by a kinswoman who was not one of the principal mourners. She laid out the body, washed it, freshly braided the hair, dressed it in its best clothing, and wrapped it in a tule mat. Among the Klamath, the body remained in the house overnight, where relatives and friends gathered for a wake, wailing and sprinkling fireplace ashes toward the west. Among the Modoc, the corpse, once prepared, was borne headfirst out the hatchway and carried to the cremation grounds. There neighbors and friends had gathered wood for the funeral pyre, on which the body was laid with its head toward the west, the direction of the afterworld. For them, the wake took place there, the widow lying beside the pyre. The Klamath brought out the body on the day of cremation; if the deceased had been prominent, time must be allowed to permit people to gather.

Meanwhile, the wealth of the deceased had been laid on the pyre; his dog and a slave, and in later days a horse, might be slain to accompany him. Relatives or friends might claim items of property, including the slave, substituting beads or promising to redeem the articles with a gift or services. After a eulogy by a leading man, the pyre was lit. When it had burned itself out, the calcined remains were raked into a hole in the ashes and covered with earth and rocks.

All those involved in the cremation were now ritually unclean. The dwelling, if an earth lodge, was dismantled; if a mat lodge or wickiup, it was burned, the family moving into a temporary wickiup. Before being reoccupied next fall, the earth lodge was fumigated with burning juniper (Klamath) or sage and cedar (Modoc). Those who had attended the funeral (children were excluded, if possible) had sweated and swum immediately afterward. The widow had her hair closely cropped and smeared her face and head with pitch, sometimes from the burning logs of the pyre, and charcoal. She wore a basket hat coated with pitch and used a scratching stick. She observed a taboo on meat, grease, or fish, and after some days in the temporary house moved for five days to the mourner's sweathouse, with an old woman for attendant, where she continued the regimen, sweating twice daily, gathering wood, wailing at the cremation grounds, perhaps seeking power in the mountains. After returning home, she continued to observe modified restrictions. For an older woman with dependent children, the demands of supporting them might curtail seclusion. Only after a year had passed did the widow return to take a final sweatbath to purify herself. She removed the pitch only at remarriage another year or more later.

The widower underwent a slightly lesser restriction, of similar sort, but at the end of the mourning year he gave away his first game or fish, as the widow gave away her first roots, and the gambler his first winnings (Spier 1930:75). Children observed still lighter restrictions on the death of their mother.

Following a death, the community at large observed a taboo on mentioning the name of the deceased before his kinsmen and, save for death in war, refrained from public festivities until the mourning ceremony. For the Klamath, this was an informal assembly of close relations of the deceased, who gathered to bewail his memory. For the Modoc, it was a communal event, akin to that of the western Achumawi (E.W. Voegelin 1942:elements 4354–4415), at which the mourners, gathered at the instance of the headman, with neighboring villagers as guests, and collectively remembered those who had died since the last ceremony. Then, purifying themselves by swimming, they feasted together, disbanding at sundown.

Games

Men contested with each other in hurling spears or shooting arrows at a target, at hoop-and-pole, at quoits, and in footraces. Women in particular played double-ball shinny: at the Lost River fishery near Olene, Klamath women played against the Modocs (E.W. Voegelin 1942:element 2201). There were dice games, with beaver or groundhog teeth as dice, played especially by women. Men played a hand game, originally using two bones, later a four-bone version from Warm Springs. Gambling was heavy and popular. Middle-aged or elderly men smoked a wild tobacco in pipes; among women the practice was restricted to shamans (E.W. Voegelin 1942:elements 2064–2072).

Mythology

To the Klamath and Modoc, the world was a disk floating on water. To the west, beyond a mountain, lay *noˑlisġeˑni*, the afterworld, where the spirits dwelt in an existence that reversed the order of earthly life. While on earth they were ghosts, and as ghosts some returned, seeking to bear away with them grieving relatives or friends. In the mountain solitudes of the earth, and particularly in the waters there, dwelt local spirits, sometimes connected with mythic beings and, like them, taking the form of birds, animals, reptiles, fish, plants, and natural phenomena. They also included anthropomorphic figures, such as Little Boy, Little Old Woman, elves, giants, and others.

In the mythic times that preceded the present order, the dominant figure had been Gmukamps, Mythic Old Man, a trickster-transformer on the order of Coyote in California and the Great Basin, but of anthropomorphic character, and thus resembling similar figures in northwestern California (Stern 1953:171–173). Though Gopher had transformed the world, Gmukamps had peopled it; in the Klamath country he had built stone fish dams and mourner's sweathouses and painted pictographs, which the Klamath retouched; and it was at his former dwelling that the Klamath held the first-sucker rite. Said to cause earthquakes today (Spier 1930:141), it was he that presided over the council at which the mythic beings announced the form each would take in the present world. At least some of the traits of Gmukamps were to be found in the Modoc figure of Coyote (Curtin 1912:51, 143); and among both peoples the two beings shared also in trickster exploits. Gmukamps was not sought out as a tutelary power; only occasionally did some Klamath pray to him in the sweathouse. Linked with him in myth was a daughter and, above all, a foster son, the heroic Aisis.

The mythology of both Klamath and Modoc, while exhibiting a covert inner consistency (Stern 1963), in the telling lacks architectonic order. In both, prominence is given to the monster-slayer, Mink, and his marplot brother, Weasel; to a form of Split-Boy, to Skunk, to Little Boy, and others. A minor but distinctive role is played by Raven, who by his laughter turned mythic beings into stone.

Power Quest and Shamanism

Among both peoples, supernatural power was sought by visiting the places where sacred beings were thought to reside and, through ritualized industry, gaining their favor. The quest was undertaken by some boys at puberty, sometimes by girls, by fathers at the birth of a child, and by those mourning a dead kinsman. The quester often sought a specific competence: luck in hunting or fishing, war, lovemaking, gambling, footracing, or—for the Klamath—curing. While a given power was not restricted to a single spirit or place, it was well known in what sites such powers were to be found. The quester went alone into the mountains where

for five days he fasted, piled rocks, and wrestled with trees; he ran, perhaps took sweatbaths, and climbed hilltops to sleep. He might swim in springs inhabited by spirit beings. If granted power, he might dream of a token of his success; for the Klamath, Spier (1930:99ff.) asserts that the spirit itself might appear. The quester awoke with blood trickling from his mouth or nose and his spirit song in his ears. The song was central: the term *swiˑs* 'song' designates as well the tutelary spirit who imparts it. The Modoc (Ray 1963:80ff.) only dreamed of the epiphany; lesser shamans, who received powers thus, cured by a laying on of hands. For major shamans, who cured by sucking, a distinctive quest was required, in which oral bleeding and the spirit song appeared.

Klamaths who sought to become shamans, both men and women, had to make repeated quests to acquire more powerful tutelaries and those in greater numbers. As among the Modoc, an occasional person might inherit the guardian spirits of a deceased relative who had been a shaman. Among the Modoc, one who sought to become a "sucking doctor" could only seek power through such deceased shamans. Having received the "call" in a dream, the aspirant visited the housepits or other sites of former shamans, there to seek the spirits that had been associated with them. Through a period of five days, they appeared to him in dreams, paired and in sequence, until with the appearance of the Ghost Spirit the aspirant fell unconscious with blood flowing from his mouth. Thereafter he was visited individually by those tutelaries that would be associated with him (Ray 1963:31–36). While Klamaths saw shamans as acting with the assistance of their tutelaries, Modocs saw the shaman as the vehicle through whom the spirits acted (Ray 1963:24, 36, 66ff.). Major shamans of both peoples might also acquire "pains" (a Californian concept), which they could use offensively.

While both men and women might become shamans, the women were less numerous and, a few individuals aside, less powerful. Before menopause, women were ineligible: indeed, the Modoc man who wished to avoid the "call" rubbed or carried menstrual blood or ashes upon his person to discourage the attention of the spirits (Ray 1963:32; cf. E.W. Voegelin 1942:element 4824).

The novice Modoc shaman arranged his initiation in the late fall, erecting his shaman's pole laden with symbols outside his dwelling or that of a relative. Inside, the houseposts were painted, the stuffed images of tutelaries propped upon the roof or suspended within. He sent out invitations and gathered foodstuffs, if possible to last five days. For the Klamath, novices were initiated together at the midwinter ceremonies, the preparations otherwise being similar, the event drawing together members of one or more local divisions, who brought food and prepared to stay for five days. Each shaman wore a fillet of woodpecker scalps; the audience was clad in traditional garb.

The shaman was assisted by several persons. One summoned the spirits; a second interpreted the utterances of the spirits as they came through the shaman. Singers led the audience in singing his sacred songs, which often referred to the amulet, *molẃas*, that represented his tutelary power (Gatschet 1890, 1:153–171; Spier 1930:131–138, for songs). After the spirits had arrived, the shaman performed the fire dance. A novice had to demonstrate his ability to swallow arrowheads and fire, after which his tutelaries spoke through him and taught the people their songs. For four days the Klamath shaman danced during the day; at night he performed sleight-of-hand marvels. Children were permitted to see only the magic, the dances being too dangerous for them. The Modoc ceremonies were held only at night, with the exhibitions of marvels on the final night, children being entirely excluded. In their exhibitions, shamans produced fish, pond-lily seeds, or blood within a basket standing at a distance; and the stuffed animals in their lodges would take on life and movement.

As curer, the shaman was again seconded by assistants and spectators. Klamath shamans, like the major Modoc shamans, cured by sucking, and they commonly possessed clairvoyance. Summoned by relatives of the patient, the shaman obtained the consent of his tutelaries and went to the house, where his retainer was already displayed. After smoking, he laid his hands on the patient and consulted his spirits. Eagle and Fishhawk, among them, aided diagnosis, and Frog searched out sickness related to foods; if necessary, the Modoc shaman consulted the Ghost Spirit (Ray 1963:57). He then sucked out the disease object and, showing it to the audience, swallowed, buried, or burned it. Usually it had been sent by another shaman, who died when the curer disposed of it. The shaman might extract several such objects. If he was unable to effect a cure, he recommended another shaman but kept his fee.

Shamans were often accused of themselves causing illness, acting out of hatred, as the hireling of a foe, or in the hope of being called in for the cure. If suspected of sorcery, the shaman might be summoned to treat the patient; and if the patient then died, his kinsmen often slew the suspect. A Modoc shaman so charged might claim that his tutelary had acted unbeknownst to him. Shamans were also endangered through their tutelary powers: his own spirits might take offense and leave him, or be enslaved by those of another shaman, and thus he might become ill or die.

There were other causes of illness. Laymen might be sickened by breaking taboos or being frightened by a spirit. In either instance, the shaman sucked out the matter produced by the illness. In wounds and fractures, shamans sucked out the blood, cauterized the wound, and turned the patients over to laymen to dress it. In rattlesnake bites, the shaman sucked out the "fang."

As clairvoyants, Klamath shamans relied upon spirits such as Bear; to find lost objects, Dog was useful. A shaman with Eagle or Weasel power could predict the outcome of an impending battle. To abate cold weather, the aid of tutelaries such as West Wind, Rain, and Thunder was invoked. Appropriate tutelaries might, upon appeal, bring snow upon enemies. During the Modoc War, a shaman acted to bring down the shielding fog against the army's advance.

History

By the time they were visited by the Hudson's Bay Company trader, Peter Skene Ogden, in 1826, both Klamath and Modoc were already involved in the Indian arms race developing about horse and gun, and the Klamath, in particular, were soon trading along the Columbia. Within a dozen years, Klamaths were working for American settlers in the Willamette Valley; thereafter, Modocs, through whose country the South Emigrant Trail ran, came to be increasingly engaged in hostilities with the newcomers. Pressure from American officials led to the recognition of paramount leaders among both peoples. In response, there developed a factionalism within both tribes, a peace party among the Klamaths led by individuals among the new chiefs who had lived for a time under White influence, while their opposites among both Klamath and Modocs also included individuals who had tasted, but repudiated, American culture (Stern 1956). A particular difficulty arose for the Modocs subject to the administrations of both Oregon and California. When they and the Klamath signed the Klamath Lake Treaty of 1864, a treaty of cession with the United States, the Modocs did so believing valid an earlier treaty made with a California official, but never ratified, guaranteeing their retention of the Tule Lake region. At the instance of Liliks, Klamath head chief, the reservation granted included Klamath heartlands, including Upper Klamath and Agency lakes, as well as the Williamson and Sprague drainages. Some Northern Paiutes were also party to the treaty.

Although the Modocs were induced to move to the new reservation, they found the Klamaths treating them like aliens and soon departed, one band under Captain Jack (Kintpuash), returning to Tule Lake, while another, under the former Modoc head chief, Schonchin, withdrew to the upper Sprague, where the Uplander Klamaths and Yahooskin Northern Paiutes were administered. Attempts to remove the Tule Lake Modocs to the reservation precipitated the Modoc War of 1872–1873, in which in the end a handful of Modocs, withdrawing to the stronghold of the lava beds south of Tule Lake, made a valiant defense against vastly superior numbers and arms (Murray 1959; E.N. Thompson 1971). Captain Jack and three others, for killing peace commissioners at a council, were hanged; and the remainder of the hostile Modocs, about 153, were exiled to Indian Territory (fig. 11) (F.D. Johnson 1939), from which survivors were permitted to return only after 1900. Others remained there (Wright 1951:184–186; L.J. Martin 1968; Tiller 1996:522).

The reservation had been created to effect the acculturation of the Indians within about a generation, when it would be

Fig. 11. Modoc War participants. top, Modocs after removal to Indian Terr. left to right, back row: Mr. Squier of the Interior Department; Hooka Jim, Shacknasty Jim, Scarface Charley, Special Commissioner Capt. M.C. Wilkinson, who brought the Modocs to Indian Terr., Bogus Charley, Faithful William, Long Jim, and Agent H.W. Jones. front row, Hooka Jim's wife; Bogus Charley's wife and boy; Scarface Charley's wife and child; Mary, Capt. Jack's sister; Lizzie, Capt. Jack's younger wife; Little George and mother; Amelia and child; and Lucy and child. Photograph by McCarty of Baxter Springs, Kans., 1873. The Modoc War was a topic of national interest, and photographers did a good business in selling these pictures. bottom left, Modoc prisoners, Schonchin John and Captain Jack in chains. Photograph by Louis H. Heller, Ft. Klamath, Oreg., before October 3, 1873, when they were executed. bottom right, Members of Alfred B. Meacham's lecture tour: standing, left to right, Modocs Shacknasty Jim, Steamboat Frank, Winema or Toby Riddle, and Scarface Charley; seated, Toby's husband, Frank Riddle, who with his wife acted as an interpreter during the peace negotiations (vol. 4:181), and their son Jeff. They are dressed in clothes that Easterners expected Indians to wear (Faulk and Faulk 1988:81–82). Photograph by Charles M. Bell, Washington, D.C., 1875.

allotted in severalty. The elevation of the Klamath Basin proved an obstacle to making the Indians farmers, and it made ranching difficult as well. By continuing to rely in part on native subsistence, supplemented by annuity rations, as well as farm labor and freighting enterprises, the Indians survived. Meanwhile, the governing officials relied at first upon the treaty chiefs, then upon younger men selected from the same background, some of whom became agency employees. As education spread, they were replaced by graduates of the schools. Slaves were freed to become equal members of the reservation, and polygyny was banned. The agency of the Bureau of Indian Affairs set out to crush shamanism and to check a succession of nativistic movements, beginning with the Ghost Dance of 1870 (Nash 1937). The evangelism of a Yakima interpreter and of other agency employees led to the development of a Methodist mission, in which some Klamath leaders served as lay preachers.

Although allotment became operative after the Dawes Severalty Act of 1887, litigation over boundary disputes held up implementation until 1895 (fig. 12), and 10 years later some tracts were still in contest. By then, the value of forests on unallotted lands was recognized, along with their unsuitability for homesteading by Whites, and they were retained for the Indians collectively. There was an influx of absentee tribal members, often highly acculturated, and a growing dependence upon income, as tribal members, from sales of timber to logging companies. Allotted lands came increasingly to be leased or sold to White ranchers. Indian anticipation of American citizenship, envisioned in the Dawes Act, led to heightened tribal activity and a search for allies in Washington to help in combatting decisions by the Bureau of Indian Affairs.

top, Klamath Co. Mus., Klamath Falls, Oreg.; bottom, Denver Public Lib., Western Hist. Dept., Colo.: 12778.
Fig. 12. Reservation life. top, Land allotment meeting. Photographed about 1895. bottom, Modocs receiving rations at the agency, Indian Terr. In the center of the photo an unidentified agency official has a slab of meat on a scale. Photograph by T.M. Concannon of Baxter Springs, Kans., 1885–1890.

The opening of tribal forests to logging, and the resultant income from revenues, did much to destroy work incentives among many Indians: thus the Indian cattle industry, which had shown promise, soon almost vanished. It brought on the reservation heavy concentrations of Whites in mill towns, and the Indians became a minority people even in their own homeland, in a legal position that at once protected and discriminated against them.

By 1954 Congress had decided to terminate government administration for certain tribes deemed capable of managing their own affairs. When termination policy was applied to the Klamath Reservation, over 70 percent of the membership elected to withdraw and receive pro rata shares of tribal holdings. Those who elected to remain under a private trust subsequently withdrew as well (Stern 1965). In 1964 the Indian Claims Commission awarded the Klamaths $2.5 million for lands ceded in 1864; an additional $4.2 million compensation was granted in 1969.

Remaining treaty rights survived termination, as demonstrated in the courts. The litigation fostered and strengthened the tribal organization. In 1975 the tribe entered into a treaty-rights protection contract with the Bureau of Indian Affairs, providing for several positions by which a Klamath Indian Game Commission administered hunting and fishing seasons for enrolled members, in accordance with agreements reached by the tribal council with the state of Oregon.

In building a tribal consensus to seek restoration, the leaders acknowledged the Modoc and Yahooskin membership. Under the new constitution of 1982, the tribal government placed dependence upon a Culture and Heritage Committee, working with a tribal specialist, to teach tribal languages (fig. 14) and customs. These measures were important to strengthen Indian identity; they were also strategic, since such shared knowledge forms one of the criteria by which the federal government assesses the Indianness of communities seeking restoration.

In 1986 the Klamath Tribe regained federal recognition of tribal status. In 1992 the tribe took over the field of health from the Indian Health Service. They have provided assistance in education beyond the local schools, for the tribal unemployment rate in 1989 was 46 percent (Haynal 1994).

Led by the Culture and Heritage Committee, the tribes reintroduced the First Sucker ceremony, modified in response to the endangered status of the fish; sweatlodge ceremonies, in which pan-Indian features have been imported; and naming and giveaway ceremonies. Powwows took pan-Indian form.

The World Championship Klamath All-Indian Invitational Basketball Tournament is a sporting event held in Chiloquin since 1954. In religion, Christianity was dominant, while shamanism was rejected as a thing of the devil.

Population

The aboriginal Klamath and Modoc are estimated to have totaled between 1,200 and 2,000 persons (Mooney 1928:18;

Fig. 13. Leaders. back row: Tom Chocktoot, Yahooskin, Klamath; Jack Palmer, Klamath; Capt. Oliver C. Applegate; Rev. Jesse Kirk, Klamath; Joe Pierce, nephew of U.S. Sen. Rice Alexander Pierce. front row: Monchnkasgitk, chief of the Upland group of Klamath; Long John, Klamath; Lilu, Klamath subchief; Chief Agency George, Modoc; Henry Blow, head chief of Klamath. Photograph by Maud Baldwin, 1903–1910.

Fig. 14. 20th-century Klamath tribal publications. left, Editors William Norval and Hiroto Zakoji in a promotional photo for the *Klamath Tribune*, published monthly from 1956 to 1961. This newspaper of the Klamath education program addressed termination matters as well as community activities (Zakoji 1961:97–103). Photographed at Chiloquin, Oreg., 1959. right, Presentation of *? at a naat stayLA* "Now we gather [roots, berries]" (Klamath Tribes 1993), a language teaching booklet, by Gordon Bettles (right) to Chief Reid David of the Klamath Council. This book was given to all Klamath and Modoc families for their personal use and is also used by Bettles in his teaching. Photograph by Taylor R. Tupper, Tribal Office, Chiloquin, Oreg., 1993.

Kroeber 1939:136–138, 1925:320), the Klamath having about twice the number of members as the Modoc. Spier (1930:5), on the basis of his settlement count, had estimated a Klamath population of 2,000; reconsidering in the light of Mooney's figure of 800, he arrived at a compromise figure of 1,200. Stern proposes an aboriginal population of 1,000 Klamath and 500 Modoc.

Population densities, following Kroeber (1939:136–138; see Stern 1965:5), indicate that the Klamath-Modoc were comparatively sparsely settled.

The Klamath and Modoc population reached nadir in the 1870s; the Modoc in particular were affected by the 1872–1873 war and the removal of the "hostile" element of the tribe to Oklahoma. At the eve of termination, the Klamath-Modoc numbered about 1,200; after tribal restoration in the mid-1980s, the figure had doubled, and in 1996 tribal enrollment on the Klamath Reservation was reported at 2,700 (table 1). The same year, the Modoc Tribe of Oklahoma numbered 200 enrolled members (table 2).

Synonymy

Klamath

The name Klamath is a borrowing from Upper Chinookan *ɬámaɬ*, literally 'they of the river, they who have a river', a designation derived from the stem -*maɬ* 'river' (Hale 1946:218; Jacobs 1958–1959, 1:204; Michael Silverstein, communication to editors 1996). Hale rendered the Chinookan form as ⟨Tlamatl⟩. The name apparently first appears in English as ⟨Clammitte⟩ in Peter Skene Ogden's journal of 1826 (Spier 1930:1); this reflects a local English pronunciation as ('klămət) attested by other early spellings, including ⟨Clamet⟩ (Hale 1946:218, 569), and still used in the twentieth century (Spier 1930:1; Janne Underriner, communication to editors 1996). The earliest form pointing to the current standard English pronunciation may be ⟨Clamouths⟩ on Gallatin's (1836) map. From the Chinookan name comes Sahaptin *ɬámaɬ* and Kalapuyan ⟨athlámeth⟩ (Gatschet 1890, 1:xxxiv). The suggestions of a derivation from Klamath (Farrand in Hodge 1907–1910, 1:712) or from an unspecified Yurok name for the Klamath River (Gatschet 1890, 1:xxxiii) are incorrect.

Gatschet (1890, 1:ii) notes that the term Klamath was applied by early Whites broadly to the dwellers about the Klamath Lakes as well as to those peoples dwelling upon the Klamath River, including the Shasta, Hupa, Karok, and Yurok. Subsequently, the phrase Klamath Lake Indians was used to distinguish the former groups and has been used in the anthropological literature at least as late as Kroeber (1939). In popular parlance, Klamath Falls Indians is also sometimes heard, identifying the people with the largest city in the region.

The Klamath term for themselves is *maqlaqs*, sometimes used with the generic meaning of 'Indian'. Significantly for

their sense of political unity, this has often to be paired with a place-name in designating Klamath. Thus the major local group, dwelling on Klamath Marsh and the Upper Williamson River, was known as *ʔewksikni· maqlaqs*, or simply *ʔewksikni·*, literally 'people of Klamath Marsh (*ʔewksi*)' (Gatschet 1890, 1:xxxiii; Barker 1963:30). From this designation and closely related terms stem Taylor's ⟨oukskenah⟩ and Steele's ⟨okshee⟩ (both cited by Farrand in Hodge 1907–1910 1:712), as well as possibly the ⟨auksi-wash⟩ that Gatschet (1890, 1:xxxiii) states was applied to the Klamath by the Shasta dwelling in the vicinity of Yreka.

Modoc

The Modoc, says Gatshet (1890, 1:xxxiv), derived their name from that for Tule Lake, *mo·waťa·k*, which he glosses 'in the extreme south' (derived from *mo·wat* 'south'), whence they were named *mo·waťa·kkni· maqlaqs*, usually abbreviated to the first term (Barker 1963a:242). Powers (1877:252) fancifully derives the term from Mo-dok-us purportedly the name of "a former chief of the tribe under whom they seceded from the Klamath Lake Indians."

The Klamath-Modoc were known variously to neighboring tribes. The Achumawi called the Tule Lake Modoc [luťwa·mi] and those of Goose Lake [lamma·wi] (Bauman 1979:26); these names are probably those given as the dialect variants ⟨lutuámi⟩ and ⟨lutmáwi⟩ by Gatschet (1890, 1:xxxiv). Hale (1846:218), erroneously taking the first term to be "the proper designation of the people in their own language," appropriated it for the Klamath (Klamath-Modoc) language. The Klamath were designated in Achumawi as ⟨alámmimakt is⟩ 'people of Upper Klamath Lake ⟨alam-mig⟩' (Gatschet 1890, 1:xxxiv) or [alammi] 'fish people' (Bauman 1979:26; Olmsted 1966), while the Ilmawi Achumawi called them the ⟨tapaádji⟩ (Jeremiah Curtin in Hodge 1907–1910, 1:712). Western Shastans termed the Klamath ⟨makaítserk⟩, while in Shasta itself the Klamath and Modoc were called *ipxa·n·á·ʔi* (Gatschet 1890, 1:xxxiii; Shirley Silver, communication to editors 1974). The Takelma of the middle Rogue River designated the Klamath *dakċa·malà·ʔ* or *dakċa·wanà·ʔ* 'those above the lakes' (Sapir 1907:255, 1909:257), while the Upland Takelma simply called them ⟨wols⟩ 'enemy' (Spier 1930:2). The Northern Paiute are said to have called the Klamath ⟨sayi⟩ (*saiʔi*) and the Modoc ⟨saidoka⟩ (Gatschet 1890, 1:xxxiii), the former a shortened form of the latter term, which Kelly (1932:70) glosses as 'tule-eaters'. The second term is Northern Paiute *saiduka·ʔa* '(those) under the tules' (Catherine S. Fowler, communication to editors 1996). The differentiation between the two forms was probably not rigid, and Stewart (1939:140, 144) observes that the shorter term has also been applied to a Northern Paiute band as well as to the Achumawi and the Nez Perce.

The Sahaptian speakers on the Columbia are said to have grouped the peoples on the Klamath Reservation (Klamath,

Table 1. Population

Date	Klamath	Modoc	Total	Source
Aboriginal	800	400	1,200	Mooney 1928:18
	1,400	600	2,000	Kroeber 1925:320
	1,200	—	—	Spier 1930:5
1864	710	339	1,049	ARCIA 1865:101–102
1872	580	67	647	ARCIA 1872:397
1880	707	151	858	ARCIA 1880:250
1900	711	238	949	ARCIA 1900:359
1910	696	282[a]	978	U.S. Bureau of the Census 1915:18–19
1920	—	—	1,132[b]	ARCIA 1920:71, 145
1945	937	329	1,266	U.S. Congress. House. Committee on Interior and Insular Affairs 1953:837
1957	—	—	2,133[c]	U.S. Department of Health, Education, and Welfare. Public Health Service. Division of Indian Health 1958:13
1960	—	—	1,185[c]	Bureau of Indian Affairs 1961:29
1989	—	—	2,313	Bureau of Indian Affairs 1989:20
1996	—	—	2,700[d]	Tiller 1996:544

[a] Includes Oklahoma.
[b] Klamath Superintendency; includes "Yahooskin" Northern Paiutes, and Achumawi.
[c] Terminated reservation total.
[d] Tribal enrollment total.

Modoc, and Northern Paiute) under the collective term ⟨aígspalu⟩ (pl. ⟨aígspaluma⟩) 'people of the chipmunks' (Gatschet 1890, 1:xxxiii). This is Sahaptin *aykʷšpal* 'Northern Paiute (of Oregon)', literally 'cottontail rabbit people' (Bruce Rigsby, communication to editors 1996), and not, as Spier (1930:2) thought, a hybrid loan combining Klamath *ʔewksi* with Sahaptian ⟨-palu⟩ 'people'.

Sources

An ethnographic treatment should exclude J. Miller (1873), despite its title, for most of the material, even where not fictitious, does not bear on the Modoc. Gatschet (1878, 1879, 1879a, 1879b, 1880, 1891, 1891a, 1894) published brief articles, some of which were incorporated within his linguistic monograph (1890); together they provide a wealth of detailed information. Hale (1892) published a brief general note.

Of general accounts, Meacham (1876) and Powers (1877) treated the Modoc, S.A. Clarke (1960) both Klamath and Modoc; and Curtis (1907–1930, 13) treated the Klamath. Kroeber (1925) included the Modoc in his survey of California peoples. Spier (1930) dealt with the Klamath in a classic ethnography, while Ray, who had (1939) included the Klamath in a comparative study of Plateau cultures, has provided (1963) a monographic treatment of the Modoc. E.W. Voegelin (1942) furnished a culture-element study of northeastern California that includes both Klamath and Modoc.

Particular aspects of the culture of the two peoples are touched upon by Barrett's (1910) study of their technology; his carefully annotated collections in the Phoebe A. Hearst (formerly R.H. Lowie) Museum at Berkeley furnish excellent documentation. W.J. Clarke (1885) had written on the stone fish dams and stone piles of the Klamath country and Franks (1874) on Modoc bow and arrows. Coville (1897, 1904) wrote on Klamath ethnobotany and in particular on the *wokas* industry. Cook (1941) included Klamath-Modoc in a study of native dietary adaptations. Hrdlička (1905) described Klamath cranial deformation. Gifford (1922)

Table 2. Modoc Population in Oklahoma, 1873–1996

Date	Total	Source
1873	153	M. Wright 1951:184
1880	99	ARCIA 1880:90
1900	49	ARCIA 1900:224, 640
1910	67[a]	ARCIA 1910:64
1920	40	ARCIA 1920:70
1929[b]	68[b]	U.S. Congress. House.Committee on Interior and Insular Affairs 1953:866
1954	55[c]	Trafzer 1994:352
1985	113	Bureau of Indian Affairs 1985:13
1996	200[d]	Tiller 1996:522

[a] For the same year, the U.S. Bureau of the Census (1915:19) listed only 33 Modocs.
[b] Allottees.
[c] Individuals losing tribal status as a result of termination
[d] Tribal enrollment total.

included the Klamath in a study of California kinship terminologies. Pearsall (1950) has dealt with Klamath childhood and education, and Spencer with Klamath slavery (1952) and with exhortation (1956). Music has been treated by de Angulo and d'Harcourt (1931), by Hall and Nettl (1955) and comparatively by Nettl (1954). Games were described by Dorsey (1901), and certain archeological sculptures by Carlson (1959). Mythological materials occur in Gatschet (1879), in Curtin (1912), Curtis (1907–1930, 13), Spencer (1952), E.E. Clark (1953), and Stern (1953, 1956a, 1963, 1963a). Gayton (1935), in a comparative study of California mythology, drew upon Klamath myths collected by Spier. Levi-Strauss (1971) has included Klamath and Modoc materials in a comparative study of mythology in South and North America.

General studies of Klamath culture change are to be found in Zakoji (1953) and for both peoples in Stern (1965). E.W. Voegelin (1955–1956), O'Callaghan (1952), and O. Johnson (1947) provide specialized historical studies. Fenton (1953) touches upon cultural stability. Religious movements among the historic Klamath and Modoc have been examined by Spier (1927) and Nash (1937); the Indian Shaker church at Klamath is included in Barnett (1957). Ames (1957) draws on Nash (1937) in a theoretical study. Psychological assessments include Clifton (1960) and Clifton and Levine (1961).

The Modoc War has its own detailed literature (Meacham 1875; Riddle 1914; Victor 1894; Murray 1959). Termination of the Klamath Indian Reservation is described by Stern (1965) and Hood (1972). For a detailed study of the restoration of tribal identity see Haynal (1994).

Demographic History Until 1990

ROBERT T. BOYD

Environmental Limits on Population

Anthropologists have assumed that the fishing and gathering populations of the Plateau culture area were limited by the abundance of naturally occurring wild food resources. Salmon has usually been considered the critical limiting resource (Sneed 1971; Hewes 1947, 1973; Schalk 1986). There is considerable variation in the salmon resource throughout the Plateau, ranging from a total lack among some upstream people to peoples along the Columbia and Fraser rivers, through whose territories all major *Onchorhyncus* species run. Comparison of the salmon resources in table 1 with the 1805–1806 population estimates presented in table 2 shows a close correlation between salmon abundance and local population size.

Although salmon abundance was important, other environmental factors influenced human population levels as well, for example, the nature of the run. The farther salmon had to travel from the ocean before spawning, the leaner they became; fall run salmon were easier to preserve for winter use than were those that ran in the spring (Hunn 1981; Schalk 1984). Both these factors favored downstream populations. Many upriver peoples, lacking salmon runs in their territories, traveled to fisheries at Kettle Falls and Priest Rapids, Washington; Musselshell Shoal, Montana; and The Dalles, Oregon; where they either fished or traded for salmon caught by others (Boyd 1985:363–366).

For some Plateau peoples, other wild food resources, particularly root crops such as camas (*Camassia quamash*) and various Lomatiums, contributed more calories than salmon to the diet (Hunn 1981) and undoubtedly also influenced human population levels. Extensive root grounds tended to be located some distance away from winter villages and were frequently used by several tribal groups. Notable camas grounds included Camas Prairie, Idaho; Latah Creek, the Kittitas Valley, and the Calispell Valley, Washington

Table 1. Salmon Resources

| | Chinook | | | | |
	spring	fall	Coho	Sockeye	Pink
Upper Chinookans	X	X	X	X	O
Sahaptins	X	X	X	X	O
Palouse	O	O	O	O	O
Cayuse	X	O	O	O	O
lower Nez Perce	X	O	X	X	O
upper Nez Perce	X	O	O	X	O
Columbia Salish	X	O	X	X	O
Okanagan	X	O	X	X	O
Sanpoil	X	O	X	O	O
Colville	X	O	X	O	O
Spokane	X	O	O	O	O
Coeur d'Alene	O	O	O	O	O
Kalispel	X	O	O	O	O
Lakes	O	O	X	O	O
Kootenai	X	O	O	O	O
Pend d'Oreille–Flathead	O	O	O	O	O
Shuswap	O	X	X	X	O
Thompson	O	X	X	X	X
Lillooet	O	X	X	X	X

X= presence; O= absence.

SOURCES: Fulton (1968, 1970) for the United States, Aro and Shepard (1967) for British Columbia.

(Thoms 1989:fig. 8). There was a concentration of Lomatiums and bitterroot (*Lewisia rediviva*) near Fossil, Oregon; Botanie Valley, British Columbia, was the largest root ground on the upper Fraser.

Most food resources were available only during the warm half of the year, when they had to be gathered in sufficient quantities to last until early spring. Methods of preparation and storage usually ensured an optimal supply of winter food (Schalk 1977; Ames and Marshall 1980). But environmental vagaries, including salmon cycles, avalanches (Hayden and Ryder 1991), ashfalls (Hunn and Norton 1984), and droughts, as well as cultural disturbances might upset this balance and lead to shortages of food in late winter and early spring, the "lean season" of the year. At this time, dietary deficiencies might contribute to higher levels of morbidity, possible malnutrition, and even starvation. These three phenomena are all reported from the lean season during the earliest period of the Hudson's Bay Company presence in the Plateau. In 1822–1823 the Okanagan were "starving" (MacLeod 1823), and in 1825 it was reported that "above the Cascade portage" there was "Starvation and many perish annually" (Merk 1931:94). At Fort Alexandria in 1827–1828 Shuswaps were experiencing starvation (J. McGillivray [1828] 1947), and at Fort Nez Perces in 1831–1832 Sahaptins were being "reduced to mere Skin & Bone" (S. McGillivray 1831–1832). Starvation is a common theme in Plateau mythology. Chances are good that, as elsewhere in the Americas, seasonal resource deprivation disproportionately affected, and caused a high death rate among, the very young. It is probable that on the Plateau, as in the Northwest Coast, Liebig's law of the minimum operated during the lean season and set an upper limit on human population levels (Hayden 1975:12).

Technological innovations increased the efficiency of resource exploitation and may have increased the potential for population expansion. Several such advances are recorded for the prehistoric period: salmon gear (Nelson 1973), salmon storage (Schalk 1984), and root processing (Thoms 1989). For the protohistoric period, the most notable advance came with the horse, which was introduced to the region after 1730 (Haines 1938). Horses allowed foraging over wider areas, thus broadening the resource base and introducing a potential for population increase (Boyd 1985:332–333; cf. Hunn 1990:25).

Paleodemography and Paleopathology

The small sample of Plateau skeletal remains has been subjected mostly to cultural analyses, such as burial patterns and grave goods distributions, not population or health studies (Campbell 1989:46). What little can be postulated about precontact demography and health comes from ethnohistorical records and paleopathological studies from adjacent culture areas.

The manuscript 1829 Fort Nez Perces report (Black 1829) is one of the most important ethnohistoric sources.

Speaking of Sahaptian peoples (mostly Walla Walla) it notes life span ("The Indians live to a good old age 50 to 60 + older, some very old..."), age at marriage ("A young Indian when he can get a wife will marry about 20."), and child-bearing period ("women continue to Bear untill 40 but at this age look very old."). A high rate of infant mortality is also noted in the historic records. Among Nez Perce: "Many births are premature occasioned by the hardships of the Women. Many children die in infancy from want of nourishment or injuries received amidst the toils of the mother moving camp or collecting roots or chopping and making firewood" (Spalding 1842). In 1840 the Reverend Asa Bowen Smith estimated that "Probably not less than half...die almost as soon as they are born" (Drury 1958:138).

The Fort Nez Perces report also contains information on prevalent diseases:

> Few diseases amongst the Indians, some sore + speckd Eyes, some Fevers from eating too many Green Roots perhaps: a Purge Cures them They are Subject to the Rash leaving Marks on the Skiin there are Cases of Phthisie [tuberculosis] which I have seen cured by a Vomit which as well as Fever I think caused by too long a use of Roots on Weak Stomachs there are also symptoms of other diseases but very Mild, very few Cases as yet of the Veneria, the Inds. are in general healthy (Black 1829).

This relative health was noted by other early observers, such as David Thompson (Glover 1962:347).

A survey of skeletal remains uncovered between 1959 and 1967 (Sprague and Birkby 1970) mentions several apparently prevalent pathologies. Osteoarthritis was common, as is true for Native Americans in general. Osteomyelitis, which is usually caused by a staphylococcus infection, was also present. Enamel hypoplasia and cribra orbitalia, both probable indicators of situational (nutritional or infectious) stress, occurred in several cases. A sample of 200 "Columbia Basin" skeletons found "bilateral separation of the neural arch," usually with evidence for spondylolisthesis, in 5 percent (Congdon 1932). On the basis of comparative evidence from neighboring culture areas, a high load of intestinal parasites is probable, as are tuberculosis and a variety of treponematosis, perhaps akin to nonvenereal syphilis (vol. 7:57; P. Walker, Lambert, and DeNiro 1989:356).

Violence

The myth of pacifism among Plateau peoples has been laid to rest on the bases of both ethnohistorical and archeological evidence (Kent 1980). Twelve of 16 skeletons from the Okanogan River, dating A.D. 330–1780, showed evidence of violent death (Chatters 1989). The evidence included bone cuts and fractures that were certainly made by stone missiles. The location of the wounds on the skeleton and the siting of the graves suggests a pattern of feuding, not full-scale war. After 1730, with the appearance of the horse, elements of the Plains warfare complex entered the Plateau (Gunther

Table 2. Population Estimates of Lewis and Clark, 1805–1806

Language or Dialect Group	Codex I	Supplement	Revision[d]	Total for Group
Molala ("Sho-Sho-nes" [part])	3,000[a]		1,000	1,000
Upper Chinookan				3,900
Cascades ("Sha-ha-la")	1,500	2,800		
Hood River ("Smack-shop")	800			
White Salmon ("Chil-luck-kit-te-quaw")	1,000	1,400		
Wishram ("E-che-lute")	600	1,000		
Northwest Sahaptin				6,880
Taitnapam ("Quath-la-poh-tle," "Shoto" [part])			900	
Klikitat			2,020	
western bands ("Sha-ha-la" [part])			1,300	
eastern bands ("Skâd-dâts, Squân-nar-oos")	320		720	
White Salmon [part]				
Yakima (total)	1,960		3,560	
"Shal-lât-tos"	100			
"Chim-nah-pum"	1,860			
Kittitas ("Shan-wap-pom")	400			
Columbia River Sahaptin				4,900
Tygh ("Sho-sho-nes" [part])			1,000	
Tenino ("E-ne-chur")	1,200		1,600	
Wayampam ("Wah-how-pum")	700			
Umatilla ("Pish-quit-pah")	1,600	2,600		
Northeast Sahaptin				4,185
Walla Walla ("Wal-low wal-low")	1,000	1,600	2,523	
Wanapam ("Sokulk" [part])	2,400[b]		400	
Palouse ("Pel-lote-pal-lah") ("Cho-pun-nish" of lower "Lewis's River" [part])	2,300[c]		1,262	
Cayuse ("Y-e-let po")	250		438	438
Nez Perce ("Cho-pun-nish" [part])	6,338		4,627	4,627
Upper Snake ("Lewis's River") ("Ki-moo-e-nim," "So-yen-now")	1,200	1,200		
Wallowa ("Wil-le-wah")	500			
Clearwater (lower "Kooskooske River")	3,600	3,600		
Lower Snake ("Cho-pun-nish" of lower "Lewis River" [part])	2,300[c]		1,038	
Coeur d'Alene and Upper Spokane ("Skeet-so-mish")	2,000		1,067	1,067
Middle Spokane ("Lar-ti-e-lo")	600		1,697	1,697

Table 2. Population Estimates of Lewis and Clark, 1805–1806 (Continued)

Language or Dialect Group	Codex I	Supplement	Revision[d]	Total for Group
Flathead				2,705
Flathead		830		
("Oate-lash-schute," "Tush-She-pah")				
Pend d'Oreille ("Ho-hil-po")	300	300	⎰ 1,875	
Kalispel ("Mick-suck-seal-tom")	300	300	⎱	
Okanagan				4,361
Colville ("Whe-el-po")	2,500	2,500	1,225	
Sanpoil ("Hi-high-e-nim-mo")	800	1,300	1,136	
Okanagan ("La-hân-na")	2,000	2,000		
Columbia Salishans				3,200
Wenatchee ("Cuts-sâh-nim")	1,200		1,200	2,100
Sinkayuse ("Sokulk" [part]	2,400[b]	2,400	1,100	
"Coospellars"[e]	600	1,600		1,600
Total				40,560

SOURCE: Boyd (1985:357–359). Some groups are identified differently in Moulton (1983–, 6:473–492).
NOTES: The figures subsumed in the total for each language or dialect group are italicized.

[a] Residing on the upper Multnomah in fall and winter. Given the geographic distribution, the total probably includes interior Sahaptins (e.g., Tygh) and Columbia drainage bands of Northern Paiute; 1,000 may be assigned to each group (Eugene Hunn, personal communication 1991).
[b] This figure probably includes both Wanapam and Sinkayuse (Columbian).
[c] This figure probably includes both Palouse and Lower Nez Perce.
[d] See Boyd (1985:366–372) for the process by which the revised estimates were determined. Because of different methodologies, numbers in the first 3 columns do not always add to the totals in the fourth column.
[e] Kootenai, Salish, or Shuswap.

1950), and there may have been an increase in deaths from violence. The Indian wars of 1847–1875 claimed hundreds of adult males, especially in the Sahaptian area, as shown by skewed sex ratios that persisted throughout the second half of the century.

Population Size

The earliest population estimate for the peoples of the Columbia Plateau is the 1805–1806 enumeration (table 2) by Meriwether Lewis and William Clark; the earliest equivalent document for the upper Fraser is the 1823 report from Fort Kamloops. Both estimates represent populations already considerably diminished from disease.

The Lewis and Clark estimates exist in two versions: "Codex I" and "Supplement" (Moulton 1983–, 6:473–488). Codex I is the earlier document, drawn up at Fort Clatsop in winter 1805; the Supplement postdates the explorers' return up the Columbia in 1806. Differences in numbers between the two versions appear to represent seasonal changes in population: the earlier winter villages and the later salmon season concentrations (Boyd 1985; Boyd and Hajda 1987). Stern (1993:43) suggests that some groups may have been absent hunting bison in the Plains. Figures from the southern Sahaptian area, which were derived from observation, are assumed to be more accurate than those from the northern Salishan zone, which were based on information from Indian informants. The identification of several of Lewis and Clark's names with historically known peoples is difficult; but by comparing the locations given in Codex I with geographic features in Clark's manuscript map of the Northwest (Moulton 1983–, 1:map 26), most can be identified with a fair degree of certainty. Similarly, given an understanding of the polyglot nature of Plateau fisheries, most discrepancies between the two estimates can be reconciled, and revised estimates closer to true winter village populations calculated.

Mooney (1928) used Lewis and Clark's data to estimate probable aboriginal (pre-1774) Columbia Plateau populations. He did not assume any pre-1805 loss from introduced disease, which makes his figures much too low for the precontact period. Although how much Plateau population declined between 1774 and 1805 is uncertain, assuming two sequential smallpox epidemics, with average mortalities (Dixon 1962:325), leads to a conservative figure of 40 percent. Assuming 40 percent decline yields an aboriginal Columbia Plateau (as defined in this volume) total of just over 68,000. Mooney based his upper

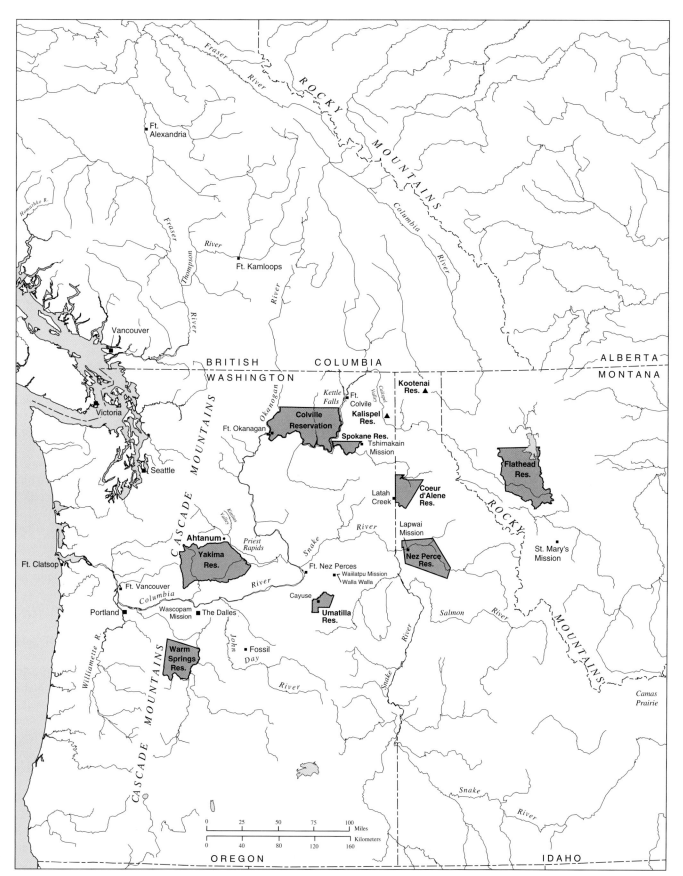

Fig. 1. Locations in the Plateau where disease has been documented in the historic period.

DEMOGRAPHIC HISTORY UNTIL 1990

Fraser estimates upon those of Teit (1900, 1906, 1909), who did consider disease mortality, and those estimates are probably more accurate. Adding the adjusted estimate for the Columbia Plateau to Teit's (1909:466, 1900:175, 1906:199) numbers—7,200 Shuswap, 5,000 Thompson, 4,000 Lillooet, plus an allowance of 2,500 for the Klamath—yields a minimal aboriginal Plateau culture area estimate of 87,000. Considering the usual mortality on "virgin soil," the number may be much higher.

Diseases and Population Decline

In common with the rest of the Americas, the Plateau culture area after 1492 was "virgin soil" for a long list of infectious diseases that had evolved in the Old World. Especially important in Plateau demographic history were smallpox, measles, influenza, colds, malaria, dysentery, and whooping cough. On first exposure to these infections, Plateau Indians had little physical resistance, either genetic or acquired, in addition to lacking knowledge of how to deal with them. The documented decline in Plateau populations in the first century of contact, 1793–1893, is largely due to cumulative mortality from introduced disease.

There is some controversy over the initial date of appearance of these diseases to the Plateau culture area. It is commonly assumed that the Rocky Mountains served as a barrier, effectively isolating the Pacific coast throughout most of its early history from cultural and epidemiological developments to the east. But interregional trade contacts did exist (Griswold 1970), and after the appearance of the horse in 1730, these contacts intensified.

Campbell (1989) raises the possibility that a high-mortality infectious disease, probably smallpox, penetrated the Plateau as early as the sixteenth century. The evidence is archeological: decline in number and size of archeological components, structured features, and shell and bone residue, all coinciding in the early 1500s in the middle Columbia drainage. The hypothesis is that this trend indicates a sharp population decline, associated with a smallpox pandemic beginning in 1519. This hypothesis does not rule out other possible causes of depopulation, such as famine or regional outmigration, and needs to be tested in comparable archeological regions in the Pacific Northwest (Campbell 1989:181,193).

In the late eighteenth century, several archeological indices once again point to population decline (Campbell 1987:26–29). This is the time period for the first documented smallpox epidemic in the Plateau culture area.

Smallpox in the 1770s

The first historically recorded smallpox epidemic in the Pacific Northwest dates to the years immediately following the first appearance of Europeans along the coast in 1774 (vol. 7:137–138; Boyd 1994a). In the Plateau culture area, the initial epidemic is reported for Colvile (fig. 1)

(Chance 1973:120), Nez Perce (A.B. Smith in Drury 1958:136–137; see also William Gray in Larsell 1947:114), Flathead (Mengarini 1977:193–194), and Kootenai (Curtis 1907– 1930, 7:119; see also Boas and Chamberlain 1918:268–271). Three of the four accounts suggest that the outbreak originated in the Plains and spread to the Plateau with the return of bison hunters. A smallpox epidemic on the Plains is firmly dated to 1780–1781 (Dobyns 1966:441), but the Plateau accounts uniformly document an earlier date which gives them contemporaniety with the Northwest Coast sources.

All the Plateau sources agree that the epidemic was severe: "a dreadful visitation;" "the most virulent form of the smallpox" (A.B. Smith in Drury 1958:137). Among the Flathead "The disease caused the growth of large red and black pustules over the entire body, particularly on the chest. Those developing red pustules died within a few days, but those who were plagued by the black pustules died almost instantly" (Mengarini 1977:194). Mortality was high: at Fort Colvile "Immense numbers...were swept off" (Work in Chance 1973:120); among the Nez Perce in the Plains "the people almost to an individual dead;" at home "very few surviving the attack of the disease" (A.B. Smith in Drury 1958:137). Among one camp of Flathead "in a very few days killed everyone with the exception of fifteen children" (Mengarini 1977:194); the Plains Kootenai band "was nearly exterminated" (Curtis 1907–1930, 7:119). The ethnohistorical evidence therefore suggests a considerable demographic impact.

In 1801–1802, a generation after its initial recorded appearance, smallpox revisited the Plateau. Two accounts (Work 1829; A.B. Smith in Drury 1958) note its presence among the Colville and Nez Perce; both also state that it caused "less destruction" and "did not prove so fatal" as the first outbreak. The reasons for the apparent lower mortality may be that the epidemic was a "milder form," that only part of the population (that segment born since the first outbreak and hence without acquired immunity) was susceptible, or both. Michel Revais, Teit's mixed-blood Flathead informant, stated that the epidemic came from the Plains and spread to the Flathead, Pend d'Oreille, Kalispel, and Spokane, on to the Colville, Lakes, Sanpoil, and stopped among the Sinkayuse (Teit 1930:212, 315–316). Circumstantial evidence suggests it occurred among the Coeur d'Alene also (de Smet 1905:525). Revais denied that the "Shahaptian tribes" were affected, but as the disease was present among peoples to the east (Nez Perce), and several others west of the Cascades (Chinookans, Chehalis, Twana, and Straits: vol. 7:138), this seems unlikely. In the Fraser drainage, the epidemic occurred among the Coast Salish (Jenness 1955:34) and Lower Thompson (Teit 1900:176). In 1808 Simon Fraser (Lamb 1960:94) noted "several Natives...marked with...smallpox" at a camp between Lytton and Spuzzum, a possible heritage of this outbreak. The Stalo account states that the disease spread "from the east," but this seems to contradict Revais's contention that most of the other southeast British Columbia peoples—Upper Thompson, Shuswap, and Okanagan—did not experience the second epidemic (Teit 1930:212). It is probable that the epidemic of 1801–1802, like that a generation earlier, occurred among all Plateau peoples.

Other Diseases

Other diseases followed smallpox over the Rockies. The first noted historically was whooping cough ("distemper"), which afflicted children in camps of Flathead, Kootenai, and Thompson in the summers of 1807 and 1808, reducing them to "skeletons" (Thompson in Glover 1962:45; Thompson in Belyea 1994:63–69, 224; Frazer in Lamb 1960:119). Once the North West Company established permanent fur-trading posts on the Plateau (at Fort Spokane 1810, Fort Okanagan 1811, Fort Kamloops 1813, Fort Nez Perces 1818, Fort Colvile 1822), the pace of introduction appears to have quickened. The posts were islands in a sparsely inhabited wilderness, connected to civilization only by the brigades of fur trappers from Red River. The attractions of the forts drew concentrations of Indians, who encamped in the vicinity throughout the year (Chance 1973:121–122). From the 1810s–1830s surviving post journals reveal a recurring pattern of what might be called "winter illnesses." Each year the fur brigades apparently brought with them a new strain of cold or influenza, which during the winter, spread among the artificial concentration of fort hangers-on, peaking during the "lean season" when food stocks, among this economically semidependent population, were low, and the Indians were most susceptible to infection. The pattern is similar to that recorded in the epidemiological literature for other isolated communities with intermittent contacts with civilization (Burnet and White 1972:132–133).

During the winter of 1824–1825 the Cayuse (Simpson in Merk 1931:127) are reported to have suffered from a "mortality" that was most often termed smallpox. Several accounts recorded from Columbia Basin native informants after 1900 may also refer to this outbreak, although the exact dating is unclear (Yakima and Wanapam: Splawn 1944:426, 393; Columbia Salish: Teit 1928:97; Okanagan and Coeur d'Alene: Teit 1930:212, 40). The low percentage of children recorded among riverbank groups in the 1827 Fort Colvile census suggests recent epidemic mortality (Boyd 1985:508–510).

In summer 1830 "fever and ague" (generally assumed to be malaria) was first recorded at Fort Vancouver. The disease reappeared annually on the lower Columbia throughout the 1830s, causing high mortality among Chinookan peoples and some Sahaptins as far as the mouth of the John Day (S. McGillivray 1831–1832). In 1805, according to Lewis and Clark, there were about 3,900 Upper Chinookans from the Cascades to The Dalles; by 1841, the total was no more than 1,000, due largely to mortality from "fever and ague" (Boyd 1985:304). Fear of the disease, found throughout the

1830–1832 Fort Nez Perces Journal, may have been a contributing factor to the surge in "Sunday dancing" that occurred outside the fort at this time (Boyd 1996). However, the only cases of fever reported upstream from John Day appear to have been imported from the lower river. The malarial vector, *Anopheles freeborni*, was absent or rare at this time throughout most of the Columbia Plateau.

Outbreak of "pneumonia" on the upper Salmon in late 1832 (Irving 1961:101–102) and "severe inflammation of the lungs" at Waiilatpu Mission in March–April 1837 (Hulbert and Hulbert 1936–1941, 1:272–273, 280) both claimed several lives. With the arrival of resident missionaries in 1836, and settlers in 1841, a new class of disease appeared on the Plateau. These were "diseases of childhood," most of which were introduced by foreign-born Euro-American children, who had been absent from the region before this time (Boyd 1994b). In spring 1840 chickenpox was first noted at Lapwai and Waiilatpu Missions, where it claimed several children (Gray in Larsell 1947:113; N. Whitman 1893:130–133). Scarlet fever appeared following the overland migration of 1843 at Lapwai, Tshimakain, and Waiilatpu Missions, but only among Whites. Whooping cough spread in late 1843 from Cayuse through Walla Walla and down the Columbia into Upper Chinookan territory where, in early 1844, it caused the deaths of several children (Boyd 1994b). Typhoid arrived with settlers in 1844 (Barclay in Dunn 1846), but like scarlet fever, was not recorded among Indians. A tropical dysentery (termed "the bloody flux"—a form of shigellosis?) was introduced by sea in summer 1844, spreading from a focus at Willamette up the Columbia at least to Wascopam Mission (The Dalles). Four hundred Indians (probably from the western band of Klikitats) died around Fort Vancouver, and several deaths were noted at both the Cascades and The Dalles (de Smet 1905:167; Brewer 1845).

The most deadly of the "diseases of childhood" was the measles epidemic of 1847–1848 (Boyd 1994b). Contrary to popular belief, measles was not brought by immigrants over the Oregon Trail but arrived with a band of mid-Columbia Indians who had been trying to acquire cattle in the vicinity of Fort Sutter in the Sacramento Valley (Heizer 1942). The trading party arrived at Fort Nez Perces on July 23, and messengers went out "in every direction...among all the neighboring tribes" with news of the disease (Kane in Harper 1971:117). By early September cases began to be reported in immigrants' journals, and by early November "The Cayuse Indians were dying very fast..." (Hulbert and Hulbert 1936–1941, 3:261). With deaths mounting rapidly, Cayuse chiefs decided to run an experiment to see if Dr. Marcus Whitman's medicines, as rumored, were causing the mortality. Three Indians were sent to ask for medicine: all died, and the Whitman Massacre followed shortly (Stanley 1847; Curtis 1907–1930, 8:81). More than 200 of an estimated 500 Cayuses died before the epidemic stopped (Craig 1858:25–27).

Fig. 2. First page of response to query 25, "What Tribe or Tribes inhabit your district, what is their present number—both of families and of individuals?" from the Fort Nez Perces report submitted by Samuel Black (1829), master of this fort in Oregon Country. Employees working for the Hudson's Bay Company received a list of 258 queries on the geography, climate, and inhabitants that they were asked to address to "the gentlemen in the interior." The tribes for which this population information was reported by Black included the Nez Perce, estimated at 500–600 men; Palouse, estimated at 60–70 men; Walla Walla, estimated 300 men; Cayuse, estimated 50–54 men; and Yakima, estimated at least 150 men. All fished near Fort Nez Perces.

By early December, the epidemic had claimed many Indians at Yakima and The Dalles (A.M. Blanchet 1978:82). The Spokane Indians appear to have picked up the disease from Nez Perce at their root grounds on Latah Creek; the epidemic among them lasted from late October through December (E. Walker 1847). Mortalities were few, apparently because the Spokane heeded the recom-mendations of the Tshimakain missionaries on how to treat measles (Teit 1930:316). At Fort Colvile the epidemic ran from December through January; Indian deaths in the vicinity were given as both 99 and 127 (Lewes 1848; E. Walker in Drury 1976:437). In mid-February, measles peaked among upper Fraser peoples; 35 "died in the vicinity" of Fort Kamloops alone, but only "6 or 8" at Fort Alexandria, where the effective imposition of "sanative regulations" apparently halted its spread (Allan 1848; Alexander Anderson 1848). At Saint Mary's Mission among the Flathead 86 died, leaving 500 survivors (Mengarini 1977:197). The total demographic impact is unknown, though two Hudson's Bay Company sources estimated it at one-ninth and one-tenth (Barclay 1848; Douglas 1848).

Table 3. Population Estimates, 1835 and 1838

	1835	1838
Shuswap	1,600 ("At Nalis")	575 (Shooshaps)
Thompson	1,100	—
Okanagan	1,200	1,050
Sanpoil	1,000	1,000
Spokane	800	800
Upper Spokane	320	—
Coeur d'Alene	640	700
Colville		
(Kettle Falls)	560	560
Lake Indians	480	500
Pend d' Oreille	1,500	2,200 (1,200?)
Flathead	500	800
Kootenai	—	1,000
Yakima	360	700
"Claaptin"	320	—
Walla Walla	400	500
Palouse	240	300
Cayuse	400	2,000
Nez Perce	1,600	2,500
Sapewell		
(Nez Perce band)	960	—
Total	13,960	14,985

SOURCES: Parker 1837, 1844.

Smallpox in the 1850s–1860s

In early 1853 smallpox was reintroduced to the Pacific Northwest at several locations along the coast from ships originating in San Francisco (vol. 7:141). An epidemic spread up the Columbia and was present at The Dalles by late May. One source stated that 257 died at Wishram village, leaving 270 survivors (Bolon 1854). In August through October, as the George B. McClellan party of the Northern Pacific Railroad Survey passed through the eastern foothills of the Washington Cascades, they encountered sick and dying Klikitats at Chequoss, Yakimas at Ahtanum, and Okanagans on the river of that name (McClellan 1853; Gibbs 1855:423, 433, 439). The explorers believed it affected "all those inhabiting the west and north sides of [the Columbia's] upper branches" (Cooper 1853:126). Sanpoil tradition stated that the disease was brought to them by a member of their tribe returning from Portland (Ray 1933:21–22). A Colville shaman who visited Sanpoil carried the disease to Kettle Falls, but as the Colville had been vaccinated by Roman Catholic missionaries, the epidemic stopped there (Joset 1854, 1860). However, the Protestant Spokane, "who said the medicine of the Fathers was a poison used only to kill them, were swept away by hundreds" (de Smet 1905:1235). The epidemic also affected the Coeur d'Alene (Teit 1928:40). The Salishan-speaking peoples of the northeast (Kalispel, Pend d'Oreille, and Flathead), vaccinated by the Catholic fathers, were spared (Suckley 1854:125), as, apparently, were the Nez Perce, many of whom had been vaccinated by Protestant missionaries in 1838–1840 (Gray in Larsell 1946:114). The French mission records from Cayuse mention several deaths in September, but from consumption not smallpox (Ricard 1853). No other statistics on mortality from this epidemic survive from the Plateau.

The last demographically significant outbreak of smallpox in the Plateau culture area was part of the great British Columbia smallpox epidemic of 1862–1863. This epidemic began in spring 1862 in Victoria and spread up the British Columbia coast. An extensive vaccination program among Coast Salish, Lower Lillooet, and Thompson by Oblates of Mary Immaculate and Anglican missionaries (*British Columbian*, May 14, 1862; *British Colonist*, June 23, 1862) apparently stalled the epidemic's entry into the interior by the Fraser River route (Ball 1862). Several Shuswaps were also vaccinated around Fort Kamloops (Manson 1862). But by midsummer smallpox penetrated the interior via the Homathco and Bella Coola rivers (*British Colonist*, Nov. 25, 1862; Palmer 1863:7–8). In addition to the Subarctic Chilcotin and Carrier, by midwinter the epidemic spread to the Shuswap (particularly the northern and western bands)

BOYD

There are 5 diff. Tribes of Indians who frequent this Establishm.
The Sahaptin or Nez Perces about 5 a 600 Men
The Palouse from or Paleushes 60 70 Men these two
Tribes reside on the lower part of the South Branch
as far as the Forks of Lewis's or Salmon River & up that
River & Red Bear River for some distance say the Palouse
reside on the lower part near the Columbea of the South Branch
The Walla Wallas about 300 Men including about 50
at Chutes in this Calculation but there are parties there
abouts living out from the River & Fish at Chutes only
The Wall Walla reside along the Columbia from Priests
Rapid to Chutes. — The Pchiwana pam a Yackama
reside on Yackama River & across the Mountains by
Mount Baker in a Line to Pugets Sound about 150 of
them Fish on this side the Mountains Often going Across
I do Not Know how many of this Tribe in all :— The
above 4 Tribes Speak a dialect of the Same Language
but do Not Know which is the Root, the Walla Walla
so perhaps. The Nez Perces the most different Not
understanding them, yet its the easiest smoothest
& finest Language & become the general Language of
the Natives in this quarter when assembled, it has
one great advantage Naming or having only one
Name for one Article & since whereas the Walla Walla
Yackumas & Paleush have several changing Names
at diff. places which makes it hard to learn
& the Whites as yet have only been able to pick up
enough to trade & settle some Occurrances about the Fort
The 5th Tribe Waylette or Cayouse (a Name given
them by the People from their living amongst the
Stones or Rocks, about the Mountains being their Lands)
These Indians Altho in appearance Manners & Customs
like the Nez Perces are altogether a distinct Tribe
& speak a Language amongst themselves totally
different from all the other Tribes in the Columbea
thats Known, & understood by None but themselves
or are they fond of others attempting it this Tribe
are the fewest about 50 a 54 Men but have great
influence over the Others Excelling in bravery hunting
& athletic exercise & the first who procured Arms
(Guns) & Ammunition for their Beaver & Horses
they are fond of domaneering & trublesome Characters among them

Table 4. Baseline Reservation Censuses

	Population	Date	Source
Fraser			
Lillooet	1,358	1884	
Thompson	1,977	1885	
Shuswap	1,637	1884	
Upper Columbia			
Kootenai			
Canada	498	1887	
U.S.	273	1865	Hutchins 1865:430
Okanagan			
Colville	616	1870	Winans 1870
Lakes	229	1870	
Okanagan (north)	768	1880	
Okanogan (south)	641	1870	
Sanpoil-Nespelem	532	1870	
Columbia Salish	1,000	1870	
Flathead			
Flathead	551	1865	Hutchins 1865:430
Pend d'Oreille	908	1865	
Kalispel	403	1870	
Spokane	716	1870	
Coeur d'Alene	450	1877	Simms 1877a:582
Middle Columbia			
Nez Perce	2,830	1865	O'Neill 1866:195
Cayuse	384	1861	Abbott 1861:775
Northeast Sahaptin			
Palouse	350	1881 estimate	Wilbur 1881:232
Walla Walla	605	1870	Boyle 1870:775
Northwest Sahaptin			
Yakima	667	1859	Lansdale 1859:780
Klikitat	663	1859	
Columbia Sahaptin			
North (Wayampam, Skin)	808	1859	
SE (Umatilla, John Day)	683	1870	Boyle 1870:519
SW (Tenino, Tygh)	682	1862	Logan 1862:432
Upper Chinookan			
Wishram-Cascades	471	1859	Lansdale 1859:780
Wasco	384	1862	Logan 1862:432
Molala	123	1851	Dart 1851:477
Klamath	1,071		Huntington 1865:269–270
Klamath	710		
Modoc	339		

(Teit 1909:463; *British Colonist*, Feb. 27, 1863), Lillooet (R.C.L. Brown 1863; Stevenson 1914:267), and Upper Thompson (Champness 1865:258; Teit 1900:176). Statistics on mortality are not available from the interior, but losses on the coast approached 20,000 (vol. 7:144).

1807–1857 Population Estimates

The demographic record for the Plateau culture area in the first half of the nineteenth century is not good. There are several unreliable estimates and partial counts. The best figures, as in the adjacent Northwest Coast culture area, come from the Hudson's Bay Company. The most comprehensive and apparently accurate of these is the compendium assembled by the Reverend Samuel Parker from Hudson's Bay sources and published in two versions (table 3).

Other sources and estimates worthy of note include the following. From the North West Company period (1808–1821) in the interior, there are several estimates of multiethnic groupings at both fisheries and rendezvous. In

June 1808, on a descent of the river that would receive his name, Simon Fraser tallied 1,240 in five villages of Thompson Indians plus 1,200 at what was probably a seasonal gathering at the root grounds of Botanie Valley, for a total of 2,440, the most complete count of these people before 1880 (Lamb 1960:86–97). Several valuable estimates include 3,000 at the Wishram summer fishery (Ross 1849:117) and 3,000 at the late spring Yakima Valley rendezvous (Ross 1956:22–23). The wording "3,000 men exclusive of women and children" is certainly wrong; it should be inclusive. The August rendezvous at the mouth of the Walla Walla was given as 1,500 (Ross 1849:126–127). Ross's (1849:290) estimate of 15 people per square mile and 600 warriors in the "Oakinakens nation" (Okanagan and Columbia Salish speakers) translates to about 5,000 people, a total very close to that of Lewis and Clark.

The 1823 Kamloops census (MacLeod 1823), though undercounting Shuswap and Thompson, gives an estimate of 450 "fighting men" among two bands of Lillooet ("Stat-lam-chee" and "Spa-chil-quah") for a probable total of 1,800, the earliest good estimate. The 1829 Fort Nez Perces census also gives only "men" for each tribe (fig. 2) but provides a total of "6,000–8,000 souls" for the district as a whole, which allows the following reconstruction (on 7,000: for computations see Boyd 1985): Nez Perce, 3,203; Walla Walla, 1,747; Palouse, 874; lower Yakima, 874; Cayuse, 303. The series of Hudson's Bay Company censuses from the Salishan area in 1827–1829 (A. McDonald [1827] 1947; Work 1829; Work in Chance 1973) are not useful as an index for total populations, as they apparently include only those peoples in regular contact with the traders. They do give breakdowns by sex and age (adult/child) and, sometimes, ancillary economic information. The censuses show sex ratios strongly skewed in favor of boys among northern bands of Shuswap, and moderately skewed in favor of women among several upstream peoples, indices that recur in counts from the 1870s (Blankinsop 1877). They also show markedly low percentages of children for southern riverine groups, a phenomenon that may be related to recent epidemic mortality (Boyd 1985:500–510).

From the 1850s, two other postepidemic counts also show low percentages of children. These are Anson Dart's 1851 treaty enumerations of eastern Klikitat ("Whulwhypum"), Wenatchee ("Piscahoose"), and Okanagan, with an aggregate 15 percent children on a total sample of 1,083 (Taylor 1974:420–422), and Albert Robie's winter 1857 counts of Wishram (22% on 199) and Wayampam ("Skein") (25% on 711) (Robie 1857:639). These counts postdate the 1848 measles epidemic and the 1853 smallpox outbreak. A second index from the early reservation period, most notable among Sahaptian peoples, is a consistently low adult sex ratio (Boyd 1985:395). The most probable explanation for this paucity of men was "the loss they have sustained in former wars" (Wilbur 1867:45). If the figures may be trusted, around 1,000 Indian men may have died in the Indian wars of the 1850s.

Early Reservation Period

The removal of most native peoples of the Plateau to reservations between 1855 and 1872 was accompanied by a dramatic shift in both prevalent diseases and demographic characteristics. Virulent epidemic diseases that affected Indian populations were replaced by "diseases of childhood" and chronic diseases as major causes of mortality; populations continued to decline, albeit at a regular, not erratic, rate.

A short-term result of sudden removal was starvation, particularly at southern reservations where uprooted populations had to be supported over winter by insufficient government rations. For example, 800 were maintained at the temporary White Salmon Reservation (A. Townsend 1857:637), and 50 Walla Wallas died of hunger in winter 1858–1859 (Cain 1859:782).

Censuses

The first apparently reliable censuses of reservation populations were, as a rule, not made until several years after the reservations were established (table 4). The numbers suggest that by 1860, the Indian population of the Plateau had dropped to a total somewhere above 20,000, but certainly not over 25,000.

There are several problems with the reservation figures. Yakima is a good example. For two decades after the establishment of the reservation, its population was estimated at around 3,500 people (S. Ross 1870:481). This may have been an overestimate. In 1859, the constituent populations totaled 2,609 (667 Yakima, 663 Klikitat, 808 Columbia River, and 471 Wishram) (Lansdale 1859). (It is possible that this total omitted several hundred Wenatchee.) When a careful tally was made in 1881, the Yakima peoples totaled 2,578 (Wilbur 1881:232). At Umatilla, a sizable portion of the population remained off-reservation. The 1870 census, which counted all constituent peoples, totaled 1,622, of whom 837 were on reservation and 785 off (Boyle 1870:519). All other enumerations from the late nineteenth century at Umatilla consistently omitted the off-reservation "Columbia River" peoples.

For both Nez Perce and Palouse there is a sizable difference between the early reservation period and post–Nez Perce war numbers. An 1865 census returned 2,830 Nez Perce; the Palouse were estimated at 350. The 1890 total was around 2,085. Josephy (1965:632–633) estimates that there were 120 Nez Perce casualties of the war; Trafzer and Scheuerman (1986:120) note a decrease of 163 among the Nez Perce and Palouse removed to Oklahoma between 1877–1885. However, if the census figures are correct, the magnitude of war-related decline was greater, perhaps as much as one-third of the pre-war total.

Discounting the undercounting of the Columbia Sahaptins and the mortality from the Nez Perce War, there was a decline of around 10 percent in Plateau populations between the beginning of the reservation period and 1890. Most of this decline was due to continuing mortality from infectious diseases plus a depressed birth rate. Although vital statistic during this time were not very reliable (births were underreported), records kept on Plateau reservations between 1879 and 1890 show an excess of deaths over births for every year except 1885. Nez Perce had the worst record, with 71 births and 130 deaths in nine years between 1879 and 1890 (three years incomplete); Klamath had 222 births and 291 deaths over 12 years. Warm Springs, on the other hand, had 176 births and 174 deaths over the same dozen years (ARCIA 1878–1890). The vital statistics are consistent with the trend in total numbers as well as the prevalence of virulent diseases and availability of health care on the reservations.

Determining the nadir date for the population of the Plateau culture area is difficult, considering the incompleteness of the record and the tendency to omit nonreservation Indians. The first year with complete Plateau coverage, 1890, shows the lowest total enrollments, 17,172. However, the actual total for this year (as well as those following) was higher—perhaps as much as 18,751 including nonenrolled Indians counted in the census. In 1900 there were about 18,103 on the rolls, and by 1910 the total was almost 19,000. In 1930 it was 20,747. Various subgroups reached their nadirs at different times. The low point for Klamath-Modoc was 1889 (769), Okanagan-speaking peoples and Coeur d'Alene 1890 (1,951 and 422), Sahaptins perhaps 1890 (2,574, a probable undercount), upper Fraser peoples 1892 (4,287), Salish speakers and Kootenai 1900 (1,961 and 771). Nez Perce reached their low point (1,387) not counting the Joseph band at Colville Reservation, in 1927. Totals for small but distinct groups resident on larger reservations (Columbia Salish, Cayuse, Wasco-Wishram, and Molala) fluctuate but on the whole show continually diminishing numbers as they became integrated into larger groups.

Health Status

Health and disease during the reservation period was dominated by minor epidemics of childhood diseases and chronic diseases such as tuberculosis. Measles recurred regularly, particularly at boarding schools. The two most deadly outbreaks occurred in 1874 in the south, where "About one hundred" Yakima and "a good many children" at Umatilla succumbed (Wilbur 1874:648; Cornoyer 1874:63) and in the Salishan area in 1887–1888, where 69 died at Colville Reservation and over 26 among the Lillooet bands (ARCIA 1888:452–453; Meason 1888). An influenza epidemic passed through the north in the winter of 1890–1891. There were at least 79 deaths among the Thompson; 10 percent of

the Lytton band died (MacKay 1891:76, 80). The Kamloops Shuswap and Lakes each lost a score. In 1891 the disease moved south, with 25 deaths recorded at Coeur d'Alene and 10 at Yakima (Cole 1891:44). In 1892, 70 deaths occurred among the Canadian Kootenai, most from influenza (Phillips 1892:247). A major smallpox scare in the winter of 1899–1900 led to quarantines at most reservations in the United States; only a few deaths occurred. But when the disease reappeared in 1901 there were nearly 500 cases recorded at Colville and Flathead reservations, and 56 deaths (Albert Anderson 1901:392–393; Smead 1901:260). The last great epidemic was the Spanish influenza in late 1918. Nearly 200 died at Kamloops and 100 at Lytton (Meighan 1919:52). In the United States there were 75 deaths at Colville, 46 at Yakima, in addition to large numbers at Nez Perce and Klamath reservations (ARCIA 1919:29–30, 140–143). Vital statistics from the nine largest reservations show an excess of 249 deaths over births for the year.

Among chronic diseases two indigenous ailments, conjunctivitis and rheumatism, were prevalent: the former particularly at Yakima and Warm Springs, the latter at those two reservations plus Colville. Malaria appeared at several reservations in the south (particularly Yakima and Warm Springs) during the late 1800s. Its increased prevalence appears to be associated with the introduction of irrigation plus a transition to permanent dwellings situated near standing water. Tuberculosis, always present in its glandular form ("scrofula"), became epidemic as respiratory disease ("consumption") by 1900. Most heavily infected were the southern reservations—Nez Perce, Yakima, and Klamath. Tuberculosis was epidemic at Nez Perce and a major reason for that tribe's continued failure to recoup early population losses. Several score children were annually kept out of school on account of the disease; in 1910 a sanitarium was established at Lapwai. In the same year the annual report noted: "The school physician thinks that at least 75% of the Nez Perce Indians have tuberculosis in some form, and that there is hardly a family on the reservation that is free from the disease. A great many families have lost from two to twelve children with tuberculosis" (Bureau of Indian Affairs 1910). The agency physicians routinely ascribed the prevalence of the disease to a decline in hygiene associated with the transition from temporary to permanent dwellings and the adoption of White clothing.

Venereal diseases are notable by their rarity on Plateau reservations at this time. There is a notable and early trend in the records to violent and accidental deaths among adult males, especially at the time and in those places where liquor became available, for example, Colville Reservation (Cole 1890:220). Several reports note problems in health care, including the difficulty of getting patients to continue taking medicines that did not yield immediate results, competition with traditional curers, low pay that made it difficult to hire and caused a high turnover among reservation physicians, and a lack of reservation hospitals.

478

In the decade preceding World War I, the United States government's health care efforts on the reservations appear to have taken hold, and results began to show in improved birth/death ratios, particularly in the Salishan area. Public health improvements were a crucial part of the government program. Field matrons, who traveled over the reservations treating ailments in the Indians' homes, also taught basics of hygiene and infant care. Several reservations ran "save the baby" campaigns and held regular "clean-up days." And there was a concerted effort at many agencies to replace ramshackle dwellings with simple but substantial structures (Bureau of Indian Affairs 1907–1914).

1934–1990

After the passage of the (United States) Indian Reorganization Act in 1934, the Bureau of Indian Affairs ceased publishing annual narrative reports and detailed statistical data from recognized reservations. Enrollment records—certainly the most accurate listings of the descendants of aboriginal populations—were maintained by the tribes themselves.

Enrollment policies, determined by the tribes, vary from one group to another. In the United States, most tribes require the following: descent from individuals named on a baseline tribal census or roll, and at least one-quarter blood in the parent tribe. There are provisions for special cases, and enrollment committees act upon individual requests. Memberships may be terminated or transferred, and people who do not qualify under the basic policy may be adopted into the tribe. Due to several clauses and changes in the enrollment policy of the Flathead Nation, for instance, people with as little as one-sixteenth blood may be enrolled; the January 1991 Flathead roll includes 1,491 people (23%) of less than one-quarter blood (enrollment offices of the Colville, Coeur d'Alene, Flathead, Nez Perce, Spokane, and Warm Springs tribes, personal communications 1991).

The degree of White admixture showed a steady increase through time and definite patterning among tribes. In 1910, the first year that blood quantum statistics were printed in the report of the commissioner of Indian affairs, 68 percent of enrolled United States Plateau Indians were listed as full-blood, 18 percent as half or more, and 14 percent as less than half. Eighty-two percent of Sahaptian tribes were full-blood, while only 53 percent of Salishan peoples were. The most highly mixed populations were Flathead and Colville (U.S. Bureau of the Census 1915:33). In 1930, 47 percent of the Plateau total, 68 percent of Sahaptians, and 33 percent of Salishans were full-blood (U.S. Bureau of the Census 1937). In 1950, 57 percent of a Sahaptian sample (Yakima, Nez Perce, and Umatilla) and 35 percent of a Salishan sample (Colville, Spokane, and Coeur d'Alene) were full-blood (U.S. Department of Health, Education, and Welfare. Public Health Service. Division of Indian Health 1958). A study of Nez Perce outbreeding showed not only a regular increase

of White admixture through time but also marked differences in blood quantum between traditional and nontraditional communities and off-reservation Indians (Walker 1967b). Statistics on blood quantum in the 1990s were generally not available, though the Flathead nation reported, on a January 1991 total of 6,580: 28 percent half or more, 49 percent one-quarter to one-half, and 23 percent less than one-quarter.

There had been a trend to migration of enrolled members away from reservations. Residence (on- versus off-reservation) statistics were first collected in 1930. In that year, a sample of United States (Colville excluded) showed 78 percent of enrolled Indians resident on identified reservations. Nez Perce and Warm Springs had 85 and 81 percent, respectively; Flathead and Spokane 74 and 78 percent (U.S. Bureau of the Census 1937). Statistics for 1991 provided by the same four reservations show: Nez Perce 59 percent, Warm Springs 81 percent, Flathead 54 percent, and Spokane 46 percent (U.S. Bureau of the Census 1991). A later trend is the presence of sizable numbers of Indians enrolled in other tribes resident on Plateau reservations. In 1980, most reservations listed 10–17 percent of total enrolled resident Indians in this category; Flathead had 31 percent (U.S. Bureau of the Census 1989).

Defining "Indian"

The United States Bureau of the Census uses a "self-identification" criterion to define Indian status. Census figures and enrollment numbers do not correspond (tables 5–7). Although the government census may pick up many nonenrolled Indians, it also tends to exclude many others who, because of low blood quantum or other reasons, identify themselves as White. Census totals have historically been lower than the totals on the tribes' own rolls; however, numbers from the 1990 census indicate a reversal of this trend (table 7). As of 1990, there were over 2,600 more self-identified Plateau Indians in the United States than there were members on the tribes' own rolls. And in the counties that make up the United States portion of the Plateau culture area there were over 11,000 more self-identified "Indians" than there were Indians enrolled in the tribes of the area. Some of this excess may include the 20 percent average in the United States who did not report tribal affiliation, but the majority probably consists of Indians belonging to non-Plateau tribes.

Two other agencies—the Bureau of Indian Affairs and the Indian Health Service—also keep records of Indian numbers. The totals for the "service populations" of these agencies differ from both enrollment and census totals.

The Canadian government defines two categories of "Indians:" status and nonstatus. The former are registered on official band rolls; the latter have been dropped for various reasons and have no legal status as "Indians" (Duff 1964:47). In Canada in 1981 the proportion of status to non-

Table 5. Population, 1890

	Reservation	Off-reservation ("taxed," by county)	Total
Fraser	4,520		4,520
Lillooet	1,171		1,171
Thompson	1,746		1,746
Shuswap	1,603		1,603
Upper Columbia			
Kootenai			1,062
Canada	600		600
U.S.	100 Idaho + circa 362 Mont.		462
Okanagan			2,417
Colville	247	340 (Stevens Co.)	587
Lakes	303		303
Okanagan (north)	660		660
Okanagan (south)	374	104 (Okanagan Co.)	478
Sanpoil-Nespelem	367	22 (Lincoln Co.)	389
Columbia Salish	743		
Wenatchee	300 ("west of Okanagan")		300
Sinkayuse	443		443
Salish			2,548
Flathead– Pend d'Oreille	1.449 (1,811 - 20% Kootenai)	165 (Missoula Co.)	1,614
Kalispel	240		240
Spokane	417 Lower	87 (Spokane Co.) + 190 Upper	694
Coeur d'Alene	422	19 (Kootenai Co.)	441
Middle Columbia			
Nez Perce	1,715 + 148 (Joseph band)	183 (Whitman, Asotin, Idaho, Nez Perce Cos.)	2,046
Cayuse	415		415
Northeast Sahaptin			494
Palouse		89 (Franklin Co.)	89
Walla Walla	405		405
Northwest Sahaptin			1,626
Kittitas		160 (Kittitas Co.)	160
Yakima	943	68 (Yakima Co.)	1,011
Klikitat	330	125 (Klickitat, Clark, Skamania Cos.)	455
Columbia Sahaptin			946
Columbia River	252 (Yakima reservation "others")		252
Umatilla–John Day	179 Umatilla + 57 John Day	28 (Gilliam Co.)	264
Tenino-Tygh	430		430
Upper Chinookan			604
Wishram-Cascades	150		150
Wasco	288	166 (Wasco Co.)	454
Molala	31		31
Klamath-Modoc	835	23 (Klamath Co.)	858
	17,172	1,579	18,751

SOURCE: U.S. Bureau of Census (1894).

Table 6. Population, 1910 and 1930

		1910		1930
	Enrolled	*Census*	*Enrolled*	*Census*
Fraser	5,260		5,538	
Lillooet	1,140			
Thompson	1,932			
Shuswap	2,188			
Upper Columbia				
Kootenai	968	1,053	1,147	
Canada	515			
U.S.	(453)	538	696	297
Okanagan	2,115		1,988	
Colville-Lakes	712	785	2,956	1,004
N. Okanagan (Canada)	631			
S. Okanogan (U.S.)	538	286		
Sanpoil-Nespelem	189+45	240+46		
Columbia Salish	587	437		1,121
Wenatchee	66	52		
Sinkayuse	521	385		
Flathead	2,507	1,693		
Flathead	1,812	486	2,318	2,046
Pend d'Oreille	(80%)	564	(80%)	
Kalispel	95		87	114
Spokane	504 + 96	643	742	629
Coeur d'Alene	537	293	605	463
Middle Columbia				
Nez Perce	1,433 + 97	1,259	1,399	
Northeast Sahaptin				
Palouse		82		
Walla Walla	461	397	195	
Cayuse	298	298	98	
Columbia Sahaptin				4,574
Umatilla	151	272	818	
Tenino-Tygh	520 (2/3)	550	501	
Columbia River				
Northwest Sahaptin	2,679		2,908 + 3!	
Yakima		1,409		
Klikitat		405		
Taitnapam				
Upper Chinookan		516		233
Wishram-Cascades		274		57
Wasco	260	242	220	166
Molala		31	5	
Klamath	1,126	978	1,172	928 (913 +
Klamath		696		15 Klamath Co.)
Modoc		282		
U.S.	12,593	10,515	15,158	11,804
Total	18,999	16,921	20,747	17,393

SOURCES: U.S. Bureau of Indian Affairs (1888–1940); Canada. Department of Indian Affairs (1910); Hawthorne et al. (1958); U.S. Bureau of the Census (1915, 1937).

Table 7. Population, 1980 and 1990

	1980 census[a] by tribe	1990 census[b] by tribe	1990-1991[c] enrollments	1990 census[d] by country
Fraser	9,411		14,828	
Lillooet	2,820		4,284	
Thompson	3,023		4,662	
Shuswap	3,568		5,882	
Upper Columbia	15,607		21,298	
Kootenai	832		764	
Canada	446		649	
U.S.	386	643	115	432
Okanagan (Canada)	1,753		2,921	
Colville	5,507	7,607	7,432	6,073
Colville	5,456		7,140	
Columbia		441		
Wenatchee	51	26		
Flathead	4,948	6,774	6,580	8,307
Salish		4,455		
Salish, Kootenai		2,319		
Kalispel	181	210	235	426
Spokane	1,753	2,118	2,118	1,822
Coeur d'Alene	684	1,048	1,248	1,293
Spokane County				5,539
Middle Columbia	12,246	16,511	15,552	20,902
Nez Perce	2,222	4,113	2,872	3,423
Umatilla	1,384	1,513	1,400	2,780
Cayuse	157	126		
Umatilla	965	1,159		
Walla Walla	262	228		
Yakima	6,813	7,887	8,002	10,894
Yakima	6,506	7,850		
Columbia River Chinook[e]	37	23		
Yakima Cowlitz		14		
Warm Springs	1,827	2,998	3,278	3,805
Warm Springs	1,336	2,715		
Wascopum	491[f]	255		
Molala		14		
Celilo		14		
Klamath	2,870	3,669	2,668	2,370
Klamath	2,107	3,097		
Modoc	763	572		
U.S.	28,963	38,580	35,968	47,164
Total	38,573	56,978	54,366	65,562

[a] U.S. Bureau of the Census (1989); Canada Department of Indian Affairs and Northern Development (1980).

[b] Paisano et al. (1992).

[c] Canadian figures for 1990 from Canada Department of Indian and Northern Affairs (1991); U.S. figures for early 1991 supplied by tribal enrollment offices.

[d] U.S. Bureau of the Census 1991.

[e] Chinookans in Klickitat Co.

[f] Chinookans in Jefferson and Wasco Cos.

status Indians nationally was approximately one to four (Thornton 1987:245). Since most of the nonstatus people are Métis, the number of non-status Indians in southeast British Columbia is probably small. Table 7 lists status Indians only for 1990.

Health Status

In 1955 the responsibility for health care of American Indians was transferred from the Bureau of Indian Affairs to the United States Public Health Service's newly created Indian

Health Service. At this time most deaths were caused by heart disease, trauma, and diseases of infancy (U.S. Department of Health, Education, and Welfare. Public Health Service. Division of Indian Health 1958).

In 1971, infant death rates had declined from almost two and one-half times the national rate to a figure slightly above the national average. Accidents and diseases of the heart remained as leading causes of death, followed by malignant neoplasm, cirrhosis, and strokes; accidents and cirrhosis far exceeded the national rate (U.S. Department of Health, Education, and Welfare. Public Health Service. Indian Health Service 1974).

In 1991 the average age of death among Plateau Indians was approximately age 40. The birthrate far exceeded the United States rate for all races. Child immunization rates exceeded 90 percent. There were occasional outbreaks of measles and hepatitis. Otitis media was common. Forty-six percent of the Indian population was below age 20 (Cecilia Delores Gregory, personal communication 1991).

Chronic illness replaced infection as the primary cause of death in adults in the 1990s. Violent death related to trauma—alcohol, homicide, suicide, and motor vehicle accidents—almost equaled deaths from chronic conditions, mainly among males aged 15–44. The high death rate among young males expressed itself demographically in skewed sex ratios in many tribes. Sexually transmitted disease, including syphilis and gonorrhea, were not uncommon. Because of the high death rate, especially of young persons, unresolved bereavement played an important role in mental and social disorder.

Dietary changes, especially those since the 1960s, resulted in much obesity with resultant Type II diabetes (Justice 1989; Freeman et al. 1989), gall bladder disease, and cardiovascular disease. Rheumatoid arthritis, a genetically linked disorder, was prevalent (Beasley, Willkens, and Bennett 1973). Tuberculosis continued to be more common than in the general population.

483

Reservations and Reserves

SYLVESTER L. LAHREN, JR.

United States Reservations

The reservation period in the United States ushered in a new era for Indian peoples that effectively ended their aboriginal way of life. This period of Plateau history marks a qualitative shift in the Indian-White relations of the area and is characterized by the assimilative design of the reservations. The first step in this process was removal of Indians from their aboriginal territory and relocation on reservations. The final phase of assimilation involved the introduction of agriculture and the development of concomitant supportive services. The results of this assimilative policy differed greatly from reservation to reservation.

After the cession of millions of acres of aboriginal lands (vol. 4:214–217), reservations were established. An important aspect of this cession process was that certain reservation boundaries were changed several times, and each time more land was ceded. More reservation land was lost through the Dawes Severalty Act, Homestead Act, rights of way and roads, and the sale of patented Indian lands. In a few instances some surplus land was restored, and certain reservations have repurchased lost reservation lands. All these factors have contributed to the land base of each reservation, which is set forth in table 1 and figure 1.

Important to an understanding of the reservations in the Plateau is the difference between treaty rights and trust responsibilities. Treaty rights refer specifically to those rights stated in the treaties. The articles of the individual treaties contain certain language that is in some cases similar and at other times different. Specific rights were given to the Indians for cession of their aboriginal territory or what is commonly referred to as ceded areas.

Trust responsibility of the federal government, on the other hand, takes the form of a parent or guardian, and the Indians were viewed as minor children. The Bureau of Indian Affairs was the agency established for this purpose. Historically, the Bureau has functioned as the administrator of all federal programs on the reservations. However, in 1975 Congress passed the Self-Determination and Education Act, which granted the Indians on the reservations the authority to administer their own federal programs. In the 1990s most federal programs were under tribal control (Lahren 1989).

Many Indian federal programs parallel those enacted for the non-Indian population. However, they are titled specifically for Indian reservations so as not to commingle the funds because they will be administered separately. Per capita payments received by the members on the individual reservations are monies the tribe has received for the settlement of land claims, violation of treaty rights, or the sale of reservation resources such as timber, mining, and so forth.

The historical development of each reservation is seminal to an understanding of their assimilative differences. The location of the reservation, size of reservation, reduction of reservation acreage, economic resources within the reservation boundary, whether treaty or executive order reservation, treaty language, constituency of cultural groups, type of aboriginal subsistence economy, religious affiliation of the cultural groups, presence of non-Indian groups, allotment act, the opening of the reservation for homestead entry, as well as other factors, have contributed significantly to the structuring of historical differences.

Treaty Reservations

The treaty period began on June 9, 1855, at Camp Stevens in the Walla Walla valley. The treaty reservations, in chronological order, are the Umatilla, Yakima, Nez Perce, Warm Springs, Flathead, and Klamath. Representing the United States government was Isaac I. Stevens, governor and superintendent of Indian affairs, Washington Territory, and Joel Palmer, superintendent of Indian affairs, Oregon Territory. These two individuals were primarily responsible for establishing the first five of these treaties. Generally, the language of these treaties was similar.

> All of the treaties included: a cession of lands; payment for the cession in annuities of beneficial objects; assistance for the Indians in the form of buildings, mills, instructors, and physicians; a reservation which the Indians were to occupy within a year after the ratification of the treaty; provision for the granting of reservation lands to the Indians in severalty; compensation to the Indians for granting rights of way for roads or railroads through their reservations; the acknowledgment by the Indians of the jurisdiction of the Federal government over them; the submission of disputes among the Indians of a band, or with other bands, or with the whites, to the Indian agent for settlement; the non-payment of debts of individual Indians from the annuities; and the reservation of fishing rights to the Indians (Coan 1922:15).

However, occasional differences in language resulted in important legal consequences. For example, Stevens's first treaty contained the following statement:

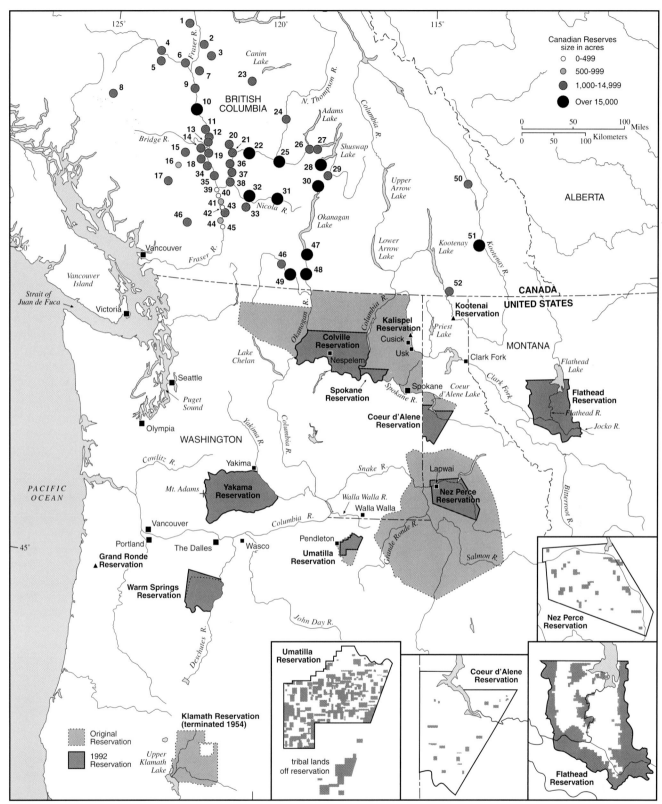

Fig. 1. Modern Plateau reservations and reserves (from Historical Atlas of Canada 1987; Bureau of Indian Affairs 1992). Insets show checkerboard effect from reservation allotments (gray areas show tribal ownership). Canadian reserves: 1, Alexandria; 2, Soda Creek; 3, Williams Lake; 4, Anaham; 5, Stone; 6, Toosey; 7, Alkali Lake; 8, Nemaiah Valley; 9, Dog Creek; 10, Canoe Creek; 11, High Bar; 12, Clinton; 13, Pavilion; 14, Bridge River; 15, Seton Lake; 16, Anderson Lake; 17, Pemberton; 18, Lillooet; 19, Fountain; 20, Bonaparte; 21, Ashcroft; 22, Deadman's Creek; 23, Canim Lake; 24, North Thompson and Canoe Lake; 25, Kamloops; 26, Adams Lake, Sahhaltkum band; 27, Little Shuswap Lake; 28, Neskainlith Halaut; 29, Spallumcheen; 30, Okanagan; 31, Upper Nicola; 32, Lower Nicola; 33, Lower Nicola, Spuzzum, Boston Bar, Boothroyd, Siska, Upper Similkameen (in common); 34, Cayoosh Creek; 35, Lytton; 36, Oregon Jack Creek; 37, Cook's Ferry; 38, Nicomen; 39, Skuppah; 40, Siska Flat; 41, Kanaka Bar; 42, Boothroyd; 43, Boothroyd, Chomok band; 44, Boston Bar; 45, Spuzzum; 46, Upper Similkameen; 47, Penticton; 48, Osoyoos; 49, Lower Similkameen; 50, Shuswap, Kinbasket's band; 51, Kootenay; 52, Lower Kootenay.

Table 1. United States Reservation Acreage

Original Reservation Acreage		1989	% of original	Tribal Trust	% of original	Individual Indian Trust	% of original
Umatilla							
1859	245,699						
1888	157,982						
1928	14,139 restored						
1928	172,121	88,550	36%	20,200	23%	68,350	77%
Yakima							
1,200,000		1,130,262	94%	904,411	80%	225,851	20%
Nez Perce							
1855	7,787,000						
1863	756,958	86,662	1%	35,106	41%	51,556	59%
by 1989,	24,000 acres						
Warm Springs							
1855	600,000						
1972	61,360 restored						
1972	661,360	643,554	107%	592,450	92%	51,104	8%
Flathead							
1,242,696		655,187	53%	611,352	93%	43,835	7%
Klamath							
1,107,847		terminated					
Colville 1872							
South half							
1,449,268		1,031,823	71%	985,263	95%	46,560	5%
Coeur d'Alene							
1867	250,000						
1873	598,000						
1889	413,000 69%	67,275	26%	21,465	32%	45,810	68%
Spokane							
1881	154,602	130,180	84%	105,383	81%	?24,797	19%
1934	139,750 90%						
Kalispel							
4,600		4,560	99%	1,970	43%	??2,587	57%
Kootenai							
1894	3,255	2,076	64%	22	1%	2,054	99%
1934	2,887						

NOTE: Figures are approximate.

That the exclusive right of taking fish in the streams running through and bordering said reservation is hereby secured to said Indians, and at all other usual and accustomed stations in common with citizens of the United States, and of erecting suitable buildings for curing the same; the privilege of hunting, gathering roots and berries and pasturing their stock on unclaimed lands in common with citizens, is also secured to them (Kappler 1904–1941, 2:694–695).

In his subsequent 1855 treaties and those of Palmer, this statement changes to "citizens of the Territory" (Kappler 1904–1941, 2:699, 703) in the treaty with the Yakima and Nez Perces, and then to "citizens of the United States" (1904–1941, 2:715) in the treaty with the tribes of middle Oregon, and then back to "citizens of the Territory" (1904–1941, 2:723) in the July 16, 1855, treaty with the Flatheads. After this treaty the entire provision was dropped.

This seemingly slight difference in language in 1855 had its most important effect in 1967–1968. The statement "citizens of the United States" provided the legal basis for the United States–Canadian fishing treaty that restructured Alaskan and Canadian ocean salmon fishing based on consideration of upriver salmon fishing rights. The language of these treaties provides the most important legal foundation for these reservations. All the treaty reservations were in existence in 1997, with the exception of the Klamath, which was terminated in 1954.

After Stevens's treaty with the Blackfoot on October 17, 1855, it was his intent to treat with the Coeur d'Alene, Spokane, Colville, and Okanagan on his return trip to Olympia, Washington. However, when the Yakima War broke out he decided to forego these negotiations. This war also delayed the ratification of these first five treaties until 1859 (Coan 1922:21, 27).

• UMATILLA RESERVATION   Governors Stevens and Palmer concluded their first treaty at Camp Stevens in the Walla Walla valley with the Walla Walla, Cayuse, and Umatilla on June 9, 1855. This treaty entailed the cession of Indian land and the creation of a "residence for said Indians," which was to become known as the Umatilla Reservation. Stevens and Palmer recognized them as one nation but did not designate a single chief as they would in subsequent treaties.

Article 1 of this treaty contained one of the most important rights and privileges of the Indians when it stated "That the exclusive right of taking fish in the streams running through and bordering said reservation is hereby secured to said Indians, and at all other usual and accustomed stations in common with citizens of the United States ..." (Kappler 1904–1941, 2:694–695). Even though the reservation was

established for the protection and exclusive use by the named Indian groups, the treaty contained certain language in Article 6 that allowed the president to survey and allot specific tracts to individuals or families (Kappler 1904–1941, 2:696).

The Walla Walla, Cayuse, and Umatilla ceded 6,400,000 acres of their aboriginal territory. As established in 1855, the Umatilla Reservation consisted of 512,000 acres; as surveyed by the U.S. government in 1859 it was 245,699. In August 1882 they ceded the Pendleton townsite.

The Slater Act of 1885, which provided for allotment of reservation land, had a significant impact upon this reservation. In 1888 the reservation was reduced to 157,982. Congress passed an act on July 1, 1902, to sell 70,000 acres that were not allotted. In May 1906, the Burke Act passed, which allowed "competent" Indians to be issued fee patents on their allotments, making the allotments marketable to non-Indians.

These laws had a severe effect toward assimilation on the Umatilla and other Plateau reservations. They had a devastating effect on the reservation land tenure system and created significant problems with the historical and contemporary management of reservation lands. This problem has become known as the "checkerboard effect." It was created by the sale or loss of Indian land. Allotment, homesteading, rights of way, and patented land sold by Indians have contributed to this "checkerboard effect."

In August 1936 Congress restored 14,139 acres to tribal control. In 1997 Indian lands on the Umatilla totaled 88,550 acres of which 20,200 were tribal and 68,350 were individually owned. This is 36 percent of the original land set aside in their treaty of 1855 (Lahren 1989).

Wash. State U. Lib., Histl. Photograph Coll., Pullman:91–126.
Fig. 2. Umatilla Indian Res., Oreg. The railroad had a major impact on the reservation and was a point of continual confrontation between Indian and non-Indian. This is probably the Oregon Railway and Navigation Company line that became part of the Union Pacific Railroad. Photograph by William H. Towne, 1883–1884.

RESERVATIONS AND RESERVES

Fig. 3. Yakima Indian Res., Wash. Protecting the reservation from non-Indian trespass, especially against sportsmen, is a reality of 20th-century life. Photograph by John W. Thompson, 1953–1955.

The Indian Reorganization Act was offered to the Umatilla Reservation in 1934. The intent of this act was to end allotment of reservation land, extend the trust period, restore surplus lands, end sales of Indian land to non-Indians, acquire lands on or off the reservation for Indian use, manage forests, and give them the right to incorporate. The Tribal Council voted not to accept the provisions of the act; however, by the 1940s they were experiencing a number of internal problems that invited reconsideration, and in November 1949 they adopted a constitution and by-laws that were accepted by the secretary of the interior. This form of government brought an end to the power of the headmen and chiefs.

In 1954 Congress passed House Concurrent Resolution 108, which became known as the Termination bill. Termination was opposed by the Umatilla Confederation. Public Law 83–280, which accompanied the Termination bill, placed criminal and civil jurisdiction under the control of state and county governments. This law was partially rescinded in 1980, and the tribe assumed jurisdiction in January 1981.

• YAKIMA RESERVATION   The second treaty completed at Camp Stevens on June 9, 1855, was with the Yakima, Palouse, Pisquouse, Wenatchee, Klikitat, Klinquit, Kowwassayee, Liaywas, Skin, Wishram, Shyiks, Ochechotes, Kahmiltpah, and Seapcat and created the Yakima Reservation. Because these groups were located in Washington Territory, Stevens negotiated this treaty alone. He recognized all these groups as one nation called Yakima and declared Kamiakan as its head chief. Being totally unaware of Plateau social organization, Stevens laid the basis for future intergroup conflict with this declaration.

The treaty was not ratified until 1859, and in the interim serious problems arose with the Yakima. Due to erroneous information, a misunderstanding occurred in which settlers thought the area had been opened to settlement and began moving into the Yakima area. The Yakimas felt that the government had violated the treaty and decided to kill anyone who trespassed on their land. After a series of confrontations the Yakima War ended in 1858 (Daugherty 1973:78–79).

When the treaty was ratified in 1859, the Yakima ceded 10,816,000 acres and were located on the Yakima Reservation, consisting of 1,200,000 acres or 10 percent of their aboriginal territory. By executive order on July 8, 1972, 21,000 acres of land on Mount Adams was returned to the Yakima (Daugherty 1973:94). In 1997 the Yakimas had 1,130,262 acres of land of which 904,411 acres were held in tribal trust (fig. 3) and 225,851 acres held by individual Indians.

• NEZ PERCE RESERVATION   On June 11, 1855, Stevens and Palmer concluded their third treaty at Camp Stevens, a treaty with the Nez Perce. When this treaty was ratified in 1859, it reduced the aboriginal territory of the Nez Perce from 13,204,000 to 7,787,000 acres.

Fig. 4. Selling Nez Perce land. left, Tribal leaders including Archie B. Lawyer, James Reuben, Jonah Hayes, James Hines, Edward J. Connor, Harrison or Khip-khip-pel-lehk-kin, James Stuart, William Wheeler, Bartholomew Moody, Is-kah-tis-ka-nihn, and Peo-peo-mukhs-mukhs and government officials represented by Robert Scheicker, James F. Allen, and Cyrus Beede pose after the signing of the agreement of May 1, 1893, which sold "surplus" lands (Slickpoo and Walker 1973:224). Photograph by J.W. Webster, 1893. right, Cashing the check after the sale, when $23,000 was on the table. left to right, Fred Brenner, Three Feathers, Samuel Martin, Red Horn, Eddie Connor, and J. Howard Howe. Photographed at Lapwai Agency, August 1895.

A second treaty was concluded with the Nez Perce on June 9, 1863, at Lapwai, Idaho (Kappler 1904–1941, 2:843–848). This treaty reduced the 1855 reservation from 7,787,000 to approximately 757,000 acres. In 1868 a third treaty was established with the Nez Perce and was ratified in 1869. The purpose of this treaty was to allow commercial harvesting of timber that was excluded under the treaty of 1863 (Kappler 1904–1941, 2:1024–1025).

The Dawes Severalty Act was agreed to on the Nez Perce Reservation, May 1, 1893 (fig. 4). The reservation was proclaimed open for settlement in 1895, and in 1905, it was opened for homestead entry. These events had a significant impact on this already greatly reduced reservation. They removed an additional 542,000 acres from the land base. The Nez Perce were allotted 182,938 acres, and 32,020 acres were left in tribal trust, for a total of 214,958 acres. During the early 1900s approximately 130,000 acres of the allotted land were fee patented and, through a variety of factors, passed out of Indian ownership. In 1989 Nez Perces owned approximately 35,000 acres of tribal trust land and 52,000 acres in individual Indian ownership. As a result of these particular historical factors, the configuration of their land ownership pattern is the "checkerboard." As of 1989 they had acquired an additional 24,000 acres.

• WARM SPRINGS RESERVATION   A fourth Plateau treaty concluded in 1855 was with the tribes of middle Oregon. On June 25, at Wasco, near The Dalles, Oregon, Joel Palmer, acting alone, began official negotiations with the Western Columbia River Sahaptin bands Tygh, Wayampam, Tenino, and John Day, and with the Upper Chinook bands of The Dalles, "Ki-gal-twal-la," and Hood River.

The 1855 treaty involved the cession of approximately 10,000,000 acres of land to the United States. The land area appropriated for them was to consist of approximately 600,000 acres located in central Oregon.

These bands were to relocate on this reservation within a year's time after ratification; be given the exclusive right of taking fish in the stream running through and bordering the reservation "in common with other citizens of the United States" at all other accustomed stations; be given the right to hunt, gather roots and berries, and pasture their stock on all unclaimed lands; and were to have monies dispensed to them for the purpose of moral improvement, education, farming, housing, etc. Article 5 provided for allotment of the reservation (Kappler 1904–1941, 2:714–719). The signing of this treaty by the Chinookan and Sahaptin groups occurred with very little opposition (French 1961:371–373).

Although the treaty was signed in 1855, these groups did not leave the protection of The Dalles until the Yakima War was in its final stages. The first group to move to the reservation was the Oregon Sahaptins in 1857. The Wascos did not relocate until 1858, allowing them the time to make sure that reservation conditions would be as the treaty had promised (French 1961:373).

To insure the success of the government's agricultural program, a second treaty was signed in 1865 and ratified in

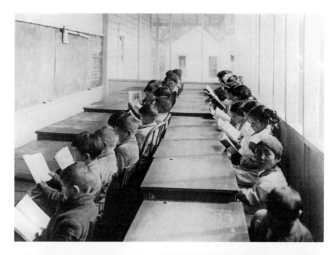

top, U. of Idaho Lib., Histl. Photograph Coll., Moscow: 5–13–7j; bottom, Idaho State Histl. Soc., Boise.
Fig. 5. Schools on the Nez Perce Res., Idaho. Run by both the Bureau of Indian Affairs and missionaries, schools greatly influenced reservation life. top, Primary school at the Ft. Lapwai Indian tuberculosis sanitorium. Photograph by John B. Wilson, about 1915. bottom, Elizabeth Wilson and playmates at the Lapwai government boarding school (Gay 1981:144–145). Photograph by E. Jane Gay, 1891.

1867. This treaty was to void all subsistence activities that would normally occur outside reservation boundaries (Kappler 1904–1941, 2:908–909). The apparent objective of this treaty was to restrict seasonal movements off the reservation thus altering aboriginal subsistence patterns, while at the same time encouraging agriculture (Lahren 1971:38).

During this early period, the reservation occupants were subjected to continual harassment by their aboriginal enemies, the Northern Paiutes. The effects of these raids were demoralizing to both the Indians and agency personnel. However, this threat was virtually eliminated as a result of the Bannock War during the late 1870s. Shortly thereafter, a group of Northern Paiutes was placed on the Warm Springs Reservation (Cliff 1942:51, 105).

The reservation was surveyed in 1871 and 1877, when a new boundary line on the west and north included an additional 61,360 acres. In 1972 the 61,360 acres were added to the Warm Springs Reservation. Another parcel was added in 1941 by the U.S. Court of Claims. Using the 1855 reservation as the land base, the addition of the 61,360 acres raised the total to 661,360 or 110 percent of the 1855 acreage as of

Fig. 6. Warm Springs Res., Oreg. top, View of the Agency. Photograph by Lee Moorhouse, 1901. bottom left, Tribal administrative building with a cast aluminum sculpture of a rootdigger by Richard Byer. Photograph by Cynthia D. Stowell, 1983. bottom right, Continuation of community native life on the reservation, shown in the "sorrow feast," or memorial ceremony at the end of a year's mourning. The longhouse had no roof at this time because it was under construction. Photograph by David and Kathrine French, at Hehe Butte, 1950.

1972. This reservation is one of the few in the Plateau that still has its original land base intact and does not suffer from the checkerboard effect. The homogeneous nature of this land base has allowed great success in reservation economic development (fig. 6).

• FLATHEAD RESERVATION On July 16, 1855, Isaac Stevens concluded a fifth treaty in the Bitterroot valley with the Flathead, Kootenai and (Upper) Pend d'Oreilles. Victor, of the Kalispel (Lower Pend d'Oreilles), did not attend this council. This treaty, which was to become known as the Hell Gate Treaty of 1855, was for cession of 12,806,000 acres and the creation of the Flathead Reservation (also referred to as the Jocko Reservation, named after a river in the Mission Valley).

From the beginning, this treaty was problematical for the groups involved. The first problem occurred in the translation of the treaty.

"Not a tenth" of the council "was actually understood by either party," due largely to incompetent interpreters. Not only were the words incompetently translated from Salish to English and from English to Salish, but the Salish mentality was completely missed. A particular element not grasped by the Whites was the limited extent of power accorded the political hierarchy of Flathead chiefs. To change the clan system with its individualistic chieftains and to defy ancient usages by placing arbitrarily all under one chief was to court trouble (Burns 1952:88).

But what about the Kootenai? Kootenai is a linguistic isolate and unrelated to the Salish. Stevens primarily used interpreters Gustav Sohon and Michael Revais, and Revais spoke some Kootenai. However, Johnson (1969:292–293) doubts that the Kootenai understood what was being said. These observations on treaty language translation can probably be generalized to some extent for all the Plateau treaties.

A second problem was created when Governor Stevens declared that these groups constituted a nation and that Victor, head chief of the Flatheads, be recognized as head chief of all the groups. Initially, Stevens wanted the reservation to be located in the upper Bitterroot valley. However, the Kalispel and Kootenai wanted the Flathead Lake area. Victor would not agree to leave the Bitterroot valley and made this known to Stevens (Bigart 1973:19). Thus, Stevens made another error by allowing Victor's group to stay in the Bitterroot valley. In Article 11 he stated that the Bitterroot valley should be surveyed and, if it proved to be better adapted for the Flathead, should be set aside for them (Kappler 1904–1941, 2:723–725). By being allowed to stay in the Bitterroot valley, Victor and his people wrongly assumed that it was set aside for them. President Ulysses Grant, by executive order in 1871, declared that it was not better suited for the Flathead and that they be removed to the Flathead Reservation (Kappler 1904–1941, 1:854–855).

In 1872 the Garfield Agreement was supposedly signed by Chief Arlee, Adolf, and Charlot, son of Victor. This agreement was for their removal from the Bitterroot valley to the Flathead Reservation. Arlee and Adolf did sign the agreement and moved to the reservation. Charlot never signed the agreement. His mark was forged, which caused extreme distrust toward the Whites. His group remained in the Bitterroot valley (Bigart 1973:21; Siefried 1968:155), and President Grover Cleveland signed into law an act of congress for Charlot's removal in 1889 (Kappler 1904–1941, 1:135–136). It was not until 1891 that his group finally moved to the reservation (Brown 1975:abstract).

Even though the reservation was established for the protection of and exclusive use by Indians, the Hell Gate Treaty contained language in Article 6 that contradicted this purpose. This article allowed the president to survey the reservation and allot specific tracts to individuals or families (Kappler 1904–1941, 2:724).

Survey of the reservation began in 1887 as a result of the passage of the Dawes Severalty Act. The survey was fraught with errors. The northern boundary was to be the midline of the lake. Since the shoreline is subject to seasonal changes, the surveyors erred, resulting in 4,000 acres being excluded. The southwest corner was to be the confluence of the Jocko and Bitterroot rivers. Somehow this was missed, and the boundary excluded another 12,000 acres. The survey was completed in 1892 and recorded as conforming to the treaty.

Bettmann Archives, N.Y.
Fig. 7. Celebration of the Confederated Salish and Kootenai Tribes of the Flathead Res. constitution. left to right, Chief Victor Vandenberg or Bear Track (Flathead); Chief Martin Charlo or Three Eagles (Flathead); unidentified man; Secretary of the Interior Harold Ickes; and Chief Kustada (Kootenai). They are looking at a war club. Photograph by an Acme newspaper photographer, Washington, D.C., 1935.

With the completion of this survey, the Flathead became eligible for allotment (Kickingbird and Ducheneaux 1973:93–94). On April 23, 1904, Congress passed into law the survey and allotment of the reservation and the sale of surplus land (33 Stats. L302, sections 2380–2381; Kickingbird and Ducheneaux 1973:96). On April 1, 1910, the Flathead, Coeur d'Alene, and Spokane reservations were opened for settlement. Shortly after the opening, President William Howard Taft signed into law a bill allowing Indians with allotments on the Flathead Reservation to sell 60 of their 80 acres. The land not claimed by this process was opened on November 1, 1910, to settlement under the homestead laws (Fahey 1974:301–307).

On October 4, 1935, the members of the Flathead Reservation voted for a constitution to become known as the Confederated Salish and Kootenai Tribes of the Flathead Reservation (fig. 7). It was reviewed by the secretary of interior and ratified by tribal members on April 25, 1936.

Since 1934, the Confederated Tribes have had a program to acquire tribal land. The original reservation was 1,242,696 acres. As of 1989, 611,352 acres are held in tribal trust and 43,835 acres are in individual Indian trust for a total of 655,187 acres. The tribe has the right of first option on these individual Indian trust lands. The tribe has 53 percent of the land that was set aside for them in the Hell Gate Treaty of 1855. Trust land is mostly forested with grazing land along the edges of the reservation. The interior of the reservation is farming land, and most of it is owned by non-Indians.

In a 1965 case, *Confederated Salish and Kootenai Tribes v. United States,* the court held that the government surveys were in error and that there were treaty lands outside the 1892 surveyed boundary. An analysis showed that 10,586 acres were eligible for inclusion with the reservation (Kickingbird and Ducheneaux 1973:99–102).

• KLAMATH RESERVATION   The final United States treaty in the Plateau was signed on October 14, 1864, with the Klamath, the Modoc, and the Yahooskin band of Northern Paiutes at Klamath Lake, Oregon. J.W. Perit Huntington, superintendent of Indian affairs in Oregon, and William Logan, Indian agent for Oregon, represented the government. The treaty ratified on July 2, 1866 (Kappler 1904–1941, 2:865–868), resulted in the cession of over 13 million acres and the creation of the Klamath Reservation. In 1869, the treaty was slightly modified, and it was ratified by Congress in 1870 (Stern 1965:42).

This treaty was not properly understood by the Indians. Charley Preston was the interpreter and used Chinook Jargon to translate English into Klamath. According to the Boundary Commission of 1896:

> The two Commissioners of the Government, with their assistants, proceeded into a country practically unknown to them to treat with an assemblage of Indians who were ignorant of the fundamental principles of the matter to be discussed, the Indian language having no words expressing the idea of direction, by equivalents of the points of the compass, or distance by measures of miles, yards, etc. To this day the older Indians can only designate direction by pointing, and distance by fractions of a day's travel; hence their topographical descriptions were very vague, unless confined to particular points. It is not surprising, therefore, that confusion should ensure when the agreement, reached after days of discussion, under such conditions was condensed into a few lines of our language (Stern 1965:41).

The original reservation consisted of 1,107,847 acres. During the allotment period, 246,911 acres were allotted and 860,936 were held in tribal trust. As the result of an act dated August 13, 1954, the Klamath Reservation initiated the process of termination and began having all federal trust controls removed. In 1958 all federal restrictions were removed from Indian-owned allotments. On August 1, 1961, the trust responsibility of the federal government was ended (Bureau of Indian Affairs 1960:26–27). Some 474 Klamaths continued to hold on to tribal status of 145,000 acres after termination; in 1974 they sold the remaining reservation (Cowger 1994).

Executive Order Reservations

A second type of Plateau reservation was created by presidential executive order. These orders did not contain any of the language found in the treaty reservations. They were short statements simply setting aside a specific tract of land for a specific group. The fiat nature of executive order reservations resulted in a major restructuring of the Colville Reservation and eventually led to the Wallowa Valley and Moses reservations being revoked.

• COLVILLE RESERVATION   The Colville Reservation was established by executive order on April 9, 1872, for the Methow, Okanagan, Sanpoil, Nespelem, Lakes, Colville,

Fig. 8. Colville Indian Agent R.D. Gwydir and some of his charges. left to right, back row: Robert Flett, Agency interpreter; R.D. Gwydir, Colville Indian Agent 1887–1889; James Gibson, Agency clerk. middle row: Billy Mason, Spokane; Seltice, chief of the Coeur d'Alene; Spokane Garry, Chief of Upper Spokane; nephew of Seltice; bottom row, Nellie, daughter of Chief Garry; child; unidentified Coeur d'Alene; and Pier Bartholemew. Photographed 1887–1889.

Kalispel, Spokane, Coeur d'Alene, and the scattered bands of the Chelan, Entiat, and Southern Okanogan. The Palouse, Moses, and Wenatchee are also recognized on the contemporary reservation. Three months later, a second executive order was issued countermanding the first; this order was to return to public domain certain areas set forth by the earlier order (Kappler 1904–1941, 1:915–916). There was considerable confusion associated with this change in orders. The second order was issued at the request of William P. Winans, then in charge of the Colville Reservation, who wanted the reservation land to include "the cold, dry highlands west of that [Columbia] river, where white men have abandoned the country after trial, and failed to farm owing to frosts and other difficulties in the way" (J.A. Ross 1968:40–61). This deception increased tensions between the cultural groups involved because, since the boundaries of their territories were not recognized, intrusive groups were placed within these boundaries. For example, the Chelan, Entiat, and Methow were the intrusive elements placed on the home territory of the Southern Okanogan, Lakes, and Sanpoil, which at that time included the total reservation.

In response to the conflict, additional executive orders were initiated in April 1879 and March 1880. These became known as the Moses Agreement and established the Columbia Reservation. The existence of these orders, although also short lived, produced similar devastating effects on intergroup relations. As a result of these orders, Chief Moses in 1883 signed an agreement to the effect that each family head may be assigned allotments of 640 acres on this reservation or they may elect to move onto the Colville Reservation. The Moses Reservation was returned to public domain by executive order in 1886. Another historical

Wash. State U. Lib., Histl. Photograph Coll., Pullman: top, 92–037; center 91–084; bottom, 92–033.
Fig. 9. Economic life on the Colville Res., Wash. top, Jon Moses helping to stack hay. center, Stimatwua hauling logs, Nespelem Agency. bottom, Building or maintaining a road in the Nespelem district to Owhi Lake. Photographs by Frank Avery, 1914.

development that produced additional tribal conflict was the introduction of an aboriginal enemy onto the reservation. In 1885 Chief Joseph's band of Nez Perce was placed on the reservation (J.A. Ross 1968:62).

In July 1892, the north half of the reservation was purchased by the United States government, and it was restored to public domain by an act of Congress. This caused additional resentment by the Colvilles who felt that the Moses-Columbia and Nez Perce had sold the land (J.A. Ross 1968; Schultz 1971).

The intergroup conflict on the Colville Reservation is a result of effects produced by executive order after an official treaty. The executive order in the Colville area tried to shift aboriginal groups within their home territory, which only resulted in causing the intergroup conflict.

The July 2, 1872, reservation consisted of approximately 2,825,000 acres. In 1906 the remaining south half, consisting of 1,449,268 acres, was allotted, and it was opened for homestead entry in 1916. Undisposed lands were withdrawn from any further disposition in 1934 and 1939. These lands remained in limbo until an act in 1956 restored 818,000 acres to tribal ownership (table 1). The groups were organized under the Indian Reorganization Act in 1938.

• COEUR D'ALENE RESERVATION   An attempt to establish a reservation for the Coeur d'Alene was initiated in 1867 when an executive order was issued for 250,000 acres. This offer was rejected by the Indians because it did not include Coeur d'Alene Lake. In 1873, an agreement was reached to establish a 598,000-acre reservation; however, this agreement was not ratified by Congress. With reference to this agreement, a second executive order was issued in 1873 that created the 598,000-acre Coeur d'Alene Reservation and resulted in the cession of 4,000,000 acres (Kappler 1904–1941, 1:835–837). The Coeur d'Alene did not accept this executive order because they wanted the reservation to be ratified by Congress so that it would have the effect of a treaty.

A second agreement reached in 1887 reaffirmed their cession of land and secured congressional approval. This agreement also allowed the nontreaty Spokane and Kalispel to settle on their reservation. However, due to political pressure from the non-Indians, the agreement was never ratified.

Another agreement was established with the Coeur d'Alene in 1889. In this agreement the tribe was to cede an additional 100,000 acres in the northeast or Wolf Creek area of the reservation. However, instead of the 100,000 acres, they in fact ceded 185,000 acres, which included most of Coeur d'Alene Lake. This reduced the executive order reservation by 31 percent (Lahren 1989; Kappler 1904–1941, 1:419–424). Within a few years, 145 Spokanes and some Kalispels from Clark Fork and Cusick moved onto the reservation (Lahren 1989; Coeur d'Alene Tribe 1989).

In 1906 Congress passed an act to allot the reservation, which was done in 1909. A total of 104,075 acres was allotted to 638 Indians. The remainder was opened for homesteads, a total of 219,767 acres. Indians began selling their allotments in 1910, and by 1967, approximately one-third (268) of the allotments had been sold. Allotments sold totaled 23,977 acres. The Coeur d'Alenes retained 67,275 acres (table 1). This reservation also suffers from the

493

checkerboard effect. In a land reacquisition program, the Indians have acquired 1,830 acres since 1974.

• SPOKANE RESERVATION   Aboriginally, the Spokane occupied about 3,000,000 acres in northeast Washington. The Spokane Reservation was created by executive order in 1881 (Kappler 1904–1941, 1:924–925) and ratified in 1892. Originally it consisted of 154,602 acres. A joint resolution of Congress was passed in 1902 to allot the reservation. The secretary of the interior was authorized to sell unallotted surplus lands in 1908, and it was opened for homestead entry in 1909. The Upper and Middle Spokane signed an agreement in 1887, ratified in 1892, to be removed to the Coeur d'Alene Reservation (Kappler 1904–1941, 1:449, 453–454). In 1958, 2,752 acres were restored to the reservation by an act of Congress.

• KALISPEL RESERVATION   Since 1855 the Lower Kalispels remained in their aboriginal territory and opposed any attempt to remove them. United States government officials tried for about 50 years to move them to the Colville, Coeur d'Alene, or Flathead reservations. Some Kalispels eventually moved to the Flathead Reservation, but a small group would not leave and stayed in the river valley near Cusick and Usk, Washington. President Woodrow Wilson issued an executive order in 1914 that created a 4,600-acre reservation for this group of Kalispels in their aboriginal territory (Kalispel Tribe 1980). The entire reservation was allotted in 1924, but the allotments were only 40 acres, in contrast to 160-acre allotments on other reservations. Sixty acres are held in tribal trust and only one 40-acre allotment has been lost to non-Indian ownership (Lahren 1989).

• KOOTENAI RESERVATION   The Kootenai Reservation is not an actual reservation, even though it is referred to as such. An act dated February 8, 1887, simply allotted to the Kootenai the land on which they were living. In 1960 the Bureau of Indian Affairs showed 3,986 acres, which consisted of 58 of the original 70 allotments. In 1989, 2,076 acres were in trust, 2,054 allotted, and 22 acres in tribal land.

• GRAND RONDE RESERVATION   The tribes on the Grand Ronde Reservation are mostly from the Northwest Coast culture area (vol. 7:182–188) but also include the Molala, one of the five Confederated Tribes of the Grand Ronde (Umpqua, Molalla, Rogue River, Kalapuya, Chasta). Established in 1857 by executive order in the Willamette Valley of northwestern Oregon, in 1901 the reservation was reduced from its original 59,000 to about 33,000 acres; the remaining land was declared "surplus" and sold to outsiders. The Confederated Tribes and the reservation were terminated in 1954 and restored in 1983 (Grand Ronde Restoration Act, 97 U.S. Stat. 1064). In 1988 Congress transferred some 9,800 acres of mostly Bureau of Land Management timber land to the Confederated Tribes for the establishment of the Grand Ronde Reservation. Timber sales have provided funds for social and development projects and the purchase of an additional 100 acres for the construction of a tribal headquarters (Tiller 1996:542–543; The Confederated Tribes of the Grand Ronde Community of Oregon 1987).

Canadian Reserves

The reserves in Canada were allocated in a partitive fashion. The Kootenai, Shuswap, Okanagan, Nicola, Thompson, and Lillooet bands were given multiple reserves that varied in size from as little as one-half acre to as much as 33,000 acres. These reserves were scattered throughout each group's aboriginal territory (fig. 1, table 2). None of the reserves was established by treaty.

The Department of Indian and Northern Affairs distinguishes four stages of Indian-government relationship. From early settlement to the Royal Proclamation of 1763 the relationship was characterized by partnership based on trade and military alliance. Partnership gave way to a policy of extinguishing Indians' occupation in advance of settlement, from 1763 to 1923. Indians, although given special protection, were relegated to the margins of Canadian society. Next, with the signing of treaties and the first Indian Act the relationship became one of imposed wardship (through the reserve system) as the government sought to assimilate Indians ("emancipation") into Canadian society. This situation covered the years 1868–1969. Indian rejection of the assimilation-oriented 1969 "White Paper" marked the end of wardship. Since 1969 the relationship has been characterized by movement toward self-sufficiency based on Indian rights and status (Department of Indian and Northern Affairs 1989).

Kootenai, Shuswap, Okanagan, Nicola, Thompson, and Lillooet consist of 53 different bands and have a total of 407 reserves (table 2). These reserves vary in size from one-half acre to 33,000 acres.

British Columbia Reserves, 1850–1871

The first reserves in colonial British Columbia were established under the direction of Gov. James Douglas in the 1850s. He took the British position that the Indians had proprietary rights to the land and these rights should be extinguished by treaty and compensation. His liberal land policy allowed Indians to select all the land they wanted (Duff 1969:61). He instructed his land commissioner in 1861 to "take measures ... for making out distinctly the Indian Reserves throughout the Colony. ... [and that] the extent of the Indian Reserves to be defined ... as they may be ... pointed out by the natives themselves" (Union of British Columbia Indian Chiefs 1974:4–5). These first reserves were located in the Shuswap Lakes area, Okanagan, Nicola Valley, Kamloops, Fraser Canyon, Fraser Valley and on southern Vancouver Island. It is due to this last statement of his policy that the reserves were established in a partitive fashion.

A major problem with these early reserves was that they were determined by the seasonal location of the groups at the particular time of the year that they were contacted by the land commissioner. If they were not using a particular area at the time the commissioner contacted them, then it was not included as a reserve location. This process did not account for land used during their entire annual cycle (Lahren 1990).

The reserve policy of Commissioner of Lands and Works Joseph Trutch was exactly the opposite of Douglas. He reduced certain reserves, was against the establishment of new reserves, and did not consider aboriginal title to be a valid claim.

> An example of Trutch's policy of reduction can be seen along the Thompson River. The Indians of Kamloops, Neskainlith and Shuswap Lake originally held a reserve along the north bank of the South Thompson River from Kamloops to Shuswap Lake. This included Little Shuswap Lake and areas around Adams Lake. In 1866 these reserves were "adjusted" by Trutch by reducing them to approximately their present size.
>
> This policy was extended to the Fraser Valley in 1867. It is difficult to get precise information on the location and size of these reductions, but it is clear that the present reserves in the Fraser Valley are only remnants of the original reserves (Union of British Columbia Indian Chiefs 1974:5).

Indian Reserve Commission, 1876–1910

In 1871 Canada changed the colony status of British Columbia to that of a province. Prime Minister John A. Macdonald, Gov. Anthony Musgrave, and Trutch were instrumental in this status change and would not treat with the Indians during this transition. Once British Columbia received provincial status, all land and resources not held in trust as Indian reserves were renamed provincial "crown lands" and were opened to non-Indian settlement. The Indians were expropriated from their lands without a treaty, which they contended was a direct violation of the Royal Proclamation of 1763 (Lahren 1990).

The federal government also assumed administrative responsibility for the Indians and their lands in 1871. Article 13 of the Terms of the Union stated:

> The charge of the Indians and the trusteeship and management of the land reserved for their use and benefit shall be assumed by the Dominion Government, and a policy as liberal as that hitherto pursued by the British Columbia Government shall be continued by the Dominion Government after the Union.
>
> To carry out such policy, tracts of land of such extent as it has hitherto been the practice of the British Columbia Government to appropriate for that purpose, shall from time to time be conveyed by local Government to the Dominion Government in trust for the use and benefit of the Indians, on application of the Dominion Government; and in case of disagreement between the two Governments respecting the quantity of such tracts of land to be so granted, the matter shall be referred for the decision of the Secretary of the State for the Colonies (Department of Indian Affairs 1924:7).

These terms pitted the provincial government against the federal government for the next 40 years. It was not in the interest of the provincial government to allow the allotment of additional Indian reserves or to recognize aboriginal title.

Prov. Arch. of B.C., Victoria: A–01772.
Fig. 10. Camp of the Joint Commission for the Settlement of Indian Reserves in the Province of B.C., at Spuzzum, enroute from Yale to Kamloops. This was the first series of meetings with the native peoples to discuss the land issue. left to right: Edward Mohun, surveyor, standing with the mules; Gilbert M. Sproat (one of 3 commissioners) standing just to the left of the flagpole with his hands behind his back; Commissioner Archibald MacKinlay to right of flagpole; George Blenkinsop, interpreter, standing right of MacKinlay; Chief Mischelle of Lytton, Thompson, wearing a suit and hat, in front of the small tent. Photograph by Richard Maynard, June 1877.

Initially, the federal government wanted to allot 80 acres per family while the provincial administration proposed that 20 acres per head of a family of five persons was sufficient (Department of Indian Affairs 1924:7).

This controversy continued until the provincial government and federal government entered into the Agreement of 1875–1876, which created the Joint Commission for the Settlement of Indian Reserves in the Province of British Columbia. The purpose of the commission was to allot and survey Indian reserves (fig. 10). There were two important conditions of this agreement, which caused further discord between the two governments. First was that in the event there was an increase or decrease in the population of a nation the reserve was to be increased or decreased in size. The second point was that any additional lands due to population increase were to come from Crown lands and that any excess land due to population loss was to revert to the province (Department of Indian Affairs 1924:7–8). The problem with allocating additional land was the provision that it be derived from available Crown lands. For example, if Crown land in a particular Indian group's aboriginal territory had passed to non-Indian title, then the additional acreage needed to adjust the reserve size due to a population increase might be allotted anywhere. Such noncontiguous allotments would represent an obstacle to a reserve management policy that fostered economic development and self-sufficiency.

The seeds for additional discord were sown when the provincial government assumed this reversionary interest. The federal government could not dispose of any reserve land without provincial government agreement.

Table 2. Plateau Reserves in British Columbia, 1987

Band and No.	Number of Reserves	Range of Acreage	Total Acreage	Total Members	On Reserve
Kootenai					
Columbia Lake 604	1		8,405	149	69
Lower Kootenay 606	8	100–1,803	6,037	105	88
St. Mary's 602	4	153–17,400	18,424	168	112
Tobacco Plains 603	1		10,570	93	79
	14		43,436	515	348
Shuswap					
Adams Lake 684	7	25–3,540	7,130	414	291
Alakali Lake 711	19	7–1,400	9,786	428	327
Bonaparte 686	6	78–2,064	4,553	423	176
Canim Lake 713	6	26–4,400	5,089	376	306
Canoe Creek 723	12	20–6,931	13,794	332	156
Clinton 702	3	3–1,223	1,397	52	42
Skeetchestn 687 (Deadman's Creek)	1		19,541	269	119
High Bar 703	3	123–2,924	3,722	9	0
Kamloops 688	5	7–32,492	32,740	507	321
Little Shuswap 689	5	60–4,265	7,747	195	136
Neskainlith 690	3	1,287–3,164	6,886	354	188
North Thompson 691	5	3–692	3,760	365	169
Shuswap 605	1		2,733	164	109
Soda Creek 716	2	1,065–4,106	5,171	177	103
Spallumcheen 600	3	195–5,602	9,650	402	244
Williams Lake 719	8	6–4,066	4,762	275	172
	89		138,461	5,072	2,859
Okanagan					
Lower Similkameen 598	9	10–16,724	37,748	237	158
Okanagan 616	5	83–25,456	26,201	960	581
Osoyoos 596	2	160–32,092	32,252	199	151
Penticton 597	2	360–33,587	33,947	445	268
Upper Similkameen 599	7	8–5,365	6,431	34	28
Westbank 601	3	5–1,583	2,395	262	203
	28		138,974	2,137	1,389
Nicola					
Coldwater 693	3	43–4,538	6,175	359	230
Lower Nicola 695	9	45–11,334	17,535	462	283
Nooaitch 699	2	1,953–2,231	4,184	112	62
Shackan 698	3	730–6,413	9,572	92	40
Upper Nicola 697	8	15–23,047	30,895	497	330
	25		68,361	1,522	945

Table 2. Plateau Reserves in British Columbia, 1987 (Continued)

Band and No.	Number of Reserves	Range of Acreage	Total Acreage	Total Members	On Reserve
Thompson					
Ashcroft 685	4	334–3,427	4,988	99	39
Boothroyd 670	19	9–413	2,775	177	71
Boston Bar 701	12	1–418	1,504	108	70
Cook's Ferry 694	24	10–4,378	10,028	179	67
Kanaka Bar 704	6	10–240	565	81	19
Lytton 705	54	3–3,839	14,778	1,125	715
Nicomen 696	16	1.5–1,520	2,905	68	33
Oregon Jack Creek 692	6	30–1,018	2,033	29	11
Siska 706	11	.5–273	790	118	32
Skuppa 707	8	20–150	522	32	17
Spuzzum 708	16	.7–313	1,572	55	16
	176		42,460	2,071	1,090
Lillooet					
Anderson Lake 556	6	18–1,469	1,987	144	77
Bridge River 590	2	140–9,597	9,737	211	117
Cayoose Creek 591	3	648–785	1,698	113	82
Douglas 561	3	.7–1,030	1,068	144	38
Fountain 592	17	11–1,082	3,885	577	351
Lillooet 593	6	3–901	1,731	143	90
Mount Currie 557	10	2–4,000	7,238	1,200	831
Pavilion 594	7	40–2,180	5,218	269	213
Samahquam 567	5	15–249	451	157	0
Seton Lake 595	6	80–1,706	4,453	415	307
Skookum Chuck 562	10	30–526	1,670	244	24
	75		39,136	3,617	2,130
Total	407		470,828	14,934	8,761

By disagreeing on the size and location of reserves and claiming a reversionary interest, the provincial government effectively nullified the work of the Joint Commission. By 1911, with both governments dissatisfied, the Indian land question was at an impasse (Department of Indian Affairs 1924:8).

McKenna-McBride Commission, 1912–1916

As a result of this conflict over Indian lands, the McKenna-McBride agreement was reached between the two governments in 1912. Richard McBride was the premier of British Columbia and J.A.J. McKenna was special commissioner appointed by the federal government to lead the negotiations in this land controversy. This Commission conducted meetings with all interested parties during the years 1913–1916 (fig. 11). After this review, the Com-mission report confirmed most of the existing reserves, recommended that approximately 87,000 acres of new reserve land be set aside and that 47,000 acres be "cut off" of 54 existing reserves (Duff 1969:68). Neither of the two governments was satisfied with the report.

The job of reconciliation fell to W.E. Ditchburn, Department of Indian Affairs, and J.W. Clark, who represented the

Royal B.C. Mus., Victoria: PN 12562.
Fig. 11. One of the Shuswap land holdings, Soda Creek Res., B.C., at the Williams Lake Agency, consisting of 1,063.77 acres. Photograph by a member of the McKenna-McBride Royal Commission, 1914.

provincial government. These men made considerable alterations to the McKenna-McBride report and finally settled on 35 reserve "cut offs" totaling 36,000 acres (Union of British Columbia Indian Chiefs 1974:18). A majority of the agencies made slight gains, but the Kootenai and Williams Lake Shuswap people lost over 6,000 and 5,000 acres respectively, and 14 cut-offs totaling 8,200 acres were saved by not allowing cut-offs in the Railway Belt (Borthwick 1975:12–13). The Ditchburn-Clark report was accepted by the two governments in 1924. This agreement gave absolute title of the reserves to the federal government and eliminated the reversionary interest of the province (Department of Indian Affairs 1924:8). It took until the 1950s to fully implement the terms of the McKenna-McBride agreement (Borthwick 1975:14).

Move Toward Self-Sufficiency

In 1968–1969, the federal government proposed the White Paper that would repeal the Indian Act, end federal responsibility for Indians, and terminate their special status (vol. 4:281–282). It was so overwhelmingly rejected by the Indian people that it was withdrawn by the government in 1969. Its introduction and subsequent withdrawal stimulated Indian nationalism in Canada. This spirit of nationalism, coupled with the federal government's policy of reestablishing Indian control over their own affairs during the 1970s and early 1980s, led to a new era in Canadian Indian-White relationships. The Department of Indian and Northern Affairs embarked on a policy of federal administrative devolution to the Indians. In 1881 the first Indian agencies were established in British Columbia, and in 1969 all Indian agents were withdrawn from Canadian reserves. This involved the transfer of their services and program administration to the Indian councils. It was during this period that the Indians began to develop an interest in economic development. In 1989 two-thirds of the budget for Indian programs of the Department of Indian Affairs and Northern Development was administered by Indians (Department of Indian and Northern Affairs 1989).

Land Claims

During this period of devolution, native land claims in Canada became an active issue. The government recognized its responsibility to the Indians and Inuit for land losses and began to review claims and negotiate settlements. Historically, the aboriginal title and treaty issue in this area is centered on the Royal Proclamation of 1763, a peace accord established by the British. It stated:

... that the several Nations or Tribes with whom we are connected, and who live under our Protection should not be molested or disturbed in the possession of such parts of our Dominions and Territories as, not having been ceded to or purchased by us, are reserved to them or any of them as their hunting grounds. ... that no Governor or Commander in Chief in any of our Colonies ... grant Warrants or Survey or pass any Patents for Lands ... which not having been ceded to or purchased by Us, are reserved to the said Indians or any of them.

And We do further strictly enjoin and require that all persons whatever who have either willfully or inadvertently seated themselves upon any lands ... not having been ceded to or purchased by Us, are still reserved to the said Indians as aforesaid, forthwith to remove themselves from such settlements (Drake-Terry 1989:325–326).

These statements clearly point out that the Indians were given exclusive title to the land and its use and that no land could be acquired from them without their permission and cession to the Crown. All the groups in the Plateau area of British Columbia cite this Proclamation as the legal basis for their native land claim cases (Lahren 1990).

There are two types of land claims in Canada. "Comprehensive claims" also referred to as "modern-day treaties" are claims that have to do with aboriginal title and are predicated on traditional use and occupancy. "Specific claims" are based on lawful obligations that were not met by the government. In 1997 there were 22 comprehensive land claims in British Columbia, involving Shuswap, Thompson, and Kootenai.

Population Changes

The registered Indian population in Canada increased from 224,164 in 1966 to 443,884 in 1988. The enactment of Bill C–31 to amend the Indian Act had an impact on these population figures. Since 1985, 52,000 people have had their status restored by Bill C–31. Even without the C–31 influence the natural growth rate was 3.4 times higher than the general population. The off-reserve population grew significantly between 1986 and 1988, primarily a result of C–31. Registered Indians in British Columbia accounted for approximately 17 percent of the 1988 population. Of the 77,153 Indians in British Columbia, 14,934 or 20 percent were registered on reserves in the Plateau (Department of Indian and Northern Affairs 1989, 1989a:4, 9) (table 2).

Even though Bill C–31 was welcomed by the Indians in general, certain individuals have expressed an important apprehension. Their concern is that increased population numbers will have a negative impact on the limited resource base of the existing reserves. They suggest that the government provide the additional resources in terms of money and land to support these new band members (Lahren 1990).

Religious Movements

DEWARD E. WALKER, JR. AND HELEN H. SCHUSTER

Dreams, visions, and associated tutelary spirit beliefs are probably the most ancient and fundamental forms of religious belief and practice in the Plateau. The vision quest, "medicine sings" or "winter spirit dances," and sweatlodge appear to form a foundation for all other traditional belief and practice throughout the region. Before participation in any activity associated with the spiritual world, people cleansed themselves in the sweatlodge, a structure used to achieve purity of body, mind, and spirit ("Yakima and Neighboring Groups," fig. 5, this vol.) (Walker 1965). Vision quest sites are scattered throughout the Plateau, especially concentrated in mountains and along rivers where stone cairns, pictographs, and petroglyphs often mark places where tutelary spirits have been encountered. Tutelary spirit power is often accompanied by a spirit sickness; trusted medicine doctors (Sahaptin *twáti*; Nez Perce *tiwét* (if a man), *tiwataʔát* (if a woman) assist in dealing with it by instructing the neophyte in proper ways to honor and employ the power they have acquired in vision quests, trance states, or other experiences.

Midwinter ceremonies provided opportunities for not only neophytes but all persons with spirit power to dramatize and honor their power through the characteristic songs and dances they received from their tutelary spirits. Although any person could attend, only those with spirit power would participate in the dances, while others in attendance cooked, served, and lent support in various tasks. Curing supernaturally caused illnesses of various types customarily took place in these ceremonies. Medicine doctors officiated during both life cycle and other calendrical ceremonies associated with the changing seasons and subsistence activities, especially with fishing, hunting, and gathering of roots and berries.

Because medicine doctors had the potential both to help or to harm, a great deal of emotional ambivalence surrounded them. The very powers that made a medicine doctor successful as a healer were also a source of potential harm. If a patient died and the medicine doctor was judged to be evil or inept in curing, he or she could be killed. In addition to curing, some healers were thought to be able to change the weather, foresee the future, impart unusual powers to inanimate objects, and possess other miraculous abilities. In addition to spirit sickness, other kinds of supernatural agents or events could cause illness such as breaking a taboo, a moral transgression, loss of the soul or spirit power, or the practice of malevolent magic. Such shamanic practices continued in the 1990s (Walker 1989; Schuster 1975).

Protohistoric Developments: The Prophet Dance

Most historians have assumed that the visits of early explorers such as Meriwether Lewis and William Clark in 1805–1806 marked the beginning of Plateau acculturation (Haines 1955; Josephy 1965), but this assumption is open to question (Spier 1935). The so-called Prophet Dance is significant in this regard, because it has been linked to later cult developments such as the Ghost Dance, the Dreamers, the Washat or Seven Drum religion, 'the ʔipnúʿcililpt cult;' the Indian Shakers; 'the Feather cult;' and by some, with certain forms of Christianity. Certain of these religous practices continued to dominate religious belief and practice in the Plateau in the 1990s. The Prophet Dance has been linked with protohistoric events in the Plateau such as epidemic disease, trade, the impact of the horse, the introduction of Christianity and other nonindigenous beliefs and practices, and the presence of various prophets seen by early explorers. Prophetic figures appeared among at least the following groups: Nez Perce, Umatilla, Spokane, Kootenai, Wanapam, Yakima, Klikitat, Wayampam (*sḱin* village), Palouse, Sanpoil-Nespelem, and probably certain Chinookan groups on the Lower Columbia. Figures such as Shuwapsa, Dla-upac, Spokane Garry, Kootenai Pelly, Nez Perce Ellis, Skolaskin, Wiletsi, Hununwe (a woman), Jim Kanine, Shramaia, Lishwailait, Ashnithlai, the Tenino Queahpahmah, Luls, the Wanapam Sahaptin Smohalla (*šmúxala*), Wiskaynatowatsanmay (a Nez Perce woman), and the Yakima Kotiahkan (Shawaway Kotiahkan) are relatively late examples of an established prophetic tradition dating from the protohistoric period (Du Bois 1938; Walker 1969, 1985).

An increasing body of evidence points to this as a time when the cultic innovations described by Spier (1935) were already underway. This is supported by: the diversity of cults and prophetic figures apparent in the Plateau at the time of contact, the archeological evidence from altered burial practices, increasing non-Indian trade goods in the region, the extinction or catastrophic reduction of various groups through epidemic disease, and oral tradition among contemporary Plateau religious leaders. The two centuries before contact and the growing intensity of contacts in the nineteenth century were probably revolutionary periods (Miller 1985; Walker 1969).

The prophet cult typically involved a dance, usually circular, and an inspired leader who made prophecies obtained in visions usually experienced during "death-like trance states" (Nez Perce *tó·ʔyaqin*), followed by a reawakening or "rebirth." The ceremonial was participated in by whole settlements, and great emphasis was placed on a creator spirit or god who reigned above the other spirits. In some cases confession of sins was emphasized, and a world-renewal message or prophecy was a virtually universal feature of the cult. Ceremonies usually were directed toward hastening the happy day. Cult activity was periodic and cyclic. Predictions would be made, an emotional heat generated, and with the failure of prophecy, interest would wane only to be regenerated at some later date (Spier 1935). The proposal that these developments were due to influences of the Iroquois who settled among the Flathead in Montana is not supported by the available evidence. The Iroquois seem to have arrived in 1820, too late to account for these events (Ruby and Brown 1989:8).

Aside from being acknowledged as a possibility by some (Du Bois 1938), and as fact by others (Ray 1936a; Herskovits 1938), Spier's hypothetical Prophet Dance received little attention until Strong (1945:254–60) hypothesized a "Ghost Cult" for the Lower Columbia River region, based on a unique artistic motif that Strong perceived as fairly recent. This exposed "herring bone" rib cage motif has since been shown to be of much older origin, depicting the shamanic trance experience, probably derived from Northeast Asia and found prehistorically at numerous New World sites.

Suttles (1957) accepted Spier's thesis concerning the aboriginal origin of the Prophet Dance and undertook a description of its diffusionary pathways among Coast Salish of the Northwest Coast. He concluded that although population decimation and the fur trade could have had something to do with outbursts of Prophet Dance activity, its "periodic reappearance" probably was related more to the poverty of political institutions among the Coast Salish. Because of their unusual, charismatic power, prophets associated with the Prophet Dance could restore order. Thus he concluded that it spread in this region because it solved problems endemic to the inadequacy of Coast Salish social structure (Suttles 1957:392–393).

Aberle (1959) maintained that the evidence is insufficient to determine whether the hypothesized Prophet Dance developed as a traditional feature of Plateau culture or in response to conditions of contact. Indirect contact with Euro-American culture could have produced several types of deprivation known to have caused movements resembling the Prophet Dance in many other parts of the world.

By employing ethnographic, ethnohistoric, and archeological research, it is possible to show that population decimation probably brought about cult activity on the Northwest Coast as well as in the Plateau and that the Nez Perce

(and probably the rest of the Plateau groups) and Northwest Coast groups were sharply affected by White influence before 1800. For example, a Cathlamet text contains a statement to the effect that the informant's grandfather had died during a smallpox epidemic, visited the afterworld, and then returned to life bringing messages, all in good Prophet Dance fashion (Boas 1901:247–251). Although the Prophet Dance custom of dying and reviving in situations of great stress is common in the Plateau and Northwest Coast generally, it is nowhere more prevalent than among the Sahaptians, where it has been explicitly related to population decimation. According to one informant:

> There was an epidemic of smallpox among the Yakima and people were dying and leaving the country. One old man, a chief, took sick and was left behind. He died. In his dream he travelled and came to a place where people were gathered eating lots of good things. He was awfully hungry. He came to a kind of gateway and asked for food. The people turned him away and told him it wasn't time for him to come in yet. So they directed him to another place a long way off. He travelled and finally he reached there. They told him when he asked for food that they didn't eat there. They looked thin and raw boned and didn't say much. They said, "We are people called angels." They told him to go back where he came from. "We can't take you in," they said. He felt bad and went back. When he came to his place he came to life again. But his people thought he was dead. He followed them. He surprised them. The first place he went to was Hell. The second place was Heaven (Spier 1935:17).

Another important bit of information suggesting a connection between epidemics and Prophet Dance activity is a Nez Perce tradition that the first knowledge of White men came from the prophecy of an old man who said they would come as a disease (Walker 1963–1964).

The Nez Perces had been visited at least a quarter century earlier by smallpox, an indirect White influence of substantial impact. Mooney's (1928) estimate of a one-third population reduction could be an exaggeration, but his estimates are largely borne out by the census conducted by Asa Smith, who talked with Nez Perce survivors of these 1820–1880 epidemics (Drury 1958:136–137). Epidemics were also felt keenly along the Columbia River valley, a main arterial for indigenous travel, exploration, and a fur trade route. Lewis and Clark observed that smallpox had made its appearance at The Dalles probably "about thirty years before" their arrival, about 1775 (Gibbs 1855:408). It was probably carried by buffalo hunters returning from the Plains (Walker 1970:157–158). Epidemics around 1800 and 1825 may have been smallpox (Teit 1928:97). Between 1829 and 1832, additional epidemics, probably of malaria, spread to the interior from the Lower Columbia (Anastasio 1972:203; Teit 1928:97; Strong 1961:97–99). In 1843, 1846, and 1852–1853, smallpox broke out again and "spread with great virulence" (Gibbs 1855:408; Smith 1953). The Yakima and Klikitat "suffered severely from smallpox," and the whole course of the Yakima is lined with the vestiges of former villages now vacant" (Gibbs

1855:408). For Kittitas and Yakima bands, with a population of 7,000 before 1805, only 2,000 survived in 1853 (Anastasio 1955:107). The Wishram were hit severely too, reduced to around 270 in 1854, having lost 257 persons to smallpox in 1853 (Gibbs 1855:418).

Plateau culture was changed dramatically by acquisition of the horse in the 1730s (Haines 1938). Horse culture brought an increased emphasis on warfare and exploitation of the buffalo. It is also clear that the Plateau tribes had been in possession of Euro-American trade goods for some time before their visit. For example, during their passage through Nez Perce territory and at The Dalles, Lewis and Clark noted the presence of rifles, Spanish coins, knives, kettles, and machine-woven cloth (Gass 1904:169, 240; Thwaites 1904–1905, 3:81, 5:23). While the horse primarily was responsible for the great increase and proliferation of new elements of material culture after 1730, Euro-American-induced cultural changes in the Plateau may have been underway by as early as 1600 (Nelson 1969).

Work on Plateau burial patterns contains evidence that the protohistoric was a time of great cultural change (Sprague 1967). Eastern Plateau burial patterns were very stable for the 1,400-year period preceding the beginning of the protohistoric, at about the time of the introduction of the horse. This relatively old, stable pattern consists of the following elements: flexed inhumations; scant grave goods, mostly attached to the corpse and not distributed throughout the grave indiscriminately; single burials in a graveyard area; no skewed distribution in old, middle-aged, or infant burials; relatively shallow graves; relatively few cairns. Usually the corpse is laid on its side. In the succeeding century and extending to about 1800, a number of pronounced changes in the pattern become apparent. They are: an increase in the number of cairns; the appearance of cedar-sided, cist burials; increased number of grave goods, some obviously thrown in; an increase in the number of talus slope burials; and a marked overall increase in pattern variability with respect to features such as type of burial, position of the corpse, and funerary ceremonies (e.g., burning of the grave goods, cremation, or absence of these).

The historic period, beginning about 1800, witnessed yet more rapid changes and is marked by the appearance of glass beads, iron goods, brass goods, woven textiles, pottery, glass, and other Euro-American manufactures. Interestingly, the historic is also marked by a reappearance of pattern stability with respect to orientation of the corpse. It is regularly extended on the back and in the majority of cases with the head oriented east or west, with east predominating. The only element in the pattern subject to much variation in this period is the direction of orientation. Apparently within very short periods, the prevailing direction would be reversed, but was, nevertheless, in the majority of instances either east or west. This, of course, is the orientation witnessed by Lewis and Clark on the Lower Columbia (Coues 1893, 2:666–697).

Although it seems plausible that protohistoric cult movements in the Plateau were related to deprivation resulting from epidemic disease, research has largely ignored yet another possible contributing factor. Protohistoric cult developments also may have contained an emphasis on acquisition of Euro-American material culture (Walker 1969). The increased awareness of technology brought by the horse and the expanded scope of Plateau peoples' universe were evident in their reactions to the first recorded Whites to arrive in their territory. Lewis and Clark were inundated with requests for demonstrations of their various devices and particularly for medicine. Among the Nez Perce, great crowds of patients desiring medical attention were present on their return trip in 1806. The Nez Perce obsession with guns, knives, watches, blankets, kettles, beads, and other trade goods was obvious even to the missionaries appearing a quarter century after Lewis and Clark. Whether the Nez Perces actually thought that performing certain rituals would produce the desired goods probably will remain undetermined. However, it is very probable that the much publicized interest of the Plateau peoples in Christianity was prompted by an interest in Euro-American material culture. Recorded prophecies indicate that this interest dates well back into the protohistoric. For example, an Upper Chinookan prophet who was supposed to have made his appearance "long before the coming of the Whites" "dreamed he saw strange people and heard new songs. Everyone, young and old, gathered to hear him and then danced for joy 'every day and every night'. He predicted the arrival of the whites and *their marvellous possessions* [italics added]" (Spier 1935:16–17). Certain "cargo" elements (Walker 1967) were observed in Plateau cult developments.

> Throughout the northern region west of the Rocky mountains one hears in almost every tribe a tradition that before the appearance of the first white man, a dreamer, or in some instances (and nearer the truth) a wandering Indian of another tribe, prophesized the coming of *a new race with wonderful implements* [italics added]. In every case the people formed a circle and began to sing according to the instructions of the prophet. At the end of the song the palms were extended outward and upward, and sometimes it closed with ... a corrupted "amen" (Curtis 1907–1930, 8:75–76).

It is apparent that the nature of influences during the Prophet Dance period were many. The revivalist religious developments that derived from these significant events included the prophets or "dreamers" of the middle Columbia plateau, so called because of the trancelike states in which they received their visions. Best known of these include the Smohalla Dreamer religion of the Wanapam, a part of Washat; the Indian Shaker Church; the Feather cult; and the Native American Church.

Washat, The Seven Drum Religion

Washat (Sahaptin *wáashat* '(Indian) dance'), also called the Longhouse or Seven Drum religion, appears to be the most direct descendant of protohistoric Prophet Dance developments. Other names for it include Sahaptin *wáashani* 'dancers' or 'dancing', Nez Perce *wa·láhsat* 'jumping up' or *ʔipnú·cililpt* 'turning around while chanting', the Dreamer religion, "Long Hair" religion, and the Sunday Dance. The term "Pom-Pom Religion," derived from the noise of the drums, is considered inappropriate and derogatory by Washat people.

Washat is a complex mixture of older elements including vision questing, tutelary spirit power, and, in some locations, shamanistic curing, along with various Christian elements, in a distinctive nativistic framework in which the tribal language, behavioral norms, morality, relations, beliefs, and customs are perpetuated. Development of the Washat religion can be traced to early description of communal worship in Plateau territory in the Lewis and Clark

journals of 1806 (Thwaites 1904–1905) and in David Thompson's journals of 1811 (Tyrell 1962). By the 1830s, influences from Christianity were being recorded with references to "the creator," worship services on Sunday, a headman to lead the prayers, and the use of a handbell "to count the songs" (Parker 1838; Townsend 1839; Gairdner 1941; Bonneville in Irving 1850); however, Washat continued to be regarded as both indigenous and Indian (Yakima Tribal Council 1955:59).

Leaders of Washat were true charismatics and thought to possess miraculous powers of visions and prophecy during trance-induced experiences. However, on the Yakima and Warm Spring reservations on the western part of the Plateau, and at off-reservation locations where the religion is celebrated, such as Priest Rapids (fig. 1), and Rock Creek, Washington, shamanistic curings or Winter Spirit Dances

top left, U. of Wash. Lib., Special Coll., Seattle: NA 706; top right, Coll. of Robert Ruby, Moses Lake, Wash.

Fig. 1. Washat religion at Priest Rapids, Wash. top left, Tule reed mat ceremonial structure in the Wanapum village, 1941. top right, Washat worship in the tule mat ceremonial house where men and women are about to begin the dance. Puck Hyah Toot, the leader, stands fifth from left, holding bell and drum. At right, all holding drums, are Tomalawash, Swakumkun, and Ihpahpahl or Jim Looney, head of the White Swan longhouse. At left are Taneighecoo, holding a drum, and M'tupum, holding a feather wand (Relander 1951). Photograph by James S. Rayner, 1951. bottom left, Root feast participants outside the longhouse built in the early 1960s. left to right, Reamona Buck and Eliza Buck (the 2 helpers), Jeanine Kahlama, Lenora Buck, Susie White, Grace Washington, Nettie Shawaway, Margaret Buck, and Shirley Wyena (the 7 root diggers), Frank Buck (the longhouse leader), and son of Frank and Margaret Buck. bottom right, Front of the longhouse showing Smohalla's flag with its 6-pointed star, one of the symbols of the Washat religion (Mooney 1896:725–726). The flag was flown only when a dance was being held. bottom left and bottom right, Photographs by Helen Schuster, March 1967.

for validation of spirit powers are not a part of Washat services. A clear distinction is made between the role of shamans or medicine doctors and that of leaders of the Washat religion. It is possible for a longhouse leader to also possess the powers of a medicine doctor; however, these roles are kept separated. Curing generally takes place in private homes.

The oldest ceremonials within this religious system are probably the first foods' feasts, ancient calendric rites held to honor the foods that sustained the people—a first roots feast in early spring, a salmon feast in mid-spring, and a berry feast at the end of summer (Schuster 1975). Common longhouse religious activities also include funeral rites, memorial ceremonies held before large annual tribal celebrations, and the Sunday Dance. In the twentieth century, community longhouses have become the popular locus of traditional rites of passage, such as namings, first dancing, first products of young people (such as a girl's first picking of berries or a boy's first shooting a deer), and public rites noting departures for the armed services or return of a veteran. Since the 1960s, a marriage rite (different from a wedding trade) has also become part of ceremonies held in the longhouse (fig. 2); high school graduation has been celebrated; and a longhouse may be used as the site of a "wedding trade."

In traditional longhouses, the entrance door is at the eastern end in the direction of the rising sun, a common feature for Indian lodges. Worshipers are usually separated by sexes, women, girls, and young children standing together along the southern wall and men and boys along the northern side, all facing the center. This order was reversed under Smohalla at Priest Rapids. Children participate in services as well as adults, and each boy dancer, regardless of age, is given an opportunity to lead the children's dance. Seven drums are usually used (seven is the sacred ritual number) by drummers standing or seated in a row at the western end of the longhouse facing the door. The bell ringer, who is the leader of Washat rituals, stands to their right, using the bell as a song counter. An interpreter sometimes stands behind the bell ringer. Drummers are seated according to each one's skill, experience, and age; the oldest, most experienced is seated next to the bell ringer. The hand drums are of a single-headed tambourine type, about three inches deep and approximately 20 inches in diameter. The drums are unpainted. A drum stick, padded at one end with cloth, is used to beat the drum. Each drummer in turn begins a song, starting with the youngest. Ideally, worshipers hold eagle feather fans in their right hands, and the people dance and sing Washat songs in time to the rhythm of the bell and drums, moving their right hands back and forth in an arc from their hearts upward toward the right. During Smohalla's priesthood at Priest Rapids, women carried eagle feathers and men carried swan feathers (fig. 3). At the end of each song series, people extend their right hands outward and upward, intoning "Aiiiiii," like an "Amen" (fig. 4) (as cited in Curtis 1907–1930, 8:75–76).

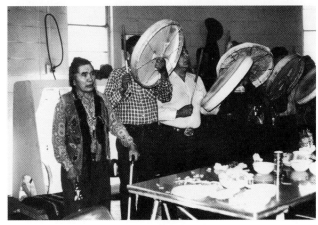

Fig. 2. Wedding ceremonies in the Toppenish Creek Longhouse, Yakima Res., Wash. top and center, Two couples, the brides first cousins, at a shared wedding. top, Ruth, wearing a cloth wingdress, and Leroy, married by the Log Church (Disciples of Christ) minister. Johnny Bill, stepfather and bell ringer, stands next to them; and an unidentified drummer is in the background. center, Celia Totus leads a Washat prayer with the characteristic raised right hand. The other groom is behind her. bottom, After dinner and speeches, Watson Totus rings the bell and the drummers stand for the final Washat prayer to be sung accompanied by drums. Photographs by Helen Schuster, top and center, Dec. 1966; bottom, Feb. 1966.

At a typical Sunday Dance, in between each series of seven songs, elders may come forward to 'speak out' in a soft, low voice with head bowed. Children and young adults are told: "Remember the teachings of your grandparents. Be of one thought and heart, that's our belief. Keep an open home. Help one another. The more you give, the more you receive; that's our Indian way. Be good to old people. Be in faith ... that's our religion" (Schuster 1965–1985). The service ends with a closing song and "friendship circle" or single file walk around the longhouse, each person turning counterclockwise at the eastern doorway ("Yakima and Neighboring Groups," fig. 11, this vol.), "To release us from Sunday worship." This is followed by a community dinner. There is nothing more binding that the sense of well-being and community that follows worshiping, celebrating, and eating together.

Certain ritual elements are ideally found in all longhouse ceremonialism: číiš or čúuš (Sahaptian) kú·s (Nez Perce) 'water', which is sipped before and after meals and at ritual feasts; the ritual number seven; handbell; seven hand drums; and tiičám (Sahaptin) 'the earth', the protective home of the people. The symbolic meaning of water is explained by elders: "Water is the element which supplies all life, all plant and animal life ... In our religion, water is our sacrament. I know that if we don't have water, there will be no life." As the ritual pattern number, seven is the sacred number for Washat; songs are always sung in a series of seven; seven hand drums are used by seven drummers; seven appointed men hunt for deer and fish for salmon for the first salmon feast; seven chosen women dig for roots or gather berries for first root and first berry feasts. The handbell is used to signal the beginning and end of

various parts of the ritual, as well as to 'count the songs'. Like water, the earth has special worth and meaning for the people, symbolized in the longhouse's traditional earthern floor on which to dance. As a sacred symbol, tiičám is the subject of a beautiful prayer. Rendered as a free translation it is: "Earth's body is ever lasting; earth's heart is ever lasting; there is ever lasting life and breath in earth" (Schuster 1965–1985).

While the patterns and gestures of the religious dance are consciously taught to youngsters in the longhouse setting after a service, there is no formal explanation or discussion of the theology or belief systems. The complex nativistic philosophy and theology of Washat remain to be fully recorded and are mainly communicated as person to person explanations and by participation in longhouse services and the oral traditions. To convey some of the traditional behavioral norms as part of a coherent moral order, Robert Jim, a longhouse leader and Yakima tribal council chairman, spoke to his sons after a special longhouse celebration in the 1960s as follows: "This is what we believe; this is what is important: Cooperation, Sharing, Hospitality, Reciprocity, and Conservation, never take more than you need." In this way, insights into participation in a cherished oral religious tradition are expressed and being passed on (Schuster 1965–1985).

For the people as a whole, the káatnam or longhouse, itself, more than any other tribal institution, represents Indian identity, the place where the Indian language, foods, dress, customs, and beliefs are maintained and perpetuated. The history of changes in the longhouse from a multifamily tule mat lodge into a community dance house and finally into a ceremonial center and community hall during the nineteenth century parallels the development of the Washat

left, Eastern Wash. State Histl. Soc., Cheney Cowles Mus., Spokane; right, Idaho State Histl. Soc., Boise:1896-B.

Fig. 3. Smohalla (b. 1815–1820, d. 1895) and his followers. left, Service at Priest Rapids, Wash., 1884. front row, left to right, 2 priests, bell boy, and Smohalla seated on a canvas-covered floor. Behind them are rows of men and boys in lines of 7, each line of men wearing shirts of the same color. On the sides on the left are a row of women in white buckskin and on the right a row of women in red (Mooney 1896:726–727). Photograph probably by J.W. MacMurray. right, Quila Lumps and White Owl, Umatilla, using the characteristic hand gestures of the Washat religion. The practice of the religion was suppressed by the Indian agents, who were sometimes also ministers, and services had to be held off the reservation. Photographer and date not recorded.

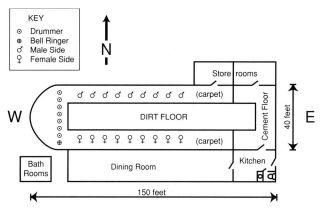

KEY
⊙ Drummer
⊕ Bell Ringer
♂ Male Side
♀ Female Side

Fig. 4. Floor plan, Toppenish Creek Longhouse, Wash., showing position of participants during a Washat ceremony (Schuster 1975).

religion itself. Originally services were regularly held in the extended family mat lodge of a headman. By the mid-nineteenth century, a special village or encampment "dance house," like an extended mat lodge, was being used (Desmond 1952:128). In an 1871 encampment at the Kittitas council and root grounds, the longhouse is described as being 100 feet in length (Splawn 1917:302). The basic structure has continued as the prototype of the contemporary wood siding or cement block community longhouse of the 1990s. As a family facility and a cultural and religious center for a group of close-knit families, each longhouse also serves in a way that is similar to an ancient village or band. In addition, many longhouses are joined together by ties of kinship and affinity. People may attend services at any of the reservation or nonreservation longhouses, with or without special invitations, and there may be invited visitors, even non-Indians.

The involvement of the Washat religion in the wars of resistance of the late nineteenth century is well known (Josephy 1965). Washat extolled the superiority of Indian culture and religion over that offered by the non-Indians. It also sanctioned a resistance to most aspects of non-Indian culture, advocating instead a maintenance of traditional subsistence practices, social organization, language, living arrangements, and sacred beliefs. During these turbulent years, the Washat leaders were opposed by both Christian missionaries and Bureau of Indian Affairs personnel on the Yakima, Warm Springs, Umatilla, and Nez Perce reservations.

Smohalla, religious leader among the Wanapam, is probably the best known nineteenth-century priest and prophet of Washat (MacMurray 1884, 1887; Mooney 1896; Relander 1956; Ruby and Brown 1989). His longhouse was located at the ancient village site of *p̓ná* below Priest Rapids on the Columbia River. His visions were received on LaLac, a sacred mountain above the rapids, and included instructions for new rituals as well as the use of flags decorated with stars and hung on flag poles, and a sacred bird, an oriole with brass tack eyes, perched on one of the poles outside the longhouse. His visions and prophecies led to his priest-

hood, and his fame increased as he eloquently preached against any "civilizing" pursuits, such as ownership of land or farming. Smohalla advocated adherence to traditional dress and subsistence patterns, protection of the earth, resistance to relocation on a reservation, and devotion to traditional spirituality, promising in return a revitalization of tribal cultures in which the dead would be brought back to life and Whites would be banished from Indian lands. Toohoolhoolzote, a disciple of Smohalla, carried his message to the rebellious Nez Perce in the 1870s. Regional variations of Washat appeared in the Plateau, including the *ʔipnú·cililpt* cult of the Nez Perce. Smohalla died around 1895, and his son Yo-Yonan (Yoyouni) assumed leadership of the Wanapam congregation. With his death in 1917, he was succeeded by his cousin Puck Hyah Toot (Johnny Buck) (fig. 1 top right), a highly regarded longhouse leader, until his death in 1956. Longhouse leadership was taken over by his sons Frank and Rex Buck, Sr. In the 1990s, Rex Buck, Jr., carried on the revered tradition at Priest Rapids.

The principal center for Washat services among the Yakimas during 1870 to 1890 was the longhouse of Kotiahkan at *páxutakyuut* (*pákyuut*), site of an extensive Indian village below Union Gap where the present town of Parker is located. Kotiahkan was a son of Shawaway, one of the brothers of the great Yakima chief Kamiakan. At one time, he is said to have been a gambler and "a very bad man." Then he was found lying in a coma, a trance state, "and the Wáashat faith came to him" (Du Bois 1938:15). Kotiahkan revived and began to preach, becoming the leader of the traditionals during the early reservation days that followed the Yakima Wars. Refusing to send his son to the Indian agency school, he served some time in chains in the tribal jail but stayed firm in his convictions of the worth of following a traditional way of life. When the Indian Agent Robert H. Milroy tried to enforce hair cutting, denying annuities to those traditionals who followed Washat religion, the traditional Indians refused to comply. When prohibited by the agent from holding Washat services on the reservation, Kotiahkan moved his mat longhouse to a site just north of the reservation boundary below Union Gap (fig. 5), out of jurisdiction of the agent, and continued to lead Washat services there. In 1884, while on a tour to investigate grievances and to assist Indians in homesteading outside the reservation after passage of the Indian Homesteading Act, Maj. J.W. MacMurray reported on the great popularity of Kotiahkan's religious services. He stated that the majority of Yakimas were "traditionals," not Christians (MacMurray 1884, 1887). Regular services took place three times a day on Sundays and for "special periodic observances" such as memorial rites and first foods' feasts (Mooney 1896:728). At this time, longhouse services were being held also at Priest Rapids, Celilo, Tumwater, the Umatilla Reservation, at Nespelem by Nez Perce on the Colville Reservation, at Simnasho on the Warm Springs Reservation, and other places. When Kotiahkan died about 1890, his priesthood was taken over by his stepson, Tianani, and his chieftainship fell to his son, Young

Fig. 5. Washat participants of Kotiahkan longhouse, south of Union Gap, Wash. top, left to right: William Stahy or Lamash with drummers: Thomas Nye, Alex Shawaway, Piahcockka Cassiat or Sukjahie, Thomas Smattie or Kitahhin, John Wynaco or Teo-an-nanee, William Charley, and Tahko Keemaer or Sheyahmenkes. bottom, William Stahy (left) with the servers at a root or berry feast. left to right, Lehops Cassiat, Umshawe Suppumwaksat or Pumshawis, Hadwesa Weanuxya or Headwesah, Saw-wasna Onepastsnute or Sun-wasnye, Minnie Smattie or Yahwenpum, Tomyeqush SweOwat, and Whye-esteh Stahy or Whol-lowish. Photograph by Andrew J. Splawn, © 1910.

Chief Kotiahkan, also known as Alex Shawaway, who led a delegation of traditionals along with an interpreter to Washington, D.C., in 1902 ("Yakima and Neighboring Groups," fig. 12, this vol.). His son, Alba Shawaway, also a leader, was married to Nettie Queahpama, daughter of the Warm Springs Tenino longhouse leader, Frank Queahpama.

By the 1930s Commissioner of Indian Affairs John Collier achieved a turnabout in the political and religious suppression of traditional Indian religious practices by missionaries and the government when he stated that interference would no longer be supported. By World War II the expanding influence of the Washat religion had become evident on most Plateau reservations. In the 1990s the Seven Drum religion, the most nativistic of all Plateau religious

developments, flourished as a focus of cultural resistance to assimilation pressures surrounding the traditional people and the reservations as a whole (fig. 6). It is at the center of a neotraditionalism that affects the Yakima, Umatilla, Warm Springs, Nez Perce, and neighboring Salishan reservations, especially the Colville, where a group of Nez Perce and Palouse have resided since 1885 and maintain Washat services at a longhouse at Nespelem.

Longhouse moral leadership also influences the political life of all Sahaptian tribal councils, where traditionals often are elected members. Their conservative influence in these councils is quite powerful. By 1832, principal Nez Perce chiefs, rather than medicine men and women, were the ceremonial leaders of longhouse religious gatherings and "religious affiliation has continued to legitimize the exercise of political authority in Nez Perce society" (Walker 1968:30, 38).

This has also been the development on the Yakima Reservation, where election and tenure on the tribal council have followed a pattern whereby the majority of council members and the council chairmen have most frequently been descendants of one of the "chiefly lineages," families that also follow the Washat religion; that maintain Indian values, traditions, language, customs, and dress; and that are committed to retention of "Indianness" as a way of life. Two-thirds of the men who have been tribal council chairmen form 1933 through 1989 were active participants in one of the Yakima reservation longhouses; of the six councilmen with greatest longevity, five were active longhouse members; all are descendants of chiefly families. However, these elected councilmen not only represent a cherished past that continues to be held in high esteem, but also support political and economic "progressivism" as these apply to maintaining self-determination, better economic security, higher standards of education, political sovereignty, and the general welfare of the Yakima Indian Nation. In the 1990s the influence of the longhouse on the Yakima Reservation was clearly as the focus of a highly regarded Indian identity; and the longhouses received support from all factions on the reservation, modernized and traditional alike. Adherence to traditional values and custom was an operative and persuasive quality, a major factor in the political arena of a modern reservation (Schuster 1989).

In the 1990s there were four active longhouses on the Yakama Reservation: the Toppenish Creek Longhouse south of White Swan; the Wapato Longhouse just outside the town; the Satus Longhouse east of Highway 22 on Satus Creek; and the Toppenish Longhouse, a new structure dedicated in 1990, south of the Yakama Nation Community Center at Toppenish. The traditional earth dance floor in the center of the hall was retained. A longhouse no longer stands at Union Gap, site of Kotiahkan's longhouse, but was moved to the Wapato site.

A longhouse was dedicated at Rock Creek, south of the reservation, in 1975. The tule mat longhouse at Priest Rapids was replaced by a wooden structure in the 1950s and again in

Fig. 6. Washat religion leaders at the Umatilla Res. They organized and formed a new longhouse there in the early 1970s. left to right: Andrew George, Palouse; Clarence Burke, Walla Walla; Amos Pond, Umatilla; Gail Shippentower, Cayuse and Walla Walla; Fermore Craig, Cayuse; Armand Minthorn, Cayuse; Ron Pond, Umatilla; Steve Sohappy, Wanapum; Dallas Dick, Wanapum, Palouse, and Nez Perce. Photograph by Joe Weinstein, Mission, Oreg., 1977.

the early 1960s, and a larger building was erected in the 1980s, in which the hard packed earthen floor was also retained.

Other longhouses in the Sahaptian part of the Plateau are located at *sk̉in* and Celilo on the Columbia River; at Simnasho on the Warm Springs Reservation in Oregon, where a larger longhouse was built in 1985, and at Warm Springs, Oregon. A longhouse was built at Umatilla Reservation in the early 1970s. Tribal halls are used for longhouse religious services on the Umatilla Reservation near Pendleton and at Cayuse, Oregon, and at Lapwai, Idaho, on the Nez Perce Reservation. A longhouse was built at Nespelem on the Colville Reservation in north-central Washington, maintained by the small community of Nez Perce–Palouse. Among Salishan tribes of the Northern Plateau longhouse activity continued on several reservations, especially among the Kootenai in both the U.S. and Canada.

By 1870, what appears to be an offshoot of the *tulím* cult was developed by the off-reservation, non-Christian faction of the Nez Perce, who were defeated in the War of 1877 and exiled to the Colville Reservation. This evolved into another nineteenth-century religious movement, the *ʔipnúˑcililpt* 'jumping' religion. Major influences came from Palouse prophets, associates of Smohalla (Du Bois 1938:12; Walker 1968:49), and a female prophet of the Nez Perce, Wiskaynatowatsanmay, who received a vision for worship services that involved "a characteristic circling and turning around form of worship" repeated seven times (Walker 1963–1964:50). At the end of the service, the worshipers held up their right hands and intoned "Aiiii," like the close of a series of Washat songs. Followers also told of their conversion experiences.

In the 1990s this group of Nez Perce followed the Washat religion, built a community longhouse in Nespelem, and regularly traveled to the Yakama Reservation to participate in first foods feasts, funerals, and other ceremonials at one of the longhouses there.

The Indian Shaker Church

By the late eighteenth century the older Plateau religions were proving incapable of dealing with the new world faced by the tribes. In addition, missionaries and other representatives of White culture were attacking native beliefs directly. Roman Catholic and Methodist missionaries had been in the Southern Coast Salish region since the 1840s. During this period of social and cultural disorganization in the Northwest, the Indian Shaker Church was founded in 1882 by John Slocum (vol. 7:633–639).

Slocum, a Squaxin (Southern Coast Salish), is said to have died, gone to heaven, and returned to life with a message from God that would bring peace and salvation. Like the Prophet Dance, this church involved certain obviously Christian elements as well as native traditions. The experiences of Slocum, the Shaker prophet, were typical. Mortality was particularly high among Indian children. He had 13 children of whom only two lived to raise children of their own (Barnett 1957:6). Shortly after Slocum prophesied that God would send a gift, he became seriously ill. Soon after his wife Mary began to tremble, and those attending concluded that Mary's "shaking" was the promised gift from God, especially since Slocum experienced a miraculous cure when she touched him. This trembling or "shaking" became a primary element in the emerging Shaker ritual (Barnett 1957), accompanied by bell-ringing, singing, and stomping. From its beginning healing has been hailed as Shakerism's greatest appeal. In the 1990s healing remained an important function; Shakers claimed

Fig. 7. Shaker Church on the Yakima Res. at White Swan, Wash. left, Photographed 1988. right, Cemetery with Indian graves at White Swan. Photograph by Homer G. Barnett, 1942.

power to help with all types of ailments and quickly responded to calls for help. Healing ceremonies were held in both the church and homes.

By 1908 Shakerism had spread to the Yakima and various other reservations on the Plateau. In 1891, a man was drowned and lost at Yakima. His body could not be found. In the presence of a crowd that had gathered for the occasion, a Shaker set up a small table on the bank of the Yakima River and put a white cloth and three lighted candles on it. Assisted by the others who rang hand bells, his extended arms began to shake. He let his hands lead him, and the rest of the people followed. They moved up and down the riverbank until evening, but without success. The next day, after making a second start, Aiyel revealed that he had located the body across the river in a clump of brush. It was found there, or in that general vicinity. This led to several rapid conversions.

Also around 1891, John Slocum along with Mud Bay Louis and three other men traveled to the Yakima Reservation to cure a Wishram woman, a sister-in-law of Alex Teio

(Spier 1935:66-69). Word of the cure and of the Shaker religion rapidly spread on the reservation to Toppenish, where Alex Teio lived, and he became one of the early converts and leaders of the Yakima Indian Shaker Church. After these preliminary conversions, other Shaker missionaries returned, to assume an important role in the growth of the church among the Yakima and in bands down to the Columbia River during salmon fishing seasons: at The Dalles, White Salmon, Hood River, and among the Wishram, Wasco, and Cowlitz (Ruby and Brown 1996:147).

The church remained traditional, that is, non-Bible using, although the Christian cross, bells and candles, robes and holy pictures, and other Christian symbolism and prayers were a regular part of services. And although formally organized as a church by 1892, for some time there was no church building in which to worship. As later seen on the Colville Reservation (Schultz and Walker 1967), the converts met in their homes and in the homes of others who invited them to the Yakima Indian Shaker Church services.

Fig. 8. Yakima Shaker Church, Satus Creek, Wash. left, Indian Full Gospel Assembly church, also known as the Independent Shaker Church of God. Photograph by Helen Schuster, 1965. right, Altar of church with an array of bells. Photograph by Rev. Earl Reisner, 1955.

Fig. 9. Wasco Shaker Church, Warm Springs Res., Oreg. left, Wasco minister dressed for a burial service. right, Wishram at Celilo Falls, Oreg., with the bells used in their service. They stand in front of a mat house, which may be where the worship took place. Photograph by Lee Moorhouse, 1898-1912.

In 1899, a prominent Yakima called Captain Simpson disavowed Methodism and offered land for a new church centrally located on the reservation about three miles east of White Swan. The members, including Enoch Abraham, who was a carpenter, contributed their labor; $200 was collected for expenses, and a new building was put up on unencumbered land in 1900. The earlier smaller building was removed from the Simpson farm to stand beside the new structure, where it was used as a kitchen and dining room at the time of conventions.

The main Yakima Shaker church was in a unique position. According to Barnett (1957), much of the credit for this was due to Enoch Abraham. As early as 1899, the year of his conversion, he realized that the Methodists and Roman Catholics on the Yakima Reservation had been confirmed in their occupancy of church lands by the provisions of the Dawes Severalty Act. He, therefore, urged his fellow Shakers to petition the Indian agent for a similar concession to them. A delegation consisting of Captain Simpson, Lincoln White, Joe Riddle, and Alex Teio appealed to agent Jay Lynch. In 1908, they were granted 79 acres of land in the center of the reservation, thus insuring the Yakima congregation of a property right that is not enjoyed by any other Shaker group. Alex Teio became the State Head Elder of the Shaker Church in 1912, when the state church convention was held on the Yakima Reservation. By 1915, Teio claimed a Shaker Church membership of around 300. Teio worked to extend the Shaker Church to the Warm Springs Reservation and to the Klamath and Modoc. Other notable Yakima leaders have been Bishop Clifford Tulee and Head

Elder Harris Teo. This place of worship, still in use in 1997, is known as the traditional Yakima "Indian Shaker Church" or "the 1910 church," the year of formal incorporation of the church (fig. 7). It has remained non-Bible using. In the 1990s there was some decline in church membership, and a young minister was reported to have left the 1910 church to join the Washat religion (Ruby and Brown 1996:134, 167, 232).

Another building, on Satus Creek in the southeastern part of the reservation, was also used for meetings. This was a Methodist church that was gradually relinquished to the Shakers as the Methodist congregation diminished through death, disinterest, and reaffiliation. It was purchased by some Shakers for $75 around 1900. In contrast to the 1910 church, this church became a Bible-reading congregation, its members separated from the original Indian Shaker Church, and it was incorporated in 1945 as the Indian Full Gospel Church at Satus (fig. 8). The original structure was replaced by a newer church house, which was built on Lizzie Shuster's allotment on Satus Creek, and was enlarged and refurbished in 1971. In 1989, Bishop David Nanamkin, a Colville from Wapato on the Yakima Reservaiton, revised the constitution of the church, inserted "Shaker" into the name to become the Indian Full Gospel Shaker Church, and "infused new life" into a congregation drawn principally from the Yakima, Umatilla, and Nez Perce reservations (Ruby and Brown 1996:206–207,263).

The schism between Bible-reading and non-Bible-reading Shakers was expressed in 1953 when a faction of "the 1910" or Indian Shaker Church separated from the original church and formed their own Bible-reading congregation in a third small church building located south of White Swan, calling themselves the Independent Shaker Church of White Swan. Justification for the split was explained as necessary for "adoption of the Bible as the basis of the church's teachings" (Ruby and Brown 1996:197). One of the original leaders, Bishop Russell Billy, was succeeded by Willey Miller, then Jasper Andy in 1991, who died in 1994 (Ruby and Brown 1996:205).

The Shaker Church quickly expanded onto most other reservations of the Plateau. As early as 1913, the state convention was held on the Warm Springs Reservation, where the Shaker religion was accepted more by the Wasco (fig. 9) than the Tenino. Harry Miller was elected State Head Elder (Ruby and Brown 1996:135, 149).

The Umatilla, near Pendleton, Oregon, heard about the Shakers at Yakima. About 1906, a Umatilla man had some property stolen and decided to apply to the Shakers for assistance in recovering it. The Presbyterians and Roman Catholics had long histories at Umatilla. As in the case of the lost body at Union Gap, Aiyel's hands led him, under power, to the hiding place of the stolen goods and the chief's house. Some of the Umatilla were interested, and later a few came to the Yakima meetings and were converted, but they never established an independent church. The Yakimas attribute this failure to the vigorous opposition of the local Christian churches. In 1912 when Enoch Abraham was asked to come to Pendleton by a delegation of Umatilla Indians, he found that he had been summoned to an inquisition by the native Presbyterian elders. According to him, they were confounded by his Christian exegesis.

There has been intermittent contact between the Nez Perce and Yakima, and as early as the 1890s George Waters, a native Methodist preacher among the Yakima, was making missionary trips to Lapwai (Walker 1985). Further exposure to the Shaker religion occurred when some of the Nez Perce, along with hundreds of other Indians, annually congregated on the Yakima and Moxee hop fields for six weeks during the summer in the 1940s. The Nez Perce, like the Umatilla, have been deterred from becoming converts by the strong influence of Christian church members. Two or three Nez Perce missionaries belonging to the Presbyterian church have covered the eastern reservation, and they have spoken against the Shaker religion and the Washat religion. In 1969 Fay Compo joined the Indian Full Gospel Church, a Bible-reading church group was established on the Nez Perce Reservation in 1979, and Compo became an ordained minister in 1984. The congregation consisted of five to seven members (Ruby and Brown 1996:207).

Shakerism was introduced on the Colville Reservation in 1914 but began to attract adherents after 1946 in the area near Malot, Washington, when two preachers from LaConner arrived. During 1953 to 1956 the movement spread to Nespelem, Washington, where a healer-teacher had gathered 30 adult congregants by 1956. From 1956 to 1961 a Bible-reading group emerged, providing alternatives in Shakerism.

The Bible was introduced in the Shaker services on the Colville Reservation by a Yakima who had been a Pentecostal minister. The church developed into a Full Gospel Shaker church. After 1961 the church again grew rapidly, and the Bible-reading Shakers became dominant over the non-Bible Shakers (Schultz and Walker 1967).

Aside from their cultural conservativeness and support for traditionalism, the Colville Shakers are in some respects distinctive from other Shaker congregations in the Pacific Northwest. For example, the factionalism so apparent between the Bible and non-Bible Shakers on other reservations has not caused a serious division there. Second, they show a pronounced Roman Catholic influence and an unusually variable interpretation of Shakerism. Third, while small, their congregation is religiously very heterogeneous. Typically, Shaker congregations are relatively large and homogeneous with respect to faiths represented in the services.

The primary reason for the lack of factional divisiveness in the Colville congregation may be that the Bible and non-Bible groups were forced to worship together because of inadequate church facilities. Worship was conducted in members' homes, usually offered on a voluntary basis. In the event that no one volunteered, a meeting place was assigned by an elder or other chuch official. This situation changed when plans to build a church house began in Nespelem in the late 1980s, and the church building was dedicated in 1992. At this time, Steven Iukes, Sr., was ordained as minister, Fred Manual as assistant minister, and Steven Iukes, Jr., as secretary (Ruby and Brown 1996:92, 102, 208). The services were presided over by both Bible and non-Bible ministers on an alternating basis. At one meeting an Indian Shaker minister conducted the services, and both groups participated. At the next, A Bible minister directed the activities. When passages from the Bible were read, the non-Bible Shakers left the room for refreshments and returned to participate again when the Bible had been removed. It was generally accepted that a successful service required many participants.

Colville Shakerism contains many Roman Catholic elements. An example is the recognition of Mary as a deity comparable to Jesus Christ rather than an intermediary in prayer. Indeed, approximately 90 percent of the Colville Shakers have been Roman Catholic at one time or another (Schultz and Walker 1967).

Noteworthy is the large percentage of non-Colvilles attending services at Nespelem. Members of the Shaker faith are noted for traveling, but on most Washington reservations, the visiting members make up only a small percentage of the congregation. At some meetings at Colville the visiting segment makes up as much as 50 percent of the worshipers.

The Colville congregation also is composed of a large percentage of non-Shakers. For example, a Shaker meeting at Nespelem may contain Bible Shakers, which includes members of the Independent Shaker Church of

Fig. 10. Warm Springs Res. Shaker Church, Oreg. left, Newly constructed church building dedicated just before the annual Root Feast in 1952. Shaker services were held throughout the Root Feast period with people participating in both. Photograph by David and Kathrine French. center, Altar. The rest of the room is bare, except for benches and one or two pictures on the wall. Photograph by Flora Warren Seymour, before 1931. right, Clarence McKinley, of Warm Springs Res., participating in the Shaker service. Photograph by Cynthia D. Stowell, 1982.

White Swan from the Yakima Reservation, non-Bible Shakers, members of Pentecostal churches, and followers of Oral Roberts.

An explanation for this variety of faiths may lie in acculturation. In Shakerism culturally conservative individuals are able to associate exclusively with Indians, to engage in essentially aboriginal religious practices, and to gain a grudging respect from the culturally progressive Indians as well as surrounding Whites. The emphasis on the dramatic transformation of the individual typical of Shakers, Pentecostals, and faith healers probably strikes a responsive chord among the many frustrated people on American Indian reservations throughout the Northwest. Not only are miraculous cures of illnesses and behavioral problems compatible with the aboriginal religion, but also they are the means of rapid adjustment to Euro-American society.

Other Plateau Shaker congregations, at Warm Springs (fig. 10) and among the Klamath and Modoc, relied on the Yakima congregation for assistance. Yakima remained the center of Plateau Shakerism.

Feather Cult

The Feather religion, or Feather cult, whose practitioners were known as *wáptasi* (from *wáptas* 'golden eagle; feather'), has also been referred to as *wáaskliki* 'Spinner cult member'. It was founded about 1904 by Jake Hunt, a Klikitat from Husum, Washington, a town on the east bank of the White Salmon River, seven miles north of the Columbia River. Hunt was born between 1860 and 1870, and is said to have been a pupil of Lishwailait and Ashnithlai, Klikitat prophets and contemporaries of Smohalla. As a young man, he had received many guardian spirit powers, including an

eagle familiar or "totem," and probably could have been a powerful shaman (Du Bois 1938:5).

Hunt was residing in Hood River, Oregon, when his third wife and son became ill with tuberculosis. A group of Shakers from the Yakima Reservation were called in to perform their cures, but the son died. While mourning at the son's grave, a niece of Hunt's had a vision, receiving a bright disk of light, like a circular mirror reflecting the sun's rays. Jake Hunt took the disk in his own hands and saw a vision of Lishwailait on the disk, dressed in buckskins and holding a tambourine hand drum. He started to shake violently, seized something between his upraised hands, and began to spin rapidly in place. He then announced that he had received Lishwailait's soul (Du Bois 1938:22-23). In spite of further ministrations by the Shakers, Hunt's wife died within one month. While the Shakers were still in his home, a sister of Hunt's had a spell and also began to spin. In deep mourning, Hunt lay on his wife's grave, fell asleep, and dreamed of a sun disk of light or land *(tiičám)*, "which was brought down from the sky by an eagle." People surrounded him, singing Washat songs. While dreaming, he was given instructions to make a hand drum and disk of light, and was then commanded to create the Feather cult in order to heal the sick, to cure drunkards, and to convert people in seven lands. He also was given a new name: "Titchám Nashat" or "Earth Thunderer," in honor of the bright disk of light that symbolized the earth, *tiičám.*

Returning to Husum, Hunt built a longhouse and, joined by his sisters, established the Feather cult, an ecstatic healing sect, with ritual and ideology influenced by both shamanism and the Washat religion. Curing was accomplished by possession of spirit power, manifested by a rapid spinning movement, with eagle feathers held aloft in the

511

right or in both hands, or sometimes tied in hair braids, and utilizing drums and songs. An eagle totem perched nearby on a pole. The disk of light was symbolized by a small round mirror worn in a fringed, buckskin container, decorated with colored beads to represent the earth and rainbow. The tambourine drum was also painted with symbols of the sun and stars, yellow the most sacred color representing the sun's rays (Du Bois 1938:22–23, 39–40).

In order to proselytize for the Feather cult, Hunt first traveled 25 miles up the Columbia River to the Wishram band at Spearfish, where he built a longhouse, cured a young girl, and gained many adherents. A year or two later he married a local Wishram woman. He next went upriver 40 miles to the Rock Creek/Fallbridge area, where he made further conversions. About 1905 the cult spread to the Yakima Reservation. Hunt held his first meeting in the longhouse belonging to Billy Wholite, three miles west of Toppenish, where it gained followers; next he spoke at the longhouse near White Swan, and finally at Kotiahkan's longhouse. In 1906 Hunt obtained more converts on the Warm Springs Reservation among the Tenino at Simnasho and among the Northern Paiute.

Hunt's greatest challenge came around 1907 when he traveled to the Umatilla Reservation to treat the wife of a Walla Walla chief at Cayuse, accompanied by Wishram, Yakima, and Warm Springs adherents. When invited to Pendleton to try to treat a Christian Nez Perce, Jim Kashkash, he was challenged by Christian Indians including an Indian judge, and by the agency doctor who had given the patient 24 hours to live. He performed his Feather religion ceremonials, but the patient died the next day. Jake Hunt was seized by the agency police, his hair was cut, his drums and regalia were destroyed, and he was left "deeply humiliated and seriously impaired." He was given a choice of imprisonment or banishment, and he returned to Wishram, losing many adherents of the Feather cult. After Hunt's death between 1910 and 1914 (Du Bois 1938:20–43), some followers carried on the curing ceremonies.

The Feather religion, like that of the Indian Shakers, is a special curing cult. Services or curing sessions are held exclusively in homes, never in a "church" or longhouse. A member of the Feather religion further explained, "Feather songs are medicine songs. Curers only come if they are called. That's not like the Shakers. And Feather curers never take any pay. They cure only if called, and for nothing." Curing rituals primarily cure alcoholism. "You should not drink if you're a Feather member" (Schuster 1965–1985). Don Umtuch, a member of the Feather religion (fig. 11), presented the following explanations in 1965,

The Feather Religion is therapy. A medicine man may join the Feather Religion; he has powers to cure and to heal, but at the same time he must cure the body of all intoxicating liquors, prohibit (the patient) from intake any longer. They took me in because I was a bad boy, indulged in drinking, which did me harm. They relieved me of something, made me quit. That's therapy treatment. They have ways and means to separate you from intoxicants, so you would dislike them, reject them.

He continued,

We use three, or five, or seven drummers. We begin by singing old Wáashat songs. Wáashat is respected as the original religion. Then we go into our own songs, medicine songs. The tempo changes, it is faster, much faster, and then they twist and spin. That's part of the power to cure. Some members have no power, they just believe.

During the service, healers form a circle around the person to be helped, moving in rhythm around the patient; they may brush the person with eagle feathers to remove evil spirits and toss them away. People also stand by the sides of the room, singing, helping. When someone starts to spin in an ecstatic state, others surround the spinner to protect them from falling. The person to be cured of drinking may also begin to spin. He is led to a corner of the room to vomit all alcohol from his system, as part of the cure from alcoholism.

Distinctions among Shakers, Washat, and the Feather cult have been pointed out by Du Bois (1938:44–45): Shakers

Fig. 11. Don Umtuch, an active participant in both the Feather cult and Washat religion. The decorated drum he is displaying was used in the Feather cult (drumheads for Washat services were undecorated). Photograph by Helen Schuster, Yakima Res., Wash., 1965.

512

use many bells; Feather and Washat only one. Feather and Shaker initiates receive powers to cure; this is not a part of Washat. Excitable movements are experienced by Shakers, such as stomping and shaking; and spinning by Feathers curers; there are none by Washat participants. Drums and feathers are used in both the Washat and Feather religions but not by Shakers.

On the Warm Springs Reservation, Isaac McKinley and his wife were early active followers, as well as Frank Winishut, Elisha Kishawa, Remi Sidwaller and his wife, Mac Quinn, Sally Ike, and Willie Jack. One held in highest regard was Andrew David, great grandson of Jake Hunt, who held services in a ceremonial addition to his home on the DesChutes River, or in homes where Feather adherents had been invited to perform healing services. He was the principal leader until his death in 1986. On the Yakima Reservation, early leaders included Thomas Umtuch near Satus, Charlie Hultucks at White Swan, and Williams Charlie at Toppenish (Du Bois 1938:26–27; Schuster 1965–1985; Stowell 1987:52–53). Louis Baker and his wife followed them, as well as Thomas Umtuch's sons George, Toney, and Don Umtuch, carrying on the Feather religion until their deaths in the 1970s and 1980s. They also were active in Washat religion. In the 1990s some families followed the Feather religion on the Yakima Reservation, but it was most actively practiced on the Warm Springs Reservation.

The Native American Church

The newest place in North America where Peyotism gained a foothold is the Plateau. In 1977, articles of incorporation were filed in the State of Washington by groups on both the Yakima Reservation and the Colville Reservation (Stewart 1987). This development represents a penetration of Plains, Southwest, and Great Basin religious influence into the Plateau, where Peyotism had long been resisted by Christian missionaries and federal agents.

The Yakima group was incorporated as the Native American Church of the State of Washington of Toppenish, Washington. Ted Strong of Yakima filed the petition (Stewart 1987). In 1970, while in Arizona, Strong had attended a Peyote meeting conducted by Truman Dailey. During the meeting, he had a vision of Mount Adams, a 12,203-foot peak on the Yakima Reservation. When Strong told of his vision, Dailey interpreted it as signifying that Peyotism would someday be established among the Yakima.

Strong continued to visit Dailey frequently in Red Rock, Oklahoma, to learn the Old Kiowa Hunting Horse way of conducting Peyote meetings. Dailey conducted a meeting at Yakima on July 30, 1977. He and his wife arrived with a large tepee as a gift for Ted Strong. Thus, it was in his own tepee at Yakima that Strong received the Hunting Horse moon from Truman Dailey and was assured that he could thenceforth conduct meetings in the correct Half Moon style.

Almost exactly at the same time this group was being organized, another was seeking incorporation on the Colville Reservation, where several young Peyotists had been arrested for possession of peyote. Peter B. ("Sonny") George was thought to be the first Colville to attend a Peyote meeting, in 1964 at Parks, Arizona, in the hogan church of Andrew Scott, the Cherokee trader who had built his church just off the Navajo reservation to accommodate the Navajo at a time when the Navajo police were vigorously enforcing the official Navajo prohibition against Peyote on the reservation (Stewart 1987). George joined an interracial and intertribal group of about 40 men and women to form a religious commune near Tahlequah, Oklahoma. Friends of George's from the Colville Reservation, George Nanamkin and Vance Robert Campbell, Sr., became Peyote adherents through him.

Led by Campbell and George, as well as Alex C. Moomaw and Danny Moomaw, the Colville Peyotists incorporated as the First Native American Church of the Colville Tribes. The purposes of this incorporation were the same as those first seen in Oklahoma in 1918: "To foster and promote religious beliefs in Almighty God... with the sacramental use of peyote for religious purposes." Friends among Sioux Peyotists were notified, and Leonard Crow Dog and Gilbert Stewart of the Rosebud Reservation and Rufus Kills Crow Indian of the Pine Ridge Reservation went to Colville with peyote to conduct the first Peyote meeting on that reservation, using the Cross Fire ritual. As a legally incorporated church, Peyotists may legally acquire eagle feathers and peyote for religious use. Individuals must be at least one-quarter Indian blood.

In 1978, Paul Small and Joe Stanley, both Cree, went to Nespelem several times to direct meetings and to teach the local leaders the order of service for the Half Moon ritual, which is somewhat simpler than the Cross Fire ceremony. Both George and Campbell were accepted as local roadmen, and there were about 30 local members of the First Native American Church who conducted Peyote meetings someplace on the Colville reservation on most weekends.

Peyotism has continued to expand among the Yakima and Colville despite State of Washington efforts to suppress it in the 1978 arrests and trial of Kenneth Little Brave (Sioux), Roger Eagle Elk (Sioux), and Robin Gunshows (Colville). After its introduction on the Yakima and Colville reservations, many meetings were held on other Plateau reservations including Nez Perce, Umatilla, Warm Springs, Spokane, Coeur d'Alene, Klamath, Salish-Kootenai, and in a variety of off-reservation settings.

Conclusion

This chapter has described religious movements of the nineteenth and twentieth centuries resulting from complex his- 513 torical and cultural processes of Indian and non-Indian contact over several centuries. For the history of Christian missions and missionaries, Drury (1936, 1937, 1940, 1949, 1958) has thoroughly documented the Presbyterian experience, and Burns (see also vol. 4:444–445, 494–500), the Roman Catholic missionary experiences in the Plateau. Other literature concentrates on the Indian players in this historic drama (Stern 1960; Ruby and Brown 1989, 1996; Miller 1985; Ray 1936a; Walker 1985; Schuster 1975). The complex interactions of missionaries and their tribal converts is a separate story.

For the Plateau as a whole, there is an evident increase in pan-Indianism and its attendant Plains-oriented religious practices, especially the Sun Dance. Many young tribal members travel to both the Plains and northern Great Basin perceiving the Sun Dance experience to be a way back to a traditional cultural orientation for which many are searching.

This summary of Plateau nineteenth and twentieth century religious movements indicates a long history of the beginnings and continuation of this search, of a remarkable creativity and innovation in response to changing times and conditions, of a functional response of selective retention and borrowing, built on religious innovation and change that continues for Plateau Indians in their ongoing pursuit of a meaningful way of life.

Kinship, Family, and Gender Roles

LILLIAN A. ACKERMAN

The Extended Family

The basic unit of traditional Plateau social organization was the extended family. The nuclear family existed, but it was a relatively weak cultural institution (Ackerman 1971:595), which was embedded within the extended family. The extended family traditionally consisted of several nuclear families and often included one or two grandparents, their sons or daughters along with their spouses and young children (Turney-High 1937:56). Collateral relatives such as siblings of the grandparents were also regarded as grandparents by all the younger members of the group, and their sons or daughters, who were classificatory brothers and sisters of their cousins, with their spouses and children were included in the family. One such extended family made up about half of the population of a winter village in the traditional culture (Ackerman 1994:299; Walker 1968:13). In the past, the extended family shared residence and economic resources. It was the economic mainspring of the society, producing all its food and other goods, providing for its members, and distributing and trading the surplus of foods and goods to nonmembers.

The eldest grandparents headed the extended family, and they were always consulted on major decisions made within it. Their influence in their grandchildren's lives often exceeded that of the parents (Ackerman 1971:595).

There is some evidence that adult members of the extended family often specialized in one particular economic task, especially if the skill was a gift given by a guardian spirit. This specialization provided a variety of food within the extended family (Walters 1938:87; Murdock 1965:203).

While most Plateau groups traced consanguineal relationships through both father and mother (bilateral reckoning), the Flathead were somewhat different. Due to incessant warfare with the neighboring Plains people, Flathead men suffered a high mortality rate. Many women married men from other groups as a consequence, but they continued to reside within their own natal families. Their children "considered themselves primarily members of their mother's families" (Turney-High 1937:92–93). Flathead society thus acquired a matricentric tendency (Anastasio 1972:193).

Variations in family organization also occurred among several groups in the western Plateau. The Lillooet were divided into clans, in which membership could be traced either through the father's or mother's line. These, then, were cognatic clans or nonunilinear descent groups. This system was said to be borrowed from their neighbors, the Coast Salish of the Northwest Coast (Teit 1906:252).

The western Shuswap borrowed social elements from the Carrier and the Chilcotin of the Subarctic. All these groups had a nascent class structure consisting of nobles, commoners, and slaves. The nobles made up from one-half to two-thirds of the population. Nobility was inherited bilaterally through either father or mother. Crest groups developed for each family of nobles along with some concept of rank (Teit 1909:575–576). The crest groups had economic and ceremonial functions and owned the right to display a crest animal or totem (Goldman 1940:337). These variations from the general Plateau pattern in family organization apparently developed beginning in the early nineteenth century (Teit 1909:581).

Marriage

First marriages were arranged for the young by their parents or grandparents. The marriage was validated through the exchange of goods in a "wedding trade" between the couple's two families, some time after the young couple took up joint residence (fig. 1). The groom's family visited the bride's family and exchanged gifts with them. Some weeks later, the bride's family visited the groom's family and repeated the process (Ackerman 1971:600; Schuster 1975:124, 126–127).

If a young man or woman found an impending arranged marriage distasteful, he or she eloped with another person. Eventually, this marriage was accepted by their families (Ackerman 1982:58).

Divorce was easy, requiring only that one of the couple departed with his or her goods. Remarriage was also easy, as it consisted of a couple taking up joint residence. The parents of the new couple had no role in choosing spouses for their children in second and subsequent marriages. A first marriage defined a person as an adult, and an adult was largely autonomous. Personal autonomy was and is

Fig. 1. Formal marriage between Justin Pinkham, Yakima from Priest Rapids, Wash., and a Palouse bride. In this first exchange, the man's family is surrounded by the woman's family. Sophie Wak-Wak, relative of the bride, is serving food. The gifts, which are stacked in bundles, include baskets, dishes, and parfleches. The wife, husband, and 3 children, who had been born before this formal exchange, are eating. Photograph by Click Relander, 1950.

one of the hallmarks of Plateau culture (Ackerman 1982:62–63).

Residence in the Plateau has been described as patrilocal (Ray 1933:140), which is a rule that men bring their brides to their parents' house to live. Residence has also been described as ambilocal, that is, a young couple had the choice to settle either with his family or hers (Mandelbaum 1938:117–118). Ambilocality seemed to be the norm throughout the Plateau, partly because kinship reckoning was bilateral. There may have been a patrilocal emphasis in some areas, as among the Nez Perce, but that appears to have been an ideal (Ackerman 1971:595) rather than an inflexible practice (McWhorter 1983:24–25).

Marriages in the Plateau were often monogamous, and a young couple took up residence with one of their sets of parents without complication or switched residence back and forth. Polygynous marriages were also acceptable, but this was more complicated. If a man had two or more unrelated wives, and he tried to establish them into one household, it was likely that the household became fraught with tension because of the jealousy of the cowives. Frequently, even usually, one or more of the wives became disgusted with the situation and left the household with her belongings. Such separation meant divorce (Mandelbaum 1938:177).

A more acceptable situation occurred if a man with plural wives left each of them with her own kin in a separate village, the husband visiting each wife in turn. This could still lead to divorce due to jealousy. Consequently, the best way to marry plural wives and have a peaceful family life was to marry sisters. Sisters almost always were compatible and mutually helpful (Mandelbaum

1938:118). Men who intended to remain married to the same women often chose this form of polygyny.

Polygynous marriages with nonsororal cowives were not always unstable. A chief usually married more than one woman, as he was expected to provide food for feasts and funerals, hosting visitors and all the people of the village. It was not easily possible for one woman to gather and prepare all the food for these events. Consequently, the labor of additional women was needed, and polygyny solved the problem. These polygynous situations were probably more stable, because of the prestige of being married to a chief (Ackerman 1982:73). Gamblers, good hunters, good fishers, and shamans also attracted and often kept plural wives because of their prestige (Ray 1933:142).

First marriages were characteristically unstable, and few Plateau people married only once (Ray 1933:143). This was partially because people married young and changed their minds, and partially because women did not need men to support them, so marriages did not have to be stable. Women could well support themselves and their children. However, as they aged most people looked for stability and settled down to one spouse. They raised their families and provided a residential anchor for the younger members of their extended families (Ackerman 1989:8).

Nonunilinear Descent Groups

There is evidence that nonunilinear descent groups have existed in the Plateau, since at least the 1900s and likely before that. The Plateau peoples recognize a kindred, which is made up of all relatives on both sides of the family (Hudson 1986:454). In addition, they trace their descent through either males or females back to the founding ancestor of their extended family, usually a well-known ancestral chief of their winter village. This group of relatives can be referred to in Okanagan as *qa?ł-* 'children of' plus the name of the common ancestor (Hudson 1986:454; Anthony Mattina, communication to editors 1997). This man may not even be a direct ancestor but may be one terminologically. The ancestor-based family is by definition a descent group. In the Plateau, the group of relatives that acknowledges each other as part of one's extended family reckons their descent from the chief who was the founder of their family. Each individual knows the ancestors who connect him or her to the founding ancestor of his extended family (Ackerman 1994:292).

The extended family provides an individual with his or her identity. This group of relatives was acquired in three ways, even in the 1990s. A person could grow up in a particular extended family that reared either his mother of father; after adulthood, a person may choose to change his affiliation from his mother's extended family to his father's extended family (or vice versa), or to some other relative; or a person may marry into a family and affiliate himself to his spouse's people. The third option does not occur automatically for either men or women. They must learn the local variations in culture and practice them (Ackerman 1994:292).

Each nonunilinear descent group is associated with a particular locality that the people regard as "home." Before the reservation period, these were the winter village areas. In the 1990s the descent groups still regarded these winter village areas as their home, even if they no longer lived there.

The nonunilinear descent groups (or extended families) were still recognized in the 1990s by others in the society. Even when a woman carries her husband's name, her descent group affiliation is known. People who meet strangers for the first time will introduce themselves as the grandchild of someone, and it is usually understood which "family" (descent group) the person belongs to.

The ancestral chiefs for whom most nonunilinear descent groups are named were born five to seven generations before the 1990s (Ackeman 1994: 293).

An important feature of the nonunilinear descent group in the Plateau is its permeability. One may be born into one descent group, but in adulthood have the choice of joining the descent groups of half-siblings or cousins (referred to as siblings) in other villages (in prereservation days) or on other reservations (in the 1990s). Mere habitual residence over the winter in the past probably changed descent group affiliation. Even ethnicity was changed if the new descent group that was joined was part of another tribe (Ackerman 1994:294).

A nonunilinear descent group was defined by the right to winter over in a certain area and exploit its resources. While the resources of the area during three seasons of the year were shared with any stranger who asked permission to use the area, those who were related to local people did not have to ask permission. Further, they had the right to winter over with their relatives, activating a claim to be part of that group. Outsiders did not have these rights: they always returned to their own places when winter came. The difference between seeking permission to extract resources and having the right to do so was considered important by the Plateau elders who discussed this subject (Ackerman 1994:297–298).

A nonunilinear descent group retained the same name over time because the name of the founding chief was handed down to his descendants. Famous names often reappear in family genealogies every other generation at least, and the family or descent group continues to be known by that name even though the original founder died several generations before. The giving of names to all children is a function of the descent group, since a child is given an ancestral name (fig. 2). Along with the name, the child is expected to behave in a general way like his ancestor of the same name. Thus, traditions, history, and

the memory of numerous ancestors are preserved within the lineage, and the extended family or nonunilinear descent group remains coherent over time (Ackerman 1994:301–302).

The kinship system provides pantribal, even panareal sodalities: it consists of a series of social groups that unite the Plateau into the area-wide integration that Anastasio (1972:177, 185) describes.

When missionaries and government agents arrived in the Plateau in the mid-nineteenth century, among the changes they sought were adjustments in family structure. Polygyny was considered a problem, and easy marriage and divorce were deplored. In other words, they sought to remold Plateau social structure into nuclear families. The social change damaged the vitality of the extended family (Ackerman 1987:64).

Some of the change was the result of building small permanent dwellings that were not expandable like the indigenous dwelling. The inflexible housing immediately

Fig. 2. Yakima name-giving ceremony. left to right, Lonnie Selam, Thomas Albert, and Theresa Selam, witness as Lonnie's son, Tracy, receives the ancestral name, Kwathlqui. Tracy is draped in blankets and other items to be given away to the elders present. Photograph by Eugene Hunn, Toppenish Community Center Longhouse, Yakima Res., Wash., 1987.

redefined the nature of a family. No longer were the dwellings sufficiently large to contain several grown siblings with their spouses and children, elderly parents, aunts, uncles, and cousins. This division of families into its nuclear components, while not destroying the extended families, did create problems that resonated on Plateau reservations in the twentieth century. The high incidence of juvenile delinquency, alcoholism, the first appearance of neglected orphans and their placement in Euro-American orphanages, incomplete socialization of children, and other social problems are rooted in the fact that extended families have been weakened (Ackerman 1987:67).

The Plateau people were persuaded to farm, and at first, many individuals took to it experimentally: planting gardens, fencing them against deer, and performing other tasks. Since people were still living in villages, this had little influence on traditional family structure. Then the Dawes Severalty Act of 1887 provided for allotments to individual Indians, with the "surplus" Indian lands being sold to Whites (Ackerman 1982:86). The allotments were effective in splitting up extended families into their nuclear components, with perhaps the very old living with their grown children.

Despite these negative influences of contact, nonunilinear descent groups appeared to be strong in the 1990s on Plateau reservations. Most people no longer farmed on their allotments since many had been lost, but they lived in settlements on the reservation, often near other members of their extended family. While most descent groups no longer lived under one roof, they maintained intense everyday contact and provided economic and emotional support for their members. There continued to be descent group celebrations, and rites of passage like weddings and funerals were attended by the entire group. At the same time, connection to kindred in other communities and on other reservations was maintained (Ackerman 1979–1990).

The Rules of Marriage and Kinship

Mandelbaum (1938:112) reports that marriage with all cousins up to the sixth degree was prohibited among the Southern Okanogan. Marriage beyond sixth cousins was supposedly preferred. However, Mandelbaum found no evidence of this in actual practice. Turney-High (1937:56) says that marriage with up to eighth cousins was prohibited among the Flathead, while Ray (1933:139) reports that fourth cousins were allowed to marry among the Sanpoil and Nespelem. In the 1990s, Plateau people noted that they did not marry any known relative, no matter how distant the relationship (Ackerman 1979–1990; Hunn 1990:217). Thus, marriages had to be geographically dispersed since about 1850 at least (Anastasio 1972:214). Other than kinship, there were no restrictions on marriage. A chief's daughter was able to marry a man from a poor family, for instance (Ray 1933:139).

The complex kinship ties in the Plateau enabled extensive visiting between relatives, because an individual could claim hospitality from any known relative. Prolonged visiting might even evolve into permanent residence. The kinship system thus aided individual mobility, and mobility facilitated intergroup relations (Ackerman 1989; Anastasio 1972:177).

The levirate and sororate occurred among many if not all Plateau tribes. The levirate required a man to marry the widow of his deceased brother or cousin. The sororate required a single woman to marry her deceased sister's husband. Ray (1933:144) reports that these classes of marriage were not obligatory. In the 1980s some elders stated that they were, so that orphaned children would be cared for and would remain in the household of their grandparents. The levirate and sororate also offered the advantage of preserving social relations between two descent groups when one of a married couple died (Ackerman 1979–1990).

The rules of hospitality among kinsmen were still followed in the 1990s. The geographically dispersed kinship system continued to promote mobility for economic and social reasons. People stayed with relatives on other reservations when they attended annual ceremonies like the First Salmon ceremony and celebrations like the powwows. They even changed their residence to that of their relatives. Visits were always welcome. Intermarriage also promoted mobility since it created new relatives in another area. Residence was so flexible that family members did not know if a person was only visiting elsewhere or had gone for good. The person himself did not know immediately if his changed residence was temporary or permanent. Thus, residence remained flexible in the 1990s and may even have resulted in a change in reservation enrollment. The ambiguities in residence noted in the 1990s were the same as those in prereservation days (Ackerman 1989).

Young people, especially before marriage, were especially prone to make long visits elsewhere. Indeed, all elements of the Plateau population moved around frequently. The only exceptions were the older people who were the anchors of the society. They provided the stable residences into which younger people moved or from which they departed (Ackerman 1989).

The Kinship System

The Plateau kinship system is bilateral; that is, people trace their relationships through both sides of their families. The terminology is of the bifurcate collateral type. Generation is stressed, resulting in a Hawaiian cousin system (Schuster 1975:60). Theoretically, relationship is traced indefinitely. No marriage is allowed between any known relatives, though lapses have occurred (Ackerman

1979–1990). Sahaptin and Salishan kinship terminology show similar structure.

In ego's generation, six terms for siblings are used that differentiate elder siblings by sex and younger siblings by sex and by the sex of the speaker. These terms are extended to all cousins and their spouses. Thus, cousins are addressed as older sister, younger brother, etc. (Murdock 1965:208). An additional two terms are reported for denoting half-siblings, which differentiate mother's children and father's children (Marshall 1977:85). A special term is used for siblings-in-law of the opposite gender, as, in the past, they were potential spouses if and when the levirate or sororate were activated (Schuster 1975:63).

In the parental or first ascending generation, mother and father are given separate terms. The parents' siblings—mother's brother, father's brother, mother's sister, and father's sister—are all differentiated from the parents and from each other. The spouses of parents' siblings are also addressed by the appropriate parent sibling terms. These terms are extended indefinitely in that generation, that is, ego addresses the cousins of one's parents and their spouses with the appropriate aunt and uncle terms. Though these relatives are distinguished terminologically from parents, consultants say that the relationship is very much parent to child.

A special relationship occurs between ego and his or her father's sister's husband. Reciprocal terms are used between these relatives, and they indulge in licensed joking (Murdock 1965:208–214), which includes making fun freely of the other person, who may not take offense.

In the grandparental or second ascending generation, all four grandparents are distinguished from each other, and the terms are used reciprocally for the grandchildren. Thus, ego and mother's mother call each other by the same term. These grandparental terms are extended to all siblings of the grandparents (Hunn 1990:206; Marshall 1977:90–91; Walter 1938:90).

One term is used for all members of the great-grandparental generation, and another for the members of the great-great grandparental generation (Walters 1938:88–89).

In the first descending generation, ego's children are distinguished from nieces and nephews. There are six terms for nieces and nephews, which are distinguished by the sex of the speaker and the sex of the connecting relative (Murdock 1965:208–209). These terms are extended out to their cousins and spouses indefinitely.

The second descending generation (grandchildren) is divided into four categories in which ego's sex is taken into account along with the sex of the connecting link. Thus, male ego's son's children are differentiated from male ego's daughter's children. Female ego's grandchildren are differentiated the same way. These terms, which are extended to all the grandchildren's cousins, are the same terms or reciprocal terms for the grandparents (Murdock 1965:208; Schuster 1975:61; Walters 1938:90).

Great-grandchildren and great-great grandchildren are all called by the same terms (reciprocals) as are great-grandparents and great-great grandparents (Marshall 1977:91)

A feature of this kinship structure is that ego has many grandchildren and many grandparents. A close relationship exists between grandparents and grandchildren. In contrast, relations between parent and child are slightly more distant. A parent sends a child to his or her grandparent for advice, comfort, or a scolding, as needed. Supportive relations exist between uncles and aunts and ego. Brothers are affectionate and cooperative; the older particularly looks after the younger siblings in the family, even in adulthood. Sisters are very close; they in the past sometimes became cowives. There was some restraint between brother and sister, probably because of incest concerns, but loyalty between them was intense (Ackerman 1979–1990; Murdock 1965:213).

Gender Roles and Relative Status

The Plateau culture area is a region where gender equality was reported by early observers (Ross 1904:280) and later by anthropologists (Ray 1939:24; Walters 1938:96). Work on the Colville Reservation (Ackerman 1982) confirmed these observations in detail by noting that gender roles on the reservation fit Schlegel's (1977:8–9) definition of gender equality. She states that gender equality is the equal access or different but balanced access of both sexes to power, authority, and autonomy in the economic, domestic, political, religious, and other social spheres. Gender status on the Colville Reservation was studied in the traditional context of foraging through the testimony of elders, and in the 1980s and 1990s, in which people work in offices and have other post-industrial types of employment. It is likely that gender equality exists throughout most of the Plateau because people from the Coeur d'Alene, Nez Perce, and Yakima reservations informally confirm its presence in their home areas.

The Economic Sphere

Plateau women shared at least equal economic power with men in the past. Women were responsible for gathering a variety of wild plants, particularly roots, which constituted a major part of the diet (fig. 3). It has been estimated that women provided 50 percent (Ackerman 1971:598; Anastasio 1972:119) to 70 percent (Hunn 1981) of the food in the diet. These foods were highly valued by all members of the society; they were judged to be as important and nutritious as the game and fish (fig. 3), which were the men's responsibilities. Rituals were performed over each gender's major foods. Men fished the great salmon runs that appeared in the Columbia River and its tributaries, and they also hunted deer and other large

Fig. 3. Women's and men's subsistence activities. top left, Yakimas Sally Dick, Rosalie Harry, and Louise Weaseltail picking huckleberries and putting them into tightly woven baskets tied around their waists. top right, Colville woman digging bitterroots, a subsistence staple. She uses the traditional style digging stick and places the roots in a woven basket. top left and top right, Photographs by John W. Thompson; left, 1953–1955; right, 1955. bottom left, Men dip-netting for salmon from platforms at Celilo Falls, Oreg. Photograph by Gladys Seufert, 1950s. bottom right, James Selam, John Day River Sahaptin, enrolled on Yakima Res., and Terry Selam, Yakima, with black-tailed deer shot above Howard Lake, Yakima Res., Wash. Photograph by Eugene Hunn, 1977.

mammals. Game and fish made up 30 to 50 percent of the diet (Hunn 1981). The varying percentages depended largely on the area. In the Southern Plateau, the camas root was especially plentiful and hunting was somewhat poor. Consequently, the people there depended more on roots. In contrast, hunting in Chelan territory was very good, and it was estimated that slightly over one-half the typical diet there consisted of meat and fish (Ackerman 1982:56, 44). Since economic productivity and power is suggested to be the basis for high gender status (Sanday 1974:194), it is not surprising that women held equal status with men in Plateau culture. A Nez Perce male elder on the Colville Reservation noted in 1980 that men hunted and fished and went to war, but women were the back-bone of the society: everything depended on them, he asserted. They did all other needed tasks and were admired for it. In the past, these tasks included making baskets (fig. 4 center left) and mats, dressing hides, and sewing clothes. They also chopped wood and packed goods. They made camp for men (fig. 4) while the men hunted, helped to surround the game, and then butchered and dried the deer meat (Ackerman 1982).

Women trained their daughters for their adult roles, and men trained their sons. The children's future economic role was recognized in a ceremony that celebrated a child's first economic accomplishments. When a boy killed his first deer or caught his first fish, a feast was held to celebrate the event. When a girl independently dug her first roots or gathered her first berries, a similar feast was held for her. These ceremonies were recognitions of a new provider for the society (Ackerman 1982:50).

Each gender was absolutely autonomous in the pursuit of his or her individual tasks. The woman's decisions were not controlled by the husband or vice versa. Indeed, the woman was considered to own all food brought into the household. She decided how and when it would be used by the family, and if there was a surplus, it was hers to trade. Each gender owned exclusive property in the form of goods and horses: a married couple owned nothing in common. Women were great traders in foodstuffs with other bands and tribes, and thus they were able to acquire horses and luxuries. Men traded horses, weapons, and fishing implements that they fashioned themselves (Ackerman 1982:56).

The Domestic Sphere

In the extended family, the oldest couple, usually the grand-parents, had the most influence over the other members of the domestic group. Very often, the grandmother's influence was more pronounced than that of her husband. Men did not exert authority over their wives without the risk of losing them. One of the traditional admonitions given to a young man marrying for the first time was that he should refrain from trying to control his wife. Indeed, women sometimes tried to control their husbands, and the divorce rate for first marriages was quite high. One consultant commented that a sensible couple gave each other advice but did not try to control each other. There was thus no institutionalization of dominance in a married couple's relationship.

In arranging a first marriage for a child, both parents had to give their consent. The decision was not made by father or mother alone.

Men and women had an equal right to divorce, which simply involved departing with one's property. Families might try to settle quarrels between a couple, but they had no right to forbid divorce. Women suffered no economic deprivation after a divorce since they were self-sufficient through their gathering, and they could trade their surplus for meat and fish if necessary. Individuals selected their second or subsequent marriage partners for their own reasons without family influence.

Both men and women in the past had the right to change their gender roles and become berdaches. A man took on the clothing and economic roles of women, and vice versa. The frequency of gender change is not known (Ackerman 1982:66).

The Political Sphere

Because only men were chiefs in most Plateau societies, it could be construed that men had more status in the political sphere than women. On the other hand, the personality and character of a prospective chief's wife was carefully evaluated when a new chief was being sought. A wife was expected to counsel the chief on his decisions, and not all women were suitable for the role of adviser. In one case, a candidate was rejected because his wife was seen as unsuitable (Ackerman 1982:67).

Women were eligible for the office of chief among the Southern Okanogan, Lakes, and possibly the Coeur d'Alene. Female chiefs were also recorded for the Shuswap and Lower Thompson, but the women of these groups inherited the office from a father without a male heir, and the daughter passed the office to her male descendant to perpetuate the line (Ray 1939:24).

Female chiefs were elected among the Southern Okanogan, the Methow, and the Chelan. These were not the head political officers of these groups; however, they wielded important advisory and judicial functions. These women were called *skʷúmalt* a 'woman of great authority'. Such a woman was always related to the chief by blood but was officially elected by the assembly (Walters 1938:95–96). Thus, in at least a few Plateau societies, women were not chiefs but exercised similar functions.

Women had other political leadership roles. In at least some groups, a chief's wife acted as chief when her husband was absent; and she nominated his successor (usually his son) when he died. Her choice was usually confirmed by the assembly, but this was not automatic. The assembly made the final decision (Ackerman 1982:72–73).

The assembly along with the chief made up the political authority of the group. Men and women participated equally in the policy debates and in the voting. Husband and wife often voted differently, and it was not an issue for discussion between them (Ackerman 1982:74–75).

The Religious Sphere

The gender roles in the above three social spheres were often complementary; that is, men and women did not perform exactly the same roles, but each role complemented the other (Schlegel's 1977:8–9 "balanced access" in her definition of gender equality). The religious sphere is the one exception to complementary access. Men and women had almost exactly the same access to this sphere, underscoring the importance that Plateau people attach to religion. All men and women in most Plateau societies sought guardian spirits as children. Both genders could aspire to become shamans or healers who were equal in power, although in some groups female shamans were not equal to male shamans in numbers. Both could become prophets, and both were resource leaders (Ackerman 1982:81).

A resource leader was a person gifted in obtaining a particular resource, like salmon or camas roots, who was elected to lead the first-foods rituals. This involved catching or gathering the resource when it first appeared during the

522

Fig. 4. Women's sphere of influence. top left, Umatilla camp where women are airing out blankets and cooking. Photograph by Arthur M. Prentiss, 1910-1932. top right, Ellen Way-maht-qua, great-grandmother of Matthew Dick and Celia Ann Campbell, Colville Confederated Tribes, in her camp. Basketmaking materials are hanging from the sun shade behind her. Photograph by John D. Wheeler, Leavenworth, Wash., 1900. center left, Thompson woman from Ruby Creek, B.C., making a split cedar root coil-constructed basket used for storing food and water. She uses a bone awl to pierce the holes through which the sewing strand is threaded. The basket she is making and the basket on the left are both decorated with imbricated geometric designs. Photograph by Charles F. Newcombe, 1903. center right, Nez Perce women breaking camp at the McWhorter ranch, Yakima, Wash. They load parfleche and sacks on horseback. Photograph by Lucullus V. McWhorter, 1908. bottom left, Louise, Flathead, making fried flatbread in an iron skillet over an open fire, while her children watch. Photograph by Edward Boos, 1899-1910. bottom right, Tsestaztko, Thompson, with baby in painted cradleboard with bag attached to the top. She wears a painted, fringed dress and cap. Taxinek is seated holding a child. Photograph by James A. Teit, Spences Bridge, B.C., 1914.

year, carrying it back to the settlement, and conducting a public ritual over it. Each resource leader had to have the proper guardian-spirit power to perform these rituals, which were designed to ensure the resource for the year. While these leadership roles can be construed to be economic roles, they were also religious ones (Ackerman 1982:81).

The 1990s

Despite acculturation, men and women have retained equality in much of Plateau society in the 1980s and 1990s (Ackerman 1982:163). To the extent that they participate in the American economic system outside the reservations, the women suffer the same discrimination that other American women do. However, those women who work in reservation offices and agencies are working within the Plateau culture. Thus, they have access to high management jobs and expe-

rience no problems with exerting authority over male employees. Men and women are equally encouraged to obtain training and employment, and the work of both genders continues to be equally valued by their families and society. Further, men and women receive equal pay for equal work within the tribal employment system. Almost all women sought employment outside the home in the 1980s (Ackerman 1982:118).

Women continued to run their households as they did in the traditional culture. They often held financial and other assets separately from their husbands and acquired loans on their own. Divorce continued to be frequent, but as women were employed, they did not regard the loss of men's economic support as an inhibiting factor in obtaining a divorce (Ackerman 1982:134).

Women sat on many of the tribal councils on the Plateau reservations, and many were tribal judges. The participation of women in politics was active on the lower levels, but young

Fig. 5. Imitating adult life through play. Dolls mimicked adult life both in their dress and the treatment of dolls as future children. left, Coeur d'Alene female doll wearing traditional Plateau deer-tail dress. center, Two Nez Perce girls playing with a doll in an elaborately beaded cradleboard similar to the ones they were held in as babies. Photograph by Edward H. Latham, Nespelem, Wash., 1890-1910. right, Coeur d'Alene male doll in buckskin shirt and leggings with a bow and quiver for arrows. Dolls collected by C.E. Babcock, Vancouver Barracks, Wash., before 1901. Height of left, 59 cm; right to same scale.

KINSHIP, FAMILY, AND GENDER ROLES

women were handicapped in serving as council members, because of having small children. It was necessary for council members to travel extensively. The traditional support network that previously helped raise children was attenuated in the 1990s. Consequently, many women put off some of their political ambitions until their children were almost grown.

Husband and wife still voted independently and often did not know how the other voted, even in federal and state elections (Ackerman 1982:136–140).

Women continued to have equal access to the traditional guardian-spirit religion as healers and prophets. They were leaders in the Indian Shaker Church, but they tended to have subordinate positions in the White churches in which they participated (Ackerman 1982:149).

Overall, the Colville Reservation's 11 tribes maintained gender equality in the economic, domestic, political, and religious spheres of their culture in the 1990s, as a legacy of their past (Ackerman 1982:163–164).

Ethnobiology and Subsistence

EUGENE S. HUNN, NANCY J. TURNER, AND DAVID H. FRENCH

Ethnobiology, in its most inclusive sense, refers to data or analysis relevant to understanding how humans relate to plants and animals by means of culture. Ethnobiological studies range from purely descriptive inventories of culturally salient species to broadly theoretical and comparative analyses (Berlin, Breedlove, and Raven 1973; Bulmer 1974; Hunn 1982; Turner 1988a). Plateau ethnobiological research has figured prominently in the development of the field.

A variety of ethnohistorical, ethnographic, and linguistic material is relevant to contemporary ethnobiology. For example, Meriwether Lewis and William Clark, the first Euro-American visitors to the Plateau to leave an extensive written record of their observations, were trained naturalists. They collected dozens of scientific specimens and annotated these discoveries with ethnographic commentary (Moulton 1983–; Burroughs 1961; Cutright 1969). Other naturalists, such as David Douglas (Davies 1980), John K. Townsend (1839), Charles A. Geyer (1845–1846), and Frederick V. Coville (1897, 1904), recorded valuable ethnobiological data. Descriptive ethnographies recorded between 1890 and 1940 include extensive sections dealing with subsistence and material culture, with data relevant to the economic perspective on ethnobiology.

Collections of myths and stories in the native languages as well as word lists and dictionaries suggest nomenclatural patterns and give some indication of which species were perceived worthy of explicit recognition. They may also suggest how each species was perceived by members of the traditional cultures. However, these data are of limited value unless knowledgeable contemporary native speakers can provide confirmation and clarification of the earlier reports; the native language names cited in the earlier sources may be inexpertly transcribed and the scientific identities of the species referred to may be ambiguous or erroneous. Collaborative research involving ethnographers, linguists, biologists, and Indian experts has produced the richest material (Turner, Bouchard, and Kennedy 1980; Turner et al. 1990; Hunn 1990).

Comprehensive inventories conducted in accordance with contemporary methodological standards reveal total inventories of named plant classes of 200–350+ folk categories (Hunn 1980a; Turner et al. 1990:293–294). Hunn has recorded 290 folk zoological taxa for Sahaptin. Hunn found only a very few plant and animal categories listed by Everette (1883) and Curtis (1907–1930) for Sahaptin that could not be verified by consultants in 1976–1992.

The majority of the plant and animal categories named in Plateau Indian languages correspond closely to scientifically recognized taxa, most often to scientific species. In some cases native terminology draws finer distinctions than recognized by Euro-American taxonomists, as in the case of serviceberries (saskatoons) (*Amelanchier alnifolia*), certain lomatiums (*Lomatium canbyi, L. farinosum*), and certain salmonid fishes (*Oncorhynchus tschawytscha, O. mykiss*) (Hunn 1980; Hunn and French 1981; Turner et al. 1990).

A feature of Plateau ethnobiological classification and nomenclature that contrasts with both Euro-American scientific classification and folk systems of indigenous tropical agriculturalists is the rarity of both life form and folk specific categories, proposed as universal ethno-biological ranks by Berlin, Breedlove, and Raven (1973). Thus, Plateau Indian taxonomies exhibit minimal hierarchic structuring. In many languages folk-specific taxa are often labeled binomially. By contrast, binomial naming of plants and animals is very rare in Plateau languages with less than 2 percent of Sahaptin folk biological categories including binomially labeled folk-specific subdivisions.

The vast majority of folk biological taxa recognized in Plateau languages are folk "generics" (Berlin, Breedlove, and Raven 1974:29), that is, they are basic level or natural categories (Rosch 1978; Hunn 1982). C.H. Brown (1985) has tested the hypothesis that hunting-gathering peoples tend to employ minimally hierarchical taxonomies because their ethnobiological inventories are not so extensive as those of agriculturalists. Plateau examples support this hypothesis.

Folk biological life-form categories also tend to be poorly developed in Plateau systems. Sahaptin and Wasco-Wishram lack terms referring to 'tree' per se; the Sahaptin term most often glossed 'tree' means literally 'that which stands upright', as is true as well of Lillooet and Thompson (Hunn 1990:180; Turner 1987:63). Widespread life-forms such as 'vine', 'grass', and 'herbaceous plant' are reduced to folk generic or "empty life-form" status in several Plateau languages (Turner 1974, 1987; Randall and Hunn 1984). Hunn and French (1984) describe a Sahaptin predilection for indicating relations among similar taxa by stressing relations of coordination rather than those of hierarchical subordination, while Turner (1987, 1989) has described a variety of nonhierarchic conceptual relationships among folk biological taxa recognized in Thompson and Lillooet.

Plateau ethnobiological research has also contributed to general theoretical debates concerning the nature of hunting-gathering modes of production. Hunn (1981) has argued that the superficial impression given by the Plateau ethnographic record concerning the relative dietary contributions of fish, game, and vegetal foods (Murdock 1967) is seriously biased. Rather than fish predominating as the primary staple food, many Plateau groups, at least in the protohistoric period, derived more than 50 percent of their food energy from starchy roots, culms, and bulbs. Plateau peoples valued vegetal foods highly, recognizing their value in narratives, and in religious and life cycle celebrations. Thus, women's economic product was not symbolically discounted in the Plateau (cf. Ackerman 1982). The perishability of "roots" in archeological contexts has made it difficult to document the antiquity of this early historic pattern (cf. Ames and Marshall 1980; Pokotylo and Froese 1983). The demonstrated importance of vegetal foods as dietary staples requires reconsideration of ecological analyses based on the assumption that fish and game were of overwhelming importance (Hewes 1973; Sneed 1971; Palmer 1975a, 1978; Kew 1976; Romanoff 1985, 1988).

Plateau ethnobiological work has also demonstrated the key role of sophisticated food harvesting and processing technologies in sustaining protohistoric population densities (Keely 1980; Konlande and Robson 1972; Kuhnlein and Turner 1986; Meilleur, Hunn, and Cox 1990; Norton et al. 1984; Turner 1977, 1981, 1988; Turner and Kuhnlein 1983; Turner, Kuhnlein, and Egger 1987). Overall Plateau population density has been estimated at the relatively high value of 0.95 people per square kilometer (Hunn 1990:135).

Turner (1988a) has used Plateau materials to develop a diagnostic tool that has been used to assess the "cultural impact" of development projects on traditional ethnobiological resources (Stoffle et al. 1990), while Hunn (1990) has documented the dense conceptual linkages between traditional ethnobiological knowledge and indigenous conceptualization of place. Plateau Indian ethnopharmacology has been studied (Stubbs 1966; D.H. French and K.S. French 1979; Turner 1984; Meilleur, Hunn, and Cox 1990).

Ethnobotany

The information on Plateau plant resources, unless otherwise specified, is summarized from the following sources: Hart (1979) for Flathead; Hart (1974, 1976) for Kootenai; Hunn (1990) for Sahaptin; Marshall (1977) for Nez Perce; D.H. French and K.S. French (1950–1992) for Wasco-

Wishram; Coville (1897, 1904) and Spier (1930) for Klamath; Palmer (1975, 1975a) for Shuswap; Turner, Bouchard, and Kennedy (1980) for Okanagan-Colville; Turner et al. (1990) for Thompson; Turner et al. (1987) and Turner (1992) for Lillooet. General discussions and illustrations of most of the Plateau food plants are given in Turner (1978) and Hunn (1990) and are discussed in a more general context by D.H. French (1965) and Kuhnlein and Turner (1991). Plants used in Plateau technology are described and illustrated in Turner (1979) and Hunn (1990).

Food Plants

Approximately 135 species of plants were utilized by Plateau peoples as sources of foods, flavorings, or beverages (fig. 1). They include "root vegetables," "green vegetables," fruits and nuts, inner bark of trees, mushrooms, one lichen species, and a variety of casual foods, sweeteners, flavorings, and beverage plants. Many were being used in the 1990s.

• ROOT VEGETABLES   Over 30 species of "root vegetables," including true roots, corms, bulbs, tubers, and rhizomes, were used in the traditional diet. There is wide regional and cultural variation in relative importance of different species. The Northern Plateau groups, including Shuswap, Thompson, and Lillooet, used two upland species, spring beauty (*Claytonia lanceolata*) and yellow avalanche lily (*Erythronium grandiflorum*) in large quantities, whereas the use of bitterroot (*Lewisia rediviva*), "wild carrot" or yampah (*Perideridia gairdneri*), false onion (*Triteleila hyacinthina*), common camas (*Camassia quamash*) (Turner and Kuhnlein 1983), and several species of lomatiums (*Lomatium canbyi, L. cous, L. farinosum, L. piperi, L. macrocarpum*) (Hunn and French 1981) predominated among the central and southern groups, the Kootenai, Okanagan-Colville, Flathead, Columbia, Sahaptin, and Nez Perce. However, bitterroot and roots of two lomatiums (*L. dissectum, L. macrocarpum*) were also used by the northern groups.

Other "root vegetables" were also eaten, but generally less intensively: wild onions (*Allium cernuum, A. douglasii, A. acuminatum, A. macrum* and related species); balsamroot (*Balsamorhiza sagittata, B. careyana,* and *B. hookeri*); triteleias (*Triteleia howellii, T. douglasii*), mariposa lily (*Calochortus macrocarpus*), wild thistles (*Cirsium undulatum, C. edule* and related species); chocolate lily (*Fritillaria lanceolata*), yellowbells (*F. pudica*), tiger lily (*Lilium columbianum*), bugleweed (*Lycopus uniflorus*), false-agoseris (*Microseris troximoides*), western sweet-cicely (*Osmorhiza occidentalis*), silverweed (*Potentilla anserina*), water-parsnip (*Sium suave*), Hoover's tauschia (*Tauschia hooveri*), edible valerian (*Valeriana edulis*), and mules-ear (*Wyethia amplexicaulis*). Most of these were collected in quantities large enough to be processed and stored for winter use.

The usual implement for harvesting roots was a pointed digging stick, made of wood (fig. 1 right), antler, or, since the late 1930s, an iron tyne from a harrow, or a section of steel rebar. A cross-piece was fixed at the top as a handle, and the implement was pushed into the ground beside the root to be dug, then pried back to loosen the turf and allow the root to be pulled out.

Several edible roots, including camas, onions, thistle, and balsamroot, contain a complex, relatively indigestible sugar, inulin, as a major portion of their carbohydrate. These were generally prepared by pit-cooking (fig. 2), which allowed the conversion of inulin to sweet-tasting, easily digestible fructose (Konlande and Robson 1972). After pit-cooking, those roots not consumed immediately were dried by spreading out on mats or threading on strings, after which they could be stored in baskets or bags. For use, they were simply soaked in water or cooked in soup to reconstitute them. Most of these inulin foods were notably sweet, "like candy," when cooked (Turner et al. 1990:122).

Dried roots, particularly bitterroots, camas, and biscuitroots, were a common trading item among Plateau peoples. For example, the Okanagan-Colville traded dried bitterroot to the Shuswap, and dried camas to the Thompson. Even in the 1980s and 1990s, a gift of dried bitterroot, biscuitroot, or camas is deeply appreciated, especially by older people who find collecting traditional foods difficult. This trade extended west of the Cascade Mountains to Coast Salish Indians, who obtained dried bitterroots, a highly valued food, from Plateau Sahaptins via intermediaries (Smith 1940:245). In exchange, Plateau peoples received valued coastal products such as dried clams and shells.

• GREEN VEGETABLES Green shoots, stems, and leaves were generally consumed only for a short time in the spring, while still mild and tender; most become tough and bitter as they mature. The young budstalks and leafstalks of cow parsnip (*Heracleum lanatum*), a large herbaceous perennial in the celery family, often called Indian celery or Indian rhubarb, were, and still are, eaten by virtually all the Plateau groups (Kuhnlein and Turner 1986). The stalks were gathered in the spring (fig. 3 right), before the flowers expand, and were always peeled, since the skin contains high concentrations of phototoxic furanocoumarins that irritate and discolor the skin in the presence of sunlight.

Other commonly eaten greens include the inner tissues of fireweed shoots (*Epilobium angustifolium*), the embryonic leaves and budstalks of balsamroot (*Balsamorhiza sagittata* and *B. careyana*), the young leaves and flower-scapes of barestem lomatium, also called Indian celery (*Lomatium nudicaule*), the sprouts of other lomatiums (*L. grayi, L. salmoniflorum, L. dissectum*), the young stems of mules-ear, and the stems of cacti (*Opuntia fragilis, O. polyacantha*, and *Pediocactus simpsonii*). Cacti were available year-round. Prickly pears (*Opuntia* spp.) were sometimes sought in times of famine, and were said to have sustained life when no other food was available (Turner et al. 1990:195). Within the historic period, many Plateau people have also used introduced greens, including common dandelion (*Taraxacum officinale*), lamb's-quarters (*Chenopodium album*), and watercress (*Rorippa nasturtium-aquaticum*).

left, Kootenai Culture Committee, Elmo, Mont.; right, Amer. Mus. of Nat. Hist., New York: 16/9295.

Fig. 1. Digging and preparing roots. left, Drawing from Kootenai coloring book *Living In Harmony* (Salish Kootenai College 1987), showing digging for bitterroots. center, left to right, Alice Starr, Wasco and Warm Springs Sahaptin; Blanche Tohet, Warm Springs Sahaptin; and Ida Wanasee peeling bitterroots (Warm Springs Sahaptin *pyaxí*, Wasco *ibyáxi*) in preparation for a root feast. A cornhusk bag in which the dug roots were packed lies on the table. Photograph by David and Kathrine French, Warm Springs, Oreg., 1951. right, Shuswap digging stick of serviceberry wood with a birch wood handle. Collected by James A. Teit, Canoe Creek, B.C., before 1903. Length, 73 cm.

ETHNOBIOLOGY AND SUBSISTENCE

Fig. 2. Preparation of camas. Elizabeth P. Wilson, Nez Perce, demonstrates the cooking of camas bulbs in a pit. The bulbs, collected in Musselshell Meadow, north of Kamiah, Idaho, were prepared in an oven pit 36 inches in diameter and 22 inches deep on the Wilson property. Layers of wood and paper were placed in the pit, and a wooden platform of wide boards was built over the entire pit. Rocks, used year after year, were then placed on the boards. top left, Drawing of camas plant. top right, Wilson's grandson Yelma Lawyer building a tepee of wood over the rocks and starting a fire. center left, Wilson's son-in-law Archie Lawyer observing as Wilson smooths out the fire surface before adding the mud around the rocks for a better surface. center right, Placing wet willow branches over the rocks, followed by clumps of wet alfalfa and rye grasses. bottom left, Wet sacks placed over 2 bags of camas bulbs. bottom center, Dirt placed on the sacks, which was tamped down. Another fire was built up over the pit and cooked all night. The camas was tested the next day; if it was not the proper dark brown color, the fire was kept going another night. bottom right, Wilson checking the freshly baked camas bulbs. The baking took 2 1/2 days (Downing and Furniss 1968). Photographs by Lloyd S. Furniss, 1966.

• FRUITS, SEEDS, AND NUTS   Throughout the Plateau region, a prominent fruit was serviceberry, or saskatoon berry as it is known in Canada (*Amelanchier alnifolia*). Several different varieties of these fruits, each with its own berry and habit characteristics, were recognized and named in Thompson, Lillooet, and other Interior Salish languages. The berries were eaten fresh and were also dried in cakes or individually like raisins, then used alone or mixed with many different foods, including other berries, bitterroot, dried fish, dried meat, and animal fat. Each year, a family group would harvest and preserve large quantities of these berries, especially in the Northern Plateau where they were the most important of all fruits. They were also an important trading item. Chokecherries (fig. 3 center) (*Prunus virginiana*) were used widely throughout the Plateau region and preserved in large quantities. Black huckleberries (*Vaccinium membranaceum*) were a preferred fruit, still very important in the 1990s. They and chokecherries are the primary fruits of the Southern Plateau.

Many Plateau families formerly traveled to the mountains for two or more weeks each summer to harvest huckleberries, and people still harvested them in quantity in the 1990s. Huckleberries were commonly dried over a slow fire set in a rotten log (Filloon 1952). Other types of huckleberries, blueberries, and cranberries (including *Vaccinium alaskaense, V. caespitosum, V. deliciosum, V. globulare, V. myrtilloides, V. ovalifolium, V. oxycoccus, V. parvifolium, V. scoparium*) were used within their ranges.

Many other types of fruits (including true berries, pomes, drupes, and aggregate fruits, all generally called "berries") were used to varying degrees: kinnikinnick (*Arctostaphylos uva-ursi*), Oregon grape (*Berberis aquifolium*; syn. *Mahonia aquifolia*), red-osier dogwood, or "red willow" (*Cornus stolonifera*; syn. *C. sericea*), hawthorn (*Crataegus douglasii, C. columbiana*), wild strawberries (*Fragaria vesca, F. virginiana*), salal (*Gaultheria shallon*), pin and bitter cherry (*Prunus pensylvanica, P. emarginata*), currant and gooseberry species (including *Ribes aureum, R. cereum, R. hudsonianum, R. irriguum, R. lacustre,* and others), rose hips (*Rosa acicularis, R. woodsii, R. nutkana* and other species), wild raspberries (*Rubus idaeus* and, in the north, *R. acaulis*), thimbleberry (*Rubus parviflorus*), blackcap (*Rubus leucodermis*), elderberries (*Sambucus cerulea,* and, to a lesser extent, *S. racemosa*), soapberry or soopolallie (*Shepherdia canadensis*), and highbush cranberry (*Viburnum edule* and *V. opulus*). Other species essentially coastal in distribution but used along the westernmost Plateau area and along the east slopes of the Cascades include: low Oregon grape (*Berberis nervosa*), salmonberry (*Rubus spectabilis*), and trailing wild blackberry (*R. ursinus*).

Wild strawberries, raspberries, thimbleberries, and blackcaps were eaten fresh or were dried for winter, like serviceberries, chokecherries, and huckleberries, if large enough quantities were obtained. Tart fruits like Oregon grapes and red-osier dogwood berries were often mixed with saskatoons or other sweeter fruits. Kinnikinnick berries, being

Fig. 3. Picking vegetables and berries. left, James Selam, John Day River Sahaptin, with corms of yellowbell just harvested. Photograph by Eugene Hunn, Canteen Flats, Wash., 1977. center, Selina Timoyakin, Northern Okanagan, picking chokecherries. Photograph by Dorothy Kennedy, Penticton Indian Res., B.C., 1976. right, Bill Edwards, Lillooet, peeling the leafstalks of cow parsnip. Photograph by Nancy Turner, Pavilion Mountain, B.C., 1984.

ETHNOBIOLOGY AND SUBSISTENCE

Fig. 4. Preserving foods. The home of Joseph Umtush, Yakima, with food surplus contained in traditional baskets and canning jars. Photograph by Robert Depue, Harrah, Wash., 1923.

somewhat dry, were usually cooked in animal fat. Hawthorn fruits, considered seedy and constipating, were seldom eaten in quantity. The outer rind of rose hips was eaten occasionally, sometimes as a famine food. Soapberries, which contain a small amount of saponin, were and still are, whipped with water into a frothy confection, sometimes referred to as "Indian ice cream." This practice seems to have originated within the Northern Plateau but in the 1990s was quite widely distributed among aboriginal peoples of British Columbia and neighboring areas (Turner 1981).

Most fleshy fruits were dried for winter use, although kinnikinnick, elderberries, highbush cranberries, soapber-

ries, and some currants and gooseberries could be stored fresh. In the late twentieth century, most fruits were preserved by freezing or canning (jarring) (fig. 4), although a few people still dried serviceberries and soapberries.

Plateau peoples did not use grains to any extent, and their use of seeds and nuts was limited to a few species, with one exception. Seeds of several coniferous tree species were harvested on occasion, but the most important were the large seeds of white-bark pine (*Pinus albicaulis*), a montane species growing near timberline. The cones were harvested in fall, then roasted or dried and the seeds extracted. These were usually cracked open and the kernels eaten as a snack, "like peanuts." Seeds (small, dry fruits) of balsamroot (*Balsamorhiza sagittata* and *B. careyana*) were harvested in some areas, then dried and pounded into meal, which was eaten alone or mixed in soup or other dishes. Hazelnuts (*Corylus cornuta*) were the only species of nut available in the region, and they were gathered and used wherever they occurred. Hazelnuts, locally abundant in some areas, were a common trading item to regions where they do not occur. Sometimes they were gathered from caches of squirrels. Acorns of garry oak (*Quercus garryana*) were also of some significance in the Columbia Gorge area, where they were baked underground after leaching in "blue" mud. An important exception to the relatively low importance of seeds in the Plateau diet is among the Klamath, who traditionally harvested and ate a wide variety of seeds, including grains of grasses, seeds of knotweeds (*Polygonum* spp.) and goosefoot species (*Chenopodium* spp.), and particularly the seeds of yellow pond-lily (*Nuphar polysepalum*). These

Fig. 5. Collecting and preparing wokas. left, Woman collecting the seeds of wokas in a shovel-nose canoe. right, Wife of Modoc Henry, Klamath, grinding wokas. Photographs by Edward S. Curtis, © 1923.

Fig. 6. Products from trees. left, Sam Mitchell, Lillooet, removing bark of lodgepole pine with a mule deer antler. Once the bark is removed, the soft inner tissue is scraped off and eaten fresh. Photograph by Nancy Turner, Pavilion Mountain, B.C., 1974. center, Louie Pichette, Colville, twisting gray willow withe, which is strong but flexible enough to use for tying. Photograph by Dorothy Kennedy, Colville Res., Wash., 1979. right, Delsie "Elsie" Albert Selam, enrolled Yakima from the village of Nawawi at Alderdale, Wash., stripping alder bark used to make a red dye. Photograph by Eugene Hunn, Alder Creek, Wash., 1986.

seeds, known as wokas (fig. 5), formed a substantial proportion of the Klamath diet (Coville 1904).

In all, about 60 species of fruits, seeds, and nuts were incorporated into the traditional diets of Plateau peoples.

• OTHER FOOD PRODUCTS In spring, the sweet, juicy cambium and secondary phloem tissues of several types of trees were sought as a food, but were apparently rarely eaten in the Southern Plateau. Lodgepole pine (*Pinus contorta*), ponderosa pine (*P. ponderosa*), and black cottonwood (*Populus balsamifera* ssp. *trichocarpa*) were three favored types. Slabs of bark were removed using a sharp implement (fig. 6 left), and the edible tissue was scraped from the outside of the wood or the inside of the bark, depending on the stage of growth of the cambium. It was generally eaten fresh and greatly enjoyed. The implement used for scraping off the edible tissue was often fashioned from the shoulder blade of a deer or other animal. A modern equivalent is made from a sharp-edged piece of tin can, whose curvature fits that of the tree. Use of this food has sharply declined within the twentieth century, partly due to prohibitions on harvesting by forestry officials.

Several species of mushrooms were eaten. These include pine mushroom (*Tricholoma magnivelare*; syn. *Armillaria ponderosa*), cottonwood mushroom (*T. populinum*), and oyster mushroom (*Pleurotus ostreatus*). They were generally harvested in mid to late fall, cooked and eaten fresh, or sliced and dried for storage. Within the twentieth century, they are often stored by freezing or canning (Turner et al. 1987).

A black, hairlike tree lichen ("Middle Columbia River Salishans," fig. 2, this vol.), known as "black moss" or "tree hair" (*Bryoria fremontii* and possibly other species), was another source of food. It was harvested from fir or pine branches in montane forests, usually in late summer, and had to be leached in running water, pounded, and then slowly pit-cooked to render it edible and digestible. It was sometimes cooked with wild onions or sweetened with serviceberry juice to enhance the flavor. It was formerly dried in flat cakes, which were cut into pieces for winter storage.

Used to thicken soups and other dishes, it was also important as a famine food (Turner 1977).

A sweet, crystalline mixture of sugars, including melezitose, was formerly obtained under special environmental conditions from Douglas fir boughs (*Pseudotsuga menziesii* var. *glauca*), but most people who recall tasting it from their childhood days say Douglas fir sugar can no longer be found (Turner et al. 1990:107–109). Larch and birch are said to yield a sweet-tasting sap, used by the Kootenai and others. A refreshing lemonadelike beverage is made from soapberries, and, as of the 1980s and 1990s, was still drunk in many Plateau households. Beverages were made from Labrador tea (*Ledum groenlandicum*, and *L. glandulosum*), mint (*Mentha arvensis*), wild bergamot (*Monarda fistulosa*), wild rose stems and flowers (*Rosa* spp.), and several other plants. The aromatic celery-flavored seeds and dried leaves of barestem lomatium were used as a flavoring for tobacco and tea. Additionally, mint, wild bergamot, and some wormwoods (*Artemisia* spp.) were used as preservatives, to repel flies and other insects from meat, fish, or berries being dried or stored. Pitch of pine, spruce, and larch were sometimes chewed as gum, as was the latex of milkweed (*Asclepias speciosa*), mountain dandelion (*Agoseris glauca*), and some other plants. Several types of plants were used to line cooking pits, serving to flavor the food as well as protect it from burning. These include Douglas fir boughs, dried needles of ponderosa pine, wild strawberry plants, fireweed stems, wild rose leaves and twigs, "red willow" branches, mountain alder branches (*Alnus incana*), shrubby pen-stemon (*Penstemon fruticosus*), and sticky geranium (*Geranium viscosissimum*).

Technologically Significant Plants

Materials from approximately 125 plant species were used in traditional Plateau technologies, including woods for fuel and construction; bark sheets for containers and canoes; root, stem, bark, and leaf fibers for cordage and weaving; and other plant materials used for dyes, preservatives, glues, caulking, scents and cleansing agents, and many other purposes.

• FUELS Almost any available type of wood could be used as a general fuel, but for specialized purposes, specific types were preferred. In the drier regions of the Plateau area, fuel was notably scarce, and people relied on driftwood or shrub-steppe species such as big sagebrush (*Artemisia tridentata*). Originally, fires were started by friction, using a hand "drill" and a "hearth." The drill was made of fairly dense, dry wood, often of pine tops or roots (*Pinus contorta*, *P. ponderosa*), black cottonwood root (*Populus balsamifera* ssp. *trichocarpa*), or willow (*Salix* spp.). In Lillooet, for example, the name for *Salix lasiandra* translates as 'match plant', alluding to its former use as fire drill material. The hearth was made of larger pieces of these materials, or of western red-cedar wood (*Thuja plicata*). Materials used specifically as tinder include: dry bracket fungus (*Fomitopsis pinicola*, *Fomes fomentarius*, and other species; apparently a modern usage); cinder conk (*Inonotus obliquus*); dried balsamroot taproot (*Balsamorhiza sagittata*), inner bark of western red-cedar, dry grass, and sagebrush bark. Douglas fir, pines (*Pinus* spp.), spruce (*Picea engelmannii*), quaking aspen (*Populus tremuloides*), and cottonwood were known as good general fuels, with green alder (*Alnus crispa*) being valued for baking and smoking fish.

• WOOD AND BARK General use of wood for construction of pit houses, frames, and various implements might sometimes have been opportunistic, but more often, preferred types of wood were used for specific purposes. For example, Douglas fir, lodgepole pine, and ponderosa pine were often employed for large construction projects, including houses and fishing platforms. Among the Kootenai and Flathead, tepee poles were often of lodgepole pine, whereas on the middle Columbia, peachleaf willow (*Salix amygdaloides*) was often used for lodgepoles. Dugout canoes, frequently of black cottonwood, were also made of western red-cedar (the usual dugout material for Northwest Coast peoples, and available as drift logs on the middle Columbia), Douglas fir, and ponderosa pine. Sapling wood of Douglas fir was used for dipnet hoops and shafts, as well as for snowshoe frames, berry drying racks, and other items. Western yew (*Taxus brevifolia*), when available, was a preferred material for bows and was also used for implement handles, digging sticks, and snowshoe frames. Rocky Mountain maple (*Acer glabrum*) was also used for such items and, in the southern area, was the preferred material for dip-net hoops. Rocky Mountain juniper (*Juniperus scopulorum*) was used for bows as well and for drum frames, as was western juniper (*Juniperus occidentalis*) in the southern Plateau. Oceanspray (*Holodiscus discolor*), serviceberry, and mock-orange (*Philadelphus lewisii*) woods were used for arrowshafts, digging sticks,

salmon-spreaders, and roasting sticks. Garry oak, which like oceanspray and mock-orange was known as an "iron wood," was also valued for its hardness in implement making. The flexible stems of red-osier dogwood and various willow species were used as spreaders in drying salmon and meat, and in constructing fishing weirs and traps, drying frames, sweatlodges, and temporary dwellings. Douglas fir boughs, and the aromatic boughs of grand fir (*Abies grandis*) and subalpine fir (*A. lasiocarpa*) were often used as "thatching" and "flooring" for these.

Large sheets of bark, cut and pried from standing trees, were important materials. The best known is paper birch (*Betula papyrifera*), used by Northern Plateau peoples for bark canoes and many types of containers, some of which were still being made by Shuswap in the 1990s. Canoes and vessels made of bark from white pine (*Pinus monticola*), Engelmann spruce (*Picea engelmannii*), and subalpine fir were also common in the northern region. Cottonwood bark was used for buckets, and bark sheets of all of these species were used for lining cache pits and as roofing.

• FIBROUS PLANTS Beautiful and intricate coiled baskets of many styles were made from the split roots of western red cedar and, sometimes, Engelmann spruce. The foundations for these were of bundles of split roots, or sometimes, thin splints of cedar sapwood. In the Northern Plateau geometric designs and patterns were made with natural colored and dyed-black cherry bark (*Prunus emarginata*, *P. pensylvanica*), with the split culms of grasses such as reed canary grass (*Phalaris arundinacea*) providing red, black, and white imbrication or overlay. In the Southern Plateau, beargrass leaves (*Xerophyllum tenax*) and, since the 1800s, corn husks, were of primary importance for basketry design. Lower Lillooet, Thompson, and Klikitat women were famous for their coiled cedar-root baskets. Klikitat berry baskets were also made from the outer bark of red cedar, folded and sewed with cedar root (Kuneki, Thomas, and Slockish 1982; Schlick 1994). Within the historic period, many supported their families by trading their baskets for food, clothing, and other necessities. They even adapted this weaving style to make European-type objects—trays, fancy tabletops, and cups with saucers—to appeal to White settlers and tourists. The art of making these baskets was still practiced in Mount Currie and some other communities of British Columbia and at Husum in Klickitat County, Washington, in the 1990s. Red cedar and spruce roots were also used for sewing and lashing, and red-cedar withes were used to make a strong rope. Hazelnut withes were used as bindings and straps.

Both tule stems (*Scirpus lacustris*; syn. *S. acutus*) and cattail leaves (*Typha latifolia*) were used to make mats and bags of various types, with tule predominating throughout (fig. 7). Mats were used as mattresses and coverings for tepees and summer lodges, as well as for berry-drying. Stems of common reed grass (*Phragmites*

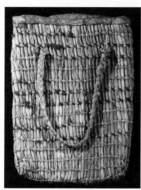

top left, Nicola Valley Mus. Arch. Assoc., Merritt, B.C.; top right, Canadian Mus. of Civilization, Que.: II–C–502 and II–C–633 (neg. 94–57); Amer. Mus. of Nat. Hist., New York: bottom left, 16/8707; bottom center, 16/9374; bottom right, Glenbow-Alberta Inst., Calgary, Alta.: 674–10.

Fig. 7. Use of fibrous plants by the Thompson. top left, People dressed in willow and cedar bark capes for a Passion Play. An adult cape required about 100 stems of Indian hemp to produce the thread and took about 2 weeks of work to gather and prepare the hemp weft (Tepper 1994:23–31). Photographed at the Nicola Ranch, Keremeos, B.C., about 1900. top right, Hat and leggings made of shredded sagebrush bark twined together with fiber. They are trimmed with buckskin strips and painted with red and brown dots. Bark hats were used sometimes by very poor people of both sexes, but more commonly by old women in rainy weather. Bark leggings were used by a very few poor old women. Collected by James A. Teit, Spences Bridge, B.C., before 1920. Height of hat 40 cm. bottom left, Model of tule canoe. Actual tule canoes were made of 2 or 3 thicknesses of tule mats overlapping the gunnel and sewn underneath. The ribs were made of light wands placed every 6–8 ins., and the floor was of bark. These canoes varied in size, but all were very lightweight and easily carried by a single person. The tules swelled when the canoe was placed in water, making the craft watertight. Collected by James A. Teit in 1901. Length 95 cm. bottom center, Fishing bag make of rushes. Collected by James A. Teit from the Upper Thompson, 1903. Length 49 cm. bottom right, Thompson River camp with sunshade and backrest made of plant fiber mats. Photograph by Frederick Dally, 1867–1868.

australis; syn. *P. communis*) were also used to make berry-drying and fish-draining mats in some areas such as along Nicola Lake, British Columbia, and in Sahaptin country. Stem fiber of Indian hemp (*Apocynum cannabinum*) was formerly a primary material for cordage ("Wasco, Wishram, and Cascades," fig. 8, this vol.), fishnets, woven bags, and capes and other types of clothing. The mature stems were harvested in the fall, split and dried, then pounded and worked to separate the fiber from the brittle, pithy stem tissues. The bundles of fiber were then hand spun into twine, usually by rolling it along the leg, with additional fiber being spliced in at intervals. Large balls of Indian-hemp twine were a valuable trading item in some areas. A "time ball" of Indian-hemp twine

was kept by a woman as a record of key events in her life, with knots signifying events tied in sequence (Leechman 1921; M.R. Harrington 1921).

The inner bark of silverberry (*Elaeagnus commutata*) was another important fiber, limited to the northern and eastern margins of the Plateau. It was woven into cordage and used for bags and capes and other clothing. Willow stems (fig. 6 center) and bark were also used for cordage, particularly sandbar willow (*Salix exigua*), known as "rope plant" in Lillooet. Sagebrush bark and black tree lichen were sometimes used for weaving clothing (fig. 7 top right; "Northern Okanagan, Lakes, and Colville," fig. 7, this vol.) but were generally regarded as suitable only for poor people. Occasionally stinging-nettle stem fiber

(*Urtica dioica*) was used, but this was far more common on the coast. Coastal peoples preferred Indian hemp twine, which they obtained through trade, to that of nettle-bark for its greater strength (Elmendorf 1960).

• DYES, STAINS AND PRESERVATIVES A reddish-brown dye obtained from alder bark (fig. 6 right) (*Alnus incana, A. crispa*) was used to color buckskin, wool, hair, feathers, porcupine quills, and other materials. Indian paint fungus (*Echinodontium tinctorium*) conks were powdered and mixed with deer fat, then applied as a face paint, by the Sahaptin and other Plateau peoples. Wolf lichen (*Letharia vulpina*) and the inner bark of Oregon grape yield bright yellow dyes. In the Southern Plateau, the rhizomes of veiny dock, *Rumex venosus*, were used to make a reddish-brown colorant for moccasins and preserved skins. Various other stains from fruits, flowers, and leaves were used to some extent (Turner et al. 1990:38). Cherry bark for basket imbrication was used in its natural reddish-brown color or dyed black by burying it in moist organic soil for several months. Alder bark apparently functioned as a preservative or tanning agent when used on hides. Other agents for curing or smoke-tanning hides include bracket fungi, rotten wood, sagebrush and wormwoods (*Artemisia* spp.), Rocky Mountain juniper (*Juniperus scopulorum*), and ponderosa pine cones. The root of chocolate tips (*Lomatium dissectum*) was used as a bleaching agent for hides at Warm Springs Reservation.

• OTHER TECHNOLOGY Various moss and lichen species, especially sphagnum moss in northern areas, were used to chink the cracks between logs of cabins; many elders recall as children collecting large quantities of moss for this purpose. Mosses and cattail and milkweed seed fluff were used as diaper material to line cradles. The rough-stalked horsetails (*Equisetum* spp.) were used as abrasives for smoothing and polishing wood and soapstone pipes. Cottonwood bud resin was used as a glue and paint base, spruce pitch as an adhesive, and prickly-pear cactus mucilage as a paint fixative. The blossoms and leaves of snowbrush (*Ceanothus velutinus*), mock-orange, and cottonwood inner bark yielded a lathery substance used as soap.

Many plants, especially coniferous trees and aromatic plants, were used for scents and cleansing agents, and a number of these were specifically applied to protect the user against illness, death, or other harmful influences. For example, juniper boughs (including Rocky Mountain and western junipers) were used almost universally in this capacity, to cleanse a household at times of severe illness and death. Subalpine fir boughs were highly regarded as a scent (Turner 1988; Hunn 1990:185). Wild rose (*Rosa* spp.) was used like juniper as a cleansing, disinfecting, and protecting agent. Among Sahaptins, it was the primary agent used against "ghosts" and "haunting." The strongly scented big sagebrush and its relatives were also used in this way. There are numerous other uses of plant materials, ranging from the use of silverberry seeds as decorative

beads, vanilla leaf (*Achlys triphylla*) as a cachet, and ponderosa pine needles to stuff mattresses and pillows, to the use of water knotweed (*Polygonum amphibium*) flowers as trout bait and of fleabane (*Erigeron* spp.) and shooting star (*Dodecatheon* spp.) flowers for patterns in basketry (Turner et al. 1990:39–40).

Medicinal Plants

The Thompson alone used at least 200 species of plants in medicinal preparations, for treating illnesses and injuries, and for the maintenance of health. Nearly 120 species of medicinal plants have been recorded for Sahaptin-speaking peoples. When the entire Plateau region is considered, medicinal plants must number somewhere between 250 and 300 species, and many of these were still being used as of the 1990s. As well as these, many plants were used as charms and "spiritual" medicines for strengthening, purification, and protection.

• CONCEPTS OF ILLNESS AND HEALTH Steedman (1930:456) provides a glossary in Thompson for a wide range of recognized ailments—colds and coughs, indigestion and loss of appetite, tumor, headache, sore feet, internal pains, swellings, constipation, retention of urine, "spreading and eating sores," vomiting, and diarrhea—virtually all of which were treated with herbal medicines. Injuries, broken bones, and aspects of menstruation, conception, and childbirth were treated with medicinal plant preparations. Various herbal preparations were applied to the maintenance of health, cleansing and purification, and "changing of the blood" in spring and fall. Palmer (1975:41) provides a comparable table of Shuswap ailments and botanical cures.

It is impossible to separate medicine and ritual practice in traditional Plateau cultures. Plants used as protective scents, and those taken internally or used externally in ritual purification, are considered to be as important in the maintenance of health and well-being as are medicines used for coughs or to alleviate constipation. Physical and "spiritual" health are not clearly divided, nor are the treatments for ailments of the body and spirit. Disorders attributed to supernatural causes may be alleviated by a shaman, or "Indian doctor," who is trained in the "magical" applications of plants and other techniques relating to the world of the supernatural. Other ailments are generally treated by a herbal specialist, or by anyone within the community having particular knowledge of medicinal plants. Even "ordinary" herbal medicines are treated with great respect, seriousness and a certain amount of ritual. It was said to bring bad luck to the user to pull up medicines in a casual or frivolous way, and medicines gathered carelessly may, it was believed, lose their ability to heal.

It is also unrealistic to separate totally "medicine" and "food" in Plateau cultures, since many foods, such as soapberry, were taken to improve health, and many medicinal preparations also provided important nutrients (Turner et al. 1990:43).

• HERBS   Herbal medicines include all parts of plants: leaves and stems, bark, roots, sap or resin, flowers, and fruits. Many of these—particularly tonics, general medicines, digestive tract medicines, medicines for colds and respiratory ailments, medicines for kidney and urinary ailments, and medicines used as gynecological aids—were in the 1990s taken internally in the form of an infusion (made by soaking the medicinal plant part in boiling water) or a decoction (made by boiling the medicine for a period of time). The decoction is considered slightly stronger. Infusions or decoctions might be drunk over a period of several days or weeks, as a replacement for other beverages. Sometimes whole parts of plants or pitch were chewed and the juice swallowed. For certain ailments such as respiratory complaints or fever, the medicine could be inhaled as a vapor, often as a steambath in a sweatlodge. Aromatic plants such as juniper (*Juniperus* spp.), wormwoods (*Artemisia* spp.), and yarrow (*Achillea millefolium*) were particularly used in this way.

External applications consisting of mashed or bruised plant parts, salves, or powdered dried or burned plants were the usual treatment for skin disorders—cuts, scrapes, boils, or burns. Counterirritants such as stinging nettle and members of the buttercup family (Turner 1984), or local anaesthetics such as the highly poisonous Indian hellebore (*Veratrum viride*), were applied externally to alleviate arthritic pain, bruises, and other subcutaneous afflictions. Arthritis, rheumatism, and muscular pains were treated with external washes of plant solutions and in the sweathouse. Palmer (1975:49) describes the use of tree fungus tissue (cinder conk) for treatment of pains, stiff and sore joints, headache, toothache, and bruises; it is ignited over the site of the pain and allowed to burn until it "pops," after which the pain vanishes.

Animals, especially horses, were commonly treated with herbal medicines; for example, the Flathead applied sticky geranium and the rhizomes of yellow pond-lily to horses' sores and cuts. Sahaptins had their winded horses inhale a vapor of chocolate-tips roots to increase their stamina. Saddle sores on horses were treated with these roots (Meilleur, Hunn, and Cox 1990).

Comprehensive lists of herbal medicines are provided by Turner et al. (1990:44–51) for Thompson, and by D.H. French and K.S. French (1979) and Hunn (1990:351–358) for Sahaptin. Table 1 lists a few examples of widely used plant medicines of Plateau peoples.

Few of these or other medicinal plants traditionally used by Plateau peoples have been thoroughly analyzed for their biochemical content or physiological effects. Initial research indicates positive correlations between medicinal use and efficacy in many cases. The effectiveness of cascara (*Rhamnus purshiana*) as a laxative is documented (Claus et al. 1970). Similarly, use of kinnikinnick as a urinary tract medicine and of Oregon grape as an eye medi-

cine are known in commercial pharmacology. The use of willows, which contain salicylic acid, a precursor to acetyl salicylic acid, or aspirin, for fevers and sores is another indication of the depth of medicinal knowledge of Plateau peoples. Chocolate tips is known for its bactericidal properties (Meilleur, Hunn, and Cox 1990).

Plateau peoples were aware of the highly toxic properties of plants such as Indian hellebore, water-hemlock (*Cicuta douglasii*), death camas (*Zigadenus venenosus*), and baneberry (*Actaea arguta*), and learned to use them, with extreme caution, as medicines. The best antidote for poisoning from these plants was said to be salmon oil or some other type of fat.

Symbolically Significant Plants

Plants, animals, and all natural objects were respected for their innate power, and their ability to influence, positively or negatively, the lives of humans. Hence, plants were important in many rituals, either in a central capacity as a recognition of their primary resource value, or in a supportive role, wherein the innate qualities of the plants enhanced the ceremony or ritual observance of a life-cycle event or the seeking of supernatural aid or power. An example of the first is in the first-fruits ceremonies that celebrate the beginning of the harvesting season for bitterroot, serviceberry, black huckleberry, and other important gathered foods (Hunn 1990; Hart 1979; Turner, Bouchard, and Kennedy 1980:152).

The second type of ritual role is reflected in the use of aromatic plants such as juniper and wormwoods as incense for ritual purification in the sweathouse, or the use of plants such as wild rose, Oregon grape, and juniper to protect bereaved friends and relatives from the spirit of a recently deceased person. Another example is the widespread use of Douglas fir boughs in puberty rites ("Thompson," fig. 8, this vol.), hunting rituals, and other ceremonies (Turner et al. 1990:109–110). Many plants, some of which could be considered toxic if taken in excess, were drunk as infusions or decoctions to cleanse one's system, as emetics and laxatives. Those seeking special protection or strong powers for hunting, fishing, or healing would often undertake such treatment. For example, an infusion of tobacco was drunk as an emetic after the death of a close relative (Hunn 1990:230).

Tobacco and smoking rituals were important in Plateau culture. Originally, native tobacco (*Nicotiana attentuata*) was the major smoking ingredient, often mixed with kinnikinnick or other substances such as red-osier dogwood bark or the seeds of red columbine (*Aquilegia formosa*). Sumac leaves (*Rhus glabra*) were smoked with kinnikinnick in some Shuswap ceremonies. Within the historic period, commercial tobacco gradually supplanted the role of native tobacco and kinnikinnick. Sweetgrass braids (*Hierochloe odorata*), widely used as incense in purifica-

Table 1. Selected Herbal Medicines

Abies lasiocarpa (subalpine fir) - liquid pitch eaten or taken in hot water for coughs, colds, influenza, tuberculosis; used externally for sores, bruises, sprains; pulverized needles as baby powder, skin salve; decoction of bark used as eyewash, drunk for gonorrhea, and as purgative; decoction of branches used as wash or drink for ritual purification in the sweathouse; boughs used as protective scent for young women at puberty.

Achillea millefolium (yarrow) - leaves and roots used as blood purifier, and for colds, diarrhea, sore eyes, toothaches, cuts, sores, and swellings, and infertility (drunk as infusion; used as external poultice or wash).

Actaea arguta (baneberry) - (toxic); infusion or decoction of roots taken with extreme caution as emetic and purgative for general sickness, arthritis, bronchitis, syphilis, rheumatism, snake bites; said to make patient very sick initially.

Anemone multifida (Pacific anemone) - fresh leaves used as counter-irritant poultice for sores, swellings, bruises, arthritis; seed fluff used to staunch nose bleeds; infusion used as wash against fleas, lice.

Arctostaphylos uva-ursi (kinnikinnick) - decoction or infusion of leaves and stems used as wash for sore eyes, burns; drunk for colds, coughs, tuberculosis, kidney ailments, and as general blood tonic, especially in "changing of the blood" (Turner, Bouchard, and Kennedy 1980).

Artemisia ludoviciana and other *Artemisia* spp. (wormwoods) - purification in sweathouse; infusion drunk for coughs, influenza, tuberculosis, arthritis, indigestion, diarrhea; wash for swellings, bruises, itches, sores, broken bones; used as purifying "disinfectant" in house or sweathouse, against illness, death, and harmful influences.

Artemisia tridentata (big sagebrush) - infusion drunk or used as external wash or inhaled for colds, laryngitis, fever, headache, tuberculosis, arthritis (some say too strong for internal use); used in house and sweathouse as purifying and protective incense.

Berberis aquifolium (Oregon grape) - infusion used as eye medicine; drunk as contraceptive, liver tonic, blood tonic, and for upset stomach and venereal disease.

Ceanothus velutinus (snowbrush) - infusion drunk for colds, fever, influenza, dull pains, weight loss, diarrhea, or general illness; powdered leaves used as a salve for burns, sores; decoction of branches used as wash or in steambath for rheumatism, arthritis, broken bones, or gonorrhea.

Chaenactis douglasii (false yarrow) - decoction drunk for swellings and as stomach tonic; used as a wash or poultice for skin ailments, burns, wounds, spider and insect bites.

Equisetum hiemale (scouring rush) - infusion or decoction drunk for urinary ailments, venereal disease, childbirth and postpartum medicine; decoction of stems, or liquid from stem segments used as eye medicine; stem ashes used as powder for burns.

Goodyera oblongifolia (rattlesnake plantain) - leaves as poultice for cuts, blisters, boils, rheumatic pains; chewed as childbirth medicine, and to determine the sex of the fetus.

Heuchera cylindrica (alumroot) - root applied to boils and sores, especially mouth sores; infusion drunk for stomach ache and diarrhea.

Juniperus communis (common juniper) - infusion drunk for colds, tuberculosis, fevers, pneumonia, aching muscles, kidney ailments, high blood pressure; used as eye wash and protective wash for hunters and others requiring purification.

Juniperus occidentalis/J. scopulorum (junipers) - boughs burned or steamed as purifying incense; infusion used as protective wash for hunters, bereaved people, and those seeking luck; used in sweathouse purification rites; infusion drunk for colds, coughs, sore throat, fever, measles, chickenpox, influenza, venereal disease, kidney ailments, and at the onset of labor in childbirth; "berries" eaten for kidney disease; decoction of boughs used as external wash for bites, stings, rheumatism, itching, and to kill ticks on horses.

Larix occidentalis (western larch) - infusion of boughs and bark drunk for tuberculosis, laryngitis, breast cancer, ulcers, poor appetite, any general illness; also used as temporary contraceptive.

Ligusticum canbyi (Canby's lovage) - root chewed for colds, sore throat, fevers, tuberculosis; used as poultice for cuts, burns.

Lomatium dissectum (chocolate tips) - infusion or poultice of root used for dandruff, lice, sores, boils; infusion drunk for colds, sore throat, fever, and as emetic; vapor used to treat winded horses.

Mentha arvensis (field mint) - infusion drunk for colds, coughs, fever, influenza; used as eye wash.

Oplopanax horridus (devil's-club) - decoction of wood drunk for tuberculosis; decoction or infusion of stem drunk for indigestion, arthritis, influenza, tuberculosis, general illness, post-partum medicine, and as tonic and blood purifier.

Paeonia brownii (Brown's peony) - infusion of root top as eye wash; root chewed or decoction drunk for worms, fever, tuberculosis.

Pinus contorta (lodgepole pine) - infusion of boughs drunk as tonic (not for pregnant women); pitch used as poultice for boils, swellings, sores.

Pinus ponderosa (ponderosa pine) - pitch as salve for burns, sores; infusion of young shoots taken for influenza (not for pregnant women).

Plantago major (broad-leaved plantain) - leaves a poultice for sores.

Rhamnus purshiana (cascara) - infusion of bark drunk as laxative and tonic.

Rhus glabra (smooth sumac) - infusion of root as eye wash or drunk for venereal disease, tuberculosis, kidney problems.

Salix spp. (willows) - leaves, shoots, bark used as poultice for cuts, wounds, sores; infusion drunk for coughs, colds.

Shepherdia canadensis (soapberry) - berry whip eaten as "health food" and for digestive tract ailments; decoction or infusion of branches and leaves drunk as purgative, laxative, tonic, stomach medicine, temporary contraceptive, and for high blood pressure; purgative properties used in ritual purification by hunters and young men at puberty.

Smilacina racemosa (false Solomon's-seal) - decoction of rhizomes drunk for colds, sore throat, lack of appetite, digestive tract and gynecological ailments, and internal injuries; decoction of leaves drunk for rheumatism.

Symphoricarpos albus (waxberry) - berries used as eye medicine; infusion of branches as wash for sores, eyewash; infusion drunk for tuberculosis, bed wetting.

Table 1. Selected Herbal Medicines (Continued)

Urtica dioica (stinging nettle) - counter-irritant for rheumatic pain, arthritis, backache, paralysis; used in sweathouse.

Valeriana sitchensis (mountain valerian) - roots chewed or drunk as a decoction for respiratory ailments (colds, coughs, tuberculosis), influenza, and digestive tract ailments such as diarrhea; mashed roots and leaves, powdered dried roots, or decoction of roots applied externally for swellings, sores and wounds.

Veratrum viride (Indian hellebore) - (toxic) root as external poultice for arthritis, rheumatism; some use for sores, scalp sores and lice, but others say do not use over open sores or cuts.

Sources: Turner 1981, 1982, 1984, 1988.

tion ceremonies by the Plains peoples, were also used by the Flathead and neighboring Plateau peoples.

Many plants were used as special charms, by virtue of their spiritual powers; these charms were said to ensure long life, obtain friendship, or bring high status, love, wealth, and success in hunting, gambling, and other endeavors. Brightly colored flowers such as red columbine, tiger lily, and calypso (*Calypso bulbosa*) were valued as charms (Turner et al. 1990:55).

Plants also featured, in both natural and supernatural roles, in many Plateau myths and stories. For example, several versions exist of a story about the origin of black tree lichen from hair of Coyote, the trickster and transformer (Turner, Bouchard, and Kennedy 1980:14–15; Bouchard and Kennedy 1979:22–23). A widely known Salishan mythical tradition concerns the long taproot of desert parsley (*Lomatium macrocarpum*), called q̓ʷəq̓ʷíle in Thompson. It is said to have been the father of one of the "transformers"—beings who traveled around the world when everything was different from its present state, using their magical powers to change things to their present condition. To this day, the q̓ʷəq̓ʷíle root is associated with fertility and fathering of children (Turner et al. 1990:155). The Shuswap myth, The Man Who Married Grizzly Bear, focuses on the long-standing importance of "root vegetables" (Teit 1909:722). Another, about a poisonous tobacco tree (Teit 1909:646), emphasizes the important role of the native wild tobacco. A Northern Okanagan myth (Turner, Bouchard, and Kennedy 1980:103) concerns the origin of black huckleberries as a gift from the mountain goats. A Klikitat story relates how Cedar Tree taught women their basketry techniques (Beavert 1974; Kuneki, Thomas, and Slokish 1982:17–19).

Ethnozoology

Primary sources for information on the knowledge and use of animals by Plateau Indian peoples are the following: in general, Ray (1942); for Lillooet, Hill-Tout (1900), Teit (1906), Kennedy and Bouchard (1975b, 1992); for Thompson, Teit (1900), Bouchard and Kennedy (1973–1981); for Shuswap, Teit (1909), Kennedy and Bouchard (1975), Palmer (1975a, 1978); for Kootenai, Schaeffer (1935), Turney-High (1941);

for Okanagan-Colville, Hill-Tout (1911), Teit (1927–1928), Ray (1933), Elmendorf (1935–1936), Spier (1938), Kennedy and Bouchard (1975a); for Middle Columbia River Salish, Teit (1928); for Coeur d'Alene, Teit (1927–1928); for Flathead, Teit (1927–1928); for Nez Perce, Spinden (1908), Walker (1967), Marshall (1977); for Sahaptin, Hunn (1976–1991, 1979, 1980, 1980a, 1990, 1991), Hunn and French (1984), Murdock (1980); for Upper Chinookans, Spier and Sapir (1930), French (1961); and for Klamath-Modoc, Spier (1930). General information on Plateau fisheries is from Craig and Hacker (1940), Hewes (1973), Cressman (1977), Schoning et al. (1951), Rostland (1952), Schalk (1977), Kew (1976), and Lovell et al. (1986).

Fishing

Most accounts of Plateau subsistence emphasize the preeminent role of anadromous salmonid fish as a dietary staple. Hunn (1981) has challenged the view that salmon supplied the bulk of food energy for Plateau peoples in protohistoric times. He argues that plant carbohydrates were at least equally important. Nevertheless, fishing technology was highly developed, and a diversity of fishing techniques is known to have been in use in the Plateau since at least 7000 B.C. (Cressman et al. 1960; Sanger 1970; Kirk and Daugherty 1978; Chance 1973). The availability of anadromous fish correlates strongly with Plateau population distributions (Sneed 1971; Kew 1976; Hunn 1990:135).

At least 35 species of freshwater fishes are native to the Columbia and Fraser river basins within the Plateau culture area (Carl, Clemens, and Lindsey 1967; Bond 1973; Wydoski and Whitney 1979). Plateau native languages may recognize nomenclaturally as many as 20 "folk species" of fish (Hunn 1982:832), most of which are used for food. Native ichthyological classification agrees closely with that of Euro-American scientists, in particular in recognizing as distinct each species of salmon (*Oncorhynchus* spp.) and sucker (*Catostomus* spp.) known to occur in local waters (Kennedy and Bouchard 1975, 1975a; Hunn 1980). In some cases local fishes are yet more precisely differentiated, as when "jack salmon" are distinguished from typical chinook salmon and when sea-run trout, or steelhead (*Onchorhynchus mykiss, O. clarki*), are distinguished from nonanadromous populations of the same species (Hunn 1980). On the other hand, the several locally occurring species of dace (*Rhinichthys* spp.) and sculpins (*Cottus* spp.) are not distinguished nomenclaturally, but are "lumped" in single basic level taxa. Most of these "underdifferentiated" species are less than 10 centimeters long and are not eaten.

Anadromous salmonids of five species (including the steelhead) spawn in Plateau rivers ("Fishing," this vol.). Collectively they are by far the most important food fishes in the region. Access to these species varied substantially within the Plateau. Quantity, quality (e.g., fat content), and diversity of salmon generally decreases upstream (Kew 1976; Hunn 1981). Peoples living near headwater streams—in particular those above salmon-blocking obstructions—might depend more on trade with downstream, better-endowed allies for their salmon stores than on fishing at sites associated with their own villages (Walker 1967). Large seasonal gatherings at key fisheries, such as The Dalles and Kettle Falls, are noted in the early historical sources (Ross 1956). Nonresident visitors at these locations numbered in the thousands.

Columbia River runs were more reliable than those of the Fraser River. For example, Fraser River sockeye (*O. nerka*) exhibit a four-year cycle, with a single year of great abundance followed by three years of relative scarcity, during which years runs were less than 5 percent of peak year abundance (Ricker 1950; Palmer 1978). No such regular and dramatic cyclic variation occurs in the Columbia system. Significant shortfalls of migrating salmon are reported for the Columbia only far upstream, as at Kettle Falls (Chance 1973). At The Dalles and Celilo Falls eight distinct runs of five salmonid species occurred each year between April and October, minimizing the impact of events affecting any single salmon population or species. Large surpluses were produced there by Upper Chinookan and Sahaptin peoples for trade throughout the Plateau and toward the coast.

Major fisheries were located at falls and rapids where migrating fish could be readily harvested with dip nets, setnets, basket traps, or spears. Fishing sites at the Cascades, The Dalles, and Celilo Falls were the "property" of families, often controlled by a group of related older men. "Ownership" did not imply a right of exclusive access, but rather the right to regulate access by granting permission to visitors to harvest for their immediate needs (Spier and Sapir 1930:175; Hunn 1982a:34–35). The Kettle Falls fishery was managed as a commons, under the direction of a salmon chief who directed the utilization of basket traps placed beneath the falls (Kane 1925:217–218; Kennedy and Bouchard 1975a).

Other anadromous fish significant as food sources were the Pacific lamprey, known locally as "eel" (*Entosphenus tridentatus*), and sturgeon (primarily if not exclusively the white sturgeon, *Acipenser transmontanus*). The large sea-run lampreys were prized throughout the Plateau, and substantial quantities were dried ("Fishing," fig. 5, this vol.). Curiously, sturgeon were disdained by most Western Columbia River Sahaptin people and by some Nez Perce (Moulton 1983–, 7:130–131; Hunn 1980; Scrimsher 1967). Chinookan speakers and the Okanagan-Colville expressed no such aversion (Spier and Sapir 1930:174; Kennedy and Bouchard 1975a).

Valuable nonanadromous food fish include suckers, of which four species are known from the Plateau. The largest species may attain a length of 60 centimeters and weigh over three kilograms. On the Columbia River above Celilo Falls large-scale (*Catostomus macrocheilus*) and bridge-lip (*C. columbianus*) suckers were snagged from pools in small tributary streams where they spawn in late winter. They helped close the late-winter "nutritional gap." Though bony, their cultural value is attested in myth and ceremony (Kennedy and Bouchard 1975a; Hunn 1980). Resident trout (*Onchorhynchus mykiss, O. clarki*) harvests were incidental to other subsistence activities but supplied fresh fish for families camped in the mountains. The Okanagan-Colville called the Spokane Indians "Rainbow trout people" due to the abundance of that species in Spokane territory (Kennedy and Bouchard 1975a:12). Dolly Varden (*Salvelinus malma*) were avoided by Western Columbia River Sahaptins for their unacceptably eclectic feeding habits (Hunn 1990:163–165), while Lillooet and Shuswap knew the Dolly Varden but did not use it. The Okanagan-Colville called the Lakes Indians "Dolly Varden people" due to the abundance of this species in Lakes territory (Kennedy and Bouchard 1975a:12). Mountain whitefish (*Prosopium williamsoni*) were harvested throughout the Plateau in midwinter or early spring through the ice. Okanagan-Colville also fished through the ice for the introduced lake whitefish (*Coregonus clupeaformis*). Native cyprinids harvested for food include the northern squawfish (to 60 cm, *Ptychocheilus oregonensis*), chiselmouth (to 30 cm, *Acrocheilus alutaceus*), peamouth (to 35 cm, *Mylocheilus caurinus*), and redside shiner (to 18 cm, *Richardsonius balteatus*). They were too bony to be preferred.

Harvest techniques documented for the protohistoric Plateau include a variety of nets and traps; spears, harpoons, leisters, and gaffhooks; hooks and chokers; and a poisonous plant, *Lomatium dissectum* (Ray 1942; Rostlund 1952). Nets were knotted of Indian hemp twine. Mesh size was systematically varied using wooden net gauges depending on the target species. Dip and set nets used bag nets attached to a hoop—typically of vine or Rocky Mountain maple (*Acer circinatum, A. glabrum*) (Davies 1980:41; Hunn 1990:184). The hoop was lashed to a pole of Douglas fir up to five meters long. The net bag might be attached to the hoop via sliding rings of mountain goat horn (Teit 1930) so that the weight of a fish in the net would close the mouth of the net. Dip nets were hand held

their house to a lodge with five fireplaces simply by singing (Sapir 1909:311–313). Personal power songs, given by the spirit guardian, augmented the individual's talent or ability—prowess for men in hunting, fishing, war; for women in digging, tanning, weaving; for both in gambling, healing, storytelling, and matters of love. The shaman's powerful songs were carried by both men and women—sometimes by a man-woman (songs 4a, 4b) (Foltin 1971:62)—depending upon the individual's fortune in gaining the songs and determination to bear the responsibilities of using them.

Instruments

The only melody instrument common throughout the Plateau was the elderberry courting flute (fig. 1) (Merriam 1951:369). It differed from that of the Plains, Northeast, and Great Basin in technique of whistle-head construction. Instead of a sliding effigy-block and gasket to cover the tone-hole, the Plateau prototype had only a pine pitch insert and rawhide wrapping to focus the air stream (Merriam 1967:50; Teit 1930:165). The usual configuration was of six finger holes with one extra hole at the bottom end for a "sweeter tone" (song 12). Later metal flutes, such as those cut from gun barrels, show the same concepts: two extra pieces added by Plains fabricators, no pieces added by Plateau makers (Olsen 1979). Extant are a few three- to six-hole wing bone flutes, which produce a particularly sweet and delicate timbre, probably also used for courting. Wing bone whistles prescribed by one's spirit guardian for specific protections in war (fig. 1) (McWhorter 1940:300, 1952:429) usually had no finger holes (Collier et al. 1942:87).

The rasp, a serrated stick scraped with a bone, was a standard accompaniment for war dances held prior to 1800 (Spinden 1908:230). Hand drums of deerhide (fig. 2) stretched over round wooden frames (averaging about 35–40 centimeters in diameter) gradually replaced the rasp; Washat ceremony hand drums of the 1860s had a greater diameter. The large war drum (fig. 3) for four to eight players came into use by about 1890, following an infusion of Plains-style war and circle dances. Shamanic healers commonly used rattles of deer hooves on a stick (fig. 4). Some were tied around the wrists and ankles of dancers. In later years trade bells replaced hooves. Shells, bear or elk teeth, and rawhide spheres with seeds inside were in widespread use. Wooden rods pounded rhythmically upon a plank, sometimes with the addition of a hand drum, propelled the songs of the stick game (fig. 5). While drums accompanied their vigorous movements, war dancers sometimes blew on

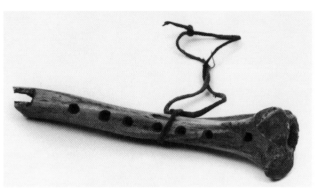

Amer. Mus. of Nat. Hist., New York: top, 16/8714 and 16/8715; center, 50.2/3854; bottom, after Wash. State U. Lib., Histl. Photograph Coll., Pullman: 82–034.

Fig. 1. Melody instruments. top, Thompson flutes made of elderwood, rawhide, and pitch. Collected by James A. Teit on the Thompson River, B.C., 1901. center, Kootenai courting flute (broken). This small flute has 7 holes and a rectangular stop that was originally bound with sinew. It was made from the leg bone of a dog. Collected by C.E. Schaeffer at Tobacco Plains, Mont., 1935. bottom, Nez Perce Yellow Wolf's war whistle made of a wing bone given to Lucullus V. McWhorter in 1909. Length of center, 23 cm; top to same scale.

547

top left, Nez Perce Natl. Histl. Park, Charles Kipp Coll., Spalding, Idaho: 350; top right, Eastern Wash. State Histl. Soc., Cheney Cowles Mus., Spokane: 1780.1035 (neg. 95.26); bottom right, Confederated Tribes of the Umatilla Indian Res., Pendleton, Oreg.

Fig. 2. Hand drums. top left, Nez Perces Bill Stevens, Jr., Charlie Wilson, and William Johnson, Sr., at a Circle Dance, Lapwai, Idaho, 1950. top right, Spokane hand drum of hide stretched over a curved wood frame and painted in red and black; manufactured about 1920; diameter 43 cm. bottom left, Washat drumming and singing preceding the meal at the Root Feast. left to right, unidentified drummer; C. Bill Moody, Warm Springs Sahaptin; Ed Welch, tribe unidentified; women singing in foreground, Blanche Tohet, Warm Springs Sahaptin and Juanita Wananawit Charging Dog, Warm Springs Sahaptin. Photograph by David and Kathrine French, Agency Longhouse, Warm Springs Res., Oreg., 1951. bottom right, Members of a Headstart preschool class participating in the groundbreaking ceremony for the Tamustalik Cultural Institute, Umatilla Indian Res., Oreg. Photograph by Debra Croswell, 1995.

whistles, but in no instance were flute and percussion, or flute and vocal melodies, sounded together.

In 1805 Plateau natives watched Meriwether Lewis and William Clark's men dance to tunes from George Gibson's fiddle, the first European musical instrument they had heard (De Voto 1953:257). A North West Company inventory at Astoria in 1813 listed Jew's harps; and its later inventories for Columbia River trade from 1814 to 1819 included "musical instruments" (Weatherford 1971:71, 72). Father Modeste Demers used the handbell in his classes in 1840 at Astoria, Oregon (Blanchet 1878:120). By 1841 a church organ was in operation at Saint Mary's on the Flathead Reservation; in the same year Father Gregory Mengarini formed an Indian band consisting of a clarinet, flute, tambourine, piccolo, cymbals, two accordions, and a bass drum (Lothrop 1977:101). Rev. Cushing Eells played his bass viol in 1842 at Tshimakain Mission among the Spokanes; and in 1846 teacher Andrew Rodgers supplied entertainment on his violin at the Oregon mission of Dr. Marcus Whitman (Drury 1973, 2:142). Through the "military band" era of the 1880s and the boarding school period of the early 1900s (fig. 6) the influx of brasses, drums, and winds was enormous.

Dance

The Okanagan legend "Snow Dance of Coyote" illustrates dimensions of power emanating from properly performed dance. Even when arrayed against all the animal spirits including the potent Bluejay, Coyote triumphs as long as he follows the directions of his *scomeq* or tutelary (Maud 1978, 1:137–139). Dance appears a persistent necessity in religious and secular Plateau Indian life, as recorded in oral and historical accounts. Upon his first hearing of the singing of Thompson Indians in 1897, Franz Boas remarked on their tendencies to add physical gesture and emotions to song. When vocalizing his song a Thompson Indian doctor gesticulated, danced, jerked, jumped, walked, and tussled (Teit 1900:362–363). When Plateau youths received songs from visionary spirit guardians, they were often given instructions as to the accompanying dance required for accessing power (Schuster 1975:26; Wickwire 1982:247). Some prophets gave directions for choreography of worship dances, such as "knee dancing," an innovation described in accounts from Yakima and Klikitat people (Schuster 1975:431; Du Bois 1938:8–9). In the 1850s upon his return from the land of the dead, the prophet Smohalla detailed to his people the Washat dance to go with his new song for restoration of Indian traditional life (Relander 1956:81–84):

> Sound of the bell, sound of the heart.
> My brothers, my sisters, I am meeting you.
> I am meeting you at the dance.

The Washat Children's Dance positioned boys on one side of the floor and girls on the other, bouncing in place. At the song's fourth verse each dancer circled counterclockwise, with hops to the right, left hand over the heart, right hand flexed and waving in time (Schuster 1975:428).

One dimension that set an Indian Shaker Church apart from other Christian denominations was the counter-clockwise stomping dance and resultant din, with full voices and bells, required for effective worship (Gunther 1949:66; Du Bois 1938:23).

In a notable equivalent to "counting coup," Nez Perce warriors stole the Crow War Dance and its songs under cover of darkness (Spinden 1908:271). The Kootenai celebrated a Plains-style Sun Dance (Turney-High 1941:178–194). The Klamath held Dream Dances evolving from a California Earth-lodge cult (Nash 1937:92). The Thompson and Shuswap borrowed dances from the Northwest Coast potlatch (Teit 1930:164). "If I hear a drum my heart just seems to be full of happiness and starts beating with the drum and dancing with the drum" (Wickwire 1982:246).

Musicality

Clark described his encounter with Middle Columbia River people in October 1805: "About 200 men singing and beeting on their drums and keeping time to the musik they formed a half circle around us and sung for some time" (DeVoto 1953:251). On their return Lewis and Clark met a combined group of Chamnapams and Walla Wallas: "The whole assemblage of Indians about 350 men and women and children sung and danced at the same time" (DeVoto 1953:367). Early missionary accounts of the Indians of the Plateau include references to their ability to memorize melodies, their love of singing, musical talent, quickness in picking up instruments never before played (Lothrop 1977:102, 164, 168, 200), positive response to hymns (Spokane Garry in Drury 1973, 1:44), and enjoyment of part-singing (Drury 1973, 1:44; 2:24; Lothrop 1977:101–102).

The pageantry of the Indian welcome at the 1836 Green River Rendezvous included the Indians'

> ...masterly horsemanship, very natural sham fights and national airs, consisting of a few striking words oft repeated, but sung in a plaintive tone, in which they were joined by a large band of young women, riding in an extended column behind, their wonderfully sweet voices keeping most excellent time, floating far throught the air ... (dresses) hung with hawk-bells and steel top thimbles, and fine bead work, hung with phylacteries of elk teeth and tin coils, producing a regular, loud, but not harsh jingle, as their fiery steeds pranced slowly along ... and all accompanied by the constant pounding of a great number of Rocky Mountain gongs, or Indian drums, the terrific screams of a number of whistles made of leg-bone of the grey eagle and swan, the constant jingle of the 'medicine rattle box' and heavy clang of hawk-bells, tin coils, bear claws and human bones trimmed with human scalps hanging upon every horse ....interrupted now and then by a terrific battle-yell, bounding off in a vibrating war-whoop, almost sufficient to curdle the blood in our veins ....They are seen already collected in a thick group hard by, bounding up and down in the scalp dance, all as one being, first upon one leg and then the other, taking three steps, keeping the most perfect time with the beat of the drum and the voices of the singers (Spalding 1836:61–62).

Father Mengarini wrote: "It is incredible how the savages like music" (Lothrop 1977:102).

Guardian-Spirit Songs

To seek a personal helper the Plateau boy or girl would, following extensive preparation by elders, set out to a distant isolated spot for several days and nights. The youngster would not eat during his sojourn, but would remain ready spiritually for the visit of a supernatural being who would communicate with him and give him a personal song (songs 2a, 4a). Although not revealed until a winter dance years in the future, the sublimated power and the proscriptions for its accession were enough to transform the youth into a responsible young adult who had experienced something unforgettable. Shamans orchestrated and encouraged the emergence of one's personal song at the Winter Dance, the major religious ceremony of the Plateau (Ray 1939:102). This song, guarded carefully by each individual who owned one, might be used thereafter to summon tutelary power in times of need. Musical examples reflecting proficiencies for buffalo hunting, weather manipulation, gambling, safety from missives in war, or escape from danger involved cryptic texts repeated in intervals of improvisation:

Fig. 3. Large drums in use. top left, War Dance at Nespelem, Wash. Nez Perce drummers left to right, Yellow Wolf (hat), Rosebush (hat), Luke Wilson, and Yakima Cleveland Kamiaken, Far right with flute is Luke Wilson's father. Photographed about 1909. top right, Elijah Williams, Nez Perce living on the Colville Res., Wash. Photographed late 1940s or early 1950s. center left, Group at Spokane fairgrounds, Wash. left to right, possibly Mrs. John Stevens; Shorty Meshell, Coeur d'Alene; Old Coyote, Coeur d'Alene; Sam Boyd, Spokane from Wellpinit; Margaret Adams, Coeur d'Alene medicine man from Worley, Idaho; Charles Smeelt, Coeur d'Alene who lived on the Kalispel Res., well-known as a storyteller. Photograph by Thomas W. Tolman about 1910. center right, left to right, John Stevens (Spokane), Paul Oyaxn, Mamie Stevens, Jackson Eli, and Martha Joshua. Photograph by Thomas W. Tolman, Spokane, Wash., 1900–1910. bottom left, Flathead drummers. left to right, around the drum, Adolph (Happy) Nine Pipe, Tony (Buck) Finley, Paul Finley, Louie Nine Pipe, Molly Big Sam. Photograph by Barbara Merriam, Victory Field, Missoula, Mont., 1950. bottom right, Eaglebear drummers and singers led by Vaughn Eaglebear (left with braided hair) during one of their songs at the Omak Stampede, Wash. All are Colville Res. residents. Photograph by Sharon Grainger, 1993.

Waila yawixne (3 times)
Wine nisu
Wax metu weinèke; Awitsnatsaka
Hila yawixne; Waila yawixne
Ēha yawixne; Waila yawixne.

This is a Nez Perce song in which 'the wolf comes' is repeated in several ways, according to Spinden (1908:263), but Nez Perce speakers in the 1960s could not interpret its words (Haruo Aoki, communication to editors 1997).

Additional power songs inherited from gifted forebears, or received after more guardian-spirit quests, might form the basis for one's becoming a shaman or healer, as with this Klamath "conjuror's song":

Tuá kînû shatashtaknû´la?	What do I remove from my mouth?
nä´paks nû shatashtaknû´la.	The disease I extract from my mouth.
tuá´kî´nû shatashtatχî´sh?	What is the thing I am taking out?
nä´paks nû shatashtatχî´sh.	It is the disease I am taking out
	(Gatschet 1890:153).

Examples of these song types are extant (songs 4a, 4b), some in the memories of Christians who have forsaken the old ways. In a few instances twentieth-century Protestants and Roman Catholics, as well as Washat worshipers have held guardian spirits secretly and still carry their songs.

Music of Revitalization

Oral tradition indicates that before contact with Whites, Plateau dreamer-prophets sang of changes that would transform their world. The Thompson prophet Kwalos, the Coeur d'Alene prophet Circling Raven, the Kalispel Woesal, Shining Shirt of the Flathead, Wat-tilki of the Wasco, Katxot of the Columbia Salish, Dla-upac at Walla Walla, Shuwapsa of the Wanapam, the Nez Perce Tawis-waikt (song 1)—all sang songs and proclaimed their visions (McBeth 1908:156; Spier 1935:5–13; Du Bois 1938:8–11; Wickwire 1982:103–107; Ruby and Brown 1989:3–15). Their words, though cryptic, told of anticipated changes to the earth, the animals, and to the people's very existence: "All people and animals! Creation as existing to be overthrown, destroyed! Buffalos exterminated! Elk and deer fenced, confined. Eagles caged from flying! Indians confined to narrow bodies of land. Liberty and happiness broken and shortened" (McWhorter 1952:84).

Suddenly harsh historical and cultural realities beset the nineteenth-century Plateau people. Explorers, trappers, and traders brought new technologies, but also epidemics, guns, and whisky. Preachers, priests, and the Bible were soon followed by gold rushes, reservations, wars, allotments, and the loss of a way of life. From the depths of despair prophetic movements arose that sought, through prayerful song and dance, to restore the old ways. The present scourge would disappear and restoration of the natural order would follow if ritual and reverence for the earth revived. The dead would return; the world's end was near; Whites and unbelievers would be destroyed.

Sacred songs and dances arising in the region drew inspiration from indigenous prophet, worship, or praying dances of old, a reservoir for each succeeding generation of seers. The christianized Prophet Dance of the 1820s and 1830s; the Washat (Dreamer or Seven Drum religion) starting in the 1850s; the Klamath Ghost Dance, Earth-lodge cult, and Dream Dance of the 1870s to the 1890s; the Yakima Indian Shakers of 1890; and the Columbia River Feather cult of 1905—all carried musical elements, in form or function, from the Plateau dreamers of old (Spier 1935; Nash 1937; Du Bois 1938; Relander 1956; Suttles 1957; Foltin 1971; Schuster 1975).

Prophets Kutaiaxen (Yakima), Smohalla (Wanapam) and Skolaskin (Sanpoil), whose influence became so powerful in the 1860s, dreamed and sang of their visions in this long-held tradition among Plateau seers (Ruby and Brown 1989). Counterparts among neighboring groups were Homlai, Luls, and Walsack, of the Umatilla; Hununwe and Nukshai of the Walla

Fig. 4. Flathead deer-hoof dance rattle. Collected in 1925 by William Wildschut on the Jocko Res. (now Flathead Res.), Mont. Length 93 cm.

top, Wash. State U. Lib., Histl. Photograph Coll., Pullman: 70–0419; bottom, *Vancouver Sun*, B.C.

Fig. 5. Stick games in progress. top, Game at Okanogan, Wash. The men are using a cut lumber pounding board and pounding sticks to maintain the rhythm for their boisterous stick game song. The side facing the photographer is hiding the bones. Photographed 1908. bottom, An evenly matched game at Indian Days on the Lake Indian Reserve, B.C., indicated by the number of counter sticks on each side. The man on the left with a hat on is blowing on a pounding stick in order to improve his ability to correctly guess the location of the unmarked bones hidden in his opponents' hands. The side on the right is singing and beating a rhythm on the log while the bones are hidden. Extra pounding sticks are in a bundle on the left, resting on the traditional lodgepole pine pounding logs. Photograph by Neil MacDonald, Vernon, B.C., 1972.

Walla; Queahpahmah and Hackney at Warm Springs; Shramaya and Paskapum of the Yakima; Thomas, Husis-Husis-Keut, Somilpilp, and Kamiakin of the Palouse (Du Bois 1938:11–19; Ruby and Brown 1989:66). Earth's songs still flourished, transformed and augmented by the reviving energy from Washat worshipers, as with this Sahaptin song (Schuster 1975:418):

> *tiičám niimí wáwnakšaš luqumyal*
> Earth   our   body   lifetime(?).

> *tiičám niimí timná luqumyal*
> Earth   our   heart   lifetime(?).

> *kwáalisim waq̓íswit ku hášwit*
> Always   soul   and breath.

The song literature of Feather religion healers was rooted in that of the Washat. Jake Hunt, the founder of the Feather religion, learned from Ashnithlai the Washat chant, "Salmon, venison, camas, huckeberry, water" (Du Bois 1938:19, 41).

The Yakima version of the Indian Shaker Church, with candles and bells, arrived directly from its origins among the Skokomish (Barnett 1957:69–73). Sunday worship and evening healing services involved full-voiced rhythmic singing, stomping of heels, and moving in a circular counterclockwise direction while ringing handbells, but no drums were played (song 13). The material of the Shaker service has retained a mixture of musical elements from Protestant, Roman Catholic, and personal spirit sources (Barnett 1957:152, 235–237; Spier 1935:53; Gunther 1949:52–60).

Styles By Area

Northern Plateau

Three types of songs originated from the spirit world: personal tutelary spirit songs including ones for doctoring, songs from the mythological age passed down through ancestors, and songs coming by way of prophets from the Chief of the Dead. Some nonspiritual songs such as lullabies and mourning songs also came through tradition from the ancestors. "Lyric songs" including laments and love songs were composed by ordinary people for emotional expression. Girls contrived such songs during puberty training, practicing them until they became satisfactory (song 14).

Among the Lillooet certain potlatch elements from the coast included the "war" or "biting" dance, singing of clan songs, and the wearing of dance masks to impersonate clan ancestors (Teit 1906:283). A religious circle dance introduced new songs from the spirit world, with instructions from people who had died temporarily but had returned to earth (Teit 1906:284–286). In the Touching Dance a young man who had reached marriageable age would step forward to touch a girl's blanket or seize her belt, and if not rejected, could thus be married (Nastich 1954:61). Adultery or theft were tried and punished by public ordeal, a group singing out the guilt of the offender (Nastich 1954:29–30). In the Lillooet salmon ceremony the shaman directed all activities including a dance to propitiate the salmon spirit (Maud 1978, 2:116–117). The first few lines of a Lillooet Bear Song text reflect this propitiatory tone: "You died first, greatest of animals. We respect you and will treat you accordingly. No woman shall eat your flesh; no dogs shall insult you. May the lesser animals all follow you" (Hallowell 1926:60).

Specific to the Nicola was a death feast, which involved food burning followed by the moving of camp; all the while the relatives sang a "low wailing chant" (Wyatt 1972:185). Since the Thompson people had virtually absorbed the Nicola by the early 1800s, no other musical characteristics of the Nicola are known (Wyatt 1972:183–186; RCIPR 1974:551–555).

Distinctive among the Thompson was a potlatch introduced from the coast in the late 1800s, which employed welcome songs, dance songs, resting songs, song contests, and farewell songs (Teit 1900:297–299; Wickwire 1982:161–163). Principal song classes included lyric, dance, war, shaman, sweathouse, mourning, prayer, gambling, and cradle songs. No actual salmon ceremony was held, but general dances for renewal occurred at a carefully prepared spring dancing ground. A Thompson River "praying dance" held in conjunction with first-foods feasts involved circling, hands extended, palms upward, ending with a quickening of tempo and heavenward gaze (Maud 1978, 1:46). At the birth of twins a grizzly bear song (song 15) and ceremony with shaman and helper insured the babies' well being (Teit 1915–1921:44). Boys on guardian-spirit quests would sing all night long; mothers with newborn babes would dance all night long when first returning to the berrying grounds. Sweathouse songs were addressed to the "Sweatbathing Grandfather Chief." Songs for curing were improvised by the shaman. Dances occurred: in preparation of war, during the war expedition by women remaining at home, and again upon its victorious conclusion (Teit 1900:309–384).

Among the western Shuswap Northwest Coast-style dance societies required a special song literature (Teit 1909:578); these dancers were adept at bird and animal imitations (Teit 1900:383). Midwinter and midsummer solstice dances were held annually. A gifted Shuswap healer could discover the cause of a patient's soul loss by singing through the songs of other shamans until he began that of the sorcerer, at which time the sorceror would become mad, relinquishing his power over the victim (RCIPR 1974:646–647). A Shuswap Youth Dance (song 16a) for recreation was extant in the 1990s (Wickwire 1982:355–357).

Kootenai

The most important ceremony for the Kootenai, their seven-day Sun Dance (song 17), was similar to that of the Plains Indians but did not involve mutilation or self-torture. The Grizzly Bear Dance, an early spring prayer for plenty, was next in significance, with the spirit of the bear present during the ceremony (Turney-High 1941:105, 184–185; Schaeffer 1966). The "Bear Foster Parent Tale" describes how the ceremony was first given to the people from the bear spirits (Schaeffer 1947; Hallowell 1926). Other Plains characteristics exhibited by the Kootenai included using medicine bundles,

Okanogan County Histl. Soc., Okanogan, Wash.

Fig. 6. St. Mary's Mission band. Photograph by George Ladd, Mission (now Omak), Wash., 1913.

MUSIC AND DANCE

counting coup, and joining exclusive societies—the Shaman Society, Crazy Dog Society or Crazy Owl Society—each of which carried its own songs and the responsibility for their use. Mimetic dances such as the Prairie Chicken and Bison Dance, and recreational ones such as the Kissing Dance (song 7) were held:

Kissing Dance
Kitamuqotl kakuwetltitkat patlke Katlkokatlmaqenamnamatikteitlne.
Drum   dance man   woman.   Kissing give.
Setis tlakitlak natkokatlmaqatlne Namatikteitlne yunakane kapsins.
Blankets, divers things,   kiss.   Give   many   things.

Medicine Song
Tamoqotlne tsitlwanuknanukanamnamne.
They beat drums,   sing very much.
Yunakapsi kapsins kEtcukwat qatkinakine.
Many   things   get,   he recovers
(RCIPR 1974:214–215).

One children's circling game with song text is extant. No midwinter ceremonials or Bluejay Dances were held by Kootenais, but after 1910 some involvement with the Flathead dances began (Turney-High 1941:188). The most powerful shaman was the "blanket shaman," who could find lost articles, foretell the future, and heal. With powerful songs and whistle blasts he called certain spirits behind his blanket and worked his magic with their help (Chamberlain 1901:96). Drum construction was the exclusive province of the shaman. Whenever the people faced famine a Fir Tree Dance was held to bring back game to the region. Smoking was a daily occurrence; at sunrise a pious man would fill his pipe with tobacco and sing (Turney-High 1941:171). Gambling was persistent among the Lower Kootenai, and one song text complains: "Many things are lost gambling—horses, blankets shirts, guns, knives, money—everything lost" (RCIPR 1974:215).

Northern Okanagan, Colville, Lakes

Among the Northern Okanagan a new pattern for trading called the Drum Dance was introduced from the Thompson and Shuswap Indians around 1900. This activity employed messenger invitations answered by trade visits. Hosts and visitors beat drums during the entire travel sequence, dancing and drumming also during the subsequent trading (Walters 1938:77). The Northern Okanagans sang war songs, and warriors described their individual war powers, displaying trophies during the dance that preceded their departure; at the scalp dance following their return, warriors told of new exploits (Walters 1938:83). A Pinto Horse Song among the Okanagan (song 16b) uses virtually the same melody as the Shuswap Youth Dance Song.

Artist Paul Kane made several paintings of the Scalp Dance among the Colville Indians (Curtis 1907–1930, 7:63) in 1846 (fig. 7) and described it vividly: "Here she commenced dancing and singing, swaying the (Blackfoot) scalp violently about and kicking it, whilst eight women, hideously painted, chanted and danced round her and the fire. The remainder of the tribe stood round in a circle, beating drums, and all singing" (Harper 1971:figs. 127–129). One Colville shamanic dance featured a performance behind a mat, similar to that of the Kootenai, but involving the hidden shaman cutting himself in two at the waist to access powers of clairvoyance (Cline 1938:152).

The Winter Dance, of two to five nights' duration, is usually held inside a shaman's house, in a large room with a central pole that only a shaman may touch. Humming by one shaman begins the ceremony, and as he sings louder he approaches the pole. When it is grasped the medicine person has become one with his spirit. As long as he holds the pole his voice is that of his spirit, whose strange language may require an interpreter for the people. The shaman moves and the people follow, shuffling, hopping, or stamping. Songs and bouncy dances continue until the first shaman, exhausted, gives up the floor to the second and so on. After midnight food is served, and the dances resume. On the final night there is gift-giving and sometimes gambling (Lerman 1953–1954). The host's purpose in calling this event may be specific to someone's needs or simply to ensure health and welfare for all the people. In 1991 it occurred among the

Fig. 7. Colville Scalp Dance. left, Dance in progress. right, Women dancers' facial decorations. Watercolors by Paul Kane, Ft. Colvile, Oreg. Country, 1847. The date appearing on the painting, 1846, was evidently placed on the painting by Kane's grandson many years after the painting was completed (Ian MacLaren, communication to editors 1996).

Okanagan, Colville, and Lakes Indians (Wickwire 1982:195, 362; Olsen 1989).

Southern Okanogan, Sanpoil, Nespelem

The Southern Okanogan Winter Dance gave opportunity for neophyte shamans to sponsor a display of their power songs, under the tutelage of an older specialist. The specialist guided an initiate's spirit back to him from hidden regions and joined the two together, enabling the novice to experience his power song accompanied by other dancers. Most people with spirit powers reiterated them at the winter dances; feet together, knees bent, they jumped rhythmically while grasping the center pole and shaking the rattles on it. A person's whole body trembled when he sang his power song. Both men and women were empowered, but a berdache was considered a "good-for-nothing," and lacking in power. Seminude Bluejay or Owl sentries with blackened faces guarded the dance hall (Ray 1933:191–193). Shamans, active in controlling the flow of events, prepared the dance floor in a counterclockwise "sweeping" with feathers or brushes; there followed the host's hopping dance at the center pole, alluding to the source of his power. Individuals with their interpreters then proceeded successively to the center pole, doing songs and dances throughout the night, each supported by the congregated viewers who sang along. With men facing women, they dance in half-circles, in rows moving opposite directions, in rows moving similar directions, or simply in place. If the people became thirsty they could make frog noises, responded to by the dancing shaman's song of permission to get water (song 18). This winter ceremony for general good health and fortune usually lasted five or six nights, with gifts distributed to all in attendance (Cline 1938:146–150).

Other Okanogan dances included the spring Chinook Dance to ensure mild weather, the Dream Dance (song 19) with its prophetic elements, the Prayer Dance for thanksgiving and renewal of resources, and a Confession Dance that often followed natural calamities. Each person entering the sweathouse prayed to "Great-grandfather" after singing the sweathouse song (song 8) (Commons 1938:194). Singing and dancing were central to shamanic power contests and curing rituals. An isolated Southern Okanogan girl at first menses rites sang "Help me, Twilight" while facing west at evening, and "Help me, Dawn" at first light, facing east. She would continue dancing in high bounces, feet together, for several nights before returning to her home and family (Mandelbaum 1938:111). Power songs were sung when the men constructed fishing weirs, and a salmon ceremony occurred during the first four days fish were taken. The Southern Okanogan had no war or scalp dances (Walters 1938:83). Returning bear hunters would carry the dead animal while singing its song, joined gradually by the voices of everyone in the camp (Cline 1938:133–176).

Sanpoil and Nespelem bear hunters were required to sing a ceremonial mourning song when a bear was killed. The melody and vocables ("*xawa...xawaxawayi...*") were fixed but the intermittent song text was improvised (Ray 1933:84,

retranscribed and translated by Anthony Mattina, communication to editors 1997):

cqpəncútmstxᵂ i ʔ-snək̓ᵂɫc̓x̣íɫ ⟨nikxulqwa⟩
'You put those like you in the same predicament you are in.'
anwí ki ʔ kᵂ-ɫtək̓ᵂməcút i ʔ-csəp̓əncútmstxᵂ,
'It's you who falls down, who hits yourself,
i ʔ-pwálxkən mi scɫək̓ᵂməncútx
and the bucks will fall down, too'.

Successful gambling required powerful songs. In the legend Grizzly and Rabbit Play the Stick Game, rabbit's song "*Qwexqwex holewea*" defeats grizzly bear (Spier 1938:247). Extemporizing occurred in sweatlodge songs (song 8), following formalized introductory song texts such as "Grandfather, do that; (make) come true what I ask. I am your grandson. Everyone who is ill, who may be injured or sick, they go to you and ask you for relief and you give happiness" (Ray 1933:179).

Among the Nespelem a girl at puberty was to dance and pray for health each evening and morning during 10 days of solitude (Curtis 1907–1930, 7:75). The Sanpoil Dream Dance (see song 19) resulted from an elder's bequest given in a vision; the people became so immersed in this dance they performed it all summer, neglecting to lay up provisions for the winter.

Middle Columbia River Salishans

Shamans were numerous and powerful, with medicine songs their main accession devices for curing or malevolence. In one singer's repertoire were his own Skunk medicine song, together with those of Pelican, Mudhen, and Loon, each belonging to a different shaman; all were sung in one instance to rid a patient of a spell (Curtis 1907–1930, 7:84). Praying dances, marrying dances, and guardian spirit dances were given among the Moses Band. In the victory dance enemy scalps were displayed on the points of sticks. Additional large dances were held periodically in which warriors related their war deeds. The round dance was introduced later from the east. A Snow Dance and a Sun Dance (not Plains) were also celebrated.

Spokane, Coeur d'Alene, and Kalispel

A Spokane novice who received salmon power songs for opening the fishing season would announce this fact at the winter dances. The next summer, as the new salmon run began, he would try his ability under the tutelage of the elder salmon chief. Deer hunting songs of a novice might result in a similar opportunity in leading a hunting party.

Among the Spokanes a January medicine dance was announced by a man singing his medicine songs. This host and others assembled for four nights in the longhouse, each performing a complete repertoire of spirit songs while grasping a central pole. Each dancer tied an offering to the pole, which at the ceremony's end was secreted high in the wilderness (Curtis 1907–1930, 7:87). Missionary Elkanah Walker commented on the persistence of these dances in 1841, writing that they closed with a feast and the handling of red-hot stones (Drury 1976:132–133). Manipulating hot stones (Curtis 1907–1930, 7:85) also was part of a Spokane sweathouse ritual; this preceded medicine dances for the departure of hunters or warriors. Spokane Garry (d. 1892), educated by Anglicans at the Red River Mission School near present-day Winnipeg, Manitoba, from 1825–1829, resisted Jesuit influences as they began to establish missions in the Spokane area. In the 1990s Garry's descendents, the Sijohn family, were leading musicians among Spokane and Coeur d'Alene Roman Catholics (song 10).

Chants and hymns of Roman Catholicism, added to the regional repertoire since the 1840s when the mission at Coeur d'Alene opened, reflect the arrival of Fathers Nicolas Point and Pierre-Jean de Smet to the Plateau (song 20). Over the years hymn translations in the Kalispel language were collected by Jesuit Fathers John Post, William Ryan, Joseph Bandini, and Tom Connolly, with the 1880 and 1953 hymnbooks resulting (Oregon Province Archives 1976:36–42). A cave near Usk, Washington, served as a chapel for Jesuit missionaries among the Kalispel in 1845. In 1989 Father Tom Connolly led Indian hymn singing in a commemorative mass in the same cave. The Cataldo Mission Centennial, August 12, 1990, involved hymn singing in Salish, a pageant reenacting the arrival of Father de Smet, and Indian dances of celebration.

Flathead and Pend d'Oreille

Dependent upon the bison and constantly fighting with the Blackfoot over horses and hunting resources, the Flathead and Pend d'Oreille shared certain Plains musical characteristics—buffalo calling songs, weather control songs, an extensive war song repertoire, wake-up songs, evening ride or parade songs, and Crazy Dog Society songs. A distinction between "real" songs from the vision quest and "make-up" songs newly composed reveals a native concept of the supernatural origins of song power (Merriam 1967:19–20). Songs may exist "floating" in a nonhuman realm and then in optimum conditions they "find" the singer (Johnny Arlee, personal communication 1991). Ceremonials included first roots, prayer, and thanksgiving dances, the Jumpin' Dance, and Bluejay Dance. Miscellaneous categories include the Bear Dance, Peace Song, Dance of the Chase, Turkey Dance, Joy Song, Thunder Song, and Grass Dance (Turney-High 1933; Merriam 1967).

"Between 1812 and 1828 a group of some 24 Iroquois, under the leadership of Ignace Lamoose, settled among the Flathead" and held a service "interspersed with singing and dancing in a great circle after the fashion of the older, native prophet dance" (Ewers 1963:7–8). The impact of Iroquois Roman Catholicism may well have altered "the entire course of Flathead history" (Merriam 1967:124). After 1841 Fathers de Smet, Point, and Mengarini became involved directly in the daily lives of the people—building and planting, leading worship, teaching and healing. They joined buffalo hunts and raid-

ing parties, offered saints in place of animal guardians, medicines for shamans, and chants for spirit songs (see Peterson 1993). The Flatheads were eager, gifted music students (Lothrop 1977:221). Musical evidences abound showing gradual but permanent changes in the religious life of the Flathead people (Trepp 1966). In the 1990s Salish language hymns enhanced the annual Saint Mary's Mission pilgrimage commemorating Jesuit beginnings and recounting the exodus northward of Flatheads from their Bitterroot Valley home. Songs to Grandfather Sweatlodge still sung in the 1990s. The Jumpin' Dance and Bluejay Dance were performed each January in Arlee, Montana.

Yakima and Neighboring Groups

Winter "sings" were held for five nights in aboriginal homes or longhouses. Indian doctors were always present to aid in bringing out initiates' songs (song 21) or in alleviating spirit sickness. Chinook Dances focused upon respite from severe winter weather. Small gifts of cloth material and food were distributed at the close of each dance. Women's songs and love songs accompanied a Klikitat girl's puberty notification dance, which lasted five nights (Ray 1939:58). The marriage dance, similar in format to that of other Plateau groups, was called *pátkʷaykašat* 'laying (stick) on (shoulder)'. In curing rituals, shamans sang power songs in sets of five, assisted by "stick beaters" or drummers (Schuster 1975:172).

The traditional Yakima longhouse religion and the Washat religion evolved from an early "praying dance" and a newer christianized Prophet Dance (Spier 1935). Seven became the new ritual number (Du Bois 1938:8), and seven drummers singing three groups of seven songs became the basic repertoire for worship in these services. A typical Washat calendar includes first foods feasts (fig. 8) (song 22), funerals, namings, first products' feasts, and first dancing rites (Schuster 1975:358–479). Indian cures were pursued through shamans, Indian Shakers (song 13), or members of the Feather religion, each with its song literature. Many Protestant and Roman Catholic congregations plus five longhouses and two Shaker churches evidence a variety of musical styles in the contemporary religious life found on the reservation. The Yakima Nation Cultural Center at Toppenish, Washington, is a focal point for educational and cultural groups such as the Weaseltail Dancers (Willard 1990). Beginning with the White Swan Longhouse New Year's Day Veterans' Dinner and extending to the Wapato Longhouse Christmas celebration, the annual calendar for the Yakima Nation is full of music and dance activities.

Mid-Columbia Northern Oregon

Among the aboriginal Wasco, Wishram, Wayampam, Tenino, Tygh, and Molala, the salmon resource was dominant, and the proper First Salmon rite imperative. The shaman

556

North Central Wash. Mus., Wenatchee, Wash.:83–67–107.

Fig. 8. Prayer-song before digging first roots used in first foods feasts. Yakimas Ellen Saluskin with a handbell, Mary Dick John of White Swan, Wash., Isabelle Meninick, and young Rudy Saluskin have root digging sticks in the ground before them. All 3 women have traditional root gathering baskets tied at their waist. Photograph by Grace Christianson Gardner Wenzel, Horse Heaven Hills, Wash., 1937 or 1947.

was involved in its protocol, as in virtually every ceremony and worship activity. Since shamans were the most powerful possessors of spirit resources, a Wishram neophyte could declare his intention to seek a tutelary spirit of such power as to make him a shaman. Upon his return from the quest a special five-night dance endorsed his objective in front of the whole community. The youth sang five songs, and his family members danced to their own spirit songs (song 23a), all under the watchful eye of an elder shaman. A horizontal pole suspended from the longhouse roof was slapped against a vertical plank—a unique percussion instrument to support the music (Spier and Sapir 1930:201, 228–229). Hand drums and rasps also were used.

A five-night dance was held during a girl's first menstrual seclusion, followed by gifts to guests while she was introduced as eligible for marriage. But among the Molala, obscene songs could be sung to the girl by a male relative (song 23b). In the Wishram and Wasco Scalp Dance (song 6), held all night immediately after a war party's return, trophies were displayed upon pointed sticks, with dancers moving in concentric circles around them. Slaves were occasionally taken, and even they could hold power songs (Song 23c). When children had their ears pierced for ornaments the process was accompanied by its song (Spier and Sapir 1930:261).

Along the Columbia River Narrows where trade funneled, Chinook Jargon songs flourished, both sacred and secular. As regional travel, missionization, and industrialization increased, worshipers and laboring people passed these songs throughout the Northwest (Swan 1857:200–202; Boas 1888; Eells 1878; Gill 1909; Howay 1943; Seaburg 1982:45–49). Boas (1888) gives three musical transcriptions and 39 song texts, one of which asks:

Ka Chali tlatowa alta?   Kyelapai nanitch naika tumtum.
Where is Charlie going now?   He comes back to see me, I think.

Pilling (1893:16–17) lists Chinook language hymnbooks, Chinook Jargon hymnbooks, and songs and song texts.

In protohistoric times the sacred number seven and dancing on knees ("you kneel and jog up and down in time") became the worship norm, following instruction from a prophetess who had come back from death (Du Bois 1938:8–9). With Smohalla's people a typical Washat funeral ceremony involved hand drums, a bell, prayers, singing, testimonials, and a children's dance—a format still in use in the 1990s in the Plateau (Schuster 1975:424–430). When Columbia River dams turned river to reservoir in 1956 the final Celilo Falls salmon ceremony was held (fig. 9), preceding social dances and a reenacted courting dance (McKeown 1959; Oregon Historical Society 1956). The Warm Springs Shaker Church and the Feather religion remained active through the 1990s. The Simnasho Longhouse had Washat worship each Sunday under the leadership of Matilda Showaway Mitchell, William John, and their families. The Agency Longhouse leaders were Prunie Williams and Art Mitchell (see Stowell 1987).

Eastern Sahaptians

The religious lives of the Nez Perce, Cayuse, Umatilla, Walla Walla, and Palouse revolved around the medicine power quest, in which songs were received. Songs could also be inherited through the male line. From the guardian spirit (Nez Perce *wéyekin*) came not only a song and dance but also instructions for a sacred package, *ʔipéˑtesˑ* Dreams and prophecies, winter dances, first foods' feasts, namings, and shamanic healing all employed song and dance.

A shaman's songs usually came from beings that inhabited the heavens, such as eagles or clouds. The doctor amassed power as he gained more songs, each vocalization representing a separate vision quest or acquisition (Walker 1968:24). Some powers were dangerous or potentially destructive. A person affected with *isxiˑp* power would behave in remarkable ways, with fits of uncontrollable dancing, self-mutilation, and divesting oneself of property (De Voto 1953:244, 245; Spinden 1908:264; Curtis 1907–1930, 8:72, 183; Walker 1968:25).

An evening farewell (song 5) preceded war expeditions, and a five-day Scalp Dance finalized them (Spinden 1908:266). Often the Scalp Dance ended with a Marriage Dance (Stevens 1900, 2:60).

New religious music began in 1830, when Spokane Garry and Kutenai Pelly returned from the Red River Mission School, preaching and singing Anglican hymns around the region. In 1836 Presbyterian missionaries ventured west to Cayuse and Nez Perce country. As soon as they arrived the missionaries began to teach hymns to the Indian people, translating them into Sahaptin with the help of native teachers. The first hymnbook in the Northwest was printed on Henry H. Spalding's Lapwai Press in 1843, containing words to 27 hymns translated into the Nez Perce language. Eventually there were 212 different hymn texts in Nez Perce

(Olsen 1980), translated between 1876 and 1967. Roman Catholic hymns also appeared in the Sahaptin tongue, some with complete musical notation (Oregon Province Archives 1976:33).

One amazing musical syncretism emerged from Kate McBeth's teaching a Christmas song to the Kamiah Nez Perces in 1890. "Have a jolly home; jolly Christmas, jolly Christmas home" emerged 70 years later among the Washat singers in Pendleton, Oregon, and Seven Drum singers in Nespelem, Washington, as "Hippa tsolly home, tsolly home"—used for an interlude between seven-song sets and termed a "Spanish Dance" from California (Olsen 1989a:22, 28). A Drop the Handkerchief Dance or Kissing Dance is remembered among elderly Indians as being used "for fun" around 1900 (song 7).

After the Nez Perce War of 1877 former combatants, returning to the northwest from exile in Canada or Oklahoma, brought with them the vibrant war dance songs of the Sioux, Blackfoot, Crow, Kiowa, and Comanche (see Hatton 1986). (An "ancient" Nez Perce war dance with several bear songs was recorded by Spinden [1908] even though the new Plains style war dance was dominant.) The circle dance came to the Nez Perces around 1900, and the owl and rabbit dances immediately thereafter. Forty-nine songs (Feder 1964) were added to the repertoire in the 1940s, some from outside sources and others from old Nez Perce war expedition songs, *kilowawia* (song 5). Regional powwows and celebrations such as Chief Joseph Days, the Pendleton Roundup (fig. 10), Chief Joseph and Warriors Memorial, Looking Glass Celebration, and Matalyma Days drew hundreds of dancers, singers, and stick-gamers in the late twentieth century in a reassertion of Indian identity.

Klamath and Modoc

Among the Klamath and Modoc, the main aboriginal song repertoire was religious, connected with personal power and shamanism. This included individual spirit songs, winter dances, novice shaman's dances, harvest ceremonies, girl's puberty ceremonies, and curing songs. A young Klamath seeking power in a secluded area would sometimes jump to the bottom of a river, return to the surface fainting, then receive a vision and a song (Foltin 1971:25). Each shaman utilized an interpreter to support the shaman's singing and clarify his sayings for the people assembled. White Sindey, a berdache, was the most renowned of shamans, functioning around 1890; several of his songs were remembered by others and recorded (songs 4a, 4b).

Other categories of songs included love, courting, satire, gambling, war, work, and children's songs (song 4a) (Gatschet 1890, 1894; Spier 1930). The repertoire later gained Chinook Jargon songs, Methodist hymns, Indian Shaker Church tunes, and songs from the Ghost Dance, Earth-lodge cult (song 4b?), and Dream Dance movements (Spier 1927, 1930; Nash 1937). In addition to common Plateau rattles, the split-stick rattle from California was employed.

A century's musical evidence reflects changes that came to the Klamath people: a shift from indigenous genres of music to borrowed ones; a music style shift from that of the Great Basin to one more northerly and westerly (Nettl 1954:297–301); a shift from spiritual to secular music; a shift from music participation to spectatorship; and a shift in the culture's musical memory process from male to female tradition bearers (Foltin 1971:125). Analyses of Leslie Spier's 1935 collection of 38 Modoc songs resulted in conclusions that place the literature in the Great Basin music genre (Hall and Nettl 1955:66).

left, Oreg. Histl. Soc., Portland: 001579.

Fig. 9. Celilo Falls Festival. left, Yakima, Umatilla, and Wayampam tribal members drumming farewell at a ceremony marking the end of the Celilo Falls traditional fishing site. Third from left is Watson Totus, Yakima. Photographed at the Wyam longhouse, Oreg., Oct. 1956. center, Drumming on a small drum placed on a larger drum. Photograph by Gladys Seufert, Celilo Village, 13 miles east of The Dalles, Oreg., 1967. right, Pierson Mitchell of Warm Springs Res., Oreg. Photograph by Gladys Seufert, 1970.

Fig. 10. Men dancing, 20th century. top, Dance in progress at the Pendleton Roundup, Oreg. First organized about 1910–1911, the Pendleton Roundup remained an annual event in the 1990s. Photographed in 1931. bottom left, Wasco dance of welcome at a Root Feast. left to right, Joe McCorkle, Wesley Smith, and Alfred Smith, all Wasco; and Teeman Heath, Warm Springs. Photograph by Bob Barber, Warm Springs Res., Oreg., 1955. bottom right, Frank Halfmoon, Nez Perce–Cayuse, at a dance demonstration at Pi-Nee-Waus Days. Photograph by Loran Olsen, Nez Perce National Historical Park, Spalding, Idaho, 1972.

By the 1990s Shaker music, Christian hymns, and the sounds of stick games and Plains-style war dances had mostly replaced indigenous Klamath and Modoc Indian music. The First Sucker ceremony held in March at Chiloquin, Oregon, under the leadership of elders and the Klamath Culture Club represents restoration of a precontact festival of thanksgiving.

559

The 1990s

In several northwest states 1989 and 1990 were centennial years. These times of celebration recalled the allotment period, 100 years before, when Plateau Indians lost much of their land base. Participating in festive events throughout the Northwest, Indian dance groups, drummers, singers, orators, and worshipers shared their traditions with mainstream communities, expressing mixed feelings about the centennial exercise (Native American Committee 1990).

At summer powwows there has been an increase in women's participation in drumming and war dancing, activities that were prohibited by custom a few generations before (Hatton 1986:208–216; J.A. Jones 1995:182–192). The Arlee Powwow, Worley Indian Days, Pi Ume Sha Treaty Days, Tinowit International Powwow, Wellpinit Indian Days, Spokane Falls Encampment, Omak Stampede (fig. 11), and Nespelem Fourth of July Powwow feature war dances, social dances, contest dances and stick games. Underlying these activities are efforts by Indian communities to rediscover their own cultural past after generations of loss, and to control academic research so that its benefit to them is insured (Colville Business Council 1981; Woodcock 1983).

Washat, Feather, and Shaker groups worshiped regularly in the 1990s in many locations on the Klamath, Warm Springs, Yakima, Umatilla, Nez Perce, and Colville Indian Reservations. A contemporary Indian funeral service may combine 21

Washat songs at the all-night wake; a children's dance; a late night traditional meal of salmon, venison, roots, and berries; an after-breakfast farewell of seven songs; a conventional Protestant or Roman Catholic church service; and graveside songs of the Washat at the burial.

On the Okanagan Reserve in British Columbia one can hear Winter Spirit Dance songs as well as Christmas carols sung in the Okanagan language (Wickwire 1982:362). Talmaks summer encampment at Mason's Butte near Winchester, Idaho, features Nez Perce translated hymns in morning and evening services (Sugden 1972). On special occasions among Coeur d'Alenes a traditional "cup dance" is presented at the communion table by Indian dancers in full regalia (Kowrach and Connolly 1990:51). The evangelical Protestant hymn "Amazing Grace" is chanted by Roman Catholic drummers as they lead the recessional from mass (Connolly 1989).

Musical Characteristics

Indigenous Plateau song is a music of improvisation, not static as might be implied from recorded examples, but dynamic—a music of motion and emotion (song 14). Human sighs or moans, animal sounds, bird calls—all are song materials for decoration and manipulation (Wickwire 1982:275–281). Motivic cells two to six notes long form the basis for melody in a majority of examples (song 10). Pentatonic (nontempered)

left, Mont. Histl. Soc., Helena.
Fig. 11. Women dancing. left, "Squaw Dance." Photograph by Norman A. Forsyth, Arlee, Mont., July 4, 1907 or 1908. right, Lolita Henry, Nez Perce from Nespelem, performing a shawl dance at the Omak Stampede, Wash. Photograph by Sharon Eva Grainger, 1995.

scalar types result from groups of these cells, transposed, and then expanded or truncated. Decorations and cadence formulas add other pitches, resulting occasionally in six- and seven-pitch (non-tempered) scales. In shamanic songs one cell often constitutes all the musical material (Densmore 1943: 25–29), forming a basis for text alteration and rhythmic manipulation—an apparent necessity in long and varied healing rituals (Foltin 1971:96–101). This reworking of the melodic cell is a hallmark of Washat and prophecy songs too. It may give a clue to the practice of testing several versions (Wickwire 1982:237–240, 277) prior to the "jelling" of a song into its permanent configuration as a ritual element (Ray 1933:84, 195).

Most personal guardian-spirit songs in recorded samples are short and continuously repetitive (songs 2a, 4a, 23a), some with texts and vocables alternating. Other dreamed songs are elaborate (songs 1, 19), reflecting the special creativity of the singers or their shaman helpers as they "brought the songs out." Stick game songs often depend upon short motives (Densmore 1943:70, 72), which are moved to higher or lower pitch locations, forming musical "slogans" that circle indefinitely (song 3) (Densmore 1943:69). It is not unusual to hear a whole melody rely upon triadic outlines (songs 2b, 21). Decorating with neighboring tones and cadential portamentos enhances the triad (songs 8, 9c, 17, 19, 22). Average ranges vary from spirit songs in the compass of a perfect fourth or perfect fifth to worship, prophecy, and Washat songs ranging an octave (songs 1, 19). The Washat songs have melodies that undulate and often descend in small intervals after upward jumps. (See comparison tables of Flathead song types in Merriam 1967:332–339.) The flute love song or its vocalized version may range a 10th or more (song 12).

Borrowed song literatures tend to utilize vocables, while rooted literatures tend to retain text. Spirit songs and shamanic healing songs tend to build upon a few syllables of text, adjusting syllables to fit the tune (song 4a), and employing catchy rhythm patterns (song 2a). A sense of syncopation to the Western ear is usual (songs 5, 6, 11, 18, 19). Regularity of pulse with freedom of meter prevails in songs accompanying dances or gambling. Generally war songs, victory songs, and canvas dance or serenade songs employ wide melody ranges averaging a ninth, beginning high and following long descending contours with some undulation and syncopation (songs 5, 6, 11). They exhibit cadence formulas with recognizable vocables surrounding low repeated notes (song 5).

For the Western ear a feeling of offbeat accent in the voice, or sometimes in the drum, is common (song 6). Frequently there is apparent vocal lagging behind the percussion pulse, giving the effect of nonchalance reminiscent of a jazz singer's style (songs 2b, 21). Polyrhythms flourish (song 9c), with subliminal triplets in the voice against drum duples (song 21) or a vocal line in total metric independence from the drum (song 23a). For both performer and listener the combination of voice with percussion is often the most interesting and challenging aspect to the music (song 17). Although canvas dances and stick game songs are performed by voices in parallel motion at the octave and occasionally at the fifth, the recordings of indigenous music hold few examples of voices in heterophony (song 15), and none in canon or counterpoint.

Sources

Of particular importance in exploring early Plateau music are wax cylinder recordings (Brady et al. 1984–, 1; Brady 1985). Text and metric notations of 286 Klamath and Modoc songs were made by linguist Albert S. Gatschet as early as 1889, but the tedious task of transcribing live Indian music by ear was a more difficult one for his musician contemporaries. Fletcher's (1893) study of Omaha Indian music and Baker's (1882) publication were accomplished using this painstaking method. Fletcher, government allotting agent among the Nez Perce, 1889–1892, made her first Plateau recordings in April 1897. At home in Washington, D.C., she preserved Nez Perce voices, including that of Chief Joseph, on seven cylinders.

Franz Boas and James Teit gathered 45 cylinders of songs at Spence's Bridge, among the Thompson Indians of British Columbia. This collection gave new impetus to the German school of comparative musicology emerging under Theodore Baker and Carl Stumpf (Herzog 1949). The Boas collection was transcribed to music (Abraham and Hornbostel 1975).

The first Plateau ethnomusicological endeavors surveyed Flathead music (Merriam and Merriam 1950). Merriam (1967; Powers 1970; Kolinsky 1970) transcribed 226 Flathead songs into musical notation and gave detailed melodic, rhythmic, and formal analyses in 17 musical parameters. Later studies investigated music of the Modoc (Hall and Nettl 1955), Nez Perce (Williams 1967; J.A. Jones 1995), Klamath (Foltin 1971), and Canadian Interior Salish (Wickwire 1988, 1982).

Melda Williams (1967) notated each of the 30 Nez Perce songs in her sample, giving a narrative analysis that included formal, melodic, and rhythmic dimensions in 11 parameters. Discussion topics include song origins, song types, instruments, musical characteristics, standards of musical excellence, and standards of performance. J.A. Jones (1995) traced the gradual alteration of the War Dance among the Nez Perce.

Foltin's (1971) thesis included notations of 145 Klamath songs and analyses. He concludes that Klamath music mirrored changes in traditional culture.

Wickwire (1982) transcribed 33 songs, all in proximate notation. Her conclusions support the benefits of avoiding a structural analysis of music in favor of one emphasizing the experiencing of music in its context (see Gourlay 1982).

There are publications dealing with sound archives, recordings, and tape collections of Plateau music (Brady et al. 1984–, 1; Briegleb 1971; Gray 1988; Lee 1984; Olsen 1989a; Seaburg 1982; Seeger and Spear 1987; Gombert 1994).

Most Plateau song collections originally on wax cylinders have been transferred to tape. Housed at the American Folklife Center of the Library of Congress (AFC); the Archives of Traditional Music at Indiana University (ATM), Bloomington; University of Washington, Seattle (UW); Washington State University, Pullman (WSU); the Lowie Museum of Anthropology (LMA) at University of California, Berkeley; and the *561*

Canadian Ethnology Service (CES), Canadian Museum of Civilization, Ottawa, they include:

1897 and 1900, Alice Fletcher—9 Nez Perce (AFC, WSU)

1897, Franz Boas and James Teit—43 Thompson (CES) (Abraham and Hornbostel 1975:309–319)

1907, Herbert Spinden—31 Nez Perce (AFC, WSU)

1907, Samuel Barrett—30 Klamath, 2 Chinook Jargon, 2 Warm Springs, 6 Wasco (LMA)

1909, Edward S. Curtis—13 Wishram, 3 Klikitat, 4 Yakima, 1 Palouse, 11 Middle Columbia River Salish, 11 Nez Perce, 18 Kootenai, 14 Flathead (ATM) (Curtis 1907–1930, 6 and 7)

1910–1912, Sam Morris—60 Nez Perce, 1 Chinook Jargon (WSU, AFC)

1912, Marius Barbeau and James Teit—40 Thompson (CES) (George 1962)

1915–1921, James Teit—233 Thompson, Shuswap, Okanagan, Lillooet (CES) (Wickwire 1988:192–196)

1926, Frances Densmore—20 Thompson (AFC) (Densmore 1943)

1927, Thelma Adamson and Franz Boas—5 Kittitas (ATM)

1927, Thelma Adamson and Melville Jacobs—6 Yakima, 7 Taitnapam, 19 Klikitat (ATM)

1929, Melville Jacobs—22 Klikitat, 3 Klamath, 1 Yakima, 16 Molala, 5 Chinook Jargon (ATM, AFC, UW) (Herzog 1950)

1931, Harry H. Turney-High—Flathead, Kootenai

1934, Claude Schaeffer—26 Flathead (AFC)

1934, Leslie Spier—38 Modoc (ATM)

1935, Leslie Spier—65 Klamath, 1 Warm Springs (ATM).

Disk recordings include:

1947 and 1949, Willard Rhodes—25 Umatilla (Nez Perce, Cayuse, Walla Walla), 2 Klamath, 1 Warm Springs (AFC, WSU)

1948, Marjorie Gellatly—2 Yakima (ATM, UW)

1949, Carling Malouf and Paul Phillips—8 Flathead (U. of Montana)

1950, Ted Stern—19 Klamath (U. of Oregon)

1950, Alan P. and Barbara W. Merriam—226 Flathead (ATM).

Tape collections include:

1950–1958, Alan P. Merriam—233 Flathead (ATM)

1956, La Monte West—5 Kootenai, 40 Nez Perce, 9 other (ATM)

1967, Melda Williams Schiemer—30 Nez Perce (U. of Idaho)

1965, Bela Foltin—66 Klamath, 13 other (U. of Illinois)

1977–1982, Wendy Wickwire—100 Thompson, Shuswap, Okanagan (UBC)

1987, Brycene Neamann—Yakima Tribal Archives Collection, Toppenish, Wash.

1989, Nez Perce Music Archive—1,000 Nez Perce, 200 other (WSU).

Compact disks include:

1995, Sam Morris Collection (denoised)—60 Nez Perce, 1 Chinook Jargon (WSU, ATM, AFC), Northwest Interpretive Association, 909 1st Ave, Ste. 630, Seattle.

1995, Heartbeat: Voices of First Nations Women—2 Wasco-Wishram (Smithsonian/Folkways).

Commercial recordings include:

1947, Nez Perce Gospel Songs; Gospel Recording, Los Angeles

1953, Songs and Dances of the Flathead Indians; Ethnic Folkways Library P445

1957, Marius Barbeau: My Life in Recording Canadian Indian Folklore; Folkways FG3502

1972, 16 Umatilla Songs; Indian Records IR1280

1972, Stick Game Songs, recording of a stick game in progress, Arlee Powwow, Montana; Canyon CR6105

1973, Ky i Yo Powwow, recorded in Missoula, Montana; Canyon CR6126

1973, Yakima; Canyon CR 6129

1973, Bad Canyon Wellpinit Singers; Canyon CR 6174–C

1974, Songs of the Warm Springs Indian Reservation; Canyon CR 6123

1975, Yakima Nation Singers of Satus Longhouse; Canyon CR 6126–C

1980, Intertribal Powwow Songs—Treaty of 1855; Canyon CR 6173–C

1981, Fraser Valley Spotted Lake Intertribal Singers; Canyon CR 9006–C

1981, Omak Pow-Wow; Canyon CR 6175–C

1984, Ya-Ka-Ma Singers; Meninick Productions, Yakima Nation

1990, The Boys, Recorded at Simnasho Longhouse, Oregon; Little Soldier Enterprise, 1725 E. Turkey, Phoenix. LS 1005

1991, Music & Word Series; Wild Sanctuary; San Francisco: Nez Perce Stories 1601, Music of the Nez Perce 1602

1993, Sacred Encounters; Lawrence Johnson Productions, Portland.

Films and Videotapes include:

1926, Sept. 26, Father Joseph Cataldo at age 90, Mass at 80th Anniversary of Construction of Old Mission (Coeur d'Alene)—10 min. (Idaho State Historical Society Library, Boise)

1928, The Shuswap Indians of British Columbia, Harlan I. Smith—12 min. (CES)

1928, The Kootenay Indians of British Columbia, Harlan I. Smith—12 min. (CES)

1956, Last Salmon Feast of the Celilo Indians—(Oregon Historical Society, Portland)

1972, Plains and Plateau Indian Drumming and Singing with Larry Parker (Flathead)—28 min. (WSU)

1973, Nee Mee Poo (Nez Perce)—32 min. (WSU)

1976, Real People Series, KSPS-TV, Spokane, Washing-ton (WSU): Awakening (Flathead)—28 min., Buffalo, Blood, Salmon, and Roots (Flathead, Kalispel, Colville)—26 min., Circle of Song (Spokane, Coeur d'Alene)—56 min., Legend of the Stick Game (Kalispel)—27 min., Mainstream (Coeur d'Alene)—27 min., Season of Grandmothers (Flathead, Coeur d'Alene, Spokane, Colville, Kalispel, Kootenai, Wenatchee)—27 min., Spirit of the Wind (Flathead, Colville, Okanagan)—27 min., Words of Life, People of Rivers (Spokane, Colville)—27 min.

1976, Kevin Alec (Lillooet)—16 min. (National Film Board of Canada)

1978, Augusta (Shuswap)—17 min. (National Film Board of Canada)

1981, Nez Perce: Portrait of a People—23 min. (Nez Perce National Historical Park)

1986, Everything Change (Wenatchee)—21 min. (Ellensburg Public Library, Washington)

1988, Changing Visions, the Art of the Salish and Kootenai—60 min. (Salish-Kutenai College, Pablo, Montana)

1990, Circle of the Spirit (Coeur d'Alene, Lummi Coast Salish)—60 min. (U.S. Catholic Conference, Washington, D.C.)

1991, The First Oregonians—10 min. (Oregon Council For the Humanities, Portland)

1993, The People Today (Flathead, Coeur d'Alene)—14 min. (Lawrence Johnson Productions, PO 14384, Portland, Oregon)

Song 1. Nez Perce Prophecy Song

Recorded by Loran Olsen, 1971
Singer: Sol Webb

TEXT:

q̇ó ʔc wáyat hiwyé·cem miyó·xat.
'The chief comes speaking from far away.'
kíye hiwyé·kcem miyó·xatom.
'The chief watches us as he comes.'

Song 2a. Taitnapam Sahaptin Medicine Song

Recorded by Melville Jacobs and Thelma Adamson, 1927
Singer: Sam Eyley, Sr.

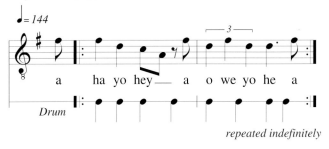

Song 2b. Taitnapam Sahaptin Lullaby

Recorded by Melville Jacobs and Thelma Adamson, 1927
Singer: Mrs. Sam Eyley, Sr.

Song 3. Palouse Hand Game Song

Recorded by Edward S. Curtis, 1909
Singer: Louis Mann

Song 4a. Klamath Medicine Song of White Sindey

Recorded by Leslie Spier, 1935
Singer: Mrs. Tom Lang

Na-no-k'as g'e-la-ka-ni-ma toʍ-go
doʍ ma wa-ba-dok dim doʍ ma-ton-
ka wa la ta nə wa-ba-dok

Note: Not all words can be identified, but the translation obtained by Spier refers to the ringing of bells *(dindan)* being heard everywhere *(na·noka·s)*.

Song 4b. Klamath Speckled Hawk Curing Song of White Sindey

Recorded by Leslie Spier, 1935 (transcribed and translated by Spier)
Singer: Tom Lang

Wi tə ga tə gei — za sai noʍko wi tə ga tə
no — lo la — wi tə ga tə
gei — za sai noʍ ko wi tə ga tə
no — la Wi tə ga tə

TEXT:

Witkotgísas gotkonólwapk 'The bird hawk' is ready to sing.

Song 5. Nez Perce Serenade Song

Recorded by Alice Fletcher, 1897 (translated by Elizabeth Wilson)
Singer: Levi Jonas

e ya ha ya hya —— e ya ha —— e ya
Drum   etc.
ha ya hya —— e ya ha —— e ya
ha —— hya —— he ya he ya e ya
ha e ya o he ya he — yo he yo I nim
ha ma wei ki et uik ce ha ma he ya
hya o ya o he ya hey he ya he ya e ya

TEXT:

ʔí·nim há·ma weye kiyé·twikce, há·ma.
'Now I go following my man, (my) husband.'

Note: Phonemic transcription and translation by Haruo Aoki.

Song 6. Wishram Victory Song

Recorded by Edward S. Curtis, 1909
Singer: Martin Spadis

A ka a q'ua-e a ko la ha
                              etc.
ya ka a q'ua-e a ko la ha

(after 5 repetitions, and whooping, tempo increases abruptly to 160)

Song 7. Nez Perce Kissing Dance

Recorded by Loran Olsen, 1972 (translated by Sol Webb)
Singer: Clarence Burke

wepesútiya timíne pe ʔní·me
' "In the way of nature" you gave me your heart.'
qe ʔciyéẃyew kawá· hímkaċaʔkt.
'Thank you, and now a kiss.'

Phonemic transcrition and translation by Haruo Aoki. The analysis of the first word is uncertain; the quoted translation is from Sol Webb.

Song 8. Kalispel Sweathouse Song

Recorded by Ignace Camille
Singer: Joe Black Bear

"He is praying to his great, great grandfather, the sweathouse — believing in it, by the tribe — calling for help — trying to be good luck, in any thing....He said he's scorched and he's hot and he's ready to run out."

—Ignace Camille

565

Song 9a. Modoc Porcupine Song

Recorded by Loran Olsen, 1991
Singer: Cecilia Langell
Notes: Phonemic transcription and translation by M.A.R. Barker

če·li če·li na·ĺs ʔam kani leĺq̓iq̓it.
'Porky, Porky, (we) wish someone would cut our wrists.'

"Porcupine wants someone to skin him and eat him."
—Cecilia Langell
Children's play song, from the dance song of the porcupines, in a legend.

Song 9b. Klamath Earth Moving Song

Recorded by Loran Olsen, 1991
Singer: Gordon Battles

ġe·la no· los danni.
'I move (?) the earth how much?'

"The moving of the earth was very sacred to the Klamath and Modoc."
—Gordon Battles

Phonemic transcription and translation derived from Barker (1963a), except for los 'move(?)'

Song 9c. Modoc Girl's Puberty Dance Song

Recorded by Leslie Spier and Earl Counts, 1934
Singer: Celia Lynch

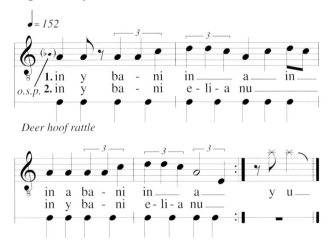

1. "Sung at beginning of dance to mark the sunset"...and again at end...
2. "to mark the midnight." — Spier

Song 10. Spokane/Coeur d'Alene Wakeup Song

Singer: Cliff Sijohn
Recorded by KSPS-TV, 1975

Song 11. Wasco Farewell Dance Song

Recorded by Samuel Barrett, 1907
Singer: Thomas Miller

Song 12. Flathead Courting Flute Song

Recorded by Loran Olsen, 1972
Player: Jerome Vanderburg

Song 13. Yakima Shaker Church Song

Recorded by Tom Connolly, 1968
Singers: Group

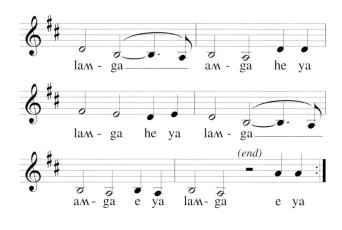

Song 14. Thompson Pubescent Girls' Dance Song

Recorded by James Teit, ca. 1915
Singer: Yiopát'ko

567

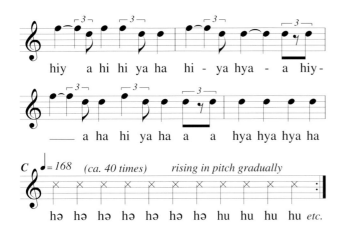

hiy   a hi hi ya ha   hi - ya hya - a hiy-

_____ a ha hi ya ha   a   a   hya hya hya ha

C ♩ = 168   *(ca. 40 times)*   *rising in pitch gradually*

hə hə hə hə hə hə hə hu hu hu hu *etc.*

Song 15. Thompson Bear Song for Twins

Recorded by James Teit, ca. 1915
Singer: Xwəlínək

o.s.p.   ə χə   χə χə χə   a χə χə   χə χə χə   *etc.*

lower voice   ə ə   ə ə   ə ə   ə ə   *etc.*

xwiw, xwiw, xwiw

xwiw,   xwiw,   xwiw

Song 16a. Shuswap Youth Dance Song

Recorded by Wendy Wickwire, 1977
Singers: Aimee August and Adeline Willard

♪ = 168

A
o.s.p.   e ya o ___ ho _____ ho _____

Drums   *etc.*

A'
e ya o   o e ya o   ho

A''
e ya ho ___ ho ___ ho ___ ho _____ ho ___ ho

_____ he ya ho ___ ha ho ___ ha

A'''
ho ___ o ho ho _____ hu _____

Song 16b. Okanogan Pinto Horse Song

Recorded by Wendy Wickwire, 1979
Singer: Mary Abel

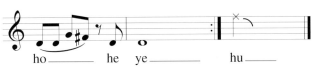

Song 17. Kootenai Sun Dance Lodge Pole Song

Recorded by LaMonte West, 1956
Singer: Baptiste Mathias

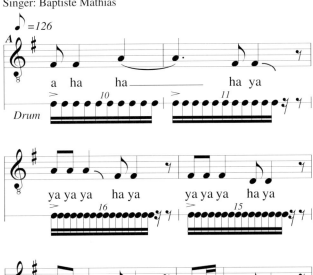

"Sung while sun dance lodge is being built—refers to the way people travel—sung for well being."
—West

569

Song 18. Kalispel Water Song (Winter Dance)

Recorded by Dan Ames, 1967
Singers: Mitch and Mary Michael, Catherine Finley,
Ignace Williams, Mary Adrian

"This song is especially for going after water during the medicine dances in the winter time."

—Mitch Michael

Song 19. Skoáxcinux (Middle Columbia) Song of Skoélik (Dream Dance)

Recorded by Edward S. Curtis
Singer: Quaiitsa

*text added here on repetitions

Song 20. Coeur d'Alene Marian Hymn

Recorded by Tom Connolly
Singer: Mary Michael

Tesčin čənt ɫ uʔ yaˤ sṫulixʷ
'I fear the dangers of this world.
miɫ sqʷn̓q̓ʷeyn̓t ɫ uʔ isnxpew̓s
So poor is my soul.
neʔ k̓ʷu mali neʔ k̓ʷu nxəmenč
You, Mary, you do love me.
u nexʷ u k̓ʷ isk̓ʷuy
You truly are my mother.
neli k̓ʷu sk̓ʷuys k̓ʷɫncutn
Because you are the mother of God.'

Notes: In the Spokane dialect, with some Coeur d'Alene features. Translation by Tom Connolly and Clarence Woodcock; phonemicized by Ivy G. Doak. The analysis of *yaˤ* and *neli* is uncertain.

Song 21. Kittitas (Pshwanwapam) Guardian—Spirit Song

Recorded by Thelma Adamson and Franz Boas, 1927
Singer: Mrs. Dan Secena

x̣áyx̣tknik inúumš tímaš.
'From the dawn the word is heard.'

Notes: Sung before the first feast of the year. Transcription and translation by Melville Jacobs and Bruce J. Rigsby.

Song 22. Klikitat First Roots Feast Song

Recorded by Thelma Adamson and Franz Boas, 1927
Singer: Joe Hunt

Song 23a. Molala Spirit Power Song

Recorded by Melville Jacobs, 1929
Singer: Victoria Howard

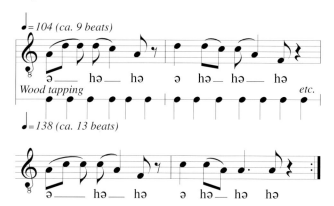

Song 23b. Molala Courtship Song
(Sung at girl's puberty ceremony)

Recorded by Melville Jacobs, 1929
Singer: Victoria Howard

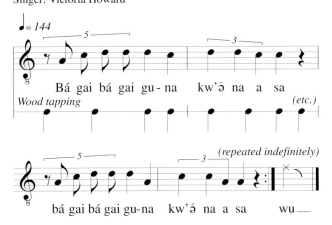

páqai páqai xu·na kwána' asa
'Only one side left of the little girl's privates.'

Note: Transcribed and translated by Melville Jacobs.

Song 23c. Molala Mole Power Song of Modoc Slave Woman

Recorded by Melville Jacobs, 1929
Singer: Victoria Howard

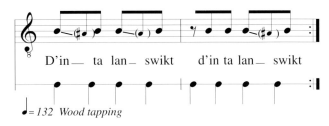

repeated 4-7 times, then raised in pitch after exclamation:

ti·nta laʌ̣wickt
'She goes throwing up dirt.'

Note: Transcribed and translated by Melville Jacobs.

The Stick Game

BILL B. BRUNTON

The Plateau stick game goes by several names, some identical or similar to designations that have been used for other games. In older ethnographies it is usually called the hand game (Culin 1907), but sometimes the stick game or bone game. The term *stick game* is the one usually employed in local English by Indian people on the Plateau, but the game is also called *slahal* in English, especially by Indians from the Northwest Coast. Among the words for the stick game in Plateau languages are Nez Perce *ló·xmit*, Kootenai *kałq̓ahał*, Klamath *nayałi·ya*, and in Salishan languages Lillooet *təkmáẃas*, Thompson *ꞓalpíx*, Columbian *sꞓlálqʷm*, and similar forms (Bruce J. Rigsby, communication to editors 1996; M. Dale Kinkade, communication to editors 1966; Barker 1963a:256). The name *slahal* is also used in English for the disk game played on the Northwest Coast, a second game that may also be called the bone game or the hand game (vol. 7:435, 495). Yet a third game with similar names is the four-stick game or bone game, considered the older game among the Klamath, who call it *sakals* (Spier 1930:77; Barker 1963a:347).

The stick game is a spirited gambling game of skill and chance that has been played throughout the Plateau and adjacent regions since aboriginal times (Brunton 1974). Its antiquity is suggested by its wide geographic distribution, integration with other aspects of culture, and early ethnic and regional variation (Culin 1907). For the Okanagan it was "the only pastime other than footracing that was mentioned for the mythical period" (Commons 1938:186).

Contests and games were a part of everyday life. They were also a major part of special occasions such as intergroup economic gatherings that took place throughout the year (Anastasio 1972; Coues 1897). For example, salmon fishing, root harvesting, and berry gathering were settings for contests of several kinds. Notable among these were footraces (later horse races), shinny, wrestling, and various games of skill and luck such as dice games, hoop and pole games (fig. 1), and guessing games.

Gambling was such a significant attribute of these contests that it led early observers such as Parker (1838) to conclude that it was a "ruling passion" for peoples of this area. Gambling was central enough to social life that it should be considered a cultural theme (Brunton 1974).

An early ethnographic account of the stick game states that: "The gambling consists in guessing in which hand one [on which a ring of bark is left] of two sticks of wood is hidden. The players sit in two rows facing each other, and a number of them keep beating on a log in front of them with sticks, while the sticks are passed from hand to hand. From time to time some of the players sing or contort their limbs in various ways" (Chamberlain 1892:561). Others (Ray 1933:155–159; Commons 1938:186–187; Turney-High 1941:160–161; Teit 1930:131, 260) offer good descriptions. Culin (1907) made a comparative survey of the stick game along with other Native American games.

Among the Yakima, the stick game was their principal gambling activity (Desmond 1952). Stick games were played between groups when they gathered for subsistence or trade purposes. Power derived from the vision quest could be used in the game. Gamblers, even "professional," were important to the large intergroup games. Among the Flathead Salish, the stick game is ancient and has central importance (Merriam 1955).

In powwow gambling of the 1960s and 1970s, the stick game was the central activity (Brunton 1974). Stick game gambling was a significant means of expressing Indian identity and of playing out important cultural paradigms.

The Setting

The stick game was played whenever friendly peoples met and camped together. For example, Okanagan (fig. 2) local bands played against each other at intertribal or interband gatherings during the summer (Commons 1938:187). Most early Kootenai gambling was in this interband setting for trade (Schaeffer 1936:81). With time and modern forms of transportation, intergroup gambling via the stick game became more extensive, with distant ethnic groups competing (Brunton 1969).

Though intragroup and even intrafamilial games were played in the late twentieth century, stick gaming occurred principally at interreservation powwows. Powwows were scheduled mainly on weekends from spring to fall, were usually located on reservations, and were often scheduled so that conflict between them was minimized. First one reservation and then another was host to such events, and some sponsored more than one. Powwows were held on the Colville, Coeur d'Alene, Kalispel, Flathead, Nez Perce, Spokane, Umatilla, Warm Springs, and Yakima reservations. Plateau people also attended powwows on reservations in adjacent areas such as the Blackfeet Reservation in Montana. Powwows

Fig. 1. Hoop and pole game, played by the Flathead and known as "playing ring." Played by 2 or more men, the ring was set rolling by one player who followed it throwing a spear. The object of the game was to throw the spear in front of the ring and make the ring fall on it (Culin 1907:420–422, 457, 491–494). Pen and brown ink on transparent paper by Gustavus Sohon, probably 1854–1855.

occurred off-reservation at events such as the Pendleton Roundup and Chief Joseph Days. During the late 1960s and early 1970s other communities, such as Soap Lake, near Spokane, Washington, and The Dalles, Oregon, sponsored powwows (Brunton 1974).

The typical powwow begins on a Friday evening and ends early Monday morning. Upon arrival, people locate and visit friends and relatives. By late Friday night stick games and other activities such as card games are in full swing. Activity usually tapers off by daybreak. There is a lull in activities throughout the morning, with small sporadic stick games, a few card games, visiting, and eating occupying people's time (Brunton 1974). By noon Saturday, activity picks up and continues throughout the afternoon and evening. The most intense activity occurs between about 10:00 p.m. Saturday and 4:00 a.m. Sunday, when several stick games, card games, and so on, occur simultaneously. Sunday is the same as Saturday except that the crowd begins to thin during the afternoon as people leave. Many have long distances, perhaps 500 miles, to travel before reaching home.

Equipment

"Bones," "counter sticks," "pounding sticks," and "pounding logs" are the main traditional equipment used. The bones are four cylindrical playing pieces, two of which are marked (fig. 3). They are made of the lower leg bone of deer, and, less frequently, of elk and bison. These are bleached and ground into smooth cylinders. Wood, and later plastic, have been substituted for bone.

Marking two of the bones is accomplished by wrapping them with one or two black painted buckskin bands. Black thread is sometimes wound on the bones, and plastic tape of various colors has come into use. In the 1930s and earlier sinew was used for this purpose. Two are left unmarked. In earlier times it was sometimes the custom to differentiate the marked and unmarked bones by sex-gender terms. For example, Spier and Sapir (1930:267) found that Wishram designated the marked bones as "men" and the unmarked ones as "women."

The usual color of bones is white, though light red and light yellow are also seen, particularly when plastic is used.

sc'lálqʷəm

tlaʔ q'sápiʔ ki
səcc'lálqʷ iʔ sqilxʷ.
łaʔ cyˁapqínməlx
iʔ sqilxʷ, yayˁát k'aʔkín xʷúyʔilx,
yˁalwísəlx, c'lálqʷməlx, walúksməlx,
t'əmk'ˁáməlx, nkʷnímməlx, wán'xməlx,
ləmtmənwíxʷəlx, məł ʔałʔíłnəlx.
ʔupənkstłnəqsálqʷ iʔ sx̌əx̌c'iʔ uł mus
iʔ sk'ʷənk'ʷán a ck'ʷúl'əmstsəlx i l
sc'lálqʷəm. ʔasíl iʔ sk'ʷənk'ʷán a
cłp'iw's, uł k'im iʔ ʔasíl t'i piq.
c'áq'ʷənt anʔawtús iʔ kilxs a cwikʷsts
iʔ piq sk'ʷənk'ʷán, łə xík'əntxʷ məł
səlmíntxʷ iʔ naqs iʔ sx̌əx̌c'íʔ, náx̌əmł
łə k'ł'amnúntxʷ, məł k'wap
anʔawtús, məł anwí kʷ nkʷnim. iʔ
piq sk'ʷənk'ʷán a ccaq'ʷəstxʷ, lut a

EN'OWKIN CENTRE   36   COPYRIGHT 1993

En'owkin Centre, Penticton, B.C.

Fig. 2. Northern Okanagan language book (En'owkin Centre 1993:36–37) that emphasizes the importance of the stick game. The translation reads: 'Stick Game: The People have been playing stick game a long time. When the People celebrate, they go lots of places. They gather, they play stick game, they play cards, they bet on cards, they sing, they dance, they enjoy each other, and they feast. They use eleven sticks and four bones for the stick game. Two of the bones are marked, and two are white. You point at the hand of your opponent that is hiding the white bone. If you miss, then you lose one stick. But, if you guess it right, your opponent stops, and you start singing. You must point to the white bone, not to the marked bone.'

They are about three inches long with a diameter of from three-quarters to one inch. The determining factor in the size of bones is that they be no larger than can be easily hidden in the clenched fist. Sometimes the intramedullary cavities are filled with cork in order to make them less fragile. They may be weighted by filling them with lead, but usually their "heft" is determined by their density. Although in the past some players wore hand coverings (fig. 4) to aid in concealing the bones (Teit 1900:276), this practice has been abandoned (Brunton 1974).

Eleven one-foot long, pointed counter sticks are used to tally the score (fig. 3). One of these, formerly valued at 10 ordinary counters, is called the kick stick. This is the first stick won in a game. Around 1900 the value of the kick stick was lowered to one point. There were also 20 regular counters at this time. Around 1945, the number of sticks used was reduced to the 11—one kick and 10 counters (Brunton 1974).

Ideally, sticks were made out of serviceberry wood because of its straightness and density. The bark was com-

pletely peeled from the counters, but only on the bottom half for the kick stick. This helped to set it apart from the others. The sticks were then painted. In the 1990s hardwood doweling is often substituted with the kick having a larger diameter than the other counters (one-quarter inch for the counters, one-half inch for the kick stick). The kick stick is often carved or painted.

Stick game songs were sung during the game. They used to be accompanied by pounding on logs with pounding sticks (fig. 5; "Music and Dance," fig. 5, this vol.). These logs were arranged parallel to each other on the ground four to six feet apart; 15 to 20-foot lodgepole pine trunks were the usual choice. These were struck with pounding sticks made of peeled serviceberry branches that measured about one inch in diameter by one foot long. In practice, anything handy would suffice as a pounding stick.

By the 1960s, the pounding logs and sticks began to be replaced by single-headed hand drums. This replacement was hastened by the appearance of folding aluminum lawn chairs, which permitted a greater degree of comfort to players who knelt on the ground to use the pounding logs. Chairs made the pounding logs difficult to reach; hand drums were well suited to chairs (fig. 6). Drums were also compatible with standing (Brunton 1974, 1985). At a powwow near Wellpinit, Washington, in the late 1980s, there were no pounding logs and sticks in use, only drums.

Stick games are often played in a gambling "shed" made of poles over which canvas or plastic tarps are stretched. Some are covered with corrugated steel roofs. Bags or pieces of cloth and buckskin are used to carry and protect bones and sticks. A scarf is used to wrap up money wagers while a game is in progress. Paper and pencil, needed to record wagers, round out the list of equipment used in the stick game.

The Play

The leading figures in the stick game are called pointers. They are the leaders of their "sides" during the game. They make all the decisions. Their selection or acceptance by fellow gamblers depended on a number of factors. Ethnicity was one important source of support for a pointer. Playing and betting with a pointer from one's ethnic group was preferred (Brunton 1985).

Gambling success was another. Each establishes a reputation, and those with high success rates receive a commensurate amount of support. Generally, pointers under 20 or over 60 years of age receive less support than those between these ages. The too-young set has not had the time to build a reputation and is thought not to have enough experience to be good. Aged people are thought to be losing their power and skills, which are connected. Pointers' behavior also is a part of their reputation. Drinking alcohol adversely affects pointers' abilities, and if they try to lead a side while intoxicated or have done so in the past, their support dwindles.

Fig. 3. Equipment for the stick game. left, Umatilla gaming set including 4 hollow bone cylinders, 2 of which are wrapped with a leather thong, and 20 willow counter sticks. Collected by Stewart Culin on the Umatilla Res., Oreg., 1900. right, Klamath game set including 4 solid bone cylinders, 2 of which are wrapped with cord cemented with black gum, and 6 red painted willow counter sticks. Collected by George A. Dorsey on Upper Klamath Lake, Oreg., 1900 (Culin 1907:291, 292). Length of left sticks 25 cm; length of right sticks 18 cm.

The stick game itself is a stream of events that begins when an eminent gambler ("pointer") sits down to play. This constitutes a challenge. Soon another noted gambler sits opposite the first. Each begins to "collect" wagers. Individuals, regardless of sex or age, place money wagers with one of these gamblers, the amount varying considerably from person to person. These money bets are noted on paper along with the person's name. They are the most frequent types of wager in the late twentieth century. Personal property such as a blanket or shawl may be wagered "in kind" between two women. These items are piled together in the middle of the area between the opposing sides (fig. 7).

Often, after sitting long enough to announce who will be playing, the noted gamblers leave the area, entrusting collecting to their gambling "partners." These are friends or family members.

From time to time the size of the pooled wagers is compared. If those on one side have significantly less than the other, they call out, "short!" This signals bystanders that more wagers are needed. Collecting can take several hours to complete. At an undetermined time, depending on how actively people are betting, the pointers decide enough has been collected. They count their respective side's collective wager, making sure they "match." If there is a small discrepancy, the pointer usually makes up the difference by increasing his or her own wager. If the difference is too large, more bets are sought. Once matched, the money is bound in a scarf and placed in the center of the area between

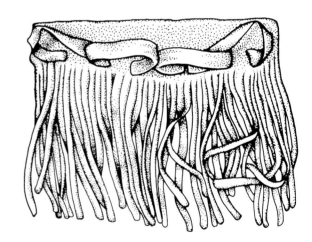

Fig. 4. Thompson knuckle-cover used during the stick game. Collected by James A. Teit on the Thompson River, B.C., 1897. Length 12 cm.

the sides. Players line up opposite each other to the left and right of their respective pointer.

At the beginning of play, each pointer produces a pair of bones. They are shuffled under a blanket, shawl, or hat, or behind the person's back, called "going under." The pointers then bring their hands out in the open with one bone clenched in each fist, called "coming out." Each pointer then guesses or "points" the other by indicating with a motion of the hand and arm in which hand he or she believes the unmarked bone to be. If both pointers "hit" (guess correctly) or "miss" (guess incorrectly), it is a standoff and the bones are rehidden. If one guesses correctly while the other does not, the former has won the kick stick, the right to use his or her bones and counter sticks in the game, and the first chance to hide both sets of bones. Those on the successful side join their pointer in a stick game song while beating out a lively rhythm. Five counter sticks are given to the other pointer who thrusts them into the ground in front of himself. Five are kept and similarly placed. The winning pointer ceremoniously lays the kick stick down in front of himself. He holds the bones, one pair in each hand, and moves his arms and body in rhythm with the song for several minutes.

The pointer then distributes the bones, one pair to each of two people noted for their skill in "bone handling." These people go under, moving in rhythm with the song. Their companions make gestures, attempting to distract the opposing pointer. When bone handlers come out, they place their arms at their sides, in their lap, or hold them over their chest resting their clenched fists against their shoulders. The song continues throughout this activity.

The opposing pointer now must decide in which hands the two opponents are concealing the unmarked bones. There are four possibilities. If the pointer believes the unmarked bones are in their left hands, the indication is a gesture made by pointing to the right with the index finger extended. If they are thought to be in their right hands, the "point" will be to the left. If the pointer believes the unmarked bone is in the left hand of the bone handler on the right, and in the right hand of the one on the left, the point is made by extending the arm with the thumb and index finger separated. If the unmarked one is thought to be in the right hand of the bone handler on the right and in the left hand of the handler on the left, the point is made by extending the arm and index finger straight out and down in front. In each case the pointing arm is clasped at the elbow by the free hand. The signal for a final binding guess or point is the exclamation, "ho!," a nodding of the head, or both.

Pointers use knowledge and strategy in playing the game. The community of gamblers is small enough to allow pointers to acquire knowledge about the habit patterns of their opponents. For instance, knowing how far opponents have traveled to attend a powwow is critical information. Persons far away from home are known to be nervous in play. Nervous bone handlers tend to "run" by changing their bones on successive guesses. This tendency is attributed to a person's concern about being caught without enough money to get back home. Confident bone handlers will "stay," repeatedly hiding in the same hands. Pointers also note idiosyncracies in the play of regular gamblers that they can then use to their advantage.

Strategy may involve the manipulation of the point itself. Until the exclamation, "ho!," or the nod of the head, a point is not final. Since the bones are won on a proper guess and are immediately thrown across, a pointer makes a series of points without the signal of finality so as to "draw out" the

opposing bone handler. A momentary flinch (showing a proper point) or a fleeting look of confidence (showing an improper point) can indicate to the pointer the true position of the unmarked bones. He or she will immediately follow feinted points with a final one. People other than the pointer also make guesses, but only the pointer's is accepted. The others are trying to "get the bone handlers to give themselves away."

In order to avoid this technique, bone handlers will often stare fixedly at the ground or over the heads of their opponents. They are told by someone sitting next to them of the pointer's final guess. Dark sunglasses may be worn to conceal the bone handler's eyes so as to prevent him from revealing information.

Good bone handlers also have techniques to increase their effectiveness. They know the habit patterns of pointers. Some pointers are stubborn; they point in the same direction time after time. Others will "chase," switching their guess each time. The tendency to chase is tied to a person's distance from home, similar to a bone handler's tendency to run.

Bone handlers may also cheat. One method is "switching" the bones. Here, the bone handler comes out with both bones in one hand and, when pointed, drops the appropriate one into the free hand in a sweeping motion as the arms are uncrossed. Another technique is the surreptitious substitution of a set of "half and halfs" (bones made so that one-half is marked and one-half is unmarked) for the regular game bones. Other ingenious techniques are reported. However, to be caught cheating is to forfeit the game and incur the wrath of all other players. This, along with more rules, and increased awareness of cheating techniques have mitigated against these practices.

Once the pointer has made a final guess, the bone handlers are obligated to "show" their bones. They do this in a variety of ways, depending upon whether the pointer has "caught" them (guessed them correctly) or not. When caught the usual practice is to open the hands, showing the position of the bones. This is all part of the fluid motion of throwing the bones across to the opposite pointer. If the pointer "misses," the bone handlers normally will expose the unmarked bone first, followed by the marked one. They do this by opening the palm slowly and extending the arm toward the opposing pointer. A miss is greeted with cheers and jeers by the hiding side. Increases in the volume and spirit of the song and body gyrations also are typical.

Taunts are used to disorganize the thoughts of opposing pointers. Pointing demands a great deal of concentration, both in terms of memory and observation. If the pointer can be angered or otherwise distracted, the elements of skill in the game no longer increase the chance of successful guessing above the 25 percent probability level that characterizes a four-bone guess. This can be the difference between winning and losing a game.

After a series of successes a bone handler may return the bones to the pointer, who rolls them in his or her hands and

577

either passes them on to someone else or back to the original bone handler. This seems a ploy to confuse the opposite pointer as well as to show deference to the pointer of the hiding side. It may also allow the bones to be recharged with the pointer's luck or power and be a demonstration of the individual's team spirit. If a bone handler continues to have success and is not caught throughout the game, he or she is said to have made a "home run."

If a pointer guesses both bone handlers correctly, the bones are won. Missing both bone handlers wins two sticks for the hiding side. One correct and one incorrect guess wins one set of bones for the guessing side and one stick for

top left, center right, and bottom left: Eastern Wash. State Histl. Soc., Cheney Cowles Mus., Spokane; top right, Field Mus., Chicago: 2834; center left, Wash. State U. Lib., Histl. Photograph Coll., Pullman: 70–0262; bottom right, Oreg. Histl. Soc., Portland: 007241.

Fig. 5. Stick games in progress. top left, Game when the pounding boards used were lumber, in place of the traditional lodgepole pine pounding logs. Photograph by Frank Palmer, Colville Res., Wash., about 1908. top right, Kootenai and Flathead game. A spectator watches the game from the sidelines, which are, in this case, on the ends of the area defined by the pounding boards. Photograph by Edward P. Allen, Bitterroot River, near Flathead Lake, Mont., 1897. center left, Nez Perce women playing at night, Sanpoil River area, Colville Res., Wash. The stick game, because it was gambling, was illegal in the state of Washington, except on the reservation, where because it was part of native culture was tolerated (Robert Dellwo, communication to editors, 1996). Photographed in 1938. center right, Nez Perce probably at a powwow. Photograph by Dick Lewis, Lapwai, Nez Perce Res., Idaho, 1935. bottom left, Colville Indians singing a stick game song as their side hides the bones from the opposing pointer. The men kneel behind pounding logs of lodgepole pine, beating out a rhythm with sticks of wood. The number of counters thrust in the ground in front of them indicates that this game was following an older style of using more than 11 counters. A container holding the collective wager is in the foreground. The number of counters on the singers' side indicates that this game was nearly over. Photograph by Wallace Gamble, Kettle Falls, Wash., 1939. bottom right, Wasco and Wishram at Celilo Falls, Oreg. The man pointing (guessing) the location of the unmarked bone in his opponent's hand holds a pair of bones himself. He has but one pair of bones to guess, and he does so by showing his opponent how he is holding his bones. If the opponent's match, he has won, and his side will have both pair of bones. The winning side will begin to pound on the pounding log, sing, and hide both pairs of bones. Three of his teammates hold their pounding sticks in anticipation of his correct guess. This anticipation communicates their confidence, a strategy that is used to undermine the confidence of the opposing pointer. Photograph by Sofie Foster, 1956.

the hiding side. All sticks won are taken from the center and laid in front of the winning pointer.

In the case where one set of bones is won by the guessing pointer, the play is changed. With but one pair of bones to guess, the pointer may use the bones already won. When the bone handler comes out, the pointer opens his or her hands showing the location of his or her bones and finalizes the point as before. A match results in winning the bones; a miss results in the hiding team winning another stick.

If the pointer has a great deal of difficulty in catching an opposing bone handler, he or she may designate someone else to point. A usual means of doing this is by giving this person the bones already won. If no bones have been won, the opposing pointer is verbally notified. The designated pointer sits more erect than before his or her change in role. If one set of bones is being hidden the designated pointer guesses only once. If two sets are involved and the designated pointer hits one and misses the other, another guess will be made. Missing both usually results in the point returning to the head pointer.

When the pointer on any guess wins either both pairs of bones or the last pair, his or her side immediately begins singing a stick game song. This song is usually led by the pointer, accompanied by percussion. Now it is their turn to hide the bones and receive sticks. Stick game songs often change every time the bones change sides. The pointer has ultimate authority over which songs from the repertory will be sung at any particular time. A close friend or relative of the pointer may also introduce a song into the game. Once in a great while a song will be introduced while a side is hiding the bones. This is done to change the luck of the side or when players are singing weakly or are not together in the song. On the other hand, if luck is running with a side, the same song will be used throughout the game.

The first sticks a side wins are the five in front of them. If their success continues, they win those in front of the opponents. Once all the sticks in the middle have been won by the two sides and are laying in front of the pointers, they move from side to side as payment for wrong guesses. The play goes back and forth until one side wins all 11.

At this point the winnings are distributed. Each winning gambler receives double the amount wagered. Those who have wagered blankets or other goods secure their own winnings. The losing side disbands, with either the same or a different pointer beginning to collect for a new contest almost immediately. If a pointer has played and won several games, a series of opponents, one after the other, will challenge.

During a game, side betting is evident. There are two ways to make a side bet. The first of these involves two people who wish to bet on the outcome of the game but who arrived too late to contribute to the collective wager or merely want to increase their wager after play has begun. The second involves wagers on the outcome of a single point. Money so wagered is twisted together and thrown in the area between the sides. Side bets made on the point are secured at the outcome of the point. Side bets made on the game are collected at its conclusion.

Professionals

Throughout the Plateau there were persons of great skill whose gambling exploits made them famous (Ray 1933:155; Commons 1938:185–186; Desmond 1952:30). They focused their economic activity on gambling, traveled extensively, and were admired. They were often wealthy and were considered excellent marriage prospects. Because of their exploits and wide travel, they became great storytellers, providing entertainment and information and serving as cultural brokers as they circulated throughout the area. Gamblers of this caliber possessed great intelligence and humor. Their personalities and exciting lives made them the focus of considerable romantic interest.

Supernaturalism

Traditional Plateau peoples live in an animistic world where all material manifestations are mirrored in spirit. It is thus understandable that the stick game is not merely a material event. The ideas of spirit and power are as much a part of the game as is strategy. An individual's personal power acquired

579

Fig. 6. Late-20th-century stick games. top, Adeline Miller, Dennis Starr, Wilson Wewa, Jr. (Northern Paiute), and Ada Sooksoit playing in a tournament at the Pi-Ume-Sha powwow. The side pictured is hiding the bones while singing a stick game song. The boisterous songs with their driving rhythm, accentuated by the use of the hand drum, help the hiding side conceal their bones from the opposing pointer. This side has all 5 of their counters remaining. Photograph by Cynthia D. Stowell, Warm Springs Indian Res., Oreg., 1981. center, Shuswap elders from the Bonaparte Band: left to right, Felix Morgan, Emily Morgan, Roger Porter, and Benny Morgan. Drums and pounding boards are being used together. Photograph by Marianne B. Ignace, Bonaparte Res., B.C., 1988. bottom, Waving newly won counters while singing and drumming boisterously, a way of taunting the opposing pointer. Lawn chairs have replaced sitting on the ground behind pounding logs or boards. Photograph by Rodney Frey, Coeur d'Alene Res., 1994.

Fig. 7. Game during the Huckleberry Feast, Warm Springs Res., Aug. 1952. top, Active players, kneeling on the ground, pounding with sticks on a board to establish a rhythm for their stick game song. Those standing behind usually have bet with them. Money wagers on the ground (one form of "side betting") are probably between individuals supporting the 2 sides. bottom, Before the game begins, matching collective wagers so that each side has identical amounts of money wagered on the outcome. Photographs by David and Kathrine French.

earlier in life through a vision quest may be invoked, especially if it is one that is specifically associated with gambling (Ray 1933:155; Commons 1938:185–186; Desmond 1952:30–31). Coyote, for example, is known to the Kootenai as one who can grant great power in gambling (Brunton 1974).

Ceremonies such as Winter Spirit Dances and Sweatlodge may be used to acquire knowledge and power for gambling.

Dreams are also a source of such power and knowledge. These divinatory experiences yield messages that contain instructions to be followed to insure success. The following account illustrates a typical spirit's message received in a Kootenai Blanket ceremony.

> Here's what happened. I went to this [ceremony] when they put up the blanket. They were putting up this blanket to get to Bonners Ferry and play with those Bonners Ferry Kootenai. I went. I sat down. Medicine was coming in. It finally came to a stop. He [the spirit] says, "You! We'll give you instructions." Everybody looked amongst each other because they were all setting there by the door. And the blanket was in the back—hanging. There was seven or eight of us sitting there. We don't know which one he meant [the spirits speak in vague terms]. Then one of 'em got up and asked him, says: "Now you are pointing to the people where they're gathered and we don't know who you're talking to or what to do." He says, "What we [the spirits] want and what we're intending to follow is him." He meant me. See, they don't go by government name. They go by your Indian name. My Indian name is Stands High. He [the spirit] says, "We're talking to Stands High." Well, that means me and I got up. He says, "When you're getting near, about one more camp before you get to Bonners Ferry, you follow a certain place and you're gonna find a saddle—White man's saddle. White man lost that saddle. He moved and he's gone. You're gonna find that saddle. When you get over there to Bonners Ferry," he said, "they'll ask you how much money you want to bet for that saddle. You tell them that you don't bet that saddle for no money. They'll ask you what you want to bet for it. Tell them that you want to bet it for a certain kind of shawl. If they bet you that shawl and if you people win, then the money comes in afterwards. You are gonna take all their money. They'll have no more and then you can come home" (Brunton 1970).

Ordinary bones may be treated with magical substances in order to make it easy for one's own pointer to guess their location, but impossible for that of the opposing side. The Kootenai also knew of a powder, which when rubbed on a set of bones, rendered them immune to other magical substances put on them by the opposition. They asserted that they no longer use such substances but attributed the practice to most Salish and the Cree. Some of these magical substances were thought to inflict injury, disease, or death. Desmond (1952:31) reported the use of a dried hummingbird by a Yakima man who touched it to his hands and the bones when hiding them.

Using gambling bones manufactured from the bones of a famous gambler made one practically unbeatable, but at a certain amount of risk. For example, a story was related in which a person made such a pair of bones from a deceased woman. He enjoyed a fantastic run of luck. However, at night the ghost of the woman appeared to him and insisted on sleeping with him. He finally was forced to get rid of the bones, after which the ghost never again appeared. Kootenai also attributed a loss of skin pigmentation to the use of such bones.

Even without assistance from supernatural beings, ordinary bones can acquire power. A set of bones that have proven lucky in play pick up an aura and are then given

"respect." This entails their being kept wrapped in cloth or buckskin when not in use. They are not to be taken out and handled, exhibited, or given to children to play with. It is felt that lack of respect will dilute their luck.

Sorcery was involved in the stick game:

> That's what happened to my wife when we were together [before she died]. We went down to Cusick [Kalispel territory]. God, we got lucky and we started winning a lot of games. And some old woman told my wife, "You want to watch your step when you go back to you home. Something will happen!" That's all she said. So we come home. She got sick. We put up a blanket. We got a powerful medicine man. When we got back we went over and got him and told him to come over to our place. We were going to put up a blanket. He was agreeable. So he came over and when the medicine was coming in the medicine told her [through the shaman], he says, "Next year you gonna be back there! That's one of the biggest surprises to that old woman who gave you this of her life because she's never failed. She gets her victim! When she told you that, if it wasn't for us, you'd never be back there again. You'd die! When she sees you it's gonna be the surprise of her life. She gave you that and you'll be over there walking around enjoying yourself like the rest."
>
> So next year we got ready and went. She told me, says, "That woman over there—that old lady coming over there, that's the one that give me that dope." She was wearing a red shawl. "Now," she says, "You just watch her actions—see what she does when she meets me. She doesn't expect me to be here." So she was walking along. When she put up her head and saw us—just kind of changed color. She was surprised to see her walking around after telling her what was gonna happen. That's my experience with that part (Brunton 1970).

Interpretations

The excitement and drama of the game are major reasons for its persistence as a principal form of gambling in the Plateau while many other aspects of culture have been lost. However, other reasons are also apparent. For example, Yakima stick gaming (and gambling in general) was functional in several ways. Desmond (1952:49–56) asserted that it was recreational, and that it provided a setting in which individuals, despite their wealth or ability, could participate. They could do so by actively playing or by betting with their group. Either brought a person a measure of prestige. This was particularly the case when persons bet beyond their means, which was viewed as a form of generosity. There were also special statuses such as that of the "professional gamblers" who were accorded high status similar to that of shamans.

Desmond (1952) argued that the stick game (and other gambling) promoted a sense of in-group solidarity and out-group rivalry, which strengthened the local group. He suggested that control mechanisms such as officials who oversaw contests mitigated against possible threats to peaceful relations between gambling opponents.

In the late 1960s and early 1970s (Brunton 1974) observed that the stick game was the centerpiece of most powwows. In-group solidarity and out-group rivalry was very much a part of stick game contests. Famous gamblers were still accorded high prestige. The game allowed everyone the opportunity to support his side, whatever the individual skill or means. And, it was and is still fun to play!

Moreover, the stick game is a metaphor and substitute for war. Historically, as warring groups established friendly relations with each other, they began to play stick games at gatherings. Their aggressive competition was rechanneled into a more innocuous form where social controls in the form of rules of the game and persons given authority prevented escalation. The level of hostility in some games between traditional enemies such as the Kootenai and Blackfoot shows that this substitution was still operating through the 1970s.

Another insight into the game's persistence came from analysis of who played with and against whom. Ethnic groups such as the Kootenai, Nez Perce, and Flathead still had salience as rallying points in game affiliation, but a shifting regional factor had entered the equation. For example, when eastern people such as the Kootenai, Blackfoot, and Flathead were near home (e.g., Arlee, Montana) they tended to play and bet against each other. However, when they were in the western country of the Yakima, or Nez Perce, they were much more likely to play and bet together against western people. Reservation mates also supported each other in this way. New social conditions bred a new type of "ethnic identity."

Finally, the stick game functions as an identity mechanism, not only in the sense of ethnic identity but also in terms of Indian identity itself. In the Plateau the stick game was added to other pan-Indian symbols that are used to identify and assert "Indianness." No matter what they do the rest of the week, the weekend powwow and stick gaming allow Plateau people to *be* Indian. It can also be considered a paradigm in that engaging in stick gaming permits a person to "work through" being Indian, thus satisfying a need to behave in a culturally salient manner.

In the late 1980s stick games were held at a powwow at Wellpinit, Washington, on the Spokane Reservation. One informant there remarked that the "sides were all mixed up"; that is, that ethnic identity was no longer very significant in forming stick game sides. This change is a result of the cultural impact of Euro-American individualism as well as the effects of pan-Indian identity.

The Drama of the Game

The following is a first-person account of a stick game at a powwow on July 4, 1970, on the Flathead Reservation.

It was late afternoon when I walked beneath the shelter of the gambling shed at the Arlee powwow grounds. It was a circular, tin-roofed pole structure without siding. I noticed three sets of pounding logs and, collecting wagers at one set

that was aligned east and west, was a close friend and informant. Hank is a Kootenai gambler who has a reputation for gambling skill and power. I walked over to him, sat in the sawdust, and asked, "who are you going to play?" He answered, "the Blackfoot [traditional enemies]. "They have been winning all day."

I asked if he wanted to use the new set of sticks and bones I had made. He replied, "If I get the kick I'll be happy to break them in for you." I left to get my equipment from my car and when I returned and unwrapped it, it caused a stir of interest among all nearby. Several gamblers tried the heft of the bones, after which we talked about how I had made them. Soon, however, interest waned and Hank left the area, asking me to collect for him during his absence.

I collected for about an hour, comparing amounts with the Blackfoot pointer from time to time. We were short, which is normal for the "losing" side. When Hank returned, he decided that it was time to match wagers. We were thirty dollars short, so Hank made up the difference. He now had 130 dollars in the game.

The collective wagers were tied in a scarf, which was placed in the center between the pounding logs. During the matching, those who had stakes in the game began kneeling behind their respective pounding logs.

Now the drama began. Hank took one pair of my bones; the Blackfoot pointer took one pair of his. Each shuffled them behind his back and "came out." They stared at each other for a moment and then the Blackfoot "pointed" him and was pointed in return. Both "hit." It was a standoff. They rehid their bones and again came out. This time Hank was successful and the Blackfoot was not. He began to sing a Kootenai stick game song as he picked up the counters, giving the Blackfoot pointer five and keeping five plus the kick. He laid the kick behind the pounding log. Each pointer thrust his five counters into the ground at an angle in front of him between the pounding logs. The Kootenai side picked up on the song and began tapping on the pounding log in rhythm. Hank held a pair of bones in each hand, swaying with the music, looking to his left and right. He finally selected an older woman and man and gave them each a pair of bones, one to his left and one to his right. These people hid the bones under cover of their clothing and came out. The Blackfoot pointed them and "caught" them. His side shouted their jubilation and waved their hands palmward at the Kootenai. Distributing his bones, the Blackfoot pointer began singing a loud, boisterous song. By this time all those playing in the game had taken their places and people had begun to gather around the game.

Hank pointed and missed both, accompanied by shouts of derision and more hand gestures from the Blackfoot side. He pointed again, and again missed both. The Blackfoot were becoming very confident and excited. Side betting was heavy. The Blackfoot pointer "made medicine" against Hank and the Kootenai side by placing the edge of his hand into the sawdust and moving it to one side, creating a small mound; this was a grave. He looked directly at Hank, smirking behind his sunglasses. The effect was powerful!

The lively song, gestures, taunts, and medicine combined to produce a kind of "energy" or "force" that seemed to emanate from the Blackfoot side. From time to time more material was added to the little symbolic grave between the pounding logs. The Kootenai continued to lose sticks, two at a time until they were down to two sticks, the kick stick and one other.

Suddenly Hank's father dove across the area between the pounding logs and wiped the grave away with his pounding stick. It was rebuilt and again he wiped it out, showing his disdain for their "power." Hank gave the point to his father who immediately pointed and caught both bone handlers. He later told me that he had been watching the Blackfoot bone handlers all day and had figured out their hiding pattern.

Hank designated his father as pointer, thus giving him control of the Kootenai side. Hank's father now led them in a different song, one given him by a spirit in a dream 50 years earlier. Hank hid one set of bones himself and gave the other pair to a middle-aged woman. They began winning sticks, two at a time. As the Blackfoot pointer made his guesses, his side would begin drumming and singing as if to anticipate the bones coming across, or perhaps to pull them across.

The Kootenai were now ecstatic. Their singing was boisterous; they taunted and gestured toward the Blackfoot side. After several "doubles" the woman bone handler was caught, leaving only Hank's pair. He hid two more times successfully, and then was caught.

The Blackfoot, who were now down to two sticks, began to sing and hide the bones. Hank's father pointed again and caught both on his first guess. The Kootenai jeered and gestured toward the Blackfoot. Women whooped in high voices. Hank's father showed total pride and confidence.

The Kootenai bone handlers remained the same as in the last inning. The Blackfoot pointer's first point caught Hank and missed the woman. They were now down to one stick! Excitement was at a feverish pitch! The outcome could be decided on the next point. The Blackfoot pointer feinted several times, but could not draw a flicker of movement from his adversary. He finally made his point, accompanied by a nod—and missed! The Kootenai hooted their derision and joy. After Hank distributed the winnings he told me that my bones had now been properly broken in.

THE STICK GAME

Mythology

RODNEY FREY AND DELL HYMES

The World of Myth People

The mythologies of the peoples of the Plateau comprise what the Klikitat and Yakima call *watítaaš* (Jacobs 1929:243), spoken narratives descriptive of the travels and the deeds, and occasional misdeeds, of a great host of beings. These are the beings the Thompson call *sptekʷɬ*, (Teit 1898:19, phonemicized) and the Nez Perce call *titwatityá·ya*, "myth people" (Aoki 1979:29; Aoki and Walker 1989:6).

The myth people are of various kinds, inclusive of many forms. Some myth people are "plants" (Turner, Bouchard, and Kennedy 1980:152) while others are objects, such as "awls," "combs," and "lassos" (Reichard 1947:59–60). Some are people without mouths (until Coyote cuts them open); and there is a myth person who does not know how to get his wife pregnant (until Coyote gladly demonstrates). Some are great monsters, such as Swallowing Monster (until slain by Coyote) or the *ƙʷaalí*, the "dangerous beings" (Jacobs 1929:243). And others are the wise Excrement Children of Coyote. Among the Okanagan and Sanpoil, Sweatlodge itself is a myth person with tremendous powers to bring forth life. Similarly, the Coeur d'Alene's Chief Child of the Root and the Okanagan and Thompson's Old One exhibit great spiritual powers that transform the world.

A vast majority of the myth people are given the names of animals. There are Salmon and Raccoon, Eagle and the Swallow Sisters, Grizzly Bear and Fox, among others; and pivotal to so many adventures, there is Coyote. These beings often possess the behavioral qualities of their animal character (Boas and Chamberlain 1918:225–231; Jacobs 1959:6–7; Reichard 1947:14). Expressed in the critical actions of the mythic beings are the particular behaviors venerated by the Indian in specific animals—Coyote as cunning or foolish, and Grizzly Bear or Wolf as wildly aggressive and dangerous.

While "no clear picture" of the physical image of the mythic beings is "offered or needed" (Phinney 1934:ix), they are often referred to in the narratives as "persons" (Jacobs 1929:182) or "man-like" (Boas and Chamberlain 1918:225–231; Phinney 1934:viii; Ray 1933:178). In a Sanpoil narrative (Ray 1933a:167–171), while attempting to win the confidence of an old couple and their granddaughter, Coyote appeared as a "chief." They noted that "his hair was long and braided all the way down and that his forelocks were carefully combed back and that the few strands

of hair in front of his ears were covered with beads. They noticed too that he was tall and strong....must be a chief of some kind." Here Coyote's appearance is in keeping with beneficent action. He provided the people with salmon as a true chief might. In other narratives, Coyote appears as an old or young man, or as a wealthy man, in order to deceive.

Throughout the narratives of the Plateau, the myth people are portrayed living in villages and kinship groupings, hunting, fishing, and gathering, dressing and offering appearances that suggest human forms. Indeed, their personalities exhibit a full range of human qualities and motives, from compassion, hospitality, and bravery, to humor, mischief and folly, to jealousy, greed, and vengeance. The myth people are thus not only inclusive of a great many expressions, but their very imagery, albeit vague and indefinite, interweaves the qualities of "animal-plant-object" with those of "humans."

In addition and certainly not blurred, the mythic beings also possess transformative-spiritual power, having "it inherently" (Ray 1933:178). The myth people are usually not seen questing for spiritual power; nevertheless, their actions presuppose and consistently demonstrate what in Salish is termed *sumix* 'sacred power' (Grim 1992). From an ability to change himself into a piece of driftwood to the slaying of giants and monsters to being brought back to life from the dead (with the help of Fox), the trickster-transformer Coyote best illustrates the spiritual power of the mythic beings.

In the collective actions of the mythic beings, the world in its entirety is indelibly transformed, rendering it meaningful and spiritually potent. The actions are those of heroes and victims, buffoons and monsters of all kinds. In their various adventures, the myth people face overwhelming challenges, find themselves deserted, engage in contests of power, seek revenge, adhere to authority and are self-sacrificing, are deceptive and self-serving and often punished for their disrespect, and are curious, playful, and sometimes foolish. Throughout, the myth people project determination and hope. As a consequence of their adventures, the landscape is molded as rivers are channeled, fish are set free, and the ways to trap and respect those fish are established. Where hunting methods, ceremonies, and social customs had been crude, and where the animals, fish, plants, and birds had been ill-defined, they are now refined and given their particular form and character. Where monsters and giants had roamed, they are now destroyed. The myth age world is not

Fig. 1. Jim Looney (Ik-pach-pall), Yakima. He is paying tribute, placing a rock in the ground, to a "fallen giantess," represented by a 30-foot marker, 9 miles south of Toppenish, Wash. This place, located on the Looney allotment, was where people went to make wishes or where favors might be granted (Helen Schuster, personal communication 1996). According to Looney's daughter, Ida Looney Bill, cannibal giants who used to eat the animal people once lived in the land. They were caught by Coyote and told to stop as "Indians are coming and you can't be eating them all the time." Two giant women thus began a journey through the Yakama valley down to the Columbia River in search of other foods. They crossed Toppenish Creek, climbed the next group of hills to the south, but before reaching Dry Creek, fell down from starvation and died. Along Highway 97 to Goldendale, Wash., 2 barren areas mark these places, one at Dry Creek and the other nearer to Status Creek (Schuster 1975). Photograph by Click Relander, 1952.

so much a world created from a void as a world already formed, though raw and dangerous, and then redefined in preparation for "the coming of the people" (Aoki 1979:4; Grim 1992; Jacobs 1929:223–227; Ray 1933a:132; Reichard 1947:57–63).

Virtually every detail of the landscape is given mythic dimension, linked with a particular myth people adventure (fig. 1). In the Coyote cycles of various Sahaptian and Salishan peoples, as Coyote goes up the Columbia River and its tributaries from west to east, he gives names to the various land forms and waterways. While describing his Cowlitz River country, Jim Yoke (Jacobs 1934–1937, 1:228–237) offers a vivid glimpse into a geography totally immersed in mythic names and meaning. "In this country, when the country had its beginning, in the myth age, he

(Coyote) ordained it (all). He named all these places in this land, (such as) the rivers, (and the) places where fish were to be obtained (and so on)" (Jacobs 1934–1937, 1:228).

As referred to in a Pend d'Oreille narrative (Teit et al. 1917:115–116) and shared by the Kootenai (Basil White, personal communication 1991), after Coyote slays the Snake Monster, specific parts of the monster can be seen along the Flathead valley—the mouth near Ravalli, heart as a butte near Jocko, tail near Evaro, and the poles Coyote brought with him while inside of the monster as two tamaracks growing near Arlee.

In a Wishram narrative (Sapir 1909:1–7), shared with the Coeur d'Alene (Reichard 1947:98–105; Teit et al. 1917:121), Colville (John Grim, personal communication 1991), Nez Perce (Aoki and Walker 1989:11–43), and Thompson (Teit 1898:27), for example, it is Coyote who is responsible for bringing fish to the rivers. Disguising himself as a child, Coyote is taken in by the Sisters who have dammed up all the fish in their pond at Celilo Falls. While the Sisters are away, Coyote breaks the dam, releasing the fish into the rivers. The Sisters are told by Coyote that they are just birds. In one Sanpoil version they are Dove Sisters, in another, Watersnipe and Killdeer; in a Kootenai version, Nighthawk and Snipe. Among the Wasco and Wishram, and Sahaptin, they are Swallows, who henceforth will announce the coming of the salmon up the river each spring. In the Nez Perce version, as Coyote travels on up the river, he leads salmon into those streams whose communities give him a woman, and "suckers" or no fish at all for those who rebuff him.

While Coyote is the primary transformer and benefactor of the world to come, his various decisions are only sometimes benevolently inspired. Much of his inspiration is derived from his own insatiable hunger (fig. 2) and amorous character. Yet Coyote's schemes to possess the "good looking girl" or have his feast usually end in himself being duped by his own deception. When his own needs are in concert with those of others, he is likely to succeed. But when his desires go against the limits of the social norm, he is just as likely to fail.

In addition, many of Coyote's decisions are inspired by others. When a situation and course of action is unclear to Coyote, he consults with, as among the Sanpoil, his companion, Fox (Ray 1933a:130). Among other groups, Coyote's advisors are his own Excrement Children (for example, Aoki and Walker 1989:42; Jacobs 1929:199; Ray 1933a:174). The narratives often unfold, to the delight of raconteurs, with Coyote unable to arrive at a decision. Coyote then brings forth his Excrement Children, who, in turn, refuse to help. But after Coyote threatens them with rain that will wash them away, they do advise him. Coyote then retorts, "That is just what I thought." Or as among the Sanpoil, Coyote says to Fox, "Oh, yes, I knew that all the time" (Ray 1933a:13).

The proper relations between the human and the animal, fish, and plant "peoples" are set forth by the mythic beings as

'Iceyeeye Tilipe'niin

'Iceyéeye tilipé'niin hitéw'yecine. Kawó' yú'cme heeyéeqcix. Kawó' 'iceyéeye hiq'oyímnaqana 'ipnalaqáaciqana. Kawó' kú'mac hi'náhpayxqana koná kaa wiwáaq'ic payaxwayikóoqana tilípe'ne yú'sne. Kaa kál'a hipewíiwuuyn láaqac. Kíi kál'awnik'ay' tilípe' hinéeke 'wáaqo' 'eeteex toláyca píik'un máat'atx.' Kawó' hitoláynikika koná hinaspaynóoya 'isíimet qíiwn haanlíisa wistitám'o kaa háacwal hixeeléewise wée'iktki 'ipnacawlatayíca koná. Konó' papaynóoya. " 'Eehé 'itúupk'eetem tilípe' kúume." "Kál'o' kíi ku'ús 'ipsqiláanx kaa 'éetx kíi paynóos." "Kúy q'uyím kaa yóx koná híiwes 'iníit. Taxc'ee koná t'awa hipú' hipst'úuy'. Hipst'úuy' núkt híiwes 'iléxni. Kál'a kem 'itúune taxc'aw'yáaxno' qó'c kál'a 'íin híitem'yekse kaa qó'c taxc'ee paynóotano'." " 'Eehé," péene. Kawó' hiq'uyímne ha'áca 'íiii 'isíimet núkt hitehémce hicapáa'laqy'awisa. Kaa hiwse'íce wáaqo' 'ilaqy'áawin' kaa sisílq'is hite'épetu. Konó' kaa hihípe hipst'úuy'. Kawó' koná páa'yaxo'ya capáaypa hipapáayna háacwal qíiwniin. Konó' kaa 'ipná'pipc'anaq'is húusus siléq'is qó'c kaa hicapáa'laqy'awisa konmá t'awa 'aláapx péene, " 'Eehé wáaqo' 'éetem hípe." " 'Eehé qe'ciy'éew'yew' wáaqo' hipst'úuy' hípe." Kawó' 'aw'laqy'áawya húukux kaa núkt pée'nike'nye koná q'o' kál'o' c'inín'is 'iséeps, "Kíi 'ee 'inéhnece," péene. "'Eehé qe'ciy'éew'yew'," tilípe'nim péene. Kawó' hi'séepe kaa hickilíine koná láwtiwaa 'iceyéeye hipaynóoya. "Kíyex 'ináhpayksa núkt kíi." "Oo qe'ciy'éew'yew'," 'iceyéeye hihíne. Kawó' tató's pe'énye kaa hipetéw'yenike kál'a hipaayáwya núkt 'iléxni hípt. Wáaqo' kaa 'ooyalá'amktacix. Kaa wáaqi koná 'iceyéeyenm péene, "Míne kaa kínye 'ew'nípe. Wáaqo' 'link'e kúuse. Oecem'íim." Kawó' péene, "Lawwlít'o 'ee kiyú'. 'Ee we wéet'u lawwlít. Qíiwn hitéew'yece máat'a. Koná 'ee paynóotano'. Wéetmet 'imáa'nahciw'atko'. 'Ee wées wéet'u c'a'a 'iceyéeye." " 'Eehé kaa 'itúupx kex 'ináa'nahciw'atko'qa." Kawó' hitoláyna hiiii hinaspaynóoya. 'Isíimet wistitám'o haanlíisa qíiwn kaa háacwal hixeeléewise wée'iktki kaa páatqa'npa'niqana kaa páapa'niqana. Kaa

34   35

U. of Alaska, Natl. Bilingual Materials Development Center, Anchorage.

Fig. 2. Text and illustration of *'Iceyéeye Tilipé'niin* (Coyote and Fox), pp. 34–35 in *Titwáatit* (Aoki 1980). This is a book of Nez Perce stories collected at Kooskia and Kamiah, Idaho, in 1960–1972 (Aoki 1979) and used in Nez Perce language and literacy programs. In the narrative a poor and hungry Fox is given meat by an old man and a boy. The generous man not only feeds Fox but also gives him a heavy bundle of food to take home. Fox shares with his friend Coyote, who soon depletes the supply and then decides to visit the people himself to get more. Coyote's greed and violence—he eats all he sees and then strikes the man—cause the meat, house, old man, and boy to become deer. Illustration by Carmen Whitman.

illustrated in a poignant Wasco narrative (Ramsey 1983:309–322; Sapir 1909:257–259). After being misguided by his father, a young man suffers the consequences of disrespecting his guardian spirit, the Elk, and of killing more than "he needed for himself and no more." He is "drawn in" by his guardian spirit to the bottom of a lake and there witnesses the bear, deer, elk: "they were all persons." The young man is asked, "Do you see our people on both sides?" The "persons" he had killed "cast him out," his guardian spirit leaves him, and the young man soon dies.

In a Sanpoil narrative (Ray 1933a:132), Sweatlodge is a "chief," with a body, head, and "able to see." After he brings forth and names all the animals and birds, Sweatlodge instructs them that they should "talk with" the children of the people who are coming. The animals will "tell" the boys that they are to be "good hunters" and "good fishermen," and the girls that "they will be able to get things easily." The "chief" then tells how he will no longer be a myth person but the Sweatlodge himself and how he will take "pity" on and "help" those people who construct him.

With the culmination of the various travels and deeds of the mythic beings, the transformers are themselves transformed. What had been a vague imagery, inclusive of animal, human, and spirit qualities, is rendered divisible and distinct. The myth people take on the particular animal, fish, plant, or object identities associated with the world of human peoples. And their spiritual powers are vested throughout the newly transformed landscape. For the Sanpoil, on his last trip, when Coyote reached Kettle Falls "he was just an ordinary animal coyote" (Ray 1933:178), though for the Wishram and Sahaptin, Coyote just "keeps on traveling." It is usually coyote and grizzly bear that are now seen roaming the landscape while the spirit of Coyote and Grizzly Bear may be embodied within the animal and come to reside with a human individual as a result of a vision quest. Coyote himself tells the myth people to take "pity" on the humans and "communicate with them through their *sumix*," giving them "guidance and direction" in "guardian spirit songs, in dreams, and in visions" (Grim 1992). The world of the myth people is the world made ready for "the coming of (Indian) people," a landscape named and inundated with mythic meanings and spiritual power.

A Wasco narrative (Sapir 1909:246–248) tells of an arrowpoint maker who becomes a cannibal. After killing and eating all the villagers, he pursues his own wife and son. The woman and child are taken in by "a very old man" who, in turn, kills the skeleton cannibal. The old

FREY AND HYMES

man and his daughter live by consuming tobacco smoke. After proving himself a great hunter of the Tobacco people, the son marries the old man's daughter. When the women, her son, and daughter-in-law become old, they are transformed into guardian spirits to help the people who are coming.

The most widely shared account of the "coming of the people" (human beings) involves Coyote and the Swallowing Monster. The motif is shared among the Coeur d'Alene (Reichard 1947:68–71; Teit et al. 1917:122), Nez Perce (Phinney 1934:18–28; Aoki 1979:23), Sahaptin (Teit et al. 1917:148–151), Thompson (Teit 1912:314), and Wishram (Sapir 1909:41–43). Having challenged Swallowing Monster to a contest of "drawing each other in" and having "lost," Coyote is inhaled into the enormous monster. Coyote proceeds to kill the monster, releasing the bird and animal peoples the monster had previously swallowed and creating the various Indian peoples. The monster's body parts are cut and thrown throughout the country, there creating the different tribes (vol. 17:189).

The World of Human People

While a vast majority of all recorded narratives can be categorized as myths, other types of spoken narratives are present. Primary among them are "tales" (Hymes 1981: ch. 5 and 7; Reichard 1947) or what the Klikitat call *txánat*, literally 'happenings or customs' (Jacobs 1929:244). Tales are narrative accounts that occur in the "historic" time, after the coming of Indian peoples to the world. The contrast between "myth" and "tale" does not suggest that "tales" lack spiritual or mythical dimensions, as such dimensions are clearly expressed in the actions of human beings (Sapir 1909:242). Among the Wishram and Sahaptin, at the end of the myth age, Coyote "keeps on traveling." There are Pend d'Oreille stories of Coyote visiting the Roman Catholic missionaries (Clarence Woodcock, personal communication 1991). The primary distinction between myth and tale is one between a world in the process of being transformed and prepared for the coming of human beings and a world rendered meaningful and spiritually potent inhabited by human beings. It is a distinction between mythic beings endowed with significance and potency and humans seeking that endowment. The mythic world necessarily precedes yet continues to reverberate through the world of tales.

Not unlike the relationship between myth and tale, the world of human beings is imbued with the world of the mythic. What is meaningful and spiritually potent in this world is grounded in the mythic world and made known through its stories. The place known as Celilo Falls, Oregon, is given its particular meaning for geographically separated peoples such as the Nez Perce, Sahaptin, and Wishram, because this is the spot where Coyote broke the dam, allowing the salmon to go upriver (fig. 3) (Aoki and Walker

1989:41; Sapir 1909:1–7). For the Wasco, the cries of the blue jay are a constant reminder of the consequences of spoiling a child as the story of Raccoon is brought to mind (Ramsey 1977:58–60). The myths are thus always close at hand, whether they are told or observed in the landscape. As the Flathead poet and playwright Vic Charlo (personal communication 1991) states, "The stories define us. When the story ended, the elder would say, 'and this is true,' pointing to that hill where the heart [of the monster] is, and you look and see, see the story; we are linked. It's a matter of just claiming that linkage."

Yet the mythic world is not readily apparent. It is a matter of "claiming that linkage." After all, the human beings are seeking that which the mythic beings have established and continue to emanate.

Raconteur: Techniques and Texts

It is during the telling of its narratives that the mythic world is rendered immediate and accessible to all, that much of the "claiming that linkage" occurs. (The linkage is also accomplished through vision quests and Winter Spirit Dances, which establish personal relationships with the myth world.) Indeed, the techniques of storytelling, perfected by the raconteur, and the structure of the narrative texts themselves, enhance the "linkage" and engage the full imagination and experiential participation of the listeners in the world of the story. It is a participation that is, in fact, overtly acknowledged by the listeners. During the narrative performance, listeners periodically respond by saying aloud, *i···*! 'yes' (Jacobs 1934–1937, 1:x; Teit 1912a:349) or as among the Pend d'Oreille, giving the hand sign of hooking the index finger and drawing it toward you as a sign for 'getting it' (Clarence Woodcock, personal communication 1991). As long as the responses are given, the telling continues. Should they cease, so too would the story.

Everyone has the potential to be a raconteur. As the Nez Perce storyteller, Mari Watters (fig. 4), the daughter of Samuel Watters, remembers, "everyone told stories, everyone was a storyteller" (personal communication 1991). Certain qualities greatly add to a raconteur's reputation. Mari Watters herself illustrated an amazing capacity for "remembering" a story just told to her. Around a campfire, a Lakota Sioux story was told by an accomplished teller, full of detail and twists, lasting over 20 minutes. Upon finishing, Watters said, "Let's see if I got it," and immediately proceeded to retell the entire narrative. While complete with the same character details and plot structure, it was not a rote memorization that was told. It was a narrative "believed in," expressive of Watters's own style, with her particular emphasis, "heart."

Typically, the long evenings of the winter months, often corresponding to the Winter Spirit Dances, are the season for storytelling (fig. 5). Particular narratives are often interwoven with each other to form longer narrative cycles, the

top, U. of Oreg. Lib., Special Coll., Eugene:M2380; left, Natl. Geographic Soc., Washington: 117512–A.

Fig. 3. Celilo Falls, Oreg., a place of mythic significance to many Plateau groups. For example, Sahaptin place-names for fishing sites at Celilo Falls often refer to mythological and ritual figues (vol. 17:187). top, Camp. Photograph by Lee Moorhouse, about 1900. bottom left, Fishing for salmon with dip nets. Photographed by a U.S. Army engineer, 1937. bottom right, Dip net fishing from a platform. Photograph by Gladys Seufert, 1950s.

telling of which could take up to two or three evenings. Clarence Woodcock, a Pend d'Oreille, remembers how his father would tell a "single story" to a group of men during each of three consecutive winter nights, from sunset until sunrise, the men sleeping only during the day (personal communication 1991).

The length of the performance is partially the consequence of stylistic phrase and sequence repetition. During the performance of the narrative, the raconteur may choose to emphasize an action or episode through repetition, though significant variation in detail, or even shortening of the successive segments can occur. The number of repetitions in a narrative depends on the dominant pattern number of a group. Throughout much of the Plateau this number is five, though four is also found, as among the Coeur d'Alene (Reichard 1947:27). Repetition of action is indeed a salient

U. of Idaho, Upward Bound, Moscow.
Fig. 4. Mari Watters, Nez Perce. Photographed at U. of Idaho, 1988.

captíkʷləm

**iʔ stəm·tímaʔtət uł
iʔ ƛ’aẋəẊƛ’ẋáptət
kʷu nʔúluʔsəntəm
məł kʷu
cəpcaptíkʷlxtəm.
q’sápiʔ iʔ sqilxʷ captíkʷləməlx məł
cxʷuy· iʔ sẋláp.**

Storytelling

Our grandmothers and grandfathers and elders gathered us around them and told us stories. Long ago the People used to tell stories all night til morning.

captíkʷləm
story_telling

iʔ	s+təm·+tímaʔ=tət	uł	iʔ	ƛ’aẋəẊ+ƛ’ẋáp-tət	kʷu
the	grandmothers-our	and	the	elders-our	us

n+ʔúluʔs+ant-əm	məł	kʷu	cəp+captíkʷl+xt-əm.	q’sápiʔ	iʔ
gather_around-they	and	us	tell_stories-they	long_ago	the

sqilxʷ	captíkʷləm-əlx	məł	c+xʷuy·	iʔ	s+ẋláp.
People	tell_stories-they	until	come	the	morning

EN'OWKIN CENTRE   39   COPYRIGHT 1993

En'owkin Centre, Penticton, B.C.
Fig. 5. Page on storytelling in a Northern Okanagan primer, *púpaʔkʷ*,
En'owkin's First Indian Language Book (En'owkin Centre 1993:39). This
book describes cultural activities and material culture items. Artist unknown.

feature. Often the plot involves a myth person doing something several times, succeeding only on the last attempt. A series of five brothers might attempt something, with only the last, usually the youngest, succeeding. It takes Coyote five separate attempts to successfully break the Swallow Sisters' dam and release the fish. Each attempt might be described in detail.

Pattern numbers also shape the organization of lines and groups of lines in the telling of a story. A raconteur will indicate by intonation contours, the rise and fall of the voice, the successive lines of his or her performance. A sentence-final intonation will indicate the end of a line or group of lines (technically, a "verse"). If the pattern number of the tradition is five, there will be sequences of three or five such verses. These sequences ("stanzas") themselves may form longer sequences ("scenes"). The whole of a story will be shaped in this way.

The Sahaptian languages, Sahaptin proper and Nez Perce, have such patterning. Table 1 gives the last scene of Chipmunk and his Grandmother, as told in Warm Springs Sahaptin by Hazel Suppah.

Notice that there are five stanzas and that each stanza has either three or five verses. The first two stanzas have three

verses, and the third has to do with the grandmother. So does the third verse of the next stanza, but here it is a pivot, ending an initial arc of three verses, and beginning another. What happens in the fourth verse is in direct response to what the grandmother has said in the third.

The same pattern occurs among the stanzas themselves. The third stanza completes the actions of the Basket Woman; she asks about Chipmunk, she looks for him, she eats him and goes away. At the same time the third stanza begins the resuscitation of Chipmunk. The grandmother prepares the possibility in the third stanza, getting Basket Woman to leave the bones whole. She brings him to life in the fourth, and in the fifth we are told what he is like henceforth. Such interlocking is common in traditions that make use of three- and five-part patterning.

The principles of patterning are the same in the Chinookan language of the Plateau, Wasco-Wishram. Table 2 gives the opening of The Deserted Boy, as told by Louis Simpson.

The three and five principle of Sahaptian and Chinookan appears to be shared with many of the Salishan languages of the Plateau. Its working out in detail, however, may vary. The Kalispel myth of Rabbit and Thunder, as dictated to Vogt (1940:82–85) by a blind octogenarian monolingual whose name is not known, has three acts, and one, three, or five scenes within each act. But the opening stanzas consist,

Table 1. Part of Chipmunk and His Grandmother, a Sahaptin Myth

ii áu,	All right,	
ináwamš áu taltaltíya áu,	she comes now, Basket Woman now,	
pá'awawiša áu. 95	she's looking for him now, 95	
áu páyanawiyáwaẋa,	Now she gets to her,	
"ái, awít,	"Oh, in-law,	
winaninm̓šaš čná,	he escaped from me here,	
ku či áu watíkš áwanainatšamš cná."	and here now his tracks are coming in here."	
"čau···mná iwá čná." 100	"He's *not* here at all." 100	
áu pá'awawiẋáika ái taltaltiyaiyáin.	Now that Basket Woman would look around for him.	
"áutya áuku čná mná iwá.	"Now he's just here somewhere.	
"čiš au áuku ánukšiša.	"I smell him now.	
"iwáštya áuku čná."	"He must be here."	
áu···ku pá'awawiẋaika áu m̓ni áu. 105	Now then she would look around for him now. 105	
áu kʷaaní káła au áwiyaičuša kʷaaná taltatíyana.	Now that grandmother is afraid of that Basket Woman.	
áuku páyaẋnẋa aukú.	Now then she finds him, then.	
áuku pátkʷataẋa áu.	Now then she eats him now.	
pá'nẋa kʷiiní tmámain,	That old woman asks her,	
"čáunamku λí pípš átkʷaitanam λíkš, 110	"Perhaps you could not eat his bones, 110	
náamn áikuš áu ánicta,	could leave him whole that way,	
kúnam áu átkʷatata áu."	when you eat him now."	
áu··· pátkʷwataẋa au,	*Now* she eats him now,	
λáa···ẋ ʷ áu,	*all* of him now,	
pípš náamn. 115	bones left whole. 115	
áuku áwinaẋa.	Now then she goes away.	
aúku či káłain áuku páwiyaunaẋa aukú,	Now then this grandmother, now then she steps over him, then,	
páwiyaunaẋa.	she steps over him.	
ánč'a páwiyaunaẋa áu.	Again she steps over him now.	
ánč'a páwiyaunaẋa áu. 120	Again she steps over him now. 120	
páẋat áu páwiyauna.	Five times she steps over him.	
wá···q̓iš ikáwa msmsyái.	Chipmunk comes to life.	
kʷaikumán íkuš áwa ẋə́lli,	That's how since that time he was stripes,	
ánačni.	on his back.	
kʷái ikuš taltatiyáin páwawapaqntka. 125	That's how Basket Woman scratched him. 125	
That's it.	That's it.	

SOURCE: V. Hymes (1972–1992).

NOTE: Raised dots indicate expressive length; phonemic length is shown by a double vowel. *áuku* is best translated as 'now then', but when it is repeated in a line to highlight it, the repeated exact translation is awkward. Here final repetitions are given as 'then'. Two medial repetitions emphasize a 'now' (*áu*) already present and are not translated separately (ll. 102–103). The medial repetition in l. 117 is given as 'now then' because the original itself foregrounds the subject (grandmother), naming her, then referring to her again with a pronoun in the verb. Final stress on a line-final occurrence (*aukú*) is always an indication of a new stanza.

not of three or five verses, but of pairs of verses. Table 3 provides the first scene and act, and the first scene of the second act.

Such patterns may carry over into narrations in English. Here is the opening of Charles Quintasket's telling of Skunk (Mourning Dove 1990a:243), reflecting the three- and five-part patterning traditional in Okanagan.

An old woman had two granddaughters,
Chipmunk and Rock Squirrel.

Table 2. Part of the Deserted Boy, a Wasco-Wishram Myth

aġa kwápt ġaɬġiúlxam iḱáškaš:		Now thén they told a boy,	
"*aġ(a) alχúya iɬkə́nkš.*"		"Now let us go for reeds."	
ġánġadix yakáml(a) iḱáškaš.		Long ago the boy was mean.	
aġa kwápt ġaɬkím:		Now thén they said,	
áġ(a) amšġiúkɬa ilkə́nkš."	5	"Now you will take him for reeds."	5
aġa kwápt ġaíḱɬúlxam:		Now thén they told them,	
"*álma kwáb(a) amšχíġidwaqɬχa.*"		"You shall abandon him there."	
aġa kwápt ġwap ġwáp ġatġí(a) idə́lxam wímaɬpa.		Now thén the people all went across the river.	
ġaɬuyá··,		They went *on,*	
ġatúyam iɬkə́nkšba.	10	they came to the reeds.	10
aġa kwápt ƛ̓ə́úp ƛ̓ə́úp ġatkɬúχ.		Now thén they cut them off.	
aġa kwápt ġaɬkím:		Now thén they said,	
"*šmániχ álma iḱáškaš aliġíma,*		"If the boy should say,	
'*mškáχaχ či?*',		'Are you there?',	
álm(a) amšġiúχwa,	15	you shall answer,	15
'*uuuuu'.*"		'*uuuuu'.*"	
aġa kwápt ġatχwáčk;		Now thén they ran off;	
náwit ġatχwá·itam,		straight home they ran,	
náwit ġwáp ġatúya:		straight across they went;	
ḱáya dan iɬġoaɬilx ġíġat,	20	not a person on this side,	20
sáqʷ ínadix.		all on that side.	
aġa kwápt yáxɬ(a) iḱáškaš ġalíkim:		Now thén that boy, too, said,	
"*aġ(a) alxḱwáyuwa.*"		"Now let's go home."	
'*uuuuu'*,		'*uuuuu'*,	
ġaɬġíux iɬkə́nkš.	25	answered the reeds.	25
kinuá·· ġaliḱínaχɬčk:		In *vain* he searched about:	
ḱáy(a) iɬġoáɬilx.		no person.	
aġa kwápt ġalíxḱwa yáχɬa		Now thén he too started home,	
ġačɬúwa qèġmtġix yáχɬa;		he too followed behind them;	
niktáia-itam:	30	he arrived running:	30
aġa, ḱáy(a) idə́lxams		now, no people.	

SOURCE: Hymes (1981:145) and an edition by Hymes of a text in Edward Sapir's 1905 field notebooks (cf. Sapir 1909:138–139).

They all lived together.
The girls had a boyfriend.
He was Fisher.

One day they heard the ominous sound of Skunk
            coming:
Phuw, phuw, phuw, phuw, phuw.
He kept breaking wind.
They could hear him coming.
The old woman hid the girls in the place they used
            for emergencies like this.

He came there
and looked around.
He said, "Where are the girls?...."

The time expression "One day" marks the opening of the action, after the five lines of introduction of actors and a situation. The second stanza has five lines (verses) from the standpoint of their perspective ("they heard"). The third stanza has three lines focused on Skunk, a kind of three-step sequence common in the region: he came, he looked, he said. Notice also the fivefold repetition of "phuw."

Klamath makes use of three and five relations also. Table 4 presents the opening of Coyote and Badger, as neatly told by Pansy Ohles (M.A.R. Barker 1963:13–15). The eye-juggler story is popular in itself and a versatile frame. The eyes are stolen, and various adventures may follow to recover them or find a substitute.

Table 3. Part of Rabbit and Thunder, a Kalispel Myth

[i] [Rabbit and his grandmother]		[i] [Rabbit and his grandmother]	
yé esq̓éy.		They dwelt.	
epłč̓čyé².		He had a grandmother.	
hóy kʷémt t nkʷá nqʷńńmis łu² č̓čyé²s,		Then one day he pitied his grandmother,	
łu² xʷÌłé sṗx̣ʷṗx̣ʷút.		because she was now old.	
cúys yé č̓čyé²s,	5	He told his grandmother,	5
"hóy čnxʷíst."		"Then I go."	
hóy łu² x̣líp		Then next morning	
u kʷńčstmíst.		he got ready.	
hóy cúys łu² č̓čyé²s,		Then he told his grandmother,	
"kʷiqsċwétštm t aqłolqʷšscútn."	10	"I will fetch for you your future helper."	10
[ii] [He sees a woman]		**[ii] [He sees a woman]**	
hóy xʷíst łi²éłttẃít.		Then the youth went.	
xʷúy łaqʷmúle²xʷ		Now he came to an open field	
łu l estíx̣ʷi t sx̣ʷe²lí.		where they were gathering camas.	
hóy łáqšlš łtrʷít.		Then the youth sat down.	
kʷémì łu² esx̣écti.	15	Now they were digging.	15
hói λ̓u²λ̓u²úsm		Then he looked around	
u ʷíčm		and he saw (someone)	
u cúti,		and he said,	
"šé²i łu²i kʷíllqs łu² iqsm²ém."		"That one in the red shirt will be my wife."	

SOURCE: Vogt (1940:82–83) retranscribed by P. Kroeber (1988).

A number of myths of the Molala are preserved in notebooks dictated by Stevens Savage to Frachtenberg (1910–1911). One salient trait is a scene, widely known in the area, in which Coyote, stumped by something that has happened, asks advice from two or more small persons he carries about in his backside. Savage uses the scene frequently and spells it out in detail. He refers to the advisors in English as Coyote's "lawyers." Another salient trait has to do with ending a myth with its actors changing into the beings they will be when the Indian people have come, as a result of a pronouncement by one of them. In the known repertoires of the region, such an ending generally is assumed but enacted only now and then. Savage enacts it again and again, with a pronouncement by Coyote. He even has Coyote require actors who have dispersed to reassemble, so that he, Coyote, can do so.

Table 4. Part of Coyote and Badger, a Klamath Myth

Badger was throwing his eyes very far (in the air).	(A)	"Is it they that thunder like that?"	
Then they made a noise like this,		"Indeed. It's just like thunder."	
"lolololok!"			
Then they fell back in.		"Indeed. Well, could I do like that too?"	15
"Ohh, I do this well," he said.	5	"Indeed. Just throw your eyes up."	
Then again,			
"lolololok!"		Then,	(C)
		"lolololok."	
Then Coyote came near,	(B)	Then they fell back in.	
came near.	10	Again he said,	
"What are you doing?"		"Ohhh, this is very good, this thing of yours."	
"I'm throwing my eyes up."			

SOURCE: M.A.R. Barker (1963:13), reanalyzed by Hymes.

Table 5. Part of Battle of the Mountains, a Molala Myth

Now in the morning they fought.   [iv]   (A)   65
Now Mt. Hood shot first.
    He shot Davis Peak.
        First shot, he made a gap there.

Then Mt. Jefferson too was hit.   (B)
Then he was hit five times.   70
    He got a big gap.
        That Mt. Rainier shot him.

Then Glass Mountain [Obsidian Cliffs?] shot too.
        (C)
    He shot Mt. Adams.
        He knocked his head off,   75
            after shooting him.
Then too he shot Glass Mountain.

Then Mt. Hood was hit,   (D)
    on the east side.
Then he got cracked forever.   80

Again Mt. Jefferson was hit.   (E)
    Five times he was hit in the same place.
        He was hit the same way five times.
Then he got a big gap.

Ten days they were fighting.   [v]   (A)   85
Then Coyote and Eagle were coming.
    They knew about it long ago.
Coyote said,
        "You are my younger brother,"
            to Eagle.   90

Then the two came to Mt. Hood.   (B)
Coyote asked Mt. Hood.
    He said,
        "What are you all doing all the time?"
Said Mt. Hood,   95
        "We were fighting yesterday.
        "We are through fighting."
Coyote said,
        "Who got killed?"
He said,   100
        "Mt. Jefferson was shot five times.
        "The one on the other side was shot five times too."

Then Coyote said,   (C)
    "Now you [mountains] will not fight.
    "Now (this) is the last time you will fight.   105
    "You [Mt. Hood], now, will never kill anybody.

    "Likewise Mt. Jefferson.
    "Likewise Mr. Three Sisters (of) the Klamath Country.
    "They will never fight again.

"Likewise Glass Mountain.   110
    "He will never fight anybody now.

"Now that's all I tell you.
"Now you will be a mountain.
"Mt. Hood will be your name.
"You will never kill anybody anymore.   115
"You will be nothing but a mountain."

To Mt. Jefferson he said likewise.
To those Three Sisters mountains he said likewise.
He, Glass Mountain, was hit.
    "Now I tell you.   120
    "You will never kill anybody.
    "You will be nothing but Glass Mountain.
        They will make (of you) arrowpoints, flint."

Then he said,
    "Now I am going to go across (the Columbia).   125
    "Other people will come here pretty soon.
    "Now we too, (I and) my younger brother, are going."

Then they two went across (the Columbia River). (D)
Then to Mt. Adams, Coyote spoke.
    He said,   130

"Now you will never fight again."

Again, he went to see Mt. St. Helens too.
    He said,
        "Now you will never fight."
Mt. Rainier he went to talk to.   135
    He said,
        "Now you will never fight."
    [—]"Now other people will come here. [to all mountains]
        "Now that's all I have to tell you.
        "Now you mountains all will be named."   140
    [—]"Now you too, my younger brother, I tell you.
                (E)
    "Now I am making the world for the last time.
    "(This) will be said by tradition,

        'Long ago Coyote said,'
            so they will say."   145
        Coyote now said.

Then he said,
    "You will be Eagle, my younger brother.
    "You will be a chief.
    "But I, now, I'm going toward the sun-rise.   150
    "Now I will never be seen.
    "Tradition will tell about me thus.

    "Now go now, my younger brother.
    "Now I too am going.
    "That's the end now of (this) tradition."   155

SOURCE: Zenk (1992), with revisions by Howard Berman.

Fig. 6. Kootenai men telling stories to James Willard Schultz, also known as Apikuni (far left). left to right: Wolf Going Out of Sight, Jack Ignatius (interpreter), Many Wolves, Water Bull, and Chief Red Horn. Photograph by Jessie Donaldson Schultz, B.C., 1930.

Savage's Molala narratives make use of three-and five-part relations, according to an analysis by Henry Zenk of Battle of the Mountains (table 5). The story has five scenes, the fourth and fifth of which are shown here. The fourth scene has 10 verses, grouped in five pairs. The fifth scene has five stanzas, mostly pronouncements by Coyote. The turns at talk in the last three stanzas (C D E) have considerable internal structure and are a fine illustration of this possibility of the narrative art of the area.

In addition to the stylistic use of repetition, other qualities mark an accomplished storyteller. These include "a fine sense of the dramatic and a particularly compelling voice" (Aoki 1979:9), "use of archaic words and speech mannerisms of various characters such as Grizzly Bear" (Aoki and Walker 1989:5), a graphic use of "intonation and gesture" (Reichard 1947:33), and a "playfulness" that would bring out the humor in the stories (Vic Charlo, personal communication 1991), all qualities that further animate the story and draw the listeners into the drama.

The animation of the stories literally occurs in the voicing of the words of the narrative. Expressed throughout the narratives of the Plateau is the understanding that words do not simply describe or refer to features or ideas in the world but may themselves have a power to bring forth that which they name. In the Wasco narrative, when five brothers desired to hold a festival, they *said*, "'Let us sing, brothers, and enlarge our house,' and they sang till they had a very large house with five fireplaces in it" (Sapir 1909:311–314). In the Nez Perce story, when Coyote *said*, "Let me look exactly like my son," and "Now let me be a Flathead man shooting grouse, wearing a blanket diagonally," Coyote was transformed into his son and then into "a man aiming at a grouse" (Aoki and Walker 1989:37, 42). In a Kootenai narrative, when the girl whimsically *said*, "This is a nice little star. I'll marry him," the Star came to her and she reluctantly was obligated to marry him (Boas and Chamberlain 1918:247–249). When a man named Wolf sang his name, "he became a wolf" (Boas and Chamberlain 1918:227).

In each of the above examples, the narratives consistently include reference to the actors *saying* what is desired, and, in turn, what is *spoken* is brought about. Among the Wasco-Wishram, after Coyote freed the salmon from the sisters who kept them dammed up, he transformed them into swallows and decreed what they would do. He did this first of all literally by naming them "Swallows" (the word for 'naming' has the force of 'pronouncing'). For the Clackamas, whose language is largely the same as their Wasco-Wishram neighbors, this understanding is voiced at the completion of a particular myth as well as an entire narrative cycle. Having spoken the names of the myth people into being, the raconteur would say, "'Now let us (the Myth Age actors) separate (and go our respective ways to the rivers, mountains, or into the air).' And they would do just that then. Some of them would become birds, some of them animals of the forests, some of them (become the creatures) in the river, some of them (especially the larger animals) in the mountains, all sorts of things (they would metamorphose into)" (Jacobs 1959:73). What had been brought about and witnessed through the storytelling is now free to return to a world mythically endowed.

The act of speaking the words of the narratives brings forth the myth people and their territory that, in turn, is to be traveled by the listeners. The story and its telling can be thought of as a "canoe journey." When a story comes to the end for a night, Mary Eyley, a Cowlitz storyteller, would say, "Now I will tie up the myth;" when the story begins again the next evening, she would say, "Now I will untie the myth;" and should the "raconteur wander from the main stream of the narrative," one of the listeners would say, "Your myth might float away" (Jacobs 1934–1937, 1:x).

Mythology as Ritual

Because the mythology is inseparably linked with the act of telling, Plateau mythology is most appropriately understood as ritual performance, as "essentially *dramatic*" (Ramsey 1977:xxv). As Jacobs (1959:7) observes, "The absence of psychological interpretation and notation of feelings in the native lines, the terse summarization of action, and the indications which we have that narrators gave dramatic renditions warrant the deduction that recitals of stories resembled plays more closely than other forms of Western literature," such as novels, short stories, or prose of any sort. The public performance of these myths is "one of the tribe's primary rituals" (Ramsey 1977:xxvi).

There are numerous instances in which myth serves as an ideational-symbolic charter for ritual behavior. The narratives, understood as a literature, can provide an infrastructure of symbolic codes, meanings, and rationale for the specific ceremonial acts. This sort of myth/ritual correspondence can be illustrated in the Sanpoil First Salmon ceremony (Ray 1933:71–75). In the Sanpoil narrative, the actions of Coyote provide a structure for and give meaning to the ceremony—explanation for the origin of the salmon, descriptions of the building of the weirs, procedures for the preparations and serving of the first fish caught, how to care for the bones, the designation and role of the Salmon Chief. The ritual acts of vision questing and the Winter Spirit Dance also have mythological correspondence as among the Kettle Falls people on the Colville Reservation (Grim 1992).

Yet the significance of mythology is not limited to its ideational replication of the behavioral world. As suggested by an appreciation of the power of words, the mythic narratives themselves reveal a world endowed with tremendous meaning, a world with a vitality and substance of its own.

As the world of guardian spirits is rendered accessible through the vision quest and Winter Dance, the formaliza-

tion and animation of that world is revealed during the ritual act of storytelling. Each ritual form carries the individual into the territory of the spiritual. In fact, the myth people witnessed during storytelling and the guardian spirits encountered during a vision quest are kindred and are often thought of as one and the same (Aoki and Walker 1989:6; Grim 1992; Ray 1932:178). When the age of transformation came to an end, the mythic beings often became the guardian spirits of the subsequent age. This affiliation is expressed during the Nez Perce and the Sanpoil Winter Dances. On the Flathead Reservation, the songs sung during storytelling are the same as those sung during the "special ceremonies" of the Winter Dances (Clarence Woodcock, personal communications 1991).

The human dancers are "actually transformed" into the form of their guardian spirit and continue to be "wild" until the dancers are "captured" and their "wild powers" are "claimed" (Ray 1933:192). The "wild powers" manifested in the dancers are understood to be those of the myth people, and for the Nez Perce, the *titwatityá·ya* (Aoki and Walker 1989:6).

What is "known," either through the storytelling or in the Winter Dances, is "essentially *one* kind of knowledge about the human order, relative to the rest of the world, natural and supernatural; not two kinds of knowing, 'ritual' as distinct from 'mythic'" (Ramsey 1977:xxvi). Indeed, any world separate from the mythic world is a world not readily conceptualized by Plateau peoples. Among the Coeur d'Alene, for instance, the reality of the "two-headed snake" is in the telling (Reichard 1947:56, 198).

Access to the mythic world through storytelling does not, of course, render the personally critical guardian spirit linkage. The ritual act of storytelling is not functionally equivalent to other ritual acts: spiritual power is not gained, a guardian spirit is not danced or a cure is not effected. But becoming familiar with the territory of the myth people through their stories is a "necessary precondition for effective participation in religion" (Aoki and Walker 1989:6). Through the participation of the stories, the particular characteristics and spiritual endowments of the tutelary spirits are made known. The howl of a guardian Wolf spirit, and its costume, dance, and song are first revealed through the telling of the narratives.

Purposes of Myths

Mythology certainly refers to a world prior to "the coming of the people," yet it is not a world of history alone, a world no longer accessible. As Vic Charlo observed, "the stories are what we have to explore with" (personal communication 1991). Through the ritual act of storytelling, the listeners are participants in the transformation of the landscape and the animals, rendering a humanity inseparably integrated with the world about it. As Archie Phinney (1934:ix), a Boasian-trained Nez Perce, so eloquently states, "Any substantial

Fig. 7. Raconteurs. left, Lawrence Aripa, Coeur d'Alene, on the Coeur d'Alene Reservation, Idaho; right, Basil White, Kootenai, on Kootenai Reservation near Bonners Ferry, Idaho. Photographs by Jane Fritz, 1990.

appreciation of these tales must come not from the simple elements of drama unfolded but from vivid feeling within oneself, feeling as a moving current all the figures and the relationships that belong to the whole mythbody." Each time the canoe is launched, traveling the territory of the myth people, the aesthetic, ethical, ontological, and pragmatic meanings and dynamics of the mythic world can be discovered, and they are reiterated and renewed in the world of the people. Outside the telling, the myths continue to be reflected upon and applied, as the world is rendered comprehensible and the various ambiguities and dilemmas encountered in daily living are offered resolution. Each time the canoe is launched, the world is kept in balance, maintaining the proper relationships with kinsmen—human, animal, and spiritual (E. Jacobs 1990:xiv).

The timing of the telling of the stories is, in part, influenced by this integrative dimension. During the summer, the mythic meanings and powers are close at hand, immediate, pervasive, and defined in the social relations, in the animals, plants, and fish, and in the well-traveled countryside. A vision quest, likely entered during the summer, may secure an even more intimate relationship with this world. During the summer, the stories are "seen" in the landscape. But during the cold and dark of winter there is a greater isolation from a landscape and the various kinships so richly

endowed with mythic meanings, from a surrounding countryside that is now not well traveled. This is the season of "spirit sickness," of a "feeling of lonesomeness and despondency" (Ray 1933:186). But through the storytelling and Winter Dances, the myth people are brought forth and witnessed, and in so doing, the vital linkage to a meaningful world is reaffirmed and renewed. During the winter, the telling of the stories brings forth a "seeing" and traveling in Coyote's landscape.

In addition to the integrative role, the act of storytelling facilitates important didactic roles. Explanations are offered and moral lessons are to be learned. For the Yakima, the Coyote narratives are the "Indian Bible, ... the core of Plateau Indian mythology [, and] embody inspired truth as is found in all great literature" (Hunn 1990:85).

While the narrative tellings are often directed at adult audiences (Ray 1933:133), children are never discouraged from listening. Indeed, among the Wishram-Wasco and Sahaptins, the most obvious occasion for the telling of stories is when children are present. Some stories are specifically intended for children and not adults, such as the Mosquito story of the Kootenai (Boas and Chamberlain 1918:v). Lawrence Aripa, a Coeur d'Alene storyteller (fig. 7), recounts how, "When I was a little boy, whenever I did something wrong, my grandfather would laugh and he would look at me and call me

Fig. 8. Warm Springs Sahaptin women portraying a myth in which a monster woman steals human children and carries them home in a basket for her own children to eat. Based on this story, Blanche Tohet, left, and her sister, Susan Moses, sometimes tried to scare their children into good behavior with commercial Halloween-style masks embellished with colored paints, which they called their "boogerman" masks. Photograph by David or Kathrine French, Warm Springs Reservation, Oreg., 1952.

Fig. 9. Elizabeth P. Wilson (b. 1882, d.1973), Nez Perce, a well-known storyteller. She had a great flair for the dramatic and was known for her compelling voice while telling myths she learned from her mother, who was a medicine woman, and other elders (Aoki 1979:8–9). Photographed in 1961.

Cosechin; ...Do you want to grow up like Cosechin?" (personal communication 1991). In the tale, Cosechin is a man who had "no respect for anything," killing too many deer and then not sharing the meat, burning down trees and laughing when the animals died, until he was finally banished by the people. And certainly, narratives such as the Klikitat story of Coyote and Deer (Jacobs 1929:199–200) and the Wasco account of the Young Man and the Elk (Sapir 1909:257–259) tell of the importance of respecting the animals and the dire consequences of not doing so. Lessons of "inspired truth" are offered. In this way children learn by the examples set forth in the actions of the mythic beings. Or sometimes, as in the instance of Coyote's antics or Cosechin, the example is of one not to emulate.

While moral and explanatory lessons are implicit and pervasive throughout Plateau narratives, they are not always the overtly stated intention for myth telling (Reichard 1947:7–8). The rendering of a particular myth is not typically followed by specific, Aesop-like, "moralistic commentary" (Ramsey 1977:xxx). Indeed, the raconteur's style of telling can also be characterized by its "dramatic terseness" (E. Jacobs 1990:xix–xx). In comparison with the often rich coloration in Western literary prose, elements of motivation, feeling, and mood are not always explicitly conveyed in the specific language of the Plateau narrative texts. Moral and explanatory meanings as well as effective characterizations are thus deeply embedded within the narratives; they are left to be *discovered* by the listeners. Truths are to be actively sought.

Storytelling also offers what Vic Charlo calls an opportunity to "lighten the load" (personal communication 1991). Experiencing the humor of the "play on words" or of the antics of Coyote brings a smile and joy. As Phinney (1934:ix) observed, "Humor is undoubtedly the deepest and most vivid element in this mythology, the element that animates all the pathos, all the commonplace and the tragic, the element that is most wasted by transliteration." The pervasiveness of humor found in the narratives invites individual expression of verbal artistry by each raconteur. The humor also serves to render the mythology more accessible. For Charlo, "With laughter you can really explore the heavy issues, like at the heavy moments at the ceremonies, the elders would light up a cigarette and say outrageous things" (personal communication 1991).

Continuity and Change

With Anglo-American contact, "canoeing" the rivers of the Plateau has taken on new dimensions. There are families who continue to travel in the same "canoe" as their grandparents. Among the Kootenai and Nez Perce, for example, particular families share the narratives in their native language. During the winter season among the Kettle Falls people on the Colville Reservation, while the stories of Coyote are shared during the day, the "revitalized" Winter Dance is held during the evening hours (Grim 1992). The mythic beings are brought forth and their territory is traveled. The "canoe journey" facilitates an intimate participation in the world, feeling the power of the river's currents and the splash of cold water on the face. On the "canoes" of others, an "outboard motor" has been added to an "enlarged canoe." In this "canoe," many more people can travel the river's territory. But in replacing the "paddle" with an "outboard motor," the splash of the cold water and power of the river's current are also less apparent. The listeners need not acknowledge their participation, as they and the narratives themselves are becoming distanced from the mythic landscape.

The mythology has reached a greatly expanded audience, an audience of Indians as well as those new to the narratives of the Plateau peoples. The project entitled *Speaking the Earth Mother* is one example. Sponsored by The Idaho Mythweaver, a non-profit organization, and the Idaho Humanities Council, and sanctioned through the specific tribal councils, the 1990–1991 project brought together several elders for a series of 14 public performances of the "traditional stories" throughout Idaho. Among the raconteurs were Basil White (fig. 7) from the Kootenai, Allen Slickpoo and Mari Watters from the Nez Perce, and Lawrence Aripa from the Coeur d'Alene. In addition to evening performances, attended by 80-200 mostly Anglo-American people, many of the stories were tape recorded and used in a series of five documentaries on how the traditional stories helped shape the natural resource heritage of Idaho's Indian peoples. The series was aired on public radio stations throughout eastern Washington and Idaho. One immediate consequence of both the public performances and the radio programs was an increase in demand by public school teachers to have the "elders" come to their classes and tell the "Indian stories."

In similar fashion, among the Flathead and Pend d'Oreille, during the winter months, a series of "Saturday potlucks" was organized by the Cultural Committee to bring together the elders and have them share the "old stories" (Clarence Woodcock, personal communication 1991). All the narratives were tape recorded in order to preserve them for use in the schools and for future generations.

Seeking to preserve a wonderful collection of Okanagan narratives, as told in English by Harry Robinson, Wendy Wickwire rendered the texts in a written format, yet in a manner that conveys "the nuance of the oral tradition" (Robinson 1989:16). The texts are presented as lines paralleling the raconteur's "emphasis on certain phrases, intentional repetition, and dramatic rhythms and pauses," on the stories as "preformed events" (Robinson 1989:16).

The didactic dimensions of the narratives are emphasized by the raconteurs. Allen Slickpoo and Mari Watters are among a handful of others who championed the vitality and applicability of their Nez Perce stories. Watters has used the narratives, told almost exclusively in English to her English-speaking Indian students, as tools for counseling in educational youth groups, such as Upward Bound. As Watters (personal communication 1991) states, "Stories of Coyote convey moral lessons, the specific issues the students face—jealousy, cheating, and true love, sharing, cooperation, their cultural values; by looking at people's hearts you do much better."

The narrative telling of Allen Slickpoo, like that of Watters, maintains much of the former style and content. Though told in English, Slickpoo skillfully brings out the humor that pervades his telling, drawing his listeners into stories such as Coyote breaking the dam at Celilo Falls or Coyote juggling his eyes. His intonation and speech patterns change as he speaks the voice of Coyote, gives the sound first of Magpie flying down to pick on Coyote's head and then of Coyote waking up, or as he sings "Coyote's happy song." The changes in his voice are augmented by Slickpoo's rich texturing of hand gestures, accentuating the action of a mythic being or pointing to the direction that Coyote went.

As the stories find their way into school and public performance settings, audience expectations and sensibilities affect the content and style of the narratives. As a didactic role increasingly predominates, narrative selection and content emphasis focus on "teaching Indian values" and on "entertaining." The stories most often requested by teachers and told by Indian raconteurs are those that explain the origins of natural phenomena and Indian customs and that offer moralistic lessons. Humor is being redefined relative to audience response, be it Indian or non-Indian, adult or child. Coyote's "obscenity" is seldom voiced publicly. The length of the narratives has been greatly condensed. Instead of relating a series of closely associated Coyote narratives, only segments are told. The embellishment and rich detail along with the stylistic use of repetition have been increasingly omitted.

The mythic narratives are often told in English, not in their native languages. A preponderance of the storytelling on the Coeur d'Alene, Flathead, and Nez Perce reservations, for example, takes place in English, though for Clarence Woodcock (personal communication 1991), when they are told in his native Pend d'Oreille language, they "make more sense and they move you back to that time." With the use of English, the understanding that words have a creative capacity is seldom appreciated and voiced by raconteurs. And correspondingly, in those communities where the practice of acquiring a personal relation with a guardian spirit has become less frequent and the desire to understand the world of mythic beings is obscured, the character of the mythology is changing. Mythology is passing from a ritual act in which the world is brought about, animated with mythic meanings and power and participated in experientially, to a mythology defined as an oral and, increasingly, written literature, descriptive of a world no longer immediate, though a literature still well-endowed with cultural values, moral lessons and a rich humor—from a mythology traveled, within oneself and one's world to a mythology viewed, in speech and on the page.

Even as early as the 1930s, Phinney (1934:viii) addressed many of these changes in the Nez Perce appreciation of their stories, stating that "the associations felt between their experiences and the ideological content, the highly imaginative quality of these tales no longer exists."

The contrast and tension between the two forms of "canoe" are brought out in a 1991 play written by Vic Charlo and Zan Agzigian, *Trickster at Dirty Corner*. At the heart of the play is the question asked, "How can we tell the stories without *telling* the stories?...Can eyes be ears?" When the protagonist, Silent Raven Sing-Too-Loud, a reservation Indian attending a college writing workshop, is asked to write and read a story, he hands the professor blank sheets of paper and proceeds to tell a story. The professor is not amused.

"We all have trickster in us," according to Charlo. Indeed, the trickster character that pervades the mythology of the Indian serves to "lighten the load" throughout this play. The challenge for Charlo is "how do we keep the stories (of Coyote and the other myth people) alive in our changing world?...how do we be faithful to the word?" And with these traditions, how do we "use them to make wise decisions?"

The performance of the play itself evokes the storytelling of a raconteur in dialogue with his listeners. "Each performance was different," as the interactions between the five-member, all-Indian cast and the audiences differed. The style of play encouraged spontaneity and interaction. As Charlo, who himself plays Silent Raven, says, "I added a line here or there," and "I asked the kids in the front row to help me guess when I played the stick game" (and they responded).

In the play, Silent Raven is haunted in his dreams by the myth people, Fox, Deer, Storyteller: "Let us out, let us out!" The play ends as Silent Raven, with a renewed confidence and conviction, reads from the paper on which he has placed the words of his stories. "You see we're all magicians; we just have to know what's in the drum and pull it out!"

MYTHOLOGY

Basketry

RICHARD G. CONN AND MARY DODDS SCHLICK

Basketry is surely one of the most significant, and least appreciated, creative and technological achievements of the world's peoples. Unlike the more-esteemed potters or bead-workers, basketmakers must create the basic form while simultaneously planning and placing the decoration correctly. The Plateau people, along with most Native Americans, realized how much skill and practice were required to make even average basketry.

In the Plateau, the principal basketry techniques practiced were coiling and twining. The third major technique—plaiting—is scarcely represented, and true weaving has not been found in the region.

By contrast with most other areas of western North America, basketry predominated in the Plateau for containers and cooking vessels. Although there were carved wooden mortars and wood or horn dishes, neither the wooden boxes of the Northwest Coast nor pottery was known.

History of Basketry

The archeological record confirms that the people of the Plateau made and used basketry for centuries before the arrival of the first European and American explorers in the region. The earliest fragments of Plateau basketry, both coiled and twined, were associated with materials thought to be at least 9,000 years old (Cressman et al. 1960:73; Krieger 1928). Both techniques were used by basketmakers the world over, but the methods of decorating the Plateau baskets were unique.

On many coiled Plateau baskets, all or part of the surface has been given a mosaiclike appearance through a folding technique known as imbrication (Mason 1904:310). Some of the earliest twined basketry was decorated in another distinctive method known as external weft wrap or false embroidery. In this process, a third element is wrapped around the outside twining weft during the actual construction. Although once known to native weavers in the Northeast (Willoughby 1905:93), after the eighteenth century false embroidery was found more often west of the Rockies. Cressman et al. (1960:73) speculate that twining with false embroidery moved northward through this region with the retreating glaciers.

Archeologists in the timbered zones of the Plateau in Washington, Oregon, and Idaho have found rectangular scars on the trunks of western red cedar (*Thuja plicata*) where slabs of bark were taken for making another type of basket. Such strips of bark were folded laterally and sewn into cylindrical containers for berries, roots, and other items. This practice has been known since before 1700 (Barbara Hollenbeck, personal communication 1984; Karl Roenke, personal communication 1987).

The relative geological stability of the Plateau region during the last 2,500 years has allowed a rich artistic and technological development. During this time, the traditional diet of fish, game, and native plant foods became well established (Aikens 1984:49, 52, 66), and making baskets for gathering and storing these foods would have been an important occupation. Those few Plateau artists who carried this tradition into the 1990s continued to use the techniques described here.

Although the rich oral traditions of the Plateau people include many references to baskets, the written record begins with the explorers. Possibly the earliest extant example was collected on Capt. George Vancouver's visit to the Northwest Coast in 1792. This twined hat (fig. 1) was collected 100 miles up the Columbia River (Wright 1989:68). Many visitors remarked about these "fez-shaped" hats worn by women in the region.

Another form of basketry mentioned by early travelers was the soft twined bag worn at the waists of native women digging root foods. Meriwether Lewis and William Clark, the first nonnatives to travel through the region above the Cascades of the Columbia, returned east in 1806 with such a gathering bag (Schlick 1979). Decorated with a network of stylized faces and quadrupeds, this bag illustrates the high level of workmanship Plateau basketmakers had attained (fig. 1).

Lewis and Clark, and others as well, mentioned a third form of twined basketry: the large flat "root bags" used to store both dried foods and various other possessions (Thwaites 1904–1905, 5:114). At the time of contact, makers were using native grasses in false embroidery to create decorative figures on such bags (Gogol 1980:6).

Those Salishan and Sahaptian groups living closest to the Cascade Mountains and other Salishan peoples farther north made coiled basketry (fig. 1 bottom left) (Wright 1989:69). Other early examples of both Cowlitz and Klikitat coiled baskets are in the National Museum of Natural History, Smithsonian Institution (catalogue nos. 2614 and 2612). These were collected by the United States Exploring Expedition, probably in 1841 (Jane Walsh, personal communication 1987).

Few of the "temporary" folded cedar bark baskets (fig. 1) have made their way into museum collections, but they remain important artifacts of Plateau material culture

top left, Smithsonian, NAA: MHN 1481–I; top right, The British Mus., Mus. of Mankind, London: VAN 197 (neg. NM031974); bottom left, The British Mus., Mus. of Mankind, London: 1842.12–10.72 (neg. MM038542); bottom right, Harvard U., Peabody Mus., Cambridge, Mass.:99–12–10/53160 (neg. 29618).

Fig. 1. Early examples of Plateau baskets. top left, Klikitat folded cedar bark baskets, used as temporary food containers when other baskets were unavailable. Watercolor by Johnson K. Duncan, 1853. top right, Earliest dated example of a Plateau woman's hat. Collected by George Hewitt on the Columbia River, 1792. bottom left, Oval-shaped coiled basket with imbricated designs of human figures on one side and 2 rows of diamonds on the other. The leather ties on the rim indicated where a lid was once attached. Collected by Edward Belcher at Ft. Vancouver, Wash. Terr., 1839. bottom right, Twined round bag with a band of plain and twill twining at the rim. The lower decorated portion of the bag is full-turned twined designs of diamond-shaped human faces and 4-legged animals. Collected by the Lewis and Clark expedition from the Pishquitpah, on the Columbia River across from the mouth of the Deschutes R., 1805–1806 (Schlick 1994:96). According to Hodge (1907–1910, 2:262), the Pishquitpah were a Yakima group residing on the north side of the Columbia. Height of top right, 13 cm; height of bottom left, 6 cm; height of bottom right, 30 cm.

("Yakima and Neighboring Groups," fig. 3 center right, this vol.), representing ingenuity of the people in creating useful and efficient containers from natural materials.

Relationships to Adjacent Regions

Although groups along the northern Pacific Coast also produced twined basketry, only the Plateau peoples seem to have made the soft round and flat bags twined of spun Indian hemp and native grass.

The twined brimless Plateau hats differed from those made both to the south and west. Plateau hats had the distinctive "fez" shape. Klamath and Modoc examples tended to be more bowl-shaped (fig. 2). Twined hats from western Washington have flaring sides that extend at the lower rim well beyond the wearers' heads (Gunther 1972:29).

The coiled basketry from western Washington also differed from Plateau examples. The former tended toward ovate bases and outwardly curved sides (Thompson and

Fig. 2. Basketry hats. These fez-shaped twined basketry hats were made and used by women of all Middle Columbia River tribes and the neighboring Nez Perce (Schlick 1994:33). Although prehistorically these hats may have been worn daily, since European settlement of the Plateau they have been reserved for use at ceremonial and social occasions, including winter dances, parades, root digging, and first-foods feasts. left, Milly Munster, Modoc, wearing a typical Modoc basketry hat, which is shorter in height than other basketry hats in the region. Photograph by Maud Baldwin, 1903–1910. right, Nez Perce woman's hat twined of Indian hemp and dyed and undyed bear grass. The 3-part zigzag or mountain peak motif is a standard design of Plateau twined hats (Schlick 1994:42). Collected by John B. Monteith in Idaho before 1876. Height 13 cm.

Marr 1983; Haeberlin, Teit, and Roberts 1928). Further, while diagonal figures were prevalent on west-slope basketry, Plateau workers favored three- or four-part zigzag figures.

Matting and Plaiting

Plateau peoples most frequently made and used matting in association with their houses. The so-called mat lodges of

both the conical and elongated types, whether built as year-round or seasonal dwellings, were fully sheathed in mats of the sewn type described below. Further, almost everywhere in the region, mats were used inside as floor coverings and insulation along lower walls (fig. 3).

The commonest kind of Plateau mat was made of many bulrush or tule stalks ("Klamath and Modoc," fig. 9, this vol.) sewn together side by side at crosswise intervals of about 15 cm. The raw edges were then finished with one or more rows of twining, all in Indian hemp cordage. The only

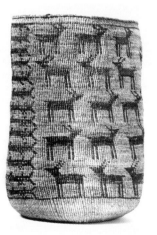

Fig. 3. Wasco and Wishram basketry. left, Wishram woman sitting in front of a large cattail mat, probably hung around the lower walls of a structure. She is making a twined cylindrical "sally" bag. Nearby is a completed sally bag, a twined basket with widely spaced wefts, and a large folded cedar bark container. At right is a tightly woven coiled basket. Photograph by Edward S. Curtis, 1909. center and right, Wasco-style twined bag (front and back) used primarily for gathering roots during root digging season, but also used for carrying and storing dried foods and household items. The designs on this bag include full human figures with hexagonal faces and "exposed ribs," large birds, fish, and deer. Collected by Roxie Shackleford at The Dalles, Oreg., 1901. Height 24 cm.

decorations were occasional colored edge twining wefts. Although surviving examples vary in size somewhat, the average dimensions for house covering mats seem to have been about 1.5 meters by 2.5 meters.

Teit (1900:188, 1906:209) illustrated examples of plaited cedar bark matting from the Lillooet and Lower Thompson. Teit assumed, probably correctly, that these mats reflected influences from adjacent Northwest Coast groups. His examples were plain plaiting with no evidence of decoration. By the 1970s the only other instances of plaiting to be found in the Plateau were placemats and similar nontraditional pieces made in school art classes.

Teit (1900:189) described one example of a twined rush mat similar to those made in the Northeast culture area. Since nothing comparable attributed to any Plateau group has been found in other collections, it seems likely that this example may have been an intrusive piece as well.

Twining

Twining is a basket weaving method in which horizontal elements known as wefts are twisted around one another as they interlace with vertical elements called warps. In Plateau twining, both the warps and the wefts are flexible, creating a soft, textilelike basket.

Working mainly during winter months, Plateau weavers used three twining techniques for their basketry: plain twining, full-turn twining, and false embroidery (fig. 4). In plain twining, also known as simple twining, two wefts are crossed only once to engage each warp in turn. In full-turn twining, also known as wrapped or full-twist twining, two wefts of different colors are used. The weaver crosses the wefts once or twice before engaging the next warp, to bring forward the desired color. This two-color technique makes it possible for the weaver to work complex designs into the basket. In false embroidery, or external weft wrap, a third element is wrapped around the outside weft strand during plain twining, creating a surface decoration as the weaving progresses. In served twined overlay, a coloring weft overlies the outside weft strand and is anchored by making a full

turn around the pair of structural wefts between each pair of warps (Fraser 1989).

Many North American Indians utilized the giant dogbane known as Indian hemp for making a strong string. Such string was essential to the people of the Plateau, who used it for snares and fish nets and to hold together the mats that served them as lodge and floor coverings. Indian hemp twine also was the major material used for the foundation of their soft basketry—hats and round and flat bags.

This plant, commonly called giant dogbane, grows near rivers and damp areas across the northern part of the continent. Native people gathered the plant in the fall, and women knee-spun the long fibers of the inner bark into twine. The strength of the fibers and the plant's insect-repellent properties (LaRea D. Johnson, personal communication 1988) offered an ideal material for food storage containers.

Other materials occasionally used by the Plateau weavers to make the twined bags were softened bark of red osier dogwood root, hazelnut brush, cattail, tule, and several varieties of native grasses. Fine strands of beargrass were used with Indian hemp for the hats, but this material is too stiff to have been a major material in the soft bags.

Strings and yarns of cotton, wool, and other fibers were utilized by Plateau weavers after being introduced by Europeans. When hop growers in the Northwest began to use cotton twine as supports for the hop vines about 1910, basketmakers who worked in the hop harvest collected the discarded string to use as the foundation for the twined bags made during the winter.

Hats

Most basket hats were made in the southern Plateau by the people who were settled on the Nez Perce, Umatilla, Warm Springs, and Yakima reservations and by the Joseph band of Nez Perce living on the Colville Reservation. Where the hats have been found among other tribes on the Plateau, they appear to have been traded from these neighbors (Haeberlin, Teit, and Roberts 1928:139). Once part of everyday clothing for women of the Plateau, the hats were brought

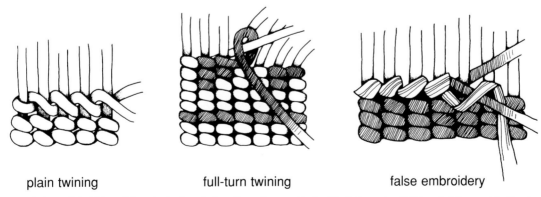

plain twining   full-turn twining   false embroidery

Fig. 4. Twining techniques. left, Plain twining, the basic technique for undecorated twined baskets. center, Full-turn twining used for 2-color decorative designs. right, False embroidery, an alternative method for creating 2-color designs.

out only for special or ceremonial occasions after the late 1800s (fig. 2).

The earlier hats were constructed in the served twined overlay technique, in which the weaver overlaid the wefts with the natural color of beargrass for background (Bill Holm, George Barth, personal communications 1995; Lehman-Kessler 1985). Darker strands of dyed grass or, when available, wool, created the distinctive three-part zigzag design. Probably in the twentieth century, weavers began using full-turn twining as well as false embroidery to create the traditional designs.

A distinctive feature of the Plateau basket hat was the hide tie the maker used to gather the warp strands together for her basket start. When the hat was finished, the maker fastened feathers, beads, bells or other decorative items to the ends of the ties, which hang from the center of the hat's crown.

Round Bags

Round twined bags were found across the Plateau wherever food roots were gathered. The most distinctive of these bags are those made by the Wasco and Wishram people of the Columbia River (fig. 3). These Wasco-style bags are recognized by the human and animal motifs or complex geometric designs that their makers worked into their fabric by means of full-turn twining.

Common figures in the bags are those of the important creatures in the weavers' environment: sturgeon, elk, deer, dogs, waterfowl, frogs, and mountain lizard ("Wasco, Wishram, and Cascades," fig. 4d, this vol.). One frequently seen motif in Wasco-style bags is a giant bird, usually described as "eagle" or "butterfly." According to Wasco elders, this bird represented the giant condor that was present in the Columbia River Gorge until the second quarter of the nineteenth century (Nelson Wallulatum, personal communication 1989; Thwaites 1904–1905, 3:232–233, 4:79–80; Gabrielson and Jewett 1970:181).

An unusual design on the Wasco-style bags is a full human figure with varying rib or garment patterning within the torso, and a hexagonal face with conventionalized features (fig. 3 right). Although small human figures were used on bags made in the twentieth century, these "exposed rib" figures appear only on older bags. Frequently the face motif from the full figure is repeated in a netlike design covering an entire bag. This face design is similar to a common motif found on the prehistoric rock and bone art in the same area of the Columbia River.

Weavers from the other groups living on the Plateau also made round twined bags for gathering roots and other foods and for storing personal and household items. Umatilla weavers and their close neighbors used the served twined overlay technique to create geometric patterns on these bags. Others used plain twining, a technique that limits the decoration to vertical, diagonal, or horizontal stripes. Some Sahaptian basketmakers in the twentieth century decorated

the round bags with naturalistic and geometric designs worked in colorful yarns applied in false embroidery.

Flat Bags

At the time of European contact, Plateau weavers twined large flat storage "sacks" of knee-spun Indian hemp (fig. 5). They used the technique of false embroidery to decorate the sacks using the lighter-colored strands of dried grass.

After corn was introduced as a food crop by the fur traders and missionaries in the nineteenth century, the softer inside husks began to replace native grass as a decorative element in the flat bags, which became known as "cornhusk" bags. With the pliable, easily dyed, and plentiful cornhusk, weavers began to cover the entire bag in false embroidery. By the late 1860s or early 1870s, the large Indian hemp sacks with false embroidery only in the design area were no longer made. In the same period, woolen yarn appeared as an embroidery medium and cotton string began to replace the native-spun Indian hemp (France D. Haines, personal communications 1962–1963).

The introduction of woolen yarn as well as commercial dyes in the late nineteenth century stimulated weavers to produce elaborately decorated bags. Although a small number of large cornhusk bags continued to be made into the twentieth century, settlement decreased the availability of native foods on traditional lands and commercial containers filled the storage needs of many Plateau families. The weavers of the Southern Plateau began to twine smaller handbags ("Molala," fig. 3 top right, this vol.) as well as horse trappings, vests, belts, and other items of clothing.

A resurgence in the use of dyed cornhusk rather than woolen yarns for the decorative elements in the flat twined bags came about during and after World War II in some areas of the Plateau "because yarns were not native" (Conn 1960–1966).

From the earliest times, the designs on the two sides of each bag were different, and it was unusual for a weaver to repeat a design on another bag. In most cases, the weavers of the Plateau cornhusk bags coordinated geometric motifs into a unified design (Miller 1986:155). Their design style may be described as formal, featuring symmetry and rhythmic repetition of motifs. In general, the earlier bags can be identified by an overall pattern, a balanced repetition of a single motif on each side. Later popular arrangements included banded designs, a unified central motif, and an organization in which a single motif is repeated five times to form a coherent design. Around 1900 a few weavers began to incorporate naturalistic designs into their bags, portraying plants and animals as well as scenes from daily life, but these were exceptions.

By the use of variations in color and internal and external elaborations of simple geometric motifs, the Plateau weavers created the endless variety of lively and dynamic designs their work is noted for.

Fig. 5. Twined flat cornhusk bags. Twined flat bags were used for storing and transporting dried foods, especially roots and personal items. Flat bags were also used as trade items in both commercial and ritual exchanges. They played a prominent role in the marriage ritual as one of the principal items exchanged between the families of the bride and groom. Along with the dried plant foods that filled them, these bags were presented by the bride's family to the family of the groom. top left and right, Front and back views of a Nez Perce flat bag. This bag is made of twined hemp and decorated with dyed cornhusks and red and black wool. Collected on the Nez Perce Res., Idaho, before 1920. bottom left and right, Front and back views of a Western Columbia River Sahaptian flat bag. This bag is also made of twined hemp and decorated with dyed cornhusks in green and yellow. Collected by E.T. Houtz, Warm Springs, Oreg., before 1899. Length of top 52 cm; bottom to same scale.

Carrying Straps

One other twined item associated with basketry in Plateau life was the forehead pad for the carrying strap or tumpline. The strap, usually formed of braided strands of string, was attached to baskets filled with the harvest of berries or roots by means of two loops at the basket's edge and a single loop on the opposite side near the base. The twined portion, the forehead pad, was about two inches wide and 10–12 inches long and decorated in simple geometric designs, often in several colors.

Coiling

The best information on coiled basketry is compiled by Haeberlin, Teit, and Roberts (1928), who give careful analyses of techniques and materials and general remarks about distribution.

Materials and Techniques

The most important single material used throughout the Plateau for coiled basketry was red cedar root, used both for foundation splints and for sewing elements. Strips were also cut from cedar sapwood by those Canadian groups working in the "slat coil" method (fig. 6). Various other plant materials were used for decoration. Some were selected for their attractive natural colors, such as pale ivory beargrass and garnet-red wild cherry. Other native plants such as Oregon grape and dogwood, as well as alkaline mud, supplied dyes with which beargrass and Phragmites reeds were dyed yellow and black respectively.

There were two basic contruction methods in general use. All the groups making coiled basketry used bundle foundations of 10 to 20 fine cedar root splints. In addition, some of the groups on the Fraser and Thompson rivers made foundations in which thin cedar wood slats combined with auxiliary splints to produce wide, flat coils (fig. 6 right). This method was usually chosen for larger baskets such as cradles and covered hampers. The most prominent decorative technique was imbrication.

Distribution

Coiled basketry was made principally by the Salishan groups in Canada and west of the Columbia River in Washington State, as well as by the Klikitat and adjacent Sahaptian groups (Haeberlin, Teit, and Roberts 1928: 335–360).

Teit (1930:223–225, 329–230) gathered information from native people indicating that most Plateau Salishan groups had made imbricated coiled basketry until some time in the early nineteenth century. By the late 1960s, knowledgeable Spokanes, Coeur d'Alenes, and Kalispels asked about this had only vague, conflicting traditions to cite. Some thought yes, others no, but all agreed that no coiled, imbricated baskets had been made by their own people within memory (Conn 1960–1966).

Several collections do contain other examples of coiled basketry identified as Spokane and Colville, but these do not have adequate documentation. Some collections also include a few examples of round coiled trays described as "Umatilla" or Warm Springs," which appear to have been trade pieces from the Great Basin.

Local and Regional Styles

Probably the best-known kind of Plateau coiled basketry is the pail shape made by the Klikitat. As shown in figure 7, it

Fig. 6. Coiled basketry of Lillooet basketmakers from Mount Currie Indian Res., Pemberton Valley, B.C. left, Mrs. Martin Williams with a bundle of split roots on her lap and more unsplit cedar roots tied together. center, Rosie Ross with a bucket in which she had soaked cherry bark in wet earth for over a year. This bark will be woven into the cedar root basket to form a decorative pattern. right, Ross starting the bottom of the basket with cedarwood splints woven with split cedar root. She soaks both well in order to make them pliable. The combination of cedar wood and coiled roots makes the baskets nearly waterproof (Wilson 1964:30). Photographs by Renate Wilson, 1963.

center, Yakama Nation Mus., Toppenish, Wash.: YIN–992–01–001 (neg. 3822–34); right, Smithsonian, Natl. Mus. of the Amer. Ind.: 15/6437.

Fig. 7. Klikitat baskets. Coiled baskets were used for berry picking, food storage, and, before metal containers were available, for holding water and cooking. left, Nettie Jackson working on a 10-gallon coiled cedar root basket. Photograph by Mary Schlick, White Salmon, Wash., 1986. center, Contemporary Klikitat basket made in the traditional fashion using cedar root for the foundation coils. The design is imbricated using bear grass and cedar root bark in their natural colors as well as colors from commercial dyes. The designs include the traditional salmon gill pattern and figures representing (visible from top to bottom) men and women, geese in flight, deer, butterflies, and, on the reverse side, dogs and horses. This basket was commissioned in 1992 by the Yakama Indian Nation from Klikitat artist Nettie Jackson, a member of the Confederated Tribes and Bands of the Yakama Nation. right, Traditional Klikitat basket. This fully imbricated coil-constructed basket was made of cedar root and decorated with dyed bear grass and the bark of cedar root. The design is a variation of the 3-peaked V or mountain motif, which is the most common design pattern used for Klikitat baskets (Schlick 1994:104). Collected in Wash. before 1927. Height of center, 43 cm; height of right, 33 cm.

has a round base with straight, flaring sides, and its height exceeds the mouth diameter. Klikitat baskets are usually fully imbricated with perhaps one or two additional bands of beading at top or bottom, often a beaded, scalloped rim. This basket form is generally described as Klikitat, but there are strong indications that women of adjacent Sahaptian groups may have made them as well (Haeberlin, Teit, and Roberts 1928:353–354).

A style less well-known was associated with the Okanagan, Wenatchee, and perhaps Methow as well. It has an oval base and flat front and back, while the sides curved outward in the lower quarter and then rose straight to the rim, spreading outward slightly if at all (fig. 8 center). Okanagan-Wenatchee baskets usually have only the decorative design imbricated as a rule with the background left open (Conn 1960–1966).

In the Canadian Plateau, there were at least three definable local basketry styles: those of the Thompson River, Upper Fraser River, and Lillooet. All had a high frequency of rectangular or square bases that set them apart from those to the south. Some of the distinctive Canadian basket forms are: those with rectangular or square bases and flat, spreading sides rising to a rectangular rim; large, rectangular covered hampers with vertical or very slightly spreading sides; and open coffin-shaped cradles. There were also some examples with round or ovate bases. The larger basketry forms, especially the hampers and cradles, were often made in the slat coil method described above.

The differences among the Canadian local styles were most evident in the placement of decoration and added elements.

The Thompson River groups tended to favor two basic decorative styles: allover imbrication with or without full background, often composed of just one or two repeated figures or else an arrangement of repeated vertical bands (fig. 9). In making hampers, these people often used the same allover pattern for both body and lid, matching the figures so that the finished baskets looked like one solid piece. On small baskets, they would maintain the idea of repeated figures, generally without background and set somewhat farther apart.

Baskets from upper Fraser River groups resemble Thompson examples closely, except that hamper lids are usually decorated in a different pattern from the body and often beaded rather than imbricated.

Lillooet baskets were decorated in zoned compositions: the upper third of the basket was as a rule fully imbricated with bolder figures than those used by the Thompson or Fraser River people. For example, figure 10 right shows a popular Lillooet design said to represent two people in conversation. The balance of a Lillooet basket's flat sides were imbricated in separated narrow vertical lines or with other small, separated figures.

Decoration

The decorations were done principally in two methods: imbrication and beading. The basic imbrication process is shown in figure 11 left. It consists of decorative strips that were folded repeatedly and slipped under successive coiling stitches as each was pulled tight. This technique was also practiced in western Washington State, but otherwise

center, Colville Confederated Tribes Mus., Robert Eddy Coll., Cashmere, Wash.

Fig. 8. Colville baskets. left, Elaine Timentwa Emerson, Methow and Wenatchee, at Omak Lake, Colville Res., Wash. Photograph by Jill Sabella, 1995. center, Lish-Lish-Tum or Johnny Baker from the Colville, Res., Wash., with a coiled basket used for storing food or household goods. Photograph by Alfred G. Simmer of Wenatchee, Wash., 1931. right, Margaret Condon, Wenatchee, with berry-picking baskets. Photograph by Jill Sabella, Colville Res., Wash., 1995.

seems to have been limited to the Plateau. Teit (1930:329–330) felt it was an Interior Salish invention that spread to adjacent regions along with knowledge of the basic coiling technique. This suggests that coiling was also invented in the Plateau, which seems unlikely. Rather, it could be proposed that coiled basketry appeared first in western North America among the Southwest and Great Basin people and gradually diffused north and west from that area. Haeberlin, Teit, and Roberts's view (1928:133–139) that imbrication was developed by Interi-

or Salishan people may be given somewhat more credit since it is found most widely among them.

The term "beading" used to define a basketry decoration has often been a source of confusion since it does not involve glass beads. Rather it is a simple over-and-under alternation of decorative material with coiling stitches (fig. 11 right). This process is associated with coiled basketry elsewhere in the world and has probably been independently invented several times. The Plateau basketmakers tended to use imbrication for large figures and to reserve beading for edgings of decorative fields or small, detached figures.

The 1990s

By the end of the twentieth century the role of basketry had changed for the people of the Plateau, but the importance of the art form had not. Although commercially made products satisfied utilitarian needs, baskets continued to have a ceremonial or sacramental place in Plateau life. The baskets' ties with a distant past offered a satisfying continuity and their fine workmanship and beauty in design continued to be a source of pride.

Matting

In many Plateau longhouses women continued to roll out tule mats on the floor for first foods feasts and other important

Amer. Mus. of Nat. Hist., New York: 16/8839.

Fig. 9. Thompson basket and lid. This hamper basket is coil-constructed of cedar root and imbricated in vertical bands of geometric designs. Collected by C.F. Briggs on the Thompson River, B.C., before 1901. Height 39 cm.

Fig. 10. Lillooet baskets. left, Woman weaving baskets. Photographed on the Fraser River, B.C., 1906. right, Coil-constructed partly imbricated basket used to hold a variety of items, most commonly roots and berries. The upper design may represent 2 heads, each with a mouth, 4 teeth, and hair along the back. Collected by James A. Teit in Lillooet, B.C., 1899. Height 28 cm.

meals. Supplemented by imported grass mats and tablecloths, the mats formed the traditional "table" for the communal feast. A few of the older women continued to make mats that occasionally were offered for sale. A Yakima elder made small versions of the twined tule mat, similar to the size used long ago for serving food, for the Yakima Nation Cultural Center shop (Cheryl Antelope, personal communication 1990).

Hats

Although a bright kerchief long since replaced the basket hat for everyday wear by the women of the Plateau, the distinctive hat continued to be worn as a part of the traditional dress on important occasions. The ceremonial root diggers or huckleberry pickers wore basket hats as they harvested and served these foods at the seasonal first foods feasts.

Occasionally a woman leader would wear a basket hat when invited to make a speech or other formal presentation. In a less ceremonial setting, an increasing number of Plateau women at tribal celebrations wore basket hats as distinctive marks of tribal identity.

From the late 1800s until the 1970s only a few basket hats were made. With renewed interest among the young people in the old ways and growing participation in tribal ceremonies and celebrations, demand for the hats increased. Many native families brought out hats handed down from earlier generations, and a small number of weavers produced new hats for sale.

Twined Bags

As the root digging areas become less accessible due to settlement and grazing, fewer Plateau families harvested the traditional foods. Those who continued to dig roots used the soft round twined bags to hold them, for no other container served the purpose so well. The twined bag could be flattened for carrying, was comfortable to wear, and expanded to hold the harvest. Most bags worn for digging in the 1990s were those made of commercial materials. Some tribal elders continued to store dried roots in flat cornhusk bags, but others preserved them in the modern counterpart, plastic bags, in the freezer. Because these large bags were no longer made, most were stored as keepsakes. Families frequently brought out these bags and the fine old round bags twined from native materials to show at fairs and other exhibitions.

Many weavers in the 1990s twined round bags and flat handbags using commercially made string and yarn. Their products could be seen in tribal shops, as gifts at wedding trades, name-givings and other giveaways. The last weaver of the distinctive Wasco and Wishram style bags with the complex geometric and human and animal motifs died in 1971 (Doreen Mahaffey, personal communication 1983). However, several young women began to study the Wasco and Wishram twining technique in the late 1980s and early 1990s in hopes of reviving their art.

Coiling

Huckleberries from the slopes of the mountains surrounding the Columbia Plateau continued to be a favorite food for the native people, and families picked their year's supply each autumn. Coiled cedar root baskets were the preferred container for the berries. Many children had their own baskets, the sizes increasing with the age of the picker.

During the ritual of the annual huckleberry feast, the ceremonial pickers brought their harvest into the longhouses on Plateau reservations in large coiled cedar root "fancy" baskets. Individual families also used coiled baskets in similar ceremonies at their campsites before beginning the harvest.

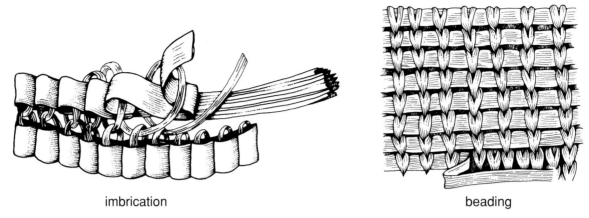

imbrication   beading

Fig. 11. Decorative techniques on coiled baskets. left, Imbrication. Decorative strips are folded and slipped under successive coiling stitches. right, Beading. In this technique, the decorative strips are simply laced over and under the coiling stitches.

Most picking baskets in use at the end of the twentieth century were old, for only a few weavers were producing them. Because of the high price of newly made coiled baskets, most were sold to collectors. Those Plateau families who did acquire new baskets displayed them in their homes or gave them as gifts. The once-utilitarian objects had become too valuable to take to the camps in the mountains.

Folded Bark

Although less intricate technically, the baskets made from a single piece of cedar bark continued to be important to many of the people of the Plateau. A few men and women made them in the 1990s, and the baskets were used by many families for picking. As with the coiled baskets, the bark baskets frequently were put away to give to children and favored relatives or hung on the walls of homes (Iris Billy-Harrison, personal communication 1983).

Is There a Revival?

The small number of weavers who have carried on the basketmaking traditions through the years of declining interest in the art have earned the respect of the Plateau people. In the 1990s many were eager to learn from those artists who remained.

Basketmaking classes on the Warm Springs and other reservations attracted elders as well as younger people. In addition to mastering the ancient arts, the students enjoyed sharing treasured family baskets with one another and learning about the place of basketry in their culture (Frances Brunoe, personal communication 1990).

No longer did basketmakers spend the winter months twining and coiling the baskets the family needed for the essentials of life. Those few who continued the traditional arts worked throughout the year to produce their basketry. Although these basketmakers received a good price for their work, the return did not compare with wages for the amount of time spent gathering and preparing materials and weaving the baskets (Nettie Jackson, personal communication 1987; Gogol 1980a:23). Only a few Plateau basketmakers were able to support themselves solely through basketmaking by the end of the twentieth century.

Whether they worked full-time at the occupation or worked only when other tasks were completed, the basketmakers expressed deep appreciation and respect for the talent that made it possible for them to carry on this part of their heritage (Schlick 1988:46). All held a strong hope that it was not too late for the art to be revived among their people (Gogol 1979a:29; Schlick 1984:29).

Rock Art

KEO BORESON

Several hundred rock art sites are scattered throughout the interior of the Pacific Northwest. These carved and painted images give an intimate glimpse into the lives of people that other archeological remains do not, a visual memory that goes a step beyond the everyday necessities of food and shelter.

Pictographs (paintings) and petroglyphs (carvings) are found on rock surfaces such as rockshelter walls, escarpments, outcrops, and boulders, generally near a permanent source of water. Pictographs are often located in out-of-the-way mountainous areas near rivers, lakes, springs, or streams. A few sites are at high elevations with a panoramic view of river valleys. Petroglyphs are frequently found at places near rivers or lakes where people congregated, often where fishing was exceptionally good (fig. 1). Painted petroglyphs or individual petroglyphs associated with pictographs are also occasionally found. This association may be related to places of environmental and economic diversity, such as the transition zone from forested mountains to grassy hills, and trade centers such as The Dalles and Kettle Falls on the Columbia River (Boreson 1976).

The notion of rock art as an element of the site complex in association with burial areas, rockshelters, fish walls, and large seasonal campsites in the southeastern Plateau (Nelson and Rice 1969:95) fits well with the location of many sites at permanent water sources. Pictographs are associated with numerous burials in The Dalles area, and both petroglyph and pictograph sites occur "not more than a mile from definite evidences of a campsite or of a fishing place" (Strong, Schenck, and Steward 1930:128). In the interior of British Columbia, most petroglyph sites appear to be associated with subsistence activities, while those located on the Fraser River are thought to be closely related to fishing (Lundy 1979:63–66).

Styles

As defined by Lundy (1974:288–289), the Interior Rock Art style consists of naturalistic designs depicted in a realistic (as opposed to stylized) manner, and rectilinear designs often of an abstract nature. Characteristic motifs, identified as belonging to the Columbia Plateau rock art tradition, consist of "stick figure humans, simple block-body animal forms, rayed arcs and circles, tally marks, abstract spirit beings or mythical figures, and geometric forms [which] are

Fig 1. Petroglyphs at the Alpowa Creek site (45AS7) in southeastern Wash., now inundated by the Lower Granite Dam. Photographed in 1972 by Keo Boreson.

combined to produce an art that is reasonably distinct from that of the neighboring areas" (Keyser 1992:16). Quadrupeds (such as mountain sheep, elk, deer, and bison) associated with anthropomorphs holding weapons suggest depictions of hunting activities (fig. 2).

Some motifs are widespread across the Plateau but occur at relatively few sites. Depictions of animal tracks, particularly of bear, are found at sites along the Columbia River and in the interior of British Columbia (Corner 1968; Loring and Loring 1982). Petroglyphs at the Cranbrook site in British Columbia include bear tracks as well as elk or deer, and dog or coyote tracks (Kennedy and Cassidy 1981). Seven petroglyph sites with bear tracks have been recorded on the islands and shoreline of Lake Pend Oreille in northern Idaho. Of the 275 documented figures, 55 percent appear to represent bear tracks, 28 percent are circles, arcs, intersected circles, or intersected arcs, and the remaining 17 percent are other forms, including a possible representation of cougar tracks (Boreson and Peterson 1985:53).

Pecked pits, or cupules, are found at sites on the lower, mid, and upper Columbia River, on the Snake River in Hells Canyon, and on the Fraser River in British Columbia. Of the five recorded sites in the interior of British Columbia with pecked pits, two are located at fishing stations. The pits are from four to 10 centimeters in diameter and from two to five centimeters deep, and some are exposed only during low water when the salmon are running. These boulders may have served as a seasonal indicator of the approaching fish runs (Lundy 1979:65). A boulder with incised lines located on the Clearwater River in central Idaho was thought to have served in the same capacity (Osmundson and Hulse 1962:13). Pecked pits, the most abundant type of petroglyph at Kettle Falls, a well known fishing locality on the Columbia River in northeastern Washington, were hypothesized to be magical or religious phenomena linked to salmon runs. The figures range from two to six centimeters in diameter and are aligned to form straight lines and half circles, are connected to make curved lines and circles, or (most frequently) occur as isolated forms (Chance and Chance 1982).

Abraded grooves that are clearly not glacial striae are also found at Kettle Falls. A local informant related that Indian women gathered quartzite and schist from bedrock ledges overlooking fishing stations for knives or scrapers and made the grooves by sharpening quartzite knives (Chance and

Chance 1982:40). Of the 14 petroglyph sites recorded in the interior of British Columbia, four have V-shaped grooves that appear to be the result of tool sharpening or tool making activity. Two of these are located at known fishing places (Lundy 1979:63–64). Similar grooves are found at site 10BR225, on Lake Pend Oreille (Boreson and Peterson 1985:46).

Incised or scratched lines have been recorded at various sites along the Snake River (Boreson 1989a; Leen 1988), which are frequently superimposed over pictographs. Characteristic designs include straight or slightly curved lines that form crosshatched grids, herringbones, chevrons, fans, parallel lines, and groups of lines at various angles.

Other modifications to rock that appear to be associated with petroglyphs and fishing locales are boulders with serrated (flaked) edges. These features have been documented at petroglyph sites at Priest Rapids, Stewart Rapids, and The Dalles on the Columbia River, in the Fraser River Valley in British Columbia, and at Buffalo Eddy (site 45AS14) on the Snake River. Three boulders at the Buffalo Eddy site have serrated edges, including one that has been modified along three sides (Boreson 1980). The modified areas are from one to two meters long and have been flaked to form saw-like edges with projections that are one to two centimeters long and from three to five centimeters apart. The appearance and position of the serrated areas suggest they were not utilized as tools (Randolph 1980).

Four rock art style areas are defined in the interior of the Pacific Northwest (fig. 3), as described in the following sections.

Western Columbia Plateau Style Area

The rayed arc was identified by Grant (1967) as the most characteristic motif from the middle Fraser River in British

drawings by Keo Boreson after Cundy 1927–1938, North Central Wash. Mus., Wenatchee.

Fig. 2. Petroglyphs from Rock Island on the Columbia River in central Wash.

Columbia to The Dalles in Washington. The distribution of this motif defines McClure's (1980) Western Columbia Plateau Style Area, described as extending from The Dalles on the lower Columbia River to the North Thompson River in British Columbia and from the Cascade Mountains to west of Kootenay Lake and south through the channeled scablands of eastern Washington. Thirty-four percent of the anthropomorphs in this area have raylike projections extending from the head or rayed arcs above the head, and arcs with rays are common nonanthropomorphic forms (McClure 1980). The motif is relatively simple in British Columbia, northern Oregon, and western Idaho; but it is a more complex design in the Yakima and Little Klickitat river valleys, along the Columbia River from near Vantage to The Dalles, and below Clarkston on the lower Snake River. More elaborate figures, called the Yakima Polychrome style, have double lines, rays, and sometimes a combination, with red, white, and occasionally green pigment, that form circles and arcs. The lines and rays sometimes surround or form the heads (some with eyes and noses) and bodies of anthropomorphs (Boreson 1991a; Grant 1967; Keyser 1992).

Other motifs or combinations of forms have a somewhat more restricted distribution. Paired anthropomorphs, also called the "brothers" or "twins," are found in the mid-Columbia region between Wenatchee and Priest Rapids, at The Dalles on the lower Columbia River (Cain 1950; Cundy 1927–1938; Keyser 1992; McClure

1978, 1979a), on the lower Snake River (Nesbitt 1968:15), and in central Oregon (Cressman 1937:17). These forms generally consist of two anthropomorphs, sometimes portraying a male and female, that are similar in size and shape with touching or interlocking hands (fig. 4).

Pictographs surrounded by an oval or circle are most commonly found in British Columbia, northeastern Washington, and northern Idaho (fig. 5), a distribution suggesting a cultural affinity across this region (Boreson 1989:7). Keyser (1992:58) noted that "vision quest symbolism in Columbia Plateau rock art often involves figures painted inside circles or ovals."

Eastern Columbia Plateau Style Area

Tally marks were used by McClure (1980) as a characteristic motif to define the Eastern Columbia Plateau Style Area, extending from Columbia Lake in British Columbia to the Middle Fork of the Salmon River in Idaho, and the eastern boundary is formed by the Continental Divide. They are common in western Montana (Keyser and Knight 1976:15) and southeastern Idaho (Erwin 1930). These dashes or dots of paint vary in number and length of lines from site to site. An unusually large number of tally marks is found near the mouth of Horse Creek (site 10IH2) on the Salmon River in east-cen-

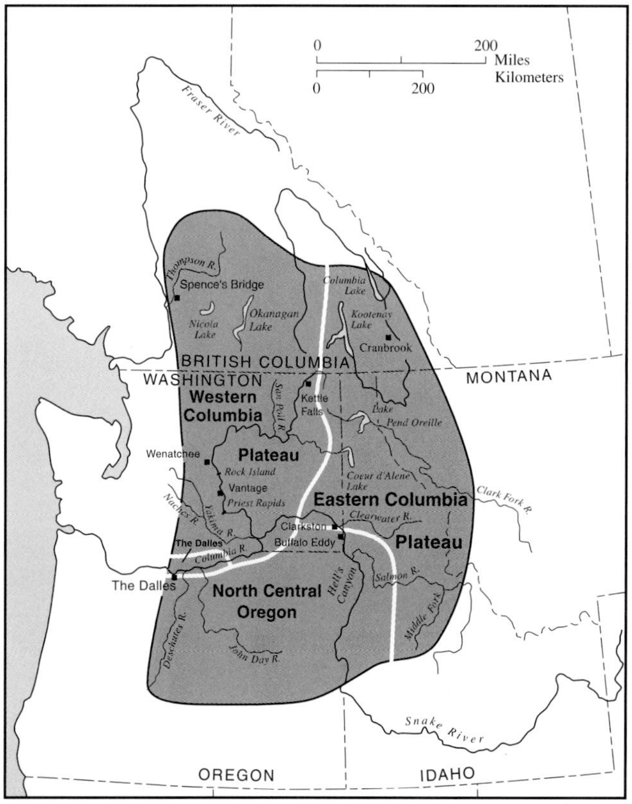

Fig. 3. Plateau rock art style areas.

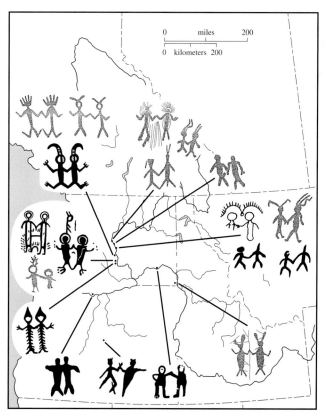

Fig 4. Distribution of paired anthropomorphs. Solid forms are pictographs; stippled figures are petroglyphs (Cain 1950; Cressman 1937; Cundy 1927–1938; McClure 1978, 1979a; Nesbitt 1968).

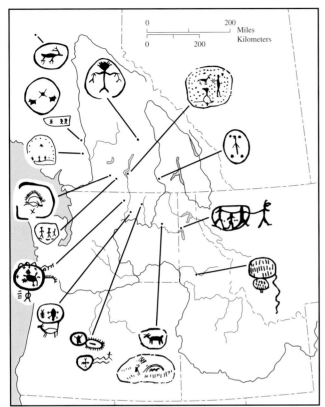

Fig. 5. Distribution of encircled motifs (Boreson 1989; Cain 1950; Corner 1968; Erwin 1930).

shield (Keyser 1975:207), often including a horned head-dress and a staff projecting from behind the shield (Keyser and Knight 1976:3). A substantial minority has a fringe of short lines projecting from the circumference of the shield (Conner and Conner 1971:14). It has been hypothesized the design originated in the Great Basin and was carried northward into the Plains by Shoshonean (Keyser 1975) or Fremont (Butler 1983a) people. Shield figures in south-central Montana have been dated to A.D. 1100, suggesting the Avonlea (thought to represent Athapaskan movements through the area during this time period) introduced the motif (Loendorf 1990:45).

North-Central Oregon Style Area

According to Cressman (1937:69–76), the pictographic motifs in north-central Oregon are clearly distinct from the rock art in the rest of Oregon and represent a style possibly intrusive from the east, south, or both directions. Cressman identified this style area as extending from the Harney-Malheur Basin and the upper Deschutes River to the Columbia River and described characteristic designs as naturalistic, including floral motifs, stars, and quadrupeds other than mountain sheep. Wellman (1979:40, 52) added rectilinear and curvilinear elements and simple anthropomorphs with and without head ornaments to this list. He thought the rock art in north-central Oregon differed noticeably from that of the Plateau and saw the area as a pictographic region with influences from the south and east, but also with some indigenous traits.

Keyser (1992:97) described the North Oregon Rectilinear style as generally resembling that of the Columbia Plateau except for the emphasis on abstract linear geometric figures and depictions of numerous lizards. He saw significant evidence attesting to the relationship between this style and the art styles common along the Columbia River. There are numerous similarities between this style and the the rock art

tral Idaho, where there are about 450 marks placed in orderly rows in groups of from six to 150 (fig. 6).

A motif that appears to be intrusive into this style area from the eastern Great Basin and the northwestern Plains is the "shield-bearing warrior" (fig. 7). The design is found at rock art sites in southeastern portion of the interior in southwestern Montana, the Middle Fork of the Salmon River, the main Salmon River, and Hells Canyon on the Snake River. The motif is described as a pedestrian warrior whose body is represented by a large circular

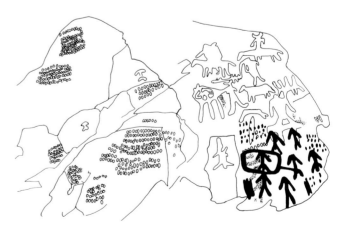

right, drawing by Keo Boreson.

Fig. 6. Pictographs at the mouth of Horse Creek on the Salmon River, east-central Idaho. left, Pictographs in 1974. Photograph by Keo Boreson. right, Illustration of pictographs. Solid figures are dark red, outlined forms are bright red, and stippled areas are light red.

614

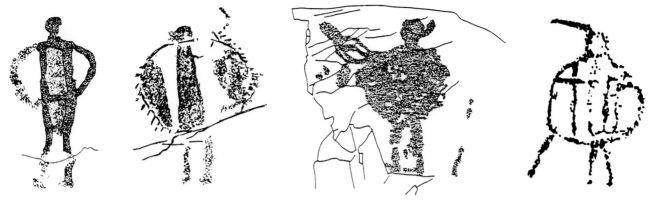

drawings by Keo Boreson; d, drawing by Keo Boreson after Leen 1988:94.

Fig. 7. Shield figures. a, Pictograph from western Mont.; b, pictograph from Middle Fork of the Salmon River, Idaho; c, pictograph from Salmon River, Idaho; d, pictograph from Hells Canyon, Snake River, Idaho.

in Hells Canyon (Leen 1988:188) and the lower Salmon River in Idaho (fig. 8) (Boreson 1984).

The Dalles Style Area

The Dalles was an important fishing place as well as a center for trade into the historic period. Archeological evidence suggests this area was occupied for more than 10,000 years. The wide variety of petroglyphs and pictographs recorded in this area has been attributed to influences from the Southwest, the Great Basin, the Northwest Coast, and the Plateau (Butler 1957; Cressman 1937; Lundy 1974; Wellman 1979; Woodward 1982). Three rock art styles in The Dalles area are defined as the Basic Coast Conventionalized style, representative of an early tradition on the Columbia River and coast and typically including circled faces and eyes and ribbed anthropomorphic and zoomorphic figures; the Columbia River Conventionalized style characterized by the grinning anthropomorphic face, elaborate headdresses, and prominent ribs; and the Interior Intrusive Rock Art style, comprised of designs typical of the interior (Lundy 1974). Rock art in this region has been called the Long Narrows style characterized by motifs regarded as mythological beings (Wellman 1979). Typical forms include grinning faces, curvilinear abstract designs, elaborate concentric spoked or rayed circles, and abstract human and animal forms with eyes, ribs, and internal organs (fig. 9)(Keyser 1992:83). The dominance of Plateau motifs, particularly the rayed arc and rayed circle, led McClure (1984) to conclude the rock art at The Dalles is basically part of the Plateau Rock Art style with some coastal attributes.

Function

Although many Indians questioned by anthropologists claimed to have no knowledge of the meaning and function of rock art or were reluctant to talk about it (Corner 1968; Erwin 1930; McClure 1979; Steve Shawley, personal communication 1980), a few ethnographic and historic sources using Indian informants with memories of events from the nineteenth and early twentieth centuries contain information about the origin and interpretation of rock art. An elderly Indian informant said pictographs at a site in the Grand Coulee in central Washington represented cattle brands used by pioneer ranchers and were used by the Indians to identify livestock ownership (McClure 1979). On the Columbia River at Vantage and on the Naches River near Yakima, Wanapam people said rock art was made by the Little People, "animal-like in appearance and inclined to the ways of evil spirits" (Relander 1956:44).

At The Dalles, on the lower Columbia River, Wishram informants indicated "the deep petroglyphs had been made by their own ancestors long ago and that they represented

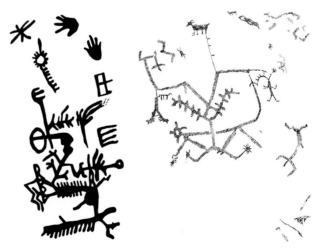

left, drawing by Keo Boreson after Cressman 1937:21; right, drawing by Keo Boreson.

Fig. 8. Characteristic rock art from the north-central Oreg. style area. The similarities between these 2 designs illustrate the eastward extent of this style. left, Pictograph from the John Day River, north-central Oreg. right, Pictograph from the lower Salmon River, Idaho.

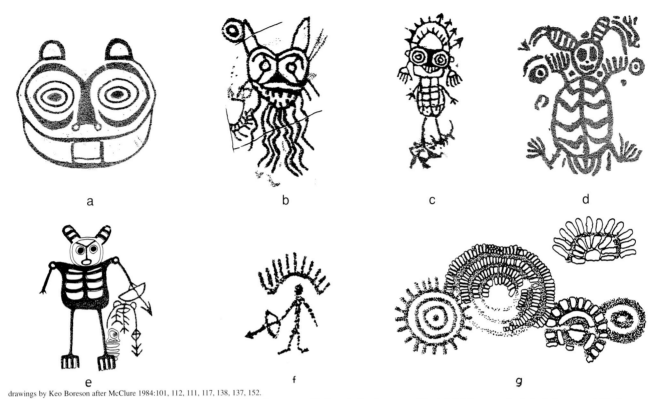

drawings by Keo Boreson after McClure 1984:101, 112, 111, 117, 138, 137, 152.

Fig. 9. Rock art from The Dalles area. a, Petroglyph with anthropomorphic face design known as Tsagiglalal; b, petroglyph depicting a masklike form; c, petroglyph depicting an anthropomorph with headdress; d, spirit guardian petroglyph; e, red and white pictograph illustrating a ribbed form with bow and arrow; f, pictograph depicting a rayed arc and an anthropomorph with a bow and arrow; g, polychrome pictographs of rayed circles and arcs. Red is indicated by stippling; outlined areas are white.

water animals who were the particular spirits of their ancestors" (Strong 1945:250). A ribbed figure (fig. 9e) was said to "represent one of the spirit-guardians of the fishing places on the narrows where salmon are caught with dip nets" (Strong 1945:250). A petroglyph known by the Wishram name of Tsagiglalal (fig. 9a), explained as "she who watches all who are coming and going" (Butler 1957:162) "from the underworld" (B. Robert Butler, personal communication 1987), is near burial areas and a village (now inundated) just above The Dalles. The petroglyph could be related to a legend that tells of a mythical woman ruler who was changed into rock by Coyote and told to watch over the people of the village of Wishram (Curtis 1907–1930, 8:145–146).

At Nicola Lake, in British Columbia, the Thompson people regard a particular rock painting as the work of the spirits and avoid looking at the place for, if they do so, the wind will immediately begin to blow. A pictograph on the east side of Okanagan Lake is said to represent a water god. During early times Indians threw animal carcasses and other things into the lake to appease the lake devil (Corner 1968:3). A point of rock on Lake Pend Oreille contained painted effigies of men and beasts thought to have been made by a preceding race of men. The Indians did not pass this point, fearing the Great Spirit would create a commotion in the water and cause them to be swallowed up in the waves (Stevens 1860:150).

Nez Perce people believe rock art sites function in a variety of ways, most important in commemorating important events, including vision quests and battles, as well as rich resource areas. Some sites were believed to be the property of individuals or families who might use them frequently for religious purposes. "Others were thought to date from ancient times, were believed to be associated with people who lived there before the Nez Perce and were avoided by the Nez Perce" (Deward Walker, personal communication 1989).

At a site on Coeur d'Alene Lake in northern Idaho, records of dreams, guardian spirits, battles, and exploits were said to have been made by young men during puberty ceremonials, occasionally by older men, and seldom by girls (Teit 1930:190). Only people with strong power painted pictures on rocks among the Southern Okanogan. The pictures assisted the painter in employing his power, especially for curing sickness (Cline 1938:138, 143–144).

Northern Okanagan, Shuswap, and Thompson adolescent boys and girls painted pictures representing the ceremonies and dreams of their training period, and the Thompson also made figures representing future wives and husbands (Teit 1900, 1909, 1930). An old woman who had made similar designs said pictographs at the Spence's Bridge site on the Thompson River in south-central British Columbia were made by girls when they

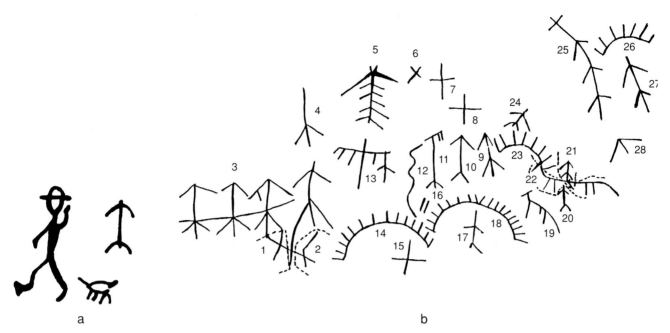

a, drawing by Keo Boreson after Corner 1968:47; b, drawing by Keo Boreson after Teit 1896:229.

Fig. 10. Pictographs near Spence's Bridge, B.C., likely made by young women as they reached puberty. a, Newer figures added to the panel of older pictographs including a human figure with a hat and a 4-legged animal. b, Older pictographs. Nos. 1, 2, 7, 8, and 15 represent the crossing of trails, a place where food might be buried. Nos. 3, 9, 10, 17, 20, 21, 27, and 28 represent fir branches, and no. 4 represents a fir branch with the needles plucked off. Nos. 5 and 11 represent a girl's lodge made of fir branches. No. 12 represents a snake. No. 13 represents sacrifices at the crossing of trails. Nos. 14, 18, 23, and 26 represent unfinished basketry. No. 16 represents 2 trenches. No. 25 represents the crossing of trails and a fir branch sacrifice. Nos. 19 and 22 represent dogs (Teit 1896:228, 230).

reached puberty (fig. 10). Designs were added to the panel through time, which accounts for the human wearing a hat, which appeared sometime between 1896 and 1968 (Corner 1968:47) and the appearance of the paintings, "some of which are quite fresh, while others appear old and indistinct" (Teit 1896:227). Thompson boys also made "round holes in rocks or in boulders with a jadeite adze, which was held in the hand. Every night he worked at these until the holes were two or three inches deep . . . . This was believed to make the arm tireless and the hand dexterous in making stone implements of any kind" (Teit 1900:320).

A Southern Okanogan child seeking a guardian spirit was sometimes sent to rock paintings that the child's father had made many years before. For each guardian spirit obtained, a short red line was made on the rock surface beside the paintings (Cline 1938:138). In northwestern Montana, a Kootenai informant related that young men would go to places where there were pictographs to receive a visitation from the spirits. There they recorded their names in pictographic form and, by means of short lines or circles, the number of days they remained at the spot (Malouf and White 1953:35).

Assessing Age

The most common method of dating rock art in the Pacific Northwest is through the use of motifs that can be identified and assigned to a particular period of time. In the interior,

depictions of Euro-American clothing, guns, and livestock brands date to the nineteenth or twentieth century. Portrayals of horses and mounted humans were made after horses were introduced to the Northwest in the early 1700s, and images of bows and arrows are no more than 2,000 years old.

Comparison of rock art motifs from 55 sites with portable dated art, ethnographic art on baskets and bowls, and depictions of horses and bows suggests that the rock art tradition at The Dalles emerged as early as 1500 B.C. out of rudimentary pit-and-groove forms. Some coastal forms, such as masklike glyphs, appear around A.D. 1000. The distinctive Tsagiglalal petroglyph motif is thought to date to the eighteenth and early nineteenth centuries because similar motifs carved on portable objects found in cremation burial sites have been dated to that time period (McClure 1984).

Superimposition, weathering, and patination have been used to suggest relative ages of rock art motifs, although little is known about site-specific environmental influences. Superimposed motifs near The Dalles were recognized as "somewhat more weathered than the overlying design. Thus it is probable that in these situations the rock art was created at different times and that the degree of difference in weathering or patination may have some relationship to the span of time separating the execution of the two designs" (McClure 1984:139). Pecked pits at Kettle Falls and in Hells Canyon were thought to be of some antiquity because of the weathering and repatination (Chance and Chance 1982:40; Leen 1988:193).

Petroglyphs at Buffalo Eddy on the Snake River in southeastern Washington were identified as belonging either to an early Naturalistic style or later Graphic style on the basis of whether designs were under desert varnish or pecked through it (Nesbitt 1968:19). However, "rock carvings located close to the water's edge are more heavily patinated than those located upslope or those situated on rock surfaces facing north" and "some glyphs depicted at Buffalo Eddy . . . have no patination at all and yet are depicted in a style that we clearly recognize as being among the oldest represented" (Lothson and Lothson 1991: 118–119).

Comparing growth rates of lichen colonies was once thought to have potential for determining the age of the underlying rock art, although later studies suggest lichenometry is an unreliable dating method since so many environmental factors influence lichen growth (Boreson 1994). For example, three colonies of lichen within six centimeters of each other were growing on pictographs at site 10VY89, on the Middle Fork of the Salmon River in central Idaho. Photographs taken in 1973 and 1989 show one colony had enlarged, one was nearly the same size, and one had disappeared over the 16-year interval (Boreson 1991).

Rock art can sometimes be dated using traditional geochronological or archeological methods. Abstract pictographs at the Long Lake site near Warner Valley in south-central Oregon (site 35LK514) were reported to be covered by a primary deposit of volcanic ash. Although the site is outside of this study area, it is worthwhile to note the tephra was identified as Mazama ash, indicating the petroglyphs are more than 6,850 years old (Cannon and Ricks 1986).

What appears to be an exfoliated basalt spall with pigment on it, found in sediment deposited more than 7,000 years ago, was recovered during test excavations at Bernard Creek Rockshelter (site 10IH483) in Hells Canyon. The red residue on the spall is not an oxidation rind nor does it look like naturally occurring iron in the rock (Charles Knowles, personal communication 1988). The artifact was located two meters below a layer of Mazama ash deposited 6,850 years ago, below charred wood dated to 7,250 ± 80 years ago (5354–5194 B.C., uncorrected date), and just above a charcoal sample dated to 7,190 ± 135 years ago (5349–5079 B.C., uncorrected date) (Randolph 1976; Randolph and Dahlstrom 1977). No intact pictographs were visible on the rockshelter walls at the time of excavation although they were reported by an earlier visitor to the site (Randolph and Dahlstrom 1977:81).

Manufacturing Techniques

The methods used to create petroglyphs include scoring, incising, abrading, and pecking with a rock, and chiseling with a hammerstone and rock chisel. Resulting alterations to the rock surface range from scratches to deeply incised grooves, sometimes a centimeter or more deep. Several hammerstones believed to have been used to make petroglyphs were collected from excavations at the Cranbrook petroglyph site (Kennedy and Cassidy 1981).

A cache of 18 modified cobbles found at site 10BR5 on Lake Pend Oreille was recovered from sediment at the base of an outcrop where numerous deeply incised petroglyphs are located. The cache included tools with bifacially modified tapered ends, striking platforms, and unifacially or bifacially modified edges. The modifications and association with the petroglyphs suggest the artifacts were used as hammers, chisels, and incising tools (Boreson and Peterson 1985:77–79).

Most pictographs appear to have been made by finger-painting, as suggested by the consistent width (from 1.0 to 1.5 cm) of the lines forming many figures and the generally simple rendition of most motifs. Occasionally very thin (from 1.0 to 2.0 mm wide) delicate lines are present that were possibly made with a pointed stick or brush. Other thin lines, with the high points of the rock surface colored and the intervening low spots untouched, suggest dry paint was applied with a crayon of natural or molded colored material. The Nez Perce boiled paint with a little glue and then dried it into disks and lumps to be used as colored pencils (Spinden 1908:222). People in the southern interior of British Columbia formed a mixture of tallow and pigment into sticks, which was then applied as greasepaint (Leechman 1932:41).

Pictographs were most commonly made with red paint, although yellow, white, green, and black colors are occasionally present. Red pigment was made from pulverized iron oxide minerals (frequently called ocher or hematite), and sometimes from clay containing iron oxide. The desired bright red color was also manufactured by baking disks of powdered yellow ocher (Leechman 1954:77). Yellow paint was made from the iron oxide minerals goethite or limonite, or from clay colored by limonite. White paint was made from burned bone, kaolin (a clay), gypsum, or diatomaceous earth; green was made from copper carbonates; and black was obtained from charcoal or graphite (Corner 1968; Erwin 1930; Grant 1967; Leechman 1932).

Mineralogical analyses of red pigment samples from various rock art sites in British Columbia identify hematite as the primary (or only) mineral constituent (Corner 1968:23; Taylor et al. 1974:34). Six red pigment samples identified by X-ray diffraction on exfoliated spalls from site 24M0505 on the Clark Fork River in western Montana indicate the presence of four iron oxide minerals, consisting of hematite, lepidocrosite, maghemite, and possibly jarosite (Boreson 1987). Hematite, maghemite, and quartz were identified in a red pigment sample from site 45AS93 in southeastern Washington. The mineralogical components of this sample are virtually identical to those of an on-site zone of oxidized sediment exposed at the base of the basalt escarpment, suggesting it was quarried for the minerals used to make the pigment. The primary minerals in two white pigment samples from the same site were identified as gypsum and quartz, with possibly a little muscovite and kaolinite in one sample (Boreson 1991a).

After obtaining properly colored minerals, organic materials were sometimes added as a binder. Ground pigment was mixed with oil or grease, then "dissolved in very thin gum or resin of the pine or fir tree, and when mixed and applied on a rock it will harden and become glazed over which will hold its bright color for a great many years, if not too much" (Erwin 1930:41). Leechman (1932:38) mentions the use of water, saliva, grease, tallow, fish oil, fish eggs, glue, and resin as vehicles for the pigment. A totally organic paint was said to have been made by the Shuswap, who mixed chokecherries with bear grease to make pictographs (Turner 1979:239). Except for a trace of carbon in a sample from site 45OK82 in north-central Washington (Boreson 1994:12), analyses have not detected organic substances in pigment collected from pictographs in the northwest (Bell 1979:43; Wainwright 1985). However, a binder identified as salmon eggs was readily detected in paint from masks from British Columbia (Wainwright 1985).

Carved and Painted Trees

Carved and painted trees have been reported in British Columbia, northeastern Washington, and northern Idaho. Anthropomorphic figures, apparently carved with a hatchet, were found on one or more sides of seven trees located on the edge of an Indian campground near the San Poil River in northeastern Washington (Walter 1969).

An early reference relates "it was not unusual to find on the small prairies [in Washington Territory] human figures rudely carved upon trees. These I have understood to have been cut by young men who were in want of wives, as a sort of practical intimation that they were in the market as purchasers" (Gibbs 1877:197). Lillooet men and adolescent boys and girls painted on trees for the same reasons they did on rocks, as records of dreams and ceremonial observations, and in some places persons passing by for the first time would paint or carve figures on trees instead of rocks (Teit 1906:282). The Okanagan also cut or burned designs into trees (Teit 1930:284), and Thompson Indians used certain trees and prominent points on mountains to observe the position of the sun in order to determine the solstice (Teit 1900:239).

When David Thompson was traveling on the Pend Oreille River in northern Idaho in 1811, Kalispel chiefs told him they "cut their arms to make the blood flow, with which they mark a Tree to apprise their enemies how far they have been in search of them, with strange figures denoting defiance" (Thompson 1916:463). Another account from northern Idaho indicates some tree carvings were made during historic times since many of the figures were "simple Latin crosses, showing the influence of the missionaries. These crosses are quite common around favorite hunting or camping spots in the mountains, and appear to be made with the object in view of warding off malign influences from the camping ground" (Leiberg 1893:156).

Fishing

GORDON W. HEWES

The Plateau fisheries constituted one of the world's leading inland aquatic food resources and in the late twentieth century remained of great economic importance. The native peoples of the Plateau depended heavily on fishing for their livelihood, especially upon the large annual salmon and steelhead runs, but also on various resident fish species. Two very large rivers, the Columbia (fig. 1) and the Fraser, their tributaries and lakes, provided the fish, once in spectacular abundance in nearly all parts of the region.

Local differences in fishing productivity did of course exist. Some rivers and lakes were inaccessible to anadromous fish, which build up their weight and nutritional value in the ocean, and which migrate upstream to spawn and die. About 95 percent of the energy requirement (and thus the caloric value) of anadromous fish such as Pacific salmon is acquired when they are feeding in the open sea (Davidson and Hutchinson 1938). The return to humans who fish in inland waters is strongly affected by local topographic or hydrographic features such as narrows, rapids, low falls, marshy places, or other constrictions that concentrate migrating fish in waters favorable for catching them. Placid lakes and slack stretches of river may facilitate the use of other kinds of gear, such as nets, or fishing from canoes. Some parts of the Columbia and Fraser basins are relatively arid, with few side streams entering the main rivers, and limited upstream or lake spawning beds.

While high mountain streams may provide sport for modern trout anglers, they are not much use to people who depend on fish for their staple food. Pacific salmon, moreover, become emaciated when they reach the vicinity of their spawning beds, and for maximal dietary value should be caught farther downstream or before they begin their upstream migration. Schalk (1977) has provided one of the most useful analyses of the anadromous fish resource of the Pacific Northwest from the standpoint of its utilization by the Indians of the region. For the once-in-a-lifetime anadromous spawners, only the upstream migrations mattered to the fishing peoples; the downstream movements of the same species are of fingerlings or smolt, generally too small to warrant significant human fishing effort.

Pacific salmon flesh is very well suited to drying or smoking for preservation and transport. Salting, and later, canning and freezing, were methods of preservation introduced by Whites. For the Indians, a critical factor in fishing productivity lay in the quantity of fish that could be dried. The men, who did nearly all the fishing, could catch more fish in a good day than the women at the adjacent fish camp or village could clean and prepare for drying before the fish would start to spoil. Large stores of dried salmon tended to limit the mobility of a given Indian community even when fishing activity was at low seasonal ebb (Schalk 1977:213). The Pacific salmon staple of the Plateau rested on five wide-ranging species (fig. 2, table 1).

Steelhead (*Oncorhynchus mykiss*) is a salmonid, often caught along with Pacific salmon, and known also as rainbow trout and Kamloops trout. Some is anadromous, some resident. The fish can weigh up to 36 pounds but averages much smaller. Unlike the Pacific salmon steelhead do not die after one spawning.

Chinook and sockeye salmon were the preferred native catch. White sport fishermen are limited in both British Columbia and the Plateau mainly to trolling in saltwater for Pacific salmon, and in freshwater, only the steelhead or rainbow is considered a genuine game fish. The upstream migrating Pacific salmon are in a fasting condition and do not rise to bait or artifical flies in freshwater.

Trout of the Plateau, including Dolly Varden (*Salvelinus malma*) and cutthroat (*Oncorhynchus clarki*), were caught in the seasons low in Pacific salmon availability by the Indians and usually eaten fresh. Dolly Varden are a lake fish, primarily. These and introduced trout have become very important in modern sport fishing wherever they can thrive. Rainbow trout may reach the size of a large salmon (15 pounds) in certain lakes.

The white sturgeon (*Acipenser transmontanus*) was the largest fish taken in fresh water, with specimens known to reach 1,000 pounds or more and a length of 13 feet. They are anadromous spawners. On the Snake River they run from March to October, on the Columbia from April to Novermber. They have been caught in Fraser and Kootenay lakes, possibly in Okanagan Lake, and as far east as the Flathead River in Montana (Scott and Crossman 1973). Large and nutritious as it is, the sturgeon was unimportant in the food economy of the Plateau Indians.

The lake whitefish (*Coregonus clupeaformis*) is widely distributed in the interior Plateau in both lakes and rivers, along with two smaller species, the pygmy and the mountain whitefish. They could be taken in winter through the ice. The burbot (*Lota lota*) also was caught through the ice and, with the whitefish, formed a useful supplement in the winter season.

Suckers (*Catostomus* spp.), which are bottom feeders, were not regarded highly as food but again were useful when

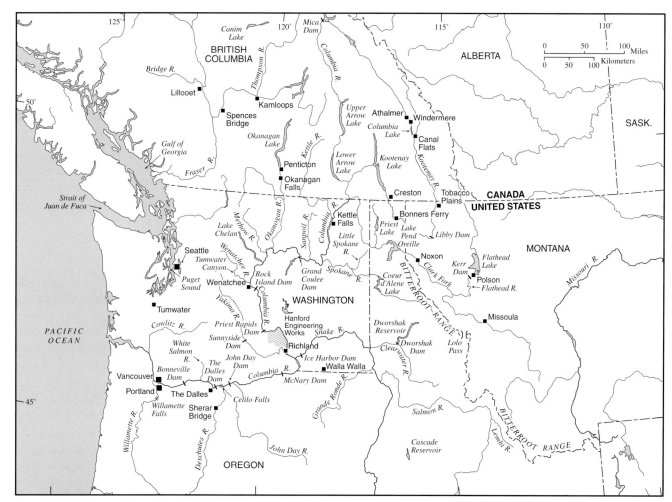

Fig. 1. Native fishing sites of the Plateau region with modern towns and drainage.

salmon and steelhead were lacking (Scott and Crossman 1973:531–535). The northern squawfish (*Ptychocheilus oregonensis*) was eaten when other fish were unavailable; it is a major predator on sockeye salmon fry. Some squawfish reached as much as five pounds.

Fish, especially ocean-feeding species, were and are valuable in the human diet, being rich in protein and fat, in vitamins, and in trace elements such as iodine likely to be lacking in the land-based wild foodstuffs on the Plateau interior. The fat content of salmon bears on its suitability for drying; overly fat fish did not preserve well (Romanoff 1988). A by-product of various fish was oil ("Lillooet," fig. 3, this vol.), often eaten with berries, and also used as skin and hair lotion.

Estimates of Aboriginal Fish Consumption

Estimates of aboriginal Plateau fish consumption have been based on some simple assumptions, such as that Indian consumers dependent upon Pacific salmon as a staple might have consumed a pound of salmon a day, or 365 pounds a year. Such guesses, to be plausible, must take into account fish other than salmon, variations in access to good fishing places, seasonal variability in runs, and the contribution to the native diet of the meat of game animals, and wild plants. Since the caloric value of salmon flesh is about 1,000 per pound, and an adequate adult human diet requires at least twice that many calories, the tendency is to raise the intake or fish per capita in such estimates, especially since adults active in cold weather usually burn more than 3,000 calories a day. Carrothers (1941) proposed that the 1879 total Indian fish consumption for all of British Columbia was 583 pounds a year per person. Craig and Hacker (1940) put the "aboriginal" Columbia River salmon catch at 365 pounds a year, presumably for some time around 1800. An estimate for Celilo Falls dip-netters, prior to the closure of that very important fishing place, was 307 pounds per fisherman per year, which did not take account of fish obtained elsewhere in the region. Using a precontact population estimate of 50,450 (1780), Hewes (1947, 1973) arrived at 438 pounds per capita (excluding the Klamath and Modoc). Walker (1967) produced an estimate of 606 pounds per capita per year for the entire Plateau. All these figures might be averaged at around 400 to 450 pounds.

621

Oncorhynchus gorbuscha (pink)

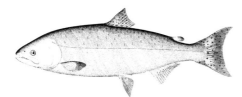

O. tshawytscha (chinook)

O. kisutch (coho)

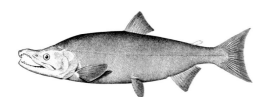

O. nerka (sockeye)

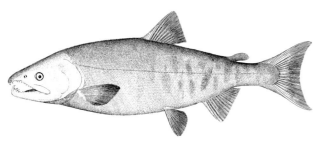

O. keta (chum)

Smithsonian, Div. of Fishes: top to bottom, P5103, P5100, P5104, P5102, P5101.
Fig 2. Salmon species most important to Plateau peoples drawn at various life stages. Sizes are not relative to maximum species weight. *Oncorhynchus gorbuscha,* drawing by S.F. Denton, 1889; *O. tshawytscha,* artist not recorded. 1884; *O. kisutch,* artist not recorded, 1881; *O. nerka,* drawing by A.H. Baldwin, about 1895; *O. keta,* artist not recorded, 1881. Length of *O. gorbuscha,* 48 cm; others to same scale.

Indian fish consumption presumably declined in some areas with the advent of firearms for hunting; establishment of subsistence agriculture; allotments of flour, beef, and other foods made to residents of many reservations in the nineteenth century; and the adoption of animal husbandry—cattle, sheep, horses, and chickens in some localities. Finally, as the Indians began to participate in the cash and credit economy of the surrounding communities, and to sell surplus fish to non-Indian consumers, they also can be assumed to have replaced fish (and wild game and plants) with foodstuffs purchased at trading posts and stores.

Fishing Methods

The fishing gear used by the Plateau peoples was remarkably similar throughout the region, probably representing centuries or millennia of exchange in techniques. Most of the devices used were rationally adapted to the environment and probably, in the majority of cases, the best technological solution available. The main technical ingredient lacking in the Indian fisheries was metal for tools; iron and steel knives, axes, and hooks were quickly adopted when they became available. Another very useful product from non-Indian sources was twine for nets and lines; the Indians had cordage of native materials, but not usually so strong as hemp, linen, or even cotton. The use of new metallic tools and other manufactured goods probably did not have much serious effect on total fishing efficiency, aside from increasing the number of fish that could be properly cleaned and prepared by a skilled worker.

Fishing methods not used, or very little used, in the Plateau were angling, except for sturgeon, use of fish poisons, use of the bow and arrow in fishing, and the plunge-basket, a conical basket, with an open bottom, placed mouth down on fish in very shallow water. The gill net was also probably not used in aboriginal times, nor the ordinary gaff. Eel pots and similar containers (for cephalopods) were not used either, nor the device known on the Northwest Coast as the herring-rake. Although the riverine and lake Indians of the Plateau all had canoes, they were not very often used for fishing, since it was usually more efficient to find a shoreside place where fish could be obtained in greater numbers in a given amount of time.

Table 1. Salmon Species Important in the Plateau

Scientific Name	English Name	Other Names	Weight
Oncorhynchus tschawytscha	chinook	king, spring	25–80 lbs.
O. keta	chum	dog	8–18
O. kisutch	coho	silver	6–12
O. nerka	sockeye	Alaska red, blueback	7, varies
O. gorbuscha	pink	humpback	3–10

Southwestern Plateau

Klamath and Modoc

This southernmost outlier of the Plateau was unlike the rest of the Plateau in several respects. Salmon did not enter the Klamath Lake and marsh area, although fish was the staple food of both the Klamath and Modoc. Salmon only ascended the Klamath River proper below Copco Marsh. Instead the fishery was based on suckers, trout, and freshwater mussels; suckers were very abundant, in this case the species *Chasmistes stomias*, which reached a length of 18 inches. Another sucker, the tswan (*Chasmistes copei*), was also important for food. Another genus of sucker, *Deltistes*, was even more useful. Residing most of the year in the deeper waters of Upper Klamath Lake, it ascends the tributary creeks in March and April in vast numbers. The flesh of this sucker was cured for winter consumption, and oil was pressed from the viscera and heads (Jordan and Evermann 1908:57).

Salmon and steelhead spawning near the outlet to Copco Marsh were taken by the Klamath with double-pronged toggle harpoons, gorge hooks, and double-pointed angle-hooks (fig. 3). The fish taken on hooks were probably all steel-

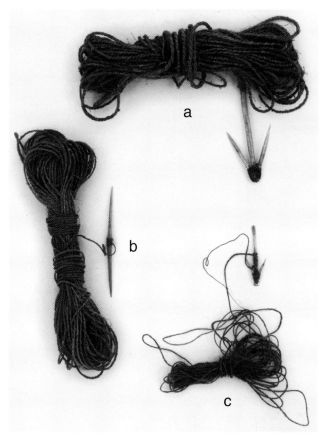

Smithsonian, Dept. of Anthr.: a, 24097; b, 24098; c. 24099 (neg. 95–20786).

Fig 3. Klamath angling equipment. a and c, Double-barbed bone fishhooks on lines made of plant fiber. b, Bone gorge on plant fiber line. Collected by L.S. Dyar at the Klamath Agency. Oreg., 1876. Length of top hook, 7 cm; others to same scale.

head, since salmon will not rise to a bait during the spawning migration. For the more productive lake sucker fishery, the Klamath and Modoc employed large A-frame dip nets, held from the prows of dugout canoes. In shallower water suckers were taken with multipointed spears, with the points being spread by a ring (Barrett 1910; Spier 1930:144–152; E.W. Voegelin 1942).

A cylindrical fish basket without an invaginated mouth was also sometimes used. Stone dams, curving out from river banks, were constructed on Williamson River, a northern affluent of Upper Klamath Lake. These seem to have been of negligible importance. Ice-fishing was carried on by the Klamath and Modoc, using hoop-framed dip nets on long poles. Fish were sometimes speared or harpooned through holes in the ice.

Central Plateau

Upper Cowlitz and Klikitat

The Upper Cowlitz and Klikitat lived mainly away from the river, though the Klikitat held a small section of the north shore; during river fishing season, they mingled freely with the Chinookan peoples (Curtis 1907–1930, 7:37). There is an important run of eulachon (*Thaleichthys pacificus*) on the Cowlitz River in spring, which was presumably exploited aboriginally. Upper Cowlitz and Klikitat salmon (and steelhead) spearing was mostly in the smaller streams during the winter and early spring (Curtis 1907–1930, 7:9, 6). The harpoon was not used (Ray 1942). Chinook salmon were the staple food of the Klikitat, but steelhead, trout, and whitefish were also utilized. In fall when streams were low, weirs were built from which fish could be caught in hoop-framed dip nets. Other nets were conical bag and gill nets. Basket traps with invaginated mouths were set by the Klikitat in streams, and open-top baskets were set at falls. Minor fishing devices were the use of poison prepared from a root, for whitefish, and horsehair sniggles, probably for trout (Ray 1942:104–116).

The Dalles and Celilo Falls

The Wasco and Wishram were Upper Chinookan peoples occupying the banks of the Columbia in the vicinity of The Dalles. The Columbia River, for a distance of about 10 miles, 180 miles from the ocean, is compressed into a bed cut through hard black rock, most confined at Celilo Falls where in a space of three miles the river pours over low falls, separating into channels and cascades, studded with rocky islands that afford good fishing places. This narrows was by far the most productive inland fishing site in native North America and was used by many groups.

Archeological evidence from the Roadcut site, Oregon, near Celilo Falls, shows abundant salmon bones, indicating

623

top left, Natl. Geographic Soc., Washington: 7784; bottom left, Oreg. Histl. Soc., Portland: 42690.
Fig. 4. Fishing at Celilo Falls on the Columbia River, Oreg. top left, Group using gaff hooks. A commercial fish wheel is upstream. Photograph by Arthur M. Prentiss, 1931. top right, Hannah Yallup cutting salmon for roasting. Photograph by Gladys Seufert, Celilo Park Festival, Oreg., 1968. bottom left, Platform fishing. Photograph by Walter Boychuk, about 1955. bottom right, Hannah Yallup (left) and Lillie Heath roasting salmon. Photograph by Gladys Seufert, Celilo Park Festival, Oreg., 1967.

the importance of that locality roughly 10,000 years ago (Daugherty 1973:6). From mid-May until the end of July, salmon ascended the narrows in huge numbers, often after the water was sufficiently high to permit them to leap the highest falls.

Before the construction of all the Columbia River dams, the runoff at The Dalles (and Celilo Falls) peaked in July. The bulk of the salmon taken at these falls was dip-netted from staging erected over the cascade (fig. 4) (vol. 17:187), preferably at eddies that would carry the bag of the net

upstream. An experienced dip-netter could take as many as 500 fish each day (Writers' Project. Oregon 1940:267). Each family had a fishing station and summer camp, which was a center of great industry during the run.

The diet of the fisherman and their families at this time consisted almost exclusively of heads, hearts, and offal from the fish being cut and dried for winter use or trade (Bancroft 1874:266). The greater part of the catch was sun-dried on scaffolding and then pounded into salmon pemmican ("Columbia River Trade Network," fig. 2, this vol.), mixed with dried roe. This concentrated powdered product was rammed into split cattail baskets lined with fishskins, each containing from 90 to 100 pounds. William Clark estimated that the annual trade in this commodity in 1806 reached 30,000 pounds (A.B. Lewis 1906:158–159). On the basis of a weight loss in drying of 60 percent, this would represent an original catch of only 75,000 pounds, probably much too low for The Dalles–Celilo Falls aboriginal pack.

The trade in dried fish centered at the Wishram village near the north end of the falls. From downstream people like the Klikitat, coastal fish, the edible tuber wapato (*Sagittaria latifolia*), other roots and berries, deer meat, and slaves were bartered; in the protohistoric period, trade goods acquired from the Whites who visited the coast were added. From the interior the Wishram obtained camas bulbs, and in later times horses from the Yakima and other groups farther east (Curtis 1907–1930, 8:94).

Salmon were harpooned and trapped elsewhere by the Wishram, but only when the river was high. Sturgeon were taken on hooks, and lampreys secured in fine-meshed dip nets (fig. 5). Trout and suckers were apparently of very little importance (Curtis 1907–1930, 7:1–34; Irving [1863] 1964:80–82). The Wasco are reported to have taken sturgeon with hook and line from canoes, as was the custom of the Chinookans farther downstream.

Tenino

Tenino fishing is fairly well known from the work of Murdock (1935). Fish were the basic food source, bulking larger than either game or wild vegetable foods. Salmon was the staple, supplemented by steelhead, which were present the year round in Columbia. Salmon runs began in late April, with a late summer run extending into October. During the salmon season, about half the Tenino were established in fishing camps. Despite the much greater productivity of the Columbia, both the John Day and Deschutes rivers had salmon fisheries of considerable importance. The falls of the Deschutes at Sherar's Bridge about 35 miles above the Columbia were visited in 1826 by Peter Skene Ogden, who found a camp of 20 families fishing there for salmon, using dip nets and single-toggle harpoons (Bancroft 1874:262; Writers' Project. Oregon 1940:268). In March there was a special mass fishing for steelhead in the lower John Day River. The Tenino caught a few sturgeon with a baited gorge hook and a strong line fastened to a tree along the shore of the Columbia. Throughout the year they caught suckers, whitefish, trout, chub, and Dolly Varden. To supplement the dwindling supplies of dried salmon from November to March, these lesser species were taken intensively, with chub exclusively in the spring.

The chief Tenino fishing implement was the single-pronged "spear," used on the Deschutes and John Day for steelhead and dog salmon; the double-pronged harpoon was for salmon and steelhead in the Columbia (Murdock 1935).

Ray (1942) denies that the Tenino had double-pronged harpoons. The "spear" was probably a true harpoon with a single toggle with a thong line, on an eight-foot pole (Bancroft 1874–1876, 1:262).

From stream banks, platforms on weirs, and at strategic sites such as Deschutes Falls, dip nets were more commonly employed. One type had a horizontal hoop on a long pole. The other was a bag suspended from a vertical pole (but without a crosspiece) to lift small fish from the faces of weirs. During spring thaw, when the water was roily, such dip nets were used for trout, whitefish, and suckers. Large seines and gill nets seem to be postcontact among the Tenino. The largest native net was only 30 feet long, and as used from a canoe, its lower corners held down by poles; it had neither floats nor sinkers. When a fish struck, the holders were notified by an alarm cord, the net was jerked upward, and the catch was clubbed with a special implement, as was common in the nuclear zone of the Salmon Area.

Basket traps were set in weirs (fig. 6). Angling with simple bone gorges or barbless J-shaped deer nasal bones on set-lines suspended from short rods for sucker, chub, and char, were minor techniques. Fish poisons were confined to very small fish in quiet pools. The unidentified root used would only stupefy an eight-inch trout. Ray (1942) lists the use of fish poisons only for the Tenino, Wenatchee, Klikitat, and possibly the Kittitas. The method was of negligible importance in the Plateau as a food producer (Murdock 1935; O. Stewart 1941:item 293).

The Tenino, and probably other tribes of the Columbia River living below The Dalles, occasionally harpooned a sea mammal, which Murdock (1935) identified as the harbor seal (*Phoca vitulina*), during the heavy salmon runs. Goode (1886–1887, 1:57) mentions the ascent of harbor seals as far as The Dalles.

The seals were taken from shore, and after the detachable harpoon head was embedded in the animal the line was fastened to a nearby post or tree, to be hauled in when the seal was exhausted. According to Murdock's (1935) informants, these seals formerly congregated on an island in the river from which they could prey on the passing salmon. Seals, and possibly sea lions, were probably fairly common visitors in the lower courses of all the larger rivers of the Pacific coast before the era of intensive commercial sealing and the spread of firearms.

Umatilla

Among the Umatilla and the other bands along the south bank of the Columbia adjoining the Tenino to the east and the Yakima, fishing methods were generally similar. Salmon was the staple food, with steelhead and whitefish secondary. The Umatilla had trident leisters that were thrust vertically from canoes for night fishing (Ray 1942).

top, Nez Perce Natl. Histl. Park, Spalding, Idaho: 0783.

Fig. 5. Fishing for lamprey. top, James Williams, Nez Perce, in dugout canoe dip-netting a lamprey. Photograph by Allen H. Hilton, Clearwater River, Idaho, 1916–1923. bottom left, Warm Springs residents Oliver Kirk and Guy Wallulatum gathering lamprey. Photograph by Cynthia D. Stowell, Willamette Falls on Willamette River, Oreg., 1980. bottom right, Blanche Tohet, Warm Springs Sahaptin, drying lamprey. In preparing lampreys for food, they are first cleaned, the notachord is removed, and then they are either roasted to be eaten immediately or are split and stretched on splints of woody plant stems to air-dry, as shown here. Photograph by David and Kathrine French, Warm Springs Res., Oreg., 1951.

top, Field Mus., Chicago: 1956; center, Okanogan County Histl. Soc., Okanogan, Wash.; bottom, Jay Miller, Seattle, Wash.

Fig. 6. Traps and weirs. top, Sahaptian fish trap. Photograph by Merton L. Miller, 1901. center, Fish corral. Photograph by Frank Matsura, Okanogan County, Wash., 1903–1913. bottom, Salmon weir across the Methow River, Twisp, Wash. Photographer and date not recorded.

Yakima

The Yakima occupied an area less favorable for fishing, but salmon was still the chief food, though some of it, in a dried form, reached them from the Upper Columbia (and from the Wishram?) in trade (Curtis 1907–1930, 7:1–34).

For the Yakima, the spring chinook run was of minor importance, and the run from late May until early July was accompanied by oil-rich sockeye; this was the peak season of Yakima fishing. From July to October or November, the main salmon were coho. Steelhead were caught most of the year (Daugherty 1973).

The main salmon gear was the dip net on a very long pole, wielded from a plank platform. Such fishing stations were inherited. The river level dropped in autumn, and the double-pronged toggle harpoon was used in clearer water (fig. 7). This device had a head of two bone barbs on the sides of a central bone point. White pebbles might be placed on the stream bed to make the moving fish easily visible. The two-pronged leister may be a later implement (Daugherty 1973:45); how it came to be among the Yakima is not known.

On small rivers and streams, weirs and traps were installed, usually with dip netting. The most common basket trap was set at a low falls. The gill net is generally regarded as a device acquired from Whites, though the Yakima informants insist they used it in the remote past. Dried salmon flesh was pulverized with mortar and pestle and then packed in baskets for storage or transport.

On a river island near the site of Priest Rapids Dam, Washington, are numerous carvings in bedrock (now flooded by the dam), suggesting a rich ceremonial importance to the former Priest Rapids as a fishery site (Daugherty 1973:23). This art style is also found along the Lower to Middle Columbia and probably dates to just before the beginning of European contact in the eighteenth century (Daugherty 1973).

Kittitas

Even the Kittitas on the Upper Yakima, who used poison for trout, were mainly dependent on salmon, rather than on hunting.

Middle Columbia River Salishans

Wenatchee and Sinkayuse took most of their salmon in dip nets from platforms with single- and double-pronged harpoons, trident leisters, and large nets dragged in the river. Traps (fig. 8) were used but were of less importance. The Wenatchee, but not the Sinkayuse, used poison for trout. Fish pemmican was prepared as at The Dalles, and oil was kept in fishskin bags (Teit 1928:118–119; Ray 1942).

Fig. 7. Yakima harpoon points made of bone and metal. Collected by T.T. Waterman, Cusick, Wash., 1921. Length of left, 12 cm.

The fishing methods of the Wenatchee, Methow, Southern Okanogan, Sanpoil, Nespelem, Colville, and Lakes were generally alike, and similar to the Plateau fishing already described, with the differences in topography taken into account. The lake in their territory, Lake Chelan, is 50 miles long, in a deeply entrenched valley, and at least 1,476 feet deep, blocked from the Columbia by a high fall, entirely inaccessible to salmon. The fauna of Lake Chelan includes the lingcods, a fish seemingly little utilized by the Wenatchee and Methow (Jordan and Evermann 1908: 517–518).

Lake fishing was mainly for whitefish and trout. Other species in this region included sturgeon, lamprey, suckers, chub, and river mussels. In the river, salmon and steelhead were chiefly caught with dip nets or harpooned in shallow places with double- or, more commonly, single-pronged implements. Trident leisters were used from canoes by torchlight, especially on lakes for trout and whitefish rather than salmon. Smaller fish were taken with hook and line.

Numerous waterfalls and lake outlets afforded sites for the use of traps, with or without weirs, and these devices were used much more commonly than farther down the Columbia.

The Sanpoil and Nespelem took salmon with single-pronged harpoons, thrust from platforms or weirs, or often simply from the river banks. Small booths or shades were sometimes erected on the smaller streams for daylight fish harpooning or spearing with the harpoon trident. The trident leister was used exclusively from canoes at night. Traps were more effective, especially those used in weirs at the mouth of the Spokane River. They were of several types. One type was an open-work twined willow basket hung a few feet from the face of a waterfall—smaller baskets of the type hung at Kettle Falls. Nets were unimportant to the Sanpoil, though in turbid water when the fish could not see them, they were useful. Both the common hoop dip net and a vertical lifting net with a crosspiece of webbing were used. Lampreys were landed in small dip nets drawn through the water (Ray 1933, 1942). Kettle Falls was second only to The Dalles–Celilo Falls in its production of salmon in the Columbia Basin. The station was visited (for trade or fishing) by all the neighboring groups, including the Lakes, but the Colville were credited with the largest salmon catch in the region (Teit 1930:246–247; Ray 1933). This fishery began somewhat later than on the Spokane, about mid-July. Here there were two falls, a few hundred meters apart.

Great quantities of salmon were speared or dip-netted and after drying (fig. 9), packed into reed baskets, often for trade to quite distant groups. The river drops about eight meters in two cascades and then flows into a stretch called the Grand Rapids. A major first salmon rite was held at Kettle Falls, by joining the Spokane, Colville, and Kettle Falls people. In 1841, an observer estimated that the annual native catch at Kettle Falls amounted to 600,000 pounds (Craig and Hacker 1940). Three weeks before the expected arrival of the salmon, the camps were occupied, and drying frames and storehouses were erected. The entire enterprise was said to be under the direction of a "chief" (ritualist?) whose basket trap was installed a month before the others could begin to fish. The gear used at the falls were large willow baskets, up to 10 feet in diameter, 12 feet deep, hung from a timber frame fixed in the rocks above (fig. 9 top left), so arranged that the leaping salmon would strike it and fall back into the basket where fishermen armed with clubs dispatched them (fig. 9 top right). One such basket is stated to have caught 5,000 pounds of fish in a day, but this must have been exceptional. These baskets were often far more efficient than harpooning or spearing (Bancroft 1874–1876, 1:261–262). Sturgeon were also numerous at Kettle Falls.

Northeastern Plateau

Spokane

The Spokane were noted in the region as salmon eaters. The Spokane could fish at Kettle Falls on the Columbia or trade

Fig. 8. Columbia Salish fish trap. Photograph by Bourbon C. Collier, Tumwater Canyon, Wenatchee River, Wash., 1902–1912.

Stark Mus. of Art, Orange, Tex.: top left, 31.78/216, WOP 19; top right, 31.78/86 WWC 87; bottom left, 31.78/50, WWC 50; bottom right, Smithsonian, Natl. Mus. of the Amer. Ind.: left 1276 and right 1275.

Fig. 9. Fishing at Kettle Falls, Wash. top left, A J-trap made of willow baskets hung from a timber frame on the east side of the falls, just south of where the Kettle River enters the Columbia River. top right, Detail of a multiple subject sketch showing speared salmon being clubbed, a woman carrying a cradleboard with a tumpline, and a decorated quiver and bow. bottom left, Part of the Colville Indian village at Kettle Falls where about 500 people lived. Drying sheds made of woven mats stretched on poles with a raised flooring made of sticks formed a shady, airy place for the salmon to dry (Harper 1971:123). Paintings by Paul Kane 1847: top left, oil; top right and bottom left, watercolors. bottom right, Wishram stone fish clubs. Collected on the Columbia River before 1904. Length of left, 51 cm.

for salmon with tribes farther downstream (O.W. Johnson 1969:60).

The Spokane fished mainly with traps, spearing, and with the salmon gaff, but the last is apparently an introduction from the Whites. Fitted with an iron hook, this modern device should be distinguished from the aboriginal gaff of the Northwest Coast and northwestern California, consisting of a pole with a simple, barbless straight point lashed at the end to form an acute angle. In a few places on the tributaries of the Spokane River, the Spokane stretched large nets across the streams to intercept the fish, instead of building weirs of stakes and brush (Teit 1930:107). Like the Sanpoil, the Spokane had tridents, the three points of which were detachable as a unit. For angling, X-shaped bone gorges were used (Curtis 1907–1930, 7:71–78). The Spokane built a rock barrier partly across the Spokane River just downstream from Little Falls, where a dam has been built. Upstream from there they built a willow-pole weir. The fish were speared and thrown to the shore. The drying took about a month, after which the dried fish were packed in baskets for underground storage (Ruby and Brown 1970:16). This fishing site attracted also Coeur d'Alenes,

Kalispels, Colvilles, Palouse, Sanpoils, and Sinkayuse. When the river dropped, the Spokane moved downriver about a mile. At the confluence of the Spokane and the Columbia was another important fishery, to which Spokanes, Sanpoils, and Sinkayuse went for salmon (this would be the site of Fort Spokane).

Where the Little Spokane River joins the main Spokane River was another important fishery, with a wing-dam or weir, in which basketry traps were set, where the fish were speared. The dried salmon were cached in pits on the hillside south of the Little Spokane. Salmon managing to escape these barriers ascended to Spokane Falls, with a fishery that lasted about six weeks. They used a rock dam, with nets. From these fisheries dried salmon was exchanged along with coastal goods such as dentalium shells and abalone, for buffalo robes (Ruby and Brown 1970:18).

Coeur d'Alene

The Coeur d'Alene territory contains no salmon, and they therefore fished with the Spokane at Spokane Falls, the highest point on that stream where the fish were available. 629

Before the arrival of the horse, it is said that they also trapped some salmon in the mountains on the northern feeders of Clearwater River, nominally a part of Nez Perce territory (Teit 1930:105–107). In Coeur d'Alene Lake, the mountain whitefish (*Prosopium williamsoni*) was present in abundant numbers. In late fall or early winter these fish leave the lake to spawn in streams (Jordan and Evermann 1908:69). Squawfish were also an important food fish in the Idaho lakes and could be taken in winter through holes in the ice; they spawn in spring or early summer in the lake affluent. Long set-nets and series of angle hooks were fixed to set-lines placed in the lake, and in winter the leister was used through ice holes. In the Coeur d'Alene whitefish and trout fishery, northern traits like the eye-shade (also found among the Thompson) are noteworthy. The salmon were caught in traps of various types, including the kind with a trap door opened by the fish on the downstream side of a weir. Also, simple weirs without gates or traps were installed to facilitate the use of the single-pronged harpoon.

Kootenai

As Plateau Indians, the Kootenai fishing emphasis set them off from their Plains neighbors, as did their use of spruce-bark canoes. They also used hide-covered bullboats and, on some lakes, reed rafts.

The Kootenai have often been regarded as a simple instance of a Plateau-Plains intermediate group, whose economy was split between fishing on the Pacific side of the Continental Divide, on the Upper Columbia and Kootenai rivers (Kootenay in Canada), and bison hunting in the Missouri Basin to the east. Walker (1985a) shows that fishing was important for the Kootenai throughout their territory. Moreover, much of their fishing took place in lakes and marshes. Their region was marked by heavy snows and freezing of lakes and rivers, leading to much ice-fishing.

The Kootenai were systematic fishermen, a trait that marked their Plains-influenced culture as still essentially of the Plateau. The Lower Kootenai, about Kootenay Lake and the lower course of the Kootenay River, were more intensive fishermen than the Upper Kootenai, whose territory was closer to the Plains, and whose people did more hunting. With the former, the seasonal round of subsistence activities began with fishing in early spring for sturgeon and trout, while the Upper Kootenai crossed the mountains eastward to hunt bison in midsummer. Salmon were caught near the outlet of Kootenay Lake with single-pronged harpoons, often by torchlight from canoes. Salmon were not trapped or taken in weirs. The Upper Kootenai though generally less dependent on fishing, apparently got more salmon, harpooning or spearing them (fig. 10) in the sloughs and marshes of the low divide (Canal Flats, or the McGillivray Portage), which separates the Kootenay from Columbia drainage, near Windermere (Turney-High 1941:51). The

salmon were sun-dried with the help of a fire. Unlike many Plateau peoples, the Kootenai did not make "salmon pemmican."

Ice fishing included the use of floating traps beneath the ice. The ice was opened with clubs and antler wedges, and the clubs were also used to drive visible fish beneath the ice to ice-holes. Gorges on lines were possibly also used for ice-fishing.

Aboriginally the Kootenai fished with neighboring groups at Arrow Lake, Kootenay Lake, Columbia Lakes, Kettle Falls, and downstream from Bonnington Falls. They also fished on Lake Pend Oreille, Priest Lake, and Flathead Lake, where members of other tribes also fished, especially the Shuswap.

The Kootenai fished for salmon at the headwaters of the Columbia, at the site of modern Athalmer, at the north end of Windermere Lake in British Columbia. They caught salmon with spears (O.W. Johnson 1969:61).

The Kootenai dried their salmon and did not smoke them. The Kootenai bands in the upper portion of the Kootenay River liked salmon and also caught trout at any time of year. The downriver Kootenai obtained fish year round, fishing in Arrow Lakes, British Columbia. The salmon could not ascend the cascade that separates Kootenay lake from the Columbia. However, the stretch between Bonner's Ferry (Idaho) and Kootenay Lake (in British Columbia) was fished especially in spring when the dropping spring floods stranded many fish in flats and marshes; they were taken in nets from canoes. The species included sturgeon, trout, but not salmon in that area.

The Kootenai salmon runs were particularly unreliable owing to natural cyclicity and their remoteness from the ocean. To make up for this, the Kootenai fished various resident species.

Amer. Mus. of Nat. Hist., New York: 50.2/3850.
Fig. 10. Kootenai fish spear point made of mountain goat horn and wound with sinew covered with pitch. A horsehair line has been attached. Collected by C.E. Schaeffer, Tobacco Plains, Mont., 1935. Length 9.5 cm.

The anadromous catch of the Kootenai, as an average, was about 300 pounds annually per capita (Walker 1985a). Anadromous species comprised less than half of the annual Kootenai catch. The Lower Kootenai probably lacked direct access to salmon in their own territory.

Pierre Jean de Smet attended a fish ritual in the late 1840s on the Lower Kootenai, held in a large grass matting shelter. The fish were stone-boiled in large baskets from heated stones drawn out of a large fire. This ritual marked the opening of the fishing season (O.W. Johnson 1969). It was apparently carried on until the early 1860s. The fishing was with traps, at weirs (fig. 11). The fish bones, carefully protected from any breaking, were returned after the cere-mony to the streams from which the fish had been taken. Bonnington Falls was a barrier to upstream migrating salmon.

Species fished for by the Kootenai, in addition to salmon, included suckers, caught in traps, also dried and smoked for winter use, squawfish, river perch, trout, peamouth chub, squawfish, eels, burbot, redside shiners, bullhead, and kokanee (landlocked salmon). One of the most prized fish was the sturgeon. The Kootenai also obtained river mussels and turtles.

At the south end of Kootenay Lake, near Creston, and on the river near Bonner's Ferry, where salmon were less abundant, the fishing was mostly for trout, sucker, whitefish, and sturgeon. The sturgeon were formerly quite numerous. Squawfish were eaten only as a last resort, but sucker were consumed in fair quantities, especially in summer. Whitefish were caught mainly in fall and continued to be taken through the ice in winter.

While salmon were caught only with spears or harpoons, other fish were trapped. Most productive of these devices was a long cylinder basket (fig. 11) ("Kootenai," fig. 7 top, this vol.) with invaginated mouth placed in a V-shaped weir, with its open end downstream, for trout. Ice fishing was done with an X-shaped bone gorge, baited; in summer such gorges were used on a cast line, but neither technique compared in efficiency to the trap and weir.

Kootenai fishing stations were more temporary than those erected as platforms farther west in the Plateau, except where salmon were taken. In river sloughs, fish could be taken readily after the spring high water had subsided. Walker (1985a) noted that of about 200 fishing sites located

Amer. Mus. of Nat. Hist., New York: 50.2/3872.
Fig. 11. Model of Kootenai closed fish trap. Closed traps were used either in shallow streams or in conjunction with a fish weir, which would funnel the fish into the trap. Collected by C.E. Schaeffer, Tobacco Plains, Mont., 1935. Length 63 cm.

in Kootenai territory, less than 50 had weirs, traps, platforms or other fixed features of the kind used in other parts of the Plateau for salmon fishing. The traps varied in form and function, some in funnel shape, others open above, and sometimes combined with stone inclines. They were usually set in weirs. For the much heavier sturgeon, composite hooks and lines were used, as well as spears.

Flathead, Pend d'Oreille, and Kalispel

Fishing was of less importance than hunting. There were no salmon in either Flathead or Pend d'Oreille territory, and they entered only a small part of Kalispel territory. On the other hand, the Flathead took enough interest in fishing to set them off sharply from the Plains peoples to the east. The southern Flathead had to go across the Bitterroot Range to obtain salmon, and they often simply traded it from the Nez Perce, or Lemhi Northern Shoshone (O.W. Johnson 1969:60).

In spring, the Flathead used to cross the Bitterroot Range via Lolo Pass to the headwaters of the Clearwater. It may be that this expedition was really for steelhead, inasmuch as the conical traps set in weirs for them were open on the upstream side. Some of the Flathead fished for salmon with the Colville, Spokane, and Nez Perce (Fahey 1974:13). By the time of the earliest White contact, the upriver or Southern Flathead obtained most of their salmon already dried, by exchange with Columbia River tribes, to whom they sent bison products (O.W. Johnson 1969:17).

For other than salmon the Flathead used angle hooks, noose and line, trident leister, ice fishing with baited horsehair set-lines, and an unusual fish trap. The trap was essentially a deadfall, placed in quiet waters, with a prop beneath stones tripped by a horsehair string. Flathead Lake was fished in winter through the ice (O.W. Johnson 1969:31).

The Pend d'Oreille and Kalispel had access to salmon only on the lower course of Clark Fork (Pend Oreille River) below the lake, but whitefish, squawfish, chub, and trout were abundant. The Kalispel also went north for salmon to the Salmon River in what is now British Columbia (O.W. Johnson 1969:61). Flathead Lake was noted for the large numbers of suckers (*Catostomus macrocheilus*) found in streams near the lake in spring and early summer. It was a food fish of some importance. The fishing of both groups was probably very similar to that of the Coeur d'Alene (Jordan and Evermann 1908:50, 72; Ray 1942:104–106; O.W. Johnson 1969:60).

Southeastern Plateau

Nez Perce

In addition to the several runs of salmon on the Snake, Clearwater, and Salmon rivers, there were steelhead, whitefish, chub, suckers, lampreys, trout, freshwater mussels, and sturgeon in Nez Perce territory. The largest specimens of white sturgeon (*Acipenser transmontanus*) ever recorded were caught along the Snake River (Irving 1961:31). Trout and similar small fish were jerked with horsehair sniggles, or taken on small gorge hooks. Seines, as long as 50 feet, with log floats were sometimes used. Sturgeon were taken on the Snake River in Idaho, some weighing up to 1,000 pounds and 13 feet long. More commonly they reached weights of 100 to 650 pounds. They appeared in the Snake on their annual upstream spawning run from March to October (Jordan and Evermann 1908:5). These huge fish were taken by the Nez Perce with lamprey-baited bone gorges six to eight inches long. From rock ledges or platforms, the platform often built in connection with brush weirs on riffles, salmon were taken with single pronged harpoons. Trident leisters were thrust vertically into the water from canoes. Both salmon and lampreys were caught from platforms in dip nets on simple two-pole frames, the base joined by a piece of willow. To remove salmon from deep pools, smaller hoop-frame dip nets on long handles were employed. The salmon gaff is a borrowing from the Whites. Traps of various types were set in weirs (fig. 12), including the trap-door type of the Coeur d'Alene. Meriwether Lewis and William Clark observed a stone fish dam with a trough-shaped matting trap (Spinden 1908:205–209). The main salmon fishing of the Lower Nez Perce was during August and September, when the people congregated in large fishing camps.

Cayuse

Among the Cayuse much fishing for salmon was carried on in the headwaters of the Grande Ronde River. There fish could be caught with the bare hands, a feasible procedure on or near the spawning beds in early fall when the salmon were in a half-dead condition, and the water was very low. The abundance of the fish at this time attracted bears and wolves, who gorged on the emaciated fish. However, the Cayuse were not primarily fishermen, and they derived most of their food from hunting and the gathering of camas bulbs. One of their regular dishes was a compote of salmon heads, camas, and sunflower seeds (Bancroft 1874–1876, 1:266).

Northern Plateau

Thompson

The banks of the Lower Thompson are mostly sagebrush covered, with scattered pines and poplar, a real dry zone, now partly in irrigated farms.

The Lower Thompson took salmon principally in long-handled dip nets, provided with horn slip-rings. These nets were wielded from rocks in the Fraser Canyon, and platforms were seldom required. Harpooning, because of the turbid water, was less profitable; when harpoons were used,

they were usually of the double-pronged type, though a simple barbed spear (without a detachable head) might be used (fig. 14). There was sometimes harpooning from canoes by torchlight ("Thompson," fig. 3, this vol.), in which case the harpooner wore a visor to shade his eyes from the glare. For trout and smaller fish, and when the river was obstructed by floating ice, trident leisters were used from canoes. Weirs and traps were seldom employed by the Lower Thompson. Angling was a technique of considerable importance for taking sturgeon, which were caught especially around Lytton, British Columbia, with a large wood and bone angle-hook on strong bark-fiber line (fig. 14), from a canoe or from shore. Small sturgeon ascended the Thompson River only as far as Spence's Bridge (Teit 1900).

The Upper Thompson made greater use of weirs and traps for salmon. Around the weirs the fish could be harpooned or speared as they milled about or else captured in slat boxes or cylindrical willow baskets set at lake outlets or water falls. The capturing method was also for taking trout. Fishing on lines with hook or gorge through ice holes was practiced by the Upper Thompson (fig. 15). Salmon oil was extracted and stored by all the peoples of the Fraser-Thompson district (Teit 1900:249–254; McIntyre 1914:472; Ray 1942:139; Perry et al. 1892:51ff.).

The Thompson Indians, according to Romanoff (1988: 157) usually had some dried salmon left by the time of the first runs of new fish in March. When the dried stores ran out, hunting was required. The Thompson River was not a particularly rich fishing ground, even for trout. The Lower Thompson, though also favored with abundant fish, spent much time hunting. Evidently hunting was considered a prestige male skill (Romanoff 1988).

Lillooet

The fishing of the Lillooet was like that of the Thompson, with a similar differentiation of intensive salmon and sturgeon fishing in the lower, muddier watercourses, and fishing for trout and whitefish in the clear upper lake and river waters (Carrothers 1941:121). Lillooet lacked the trident leister but had both single- and double-pronged harpoons.

The Lillooet usually caught more chinook than sockeye (Romanoff 1988:165). Sockeye fishing usually involved more concentrated fishing places than in the case of chinook fishing. The Lillooet depended on chinook and sockeye salmon, especially easily caught at Bridge River Falls, where Simon Fraser reported seeing 1,000 Indians encamped in 1808, which may have been an unusually productive season (Romanoff 1988).

Among the Lillooet, nearly all males were expected to fish for sockeye. Chinook salmon were caught from special rocks, owned by particular individuals. In terms of prestige, hunting ranked highest, then chinook fishing, and finally sockeye fishing (Romanoff 1988). The chinook were taken from platforms built out over special rocks, sockeye at falls, though both in dip

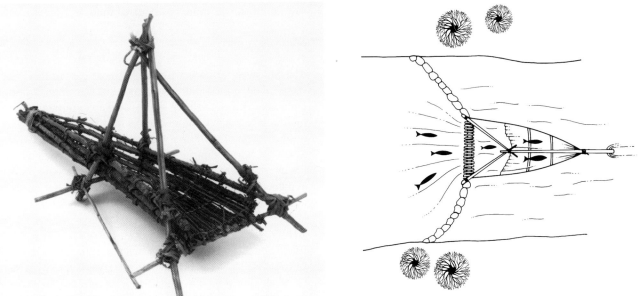

top, Idaho State Histl. Soc., Boise: 63–221.222; bottom left. Amer. Mus. of Nat. Hist., New York: 50.2/3871; bottom right, after Walker 1973: fig. 15.

Fig. 12. Open fish trap used at small falls or weirs in shallow streams to catch fish as they swam downstream over the falls or through the weir. top, Nez Perce fish trap with a stone V-shaped weir. Photograph by E. Jane Gay, Lapwai, Idaho, 1889–1892. bottom left, Model of Kootenai fish trap. Collected by C.E. Schaeffer, Tobacco Plains, Mont., 1935. bottom right, Plan view drawing of an open fish trap showing how fish are funneled into the trap. Length of bottom left, 49 cm.

nets (fig. 16). Sockeye dip nets varied according to the characteristics of the falls where they were used. Sockeye fishing usually involved several men taking turns at the task, rather than individual expertise by the owner of a certain rock. The abundance of fish attracted Indians from a wide area to these centers. The only weir fishing for the Lillooet was at a trout weir in Shuswap territory (Romanoff 1988:160). The sites for trout were at lakes, in spring and autumn.

The interior Lillooet, especially near the confluence of the Fraser and Thompson, lacked a suitable rapids in which to

Fig 13. Annie Johnson, Cayuse, processing salmon. Photographs by Dan Warren, 1962. Left, Drying the fish over a modern stove; center, grinding the fish flesh in a wooden mortar with pestle; right, Walla Walla wooden mortar and stone pestle use for pulverizing dried fish, berries, or roots. This mortar, in the Burke family for several generations, was probably manufactured in the early 19th century. Length 74 cm.

fish, and despite large volumes of migrating salmon, might undergo near starvation in some lean years (Romanoff 1988:156). To offset this risk, the Lillooet "buried" some dried fish in storage pits, in addition to keeping it in above-ground structures; in pits, it would keep as long as two years.

In very bad years, Lillooet fishermen might take as little as one fish a day in their dip nets. For the Thompson Indians proper, they estimated a 30 percent deficit for the two middle years of the four-year cycle. If these estimates are even approximately correct, the Lillooet, Shuswap, and Thompson inhabitants alternated their food economy dramatically in rich and in lean years with regard to salmon, making up for the deficits by greatly intensified hunting. The Lillooet lived through the winter mainly on dried salmon. Chinook were caught from riverside rocks in summer, while in autumn the chief catch was sockeye, taken in the Bridge River Rapids. The dry summers are a definite aid to the drying of salmon. Their chief winter-stored food was dried pulverized salmon (Hill-Tout 1905:126–218; Ray 1942). Drying sockeye was easier than drying chinook, which were bigger and fatter. Both dried chinook and sockeye were traded to other groups by the Lillooet. The biggest proportion of dried salmon for trade consisted of sockeye toward the end of the run.

In any case, planning for both required construction of a drying rack, in advance of the run if possible. Stored salmon allowed the Lillooet to winter in a permanent village. Despite the great dietary importance of salmon, the feasting centered on distributions of deer meat (Romanoff 1988:150). Dried fish was also distributed at some Lillooet feasts. Following the salmon season, hunting became

prominent in late autumn into November. Deer meat was a secondary food among the Fraser Lillooet; the staple was salmon. Fish was more easily dried than deer meat.

Shuswap

The Shuswap territory was for the most part in the Fraser Basin, though the small eastern portion was drained by the Columbia River. Salmon were available throughout the region, save in the Canim Lake district. The best fishing was in the section of the Fraser Canyon occupied by the Western Shuswap, where slip-ring dip nets were mainly used. On the upper courses of the river, various traps were employed in conjunction with weirs; some of these devices were for fish other than salmon—steelhead, trout, or whitefish. At other concentration points, the fish were speared or gaffed (Teit 1914:301; Ray 1942:111; Perry et al. 1892:51ff.). Often, scaffolding or catwalks were built to facilitate the removal of fish from such sites. Shuswap methods of lake fishing were quite elaborate. For trout and whitefish, long series of hooks were used, or gill nets, and bag nets were set at the ends of oblique weirs or wing dams. In winter, there was angling through ice holes, sometimes with short rods tipped with eyelets, similar to Eskimo fishing rods. Other elaborations of possibly northern origin were special chisels for cutting ice holes, and scoops to remove ice chips (fig. 15) (Teit 1909:526).

Fishing places were inherited. The Shuswap were allowed to use the same rocks; the dip nets were usually left at the rocks and falls. Both Lillooet and Shuswap experienced major fish deficits in the year before the sockeye maximum. It is estimated that this is a four-year salmon cycle.

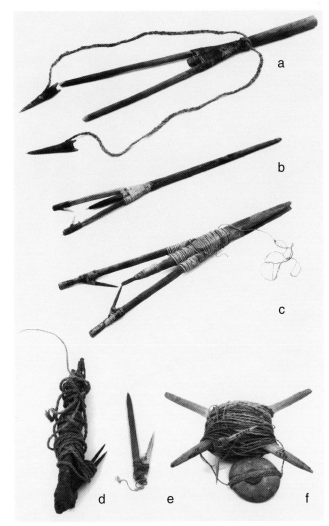

Amer. Mus. of Nat. Hist., New York: a, 16/1050; b, 16/1049; c, 16/9324; d, 16/5966; e, 16/1028; f, 16/4834.

Fig. 14. Fishing equipment of the Northern Plateau. a, Thompson spear head used for salmon. The detachable darts are made of buck horn, and the lashing of bark twine has been smeared over with pitch. Handles for spear heads of this type vary in length from 1.8 to 4.6 m. b, Thompson leister for spearing small fish with buck horn prongs affixed with bark lashing and pitch. Handles for this type of spear head were 1.4 to 1.8 m in length. a-b Collected by James A. Teit on the Thompson River, B.C., 1895. c, Shuswap leister head for spearing large fish. Collected by James A. Teit in Kamloops, B.C., 1903. d, Lillooet fishhooks with points of brass and copper, collected by James A. Teit in 1899. e, Thompson fishook made of rosewood and deer bone fastened with bark twine, collected by James A. Teit at Spences Bridge, B.C., 1895. f, Thompson reel with fishing line made of spatsan bark, a bone hook, and a stone sinker. Collected by James A. Teit from the Upper Thompson, 1898. Length of a, 56 cm; b and c to same scale. Length of d, 8 cm; e and f to same scale.

Changes After Contact

Early Eighteenth Century to 1855

The effects of European contact on the fishing of the Indians of the Plateau was indirect at first. European ships had visited the coast well before 1780, introducing the native peoples there to iron and steel tools, some of which found their way inland as replacements for stone cutting implements in preparation of fish. From the east, overland, the use of horses reached the Indians of the Plateau possibly as early as 1730. Although horses were not used in fishing as such, they proved to be very useful in transporting heavy basket loads of dried salmon in the trading orbit of the Columbia River tribes, from productive fishing centers such as Celilo Falls or Kettle Falls (Daugherty 1973:22).

The spread of firearms presumably increased the importance of hunting and may have slightly decreased dependence in some groups on a steady fish diet. Another effect of European contact was the spread of infectious diseases, especially smallpox and measles. Groups such as the Spokane may have lost 50 percent of their population in the smallpox epidemic of 1782 (Ruby and Brown 1970:29). The removal of so many fisherman, and especially, of women who prepared the fish for preservation, would have decreased the pressure on the natural fish resource (Ruby and Brown 1970:29). European contacts along the coast may have initiated more interaction between coastal Indians and the Plateau dwellers, because the coastal people then had new kinds of goods to trade, supplementing their traditional commodities such as dentalium and abalone shell. The spread inland of toggle-harpoons, leisters, and large nets (as indicated by finds of net-gauges), and coastal forms

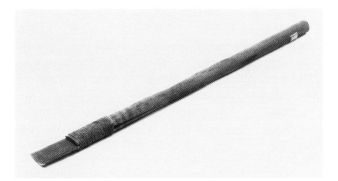

Amer. Mus. of Nat. Hist., New York: top, 16/7993; bottom, 16/9369.

Fig. 15. Thompson winter fishing implements. top, Ice breaker with steel head and wooden handle. Older ice breakers had heads of stone or elk antler. bottom, Ice scooper made of bark string and wood used for removing ice from fishing holes. Length of top, 3 cm; length of bottom, 35 cm.

of the club used to stun large salmon (Daugherty 1973:22) may antedate direct White penetration of the Plateau.

The first White commercial transaction involving Columbia River salmon occurred at the mouth of the river in 1792, when chinook were exchanged for common iron nails. Salmon were not so valuable as furs in the fur-trading era, but they were frequently welcome at White outposts in the Plateau. The Hudson's Bay Company found the Indians of the Plateau good customers for iron fishhooks, knives, and possibly strong twine for netting.

Pacific salmon ascend as far as the Lemhi, a tributary of the Salmon River in Idaho, where the fish were first seen by Lewis and Clark. The explorers noted more and more salmon and Indians engaged in fishing as they moved westward.

Large parts of the Plateau soon came to be well known to Whites engaged in beaver trapping and trade. The eventual reduction of beaver populations in some parts of the region may have affected fishing, both positively and negatively. Beaver dams create ponds and slack water, decreasing the rate of run-off, a disadvantage to salmon fry on their way to the ocean. In some areas, the work of beaver contributes to watershed stability (D. Cook 1940). One by-product of the economic importance of the beaver trade was that the river systems of the Plateau were explored and mapped in detail.

White settlement in the Plateau led in favorable areas to early commercialization, especially in the Lower Columbia and Lower Fraser. The Hudson's Bay post at Fort Vancouver, Washington, salted salmon for export in the 1830s, shipping some barrels of it to the Hawaiian Islands (Hutchinson 1950:286); a similar salmon business arose on the Lower Fraser during the 1840s, with the Hawaiian market its chief outlet. Salted salmon was to be no match for canned salmon.

Canning of Pacific salmon began on the Sacramento River in California in the 1860s but soon spread to the richer salmon fisheries of Oregon, Washington, and British Columbia. It was during this same period that the Indian populations of the Plateau were declining as a result of economic dislocation due to the concentration of remaining Indians on a few reservations in the United States; the spread of White agriculture and ranching, logging, mining; the proliferation of towns; and the still serious consequences of infectious diseases, as well as several military conflicts (Waldman 1985:maps 5.15 and 6.1).

The drop in Indian population was not evenly distributed in the Plateau, but it was perhaps significant enough to lead to a decline in the Indian fishing effort, not yet made up for by the growth of commercial fishing, and especially of salmon canning business, which started on the Columbia in 1866. If true, the Indian fishing decline might have misled those who made initial estimates of the total salmon resource of the Columbia Basin, and perhaps less so in the case of the Fraser River sockeye fishery.

Meanwhile, in addition to Europeans, the nonnative population in the Plateau was augmented by importations of

top, Royal B.C. Mus., Victoria: PN 6623; bottom, Amer. Mus. of Nat. Hist., New York: 16/1024.

Fig.16. Dip-netting. top, Lillooet man taking a large salmon from the Fraser River, near Lillooet, B.C. Photograph by John Pease Babcock, 1901–1910. bottom, Thompson dip net for catching salmon and large trout. The wooden handle and hoop are made of fir, and the netting and string are made of spatsan bark. Collected by James A. Teit at Spences Bridge, B.C., 1895. Length of bottom, 229 cm.

Canadian Indians—Ojibwa and Cree—to supply labor at the fur trading posts, and eventually by Chinese immigrants who worked at first on the railroads, and in gold mining, but came to be the principal employees for processing fish in the canneries.

Indigenous concern for the fisheries was still being shown by the Plateau Indians. In the late 1840s, Indians were encamped at Kettle Falls, spearing, dip-netting, and processing salmon. The Celilo Falls fishery was seemingly as busy and productive as ever, although Whites began taking salmon in gill nets on the Lower Columbia in 1853. For a time, horses were used to haul some very large nets on to the shore.

Growing White settlement and pressure to diminish conflicts over land led Gov. Isaac I. Stevens of Washington Territory on a treaty-making project, which has had reverberations into the last decade of the twentieth century. Stevens also was made Indian commissioner, and his work resulted in the establishment of a few large reservations, and to promises on the part of the government to respect traditional Indian fishing rights and access to customary sites for fishing and curing of salmon. The major councils that led to the "Stevens treaties" were held at Walla Walla (September 12, 1856) and Hell Gate, near Missoula, Montana, in 1855. The tribes involved included the Yakima, Flathead, Kootenai, Kalispel, Spokane, and Umatilla.

No such drastic relocation occurred in the Plateau territory now in British Columbia, where small reservation communities were recognized, usually in the same areas of traditional villages. Indians were, on the whole, confirmed more effectively in their traditional fishing rights in Canada.

Threat to the Fisheries Productivity, 1856–1900

Threats to the abundance of salmon and other fish led to the first closed fishing season in Washington Territory as early as 1877, and in Oregon in 1878. At this period, Indian fishing rights, although guaranteed by treaty or other agreements, were often disregarded by local government authorities.

The sturgeon fishery, never a very important item, peaked in the 1890s. Before the 1880s it had been left to the Indians, but a market in the eastern United States was eventually found, particularly for smoked sturgeon (and for caviar!).

The commercial salmon catch was enhanced with the introduction of giant fish wheels, first installed in 1879 (Holbrook 1956:248). The Indians continued to fish with dip nets and did not benefit from the fish wheels or gill net operations. The peak canned pack of Columbia salmon was reached in 1883—630,000 cases—representing 19,500,000 kilograms of fish, a figure not matched for that river until 1899, when ocean-caught salmon were included in the pack statistics. By 1900 there were 76 wheels working (fig. 4) some of which could catch 3,000 salmon a day. Even so, it is believed that their total catch never exceeded that of the White gill-netters farther downstream, operating out of Astoria.

Some modifications in the Columbia River systems were made to accommodate river steamship operation, probably only marginally impeding fish migration, as at The Dalles, and far inland as at Canal Flats (1889) where a short canal linked the Upper Columbia and the Kootenay.

The first serious legal case involving a Plateau Indian, a Yakima, occurred at Tumwater, near Olympia, west of the Plateau, in 1887. A White settler had fenced land, blocking Indian access to a traditional fishing site. The local courts were overruled by the federal court (at Tacoma), upholding the right of Indian access by treaty (Cohen 1986:54–55).

In 1894 the U.S. commissioner of fisheries warned that the Columbia salmon fishery was threatened by overfishing. The danger was seen at the time to come from excessive catches, and not the encroachment of river pollution from a variety of causes.

Twentieth Century—Fishing Rights Disputes

Commercial salmon production became more efficient through more central organization of the canning industry shortly after 1900. The Yakima brought a case in 1905 against the operator of one of the fish wheels on the Columbia, one Winans, licensed by the state of Washington, but installed at a traditional Indian fishing site. Indian fishing rights were upheld, although the court did not exempt Indians from enforcement of all fishing regulations.

The first United States–Canadian negotiation over Plateau fisheries dates from 1908, but continued United States objections led Canada to abandon the effort in 1914. Meanwhile, the river environment along the Fraser was very seriously disturbed starting in 1911–1912, when the Canadian Northern Railroad builders allowed large quantities of rubble to slide into a narrow gorge. This increased stream velocity, interfering with the upstream migration of sockeye salmon. A much more devastating slide occurred in 1914 at a tunnel site on the left bank of the canyon, blocking nearly half the channel. Construction of a wooden flume bypass for migrating fish did not solve the problem. The Fraser sockeye runs were being depleted at the same time by commercial trolling in the Gulf of Georgia and Puget Sound. Rock removal alleviated the Fraser Gorge situation, and in 1917 about four million salmon were caught upstream, one quarter of what it had been in 1913. An interstate river pact was negotiated by Washington and Oregon in 1918, ratified by the United States Congress. Fishing rights were part of the agenda. A Washington State court in 1916 had meanwhile rejected Indian claims of sovereignty in fishing cases brought by the Yakima.

A navigation canal with locks, completed at Celilo Falls in 1915, did not significantly diminish the traditional Indian dip-net fishery there. Soon thereafter, a positive factor was the construction of a paved highway along the Columbia, on the Oregon side, creating a roadside market in fresh-caught salmon with tourists. Indian fishing in off-reservation sites was again upheld in a United States court in 1919.

Continued dissension over Columbia River fishing led to an Oregon initiative proposal to ban all fixed fishing devices (including traps and wheels) on the Columbia, except for Indian uses, passed in 1926, but was overturned by the Oregon legislature in 1934. Fish wheels were outlawed in 1927 in Oregon in a separate action. In Washington, all traps, fish wheels, set-nets, and drag seines were banned in 1934, again excepting Indian traditional fisheries.

The major modification of the Columbia River system was to begin in 1931 with the completion of the first dam for hydroelectric power, at Rock Island, below Wenatchee, Washington. So far the damage to fishing seemed minimal. More important for United States Plateau Indian fishing was the passage of the Indian Reorganization Act of 1934, which led to improvement in the legal status of tribal governments, some of which soon adopted new fishing regulations

(Cohen 1986:62). A huge dam was begun in 1933, at Bonneville, just below the Columbia Cascades, which began to deliver power in 1938. Three fishways were included, along with a succession of pools, and fish counting stations. More than nine million salmon and steelhead were counted during the first decade of the dam's operation, providing for the first time a fairly accurate measure of what survived of the Columbia fish resource.

A Yakima Indian was arrested in 1939 for dip-netting salmon without a license in Washington. Though the original charge was dismissed, the U.S. Supreme Court ruled in 1942 that Indian fishing could be regulated for conservation purposes (Cohen 1986). Grand Coulee Dam construction led the Spokane, who lived upstream from it, to enact a fish and wildlife code in 1944 (Ruby and Brown 1970). Generally unknown to the public, both Indian and non-Indian at the time, a new threat arose to Columbia River fishing in the form of the Hanford Engineering Works, upstream from Richland, Washington, a unit of the newly established nuclear industry. After World War II, a nuclear power station was added to the plutonium processing plant. These installations, which became public, produced warm water effluent from cooling towers; the danger to consumers from possibly radioactive residue in the fish was not perceived as a serious problem.

On the Fraser River, the upstream migrating sockeye were still hampered by excessive water depths produced by channel narrowing; a new fishway system was devised in 1944–1945, with a further one at Bridge River Rapids. By the mid- and late twentieth century, specially owned fishing rocks were generally unclaimed, though still often referred to as having belonged to someone.

Hatcheries were built at Grand Coulee Dam to replenish the fish supply. In 1949 Washington State declared the Lower Columbia tributaries a fish sanctuary until stocks could be restored.

The early 1950s saw the emergence of further problems for Indian fishing in the United States, with the rising congressional support for reservation terminations. When the Klamath Reservation was terminated in 1954, the Indians there retained fishing rights on former reservation land. British Columbia Indians were still protected by regulations forbidding salmon fishing for non-Indians except in fresh water, such as the Gulf of Georgia.

The year 1956 saw the last First Salmon ceremony celebrated at Celilo Falls, which was about to be inundated by The Dalles Dam. This dam not only eliminated the famous Celilo Falls dip-net fishery but also led to rules permitting only Indians to fish between Bonneville Dam and McNary Dam. Non-Indian commercial Columbia River fishing was permitted only downstream from Bonneville (Zucker, Hummel, and Høgfoss 1983:169).

These complications led to widespread dissatisfaction on the part of Indian communities, commercial fishing groups, and sport fishing organizations, to say nothing of hydroelectric power consumers and agricultural interests, all of whom were affected by the possibility of further measures to conserve the fish resources of the Columbia Basin. A United States Senate resolution (not enacted) sought in 1962 to buy out Indian off-reservation fishing rights, or to declare Indians fully subject to state regulations off-reservation. In part this action failed because the total Indian fish catch apparently only amounted to about 5 percent of the total. This effort had arisen not in the Columbia Basin, in fact, but in the Puget Sound and Strait of Juan de Fuca areas of Washington State.

Indian opposition to the policies regarding their traditional fishing rights, as secured by treaty, led in the 1960s to several "fish-ins"—demonstrations in which groups of Indians fished in deliberate violation of local and state regulations at traditional sites. Outside organizations supporting the Indian position included the American Friends Service Committee and the American Civil Liberities Union. Adding to the conflict was the fact that United States federal agencies found themselves on opposite sides of the fishing controversy, notably the Department of Commerce and the Department of the Interior. The fish-ins were not entirely new; three Umatilla Indians had staged such a fish-in in 1958. The Stevens treaty rights, in respect to off-reservation fishing by Indians, were upheld again in 1963 (Cohen 1986). The Confederated Tribes of the Umatilla Reservation won a case involving off-reservation fishing rights in 1963, followed by another in 1977.

Despite all these difficulties, the United States-Canadian treaty of 1961 provided for more dams to be built on the Upper Columbia in Canada, three with navigation locks, but two with no fishways. In Montana, the Libby Dam on the Kootenay was completed, which formed a long narrow lake, Lake Koocanusa, altering another natural fish resource, though probably expanding its population of resident species. The Kootenai Indians strove to limit the damage to their traditional fishery at Kootenai Falls, where a dam project was undertaken by the Northern Lights Power Company.

Other dams were constructed on the Clark Fork, upstream from Lake Pend Oreille, and at Noxon Rapids, in Montana. Fishing disputes delayed construction of the Ice Harbor Dam for 11 years after its authorization in 1962 (Petersen 1991).

Conservationists were concerned not only with blocking the upstream spawning migrations, but also with the deleterious effects of dams and the reservoirs they create on downstream moving salmon and steelhead fry. Paradoxically, two contrary effects are destructive of small fish: in the foamy passage at the dam sites themselves, the water is supersaturated with atmospheric nitrogen, which produces a condition analogous to the "bends" in human divers. The slack, and warmer waters backed by the dams are not conducive to survival of fry or fingerlings, which are more easily preyed upon by resident fish predators such as the squawfish, and by fish-eating birds.

top left, Mont. State U., Mus. of the Rockies, Bozeman: 83.13.492; top right, U.S. Dept. of Interior, Bureau of Reclamation, Boise, Idaho; bottom left, Oreg. Histl. Soc., Portland: 77487; bottom right, Bureau of Ind. Affairs, SMC Cartographic Section, Concho, Okla.

Fig. 17. 20th-century responses to changing fish resources. top left, Staged photo at Kerr Dam, Polson, Mont., which gave the impression that Native Americans were supportive of the dam programs. The dams, in fact, have created havoc with the fish resources. left to right, Stmilx or Eneas Quequesah; Little Martin; Louis Hammer; Mose Michel; Snilyaqn; and Pete Beaverhead, all Pend d'Oreille. Photograph by C. Owen Smithers, Aug. 1938, when the dam was dedicated. top right, Yakima man net fishing from the Sunnyside Diversion Dam, on the Yakima River, Wash. He has set up a fishing platform on the dam just as his ancestors set up platforms on rocks above falls. Photograph by Glade Walker, 1976. bottom left, Distribution by federal government officials of spawned out tule salmon at the White Salmon River, Wash., hatchery to Yakima Indians. This fish hatchery was built in 1896 to supplement the run of the fall chinook salmon. By 1985 that run was so poor that rearing of this native stock was abandoned. In the 1990s efforts were solely to rear transplanted stock (Nelson and Bodle 1990). Photograph by Robert L. Hacker, 1960. bottom right, Incubation box site for fish stocking project, on the Umatilla Res., a Bureau of Indian Affairs project. Salmon runs in the Umatilla River had stopped as the result of dam building (Bureau of Indian Affairs. Branch of Land Operations 1966). In 1996 the Umatilla River fisheries restoration program had produced enough adult chinook salmon returning to permit a fishery. Photographed in 1966.

Both railroad and highway construction leads to a proliferation of culverts, frequently placed too high for upstream migrants to overcome. Agricultural development is also unfavorable to fish, from diversion of waters into irrigation systems, from silty runoff from plowed lands, and chemical herbicide and pesticide residues. Proposals to draw down water levels in the many reservoirs of the region in order to assist the downstream passage of young fish adversely affect both irrigation farmers and managers of hydroelectric facilities.

In the Kootenay Range of British Columbia extensive strip-mining of coal also had a damaging effect on fish resources. Only small areas of British Columbia were developed agriculturally, such as the Okanogon Valley. In British Columbia, accelerated exploitation of forests began in the 1940s, notably with pulp mills, in addition to the former small-scale timber sawmills. Paper pulp effluent is dangerously polluting to fish.

Indian off-reservation fishing rights were upheld in a Umatilla case in 1958. In 1969 a more far-reaching decision was handed down by Judge Robert C. Belloni in a Washington case involving the Yakima (Cohen 1986:120). Fishing zones were set up on the Columbia, permitting gill-netting from the river mouth up to Bonneville Dam, and another zone, from Bonneville up to the McNary Dam for only Indian fishing, in which set-nets could be used. Another case, arising in the Northwest Coast, but affecting the Plateau, was *United States* v. *State of Washington* (384 F. Supp. 312), decided in 1974. It held that Indians were permitted to catch up to 50 percent of the harvestable fish from their customary fishing sites. The state was allowed to regulate Indian off-reservation fishing only for conservation purposes (vol. 7:176–178).

These cases met with considerable non-Indian opposition, and even some Indians objected that the 50 percent provision limited them in ways contrary to the 1855–1856 Stevens treaties. A 1974 refinement related the allotment specifically to chinook salmon (Cohen 1986; Marsh and Johnson 1985). In a further attempt to settle these matters, a five-year plan was set up in 1977, setting the Indian allotment to 60 percent of the autumn chinook run, including ceremonial use of the salmon. The plan had envisaged runs similar to the salmon and steelhead of about the size of the 1975–1979 runs, but the catches had fallen further. In 1977 all commercial spring salmon was banned for both Indians and non-Indians. The State of Washington sought to appeal the ruling of 1979, which had also restricted the United States share of the pelagic salmon fishery out to the 200-mile international limit. The affected Plateau tribes—Nez Perce, Umatilla, Warm Springs, and Yakima—formed the Columbia River Inter-Tribal Fish Commission, with headquarters in Portland, Oregon. Meanwhile, a claim for damage to fisheries by the Warm Springs tribes was dismissed, and that of the Umatilla resulted in a compromise settlement. While this litigation was underway, still more dams were completed, such as the Dworshak, in 1973, which blocked both steelhead and salmon passage (Cohen 1986; Zucker, Hummel, and Høgfoss 1983). In British Columbia, the Fraser is less seriously beset with blockage and other problems created by dams.

The 1970s was a decade of intensive legislative and legal activity affecting Indian fishing interests in the Plateau. The United States Indian Claims Commission ended in 1978, establishing data bases for fiscal awards to tribal groups, including losses to their former fishing resource. Meanwhile, the Pacific salmon caught on the Columbia, which had reached 1,200,000 fish actually counted or carefully estimated in their upstream migration, had dropped by 1978 to 24,000 (Zucker, Hummel, and Høgfoss 1983:166).

Fig 18. Columbia River Indians protesting the 50th anniversary celebration of Bonneville Dam, Oreg. Photograph by Chuck Williams, 1987.

In both the United States and Canada, the growth of the sports fishery had entailed investment in accommodations and marinas, not only in "pristine" trout streams and lakes but also in the reservoirs created by dams. The non-Indian public monitored the fishing resources of the Plateau with as much zeal as the Indians for whom fishing remained an economic activity. Major commercial fishing became largely a matter of far downstream operations. The inland salmon and steelhead have been obtained by offshore fishing enterprises based in Asia.

The Belloni decision and *United States* v. *State of Washington* did not end the harassment of Indians fishing off-reservation. Organizations opposed to Indian fishing rights in Washington State initiated a measure based on the contention that special rights for Indians violated the civil rights of other citizens; this was passed in 1984. A Columbia River Fish Management Plan was approved in 1988, along with the much debated Pacific Salmon treaty between the United States and Canada in 1985.

Predation by the squawfish was blamed by 1988 for 30 percent of the kill of salmon and steelhead smolts per year in the Columbia-Snake Basin. Accordingly, the Bonneville Power Administration in its role as protector of aquatic life authorized in 1991 the unusual measure of a three-dollar payment per squawfish over 11 inches long to anyone presenting the fish at one of a series of checkpoints. Meanwhile, the same unwanted fish could be caught with long multihook set-lines by Indians in the Bonneville Reservoir itself, with a payment of four dollars per fish (*The Spokesman-Review* and *Spokane Daily Chronicle*, May 12, 1991:B10).

The problems regarding fishing facing Plateau Indians are seen in the perspective of one great river system studded with huge dams and reservoirs, none of them contributing to the survival of anything like the precontact fishery. Further, there are pollution threats, almost none of which arises from activities of the Indian population, on or off-reservation.

Columbia River Trade Network

THEODORE STERN

Native Trade Patterns

The drainage of the Columbia River, that great avenue of communication, from aboriginal times has been the locus of an exchange system that formed one of the expressions of Plateau culture. It drew in turn upon regions beyond that drainage; within the Plateau, it drew from proximate segments of the Thompson-Fraser river system to the north: on the west, it ranged both north and south along the Pacific coast within the cultural province of the Northwest Coast; in the south, it drew upon the fringe regions belonging to the provinces of California and the Great Basin: while on the east, particularly after the advent of the horse, it reached across the Rockies into the Missouri drainage of the Plains (fig. 1). Eventually it had continental extensions (Wood 1972).

Meriwether Lewis and William Clark described the system in 1805–1806. Five regionally distinct entities participated in the exchange, of which four were Indian. There were those dwelling in villages where the river cuts through the Cascades, who dominated portages around falls, and thus controlled passage; those on the lower river and coast, who traded with them; and those who came seasonally to trade—one from the western Plateau and one from the mountainous country east of them in the foothills of the Rockies (Lewis and Clark 1902, 2:148–154). The fifth group was coastal traders, by that time largely American, whose seasonal calls, in the words of the explorers, formed "the soul of this trade." They cannot have been responsible for initiating the exchange network: they had only breached into a traffic already in existence.

At the center lay those villages situated along the Columbia between Celilo Falls, just upriver from The Dalles, and the Cascades, a distance of roughly 50 miles. These were first the villages of the Western Columbia River Sahaptin bands and the Chinookan-speaking Wasco, Wishram, and White Salmon. Not only did these villages dominate passage along the river, strewn as it was with obstacles, but they were favored with local conditions within which they had developed the production of salmon pemmican, both for their own use and for trade. Yearly, they dried and pulverized salmon (fig. 2), packing it in baskets lined with salmon skin, holding some 100 pounds apiece. Stored in stacks of 12, the pemmican baskets provided the captains, and subsequent scholars, the basis for calculating the total amount

consigned each year to trade, which Griswold (1970:21) estimated to have been a million pounds. This delicacy, still recalled with pleasure by elderly Indians, was traded in several directions. It was highly sought on the lower river, for the fresh-run salmon caught there in abundance were too fat, and the climate too humid, to produce a satisfactory pemmican. Above The Dalles to the mouth of the Snake, where other conditions were favorable, the dearth of firewood, said the captains, made it often necessary to burn dried salmon for fuel; and not enough was left for pemmican (cf. Hunn 1990:184f.). Klamath, trading northward from their well-stocked lakes and marshes, found the pemmican so admirable an article that they seem to have copied it in their local whitefish (Gatschet 1890, 2:116). Finally, even Plains tribes seem to have traded for it.

This was but a single item in a complex exchange of products. In local environments there flourished plants and animals that entered into the stream of trade. Such, for example, was wapato root in the lower valley, berries in numerous localities, or on the coast sea fish, eulachon oil, and whale oil and blubber. There were shells from the coast and other raw materials elsewhere. Moreover, there were a myriad of local manufactures that were eagerly sought in trade. Thus, the trading network had the consequence not only of enlarging local diets and enriching local cultures but also of encouraging local specialization in production while, through the dissemination of foods, material, and products, it diminished the cultural distinctiveness of participant peoples (Wood 1972:164).

The Dalles, which lay at the juncture of the Northwest Coast and the Plateau, was the great center for inter- and intra-regional exchange. There, diverse peoples congregated from late springtime into late summer, bringing with them their trading goods (Lewis and Clark 1902, 2:150; cf. Murdock 1980:132). Lewis and Clark observed that those from the western Plateau brought skins, mats, silk grass, and bread made from couse root (Cutright 1989:410), which they exchanged for wapato, horses, beads, and items from the coastal traders, now retraded. Those from the foothills of the Rockies, such as the Nez Perces, brought beargrass, horses, camas root, as well as buffalo robes and other skins (fig. 3) that they had secured, either through their own hunting or in trade with the Flathead. These they exchanged for wapato, salmon pemmican, and trade beads.

From the south, in the nineteenth century, came Klamath who, together with the related Modoc, raided Shas-

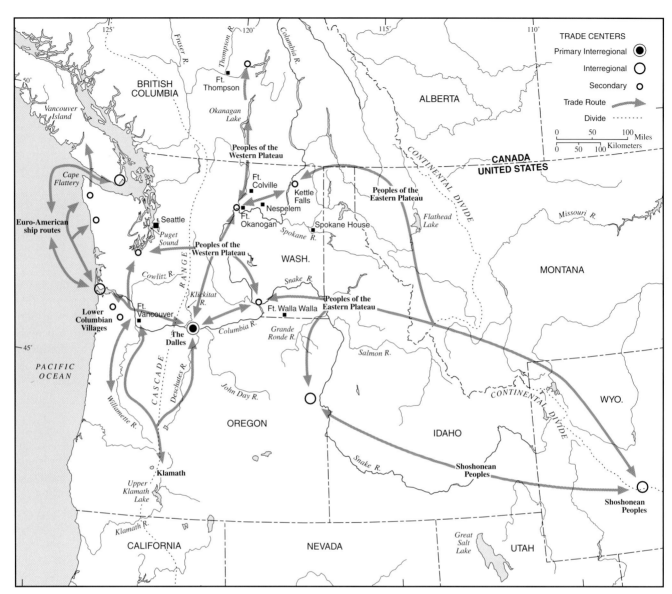

Fig. 1. The Columbia River trade network, with major trade centers and routes.

ta, as well as the Achumawi and Atsugewi of the Pit River drainage, carrying off women and children as slaves, together with loot such as bows and watertight baskets. Together with wokas (pond lily seeds) and other local products, Klamath traders brought these articles northward along the Klamath Trail to trade, either with the Chinookan tribes at the falls of the Willamette or, making their way to the Tygh Valley villages on the Deschutes, traded with the Wasco for horses, parfleches, and salmon pemmican. Slaves were a commodity much sought on the lower Columbia, as well as along the northern reaches of the Northwest Coast. To secure them, Lower Chinook, at the mouth of the Columbia, raided southward along the Oregon coast (Ray 1938:52).

The Lower Chinook sought to dominate all trade with the coastal traders. Their own trading parties made their way north to the Makah, at Cape Flattery, through whom they acquired both Makah products and items traded south from

the related Nootka, of southern Vancouver Island. Among products from this quarter were dentalium shells (fig. 4), slaves, and Nootka canoes.

Within the network, many of the participant peoples exchanged not only their own products but also surplus stocks of items received in trade from others. When a whale washed up on the Tillamook coast, south of the mouth of the Columbia, Clark met parties of Lower Chinook and Clatsop from the lower river trading with the Tillamook for whale oil and blubber. In turn, the Clatsop received a party of Cathlamet, from above them on the Columbia, who bartered wapato for at least part of their stock of the whale. "In this manner," wrote Lewis, "there is a trade continually carried on by the natives of the river each trading some article or other with their neighbors above and below them; and thus articles which are vended by the whites at the entrance of this river, find their way to the most distant nations inhabiting it's [sic] waters" (Thwaites 1904–1905, 3:329, 338). At

Fig. 2. Salmon pemmican. "Sugar" salmon, so called because of its texture, being dried on a tule mat to absorb the excess oil, by Blanche Tohet, Warm Springs Sahaptin. After being air-dried, the salmon flesh could be pulverized and packed into baskets to be traded. Photograph by David and Kathrine French, Warm Springs Res., Oreg., 1951.

The Dalles, the Klikitat, inveterate traders, sold their imbricated baskets ("Basketry," fig. 7, this vol.) to the Nez Perce for buffalo robes, in turn bartering the robes with the Wishram for salmon pemmican (Spier and Sapir 1930:227). The villagers at The Dalles readily bought goods for resale (Teit 1928:122).

Middlemen

Among trading peoples were those entrepreneurs who more largely served as middlemen, as carriers more profoundly immersed in the trade. Among the Cathlamet were traders who bore goods between the falls and the lower tribes, as well as to the trading ships at the mouth of the Columbia. For those vessels that traded into Puget Sound, the Chehalis (Southwestern Coast Salish), among others, served as intermediaries to the lower Columbia. The routinization of practice of such traders is illustrated by the account of one man, perhaps a Wishram, whom Lewis and Clark encountered at The Dalles as he was returning upriver. On trading trips to the lower river, he told them, his party left their canoes at the head of The Narrows, a difficult and dangerous passage, portaging their goods to the foot of that obstacle, where they rented or borrowed craft from the local villagers to continue their journey. On their return, they reversed the procedure (Lewis and Clark 1902, 2:249).

Within the Plateau, the Klikitat were notable middlemen after the advent of the horse, carrying not only to The Dalles but also overland to the tribes of the coast. The Sinkayuse and Wenatchee bands of Columbia Salish journeyed annually in large trading parties to The Dalles and

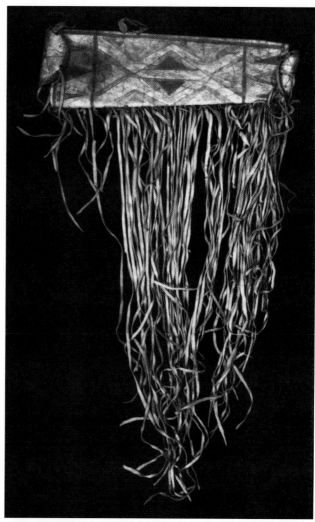

Smithsonian, Dept. of Anthr.: 204243.

Fig. 3. Quiver made of buffalo rawhide and painted in geometric designs, collected from a Wasco on the Warm Springs Res., Oreg. This item was either manufactured elsewhere and traded along the Columbia River or made locally from hide obtained through trade. Collected by E.T. Houtz before 1899. Length of case 58 cm.

below; the Wenatchee also went via mountain passes to trade with Coast Salish peoples. Major middlemen from the northeast were the Spokane, who carried from the fishery at Kettle Falls, a trading center of great importance in the northeast, and the Southern Okanogan, west of them, both of whom carried down to the mouth of the Snake. It was from the Spokane that the Walla Walla, in their largely treeless area, are said to have procured their dugout canoes (Gibbs 1855:403). Almost annually, the Spokane descended to The Dalles, while later they would make their way to Fort Vancouver. As for the Southern Okanogan, they and the Northern Okanagan separately traded eastward into Thompson country, where they exchanged Indian hemp and dressed deerskins for salmon pemmican and dentalia, as well as north into Kamloops, above the Thompson, to trade with the Shuswap (Teit 1930:250f.; Walters in Spier 1938:74).

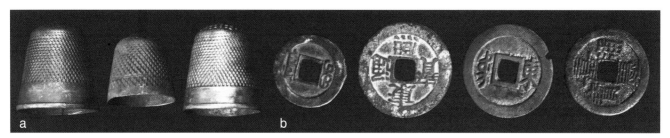

Fig. 4. Clothing and jewelry used to display wealth. top left, Wishram woman in clothing worn on special occasions between puberty and marriage, when display of wealth was customary. She wears items obtained through the Columbia River trade network, including dentalium and olivella shells on her headdress, clamshell wampum necklace, glass beads, Chinese coins in her headpiece, and a beaded buckskin dress and belt of the Plains type. Photograph by Edward S. Curtis, © 1910. top right, Klikitat wedding veil made of glass and metal beads, dentalium shells, thimbles, bells, and Chinese coins. The thimbles symbolize a bride's domestic skills and the coins represent her wealth. This veil was worn by Towlistia in the 1880s and was passed down through her family for generations. Length 56 cm. center right, Yakima hair ornaments made of dentalia, glass beads, and Chinese coins. Length 24 cm. Collected on the Yakima Res., Wash., 1932. a, Perforated brass thimbles used for decoration; b, Chinese coins minted between 1662 and 1820 used for ornamentation. Collected by Herbert W. Krieger, Sullivan's Island, Wash., 1934. Height of leftmost thimble, 2 cm; others to same scale.

Trade with the Plains grew greatly with the introduction of the horse into the Plateau, initially through the Northern Shoshone. Cayuse tradition has it that their first horses were secured by a joint Cayuse-Umatilla war party against the Shoshone in country below the Grande Ronde. When they spied the animals, the raiders hastily withdrew, amassed all the property they could, and returned to barter for a stallion and a mare (Donald McKay in McKay 1839–1892). The Nez Perce claim to have secured their first horses from the same people (Haines 1964:79), probably about 1730 (Haines 1938:map). In time, the herds of the eastern Plateau became the initial source for the Crow (Haines 1938:436). From the upper Columbia the Kootenai and Flathead had early extended upon the Northern Plains until, ravaged by smallpox, they were driven back by the Blackfoot. They still ventured there to hunt and to trade. With the development of the Shoshone trading rendezvous in southwestern Wyoming (vol. 11:504, 518), the Plateau tribes tended to travel there to trade. The Crow were important middlemen in Plains trade, ranging eastward to the farming villages of their relatives, the Hidatsa, and the neighboring Mandan on the upper Missouri River. In traffic with the Crow, Cayuse and Nez Perce exchanged roots, horses, and horn bows for Plains clothing, tepees, parfleches, women's saddles, and other items, including Euro-American trade items procured at the Hidatsa villages. The Crow were noted for their ornamented buffalo robes, and the Sioux for their feather bonnets (Teit 1930:114); here, then, as in the Plateau, there seem to have been items made expressly for the trade. While the Shoshone rendezvous is said to have been a common center for Plateau trading with Plains tribes, in the early 1800s a handful of Nez Perces, seeking to buy firearms and other weapons, made their way eastward to the upper Missouri, to the Hidatsa villages, arriving just after the exploring party of Meriwether Lewis and William Clark had departed toward the Rockies, and brought back six guns, the first obtained by their people (Thwaites 1904–1905, 5:22–23). Anastasio (1972:185) quite properly calls attention to the trading range of the Nez Perces, some members of whom traded regularly at The Dalles, while others were represented at the Shoshone rendezvous. Closer to home, they, the Cayuse, and allied tribes, such as the Walla Walla and Umatilla, met the Shoshone in the Grande Ronde, where in 1841 the Cayuse exchanged salmon and horses for roots, tepees, and elk and buffalo meat (Wilkes 1845, 4:394).

The introduction of the horse into the Plateau greatly affected the Columbia trade network. In the days when trade had been conducted by canoe or overland afoot, the articles carried had been of necessity light and of relatively high value, while trading parties had been small and their travels infrequent. With the advent of the horse, all this was changed: both the volume and variety of goods carried increased, being extended to include raw and semiprocessed

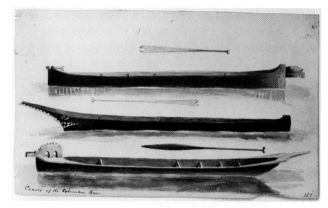

top, Stark Mus. of Art, Orange, Tex.:31.78/2, WWC 2; bottom, Oreg. Histl. Soc., Portland: 36828.
Fig. 5. Dugout canoes on the Columbia River. top, Drawing of canoes and paddles identified from top to bottom, as Klikitat or Cowlitz, Chinook, and Cowlitz. The types seem to be Lewis and Clark's sea-going "Kilamox" canoe used below The Dalles and as big as 50 ft. long; the large "Chinook" canoe with a raised prow, which ranged from 20–40 ft. long and was found up to the Klickitat River; and the medium sized canoe found up to The Dalles (Boyd 1996: 61, pl. II). Watercolor by Paul Kane, 1847. bottom, Man, possibly Wasco or Wishram, in a dugout canoe at The Dalles, Columbia River, Oreg. It appears to be a shovel-nose type canoe. Photograph by Benjamin Gifford, 1897.

materials. Routes became direct and led overland through open grasslands and prairies, such as the Klikitat Trail in southern Washington (Norton, Boyd, and Hunn 1983), while parties grew in size and their trading ventures in frequency (Teit 1930:150). Moreover, horses themselves became a new source of wealth and an important commodity in trade.

The major nodes within the network largely continued as before: within the Columbia Plateau, ranging from the north to south, they included the fishery at Kettle Falls on the upper Columbia, within the country of the Colville tribe; the mouth of the Okanogan River, downstream; the mouth of the Snake; and The Dalles. There were also lesser centers, where transient gatherings came together seasonally, numbering several thousands from several tribes, at which trading, among other activities, was transacted. In the vicinity of the mouth of the Snake, one such center lay within Yakima country, another within that of the Walla Walla. The routes by which tribesmen—in particular, middlemen—traveled between those trading centers provide a geographical delineation of that network.

Media of Exchange

A trade system is much facilitated by a medium of exchange in terms of which items may be evaluated. On the lower river, dentalium shells from the Nootka constituted such a medium (fig. 4), the horn-shaped shells being strung by uniform size in fathom lengths, with 40 shells of the largest grade to the string. Griswold (1970:33–35) asserts that beyond The Dalles dentalia were no longer a medium of exchange but were valued as articles of wealth and adornment, entering widely into Plateau and Plains costume. By contrast, other shells, such as olivella, clamshell, and abalone, were valued solely for adornment (fig. 6). Dentalia were highly valued and standarized in northwestern California, from where the Klamath received them (Spier 1930:216). In the early twentieth century, a Umatilla journeyed south with a party from the Columbia to the Klamath to trade for dentalia and clamshell wampum. No doubt this was then necessitated because of the near extinction of those peoples on the lower river who had been their former source (Stern 1953–1968).

Without standard weights and measures, it is doubtful that the dentalium fathom provided more than a general approximation of value. At the time the Pacific Fur Company founded Fort Astoria in 1811, it used as standard in pricing its trade goods either the dentalium fathom or the new medium, the beaver skin (Ross 1923:79f.). As the Hudson's Bay Company phrased that item, the Made Beaver was a prime adult pelt, taken in winter. In 1829, Samuel Black, manager of Fort Nez Perces, reported the Made Beaver was locally equivalent to the double fathom of dentalia. (Thus the value of trade goods had doubled the Astorian price.) The values he gave for items locally made, so-called "country produce," included that for a set of garments, which was valued at 10–40 skins, "according to the garnishd work about it" (S. Black 1829: query 101). In the Indian network articles must often have been evaluated individually, rather than simply as members of a category, with qualities such as rarity, workmanship, condition, and personal appeal being weighed in. That same variable value is seen also in horses, a major item of trade at Fort Nez Perces. As Simon McGillivray, Jr., manager a few years after Black, wrote, "a good moderate Horse will always cost ... the amount of 20 to 22 skins ... a Stout one will come up to 30 to 35/+ Ea: and a Known Racer is invaluable to an Indian. He will scarcly part with him, without an exhorbitant price" (McGillivray and Kittson 1831–1832: entry for March 30, 1831).

Communication and Trading

As a multitribal exchange system, the Columbia River network benefited from the use of contact languages and other means of intergroup communication. In addition to local bilingualism between neighboring tribes, regional trade language came into use in the lower drainage of the river and along the coast, Chinook Jargon. This was a pidgin language with simple grammar and a small vocabulary, derived from several languages (Hale 1890:18f.; Thomason 1983;

left. Okanogan County Histl. Soc., Okanogon, Wash.; Smithsonian, Dept. of Anthr.: center, 129677; right, 24110.

Fig. 6. Shell necklaces. left, Cecile Joe, Colville, wearing a cloth wing dress cut in traditional style and decorated with beads, bells, fur strips, and 2 photograph pins. Her necklace is made of strands of Anomia shells, with a shell of Trachycardium near the bottom and one of Saxidomus on the bottom. All 3 mollusks were traded from the Northwest Coast area. Photograph by Frank Matsura, 1903–1913. center, Spokane necklace made from olivella shells from the coast and traded inland along the Columbia River. Collected in Wash. before 1888. right, Necklace of clamshell wampum strung on a fiber cord. The value of these wampum at the time they were collected was 4 dollars. Collected by L.S. Dyar, Klamath Agency, Oreg., before 1876. Length of center, 26 cm; length of right, 60 cm.

vol. 17:127–130). Judging by the Indian component of its vocabulary, largely Chinookan, with some Nootka and Chehalis, it may have sprung up in the coastal trade with the north, possibly among middlemen in the trade (cf. Hymes 1980:417). The vocabulary includes large components drawn from English and French, leading some authorities to conclude that it originated only in postcontact days from White-Indian intercourse (Silverstein 1972). Hymes (1980) has summarized the evidence for concluding that it had aboriginal roots, while Samarin (1988) posits an earlier Nootka Jargon in the coastal fur trade. Hancock (1860), who traded with the Indians of the Washington coast in the 1850s, also saw the genesis of Chinook Jargon in the fur trade and thought it recent, since "very few of the old Indians learn much of it."

There were other contact languages available. Among the Kalapuyans, Chinook Jargon is said to have replaced an earlier sign language (Mallery 1881:312f.). At least among the Salishan peoples of the Plateau, a local sign language was in existence, later replaced by a form of Plains sign language, learned particularly through the Crow (Teit 1930:135f.; cf. 261, 273). Among Sahaptian speakers, the Crow form is attested. What is clear is that Chinook Jargon was late in coming to the Plateau. At Fort Nez Perces, the interpreter was a French Canadian, a veteran of the trade, with a Walla Walla wife, and there is evidence that he employed her language in discharging his office (McGillivray and Kittson 1831–1832). Among the Salishan peoples to the north, Chinook Jargon seems to have been introduced in the fur trade about 1840, by traders from the lower river. It did not replace signing and bilingualism in French as a medium of communication in the fur trade (Teit 1930:136, 261, 373).

The Social Context of Trading

That exchange was deeply embedded in social relationships is clear. Something of its complex nature may be seen in the career of Kammach, in the first half of the nineteenth century. Son of a headman of the Tualatin Kalapuyans, who dwelt above the falls of the Willamette, he was destined to become a headman himself. Trade such as his brought to the Kalapuya Klikitat baskets, woven goat-wool blankets from the Wenatchee and other Salishan tribes of the western Plateau, and buffalo robes from the Plains. Kammach had early aligned himself with the interests of Casino, the Multnomah Chinookan chief who dominated the Columbia around the mouth of the Willamette. When Kammach thereafter married the daughter of a Chinookan headman, of either Clackamas or Wishram-Wasco affiliation, his father paid a bride price of 20 slaves and 10 guns to her family. Annually thereafter, Kammach visited friends—in all likelihood, trading partners—among the Luckiamute and Mary's River bands of Kalapuyans, as well as the Alsea on the coast, in tours that might last six months. He took them horses and dentalia, together with guns, blankets, coats,

tobacco, and gunpowder. From them he received slaves, beaver and otter pelts, and buckskins, all of which he handed over to his father-in-law. Perhaps they were a supplement to the bride price, but surely something more was involved: for his father-in-law was probably the source of his trading goods, and in all likelihood traded the pelts and deerskins at Fort Vancouver, while trading the slaves within the native network (Gatschet, Frachtenberg, and Jacobs 1945:160–163).

The social dimensions of trading can develop at different levels (Sahlins 1965). Exchange among kinsmen and friends is likely to be characterized by "generalized reciprocity." Thus among the Southern Okanogan, friends were said to borrow each others' horses or other property freely, though considerably leaving the best items for the owner (Mandelbaum in Cline et al. 1938:126). Among more distant tribesmen, and with friendly Plateau neighbors, exchange might be expected to follow the lines of "balanced reciprocity," with a fair, but somewhat impersonal, calculation of values. At a greater degree of removal, in dealing with peoples with whom one does not marry, but instead may wage intermittent warfare, trading relations are likely to become volatile, to say the least, at times taking on the character of trickery, bluff, and force, which Sahlins denominates "negative reciprocity." For where goods that are traded may alternatively be seized by coercion or as loot, exchange may take on a myriad of colorations. Such was the Cayuse traffic with the Northern Shoshone (S. Black to John McLoughlin, July 25, 1826).

So frequently did Plateau tribes, or segments thereof, participate together in various activities that Anastasio (1972:185) has characterized the entire congeries as a social entity, unified by consensus and reciprocal interaction. By way of example, Cayuse bands associated most intimately with those of the lower Nez Perces, with whom they had intermarried and whose language had become their public tongue, as well as with the equestrian elements of the Walla Walla and Umatilla. Combined parties from among those peoples sometimes camped together at Cayuse fishing stations in the Grande Ronde or in Nez Perce country on the Wallowa River. From among them, joint war parties went forth against the Northern Shoshone to the south; and joint parties formed part of the large entourages, which included Flathead and other Salishan tribes, that crossed the Rockies, "going to buffalo" in the upper Yellowstone. Locally, the Cayuse, Nez Perce, and others joined with the Yakima in their country in the springtime, and with the Walla Walla in their country in late summer. Aside from engaging, when seasonally appropriate, in fishing or root digging, they celebrated together the thanksgiving ceremonies for first fruits, discussed political concerns and gossiped, renewed friendships, and courted; as well, they traded, raced horses, and gambled. Such was the permeability of ethnic boundaries that villages on the border of adjacent amicable groups often had a composite population drawn from both (Ray 1936). Notwithstanding such fusing at the boundaries, the retention of distinctive dialects and characteristic local cultural traditions testify to the persistence of a sense of ethnic identity.

Within the context of such relationships, exchange might well take place at the local level, when one individual had a surplus, and another a need for, an item in common use. As Teit (1930:255) instances of the Northern Okanagan, trading was commonplace between families within the same band, or comrades, or neighbors. Women bartered for staple articles such as Indian hemp, twined or in its raw state, and for dressed deerskins. "All commodities," he observes, "could be bought for them." Among the Flathead, men "swapped" with each other, women with women, the women in foods and feminine garments. The verb for 'trading' implies "coaxing, as if one were being kind, respectful, and suave towards the other party of the trade with intent of drawing him out" (Turney-High 1937:136).

Relations between the Flathead and Nez Perce are instructive. Flatheads valued the watertight bags and tasty roots of the Nez Perce, who in turn found superior the dried meat and dressed deerskins produced by the Flathead. When the Nez Perce came visiting, they were warmly received; but if the parties were not well acquainted they haggled over the exchange. Flathead men and women sat outside their lodges with meat and buckskin wares displayed, and Nez Perce visitors with baskets and bowls of roots would stroll about, then set to bargaining. If the two were long-time friends, they became in essence trading partners. The visitor entered the Flathead's lodge and placed his goods on the floor as a gift; upon his departure, his partner made his return prestation (Turney-High 1937:136–138). Among the Southern Okanogan, men and women had particular friends, 'partners', of the same sex, with whom they observed a gift exchange, for example, of foods or moccasins. Often they had partners in neighboring tribes, and would help each other, particularly if a partner had bankrupted himself by gambling. "Friends seldom buy from each other while visiting. If a host sees that his guest is in need of moccasins, clothes, etc., he would try to find some to present when the latter leaves. Begging was some to considered contemptible, however. A guest presented with moccasins, for example, would feel that he owed his host a present in return, but the donor would not think so." Thus, Southern Okanogan and Wenatchee men who agreed to be partners would thereafter exchange gifts and hospitality. "Each would insist on the worthlessness of the things he was giving. They all tried to return more than they were giving" (Mandelbaum in Cline et al. 1938:126).

The trading partnership is a frequent institution between two peoples. In the early days of the Umatilla Reservation, such a connection was formed between one Cayuse cattleman and a Umatilla fisherman, who periodically, when a beef had been slaughtered or the salmon were running, would bring each other gifts of flesh. The two men called each other 'Brother' throughout their lifetime; and after death of the Cayuse his children continued to address the

Umatilla as 'Uncle.' The bond was sometimes strengthened by marriage: indeed in giving the Nez Perce term by which the parents of a couple referred to each other, one person glossed it as 'my trading partner' (Stern 1953–1968).

It is in a gift exchange between nominal kinswomen of a bride and groom that what is formally termed "trading" exists in the 1990s on reservations within the Plateau. It is marked by an exchange of feasts between the two parties, each member of which is paired for the trade with a member of the opposite party. While pots, chinaware, and flatware are also involved, the prinicpal articles traded are symbolic of the roles of groom and bride. Typically, a woman on the groom's side gives her trading partner a parfleche holding a blanket, shawl, dress materials, and perhaps moccasins and other items, reflecting the man's ability to provide. At the return feast, her trading partner may return cornhusk bags of dried roots (fig. 7), a beaded buckskin dress, and strings of shell beads, betokening the bride's industry and skill. One Umatilla woman who had recently traded on the groom's side expressed satisfaction that the "bride's bundle" she had presented her partner had been so well appreciated that the groom had made an even more generous return. There may be repeated exchanges, and in the 1990s trading may be extended to celebrate the birth of the first child, and even of each successive offspring (Stern 1953–1968).

Haggling generally occurred between parties who were not on close personal terms. Time thus spent would often seem to have been enjoyed in and of itself. Lewis and Clark (1902, 1:148f.) wrote of the Chinookans, "They begin by asking double or treble the value of their merchandise, and

Fig. 7. A wedding trade. Marriages were validated by a series of exchanges of valued goods and products between the families of the spouses. This second "wedding trade" shows the relatives of a Yakima woman who was marrying a Warm Springs man. Gifts include fresh and canned food and cornhusk bags of roots. These items are symbolic of the women's subsistence role. Photograph by David and Kathrine French, Hehe Butte, Warm Springs Res., Oreg. 1951.

lower the demand in proportion to the ardor or experience in trade of the purchaser; and if he expresses any anxiety, the smallest article, perhaps a handful of roots, will furnish a whole morning's negotiations." Haines (1964:80) thus describes the horse trading between Nez Perces and Spokane near the mouth of the Little Spokane River:

> The Nez Percé lined up on one side, each man holding the lead rope of his 'trading' horse. Each Spokane came forward and placed his pile of trade goods in front of the horse he liked. If the Nez Percé was satisfied, he handed over the lead rope and took the goods. If not, he might try for an extra article, or he might lead his horse to some other pile which interested him. It might take all of a pleasant summer day to trade forty horses, but this seemed to worry nobody.

The role of women in trading should not be understated. Among the Lower Chinook in 1824–1825, the discerning eye of the Hudson's Bay Company's George Simpson (1931:98) noticed a social practice. "[I]n order to strengthen their commercial relations," he wrote, "men of consequence or extensive traders have sometimes as many as half a Doz Wives selected from among the best Families of the Neighbouring tribes and each of those is entrusted with a small Outfit [of goods] and sent on trading excursions to Her Friends & relatives and this is her constant employment." Kammach, the Kalapuyan married to the daughter of a high-born Chinookan, may well have played out a variant of this arrangement.

Among the Southern Okanogan, when men visited their trading partners, they often journeyed in large groups, the women, so it was said, going along to carry burdens and care for the food. In fact, much of the goods traded was the property of the women, who carried on their trading while the men gambled with their hosts (Spier 1938:126).

The understated role of women may in part account for a certain distortion in perspective concerning the trading at The Dalles. The fur trader Alexander Ross was struck by the turbulence of the gatherings at that spot, where some hundred Wayampam in their village at Celilo Falls were virtually swamped during the spring salmon run by the descent of 3,000 members of diverse Plateau tribes—many of them probably in some way related to Wayampam or linked by trading partnerships—there for the salmon, the good times, and the trade. "Now all these articles," declares Ross (1923:127f.), "generally change hands through gambling, which alone draws so many vagabonds together at this place because they are always sure to live well here . . . the long narrows, therefore, is the great emporium or mart of the Columbia, and the general theatre of gambling and roguery." Murdock (1980:132) provides another piece of the picture, explaining that "the visitors," doubtless their womenfolk, "went from house to house, bartering with the local women."

Yet, after the introduction of European goods—in particular, weapons—the stretch from the Cascades to The Dalles often became characterized by negative reciprocity, as the villages at the portages sought to prevent those commodities from passing upriver. "Look at all these bales of goods going to our enemies," Ross (1924:119) quotes a villager as saying. Alexander Henry, of the North West Company, remarked that the Chinookans at the Cascades sought to acquire firearms to use against their foes in the Plateau, and they wanted revenge upon those traders who had gone above and traded weapons to their enemies (Coues 1897:1409–1410). It is evident that animosities of long standing had been exacerbated by these developments.

On their part, the Nez Perce and Cayuse, among others of the Plateau, resented the throttlehold exercised by the villages of the portages for withholding those arms. As David Thompson was told in 1811 by a Cayuse or Walla Walla chief, his people were feeling pressure in the south from the "Straw Tent" Snakes (Northern Paiute or Bannock?) (Thompson 1962:352), and they wanted weapons to withstand them and drive them back. Once they had acquired firearms, the Nez Perce and Cayuse sought to to open up the constriction of trade from the Cascades to The Dalles. In 1814 they went to war on "the tribes at the Falls, killing a great many, and carried off a number of slaves, which has caused the natives to abandon their villages and fly to the woods in a panic" (Coues 1897, 2:853, 856, 897). A joint war party went further, to Casino's village, probably on the Kalama River (Work 1909:304).

Missionaries at The Dalles recorded winter visits by Cayuse, Nez Perce, and Walla Walla, and portrayed them as domineering over the local tribes. In purchasing salmon, the visitors "buy at their own price, compelling them to sell even their own stock of provisions, so as to have little to subsist on themselves" (Lee and Frost 1844:176–177; Brown 1966:269). They make no reference to intermarriage or trading partnerships, such as were maintained with Sahaptin-speaking Wayampam.

Trading on the Plains was also often characterized by negative reciprocity, for many Plains tribes resented the intrusion of Plateau tribes upon buffalo grounds they deemed their own. Griswold (1970:67f.) says that in such trading Plains ceremonialism invested the proceedings with a greater degree of formality and control than within the Plateau. The Blackfoot, who had driven back the Kootenai and Flathead on the Northern Plains, on occasion traded with them, and with allied tribes. With the Crow, at the Shoshone rendezvous, the trading partnership prevailed. Recalled one man of Palouse–Nez Perce ancestry, when the Plateau party arrived, "the Crow chief would indicate to us the place where our people were to pitch their separate camp circle. Each man had a trading partner who put by goods to trade" against the time they came together (Stern 1953–1968). When the Coeur d'Alene and others encountered erstwhile foes on the prairies, leaders of the two sides might smoke together, then announce a trading truce for a set period. During that time, then, members of the two parties danced, gambled, and traded together. Often, less than a day after the groups had once more separated, members on either side might already be engaged in trying to cut off stragglers or run off horses from their opposites (Teit 1930:112).

The ambivalence of negative reciprocity also character-izes the activities of some of those carriers, or middlemen, whose course necessarily took them through the territory of alien peoples. Klamath traders, journeying northward down the Willamette Valley toward the Tualatin and Clackamas country with goods to trade, pounced upon Kalapuyan vil-lages along the way for booty and slaves (Mackey 1974:29f.). The Spokane, whose parties were middlemen down the Columbia to The Dalles, raided there as well, and warred with the Yakima, who termed them "robbers" (Teit 1930:360). It is no wonder their trading parties were said to have been heavily armed. In similar manner, the Klikitat, having gained dominance over Western Oregon tribes, combined the roles of mobile traders and opportunistic raiders (Clarke 1905, 1:313; Hodge 1907–1910, 1:713).

Trade with the Fur Companies

The Columbia River trade network coexisted with, and interacted with, a developing Euro-American trade. The coastal traders at first merely supplemented the goods of the indigenous network with their novel and desirable articles and their demand upon a narrow segment of native prod-ucts. They soon intervened as middlemen, as Spanish ships imported abalone shell from Monterey Bay (Heizer 1940, cited by Griswold 1970:14). When the lower Columbia and the coast had been largely depleted of sea otter, American traders took to buying elkskin armor from the Lower Chi-nook for resale to the Nootka, Haida, and others to the north; and they also took up the trade in eulachon oil and slaves (Ruby and Brown 1976:61f., 115f.). From the Noot-ka, they bought dentalium shells, partially supplanting native carriers.

At the time of Lewis and Clark, coastal traders seem to have mounted a challenge to dentalium as a medium of exchange. The captains found on the lower river that blue or white beads from the China trade were the most highly sought commodity, "which are strung on strands by the yard or the length of both arms"—that is, treated like dentalium. "Of these, blue beads, which are called tia commashuck, or chief beads, hold the first rank in their ideas of relative value; the most inferior kind are esteemed beyond the finest wampum. . . . These beads are . . . at once beautiful orna-ments for the person and the greatest circulating medium of trade with all the nations on the Columbia" (Lewis and Clark 1902, 2:152). Although trade beads continued to be highly valued, they failed in the end to displace dentalium as a medium of exchange. Indeed, the fur companies con-tinued to deal in dentalia, as they did in other native prod-ucts.

When fur companies established themselves on land, they frequently sought sites close to native trading centers: thus for example, Spokane House, Fort Okanogan, Fort Nez Perces/Walla Walla, Fort Thompson/Kamloops, and Fort Colville. Tribes often welcomed the establishment of posts in

Okanogan County Histl. Soc., Okanogan, Wash.
Fig. 8. Bill Friedlander, Sinkayuse, with furs. Photographed possibly at Nespelem, Wash., about 1912.

their vicinity and when company considerations prompted the closing of "their" post, vigorously resisted the move.

Such companies were mercantilistic, rationalized in per-spective, and hierarchical in organization. Their trading posts were small and dispersed, fortified, and dependent upon watercraft or the horse for transportation. Fort Nez Perces, an interior post on the east bank of the Columbia below the mouth of the Snake, traded for both furs and hors-es, drawing the horses principally from the Cayuse and Nez Perce tribes. In a service area extending westward from the Nez Perce to The Dalles, Samuel Black in 1829 estimated a fighting strength of some 1,100 warriors (Black 1829:query 25; see "Demographic History Until 1990," fig. 2, this vol.); yet two years earlier he had just seven men to man his post. Forced by economic necessity to operate with so small a staff, the Company required great tact, diplomacy, and firm-ness to maintain a local order among independent tribes.

Moreover, as had its local predecessor and rival, the North West Company, with which it had amalgamated in 1821, the Hudson's Bay Company sought to trade beyond its district with the Northern Shoshone and Northern Paiute, with which the fort tribes were engaged in intermittent hos-tilities. The leading tribes of the district, the Cayuse and Nez Perce, from the outset had each split over engaging in such trade. Their leaders had initially welcomed David Thomp-son's proposal in 1811 to build a post in their country because of the need for weapons to drive the "Straw Tent" band of Northern Paiutes out of the southern part of their country (Thompson 1962:350–352). Donald McKenzie, who had built Fort Nez Perces, promptly encouraged the development of a trading peace with the Northern Shoshone, for he was impressed with the low price for which furs could be obtained by trading directly with them. Leaders of a Cayuse faction, led probably by Wilewmutkin and his relative, Alokwat, set forth in person to conclude their own peace. They seem already to have been known to the Northern Shoshone (Wilkes 1845, 4:394–395), and, as middlemen, their markup had added to the relatively high prices of the furs they brought back. In addition, with beaver traps purchased from the Company, they had trapped beaver themselves. Meanwhile, a rival faction, under Hiyumtipin (Umtippe) and his brothers, continued their traditional hostility to the "Snakes." As one trader observed in 1831 (McGillivray and Kittson 1831–1832), through the traffic in firearms by the Cayuse middlemen, the "Snakes" were rapidly overcoming the advantage in firearms that the Cayuse enjoyed. Both Cayuse factions were united in seeking to block Northern Shoshone from trading directly with the fort.

For years, the Company also trapped directly in Shoshonean territory by means of the Snake Country brigade, operating out of Fort Nez Perces in rivalry with American trappers expanding their activities westward across the Rockies. In time, this led to posts in the valley of the upper Snake River, Forts Boise and Hall, which by 1837 were both owned by the Company. Thereafter, the Company organized them into a separate Snake District, within which the Company traded directly with the Shoshone. Thus, after somewhat less than two decades of activity, the role of Indian middleman at Fort Nez Perces was largely eliminated.

In addition to serving as middlemen, a few Indians traveled with the Snake Country brigade as freemen, receiving equipment on credit against the pelts they would bring in. A few tribal members simply rode with the brigade for adventure.

Matters stood differently as concerned the local Indians known as Home Guard Indians, a small band of Walla Wallas resident on the Little Walla Walla River, near the fort. In 1831–1832, when Simon McGillivray, Jr., was manager of the post, three of his nine men had wives from this band, who dwelt with their husbands and children in the fort. Their brothers and fathers, as well as other members of the band, were employed as horseherds, messengers, and occasional laborers in fort activities. On New Year's Day, the Home Guard, alone among the Indians served by the post, gathered before its gates, where McGillivray, through their headmen, presented them with a gift of tobacco, salmon pemmican, and dried salmon.

Post society was dominated by British sentiments of class and race. Officers—chief traders and clerks—were usually of English or Scottish origin, the men of French-Canadian, Métis, Indian, or Hawaiian descent. Regulations enforced sumptuary distinctions: thus, officers were not to eat with the men. McGillivray was himself a Métis, brought up in the officers' culture, a domineering and aggressive man, who thrashed his Home Guard horseherds on occcasion and, when one defied him, shot and wounded him. That the Home Guard Indians placed themselves under the orders of these foreigners seems to have awakened the contempt of their tribal brethren.

For the women married to men of the post, their status was complicated. They were at once Indian and of the fort. As Indians, they could own horses and slaves, which their husbands could not. As part of the families of the post, they received rations, and McGillivray could send them out to help their husbands plant potatoes or perform other routine chores.

Between the Indians of the district and the traders of the post, Samuel Black detected an underlying animosity. Having delineated the character of the Indians in generally favorable terms, Black (1829:query 66) described Indians as aggressive traders, *"With Traders Whites and even amongst themselves the Demon of Avarice Reignes, Hectoring Domineering pillaging Thieving & all Kinds of Tricks to draw property from the Whites."*

Here, after all, was a post planted with Indian permission on tribal soil, using local resources, with staff even married to tribal women, yet from the Indian perspective stingy with the wealth of goods in which they dealt. From the first, the young men had badgered Alexander Ross (1924:221f.) for such contravention of Indian norms. When the expectation is of a generalized reciprocity, the relatively balanced and impersonal behavior of the Company took on negative coloring. On several occasions, Hiyumtipin mounted plots to seize the post, and Black himself was involved in a fight with that Cayuse chief in the Indian store (McGillivray and Kittson 1831–1832). In the end, identified too closely with the Americans who had forced an unpopular treaty of cession upon the tribes, the fort was finally sacked by Piupiumaksmaks, son of the Walla Walla leader who had in the beginning so welcomed its construction.

Considering the wealth of social values in which Columbia River trading had been imbued, it is no wonder that the fur trade did not supplant it.

Yet the Hudson's Bay Company sought to accommodate its operations to the local scene. McGillivray waited patiently until, having performed the ritual welcoming of the spring salmon, the Walla Walla salmon chief thereafter brought him what might be termed the first secular salmon of the year, thus opening the season for that fish. Judging by McGillivray's journal, there were two main gatherings at the fort for trade, in late March and in November, with the sporadic visits between, the winter months being relatively quiet. It is probable that the March gathering coincided with a thanksgiving feast, perhaps a root feast, while the gathering for the "clothing of the chiefs" took place at the time of a "grand feast and dance," a ceremony that may have celebrated the end of fall hunting and the return to winter quarters.

The clothing of chiefs merely recognized leaders already chosen by their tribesmen. A local successor to those ceremonies initiated at York Factory, on Hudson's Bay, for the "captains" of the Indian flotilla of canoes bringing down the take of furs from the interior (A.J. Ray and Freeman 1978:53–75), this ceremony stabilized relationships with client chiefs and encouraged them to zeal in gathering peltries. In McGillivray's time, with the death of the younger Wilewmutkin the Cayuse lost the leader of that faction that had so long favored trading with the "Snakes," and his successor by tribal custom was that very Hiyumtipin who had so long opposed those things. McGillivray, though disapproving, did not contest the choice.

In the ceremony of "clothing the chiefs," each tribe approached the fort, sending ahead a messenger to apprise the trader of their arrival. The trader sent back a welcome, along with a gift of tobacco for the chief. Approaching the fort, the Indians saluted it with a volley from their guns, answered by the discharge of a cannon, then pitched camp on the grounds nearby. When they had dressed in their best, they made their way to the Indian hall, leaving their weapons behind. There the trader welcomed them and smoked with their chief, after which he gave him tobacco to be distributed within the tribe. Later, the principal chiefs withdrew with the trader to his sitting room, where they discussed current events over pipes and tea laced with rum.

The clothing of chiefs itself took place before the Indian feast. Assembled in the square of the fort, the chiefs were each clothed in a costume usually including a semimilitary jacket or capote and a beaver hat or other headgear adorned with ribbons and feathers. Headmen were acknowledged with lesser gifts. As the chiefs marched out of the fort to their people, two cannons were fired in salute.

The Indians were thereafter preoccupied with their own ceremony. Although the trader was ordinarily a guest at the last day of the ritual dance, McGillivray reported that he was not so honored. Thereafter, each chief brought in a horse to the "yard" of the fort as a gift to the trader. Ostensibly, it may have been deemed a return for the clothing, drawing upon the convention of the trading partnership; but to ensure future goodwill, the trader set out a bundle of trade goods equal to the value of the steed. When one Cayuse chief, a brother of Hiyumtipin, spurned the goods as inadequate, McGillivray sent back his horse. Relenting, the chief returned his animal to the yard, and the matter was closed. (The goods were, of course, Company property, and the horses likewise: private trading by Company personnel was forbidden.)

It was only after these formalities had ended that regular trading opened, horses being purchased in the yard and peltries and other goods in the Indian store. Soon thereafter, about two weeks after they had arrived, the tribes individually broke camp and were on their way.

In general, Company trading, with its set prices for its stock in trade, had room for bargaining only on the peltries and other "country produce" the Indians brought in for sale. Some trade items, such as guns, were supposed to be sold only for a horse, while there were minor articles, such as gunflints and vermillion, that were added as a gift at the end of a sale. When a Walla Walla tried to trade a dried salmon for a cotton shirt, McGillivray threw his fish out of the store. "They have no sense of shame," he wrote indignantly, "for they know our Tariff very well, but will always try to prize their Salmon high" (McGillivray and Kittson 1831–1832). The nicety of Company rules governing trade articles must have been difficult for the Indians to appreciate.

From the beginning, Plateau tribes had shown a desire to play off competing companies against one another. When American fur traders, and later American missionaries, entered the scene, Cayuses and Nez Perces greeted them as potential competitors to the Hudson's Bay Company; and upon the appearance of emigrant caravans, they bartered freely with them (Minto 1901:224–229). The tribes at The Dalles, as well as the Kalapuyans, were always in some measure hostile to the White traders, who had eliminated their middleman role (Teit 1928:122). By 1850, when the English traveler, Henry J. Coke (1852:294), sought to buy a horse from a Cayuse, and held out some gold to tempt him, the Indian flourished his own bag of five-dollar gold pieces and proclaimed that, " 'The Kayuses were very rich, and wanted nothing. They had plenty of cattle, plenty of corn, plenty of potatoes. When they wanted money, or cloth, or blankets, or paint, they bartered their horses for those at [Fort] Wallah-Wallah or [the American settlements in the] Willamette.' " Elsewhere, and for years to come, wherever Indian peoples gathered together, they would continue to trade in the traditional manner.

Contributors

This list gives the academic affiliations of authors at the time this volume went to press. The dates following the entries indicate when each manuscript was (1) first received in the General Editor's office; (2) accepted by the General Editor's office; and (3) sent to the author (or, if deceased, a substitute) for final approval after revisions and editorial work.

ACKERMAN, LILLIAN A., Department of Anthropology, Washington State University, Pullman. Kinship, Family, and Gender Roles: 6/3/91; 6/11/96; 2/28/97.

AMES, KENNETH M., Department of Anthropology, Portland State University, Oregon. Prehistory of the Southern Plateau: 10/9/92; 7/10/97; 8/11/97.

AOKI, HARUO (emeritus), Department of East Asian Languages, University of California, Berkeley. Languages: 10/8/91; 7/18/96; 7/3/97.

BECKHAM, STEPHEN DOW, Department of History, Lewis and Clark College, Portland, Oregon. History Since 1846: 5/29/97; 6/9/97; 9/11/97.

BORESON, KEO, Archaeological and Historical Services, Eastern Washington University, Cheney. Rock Art: 5/9/91; 5/24/96; 1/6/97.

BOUCHARD, RANDALL T., British Columbia Indian Language Project, Victoria. Lillooet: 3/4/92; 12/6/96; 5/19/97. Northern Okanagan, Lakes, and Colville: 8/5/91; 5/16/97; 7/9/97.

BOYD, ROBERT T., Northwest Ethnohistorical Research Associates, Portland, Oregon. Demographic History Until 1990: 7/15/91; 6/11/96; 12/9/96.

BRUNTON, BILL B., Department of Sociology-Anthropology, North Dakota State University, Fargo. Kootenai: 8/5/74; 4/24/97; 6/19/97. The Stick Game: 7/20/92; 5/10/96; 1/10/97.

CHATTERS, JAMES C., Applied Paleoscience, Richland, Washington. Environment: 10/7/92; 5/20/96; 8/1/97. Prehistory: Introduction: 3/20/95; 6/26/97; 7/10/97.

CONN, RICHARD G. (emeritus), Denver Art Museum, Colorado. Basketry: 6/4/91; 5/24/96; 4/2/97.

DUMOND, DON E. (emeritus), Department of Anthropology, University of Oregon, Eugene. Prehistory of the Southern Plateau: 10/9/92; 7/10/97; 8/11/97.

ELMENDORF, WILLIAM W. (research associate), Department of Anthropology, University of California, Davis. Languages: 10/8/91; 7/18/96; 7/3/97.

FRENCH, DAVID H. (deceased), Department of Anthropology, Reed College, Portland, Oregon. Wasco, Wishram, and Cascades: 1/24/94; 9/27/95; 2/13/97. Western Columbia River Sahaptins: 7/30/91; 11/3/95; 3/21/97. Ethnobiology and Subsistence: 11/25/92; 8/2/96; 4/17/97.

FRENCH, KATHRINE S. (adjunct faculty), Department of Anthropology, Reed College, Portland, Oregon. Wasco, Wishram, and Cascades: 1/24/94; 9/27/95; 2/13/97.

FREY, RODNEY, Department of Social Sciences, Lewis-Clark State College, Coeur d'Alene, Idaho. Mythology: 10/28/91; 6/5/96; 11/18/96.

GALM, JERRY R., Department of Geography and Anthropology, Eastern Washington University, Cheney. Prehistory of the Southern Plateau: 10/9/92; 7/10/97; 8/11/97.

HACKENBERGER, STEVEN, Department of Anthropology, Central Washington University, Ellensburg. Prehistory of the Eastern Plateau: 3/27/95; 7/27/97; 8/27/97.

HEWES, GORDON W. (deceased), Department of Anthropology, University of Colorado, Boulder. Fishing: 7/30/91; 6/29/96; 2/24/97.

HUNN, EUGENE S., Department of Anthropology, University of Washington, Seattle. Western Columbia River Sahaptins: 7/30/91; 11/3/95; 3/21/97. Ethnobiology and Subsistence: 11/25/92; 8/2/96; 4/17/97.

HYMES, DELL, Department of Anthropology, University of Virginia, Charlottesville. Mythology: 10/28/91; 6/5/96; 11/18/96.

IGNACE, MARIANNE BOELSCHER, Secwepemc Cultural Education Society, Kamloops, British Columbia. Shuswap: 5/27/92; 5/9/96; 4/23/97.

KENNEDY, DOROTHY I.D., British Columbia Indian Language Project, Victoria. Lillooet: 3/4/92; 12/6/96; 5/19/97. Northern Okanagan, Lakes, and Colville: 8/5/91; 5/16/97; 7/9/97.

KINKADE, M. DALE (emeritus), Department of Linguistics, University of British Columbia, Vancouver. Languages: 10/8/91; 7/18/96; 7/3/97.

LAHREN, SYLVESTER L., JR., Elbert, Colorado. Kalispel: 11/20/91; 5/14/97; 6/4/97. Reservations and Reserves: 11/9/90; 2/20/97; 4/8/97.

LOHSE, E.S., Department of Anthropology, Idaho State University, Pocatello. History of Research: 4/2/97; 4/11/97; 9/23/97.

MALOUF, CARLING I. (emeritus), Department of Anthropology, University of Montana, Missoula. Flathead and Pend d'Oreille: 9/15/72; 6/26/97; 9/22/97.

MILLER, JAY, Prince Rupert, British Columbia. Middle Columbia River Salishans: 10/17/96; 6/25/97; 7/29/97.

MINOR, RICK, Heritage Research Associates, Inc., Eugene, Oregon. Prehistory of the Southern Plateau: 10/9/92; 7/10/97; 8/11/97.

MITCHELL, DONALD (emeritus), Department of Anthropology, University of Victoria, British Columbia. Prehistory of the Northern Plateau: 8/2/91; 8/4/97; 8/29/97.

OLSEN, LORAN (emeritus), School of Music and Theater Arts, Washington State University, Pullman. Music and Dance: 7/30/91; 5/16/96; 2/12/97.

PALMER, GARY B., Department of Anthropology and Ethnic Studies, University of Nevada, Las Vegas. Coeur d'Alene: 6/10/82; 5/13/96; 6/12/97.

POKOTYLO, DAVID L., Department of Anthropology and Sociology, University of British Columbia, Vancouver. Prehistory: Introduction: 3/20/95; 6/26/97; 7/10/97. Prehistory of the Northern Plateau: 8/2/91; 8/4/97; 8/29/97.

RIGSBY, BRUCE, Department of Anthropology and Sociol-ogy, University of Queensland, Australia. Languages: 10/8/91; 7/18/96; 7/3/97. Molala: 1/23/92; 5/3/96; 12/10/96.

ROLL, TOM E., Department of Sociology, Montana State University, Bozeman. Prehistory of the Eastern Plateau: 3/27/95; 7/27/97; 8/27/97.

ROSS, JOHN ALAN, Department of Geography and Anthropology, Eastern Washington University, Cheney. Spokane: 9/30/91; 5/13/96; 6/6/97.

SCHLICK, MARY DODDS (adjunct curator), Native American Collections, Maryhill Museum of Art, Goldendale, Washington. Basketry: 6/4/91; 5/24/96; 4/2/97.

SCHUSTER, HELEN H. (emerita), Department of Anthropology, Iowa State University, Ames. Yakima and Neighboring Groups: 10/11/91; 9/11/95; 4/10/97. Religious Movements: 8/13/96; 1/27/97; 2/26/97.

SPRAGUE, RODERICK (emeritus), Laboratory of Anthropology, University of Idaho, Moscow. History of Research: 4/2/97; 4/11/97; 9/23/97. History Until 1846: 8/5/96; 6/9/97; 9/17/97. Palouse: 6/14/78; 1/9/97; 2/25/97.

STERN, THEODORE (emeritus), Department of Anthropology, University of Oregon, Eugene. Cayuse, Umatilla, and Walla Walla : 12/10/75; 5/6/96; 1/13/97. Klamath and Modoc: 9/18/72; 5/31/96; 12/6/96. Columbia River Trade Network: 9/17/91; 2/28/97; 4/8/97.

TURNER, NANCY J., School of Environmental Studies, University of Victoria, British Columbia. Ethnobiology and Subsistence: 11/25/92; 8/2/96; 4/17/97.

WALKER, DEWARD E., JR., Department of Anthropology, University of Colorado, Boulder. Introduction: 7/17/97; 8/18/97; 9/11/97. History Until 1846: 8/5/96; 6/9/97; 9/17/97. Nez Perce: 3/28/96; 9/23/96; 1/15/97. Religious Movements: 8/13/96; 1/27/97; 2/26/97.

WYATT, DAVID, Department of Anthropology, University College of the Fraser Valley, Abbotsford, British Columbia. Thompson: 6/1/73; 5/14/96; 4/24/97. Nicola: 3/20/73; 5/15/96; 3/26/97.

ZENK, HENRY B., Portland, Oregon. Molala: 1/23/92; 5/3/96; 12/10/96.

List of Illustrations

This list identifies the subjects of all illustrations, organized by chapter. All artists, photographers, and some individuals depicted (but not collectors) are included. Every identified individual depicted is found in the index, but not the photographers.

Bibliography

This list includes all references cited in the volume, arranged in alphabetical order according to the names of the authors as they appear in the citations in the text. It also includes works submitted by the contributors but not cited in their chapters. Multiple works by the same author are arranged chronologically; second and subsequent titles by the same author in the same year are differentiated by letters added to the dates. Where more than one author with the same surname is cited, one has been arbitrarily selected for text citation by surname alone throughout the volume, while the others are always cited with added initials; the combination of surname with date in text citations should avoid confusion. Where a publication date is different from the series date (as in some annual reports and the like), the former is used. Dates, authors, and titles that do not appear on the original works are enclosed by brackets. For manuscripts, dates refer to time of composition. For publications reprinted or first published many years after original composition, a bracketed date after the title refers to the time of composition or the date of original publication.

ARCIA = Commissioner of Indian Affairs
1824–1848   Annual Reports of the Commissioner of Indian Affairs to the Secretary of War. [Issued both as *House* and *Senate* Documents.] Washington: Government Printing Office.

1849-   Annual Reports of the Commissioner of Indian Affairs to the Secretary of the Interior. Washington: Government Printing Office. (Reprinted: AMS Press, New York, 1976–1977; orig. issued both as *House* and *Senate Documents*, and as Department of the Interior separate publications; *see*: Key to the Annual Reports of the United States Commissioner of Indian Affairs, by J.A. Jones. *Ethnohistory* 2(1):58–64, 1955.)

Aaberg, Stephen A.
1985   County Line (24MO197): A Warex/Avonlea Phase Site on the Blackfoot River near Its Confluence with the Clearwater River, Missoula County, Montana. *Archaeology in Montana* 26(1):52–71.

Abbot, Henry L. [1855] *see* 1857

1857   Report of Lieut. Henry L. Abbot, Corps of Topographical Engineers upon Explorations for a Railroad Route, from the Sacramento Valley to the Columbia River, ... 1855. In Vol. VI of: Reports of Explorations and Surveys, To Ascertain the Most Practicable and Economical Route for a Railroad from the Mississippi River to the Pacific Ocean. Made under the Direction of the Secretary of War, in 1854–5, According to Acts of Congress of March 3, 1853, May 31, 1854, and August 5, 1854. *33d Congress. 2d Session. House Executive Document* 91. Washington.

Abbott, George H.
1861   [Letter of September 10, 1861, Umatilla Agency, Oreg.] Pp. 774–776 in *37th Congress, 2d. Session. Senate Executive Document* 1. (Serial No. 1117). Washington. (See also pp. 164–166 in ARCIA for 1861.)

Aberle, David F.
1959   The Prophet Dance and Reactions to White Contact. *Southwestern Journal of Anthropology* 15(1):74–83.

Abraham, Otto, and Erich M. von Hornbostel
1975   Indian Melodies from British Columbia Recorded on the Phonograph. Richard Campbell, trans. Pp. 301–322 in *Hornbostel Opera Omnia* 1. The Hague: M. Nijhoff. (Original: Phonographirte Indianermelodieen aus British Columbia. Berlin and New York, 1906.)

Ackerman, Lillian A.
1971   Marital Instability and Juvenile Delinquency Among the Nez Perces. *American Anthropologist* 73(3):595–603.

1979–1990   [Ethnographic notes from fieldwork on the Colville Indian Reservation in Washington State and the Coeur d'Alene Reservation in Idaho.] (Manuscripts in Ackerman's possession.)

1982   Sexual Equality in the Plateau Culture Area. (Ph.D. Dissertation in Antropology, Washington State University, Pullman. Microfilm: University Microfilms International, Ann Arbor, Mich., 1982.)

1987   The Effect of Missionary Ideals on Family Structure and Women's Roles in Plateau Indian Culture. *Idaho Yesterdays* 31(1–2):64–73. Boise.

1989   Residential Mobility among the Colville Indians. (Report to the Center for Survey Methods. U.S. Census Bureau, Department of Commerce, Washington.

1991   [Descent and Clan in the Plateau Culture Area.] (Manuscript in Ackerman's possession.)

1994   Nonunilinear Descent Groups in the Plateau Culture Area. *American Ethnologist* 21(2):286–309.

1996   A Song to the Creator: Traditional Arts of Native American Women of the Plateau. Norman and London: University of Oklahoma Press.

1996a   Ethnographic Overview and Assessment of Federal and Tribal Lands in the Lake Roosevelt Area Concerning the Confederated Tribes of the Colville Indian Reservation. *Washington State University. Department of Anthropology. Project Report* 30. Pullman.

Adams, Barbara
1958   The Cascade Indians: Ethnographic Notes and an Analysis of Early Relations with Whites. (B.A. Thesis in Anthropology, Reed College, Portland, Oreg.)

Adams, E. Charles
1984   Archaeology and the Native American: A Case at Hopi. Pp. 236–242 in Ethics and Values in Archaeology. E.L. Green, ed. New York: Free Press.

Adams, William H.
1972   Component I at Wawawai (45WT39): The Ethnographic Period Occupation. (M.A. Thesis in Anthropology, Washington State University, Pullman.)

1977   Second Annual Northwest Anthropological Conference Symposium on Historical Archaeology. *Northwest Anthropological Research Notes* 11(2). Moscow, Idaho.

Adler, Fred W.
1961   A Bibliographical Checklist of Chimakuan, Kutenai, Ritwan, Salishan, and Wakashan Linguistics. *International Journal of American Linguistics* 27(3):198–210.

Adolph, Thomas, et al.
1922   Petition of Lillooet Chiefs. (Manuscript in National Archives of Canada, RG 10, Volume 10895, File 167/1907–21, Part 2.)

Aikens, C. Melvin
1978   The Far West. Pp. 131–181 in Ancient Native Americans. Jesse D. Jennings, ed. San Francisco: W.H. Freeman.

1984   Archaeology of Oregon. Portland, Oreg.: U.S. Department of the Interior, Bureau of Land Management, Oregon State Office.

1993   Archaeology of Oregon. 3d ed. Portland, Oreg.: U.S. Department of the Interior, Bureau of Land Management.

Akersten, William
1989   Jaguar Cave Revisited and Re-evaluated. (Paper presented at the 16th Annual Conference of the Idaho Archaeological Society, Boise.)

Alexander, Diana
1992   A Reconstruction of Prehistoric Land Use in the Mid-Fraser River Area Based on Ethnographic Data. Pp. 47–98 in A Complex Culture of the British Columbia Plateau: Traditional *Stl'átl'imx* Resource Use. Brian Hayden, ed. Vancouver: UBC Press.

Alexander, Diana, and R.G. Mason
1987   Report on the Potato Mountain Archaeological Project (1985). (Manuscript, Laboratory of Archaeology, University of British Columbia, Vancouver.)

Allan, G.T.
1848   [Fort Alexandria Journal, 1848.] (Manuscript B. 5/a/7, Hudson's Bay Company Archives, Winnipeg, Man.)

Allen, A.J. comp.
1848   Ten Years in Oregon. Travels and Adventures of Doctor E. White and Lady, West of the Rocky Mountains, [etc.]. 2d. ed. Ithaca, N.Y.: Mack, Andrus, and Co.

Allen, Paul, ed. 1814 *see* Lewis, Meriwether, and William Clark 1814

Alley, Neville F.
1976   The Palynology and Paleoclimatic Significance of a Dated Core of Holocene Peat, Okanogan Valley, Southern British Columbia. *Canadian Journal of Earth Sciences* 13:1131–1144. Ottawa.

Allison, Susan L. (Mrs. S.S. Allison)
1892   Account of the Similkameen Indians of British Columbia. *Journal of the [Royal] Anthropological Institute of Great Britian and Ireland* 21(3):305–318. London.

————
1970   Allison Pass Memoirs, Part 3. *Canada West* 2(2):20–33. Summerland, B.C.

Alvord, Benjamin
1857   Report of Brevet Major Benjamin Alvord, Captain 4th Infantry ... Concerning the Indians of the Territories of Oregon and Washington, East of the Cascades, etc. [1853]. In *34th Congress. House Executive Document 76, Report 3S*: Indian Affairs on the Pacific. Washington: Government Printing Office.

————
1884   The Doctor-killing in Oregon. *Harper's New Monthly Magazine* 68(405):364–366.

American Indian Defense Association
1923–1936 [Papers and correspondence files, 1923–1936.] (Boxes 16, 17, 18, in the John Collier Papers, 1922–1956, Sterling Memorial Library, Manuscripts and Archives, Yale University, New Haven, Conn.)

American Indian Policy Review Commission
1976   Report on Terminated and Nonfederally Recognized Indians, Task Force Ten: Terminated and Nonfederally Recognized Indians, American Indian Policy Review Commission. Washington: Government Printing Office.

Ames, Kenneth M.
1980   A Prehistory of the Clearwater River and Adjacent Portions of the Columbia Plateau. (Manuscript, Idaho State Historic Preservation Office, Boise.)

————
1982   Archaeological Investigations in the Payette River Drainage, Southwestern Idaho. *Boise State University. Archaeological Reports* 11. Boise, Idaho.

————
1982a   Comments on the Tucannon Phase. *Idaho Archaeologist* 5(3):1–8. Caldwell.

————
1985   Hierarchies, Stress and Logistical Strategies among Hunter-gatherers in Northwestern North America. Pp. 55–80 in Prehistoric Hunter-gatherers: The Emergence of Cultural Com-plexity. T.D. Price and J.D. Brown, eds. New York: Academic Press.

————
1988   Early Holocene Forager Mobility Strategies on the Southern Coumbia Plateau. Pp. 325–360 in Early Human Occupation in Far Western North America: The Clovis: Archaic Interface. Judith A. Willig, C. Melvin Aikens, and John L. Fagan, eds. *Nevada State Museum Anthropological Papers* 21. Carson City, Nev.

————
1990   The Archaeology of Hatwai (10NP143) and the Southeastern Coumbia Pleateau. (Manuscript in K. Ames's possession.)

————
1991   Sedentism: A Temporal Shift or a Transitional Change in Hunter-Gatherer Mobility Patterns. Pp. 108–134 in Between Bands and States. Susan Gregg, ed. *Southern Illinois University at Carbondale. Center for Archaeological Investigations. Occasional Paper* 9. Carbondale.

Ames, Kenneth M., and Alan G. Marshall
1980   Villages, Demography and Subsistence Intensification on the Southern Columbia Plateau. *North American Archaeologist* 2(1):25–52. Farmingdale, N.Y.

Ames, Kenneth M., James P. Green, and Margaret Pfoertner
1981   Hatwai (10NP143): Interim Report. *Boise State University. Archaeological Reports* 9. Boise, Idaho.

Ames, Michael
1956   Fountain in a Modern Economy: A Study of Social Structure, Land Use and Business Enterprise in a British Columbia Indian Community. (B.A. Essay in Economics, Political Science and Sociology, University of British Columbia, Vancouver.)

————
1957   Reaction to Stress. *Journal of Anthropology* 3:17–30

Anastasio, Angelo
1955   Intergroup Relations in the Southern Plateau. (Ph.D. Dissertation in Anthropology, University of Chicago, Chicago; publ. in *NARN* 6(2):109–229. Moscow, Idaho, 1972.)

————
1972   The Southern Plateau: An Ecological Analysis of Intergroup Relations. *Northwest Anthropological Research Notes* 6(2):109–229. Moscow, Idaho. (Reprinted, with minor revisions: University of Idaho, Laboratory of Anthropology, Moscow, 1975, 1985.)

Anderson, Albert
1901   [Letter of September 12, 1901, Colville Agency, Wash.] Pp. 384–385 in *57th Congress. 1st Session. House Document* 5, Pt. 1. (Serial No. 4290). Washington.

Anderson, Alexander C.
1846   Journal of an Expedition Under Command of Alex C. Anderson of the Hudson's Bay Company, Undertaken with the View of Ascertaining the Practicability of a Communication with the Interior for the Import of the Annual Supplies. (Manuscript B. 97/a/3 in Hudson's Bay Company Archives, Provincial Archives of Manitoba, Winnipeg.)

————
1848   [Letter of February 24, 1848, from Fort Alexandria, B.C., to George Simpson.] (Manuscript D.5/21, folio 294, Hudson's Bay Company Archives, Provincial Archives of Manitoba, Winnipeg.)

————
1863   Notes on the Indian Tribes of British North America and the North West Coast. *Historical Magazine*, 1st ser. 7(3). New York and London.

————
1867   [Map of a Portion of the Colony of British Columbia, compiled from Various Sources, including Original Notes from Personal Explorations between the Years 1832 and 1851.]

(Original in British Columbia Archives and Record Service, Victoria.)

1876   Notes on North-western America. (Descriptive Matter Intended to Accompany a 'Skeleton Map of North-West America'; Prepared by Mr. Anderson to Send to the Philadelphia International Exhibition of 1876.) Montreal: Mitchell and Wilson.

Angulo, Jaime de, and Marguerite Béclard d'Harcourt
1931   La musique des Indiens de la Californie du Nord. *Journal de la Société des Américanistes de Paris*, n.s. 23(1):189–228. Paris.

Angus, Henry F., ed.
1942   British Columbia and the United States: The North Pacific Slopes from the Fur Trade to Aviation. Toronto: The Ryerson Press; New Haven, Conn.: Yale University Press, [etc.], for the Carnegie Endowment for International Peace, Division of Economics and History.

Anonymous
1859   [Report of Mullan at the Mount of the Palouse River.] *Pacific Christian Advocate*, 4 June. Portland, Oreg.

1862   [Article on smallpox epidemic.] *The British Colonist*, June 23. Victoria, V.I.

1862a   [Article on vaccination program by Leon Fouquet.] *The British Columbian*, May 14. New Westminster, B.C.

1863   [Article on smallpox epidemic.] *The British Colonist*, February 27. Victoria, V.I.

1893   King Without a Country. *The Spokane Review,* 1 May:5. Spokane, Wash.

1903   On the Road to Moses Lake. *Spokesman-Review,* 24 April:8. Spokane, Wash.

1911   Chief Big Sunday Begs Judge to Stop Pillaging of Indian Graves. *Spokesman-Review,* 29 May:7. Spokane, Wash.

1913   Wanamaker Party Now With Pueblos. *New York Times*, June 29. New York.

1937   De Smet Sixty Years Ago, 1878. *The Coeur d'Alene Teepee* 1(1):6. DeSmet, Idaho: Sacred Heart Mission. (Reprinted: Serento Press, Plummer, Idaho, 1981.)

Antelope, Morris
1938   History of Morris Antelope of the Coeur d'Alenes. *Coeur d'Alene Teepee* 1:17–18. DeSmet, Idaho: Sacred Heart Mission. (Reprinted: Serento Press, Plummer, Idaho, 1980.)

1938a   Indian Pipes. Coeur d'Alene Teepee 1:18. DeSmet, Idaho: Sacred Heart Mission. (Reprinted: Serento Press, Plummer, Idaho, 1980.)

Aoki, Haruo
1962   Nez Perce and Northern Sahaptin: A Binary Comparison. *International Journal of American Linguistics* 28(3):172–182.

1963   On Sahaptian-Klamath Linguistic Affiliations. *International Journal of American Linguistics* 29(2):107–112.

1963a   Reduplication in Nez Perce. *International Journal of American Linguistics* 29(1):42–44.

1966   Nez Perce and Proto-Sahaptian Kinship Terms. *International Journal of American Linguistics* 32(4):357–38.

1966a   Nez Perce Vowel Harmony and Proto-Sahaptian Vowels. *Language* 42(4):759–767.

1967   "Chopunnish" and "Green Wood Indians": A Note on Nez Perce Tribal Synonymy. *American Anthropologist* 69(5):505–506.

1968   Toward a Typology of Vowel Harmony. *International Journal of American Linguistics* 34(3):142–145.

1970   Nez Perce Grammar. *University of California Publications in Linguistics* 62. Berkeley.

1975   The East Plateau Linguistic Diffusion Area. *International Journal of American Linguistics* 41(3):183–199.

1978   Coyote and Fox. Pp. 26–31 in Coyote Stories. William Bright, ed. *International Journal of American Linguistics. Native American Text Series. Monograph* 1. Chicago: The University of Chicago Press.

1979   Nez Perce Texts. *University of California Publications in Linguistics* 90. Berkeley.

1980   Titwáatit (Nez Perce Stories). Anchorage: University of Alaska, National Bilingual Materials Development Center. (Rev. and repr. from : Pp. 14–81 in Nez Perce Texts, by Haruo Aoki. Berkeley, 1979.)

1994   Nez Perce Dictionary. *University of California Publications in Linguistics* 122. Berkeley.

1994a   Symbolism in Nez Perce. Pp. 15–22 in Sound Symbolism. Leanne Hinton, Johanna Nichols, and John J. Ohala, eds. Cambridge: Cambridge University Press.

Aoki, Haruo, and Tupou L. Pulu
1981   Nez Perce Unit of Study: Clothing Level One Sám'qit. Assisted by Josephine Ramsey, et al.; J. Leslie Boffa, illus. Anchorage: University of Alaska, Rural Education, National Bilingual Materials Development Center.

Aoki, Haruo, and Deward E. Walker, Jr.
1989   Nez Perce Oral Narratives. *University of California Publications in Linguistics* 104. Berkeley.

Applegate, Jesse A.
1907   The Yangoler Chief. Roseburg, Oreg.: Review Publishing Company.

Arcas Associates
1985   Excavations at the Rattlesnake Hill Site (EeRh 61), Ashcroft, B.C. (Manuscript, Archaeology Branch, Victoria, B.C.)

1986   Archaeological Excavations at Valley Mine, Highland Valley, B.C. 2 vols. Port Moody, B.C.: Arcas Associates.

Archer, David
1971   The Monck Park Site: EbRd 3, Summary Report. (Manuscript, Archaeology Branch, Victoria, B.C.).

Arnold, Quentin Mark
1984   Prehistory of Long Valley, Idaho; with an Appendix on the Carbon Materials by Jerry Wylie. *USDA Forest Service. Intermountain Region. Cultural Resource Report* 10. Ogden, Utah. (Originally presented as the Author's M.A. Thesis in Anthropology under title: Preliminary Research into the Prehistory of Long Valley, Idaho. University of Idaho, Moscow.)

Aro, K.V., and M.P. Shepard
1967   Pacific Salmon in Canada. Pp. 225–327 in Salmon of the North Pacific Ocean, Part IV: Spawning Populations of North

Pacific Salmon. *International North Pacific Fisheries Commission Bulletin* 23. Vancouver, B.C.

Arrowsmith, John
1857   Map of North America. (Drawn by J. Arrowsmith: Ordered by the House of Commons to be printed 31st July & 11th August, 1857.) London: J. Arrowsmith; Henry Hansard, Printer. (Copy in Oregon Historical Society Library, Maps Department, Portland, Oreg.)

Arthur, Chester A.
1883   Message from the President of the United States Transmitting a Letter from the Secretary of the Interior Respecting the Ratification of an Agreement with the Confederated Tribes of Flathead, Kootenay, and Upper Pend d'Oreilles Indians, for the Sale of a Portion of Their Reservation in Montana Territory. *47th Congress. 2d Session. Senate Executive Document* 44. (Serial No. 2076). Washington.

Artz, Joe Alan
1983   An Evaluation of the Cultural Resources of the Montour Wildlife/Recreation Area Gem Country, Idaho. *University of Kansas Museum of Anthropology. Project Report Series* 51. Lawrence.

Atkinson, C.E., J.H. Rose, and T.O. Duncan
1967   Pacific Salmon in the United States. Pp. 43–223 in Salmon of the North Pacific Ocean, Part IV: Spawning Populations of North Pacific Salmon. *International North Pacific Fisheries Commission Bulletin* 23. Vancouver, B.C.

Atkinson, Reginald N.
1952   Burial Grounds of the Okanagan Indians. Pp. 5–12 in *16th Annual Report of the Okanagan Historical Society*. Vernon, B.C.

Atwater, Brian F.
1986   Pleistocene Glacial-Lake Deposits of the Sanpoil River Valley, Northeastern Washington. *U.S. Geological Survey Bulletin* 1661. Washington.

Atwell, Ricky G.
1989   Subsistence Variability on the Columbia Plateau. (M.A. Thesis in Anthropology, Portland State University, Portland, Oreg.)

Baars, Patricia R.
[1982]   Near Neighbors: Cross-Cultural Friendships in Dickey Prairie and South Molalla. (Text accompanying an exhibits project funded by The Oregon Committee for the Humanities; copy in Molalla Area Historical Society, Molalla, Oreg., and in Clackamas County Historical Society, Oregon City, Oreg.)

Bacon, Charles R.
1983   Eruptive History of Mount Mazama and Crater Lake Caldera, Cascade Range, U.S.A. *Journal of Volcanology and Geothermal Research* 18(1/4):57–115. Amsterdam and New York.

Baenan, James A.
1965   Hunting and Fishing Rights of Nez Perce Indians: A Chapter in Recent Ethno-history. (M.A. Thesis in Anthropology, Washington State University, Pullman.)

Bagley, Clarence B.
1930   Indian Myths of the Northwest. Seattle: Lowman and Hanford Company.

Bagshaw, Roberta L.
1996   No Better Land: The 1860 Diaries of the Anglican Colonial Bishop George Hills. Victoria, B.C.: Sono Nis Press.

Bahar, Hushang
1955   Pend d'Oreille Kinship. (M.A. Thesis in Anthropology, University of Montana, Missoula.)

Bailey, Liberty H.
1914   The Standard Cyclopedia of Horticulture. Rev. and enl. ed. 6 vols. [vol. 2: C-E] New York: The Macmillan Company.

Bailey, Vernon
1936   The Mammals and Life Zones of Oregon. *U.S. Department of Agriculture. Bureau of Biological Survey. North American Fauna* 55. Washington.

Baker, Richard G.
1983   Holocene Vegetational History of the Western United States. Pp. 109–127 in Vol. 2 of Late-Quaternary Environments of the United States. H.E. Wright, Jr., ed. 2 vols. Minneapolis: University of Minnesota Press.

Baker, Theodore
1882   Über die Musik der nordamerikanischen Wilden. Leipzig: Breitkopf und Härtel. (Reprinted as: On the Music of the North American Indians. Ann Buckley, trans. Buren, The Netherlands: F. Kunf; New York: [obtainable from] W.S. Heinman, 1976.)

Balf, Mary
1989   Kamloops: A History of District Up To 1914. 2d ed. Kamloops, B.C.: Kamloops Museum Association.

Ball, Henry M.
1862   [Letter of July 2, 1862.] (Colonial Correspondence F96, Royal British Columbia Archives, Victoria.)

Ballou, Howard Malcolm
1922   The History of the Oregon Mission Press. *Oregon Historical Quarterly* 23(1):39–52, (2):95–110.

Bancroft, Hubert Howe
1874–1876   The Native Races of the Pacific States of North America. 5 vols. New York: D. Appleton.

————
1886   History of the Northwest Coast. Vol. I: 1543–1800; Vol. II: 1800–1846. (*The Works of Hubert Howe Bancroft* 27, 28). San Francisco: The History Company.

————
1887   History of British Columbia, 1792–1887. San Francisco: The History Company.

————
1890   History of Washington, Idaho, and Montana, 1845–1889. (*The Works of Hubert Howe Bancroft* 31). San Francisco: The History Company.

Baravelle, Richard
1981   Final Report on a Survey of Kootenay Lake Pictograph Sites. (Report submitted to the Heritage Advisory Board of British Columbia, Victoria.)

Barbeau, C. Marius
1914   On Interior Salish Work, 1912. Pp. 461–463 in *Canada. Department of Mines. Summary Report of the Geological Survey*. Ottawa.

————
1957   My Life in Recording: Canadian-Indian Folk-Lore. (Article [Inside title varies: My Life with Indian Songs] enclosed with Folkways Records Album No. FG 3502). New York City: Folkways Records and Service Corp.

Barclay, Forbes
1848   [Letter of March 18, 1848.] (Manuscript D.5/21, fol. 541 in Hudson's Bay Company Archives, Winnipeg, Man.)

Barker, M.A.R.
1963   Klamath Texts. *University of California Publications in Linguistics* 30. Berkeley. (Reprinted: Kraus Reprint, Millwood, N.Y., 1981.)

————
1963a   Klamath Dictionary. *University of California Publications in Linguistics* 31. Berkeley. (Reprinted: Kraus Reprint, Millwood, N.Y., 1981.)

1964   Klamath Grammar. *University of California Publications in Linguistics* 32. Berkeley. (Reprinted: Kraus Reprint, Millwood, N.Y., 1981.)

Barlee, Kathleen, comp. and ed.
1988   The Central Okanagan Records Survey. Duane Thomson, Maurice Williams, and Kathleen Barlee, co-investigators. Kelowna, B.C.: Okanagan College Press.

Barnett, Homer G.
1938   The Nature and Function of the Potlatch. (Ph.D. Dissertation in Anthropology, University of California, Berkeley. Reprinted: University of Oregon, Department of Anthropology, Eugene, 1968.)

1957   Indian Shakers: A Messianic Cult of the Pacific Northwest. Carbondale: Southern Illinois University Press. (Reprinted in 1972.)

Barnier, Cecil D.
1971   Archaeological Survey of the National Bison Range and other Portions of the Lower Flathead Basin, Montana. *Archaeology in Montana* 12(4). Bozeman.

Barnosky, Cathy W.
1985   Late Quaternary Vegetation in the Southwestern Columbia Basin, Washington. *Quaternary Research* 23(1):109–122. New York.

Barnosky, Cathy W., Patricia M. Anderson, and Patrick J. Bartlein
1987   The Northwestern U.S. During Deglaciation; Vegetational History and Paleoclimatic Implications. Pp. 289–321 in North America and Adjacent Oceans During the Last Deglaciation. William F. Ruddiman and Herbert E. Wright, Jr., eds. Boulder, Colo.: The Geological Society of America.

Barrett, Samuel A.
1910   The Material Culture of the Klamath Lake and Modoc Indians of Northeastern California and Southern Oregon. *University of California Publications in American Archaeology and Ethnology* 5(4):239–292. Berkeley. (Reprinted: Kraus Reprint, New York, 1964.)

Barry, Roger G., and Richard J. Chorley
1968   Atmosphere, Weather, and Climate. London: Methuen. (Reprinted, 7th ed.: Routledge, New York, 1992.)

Bartholomew, Michael J.
1982   Pollen and Sediment Analyses of Clear Lake, Whitman County, Washington: The Last 600 Years. (M.A. Thesis in Anthropology, Washington State University, Pullman.)

Bates, Dawn, and Barry F. Carlson
1992   Simple Syllables in Spokane Salish. *Linguistic Inquiry* 23(4):653–659.

1997   Spokane (Npoqínišcn) Syllable Structure and Reduplication. Pp. 99–123 in Salish Languages and Linguistics: Theoretical and Descriptive Perspectives. Ewa Czaykowska-Higgins and M. Dale Kinkade, eds. (*Trends in Linguistics. Studies and Monographs* 107). Berlin and New York: Mouton de Gruyter.

Bauman, James J., with Ruby Miles, and Ike Leaf, comps.
1979   Pit River Teaching Dictionary. Anchorage: University of Alaska, National Bilingual Materials Development Center.

Baumhoff, Martin A.
1963   Ecological Determinants of California Aboriginal Populations. *University of California Publications in American Archaeology and Ethnology* 49(2):155–236. Berkeley.

Baumhoff, Martin A., and David L. Olmsted
1963   Palaihnihan: Radiocarbon Support for Glottochronology. *American Anthropologist* 65(2):278–284.

Beach, Margery Ann
1985   The Waptashi Prophet and Feather Religion: Derivative of the Washani. *American Indian Quarterly* 9(3):325–333.

Beal, Merrill D.
1963   "I Will Fight No More Forever": Chief Joseph and the Nez Perce War. Seattle: University of Washington Press.

Beall, Thomas B.
1917   Pioneer Reminiscenes. *Washington Historical Quarterly* 8(2):83–90.

Bear, Sterns, and Company
1997   Global Gaming Almanac. New York: Bear, Sterns & Company.

Beasley, R. Palmer, Robert Wilkens, and Peter Bennett
1973   High Prevalence of Rheumatoid Arthritis in Yakima Indians. *Arthritis and Rheumatism* 16(6):743–748.

Beavert, Virginia R.
1974   The Way It Was, *Anaku Iwacha*: Yakima Legends. Deward E. Walker, Jr., technical advisor. Yakima, Wash.: Franklin Press; [for the] Consortium of Johnson O'Malley Comittees of Region IV, State of Washington.

Beavert, Virginia R., and Bruce Rigsby, eds.
1975   Yakima Language Practical Dictionary. Toppenish, Wash.: Consortium of Johnson-O'Malley Committees of Region IV, State of Washington.

Beavert Martin, Virginia R., and Deward E. Walker, Jr.
1992   The Ellen Saluskin (*hápteliks sáwyalilx̲*) Narratives 1992: Traditional Religious Beliefs and Practices. [2 Pts.; 1] Traditional Religious Beliefs and Practices; [2] The Yakima River People. *Northwest Anthropological Research Notes* 26(2):209–213, 214–216. Moscow, Idaho.

Beck, Warren A., and Ynez D. Hasse
1989   Historical Atlas of the American West. Norman: University of Oklahoma Press.

Beckham, Stephen Dow
1985   Exercise of Congressional Plenary Power, Presidential Authority, and Bureau of Indian Affairs Procedures, Colville Indian Reservation, 1872–1944. (Report to U.S. Department of Justice, Docket 181-D, Colville Tribe v. U.S.; U.S. Claims Court, Washington, D.C.)

Begbie, Matthew B.
1861   Journey into the Interior of British Columbia. *Journal of the Royal Geographic Society* 31:237–248. London.

Belden, G.
1855   Sketch Map of Oregon Territory, Exhibiting the Locations of the Various Indian Tribes, the Districts of Country Ceded by Them, with the Dates of Purchases and Treaties, and the Reserves of the Umpqua and Rogue River Indians. (Map 234, tube 451, Cartographic Records Division, National Archives, Washington. Redrafted, p. 58 in *53d Congress. 1st Session. Executive Document* 25. Washington, 1893.)

Bell, Joy F.
1979   The Pictographs of Slocan Lake. Pp. 23–48 in Papers from the Fourth Biennial Conference of the Canadian Rock Art Research Associates. Doris Lundy, ed. *British Columbia Provincial Museum. Heritage Record* 8. Victoria.

Bellrose, Frank C.
1976   Ducks, Geese and Swans of North America. Harrisburg, Pa.: Stackpole Books. (Reprinted, 3d ed., 1980.)

Belyea, Barbara, ed. 1994 *see* Thompson, David 1994

Bennett, Kenneth A.
1972   Lumbosacral Malformation and Spina Bifida Occulta in a Group of Proto-historic Modoc Indians. *American Journal of Physical Anthropology* 36(3):435–439.

Bense, Judith Ann
1971   Cultural Stability on the Lower Snake River during the Altithermal. Pp. 37–42 in Great Basin Anthropological Con-

ference, 1970: Selected papers. C. Melvin Aikens, ed. *University of Oregon Anthropological Papers* 1. Eugene.

1972   The Cascade Phase: A Study in the Effect of the Altithermal on a Cultural System. (Ph.D. Dissertation in Anthropology, Washington State University, Pullman. Facsimile/microfilm-xerography: University Microfilms International, Ann Arbor, Mich., 1978.)

Benson, Eva M., Jean M. Peters, Margaret A. Edwards, and Louise A. Hogan
1973   Wild Edible Plants of the Pacific Northwest. *Journal of the American Dietetic Association* 62:143–147. Chicago.

Benson, Michael P., Ruthann Knudson, Thomas Dechert, and Richard C. Waldbauer
1979   A Preliminary Outline of the Cultural Resources of the Wilderness Gateway Recreation Area, Clearwater National Forest, Idaho. *University of Idaho. Anthropological Research Manuscript Series* 56. Moscow.

Benson, Robert L.
1973   [The Molalla.] (Typewritten abstract in Henry Zenk's possession.)

Beram, Luisa J.
1990   The Capital Regional District Parks: A Case Study in Archaeological Resource Management. (M.A. Thesis in Antrhopology, Simon Fraser University, Burnaby, B.C.; National Library of Canada, Ottawa, 1991.)

Beresford, William
1789   A Voyage Round the World; But More Particularly to the Northwest Coast of America; Performed in 1785, 1786, 1787, and 1788, in the King George and Queen Charlotte ... 2d ed. George Dixon, ed. London: George Goulding. (Reprinted: *Biblioteca Australiana* 37, Da Capo Press, New York, 1968.)

Berkhofer, Robert F., Jr.
1965   Salvation and the Savage: An Analysis of Protestant Missions and American Indian Response, 1787–1862. Lexington: University of Kentucky Press. (Reprinted: Athaneum, New York, 1972; also, Greenwood Press, Westport, Conn., 1977.)

Berlin, Brent, Dennis E. Breedlove, and Peter H. Raven
1973   General Principles of Classification and Nomenclature in Folk Biology. *American Anthropologist* 75(1):214–242.

1974   Principles of Tzeltal Plant Classification: An Introcution to the Botanical Ethnography of a Mayan-Speaking People of Highland Chiapas. New York: Academic Press.

Berman, Howard
1996   The Position of Molala in Plateau Penutian. *International Journal of American Linguistics* 62(1):1–30.

Berreman, Joel V.
1937   Tribal Distribution in Oregon. *Memoirs of the American Anthropological Association* 47. Menasha, Wis.: George Banta. (Reprinted: Kraus Reprint, New York, 1969.)

1944   Chetco Archaeology: A Report of the Lone Ranch Creek Shell Mound on the Coast of Southern Oregon. *General Series in Anthropology* 11. Menasha, Wis.

Berry, Kevin L.
1991   Where Have All The Salmon Run? Radiographic Examinations of Salmon Remains from the Keatley Creek Site in the Upper Fraser Canyon. (Paper presented at the 44th Annual Northwest Anthropological Conference, Missoula, Mont., 28–30 March 1991.)

Berven, Irene M.
1959   History of Indian Education on the Flathead Reservation. (M.A. Thesis in Education, Montana State University, Missoula.)

Bessell, Nicola J.
1992   Towards a Phonetic and Phonological Typology of Post-Velar Articulation. (Ph.D. Dissertation in Linguistics, University of British Columbia, Vancouver.)

1997   Phonetic Aspects of Retraction in Interior Salish. Pp. 125–152 in Salish Languages and Linguistics: Theoretical and Descriptive Perspectives. Ewa Czaykowska-Higgins and M. Dale Kinkade, eds. (*Trends in Linguistics. Studies and Monographs* 107). Berlin and New York: Mouton de Gruyter.

Bessell, Nicola J., and Ewa Czaykowska-Higgins
1992   Interior Salish Evidence for Placeless Laryngeals. *Northeast Linguistic Society Proceedings* 22:35–49.

1993   The Phonetics and Phonology and Postvelar Consonants in Moses-Columbia Salish (*Nxaʔamxcín*). Pp. 35–48 in *Toronto Working Papers in Linguistics*, CLA Proceedings. Toronto.

Bicchieri, Barbara
1975   Units of Culture and Units of Time: Periodization and Its Use in Syntheses of Plateau Prehistory. *Northwest Anthropological Research Notes* 9(2):246–266. Moscow, Idaho.

Biddle, Henry J.
1926   Wishram. *Oregon Historical Quarterly* 27(1):113–130.

Biddle, Nicholas 1814 *see* Lewis, Meriwether, and William Clark 1814

Bigart, Robert
1973   The Salish Flathead Indians, 1850–1891. *Idaho Yesterdays* 17(3):18–28.

Bigart, Robert, and Clarence Woodcock
1981   St. Ignatius Mission, Montana: Reports from Two Jesuit Missionaries, 1885 and 1900–1901. 2 Pts. *Arizona and the West* 23(2):149–172, (3):267–278.

1996   In the Name of the Salish & Kootenai Nation: The 1855 Hell Gate Treaty and the Origin of the Flathead Indian Reservation. Pablo, Mont.: Salish Kootenai College Press; distrib. by University of Washington Press, Seattle.

Bigart, Robert, et al.
1981   Salish and Kootenai Tribes Bibliography: An Annotated and Indexed Bibliography of General Interest Materials Dealing with the History and Culture of the Tribes. Pablo, Mont.: The Steve Matt, Sr., Fund for Indian Education, Salish Kootenai Community College, and Two Eagle River School, Dixon Sub-Agency, Dixon, Mont.

Bigcrane, Robert, and Thompson Smith
1991   The Place for Falling Waters. Three-part film history of the Flathead Reservation and Kerr Dam. Pablo, Mont.: Salish Kootenai College.

Binford, Lewis R.
1967   [Comment on K.C. Chang's *Major Aspects of the Interrelationship of Archaeology and Ethnology*.] *Current Anthropology* 8(3):234–235.

Binford, Lewis R.
1980   Willow Smoke and Dog's Tails: Hunter-gatherer Settlement Systems and Archaeological Site Formation. *American Antiquity* 45(1):4–20.

Bischoff, William N.
1945   The Jesuits in Old Oregon, 1840–1940. Caldwell, Idaho: The Caxton Printers.

1949   The Yakima Campaign of 1856. *Mid-America* 31:163–208.

1950   The Yakima Indian War:1855–1856 (Ph.D. Dissertation in History, Loyola University, Chicago.)

667

Bishop, Charles
1794–1796 [Commercial Journal; copy of Letters, and Acts of Ship Ruby's Voyage to NW Coast of America and China, 1794–5–6.] (Typewritten [carbon] copy.)

_____
1967 The Journal and Letters of Captain Charles Bishop on the North-West Coast of America, in the Pacific and in New South Wales, 1794–1799. Michael Roe, ed. *Works Issued by the Hakluyt Society*, 2d ser., 131. Cambridge: Published for the Hakluyt Society at University Press.

Black, Samuel
1826 [Letter to John McLoughlin, Nez Perces, 25 July 1826.] (Manuscript B. 223/b/2, fos. 41–43, here 41d. Hudson's Bay Company Archives, Provincial Archives of Manitoba, Winnipeg.)

_____
1829 [Report by Chief Trader Samuel Black to the Governor and Committee of the Hudson's Bay Company, dated 'Willa Willa', 25 March 1829.] (Manuscript B. 146/e/2, fo. 20(N3216), in Hudson's Bay Company Archives, Provincial Archives of Manitoba, Winnipeg.)

_____
[1833] [Manuscript Map of Thompson's River District, attributed to Samuel Black of the Hudson's Bay Company.] (Map, Accession No. 13,660, in British Columbia Archives and Records Service, Victoria.)

Blades, Thomas E., and John W. Wike
1949 Fort Missoula. *Military Affairs* 13(1):29–36. Washington.

Blanchet, Augustine Magloire
1978 Journal of a Catholic Bishop on the Oregon Trail: The Overland Crossing of the Rt. Rev. A.M.A. Blanchet, Bishop of Walla Walla, from Montreal to Oregon Territory, March 23, 1847 to January 23, 1851. Blackrobe Buries Whitmans. J.B.A. Brouillet. [Trans. from the French manuscript and ed. by] Edward J. Kowrach. Fairfield, Wash.: Ye Galleon Press.

Blanchet, Francis N.
1878 Historical Sketches of the Catholic Church in Oregon during the Past Forty Years (1838–1878). Portland, Oreg.: Catholic Centennial Press. (Reprinted: Ye Galleon Press, Fairfield, Wash., 1983.)

Blandau, Richard L.
1972 Nez Perces on the Colville Reservation: An Investigation of the Inception and Maintenance of a Socio-Cultural Isolate, 1885–1968. (M.A. Thesis in Anthropology, Washington State University, Pullman.)

Blenkinsop, George
1877 [Census of the] Shuswap Tribe. (Manuscript GR494, File 46, in Royal British Columbia Archives, Victoria.)

Boas, Franz
1887 Museums of Ethnology and Their Classification. *Science* 9(228):587–589.

_____
1888 Chinook Songs. *Journal of American Folk-Lore* 1(3):220–226.

_____
1890 First General Report on the Indians of British Columbia. Pp. 801–893 in *59th Annual Report of the British Association for the Advancement of Science for 1889*. London. (Also issued as separate publ. with new pagination.)

_____
1890a English-Thompson Lexicon. (Manuscript 497.3.B63c, [30(S1b.10)], Boas Collection, Library of the American Philosophical Society, Philadelphia.)

_____
1890b [Molala fieldnotes.] (Manuscripts No. 999 in National Anthropological Archives, Smithsonian Institution, Washington.)

_____
1891 Second General Report on the Indians of British Columbia. [Incl. Pt. IV, pp. 632–647:The Shuswap.] Pp. 562–715 in *60th Annual Report of the British Association for the Advancement of Science for 1890*. London. (Also issued as separate publ. with new pagination.)

_____
1892 Physical Characteristics of the Tribes of the North Pacific Coast. Pp. 424–449 in *61st Annual Report of the British Association for the Advancement of Science for 1891*. London (Also issued as separate publ. with new pagination.)

_____
1892a [Upper Chinookan texts and vocabulary, from Wasco and Clackamas fieldwork, Grand Ronde Reservation, Oreg.] (Manuscripts in the Library of the American Philosophical Society, Philadelphia.)

_____
1894 Chinook Texts. *Bureau of American Ethnology Bulletin* 20. Washington.

_____
1895 Fifth Report on the Indians of British Columbia. Pp. 522–592 in *65th Annual Report of the British Association for the Advancement of Science for 1895*. London. (Also issued as separate publ. with new pagination.)

_____
1899 Summary of the Work of the Committee in British Columbia. Pp. 667–682 in *68th Annual Report of the British Association for the Advancement of Science for 1898*. London. (Also issued as separate publ. with new pagination.)

_____
1900 [Okanagan materials.] (Manuscripts in Boas Collection, Library of the American Philosophical Society, Philadelphia; copy, microfilm No. A248, in British Columbia Archives and Record Service, Victoria.)

_____
1901 Kathlamet Texts. *Bureau of American Ethnology Bulletin* 26. Washington (Reprinted: Scholarly Press, St. Clair Shores, Mich., 1977.)

_____
1902 Some Problems in North American Archaeology. *American Journal of Archaeology*, 2d ser. 6:1–6.

_____
1905 The Jesup North Pacific Expedition. Pp. 90–100 in *Proceedings of the 13th International Congress of Americanists, New York, 1902*. Easton, Pa.: Eschenbach. (Reprinted: Kraus Reprint, Nendeln, Liechtenstein, 1968.)

_____
1909 Coyote and Eagle, a Wasco Text. Pp. 232–233 in Wishram Texts, by Edward Sapir. *Publications of the American Ethnological Society* 2. Leyden. (Reprinted: AMS Press, New York, 1974; Mouton de Gruyter, New York and Berlin, 1990.)

_____
1909a [Editor's note on Basketry.] Pp. 487–488 in The Shuswap, by James A. Teit. *Memoirs of the American Museum of Natural History* 4(7); *Publications of the Jesup North Pacific Expedition* 2(7). Leiden and New York.

_____
1911 Introduction. Pp. 5–83 in Pt. 1 of Handbook of American Indian Languages. Franz Boas, ed. *Bureau of American Ethnology Bulletin* 40. Washington. (Reprinted as: Introduction to *Handbook of American Indian Languages*, with J.W. Powell's Indian Linguistic Families of America North of Mexico. Preston Holder, ed. University of Nebraska Press, Lincoln, 1966.)

_____
1911a Chinook. Pp. 559–677 in Pt. 1 of Handbook of American Indian Languages. Franz Boas, ed. *Bureau of American Ethnology Bulletin* 40. Washington. (Pp. 673–677 is: Wishram Text, by Edward Sapir.)

1917   Folk-tales of Salishan and Sahaptin Tribes. Collected by James A. Teit, Marian K. Gould, Livingston Farrand, and Herbert J. Spinden. *Memoirs of the American Folk-Lore Society* 11. Lancaster, Pa. (Reprinted: Kraus Reprint, New York, 1969.)

1918   Kutenai Tales; Together with Texts Collected by Alexander Francis Chamberlain. *Bureau of American Ethnology Bulletin* 59. Washington.

1919   Kinship Terms of the Kutenai Indians. *American Anthropologist*, n.s. 21(1):98–101.

1920   The Classification of American Languages. *American Anthropologist*, n.s. 22(4):367–376. (Reprinted: Pp. 211–218 in Race, Language and Culture, by Franz Boas. Macmillan, New York, 1940.)

1922   James A. Teit. *American Anthropologist*, n.s. 24(4):490–492.

1924   Vocabulary of an Athapascan Tribe of Nicola Valley, British Columbia. *International Journal of American Linguistics* 3(1):36–38.

1926   Additional Notes on the Kutenai Language. [Appended to: Grammar of the Kutenai Language, by Pater Philippo Canestrelli.] *International Journal of American Linguistics* 4(1):85–104.

1927   Primitive Art. Cambridge, Mass.: Harvard University Press. (Reprinted: Dover Publications, New York, 1955.)

1929   Classification of American Indian Languages. Language 5(1):1–7. (Reprinted: Pp. 219–225 in Race, Language and Culture, by Franz Boas. Macmillan, New York, 1940.)

Boas, Franz, and Alexander F. Chamberlain 1918 *see* Boas, Franz, 1918

Boas, Franz, and Herman K. Haeberlin
1927   Sound Shifts in Salishan Dialects. *International Journal of American Linguistics* 4(2–4):117–136.

Boas, Franz, et al.
1915   Anthropology in North America. New York: G.E. Stechert. (Reprinted: Kraus Reprint, New York, 1972.)

Boelscher, Marianne Ignace
1986   Setsintens re Simpcw: Songs of the North Thompson Shuswap. British Columbia: North Thompson Indian Band.

Bolon, Gustavus
1854   [Report to Isaac I. Stevens, September 3, 1854.] (Manuscript in Records of the Washington Superintendency of Indian Affairs, 1853–1874, Record Group 75, National Archives, Washington.)

Bond, Carl E.
1973   Keys to Oregon Freshwater Fishes: Rev. ed. *Oregon Agricultural Experiment Station Technical Bulletin* 58. Corvallis.

Bonnichsen, Robson
1977   Models for Deriving Cultural Resource Information from Stone Tools. *Canada. National Museum of Man. Mercury Series. Ethnology Service Paper* 60. Ottawa.

Booth, Margaret, ed.
1928   Overland from Indiana to Oregon, The Dinwiddie Journal. *Sources of Northwest History* 2. Missoula: University of Montana.

Borden, Charles E.
1950   Preliminary Report on Archaeological Investigations in the Fraser Delta Region. *Anthropology in British Columbia* 1:13–27. Victoria.

1952   Results of Archaeological Investigations in Central British Columbia. *Anthropology in British Columbia* 3:31–43. Victoria.

1952a   A Uniform Site Designation Scheme for Canada. *Anthropology in British Columbia* 3:44–48. Victoria.

1954   Some Aspects of Prehistoric Coastal-Interior Relations in the Pacific Northwest. *Anthropology in British Columbia* 4:26–32. Victoria.

1956   Two Surveys in the East Kootenai Region. Pp. 71–101 in Northwest Archaeology Number, by Richard D. Daugherty et al. *Research Studies of the State College of Washington* 24(1). Pullman, Wash.

1960   DjRi3, An Early Site in the Fraser Canyon, British Columbia. Pp. 101–118 in Contributions to Anthropology 1957. *National Museum of Canada. Bulletin* 162; *Anthropological Series* 45. Ottawa.

1962   West Coast Crossties with Alaska. Pp. 9–19 in Prehistoric Cultural Relations between the Arctic and Temperate Zones of North America. John M. Campbell, ed. *Arctic Institute of North America, Technical Papers* 11. Montreal. (Reprinted: Johnson Reprint, New York, 1972.)

1975   Origins and Development of Early Northwest Coast Culture, to About 3000 B.C. *Canada. National Museum of Man. Mercury Series. Archaeological Survey Paper* 45. Ottawa.

Boreson, Keo
1975   Rock Art of the Pacific Northwest. (M.A. Thesis in Anthropology, University of Idaho, Moscow; published in NARN 10(1):90–122. Moscow, Idaho, 1976.)

1976   Rock Art of the Pacific Northwest. *Northwest Anthropological Research Notes* 10(1):90–122. Moscow, Idaho. (Originally presented as the author's M.A. Thesis in Anthropology, 1975.)

1976a   A Bibliography of Petroglyphs/Pictographs in Idaho, Oregon, and Washington. *Northwest Anthropological Research Notes* 10(1):123–146. Moscow, Idaho.

1979   Archaeological Test Excavations at 10-VY-156, South Fork Salmon River Satellite Facility, Valley County, Idaho. *University of Idaho. Anthropological Research Manuscript Series* 57. Moscow, Idaho.

1980   Serrated Edges on Petroglyph Boulders. (Paper presented at the 33d Annual Northwest Anthropological Conference, Bellingham, Wash.)

1984   The Rock Art of the Lower Salmon River. (Report prepared for the Bureau of Land Management, Cottonwood Resource Area, Cottonwood, Idaho.)

1987   Documentation of the Alberton Pictograph Site (24MO505) in Western Montana. (Report prepared for the Bonneville Power Administration, Archaeological and Historical Services, Eastern Washington University, Cheney.)

1989   Documentation and Management Recommendations of the Treaty Rock Site (10KA44), Kootenai County, Idaho. *Eastern Washington University. Archaeological and Historical Services. Short Report* 176. Cheney.

1989a   Documentation of Rock Art Site (10NP287), Nez Perce County, Idaho. *Eastern Washington University. Archaeological and Historical Services. Short Report* 182. Cheney.

1990   Documentation of Rock Art Site (45AS93), Asotin County, Washington. (Report submitted to the U.S. Army Corps of Engineers, Walla Walla District, Wash.)

1990a   Rock Art. Pp. 80–133 in A Culture Resources Overview, Sampling Survey, and Management Plan, Colville Indian Reservation, Okanogan and Ferry Counties, Washington. Stan Gough, ed. *Eastern Washington University. Reports in Archaeology and History* 100–74. Cheney.

1991   The Rock Art of the Middle Fork of the Salmon River: Custer, Idaho, Lemhi, and Valley Counties, Idaho. *Eastern Washington University. Reports in Archaeology and History* 100–76. Cheney.

1991a   Documentation of the Rock Art of Moon Cave, Asotin County, Washington. *Archeology in Washington* 3:75–86. Bellingham: Association for Washington Archaeology.

1994   Documentation of Pictographs at Sites 450K82, 450K392, and 450K603, Okanogan National Forest, Washington. (Report prepared for the Okanogan National Forest, Okanogan, Wash.)

Boreson, Keo, and Jerry R. Galm
1997   Archaeological Investigations at the Stemilt Creek Village Site (45CH302), Chelan County, Washington. *Eastern Washington University. Reports in Archaeology and History.* Cheney, Wash.

Boreson, Keo, and Warren R. Peterson
1985   The Petroglyphs at Lake Pend Oreille, Bonner County, Northern Idaho. *Eastern Washington University. Reports in Archaeology and History* 100–149. Cheney. (Technical report published jointly with the U.S. Army Corps of Engineers, Seattle District.)

Borthwick, David
1975   Indian Reserves in British Columbia: An Overview of a Century of Conflict. (Manuscript in D. Borthwick's possession.)

Bouchard, Randall T. (Randy)
1966–1970   [Okanagan-Colville mythology.] (Manuscript in British Columbia Indian Language Project, Victoria.)

1966–1991   [Okanagan-Colville ethnographic and linguistic fieldnotes.] (Manuscript in British Columbia Indian Language Project, Victoria.)

1968–1991   [Lillooet ethnographic and linguistic fieldnotes.] (Manuscript in British Columbia Indian Language Project, Victoria.)

1971–1981   [Squamish ethnographic and linguistic fieldnotes.] (Manuscript in British Columbia Indian Language Project, Victoria.)

1978   Okanagan Indian Legends. Pp. 10–20 in *2d Annual Report of the Okanagan Historical Society.* Vernon, B.C.

Bouchard, Randall T. (Randy), and Dorothy I.D. Kennedy
1973–1981   [Thompson (Lytton) ethnobotanic fieldnotes.] (Manuscript in British Columbia Indian Language Project, Victoria.)

1977   Lillooet Stories. [Text and 1 sound cassette.] *Sound Heritage* 6(1). Victoria: Provincial Archives of British Columbia.

1979   Shuswap Stories: Collected 1971–1975. Vancouver, B.C.: CommCept Publishing Ltd.

1984   Indian Land Use and Occupancy in the Franklin D. Roosevelt Lake Area of Washington State. (Report prepared for the Colville Confederated Tribes, Washington, and the United States Bureau of Reclamation, Seattle, Wash.)

1984a   Indian History and Knowledge of the Lower Similkameen River-Palmer Lake Area, Okanogan County, Washington. (Report to the U.S. Army Corps of Engineers, Seattle District, North Pacific Division. Manuscript in British Columbia Indian Language Project, Victoria.)

1985   Lakes Indian Ethnography and History. (Report prepared for the British Columbia Heritage Conservation Branch, Victoria.)

1985a   Indian History and Knowledge of the Merritt to Surey Lake Corridor of the Proposed Coquihalla Highway. (Manuscript in British Columbia Indian Language Project, Victoria.)

1985b   Indian Knowledge and Utilization of the Sicamous-Revelstoke Area. (Appendix 1:71–90 in Highway 1 — Four Laning Project, Cambie to Revelstoke, B.C., Detailed Heritage Resource Inventory and Impact Assessment.) Victoria: Arcas Associates for the Heritage Conservation Branch, Ministry of Provincial Secretary and Government Services, Victoria, and the Designs and Surveys Branch, Ministry of Transportation and Highways, Victoria.

1988   Indian Land Use and Indian History of the Stein River Valley, British Columbia. Pp. 104–197 (Appendix One) in Stein River Haulroad, Heritage Resources Inventory and Impact Assessment, by Ian Wilson. Report prepared for B.C. Forest Products Limited, Boston Bar Division, by I.R. Wilson Consultants, Brentwood Bay, B.C. (Copy in the Library of the B.C. Ministry of Tourism and Ministry Responsible for Culture, Victoria.)

1995   Ethnographic Examination of Scheidam Flats Land Use. Victoria: British Columbia Indian Language Project.

Bouchard, Randall T. (Randy), and Sam Mitchell
1975   Fraser River Lillooet Classfied Word List. (Manuscript in British Columbia Indian Language Project, Victoria.)

Bouchard, Randall T. (Randy), and Lary Pierre
1973   How to Write the Okanagan Language. (Manuscript in British Columbia Indian Language Project, Victoria.)

Bouchard, Randall T. (Randy), Charlie Mack, and Baptiste Ritchie
1974   Mount Currie Lillooet Classifed Word List. (Manuscript in British Columbia Indian Language Project, Victoria.)

1974a   How to Write the Lillooet Language (Mount Currie Dialect). Rev. version. (Manuscript in British Columbia Indian Language Project, Victoria.)

Bouchard, Randall T. (Randy), Sam Mitchell, and Bill Edwards
1973   How to Write the Lillooet Language (Fraser River Dialect). Rev. version. (Manuscript in British Columbia Indian Language Project, Victoria.)

Bouchard, Randall T. (Randy), Lary Pierre, and Martin Louie
1973   Classified Word List for the Okanagan Language. (Manuscript in British Columbia Indian Language Project, Victoria.)

Bowers, Alfred W.
1952   [Oral Testimony, before the Indian Claims Commission, 16 January 1952.] (Transcript of oral testimony, pp. 526–564 in Docket 81, Indian Claims Commission, National Archives, Washington.)

1964   Archaeological Reconnaissance in the Sawtooth Mountain Study Area. (Manuscript, Pacific Northwest Anthropological Archive, Moscow, Idaho.)

1967   Archaeological Excavations in the Spangler Reservoir and Surveys in Washington County, Idaho. (Manuscript, National Park Service and Idaho Bureau of Mines and Geology, Moscow.)

Boyd, Robert
1985   The Introduction of Infectious Dieases among the Indians of the Pacific Northwest, 1774–1874. (Ph.D. Dissertation in Anthropology, University of Washington, Seattle. Photocopy: University Microfilms International, Ann Arbor, Mich., 1985.)

1994   Smallpox in the Pacific Northwest: The First Epidemics. *BC Studies* 101:5–40.

1994a   The Pacific Northwest Measels Epidemic of 1847–1848. Oregon Historical Quarterly 95(1):6–47. (Special Issue: Early Contacts between Euro-Americans and Native Americans.)

1994b   The Columbia River as a Corridor for Disease Introduction: 'New Diseases' of the 1840's in the Pacific Northwest. (To appear in Essays in Columbia River History and Culture. William Lang and Robert Carriker, eds. Seattle: University of Washington.) (In press.)

1996   People of The Dalles: The Indians of Wascopam Mission. A Historical Ethnography Based on the Papers of the Methodist Missionaries. Lincoln and London: University of Nebraska Press; In cooperation with the American Indian Studies Research Institute, Indiana University, Bloomington.

Boyd, Robert, and Yvonne Hajda
1987   Seasonal Population Movement along the Lower Columbia River: The Social and Ecological Context. *American Ethnologist* 14(2):309–26.

Boyer, David S.
1974   Powerhouse of the Northwest. *National Geographic Magazine* 146(6):821–847. Washington.

Boyle, W.H.
1870   [Letter of August 15, 1870, Umatilla Indian Agency, Oregon.] Pp. 519–522 in *41st Congress. 3d Session. House Executive Document* 1. (Serial No. 1449). Washington. (See also pp. 55–58 in ARCIA for 1870.)

Brady, Erika
1985   The Box That Got the Flourishes: The Cylinder Phonograph in Folklore Fieldwork, 1890–1937. (Ph.D. Dissertation in Anthropology, Indiana University, Bloomington.)

Brady, Erika, et al.
1984–   The Federal Cylinder Project: A Guide to Field Cylinder Collections in Federal Agencies 5 vols. through 1990. Vol. 1: Introduction and Inventory. Erika Brady, Maria La Vigna, Dorothy S. Lee, and Thomas Vennum, eds., 1984. Vol. 8: Early Anthologies. Dorothy S. Lee, ed., 1984. Vol. 2: Northeastern Indian Catalog; Southeastern Indian Catalog. Judith A. Grey and Dorothy S. Lee, eds., 1985. Vol. 3: Great Basin/Plateau Indian Catalog; Northwest Coast/Arctic Indian Catalog. Judith A. Gray, ed., 1988. Vol. 5: California Indian Catalog; Middle and South American Indian Catalog; Southwestern Indian Catalog, 1. Judith A. Grey and Edwin J. Schupman, Jr., eds., 1990. Washington: American Folklife Center, Library of Congress.

Brauner, David R.
1975   Archaeological Salvage of the Scorpion Knoll Site, 45AS41, Southeastern Washington. *Washington State University.*

Archaeological Research Center. Project Reports 23. Pullman.

1976   Alpowai: The Culture History of the Alpowa Locality. 2 vols. (Ph.D. Dissertation in Anthropology, Washington State University, Pullman. Conducted through contracts between the National Park Service and Washington State University; Frank C. Leonhardy, principal investigator.)

1985   Early Human Occupation in the Uplands of the Southern Plateau: Archaeological Excavations at the Pilcher Creek Site (35UN147), Union County, Oregon. (Report of the Department of Anthropology, Oregon State University, to the U.S.D.A. Soil Conservation Service and the National Geographic Society, Washington.)

Brauner, David R., and Nahani Stricker
1990   Archaeological Test Excavations and Evaluation of the Proposed Clearwater Fish Hatchery Site (10CW4), Clearwater County, Idaho: Phase II. Corvallis: Oregon State University, Department of Anthropology. (Report prepared for the Walla Walla District, Army Corps of Engineers, Walla Walla, Wash.)

Brewer, Laura
1845   [Letter of August 15, 1845, Wascopam Mission.] (Manuscript in Washington State Historical Society, Tacoma.)

Briegleb, Ann, ed.
1981   Directory of Ethnomusicological Sound Recording Collections in the U.S. and Canada. *Society for Ethnomusicology. Special Series* 2. Ann Arbor, Mich.

Bright, R.C.
1964   Pollen and Seed Stratigraphy of Swan Lake, Southeastern Idaho. *Tebiwa: Journal of the Idaho State University Museum* 9(2):1–47. Pocatello.

Bright, Ruth M.
1980   Harney Area Cultural Resources Class I Inventory: A Cultural Resources Overview. (M.A. Thesis in Anthropology, Portland State University, Portland, Oreg.)

British Columbia
1866   Columbia River Exploration, 1865–6: Instructions, Reports, & Journals Relating to the Government Exploration of the Country Lying between the Shuswap and Okanagan Lakes and the Rocky Mountains. W. Moberly in charge of Exploration. New Westminster, B.C.: Government Printing Office.

1869   Columbia River Exploration, 1866: Instructions, Reports, & Journals Relating to the Government Exploration of the Country Lying between the Shuswap and Okanagan Lakes and the Rocky Mountains. W. Moberly in charge of Exploration. New Westminster, B.C.: Government Printing Office.

1872   Map of British Columbia; Being a Geographical Division of the Indians of the Province, According to their Nationality or Dialect. Victoria, B.C.

British Columbia. Department of Health Services and Hospital Insurance
1956   Numerical List by School District of Residence of Indian Bands and Population as at December 31, 1956. (Manuscript in Vital Statistics Division, Department of Health Services and Hospital Insurance, Victoria, B.C.)

British Columbia. Indian Reserve Commission
1875   Papers Connected with the Indian Land Question, 1850–1875. Victoria, B.C.: R. Wolfenden.

Brockmann, Charles Thomas
1968   The Modern Social and Economic Organization of the Flathead Reservation. (Ph.D. Dissertation in Anthropology, University of Oregon, Eugene.)

1971   Reciprocity and Market Exchange on the Flathead Reservation. *Northwest Anthropological Research Notes* 5(1):77–93. Moscow, Idaho.

Brouillet, J.B.A.
1858   Account of the Murder of Dr. Whitman and the Ungrateful Calumnies of Henry H. Spalding, Protestant Missionary. *35th Congress. 1st Session. House Executive Document* 38. Washington.

Brow, Catherine Judith
1967   A Socio-Cultural History of the Alkali Lake Shuswap 1882–1966. (M.A. Thesis in Anthropology, University of Washington, Seattle.)

Brownam, David L., and David A. Munsell
1969   Columbia Plateau Prehistory: Cultural Development and Impinging Influences. *American Antiquity* 34(3):249–264.

1972   Columbia Plateau Prehistory: Some Observations. *American Antiquity* 37(4):546–548.

Brown, Cecil H.
1985   Mode of Subsistence and Folk Biological Taxonomy. *Current Anthropology* 26(1):43–46.

Brown, Ellsworth Howard
1975   The History of the Flathead Indians in the Nineteenth Century. (Ph.D. Dissertation in History, Michigan State University, East Lansing.)

Brown, Mark H.
1967   The Flight of the Nez Perce. New York: G.P. Putnam's Sons.

Brown, R.C. Lundin
1863   [Letter of February 3, 1863.] (Colonial Correspondence F214, Royal British Columbia Archives, Victoria.)

Brown, William C.
1961   The Indian Side of the Story; Being a Concourse of Presentations Historical and Biographical in Character Relating to the Indian Wars, and the Treatment Accorded the Indians, in Washington Territory East of the Cascade Mountains during the Period from 1853 to 1889, [etc.]. Spokane, Wash.: C.W. Hill Printing.

Browne, John Ross
1858   Indian War in Oregon and Washington Territories: Special Report to the Secretary of War, and the Secretary of the Interior, Dated December 4, 1857. Pp. 1–66 in *35th Congress. 1st Session. House Executive Document* 38. (Serial No. 955). Washington. (Issued also in *Senate Executive Document* 12, Pt. 4.)

Brunot, Felix R.
1871   Yakama Indians; Minutes of a Council Held with Simcoe Indians, at Their Reservation, Washington Territory [...] Monday, July 31, 1871. Thomas K. Cree, Clerk Pp. 131–135 in ARCIA for the Year 1871. Washington: Government Printing Office.

Brunton, Bill B.
1966   [Ethnographic fieldnotes on Plateau intergroup ceremonialism.] (Manuscripts in Brunton's possession.)

1968   Cermonial Integration in the Plateau of Northwestern North America. *Northwest Anthropological Research Notes* 2(1):1–28. Moscow, Idaho.

1969   [Ethnographic fieldnotes on Kootenai intergroup ceremonialism and the stick game.] (Manuscript in Brunton's possession.)

1970   [Ethnographic fieldnotes on Kootenai stick gaming and related cultural domains.] Manuscript in Brunton's possession.

1974   The Stick Game in Kutenai Culture. (Ph.D. Dissertation in Anthropology, Washington State University, Pullman. Photocopy: University Microfilms International, Ann Arbor, Mich., 1984.)

1983   [Information gained through consulting work for the Kootenai.] (Manuscript in Brunton's possession).

1985   [Ethnographic fieldnotes on Kootenai shamanism and contemporary reservation life.] (Manuscript in Brunton's possession.)

1988   [Ethnographic fieldnotes on Kootenai shamanic healing] (Manuscript in Brunton's possession.)

Bryan, Alan L., and Donald R. Tuohy
1960   A Basalt Quarry in Northeastern Oregon. *Proceedings of the American Philosophical Society* 104(5):485–510. Philadelphia.

Buan, Carolyn M., and Richard Lewis, eds.
1991   The First Oregonians: An Illustrated Collection of Essays on Traditional Lifeways, Federal-Indian Relations, and The State's Native People Today. Portland, Oreg.: Oregon Council for the Humanities.

Bucy, Douglas
1974   A Technological Analysis of a Basalt Quarry in Western Idaho. *Tebiwa: Journal of the Idaho State University Museum* 16(2):1–45. Pocatello.

Buechel, Eugene
1970   A Dictionary of the Teton Dakota Sioux Language: Lakota-English, English-Lakota; with Considerations Given to Yankton and Santee [etc.]. Paul Manhart, ed. Pine Ridge, S. Dak.: Red Cloud Indian School, Inc., Holy Rosary Mission. (Reprinted in 1984.)

Bulmer, Ralph N.H.
1974   Folk Biology in the New Guinea Highlands. *Social Science Information* 13(4–5):9–28. The Hague, Netherlands.

Bunnell, Clarence O.
1933   Legends of the Klickitats: a Klickitat Version of the Story of the Bridge of the Gods. Portland, Oreg.: Metropolitan Press.

Bureau of Indian Affairs
1886–1939   [Indian Census Rolls, 1885–1940: Flathead, Kutenai, Pend d'Oreille, and Kalispel Indians, 1886–1939.] (Microfilms in Records of the Bureau of Indian Affairs, Record Group 75, National Archives, Washington.)

1887   [Letters Received, 1887.] (Document No. 5858 in Records of the Bureau of Indian Affairs, Record Group 75, National Archives, Washington.)

1887a   [Letters Received, 1887a.] (Document No. 28329 in Records of the Bureau of Indian Affairs, Record Group 75, National Archives, Washington.)

1888   [Letters Received, 1888.] (Document No. 15665 in Records of the Bureau of Indian Affairs, Record Group 75, National Archives, Washington.)

1888–1940   [American Indian Census Rolls: Plateau Tribes]. (Microfilms in Records of the Bureau of Indian Affairs, Record Group 75, National Archives, Washington.)

1889   [Letters Received, 1889.] (Document No. 32102 in Records of the Bureau of Indian Affiars, Record Group 75, National Archives, Washington.)

1889a   [Letters Received, 1889a.] (Documents Nos. 22118, 33895 in Records of the Bureau of Indian Affairs, Record Group 75, National Archives, Washington.)

1891   [Letters Received, 1891.] (Documents Nos. 37294, 38181, 39214, 39445 in Records of the Bureau of Indian Affairs, Record Group 75, National Archives, Washington.)

1894   [Letters Received, 1894.] (Document No. 5625 in Records of the Bureau of Indian Affairs, Record Group 75, National Archives, Washington.)

1894a   [Letters Received, 1894a.] (Document No. 24446 in Records of the Bureau of Indian Affairs, Record Group 75, National Archives, Washington.)

1896   [Letters Received, 1896.] (Document No. 15291 in Records of the Bureau of Indian Affairs, Record Group 75, National Archives, Washington.)

1897   [Letters Received, 1897.] (Document No. 51868 in Records of the Bureau of Indian Affairs, Record Group 75, National Archives, Washington.)

1904   [Letters Received, 1904.] (Document No. 86566 in Records of the Bureau of Indian Affairs, Record Group 75, National Archives, Washington.)

1907   [Central Classified Files, 1907.] (Documents Nos. 75954, 76667 in Records of the Bureau of Indian Affairs, Record Group 75, National Archives, Washington.)

1907–1914 [Reports of Superintendents.] (Annual Narratives and Statistical Reports from Field Jurisdictions of the Bureau of Indian Affairs, 1907–1938; M 1011, Roll 51, Record Group 75, National Archives, Washington.)

1908   [Central Classified Files, 1908.] (Document No. 51017 in Records of the Bureau of Indian Affairs, Record Group 75, National Archives, Washington.)

1908a   [Central Classified Files, 1908a.] (Document No. 72298–08–Flathead–175 in Records of the Bureau of Indian Affairs, Record Group 75, National Archives, Washington.)

1909   [Central Classified Files, 1909.] (Documents Nos. 34513, 47604 in Records of the Bureau of Indian Affairs, Record Group 75, National Archives, Washington.)

1910   [Central Classified Files, 1910.] (Document No. 30635 in Records of the Bureau of Indian Affairs, Record Group 75, National Archives, Washington.)

1910a   [Superintendent's Report: Fort Lapwai Sanitarium and School, 1910.] (Annual Narratives and Statistical Reports from Field Jurisdictions of the Bureau of Indian Affairs, 1907–1938; M 1011, Roll 51, Record Group 75, National Archives, Washington.)

1920   [Klamath Superintendency: Superintendent's Annual Report, 1920.] (Manuscript in Records of the Bureau of Indian Affairs Record Group 75, National Archives, Seattle Repository, Seattle, Wash.)

1938   Statistical Supplement to the Annual Report of the Commissioner of Indian Affairs. Washington: Government Printing Office.

1945   [Population Report, 1945.] Washington: U.S. Department of the Interior, Bureau of Indian Affairs.

1946   Indian Tribes, Bands and Communities Which Voted to Accept or Reject the Terms of the Indian Reorganization Act, the Dates When Elections Were Held and the Votes Cast. *Bureau of Indian Affairs Tribal Relations Pamphlet* 1A. Washington: Government Printing Office.

1960   Indian Reservations of the Northwest. E.L. Wight, Mary Mitchell, and Marie Schmidt, comps. and eds.; Lester Beal, illus. Portland, Oreg.: U.S. Department of the Interior, Bureau of Indian Affairs, Portland Area Office.

1961   United States Indian Population and Land, 1960–1961. Washington: U.S. Department of the Interior, Bureau of Indian Affairs.

1964   Flathead Indian Reservation 10 Year Plan: Poverty, Illiteracy & Ill Health Breed Dependency, Delinquency and Discrimination. (Typescript in Records of the Bureau of Indian Affairs, Record Group 75, National Archives, Washington. Cover title reads: The Long Trail from Poverty, Illiteracy & Stagnation; the Vanguard to Self-sufficiency, Education & Dynamism. Second set of leaves consists of: Addendum to Flathead Agency Ten-year Report; Index of Report for the Flathead Irrigation and Power Project.)

1966   Developing Recreation Resources: 1966 Narrative Highlights, Umatilla Sub-Agency. Portland, Oreg.: U.S. Department of the Interior, Bureau of Indian Affairs, Branch of Land Operations, Umatilla Sub-Agency.

1983   Local Estimates of Resident Indian Population and Labor Force Status: January 1983. Washington: U.S. Department of the Interior, Bureau of Indian Affairs.

1985   Local Estimates of Resident Indian Population and Labor Force Status, January 1985. Washington: U.S. Department of the Interior, Bureau of Indian Affairs.

1987   Indian Service Population and Labor Force Estimates: Local Estimates of Resident Indian Population and Labor Force Status, January 1987. Washington: U.S. Department of the Interior, Bureau of Indian Affairs.

1989   Indian Service Population and Labor Force Estimates, January 1989. Washington: U.S. Department of the Interior, Bureau of Indian Affairs.

1990   Acreage Recapitulation by Agency. Portland, Oreg.: U.S. Department of the Interior, Bureau of Indian Affairs, Portland Area Office.

1991   Indian Service Population and Labor Force Estimates: Local Estimates of Resident Indian Population and Labor Force Status, January 1991. Washington: U.S. Department of the Interior, Bureau of Indian Affairs.

1992   Indian Land Areas. (Indian Lands 1992). Map; compiled by the Handbook of North American Indians (Smithsonian Institution) in cooperation with the Bureau of Indian Affairs. Reston, Va.: U.S. Geological Survey.

1993   Indian Service Population and Labor Force Estimates. Washington: U.S. Department of the Interior, Bureau of Indian Affairs.

1994   [Draft: Enrollment, Reservpop., Census80, Census90, ICWANO.] (Printout of comparative population and enrollment figures, Office of Tribal Enrollment/Tribal Relations, Bureau of Indian Affairs; Lathel F. Duffield, Ph.D., Branch Chief, Washington.)

Burke, R.M., and P.W. Birkeland
1983   Holocene Glaciation in the Mountain Ranges of the Western United States. Pp. 3–11 in Vol. 2 of Late-Quaternary Environments of the United States. H.E. Wright, Jr., ed 2 vols. Minneapolis: University of Minnesota Press.

Burnet, MacFarlane, and David White
1972   Natural History of Infectious Diseases. New York: Cambridge University Press.

Burnett, Peter H.
1904   Recollections and Opinions of an Old Pioneer. *Oregon Historical Quarterly* 38(4):5(1):64–99.

Burns, Robert Ignatius
1947   Pere Joset's Account of the Indian War of 1858. *Pacific Northwest Quarterly* 38(4):285–314.

1952   A Jesuit at the Hell Gate Treaty of 1855. *Mid-America* 34(2):87–114. Chicago.

1966   The Jesuits and the Indian Wars of the Northwest. *Yale Western Americana Series* 11. New Haven, Conn.: Yale University Press. (Reprinted: University of Idaho Press, Moscow, 1986.)

Burroughs, Raymond D.
1961   The Natural History of the Lewis and Clark Expedition. East Lansing, Mich.: Michigan State University Press.

Burrows, James K.
1986   'A Much Needed Class of Labour,' The Economy and Income of the Southern Plateau Indians, 1897–1910. *BC Studies* 71(Autumn). Vancouver.

Bussey, Jean
1983   Alexis Creek Archaeological Investigations. (Manuscript on file, Archaeology Branch, Victoria, B.C.)

Butler, B. Robert
1957   Art of the Lower Columbia Valley. *Archaeology* 10(3):158–165.

1958   Archaeological Investigations on the Washington Shore of The Dalles Reservoir, 1955–1957; with an Appendix by Rodger Heglar. (Report on a joint archaeological project carried out under terms of a contract /No. 14–10–434–126/ between the U.S. National Park Service and the University of Washington). 2 vols. [Seattle: University of Washington to the U.S. National Park Service.]

1958–1959   The Prehistory of the Dice Game in the Southern Plateau. *Tebiwa: Journal of the Idaho State University Museum* 2(1):65–71. Pocatello.

1959   Lower Columbia Valley Archaeology: A Survey and Appraisal of Some Major Archaeological Resources. *Tebiwa: Journal of the Idaho State University Museum* 2(2):6–24. Pocatello.

1960   The Physical Stratigraphy of Wakemap Mound: A New Interpretation. (M.A. Thesis in Anthropology, University of Washington, Seattle.)

1961   The Old Cordilleran Culture in the Pacific Northwest. With an Appendix by Earl H. Swanson, Jr. *Occasional Papers of the Idaho State College Museum* 5. Pocatello.

1962   Contributions to the Prehistory of the Columbia Plateau; A Report on Excavations in the Palouse and Craig Mountain

Sections. *Occasional Papers of the Idaho State College Museum* 9. Pocatello. (Photocopy: Library Photographic Service, University of California, Berkeley, 1987.)

1962a   The B. Stewart and the Cradleboard Mortuary Sites: A Contribution to the Archaeology of The Dalles Region of the Lower Columbia Valley. *Tebiwa: Journal of the Idaho State University Museum* 5(1):30–40. Pocatello.

1963   An Early Man Site at Big Camas Prairie, South-central Idaho. *Tebiwa: Journal of the Idaho State University Museum* 6(1):22–23. Pocatello.

1965   The Structure and Function of the Old Cordilleran Culture Concept. *American Anthropologist* 67(5):1120–1131.

1965a   Perspectives on the Prehistory of the Lower Columbia Valley. *Tebiwa: Journal of the Idaho State University Museum* 8(1):1–16. Pocatello.

1965b   Contributions to the Archaeology of Southeastern Idaho. *Tebiwa: Journal of the Idaho State University Museum* 8(1):41–48. Pocatello.

1966   A Guide to Understanding Idaho Archaeology. 1st ed. Pocatello: Idaho State University Museum.

1968   A Guide to Understanding Idaho Archaeology. 2nd rev. ed. Pocatello: Idaho State University Museum.

1968a   An Introduction to the Archaeoogical Investigations in the Pioneer Basin Locality of Eastern Idaho. *Tebiwa: Journal of the Idaho State University Museum* 11(1):1–30. Pocatello.

1969   The Earlier Cultural Remains at Cooper's Ferry. *Tebiwa: Journal of the Idaho State University Museum* 12(2):35–50. Pocatello.

1971   A Bison Jump in the Upper Salmon River Valley of Eastern Idaho. *Tebiwa: Journal of the Idaho State University Museum* 14(1):4–32. Pocatello.

1972   Folsom Points from the Upper Salmon River Valley. *Tebiwa: Journal of the Idaho State University Museum* 15(1):72. Pocatello.

1973   Folsom and Plano Points from the Peripheries of the Upper Snake River Country. *Tebiwa: Journal of the Idaho State University Museum* 16(1):69–72. Pocatello.

1978   A Guide to Understanding Idaho Archaeology: The Upper Snake and Salmon River Country. Third edition. Boise: Idaho State Historic Preservation Office.

1978a   An Alternative Explanation of the Large Pithouse Villages on the Middle Fork of the Salmon River. (Paper presented at the 6th Annual Meeting of the Idaho Archaeological Society, Boise.)

1979   A Fremont Culture Fontier in the Upper Snake and Salmon River Country? *Tebiwa: Miscellaneous Papers of the Idaho State University Museum of Natural History* 18. Pocatello.

1979a   The Native Pottery of the Upper Snake and Salmon River Country. (Paper presented at the 32d Annual Northwest Anthropological Conference, Eugene, Oreg.)

1981   Late Period Cultural Sequences in the Northeastern Great Basin Subarea and their Implications for the Upper Snake and Salmon River Country. *Journal of California and Great Basin Anthropology* 3(2):245–256.

1981a   When Did the Shoshoni Begin to Occupy Southern Idaho? Essay on Late Prehistoric Cultural Remains from the Upper Snake and Salmon River Country. *Occasional papers of the Idaho State University Museum of Natural History* 32. Pocatello.

1983   The Quest for the Historic Fremont; and A Guide to the Prehistoric Pottery of Southern Idaho. *Occasional Papers of the Idaho State University Museum of Natural History* 33. Pocatello.

1983a   Shield-Bearing Warriors, Horned Figures, and Great Salt Lake Gray Wares: Whither the Fremont after A.D. 1300? (Paper presented at the 11th Annual Idaho Archaeological Society Conference, Boise.)

Butler, Virginia L.
1993   Natural Versus Cultural Salmonid Remains: Origin of The Dalles Roadcut Bones, Columbia River, Oregon, U.S.A. *Journal of Archaeoogical Science* 20(1):1–24. London and New York.

Butler, Virginia L., and James C. Chatters
1994   The Role of Bone Density in Structuring Prehistoric Salmon Bone Assemblages. *Journal of Archaeological Science* 21(3):413–424. London and New York.

Butler, Virginia L., and Randall F. Schalk
1986   Holocene Salmonid Resources of the Upper Columbia. Pp. 232–252 in Vol. 1 of The Wells Reservoir Archaeological Project. James E. Chatters, ed. *Central Washington University. Archaeological Survey Report* 86–6. Ellensburg, Wash.

CRITFC *see* Columbia River Inter-Tribal Fish Commission

Cain, A. John
1859   [Letter of August 2, Indian Agency Office, Walla Walla Valley.] Pp. 781–785 in *36th Congress. 1st Session. Senate Executive Document* 2. (Serial No. 1023). Washington.

Cain, H. Thomas
1950   Petroglyphs of Central Washington. Seattle: University of Washington Press.

Caldwell, Warren W.
1956   The Archaeology of Wakemap: A Stratified Site near The Dalles of the Columbia. (Ph.D. Dissertation in Anthropology, University of Washington, Seattle.)

1968   The View from Wenas: A Study in Plateau Prehistory. *Occasional Papers of the Idaho State University Museum* 24. Pocatello.

Caldwell, Warren W., and Oscar L. Mallory
1967   Hells Canyon Archeology. Jerome E. Petsche, ed. *River Basin Surveys. Publications in Salvage Archaeology* 6. Washington: Smithsonian Institution.

Caldwell, Warren W., et al.
1967   Lake Sharpe; Big Bend Dam: Archaeology, History, Geology, Richard B. Johnston, ed. Washington: Smithsonian Institution.

Cameron, Catherine
1984   An Archaeological Reconnaissance of the Nevada Creek Drainage, Powell County, Montana. (Draft report submitted to the Montana State Historic Preservation Office; rev. in 1985.)

Campbell, Sarah K.
1984   Report of Burial Relocation Projects, Chief Joseph Dam Project, Washington. Seattle: Office of Public Archaeology, Institute for Environmental Studies, University of Washington.

1984a   Archaeological Investigations at Sites 45-OK-2 and 45-OK-2A, Chief Joseph Dam Project, Washington. Seattle: Office of Public Archaeology, Institute for Environmental Studies, University of Washington.

1984b   Research Design for the Chief Joseph Dam Cultural Resources Project. Seattle: Office of Public Archaeology, Institute for Environmental Studies, University of Washington.

1985   Summary of Results, Chief Joseph Dam Cultural Resources Project, Washington. Seattle: Office of Public Archaeology, Institute for Environmental Studies, University of Washington.

1985a   Sedimentary Sequence at Excavated Sites and Regional Paleoenvironmental Reconstruction. Pp. 149–178 in Summary of Results, Chief Joseph Dam Cultural Resources Project, Washington. Sarah K. Campbell, ed. Seattle: Office of Public Archaeology, Institute for Environmental Studies, University of Washington.

1985b   Selected Aspects of the Artifact Assemblage. Pp. 287–316 in Summary of Results, Chief Joseph Dam Cultural Resources Project, Washington. Sarah K. Campbell, ed. Seattle: Office of Public Archaeology, Institute for Environmental Studies, University of Washington.

1985c   Discussion and Conclusions. Pp. 483–514 in Summary of Results, Chief Joseph Dam Cultural Resources Project, Washington. Sarah K. Campbell, ed. Seattle: Office of Public Archaeology, Institute for Environmental Studies, University of Washington.

1985d   Synthesis. Pp. 481–511 in Summary of Results: Chief Joseph Dam Cultural Resources Project. Sarah K. Campbell, ed. Seattle: Office of Public Archaeology, Institute for Environmental Studies, University of Washington.

1987   A Resource Protection Planning Process Identification Component for the Eastern Washington Protohistoric Study Unit. Olympia: Washington State Office of Archaeology and Historic Preservation.

1989   PostColumbian Culture History in the Northern Columbia Plateau: A.D. 1500–1900. (Ph.D. Dissertation in Anthropology, University of Washington, Seattle. Published: Garland Publishing Co., New York, 1990.)

Canada. Department of Indian Affairs
1893   [Annual Report, 1892.] Ottawa: Canada. Department of Indian Affairs.

1896   [Annual Report, 1895.] *Canada. Sessional Paper 14*. Ottawa.

1910   [Census Return, 1910.] *Canada. Sessional Paper 27*. Ottawa.

1915   [Annual Report, 1915.] Ottawa: Canada. Department of Indian Affairs.

1924   [Annual Report, 1924.] *Canada. Sessional Paper 14*. Ottawa.

1929   [Annual Report, 1929.] Ottawa: Canada. Department of Indian Affairs.

Canada. Department of Indian Affairs and Northern Development
1960   List of Indian Agencies and Bands in British Columbia and
            Yukon Region as of June 30, 1960. (Manuscript at Union of
            British Columbia Indian Chiefs, Vancouver.)

1972   Registered Indian Membership by Band and Agency or Dis-
            trict within Regions. (Manuscript at Department of Indians
            Affairs and Northern Development, Vancouver.)

1980   Linguistic and Cultural Affiliations of Canadian Indian
            Bands. Ottawa: Department of Indian Affairs and Northern
            Development.

1997   Registered Indian Population. Ottawa: Department of Indian
            Affairs and Northern Development.

Canada. Department of Indian Affairs and Northern Development. Indian
Affairs Branch
1970   Linguistic and Cultural Affiliations of Canadian Indian
            Bands. G.W. Neville, comp. and ed. Ottawa: Department of
            Indian Affairs and Northern Development, Indian Affairs
            Branch; Queen's Printer for Canada.

Canada. Department of Indian and Northern Affairs
1986   The Canadian Indian. Ottawa: Department of Indian and
            Northern Affairs.

1989   Basic Departmental Data; December 1989. Ottawa: Depart-
            ment of Indian and Northern Affairs.

1989a   Departmental Overview; June 1989. Ottawa: Department of
            Indian and Northern Affairs.

Canada. Department of Mines and Resources
1939   Census of Indians in Canada. Ottawa: Canada. Department of
            Mines and Resources.

Canada. Indian and Northern Affairs
1991   Indian Register Population by Sex and Type of Residence by
            Group, Responsibility Centre and Region, 1990. Ottawa:
            Minister of Government Services Canada.

1992   Schedule of Indian Bands, Reserves and Settlements, Includ-
            ing - Membership and Populatin Location and Area in
            Hectares, December 1992. Ottawa: Minister of Government
            Services Canada.

1996   Indian Register Populations by Sex and Residence 1996.
            Ottawa: Ministry of Indian Affairs and Northern Develop-
            ment.

Canada. Indian Reserve Commission
1881–1908   Indian Reserve Commission: Minutes of Decision and Corre-
            spondence, Books No. 4, 6–7, 8, and 22–23. (Documents in
            Indian Land Registry Branch of Lands, Revenues and Trusts.
            Indian and Northern Affairs Canada, British Columbia
            Regional Office, Vancouver.)

Canada. Royal Commission on Indian Affairs
1916   Report of the Royal Commission on Indian Affairs for the
            Province of British Columbia. [The McKenna-McBride Com-
            mission.] 4 vols. Victoria, B.C.: Acme Press.

Canada. Superintendent of Indian Affairs
1879   Report 15 of the Deputy Superintendent General of Indians
            Affairs, 1876–1879. Ottawa: Canada. Superintendent of Indian
            Affairs.

Canestrelli, Phillip (Filippo)
1894   Linguae Ksanka (Kootenai): Elementa Grammaticae. Santa
            Clara, Calif.: N.H. Downing. (Reissued: A Kootenai Gram-
            mar, Gonzaga University, Spokane, 1959.)

1926   Grammar of the Kutenai Language. Franz Boas, ed. *Interna-
            tional Journal of American Linguistics* 4(1):1–84.

Cannon, Aubrey
1992   Conflict and Salmon on the Interior Plateau of British Colum-
            bia. Pp. 506–524 in A Complex Culture of the British Colum-
            bia Plateau: Traditional *Stl'átl'imx* Resource Use. Brian Hay-
            den, ed. Vancouver: UBC Press.

Cannon, William J., and Mary F. Ricks
1986   The Lake Country Oregon Rock Art Inventory: Implications
            for Prehistory Settlement and Land Use Patterns. Pp. 1–23 in
            Contributions to the Archaeology of Oregon 1983–1986. Ken-
            neth Ames, ed. *Association of Oregon Archaeologists. Occa-
            sional Papers* 3. Portland.

Carl, G. Clifford, Wilbert A. Clemens, and Casimir C. Lindsey
1959   The Fresh-water Fishes of British Columbia. 3d rev. ed.
            *British Columbia Provincial Museum. Department of Recre-
            ation and Conservation. Handbook* 5. Victoria.

1967   The Fresh-water Fishes of British Columbia. 4th ed. *British
            Columbia Provincial Museum, Department of Recreation and
            Conservation. Handbook* 5. Victoria. (Reprinted in 1973).

Carley, Caroline D.
1981   Water Line Trench Emergency Excavations, 1979–1980. *Uni-
            versity of Idaho. Anthropological Research Manuscript Series*
            14. Moscow.

Carley, Caroline D., and Robert Lee Sappington
1984   Archaeological Investigations on the East Fork of the Salmon
            River, Custer Country, Idaho. *University of Idaho. Anthropo-
            logical Research Manuscript Series* 79. Moscow.

Carlson, Barry F.
1972   A Grammar of Spokan: A Salish Language of Eastern Wash-
            ington. *University of Hawaii Working Papers in Linguistics*
            4(4). Honolulu.

1976   The n-shift in Spokane Salishan. *International Journal of
            American Linguistics* 42(2):133–139.

1978   Coyote and Gopher (Spokane). Pp. 3–14 in Coyote Stories.
            William Bright, ed. *International Journal of American Lin-
            guistics. Native American Text Series. Monograph* 1. Chicago.
            The University of Chicago Press.

1980   Spokane -e-. *International Journal of American Linguistics*
            46(2):78–84.

1980a   Two-goal Transitive Stems in Spokane Salish. *International
            Journal of American Linguistics* 46(1):21–26.

1989   Reduplication and Stress in Spokane. *International Journal of
            American Linguistics* 55(2):204–213.

1990   Compounding and Lexical Affixation in Spokane. *Anthropo-
            logical Linguistics* 32(1–2):69–82.

1993   Strong and Weak Root Inchoatives in Spokane. Pp. 37-46 in
            American Indian Linguistics and Ethnography in Honor of
            Laurence C. Thompson. Anthony Mattina and Timothy
            Montler, eds. *University of Montana Occasional Papers in
            Linguistics* 10. Missoula.

Carlson, Barry F., and Pauline Flett, comps.
1989   Spokane Dictionary. *University of Montana Occasional
            Papers in Linguistics* 6. Missoula.

Carlson, Barry F., and Laurence C. Thompson
1982   Out-of-control in Two (Maybe More) Salish Languages.
            Anthropological Linguistics 24(1):51–65.

Carlson, Roy L.
1959　　Klamath Henwas and Other Stone Sculpture. *American Anthropologist* 61(1):88–96.

———
1970　　Archaeology of British Columbia. *BC Studies* 6–7:7–17. Vancouver.

———
1991　　The Northwest Coast Before A.D. 1600. Pp. 109–136 in Proceedings of the Great Ocean Conferences, Vol. 1, the North Pacific to 1600. Portland, Oreg.: Oregon Historical Society Press.

———
1996　　The Later Prehistory of British Columbia. Pp. 215–226 [vol. bib., pp. 227–256] in Early Human Occupation in British Columbia. Roy L. Carson and Luke Dalla Bona, eds. Vancouver, B.C.: UBC Press.

Carlson, Roy L., and Luke Dalla Bona, eds.
1996　　Early Human Occupation in British Columbia. Vancouver, B.C.:UBC Press.

Carriker, Eleanor, Robert C. Carriker, Clifford A. Carroll, and W.L. Larsen
1976　　Guide to the Microfilm Edition of the Oregon Province Archives of the Society of Jesus Indian Language Collection: The Pacific Northwest Tribes. Spokane, Wash.: Gonzaga Univeristy.

Carroll, James W.
1959　　Flatheads and Whites: A Study of Conflict. (Ph.D. Dissertation in Sociology and Social Institutions, Univeristy of California, Berkeley.)

Carrothers, Beulah Harden
1959　　Indian Lore. *Lane Country Historian* 4(2):42–44. Eugene, Oreg.

Carrothers, W.A.
1941　　The British Columbia Fisheries. Foreword by H.A. Innis. *Political Economy Series* 10. Toronto: University of Toronto Press.

Carstens, Peter
1987　　Leaders, Followers, and Supporters: The Okanagan Experience. *Anthropologica* 29(1):7–19.

———
1991　　The Queen's People: A Study of Hegemony, Coercion, and Accomodation among the Okanagan of Canada. Toronto: University of Toronto Press.

Chalfant, Stuart A.
1974　　Ethnohistorical Reports on Aboriginal Land Use and Occupancy: Spokan Indians, Palus Indians, Columbia Salish, Wenatchi Salish. Pp. 25–142 [Spokane], 175–227 [Palouse], 229–313 [Columbian Salish], 315–375 [Wenatchee Salish] In Interior Salish and Eastern Washington Indians IV. *American Indian Ethnohistory: Indians of the Northwest*. New York: Garland.

———
1974a　　Aboriginal Territory of the Kalispel Indians. pp. 169–231 in Interior Salish and Eastern Washington Indians III. *American Indian Ethnohistory: Indians of the Northwest*. New York: Garland.

———
1974b　　Aboriginal Territories of the Flathead, Pend d'Oreille and Kutenai Indians of Western Montana. Pp. 25–116 in Interior Salish and Eastern Washington Indians II. *American Indian Ethnohistory: Indians of the Northwest*. New York: Garland.

———
1974c　　Ethnological Field Investigation and Analysis of Historical Material Relative to Coeur d'Alene Indian Aborginal Distribution. Pp. 37–96 in Interior Salish and Eastern Washington Indians I. *American Indian Ethnohistory: Indians of the Northwest*. New York: Garland.

Chalmers, Harvey II
1862　　The Last Stand of the Nez Perce: Destruction of a People. (Contains, in alternating chapters, an account of the events leading up to the outbreak of the war, based on historical records, by the author and an account of the same events as told by the Yellow Wolf [through an interpreter] to L.V. McWhorter). New York: Twayne Publishers. (Microfilm: University of Washington Libraries, Seattle, 1982.)

Chamberlain, Alexander F.
1893　　Report on the Kootenay Indians. pp. 549–617 in *62d Annual Report of the British Association for the Advancement of Science for 1892*. London. (Reprinted in: Northwest Anthropological Research Notes 8(1–2):208–247. Moscow, Idaho, 1974.)

———
1901　　Kootenai "Medicine-Men". *Journal of American Folk-Lore* 14–(53):95–99.

———
1907　　Kutenai. Pp. 740–742 in Pt. 1 of Handbook of American Indians North of Mexico. Frederick W. Hodge, ed. 2 Pts. *Bureau of American Ethnology Bulletin* 30. Washington.

Champnes, W.
1865　　To Cariboo and Back. (To Cariboo and Back, and Emigrant's Journey to the Gold-fields in British Columbia. Adventure with the Indians of Oregon.) 6 Pts. The Leisure Hour 692–695 (April 1, 8, 15, 22):[193]-275; [and] 708–709 (July 22, 29):[449]-480. London.

Chance, David H.
1968　　Survey of Antiquities Management on Bureau of Land Management Lands in Oregon, 1968. (Report submitted to the Bureau of Land Management, Portland, Oreg.)

———
1973　　Influences of the Hudson's Bay Company on the Native Cultures of the Colville District. *Northwest Anthropological Research Notes* 7(1, Pt. 2); *Memoir* 2. Moscow, Idaho.

———
1978　　Archaeological Tests and Excavations at the Agency Office Area, Spalding, Idaho. A Summary of Work of July and August 1978. (Report on file, Laboratory of Anthropology, University of Idaho, Moscow.)

———
1978a　　Interim Report of the Fall Excavations at Spalding, Idaho, in 1978. (Report on file, Laboratory of Anthropology, University of Idaho

———
1979　　First Summary of the Fall Excavations at Spalding, Idaho, during the Spring of 1979. (Report on file, Laboratory of Anthropology, University of Idaho, Moscow.)

———
1980　　Research Questions and Approaches for the Middle Columbia River Area. Moscow, Idaho: Alfred W. Bowers Laboratory of Anthropology, University of Idaho.

———
1981　　The Kootenay Fur Trade and Its Establishments, 1795–1871. Seattle: Submitted to the U.S. Army Corps of Engineers, Seattle District.

———
1986　　People of the Falls. Colville, Wash.: Kettle Falls Historical Society.

Chance, David H., and Jennifer V. Chance
1977　　Kettle Falls 1976: Salvage Archaeology in Lake Roosevelt. *University of Idaho. Laboratory of Anthropology. Anthropological Research Manuscript Series* 39. Moscow, Idaho.

———
1979　　Kettle Falls 1977: Salvage Archaeology in and beside Lake Roosevelt. *University of Idaho. Laboratory of Anthropology. Anthropological Research Manuscript Series* 53. Moscow, Idaho.

1982 Kettle Falls, 1971 and 1974: Salvage Archaeology in Lake Roosevelt. *University of Idaho. Laboratory of Anthropology. Anthropological Research Manuscript Series* 69. Moscow, Idaho.

1985 Kettle Falls, 1978: Further Archaeological Excavations in Lake Roosevelt. With Appendices by Richard W. Casteel [et al.]. *University of Idaho. Laboratory of Anthropology. Anthropological Reports* 84. Moscow.

1985a Archaeology at Spalding, 1978–1979. Appendices by Elaine Anderson ... [et al.]. *University of Idaho. Laboratory of Anthropology. Anthropological Reports* 85. Moscow.

Chance, David H., et al.
1989 Archaeology of the Hatiuhpuh Village. Moscow: Alfred W. Bowers Laboratory of Anthropology, University of Idaho.

Chang, Kwang-chih
1967 Rethinking Archaeology. (Lectures delivered at an anthropology seminar at Yale University in 1966.) *Studies in Anthropology* AS 6. New York: Random House.

Chapman, James
[1940] [Notes and Photographs of Rock Art Sites Located along the Snake River South of Clarkston, Washington, and Lewiston, Idaho.] (Manuscript notebooks and photographs in Luna House Museum, Lewiston, Idaho, and the Idaho State Historical Society, Boise.)

Chatters, James C.
1976 Pahsimeroi Valley Longitudinal Subsistence-Settlement and Land use Study. *United States Department of Agriculture. Forest Service. Intermountain Region Archaeological Report* 4. Ogden, Utah.

1980 Cultural Resources of the Columbia Basin Project: An Inventory of Selected Parcels. *University of Washington. Office of Public Archaeology. Institute for Environmental Studies. Reconnaissance Report* 32. Seattle.

1982 Evolutionary Human Paleoecology: Climatic Change and Human Adaptation in the Pahsimeroi Valley, Idaho, 2500 BP to the Present. (Ph.D. Dissertation in Anthropology, University of Washington, Seattle. Microfiche: University Microfilms International, Ann Arbor, Mich., 1983.)

1984 Dimensions of Site Structure: The Archaeological Record from Two Sites in Okanogan County, Washington. With Contributions by Carol Ellick, et al. Seattle: Central Washington University. Central Washington Archaeological Survey for the Seattle District, U.S. Army Corps of Engineers.

1984a Human Adaptation along the Columbia River 4700–1600 B.P.: A Report of Test Excavations at River Mile 590, North Central Washington. *Central Washington University. Occasional Paper* 1; *Office of Graduate Studies and Research. Research Report* 84–1. Ellensburg.

1986 The Wells Reservoir Archaeological Project. Volume 1: Summary of Findings. With contributions by Virginia Butler, Guy Moura, David Rhode, Stephen R. Samuels, and Randall F. Schalk. Volume 2: Site Reports, by James R. Benson, Gregory C. Cleveland, John A Draper, Guy Moura, and Guy Marden. *Central Washington University. Central Washington Archaeological Survey. Archaeological Report* 86–6. Ellensburg.

1987 Hunter-Gatherer Adaptations and Assemblage Structure. *Journal of Anthropological Archaeology* 6(4):336–375.

1988 Pacifism and the Organization of Conflict in the Plateau of Northwestern America. Pp. 241–252 in Cultures in Conflict: Current Archaeological Perspectives. Proceedings of the Twentieth Annual Conference of the Archaeological Association of the University of Calgary. Diana Claire Tkaczuk and Brian C. Vivian, eds. Calgary, Alta: University of Calgary Archaeological Association.

1989 Resource Intensification and Sedentism on the Southern Plateau. *Archaeology in Washington* 1:3–19. Bellingham, Wash.

1989a Hanford Cultural Resources Management Plan (PNL-6942). (Report in Chatters's possession.)

1991 Paleoecology and Paleoclimates of the Columbia Basin, Northwest America. PNL-SA-18715. Richland, Wash.: Pacific Northwest Laboratory.

1992 A History of Cultural Resources Management at the U.S. Department of Energy's Hanford Site, Washington. *Northwest Anthropological Research Notes* 26(1):73–88. Moscow, Idaho.

1992a Freshwater Biota as Proxy Indicators for Temperature and Flow Characteristics of Ancient Fluvial Systems. (Paper presented at the INQUA Symposium on Global Continental Paleohydrology, Krakow, Poland, September 10–12, 1992.)

1995 Population Growth, Climatic Cooling, and the Development of Collector Strategies on the Southern Plateau, Western North America. *Journal of World Prehistory* 9(3):341–400. New York.

Chatters, James C., and K.A. Hoover
1992 The Response of the Columbia River Fluvial System to Holocene Climatic Change. *Quaternary Research* 37(1):42–59.

Chatters, James C., and Matthew K. Zweifel
1987 Archaeology of Eight Sites in the Multipurpose Range Complex, Yakima Firing Center, Washington. *Central Washington University. Central Washington Archaeological Survey Report* 87–2. Ellensburg.

Chatters, James C., D.N. Neitzel, M.B. Scott, and S.A. Shankle
1991 Potential Impacts of Global Climate Change on Pacific Northwest Spring Chinook Salmon (*Oncorhynchus tschawytscha*): An Exploratory Case Study. *The Northwest Environmental Journal* 7(1)71–92. Seattle.

Chatters, James C., et al.
1995 A Paleoscience Approach to Estimating the Effects of Climatic Warming on the Salmonid Fisheries of the Columbia River Basin. V.L. Butler, M.J. Scott, D.M. Anderson, and D.A. Neitzel Pp. 489–496 in Climate Change and Northern Fish Populations. R.J. Beamish, ed. *Canadian Special Publication of Fisheries and Aquatic Sciences* 121. Ottawa.

Chatters, James C., et al.
1995a Bison Procurement in the Far West: A 2,100-Year-Old Kill Site on the Columbia Plateau. Sarah K. Campbell, Grant D. Smith, and Phillip E. Minthorn, Jr. *American Antiquity* 60(4):751–763.

Cheek, Annetta L., and Bennie C. Keel
1984 Value Conflicts in Osteo-Archaeology. Pp. 194–207 in Ethics and Values in Archaeology. E.L. Green, ed. New York: Free Press.

Cheney Cowles Memorial Museum
1990 Traditions: Beadwork of the Native American. Text by Lynn Harrison. Spokane, Wash.: Cheney Cowles Museum, Eastern Washington State Historical Society.

678

Chief Joseph
1879   An Indian's View of Indian Affairs. By Young Joseph, Chief
         of the Nez Percés. With an Introduction by the Right Rev.
         W.H. Hare, D.D. *North American Review* 128(269):412–433.

Chisholm, Brian S.
1986   Reconstruction of Prehistoric Diet in British Columbia Using
         Stable-Carbon Isotopic Analysis. (Ph.D. Dissertation in
         Archaeology, Simon Fraser University, Burnaby, B.C.; Micro-
         fiche: Canadian Theses Service, National Library of Canada,
         Ottawa, 1988.)

Chisholm, Brian S., and D. Erle Nelson
1983   An Early Human Skeleton from South-Central British
         Columbia: Dietary Inference from Carbon Isotopic Evidence.
         Canadian Journal of Archaeology 7(1):85–86. Ottawa.

Chittenden, Hiram M., and Alfred T. Richardson, eds. *see* de Smet, Pierre-
Jean 1905

Chomsky, Noam, and Morris Halle
1968   The Sound Pattern of English. New York: Harper and Row.

Choquette, Wayne
1971   Archaeological Salvage Operations within the Libby Dam
         Pondage, 1971. (Report submitted to the Archaeological Sites
         Advisory Board of British Columbia, Vancouver.)

————
1972   Preliminary Report, Libby Reservoir Archaeological Salvage
         Project. (Report submitted to the Archaeologist Sites Adviso-
         ry Board of British Columbia, Vancouver.)

————
1973   Archaeological Site Survey in the Kootenay River Drainage
         Region, 1972. (Report submitted to the Archaeological Sites
         Advisory Board of British Columbia, Vancouver.)

————
1974   Archaeological Fieldwork in the East Kootenay, 1973 Season.
         The Midden 6(1):6–9. Vancouver, B.C.

————
1984   A Proposed Cultural Chronology for the Kootenai Region.
         Pp. 303–316 in Cultural Resource Investigations of the Bon-
         neville Power Administration's Libby Integration Project,
         Northern Idaho and Northwestern Montana. Stan Gough, ed.
         *Eastern Washington University. Archaeology and Historical
         Services. reports in Archaeology and History* 100–29.
         Cheney, Wash.

————
1987   Archaeological Investigations in the Middle Kootenai Region
         and Vicinity. Pp. 57–120 in Prehistoric Land Use in the North-
         ern Rocky Mountains: A Perspective from the Middle Koote-
         nai River. Alston V. Thoms and Greg Burtchard, eds. *Wash-
         ington State University. Center for Northwest Anthropology.
         Project Report* 4. Pullman.

Choquette, Wayne, and Craig Holstine
1980   A Cultural Resource Overview of the Bonneville Power
         Administration's Proposed Transmission Line From Libby
         Dam, Montana to Rathdrum, Idaho. *Washington State Uni-
         versity. Washington Archaeological Research Center. Project
         Report* 100. Pullman.

————
1982   An Archaeological and Historical Overview of the Bonneville
         Power Administration's Proposed Garrison-Spokane Trans-
         mission Line Corridor, Western Montana, Northern Idaho,
         and Eastern Washington. *Eastern Washington University.
         Bonneville Cultural Resources Group. Reports in Archaeolo-
         gy and History* 100–20. Cheney, Wash.

Choquette, Wayne, Sheila J. Bobalik, Stan Gough, and Craig Holstine
1984   Results of Investigations. Pp. 33–301 in Cultural Resource
         Investigations of the Bonneville Power Administration's Lib-
         by Integration Project, Northern Idaho and Northwestern
         Montana. Stan Gough, ed. *Eastern Washington University.*

*Archaeology and Historical Services. Reports in Archaeology
and History* 100–29. Cheney, Wash.

Christie, J.H., and Robert L. de Pfyffer
1990   Okanagan Indians Non-Registered: The Reason Why. Pp.
         77–91 in *54th Annual Report of the Okanagan Historical
         Society.* Vernon, B.C.

Clague, John J.
1981   Late Quaternary Geology and Geochronology of British
         Columbia. Part 2: Summary and Discussion of Radiocarbon-
         dated Quaternary History. *Canada. Geological Survey Paper*
         80–35. Ottawa. (Summary in French.)

Clague, John J., and Rolf W. Mathewes
1989   Early Holocene Thermal Maximum in Western North Ameri-
         ca: New Evidence from Castle Peak, British Columbia. *Geol-
         ogy* 17(3):277–280.

Clark, Ella E.
1953   Indian Legends of the Pacific Northwest. Berkeley and Los
         Angeles: University of California Press. (Reprinted in 1958,
         1963, 1966, title varies.)

————, ed. 1955–1956 *see* Gibbs, George 1955–1956

————
1966   Indian Legends from the Northern Rockies. Norman: Univer-
         sity of Oklahoma Press.

Clark, Gerald R.
1971   The Public Image of Archaeology in Washington State: A
         Pilot Study. (M.A. Thesis in Anthropology, Washington State
         University, Pullman.)

Clark, Keith, and Donna Clark
1978   William McKey's Journal 1866–67: Indian Scouts, Part I, Part II.
         Oregon Historical Quarterly 79(2):[120]-171, 79(3):[268]-333.

Clarke, Samuel A.
1885   Pioneer Days: Battle of the Abiqua—A Story Never Before
         Fully Told. *Sunday Oregonian,* Sept. 6, 1885. Portland.

————
1905   Pioneer Days of Oregon History. 2 vols. Portland, Oreg.: J.K.
         Gill; also, Cleveland, Ohio: Arthur H. Clark.

————
1960   [The Samuel A. Clarke] Papers [1873]; with an Appendix
         Compiled from Material in Clarke's Scrapbook. B.K. Swartz,
         Jr., ed. *Klamath County Museum. Research Papers* 2. Kla-
         math Falls, Oreg.

Clarke, William J.
1885   Rock Piles and Ancient Dams in the Klamath Valley. *Ameri-
         can Antiquarian and Oriental Journal* 7(1):40–41.

Claus, Edward P., Varro E. Tyler, and Lynn R. Brady
1970   Pharmacognosy; 6th ed. Philadelphia: Lea and Febiger.

Cleveland, Gregory C., ed.
1976   Preliminary Archaeological Investigations at the Miller Site,
         Strawberry Island, 1976: A Late Prehistoric Village Near Bur-
         bank, Franklin County, Washington. *Washington State Uni-
         versity. Washington Archaeological Research Center. Project
         Report* 46. Pullman.

Cleveland, Gregory C., B. Cochran, J. Giniger, and H.H. Hammatt
1976   Archaeological Reconnaissance on the Mid-Columbian and
         Lower Snake Reservoirs for the Walla Walla District, Corps of
         Engineers. *Washington State University. Washington Archaeo-
         logical Research Center. Project Report* 27. Pullman.

Cliff, Thelma Drake
1942   A History of the Warm Springs Reservation 1855–1900.
         (M.A. Thesis in History, University of Oregon, Eugene.)

Clifton, James A.
1960   Explorations of Klamath Personality. (Ph.D. Dissertation in
         Anthropology, University of Oregon, Eugene.)

Clifton, James A., and David Levine

1961   Klamath Personalities: Ten Rorschach Case Studies. Eugene: University of Oregon Press. (Reprinted: Department of Sociology and Anthropology, University of Kansas, Lawrence, 1963.)

Cline, Walter

1938   Religion and World View. Pp. 131–182 in The Sinkaietk or Southern Okanagon of Washington. Leslie Spier, ed. *General Series in Anthropology* 6, *Contributions from the Laboratory of Anthropology* 2. Menasha, Wis.: George Banta.

————— , et al. 1938 *see* Spier, Leslie, ed. 1938

Coale, George L.

1956   Ethnohistorical Sources for the Nez Perce Indians. *Ethnohistory* 3(3):246–255, (4):346–360.

—————

1958   Notes on the Guardian Spirit Concept among the Nez Perce. *International Archives of Ethnography* 48(pt. 2):135–148. Leiden.

Coan, Charles F.

1922   The Adoption of the Reservation Policy in Pacific Northwest, 1853–1855. Oregon Historical Quarterly 23(1):1–38. (Reprinted: The Ivy Press, Portland, Oreg., 1922.)

Cobb, John N.

1930   Pacific Salmon Fisheries. 4th ed. Pp. 409–704 in *U.S. Bureau of Fisheries. Report of the Commissioner of Fisheries for 1930*, (Appendix XIII); *U.S. Bureau of Fisheries. Document* 1092. Washington.

Coburn, Larry W.

1975   A Theoretical Framework for Investigating the Relationship of Pictographs to Mythology in the Northern Plateau. (M.A. Thesis in Anthropology, Washington State University, Pullman.)

Cochran, Bruce D.

1988   Significance of Holocene Alluvial Cycles in the Pacific Northwest Interior. (Ph.D. Dissertation in Geology, University of Idaho, Boise.)

—————

1991   Geomorphic Context and Site Formation Processes. Pp. 54–143 in Prehistory and Paleoenvironments at Pittsburg Landing: Data Recovery and Test Excavation at Six Sites in Hells Canyon National Recreation Area, West Central Idaho. Kenneth C. Reid, ed. *Washington State University. Center for Northwest Anthropology. Project Report* 15. Pullman.

Coeur d'Alene Teepee

1939   An Old Time Indian's Story. *The Coeur d'Alene Teepee* 2:307–308. DeSmet, Idaho: Sacred Heart Mission. (Reprinted: Serento Press, Plummer, Idaho, 1980.)

Coeur d'Alene Tribe

1961   Constitution and By-Laws of the Coeur d'Alene Tribe, Idaho. Revised February 3, 1961. Plummer, Idaho: Coeur d'Alene Tribe.

—————

1979   Resource Development Project Annual Progress Report. Plummer, Idaho: Coeur d'Alene Tribe.

—————

1989   Coeur d'Alene Tribe of Idaho Comprehensive Plan Update: December 1988-March 1989; Section II: History. Plummer, Idaho: Coeur d'Alene Tribe.

Coffey, John, et al.

1990   Shuswap History: the First 100 Years of Contact. Kamloops, B.C.: Secwepemc Cultural Education Society.

Cohen, Fay G., ed.

1986   Treaties on Trial: The Continuing Controversy Over Northwest Indian Fishing Rights. (A Report prepared for the American Friends Service Committee). Seattle: University of Washington Press.

Coke, Henry J.

1852   A Ride Over the Rocky Mountains to Oregon and California. London: Richard Bentley.

Cole, David L.

1954   A Contribution to the Archaeology of The Dalles Region, Oregon. M.S. Thesis in Anthropology, University of Oregon, Eugene.)

—————

1958   A Report on the Disinterment of Burials on Grave and Memaloose Islands in The Dalles Dam Reservoir Area. (Report to the U.S. Army Corps of Engineers and the National Park Service, on file at the Oregon State Museum of Anthropology, University of Oregon, Eugene.)

—————

1966   Report on Archaeological Research in the John Day Dam Reservoir Area — 1965. Interim Report 1965–66. Eugene: University of Oregon, Museum of Natural History.

—————

1967   Archaeological Research of Site 35SH23, the Mack Canyon Site. (Interim report to the Bureau of Land Management, on file at the Oregon State Museum of Anthropology, University of Oregon, Eugene.)

—————

1969   1967 and 1968 Archaeological Excavations of the Mack Canyon Site: Interim Report 1968. Eugene: University of Oregon, Museum of Natural History.

—————

1973   Survey of the Proposed Catherine Creek Dam Reservoir and Lower Grande Ronde Reservoir in Union County, Oregon. (Order No. 4970L20413 between The National Park Service and the University of Oregon Museum of Natural History.)

Cole, Douglas, and Bradley Lockner, eds.

1989   The Journals of George M. Dawson: British Columbia, 1875–1878. 2 vols. Vancouver: University of British Columbia Press.

Cole, Hal

1890   [Letter of August 11, 1890, Colville Indian Agency, Wash.] Pp. 216–222 in *51st Congress. 2d Session. House Executive Document* 1. (Serial No. 2841). Washington.

—————

1891   [Letter of August 15, 1891, Colville Indian Agency, Wash.] Pp. 440–441 in *52d Congress. 1st Session. House Executive Document* 1. (Serial No. 2934). Washington.

Cole, Jean M.

1979   Exile in the Wilderness: The Biography of Chief Factor Archibald McDonald, 1790–1853. Don Mills, Ont.: Burns and McEachern Ltd.

Collier, Donald, Alfred E. Hudson, and Arlo Ford

1942   Archaeology of the Upper Columbia Region. *University of Washington Publications in Anthropology* 9(1). Seattle.

Collins, Mary B., and William Andrefsky, Jr.

1995   Archaeological Collections Inventory and Assessment of Marmes Rockshelter (45FR50) and Palus Sites (45FR36A,B,C): A Compliance Study for the Native American Graves Protection and Repatriation Act. *Washington State University. Department of Anthropology. Center for Northwest Anthropology. Project Report* 28. Pullman.

Columbia River Inter-Tribal Fish Commission

1988   [CRITFC Special Report.] Portland, Oreg.: Columbia River Inter-Tribal Fish Commission.

—————

1990   [CRITFC Special Issue.] Portland, Oreg.: Columbia River Inter-Tribal Fish Commission.

—————

1992   [CRITFC Annual Report.] Portland, Oreg.: Columbia River Inter-Tribal Fish Commission.

Colville Business Council
1981   Research Regulation Ordinance. Nespelem, Wash.: Colville Confederated Tribes.

Combes, John D.
1968   Burial Practices as an Indicator of Cultural Change in the Lower Snake River Region. (M.A. Thesis in Anthropology, Washington State University, Pullman.)

Commission = Commission to Investigate Irrigation Projects on Indian Lands
1914   Report of Commission to Investigate Irrigation Projects on Indian Lands. *63d Congress. 3d Session. House Executive Document* 1215. (Serial No. 6888). Washington.

Commissioner of Indian Affairs
1856   Indian Disturbances in Oregon and Washington. *34th Congress. 1st Session. House Executive Document* 48. (Serial No. 853). Washington: Cornelius Wendell.

Commons, Rachel S.
1938   Diversions. Pp. 183–194 in The Sinkaietk or Southern Okanagon of Washington. Leslie Spier, ed. *General Series in Anthropology* 6. Menasha, Wis.: George Banta.

Confederated Tribes of The Grand Ronde Community of Oregon
1987   Grand Ronde Reservation Plan: Supplement, April 1987. (Prepared under a Grant from the Bureau of Indian Affairs, U.S. Department of the Interior.) Grand Ronde, Oreg.: The Confederated Tribes of The Grand Ronde Community of Oregon.

Confederated Tribes of The Umatilla Reservation
1959   Petitioner's Proposed Findings of Fact and Brief. (Document submitted to the Indian Claims Commission, Docket No. 264, Washington.)

Confederated Tribes of The Warm Springs Reservation of Oregon
1984   The People of Warm Springs. Warm Springs: The Confederated Tribes of the Warm Springs Reservation of Oregon.

Congdon, Russell
1932   Spondylolisthesis and Vertebral Anomalies in Skeletons of American Aborigines, with Clinical Notes on Spondylolisthesis. *Journal of Bone and Joint Surgery* 14:511–524.

Conklin, Harold C.
1954   The Relation of Hanunóo Culture to the Plant World. (Ph.D Dissertation in Anthropology, Yale University, New Haven, Conn. Microfilm-xerography: University Microfilms International, Ann Arbor, Mich., 1978.)

Conn, Richard G.
1960–1966   [Ethnographic notes from visits to the Coeur d'Alene, Spokane, Colville, and Kalispel, Washington and Idaho.] (Manuscripts in Conn's possession.)

Conner, Stuart, and Betty Lu Conner
1971   Rock Art of the Montana High Plains. (Catalogue of an exhibition for the Art Galleries, University of California, Santa Barbara.)

Connolly, Thomas E.
1989   [Sunday Mass.] (Videotape in T.E Connolly's possession, Sacred Heart Mission, DeSmet, Idaho.)

————
1990   A Coeur d'Alene Indian Story. (Young tribal member Reno Steusgar learns about Coeur d'Alene history, legends and customs from his grandmother, Keena.) Fairfield, Wash.: Ye Galleon Press. A Centennial publication of the Coeur d'Alene Tribe in conjunction with the Idaho Indian Centennial Committee, 1890–1990.

Connolly, Thomas E., and Gary B. Palmer
1983   Making Traditional Values Work in the 20th Century. Pp. 8–10 in Wealth and Trust: A Lesson from the American West. Special Publication. Sun Valley, Idaho: Institute of the American West.

Connolly, Thomas J.
1995   Human and Environmental Holocene Chronology in Newberry Crater, Central Oregon. (Report to the Oregon Department of Transportation, Salem, Oreg.; State Museum of Anthropology, University of Oregon, Eugene.)

Cook, David B.
1940   Beaver-trout Relations. *Journal of Mammalogy* 21:395–401. Baltimore, Md.: American Society of Mammalogists.

Cook, Sherburne F.
1941   The Mechanism and Extent of Dietary Adaptation among Certain Groups of California and Nevada Indians. *Ibero-Americana* 18:1–59. Berkeley.

————
1955   The Epidemic of 1830–1833 in California and Oregon. *University of California Publications in American Archaeology and Ethnology* 43(3):303–326. Berkeley.

Cook, Warren L.
1973   Flood Tide of Empire: Spain and the Pacific Northwest, 1543–1819. *Yale Western Americana Series* 24. New Haven: Yale University Press.

Cooper, James
1853   [Notebook, Northern Pacific R.R. Survey, June 13-December 29.] (Manuscript in Smithsonian Institution Archives, Record Unit 7067, Washington.)

Copp, Stanley A.
1979   Archaeological Excavations at the McCall Site, South Okanagan Valley, British Columbia. (M.A. Thesis in Archaeology, Simon Fraser University, Barnaby, B.C.; Microfiche: *Canadian Theses on Microfiche* 44875, National Library of Canada, Ottawa, 1981.)

————
1996   The 1995 Excavations of the Stirling Creek Bridge Site (DiRa-09): A Final Report of Investigations. (Report submitted to the Upper Similkameen Indian Band, The Archaeology Branch [Ministry of Small Business, Tourism and Culture] and the Ministry of Highways; Permit # 1995–148, [Ottawa].)

Corliss, David W.
1972   Neck Width of Projectile Points: An Index of Culture Continuity and Change. *Occasional Papers of the Idaho State University Museum* 29. Pocatello.

Corliss, David W., and Joesph G. Gallagher
1972   Final Report, 1970–1971 Archaeological Survey of the Dworshak Reservoir. (Report on file, Pacific Northwest Region Office, National Park Service, Seattle, Wash.)

Cornelius, Thomas R.
1856   [Letter of April 2d, 1856, from Thomas R. Cornelius, Col., Headquarters, 1st Regiment, Oregon Mounted Volunteers, to George L. Curry, Governor-Commander in Chief, Salem, Oregon Territory.] (Manuscript in records of the War Department, Letter Received 1854–1858, Record Group 94, National Archives, Washington.)

Corner, John
1968   Pictographs (Indian Rock Paintings) in the Interior of British Columbia. Vernon, B.C.: Wayside Press.

Cornoyer, N.A.
1874   [Letter of September 17, 1874, Umatilla Indian Agency.] Pp. 630–631 in *43d Congress. 2d Session. House Executive Document* 1. (Serial No. 1639.) Washington.

Cosminsky, Sheila Claire
1964   An Analysis of Wasco-Wishram Mythology. (M.A. Thesis in Anthropology, Washington State University, Pullman.)

Cotroneo, Ross R., and Jack Dozier
1974   A Time of Disintegration: The Coeur d'Alene and the Dawes Act. *The Western Historical Quarterly* 5(4):405–419.

Coues, Elliott, ed.
1893   History of the Expedition Under the Command of Lewis and
            Clark; to the Sources of the Missouri River, Thence Across
            the Rocky Mountains and Down the Columbia River to the
            Pacific Ocean, Performed During the Years 1804–5–6. New
            ed. 4 vols. New York: Francis P. Harper. (Reprinted in 3 vols.:
            Dover Publications, New York, 1965.)

_____ , ed.
1897   New Light on the Early History of the Greater Northwest: The
            Manuscript Journals of Alexander Henry, Fur Trader of the
            Northwest Company, and of David Thompson, Official Geo-
            grapher and Explorer of the Same Company, 1799–1814.
            Exploration and Adventure among the Indians on the Red,
            Saskatchewan, Missouri, and Columbia Rivers. 3 vols. New
            York: Francis P. Harper. (Reprinted in 3 vols.: Ross and
            Haines, Minneapolis, 1965.)

Coville, Frederick V.
1897   Notes on the Plants Used by the Klamath Indians of Oregon.
            U.S. Department of Agriculture. Division of Botany. Contri-
            butions from the United States National Herbarium
            5(2):87–108. Washington.

1904   Wokas, A Primitive Food of the Klamath Indians. Pp.
            725–739 in Annual Report of the U.S. National Museum for
            1902. Washington.

Cowan, Ian McTaggart, and Charles J. Guiguet
1973   The Mammals of British Columbia. 5th ed. British Columbia
            Provincial Museum. Handbook 11. Victoria.

Cowger, Thomas W.
1994   Klamath Pp. 292–293 in Native America in the Twentieth
            Century, An Encyclopedia. Mary B. Davis, ed. (Garland Ref-
            erence Library of Social Science 452). New York: Garland.

Cox, Ross
1831   Adventures on the Columbia River, Including the Narrative of
            a Residence of Six Years on the Western Side of the Rocky
            Mountains among Various Indian Tribes Hitherto Unknown,
            Together with a Journal Across the American Continent. 2
            vols. [1st ed.] London: Henry Colburn and Richard Bentley.
            (Reprinted: Binfords and Mort, Portland, Oreg., 1975.)

1832   Adventures on the Columbia River, Including the Narrative of
            a Residence of Six Years on the Western Side of the Rocky
            Mountains among Various Indian Tribes Hitherto Unknown,
            Together with a Journal Across the American Continent. 2
            vols. [American ed.] New-York: J.&J. Harper. (Orig. publ.:
            Henry Colburn and Richard Bentley, London, 1831.)

1957   The Columbia River; or, Scenes and Adventures on the West-
            ern Side of the Rocky Mountains, [etc.]. Edgar I. Stewart and
            Jane R. Stewart, eds. Norman: University of Oklahoma Press.
            (Orig. publ.: Henry Colburn and Richard Bentley, London,
            1831; also, J.&J. Harper, New-York, 1832.)

Cox, Thomas R.
1979   Tribal Leadership in Transition: Chief Peter Moctelme of the
            Coeur d'Alenes. Idaho Yesterdays 23(1):2–9, 25–31. Boise,
            Idaho.

1980   Weldon Heyburn, Lake Chatkolet, and the Evolving Con-
            cept of Public Parks. Idaho Yesterdays 24(2):2–15. Boise,
            Idaho.

Cox, William G.
1861   [Letter and report to James J. Young, October 19, 1861.]
            (Government Record 1372, File F/376/24, in British Colum-
            bia Archives and Records Service, Victoria.)

Craig Joseph A., and Robert L. Hacker
1940   The History and Development of the Fisheries of the Colum-
            bia River. U.S. Bureau of Fisheries Bulletin 49(32):133–216.
            Washington.

Craig, William
1858   [Statement of July 11, 1858.] Pp. 25–27 in Indian War in
            Oregon and Washington Territories. 35th Congress. 1st Ses-
            sion. House Executive Document 30(Vol. 9:1–66). Wash-
            ington.

Cram, Thomas J.
1859   Topographical Memoir of the Department of the Pacific. Let-
            ter from the Secretary of War, Transmitting the Topographical
            Memoir and Report of Captain T.J. Cram, Relative to the Ter-
            ritories of Oregon and Washington, in the Military Depart-
            ment of the Pacific, [etc.]. 35th Congress. 2d Session. House
            Executive Document 114. Washington.

Cressman, Luther S.
1937   Petroglyphs of Oregon. University of Oregon Monographs.
            Studies in Anthropology 2. Eugene.

1937a   The Wikiup Damsite No. 1 Knives. American Antiquity
            3(1):53–67.

1940   Studies on Early Man in South Central oregon. Pp. 300–306
            in Carnegie Institution of Washington, Yearbook 39. Wash-
            ington.

1948   Odell Lake Site: A New Paleo-Indian Campsite in Oregon.
            American Antiquity 14(1):57–60.

1950   Archaeological Research in the John Day Region of North
            Oregon. Proceedings of the American Philosophical Society
            94(4):369–390. Philadelphia.

1956   Klamath Prehistory: the Prehistory of the Culture of Klamath
            Lake Area, Oregon. Transactions of the American Philosoph-
            ical Society, n.s. 46(4):375–513. Philadelphia. (Microfilm:
            University Microfilm, Ann Arbor, Mich., 1975.)

1962   The Sandal and the Cave: The Indians of Oregon. Portland,
            Oreg.: Beaver Books. (Reprinted: Oregon State University
            Press, Corvallis, 1962.)

1977   Prehistory of the Far West: Homes of Vanished Peoples. Salt
            Lake City: University of Utah Press.

Cressman, Luther S., with Frank C. Baker, Paul S. Conger, Henry P.
Hansen, and Robert F. Heizer
1942   Archaeological Researches in the Northern Great Basin.
            Carnegie Institution of Washington Publication 538. Wash-
            ington. (Microfilm: Photoduplication Service, Library of
            Congress, Washington, 1959.)

Cressman, Luther S., with David L. Cole, Wilbur A. Davis, Thomas M.
Newman, and Daniel J. Scheans
1960   Cultural Sequences at The Dalles, Oregon: A Contribution to
            Pacific Northwest Prehistory. Transactions of the American
            Philosophical Society, n.s. 50(10). Philadelphia.

Crosby, Thomas
1907   Among the An-ko-me-nums, or Flathead Tribes of Indians of
            the Pacific Coast. Toronto: William Briggs.

Crow, Flathead etc. Commission
1901   Proceedings of a General Council Held with Indians of the
            Flathead Reservation at Saint Ignatius, Montana, April 3,
            1901 (Wednesday). [Commissioners McNeely (Chairman),
            Hoyt, and McIntire.] (Typescript in Records of the Bureau of
            Indian Affairs, Record Group 75, Letters Received 1901,
            24033, National Archives, Washington.)

Crowell, Sandra A., and David O. Aleson
1980   Up the Swiftwater: A Pictorial History of the Colorful Upper St. Joe River Country, Published by the Authors. Spokane, Wash.: A. and P. Business Service Printers.

Crutchfield, James A., and Giulio Pontecorvo
1969   Pacific Salmon Fisheries: A Study of Irrational Conservation. Baltimore: Johns Hopkins Press.

Culin, Stewart
1901   A Summer Trip among the Western Indians: The Wanamaker Expedition. 3 Pts. *Bulletin of the Free Museum of Science and Art of the University of Pennsylvania* 3(1):1–22, (2):88–122, (3):143–175. Philadelphia.

1907   Games of the North American Indians. Pp. 3–809 in *24th Annual Report of the Bureau of American Ethnology for 1902–1903*. Washington. (Reprinted: Dover Publications, New York, 1975; also, University of Nebraska Press, Lincoln, 1992.)

Cundy, Harold J.
1927–1938   [Field drawings and notes.] (Manuscript notes and drawings on file, Heritage Reference Center, North Central Washington Museum, Wenatchee, Wash.)

1938   Petroglyphs of North Central Washington. Wenatchee, Wash.: Privately printed.

Curtin, Jeremiah
1909   Wasco Tales and Myths. Collected by Jeremiah Curtin [1885]. Edward Sapir, ed. Pp. [237]-314 in Wishram Texts, by Edward Sapir. *Publications of the American Ethnological Society* 2. Leyden. (Reprinted: AMS Press, New York, 1974; Mouton de Gruyter, New York and Berlin, 1990.)

1912   Myths of the Modocs. London: Low, Marston and Co.; Boston: Little, Brown. (Reprinted: B. Blom, New York, 1971.)

Curtis, Edward S.
1907–1930   The North American Indian: Being a Series of Volumes Picturing and Describing the Indians of the United States, the Dominion of Canada, and Alaska. Frederick W. Hodge, ed. 20 vols. Norwood, Mass.: Plimpton Press. (Reprinted: Johnson Reprint, New York, 1970.)

1909   [Yakima fieldnotes.] (Manuscript in Archive of Traditional Music, Indiana University, Bloomington.)

Cutright, Paul Russell
1969   Lewis and Clark, Pioneering Naturalists. [1st ed.] Urbana, Ill.: University of Illinois Press.

1989   Lewis and Clark: Pioneering Naturalists [Repr. ed.] Lincoln and London: University of Nebraska Press.

Cybulski, Jerome S.
1983   Paleopathology in the Northwest. (Manuscript, No. 86–2631, in Scientific Records Section, Archaeological Survey of Canada, National Museum of Man, Ottawa.)

Cybulski, Jerome S., Donald E. Howes, and James C. Haggarty
1981   An Early Human Skeleton from South-Central British Columbia: Dating and Bioarchaeology Inference. *Canadian Journal of Archaeology* 5:49–59. Ottawa.

Czaykowska-Higgins, Ewa
1991   Cyclicity as a Morphological Diacritic: Evidence from Moses-Columbia Salish (Nxaʔamxcin). *Proceedings of the Northeast Linguistic Society* 21:65–79.

1993   Cyclicity and Stress in Moses-Columbia Salish (Nxaʔamxcin). *Natural Language and Linguistic Theory* 11(2):197–278. Dordrecht, The Netherlands.

1993a   The Phonology and Semantics of CVC Reduplication in Moses-Columbian Salish. Pp. 47–72 in American Indian Linguistics and Ethnography in Honor of Laurence C. Thompson. Anthony Mattina and Timothy Montier, eds. *University of Montana Occasional Papers in Linguistics* 10. Missoula.

1997   The Morphological and Phonological Constituent Structure of Words in Moses-Columbia Salish (Nxaʔamxcín). Pp. 153–195 in Salish Languages and Linguistics: Theoretical and Descriptive Perspectives. Ewa Czaykowska-Higgins and M. Dale Kinkade, eds. (*Trends in Linguistics. Studies and Monographs* 107). Berlin and New York: Mouton de Gruyter.

Czaykowska-Higgins, Ewa, and M. Dale Kinkade
1997   Salish Languages and Linguistics. Pp. 1–68 in Salish Languages and Linguistics: Theoretical and Descriptive Perspectives. Ewa Czaykowska-Higgins and M. Dale Kinkade, eds. (*Trends in Linguistics. Studies and Monographs* 107). Berlin and New York: Mouton de Gruyter.

Dahl, Kathleen A.
1990   Sovereignty, Environmental Use and Ethnic Identity on the Colville Indian Reservation. (Ph.D. Dissertation in Anthropology, Washington State University, Pullman.)

Dahlstrom, Max
1972   Results of the Archaeological Reconnaissance for the Idaho Primitive Area, 1971. (Manuscript on file at Boise State University, Department of Sociology and Anthropology, Boise, Idaho.)

Dalan, Rinita
1985   Pollen Analysis of a Core from Goose Lake, Okanogan County, Washington. Pp. 113–129 in Summary of Results, Chief Joseph Dam Cultural Resources Project, Washington. Sarah K. Campbell, ed. Seattle: Office of Public Archaeology, Institute for Environmental Studies, University of Washington.

Dalquest, Walter W.
1948   Mammals of Washington. *University of Kansas. Museum of Natural History. Publications* 2. Lawrence.

Dancey, William S.
1973   Prehistoric Land Use and Settlement Patterns in the Priest Rapids Area, Washington. (Ph.D. Dissertation in Anthropology, University of Washington, Seattle. Photocopy: University Microfilms International, Ann Arbor, Mich., 1973.)

1974   The Wood Box Spring Site (45–KT–209): A Preliminary Report. [Columbus]: Ohio State University, Department of Anthropology. *University of Washington. Office of Public Archaeology. Report in Highway Archaeology* 1. Seattle.

Dart, Anson
1851   Report to the Commissioner of Indian Affairs; [including] Articles of a Treaty, Made and Concluded at Tansey Point, Near Clatsop Plains, This 9th Day of August 1851. Pp. 472–483 in *32d Congress. 1st Session. House Executive Document* 2(68). (Serial No. 636). Washington.

Daubenmire, Rexford F. [1968] *see* [1970]

1969   Ecological Plant Geography of the Pacific Northwest. *Madroño: A West American Journal of Botany* 20(3):111–128. Berkeley.

[1970]   Steppe Vegetation of Washington. *Washington State University. Washington Agricultural Experiment Station. Technical Bulletin* 62. Pullman. (Revised ed.: *Washington State University Cooperative Extension* EB1446, Pullman, 1988.)

Daubenmire, Rexford F., and Jean B. Daubenmire
1968   Forest Vegetation of Eastern Washington and Northern Idaho. *Washington State University. Washington Agricultural Experiment Station. Technical Bulletin* 60. Pullman. (Reprinted: Washington State University, Cooperative Extension Service, Pullman, 1976, 1984.)

Daugherty, Richard D.
1952   Archaeological Investigation of O'Sullivan Reservoir, Grant County, Washington. *American Antiquity* 17(4):374–386.

———
1956   Early Man in the Columbia Intermontane Province. *University of Utah Anthropological Papers* 24. Salt Lake City.

———
1956a   Archaeology of the Lind Coulee Site, Washington. *Proceedings of the American Philosophical Society* 100(3):223–278. Philadelphia.

———
1956b   Survey of Rocky Reach Reservoir. Pp. 1–16 in Northwest Archaeology Number, by Richard D. Daugherty et al. *Research Studies of the State College of Washington* 24(1). Pullman, Wash.

———
1959   Early Man in Washington. *State of Washington. Department of Conservation. Division of Mines and Geology. Information Circular* 32. Olympia.

———
1959a   A Tentative Cultural Sequence for the Lower Snake River Region. (Paper presented at the 24th Annual Meeting of the Society for American Archaeology, Salt Lake City.)

———
1962   The Intermontane Western Tradition. *American Antiquity* 28(2):144–150.

———
1973   The Yakima People. Phoenix, Ariz.: Indian Tribal Series.

Daugherty, Richard D., Barbara A. Purdy, and Roald Fryxell
1967   The Descriptive Archaeology and Geochronology of the Three Springs Bar Archaeological Site, Washington. *Washington State University. Laboratory of Anthropology. Report of Investigations* 40. Pullman.

Daugherty, Richard D., et al.
1956   Northwest Archaeology Number. [Articles by: Richard D. Daugherty; Warren A. Snyder; Douglas Osborne; Carling Malouf; Herbert C. Taylor, Jr.; Herbert C. Taylor, Jr., and Wilson Duff; Wilson Duff; Charles E. Borden.] *Research Studies of the State College of Washington* 24(1). Pullman, Wash. (See separate articles under each contributor's name.)

Davenport, T.W.
1907   Recollections of an Indian Agent. *Oregon Historical Quarterly* 8(1):1–41, (2):95–128, (3):231–264, (4):353–374.

Davidson, Frederick A., and Samuel J. Hutchinson
1938   The Geographic Distribution and Environmental Limitations of the Pacific Salmon (genus *Oncorhynchus*). *Bulletin of the United States Bureau of Fisheries* 48(26):667–692. Washington: Government Printing Office. (Whole *Bulletin* 48 has inprint date 1940.)

Davidson, John
1915   Botanical Exploration of the Province. Headwaters of Skoonton, Botanie, Laluwissin, Murray and Twaal Creeks, between the South Thompson and Fraser Rivers. Pp. 44–50 in *Second Annual Report of the Botanical Office.* Vancouver, B.C.

———
1916   Botanical Exploration of the Bitter-root Grounds and the "Three Sisters" Valley Between the Spences Bridge and Ashcroft. Pp. 134–136 in *Third Annual Report of the Botanical Office.* Vancouver, B.C.

———
1919   Douglas Fir Sugar. *The Canadian Field Naturalist* 33(April):6–9.

———
1980   Douglas of the Forests: The North American Journals of David Douglas. Seattle: University of Washington Press.

Davis, Carl M., and Sara A. Scott
1991   The Lava Butte Site Revisited. *Journal of California and Great Basin Anthropology* 13(1):40–59. Banning.

Davis, Clark
1975   Some Notes on Plateau Athapaskans. Pp. 620–629 in Proceedings: Northern Athapaskan Conference, 1971. Vol. 2. A. McFadyen Clark, ed. *Canada. National Museum of Man. Mercury Series. Ethnology Service Paper* 27. Ottawa.

Davis, Leslie B.
1982   Montana Archaeology and Radiocarbon Chronology: 1962–1981. *Archaeology in Montana*, (Special issue) 3. Bozeman.

Davis, Leslie B., and Sally T. Greiser
1992   Indian Creek Paleoindians: Early Occupation of the Elkhorn Mountains' Southeast Flank, West-Central Montana. Pp. 225–283 in Ice Age Hunters of the Rockies. Dennis J. Stanford and Jane S. Day, eds. [Denver]: Denver Museum of Natural History; Niwot, Colo.: University Press of Colorado.

Davis, Leslie B., Sally T. Greiser, and T. Weber Greiser
1987   Spring Cleanup at a Folsom Campsite in the Northern Rockies. *Current Research in the Pleistocene* 4:5–6. Orono, Maine.

Davis, Mary Anne
1987   Archaeological Investigation at Patrol Point (10–IH–1603), A Site in the Mountains of the Nez Perce National Forest. *Idaho Archaeologist* 10(2):27–34. Caldwell.

Davis, Philip T.
1988   Holocene Glacier Fluctuations in the American Cordillera. *Quaternary Science Reviews* 7(2):129–157. Oxford and New York.

Davis, Ray J.
1952   Flora of Idaho. Provo, Utah: Brigham Young University Press.

Davis, William Lyle
1954   A History of St. Ignatius Mission: An Outpost of Catholic Culture on the Montana Frontier. Spokane, Wash.: C.W. Hill Printing.

Dawson, George M.
1877   General Note on the Mines and Minerals of Economic Value of British Columbia; with a List of Localities. Ottawa: Geological Survey of Canada. (Reprinted, with alterations from the Canadian Pacific Railway Report, 1877.)

———
1892   Notes on the Shuswap People of British Columbia. Pp. 3–44 in *Proceedings and Transactions of the Royal Society of Canada for the Year 1891*, ser. 1, vol. 9(Sect. 2: Papers for 1891). Montreal.

———
1895   [Kamloops,] British Columbia: Kamloops Sheet. Montreal: The Canada Eng. & Litho. Co.

de Angulo, Jaime *see* Angulo, Jaime de

Deaver, Sherri, and Ken Deaver
1986   An Archaeological Overview of Butte District Prehistory. Leslie B. Davis, vol. ed. *U.S. Bureau of Land Management. Montana State Office. Cultural Resource Series* 2. Billings.

DeBloois, Evan I.
1977   Evaluation Report, Cultural Resource Management: An Investigation of Cultural Resources at the Boundary Creek Boat Launching Facility, Challis National Forest, Idaho. (Manuscript on file at United States Forest Service, Intermountain Region, Ogden, Utah.)

Decker, Frances, Margaret Fougberg, and Mary Ronayne
1977   Pemberton: The History of a Settlement. Pemberton, B.C.:
            Pemberton Pioneer Women.

Dehart, Shelagh
[1985]   The Shuswaps: Their Move to the Columbia Valley. (Manu-
            script in Dehart's possession.)

DeLancey, Scott
1987   Klamath and Wintu Pronouns. *International Journal of Amer-
            ican Linguistics* 53(4):461–464.

1987a   Morphological Parallels between Klamath and Wintu. Pp.
            50–60 in Proceedings of the 1987 Hokan-Penutian Confer-
            ence. J. Redden, ed. Carbondale: Southern Illinois University,
            Department of Linguistics.

1988   Klamath Stem Structure in Genetic and Areal Perspective. In
            Papers from the 1988 Hokan-Penutian Workshop. Scott
            Delancey, ed. Eugene: University of Oregon, Department of
            Linguistics.

1991   Chronological Strata of Suffix Classes in the Klamath Verb.
            International Journal of American Linguistics
            57(4):426–445.

1992   Klamath and Sahaptian Numerals. *International Journal of
            American Linguistics* 58(2):235–239.

DeLancey, Scott, Carol Genetti, and Noel Rude
1988   Some Sahaptian-Klamath-Tsimshianic Lexical Sets. Pp.
            195–224 in In Honor of Mary Haas: From the Haas Festival
            Conference on Native American Linguistics. William Shipley,
            ed. Berlin, New York, and Amsterdam: Mouton de Gruyter.

Delwo, Robert D.
1975   Legal Analysis and Report and Recommendation for Litiga-
            tion Concerning the Water Rights of the Coeur d'Alene Indi-
            an Tribe in the Waters of the Hangman Creek Basin. (Unpub-
            lished brief owned by Delwo, Rudolf, and Schroeder.
            Spokane, Wash.)

Dempsey, Hugh A.
1965   Thompson's Journey to the Red Deer River. *Alberta Histori-
            cal Review* 13(1):1–8. Calgary.

Densmore, Frances
1943   Music of the Indians of British Columbia. *Anthopological
            Papers* 27, *Bureau of American Ethnology Bulletin* 136.
            Washington. (Reprinted: Da Capo Press, New York, 1972.)

Department of Indian Affairs 1896, 1924 *see* Canada. Department of Indian Affairs 1896, 1924.

Department of Indian Affairs and Northern Development. Indian Affairs
Branch *see* Canada. Department of Indian Affairs and Northern Development. Indian Affairs Branch 1970

Department of Indian and Northern Affairs 1986, 1989, 1989a *see* Canada.
Department of Indian and Northern Affairs 1986, 1989, 1989a

de Smet, Pierre-Jean
1843   Letters & Sketches: With a Narrative of a Year's Residence
            Among the Indian Tribes of the Rocky Mountains,
            1841–1842. Philadelphia: M. Fithian.

1847   Oregon Missions and Travels Over the Rocky Mountains in
            1845–46. New York: E. Dunigan.

1859   Western Missions and Missionaries: A Series of Letters. New
            York: P.J. Kenedy.

1863   New Indian Sketches. New York: D. and J. Sadler.

1895   New Indian Sketches. New York: P.J. Kenedy.

1905   Life, Letters and Travels of Father Pierre-Jean de Smet, S.J.,
            1801–1873; Missionary Labors and Adventures Among the
            Wild Tribes of North American Indians. Edited from the Orig-
            inal Unpublished Manuscript Journals and Letter Books and
            from His Printed Works with Historical, Geographical, Ethno-
            logical and Other Notes; Also a Life of Father de Smet. Hiram
            M. Chittenden and Alfred T. Richardson, eds. 4 vols. New York:
            Francis P. Harper. (Reprinted: Arno Press, New York, 1969.)

De Smet/DeSmet, Pierre Jean *see* de Smet, Pierre-Jean

Desmond, Gerald R.
1952   Gambling among the Yakima. *The Catholic University of
            America. Anthropological Series* 14. Washington.

De Voto, Bernard A.
1947   Across the Wide Missouri. Illustrated with Paintings by Alfred
            Jacob Miller and Charles [i.e., Karl] Bodmer. Boston: Houghton
            Mifflin, (Several reprints, incl. 1964, 1967, 1970, 1975, 1987.)

1953   The Journals of the Lewis and Clark Expedition. Boston:
            Houghton Mifflin. (Reprinted: Franklin Library, Franklin
            Center, Pa., 1982.)

Dewdney, Selwyn
1964   Writings on Stone along Milk River. *The Beaver* 295(Win-
            ter):22–29. Winnipeg, Man.

Diomedi, Alexander
1879   Sketches of Modern Indian Life. St. Ignatius, Mont.: St.
            Ignatius Mission Press. (Reprinted: *Woodstock Letters* 22–23,
            Woodstock, Md., 1893–1894; also, Ye Galleon Press, Fair-
            field, Wash., 1978.)

1890   [Short notice about the Mission of the Sacred Heart.] (Manu-
            script in Sacred Heart Mission Papers, Foley Library, Gonza-
            ga University, Spokane, Wash.)

1978   Sketches of Indian Life in the Pacific Northwest. Edward J.
            Kowrach, ed. Fairfield, Wash.: Ye Galleon Press. (Originally
            publ. in: *Woodstock Letters* 22–23, Woodstock, Md.,
            1893–1894.)

Dionne, Gabriel
1947   Histoire des méthodes missionnaires utilisées par les Oblats
            de Marie Immaculée dans l'évangélisation des Indiens de
            'Versant Pacifique' au dix-neuvième siècle. (Thèse présentée
            á la Faculté des Arts de l'Université d'Ottawa en vue de l'ob-
            tention de la Maîtrise des Arts / M.A. Thesis, Ottawa Univer-
            sity, Ottawa.)

Dixon, Cyril W.
1962   Smallpox. London: J. and A. Churchill.

Dixon, George, ed. *see* Beresford, William

Dixon, Roland B., and Alfred L. Kroeber
1913   New Linguistic Families in California. *American Anthropolo-
            gist* 15(4):647–655.

1919   Linguistic Families of California. *University of California
            Publications in American Archaeology and Ethnology*
            16(3):47–118. Berkeley.

Doak, Ivy G.
1983   The 1908 Okanagan Word Lists of James Teit. *University of
            Montana Occasional Papers in Linguistics* 3. Missoula.

1989   Harmony in Coeur d'Alene. (Manuscript in Ivy Doak's pos-
            session.)

1991   Coeur d'Alene Rhetorical Structure. *Texas Linguistic Forum: Discourse* 33:43–70. Austin: University of Texas, Department of Linguistics.

1992   Another Look at Coeur d'Alene Harmony. *International Journal of American Linguistics* 58(1):1–35.

1993   Discourse Use of the Coeur d'Alene -st(u)- Transitivizer. Pp. 73–91 in American Indian Linguistics and Ethnography in Honor of Laurence C. Thompson. Anthony Mattina and Timothy Montler, eds. *University of Montana Occasional Papers in Linguistics* 10. Missoula.

1997   Coeur d'Alene Grammatical Relations. (Ph.D. Dissertation in Linguistics, The University of Texas, Austin.)

Dobyns, Henry
1966   Estimating Aboriginal American Population, 1: An Appraisal of Techniques with a New Hemispheric Estimate. *Current Anthropology* 7(4):395–416.

Dolby, Elizabeth
1973   The Fur Trade and Culture Change among the Okanagan Indians. Pp. 134–135 in *37th Annual Report of the Okanagan Historical Society.* Vernon, B.C.

Donald, Leland
1996   Slavery and Captivity: A Comparison of Servitude on the Northwest Coast and Among Interior Salish. Pp. 75–86 in Chin Hills to Chiloquin: Papers Honoring the Versatile Career of Theodore Stern. With a Note of Personal Appreciation by Patrick M. Haynal. Don E. Dumond, ed. *University of Oregon Anthropological Papers* 52. Eugene.

Donaldson, Ivan J., and Frederick K. Cramer
1971   Fishwheels of the Columbia. Portland, Oreg.: Binfords and Mort.

Donnelly, Joseph P., ed. *see* Point, Nicolas

Dorn, Ronald I.
1990   Rock Varnish Dating of Rock Art: State of the Art Perspective. *La Pintura* 17(2):1–2, 9–11.

Dorsey, George A.
1901   Certain Gambling Games of the Klamath Indians. *American Anthropologist,* n.s. 3(1):14–27.

Dort, Wakefield, Jr.
1964   Laboratory Studies in Physical Geology. 2d ed. Minneapolis: Burgess Publishing Co.

1975   Archaeo-geology of Jaguar Cave, Upper Birch Creek Valley, Idaho. *Tebiwa: Journal of the Idaho State University Museum* 17(2):33–58. Pocatello.

Doty, James 1855, 1855–1856 *see* Doty, James 1978

1860   Report of Mr. James Doty, of a Reconnaissance from Fort Benton to Cantonment Stevens, and of a Survey from Fort Benton to Olympia. Pp. 550–565 in Vol. 1 of Reports of Explorations and Surveys, to Ascertain the Most Practicable and Economical Route for a Railroad from the Mississippi River to the Pacific Ocean. *36th Congress. 1st Session. House Executive Document* 11 (Pt. 1, No. 56). (Serial No. 1054); and *Senate Executive Document* 78. Washington.

1978   Journal of Operations of Governor Isaac Ingalls Stevens of Washington Territory in 1855. Edward J. Kowrach, ed. Fairfield, Wash.: Ye Galleon Press. (From the original manuscript, T–494, Roll 5, Item 9, Record Group 75, National Archives, Washington.)

Douglas, David
1904–1905   Sketch of a Journey to the Northwestern Parts of the Continent of North America, during the Years 1824–'25–'26–'27. *Oregon Historical Quarterly* 5(3):230–271, (4):325–369; 6(1):76–97, (2):206–227. (Reprinted from: *The Companion to the Botanical Magazine,* vol. II; London, 1836.)

Douglas, David
1914   Journal Kept by David Douglas during His Travels in North America, 1823–1827. Together with A Particular Description of Thirty-three Species of American Oaks and Eighteen Species of *Pinus*, with Appendices containing a List of the Plants Introduced by Douglas and an Account of His Death in 1834. Publ. under the direction of the Royal Horticultural Society. London: W. Wesley and Son. (Reprinted: Antiquarian Press, New York, 1959.)

1959   Journal Kept by David Douglas during His Travels in North America, 1823–1827. Repr. ed. New York: Antiquarian Press. (Orig. publ.: W. Wesley and Son, London, 1914.)

Douglas, James
1848   [Letter of March 16, 1848.] (Manuscript D.5/10, folders 474, 479, in Hudson's Bay Company Archives, Provincial Archives of Manitoba, Winnipeg.)

1856   [Letter to W. McNeill, July 30, 1856.] (Country Letterbook 1855–1856 [B.226/b12 fo. 93d–94d] in Hudson's Bay Company Archives, Provincial Archives of Manitoba, Winnnipeg.)

1860   [Despatch No. 13 to the Duke of Newcastle, October 9th, 1860.] *British Parliamentary Papers* 23. Shannon: Irish University Press.

Down, Robert Horace
1926   A History of the Silverton Country. Portland, Oreg.: The Berncliff Press.

Downie, William
1858   [Report of October 2d, 1858, to Governor James Douglas.] (Document GR 1372, File 487/2a, in British Columbia Archives and Records Service, Victoria.)

Downing, Glenn R., and Lloyd S. Furniss
1968   Some Observations on Camas Digging and Baking among Present-Day Nez Perce. *Tebiwa: Journal of the Idaho State University Museum* 11(1):48–59. Pocatello.

Dozier, Jack
1961   History of the Coeur d'Alene Indians to 1900. (M.A. Thesis in History, University of Idaho, Moscow, Idaho.)

1962   The Coeur d'Alene Country: The Creation of the Coeur d'Alene Reservation in Northern Idaho. *Idaho Yesterdays* 6:2–7. Boise.

Drake-Terry, Joanne
1989   The Same As Yesterday: The Lillooet Chronicle the Theft of Their Lands and Resources. Lillooet, B.C.: Lillooet Tribal Council.

Draper, John A.
1987   Appendix B, Description of Stone Tools and Debitage. Pp. B1–B44 in Prehistoric Land Use in the Northern Rocky Mountains: A Perspective from the Middle Kootenai River Valley. Alston V. Thoms and Greg C. Burtchard, eds. *Washington State University. Center for Northwest Anthropology. Project Report* 4. Pullman.

1990   An Intensive Cultural Resources Inventory Survey of the Dworshak Reservoir Drawdown Zone, North Fork Clearwater River, West-Central Idaho. With contributions by Deborah L. Olson. *Washington State University. Center for Northwest Anthropology. Project Report* 11, (2d ed.). Pullman.

Draper, John A., and Gordon A. Lothson
1990   Test Excavations at 10NP143 and 10NP292, Lower Clearwater River, West-central Idaho. *Washington State University. Center for Northwest Anthropology. Project Report* 12. Pullman.

Drews, Robin A.
1938   Cultural Sequences in the Middle Columbia Region. (Honors Thesis in Anthropology, University of Oregon, Eugene.)

Driver, Harold E.
1969   Indians of North America. 2d ed. Chicago: University of Chicago Press. (Reprinted in 1973.)

Driver, Harold E., and James L. Coffin
1975   Classification and Development of North American Indian Cultures: A Statistical Analysis of the Driver-Massey Sample. *Transactions of the American Philosophical Society*, n.s. 65(Pt. 3). Philadelphia.

Driver, Harold E., and William C. Massey
1957   · Comparative Studies of North American Indians. *Transactions of the American Philosophical Society*, n.s. 47(Pt. 2). Philadelphia.

Drucker, Philip
1934   [Clackamas Chinookan ethnographic fieldnotes (copy).] (Philip Drucker Papers, Manuscript No. 4516 (82), National Anthropological Archives, Smithsonian Institution, Washington.)

_____
1934a   [Molala ethnographic fieldnotes.] (Philip Drucker Papers, Manuscript No. 4516(78), National Anthropological Archives, Smithsonian Institution, Washington.)

_____
1943   Archaeological Survey on the Northern Northwest Coast. *Anthropological Papers* 20, *Bureau of American Ethnology Bulletin* 133. Washington. (Reprinted: Shorey Book Store, Seattle, Wash., 1972.)

_____
1948   Appraisal of the Archaeological Resources of Cascade Smith's Ferry, Scriver Creek and Garden Valley Reservoirs, Upper Payette River Basin, Idaho. Eugene, Oreg.: Columbia Basin Project, River Basin Surveys.

_____
1948a   An Appraisal of the Archaeological Resources of the McNary Reservoir, Oregon-Washington. Washington: Columbia Basin Project, River Basin Surveys, Smithsonian Institution.

_____
1965   Cultures of the North Pacific Coast. San Francisco: Chandler Publishing Company.

Drury, Clifford M.
1936   Henry Harmon Spalding, Pioneer of Old Oregon. Caldwell, Idaho: The Caxton Printers.

_____
1937   Marcus Whitman, M.D., Pioneer and Martyr. Caldwell, Idaho: The Caxton Printers.

_____
1940   Elkanah and Mary Walker, Pioneers among the Spokanes. Caldwell, Idaho: The Caxton Printers.

_____
1949   A Teepee in His Front Yard; A Biography of H.T. Cowley, One of the Four Founders of the City of Spokane, Washington. Portland, Oreg.: Binfords and Mort.

_____, ed.
1958   The Diaries and Letters of Henry H. Spalding and Asa Bowen Smith Relating to the Nez Perce Mission, 1838–1842. Glendale, Calif.: Arthur H. Clark.

_____, ed.
1963–1966 First White Women Over the Rockies; Diaries, Letters, and Biographical Sketches of Six Women of the Oregon Mission Who Made the Overland Journey in 1836 and 1838. 3 vols. Glendale, Calif.: Arthur H. Clark.

_____, ed.
1973   Marcus and Narcissa Whitman, and the Opening of Old Oregon. 2 vols. Glendale, Calif.: Arthur H. Clark.

_____, ed.
1976   Nine Years with the Spokane Indians. The Diary, 1838–1848, of Elkanah Walker. Glendale, Calif.: Arthur H. Clark.

Druss, Mark
1983   Radiocarbon Dating of Two Charcoal Samples from the Doublesprings Archaeological Site (10CR29), East-Central Idaho. (Unpublished report in M. Druss's possession.)

Dryden, Cecil
1968   Dryden's History of Washington. Portland, Oreg.: Binfords and Mort.

Dryer, Matthew S.
1991   Subject and Inverse in Kutenai. Pp. 183–202 in Papers from the American Indian Languages Conferences, Held at the University of California, Santa Cruz, July and August 1991. James E. Redden, ed. *Occasional Papers on Linguistics* 16. Carbondale: Southern Illinois University, Department of Linguistics.

_____
1992   A Comparison of the Obviation Systems of Kutenai and Algonquian. Pp. 119–163 in Papers of the Twenty-Third Algonquian Conference. William Cowan, ed. Ottawa: Carleton University.

_____
1994   The Discourse Function of the Kutenai Inverse. Pp. 65–99 in Voice and Inversion. T. Givón, ed. *Typological Studies in Language* 28. Amsterdam and Philadelphia: John Benjamins.

_____
1996   Grammatical Relations in Ktunaxa (Kutenai). *The Belcourt Lecture*, delivered before the University of Manitoba on 24 February 1995. Winnipeg, Man.: Voices of Rupert's Land.

Du Bois, Cora
1938   The Feather Cult of the Middle Columbia. *General Series in Anthropology* 7. Menasha, Wis.: George Banta.

_____
1939   The 1870 Ghost Dance. *University of California Anthropological Records* 3(1). Berkeley. (Reprinted: Kraus Reprint, Millwood, N.Y., 1976.)

Duff, Wilson
1952   The Upper Stalo Indians of the Fraser Valley, British Columbia. *Anthropology in British Columbia. Memoir* 1. Victoria. (Reprinted in 1973.)

_____
1956   An Unusual Burial at the Whalen Site. Pp. 67–72 in Northwest Archaeology Number, by Richard D. Daugherty, et al. *Research Studies of the State College of Washington* 24(1). Pullman, Wash.

_____
1964   The Indian History of British Columbia, Volume 1: The Impact of the White Man. *Anthropology in British Columbia. Memoir* 5. Victoria. (Reprinted, 2d ed., 1969; also in 1992.)

_____
1969   The Indian History of British Columbia, Volume 1: The Impact of the White Man. 2d ed. *Anthropology in British Columbia. Memoir* 5. Victoria: British Columbia Provincial Museum. (Reprinted: Royal British Columbia Museum, Victoria, 1992.)

687

1975   Images, Stone, B.C.: Thirty Centuries of Northwest Coast Indian Sculpture. Seattle: University of Washington Press.

Dumond, Don E., and Rick Minor
1983   Archaeology in the John Day Reservoir: The Wildcat Canyon Site, 35–GM–9. *University of Oregon Anthropological Papers* 30. Eugene.

Dunbar, Seymour, and Paul C. Phillips, eds. 1927 *see* Owen, John 1927

Dunn, J.R.
1846   [Journal on H.M.S. Fisgard.] (Manuscript Adm. 101/100/4XC/A/3930 in the Public Record Office, Kew, Surrey, England.)

Dunn, Jacob P., Jr.
1886   Massacres of the Mountains; A History of the Indian Wars of the Far West, 1815–1875. New York: Harper and Brothers. (Reprinted: Archer House, New York, 1958.)

Dunnell, Robert C.
1979   Trends in Current Americanist Archaeology. *American Journal of Archaeology* 83(4):437–449.

Dunwiddie, Peter W.
1986   A 6000-Year Record of Forest History on Mount Rainier, Washington. *Ecology* 67:58–68. Tempe, Ariz.

Dusenberry, J. Verne
1959   Visions among the Pend d'Oreille Indians. *Ethnos* 24(1–2):52–57.

1979   Samples of Pend d'Oreille Oral Literature and Salish Narratives. Pp. 109–120 in Lifeways of Intermontane and Plains Montana Indians: In Honor of J. Verne Dusenberry. Leslie B. Davis, ed. *Occasional Papers of the Museum of the Rockies* 1. Bozeman: Montana State University.

Dyck, Ian George
1976   The Harder Site: A Middle Period Bison Hunters' Campsite in the Northern Great Plains. (Ph.D. Dissertation in Anthropology, University of Alberta, Edmonton.)

Dyk, Walter
1930–1933   [Wishram linguistic notes, from fieldwork at Spearfish, Wash., and subsequent work at Yale University with Philip Kahclamat, a Wishram.] (Manuscripts in the Library of the American Philosophical Society, Philadelphia.)

1931   Verb Types in Wishram. (M.A. Thesis in Anthropology, University of Chicago, Chicago.)

1933   A Grammar of Wishram. (Ph.D. Dissertation in Anthropology, Yale University, New Haven, Conn.)

Dyk, Walter, and Dell H. Hymes
1956   Stress Accent in Wishram Chinook. *International Journal of American Linguistics* 22(4):238–241.

ERTEC = Ertec Northwest, Inc.
1982   A Cultural Resources Overview and Scenic and Natural Resources Assessment for the Skagit-Hanford Nuclear Power Project. Seattle, Wash.: Ertec Northwest, Inc.

Edwards, Irene
1978   Short Portage to Lillooet. Lillooet, B.C.: Irene Edwards.

Edwards, T.A.
1881   Daring Donald McKay; or, The Last War-Trail of the Modocs: The Romance of the Life of Donald McKay, Government Scout, and Chief of the Warm Spring Indians. 1st ed. Chicago: Rounds Brothers, Printers. (Reprinted in 1884, 1889 and 1893; also, Edited with Introd. and Notes by Keith and Donna Clark: Oregon Historical Society, Portland, Oreg., 1971.)

1884   Daring Donald McKay; or, The Last War Trail of the Modocs: The Romance of the Life of Donald McKay, Government Scout, and Chief of the Warm Spring Indians. 3d ed. Erie, Pa.: Herald Printing and Publishing Co. (Reprinted in 1889 and 1893; also, Edited with Introd. And Notes by Keith and Donna Clark: Oregon Historical Society, Portland, Oreg., 1971.)

Eells, Myron
1878   Hymns in the Chinook Jargon Language. Portland, Oreg.: G.H. Himes. (Reprinted: 2d ed., rev. and enl. D. Steel, Portland, Oreg., 1889.)

1894   Father Eells: A Bibliography of Rev. Cushing Eells. Boston: Congregational Sunday School and Publishing Society.

Egesdal, Steven M.
1984   Stylized Characters' Speech in Thompson Salish Narrative. (Ph.D. Dissertation in Linguistics, University of Hawaii, Honolulu. Published: *University of Montana Occasional Publications in Linguistics* 9. Missoula, 1992.)

1992   Stylized Characters' Speech in Thompson Salish Narrative. *University of Montana Occasional Papers in Linguistics* 9. Missoula.

Egesdal, Steven M., and M. Terry Thompson
1994   Hilda Austin's Telling of "qʷíqʷλ'qʷəλ't: A Traditional Nɬeʔképmx Legend." Pp. 313–331 in Coming to Light: Contemporary Translations of the Native Literatures of North America. Brian Swann, ed. New York: Random House.

Eijk, Jan P. van
1978   A Classified English-Lillooet Wordlist. Lisse: Peter de Ridder Press.

1978a   Ucwalmícwts. Mount Currie, B.C.: The Tŝzil Publishing House.

1981   Cuystwí malh Ucwalmícwts (Teach Yourself Lillooet) / Ucwalmícwts Curriculum for Advanced Learners. Mount Currie, B.C.: The Tŝzil Publishing House.

1985   The Lillooet Language: Phonology, Morphology, Syntax. (Doctoral Dissertation in Linguistics, University of Amsterdam, The Netherlands. Published: University of British Columbia Press, Vancouver, 1997.)

————, comp.
1990   Lillooet - English Dictionary. (Manuscript in van Eijk's possession; Saskatchewan Indian Federated College, Regina.)

1993   CVC Reduplication and Infixation in Lillooet. Pp. 317–326 in American Indian Linguistics and Ethnography in Honor of Laurence C. Thompson. Anthony Mattina and Timothy Montler, eds. *University of Montana Papers in Linguistics* 10. Missoula.

1997   CVC Reduplication in Salish. Pp. 453–475 in Salish Languages and Linguistics: Theoretical and Descriptive Perspectives. Ewa Czaykowska-Higgins and M. Dale Kinkade, eds. (*Trends in Linguistics. Studies and Monographs* 107). Berlin and New York: Mouton de Gruyter.

1997a   The Lillooet Language: Phonology, Morphology, Syntax. Vancouver: University of British Columbia Press. (Orig. presented as the Author's Doctoral Dissertation, 1985.)

Eijk, Jan P. van, and Thom Hess
1986   Noun and Verb in Salish. *Lingua: International Review of General Linguistics* 69(4):319–331. Amsterdam.

Eijk, Jan P. van, and Lorna Williams, eds.
1981   Cuystwí malh Ucwalmícwts: Lillooet Legends and Stories.
            Storytellers: Martina Larochelle, Adelina Williams, Rosie
            Joseph, Sam Mitchell, Bill Edwards. Developed by Mount
            Currie Cultural Centre. Mount Currie, B.C.: The Tŝzil Pub-
            lishing House.

Ekland, Roy E.
1969   The 'Indian Problem': Pacific Northwest, 1879. *Oregon His-
            torical Quarterly* 70(2):101–138.

Eldridge, Morley
1974   Recent Archaeological Investigations near Chase, B.C. *Cari-
            boo College Papers in Anthropology* 2. Kamloops, B.C.

────────
1984   Vallican Archaeological Site (DjQi 1): a Synthesis and Man-
            agement Report. (Unpublished manuscript on file, Archaeol-
            ogy Branch, Victoria, B.C.)

Eldridge, Morley, and Ann Eldridge
1980   An Evaluation of the Heritage Resource Potential of the Dean
            River Valley. (Unpublished manuscript on file, Archaeology
            Branch, Victoria, B.C.)

Elliott, William
1931   Lake Lillooet Tales. *Journal of American Folk-Lore*
            44(171):166–181.

Elliott, T.C., ed. 1909, 1912, 1912a, 1913, 1914, 1914a, 1914b, 1915 *see*
Work, John 1909, 1912, 1912a, 1913, 1914, 1914a, 1914b, 1915

──────── , ed.
1909–1910 *see* Ogden, Peter Skene 1909–1910

──────── , .ed
1914c, 1917, 1920 *see* Thompson, David 1914, 1917, 1920

────────
1915   The Dalles-Celilo Portage; Its History and Influence. *Oregon
            Historical Quarterly* 16(2):135–174.

Elmendorf, William W.
1935–1936 [Lakes and Spokane ethnographic and linguistic fieldnotes.]
            (Manuscripts in Elmendorf's possession.)

────────
1949   [Wenatchee and Columbia ethnographic and linguistic field-
            notes.] (Manuscripts in Elmendorf's possession.)

────────
1960   The Structure of Twana Culture; With Comparative Notes on
            the Structure of Yurok Culture, by A.L. Kroeber. *Washington
            State University. Research Studies. Monographic Supplement*
            2. Pullman.

────────
1961   System Change in Salish Kinship Terminologies. *Southwest-
            ern Journal of Anthropology* 17(4):365–382.

────────
1962   Relations of Oregon Salish as Evidenced in Numerical Stems.
            Anthropological Linguistics 4(2):1–16.

────────
1965   Linguistic and Geographic Relations in the Northern Plateau
            Area. *Southwestern Journal of Anthropology* 21(1):63–78.

────────
1965a   Some Problems in the Regrouping of Powell Units. *Cana-
            dian Journal of Linguistics* 10(2–3):93–107. (With discus-
            sion by Wallace Chafe, William Elmendorf, Mary Haas,
            Morris Swadesh, Harry Hoijer, and Carl Voegelin, pp.
            104–107.)

En'owkin Centre
1993   púpaʔkʷ: En'owkin's First Indian Language Book. Anthony
            Mattina, ed. Penticton, B.C.: En'owkin Centre.

Endacott, Neal A.
1992   The Archaeology of Squirt Cave: Seasonality, Storage, and
            Semisedentism. (M.A. Thesis in Anthropology, Washington
            State University, Pullman.)

Endzweig, Pamela E.
1994   Late Archaic Variabilty and Change on the Southern Colum-
            bia Plateau: Archaeological Investigations in the Pine Creek
            Drainage of the Middle John Day River, Wheeler County,
            Oregon. (Ph.D. Dissertation in Anthropology, University of
            Oregon, Eugene. Microfilm: University Microfilms Interna-
            tional, Ann Arbor, Mich., 1994.)

Engle, P.M.
1861   Appendix L to Military Road from Fort Benton to Fort Walla
            Walla, pp. 137–40. *36th Congress. 2d Session. House Execu-
            tive Document* 44. (Serial No. 1099). Washington.

Epperson, Terrence W.
1977   Final Report on the 1976 Archaeological Evaluation of
            Bureau of Reclamation Upper Snake River Project, Salmon
            Falls Division, Twin Falls and Cassia Counties, Idaho.
            *Archaeological Reports of the Idaho State Museum of Natur-
            al History* 9. Pocatello.

Erickson, Kevin
1983   Marine Shell Utilization in the Plateau Culture Area. (M.A.
            Thesis in Anthropology, University of Idaho, Moscow.)

Erwin, L.T.
1897   [Report on the Condition of the Palouse Indians from Yakima
            Agency, to Commissioner of Indian Affairs, April 5, 1897.]
            (Manuscript in Commissioner of Indian Affairs, Letters
            Received 1897, Records of the Bureau of Indian Affairs,
            Record Group 75, National Archives, Washington.)

Erwin, Richard P.
1930   Indian Rock Writing in Idaho. Pp. 2, 35–111 in *12th Biennial
            Report of the State Historical Society of Idaho for the Years
            1929–30.*

Evans, Lucylle H.
1981   Good Samaritan of the Northwest: Anthony Ravalli, S.J.,
            1812–1884. (*University of Montana Publications in History*).
            Stevensville, Mont.: Montana Creative Consultants.

Evans, Steven Ross
1996   Voice of the Old Wolf: Lucullus Virgil McWhorter and the
            Nez Perce Indians. Pullman, Wash.: Washington State Uni-
            versity Press.

Everette, Willis E.
1883   [Words, phrases and sentences in the language of the
            Qwǜŝwaipüm or Yákima Indians, with an account of their cus-
            toms, habits, etc.; collected at Ft. Simcoe, Washington Territory,
            June 4, 1883.] (Manuscript No. 698 in National Anthropologi-
            cal Archives, Smithsonian Institution, Washington.)

────────
1883a   [Words, phrases and sentences in the language of the Nez Per-
            cés of Nǜ'mípotitókěn, collected at the mouth of Làpwé
            Creek, on Clearwater River, Idaho Territory, March 30, 1883.]
            (Manuscript No. 677 in National Anthropological Archives,
            Smithsonian Institution, Washington.)

Ewers, John C.
1946   Identification and History of the Small Robes Band of the Pie-
            gan Indians. *Journal of the Washington Academy of Sciences*
            36(12):397–401. Washington.

────────
1948   Gustavus Sohon's Portraits of Flathead and Pend d'Oreille
            Indians, 1854. *Smithsonian Miscellaneous Collections*
            110(7). Washington. (Reprinted: Pp. 67–120 in In the Name
            of the Salish & Kootenai Nation: The 1855 Hell Gate Treaty
            and the Origin of the Flathead Indian Reservation. Robert
            Bigart and Clarence Woodcock, eds. Salish Kootenai College
            Press, Pablo, Mont. 1996.)

────────
1955   The Horse in Blackfoot Indian Culture: With Comparative
            Material from Other Western Tribes. *Bureau of American Eth-
            nology Bulletin* 159. (Reprinted: Smithsonian Institution
            Press, Washington, 1980.)

689

1958   The Blackfeet: Raiders on the Northwestern Plains. Norman: University of Oklahoma Press. (Reprinted in 1967, 1976, 1988.)

1963   Iroquois Indians in the Far West. *Montana: The Magazine of Western History* 13(2):2–10. Helena.

1968   The Indian Trade of the Upper Missouri Before Lewis and Clark. Pp. 14–33 in Indian Life on the Upper Missouri. Norman: University of Oklahoma Press. (Reprinted with revisions from: *Bulletin of the Missouri Historical Society* 10(4), St. Louis, Mo., 1954.)

1975   Intertribal Warfare as the Precursor of Indian-White Warfare on the Northern Great Plains. *The Western Historical Quarterly* 6(4):397–410.

Ewing, Shirley, and Bonnie Grossen
1978   Skitswish Tales of the Ancient Coeur d'Alene Indians. DeSmet, Idaho: Coeur d'Alene Indian Tribal School.

Fahey, John
1974   The Flathead Indians. Norman: University of Oklahoma Press.

1986   The Kalispel Indians. Norman: University of Oklahoma Press.

Farley, Albert L.
1979   Atlas of British Columbia: People, Environment, and Resource Use. Vancouver: University of British Columbia Press.

Farmer, Judith A., with Daniel B. Karnes, G. Thomas Babich, and Thompson P. Porterfield
1973   An Historical Atlas of Early Oregon. Text by Kenneth L. Holmes. Portland, Oreg.: Historical Cartographic Publications.

Farnham, Thomas J.
1843   Travels in the Great Western Prairies, the Anahuac and Rocky Mountains, and in the Oregon Territory. 2 vols. New York: Greeley and McElrath. (Reprinted: Vols. 28–29 of Early Western Travels, Reuben G. Thwaites, ed., Arthur H. Clark, Cleveland, Ohio, 1906.)

Farrand, Livingston
1899   The Chilcotin. Pp. 645–648 in *68th Annual Report of the British Association for the Advancement of Science for 1898.* London. (Reprinted in: *Northwest Anthropological Research Notes* 8(1–2):338–340. Moscow, Idaho, 1974.)

———— 1907–1910 *see* Hodge, Frederick W., ed. 1907–1910

1917   Sahaptin Tales. Pp. 135–179 in Folk-tales of Salishan and Sahaptin Tribes. Franz Boas, ed. *Memoirs of the American Folk-Lore Society* 11. Lancaster, Pa., and New York.

Faulk, Odie B., and Laura E. Faulk
1988   The Modoc. *(Indians of North America).* New York: Chelsea House Publishers.

Feder, Norman
1964   Origin of the Oklahoma Forty-Nine Dance. *Ethnomusicology* 8(3):290–294.

1971   Two Hundred Years of North American Indian Art. New York: Praeger Publishers in association with the Whitney Museum of American Art.

Fee, Chester A.
1936   Chief Joseph: The Biography of a Great Indian. New York: Wilson-Erickson.

Fenton, William N.
1953   Cultural Stability and Change in American Indian Societies. *Journal of the Royal Anthropological Institute of Great Britain and Ireland* 83(2):169–174. London.

Ferguson, T.J.
1984   Archaeological Ethics and Values in a Tribal Cultural Resource Management Program at the Pueblo of Zuni. Pp. 224–235 in Ethics and Values in Archaeology. Ernestene L. Green, ed. New York: Free Press.

Ferris, Warren Angus
1940   Life in the Rocky Mountains, 1830–1835, by Warren Angus Ferris; arranged by Herbert S. Auerback, annotated by J. Cecil Alter. Salt Lake City: Rocky Mountain Book Shop. (Orig. publ. in the *Western Literary Messenger*, July 13, 1842–May 18, 1844; reprinted in 1983.)

Filloon, Ray M.
1952   Huckleberry Pilgrimage. *Pacific Discovery* 5(3):4–13. San Francisco, Calif.

Finley, James B.
1840   History of the Wyandott Mission at Upper Sandusky, Ohio, under the Direction of the Methodist Episcopal Church. Cincinnati: Wright and Swormstedt.

Finster, David E.
1973   Beadwork of the Nez Perce Indians. (M.A. Thesis in Anthropology, Washington State University, Pullman.)

Fisher, Robin
1977   Contact and Conflict: Indian-European Relations in British Columbia, 1774–1890. Vancouver: University of British Columbia Press.

Fitch, James B.
1974   Economic Development in a Minority Enclave: The Case of the Yakima Indian Nation, Washington. (Ph.D. Dissertation in Anthropology, Stanford University, Stanford, Calif.; Photocopy: University Microfilms International, Ann Arbor, Mich., 1978.)

Fitzpatrick, Darleen Ann
1968   The 'Shake': The Indian Shake Curing Ritual among the Yakima. (M.A. Thesis in Anthropology, University of Washington, Seattle.)

Fladmark, Knut R.
1979   Review of "The Athapaskan Question". *Canadian Journal of Archaeology* 3:250–254. Ottawa.

1981   Paleoindian Artifacts from the Peace River District. Pp. 124–135 in Fragments of the Past: British Columbia Archaeology in the 1970s. Knut R. Fladmark, ed. *BC Studies* (Special Issue):48. Vancouver.

1982   An Introduction to the Prehistory of British Columbia. *Canadian Journal of Archaeology* 6:95–156. Ottawa.

1986   British Columbia Prehistory. Ottawa: Archaeological Survey of Canada, National Museum of Man, National Museums of Canada.

Fladmark, Knut R., Jonathan C. Driver, and Diana Alexander
1988   The Paleoindian Component at Charlie Lake Cave (HbRf 39), British Columbia. *American Antiquity* 53(2):371–384.

Flathead Culture Committee
1983   A Brief History of the Flathead Tribes. 3d ed. Clarence Woodcock, director ... [et al.]. St. Ignatius, Mont.: Flathead Culture Committee of the Confederated Salish and Kootenai Tribes.

Fleming, R. Harvey, ed.
1976   Minutes of Council, Northern Department of Rupert Land, 1821–31. With an Introduction by H.A. Innis; E.E. Rich, gen. ed. *Publications of the Champlain Society. Hudson's Bay Company Series* 3. Toronto: The Champlain Society.

Flemming, Edward, Peter Ladefoged, and Sarah Thomason
1994   Phonetic Structure of Montana Salish. *UCLA Working Papers in Phonetics* 87:1–33; (*Fieldwork Studies of Targeted Languages* 2). Los Angeles.

Fletcher, Alice C.
1891   Ethnologic Gleanings among the Nez Percés. (Manuscript No. 4558/57, Fletcher-La Flesche Papers, National Anthropological Archives, Smithsonian Institution, Washington; see also: Sappington, Robert Lee, and Caroline D. Carley, 1995.)

─────   The Nez Perce Country. [Typescript accompanying a map of
1891a   the Nez Perce Country drawn by Billy Williams, a Nez Perce.] (Manuscript No. 4558/58–59, Fletcher-La Flesche Papers, National Anthropological Archives, Smithsonian Institution, Washington.)

─────   A Study of Omaha Music; by Alice C. Fletcher, aided by
1893   Francis La Flesche. With a Report on the Structural Peculiarities of the Music by John Comfort Fillmore. *Harvard University. Archaeological and Ethnological Papers of the Peabody Museum* 1 (5). Cambridge, Mass. (Reprinted: Kraus Reprint, New York, 1978; also, University of Nebraska Press, Lincoln and London, 1994.)

Flett, Nancy
1974   [Oral History file 432–A, Eastern Washington State Historical Society, Spokane, Wash.]

Flint, Patricia Robins
1982   The Northern Rocky Mountain Region: Environment and Culture History. (Ph.D. Dissertation in Anthropology, University of Oregon, Eugene. Microfiche: University Microfilms International, Ann Arbor, Mich., 1984.)

Flyn, Frank
1976   A Temporal Classification of Folklore of the Okanagan Indians. (M.A. Thesis in Anthropology, University of British Columbia, Vancouver.)

Foltin, Béla, Jr.
1971   Continuity and Change in Klamath Indian Music and Musical Culture. (M.A. Thesis in Music, University of Illinois, Urbana - Champaign.)

Foor, Thomas Allyn
1981   Cultural Continuity on the Northwestern Great Plains: 1300 B.C. to A.D. 100, the Pelican Lake Culture. (Ph.D. Dissertation in Anthropology, University of California, Santa Barbara. Photocopy: University Microfilms International, Ann Arbor, Mich., 1984.)

Forbes, Jeffrey
1987   Carbon and Oxygen Isotopic Composition of Holocene Lake Sediments from Okanogan County, Washington. (M.S. Thesis in Geology, University of Washington, Seattle.)

Forbis, Richard G.
1950   Religious Acculturation of the Flathead Indians. (M.A. Thesis in Anthropology, Montana State University, Bozeman.)

─────   The Flathead Apostacy. *Montana Magazine of History*
1951   1(4):35–40. Helena.

─────   The Old Women's Buffalo Jump, Alberta. *National Museum*
1960   *of Canada Bulletin* 180:56–123; *Contributions to Anthropology, 1960.* Ottawa.

Ford, Pat
1991   Salmon Do Not Swim to the Ocean: Regional Economies Cannot Afford Not to Save Salmon. *Palouse Journal* 45(Spring): 14–16. Moscow, Idaho.

Fort Lapwai Agency
1910   [Annual Narrative Report, 1910.] (Microfilm in Records of the Bureau of Indian Affairs, Record Group 75, National Archives, Washington.)

Fortier, Theodore N.
1995   Piercing Hearts: Coeur d'Alene Indians and Jesuit Priests on the Columbia Plateau. (Ph.D. Dissertation in Anthropology, Washington State University, Pullman.)

Fortune, A.L.
1910   Report on Overlanders Expedition. (Manuscript in British Columbia Provincial Archives, Victoria.)

Fowler, Nancy J.
1982   Wasco-Wishram Noun Plurals. (B.A. Thesis in Anthropology, Reed College, Portland, Oreg.)

Frachtenberg, Leo J.
1910–1911   [Molala texts (9 vols.), notes to texts (3 vols.), grammatical notes (2 vols.), ethnological notes (1 vol.).] (Manuscript No. 2517 in National Anthropological Archives, Smithsonian Institution, Washington.)

─────   Comparative Studies in Takelman, Kalapuyan, and Chi-
1918   nookan Lexicography, a Preliminary Paper. *International Journal of American Linguistics* 1(2):175–182.

Franchère, Gabriel
1854   Narrative of a Voyage to the Northwest Coast of America in the Years 1811, 1812, 1813, and 1814. J.V. Huntington, trans. and ed. New York: Redfield. (Reprinted in Vol. 6 of Early Western Travels, 1748–1846, by Reuben G. Thwaites, ed.; Arthur H. Clark, Cleveland, 1904–1907; also, AMS Press, New York, 1966.)

Franklin, Jerry F., and C.T. Dyrness
1969   Vegetation of Oregon and Washington. *USDA Forest Service Research Paper* PNW-80. Portland, Oreg.

─────   Natural Vegetation of Oregon and Washington. *USDA Forest*
1973   *Service Technical Report* PNW-8. Portland, Oreg. (Reprinted, rev. and enl. ed.: Oregon State University Press, Corvallis, 1988.)

Franks, A.W.
1874   A Bow and Two Arrows of the Modocs. *Journal of the Royal Anthropological Institute of Great Britain and Ireland* 3:204–205. London.

Franz, Donald G., and Norma J. Russell
1989   Blackfoot Dictionary of Stems, Roots, and Affixes. Toronto: University of Toronto Press. (New ed. in 1995.)

Franz, William
1979   The Colossus of Staten Island: A Ponderous Memorial to a People Who Refused to Vanish. *American Heritage* 30(3):96–99.

Fraser, David W.
1989   A Guide to Weft Twining and Related Structures with Interacting Wefts. Philadelphia: University of Pennsylvania Press.

Fraser, Simon
1889   Journal of a Voyage from the Rocky Mountains to the Pacific Coast, 1808. Pp. 156–221 in vol. 1 of Les Bourgeois de la Compagnie du Nord-ouest. Louis R. Masson, ed. 2 vols. Quebec: A. Coté. (Reprinted, 2 vols.: Arno Press, New York, 1960.)

─────   The Letters and Journals of Simon Fraser 1806–1808. W.
1960   Kaye Lamb, ed.; maps by C.C.J. Bond. Toronto: Macmillan.

Fredlund, Dale E.
1970   Archaeology in the Sapphire and Bitterroot Mountains of Western Montana. (AMQUA Field Conference C, August 29, 1970: First Biennial Meeting, American Quaternary Associa-

tion, Yellowstone Park and Bozeman, Montana, August 29–September 1, 1970.) *AMQUA Abstracts* 1:48. [Springfield, Ill.]

Fredlund, Dale E., and Lynn B. Fredlund
1970   Archaeological Survey of the Forks of the Flathead River: A Preliminary Report. *Archaeology in Montana* 11 (4):15–29. Bozeman.

Fredlund, Dale E., and William LaCombe
1971   Alpine Archaeology in the Bitterroot Mountains of Montana. Preliminary report. (University of Montana, Faculty Research Grant No. 925, Missoula.)

Fredlund, Lynn B.
1979   Archaeological Investigations at the Big Creek Lake Site (24RA34). *Montana Tech Alumni Foundation. Mineral Research Center. Cultural Resources Division. Reports of Investigations* 10. Butte.

Freeman, John F.
1966   A Guide to Manuscripts Relating to the American Indian in the Library of the American Philosophical Society. *Memoirs of the American Philosophical Society* 65. Philadelphia.

Freeman, Otis W., and Howard H. Martin, eds.
1942   The Pacific Northwest: A Regional, Human, and Economic Survey of Resources and Development. New York: J. Wiley and Sons; London: Chapman and Hall.

Frémont, John C.
1845   Report of the Exploring Expedition to the Rocky Mountains in the Year 1842, and to Oregon and North California in the Years 1843–44. By Brevet Capt. J.C. Frémont ... under the Orders of Col. J.J. Abert, Chief of Topographical Bureau [etc.]. *28th Congress. 2d Session. House Executive Document* 166; *Senate Executive Document* 174. Washington: Blair and Rives; [also] Gales and Seton.

French, David H.
1957   An Exploration of Wasco Ethnoscience. Pp. 224–226 in *American Philosophical Society Year Book 1956*. Philadelphia.

1957a   Aboriginal Control of Huckleberry Yield in the Northwest. (Manuscript in Kathrine French's possession.)

1958   Cultural Matrices of Chinookan Non-casual Language. *International Journal of American Linguistics* 24(4):258–263.

1961   Wasco-Wishram. Pp. 337–430 in Perspectives in American Indian Culture Change. Edward H. Spicer, ed. Chicago: University of Chicago Press.

1965   Ethnobotany of the Pacific Northwest Indians. *Economic Botany* 19(4):378–382. New York.

1979   The Columbia-Fraser Plateau: A Little-known Part of the World. (Paper presented at the 32d Annual Northwest Anthropological Conference, Eugene, Oreg. Manuscript in Kathrine French's possession.)

1981   Neglected Aspects of North American Ethnobotany. *Canadian Journal of Botany* 59(11):2326–2330. Ottawa: National Research Council of Canada.

1985   Zebras Along the Columbia River: Imaginary Wasco-Wishram Names for Real Animals. *International Journal of American Linguistics* 51(4):410–412.

French, David H., and Kathrine S. French
1949–1993 [Ethnographic and linguistic notes from fieldwork among Sahaptin-speaking residents on the Warm Springs Reserva-

tion and elsewhere in Oregon; also in Washington State.] (Manuscript in Kathrine French's possession.)

1950–1993 [Ethnographic and linguistic notes from fieldwork among Wasco, Wishram, and Cascade residents at Warm Springs, Oreg., Yakima, Wash., and along the Columbia River.] (Manuscript in Kathrine French's possession.)

1979   Warm Springs Sahaptin Medicinal Plants: A Summary. (Manuscript in Kathrine French's possession.)

1989   [Some Wasco-Wishram terms dealing with plants.] (Manuscript in Kathrine French's possession.)

French, Kathrine S.
1955   Culture Segments and Variation in Contemporary Social Ceremonialism on the Warm Springs Reservation, Oreg. (Ph.D. Dissertation in Anthropology, Columbia University, New York City.)

Frenkel, Robert E.
1985   Vegetation. Pp. 58–66 in Atlas of the Pacific Northwest. A. Jon Kimberling and Philip L. Jackson, eds. 7th ed. Corvallis: Oregon State University Press.

Frey, Rodney, ed.
1995   Stories That Make the World: Oral Literature of the Indian Peoples of the Inland Northwest; As Told by Lawrence Aripa, Tom Yellowtail, and Other Elders. Norman and London: University of Oklahoma Press.

Frison, George C.
1991   Prehistoric Hunters of the High Plains. 2d ed. San Diego: Academic Press.

Frison, George C., and Dennis J. Stanford, eds.
1982   The Agate Basin Site: A Record of the Paleoindian Occupation of the Northwestern High Plains. New York: Academic Press.

Fritz, Henry E.
1963   The Movement for Indian Assimilation, 1860–1890. Westport, Conn.: Greenwood Press.

Froben, Minnie 1877 *see* Gatschet, Albert S. 1877c

Fryxell, Roald
1963   Late Glacial and Post Glacial Geological and Archaeological Chronology of the Columbia Plateau, Washington. (Interim Report to the National Science Foundation, 1962–1963. Washington State University, Pullman.)

Fryxell, Roald, and Richard D. Daugherty
1962   Interim Report: Archaeological Salvage in Lower Monumental Reservoir. *Washington State University. Laboratory of Anthropology and Geochronology. Report of Investigations* 21. Pullman.

1963   Late Glacial and Post Glacial Geological and Archaeological Chronology of the Columbia Plateau, Washington: An Interim Report to the National Science Foundation, 1962–1963. *Washington State University. Laboratory of Anthropology. Report of Investigations* 23. Pullman.

Fryxell, Roald, and Bennie C. Keel
1969   Emergency Salvage Excavations for the Recovery of Early Human Remains and Related Scientific Materials from the Marmes Rockshelter Archaeological Site, Southeastern Washington, May 3–Dec. 15, 1968. (Final Report to the Walla Walla District, U.S. Army Corps of Engineers, Laboratory of Anthropology, Washington State University, Pullman.)

Fryxell, Roald, Tadeusz Bielicki, Richard D. Daugherty, Carl E. Gustafson, Henry T. Irwin, and Bennie C. Keel
1968   A Human Skeleton from Sediments of Mid-Pinedale Age in Southeastern Washington. *American Antiquity* 33(4):511–515.

Fuller, George W.
1928   The Inland Empire of the Pacific Northwest, A History.
            Spokane: H.G. Linderman.

———
1931   A History of the Pacific Northwest. New York: A. Knopf.
            (Several reprints, incl.: 1938, 1948, 1958, 1966; also, AMS
            Press, New York, 1976.)

Fulton, Leonard A.
1968   Spawning Areas and Abundance of Chinook Salmon
            (Oncorhynchus tshawytscha) in the Columbia River Basin:
            Past and Present. *U.S. Fish and Wildlife Service. Special Sci-
            entific Report—Fisheries* 571. Washington.

———
1970   Spawning Areas and Abundance of Steelhead Trout and
            Coho, Sockeye, and Chum Salmon in the Columbia River
            Basin-Past and Present. *U.S. Department of Commerce.
            National Oceanic and Atmospheric Administration. National
            Marine Fisheries Service. Special Scientific Report—Fish-
            eries* 618. Washington.

Furniss, Elizabeth M.
1987   A Sobriety Movement among the Shuswap Indians of Alkali
            Lake. (M.A. Thesis, Department of Anthropology and Sociol-
            ogy, University of British Columbia, Vancouver.)

Furste, Edward, coll.
1857   Message of the Governor of Washington Territory; Also, the
            Correspondence with the Secretary of War, Major Gen.
            Wool, the Officers of the Regular Army, and the Volunteer
            Service of Washington Territory. Olympia, Wash.: Edward
            Furste.

Gaarder, Lorin R.
1967   A Report of Test Excavations on Cunningham Bar
            (10LH125). (Manuscript on file at Salmon National Forest,
            Salmon, Idaho.)

———
1967a   Excavation at a Campsite on Eagle Creek (North Central Ida-
            ho). *Tebiwa: Journal of the Idaho State University Museum*
            10(2):39–61. Pocatello.

———
1968   A Report on Archaeological Testing of Site 10-CW-5, Clear-
            water River, North Central Idaho. *Tebiwa: Journal of the Ida-
            ho State University Museum* 11(1):60–71. Pocatello.

Gabriel, Louise
1954   Food and Medicines of the Okanakens. Pp. 24–29 in *18th
            Annual Report of the Okanagan Historical Society*. Vernon,
            B.C.

Gabrielson, Ira N., and Stanley G. Jewett
1970   Birds of the Pacific Northwest. New York: Dover Publica-
            tions.

Gairdner, Meredith
1841   Notes on the Geography of the Columbia River. *Journal of the
            Royal Geographical Society of London* 11(2):250–257. London.

Gallagher, Joseph G.
1972   Preliminary Report, Archaeological Excavations at the Basin
            Creek Site (10CR213). (Manuscript on file at Idaho State
            University Museum, Pocatello.)

———
1973   [Fieldnotes, Basin Creek (10CR213) Site.] (Manuscript on
            file at Idaho State University Museum, Pocatello.)

———
1975   The Archaeology of the Sheepeater Battleground and Redfish
            Overhang Sites: Settlement Model for Central Idaho. (M.A.
            Thesis in Anthropology, Idaho State University, Pocatello.
            Published, slightly rev.: *USDA Forest Service. Intermountain
            Region. Archeological Report* 5. Ogden, Utah, 1979.)

Gallatin, Albert
1836   A Synopsis of the Indian Tribes Within the United States East
            of the Rocky Mountains, and in the British and Russian Pos-
            sessions in North America. Pp 1–422 in Archaeologia Ameri-
            cana: *Transactions and Collections of the American Anti-
            quarian Society* 2. Cambridge, Mass.

———
1848   Hale's Indians of North-West America, and Vocabularies of
            North America: With an Introduction. Pp. xxiii-clxxxviii,
            1–130 in *Transactions of the American Ethnological Society*
            2. New York.

Galm, Jerry R.
1994   Prehistoric Trade and Exchange in the Interior Plateau of North-
            western North America. Pp. 275–305 in Prehistoric Exchange
            Systems in North America. Timothy G. Baugh and Jonathon E.
            Ericson, eds. New York and London: Plenum Press.

Galm, Jerry R., and Glenn D. Hartmann
1975   Archaeological Reconnaissance of the Saddle Mountains,
            Washington. (Report submitted to the U.S. Bureau of Land
            Management, Seattle, Wash.)

Galm, Jerry R., and Ruth A. Masten, eds.
1985   Avey's Orchard: Archaeological Investigation of a Late Pre-
            historic Columbia River Community. *Eastern Washington
            University. Archaeological and Historical Services. Reports
            in Archaeology and History* 100–142. Cheney.

———
1988   A Management Plan for Cultural Resources at the Rock
            Island Hydroelectric Project, Chelan and Douglas Counties,
            Washington. *Eastern Washington University. Archaeological
            and Historical Services. Reports in Archaeology and History*
            100–66. Cheney.

Galm, Jerry R., Glenn D. Hartmann, Ruth A. Masten, and Garry O.
Stephenson
1981   A Cultural Resource Overview of Bonneville Power Admin-
            istration's Mid-Columbia Project, Central Washington. *East-
            ern Washington University. Archaeological and Historical
            Services. Reports in Archaeology and History* 100–116.
            Cheney.

Gannon, Brian L.
1976   Synopsis of Archaeological Research in the Clarno Basin,
            North-Central Oregon: 35-WH-13 and 35-WH-21. In: An
            Introduction to the Natural History of Camp Hancock and the
            Clarno Basin, North-Central Oregon. John H. Atherton and
            Michael C. Houck, eds. Portland: Oregon Museum of Science
            and Industry.

Garbarino, Merwyn S., and Robert F. Sasso
1994   Native American Heritage. 3d ed. Prospect Heights, Ill.:
            Waveland Press.

Gardiner, Dwight G.
1993   Structural Asymmetries and Preverbal Positions in Shuswap.
            (Ph.D. Dissertation in Linguistics, Simon Fraser University,
            Burnaby, B.C.; Microfiche: Canadian Theses on Microfiche,
            National Library of Canada, Ottawa, 1994.)

———
1997   Topic and Focus in Shuswap (Secwepemctsín). Pp.
            275–304 in Salish Languages and Linguistics: Theoretical
            and Descriptive Perspectives. Ewa Czaykowska-Higgins
            and M. Dale Kinkade, eds. (*Trends in Linguistics. Studies
            and Monographs* 107). Berlin and New York: Mouton de
            Gruyter.

Gardiner, Dwight G., and Ross Saunders
1991   Split Ergativity in Shuswap Salish. *Amérindia* 16:79–101.

Garfield, James A.
1934   James A. Garfield's Diary of a Trip to Montana in 1872. Oliv-
            er W. Holmes, ed. *State University of Montana. Historical
            Reprints. Sources of Northwest History* 21. Missoula.

Garraghan, Gilbert J.
1938   The Jesuits of the Middle United States. 3 vols. New York: America Press. (Reprinted: Arno Press, New York, 1978.)

Garrand, Victor
1977   Augustine Laure, S.J., Missionary to the Yakimas. Edward J. Kowrach, ed. Fairfield, Wash.: Ye Galleon Press.

Garrecht, Francis A.
1928   An Indian Chief. *Washington Historical Quarterly* 19(3):165–180.

Garth, Thomas
1952   The Middle Columbia Cremation Complex. *American Antiquity* 18(1):40–56.

1964   Early Nineteenth Century Tribal Relations in the Columbia Plateau. *Southwestern Journal of Anthropology* 20(1):43–57.

1964a   Further Comment on the Sheep Island Site, McNary Reservoir, Washington. *American Antiquity* 30(1):100–103.

1965   The Plateau Whipping Complex and its Relationship to Plateau-Southwestern Contacts. *Ethnohistory* 12(2):141–170.

Garvin, Paul L.
1948   Kutenai I: Phonetics. *International Journal of American Linguistics* 14(1):37–42.

1948a   Kutenai II: Morpheme Variations. *International Journal of American Linguistics* 14(2):87–90.

1948b   Kutenai III: Morpheme Distributions (Prefix, Theme, Suffix). *International Journal of American Linguistics* 14(3):171–187.

1951   Kutenai IV: Word Classes. *International Journal of American Linguistics* 17(2):84–97.

1951a   L'obviation en Kutenai: Échantillon d'une catégorie grammaticale amérindienne. *Bulletin de la Société de Linguistique de Paris* 47(1):166–212. Paris.

1953   Short Kutenai Texts: *International Journal of American Linguistics* 19(4):305–311.

1954   Colloquial Kutenai Text: Conversation II. *International Journal of American Linguistics* 20(4):316–334.

Gass, Patrick
1807   A Journal of the Voyages and Travels of a Corps of Discovery; Under the Command of Capt. Lewis and Capt. Clarke of the Army of the United States; from the Mouth of the River Missouri through the Interior Parts of North America to the Pacific Ocean, during the Years 1804, 1805 & 1806. Philadelphia: Printed for Mathew Carey. (Reprinted: Ross and Haines, Minneapolis, 1958.)

1904   Gass's Journal of the Lewis and Clark Expedition. Introduction and Index by James K. Hosmer. Chicago: A.C. McClung.

1958   A Journal of the Voyages and Travels of a Corps of Discovery, Under the Command of Capt. Lewis and Capt. Clarke ..., during the Years 1804, 1805 and 1806 [1807]. Minneapolis: Ross and Haines.

Gates, Charles M., ed.
1940   Message of the Governors of the Territory of Washington to the Legislative Assembly, 1854–1889. [Map of Yakima Treaty ceded lands, pp. 22–23.] Seattle: University of Washington Press. (Map of Yakima Treaty ceded lands, pp. 22–23.)

Gatschet, Albert S.
1877   [Mólale: Waïïlatpuan Family (Hale). Vocabulary and texts (collected at) Grande Ronde Reserve, Yamhill & Polk Cos., Oregon. In J.W. Powell's schedule *Introduction to the Study of Indian Languages, with Words, Phrases, and Sentences To Be Collected*. Government Printing Office, Washington, 1877.] (Manuscript No. 1000 in National Anthropological Archives, Smithsonian Institution, Washington.)

1877a   [Molale language: Words, sentences and various texts collected at the Grande Ronde Agency northwest'n Oregon, in November & Decb., 1877. Incl.: Molala words and sentences; "Marriage Ceremonies"; "Myth of the Coyote"; and, "The Molale tribe raided by the Cayuse". The three texts were copied by Gatschet, attributed to Stephen Savage, and separately cataloged as Manuscript No. 998.] (Manuscript No. 2029 in National Anthropological Archives, Smithsonian Institution, Washington; see also Manuscript No. 998.)

1877b   [Three Molale texts with interlinear English translations, from informant Stephen Savage, Grande Ronde Reserve, Oreg., Dec. 1877. Incl.: "Marriage Ceremonies"; "Myth of the Coyote"; and, "The Molale tribe raided by the Cayuse". Texts copied by Gatschet.] (Manuscript No. 998 in National Anthropological Archives, Smithsonian Institution, Washington; see also Manuscript No. 2029.)

1877c   [Klamath Material, Vol. 1: Gathered at Klamath Agency, Southwestern Oregon, in September and October 1877.] (Manuscript No. 1581 in National Anthropological Archives, Smithsonian Institution, Washington.)

1877d   [Wasco Vocabulary.] (Manuscript No. 401 in National Anthropological Archives, Smithsonian Institution, Washington.)

1877e   [Texts, Sentences, and Vocables of the Atfalati Dialect of the Kalapuya Language of Willamet [*sic*] Valley, Northwestern Oregon.] (Manuscript No. 472-a in National Anthropological Archives, Smithsonian Institution, Washington.)

1878   Sketch of the Klamath Language. *American Antiquarian and Oriental Journal* 1(2):81–84.

1879   Mythologic Text in the Klamath Language of Southern Oregon. *American Antiquarian and Oriental Journal* 1(3):161–166.

1879a   Volk und Sprache der Máklaks im südwestlichen Oregon. *Globus: Illustrirte Zeitschrift für Länder- und Völkerkunde* 35:167–171. Braunschweig, Germany.

1879b   Adjectives of Color in Indian Languages. *American Naturalist* 13(8):475–485.

1880   The Numerical Adjectives in the Klamath Language. *American Antiquarian and Oriental Journal* 2:210–217.

1885   [Okinagan (Okinakane) vocabulary; Band names of the Northwest.] (Manuscript No. 1565 in National Anthropological Archives, Smithsonian Institution, Washington.)

1890   The Klamath Indians of Southwestern Oregon. 2 Pts. *Contributions to North American Ethnology* 2(1–2). Washington: U.S. Geographical and Geological Survey of the Rocky Mountain Region. (Pt. 1, Ethnographic Sketch, reprinted: Shorey Book Store, Seattle, Wash., 1966.)

1891   Die Windhosen: ein Mythus der Modoc-Indianer. *Am Ur-Quell* 2:1–3. Hamburg: G. Kramer.

1891a   Oregonian Folk-Lore. *Journal of American Folk-Lore* 4(13):139–143.

1894   Songs of the Modoc Indians. *American Anthropologist*, o.s. 7(1):26–31.

Gatschet, Albert S., L.J. Franchtenberg, and M. Jacobs *see* Jacobs, Melville 1945

Gay, E. Jane
1981   With the Nez Perces: Alice Fletcher in the Field, 1889–92. Edited, with an Introd. by Frederick E. Hoxie and Joan T. Mark. Lincoln: University of Nebraska Press. (Reprinted in 1987.)

Gayton, Anna H.
1935   Areal Affiliations of California Folktales. *American Anthropologist* 37(4):582–599.

Genealogical Forum of Portland, Oregon
1957–1982 Genealogical Material in Oregon Donation Land Claims. 5 vols. Portland, Oreg.: Genealogical Forum of Portland, Oregon.

George, Graham
1962   Songs of the Salish Indians of British Columbia. *Journal of the International Fold Music Council* 14:22–29.

Geyer, Charles A.
1845–1846 Notes on the Vegetation and General Characteristics of the Missouri and Oregon Territories...During the Years 1843 and 1844. *London Journal of Botany* 4:479–492, 653–622, 5:22–41, 198–208, 285–310, 509–524. London.

Gibbs, George
1851   [Molala vocabulary.] (Manuscript No. 995-a-b in National Anthropological Archives, Smithsonian Institution, Washington.)

1855   Report of Mr. George Gibbs to Captain Mc'Clellan, on the Indian Tribes of the Territory of Washington. [Dated] Olympia, Washington Territory, March 4, 1854. Pp. 402–434 in Report of Explorations for a Route for the Pacific Railroad, near the Forty- seventh and Forty-ninth Parallels of North Latitude, from St. Paul to Puget Sound; by I.I. Stevens, Governor of Washington Territory. In Vol. 1 of Reports of Explorations and Surveys...from the Mississippi River to the Pacific Ocean...1853–4, [etc.]. *33d Congress. 2d Session. Senate Executive Document* 78. (Serial No. 758). Washington: Beverly Tucker, Printer. (Reprinted: Ye Galleon Press, Fairfield, Wash., 1972.)

1857   [Letter to James G. Swan, dated 7 January 1857.] Pp 426–429 in The Northwest Coast; or, Three Year's Residence in Washington Territory. James G. Swan, ed. New York: Harper and Bros. (Reprinted: University of Washington Press, Seattle, 1972.)

1858   [Letter to John G. Parke, dated 4 September 1858.] (Northwest Boundary Survey Reports, 1857–1862, Entry 198, Box 5, RG 76, National Archives II, College Park, Md.)

1862   Preface. Pp. vii-viii in Grammar and Dictionary of the Yakama Language, by Rev. Marie-Charles Pandosy, O.M.I.; George Gibbs and John Gilmary Shea, trans. *Shea's Library of American Linguistics* 6. New York: Cramoisy Press. (Reprinted: AMS Press, New York, 1970.)

1865   Instructions Relative to the Ethnology and Philology of America. *Smithsonian Miscellaneous Collections* 7. Washington.

1873   Comparative Vocabularies. Family xxiii: Selish (Eastern Branches). (Manuscript in National Anthropological Archives, Smithsonian Institution, Washington.)

1877   Tribes of Western Washington and Northwestern Oregon. Pp. 157–361 in *Contributions to North American Ethnology* 1(2). John Wesley Powell, ed. Washington: U.S. Geographical and Geological Survey of the Rocky Mountain Region. (Reprinted: Shorey Bookstore, Seattle, Wash., 1970.)

1955–1956 George Gibbs' Account of Indian Mythology in Oregon and Washington Territories. Ella Clark, ed. *Oregon Historical Quarterly* 56(4):293–325 (Part 1); 57(2):125–167 (Part 2).

Gibson, James A.
1973   Shuswap Grammatical Structure. (Ph.D. Dissertation in Linguistics, University of Hawaii, Honolulu. Photocopy: University Microfilms International, Ann Arbor, Mich., 1977.)

Gidley, M. (Mick)
1981   Kopet: A Documentary Narrative of Chief Joseph's Last Years. Seattle: University of Washington Press.

1985   With One Sky Above Us: Life on an Indian Reservation at the Turn of the Century. Photographs by Dr. Edward H. Latham, U.S. Indian Agency Physician. Seattle: University of Washington Press. (Orig. publ.: Putnam, New York, 1979.)

Gifford, Edward W.
1922   California Kinship Terminologies. *University of California Publications in American Archaeology and Ethnology* 18(1):1–285. Berkeley. (Reprinted: Kraus Reprint, New York, 1965.)

1926   California Anthropometry. *University of California Publications in American Archaeology and Ethnology* 22(2):217–390. Berkeley. (Reprinted: Kraus Reprint, New York, 1965.)

Gilbert, Frank T.
1882   Historic Sketches of Walla Walla, Whitman, Columbia and Garfield Counties, Washington Territory, and Umatilla County, Oregon. Portland, Oreg.: A.G. Walling.

Gill, John K., comp.
1909   Gill's Dictionary of the Chinook Jargon; With Examples of Use in Conversation and Notes upon Tribes and Tongues, English-Chinook and Chinook-English. 18th ed. Portland, Oreg.: J.K. Gill.

Giniger, Judith E.
1977   Aboriginal Female Status and Autonomy of the Columbia Plateau. (M.A. Thesis in Anthropology, Washington State University, Pullman.)

Giorda, Joseph, Joseph Bandini, Joseph Guidi, Gregory Mengarini, and Leopold Van Gorp
1877–1879 A Dictionary of the Kalispel or Flat-head Indian Language. Compiled by the Missionaries of the Society of Jesus. Pt. I: Kalispel-English; Pt. II: English-Kalispel. St. Ignatius, [Mont. Terr.]: St. Ignatius Print.

Gjessing, Gutorem
1952   Petroglyphs and Pictographs in British Columbia. Pp. 66–79 in Indian Tribes of Aboriginal America. Sol Tax, ed. (Selected Papers of the *29th International Congress of Americanists*.) Chicago: University of Chicago Press.

Glauert, Earl T., and Merle H. Kunz, eds.
1972   The Kittitas Indians. Ellensburg, Wash.: Ellensburg Public Library.

1976   Kittitas Frontiersman. Ellensburg, Wash.: Ellensburg Public Library.

Glenmore, Josephine Stands in Timber, and Wayne Leman
1984   Cheyenne Topical Dictionary. Busby, Mont.: Cheyenne Translation Project. (Rev. ed. in 1985.)

Glover, Richard, ed. 1962 *see* Thompson, David 1962

Goddard, Ives, comp.
1996   Native Languages and Language Families of North America. Map, to accompany: *Handbook of North American Indians*, vol. 17: *Languages.* Ives Goddard, vol. ed.; William C. Sturtevant, gen. ed. Washington: Smithsonian Institution.

Godfrey, W. Earl
1986   The Birds of Canada. Ottawa: National Museums of Canada.

Gogol, John M.
1979   Columbia River Indian Basketry. *American Indian Basketry Magazine* 1(1):4–9. Portland, Oreg.

1979a   Elsie Thomas Shows How to Make a Traditional Klickitat Indian Basket. *American Indian Basketry Magazine* 1(1):18–29. Portland, Oreg.

1980   Cornhusk Bags and Hats of the Columbia Plateau Indians. *American Indian Basketry Magazine* 1(2):4–10. Portland, Oreg.

1980a   Rose Frank Shows How to Weave a Nez Perce Cornhusk Bag. *American Indian Basketry Magazine* 1(2):22–30. Portland, Oreg.

1983   Klamath, Modoc, and Shasta Basketry. *American Indian Basketry* 3(2/Whole Issue No. 10):4–17. Portland, Oreg.

1985   Columbia River/Plateau Indian Beadwork. Part I: Yakima, Warm Springs, Umatilla, Nez Perce. *American Indian Basketry and Other Native Arts* 5(2/Whole Issue No. 18):3–27. Portland, Oreg.

1985a   Cowlitz Indian Basketry. *American Indian Basketry and Other Native Arts* 5(4/Whole Issue No. 22):4–20. Portland, Oreg.

Goldman, Irving
1940   The Alkatcho Carrier of British Columbia. Pp. 333–389 in Acculturation in Seven American Indian Tribes. Ralph Linton, ed. New York: D. Appleton-Century.

Gombert, Greg, comp. and ed.
1994   A Guide to Native American Music Recordings. Fort Collins, Colo.: Multi Cultural Publishing.

Good, John Booth
1878   The Morning and Evening Prayer, and Litany, with Prayers and Thanksgivings, Translated into the Neklakapamuk Tongue, for the Use of the Indians of the St. Paul's Mission, Lytton, British Columbia. Victoria, B.C.: St. Paul's Mission Press.

1878a   The Office of the Holy Communion Translated into the Neklakapamuk Tongue, for the Use of the Indians in the St. Paul's Mission, Lytton, British Columbia. Victoria, B.C.: St. Paul's Mission Press.

1879   The Office for Public Baptism and the Order of Confirmation, with Select Hymns and Prayers Translated into the Neklakapamuk or Thompson Tongue for the Use of the Indians of the St. Paul's Mission, Lytton, British Columbia. Victoria, B.C.: St. Paul's Mission Press.

1880   Offices for the Solemnizat[i]on of Matrimony, the Visitation of the Sick, and the Burial of the Dead. Translated into the Nitlakapamuk or Thompson Indian Tongue. Victoria, B.C.: St. Paul's Mission Press.

1880a   A Vocabulary and Outlines of Grammar of the Nitlakapamuk or Thompson Tongue... Together with a Phonetic Dictionary, Adapted for Use in the Province of British Columbia. Victoria, B.C.: St. Paul's Mission Press.

Goode, George Brown, ed.
1884–1887   The Fisheries and Fishery Industries of the United States. Prepared through the Co-operation of the Commissioner of Fisheries and the Superintendent of the Tenth Census by George Brown Goode, [etc.]. 8 vols. in 7. Washington: Government Printing Office, U.C. Commission of Fish and Fisheries.

Gormly, Mary
1977   Early Culture Contact on the Northwest Coast, 1774–1795, Analysis of Spanish Source Material. *Northwest Anthropological Research Notes* 11(1):1–80. Moscow, Idaho.

Gough, Stan, ed.
1984   Cultural Resource Investigations of the Bonneville Power Administration's Libby Integration Project, Northern Idaho and Northwestern Montana. *Eastern Washington University. Archaeology and Historical Services. Reports in Archaeology and History* 100–29. Cheney, Wash.

1990   A Cultural Resources Overview, Sampling Survey, and Management Plan, Colville Indian Reservation, Okanogan and Ferry Counties, Washington. *Eastern Washington University. Reports in Archaeology and History* 100–74. Cheney: Archaeological and Historical Services.

Gould, Marian K.
1917   Okanogan Tales; Sanpoil Tales. Pp. 98–100 [Okanogan]; 101–113 [Sanpoil] in Folk-Tales of Salishan and Sahaptin Tribes. Franz Boas, ed. *Memoirs of the American Folk-Lore Society* 11. Lancaster, Pa., and New York. (Reprinted: Kraus Reprint, New York, 1969.)

Gourlay, Kenneth A.
1982   Towards a Humanizing Ethnomusicology. *Ethnomusicology.* 26(3):411–420.

Grabert, Garland F.
1968   North-Central Washington Prehistory; A Final Report on Salvage Archaeology in the Wells Reservoir—Part 1. *University of Washington. Department of Anthropology. Reports in Archaeology* 1. Seattle.

Grabert, Garland F.
1971   Some Implications of Settlement Variation in the Okanagan Region. Pp. 153–167 in Aboriginal Man and Environments on the Plateau of Northwest America. Arnoud H. Stryd and Rachel A. Smith, eds. Calgary, Alta.: The University of Calgary Student's Press.

1974   Okanagan Archaeology: 1966–67. *Syesis* 7 (Suppl. 2):1–82. Victoria, B.C.

Grant, Campbell
1967   Rock Drawings of the American Indian. New York: Crowell.

Grant, George M.
1967   Ocean to Ocean: Sanford Fleming's Expedition through Canada in 1872. Enl. and rev. ed. Rutland, Vt.: Charles E. Tuttle.

Grater, Barbara A.
1966   The Archeology of the Votaw Site: Lower Snake River, Washington. (M.A. Thesis in Anthropology, San Francisco State University, San Francisco.)

Gray, Judith A. 1988 *see* Brady, Erika, et al. 1984–

Greaves, Sheila
1991   The Organization of Microcore Technology in the Canadian Southern Interior Plateau. (Ph.D. Dissertation in Anthropology, University of British Columbia, Vancouver.)

Green, Jonathan S.
1915   Journal of a Tour on the North West Coast of America in the Year 1829; Containing a Description of a Part of Oregon, California and the North West Coast and the Numbers, Manners and Customs of the Native Tribes. (*Heartman's Historical Series* 10.) New York: Chas. Fred. Heartman. (Reprinted from the *Missionary Herald*, Nov. 1830, together with extracts from earlier issues of the same periodical, 1821, 1830.)

Green, Thomas
1988   Aboriginal Structures in Southern Idaho. (Paper presented at the 41st Annual Northwest Anthropological Conference, Tacoma, Wash.)

Green, Thomas, Max G. Pavesic, J. Woods, and G. Titmus
1986   The Demoss Burial Locality: Preliminary Observations. *Idaho Archaeologist* 9(2):31–40. Caldwell, Idaho.

Green, Thomas, B. Cochran, M.A. Davis, T. Fenton, S. Miller, G. Titmus, and J. Woods
1992   Buhl Burial: The Recovery and Reburial of a Paleoindian from Southern Idaho. (Paper presented at the 23d Biennial Meeting, Great Basin Anthropological Conference, Boise, Idaho.)

Greenberg, Joseph H.
1987   Language in the Americas. Stanford, Calif.: Stanford University Press.

Greene, Glen S.
1975   Prehistoric Utilization in the Channeled Scablands of Eastern Washington. (Ph.D. Dissertation in Anthropology, Washington State University, Pullman. Microfiche: University Microfilms International, Ann Arbor, Mich., 1976.)

Greengo, Robert E.
1986   Prehistory of the Priest Rapids—Wanapum Region, Columbia River, Washington. 3 vols. *B.A.R. International Series* 290(i-iii). Oxford, England: B.A.R. [British Archaeological Reports.] (Spine title: Priest Rapids—Wanapum Prehistory.)

———
1986a   The Prehistory of the Priest Rapids—Wanapum Region: A Summary. *Burke Museum Contributions in Anthropology and Natural History* 2. Seattle: Thomas Burke Memorial Washington State Museum, University of Washington. (Running title: Priest Rapids—Wanapum Prehistory.)

Greiser, Sally T., T. Weber Greiser, and Susan M. Vetter
1985   Middle Prehistoric Period Adaptations and Paleoenvironment in the Northwestern Plains: The Sun River Site. *American Antiquity* 50(4):849–877.

Grim, John
1992   Cosmogony and the Winter Dance: Native American Ethics in Transition. *Journal of Religious Ethics* 20(Fall):389–413.

Griswold, Gillett
1954   Aboriginal Patterns of Trade between the Columbia Basin and the Northern Plains. (M.A. Thesis in Anthropology, Montana State University [now University of Montana], Missoula; publ. in 1970.)

———
1970   Aboriginal Patterns of Trade between the Columbia Basin and the Northern Plains. *Archaeology in Montana* 11(2–3):1–96. Missoula. (Orig. issued as the author's M.A. Thesis in Anthropology, Montana State University, Missoula, 1954.)

Grover, C.
1855   Final Report of Lieutenant C. Grover, of His Examinations on a Trip from the Headwaters of the Missouri to the Dalles of the Columbia. Pp. 498–515 in Reports of Explorations for a Route ... by I.I. Stevens. In Vol. 1 of Report of Explorations and Surveys ... 1853–4. *33d Congress. 2d Session. Senate Executive Document* 78. (Serial No. 758). Washington: Beverly Tucker, Printer.

Gudschinsky, Sarah C.
1956   The ABC's of Lexicostatistics (Glottochronology). *Word* 12(2):175–210.

Guie, Heister Dean
1937   Tribal Days of the Yakimas. Yakima, Wash.: Republic Publishing.

———
1956   Bugles in the Valley: Garnett's Fort Simcoe. [1st ed.] Yakima, Wash.: Republic Press. (Revised ed.: Oregon Historical Society, Portland, 1977.)

———
1977   Bugles in the Valley: Garnett's Fort Simcoe. Rev. ed. Portland, Oreg.: Oregon Historical Society.

Gulick, Bill
1985   Chief Joseph Country: Land of the Nez Perce. Caldwell, Idaho: The Caxton Printers.

Gunkel, Alexander
1978   Culture in Conflict: A Study of Contrasted Interrelations and Reactions between Euroamericans and the Wallawalla Indians of Washington State. (Ph.D. Dissertation in Anthropology, Southern Illinois University at Cardondale; facsimile reprod.: University Microfilms International, Ann Arbor, Mich., 1980.)

Gunther, Erna
1928   A Further Analysis of the First Salmon Ceremony. *University of Washington Publications in Anthropology* 2(5):129–173. Seattle.

———
1936   A Preliminary Report on the Zoological Knowledge of the Makah. Pp. 105–118 in Essays in Anthropology Presented to A.L. Kroeber. Robert Lowie, ed. Berkeley: University of California Press.

———
1942   Reminiscences of a Whaler's Wife. *Pacific Northwest Quarterly* 3(1):65–69.

———
1949   The Shaker Religion of the Northwest. Pp. 37–76 in Indians of the Urban Northwest. Marian W. Smith, ed. New York: Columbia University Press. (Reprinted: AMS Press, New York, 1969.)

———
1950   The Westward Movement of Some Plains Traits. *American Anthropologist* 52(2):174–180.

———
1962   Northwest Coast Indian Art: An Exhibit at the Seattle World's Fair Fine Arts Pavilion, Apr. 21-Oct. 21. Seattle: Century 21 Exposition.

———
1972   Indian Life on the Northwest Coast of North America. Chicago: University of Chicago Press.

Gustafson, Carl E.
1972   Faunal Remains from the Marmes Rockshelter and Related Archaeological Sites in the Columbia Basin. (Ph.D. Dissertation in Anthropology, Washington State University, Pullman.)

Haas, Mary R.
1965   Is Kutenai Related to Algonkian? *Canadian Journal of Linguistics* 10(2–3):77–92. Toronto.

———
1969   The Prehistory of Languages. *Janua Linguarum. Series Minor* 57. The Hague: Mouton.

Hackenberger, Steven
1984   Cultural Ecology and Economic Decision Making of Mon-
            tane Hunter-Gatherers in Central Idaho. (M.A. Thesis in
            Anthropology, Washington State University, Pullman.)

1988   Cultural Ecology and Evolution in Central Montane Idaho.
            (Ph.D. Dissertation in Anthropology, Washington State Uni-
            versity, Pullman.)

Hackenberger, Steven, and Daniel S. Meatte
1991   The Salmon River and Western and Eastern Snake River
            Basins. Pp. 161–190 in An Overview of Cultural Resources in
            the Snake River Basin: Prehistory and Paleoenvironments.
            K.C. Reid, ed. *Washington State University. Center for North-
            west Anthropology. Report* 13. Pullman.

Hackenberger, Steven, David A. Sisson, and Bruce R. Womack
1989   Middle and Late Prehistoric Residential Strategies, Central
            Idaho: House Frequency and Size on the Middle Snake,
            Salmon and Middle Fork Rivers. Pp. 133–142 in Households
            and Communities: Proceedings of the Twenty-first Annual
            Conference of the Archaeological Association of the Univer-
            sity of Calgary, Scott MacEachern, David J.W. Archer, and
            Richard D. Garvin, eds. Calgary, Alta.: University of Calgary,
            Archaeological Association.

Haeberlin, Hermann K.
1918   Types of Reduplication in the Salish Dialects. *International
            Journal of American Linguistics* 1(2):154–174.

1974   Distribution of the Salish Substantival (Lexical) Suffixes. M. Ter-
            ry Thompson, ed. *Anthropological Linguistics* 16(6):219–350.

Haeberlin, Hermann K., James A. Teit, and Helen H. Roberts
1928   Coiled Basketry in British Columbia and Surrounding
            Region. Pp. 119–484 in *41st Annual Report of the Bureau of
            American Ethnology for 1919–1924.* Washington.

Haig-Brown, Celia
1988   Resistance and Renewal: Surviving the Indian Residential
            School. Vancouver, B.C.: Tillacum Library. (Reprinted in
            1991, 1993.)

Haines, Francis
1937   The Nez Perce Delegation to St. Louis in 1831. *Pacific His-
            torical Review* 6(1):71–78.

1938   Where Did the Plains Indians Get Their Horses? *American
            Anthropologist* 40(1):112–117.

1938a   The Northward Spread of Horses among the Plains Indians.
            American Anthropologist 40(3):429–437.

1939   Red Eagles of the Northwest: The Story of Chief Joseph and
            His People. Portland, Oreg.: The Scholastic Press. (Reprint-
            ed: AMS Press, New York, 1980.)

1954   Chief Joseph and the Nez Perce Warriors. *Pacific Northwest
            Quarterly* 45(1):1–7.

1955   The Nez Percés: Tribesmen of the Columbia Plateau. Nor-
            man: University of Oklahoma Press. (Reprinted in 1972;
            revised in 1982.)

1964   How the Indians Got the Horse. *American Heritage*
            15(2):16–22, 78–81.

1964a   The Nez Perce Tribe versus the United States. *Idaho Yester-
            days* 8(1):18–25.

1976   The Plains Indians. New York: Thomas Y. Crowell.

Hajda, Yvonne
1991   The Confederate Tribes of the Grand Ronde Community of
            Oregon. Pp. 95–100 in The First Oregonians. Carolyn M.
            Buan and Richard Lewis, eds. Portland: Oregon Council for
            the Humanities.

Hale, Horatio
1846   Ethnography and Philology. (With Map.) Vol. 6 of United
            States Exploring Expedition; During the Years 1838, 1839,
            1840, 1841, 1842. Under the Command of Charles Wilkes,
            U.S.N. 5 vols. And Atlas. Philadelphia: Lea and Blanchard.
            (Reprinted: The Gregg Press, Ridgewood, N.J., 1968.)

1890   An International Idiom. A Manual of the Oregon Trade Lan-
            guage, or 'Chinook Jargon.' London: Whittaker & Co.

1892   The Klamath Nation. *Science,* o.s. 19(465):6–7, (466):20–21,
            (467):29–31.

Hall, Eugene R.
1981   The Mammals of North America. 2d ed. New York: John
            Wiley.

Hall, Jody C., and Bruno Nettl
1955   Musical Style of the Modoc. *Southwestern Journal of Anthro-
            pology* 11(1):58–66.

Haller, Granville O.
1855–1856   [Kamiakin—In History: Memoir of the War, in the Yakima
            Valley, 1885–1856.] (Pacific Manuscript A128. H.H. Bancroft
            Collection, Bancroft Library, University of California, Berke-
            ley.)

1855–1856a [The Indian War of 1855–1856 in Washington and Oregon.]
            (Copy in G.O. Haller Box 2, Folder 5, Manuscripts Collec-
            tion, Documents Section, University of Washington Library,
            Seattle.)

Hallowell, A. Irving
1926   Bear Ceremonialism in the Northern Hemisphere. *American
            Anthropologist* 28(1):1–175.

Ham, Leonard C.
1976   Shuswap Settlement Patterns. (M.A. Thesis in Archaeology,
            Simon Fraser University, Burnaby, B.C.)

Hamilton, W.T.
1900   A Trader's Expedition among the Indians from Walla Walla to
            the Blackfeet Nation and Return in the Year 1858. *Contribu-
            tions to the Historical Society of Montana* 3:33–123. Helena.

Hammatt, Hallett H.
1977   Late Quaternary Stratigraphy and Archaeological Chronology
            in the Lower Granite Reservoir, Lower Snake River, Wash-
            ington. (Ph.D. Dissertation in Anthropology, Washington
            State University, Pullman. Photocopy: University Microfilms
            International, Ann Arbor, Mich., 1982.)

Hampton, Bruce
1994   Children of Grace: The Nez Perce War of 1877. New York:
            Henry Holt.

Hancock, Samuel
1860   Account of His Pioneer Experiences. Whidby's Island, W.T.,
            February 17, 1860. (Box 21, Vol. 1A, Miscellaneous Selec-
            tions, Clarence B. Bagley Papers, Manuscript and University
            Archives Division, University of Washington Library, Seat-
            tle.)

Hanley, Phillip M.
1993   History of the Catholic Ladder. Edward J. Kowrach, ed. Fair-
            field, Wash.: Ye Galleon Press.

Hanna, Darwin, and Mamie Henry, comps. and eds.
1995   Our Tellings: Interior Salish Stories of the Nlha7kápmx Peo-
            ple. Vancouver: UBC Press.

698

Hansen, Bert B., and C.C. Wright
1947   A Discussion of the Problems of the Full Blood Flathead Indians, Past and Present. Pete Vanderberg and Pierre Pichette, interpreters. 1 vol., various pagings. (Mimeographed; presented on April and May, 1947, at Jocko, former headquarters of the Flathead Reservation, Mont.)

Harbinger, Lucy J.
1964   The Importance of Food Plants in the Maintenance of Nez Perce Cultural Identity. (M.A. Thesis in Anthropology, Washington State University, Pullman.)

Harmon, Ray
1971   Indian Shaker Church: The Dalles. *Oregon Historical Quarterly* 72(2):148–158.

Harper, J. Russell, ed.
1971   Paul Kane's Frontier. Including *Wanderings of an Artist among the Indians of North America*, by Paul Kane. Edited with a Biographical Introduction and a Catalogue Raisonné by J. Russell Harper. Austin and London: The University of Texas Press for the Amon Carter Museum, Fort Worth, and the National Gallery of Canada, Ottawa.

Harrington, John Peabody
1941   [Fieldnotes on Nicola Valley Athapaskan/Thompson River Salish.] (Manuscript in John Peabody Harrington Papers, Alaska/Northwest Coast, National Anthropological Archives, Smithsonian Institution, Washington.)

_____
1943   Pacific Coast Athapaskan Discovered To Be Chilcotin. *Journal of the Washington Academy of Sciences* 33(7):203–213.

Harrington, Mark R.
1921   Some String Records of the Yakima. *Museum of the American Indian. Heye Foundation. Indian Notes and Monographs* 16:48–64. New York.

Harris, Lorraine
1977   Halfway to the Goldfields: A History of Lillooet. Vancouver, B.C.: J.J. Douglas.

Harris, R. Cole, ed., and Geoffrey J. Matthews, cartog.
1987   Historical Atlas of Canada, Volume I: From the Beginning to 1800. Toronto: University of Toronto Press.

Harrison, Lynn 1990 *see* Cheney Cowles Memorial Museum 1990

Harrison, Richard R.
1972   The Final Report of the 1971 Salmon River Archaeological Survey. (Manuscript, USDA Forest Service, Intermountain Region, Ogden, Utah.)

Hart, Jeffrey A.
1974   Plant Taxonomy of the Salish and Kootenai Indians of Western Montana. (M.A. Thesis in Botany, University of Montana, Missoula.)

_____
1976   Montana - Native Plants and Early Peoples. Helena: The Montana Historical Society and the Montana Bicentennial Administraiton.

_____
1979   The Ethnobotany of the Flathead Indians of Western Montana. *Harvard University. Botanical Museum Leaflets* 27(10):261–307. Cambridge, Mass.

Hartmann, Glenn D.
1975   The Archaeology of the Cox's Pond Site (45DO172). *Washington State University. Laboratory of Archaeology and History. Project Report* 17. Pullman.

Harvey, Athelstan George
1947   Douglas of the Fir: A Biography of David Douglas, Botanist. Cambridge: Harvard University Press.

Hatton, Orin T.
1986   In the Tradition: Grass Dance Musical Style and Female Powwow Singers. *Ethnomusicology* 30(2):197–222.

Hawthorn, Harry B., C.S. Belshaw, and S.M. Jamieson
1958   The Indians of British Columbia: A Study of Contemporary Social Adjustment. Berkeley: University of California Press.

Hayden, Brian
1975   The Carrying Capacity Dilemma: An Alternative Approach. Pp. 11–21 in Population Studies in Archaeology and Biological Anthropology: A Symposium. Alan C. Swedlund, ed. *Society for American Archaeology Memoir* 30. Salt Lake City.

_____ , ed.
1992   A Complex Culture of the British Columbia Plateau: Traditional *Stl'átl'imx* Resource Use. Vancouver: UBC Press.

_____
1997   The Pithouses of Keatley Creek: Complex Hunter-Gatherers of the Northwest Plateau. (*Case Studies in Archaeology*.) Fort Worth, Tex.: Harcourt Brace College Publ.

Hayden, Brian, and June M. Ryder
1991   Prehistoric Cultural Collapse in the Lillooet Area. *American Antiquity* 56(1):50–65.

Hayden, Brian, and James Spafford
1993   The Keatley Creek Site and Corporate Group Archaeology. *BC Studies* 99 (Autumn):106–139. Vancouver.

Hayden, Brian, Diana Alexander, and Karla Kusmer
1986   Report on the 1986 Excavations at Keatley Creek. (Manuscript, Department of Archaeology, Simon Fraser University, Burnaby, B.C.)

Hayden, Brian, John Breffitt, and Pierre Friele
1987   Report on the 1987 Excavations at Keatley Creek. (Manuscript, Department of Archaeology, Simon Fraser University, Burnaby, B.C.)

Hayden, Brian, Morley Eldridge, and Ann Eldridge
1985   Complex Hunter-Gatherers in Interior British Columbia. Pp. 181–199 in Prehistoric Hunter-Gatherers. T. Douglas Price and J. Brown, eds. New York: Academic Press.

Hayden, Ferdinand Vandeveer
1862   Contributions to the Ethnography and Philology of the Indian Tribes of the Missouri Valley. Prepared under the Direction of Capt. William F. Raynolds, T.E.U.S.A., and published by permission of the War Department. *Transactions of the American Philosophical Society*, n.s. 12, Pt. 2:231–461. Philadelphia.

Haynal, Patrick Mann
1994   From Termination Through Restoration and Beyond: Modern Klamath Cultural Identity. (Ph.D. Dissertation in Anthropology, University of Oregon, Eugene.)

Hebda, Richard J.
1981   Paleoecology of Bluebird Lake Core, Rocky Mountain Trench, South East British Columbia. (Report to British Columbia Heritage Conservation Branch, Resource Management Division, Victoria.)

_____
1982   Postglacial History of Grasslands of Southern British Columbia and Adjacent Regions. Pp. 157–194 in Grassland Ecology and Classification Symposium Proceedings (1982, Kamloops, B.C.). A.C. Nicholson, A. McLean, and T.E. Baker, eds. *Ministry of Forests Publication* R28–82060. Victoria, B.C.

Hébert, Yvonne M.
1982   Aspect and Transitivity in (Nicola Lake) Okanagan. Pp. 195–215 in Syntax and Semantics. Vol. 15: Studies in Transitivity. Paul J. Hopper and Sandra A. Thompson, eds. New York: Academic Press.

699

Heizer, Robert F.
1940   The Introduction of Monterey Shells to the Indians of the Northwest Coast. *Pacific Northwest Quarterly* 31(4):339–402.

———
1941   Oregon Prehistory: Retrospect and Prospect. *Commonwealth Review* 23:30–40.

———
1942   Walla Walla Indian Expeditions of the Sacramento Valley, 1844–1847. *California Historical Quarterly* 21(1):1–7.

———
1970   Ethnographic Notes on the Northern Paiute of Humbolt Sink, West Central Nevada. Pp. 232–245 in Languages and Cultures of Western North America: Essays in Honor of Sven Liljeblad. Earl H. Swanson, ed. Pocatello: Idaho State University Press.

Helland, Maurice
1975   They Knew Our Valley, Yakima, Wash.: Printed by the Author.

Helmer, James W.
1977   Points, People and Prehistory: A Preliminary Synthesis of Culture History in North Central British Columbia. Pp. 90–96 in Problems in the Prehistory of the North American Subarctic: The Athapaskan Question. J.W. Helmer, S. Van Dyke, and F.J. Kense, eds. Calgary, Alta.: University of Calgary Archaeological Association.

Helmer, James W., S. Van Dyke, and F.J. Kense, eds.
1977   Problems in Prehistory of the North American Subarctic: The Athapaskan Question. Calgary, Alta.: University of Calgary Archaeological Association.

Hemphill, Martha L.
1983   Fire, Vegetation, and People—Charcoal and Pollen Analysis of Sheep Mountain Bog, Montana, the Last 2800 Years. (M.A. Thesis in Anthropology, Washington State University, Pullman.)

Henley, Thom
1989   Rediscovery: Ancient Pathways, New Directions: A Guide to Outdoor Education. Vancouver, B.C.: Western Canada Wilderness Committee.

Henshaw, Henry W.
1888   [Vocabulary of the Kayus (Waiilatpuan Family) called the 'Old Cayuse' language.] (Manuscript No. 190 in National Anthropological Archives, Smithsonian Institution, Washington.)

Herskovits, Melville J.
1938   Acculturation: The Study of Culture Contact. New York: J.J. Augustin.

Herzog, George
1949   Salish Music. *Indians of the Urban Northwest, Columbia University Contributions to Anthropology* 36:93–110.

———
[1950]   [Musical transcriptions.] (Transcripts with text, Melville Jacobs Collection No. 54–185–F; songs by Victoria Howard, Archives of Traditional Music, Indiana University, Bloomington.)

Hewes, Gordon W.
1942   The Ainu Double Foreshaft Toggle Harpoon and Western North America. *Journal of the Washington Academy of Sciences* 32(4):93–104. Washington.

———
1947   Aboriginal Use of Fishery Resources in Northwestern North America. (Ph.D. Dissertation in Anthropology, University of California, Berkeley.)

———
1973   Indian Fisheries Productivity in Pre-contact Times in the Pacific Salmon Area. *Northwest Anthropological Research Notes* 7(2):133–155. Moscow, Idaho.

Hibbert, Dennis M.
1985   Quaternary Geology and the History of the Landscape Along the Columbia River Between Chief Joseph and Grand Coulee Dams. Pp. 85–111 in Summary of Results, Chief Joseph Dam Cultural Resources Project, Washington. Sarah K. Campbell, ed. Seattle: Office of Public Archaeology, Institute for Environmental Studies, University of Washington.

Hill, Richard D.
1974   Final Report of the 1973 Lower Salmon River Archaeological Excavations. (Manuscript, Idaho State University Museum, Pocatello.)

Hill, William Lair, ed.
1887   The Codes and General Laws of Oregon. Vol. 1. San Francisco, Calif.: Bancroft-Whitney Company.

Hill-Tout, Charles
1895   Later Prehistoric Man in British Columbia. *Transactions of the Royal Society of Canada*, 2d ser., Vol. 1(2):103–122. Ottawa.

———
1900   Notes on the N'tlaka´pamuQ of British Columbia, a Branch of the Great Salish Stock of North America. Pp. 500–584 in *69th Annual Report of the British Association for the Advancement of Science for 1899*. London (Reprint: Pp. 41–129 in The Salish People, Vol. I: The Thompson and the Okanagan. Ralph Maud, ed. Talonbooks, Vancouver, B.C., 1978.)

———
1904   Report on the Ethnology of the Síciatl of British Columbia , a Coast Division of the Salish Stock. *Journal of the [Royal] Anthropological Institute of Great Britain and Ireland* 34(January-June):20–91. London. (Reprinted: Pp. 93–125 in The Salish People, Vol. IV: The Sechelt and the South-Eastern Tribes of Vancouver Island. Ralph Maud, ed. Talonbooks, Vancouver, B.C., 1978.)

———
1904a   Ethnological Report on the Stseélis and Sk·aúlits Tribes of Halkomelem Division of the Salish of British Columbia. *Journal of the [Royal] Anthropological Institute of Great Britain and Ireland* 34:311–376. London. (Reprinted: Pp. 95–158 in The Salish People, Vol. III: The Mainland Halkomelem. Ralph Maud, ed. Talonbooks, Vancouver, B.C., 1978.)

———
1905   Report on the Ethnology of the StlatlumH of British Columbia. *Journal of the [Royal] Anthropological Institute of Great Britain and Ireland* 35(January-June):126–218. London. (Reprinted: Pp. 99–155 in The Salish People, Vol. II: The Squamish and the Lillooet. Ralph Maud, ed. Talonbooks, Vancouver, B.C., 1978.)

———
1911   Report on the Ethnology of the Okanák·ēn of British Columbia, an Interior Division of the Salish Stock. *Journal of the [Royal] Anthropological Institute of Great Britain and Ireland* 41:130, 137–144. London. (Reprinted: Pp. 131–159 in The Salish People, Vol. I: The Thompson and the Okanagan. Ralph Maud, ed. Talonbooks, Vancouver, B.C., 1978.)

———
1978   The Salish People: The Local Contribution of Charles Hill-Tout. 4 vols. I: The Thompson and the Okanagan; II: The Squamish and the Lillooet; III: The Mainland Halkomelem; IV: The Sechelt and the South-Eastern Tribes of Vancouver Island. Ralph Maud, ed. Vancouver, B.C.: Talonbooks.

Hills, L.V.
1971   A Talus Burial (EqQw 1) Skwaam Bay, Adams Lake, British Columbia. Pp. 27–35 in Aboriginal Man and Environments on the Plateau of Northwest America. Arnoud H. Stryd and Rachel A. Smith, eds. Calgary: The University of Calgary Student's Press.

Hines, Donald M.
1991   Some Southern Plateau Tribal Tales Recounting the Death Journey Vision. *Northwest Anthropological Research Notes* 25(1):31–56. Moscow, Idaho.

————
1996   Celilo Tales: Wasco Myths, Legends, Tales of Magic and the Marvelous. Issaquah, Wash.: Great Eagle Publishing.

Hines, Gustavus
1881   Wild Life in Oregon. New York: Hurst and Co.

Hinsley, Curtis M.
1981   Savages and Scientists: The Smithsonian Institution and the Development of American Anthropology. Washington: Smithsonian Institution.

Hirabayashi, James
1954   Aspects of Farming, Politics, and Factionalism in Okanagan. (Manuscript in Harry Hawthorn Papers, Special Collections Division, University of British Columbia, Vancouver.)

Hoard, James E.
1971   Problems in Proto-Salish Pronoun Reconstruction. Pp. 70–90 in Studies in Northwest Indian Languages. James E. Hoard and Thos. M. Hess, eds. *Sacramento Anthropological Society Paper* 11. Sacramento.

Hodge, Frederick W., ed.
1907–1910 Handbook of American Indians North of Mexico. 2 Pts. *Bureau of American Ethnology Bulletin* 30. Washington. (Reprinted: Rowman and Littlefield, New York, 1971.)

Hofmeister, Jon Fredrick
1968   A Statistical Analysis of Culture Change among Fourteen Plateau and California Indian Groups. (M.A. Thesis in Anthropology, University of Oregon, Eugene.)

Hogan, Bonnie H.
1974   Two High Altitude Game Trap Sites in Montana. (M.A. Thesis in Anthropology, University of Montana, Missoula.)

Hoijer, Harry
1956   The Chronology of the Athapaskan Languages. *International Journal of American Linguistics* 22(4):219–232.

Holbrook, Stewart H.
1956   The Columbia (*Rivers of America*). New York: Rinehart and Winston. (Reprinted in 1974; also, new ed.: Comstock Editors, San Francisco, Calif., 1990.)

Holland, Stuart S.
1964   Landforms of British Columbia: A Physiographic Outline. *British Columbia Department of Mines and Petroleum Resources Bulletin* 48. Victoria.

Hollenbeck, Jan L.
1987   A Cultural Resource Overview: Prehistory, Ethnography and History: Mt. Baker-Snoqualmie National Forest. Program Assessment by Madonna Moss. Portland, Oreg.: U.S. Department of Agriculture, Forest Service, Pacific Northwest Region.

Holm, Bill
1965   Northwest Coast Indian Art: An Analysis of Form. *Thomas Burke Memorial Washington State Museum Monograph* 1. Seattle: University of Washington Press (Reprinted in 1970.)

————
1972   Heraldic Carving Styles of the Northwest Coast. Pp. 77–83 in American Indian Art: Form and Tradition. (An exhibition organized by [the] Walker Art Center, Indian Art Association, and the Minneapolis Institute of Art, 22 October- 31 December 1972) Minneapolis: Walker Art Center and the Minneapolis Institute of Arts.

————
1981   The Crow-Nez Perce Otterskin Bowcase-Quiver. *American Indian Art Magazine* 6(4):60–70.

Holm, Bill, and Bill Reid
1975   Indian Art of the Northwest Coast: A Dialogue on Craftsmanship and Aesthetics. Seattle: University of Washington Press. (Originally publ. as: Form and Freedom: A Dialogue on Northwest Coast Indian Art, Rice University Press, Houston, Tex.)

Holmer, Richard N.
1988   Preliminary Report: The 1988 Excavation at Dagger Falls. *Swanson/Crabtree Anthropological Research Laboratory. Reports of Investigations* 88–10. Pocatello: Idaho State University.

————
1990   Fort Hall and the Shoshone-Bannock. *Rendezvous: Idaho State University Journal of Arts and Letters* 26(1). Pocatello.

Holmer, Richard N., and Lael Suzann Henrikson
1988   Archaeological Investigations on the Middle Fork of Salmon River-A General Research Design. Pp. 32–47 in Preliminary Report: The 1988 Excavation at Dagger Falls. Richard N. Holmer, ed. *Swanson/Crabtree Anthropological Research Laboratory. Reports of Investigations* 88–10. Pocatello: Idaho State University.

Holmer, Richard N., and Jeffrey W. Ross
1985   Excavations at Corn Creek. *Swanson/Crabtree Anthropological Research Laboratory. Reports of Investigations* 84–08. Pocatello: Idaho State University.

————
1986   The Temporal Distribution of Artifact Types in the Salmon River Mountains. (Paper presented at the 39th Annual Northwest Anthropological Conference.)

Holmes, Oliver W., ed. 1934 *see* Garfield, James A. 1934

Holmes, William H.
1914   Areas of American Culture Characterization Tentatively Outlined as an Aid in the Study of the Antiquities. *American Anthropologist,* n.s. 16(3):413–446. (Reprinted: Pp. 42–75 in Anthropology in North America, by Franz Boas, et al. G.E. Stechert, New York, 1915.)

————
1919   Handbook of Aboriginal American Antiquities; Part 1, Introductory, The Lithic Industries. *Bureau of American Ethnology Bulletin* 60. Washington.

Hood, Susan
1972   Termination of the Klamath Indian Tribe of Oregon. *Ethnohistory* 19(4):379–392.

Hopkins, Sarah Winnemucca
1883   Life Among the Paiutes: Their Wrongs and Claims. New York: G.P. Putnam's Sons.

Howard, Helen Addison
1952   War Chief Joseph. Caldwell, Idaho: The Caxton Printers.

Howard, Oliver Otis
1881   Nez Perce Joseph: An Account of His Ancestors, His Lands, His Confederates, His Enemies, His Murders, His War, His Pursuit and Capture. Boston: Lee and Shepard; also, New York: Charles T. Dillingham.

Howay, Frederick W.
1943   Origin of the Chinook Jargon on the North West Coast. *Oregon Historical Quarterly* 44(1):27–55.

Howell, Nancy
1979   Demography of the Dobe !Kung. San Francisco: Academic Press.

Howett, Catherine D.
1993   On the Classification of Predicates in Nłeʔképmx (Thompson River Salish). (M.A. Thesis in Linguistics, University of British Columbia, Vancouver.)

Hrdlička, Aleš
1905   Head Deformation among the Klamath. *American Anthropologist,* n.s. 7(2):360–361.

701

Hudson, Douglas
1986   The Okanagan Indians. Pp. 445–465 in Native Peoples: The Canadian Experience. R. Bruce Morrison and C. Roderick Wilson, eds. Toronto: McCelland and Stewart.

_____
1990   The Okanagan Indians of British Columbia. Pp. 54–89 in Okanagan Sources. Jean Webber and The En'owkin Centre, eds. Penticton, B.C.: Theytus Books.

Hudson, Lorelea, et al.
1978   Cultural Resource Overview of the Malheur, Umatilla, and Wallowa-Whitman National Forests, Northeast Oregon. Cultural Resource Management Report, John Day, Oreg.

_____ , et al.
1981   A Cultural Resource Overview for the Colville and Idaho Panhandle National Forests and the Bureau of Land Management, Spokane and Coeur d'Alene Districts: Northeastern Washington, Northern Idaho. 2 vols. in 3. Sandpoint, Idaho: Cultural Resource Consultants.

Hughes, Richard E.
1986   Diachronic Variability in Obsidian Procurement Patterns in Northeastern California and Southcentral Oregon. University of California Publications in Anthropology 17. Berkeley.

Hulbert, Archer Butler, and Dorothy Printup Hulbert, eds.
1936–1941   Marcus Whitman, Crusader. 3 Pts. Pt. 1: 1802 to 1839; Pt. 2: 1839 to 1843; Pt. 3: 1843–1847. Overland to the Pacific 6, 7, and 8. Colorado Springs: The Stewart Commission of Colorado College and The Denver Public Library.

Hungry Wolf, Adolf
1974   Charlo's People: The Flathead Tribe of Montana. (Good Medicine Books 10). Invermere, B.C.: Good Medicine Books.

Hunn, Eugene 1976–1991 see 1976–1993 (inclusive)

_____
1976-1993   [Sahaptin ethnobiological fieldnotes.] (Manuscripts in E. Hunn's possession.)

_____
1977   Tzeltal Folk Zoology: The Classification of Discontinuities in Nature. New York: Academic Press.

_____
1979   Sahaptin Folk Zoological Classification: A Persistent Paradigm. Folk Classification Bulletin 3(1):3–4.

_____
1980   Sahaptin Fish Classification. Northwest Anthropological Research Notes 14(1):1–19. Moscow, Idaho.

_____
1980a   Final Project Report, BNS 76–16914. (National Science Foundation, Washington, D.C.)

_____
1981   On the Relative Contribution of Men and Women to Subsistence among Hunter-Gatherers of the Columbia Plateau: A Comparison with Ethnographic Atlas Summaries. Journal of Ethnobiology 1(1):124–134.

_____
1982   The Utilitarian Factor in Folk Biological Classification. American Anthropologist 84(4):830–847.

_____
1982a   Mobility as a Factor Limiting Resource Use in the Columbia Plateau of North America. Pp. 17–43 in Resource Managers: North American and Australian Hunter-Gatherers. Nancy M. Williams and Eugene S. Hunn, eds. Boulder, Colo.: Westview Press. (Reprinted: Australian Institute of Aboriginal Studies, Canberra, 1986.)

_____
1990   The Plateau Culture Area. Pp. 361–385 in Native North Americans: An Ethnohistorical Approach. D.L. Boxberger, ed. Dubuque, Iowa: Kendall/Hunt Publishing Company.

_____
1990a   [Semantic cross-referencing between nature and society in folk-biological classification.] (Manuscript in E. Hunn's possession.)

_____
1991   Native Place Names on the Columbia Plateau. Pp. 170–177 in A Time of Gathering: Native Heritage in Washington State. Robin K. Wright, ed. Thomas Burke Memorial Washington State Museum Monograph 7. Seattle: Burke Museum and University of Washington Press.

_____
1991a   [Plants and animals as semantic points of reference in Sahaptin ethnotopography.] (Manuscript in E. Hunn's possession.)

Hunn, Eugene S., and David H. French
1981   Lomatium: A Key Resource for Columbia Plateau Native Subsistence. Northwest Science 55(2):87–94.

_____
1984   Alternatives to Taxonomic Hierarchy: The Sahaptin Case. Journal of Ethnobiology 4(1):73–92.

Hunn, Eugene S., and Helen H. Norton
1984   Impact of Mt. St. Helens Ashfall on Fruit Yield of Mountain Huckleberry, Vaccinium membranaceum, Important Native American Food. Economic Botany 38(1):121–127.

Hunn, Eugene S., with James Selam and Family
1990   Nch'i-Wána, "The Big River": Mid Columbia Indians and Their Land. Seattle and London: University of Washington Press.

Hunt, Charles B.
1974   Natural Regions of the United States and Canada. San Francisco: W.H. Freeman.

Hunt, Clair
[1936]   [Manuscript on file with Dellwo, Rudolf, and Schroeder, P.S.; Spokane, Wash.]

Hunter, George
1887   Reminiscences of an Old Timer. San Francisco: H.S. Crocker.

Huntington, J.W. Perit
1865   [Letter of December 10, 1865, Office of the Superintendent of Indian Affairs, Salem, Oreg.] Pp. 269–272 in 39th Congress. 1st Session. House Executive Document 1. (Serial No. 1248). Washington.

_____
1867   [Annual Report of J.W.P. Huntington, Superintendent, Oregon Superintendency.] Pp. 61–103 in Message of the President of the United States and Accompanying Documents to the Two Houses of Congress...; Report of the Secretary of the Interior, Part II. 40th Congress. 2d Session. House Executive Document 1. Washington: Government Printing Office.

Husted, Wilfred M., and Robert Edgar
1970   The Archaeological Mummy Cave Wyoming: An Introduction to Shoshonean Prehistory. (Manuscript on file at Buffalo Bill Historical Center, Cody, Wyo.)

Husted, Wilfred M., and Oscar L. Mallory
1967   The Fremont Culture: Its Derivation and Ultimate Fate. Plains Anthropologist 12(36):222–232.

Hutchins, Charles
1865   [Letter of June 30, 1865: Office of Flathead Indian Agency, Jocko, Montana.] Pp. 429–432 in 39th Congress. 1st Session. House Executive Document 1. (Serial No. 1248). Washington.

Hutchinson, Bruce
1950   The Fraser. (Rivers of America). New York: Rinehart and Winston. (Reprinted: Clarke, Irwin and Co., Toronto, 1982.)

Hymes, Dell H.
1951–1990   [Upper Chinookan Linguistic and Ethnographic Notes, from Fieldwork at Warm Springs, Oreg.] (Manuscript in Hymes's possession.)

702

BIBLIOGRAPHY

1953 Two Wasco Motifs. *Journal of American Folklore* 66(259):69–70.

1957 A Note on Athapaskan Glottochronology. *International Journal of American Linguistics* 23(4):291–297.

1957a Some Penutian Elements and the Penutian Hypothesis. *Southwestern Journal of Anthropology* 13(1):69–87.

1958 Linguistic Features Peculiar to Chinookan Myths. *International Journal of American Linguistics* 24(4):253–257.

1960 Lexicostatistics So Far. *Current Anthropology* 1(1):3–34, 41–44.

1961 On Typology of Cognitive Styles in Language (with Examples from Chinookan). *Anthropological Linguistics* 3(1):22–54.

1964 Evidence for Penutian in Lexical Sets with Initial *c- and *s-. *International Journal of American Linguistics* 30(3):213–242.

1964a The Problem of Penutian. Pp. 453–456 in Vol. 2 of *XXXV Congreso Internacional de Americanistas, Mexico, 1962: Actas y Memorias*. 3 vols. Mexico.

1966 Two Types of Linguistic Relativity; with Examples from Amerindian Ethnography. Pp. 114–167 in Sociolinguistics: Proceedings of the UCLA Sociolinguistics Conference, 1964. William Bright, ed. The Hague and Paris: Mouton.

1972 On Personal Pronouns: 'Fourth' Person and Phonesthematic Aspects. Pp. 100–121 in Studies in Linguistics in Honor of George L. Trager., M. Estellie Smith, ed. The Hague and Paris: Mouton.

1973 An Introduction to Saying and Writing Wasco Words. (Manuscript, duplicated; copies in Hymes's possession and at the Education Department of The Confederated Tribes of the Warm Springs Reservation, Oreg.)

1973a Sapir Files and Manuscripts. *International Journal of American Linguistics* 39(2):105–106.

1975 Breakthrough into Performance. Pp. 11–74 in Folklore: Performance and Communication. Dan Ben-Amos and Kenneth S. Goldstein, eds. The Hague, Paris: Mouton. (Reprinted: Pp. 79–141 in "In Vain I Tried to Tell You": Essays in Native American Ethnopoetics, by Dell H. Hymes. University of Pennsylvania Press, Philadelphia, 1981.)

1975a From Space to Time in Tenses in Kiksht. *International Journal of American Linguistics* 41(4):313–329.

1976 Louis Simpson's 'The Deserted Boy'. *Poetics* 5(2):119–155. (Reprinted: Pp. 142–183 in "In Vain I Tried To Tell You": Essays in Native American Ethnopoetics, by Dell H. Hymes, University of Pennsylvania Press, Philadelphia, 1981.)

1980 Commentary. Pp. 389–423 in Theoretical Orientations in Creole Studies: Proceedings of a Symposium, St. Thomas, U.S. Virgin Islands, March 1979. Albert Valdman and Arnold Highfield, eds. New York: Academic Press.

1980a Verse Analysis of a Wasco Text: Hiram Smith's "At'unaqa." *International Journal of American Linguistics* 46(2):65–77. (Reprinted in: "In Vain I Tried To Tell You": Essays in Native American Ethnopoetics, by Dell H. Hymes. University of Pennsylvania Press, Philadelphia, 1981.)

1981 "In Vain I Tried To Tell You": Essays in Native American Ethnopoetics. *Studies in Native American Literature* 1. Philadelphia: University of Pennsylvania Press.

1984 Bungling Host, Benevolent Host: Louis Simpson's 'Deer and Coyote.' *American Indian Quarterly* 8(3):171–198.

Hymes, Virginia
1972–1992 [Fieldwork with speakers of Warm Springs Sahaptin, especially Verbena Green, Susan Moses, Ellen Squiemphen, Hazel Suppah, Linton Winishut.] (Manuscripts in V. Hymes's possession.)

1976 Word and Phrase List of Warm Springs Sahaptin. (Duplicated manuscripts distributed by Warm Springs Confederated Tribes, Warm Springs, Oregon. Original version, 1973.)

1987 Warm Springs Sahaptin Narrative Analysis. Pp 62–102 in Native American Discourse: Poetics and Rhetoric. Joel Sherzer and Anthony C. Woodbury, eds. *Cambridge Studies in Oral and Literate Culture* 13. Cambridge and New York.

Ice, Dennie M.
1962 Archaeology of the Lava Butte Site, Deschutes County, Oregon. *Washington State University. Laboratory of Anthropology. Report of Investigations* 15. Pullman.

Idsardi, William J.
1991 Stress in Interior Salish. Pp. 246–260 in CLS 27: Papers from the 27th Regional Meeting of the Chicago Linguistic Society. Part I: The General Session. Lisa M. Dobrin, Lynn Nichols, and Rosa M. Rodriguez, eds. Chicago: CLS

Ignace, Marianne Boelscher
1984–1992 [Ethnographic and linguistic notes from fieldwork among the Secwepemc People of North Thompson, Skeetchestn, Bonaparte, Kamloops, Neskainlith, Adams Lake, Whispering Pines and Canoe Creek Bands, British Columbia.] (Manuscripts in Ignace's possession and on file with respective Bands.)

1992 Aboriginal Territories of the Shuswap Nation. Kamloops, B.C.: Shuswap Nation Tribal Council.

Ignace, Ronald E.
1980 Kamloops Agency and the Indian Reserve Commission of 1912–1916. (M.A. Thesis in Anthropology, University of British Columbia, Vancouver.)

[1985] Roots of Shuswap Impoverishment. (Manuscript, Secwepemc Cultural Education Society, Kamloops, B.C.)

In-SHUCK-ch
1993 Statement of Intent to Negotiate a Treaty, December 15th, 1993. (Document on file with the British Columbia Treaty Commission, Vancouver.)

Indian and Northern Affairs Canada 1992, 1996 *see* Canada. Indian and Northern Affairs 1992, 1996

Indian Claims Commission
1974 Commission Findings: The Chinook Tribe and Bands of Indians, Petitioner, vs. The United States of America, Defendant. Decided April 16, 1958. Findings of Fact and Opinion of the Commission. Pp. 257–311 in Oregon Indians, I. *American Indians Ethnohistory: Indians of the Northwest*. New York: Garland.

1979 United State Indian Claims Commission Final Report, August 13, 1946-September 30, 1978. Washington: U.S. Government Printing Office.

Ingles, Lloyd G.
1965 Mammals of the Pacific States: California, Oregon and Washington. Palo Alto, Calif.: Stanford University Press.

Ingram, W.J.
1948 The Larger Freshwater Clams of California, Oregon and Washington. *Journal of Ethology and Zoology* 40:72–92.

703

Innis, Harold A.
1930   The Fur Trade in Canada: An Introduction to Canadian Eco-
        nomic History. New Haven, Conn.: Yale University Press.
        (Revised ed., 1956, 1962; reprinted: Toronto University Press,
        Toronto, 1973.)

Irving, Washington
1834   The Adventures of Captain Bonneville. New York: G.P. Put-
        man. (Reprinted in 1836.)

————

1836   The Adventures of Captain Bonneville, U.S.A., in the Rocky
        Mountains and the Far West. New York: G.P. Putnam. (Sever-
        al reprints, incl.: 1850, 1868; also, ed. by Edgeley W. Todd,
        University of Oklahoma Press, Norman, 1961; and, Twayne,
        New York, 1977.)
————   1850, 1868, 1961 see 1836
————   1951, 1964, see 1895

1895   Astoria: or, Anecdotes of an Enterprise Beyond the Rocky
        Mountains [1836]. 2 vols. New York: G.P. Putnam's Sons.
        (Title page has 1897 date for "Tacoma Edition".)

Irwin, Ann M., and Ula L. Moody
1978   The Lind Coulee Site (45GR97). Washington State Universi-
        ty. Washington Archaeological Research Center. Project
        Report 56. Pullman.

Isham, Dana A.
1974   Conflict and Compromise: The American Indian and the
        Archaeologist. (M.A. Thesis in Anthropology, San Diego
        State University, San Diego, Calif.)

Isselstein, Karl H.
1965   Ancient Cataclysms Which Changed the Earth's Surface.
        Mokelumne Hill, Cal.: Health Research.

Iverson, Thomas M.
1975   [Prehistory.] In: Rock Creek, a Recreational Resource Inven-
        tory and Analysis, Twin Falls County, Idaho. Moscow: Uni-
        versity of Idaho.

Ives, John W.
1990   A Theory of Northern Athapaskan Prehistory. Boulder, Colo.:
        Westview Press.

JP = Joset Papers
1890   [The Older Coeur d'Alene Mission and Its Church.] (Manu-
        script, Joseph Joset Papers, Oregon Province Archives of the
        Society of Jesus, Foley Library, Gonzaga University,
        Spokane.)

Jackson, Donald D., ed.
1978   Letters of the Lewis and Clark Expedition with Related Doc-
        uments, 1783–1854. 2d ed., with Additional Documents and
        Notes. 2 vols. Urbana, Chicago, London: University of Illi-
        nois Press.

Jackson, J. Brantley, and Glenn D. Hartmann
1977   Archaeological Survey from Lower Monumental Substation
        to Ashe Substation. Washington State University. Washington
        Archaeological Research Center. Project Report 38. Pullman.

Jackson, Philip L.
1985   Climate. Pp. 48–57 in Atlas of the Pacific Northwest. A. Jon
        Kimberling and Philip L. Jackson, eds. 7th ed. Corvallis: Ore-
        gon State University Press.

Jacobs, Elizabeth D.
1990   Nehalem Tillamook Tales; Told by Clara Pearson. Melville
        Jacobs, ed. Corvallis: Oregon State University Press. (Orig.
        publ.: University of Oregon Monographs. Studies in Anthro-
        pology 5. Eugene, 1959.)

Jacobs, Melville
1927–1930 [Molala: texts, vocabulary, comparative and ethnographic
        notes.] (Notebooks 32–35, 37–40 in Melville Jacobs Collec-
        tion, University of Washington Libraries, Seattle.)

————   1928, 1928a see 1927–1930 (inclusive)

1928–1936 [Tualatin and Santiam Kalapuyan linguistic and ethnographic
        notes.] (Notebooks 33–37, 46, 47, 76–90, 122–125 in
        Melville Jacobs Collection, University of Washington
        Libraries, Seattle.)

————

1929   Northwest Sahaptin Texts, Pt. 1. University of Washington
        Publications in Anthropology 2(6):175–244. (Reprinted:
        Columbia University Press, New York, 1934.)

————

1929–1930 [Clackamas Chinookan Linguistic and Ethnographic Notes
        (including Molala items).] (Notebooks 51–69 in Melville
        Jacobs Collection, University of Washington Libraries, Seat-
        tle.)

————

1931   A Sketch of Northern Sahaptin Grammar. University of Wash-
        ington Publications in Anthropology 4(2). Seattle.

————

1932   Northern Sahaptin Kinship Terms. American Anthropologist,
        n.s. 34(4):688–693.

————

1934–1937 Northwest Sahaptin Texts. 2 Pts. Part 1: English; Part 2:
        Sahaptin. Columbia University Contributions to Anthropolo-
        gy 19(1–2). New York. (Reprinted: AMS Press, New York,
        1969.)

————

1936   Texts in Chinook Jargon. University of Washington Publica-
        tions in Anthropology 7(1):1–27. Seattle.

1937   Historic Perspectives in Indian Languages of Oregon and
        Washington. Pacific Northwest Quarterly 28(1):55–74.

————

1939   Coos Narrative and Ethnologic Texts. University of Washing-
        ton Publications in Anthropology 8(1):1–125. Seattle.

————

1945   Kalapuya Texts. Pt. 1: Santiam Kalapuya Ethnologic Texts,
        by M. Jacobs. Pt. 2: Santiam Kalapuya Myth Texts, by M.
        Jacobs. Pt. 3: Kalapuya Texts, by A.S. Gatschet, L.J. Fracht-
        enberg, and M. Jacobs. University of Washington Publications
        in Anthropology 11. Seattle.

————

1954   The Areal Spread of Sound Features in the Languages North
        of California. Pp. 46–56 in Papers from the Symposium on
        American Indian Linguistics, Held at Berkeley, July 7, 1951.
        University of California Publications in Linguistics 10.
        Berkeley

————

1955   A Few Observations on the World View of the Clackamas
        Chinook Indians. Journal of American Folklore
        68(269):283–289.

————

1958–1959 Clackamas Chinook Texts. 2 Pts. Publications of the Indiana
        University Research Center in Anthropology, Folklore, and
        Linguistics 8,11; International Journal of American Linguis-
        tics 24(2, Pt. 2), 25(2, Pt. 2). Bloomington.

————

1959   The Content and Style of an Oral Literature: Clackamas Chi-
        nook Myths and Tales. Viking Fund Publications in Anthro-
        pology 26. New York: Wenner-Gren Foundation for Anthro-
        pological Research.

————

1962   The Fate of Indian Oral Literatures in Oregon. Northwest
        Review 5(3):90–99. Eugene: University of Oregon.

Jacobs, Melville, Verne F. Ray, and Morris Swadesh
1930   [Cayuse linguistic note from fieldwork on the Umatilla Indi-
        an Reservation, Oreg.] (Manuscript copy in Bruce Rigsby's
        possession.)

Jacobsen, William H., Jr.
1968   On the Prehistory of Nez Perce Vowel Harmony. *Language* 44(4):819–829.

Jaehnig, Manfred E.W.
1983   Archaeological Investigations at Site 45–OK–258, Chief Joseph Dam Project. Seattle: Office of Public Archaeology, University of Washington.

1983a   Chief Joseph Dam Cultural Resources Project: Preliminary Report of Field Investigations, 1978–1980. Seattle: Office of Public Archaeology, University of Washington.

1984   Archaeological Investigations at Site 45–DO–273, Chief Joseph Dam Project. Seattle: Office of Public Archaeology, University of Washington.

1984a   Archaeological Investigations at Site 45–OK–18, Chief Joseph Dam Project, Washington. Seattle: Office of Public Archaeology, University of Washington.

James, Caroline
1996   Nez Perce Women in Transition, 1877–1990. Moscow: University of Idaho Press.

Jenness, Diamond
1932   The Indians of Canada. *National Museum of Canada Bulletin* 65; *Anthropological Series* 15. Ottawa. (Reprinted in 1934.)

1939   The "Snare" Indians. *Proceedings and Transactions of the Royal Society of Canada*, ser. 3, 33(2):103–105. Ottawa.

1943   The Carrier Indians of the Bulkley River: Their Social and Religious Life. *Anthropological Paper* 25, *Bureau of American Ethnology Bulletin* 133. Washington.

1955   The Faith of a Coast Salish Indian. *Anthropology in British Columbia. Memoir* 3. Victoria.

Jennings, Jesse D.
1968   Prehistory of North America. San Francisco: W.H. Freeman.

1989   Prehistory of North America. 3d ed. San Francisco: W.H. Freeman.

Jermann, Jerry V., and Stephen A. Aaberg
1976   Archaeological Reconnaissance in the Libby Reservoir-Lake Koocanusa Area, Northwestern Montana. (Report submitted to U.S. Army Corps of Engineers, Seattle District, Seattle.)

Jermann, Jerry V., and K.A. Whittlesey
1978   Chief Joseph Dam Cultural Resources Project: Plan of Action, 1978. Seattle: Office of Public Archaeology, University of Washington. (Report submitted to the U.S. Army Corps of Engineers, Seattle District, Seattle.)

Jermann, Jerry V., Leon L. Leeds, Linda A. Leeds, and K.A. Whittlesey
1980   Paleokistic Studies of Hunter-gatherer Groups in the Big Bend Region, Upper Columbia River, Washington: A Research Proposal. Seattle: Office of Public Archaeology, University of Washington. (Report submitted to the U.S. Army Corps of Engineers, Seattle District, Seattle.)

Jessett, Thomas E.
1960   Chief Spokan Garry, 1811–1892: Christian, Statesman, and Friend of the White Man. Minneapolis: T.S. Denison. (Microfilm: *Book Collection on Microfilm Relating to the North American Indian, Reel* 7, Glen Rock, N.J., 1973.)

Jilek, Wolfgang, and Louise Jilek-Aall
1974   Meletinsky in the Okanagan: An Attempt to Apply Meletinsky's Analytic Criteria to Canadian Indian Folklore. Pp. 143–149 in Soviet Structural Folkloristics: Texts by Meletinsky [et al.]. With Tests of the Approach by Jilek [et al.]. Introduced and edited by Pierre Maranda. *Approaches to Semiotics* 42. The Hague: Mouton.

Jimmie, Mandy Na'zinek B.D.
1994   A Prosodic Analysis of Nłeʔkepmx Reduplication. (M.A. Thesis in Linguistics, University of British Columbia, Vancouver. Microfiche: Precision Micrographics, Vancouver, 1994.)

Joe, Mary
1981   Food of the Okanagan Indian. Pp. 72–73 in *45th Annual Report of the Okanagan Historical Society*. Vernon, B.C.

Johansen, Dorothy O., ed. 1959 *see* Newell, Robert 1959

Johansen, Dorothy O., and Charles M. Gates
1967   Empire of the Columbia: A History of the Pacific Northwest. 2d ed. New York: Harper and Row. (Orig. pub. In 1957.)

Johnsgard, Paul A.
1973   Grouse and Quails of North America. Lincoln: University of Nebraska Press.

Johnson, Francis
1986   We Made Our Lives Good: The Struggle and Success of the People of Alkali Lake against Their Alcohol Problem 1950–86. (M.A. Thesis in Education, University of British Columbia, Vancouver.)

Johnson, Frank Davis
1939   The Modoc Indians and Their Removal to Oklahoma. (M.A. Thesis in History, University of Oklahoma, Norman.)

Johnson, LeRoy, Jr.
1969   Obsidian Hydration Rate for the Klamath Basin of California and Oregon. *Science* 165(1300):1354–1355.

Johnson, LeRoy, Jr., and David L. Cole
1969   A Bibliographical Guide to the Archaeology of Oregon and Adjacent Regions. Eugene: Special Publication of the Museum of Natural History, University of Oregon.

Johnson, Olga Weydemeyer
1969   Flathead and Kootenay: The Rivers, the Tribes and the Region's Traders. *Northwest Historical Series* 9. Glendale, Calif.: Arthur H. Clark.

Johnson, Otis
1947   The History of the Klamath Indian Reservation, 1864–1900. (M.A. Thesis in History, University of Oregon, Eugene.)

Johnson, Robert E.
1975   The Role of Phonetic Detail in Coeur d'Alene Phonology. (Ph.D. Dissertation in Linguistics, Washington State University, Pullman.)

Johnston, Robbin T.
1987   Archaeological Evidence of Fishing in the Southern Plateau, a Cultural Area of the Columbia Plateau. (M.S. Thesis in Anthropology, University of Idaho, Moscow.)

Joint Reserve Commission *see* British Columbia. Indian Reserve Commission

Jones, Judith Ann
1995   "Women Never Used to War Dance:" Gender and Music in Nez Perce Culture Change. (Ph.D. Dissertation in Interdisciplinary Studies, Washington State University, Pullman. Photocopy: University Microfilms International, Ann Arbor, Mich., 1997.)

Jonkel, Charles J.
1967   Black Bear Population Studies: Final Report. [Helena]: Montana Fish and Game Commission.

Jordan, David Starr, and Barton Warren Evermann
1898–1900   The Fishes of North and Middle America: A Descriptive Catalog of Fish-like Vertebrates Found in the Waters on North America, North of the Isthmus of Panama. 4 vols. *Smithsonian Institution. United States National Museum Bulletin* 47. Washington.

705

1908   American Food and Game Fishes: A Popular Account of All the Species Found in America North of the Equator; [etc.]. Garden City, N.Y.: Doubleday. (Reprinted in 1923; also, Dover Publications, New York, 1969.)

Jorgensen, Joseph G.
1969   Salish Language and Culture: A Statistical Analysis of Internal Relationships, History, and Evolution. *Language Science Monographs* 3. Bloomington: Indiana University.

1980   Western Indians: Comparative Environments, Languages, and Cultures of 172 Western American Indian Tribes. Research collaborators, Harold E. Driver...[et at.]. San Francisco: W.H. Freeman and Company.

Joseph, Marie, Jan P. van Eijk, Gordon Turner, and Lorna Williams, eds.
1979   Cuystwí malh Ucwalmícwts / Ucwalmícwts Curriculum for Beginners. Mount Currie, B.C.: The Tŝzil Publishing House.

Josephy, Alvin M., Jr.
1955   The Naming of the Nez Perce. *Montana* 5:1–18. Helena.

1962   Origins of the Nez Perce Indians. *Idaho Yesterdays* 6(1):2–13. Boise.

1965   The Nez Perce Indians and the Opening of the Northwest. New Haven, Conn.: Yale University Press. (Reprinted: Houghton Mifflin, Boston, 1997.)

1983   The People of the Plateau. In: Nez Perce Country: A Handbook for the Nez Perce National Historical Park. Washington: National Park Service.

Joset, Joseph
1854   [Letter of August 18, 1854.] (Manuscript, Joseph Joset Papers, Oregon Province Archives of the Society of Jesus, Foley Library, Gonzaga University, Spokane.)

1860   [Rocky Mountains: The History of the Colville Mission. Translated from the French by Bernard Thomas.] (Manuscript, Joseph Joset Papers, Oregon Province Archives of the Society of Jesus, Foley Library, Gonzaga University, Spokane.)

Justice, James
1989   Twenty Years of Diabetes on the Warm Springs Indian Reservation, Oregon. *American Indian Culture and Research Journal* 13(3–4):49–81.

Kahclamat, Philip, and Dell H. Hymes
1977   Iyagiximnihl. *Alcheringa: Ethnopoetics* 3(2):8–9.

Kalispel Tribe
1980   The Kalispels: People of the Pend Oreille. Glen Nenema, Tribal Chairman, O.J. Cotes, ed. [Usk, Wash.: Kalispel Tribe.]

Kane, Paul
1856   Notes on Travels among the Walla Walla Indians. *Canadian Journal*, n.s. 1(5):417–424.

1859   Wanderings of an Artist Among the Indians of North America, from Canada to Vancouver's Island and Oregon Through the Hudson's Bay Territory and Back Again. London: Longmans Brown, [etc.]. (Reprinted: The Radisson Society of Canada, Toronto, 1925.; also: Pp. 49–157 in Paul Kane's Frontier, ed. by J. Russell Harper. University of Texas Press for the Amon Carter Museum, Fort Worth, Tex., and the National Gallery of Canada, Ottawa; Austin and London, 1971.)

1925   Wanderings of an Artist Among the Indians of North America, from Canada to Vancouver's Island and Oregon.... Toronto: The Radisson Society of Canada. (Reprinted: C.E. Tuttle,

Rutland, Vermont, 1968; also, Hurtig Publishers, Edmonton, Alta., 1974.)

1971   Paul Kane, The Columbia Wanderer, 1846–7. Sketches and Paintings of the Indians and His Lecture, "The Chinooks". Edited with an Introduction by Thomas Vaughan. Portland: Oregon Historical Society.

1974   Wanderings of An Artist among the Indian of North America. Edmonton: Hurtig Publishers.

Kapoun, Robert W., with Charles J. Lohrmann
1992   Language of the Robe: American Indian Trade Blankets. Salt Lake City: Peregrine Smith Books.

Kappler, Charles J., comp. and ed.
1904–1941 Indian Affairs: Laws and Treaties. 5 vols. (Vols. I–V). Washington: U.S. Government Printing Office. (Reprinted: AMS Press, New York, 1971; see also Kappler 1904–1979.)

————— , comp. and ed.
1904–1979 Indian Affairs: Laws and Treaties. 7 vols. Vols. I–V, reprinted [plus:] Kappler's Indian Affairs: Laws and Treaties. 2 vols.: Vols. VI–VII, prepared under the direction of Deputy Solicitors Raymond C. Coutler and David E. Lindgren. Washington: U.S. Department of the Interior; U.S. Government Printing Office. (Reprinted, 7 vols.: William S. Hein and Co., New York, [1990].)

Kasahara, Hiroshi
1963   Catch Statistics for North Pacific Salmon. Pp. 7–82 in Salmon of the North Pacific Ocean, Part I. *International North Pacific Fisheries Commission Bulletin* 12. Vancouver, B.C.

Kawamura, Hiroaki
1995   Nez Perce Ethnic Identification: Selection and Interpretation of Symbols. (M.S. Thesis in Anthropology, University of Idaho, Moscow.)

Kean, Mary-Louise
1973   Non-global Rules in Klamath Phonology. *Quarterly Progress Report of the Research Laboratory of Electronics* 108:288–309. Cambridge: Massachusetts Institute of Technology.

Keane, A.H.
1878   Ethnography and Philology of America. In Stanford's Compendium of Geography and Travel: Central America, and West Indies, and South America, by H.W. Bates. London.

Keeler, Robert W.
1973   An Upland Hunting Camp on the North Fork of the Clearwater River, North-Central Idaho. *Occasional Papers of the Idaho State University Museum* 30. Pocatello.

Keely, Patrick B.
1980   Nutrient Composition of Selected Important Plant Foods of the Pre-Contact Diet of the Northwest American Peoples. (M.S. Thesis in Nutritional Science, University of Washington, Seattle.)

Keely, Patrick B., Charlene S. Martinsen, Eugene S. Hunn, and Helen H. Norton
1982   Composition of Native American Fruits in The Pacific Northwest. *Journal of the American Dietetic Association* 81:568–572.

Kehoe, Thomas F.
1955   Some Chipped Stone Artifacts from Southwestern Idaho. *Plains Anthropologist* 3(April):13–18.

1966   The Small Side-Notched Point System of the Northern Plains. *American Antiquity* 31(6):827–841.

Kelly, Gail M.
1955   Themes in Wasco Culture. (B.A. thesis in Anthropology, Reed College, Portland, Oreg.)

Kelly, Gerald Lee
1954   The History of St. Ignatius Mission, Montana. (M.A. Thesis in History, University of Montana, Missoula.)

Kelly, Isabel T.
1932   Ethnography of the Surprise Valley Paiute. *University of California Publications in American Archaeology and Ethnology* 31(3). Berkeley. (Reprinted: Kraus Reprint, New York, 1965.)

Kelly, Marcia K.
1982   A Technical Analysis of a Microblade Industry from Southwestern Washington. (Paper presented at the 35th Annual Northwest Anthropological Conference, Burnaby, B.C.)

Kelly, Plymton J.
1976   We Were Not Summer Soldiers: The Indian War Diary of Plympton J. Kelly, 1855–1856. Introduction and Annotations by William N. Bischoff, S.J. Tacoma: Washington State Historical Society.

Kelly, Robert L., and Lawrence C. Todd
1988   Coming into the Country: Early Paleoindian Hunting and Mobility. *American Antiquity* 53(2):231–244.

Kenaston, Monte R.
1966   The Archaeology of the Harder Site, Franklin County, Washington. *Washington State University. Laboratory of Anthropology. Report of Investigations* 35. Pullman.

Kennedy, Alexander
1823   [Spokan House Report, 1822–1823.] (Manuscript B 208/e/1, in Hudson's Bay Company Archives, Provincial Archives of Manitoba, Winnipeg.)

————   1824–1825 [Fort George District, Columbia Department Report, 1824–1825.] (Manuscript B.7/b/e in Hudson's Bay Company Archives, Provincial Archives of Manitoba, Winnipeg.)

Kennedy, Barbara, and Steve Cassidy
1981   The Cranbrook Petroglyphs. *Datum: Heritage Conservation Branch Newsletter* 6(2):6–7. Victoria.

Kennedy, Dorothy I.D.
1971–1991 [Lillooet ethnographic fieldnotes. Okanagan-Colville ethnographic fieldnotes.] (Manuscripts in British Columbia Indian Language Project, Victoria.)

————   1975–1976 [Ethnobotanical excerpts from discussion of Thompson fishing and hunting with Louis Phillips.] (Manuscript in British Columbia Indian Language Project, Victoria.)

————   1976 [Ethnobotanical excerpts from discussion of Thompson fishing technology with the Late Walter Isaac and the Late Jenny Charlies of Boothroyd, March 1976.] (Manuscript in British Columbia Indian Language Project, Victoria.)

————   1976a [Ethnobotanical excerpts from discussion of fishing technology in Merritt Area with Mable Joe, March 1976.] (Manuscript in British Columbia Indian Language Project, Victoria.)

————   1976b [Discussion of birds among the Upper and Lower Lillooet, with Sam Mitchell, Charlie Mack and Baptiste Ritchie.] (Manuscript in British Columbia Indian Language Project, Victoria.)

————   1984 The Quest for a Cure: A Case Study in the Use of Health Care Alternatives. *Culture* 4(2):21–31.

————   1986 [Stl'atl'imx (Fraser River Lillooet) fishing.] (Manuscript in British Columbia Indian Language Project, Victoria.)

Kennedy, Dorothy I.D., and Randall T. (Randy) Bouchard
1975   Utilization of fish by the Chase Shuswap Indian People of British Columbia.] (Manuscript in British Columbia Indian Language Project, Victoria.)

————   1975a [Utilization of fish by the Colville Okanagan Indian People.] (Manuscript in British Columbia Indian Language Project, Victoria.)

————   1975b [Utilization of fish by the Mount Currie Lillooet Indian People of British Columbia.] (Manuscript in British Columbia Indian Language Project, Victoria.)

————   1977 [Discussions of Upper and Lower Lillooet ethnography, with Sam Mitchell, Slim Jackson, Charlie Mack, and Baptiste Ritchie.] (Manuscript in British Columbia Indian Language Project, Victoria.)

————   1978 Fraser River Lillooet: An Ethnographic Summary. Pp. 22–55 in Reports of the Lillooet Archaeological Project, No. 1: Introduction and Setting. A.H. Stryd and S. Lawhead, eds. *Canada. National Museum of Man. Mercury Series. Archaeological Survey Paper* 73. Ottawa.

————   1984 [Indian history and knowledge of the Merritt to Surrey Lake portion of the proposed Coquihalla Highway.] (Kamloops, B.C.: Arcas Associates Heritage Resources Consultants.)

————   1985 Interior Salish. *The Canadian Encyclopedia* 3:1631. Edmonton: Hurtig Publishers.

————   1992 *Stl'átl'imx* (Fraser River Lillooet) Fishing. Pp. 266–354 in A Complex Culture of the British Columbia Plateau: Traditional *Stl'á'tl'imx* Resource Use. Brian Hayden, ed. Vancouver: UBC Press.

Kennedy, Hal K.
1976   Examination of the Tucannon Phase as a Valid Concept. (M.A. Thesis in Anthropology, University of Idaho, Moscow.)

Kenny, Ray A.
1972   Preliminary Report, Deep Creek Site (FbRn 13). (Report on file, Archaeology Branch, Victoria, B.C.)

Kent, Susan
1980   Pacifism—A Myth of the Plateau. *Northwest Anthropological Research Notes* 14(2):125–134. Moscow, Idaho.

Kew, Michael
1976   Salmon Abundance, Technology and Human Populations on the Fraser River Watershed. (Manuscript in Department of Anthropology, University of British Columbia, Vancouver.)

————   1992 Salmon Availability, Technology, and Cultural Adaptation in the Fraser River Watershed. Pp. 177–221 in A Complex Culture of the British Columbia Plateau: Traditional *Stl'átl'imx* Resource Use. Brian Hayden, ed. Vancouver: UBC Press.

Keyes, Erasmus d.
1884   Fifty Years' Observation Men and Events, Civil and Military. New York: Charles Scribner's Sons. (Reprinted: Ye Galleon Press, Fairfield, Wash., 1988.)

Keyser, James D.
1975   A Shoshonean Origin for the Plains Shield Bearing Warrior Motif. *Plains Anthropologist* 20(69):207–215.

————   1992 Indian Rock Art of the Columbia Plateau. Seattle: University of Washington Press.

Keyser, James D., and George C. Knight
1976   The Rock Art of Western Montana. *Plains Anthropologist* 21(71):1–12.

Kickingbird, Kirke, and Karen Ducheneaux
1973   One Hundred Million Acres. New York: Macmillan.

Killoren, John J.
1994   "Come Blackrobe": De Smet and the Indian Tragedy. Norman: University of Oklahoma Press.

Kimball, Patricia C.
1976   Warm Creek Spring: A Prehistoric Lithic Workshop. *Archaeological Reports of the Idaho State University Museum of Natural History* 8. Pocatello.

Kingston, C.S.
1932   Buffalo in the Pacific Northwest. *Washington Historical Quarterly* 23(3):163–172.

Kinkade, M. Dale
1967   On the Identification of the Methows (Salish). *International Journal of American Linguistics* 33(3):193–197.

———
1967a   Uvular-Pharyngeal Resonants in Interior Salish. *International Journal of American Linguistics* 33(3):228–234.

1975   The Lexical Domain of Anatomy in Columbian Salish. Pp. 423–443 in Linguistics and Anthropology: In Honor of C.F. Voegelin. M. Dale Kinkade, Kenneth L. Hale, and Oswald Werner, eds. Lisse, The Netherlands: Peter de Ridder Press. (Separately printed: *Publications on Salish Languages* 1. Lisse, The Netherlands: Peter de Ridder Press, 1975.)

1978   "Coyote and Rock" (Columbian Salish). Pp. 15–20 in Coyote Stories. William Bright, ed. *International Journal of American Linguistics. Native American Text Series. Monograph* 1. Chicago: University of Chicago Press.

1980   Columbian Salish -xí, -xl, -túl. *International Journal of American Linguistics* 46(1):33–36.

———, comp.
1981   Dictionary of the Moses-Columbia Language. Nespelem, Wash.: Colville Confederate Tribes.

1981a   Interior Salishan Particles. *Anthropological Linguistics* 23(8):327–343.

1982   Columbian (Salish) C2-Reduplication. *Anthropological Linguistics* 24(1):66–72.

1982a   Transitive Inflection in (Moses) Columbian Salish. *Kansas Working Papers in Linguistics (Studies in Native American Languages* 1), 7:49–62.

1983   The Non-perfective Suffix(es) of Columbian (Salish). *Amérindia: Revue d'Ethnolinguistique Amérindienne* 8:7–15. Paris.

1983a   Salish Evidence against the Universality of 'Noun' and 'Verb'. *Lingua: International Review of General Linguistics* 60(1):25–39. Amsterdam.

1988   Proto-Salishan Colors. Pp. 433–466 in In Honor of Mary Haas: From the Haas Festival Conference on Native American Linguistics. William Shipley, ed. Berlin: Mouton de Gruyter.

1990   Sorting Out Third Persons in Salishan Discourse. *International Journal of American Linguistics* 56(3):341–360.

———, comp.
1991   Upper Chehalis Dictionary. *University of Montana Occasional Papers in Linguistics* 7. Missoula.

1991a   Prehistory of the Native Languages of the Northwest Coast. Pp. 137–158 in Proceedings of the Great Ocean Conferences. Vol. 1: The North Pacific to 1600. Portland: Oregon Historical Society Press.

1993   Salishan Words for "Person, Human, Indian, Man." Pp. 163–183 in American Indian Linguistics and Ethnography in Honor of Laurence C. Thompson. Anthony Mattina and Timothy Montler, eds. *University of Montana Occasional Papers in Linguistics* 10. Missoula.

1994   Native Oral Literature of the Northwest Coast and the Plateau. Pp. 33–45 in Dictionary of Native American Literature. Andrew Wiget, ed. *Garland Reference Library of the Humanities* 1815. New York and London: Garland.

Kinkade, M. Dale, and Clarence Sloat
1972   Proto-Eastern Interior Salish Vowels. *International Journal of American Linguistics* 38(1):26–48.

Kinkade, M. Dale, and Laurence C. Thompson
1974   Proto-Salish *r. *International Journal of American Linguistics* 40(1):22–28.

Kinney, Jay P.
1973   Facing Indian Facts. Laurens, N.Y.: Press of the Village Printer.

Kip, Lawrence
1855   The Indian Council in the Valley of the Walla Walla. San Francisco: Whitton, Towne. (Reprinted: W. Abbatt, Terrytown, New York, 1915.)

1859   Army Life on the Pacific; A Journal of the Expedition against the Northern Indians, the Tribes of the Coeur d'Alenes, Spokans, and Pelouzes, in the Summer of 1858. New York: Redfield. (Reprinted: W. Abbatt, Terrytown, New York, 1914.)

1897   The Indian Council at Walla Walla, May and June, 1855. A Journal. *Sources of the History of Oregon* 1(2). Eugene: Star Job Office.

Kiparsky, Paul
1982   How Abstract Is Phonology? Pp. 119–163 in Explanation in Phonology. Paul Kiparsky, ed. *Publications in Language Science* 4. Dordrecht, The Netherlands: Foris Publishers.

Kirk, Donald R.
1975   Wild Edible Plants of the Western United States, Including also most of Southwestern Canada and Northwestern Mexico. Illus. By Janice Kirk. Happy Camp, Calif.: Naturegraph Publishers. (Originally publ. in 1970.)

Kirk, Ruth, with Richard D. Daugherty
1978   Exploring Washington Archaeology. Seattle: University of Washington Press.

Kirkwood, Charlotte M.
1928   The Nez Perce Indian War Under Chief Joseph and White Bird. Grangeville: Idaho County Free Press.

Kisseberth, Charles W.
1972   Cyclical Rules in Klamath Phonology. *Linguistic Inquiry* 3(1):3–33. Cambridge, Mass.

Kisseberth, Charles W.
1973   On the Alternation of Vowel Length in Klamath: A Global Rule. Pp. 9–26 in Issues in Phonological Theory: Proceedings of the Urbana Conference on Phonology. Michael J. Kenstowicz and Charles W. Kisseberth, eds. The Hague: Mouton.

1973a   The 'Strict Cyclicity' Principle: The Klamath Evidence. Pp. 179–195 in Studies in Generative Phonology. Charles W.

708

Kisseberth, ed. Edmonton, Alta.: Linguistic Research Incorporated.

Kittson, William
1826   [Letter for William Kittson to John Dease, September 5th, 1826.] (Document D.4/120/11–12 in Hudson's Bay Company Archives, Provincial Archives of Manitoba, Winnipeg.)

Klamath Tribes
1993   / ? At a naat stay LA / ("Now we gather [roots, berries]"). A Treatment of Indigenous Plants in the Klamath Basin. [Chiloquin, Oreg.]: Klamath Tribes in cooperation with the U.S. Forest Service and Chiloquin High School.

Klein, Laura, and Lillian Ackerman
1995   Woman and Power in Native North America. Norman: University of Oklahoma Press.

Kniffen, Fred B.
1928   Achomawi Geography. *University of California Publications in American Archaeology and Ethnology* 23(5):297–332. Berkeley.

Knight, George C.
1989   Overview: Ecological and Cultural Prehistory of the Helena and Deerlodge National Forests, Montana. [Mont.]: Helena and Deerlodge National Forests.

Knight, Rolf
1978   Indians at Work: An Informal History of Native Indian Labour in British Columbia 1858–1930. Vancouver, B.C.: New Star Books.

Knudson, Ruthann
1977   Archaeological Investigation of the Proposed Kelly Creek Gravel Source, Clearwater National Forest, Idaho. *University of Idaho. Laboratory of Anthropology. Anthropological Research Manuscript Series* 40. Moscow.

Knudson, Ruthann, and Duane Marti
1978   Cultural Resources Reconnaissance and Survey, Hayden Lake Wastewater Facilities Phase I, Spring 1977. *University of Idaho. Laboratory of Anthropology. Anthropological Research Manuscript Series* 45. Moscow, Idaho.

Knudson, Ruthann, and Robert Lee Sappington
1977a   Archaeological Investigation of the Wilderness Gateway Recreation Area, Clearwater National Forest, Idaho. *University of Idaho. Laboratory of Anthropology. Anthropological Research Manuscript Series* 41. Moscow.

Knudson, Ruthann, Robert Lee Sappington, and M.A. Pfeiffer
1977   Assessment of the Archaeological Resources Within the Dworshak Reservoir Project Boundaries, 1976. (Report to the U.S. Army Corps of Engineers, Walla Walla District, Walla Walla, Wash.)

Knudson, Ruthann, Darby Stapp, Steven Hackenberger, William D. Lipe, and Mary P. Rossillon
1982   A Cultural Resource Reconnaissance in the Middle Fork Salmon River Basin, Idaho, 1978. *University of Idaho. Laboratory of Anthropology. Anthropological Research Manuscript Series* 67. Moscow.

Kolinsky, Mieczyslaw
1970   Review Essay (on Alan P. Merriam's Ethnomusicology of the Flathead Indians). *Ethnomusicology* 14(1):77–99. Middletown, Conn.

Konlande, James E., and John R.K. Robson
1972   The Nutritive Value of Cooked Camas as Consumed by Flathead Indians. *Ecology of Food and Nutrition* 2:193–195. New York.

Kootenai Culture Committee
1984   Kootenai Legends. Pablo, Mont.: Char-Koosta Printing.

1989   Ksanka K¢xamali̵ / Kootenai Hymns and Prayers. Nancy Joseph and Sarah Bufton, trans. and eds. Elmo, Mont.: The Kootenai Culture Committee.

Kowrach, Edward J., ed. 1978 *see* Doty, James 1978

Kowrach, Edward J., and Thomas E. Connolly, eds.
1900   Saga of the Coeur d'Alene Indians: An Account of Chief Joseph Seltice. Fairfield, Wash.: Ye Galleon Press.

Krajina, Vladimir J.
1970   Ecology of Forest Trees in British Columbia. Pp. 1–146 in *Ecology of Western North America* 2(1). V.J. Krajina and R.C. Brooke, eds. Vancouver: University of British Columbia, Department of Botany.

———
1973   Biogeoclimatic Zones of British Columbia. (Map). Victoria: British Columbia Ecological Reserves Committee.

———
1976   Biogeoclimatic Zones of British Columbia. Vancouver: VanDusen Botanical Gardens.

Krause, Marilyn L.
1969   A Study of Drinking on a Plateau Indian Reservation. (M.A. Thesis in Anthropology, University of Washington, Seattle.)

Krauss, Michael E.
1973   Na-Dene. Pp. 903–978 in Current Trends in Linguistics, Vol. 10: Linguistics in North America (Pt. 2). Thomas A. Sebeok, ed. The Hague: Mouton. (Reprinted: Plenum Press, New York, 1976.)

———
1979   Na-Dene and Eskimo-Aleut. Pp. 803–901 in The Languages of Native America: Historical and Comparative Assessment. Lyle M. Campbell and Marianne Mithun, eds. Austin: University of Texas Press.

Krieger, Alex D.
1939   Environment, Population, and Prehistory in the Northwestern United States. (M.A. Thesis in Anthropology, University of Oregon, Eugene.)

Krieger, Herbert W.
1928   [Letter to H.W. Dorsey, January 20, 1928.] (Manuscript in Herbert W. Krieger Papers, National Anthropological Archives, Smithsonian Institution, Washington.)

———
1928a   A Prehistoric Pit House Village Site on the Columbia River at Wahluke, Grant County, Washington. *Proceedings of the United States National Museum* 73(2732/11):1–29. Washington.

———
1928b   Prehistoric Inhabitants of the Columbia River Valley. Pp. 133–140 *Explorations and Field-work of the Smithsonian Institution in 1927*. Washington.

Kroeber, Alfred L.
1923   Anthropology. New York: Harcourt, Brace and Company. (Several reprints, incl.: 1933, 1936, 1948.)

———
1923a   American Culture and the Northwest Coast. *American Anthropologist*, n.s. 25(1):1–20.

———
1925   Handbook of the Indians of California. *Bureau of American Ethnology Bulletin* 78. Washington. (Reprinted: Book Company, Berkeley, Calif., 1953, 1970; also, Dover Publications, New York, 1976.)

———
1931   The Culture-area and Age-area Concepts of Clark Wissler. Pp. 248–265 in Methods in Social Science. S. Rice, ed. Chicago: University of Chicago Press.

1935   History and Science in Anthropology. *American Anthropologist*, n.s. 37(4):539–569.

1939   Cultural and Natural Areas of Native North America. *University of California Publications in American Archaeology and Ethnology* 38:1–242. Berkeley. (Reprinted: University of California Press, Berkeley, 1963; also, Kraus Reprint, Millwood, N.Y., 1976.)

Kroeber, Alfred L., and Harold Driver
1932   Quantitative Expression of Cultural Relationships. *University of California Publications in American Archaeology and Ethnology* 31(4):211–256.

Kroeber, Paul D.
1988   Rhetorical Structure of a Kalispel Narrative. (Paper presented at the Annual Meeting of the American Anthropological Association held in Phoenix, Ariz., Nov. 16–20, 1988.)

1991   Comparative Syntax of Subordination in Salish. (Ph.D. Dissertation in Linguistics, University of Chicago, Chicago.)

Krueger, John R.
1960   Miscellanea Selica I: A Flathead Supplement to Vogt's Salishan Studies. *Anthropological Linguistics* 2(7):33–38.

1961   Miscellanea Selica II: Some Kinship Terms of the Flathead Salish. *Anthropological Linguistics* 3(2):11–18.

1961a   Miscellanea Selica III: Flathead Animal Names and Anatomical Terms. *Anthropological Linguistics* 3(9):43–52.

1967   Miscellanea Selica IV: An Interim Moses' Columbia (Wenatchee) Salishan Vocabulary. *Anthropological Linguistics* 9(2):5–11.

1967a   Miscellanea Selica V: English-Salishan Index and Finder List. *Anthropological Linguistics* 9(2):12–25.

Küchler, August Wilhelm
1949   Physiognomic Classification of Vegetation. *Annals of the Association of American Geographers* 39(3):201–210.

1964   Potential Natural Vegetation of the Conterminous United States. (Col. map, with Manual to accompany the map.) *American Geographic Society Special Publication* 36. New York. (Reprinted, 2d ed., 1975. Revised: U.S. Geological Survey, Reston, Va., 1985.)

Kuhnlein, Harriet V., and Nancy J. Turner
1986   Cow-Parsnip (*Heracleum lanatum* Michx.): An Indigenous Vegetable of Native People of Northwestern North America. *Journal of Ethnobiology* 6(2):309–324.

1991   Traditional Food Plants of Canadian Indigenous Peoples: Nutrition, Botany and Use. Volume 8 of: Food and Nutrition in History and Anthropology. Solomon H. Katz, ed. New York: Gordon and Breach Science Publishers.

Kuijt, Ian
1989   Subsistence Resource Variability and Culture Change during the Middle-Late Prehistoric Cultural Transition on the Canadian Plateau. *Canadian Journal of Archaeology* 13:97–118. Ottawa.

Kuipers, Aert H.
1970   Toward a Salish Etymological Dictionary. *Lingua: International Review of General Linguistics* 26(1):46–72. Amsterdam.

1974   The Shuswap Language: Grammar, Texts, Dictionary. *Janua Linguarum. Series Practica* 225. The Hague: Mouton.

1975   A Classified English-Shuswap Word-List. *Publications on Salish Languages* 3. Lisse, The Netherlands: Peter de Ridder.

1978   On the Phonological Typology of Proto-Salish. Pp. 607–621 in vol. 4 of *Proceedings of the 42d International Congress of Americanists*. Paris.

1981   On Reconstructing the Proto-Salish Sound System. *International Journal of American Linguistics* 47(4):323–335.

1982   Toward a Salish Etymological Dictionary II. *Lingua: International Review of General Linguistics* 57(1):71–92. Amsterdam.

1983   Shuswap-English Dictionary. Leuven, Belgium: Peeters.

1989   A Report on Shuswap, With a Squamish Lexical Appendix. *Langues et Société d'Amérique Traditionelle* 2. SELAF 310. Paris: Peeters-SELAF.

1993   Irregular Stress in Shuswap. Pp. 185–189 in American Indian Linguistics and Ethnography in Honor of Laurence C. Thompson. Anthony Mattina and Timothy Montler, eds. *University of Montana Occasional Papers in Linguistics* 10. Missoula.

Kuipers, Aert H., and May Dixon
1974   [A Shuswap Course.] (Manuscript, University of Leiden, Leiden, The Netherlands.)

Kulesza, Michael
1982   A Cultural Resource Reconnaissance in the Middle Fork Salmon River Basin Uplands, River of No Return Wilderness, Idaho 1981–1982. (Manuscript on file at Salmon National Forest, Salmon, Idaho.)

Kuneki, Nettie J., Elsie Thomas, and Marie Slockish
1982   The Heritage of Klickitat Basketry: A History and Art Preserved. Portland: Oregon Historical Society Press.

Kutzbach, John E.
1987   Model Simulations of the Climate Patterns during the Deglaciation of North America. Pp. 425–446 in North America and Adjacent Oceans During the Last Deglaciation. W.F. Ruddiman and Herbert E. Wright, Jr. eds. Boulder, Colo.: The Geological Society of America.

Kutzbach, John E., and P.J. Geuter
1986   The Influence of Changing Orbital Parameters and Surface Boundary Conditions on Climate Simulations for the Past 18,000 Years. *Journal of the Atmospheric Sciences* 43:1726–1759. Boston.

Kuykendall, George P.
1889   A Graphic Account of the Religions or Mythology of the Indians of the Pacific Northwest: Including a History of Their Superstitions, Marriage Customs, Moral Ideas and Domestic Relations, and Domestic Relations, and Their Conception of a Future State, and the Re-habiliment of the Dead. Pp. 60–95 in Vol. 2 of History of the Pacific Northwest: Oregon and Washington, by Elwood Evans, et al. Portland, Oreg.: North Pacific History Company. [The above title is from the Table of Contents; the title of the article (Chapt. 60) differs.]

Laforet, Andrea
1981   [Notes on: Songs of the Indians of British Columbia, collected by James Teit, 1912–1921.] (Manuscript in Canadian Museum of Civilization, Hull, Que.)

Laforet, Andrea, and Annie Z. York
1981   Notes on the Thompson Winter Dwelling. Pp. 115–122 in The World Is As Sharp As a Knife: An Anthology in Honour of Wilson Duff. Donald N. Abbott, ed. Victoria: British Columbia Provincial Museum.

710

Laforet, Andrea, Nancy J. Turner, and Annie Z. York
1991   Traditional Foods of the Fraser Canyon Nłeʔkepmx. (Manuscript in N.J. Turner's possession.)

Lahren, Sylvester L., Jr.
1971   The Warm Springs and Colville Indian Reservations: A Comparative Study of Their History and Politics. (Honors Thesis in Anthropology, Oregon State University, Corvallis.)

————
1989   [Fieldnotes.] (Manuscripts in Lahren's possession.)

————
1990   [Fieldnotes.] (Manuscripts in Lahren's possession.)

Lahren, Sylvester L., Jr., and John L. Schultz
1973   New Light on Old Issues: Plateau Political Factionalism. *Northwest Anthropological Research Notes* 7(2):156–184. Moscow, Idaho.

Lamar, Howard R., ed.
1979   The Reader's Encyclopedia of the American West. New York: Thomas Y. Crowell.

Lamb, W. Kaye, ed. 1960 *see* Fraser, Simon 1960

Landar, Herbert
1973   The Tribes and Languages of North America: A Checklist. Pp. 1253–1441 in Current Trends in Linguistics, Vol. 10: Linguistics in North America. Thomas A. Sebeok, ed. The Hague: Mouton. (Reprinted: Plenum Press, New York, 1976.)

————
1980   American Indian Linguistic Contributions of Gladys A. Reichard: A Bibliography. *International Journal of American Linguistics* 46(1):37–40.

Lane, Harrison
1982   The Long Flight: A History of the Nez Perce War. Havre, Mont.: H. Earl Clack Memorial Museum.

Lane, Robert B.
1953   Cultural Relations of the Chilcotin Indians of West Central British Columbia. (Ph.D. Dissertation in Anthropology, University of Washington, Seattle. Microfiche: *Canadian Theses on Microfiche* 44875, National Library, Ottawa, 1980; also, University Microfilms International, Ann Arbor, Mich., 1983.)

Lang, Samuel V., Jr.
1965   Children of the Flathead: A Study of Culture-and-Personality in a Changing Society. (M.A. Thesis in Anthropology, University of Montana, Missoula.)

————
1979   Cultural Ecology and the Horse in Flathead Culture. Pp. 63–72 in Lifeways of Intermontane and Plains Montana Indians: In Honor of J. Verne Dusenberry. Leslie B. Davis, ed. *Occasional Papers of the Museum of the Rockies* 1. Bozeman: Montana State University.

————
1979a   The Belief in Immanent Justice among Contemporary Flathead Indian Children. Pp. 87–98 in Lifeways of Intermontane and Plains Montana Indians: In Honor of J. Verne Dusenberry. Leslie B. Davis, ed. *Occasional Papers of the Museum of the Rockies* 1. Bozeman: Montana State University.

Lansdale, Richard
1859   [Letter of August 1, 1859, Fort Simcoe.] Pp. 777–781 in *36th Congress. 1st Session. Senate Executive Document* 2. (Serial No. 1023). Washington.

Lansing, Ronald
1993   Juggernaut: the Whitman Massacre Trial, 1850. Pasadena, Calif.: Ninth Judicial Circuit Court Historical Society.

Larrison, Earl J.
1981   Birds of the Pacific Northwest: Washington, Oregon, Idaho and British Columbia. Moscow: University of Idaho Press.

Larsell, Olov
1947   The Doctor in Oregon: A Medical History. Portland: Binfords and Mort for the Oregon Historical Society.

Larsen, Patricia B., and Sandra L. Nisbet, eds.
1986   Everything Change, Everything Change: Recollections of Ida Nason, an American Indian Elder. (Videorecording.) [Seattle: University of Washington, Instructional Media Services.]

Latham, Robert G.
1850   The Natural History of the Varieties of Man. London: J. Van Voorst.

Lavender, David
1992   Let Me Be Free: The Nez Perce Tragedy. New York: Harper Collins.

Lawhead, Stephen, and Arnoud H. Stryd
1983   The Quiltanton Complex: A New Archaeological Unit for the British Columbia Southern Interior. (Manuscript, Arcas Associates, Kamloops, B.C.)

Layman, William D.
1984   The Rock Art of Rock Island Rapids: An Historical Overview. (Paper presented at the Tenth Annual Rock Art Symposium, American Rock Art Research Association, Boulder City, Nev.)

Le Jeune, Jean-Marie Raphael
1890   A ha a skoainjwts a Jesu-Kri oa Ste. Marguerite-Marie Alacoque. A joat k'oe iamit oa N'jhoakwk. Dayton, Ohio: P.A. Kemper.

————
1892   Prayers in Thompson or Mtlakapmah. Morning Prayers. Kamloops, B.C.: [St. Louis Mission.]

————
1896   Shuswap Manual; or, Prayers, Hymns and Catechism in Shuswap. Kamloops, B.C.: [St. Louis Mission.]

————
1897   Lillooet Manual; or, Prayers, Hymns and the Cathechism in the Lillooet or Stlatliemoh Language. Kamloops, B.C.: [St. Louis Mission.]

————
1897a   Okanagan Manual; or, Prayers and Hymns and Catechism in the Okanagan Language. Kamloops, B.C.: [St. Louis Mission.]

————
1897b   Thompson Manual; or, Prayers, Hymns and Catechism in the Thompson or Ntla Kapmah Language. Kamloops, B.C.: [St. Louis Mission.]

————
1925   Studies on Shuswap. Kamloops, B.C.: [St. Louis Mission.]

Lee, Daniel
1840   A Vocabulary of The Dalls [Dalles] Indians Language [Wasco-Wishram]. (Manuscript notebook; duplicated copy in Kathrine S. French's possession.)

Lee, Daniel, and J[oseph] H. Frost
1844   Ten Years in Oregon. New York: Published for the Authors by J. Collord. (Reprinted: Ye Galleon Press, Fairfield, Wash., 1968; also, Arno Press, New York, 1973.)

Lee, Dorothy S. 1984 *see* Brady, Erika, et al. 1984–

Leechman, Douglas
1921   String Records of the Northwest. *Museum of the American Indian. Heye Foundation. Indian Notes and Monographs* 16:5–47. New York.

————
1932   Aboriginal Paints and Dyes in Canada. *Proceedings and Transactions of the Royal Society of Canada*, 3d ser., Vol. 26, Sect. 2:37–42. Ottawa.

————
1954   Some Pictographs of Southeastern British Columbia. *Proceedings and Transactions of the Royal Society of Canada*, 3d ser., Vol. 48, Sect. 2:77–85. Ottawa.

Leeds, Leon L.
1985   Implications of Environment and Site Distribution: A Preliminary Investigation of Hunter-gatherer Adaptations in the Chief Joseph Dam Project Area. Pp. 223–247 in Summary of Results, Chief Joseph Dam Cultural Resources Project, Washington, Sarah K. Campbell, ed. Seattle: Office of Public Archaeology, Institute for Environmental Studies. University of Washington.

Leeds, Leon L., Linda A. Leeds, and Karen A. Whittlesey
1985   Model Building as an Approach to Explaining Evolution of Hunter-gatherer Adaptations on the Columbia Plateau. Pp. 3–81 in Summary of Results, Chief Joseph Dam Cultural Resources Project, Washington. Sarah K. Campbell, ed. Seattle: Office of Public Archaeology, Institute for Environmental Studies, University of Washington.

Leeds, Leon L., William S. Dancey, Jerry V. Jermann, and R.L. Lyman
1981   Archaeological Testing at 79 Prehistoric Habitation Sites in the Chief Joseph Reservoir Area: Subsistence Strategy and Site Distribution. *Chief Joseph Dam Cultural Resources Survey Reports* 3. Seattle: Office of Public Archaeology, Institute for Environmental Studies, University of Washington.

Leen, Daniel
1984   Rock Art Sites. Pp. 13–60 in Archaeological Investigations at Nonhabitation and Burial Sites Chief Joseph Dam Project, Washington, by Sarah Campbell. (Report submitted to the U.S. Army Corps of Engineers, Seattle District. Office of Public Archaeology, Institute for Environmental Studies, University of Washington, Seattle.)

————
1988   An Inventory of Hells Canyon Rock Art, Vol. 1. (Manuscript, Hells Canyon National Recreation Area, Wallowa-Whitman National Forest, Enterprise, Oreg.)

Lehman-Kessler, Marcia N.
1985   The Traditional Nez Perce Basketry Hat: Its Modal Style and Cultural Significance. (M.A. Thesis in Anthropology, Washington State University, Pullman.)

Leiberg, John B.
1893   Petroglyphs at Lake Pend d'Oreille, Idaho. *Science* 22(555):156.

Leighton, Caroline C.
1884   Life at Puget Sound: with Sketches of Travel in Washington Territory, British Columbia, Oregon and California, 1865–1881. Boston: Lee and Shepard. (Reprinted: Ye Galleon Press, Fairfield, Wash., 1980.)

Lemert, Edwin M.
1954   The Life and Death of an Indian State. *Human Organization* 13(3):23–27.

Leonhardy, Frank C.
1968   An Opinion on Archaeological Interpretation in the Plateau. Pp. 27–31 in Archaic Prehistory in the Western United States: A Symposium of the Society for American Archaeology, Santa Fe, 1968. C. Irwin-Williams, ed. *Eastern New Mexico University Contributions in Anthropology* 1(3). Portales.

————
1970   Artifact Assemblages and Archaeological Units at Granite Point Locality 1 (45WT41), Southeastern Washington. (Ph.D. Dissertation in Anthropology, Washington State University, Pullman.)

————
1987   Archaeological Research in the Big Creek Ranger District, Payette National Forest, Idaho. (Manuscript, Laboratory of Anthropology, University of Idaho, Moscow.)

Leonhardy, Frank C., and R. Johnston
1984   An Archaeological Survey in the Big Creek Ranger District, Payette National Forest, Idaho. *University of Idaho. Laboratory of Anthropology. Letter Report* 84–13. Moscow.

Leonhardy, Frank C., and David G. Rice
1970   A Proposed Culture Typology for the Lower Snake River Region, Southeastern Washington. *Northwest Anthropological Research Notes* 4(1):1–29. Moscow, Idaho.

Leonhardy, Frank C., Gerald C. Schroedl, Judith A. Bense, and Seth Beckerman
1971   Wexp'usnime (45GA61): Preliminary Report. Washington State University. *Laboratory of Anthropology. Report of Investigations* 49. Pullman.

Lerman, Norman
1952–1954 [Okanogan ethnographic fieldnotes.] (Manuscripts in Melville Jacobs Collection, Suzzallo Library, University of Washington, Seattle; copy in British Columbia Indian Language Project, Victoria.)

————
1954   An Okanagan Winter Dance. *Anthropology in British Columbia* 4:35–36. Victoria.

Lerner, Andrea
1991   Relearning the Past: A Language Project of the Klamath Tribe. Pp. 101–104 in The First Oregonians: An Illustrated Collection of Essays on Traditional Lifeways, Federal-Indian Relations, and the State's Native People Today. Carolyn M. Buan and Richard Lewis, eds. Portland: Oregon Council for the Humanities.

Lesser Alexander
1935   Functionalism in Social Anthropology. *American Anthropologist* 37(3):387–393.

Lévi-Strauss, Claude
1964–1971 Mythologiques. 4 vols. [Vol. 4: L'Homme Nu.] Paris: Librairie Plon.

———— 1971 *see* 1964–1971

————
1985   Cosmopolitanism and Schizophrenia. Translated by Joachim Neugroschel and Phoebe Hoss. Pp. 177–185 in The View from Afar. Oxford: Basil Blackwell.

Lewarch, Dennis E., and J.R. Benson
1989   Horseshoe Bend Archaeological Project: Results of Data Recovery Excavations at Sites 10–BO–418 and 10–BO–419, Boise County, Idaho. (Manuscript, Idaho State Highway/Transportation Department, Boise.)

Lewarch, Dennis E., J.R. Benson, and C. Miss
1988   Archaeological Excavations at Two Upland Sites Near Horseshoe Bend, Boise County, Idaho. (Manuscript, Idaho State Highway/Transportation Department, Boise.)

Lewes, John
1848   [Letter of February 10, 1848.] (Manuscript No. 1204 in Elkanah and Mary Walker Papers, Oregon Historical Society, Portland.)

Lewis, Albert Buell
1906   Tribes of the Columbia Valley and the Coast of Washington and Oregon. *Memoirs of the American Anthropological Association* 1(2):147–209. Lancaster, Pa. (Reprinted: Kraus Reprint, New York, 1964; [and] Millwood, N.Y., 1983.)

Lewis, Meriwether, and William Clark
1814   History of the Expedition Under the Command of Captains Lewis and Clarke, to the Sources of the Missouri; Thence Across the Rocky Mountains and Down the River Columbia to the Pacific Ocean; Performed during the Years 1804–5–6. [1st Nicholas Biddle edition.] Paul Allen, ed. Philadelphia: Bradford and Inskeep. (Reprinted in 1817; also, A.C. McClurg, Chicago, 1902; J.B. Lippincott Company, Philadelphia, 1961.)

————1817 *see* 1814

————
1902   History of the Expedition Under the Command of Captains Lewis and Clark, 1804–5–6. 2 Vols. Elliott Coues, ed. Chicago: A.C. McClurg.

———— 1904–1905 *see* Thwaites, Reuben G., ed. 1904–1905

———— 1953 *see* De Voto, Bernard A., ed. 1953

1961   The Lewis and Clark Expedition. The 1814 Edition, Unabridged in Three Volumes; Introduction by Archibald Hanna. Philadelphia and New York: J.B. Lippincott.

———— 1983– *see* Moulton, Gary A., ed. 1983–

Lewis, Thomas H.
1985   Bears and Bear Hunting in Prehistory: The Rock Art Recorded on the Yellowstone. *Northwest Anthropological Research Notes* 19(2):208–245. Moscow, Idaho.

Lewis, William S.
1917   The Case of Spokane Garry; Being a Brief Statement of the Principal Facts Connected with His Career; and a Review of the Charges Made Against Him. *Bulletin of the Spokane Historical Society* 1(1). Spokane, Wash. (Reprinted: Ye Galleon Press, Fairfield, Wash., 1987.)

Lewis, W.S., and J.A. Meyers, eds. 1920 *see* Work, John 1920

Lindburg, Donald G.
1962   Social Organization of the Kutenai. (M.A. Thesis in Anthropology, University of Chicago, Chicago.)

Linderman, Frank Bird
1926   Kootenai Why Stories. New York: Charles Scribner's Sons.

Livingston, Stephanie
1985   Summary of Faunal Data. Pp. 365–419 in Summary of Results, Chief Joseph Dam Cultural Resources Project, Washington. Sarah K. Campbell, ed. Seattle: Office of Public Archaeology, Institute for Environmental Studies, University of Washington.

Lobb, Allen
1978   Indian Baskets of the Northwest Coast. Portland, Oreg.: C.H. Belding.

Locke, S.B.
1929   Whitefish, Grayling Trout, and Salmon of the Intermountain Region. Pp. 173–190 in U.S. Bureau of Fisheries. Report of the Commissioner of Fisheries for 1929, (Appendix V). Washington.

Lockley, Fred
1928   History of the Columbia River Valley from the Dalles to the Sea. 3 vols. Chicago: S.J. Clarke.

Loeb, Barbara
1983   Classic Intermontane Beadwork. (Ph.D. Dissertation in Art History, School of Art, Division of Art History, University of Washington, Seattle.)

————
1991   Dress Me in Color: Transmontane Beading. Pp. 197–201 in A Time of Gathering: Native Heritage in Washington State. Robin K. Wright, ed. *Thomas Burke Memorial Washington State Museum. Monograph* 7. Seattle: Burke Museum; Seattle and London: University of Washington Press.

Loendorf, Lawrence L.
1990   A Dated Rock Art Panel of Shield Bearing Warriors in South Central Montana. *Plains Anthropologist* 35(127):45–54.

Logan, William
1862   [Letter of July 28, 1862, Warm Springs Reservation, Oreg.] *37th Congress. 3d Session. House Executive Document* 1. (Serial No. 1157). Washington.

Lohse, Ernest S.
1984   Archaeological Investigations at Site 45–DO–11, Chief Joseph Dam Project. Seattle: University of Washington, Office of Public Archaeology.

————
1984a   Archaeological Investigations at Site 45–DO–211, Chief Joseph Dam Project. Seattle: University of Washington, Office of Public Archaeology.

————
1984b   Archaeological Investigations at Site 45–DO–242/243, Chief Joseph Dam Project. Seattle: University of Washington, Office of Public Archaeology.

————
1984c   Archaeological Investigations at Site 45–DO–282, Chief Joseph Dam Project. Seattle: University of Washington, Office of Public Archaeology.

————
1984d   Archaeological Investigations at Site 45–DO–326, Chief Joseph Dam Project. Seattle: University of Washington, Office of Public Archaeology.

————
1984e   Archaeological Investigations at Site 45–OK–11, Chief Joseph Dam Project. Seattle: University of Washington, Office of Public Archaeology.

————
1985   Rufus Woods Lake Projectile Point Chronology. Pp. 317–364 in Summary of Results: Chief Joseph Dam Cultural Resources Project, Washington. Sarah K. Campbell, ed. Seattle: University of Washington, Office of Public Archaeology, Institute for Environmental Studies.

————
1994   The Southeastern Idaho Prehistoric Sequence. *Northwest Anthropological Research Notes* 28(2):135–156. Moscow, Idaho.

Lohse, Ernest S., and Dorothy Sammons-Lohse
1986   Sedentism on the Columbia Plateau: A Matter of Degree Related to the Easy and Efficient Procurement of Resources. *Northwest Anthropological Research Notes* 20(2):115–136. Moscow, Idaho.

Longmire, David
1917   First Immigrants to Cross the Cascades. *Washington Historical Quarterly* 8(1):22–28.

Longmire, David, and James Longmire
1932   Narrative of James Longmire, a Pioneer of 1853. *Washington Historical Quarterly* 23(1):47–60, (2):138–150.

Lord, John K.
1866   The Naturalist in Vancouver Island and British Columbia. 2 vols. London: Richard Bentley.

Loring, J. Malcolm, and Louise Loring
1982   Pictographs and Petroglyphs of the Oregon Country. Part 1: Columbia River and Northern Oregon. *University of California. Institute of Archaeology. Monograph* 21. Los Angeles. (Reprinted, 2d ed. In 1996.)

Lothrop, Gloria Ricci, ed. and trans. 1977 *see* Mengarini, Gregory 1977

Lothson, Gordon A., and Bruce L. Lothson
1991   Phase I. Archaeological Reconnaissance and Shovel Testing of the Proposed Buffalo Eddy-Buffalo Bar Bypass Road Realignment, Asotin County, Washington. Vol. 1. *Reports of Investigations* 17. Pullman, Wash.: Cougar Consulting.

Lovell, N.C., Brian C. Chisholm, D. Erie Nelson, and Henry P. Schwarcz
1986   Prehistoric Salmon Consumption in Interior British Columbia. *Canadian Journal of Archaeology* 10:99–106. Ottawa.

Lowe, Thomas
1847   [Thomas Lowe Journal, 1847.] (Manuscript A/B/20.4/L95A, British Columbia Provincial Archives, Victoria.)

Loy, Thomas H.
1986   Appendix III: Microscopic and Chemical Analysis of Selected Tool Edges. Pp. 301–305 in Archaeological Excavations at Valley Mine, Highland Valley, B.C. (Report on file, Archaeology Branch, Arcas Associates, Victoria, B.C.)

Loy, Thomas H., and G. Robert Powell
1977   Archaeological Data Recording Guide. *British Columbia Provincial Museum. Heritage Record* 3. Victoria.

Loy, Thomas H., D.E. Nelson, Betty Meehan, John Vogel, John Southon, and Richard Cosgrove
1990   Accelerator Radiocarbon Dating of Human Blood Proteins in Pigments from Lake Pleistocene Art Sites in Australia. *Antiquity* 64(242):110–116.

Luckman, B.H., and M.S. Kearney
1986   Reconstruction of Holocene Changes in Alpine Vegetation and Climate in the Maligne Range, Jasper National Park, Alberta. *Quaternary Research* 26(2):244–261. New York.

Ludowicz, Deanna
1983   Assemblage Variation Associated with Southwestern Interior Plateau Microblade Technology. (M.A. Thesis in Anthropology, University of British Columbia, Vancouver.)

Lugenbeel, Pinkney
1859   [Letter to E.R. Geary, dated July 16, 1859.] (Manuscript in Record Group 75, Records of the Bureau of Indian Affairs, Washington Superintendency [Letters Received from Colville Valley], National Archives, Washington.)

Lundsgaarde, Henry P.
1967   Structural Analysis of Nez Perce Kinship. *[Washington State University.] Research Studies of Washington State College* 35(1):48–77. Pullman.

Lundy, Doris
1974   The Rock Art of the Northwest Coast. (M.A. Thesis in Anthropology, Simon Fraser University, Vancouver, B.C.)

_____
1979   The Petroglyphs of the British Columbia Interior. Pp. 49–70 in Papers from the Fourth Biennial Conference of the Canadian Rock Art Research Associates. Doris Lundy, ed. *British Columbia Provincial Museum. Heritage Record* 8. Victoria.

Lutz, Frank W., and Donald A. Barlow
1981   School Boards and the Process of Native American Influence on the Education of Native American Children. *Journal of Educational Equity and Leadership* 1:90–97. Columbus, Ohio.

Lyman, Richard Lee
1976   A Cultural Analysis of Faunal Remains from the Alpowa Locality. (M.A. Thesis in Anthropology, Washington State University, Pullman.)

_____
1980   Inferences from Bone Distributions in Prehistoric Sites in the Lower Granite Reservoir Area, Southeastern Washington. *Northwest Anthropological Research Notes* 14(1):107–123. Moscow, Idaho.

_____
1980a   Freshwater Bivalve Molluscs and Southern Plateau Prehistory: A Discussion and Description of Three Genera. *Northwest Science* 54(2):121–136. Pullman, Wash.

_____
1984   A Model of Large Freshwater Clam Exploitation in the Prehistoric Southern Columbia Plateau Culture Area. *Northwest Anthropological Research Notes* 18(1):97–107. Moscow, Idaho.

_____
1985   The Paleozoology of the Avey's Orchard Site. Pp. 243–319 in Avey's Orchard: Archaeological Investigation of a Late Prehistoric Columbia River Community. Jerry R. Galm and Ruth A. Masten, eds. *Eastern Washington University. Archaeological and Historic Services. Reports in Archaeology and History* 100–42. Cheney.

_____
1985a   Culture Resource Management and Archaeological Research in the Interior Pacific Northwest: A Note to NARN Readers on the Translucency of Northwest Archaeology. *Northwest Anthropological Research Notes* 19(2):161–168. Moscow, Idaho.

Lyman, Richard Lee, and Stephanie D. Livingston
1983   Late Quaternary Mammalian Zoogeography of Eastern Washington. *Quaternary Research* 20(3):360–373. New York.

Lyman, William Denison
1919   History of the Yakima Valley, Washington: comprising Yakima, Kittitas, and Benton Counties. 2 vols. Chicago: S.J. Clarke.

Lynch, Alice J.
1976   An Archaeological Test of an Aboriginal Burial Site Near Richland, Washington. *University of Idaho. Anthropological Research Manuscript Series* 28. Moscow.

Lyons, Perry J.
1906   [Letter as Inclosure I with Letter from Levi Ankeny to Commissioner of Indian Affairs, 11 January, 1906.] (Manuscript in Commissioner of Indian Affairs, Letters Received 1906/3535, Records of the Bureau of Indian Affairs, Record Group 75, National Archives, Washington.)

McBeth, Kate C.
1908   The Nez Perces Since Lewis and Clark. New York: Fleming H. Revell.

McClellan, George B.
1853   [Journal, May 20 to December 15, 1853.] (Manuscript in Manuscript Division, Library of Congress, Washington. Available on microfilm A228, University of Washington Library, Seattle.)

_____
1855   General Reports of the Survey of the Cascades: General Report of Captain McClellan, Corps of Engineers, U.S.A., in Command of the Western Division, Olympia, W.T. February 25, 1853. Pp. 188–202 in *33d Congress. 2d Session. Senate Executive Document* 78; [also] *House Executive Document* 91. (Serial No. 791). Washington.

McClure, Richard H., Jr.
1978   An Archaeological Survey of Petroglyph and Pictograph Sites in the State of Washington. *The Evergreen State College. Archaeological Reports of Investigations* 1. Olympia, Wash.

_____
1979   Dating Petroglyphs and Pictographs in Washington. (Paper presented at the 32d Annual Northwest Anthropological Conference, Eugene, Oreg.)

_____
1979a   Paired Anthropomorphs of Central Washington. (Paper presented at the 5th Annual Rock Art Symposium, American Rock Art Research Association, Bottle Hollow, Utah.)

_____
1980   Anthropomorphic Motifs and Style in Plateau Rock Art. (Selected Papers from the 33d Annual Northwest Anthropological Conference, Bellingham, Washington). Department of Anthropology, Washington University.

_____
1984   Rock Art of the Dalles-Deschutes Region: A Chronological Perspective. (M.A. Thesis in Anthropology, Washington State University, Pullman.)

_____
1987   Alpine Obsidian Procurement in the Goat Rocks Wilderness: Preliminary Research. (Paper presented at the 40th Annual Northwest Anthropological Conference, Gleneden Beach, Salishan Lodge, Oreg.)

_____
1989   Alpine Obsidian Procurement in the Southern Washington Cascades: Preliminary Research. *Archaeology in Washington* 1:59–69. Bellingham, Wash.

McDermott, Louisa
1901   Folk-lore of the Flathead Indians of Idaho: Adventures of Coyote. *Journal of American Folk-lore* 14(55):240–251.

_____
1904   Ethnology and Folklore of Selish Proper. (M.S. Thesis [in Anthropology], University of California, Berkeley.)

McDonald, Angus
1917   Angus McDonald: A Few Items of the West. F.W. Howay,
            William S. Lewis, and Jacob A. Meyers, eds. *Washington His-
            torical Quarterly* 8(3):188–229.

McDonald, Archibald
1826–1827   [Journal of Occurrences at Thompson's River (Fort Kam-
            loops), 1826–1827.] (Manuscript B. 97/a/2 in Hudson's Bay
            Company Archives, Provincial Archives of Manitoba, Win-
            nipeg.)

1827   [A Sketch of the Thompson River District.] (Microfiche of
            map in the Provincial Archives of British Columbia.
            CM/A354, Victoria.)

1947   Thompson River District Report [1827]. Pp. 224–233 in Part
            of Dispatch from George Simpson... 1829. E.E. Rich, ed.
            (*Hudson's Bay Record Society* 10.) London: Hudson's Bay
            Record Society.

1971   Peace River: A Canoe Voyage from Hudson's Bay to the
            Pacific by the Late Sir George Simpson (Governor Hon. Hud-
            son's Bay Company) in 1828; Journal of the Late Chief Fac-
            tor, Archibald McDonald (Hon. Hudson's Bay Company)
            Who Accompanied Him. Edmonton, Alta.: M.G. Hurtig.
            (Originally publ.: Durie & Son, Ottawa, 1872.)

McDonald, Donald
1927   [Testimony of Donald McDonald, 22 December 1927,
            Spokane City, Wash.] (Manuscript in Record Group 75, No.
            2295, Records of the Bureau of Indian Affairs, National
            Archives, Washington.)

McDonald, James A.
1982   Targhee National Forest Cultural Resources Overview.
            (Report on file, Targhee National Forest, Idaho.)

McDonald, Jo, Kelvin Officer, Tim Jull, Doug Donahue, John Head, and
Bruce Ford
1990   Investigating 14C AMS: Dating Prehistoric Rock Art in the
            Sydney Sandstone Basin, Australia. *Rock Art Research: The
            Journal of the Australian Rock Art Research Association*
            7(2):83–92. Melbourne.

McDonnel, Roger F.
1965   Land Tenure among the Upper Thompson Indians. (M.A.
            Thesis in Anthropology, University of British Columbia, Van-
            couver.)

McFee, Malcolm
1972   The Modern Blackfeet: Montanans on a Reservation. New
            York: Holt, Rinehart and Winston. (Reprinted: Waveland
            Press, Prospect Heights, Ill., 1986.)

McGeorge, Alice Sutton
1939   Kamaiwea: The Coeur d'Alene. Kansas City: Burton Publish-
            ing Company.

McGillivray, Joseph
1947   Report of Fort Alexandria [1828]. Pp. 188–221 in Part of Dis-
            patch from George Simpson... 1829. E.E. Rich, ed. (*Hudson's
            Bay Record Society* 10.) London: Hudson's Bay Record Society.

McGillivray, Simon, Jr., and William Kittson
1831–1832   [Journal: Fort Nez Perces, Outfit 1831.] (Manuscript B.
            146/a/1, Hudson's Bay Company Archives, Provincial
            Archives of Manitoba, Winnipeg.)

M'Gonigle, Michael, and Wendy Wickwire
1988   Stein, the Way of the River. Vancouver, B.C.: Talon Books.

MacGregor, James G.
1966   Peter Fidler: Canada's Forgotten Surveyor, 1769–1822.
            Toronto: McClelland and Stewart.

1974   Overland by the Yellowhead. Saskatoon, Sask.: Western Pro-
            ducer Book Service.

McGuire, Randall H.
1992   Archaeology and the First Americans. *American Anthropolo-
            gist* 94(4):816–836.

McIntyre, D.N.
1914   The Fisheries. *Canada and Its Provinces* 23(Pt. II):445.
            Toronto.

Mack, Richard N., N.W. Rutter, and S. Valastro
1978   Late Quaternary Pollen Record from the Sanpoil River Valley,
            Washington. *Canadian Journal of Botany* 56:1642–1650.
            Ottawa.

1979   Holocene Vegetation History of the Okanogan Valley, Wash-
            ington. *Quaternary Research* 12(2):212–225. New York.

1983   Holocene Vegetational History of the Kootenai River Valley,
            Montana. *Quaternary Research* 20(2):177–193. New York.

Mack, Richard N., N.W. Rutter, Vaughn M. Bryant, Jr., and S. Valastro
1978   Late Quaternary Pollen Record from Big Meadow, Pend Oreille
            County, Washington. *Ecology* 59(5):956–965. Tempe, Ariz.

1978a   Reexamination of Post Glacial Vegetation History in Northern
            Idaho. *Quaternary Research* 10(2):241–255. New York.

McKay, J.W.
1858   [Report of a Journey Through a Part of the Fraser's River,
            1858.] (Manuscript A/C/20M191.1 in British Columbia
            Archives and Records Service, Victoria.)

MacKay, Joseph W.
1891   [Letter of August 25, 1891.] Pp. 76–87 in *Canadian Session-
            al Papers* 24(18). Ottawa.

1895   [Letter to James A. Teit; Postal card dated June 11, 1895.]
            (Manuscript No. 31 [Freeman No. 2480] in the American
            Philosophical Society Library, Philadelphia.)

1899   The Indians of British Columbia: A Brief Review of Their
            Probable Origin, History and Customs. Victoria and Vancou-
            ver: The British Columbia Mining Record.

McKay, William C.
1839–1892   [William Cameron McKay Papers, 1839–1892.] (Microfilm
            copy in Special Collections, University of Oregon Library, of
            originals copied by permission of the late J.R. Raley, Pendle-
            ton, Oreg.)

1871   [Report of William Cameron McKay to Superintendent A.B.
            Meacham, 1871.] (Manuscript D.20/71, Umatilla County
            Library, Pendleton, Oreg.)

McKelvie, Bruce A.
1947   Fort Langley: Outpost of Empire. Vancouver, B.C.: Vancouver
            Daily Province. (Reprinted: Nelson and Sons, Toronto, Ont.,
            1957.)

McKenna-McBride Commission *see* Canada. Royal Commission on Indian
Affairs

Mackenzie, Sir Alexander
1801   Voyages from Montreal, on the River St. Lawrence, Through
            the Continent of North America, to the Frozen and Pacific
            Oceans; in the Years 1789 and 1793. London: Printed for T.
            Cadell, Jr. (Reprinted: [in] The Journals and Letters of Sir
            Alexander Mackenzie. W. Kaye Lamb, ed. Cambridge Uni-
            versity Press, Cambridge, Mass., 1970.)

1902   Alexander Mackenzie's Voyage to the Pacific Ocean in 1793.
            London: J. Lee. (Reprinted: Citadel Press, New York, 1967.)

McKeown, Martha F.
1959   Come to Our Salmon Feast. Portland, Oreg.: Binfords and Mort.

Mackey, Harold
1974   The Kalapuyans: A Sourcebook on the Indians of the Willamette Valley. Salem, Oreg.: Mission Mill Museum Association.

MacKinnon, Andy, Dellis Meidinger, and Karel Klinka
1992   Use of the Biogeoclimatic Ecosystem Classification System in British Columbia. *Forestry Chronicle* 68(1):100–120. Oshawa, Ont.

MacLaury, Robert E.
1987   Color-Category Evolution and Shuswap Yellow-with-Green. *American Anthropologist* 89(1):107–124.

McLeod, C. Milo, and Douglas A. Melton
1984   An Examination and Test Excavation of Archaeological Sites within the Magruder Corridor and Selway River Drainage Bitterroot National Forest, Idaho County, Idaho, or Snakes along the Selway. Missoula, Mont.: Bitterroot National Forest.

_____   The Prehistory of the Lolo and Bitterroot National Forests
1986   (An Overview) : or "Making It in a Marginal Environment the Past 10,000 Years!". (USDA Forest Service, Northern Region, Lolo and Bitterroot National Forests, Idaho and Mont.)

McLeod, John
1823   [Report: Kamloops, April 1823.] (In: Alexander Kennedy's Spokan House Report, 1822–1823; Manuscript B.208/e/1 in Hudson's Bay Company Archives, Provincial Archives of Manitoba, Winnipeg.)

McLoughlin, John
1941–1944   The Letters of John McLoughlin from Fort Vancouver to the Governor and Committee. 3 vols. Toronto: The Champlain Society.

_____   Letters of Dr. John McLoughlin, Written at Fort Vancouver,
1948   1829–1832. Burt Brown Baker, ed. Portland, Oreg.: Binfords and Mort for the Oregon Historical Society.

MacMurray, J.W.
1884   [Reports of August 26th and September 19th, 1884, to the Acting Assistant Adjutant General, Department of the Columbia.] (Manuscripts in Record Group 94, Letters Received, National Archives, Washington.)

_____   The "Dreamers" of the Columbia River Valley, in Washington
1887   Territory. *Transactions of the Albany Institute* 11:241–248. Albany: Webster and Skinners.

MacNab, Gordon
1972   A History of the McQuinn Strip. [Warm Springs, Oreg.: Tribal Council of the Confederated Tribes of the Warm Springs Reservation.]

McNickle, D'Arcy
1936   The Surrounded. New York: Dodd, Mead. (Reprinted: University of New Mexico Press, Albuquerque, 1978, 1994.)

McPhail, J.D., and C.C. Lindsey
1986   Zoogeography of the Freshwater Fishes of Cascadia (The Columbia System and Rivers North to the Stikine). Pp. 615–638 in the Zoogeography of North American Freshwater Fishes. C.H. Hocutt and E.O. Wiley, eds. New York: John Wiley.

McPherson, Penny J., Carol A. Coe, Lois Ann Day, David M. Hall, and Vincent J. McGlone
1981   Archaeological Excavation in the Blue Mountains: Mitigation of Sites 35UN52, 35UN74, and 35UN95 in the Vicinity of Ladd Canyon, Union County, Oregon. (Report of Western Cultural Resource Management, Inc., to Northwest Pipeline Corporation.)

McWhorter, Lucullus Virgil
1913   The Crime Against the Yakimas. North Yakima, Wash.: Republic Print. (Reprinted: Shorey Book Store, Seattle, 1965.)

_____   The Continued Crime against the Yakimas. *American Patriot*.
1916

_____   The Discards: By He-Mene Ka-Wan, "Old Wolf." [Yakima,
1920   Wash.]: L.V. McWhorter.

_____   Tragedy of Wahk-Shum: Prelude to the Yakima Indian War,
1937   1855–1856. Yakima, Wash.: L.V. McWhorter. (Reprinted: Ye Galleon Press, Fairfield, Wash., 1968.)

_____   [Report by Lucullus Virgil McWhorter to the Washington
1939   State Historical Society concerning a Visit to the Mouth of the Palouse River in July, 1939.] (Manuscript in Lucullus Virgil McWhorter Collection, File No. 1529, Washington State University, Holland Library Archives, Pullman.)

_____   Yellow Wolf: His Own Story. Caldwell, Idaho: The Caxton
1940   Printers.

_____   Hear Me, My Chiefs! Nez Perce History and Legend. Ruth
1952   Bordin, ed. Caldwell, Idaho: The Caxton Printers.

_____   Yellow Wolf: His Own Story. Reprint ed. Caldwell, Idaho:
1983   The Caxton Printers.

Maddock, J.G.
1895   The Klickitat Indians. *Northwest Miscellany* 1(20):306–311. New York.

Magne, Martin
1984   Taseko Lakes Prehistory Project: Report on a Preliminary Survey. (Report on file, Laboratory of Archaeology, University of British Columbia, Vancouver.)

_____   Taseko Lakes Prehistory Project Phase II: Preliminary Exca-
1985   vations. (Report on file, Laboratory of Archaeology, University of British Columbia, Vancouver.)

Magne, Martin, and R.G. Matson
1982   Identification of 'Salish' and 'Athapaskan' Side-Notched Points from the Interior Plateau of British Columbia. Pp. 57–80 in Approaches to Algonquian Archaeology. M.G. Hanna and B. Kooyman, eds. Calgary: University of Calgary Archaeological Association.

_____   Athapaskan and Earlier Archaeology at Big Eagle Lake,
1984   British Columbia. (Manuscript, Laboratory of Archaeology, University of British Columbia, Vancouver.)

_____   Projectile Point and Lithic Assemblage Ethnicity in Interior
1987   British Columbia. Pp. 227–242 in Ethnicity and Culture: Proceedings of the Eighteenth Annual Conference of the Archaeological Association of the University of Calgary. R. Auger, M.F. Glass, S. MacEachern, and P.H. McCartney, eds. Calgary, Alta.: University of Calgary Archaeological Association.

Majors, Harry M.
1981   John McClellan in the Montana Rockies 1807: The First Americans after Lewis and Clark. *Northwest Discovery* 2(9):554–630.

Malan, Vernon D.
1948   Language and Social Change among the Flathead Indians. (M.A. Thesis in Sociology, University of Montana, Missoula.)

Mallery, Garrick
1881   Sign Language among North American Indians; Compared with That among Other Peoples and Deaf-Mutes. Pp. 263–552 in *1st Annual Report of the Bureau of [American]*

Ethnology for 1879-'80. Washington. (Reprinted, with articles by A.L. Kroeber and C.F. Voegelin in: *Approaches to Semiotics* 14. Mouton, The Hague, 1972.)

1886   Pictographs of the North American Indians: A Preliminary Paper. Pp. 3–256 in *4th Annual Report of the Bureau of [American] Ethnology for 1882–1883*. Washington.

1893   Picture-Writing of the American Indians. Pp. 3–822 in *10th Annual Report of the Bureau of [American] Ethnology [for] 1888–1889*. Washington. (Reprinted, 2 vols.: Dover Publications, New York, 1972.)

Mallory, Oscar L.
1961   An Archaeological Survey of Pacific Gas Transmission Company's Alberta to California Pipeline System: MP 108.0 to MP 722.0. *Washington State University. Laboratory of Anthropology. Report of Investigations* 12. Pullman.

Maloney, Alice B., ed.
1945   Fur Brigade to the Bonaventura: John Work's California Expedition, 1832–1833, for the Hudson's Bay Company. San Francisco: California Historical Society.

Malouf, Carling I.
1954   Turn the Indians Loose? (Mimeograph, Montana State University [now University of Montana], Missoula.)

1956   Montana Western Region. Pp. 45–52 in Northwest Archaeology Number, by Richard D. Daugherty et al. *Research Studies of the State College of Washington* 24(1). Pullman, Wash.

1956a   The Cultural Connections Between the Prehistoric Inhabitants of the Upper Missouri and Columbia River Systems. (Ph.D. Dissertation in Anthropology, Colombia University, New York City.)

1957   Louis Pierre's Affair. In: Historical Essays on Montana and the Northwest. J.W. Smurr and K. Ross Toole, eds. A *Publication of the Western Press* 1. Helena, Mont.

1974   Economy and Land Use by the Indians of Western Montana. Pp. 117–178 in Interior Salish and Eastern Washington Indians II. *American Indian Ethnohistory: Indians of the Northwest*. New York: Garland.

1982   A Study of the Prehistoric and Historic Sites along the Lower Clark Fork River Valley, Western Montana. *University of Montana. Contributions to Anthropology* 7. Missoula.

Malouf, Carling I., and Thain White
1953   Kutenai Calendar Records. *Montana Magazine of History* 3(2):34–39. Helena.

Mandelbaum, May
1938   The Individual Life Cycle. Pp. 101–129 in the Sinkaietk or Southern Okanagon of Washington. Leslie Spier, ed. *General Series in Anthropology* 6; *Contributions from the Laboratory of Anthropology* 2. Menasha, Wis.: George Banta.

Manion, Elizabeth
1981   Faunal Analysis of Big Creek Cave, Idaho: Preliminary Report (10VY67). (Manuscript, USDA Forest Service, Intermountain Region, Ogden, Utah.)

Manring, Benjamin F.
1912   The Conquest of the Coeur d'Alenes, Spokanes and Palouses: The Expeditions of Colonels E.J. Steptoe and George Wright against the "Northern Indians" in 1858. Spokane, Wash.: Inland Printing. (Reprinted: Ye Galleon Press, Fairfield, Wash., 1975.)

Mansfield, Joseph K.F.
1963   Mansfield on the Condition of the Western Forts, 1853–1854. Robert W. Fraser, ed. Norman: University of Oklahoma Press.

Manson, William
1862   [Fort Kamloops Journal, 1859–1862.] (Manuscript A C20 K12–A in Royal British Columbia Archives, Victoria.)

Manzione, Joseph A.
1991   "I am looking to the north for my life": Sitting Bull, 1876–1881. *University of Utah Publications in the American West* 25. Salt Lake City: University of Utah Press. (Reprinted, paperback ed., 1994.)

Mark, Joan T.
1988   A Stranger in Her Native Land: Alice Fletcher and the American Indians. Lincoln: University of Nebraska Press.

Markos, Jeffery A., J. Gallison, J.J. Flenniken, and T. Ozbun
1990   Results of Archaeological Testing and Evaluation of the Russel Bar Site, 10IH58. (Manuscript on file, Nez Perce National Forest, Grangeville, Idaho.)

Marr, John Paul
1941   [Molala Sound Recording.] (Aluminum discs, Nos. 1178–1185, in John Peabody Harrington Collection, National Anthropological Archives, Smithsonian Institution, Washington.)

Marshall, Alan G.
1977   Nez Perce Social Groups: An Ecological Interpretation. (Ph.D. Dissertation in Anthropology, Washington State University, Pullman. Photocopy: University Microfilms International, Ann Arbor, Mich., 1981.)

Martin, Lucille J.
1968   Modoc Assimilation: An Acculturation Study of the Modoc Indians in the Mid-Western States. (M.A. Thesis in Anthropology, Wichita State University, Wichita, Kans.)

Mason, Otis Tufton
1887   The Occurrence of Similar Inventions in Areas Widely Apart. *Science* 9(226):534–535.

1896   Influence of the Environment upon Human Industries or Arts. Pp. 639–665 in *Annual Report of the ... Smithsonian Institution ... to July 1895*. Washington.

1904   Aboriginal American Indian Basketry. Washington: Government Printing Office. (Reprinted: P. Smith, Santa Barbara, Calif., 1976.)

1907   Environment. Pp. 427–430 in Pt. 1 of Handbook of American Indians North of Mexico. Frederick W. Hodge, ed. 2 Pts. *Bureau of American Ethnology Bulletin* 30. Washington. (Reprinted: Rowman and Littlefield, New York, 1971.)

Masterson, James R.
1946   The Records of the Washington Superintendency of Indian Affairs, 1853–1874. *Pacific Northwest Quarterly* 37(1):31–57.

Mathewes, Rolf W.
1978   The Environment and Biotic Resources of the Lillooet Area. Pp. 68–99 in Reports of the Lillooet Archaeological Project, No. 1: Introduction and Setting. A.H. Stryd and S. Lawhead, eds. *Canada. National Museum of Man. Mercury Series. Archaeological Survey Paper* 73. Ottawa.

1985   Paleobotanical Evidence for Climatic Change During Lateglacial and Holocene Time. Pp. 397–422 in Climatic Change in Canada, 5: Critical Periods in the Quaternary Climatic History of Northern North America. C.R. Harrington, ed. *Syllogeus* 55. Ottawa: National Museums of Canada, National Museum of Natural Sciences. (Prefatory material in French.)

Mathewes, Rolf W., and Miriam King
1989   Holocene Vegetation, Climate, and Lake-level Changes in the Interior Douglas-Fir Biogeoclimate Zone, British Columbia. *Canadian Journal of Earth Sciences* 26(9):1811–1825. Ottawa.

717

Mathewes, Rolf W., and C.E. Rouse
1975   Palynology and Paleoecology of Postglacial Sediments from the Lower Fraser Canyon of British Columbia. *Canadian Journal of Earth Sciences* 12:745–756. Ottawa.

Mathews, Stephen B., and Henry C. Wendler
1968   Economic Criteria for Decision to Catch Between Sport and Commercial Fisheries with Special Reference to Columbia River Chinook Salmon. *U.S. Department of Fish and Fish Resources* 3(1):93–105. Washington.

Matson, R.G.
1982   The Parallel Direct Historical Approach: Ethnic Identification at Eagle Lake, B.C. Pp. 233–242 in Approaches to Algonquian Archaeology. M.G. Hanna and B. Kooyman, eds. Calgary, Alta.: University of Calgary Archaeological Association.

Matson, R.G., L.C. Ham, and D.E. Bunyan
1984   Prehistoric Settlement Patterns at the Mouth of the Chilcotin River. (Manuscript, Laboratory of Archaeology, University of British Columbia, Vancouver.)

Matt, Clayton
1997   [Statistical Information from Archival Research conducted by Natural Resources Department, Confederated Salish and Kootenai Tribes, Pablo, Mont.]

Matthewson, Lisa
1996   Determiner Systems and Quantificational Strategies: Evidence from Salish. (Ph.D. Dissertation in Linguistics, University of British Columbia, Vancouver.)

Mattina, Anthony
1973   Colville Grammatical Structure. (Ph.D. Dissertation in Linguistics, University of Hawaii, Honolulu. Published in the series: *University of Hawaii Working Papers in Linguistics* 5(4). Honolulu, 1973.)

————
1979   Pharyngeal Movement in Colville and Related Phenomena in the Interior Salishan Languages. *International Journal of American Linguistics* 45(1):17–24.

————
1980   Imperative Formations in Colville-Okanagan and in the Other Interior Languages. Pp. 208–228 in *15th International Conference on Salish Languages.* Vancouver, B.C.

————, ed. 1985 *see* Seymour, Peter J. 1985

————
1987   Colville-Okanagan Dictionary. *University of Montana Occasional Papers in Linguistics* 5. Missoula.

————
1993   (V)C₂ Reduplication in Colville-Okanagan, with Historical Notes. Pp. 215–235 in American Indian Linguistics and Ethnography in Honor of Laurence C. Thompson. Anthony Mattina and Timothy Montler, eds. *University of Montana Occasional Papers in Linguistics* 10. Missoula.

————, ed. 1993a see En'owkin Centre 1993

————
1994   Blue Jay and His Brother-in-Law Wolf. Pp. 332–345 in Coming to Light: Contemporary Translations of the Native Literatures of North America. Brian Swann, ed. New York: Random House.

Mattina, Anthony, and Clara Jack
1990   Okanagan Communication and Language. Pp. 143–165 in Okanagan Sources. Jean Webber and The En'owkin Centre, eds. Penticton, B.C.: Theytus Books.

————
1992   Okanagan-Colville Kinship Terms. *Anthropological Linguistics* 34(1–4):117–137.

Mattina, Anthony, and Timothy Montler, eds.
1993   American Indian Linguistics and Ethnography in Honor of Laurence C. Thompson. *University of Montana Occasional Papers in Linguistics* 10. Missoula.

Mattina, Nancy J.
1996   Aspect and Category in Okanagan Word Formation. (Ph.D. Dissertation in Linguistics, Simon Fraser University, Burnaby, B.C.)

Mattson, Daniel M.
1983   Cultural Resource Investigations of the Dworshak Reservoir Project, North Fork Clearwater River, Northern Idaho. With Contributions by Ruthann Knudson, Robert Lee Sappington, and Michael A. Pfeiffer. *University of Idaho. Anthropological Research Manuscript Series* 74. Moscow.

————
1984   The Occurrence of Peripherally-Flaked Cobble Tools in the Clearwater River Valley, North Central Idaho. (M.A. Thesis in Anthropology, University of Idaho, Moscow.)

Mattson, Daniel M., et al. 1983 *see* Mattson, Daniel M. 1983

Matzke, Gordon F.
1985   Hunting and Fishing. Pp. 132–135 in Atlas of the Pacific Northwest. A. Jon Kimberling and Philip L. Jackson, eds. 7th ed. Corvallis: Oregon State University Press.

Maud, Ralph, ed. 1978 *see* Hill-Tout, Charles 1978

May, Robert
1969   Homicide of a Community: Termination This Time for the Colville Indians. Pp. 817–849 in The Education of American Indians, Vol. 4: The Organization Question. *91st Congress. 1st Session. Committee Print.* 4 vols. Washington: United States Senate, Committee on Labor and Public Welfare.

Mayne, Richard C.
1862   Four Years in British Columbia and Vancouver Island: An Account of Their Forests, Rivers, Coasts, Gold Fields and Resources for Colonisation. London: J. Murray. (Reprinted: Johnson Reprint, New York, 1969.)

Meacham, Alfred B.
1875   Wigwam and War-path; or, The Royal Chief in Chains. 2d and rev. ed. Boston: John P. Dale and Co.

————
1876   Wi-ne-ma (The Woman-Chief) and Her People. Hartford, Conn.: American Publishing. (Reprinted: AMS Press, New York, 1980.)

————
1883   The Tragedy of the Lava Beds: A Lecture Delivered by Alfred B. Meacham, in Park Street Church, Boston, Massachusetts, May 24, 1874. Washington: Bland Publishers. (Originally publ. by The Author, Hartford, Conn, 1877.)

Meason, William
1888   [Letter of September 15, 1888.] Pp. 112–113 in *Canadian Sessional Papers* 22(16). Ottawa.

Meatte, Daniel S.
1989   Prehistory of the Western Snake River Basin: An Overview. (M.A. Thesis in Anthropology, Idaho State University, Pocatello. Published: *Occasional Papers of the Idaho Museum of Natural History* 35. Pocatello.)

Medicine Horse, Mary Helen (Ishtaléeschia Báachiia Héeleetaalawe), comp.
1987   A Dictionary of Everyday Crow: Crow-English / English-Crow. Rev. ed. Preface by G.H. Matthews. Crow Agency, Mont.: Bilingual Materials Development Center. (First ed. publ. in 1979.)

Mehringer, Peter J., Jr.
1985   Late-Quaternary Pollen Records from the Interior Pacific Northwest and Northern Great Basin of the United States. Pp. 167–189 in Pollen Records of Late-Quaternary North American Sediments. Vaughn A. Bryant, Jr., and R.G. Holloway, eds. Dallas: American Association of Stratigraphic Palynologists.

1985a   Late-Quaternary Vegetation and Climates of South-Central Washington. (Report to Battelle/Pacific Northwest Laboratories, Richland, Wash.)

1989   Age of the Clovis Cache at East Wenatchee, Washington. (A Report to the Washington State Historic Preservation Office.) Pullman: Washington State University, Department of Anthropology.

1991   [Unpublished data on the Late Pleistocene and Early Holocene palynology of Wild Lake, Washington.] (Prepared for Pacific Northwest Laboratory, Richland, Wash.)

Mehringer, Peter J., Jr., Stephen F. Arno, and Kenneth L. Petersen
1977   Postglacial History of Lost Trail Pass Bog, Bitterroot Mountains, Montana. *Arctic and Alpine Research* 9(4):345–368. Boulder, Colo.

Meidinger, Dellis V., and Jim Pojar, comps. and eds.
1991   Ecosystems of British Columbia. *British Columbia. Ministry of Forests. Special Report Series* 6. Victoria.

Meighan, Arthur
1919   Annual Report of the Department of Indian Affairs for the Year Ended March 31, 1919. *Canadian Sessional Papers* 27(56/8). Ottawa.

Meighan, Clement W.
1984   Archaeology: Science or Sacrilege? Pp. 208–223 in Ethics and Values in Archaeology. E.L. Green, ed. New York: Free Press.

Meilleur, Brien A., Eugene S. Hunn, and Rachel L. Cox
1990   *Lomatium dissectum* (Apiaceae): Multi-Purpose Plant of the Pacific Northwest. *Journal of Ethnobiology* 10(1):1–20.

Meinig, Donald W.
1968   The Great Columbia Plain: A Historical Geography, 1805–1910. (*The Emil and Kathleen Sick Lecture-book Series in Western History and Biography*). Seattle: University of Washington Press. (Reprinted in 1995/1996, with a Foreword by William Cronon, and a New Preface by the Author.)

Melton, Douglas A.
1983   Review of "Archaeological Investigations in the Avon Valley" by Lewis K. Napton. *Archaeology in Montana* 24(2):153–155. Bozeman.

1984   From the Plains to Palouse, the Basin to the Boreal: An Essay on the Cultural Chronology of the Central Northern Rockies. (In: An Archaeological Reconnaissance of the Nevada Creek Drainage, Powell County, Montana. C. Cameron, ed. Draft report submitted to the Montana State Historic Preservation Office. Rev. in 1985.)

Menefee, Leah Collins, and Lowell Tiller
1977   Cutoff Fever, II. *Oregon Historical Quarterly* 78(1)41–72.

Mengarini, Gregory
1861   A Selish or Flat-head Grammar. [Added t.p.: Grammatica linguae selicae.] *Shea's Library of American Linguistics* 2. New York: Cramoisy Press. (Reprinted: AMS Press, New York, 1970.)

1938   Mengarini's Narrative of The Rockies: Memoirs of Old Oregon, 1841–1850, and St. Mary's Mission. *Historical Reprints, Sources of Northwest History* 25. Missoula: State University of Montana.

1977   Recollections of the Flathead Mission: Containing Brief Observations Both Ancient and Contemporary Concerning This Particular Nation; by Gregory Mengarini. Gloria Ricci Lothrop, trans. and ed. Glendale, Calif.: Arthur H. Clark.

Merbs, Charles
1989   Patterns of Health and Sickness in the Precontact Southwest. Pp. 41–55 in Columbian Consequences, Volume 1: Archaeo-logical and Historical Perspectives on the Spanish Borderlands West. David Hurst Thomas, ed. Washington: Smithsonian Institution Press.

Merk, Frederick, ed. 1931 *see* Simpson, Sir George 1931

1963   Manifest Destiny and Mission in American History: A Reinterpretation. New York: A. Knopf.

Merriam, Alan P.
1951   Flathead Indian Instruments and Their Music. *Musical Quarterly* 37:368–375.

1953   Introduction to Song and Dances of the Flathead Indians. *Ethnic Folkways Library*, recording P445.

1955   The Hand Game of the Flathead Indians. *Journal of American Folklore* 68(269):313–324.

1965   The Importance of Song in the Flathead Indian Vision Quest. *Ethnomusicology* 9(2):91–99. Middletown, Conn.

1967   Ethnomusicology of the Flathead Indians. *Viking Fund Publications in Anthropology* 44. New York: Wenner-Gren Foundation for Anthropological Research.

Merriam, Alan P., and Barbara W. Merriam
1950   Flathead Indian Music: Report on Field Research, Summer 1950. (Typescript; copy in Anthropology Library, National Museum of Natural History, Smithsonian Institution, Washington.)

Merriam, H.G., ed. 1973 *see* Ronan, Mary 1973

Mierendorf, Robert R.
1984   Radiocarbon Dates. Pp. 591–592 in Cultural Resources Investigations for Libby Reservoir, Northwest Montana. Vol. 1: Environment, Archaeology, and Land Use Patterns in the Middle Kootenai River Valley. Alston V. Thoms, ed. *Washington State University. Center for Northwest Anthropology. Project Report* 2(1). Pullman.

Miller, C. Daniel
1969   Chronology of Neoglacial Moraines in the Dome Park Area, North Cascade Range, Washington. *Arctic and Alpine Research* 1(1):49–66. Boulder, Colo.

Miller, C. Marc
1956   [Appraisal of Coeur d'Alene Tract, Idaho and Washington, 1873, 1887, 1891. Case Number 81 before the Indian Claims Commission.] (Report prepared for the Lands Division, U.S. Department of Justice, Washington. Microfilm in Idaho State Historical Society, Boise.)

Miller, Christopher L.
1985   Prophetic Worlds: Indians and Whites on the Columbia Plateau. New Brunswick, N.J.: Rutgers University Press.

Miller, G. Lynette
1986   Flat Twined Bags of the Plateau. (M.A. Thesis in Anthropology, University of Washington, Seattle.)

Miller, Harriet, and Elizabeth Harrison
1974   Coyote Tales of the Montana Salish. Pierre Pichette, narrator; Fred E. Rouiller, illus. Rapid City, S. Dak.: Tipi Shop.

Miller, Jay
1977–1996   [Colville Interior Salish fieldnotes.] (Manuscripts in J. Miller's possession.)

1985   Salish Kinship: Why Decedence? *Proceedings of the 20th International Conference on Salish and Neighboring Languages, August 15–17, 1985.* Vancouver, B.C.

1989   Mourning Dove: The Author as Cultural Mediator. Pp. 160–182 in Being and Becoming Indian: Biographical Studies of North American Frontiers. James Clifton, ed. Chicago: Dorsey Press.

1989a   An Overview of Northwest Coast Mythology. *Northwest Anthropological Research Notes* 23(2):125–141. Moscow, Idaho.

———, ed. 1990 *see* Mourning Dove 1990

1992   Earthmaker: Tribal Stories from Native North America. New York: Perigee Books.

Miller, Joaquin
1873   Life amongst the Modocs: Unwritten History. London: R. Bentley and Son. (Also pub. with titles: Unwritten History; Paquita, the Indian Heroine; My Own Story; [etc.].)

Miller, Tom O., Jr.
1954   Four Burials from the Coeur d'Alene Region, Idaho. *American Antiquity* 19(4):389–390.

1959   Archaeological Survey of Kootenai Country, North Idaho. *Tebiwa: Journal of the Idaho State University Museum* 2:38–51. Pocatello.

Miller, Wick R.
1966   Anthropological Linguistics in the Great Basin. Pp. 75–112 in The Current Status of Anthropological Research in the Great Basin: 1964. Warren L. d'Azevedo et al., eds. *University of Nevada. Desert Research Institute. Social Sciences and Humanities Publications* 1. Reno.

Millstein, Henry Morrison
1979–1993   [Linguistic and ethnographic notes, from fieldwork among Warm Springs Reservation Sahaptins, Wascos, and Paiutes, Oreg.] (Manuscript in Millstein's possession and on file with The Confederated Tribes of the Warm Springs Reservation.)

1991   Giving the Past a Voice: The Confederated Tribes of the Warm Springs Reservation. Pp. 115–122 in The First Oregonians: An Illustrated Collection of Essays on Traditional Lifeways, Federal-Indian Relations, and the State's Native People Today. Carolyn M. Buan and Richard Lewis, eds. Portland: Oregon Council for the Humanities.

Milton, William F., and Walter B. Cheadle
1865   The North-west Passage by Land: Being the Narrative of an Expedition from the Atlantic to the Pacific, Undertaken with the View of Exploring a Rout Across the Continent to British Columbia.... By Viscount Milton and W.B. Cheadle. London: Cassell, Petter, and Galpin. (Reprinted, 8th ed.: Canadiana House, Toronto, 1969.)

Ministry of Aboriginal Affairs
1991   Treaty Negotiation and Openness Principles. Victoria, B.C.: Ministry of Aboriginal Affairs.

1995   Information About Landmark Court Cases. Victoria, B.C.: Ministry of Aboriginal Affairs.

1995a   Information About Treaty Negotiations in B.C. Victoria, B.C.: Ministry of Aboriginal Affairs.

1995b   Information About Interim Measures. Victoria, B.C.: Ministry of Aboriginal Affairs.

1997   First Nations in the Six-Step Process. Victoria, B.C.: Ministry of Aboriginal Affairs.

1997a   Glossary of Treaty-Related Terms. Victoria, B.C.: Ministry of Aboriginal Affairs.

Minor, Rick, and Brian E. Hemphill
1990   Archaeological Assessment of the Crates Point Site (35WS221), Wasco County, Oregon. *Heritage Research Associates Report* 90. Eugene, Oreg.

Minor, Rick, and Kathryn Anne Toepel
1984   Lava Island Rockshelter: An Early Hunting Camp in Central Oregon. With Appendices by Becky Saleeby ... [et al.]. *Occasional Papers of the Idaho Museum of Natural History* 34. Pocatello.

1986   Archaeological Assessment of the Bob's Point Site (45KL219), Klickitat County, Washington. With Contributions by Ruth L. Greenspan, Patricia F. McDowell. 2 vols. *Heritage Research Associates Report* 42. Eugene, Oreg.

1986a   Archaeological Investigations for the Old Town Umatilla Bank Revetment Project, Umatilla County, Oregon. *Heritage Research Associates Report* 47. Eugene, Oreg.

Minto, John
1901   Reminiscences of Honorable John Minto, Pioneer of 1844. (Introd. by H.S. Lyman.) 2 Pts. Pt. 1: The Oregon Trail in 1844; Pt. 2: Reminiscences of Experiences on the Oregon Trail in 1844. *Oregon Historical Quarterly* 2(2):119–167, (3):209–254.

Miss, Christian J.
1984   Archaeological Investigations at Site 45–DO–214, Chief Joseph Dam Project, Washington. Seattle: Office of Public Archaeology, University of Washington.

1984a   Archaeological Investigations at Site 45–DO–285, Chief Joseph Dam Project, Washington. Seattle: Office of Public Archaeology, University of Washington.

1984b   Archaeological Investigations at Site 45–OK–250/4, Chief Joseph Dam Project, Washington. Seattle: Office of Public Archaeology, University of Washington.

1984c   Archaeological Investigations at Site 45–OK–287/288, Chief Joseph Dam Project, Washington. Seattle: Office of Public Archaeology, University of Washington.

1985   Site Frequency, Intensity of Use, and Differentiation Through Time. Pp. 269–286 in Summary of Results, Chief Joseph Dam Cultural Resources Project, Washington. Sarah K. Campbell, ed. Seattle: Office of Public Archaeology, Institute for Environmental Studies, University of Washington.

1990   Test Excavations at Butcher Bar on the Lower Salmon River Idaho County, Idaho. (Manuscript, Salmon District Bureau of Land Management Office, Cottonwood, Idaho.)

Miss, Christian J., and Nancy Vaughan Anderson
1984   Archaeological Investigations at 10–CR–60, An Upland Spring Site in South-Central Idaho. (Manuscript, Salmon District Bureau of Land Management Office, Salmon, Idaho.)

Miss, Christian J., and Lorelea Hudson
1987   Cultural Resources Reconnaissance of the Albeni Falls Project, Northern Idaho. Sandpoint, Idaho: [CRC] Cultural Resource Consultants for the Seattle District, U.S. Army Corps of Engineers.

Mitchell, Darcy Anne
1977   The Allied Tribes of British Columbia: a Study in Pressure Group Behaviour. (M.A. Thesis in History, University of British Columbia, Vancouver.)

Mitchell, Donald H.
1970   Excavations on the Chilcotin Plateau: Three Sites, Three Phases. *Northwest Anthropological Research Notes* 4(1):99–116. Moscow, Idaho.

720

1970a   Archaeological Investigation on the Chilcotin Plateau, 1968. *Syesis* 3:45–65. Victoria, B.C.

Moberly, Walter
1885   The Rocks and Rivers of British Columbia. London: H. Blacklock. (Reprinted in 1926.)

Moeller, Bill, and Jan Moeller
1995   Chief Joseph and the Nez Perce: A Photographic History. Missoula, Mont.: Mountain Press Publishing Company.

Mohr, Albert, and L.L. Sample
1983   Upper Chinookan Fire Planes: Two New North American Fire-making Techniques. *Ethnology* 22(3):253–262.

Mohs, Gordon
1980   The Heritage Resources of the Western Shuswap Basin. An Inventory and Evaluation. *Heritage Conservation Branch Occasional Paper* 8. Victoria, B.C.

1982   Final Report on Excavations at (DjQi 1), Slocan Valley, British Columbia. (Report on file, Archaeology Branch, Victoria, B.C.)

1987   Spiritual Sites, Ethnic Significance and Native Spirituality: The Heritage and Heritage Sites of the Sto:Lo Indians of British Columbia. (M.A. Thesis in Anthropology, Simon Fraser University, Burnaby, B.C.)

Monroe, Robert D.
1982   The Earliest Pacific Northwest Indian Photograph (1860). Pp. [12] 13–20, 39–40 in Three Classic American Photographs, Texts and Contexts. Mick Gidley, ed. (*American Arts Pamphlet Series*). Exeter, England: American Arts Documentation Centre, University of Exeter.

Monteith, J.B.
1872   [Letter from J.B. Monteith to Hon. F.A. Walker, Lapwai, Idaho Territory, 13 August 1872.] (Manuscript in John A. Simms Papers, Box 1, File 5, Washington State University, Holland Library Archives, Pullman.)

Moodie, D. Wayne, and Barry Kaye
1977   The Ac Ko Mok Ki Map. *The Beaver: Magazine of the North* (Spring Issue):4–15. Winnipeg, Man.

Moody, Ula L.
1978   Microstratigraphy, Paleoecology, and Tephrochronology of the Lind Coulee Site, Central Washington. (Ph.D. Dissertation in Anthropology, Washington State University, Pullman.)

Mooney, James
1896   The Ghost-dance Religion and the Sioux Outbreak of 1890. Pp. 641–1136 in Pt. 2 of *14th Annual Report of the Bureau of American Ethnology for 1892–'93*. Washington. (Reprinted: Dover Publications, New York, 1973; also, with an Introduction by Raymond J. DeMallie, University of Nebraska Press, Lincoln, 1991.)

1928   The Aboriginal Population of America North of Mexico. John R. Swanton, ed. *Smithsonian Miscellaneous Collections* 80(7). Washington.

Moore, Joseph M., and Kenneth M. Ames
1979   Archaeological Inventory of the South Fork of the Payette River, Boise County, Idaho. (Report in Moore and Ames's possession.)

Moore, Robert E.
1980   How Coyote Thinks: Exploration of a Linguistic and Narrative Option in Upper Chinookan. (B.A. Thesis in Anthropology, Reed College, Portland, Oreg.)

1983–1993   [Linguistic and ethnographic notes from fieldwork among Wasco-Wishram speakers in Oregon and Washington.] (Manuscript in R. Moore's possession.)

1986   Code-switching, Performance, and Text in a Wasco Coyote from the Contemporary Reservation Period. (M.A. Thesis in Anthropology, University of Chicago, Chicago.)

1986a   Coyote and Five Sisters. *Studies in American Indian Literatures* 10(1):1–15.

1988   Lexicalization Versus Lexical Loss in Wasco-Wishram Language Obsolescence. *International Journal of American Linguistics* 54(4):453–468.

1993   Performance Form and the Voices of Characters in Five Versions of the Wasco Coyote Cycle. Pp. 213–240 in Reflexive Language: Reported Speech and Metapragmatics. John A. Lucy, ed. Cambridge: Cambridge University Press.

Moorhouse, (Major) Lee
1906   Souvenir Album of Noted Indian Photographs. 2d ed. Pendleton, Oreg.: East Oregonian Print.

Morgan, Lawrence R.
1980   Kootenay-Salishan Linguistic Comparison: A Preliminary Study. (M.A. Thesis in Linguistics, University of British Columbia, Vancouver. Microfiche: National Library of Canada, Ottawa, 1982).

1991   A Description of the Kutenai Language. (Ph.D. Dissertation in Linguistics, University of California, Berkeley.)

Morgan, Thomas J. *see* ARCIA for 1890

Morgan, Vincent
1981   Archaeological Reconnaissance of the North Richland Toll Bridge and Associated Access Roads (L6909). Cheney, Wash.: Archaeological and Historical Services, Eastern Washington University.

Morgolis, L., F.C. Cleaver, Y. Fukuda, and H. Godfrey
1966   Sockeye Salmon in Offshore Waters. Pp. 1–70 in Salmon of the North Pacific Ocean, Part 6. *International North Pacific Fisheries Commission Bulletin* 20. Vancouver, B.C.

Morrill, Allen, and Edith D. Morrill
1978   Out of the Blanket: The Story of Sue and Kate McBeth, Missionaries to the Nez Perces. Moscow: University of Idaho Press.

Moulton, Gary E., ed.
1983   The Journals of the Lewis and Clark Expedition. 11 vols. through 1997. Lincoln and London: University of Nebraska Press.

Mourning Dove (Humishuma, or Christine Quintasket)
1927   Co-ge-we-a, the Half Blood: A Depiction of the Great Montana Cattle Range ... given through Show-pow-tan, with Notes and Biographical Sketch by Lucullus Virgil McWhorter. Boston: The Four Seas Company. (Reprinted, with an Introduction by Dexter Fisher: University of Nebraska Press, Lincoln, 1981.)

1933   Coyote Stories. Heister Dean Guie, ed. and illus.; Notes by L.V. McWhorter (Old Wolf); Foreword by Chief Standing Bear. [1st ed.] Caldwell, Idaho: Caxton Printers. (Reprinted: Ye Galleon Press, Fairfield, Wash., 1976; also, AMS Press, New York, 1984; and, with Introd. and Notes by Jay Miller, University of Nebraska Press, Lincoln, 1990.)

1990   Mourning Dove: A Salishan Autobiography. Jay Miller, ed. Lincoln: University of Nebraska Press.

1990a   Coyote Stories, by Mourning Dove (Humishuma). Heister Dean Guie, ed. and illus.; Notes by L.V McWhorter (Old Wolf) and a Foreword by Chief Standing Bear; Introd. And Notes by Jay Miller. [Repr. ed.] Lincoln: University of Nebraska Press. (Originally publ.: Caxton Printers, Caldwell, Idaho, 1933.)

Muck, Lee
1926   Management Plan, Klamath Indian Forests. (Item 3 in A Forest in Trust. Alan S. Newell et al. Washington: U.S. Department of the Interior, Bureau of Indian Affairs Division of Forestry.)

Muckleston, Keith W.
1985   Water Resources. Pp. 71–79 in Atlas of the Pacific Northwest. A. Jon Kimberling and Philip L. Jackson, eds. 7th. ed. Corvallis: Oregon State University Press.

Mullan, John
1861   United States Millitary Road Expedition from Fort Walla-Walla to Fort Benton, W.T., by Lieutenant John Mullan, 2nd Artillery. Appendix 17, pp. 549–569 in Report of the Secretary of War for 1861. *37th Congress. 2d Session. Senate Executive Document* 2(1). (Serial No. 1118). Washington.

1863   U.S. Army Corps of Engineers Report on the Construction of a Military Road from Fort Walla-Walla to Fort Benton. *37th Congress. 3d Session. Senate Executive Document* 43, ("The Mullan Report"). Washington: Government Printing Office.

Mulloy, William
1952   The Northern Plains. Pp. 124–138 in Archaeology of the Eastern United States. James Griffin, ed. Chicago: University of Chicago Press.

1958   A Preliminary Historical Outline for the Northwestern Plains. *University of Wyoming Publications* 22(1). Laramie.

Munger, Benjamin S.
1993   High Country Archaeology in the Bitterroot Mountains. *Archaeology in Montana* 34(1):1–6. Bozeman.

1993a   Whitebark Pine: A Prehistoric Food Source at Timberline in the Bitterroot Mountains of Montana. (M.A. Thesis in Anthropology, University of California, Santa Barbara.)

Munnick, Harriet D., and Adrian R. Munnick, eds.
1989   Catholic Church Records of the Pacific Northwest: Missions of St. Ann and St. Rose of the Cayouse, 1847–1888, Walla Walla and Frenchtown, 1859–1872, Frenchtown, 1872–1888. Portland, Oreg.: Binford and Mort.

Munsell, David A.
1968   The Ryegrass Coulee Site. (M.A. Thesis in Anthropology, University of Washington, Seattle.)

Murdock, George Peter
1935   [Unpublished manuscript, Yale University Cross-Cultural Survey.] (Manuscript in Human Relations Area Files, Yale University, New Haven, Conn.)

1938   Notes on the Tenino, Molala, and Paiute of Oregon. *American Anthropologist* 40(3):395–402.

1938a   [Review of: *Tribal Distribution in Oregon*, by Joel V. Berreman.] *Pacific Northwest Quarterly* 29(3):316–317.

1941   Ethnographic Bibliography of North America. [1st ed.] *Yale Anthropological Studies* 1. New Haven, Conn.

1949   Social Structure. New York: Macmillan.

1953   Ethnographic Bibliography of North America. 2d ed. New Haven, Conn.: Human Relations Area Files.

1958   Social Organization of the Tenino. Pp. 299–315 in Miscellanea Paul Rivet Octogenario Dicata. [Mexico, D.F.]: Universidad Nacional Autónoma de México, XXXI Congreso Internacional de Americanistas. (Reprinted: Pp. 199–216 in Culture and Society: Twenty-Four Essays, by G.P. Murdock, University of Pittsburgh Press, Pittsburgh, 1965.)

1965   Culture and Society: Twenty-Four Essays. Pittsburgh: University of Pittsburgh Press.

1965a   Tenino Shamanism. *Ethnology* 4(2):165–171.

1967   Ethnographic Atlas. Pittsburgh: University of Pittsburgh Press.

1972   Ethnographic Bibliography of North America. 3d ed. New Haven, Conn.: Human Relations Area Files.

1980   The Tenino Indians. *Ethnology* 19(2):129–149.

Murdock, George Peter, and Timothy J. O'Leary
1975   Ethnographic Bibliography of North America. 4th ed. 5 vols. *Behavior Science Bibliographies*. New Haven, Conn.: Human Relations Area Files Press.

Murray, Audrey L., James K. Keyser, and Floyd W. Sharrock
1977   A Preliminary Shoreline Survey of the Lima Reservoir: Archaeology in the Centennial Valley of Southwestern Montana. *Plains Anthropologist* 22(75):51–57.

Murray, Keith A.
1959   The Modocs and Their War. Norman: University of Oklahoma Press. (Reprinted in 1984.)

Musil, Robert R.
1984   Hobo Cave: A Resurrection. (Manuscript, Oregon State Museum of Anthropology, University of Oregon, Eugene.)

Muto, Guy R.
1972   A Technological Analysis of the Early States in the Manufacture of Lithic Artifacts. (M.A. Thesis in Anthropology, Idaho State University, Pocatello.)

1976   The Cascade Technique: An Examination of a Levallois-like Reduction System in Early Snake River Prehistory. (Ph.D. Dissertation in Anthropology, Washington State University, Pullman. Microfilm-xerography: University Microfilms International, Ann Arbor, Mich., 1978.)

Nance, Charles R.
1966   45WT2: An Archaeological Site on the Lower Snake River. (M.A. Thesis in Anthropology, Washington State University, Pullman.)

Nash, Philleo
1937   The Place of Religious Revivalism in the Formation of the Intercultural Community on Klamath Reservation. Pp. 377–442 in Social Anthropology of North American Tribes. Fred Eggan, ed. Chicago: The University of Chicago Press.

Nastich, Milena
1954   The Lillooet: An Account of the Basis of Individual Status. (M.A. Thesis, Department of Economics, Political Science and Sociology, University of British Columbia, Vancouver.)

National Archives
1854–1856   Records of the Washington Superintendency of Indian Affairs. (Records of the Bureau of Indian Affairs, Record Group 75, Roll 20, National Archives, Washington.)

National Park Service
1981   Resources Management Plan and Environmental Assessment for Nez Perce National Historic Park. Washington: U.S. Department of the Interior, National Park Service.

1993   Federal Historic Preservation Laws. Washington: U.S. Department of the Interior, National Park Service, Cultural Resources Program.

Native American Committee
1990   Idaho Indians: Tribal Histories. Boise: Idaho Centennial Commission.

Nehl, Steve
1994   Donald Sampson Old Traditions New Ways. *The Oregonian*, August 28. Portland, Oreg.

Nelles, Wayne C.
1984   Archaeology, Myth, and Oral Tradition: A Problem in Specialization, Consciousness, and the Sociology of Archaeological Knowledge. (M.A. Thesis in Anthropology, Simon Fraser University, Burnaby, B.C.)

Nelson, Charles G.
1957   The Osborne Case: A Report from the President. *Washington Archaeologist* 1(7):193–263.

Nelson, Charles M.
1966   A Preliminary Report on 45CO1, a Stratified Open Site in the Southern Columbia Plateau. *Washington State University. Laboratory of Anthropology. Report of Investigations* 39. Pullman.

1969   The Sunset Creek Site (45–KT–28) and its Place in Plateau Prehistory. *Washington State University. Laboratory of Anthropology. Report of Investigations* 46. Pullman.

1973   Prehistoric Culture Change in the Intermontane Plateau of Western North America. Pp. 371–390 in The Explanation of Culture Change: Models in Prehistory. Proceedings of a Meeting of the Research Seminar in Archaeology and Related Subjects, Held at the University of Sheffield, 1971. Collin Renfrew, ed. London: Duckworth.

Nelson, Charles M., and David G. Rice
1969   Archaeological Survey and Test, Asotin Dam Reservoir Area, Southeastern Washington. (Report on file, Washington State University, Laboratory of Anthropology, Pullman.)

Nelson, Denys
1928   Yakima Days. *Washington Historical Quarterly* 19(1):45–51, (2):117–133, (3):181–192.

Nelson, William R., and Jack Bodle
1990   Ninety Years of Salmon Culture at Little White Salmon National Fish Hatchery. *U.S. Department of the Interior. Fish and Wildlife Service. Biological Report* 90(17). Washington.

Nero, Robert W., and Bruce A. McCorquodale
1958   Report on an Excavation at the Oxbow Dam Site. *The Blue Jay* XVL(2):82–90.

Nesbitt, Paul Edward
1968   Stylistic Locales and Ethnographic Groups: Petroglyphs of the Lower Snake River. *Occasional Papers of the Idaho State University Museum* 23. Pocatello.

Nettl, Bruno
1954   North American Indian Musical Styles. *Memoirs of the American Folklore Society* 45. Philadelphia.

Neville, G.W. 1970 *see* Canada. Department of Indian and Northern Development. Indian Affairs Branch 1970

Nevins, Albert J., comp. and ed.
1965   The Maryknoll Catholic Dictionary. Preface by Donald Attwater. New York: Dimension Books / Grosset and Dunlap.

Newell, Alan S., Richmond L. Clow, and Richard N. Ellis
1986   A Forest in Trust: Three-Quarters of a Century of Indian Forestry, 1914–1986. Washington: U.S. Department of Interior, Bureau of Indian Affairs, Division of Forestry.

Newell, Robert
1959   Robert Newell's Memoranda: Travels in the Teritory of Missourie; Travle to the Kayuse War; together with A Report on the Indians South of the Columbia River. Edited, with Notes and Introduction, by Dorothy O. Johansen. Portland, Oreg.: Champoeg Press.

Newman, Stanley S.
1976   Salish and Bella Coola Prefixes. *International Journal of American Linguistics* 42(3):228–242.

1979   A History of the Salish Possessive and Subject Forms. *International Journal of American Linguistics* 45(3):207–223.

1979a   The Salish Object Forms. *International Journal of American Linguistics* 45(4):299–308.

1980   Functional Changes in the Salish Pronominal System. *International Journal of American Linguistics* 46(3):155–167.

Newman, Thomas M.
1966   Cascadia Cave. *Occasional Papers of the Idaho State University Museum* 18. Pocatello.

Nickman, Rudy J. and E. Leopold
1985   A Postglacial Pollen Record from Goose Lake, Okanogan County, Washington: Evidence for an Early Holocene Cooling. Pp. 131–147 in Summary of Results, Chief Joseph Dam Cultural Resources Project, Washington. Sarah K. Campbell, ed. Seattle: Office of Public Archaeology, Institute for Environmental Studies, University of Washington.

Nicodemus, Lawrence G.
1975   Snchitsu'umshtsn: The Coeur d'Alene Language. 2 vols. And 6 sound cassettes. Vol. 1: The Grammar, Coeur d'Alene-English Dictionary. Vol. 2: English-Coeur d'Alene Dictionary. Plummer, Idaho: Coeur d'Alene Tribal Council; Spokane, Wash.: University Press.

1975a   Snchitsu'umshtsn: The Coeur d'Alene Language. A Modern Course. Plummer, Idaho: Coeur d'Alene Tribe.

Nicol, C.S.
1859   [Letters to the Colonial Secretary, April 1859.] (Original manuscripts, GR 1372, file 1248, in British Columbia Archives and Records Service, Victoria.)

Noelke, Virginia H.
1974   The Origin and Early History of the Bureau of American Ethnology, 1879–1910. (Ph.D. Dissertation in Anthropology, University of Texas at Austin.)

Norton, Helen H., Robert Boyd, and Eugene S. Hunn
1983   The Klickitat Trail of South-Central Washington: A Reconstruction of Seasonally Used Resource Sites. Pp. 121–152 in Prehistoric Places on the Southern Northwest Coast. Robert E. Greengo, ed. Seattle: Thomas Burke Memorial Museum, University of Washington.

Norton, Helen H., E.S. Hunn, C.S. Martinsen, and P.B. Keely
1984   Vegetable Food Products of the Foraging Economies of the Pacific Northwest. *Ecology of Food and Nutrition* 14(3):219–228.

Oblate Missions of British Columbia
1971   [Letters and Papers by Fa. Grandidlier, O.M.I., 1866–74, St. Peter's Province Holy Rosary Scholasite, Ottawa.] (Microfilm on file at University British Columbia, Vancouver.)

O'Callaghan, Jerry A.
1952   Klamath Indians and the Oregon Wagon Road Grant. *Oregon Historical Quarterly* 53(1):23–28.

Oetting, Albert C.
1986   Archaeological Investigations at Area 3 of the Alderdale Site, 45KL5. (Manuscript on file at the Oregon State Museum of Anthropology, University of Oregon, Eugene.)

Ogden, Peter Skene
1853   Traits of American Indian Life and Character, by a Fur Trader. London: Smith, Elder. (Reprinted: Grabhorn Press, San Francisco, 1933; also, Ye Galleon Press, Fairfield, Wash., 1986.)

1909–1910   The Peter Skene Ogden Journals. T.C. Elliott, ed. *Oregon Historical Quarterly* 10(4):331–365; 11(2):201–222, (4):355–396.

1933   Traits of American Indian Life & Character, by a Fur Trader [1853]. San Francisco: Grabhorn Press.

1950   Snake Country Journals, 1824–25 and 1825–26. E.E. Rich, ed., assisted by A.M. Johnson, with an Introd. by Burt Brown Baker. *Publications of the Hudson's Bay Company Record Society* 13. London.

1961   Snake Country Journal, 1826–27. K.G. Davies, ed., assisted by A.M. Johnson, with an Introd. by Dorothy O. Johansen. *Publications of the Hudson's Bay Company Record Society* 23. London.

1971   Peter Skene Ogden's Snake Country Journals, 1827–28 and 1828–29. Glyndwr Williams, ed., with an Introd. and Notes by David E. Miller and David H. Miller. *Publications of the Hudson's Bay Company Record Society* 28. London.

Olmsted, David L.
1966   Achumawi Dictionary. *University of California Publications in Linguistics* 45. Berkeley.

Olsen, A. Loran
1972   Nez Perce Songs of Historical Significance, as Sung by "Sol" Webb. Lapwai, Idaho: Nez Perce Tribe.

1974   External Influences in Nez Perce Song. (Manuscript in Olsen's possession.)

1979   The Nez Perce Flute. *Northwest Anthropological Research Notes* 13(1):36–44. Moscow, Idaho.

1980   Nez Perce Hymns. (Manuscript in Olsen's possession.)

1989   [Inchelium fieldnotes.] (Manuscript in Olsen's possession.)

1989a   Guide to the Nez Perce Music Archive: An Annotated Listing of Songs and Musical Selections Spanning the Period 1897–1974. Pullman: Washington State University, School of Music and Theatre Arts.

Olson, Deborah
1984   Faunal Analysis. Pp. 215–237 in Environment, Archaeology, and Land Use Patterns in the Middle Kootenai River Valley, Vol. 1. Alston V. Thoms, ed. *Washington State University. Center for Northwest Anthropology. Project Report* 2. Pullman.

Olson, Tracy
1994   Confederated Tribes of Grand Ronde. Pp. 135–137 in Native America in the Twentieth Century: An Encyclopedia. Mary B. Davis, ed. New York: Garland.

O'Neal, Jerome Scott
1968   Flathead Law: Past and Present. (M.A. Thesis in Anthropology, University of Montana, Missoula.)

O'Neill, James
1866   [Letter of July 20, 1866, Lapwai, Idaho.] Pp. 193–195 in *39th Congress. 1st Session. House Executive Document* 1. (Serial No. 1284). Washington.

O'Nell, Theresa DeLeane
1996   Disciplined Hearts: History, Identity, and Depression in an American Indian Community. Berkeley: University of California Press.

Oregon Archaeological Society
1959   Wakemap Mound and Nearby Sites on the Long Narrows of the Columbia River. *Oregon Archaeological Society Publication* 1.

Oregon Historical Society
1956   Last Salmon Feast of the Celilo Indians. Portland: Oregon Historical Society Film Archives.

Oregon Legislature
1955   Oregon Laws. Salem, Oreg.: State Printer.

Oregon Pioneer Association
1885   Transactions of the Twelfth Annual Re-Union of the Oregon Pioneer Association for 1884. Salem, Oreg.: E.M. Waite.

1893   Transactions of the Nineteenth Annual Reunion of the Oregon Pioneer Association for 1891. Portland, Oreg.: A. Anderson.

1894   Transactions of the Twenty-first Annual Reunion of the Oregon Pioneer Association for 1893. Portland, Oreg.: G.H. Hines.

Oregon Province Archives [of the Society of Jesus] *see* Carriker, Eleanor, et al. 1976

Oregon Superintendency of Indian Affairs
1851–1856   Records of the Oregon Superintendency of Indian Affairs; Records Pertaining to Relations with the Indians, January 24, 1851–November 18, 1856. (Microcopy No. M–2, Roll 28, National Archives, Washington.)

Oregon Territorial Legislature
1854   The Statutes of Oregon, Enacted and Continued in Force by the Legislative Assembly, at the Session Commencing 5th December, 1853. Salem, Oreg.: Asahel Bush, Public Printer.

Orser, Brenda I.L.
1993   Stem-Initial Pharyngeal Resonants in Spokane, Interior Salish. (M.A. Thesis in Linguistics, University of Victoria, Victoria, B.C.)

Osborn, Gerald, and Brian H. Luckman
1988   Holocene Fluctuations in the Canadian Cordillera (Alberta and British Columbia). *Quaternary Science Reviews* 7(2):115–128. Oxford, [and] New York.

Osborne, Douglas D.
1950   An Archaeological Survey of the Benham Falls Reservoir, Oregon. *American Antiquity* 16(2):112–120.

1955   Nez Perce Horse Castration—A Problem in Diffusion. *Davidson Journal of Anthropology* 1(2):113–122. (Reprinted: *Northwest Anthropological Research Notes* 21(1/2):121–130. Moscow, Idaho, 1987.)

1956   Early Lithic in the Pacific Northwest. Pp. 38–44 in Northwest Archaeology Number, by Richard D. Daugherty et al. *Research Studies of the State College of Washington* 24(1). Pullman, Wash.

1957   Excavations in the McNary Reservoir Basin Near Umatilla, Oregon. With Appendixes by Marshall T. Newman ... [et al.]. *Bureau of American Ethnology Bulletin* 166; *River Basin Surveys Paper* 8. Washington.

1959   Archaeological Tests in the Lower Grand Coulee, Washington. Excavations Conducted by a Washington State College-State Department of Conservation and Development Field Party During the Months of July and August 1958. *Washing-*

ton State University. Laboratory of Anthropology. Report of Investigations 5. Pullman.

Osborne, Douglas D., Alan Bryan, and Robert H. Crabtree
1961   The Sheep Island Site and the Mid-Columbia Valley. *Bureau of American Ethnology Bulletin* 179; *River Basin Surveys Paper* 24. Washington.

Osborne, Douglas D., Warren W. Caldwell, and Robert H. Crabtree
1956   The Problem of Northwest Coastal-Interior Relationships As Seen from Seattle. *American Antiquity* 22(2):117–128.

Osmundson, John, and Christopher Hulse
1962   Preliminary Report on an Archaeological Survey of the Bruces Eddy Reservoir, North-Central Idaho, 1961. *Tebiwa: Journal of the Idaho State University Museum* 5(1):11–29. Pocatello.

Ostrom, Vincent, and Theodore Stern
1959   A Case Study of the Termination of Federal Responsibilities Over the Klamath Reservation. Report to the Commission on the Rights, Liberties, and Responsibilities of the American Indian. Eugene, Oreg.: [hectographed.]

Oswald, Dixie Y.
1975   A Direct Historic Approach to Slate Creek Site 10–IH–94. (M.A. Thesis in Anthropology, Idaho State University, Pocatello.)

Overmeyer, Philip H.
1941   George B. McClellan and the Pacific Northwest. *Pacific Northwest Quarterly* 32(1):3–60.

Owen, John
1927   The Journals and Letters of Major John Owen, Pioneer of the Northwest, 1850–1871; Embracing His Purchase of St. Mary's Mission, the Building of Fort Owen, His Travels, His Relation with the Indians, His Work for the Government, and His Activities as a Western Empire Builder for Twenty Years. Transcribed and edited [...] by Seymour Dunbar; and with Notes [...] by Paul C. Phillips. 2 vols. New York: Edward Eberstadt.

Owens, Patrick Allen
1976   An Historical and Theoretical Examination of Nativistic Phenomena. (M.A. Thesis in Anthropology, University of Idaho, Moscow.)

Pac, David F., Richard J. Mackie, and Henry E. Jorgensen
1991   Mule Deer Population Organization, Behavior, and Dynamics in a Northern Rocky Mountain Environment. Bozeman: Montana Department of Fish, Wildlife, and Parks.

Pace, Robert E., comp.
1977   The Land of the Yakimas. Edited by Kamiakin Research Institute. Toppenish, Wash.: Yakima Indian Nation Tribal Council.

Paige, George A.
1866   [Report of George Paige to W. Waterman, dated September 19th, 1866.] (Manuscript in Letters Received, M234, Reel 909, Records of the Bureau of Indian Affairs, Record Group 75, National Archives, Washington.)

Painter, H.M.
1946   The Coming of the Horse. *Pacific Northwest Quarterly* 37(2):155–157.

Paisano, Edna, et al.
1992   American Indian Population by Tribe... 1990. (CPH–L–99.) Washington: Racial Statistics Branch, Population Division, Bureau of the Census.

Palladino, Lawrence B.
1922   Indian and White in the Northwest; A History of Catholicity in Montana, 1831–1891. Introd. by Right Reverend John B. Brondel. 2d ed., rev. and enl. Lancaster, Pa.: Wickersham Publishing Co.

Palmer, Gary B.
1975   Shuswap Indian Ethnobotany. *Syesis* 8:29–81. Victoria, B.C.

———
1975a   Cultural Ecology in the Canadian Plateau: Pre-Contact to the Early Contact Period in the Territory of the Southern Shuswap Indians of British Columbia. *Northwest Anthropological Research Notes* 9(2):199–245. Moscow, Idaho.

———
1978   Cultural Ecology in the Canadian Plateau: Estimates of Shuswap Indian Salmon Resources in Pre-Contact Times. *Northwest Anthropological Research Notes* 12(1):5–8. Moscow, Idaho.

———
1981   The Coeur d'Alene Migration to *Ni'lokhwalqw* (DeSmet). (Paper presented at the 80th Annual Meeting of the American Anthropological Association, Los Angeles, California, December 2–6, 1981.)

———
1981a   Indian Pioneers: Coeur d'Alene Mission Farming from 1842 to 1876. *Papers in Anthropology* 22(1):65–92.

———
1981b   Light Shining on the Mountain, A Thumbnail Biography of Louis Victor. *Idaho Humanities Forum* (Spring):2, 12.

———
1988   The Language and Culture Approach in the Coeur d'Alene Language Preservation Project. *Human Organization* 47(4):307–317.

———
1989   The Gobbler. *The World and I* (March):652–659.

———
1990   "Where There are Muskrats": The Semantic Structure of Coeur d'Alene Place Names. *Anthropological Linguistics* 32(3–4):263–294.

———
1991   Ethnohistorical Report on Columbia, Entiat, Chelan, and Wenatchi Peoples of the Colville Confederated Tribes. (Prefile Testimony, June 18, 1991; U.S. v. Oregon, U.S. District Court, District of Oregon; Civ. No. 68–513–MA.)

———
1992   Concurrent Application of Language Research. Pp. 135–164 in Amerindian Languages and Informatics: The Pacific Northwest / Langues amérindiennes et informatique: Le Pacifique nord-ouest. Guy P. Buchholtzer, ed. *Amerindia: Revue d'Ethnolinguistique Amérindienne*, numéro spécial 7. Paris.

———
1997   Foraging for Patterns in Interior Salish Semantic Domains. Pp. 349–386 in Salish Languages and Linguistics: Theoretical and Descriptive Perspectives. Ewa Czaykowska-Higgins and M. Dale Kinkade, eds. (*Trends in Linguistics. Studies and Monographs* 107). Berlin and New York: Mouton de Gruyter.

Palmer, Gary B., Lawrence N. Nicodemus, and Lavinia Felsman
1985   Workbooks in the Coeur d'Alene Language. 2 vols. Plummer, Idaho: Coeur d'Alene Tribe of Idaho.

———
1987   *Khwi'Khwe Hntmikhw'lumukhw*: This is My Land. Plummer, Idaho: Coeur d'Alene Tribe of Idaho.

Palmer, H. Spencer
1861   Report [read December 12th, 1859] on the Harrison and Lillooet Route, from the Junction of the Fraser and Harrison rivers to the Junction of the Fraser and Kayosch rivers, with Notes on the Country beyond, as far as Fountain. *The Journal of the Royal Geographical Society* 31:213–214, 224–234. London.

Palmer, H. Spencer
1863   Report of a Journal of a Survey from Victoria to Fort Alexandria, via North Bentinck Arm. New Westminster, B.C.: Royal Engineer Press.

Palmer, Joel
1847   Journal of Travels Over the Rocky Mountains to the Mouth of the Columbia River: Made During the Years of 1845 and 1846. Cincinnati: J.A. and V.P. Janes.

725

1855   [Letter transmitting Ratified Treaty No. 282, concluded with Bands of Indians in the Willamette Valley.] (Original document in Ratified and Unratified Treaties with Indian Tribes, 1801–1869, National Archives, Washington.)

1856   [Letter to J. Cain, Acting Superintendent of Indian Affairs, Washington, dated October 3d, 1855.] *34th Congress. 1st Session. House Executive Document* 93. (Serial No. 858). Washington.

Pambrun, Andrew Dominique
1979   Sixty Years on the Frontier in the Pacific Northwest. Edward J. Kowrach, ed. Fairfield, Wash.: Ye Galleon Press.

Pandosy, Marie-Charles
1862   Grammar and Dictionary of the Yakama Language. George Gibbs and John Gilmary Shea, trans. *Shea's Library of American Linguistics* 6. New York: Cramoisy Press. (Reprinted: AMS Press, New York, 1970.)

Parker, Samuel
1837   Rocky-Mountain Indians: Letter from Mr. Parker, dated on Green River, Aug. 17th, 1835. *Missionary Herald* 33(8):348–349. St. Louis.

1838   Journal of an Exploring Tour Beyond the Rocky Mountains; Under the Direction of the A.B.C.F.M., Performed in the Years 1835, 1836, and 1837. Ithaca, N.Y.: Published by the Author. (Reprinted in 1840, 1844; also, Ross and Haines, Minneapolis, 1967; and, University of Idaho Press, Moscow, 1990.)

1840   Journal of an Exploring Tour Beyond the Rocky Mountains; Under the Direction of the A.B.C.F.M., Containing a Discription of the Geography, Geology, Climate, Productions of the Country, and the Numbers, Manners, and Customs of the Natives: with a Map of Oregon Territory. Ithaca, N.Y.: The Author, Mack, Andrus, and Woodruff. (Reprinted in 1844; also, Ross and Haines, Minneapolis, 1967; University of Idaho Press, Moscow, 1990.)

1844   Journal of an Exploring Tour Beyond the Rocky Mountains; Under the Direction of the A.B.C.F.M., Containing a Discription of the Geography, Geology, Climate, Productions of the Country, and the Numbers, Manners, and Customs of the Natives: with a Map of Oregon Territory. 4th ed. Ithaca, N.Y., Andrus, Woodruff, and Gauntlett; also Boston: Crocker and Brewster. (Reprinted: Ross and Haines, Minneapolis, 1967; University of Idaho Press, Moscow, 1990.)

Partoll, Albert J.
1937   The Blackfoot Indian Peace Council: a Document of the Official Proceedings of the Treaty Between the Blackfoot Nation and Other Indians and the United States, in October, 1855. *Frontier and Midland* 17(3):199–207. Missoula, Mont.

1938   The Flathead Indian Treaty Council of 1855. *Pacific Northwest Quarterly* 29(3):283–314.

1939   Fort Connah: A Frontier Trading Post, 1847–1871. *Pacific Northwest Quarterly* 30(4):399–415.

1951   The Flathead-Salish Indian Name in Montana Nomenclature. *Montana Magazine of History* 1(1):37–48.

Patterson, Ida Smith
1981   Montana Memoirs: The Life of Emma Magee in the Rocky Mountain West, 1866–1950. With a Biography of the Author by Grace Patterson McComas. Pablo, Mont.: Steve Matt, Sr., Memorial Fund, Salish Kootenai Community College.

Pattison, Lois C.
1978   Douglas Lake Okanagan: Phonology and Morphology. (M.A. Thesis in Linguistics, University of British Columbia, Vancouver.)

Pavesic, Max G.
1966   A Projectile Point "Blank" Cache from Southeastern Idaho. *Tebiwa: Journal of the Idaho State University Museum* 9(1):52–57. Pocatello.

1971   The Archaeology of Hells Canyon Creek Rockshelter, Wallowa County, Oregon. (Ph.D. Dissertation in Anthropology, University of Colorado, Boulder.)

1978   Archaeological Overview of the Middle Fork of the Salmon River Corridor, Idaho Primitive Area. *Boise State University Archaeological Report* 3. Boise, Idaho.

1979   Public Archaeology in Weiser Basin and Vicinity: A Narrative Report. Boise, Idaho: Boise State University.

1985   Cache Blades and Turkey Tails: Piecing Together the Western Idaho Archaic Burial Complex. Pp. 55–89 in Stone Tool Analysis; Essays in Honor of Don E. Crabtree. Mark G. Plew, James C. Woods, and Max G. Pavesic, eds. Albuquerque: University of New Mexico Press.

1986   Descriptive Archaeology of Hells Canyon Creek Village. Illus. by James C. Woods; Appendices by Susanne J. Miller, E. Bentley. *Boise State University Archaeological Reports* 14. Boise, Idaho.

1991   Death and Dying in the Western Idaho Archaic. In: Proceedings of the Annual Chacmool Conference. Calgary, Alta.: University of Calgary Archaeological Association.

Pavesic, Max G., Mark G. Plew, and Roderick Sprague
1979   A Bibliography of Idaho Archaeology, 1889–1976. *Northwest Anthropological Research Notes. Memoir* 5. Moscow, Idaho.

1981   A Bibliography of Idaho Archaeology, 1977–1979. *Northwest Anthropological Research Notes* 15(2):248–260. Moscow, Idaho.

Pearsall, Marion
1950   Klamath Childhood and Education. *University of California Anthropological Records* 9(5). Berkeley. (Reprinted: Kraus Reprint, Millwood, N.Y., 1976.)

Peltier, Jerome
1975   Manners and Customs of the Coeur d'Alene Indians. Spokane, Wash.: Peltier Publications.

Peltier, Jerome, and B.C. Payette
1972   Warbonnets and Epaulets: With Pre- and Post Factors, Documented, of the Steptoe-Wright Indian Campaigns of 1858 in Washington Territory. Montreal: Payette Radio.

Pembroke, Timothy R.
1976   An Anthropological Analysis of Conflict and Confrontation among the Lower Kootenai of Bonners Ferry, Idaho. (M.A. Thesis in Anthropology, Washington State University, Pullman.)

Perkins, Henry W.K.
[1838–1844] [The Wascopam Mission Papers of Henry Perkins, 1838–1844.] (Manuscripts at the University of Puget Sound and the Washington State Historical Society, Tacoma; the Oregon Historical Society, Portland; and other collections.)

[1843]   [Diary and Letters, 1843.] (Manuscript edited by Robert T. Boyd, Pacific Lutheran University, Tacoma, Wash.)

Perry, Jay
1939   Notes on a type of Indian Burial Found in the Mid-Columbia
            River District of Central Washington. *New Mexico Anthropol-
            ogist* 3(5):80–82.

Perry, W.A. ("Sillalicum"), A.A. Mosher, W.H.H. Murray, et al.
1892   American Game Fishes, Their Habits, Habitat, and Peculiari-
            ties; How, When and Where to Angle for Them. George O.
            Shields, ed. Chicago and New York: Rand and McNally.

Petersen, Keith C.
1991   Idaho's Embattled Snake River Salmon. *Idaho, the Universi-
            ty*, (Spring): 12–15. Pocatello.

Petersen, Kenneth L.
1990   Projecting Long-Term Climate Change to Assess Potential
            Effects on Water Infiltration in Southeastern Washington, U.S.A.
            American Quaternary Association Program and Abstracts, June
            4–6, 1990. Waterloo, Ont.: University of Waterloo.

Peterson, Jacqueline, with Laura Peers
1993   Sacred Encounters: Father De Smet and the Indians of the
            Rocky Mountains West. Norman and London: The De Smet
            Project, Washington State University [Pullman] in association
            with the University of Oklahoma Press.

Pethick, Derek
1976   First Approaches to the Northwest Coast. Vancouver: J.J.
            Douglas.

Pettigrew, Richard M.
1981   A Prehistoric Culture Sequence in the Portland Basin of the
            Lower Columbia River. *University of Oregon Anthropological
            Papers* 22. Eugene.

_____
1982   Archaeological Investigations in Mill Creek Valley, Crook
            County, Oregon. *University of Oregon Anthropological
            Papers* 26. Eugene.

Phair, A.W.A.
1959   The History of Lillooet. (Unpublished manuscript, British
            Columbia Archives and Records Service, Victoria. Add. ms. 275.)

Phebus, George E.
1978   The Smithsonian Institution 1934 Bonneville Reservoir Sal-
            vage Archaeology Project. *Northwest Anthropological
            Research Notes* 12(2):113–117. Moscow, Idaho.

Philips, Susan U.
1983   The Invisible Culture: Communication in Classroom and
            Community on the Warm Springs Indian Reservation. New
            York: Longman. (Reprinted: Waveland Press, Prospect
            Heights, Ill., 1993.)

Phillips, Earl L.
1965   Climates of the States: Washington. *Climatography of the
            United States No.* 60–45. Washington.U.S. Department of
            Commerce, Weather Bureau.

Phillips, Michael
1892   [Letter of June 30, 1892.] Pp. 245–247 in *Canadian Session-
            al Papers* 14. Ottawa.

Phillips, Paul C.
1929   The Battle of the Big Hole; an Episode in the Nez Perce War.
            Historical Reprints, Sources of Northwest History 8. Mis-
            soula: State University of Montana.

_____
1930   The Oregon Missions as Shown in the Walker Letters,
            1839–1851. *Frontier* 11(1):74–89. (Reprinted: Pp. 101–119
            in *Frontier Omnibus*. John W. Hakola, ed. Montana State Uni-
            versity [University of Montana], Missoula, 1962.)

_____ [1950] *see* 1974

_____ 1962 *see* 1930

1974   History of the Confederated Salish and Kootenai Tribes of the
            Flathead Reservation, Montana. [Docket No. 61, Pet. Ex. 1.,
            1950.] Pp. 233–305 in Interior Salish and Eastern Washington
            Indians III. *American Indian Ethnohistory, Indians of the
            Northwest*. New York: Garland.

Phillips, Yvonne E.
1955   A Study of the Distribution of Wishram Indian Myths. (B.A.
            Thesis in Anthropology, Reed College, Portland, Oreg.)

Philp, Kenneth R.
1977   John Collier's Crusade for Indian Reform, 1920–1954. Fore-
            word by Francis Paul Prucha. Tucson: The University of Ari-
            zona Press.

Phinney, Archie
1934   Nez Percé Texts. *Columbia University Contributions to
            Anthropology* 25. New York. (Reprinted: AMS Press, New
            York, 1969.)

Phinney, Edward S.
1963   Alfred B. Meacham: Promoter of Indian Reform. (Ph.D. Dis-
            sertation in History, University of Oregon, Eugene. Photocopy:
            University Microfilms International, Ann Arbor, Mich., 1983.)

Pickering, Charles
1895   The Races of Man; and Their Geographical Distribution. New
            Edition to Which is Prefixed, An Analytical Synopsis of the
            Natural History of Man, by John Charles Hall. London:
            George Bell & Sons. (Rev. of the work issued as Vol. 9 of the
            U.S. Exploring Expedition publications; originally publ.,
            London, H.G. Bohn, 1850.)

Pierre, Larry
1970   The Okanagan Winter Dance. [Text in Northern Okanagan
            and translated into English.] (Manuscript in British Columbia
            Indian Language Project, Victoria.)

Pilling, James Constantine
1885   Proof-sheets of a Bibliography of the Languages of the North
            American Indians. *Bureau of [American] Ethnology Miscel-
            laneous Publication* 2. Washington. (Reprinted: Central Book
            Co., Brooklyn, N.Y., 1966.)

_____
1893   Bibliography of the Chinookan Languages (Including the
            Chinook Jargon). *Bureau of [American] Ethnology Bulletin*
            15. Washington. (Reprinted as vol. 3, pt. 3 of 3 vols.: AMS
            Press, New York, 1973.)

_____
1893a   Bibliography of the Salishan Languages. *Bureau of [Ameri-
            can] Ethnology Bulletin* 16. Washington. (Reprinted as vol. 3,
            pt. 8 of 3 vols.: AMS Press, New York, 1973.)

Pippin, Lonnie C., and Jonathan O. Davis
1980   A Study of Cultural Resources Inundated by Island Park
            Reservoir, Fremont County, Idaho. Reno: University of Neva-
            da, Desert Research Institute, Social Science Center.

Plew, Mark G.
1976   Shield-Bearing Warrior Motif Petroglyphs from Southwestern
            Idaho. *The Masterkey* 50(3):112. Los Angeles.

_____
1977   A Final Report on the Archaeological Evaluations at Sites
            10–VY–95, 96 and 97, Valley County, Idaho. (Report on file,
            Boise National Forest, Boise, Idaho.)

_____
1981   Southern Idaho Plain: What are the Facts? A Reply to Butler.
            Plains Anthropologist 26(92):161–164.

Plew, Mark G., Kenneth M. Ames, and C. Fuhrman
1984   Archaeological Excavations at Silver Bridge (10–BO–1),
            Southern Idaho. *Boise State University. Archaeological
            Reports* 12. Boise, Idaho.

727

Point, Nicolas
1967   Wilderness Kingdom: Indian Life in the Rocky Mountains: 1840–1847: The Journal and Paintings of Nicolas Point, S.J. Translated and introduced by Joseph P. Donnelly, S.J. With an appreciation by John C. Ewers. New York, Chicago, San Francisco: Holt, Rinehart and Winston.

Pokotylo, David L.
1978   Lithic Technology and Settlement Patterns in the Upper Hat Creek Valley, B.C. (Ph.D. Dissertation in Anthropology, University of British Columbia, Vancouver. Microfiche of typescript: *Canadian Theses on Microfiche* 40759, National Library of Canada, Ottawa, 1980.)

_____
1983   Blood from Stone: Making and Using Stone Tools in Prehistoric British Columbia. *University of British Columbia. Museum of Anthropology. Museum Note* 11. Vancouver.

Pokotylo, David L., and Patricia D. Froese
1983   Archaeological Evidence for Prehistoric Root Gathering on the Southern Interior Plateau of British Columbia: A Case Study from Upper Hat Creek Valley. *Canadian Journal of Archaeology* 7(2):127–157. Ottawa.

Pokotylo, David L., Marian E. Binkley, and A. Joanne Curtin
1987   The Cache Creek Burial Site (EeRh 1), British Columbia. *British Columbia Provincial Museum. Contributions to Human History* 1. Victoria.

Pope, Richard K.
1953   The Indian Shaker Church and Acculturation at Warm Springs Reservation. (B.A. Thesis in Anthropology, Reed College, Portland, Oreg.)

Post, John A.
1904   Kalispel Grammar. (Manuscript in Oregon Province Archives of the Society of Jesus, Gonzaga University, Spokane, Wash.)

Poston, Richard Waverly
1950   Small Town Renaissance: a Story of the Montana Study. New York: Harper and Brothers.

Powell, John Wesley
1872   [Map of British Columbia, Being a Geographical Division of the Indians of the Province According to Their Nationality or Dialect.] (Original map, RG10m, Accession 901–10, Drawer D3950, Folder F3, in National Archives of Canada, Ottawa.)

_____
1877   Introduction to the Study of Indian Languages, with Words, Phrases, and Sentences To Be Collected. Washington: U.S. Government Printing Office. (2d ed. in 1880.)

_____
1891   Indian Linguistic Families of America North of Mexico. Pp. 1–142 in *7th Annual Report of the Bureau of [American] Ethnology for 1885–1886.* With map. Washington. (Reprinted: with Franz Boas's Introduction to *Handbook of American Indian Languages.* Preston Holder, ed. University of Nebraska Press, Lincoln, 1966.)

Powers, Stephen
1877   Report on the Tribes of California. *Contributions to North American Ethnology* 3. Washington: U.S. Geographical and Geological Survey of the Rocky Mountain Region. Government Printing Office.

Powers, William K.
1970   [Review Essay: Alan P. Merriam's Ethnomusicology of the Flathead Indians.] *Ethnomusicology* 14(1):67–76.

Price, Mark
1982   A Cultural Resource Reconnaissance of the Campgrounds on the Main Salmon River Corridor, 1982. (Report No. SL–82–254. Manuscript on file at Salmon National Forest, Salmon, Idaho.)

Quaife, Milo M., ed.
1916   The Journals of Captain Meriwether Lewis and Sergeant John Ordway, Kept on the Expedition of Western Exploration, 1803–1806. Madison, Wis.: The State Historical Society of Wisconsin. (Reprinted in 1965.)

Quill Point, Inc.
1984   The People of Warm Springs. Profile: The Confederated Tribes of the Warm Springs Reservation of Oregon. [Warm Springs, Oreg.]: Confederated Tribes of the Warm Springs Reservation of Oregon.

Quimby, George I.
1948   Culture Contact on the Northwest Coast, 1785–1795. *American Anthropologist* 50(2):247–255.

Quinn, Robert R.
1984   Climate of the Northern Columbia Plateau. In Northern Columbia Plateau Landscapes: Narrative and Field Guide. Michael M. Folsom, ed. Cheney, Wash.: Eastern Washington University Press.

Rabel, Eduardo
1993   Artist in Resistance: Corwin Clairmont Makes Indian History a Contemporary Concern. *Tribal College: Journal of the American Indian Higher Education* 5(1):12–17. Chestertown, Md.

Radcliffe-Brown, A.R.
1958   Method in Social Anthropology: Selected Essays by A.R. Radcliffe-Brown. M.N. Srinivas, ed. Chicago: The University of Chicago Press.

Ramsey, Jarold
1972   Three Warm Springs-Wasco Stories. *Western Folklore* 3:116–119. (Reprinted: [the narrations] in Coyote Was There: Indian Literature of the Oregon Country. Jarold Ramsey, ed., University of Washington Press, Seattle, 1977.)

_____
1977   Coyote Was Going There: Indian Literature of the Oregon Country. Seattle and London: University of Washington Press. (Reprinted in 1980.)

_____
1983   'The Hunter Who Had an Elk for a Guardian Spirit,' and the Ecological Imagination. Pp. 309–322 in Smoothing the Ground: Essays on Native American Oral Literature. Brian Swann, ed. Berkeley, Los Angeles, and London: University of California Press.

_____
1983a   Reading the Fire: Essays in the Traditional Indian Literatures of the Far West. Lincoln and London: University of Nebraska Press.

Randall, Robert A., and Eugene S. Hunn
1984   Do Life-forms Evolve or Do Uses for Life? Some Doubts about Brown's Universals Hypotheses. *American Ethnologist* 11(2):329–349.

Randolph, Joseph
1976   Field Catalog and Collection Artifacts from Site 10IH483. (Catalog No. 794, Artifact Box 123 in Alfred A. Bowers Laboratory of Anthropology, University of Idaho, Moscow.)

_____
1980   A Preliminary Description of the Lithic Technology of the Serrated Boulders at Buffalo Eddy (45AS14). (Paper presented at the 33d Annual Northwest Anthropological Conference, Bellingham, Wash.)

Randolph, Joseph, and Max Dahlstrom
1977   Archaeological Test Excavations at Bernard Creek Rockshelter. *University of Idaho. Laboratory of Anthropology. Anthropological Research Manuscript Series* 42. Moscow, Idaho.

Ranere, Anthony J.
1971   Birch Creek Papers No. 4: Stratigraphy and Stone Tools from Meadow Canyon, Eastern Idaho. *Occasional Papers of the Idaho State University Museum* 27. Pocatello.

Rankin, Del, comp.
[1977]   Index to The Relander Archives in the Yakima Valley Region-
            al Library: A Calendar of Pacific Northwest Americana, with
            Emphasis on Indians of the Columbia Basin. Yakima, Wash.:
            Yakima Valley Regional Library.

Rasmussen, Donald L.
1974   New Quaternary Mammal Localities in the Upper Clark Fork
            River Valley, Western Montana. *Northwest Geology* 3:62–70.
            Missoula, Mont.

Raufer, (Sister) Maria Ilma
1966   Black Robes and Indians on the Last Frontier, a Story of
            Heroism. Milwaukee, Wis.: The Bruce Publishing Company.

Ray, Arthur J.
1978   Competition and Conservation in the Early Subarctic Fur
            Trade. *Ethnohistory* 25(4):347–357.

––––––––
1980   Indians as Consumers in the Eighteenth Century. Pp. 255–271
            in Old Trails and New Directions: Papers of the Third North
            American Fur Trade Conference. C.M. Judd and A.J. Ray,
            eds. Toronto: University of Toronto Press.

––––––––
1984   The Northern Great Plains: Pantry of the Northwestern Fur
            Trade, 1774–1885. *Prairie Forum* 9(2):263–280.

Ray, Arthur J., and Donald B. Freeman
1978   'Give Us Good Measure': An Economic Analysis of Relations
            Between the Indians and the Hudson's Bay Company Before
            1763. Toronto: University of Toronto Press. (Reprinted: U-M-
            I Out-of-Print Books on Demand, Ann Arbor, Mich., 1990.)

Ray, Verne F. [1932] *see* 1933

––––––––
1933   The Sanpoil and Nespelem: Salishan Peoples of Northeastern
            Washington. *University of Washington Publications in
            Anthropology* 5. Seattle. (Reprinted: Human Relations Area
            Files, New Haven, Conn., 1954; also, AMS Press, New York,
            1980.)

––––––––
1933a   Sanpoil Folk Tales. *Journal of American Folk-Lore*
            46(180):129–187.

––––––––
1936   Native Villages and Groupings of the Columbia Basin. *Pacif-
            ic Northwest Quarterly* 27(2):99–152.

––––––––
1936a   The Kolaskin Cult: A Prophet Movement of 1870 in North-
            eastern Washington. *American Anthropologist* 38(1):67–75.

––––––––
1937   The Bluejay Character in the Plateau Spirit Dance. *American
            Anthropologist* 39(4, Pt. 1):593–601.

––––––––
1938   Lower Chinook Ethnographic Notes. *University of Washing-
            ton Publications in Anthropology* 7(2). Seattle.

––––––––
1939   Cultural Relations in the Plateau of Northwestern America.
            *Publications of the Frederick Webb Hodge Anniversary Pub-
            lication Fund* 3. Los Angeles: Southwestern Museum.
            (Reprinted: AMS Press, New York, 1978.)

––––––––
1941   Historic Backgrounds of the Conjuring Complex in the Plateau
            and the Plains. Pp. 204–216 in Language, Culture, and Person-
            ality. Leslie Spier, A. Irving Hallowell, and Stanley Newman,
            eds. Menasha, Wis.: Sapir Memorial Publication Fund.

––––––––
1942   Culture Element Distributions: XXII, Plateau. *University of Cal-
            ifornia Anthropological Records* 8(2):99–258[+4]. Berkeley.

––––––––
1954   The Nez Perce Tribe: Preliminary Report of Columbia River
            Salmon Fishing. (Manuscript in Verne F. Ray's possession.)

––––––––
1954a   [Testimony before the Indian Claims Commission, Docket
            No. 181, The Confederated Tribes of the Colville Reservation
            et al. *v.* The United States of America.] (Microfiche). New
            York: Clearwater Publishing.

––––––––
1959   Tribal Territories and Village Locations of the Walla Walla,
            Cayuse and Umatilla Tribes. Map. Together with Testimony
            in Confederated Tribes of the Umatilla Indian Reservation v.
            United States of America; Petitioner's Proposed Findings of
            Fact and Brief. Docket No. 264, before the Indian Claims
            Commission. (Published, pp. 333–534 in Oregon Indians II.
            Garland, New York, 1974.)

––––––––
1960   The Columbia Indian Confederacy: A League of Central
            Plateau Tribes. Pp. 771–789 in Culture in History: Essays in
            Honor of Paul Radin. Stanley Diamond, ed. New York:
            Columbia University Press.

––––––––
1960a   [Testimony before the Indian Claims Commission, Dockets
            161 and 222, in the matter of The Confederated Tribes of the
            Colville Indian Reservation, as the Representative of the
            Palus Band.] (Microfiche). New York: Clearwater Publishing.

––––––––
1963   Primitive Pragmatists: The Modoc Indians of Northern Cali-
            fornia. *Monograph of the American Ethnological Society* 38.
            Seattle: University of Washington Press.

––––––––
1971   Tribes of the Columbia Confederacy and the Palus. (Plaintiff
            Exhibit No. 113, The Confederated Tribes of the Colville
            Reservation v. the Yakima Tribes of the Indians of the Yakima
            Reservation; U.S. Court of Claims, Docket No. 261–270,
            Washington.)

––––––––
1971a   Lewis and Clark and the Nez Perce Indians. *Potomac Corral
            of The Westerners. The Great Western Series* 10. [Washington,
            D.C.]

––––––––
1974   Ethnohistorical Notes on the Columbia, Chelan, Entiat, and
            Wenatchee Tribes. Pp. 377–435 in Interior Salish and Eastern
            Washington Indians IV. *American Indian Ethnohistory: Indi-
            ans of the Northwest*. New York: Garland.

––––––––
1975   Chief Joseph Dam Visitors Facilities. Cultural Report.
            (Report prepared for the U.S. Army Corps of Engineers, Seat-
            tle District, Seattle, Wash.)

––––––––
1975a   Final Report: Colville Interpretive Theme. 2 vols. Nespelem,
            Wash.: Colville Confederated Tribes.

––––––––
1975b   [Testimony, Docket 81: Coeur d'Alenes, Records of the Indian
            Claims Commission, Record Group 279, National Archives,
            Washington.] (Microfiche). New York: Clearwater Publishing.

––––––––
1977   Ethnic Impact of the Events Incident to the Federal Power
            Development on the Colville and Spokane Indian Reserva-
            tions. (Report prepared for The Confederated Tribes of the
            Colville Reservation and The Spokane Tribe of Indians,
            Nespelem, Wash.)

Ray, Verne F., and Nancy O. Lurie
1954   The Contribution of Lewis and Clark to Ethnography. *Journal
            of the Washington Academy of Sciences* 44(11):358–370.
            Washington.

Ray, Verne F., et al.
1938   Tribal Distribution in Eastern Oregon and Adjacent Regions.
            American Anthropologist 40(3):384–415.

RCIPR = Sprague, Roderick, and Deward E. Walker, Jr.

1974 Report of the Committee for Investigating and Publishing Reports on the Physical Characteristics, Languages, and Industrial and Social Condition of the North-western Tribes of the Dominion of Canada, 1886–1889. [Reprinted in:] *Northwest Anthropological Research Notes* 8(1/2):1–384. Moscow, Idaho.

Rebillet, S.J.
1981 Final Report on the South Fork of the Salmon River: The Place and the People. (Manuscript on file, Idaho State Historical Society, Boise.)

Reeves, Brian O.K.
1969 The Southern Alberta Paleo-Cultural Paleo-Environmental Sequence. Pp. 6–46 in Post-Pleistocene Man and His Environment on the Northern Plains. R.G. Forbis, L.B. Davis, O.A. Christensen, and G. Fedirchuk, eds. Calgary, Alta.: The Student Press.

————
1970 Culture Change in the Northern Plains, 1000 B.C.–A.D. 1000. (Ph.D. Dissertation in Anthropology, University of Calgary, Calgary, Alta.; Published: *Archaeological Survey of Canada. Occasional Paper* 20. Edmonton.

————
1973 The Concept of an Altithermal Cultural Hiatus in Northern Plains Prehistory. *American Anthropologist* 75(5):1221–1253.

Reichard, Gladys A.
1933–1938 Coeur d'Alene. Pp. 517–707 in Pt. 3 of Handbook of American Indian Languages. Franz Boas, ed. Glückstadt-Hamburg-New York: J.J. Augustin.

————
1934 The Style of Coeur d'Alêne Mythology. Pp. 243–253 in *Proceedings of the 24th International Congress of Americanists, Hamburg, 7–13 September 1930.* Hamburg: Friederichsen, De Gruyter.
———— 1938 *see* 1933–1938
————
1939 Stem-List of the Coeur d'Alene Language. *International Journal of American Linguistics* 10(2–3):92–108.

————
1943 Imagery in an Indian Vocabulary. *American Speech* 9:96–102.

————
1945 Composition and Symbolism of Coeur d'Alene Verb-stems. *International Journal of American Linguistics* 11(1):47–63.

————
1946 Coeur d'Alene Texts, Part II, XVIII-XXIV. (Manuscript in Archives of Languages of the World, University of Indiana, Bloomington.)

————
1947 An Analysis of Coeur d'Alene Indian Myths. *Memoirs of the American Folk-lore Society* 41. Philadelphia.

————
1958–1960 A Comparison of Five Salish Languages. 6 Pts. Florence M. Voegelin, ed. *International Journal of American Linguistics* 24(4):293–300; 25(1):8–15, (2):90–96, (3):154–167, (4):239–253; 26(1):50–61.

Reichwein, Jeffrey C.
1988 Native American Response to Euro-American Contact in the Columbia Plateau of Northwestern North America, 1840 to 1914: An Anthropological Interpretation Based on Written and Pictorial Ethnohistorical Data. (Ph.D. Dissertation in Anthropology, Ohio State University, Columbus.)

————
1990 Emergence of Native America Nationalism in the Columbia Plateau. (*The Evolution of North American Indians Series*). New York: Garland Press.

Reid, Kenneth C.
1988 Downey Gulch Archaeology: Excavations at Two Seasonal Camps on the Joseph Upland, Wallowa County, Oregon. *Washington State University. Center for Northwest Anthropology. Contributions in Cultural Resource Management* 22. Pullman.

————, ed.
1991 Prehistory and Paleoenvironments at Pittsburg Landing: Data Recovery and Test Excavations at Six Sites in Hells Canyon National Recreation Area, West Central Idaho. *Washington State University. Center for Northwest Anthropology. Project Report* 15. Pullman.

————, ed.
1991a An Overview of Cultural Resources in the Snake River Basin: Prehistory and Paleoenvironments. *Washington State University. Center for Northwest Anthropology. Project Report* 13. Pullman.

————
1992 Housepits and Highland Hearths: Comparative Chronologies for the Snake River and Blue Mountains. (Paper presented at the 45th Annual Northwest Anthropological Conference, Burnaby, B.C., April 16–18.)

Reid, Kenneth C., and James D. Gallison
1992 Site Testing and Data Recovery Plan, Crane Flats Site (FS 8–35.5–1–/1), North Fork John Day District, Umatilla National Forest, Grant County, Oregon. *Rain Shadow Research Project Report* 2. Pullman, Wash.

————
1993 Test Excavations at Cache Creek (FS 6N47E–23–07), Oregon, and Kirkwood Bar (10IH699), Idaho, Hells Canyon National Recreation Area, Wallowa Whitman National Forest. *Rain Shadow Research Project Report* 15. Pullman, Wash.

Reid, Kenneth C., John A. Draper, and Peter E. Wigand
1989 Prehistory and Paleoenvironments of the Silvies Plateau, Harney Basin, Southeastern Oregon. *Washington State University. Center for Northwest Anthropology. Project Report* 8. Pullman.

Reimers, Henry L.
1947 Half-Way House by the Trail. (M.A. Thesis in History, Eastern Washington University, Cheney, Wash.)

————
1987 The Secret Saga of Five-Sack. Fairfield, Wash.: Ye Galleon Press. (Publ. in 1975; taken from the Wes Lloyd manuscript; it also appeared in an unpubl. manuscript titled *Tumbleweed Trails*, by Helga Travis, Prescott, Wash.)

Relander, Click (Now Tow Look)
1949 [Yakima Indians: Curing Hides; source: Mrs. Sophia Williams, known as Mrs. Wak Wak; Toppenish, Wash., Nov. 20, 1949.] (Typescript, Box 58–7, Click Relander Archives, Yakima Valley Regional Library, Yakima, Wash.)

————
1951 [Field trip to Priest Rapids made with Roger Chute, May 13, 1951.] (Typescript, Box 58–20, Click Relander Archives, Yakima Valley Regional Library, Yakima, Wash.)
————, ed. 1955 *see* Yakima Tribal Council 1955
————
1956 Drummers and Dreamers: the Story of Smowhala the Prophet and His Nephew Puck Hyah Toot, the Last Prophet of the Nearly Extinct River People, the Last Wanapums. With a Foreward by Frederick Webb Hodge. Caldwell, Idaho: The Caxton Printers. (Reprinted: Pacific Northwest National Parks and Forests Association, Seattle, Wash., 1986.)

————
1962 Strangers on the Land; a Historiette of a Longer Story of the Yakima Indian Nation's Efforts To Survive against Great Odds. Yakima, Wash.: Franklin Press.

Remnant, Daphne E.
1990 Tongue Root Articulations: A Case Study of Lillooet. (M.A. Thesis in Linguistics, University of British Columbia, Vancouver.)

Ricard, Pascal
1853   [Letters of September 5, and October 10, 1853; Oblates of Mary Immaculate, O.M.I.] (Manuscript 1581 in Oregon Historical Society Archives, Portland.)

Ricci, Gloria Lothrop, trans. and ed. 1977 *see* Mengarini, Gregory 1977

Rice, David G.
1968   Archaeological Reconnaissance: Ben Franklin Reservoir Area, 1968. Pullman: Washington State University, Laboratory of Anthropology.

———
1968a   Archaeological Reconnaissance: Hanford Atomic Works. (Report submitted to the U.S. Atomic Energy Commission and National Park Service from Washington State University, Laboratory of Anthropology, Pullman, Wash.)

———
1969   Preliminary Report: Marmes Rockshelter Archaeological Site, Southern Columbia Plateau. Pullman: Washington State University, Laboratory of Anthropology.

———
1971   Preliminary Report: Excavations at Old Umatilla (35UM35), Umatilla County, Oregon. *Mid-Columbia Archaeological Society. Report for 1970–1971.* Pasco, Wash.

———
1972   The Windust Phase in Lower Snake River Region Prehistory. *Washington State University. Laboratory of Anthropology. Reports of Investigations* 50. Pullman.

———
1978   An Archaeological Burial Relocation at Old Umatilla, Oregon. (Report submitted to the Portland District, U.S. Army Corps of Engineers from the Laboratory of Anthropology, University of Idaho.)

———
1980   Cultural Resources Assessment of the Hanford Reach of the Columbia River, State of Washington. (Report submitted to the Seattle District, Corps of Engineers, Seattle.)

———
1980a   Overview of Cultural Resources on the Hanford Reservation in South Central Washington State. (Report submitted to the Seattle District, Corps of Engineers, Seattle.)

———
1983   Archaeological Investigations at Washington Public Power Supply System Nuclear Plants on the Hanford Reservation, Washington. (Report submitted to Washington Public Power System, Richland, Wash.)

———
1985   A Resource Protection Planning Process Identification and Evaluation for Prehistoric Archaeological Resources of the Paleoindian Study Unit. (Manuscript on file, Archaeological and Historical Services, Eastern Washington University, Cheney.)

———
1987   Resource Protection Planning Process, Paleoindian Study Unit. Seattle, Wash.: Office of Archaeology and Historic Preservation.

Rice, David G., M. Giddings, and S. Johnson
1974   An Overview of Archaeological Resources in Region One National Forests in Northern Idaho. Final Report: Salmon River to the Canadian Line. *University of Idaho. Anthropological Research Manuscript Series* 15. Moscow.

Rice, Harvey S.
1965   The Cultural Sequence at Windust Caves. (M.A. Thesis in Anthropology, Washington State University, Pullman.)

———
1985   Native American Buildings and Attendant Structures on the Southern Plateau. *Eastern Washington University. Archaeological and Historical Services, Reports in Archaeology and History* 100–44. Cheney.

Rich, E.E., ed. 1947 *see* Simpson, Sir George 1947

———
1958–1960   The History of the Hudson's Bay Company, 1670–1870. With a Foreword by Winston Churchill. 3 vols. Vol. 1: 1670–1763; Vol. 2: 1763–1820; Vol. 3: 1821–1870. Toronto: McClelland and Stewart. (Also: Macmillan, New York, 1960–1961.)

Richard, Jim Earl
1964   A Study of the Big Game Animals of the Flathead Indian Reservation, Montana. (M.A. Thesis, School of Forestry, Wildlife Biology Program, University of Montana, Missoula.)

Richards, Kent D.
1979   Isaac I. Stevens: Young Man in a Hurry. Provo, Utah: Brigham Young University Press.

Richards, Thomas H.
1978   Excavations at EeRl 171. (Manuscript on file, Archaeology Branch, Victoria, B.C.)

Richards, Thomas H., and Michael K. Rousseau
1982   Archaeological Investigations on Kamloops Indian Reserve Number 1. (Manuscript on file, Archaeology Branch, Victoria, B.C.)

———
1987   Late Prehistoric Cultural Horizons on the Canadian Plateau. *Simon Fraser University. Department of Anthropology. Publication* 16. Burnaby, B.C.

Ricker, William E.
1950   Cycle Dominance among the Fraser Sockeye. *Ecology* 31(1):6–26.

Riddle, Jeff C.
1914   The Indian History of the Modoc War and the Causes That Led to It; by Jeff C. Riddle, the Son of Winema (the Heroine of the Modoc War). [San Francisco: privately printed.] (Reprinted: Pine Cone Publishers, Medford, Oreg., 1973.)

Riggs, Stephen R.
1890   A Dakota-English Dictionary. James Owen Dorsey, ed. *Contributions to North American Ethnology* 7. Washington: U.S. Geographical and Geological Survey of the Rocky Mountain Region.

Rigsby, Bruce J.
1964   [Phonetic transcript of Penutian Vocabulary survey tape (Swadesh 1954): Molala.] (Manuscript in Rigsby's possession.)

———
1965   Linguistic Relations in the Southern Plateau. (Ph.D. Dissertation in Anthropology, University of Oregon, Eugene. Photocopy: University Microfilms International, Ann Arbor, Mich., 1980.)

———
1965a   Continuity and Change in Sahaptian Vowel Systems. *International Journal of American Linguistics* 31(4):306–322.

———
1966   On Cayuse-Molala Relatability. *International Journal of American Linguistics* 32(4):369–378.

———
1969   The Waiilatpuan Problem: More on Cayuse-Molala Relatability. *Northwest Anthropological Research Notes* 3(1):68–146. Moscow, Idaho.

———
1971   Some Pacific Northwest Native Language Names for the Sasquatch Phenomenon. *Northwest Anthropological Research Notes* 5(2):153–156. Moscow, Idaho.

———
1972   [Review of: *Nez Perce Grammar*, by Haruo Aoki.] *Language* 48(3):737–742.

———
1978   Coyote and the Dogs (Sahaptin). Pp. 21–25 in Coyote Stories. William Bright, ed. *International Journal of American Linguistics. Native American Text Series. Monograph* 1. Chicago: The University of Chicago Press.

731

1996 Some Aspects of Plateau Linguistic Prehistory: Sahaptian/Interior Salish Relations. Pp. 141–146 in Chin Hills to Chiloquin: Papers Honoring the Versatile Career of Theodore Stern. Don E. Dumond, ed. *University of Oregon Anthropological Papers* 52. Eugene.

Rigsby, Bruce J., and Michael Silverstein
1969 Nez Perce Vowels and Proto-Sahaptian Vowel Harmony. *Language* 45(1):45–59.

Riley, Robert J.
1961 The Nez Perce Struggle for Self-Government: A History of Nez Perce Governing Bodies, 1842–1960. (M.A. Thesis in History, University of Idaho, Moscow.)

Rivera, Trinita
1949 Diet of a Food-Gathering People, with Chemical Analysis of Salmon and Saskatoons. Pp. 19–36 in Indians of the Urban Northwest. Marian W. Smith, ed. New York: Columbia University Press. (Reprinted: AMS Press, New York, 1969.)

Roberts, Daniel G.
1976 Final Report on the 1974–1975 Camas Creek—Little Grassy Archaeological Survey. *Idaho State University Museum of Natural History. Archaeological Report* 5. Pocatello.

Roberts, Taylor
1994 Subject and Topic in St'át'imcets (Lillooet Salish). (M.A. Thesis in Linguistics, University of British Columbia, Vancouver.)

Robie, Albert H. 1857 *see* ARCIA For 1857

Robinson, Harry
1989 Write It on Your Heart: The Epic World of an Okanagan Storyteller. Wendy Wickwire, ed. Vancouver, B.C.: Talonbooks/Theytus.

Rochford, Thomas M.
1996 Father Nicolas Point: Missionary and Artist. *Oregon Historical Quarterly* 97(1):46–69.

Roe, Frank G.
1955 The Indian and the Horse. Norman: University of Oklahoma Press. (Reprinted in 1968 and 1974.)

Roe, Joann
1981 Frank Matsura, Frontier Photographer. Introd. by Murray Morgan. Seattle, Wash.: Madrona Publishers.

Roehrig, F.L.O.
[1870] [Three comparative vocabularies of the Salish languages. One dated Nov. 15, 1870, Ithaca, N.Y.] (Manuscript No. 3072, 3 Pts., National Anthropological Archives, Smithsonian Institution, Washington.)

Roll, Tom E.
1979 Additional Archaeological Assessment of the Fisher River Site (24LN10), Northwestern Montana. *Archaeology in Montana* 20(2):79–106. Bozeman.

————, ed.

1982 Kootenai Canyon Archaeology: The 1979 LAURD Project, Final Mitigation Report. Bozeman, Mont.: Department of Sociology, Montana State University.

1988 Focus on a Phase: Expanded Geographical Distribution and Resultant Taxonomic Implications for Avonlea. Pp. 237–250 in Avonlea Yesterday and Today: Archaeology and Prehistory. Leslie B. Davis, ed. Regina: Saskatchewan Archaeological Society.

Roll, Tom E., and Marylin J. Bailey
1979 Archaeological Investigations of Selected Recreation Sites on Koocanusa Reservoir—Spring 1979. Bozeman: Montana State University.

Roll, Tom E., and William L. Singleton
1982 Introduction to the LAURD Project. Pp. 1–137 in Kootenai Canyon Archaeology: The 1979 LAURD Project, Final Mitigation Report. Tom E. Roll, ed. Bozeman: Department of Sociology, Montana State University.

Romanoff, Steven
1971 Fraser Lillooet Salmon Fishing. (B.A. Thesis in History and the Social Sciences, Reed College, Portland, Oreg.)

1985 Fraser Lillooet Salmon Fishing. *Northwest Anthropological Research Notes* 19(2):119–160. Moscow, Idaho.

1988 The Cultural Ecology of Hunting and Potlatches among the Lillooet Indians. *Northwest Anthropological Research Notes* 22(2):145–174. Moscow, Idaho.

1992 The Cultural Ecology of Hunting and Potlatches among the Lillooet Indians. Pp. 470–505 in A Complex Culture of the British Columbia Plateau: Traditional *Stl'átl'imx* Resource Use. Brian Hayden, ed. Vancouver: UBC Press.

1992a Fraser Lillooet Salmon Fishing. Pp. 222–265 in A Complex Culture of the British Columbia Plateau: Traditional *Stl'átl'imx* Resource Use. Brian Hayden, ed. Vancouver: UBC Press.

Ronan, Mary
1973 Frontier Woman: The Story of Mary Ronan as Told to Margaret Ronan. H.G. Merriam, ed. Missoula: University of Montana Publications in History.

Ronan, Peter
1890 Historical Sketch of the Flathead Indian Nation; from the Year 1813 to 1890. Embracing the History of the Establishment of St. Mary's Indian Mission in the Bitter Root Valley, Mont.; With Sketches of the Missionary Life of Father Ravalli and Other Early Missionaries. Wars of the Blackfeet and Flatheads; And Sketches of History, Trapping and Trading in the Early Days, with Illustrations. Helena, Mont.: Journal Publishing Co. (Reprinted under title: History of the Flathead Indians; Ross and Haines, Minneapolis, 1965.)

Ronda, James P.
1984 Lewis and Clark among the Indians. Lincoln and London: University of Nebraska Press.

Rosch, Eleanor
1978 Principles of Categorization. Pp. 27–48 in Cognition and Categorization. Eleanor Rosch and Barbara B. Lloyd, eds. Hillsdale, N.J.: Lawrence Erlbaum Associates.

Roscoe, Ernest J., and S. Redelings
1964 The Ecology of the Freshwater Pearl Mussel, *Margaritifera margaritifera* (L.). *Sterkiana* 16:19–32. Columbus, Ohio.

Rosenfeld, Charles L.
1985 Landforms and Geology. Pp. 40–47 in Atlas of the Pacific Northwest. A. Jon Kimberling and Philip L. Jackson, eds. 7th ed. Corvallis: Oregon State University Press.

Ross, Alexander
1821 [Map of Western North America from the British Museum Archives, London.] (Reproduction: Map No. 19, Washington State University, Holland Library Archives, Pullman.)

1849 Adventures of the First Settlers on the Oregon or Columbia River: Being a Narrative of the Expedition Fitted Out by John Jacob Astor, to Establish the "Pacific fur company"; with an Account of Some Indian Tribes on the Coast of the Pacific. By Alexander Ross, One of the Adventurers. London: Smith, Elder. (Reprinted: Vol. 7 of Early Western Travels, 1748–1846. Reuben G. Thwaites, ed. Arthur H. Clark, Cleveland, 1904; also, Milo M. Quaife, ed. Lakeside Press, Chicago, 1923; The Citadel Press, New York, 1969.)

1855   The Fur Hunters of the Far West: A Narrative of Adventures in the Oregon and Rocky Mountains. 2 vols. ("Vocabulary of the Languages Spoken by the Nez Percés" in Vol. 1, pp. 313–323). London: Smith, Elder. (Reprinted: Kenneth A. Spaulding, ed. University of Oklahoma Press, Norman, 1956.)

1904   Adventures of the First Settlers on the Oregon or Columbia River, 1810–1813. Vol. 7 of Early Western Travels, 1748–1846. Reuben G. Thwaites, ed. Cleveland: Arthur H. Clark. (Orig. publ.: Smith, Elder, London 1849.)

1913   Journal of Alexander Ross. T.C. Elliott, ed. *Oregon Historical Quarterly* 14(3):366–385.

1923   Adventures of the First Settlers on the Oregon or Columbia River: Being a Narrative of the Expedition Fitted Out by John Jacob Astor, to Establish the "Pacific fur company"; with an Account of Some Indian Tribes on the Coast of the Pacific. By Alexander Ross, One of the Adventurers. Milo M. Quaife, ed. Chicago: Lakeside Press. (Orig. publ.: Smith, Elder, London, 1849.)

1924   The Fur Hunters of the Far West: A Narrative of Adventures in the Oregon and Rocky Mountains. Milo M. Quaife, ed. Chicago: Lakeside Press. (Orig. Publ.: Smith, Elder, London, 1855.)

1956   The Fur Hunters of the Far West: A Narrative of Adventures in the Oregon and Rocky Mountains. Kenneth A. Spaulding, ed. Norman: University of Oklahoma Press. (Orig. publ.: Smith, Elder, London, 1855.)

1969   Adventures of the First Settlers on the Oregon or Columbia River. New York: Citadel Press. (Orig. publ.: Smith, Elder and Co., London, 1849.)

Ross, John Alan
1964–1991   [Ethnographic notes from Spokane and Coeur d'Alene consultants.] (Manuscripts in J.A. Ross's possession.)

1967   Factionalism on the Colville Reservation. (M.A. Thesis in Anthropology, Washington State University, Pullman.)

1968   Political Conflict on the Colville Reservation. *Northwest Anthropological Research Notes* 2(1):29–91. Moscow, Idaho.

1981   Controlled Burning: A Case of Aboriginal Resource and Forest Management in the Columbia Basin. (Paper presented at the 66th Northwest Scientific Association Annual Meeting, 24–26 March, Oregon State University, Corvallis.)

1982   The Significance of the Bluejay Ceremony in Columbia Plateau Syncretic Medicine. (Paper presented at the 35th Northwest Anthropological Conference, 7–9 April, Simon Fraser University, Burnaby, B.C.)

1984   The Occurrence and Significance of the Berdache among the Southern Plateau Salish. With Kavan di Pignatelli. (Paper presented at the 37th Northwest Anthropological Conference, 21–23 March, Spokane, Wash.)

1988   Games of the Plateau Indians. *The Journal of Physical Education, Recreation, and Dance* 59(9).

1989   Indian Shamans of the Plateau: Past and Present. *Medical Journal* 62(3).

Ross, Lester A., ed.
1975   Historical Archaeological Research within the Pacific Northwest. *Northwest Anthropological Research Notes* 9(1). Moscow, Idaho.

Ross, Richard E.
1963   Prehistory of the Round Butte Area, Jefferson County, Oregon. (M.A. Thesis in Anthropology, University of Oregon, Eugene.)

Ross, Robert L., and Harold E. Hunter
1976   Climax Vegetation of Montana; Based on Soils and Climate. Bozeman, Mont.: U.S. Department of Agriculture, Soil Conservation Service.

Ross, Samuel
1870   [Letter of September 1, 1870.] Pp. 480–494 in *41st Congress. 3d Session. House Executive Document* 1. (Serial No. 1449). Washington.

Rossillon, Mary P.
1982   Cultural Resource Overview for the Salmon National Forest. (Manuscript on file, Salmon National Forest, Salmon, Idaho.)

Rostlund, Erhard
1952   Freshwater Fish and Fishing in Native North America. *University of California Publications in Geography* 9. Berkeley. (Reprinted: Johnson Reprint Co., New York, 1968.)

Rothermich, Albert E., ed.
1936   Early Days at Fort Missoula. *Frontier and Midland* 16(3):225–235. Missoula, Mont. (Reprinted: *Historical Reprints, Sources of Northwest History* 23. Missoula: State University of Montana.)

Rounsefell, George A., and George B. Kelez
1938   The Salmon and Salmon Fisheries of Swiftsure Bank, Puget Sound, and the Fraser River. *U.S. Bureau of Fisheries. Bulletin* 48(27):693–823. Washington. (Whole *Bulletin* 48 has imprint date 1940.)

Rousseau, Michael K.
1982   An Interpretive and Descriptive Analysis of Lithic Artifacts from Site (DiQj 1), Vallican, Slocan Valley. (Manuscript on file, Archaeology Branch, Victoria, B.C.)

1990   Changes in Human Sedentism, Mobility, and Subsistence during the Plateau Pithouse Tradition on the Canadian Plateau. (Paper presented at the 1990 meeting of the American Anthropological Association, Las Vegas.)

1993   Early Prehistoric Occupation of South-Central British Columbia: A Review of the Evidence and Recommendations for Future Research. *BC Studies* 99(Autumn):140–183. Vancouver.

Rousseau, Michael K., and Geordie Howe
1987   Scheidam Flats: A Prehistoric Root Roasting Area near Kamloops. *The Midden* 19(2):7–10. Vancouver.

Rousseau, Michael K., and Thomas H. Richards
1985   A Culture-Historical Sequence for the South Thompson River-Western Shuswap Lakes Region of British Columbia. *Northwest Anthropological Research Notes* 19(1):1–32. Moscow, Idaho.

1988   The Oregon Jack Creek Site (EdRi–6): A Lehman Phase Site in the Thompson River Valley, British Columbia. *Canadian Journal of Archaeology* 12:39–63. Ottawa.

Rousseau, Michael K., Robert J. Muir, and Diana Alexander
1991   The 1990 Archaeological Investigations Conducted at the Fraser Bay Site (EfQt 1), Shuswap Lake, South-Central B.C. (Manuscript on file, Archaeology Branch, Victoria, B.C.)

1991a   Results of the 1990 Archaeological Investigations Conducted in the Oregon Jack Creek Locality, Thompson River Region, South-Central British Columbia. (Manuscript on file, Archaeology Branch, Victoria, B.C.)

733

Rousseau, Michael K., R.J. Muir, D. Alexander, J. Breffitt, S. Woods, K. Berry, and T. Van Galen
1991   Results of the 1989 Archaeological Investigations Conducted in the Oregon Jack Creek Locality, Thompson River Region, South- Central British Columbia. Burnaby, B.C.: Simon Fraser University.

Roy, Prodipto
1961   Assimilation of the Spokane Indians. *Washington [State] Agricultural Experiment Stations. Institute of Agricultural Sciences. Washington State University Bulletin* 628. Pullman.

Royce, Charles C., comp.
1899   Indian Land Cessions in the United States. Pp. 521–997 in Pt. 2 of *18th Annual Report of the Bureau of American Ethnology for 1896–1897.* Washington. (Reprinted: Arno Press, New York, 1971; also, AMS Press, New York, 1973.)

Ruby, Robert H.
1966   A Healing Service in the Shaker Church. *Oregon Historical Quarterly* 67(4):347–355.

Ruby, Robert H., and John A. Brown
1965   Half-Sun on the Columbia: A Biography of Chief Moses. Norman: University of Oklahoma Press.

1970   The Spokane Indians, Children of the Sun. With a Foreword by Robert L. Bennett. Norman: University of Oklahoma Press.

1972   The Cayuse Indians: Imperial Tribesmen of Old Oregon. Foreword by Clifford M. Drury. Norman: University of Oklahoma Press.

1976   The Chinook Indians: Traders of the Lower Columbia River. Norman: University of Oklahoma Press.

1981   Indians of the Pacific Northwest: A History. With a Foreword by Alvin M. Josephy, Jr. Norman: University of Oklahoma Press.

1986   A Guide to the Indian Tribes of the Pacific Northwest. Norman: University of Oklahoma Press.

1989   Dreamer-Prophets of the Columbia Plateau: Smohalla and Skolaskin. Foreword by Herman J. Viola. Norman: University of Oklahoma Press.

1996   John Slocum and the Indian Shaker Church. Norman: University of Oklahoma Press.

Rude, Noel
1982   Promotion and Topicality of Nez Perce Objects. Pp. 283–301 in *Proceedings of the Eighth Annual Meeting of the Berkeley Linguistic Society.* Monica Macaulay et al., eds. Berkeley.

1985   Studies in Nez Perce Grammar and Discourse. (Ph.D. Dissertation in Linguistics, University of Oregon, Eugene. Photocopy: University Microfilm International, Ann Arbor, Mich., 1987.)

1986   Discourse-Pragmatic Context for Genitive Promotion in Nez Perce. *Studies in Language* 10:109–136.

1986a   Topicality, Transitivity, and the Direct Object in Nez Perce. *International Journal of American Linguistics* 52(2):124–153.

1987   Some Klamath-Sahaptian Grammatical Correspondences. *Kansas Working Papers in Linguistics* 12(1):67–83. Lawrence.

1988   Ergative, Passive, and Antipassive in Nez Perce: A Discourse Perspective. Pp. 547–560 in Passive and Voice. Masayoshi

Shibatani, ed. *Typological Studies in Language* 16. Amsterdam: John Benjamins Publishing Company.

1988a   Semantic and Pragmatic Objects in Klamath. Pp. 51–673 in In Honor of Mary Haas: From the Haas Festival Conference on Native American Linguistics. William Shipley, ed. Berlin: Mouton de Gruyter.

1989   The Grammar of Kinship Terms in Sahaptin. Pp. 87–95 in Papers from the 1989 Hokan-Penutian Languages Workshop. Scott DeLancey, ed. Eugene: University of Oregon.

1991   On the Origin of the Nez Perce Ergative NP Suffix. *International Journal of American Linguistics* 57(1):24–50.

1991a   Verbs to Promotional Suffixes in Sahaptian and Klamath. Pp. 185–199 in Approaches to Grammaticalization. Elizabeth Closs Traugott and Bernd Heine, eds. *Typological Studies in Language* 19, Pt. 2. Amsterdam and Philadelphia: John Benjamins.

1991b   [Linguistic fieldnotes, Warm Spring Reservation, Oreg.] (Manuscripts in Rude's possession.)

1992   Dative Shifting in Sahaptin. *International Journal of American Linguistics* 58(3):316–321.

1992a   Word Order and Topicality in Nez Perce. Pp. 193–208 in Pragmatics of Word Order Flexibility. Doris L. Payne, ed. *Typological Studies in Language* 22. Amsterdam and Philadelphia: John Benjamins.

1994   Direct, Inverse and Passive in Northwest Sahaptin. Pp. 101–119 in Voice and Inversion. T. Givón, ed. *Typological Studies in Language* 28. Amsterdam and Philadelphia: John Benjamins.

1996   The Sahaptian Inflectional Suffix Complex. In: *Proceedings of the 1994–1995 Hokan-Penutian Workshops, Survey of California and Other Indian Languages, Report* 9. Berkeley: University of California, Department of Linguistics.

1997   On the History of Nominal Case in Sahaptian. *International Journal of American Linguistics* 63(1):113–143.

Ruebelmann, George N.
1973   The Archaeology of the Mesa Hill Site: A Prehistoric Workshop in the Southeastern Columbia Plateau. The Final Report on Archaeological Salvage Excavations of Federal Highway Project F–3112(21) Mesa North, Adams County, Idaho. *University of Idaho. Laboratory of Anthropology. Anthropological Research Manuscript Series* 9. Moscow.

1978   The Weis Rockshelter: A Problem in Southeastern Plateau Chronology. *Northwest Anthropological Research Notes* 12(1):9–16. Moscow, Idaho.

Rust, Henry J.
1912   A Brief Historical and Archaeological Sketch of Lake Coeur d'Alene, Kootenai County, Idaho. *The Archaeological Bulletin* 3(2):46–48.

Ryan, Jerome
1977   An Archaeological Survey of the Middle Clark Fork River Valley: Missoula to Superior, Montana. (M.A. Thesis in Anthropology, University of Montana, Missoula.)

Ryder, June M.
1978   Geomorphology and Late Quaternary History of the Lillooet Area. Reports of the Lillooet Archaeological Project, 1: Introduction and Setting. A.H. Stryd and S. Lawhead, eds. Pp. 56–67 in *Canada. National Museum of Man. Mercury Series. Archaeological Survey Paper* 73. Ottawa.

Ryder, June M., and B. Thompson
1986 Neoglaciation in the Southern Coast Mountains of British Columbia: Chronology Prior to the Late Glacial Maximum. *Canadian Journal of Earth Sciences* 23(3):273–287. Ottawa.

Sadek-Kooros, Hind
1965 Appendix: Distribution of the Bird Remains at Jaguar Cave. *Tebiwa: Journal of the Idaho State University Museum* 8(1):20–28. Pocatello.

———— 1966 Jaguar Cave: An Early Man Site in the Beaverhead Mountains of Idaho. (Ph.D. Dissertation in Anthropology, Harvard University, Cambridge, Mass.)

———— 1972 The Sediments and Fauna of Jaguar Cave: 1-The Sediments. *Tebiwa: Journal of the Idaho State University Museum* 15(1):1–20. Pocatello

Sahlins, Marshall D.
1965 On the Sociology of Primitive Exchange. Pp. 139–236 in The Relevance of Models for Social Anthropology. Michael Banton, ed. *ASA Monographs* 1. London: Tavistock.

St. Onge, Louis Napoléon
1872 Alphabet yakama, contenant les prières, les cantiques et le catéchisme dans la même langue. Montreal: Imprimé à la Providence.

Salish Culture Committee
1975- [Taped interviews, mainly in Salish, conducted with Tribal Elders; most translated into English.] (Tapes in Selis-Qlispé Oral History and Culture Archives, St. Ignatius, Mont.; written permission of Salish Culture Committee needed to access tapes and transcripts.)

———— 1996 Skʷskʷstulexʷ Sqelixʷ — Names Upon the Land: a Tribal Geography of the Salish and Pend d'Oreille People. (Unpublished manuscript.) St. Ignatius, Mont.: Confederated Salish and Kootenai Tribes.

Salish Kootenai College
1987 Living in Harmony Color Book. Pablo, Mont.: Salish Kootenai College.

———— 1995–1997 1995–1997 College Catalog. Pablo, Mont.: Salish Kootenai College.

Salish Kootenai College (and U.S. Soil Conservation Service)
1987 Living in Harmony Color Book. Dwight Billedeaux, Patrick Chief Stick, Jr., Sam Sandoval, and Corwin Clairmont, illus.; Corwin Clairmont, art dir. Elmo, Mont.: Salish Kootenai College.

Salo, Lawr V.
1985 Large Scale Analytic Units: Chronological Periods and Types. Pp. 183–222 in Summary of Results, Chief Joseph Dam Cultural Resources Project, Washington. Sarah K. Campbell, ed. Seattle: Office of Public Archaeology, Institute for Environmental Studies, University of Washington.

———— 1985a Site Clustering. Pp. 249–268 in Summary of Results, Chief Joseph Dam Cultural Resources Project, Washington. Sarah K. Campbell, ed. Seattle: Office of Public Archaeology, Institute for Environmental Studies, University of Washington.

Salzmann, Zdeněk, comp.
1983 Dictionary of Contemporary Arapaho Usage. *Arapaho Language and Culture Instructional Materials Series* 4. William J. C'Hair, gen. ed. Wind River Reservation, Wyo.

Samarin, William J.
1988 Jargonization Before Chinook Jargon. *Northwest Anthropological Research Notes* 22(2):219–238. Moscow, Idaho.

Sammons-Lohse, Dorothy
1985 Features. Pp. 455–480 in Summary of Results, Chief Joseph Dam Cultural Resources Project, Washington. Sarah K. Campbell, ed. Seattle: Office of Public Archaeology, Institute for Environmental Studies, University of Washington.

Sample, Laetitia L., and Albert Mohr
1980 Wishram Birth and Obstetrics. *Ethnology* 19(4):427–445.

Sampson, C. Garth
1985 Nightfire Island: Late Holocene Lakemarsh Adaptation on the Western Edge of the Great Basin. *University of Oregon Anthropological Papers* 3. Eugene.

Sanday, Peggy R.
1974 Female Status in the Public Domain. Pp. 189–206 in Woman, Culture and Society. Michelle Zimbalist Rosaldo and Louise Lamphere, eds. Stanford, Calif.: Stanford University Press.

Sanders, Paul H., and Deborah L. Olson
1992 Analysis of Archaeological Assemblage. In: Archaeological Investigations Along the Pend d'Oreille River: Site 24PO149. Paul H. Sanders, ed. *Washington State University. Department of Anthropology. Center for Northwest Anthropology. Project Report* 18. Pullman.

Sanger, David
1964 Excavations at Nesikep Creek (EdRk:4), a Stratfied Site Near Lillooet British Columbia: Preliminary Report. Pp 130–161 in Contributions to Anthropology, 1961–1962 (Pt.1). *National Museum of Canada Bulletin* 193. Ottawa.

———— 1966 Excavations in the Lochnore-Nesikep Creek Locality, British Columbia: Interim Report. *Canada. National Museum. Anthropology Papers* 12. Ottawa.

———— 1967 Prehistory of the Pacific Northwest Plateau as Seen from the Interior of British Columbia. *American Antiquity* 32(2):186–197.

———— 1968 The Texas Creek Burial Site Assemblage, British Columbia. *Canada. National Museum. Anthropology Papers* 17. Ottawa.

———— 1968a Prepared Core and Blade Traditions in the Pacific Northwest. *Arctic Anthropology* 5(1):92–120. Madison, Wis.

———— 1969 Cultural Traditions in the Interior of British Columbia. *Syesis* 2:189–200. Victoria, B.C.

———— 1969a The Chase Burial Site (EeQw:1), British Columbia. Pp 85–185 in Contributions to Anthropology VI: Archaeology and Physical Anthropology. *Canada. National Museum Bulletin* 224. Ottawa. (Incl. a Summary in French, p. 86.)

———— 1970 The Archaeology of the Lochnore-Nesikep Locality, British Columbia. *Syesis* 3 (Suppl. 1):1–146. Victoria, B.C.

———— 1970a Mid-latitude Core and Blade Traditions. *Arctic Anthropology* 7(1):106–117. Madison, Wis.

Sapir, Edward
1905 [Unpublished Wishram and Cascade linguistic and ethnographic notes and manuscripts, from two months' fieldwork on the Yakima Reservation, Wash.; also, Correspondence with Peter McGuff, Cascades/Wishram.] (Manuscripts in Franz Boas Collection, American Philosophical Society Library, Philadelphia.)

———— 1907 Notes on the Takelma Indians of Southwest Oregon. *American Anthropologist*, n.s. 9(2):251–275.

———— 1907a Preliminary Report on the Language and Mythology of the Upper Chinook. *American Anthropologist*, n.s. 9(3):533–544.

———— 1907–1910 *see* Hodge, Frederick W., ed. 1907–1910.

735

1909   Wishram Texts. Together with Wasco Tales and Myths, collected by Jeremiah Curtin and ed. by Edward Sapir. *Publications of the American Ethnological Society* 2. Leyden. (Reprinted: AMS Press, New York, 1974; also, pp. 17–340 in The Collected Works of Edward Sapir, Vol. 7: Wishram Texts and Ethnography. William Bright, ed. Mouton de Gruyter, Berlin and New York, 1990.)

1909a   Takelma Texts. *University of Pennsylvania. University Museum. Anthropological Publications* 2(1). Philadelphia.

1911   Diminutive and Augmentative Consonantism in Wishram. Pp. 638–645 in Pt. 1 of Handbook of American Indian Languages. Franz Boas, ed. *Bureau of American Ethnology Bulletin* 40. Washington. (Reprinted: Scholarly Press, St. Clair Shores, Mich., 1976.)

1911a   Post-positions in Wishram. Pp. 650–654 in Pt. 1 of Handbook of American Indian Languages. Franz Boas, ed. *Bureau of American Ethnology Bulletin* 40. (Reprinted: Scholarly Press, St. Clair Shores, Mich., 1976.)

1913   A Note on Reciprocal Terms of Relationship in America. *American Anthropologist*, n.s. 15(1):132–138.

1916   Time Perspective in Aboriginal American Culture: A Study in Method. *Canada. Department of Mines. Geological Survey Memoir* 90 *Anthropological Series* 13,. Ottawa. (Reprinted: Pp. 389–462 in Selected Writings of Edward Sapir in Language, Culture and Personality. David G. Mandelbaum, ed. University of California Press, Berkeley and Los Angeles, 1949, 1963; also, Johnson Reprint, New York, 1968.)

1916a   Terms of Relationship and the Levirate. *American Anthropologist*, n.s. 18(3):327–337.

1918   Kinship Terms of the Kootenay Indians. *American Anthropologist*, n.s. 20(4):414–418.

1921   A Bird's-eye View of American Languages North of Mexico. *Science*, n.s. 54(1400):408. (Reprinted: Pp. 93–94 in The Collected Works of Edward Sapir, Vol. 5: American Indian Languages. William Bright, ed. Mouton de Gruyter, Berlin and New York, 1990.)

1921a   A Characteristic Penutian Form of Stem. *International Journal of American Linguistics* 2(1–2):58-67.

1921b   Language: An Introduction to the Study of Speech. New York: Harcourt, Brace. (Reprinted in 1949, 1957.)

1926   A Chinookan Phonetic Law. *International Journal of American Linguistics* 4:105–110. (Reprinted: Pp 197–205 in Selected Writings of Edward Sapir in Language, Culture and Personality. David G. Mandelbaum, ed. University of California Press, Berkeley, 1949, 1963; also, Johnson Reprint, New York, 1968.)

1929   Central and North American Languages. Pp. 138–141 in Vol. 5 of Encyclopaedia Britannica. 14th ed. London and New York: Encyclopaedia Britannica Company. (Reprinted: Pp. 169–178 in Selected Writings of Edward Sapir in Language, Culture and Personality. David G. Mandelbaum, ed. University of California Press, Berkeley and Los Angeles, 1949, 1963; also, Johnson Reprint, New York, 1968.)

Sapir, Edward, and Morris Swadesh
1939   Nootka Texts: Tales and Ethological Narratives, with Grammatical Notes and Lexical Material. Philadelphia: University of Pennsylvania, Linguistic Society of America. (Reprinted: AMS Press, New York, 1978.)

1953   Coos-Takelma-Penutian Comparisons. *International Journal of American Linguistics* 19(2):132–137.

1955   Native Accounts of Nootka Ethnography. *Indiana University. Research Center in Anthropology, Folklore and Linguistics. Publications* 1:1–457. Bloomington. (Reprinted: AMS Press, New York, 1978.)

Sappington, Robert Lee
1981   A Progress Report on the Obsidian and Vitrophyre Sourcing Project. *Idaho Archaeologist* 4(4):4–17.Caldwell.

1984   Procurement Without Quarry Production: Examples from Southwestern Idaho. Pp. 23–34 in Prehistoric Quarries and Lithic Production. Jonathon E. Ericson and Barbara A. Purdy, eds. Cambridge and New York: Cambridge University Press.

1985   Archaeological Investigations at 10 Sites Along the Lower Snake and Clearwater Rivers. *University of Idaho. Alfred W. Bowers Laboratory of Anthropology. Letter Report* 85–24. Moscow.

1988   Archaeological Test Excavation and Evaluation of the Proposed Clearwater Fish Hatchery Site (10-CW-4), on the North Fork of the Clearwater River, North Central Idaho. With Contributions by Bruce Cochran and Terry L. Ozbun. *University of Idaho. Alfred W. Bowers Laboratory of Anthropology. Anthropological Reports* 88. Moscow.

1989   The Lewis and Clark Expedition among the Nez Perce Indians: The First Ethnographic Study in the Columbia Plateau. *Northwest Anthropological Research Notes* 23(1):1–33. Moscow, Idaho.

1990   Archaeological Investigations at the Ahsahka Sportsmen's Access Site (10-CW-5), Clearwater River, North Central Idaho. With Contributions by M.A. Fosberg, D.L. Olson, J. Flenniken, and T.L. Olson. *University of Idaho. Alfred W. Bowers Laboratory of Anthropology. Anthropological Reports* 90. Moscow.

1990a   Preliminary Report Concerning Additional Test Excavation at the Canoe Camp Site. *University of Idaho. Alfred W. Bowers Laboratory of Anthropology. Letter Report* 90–11. Moscow

1991   The Clearwater Basin. Pp. 161–190 in An Overview of Cultural Resources in the Snake River Basin: Prehistory and Paleoenvironments. K.C. Reid, ed. *Center for Northwest Anthropology, Project* 13. Pullman: Washington University.

1991a   Results of Archaeological Investigations at Tuhkaytahs'peh, The Maggies Bend Site (10-IH-10009), Middle Fork of the Clearwater River, Idaho. *University of Idaho. Alfred W. Bowers Laboratory of Anthropology. Letter Report* 91–7. Moscow.

1993   Results of Archaeological Test Investigations at the Kooskia National Fish Hatchery, Middle Fork Clearwater River, North Central Idaho. With Contributions by R. Tracy, J. Flenniken, J. Markos, T.L. Ozbun, and N. Stricker. *University of Idaho. Alfred W. Bowers Laboratory of Anthropology. Letter Report* 93–9. Moscow.

1994   The Prehistory of the Clearwater River Region, North Central Idaho. *University of Idaho. Alfred W. Bowers Laboratory of Anthropology. Letter Report* 95. Moscow.

Sappington, Robert Lee, and Caroline D. Carley
1983   Results of Archaeological Test Excavations along the Clearwater River, North Central Idaho. *University of Idaho. Alfred*

736

W. Bowers Laboratory of Anthropology. *Report to the Idaho Transportation Department.* E-124. Moscow.

1986   Archaeological Investigations at Eight Locations along the Lochsa River, North Central Idaho. *University of Idaho. Alfred W. Bowers Laboratory of Anthropology. Letter Report* 86–8. Moscow.

1987   Archaeological Investigations at the Kooskia Bridge Site (10-IH-1395), Middle Fork, Clearwater River, North Central Idaho. *University of Idaho, Alfred W. Bowers Laboratory of Anthropology. Anthropological Reports* 87. Moscow.

1989   Archaeological Investigations at the Beaver Flat and Pete King Creek Sites, Lochsa River, North Central Idaho. *University of Idaho. Alfred W. Bowers Laboratory of Anthropology. Anthropological Reports* 89. Moscow.

1995   Alice Cunningham Fletcher's "Ethnologic Gleanings among the Nez Perces". *Northwest Anthropological Research Notes* 29(1):1–50. Moscow, Idaho.

Sappington, Robert Lee, and Priscilla Wegars
1988   Results of Archaeological Test Excavations at Canoe Camp, Nez Perce National Historical Park, near Orofino, Idaho. *University of Idaho. Alfred W. Bowers Laboratory of Anthropology. Letter Report* 88–15. Moscow.

Sappington, Robert Lee, et al.
1989   Archaeological Investigations at the Beaver Flat and Pete King Creek Sites, Lochsa River, North Central Idaho. Moscow: Alfred W. Bowers Laboratory of Anthropology, University of Idaho.

Sargeant, Kathryn E.
1973   The Haskett Tradition: A View from Redfish Overhang. (M.A. Thesis in Anthropology, Idaho State University, Pocatello.)

Schaeffer, Claude E.
1930   Material Culture and Annual Economic Cycle of the Flatheads. (M.A. Thesis in Anthropology, Yale University, New Heaven, Conn.)

1935   [Fieldnotes from ethnographic work among the Kootenai, 1935 to 1969, concentrated primarily in 1935–1937.] (Manuscripts in the Glenbow Foundation, Calgary, Alta., and in the American Museum of Natural History, New York.)

1935a   Flathead (Sélic) Medicine Ceremony: Notes Secured Winter of 1935 at Flathead Reservation, Montana. (Typescript.)

1936   An Acculturation Study of the Indians of the Flathead Reservation of Western Montana. (Report submitted to the Commissioner of Indian Affairs, U.S. Department of the Interior, Washington.)

1937   Kutenai Ethnographic Notes. Calgary, Alta.: Glenbow Foundation.

1940   The Subsistence Quest of the Kutenai: A Study of the Interaction of Culture and Environment. (Ph.D. Dissertation in Anthropology, University of Pennsylvania, Philadelphia.)

1947   The Bear Foster Parent Tale: A Kutenai Version. *Journal of American Folk-Lore* 60 (237):286–288.

1949   Wolf and Two-Pointed Buck: A Lower Kutenai Tale of the Supernatural Period. *Primitive Man* 22(1–2):1–22. (Reprinted: Pp. 107–118 in The Last Best Place: A Montana Anthology. William Kittredge and Annick Smith, eds. Helena: Montana Historical Society, 1988.)

1952   Conjuring. Vancouver, B.C.: West Canadian Graphics Industrie Limited.

1959   Indian Tribes and Languages of the Old Oregon Country. Map, 2d ed. Portland: Oregon Historical Society.

1964   The Plains Kutenai: An Ethnological Evaluation. (Manuscript in the Glenbow Foundation, Calgary, Alta.)

1966   Bear Ceremonialism of the Kutenai Indians. *Studies in Plains Anthropology and History* 4. Browning, Mont.: U.S. Dept. of Interior, Indian Arts and Crafts Board.

1966a   Le Blanc and La Gasse: Predecessors of David Thompson in the Columbian Plateau. *Studies in Plains Anthropology and History* 3. Browning, Mont.: Museum of the Plains Indian, Indian Arts and Crafts Board, U.S. Department of the Interior.

Schalk, Randall F.
1977   The Structure of an Anadromous Fish Resource. Pp. 207–249 in For Theory Building in Archaeology. Louis R. Binford, ed. Orlando, Fla.: Academic Press.

————, ed.
1980   Cultural Resource Investigations for the Second Powerhouse Project at McNary Dam, Near Umatilla, Oregon. *Washington State University. Laboratory of Archaeology and History. Project Report* 1. Pullman.

1980a   Land Use of the Ethnographic Umatilla. Pp. 47–52 in Cultural Resource Investigations for the Second Powerhouse Project at McNary Dam, Near Umatilla, Oregon. Randall F. Schalk, ed. *Washington State University. Laboratory of Archaeology and History. Project Report* 1. Pullman.

1983   The 1978 and 1979 Excavations at Strawberry Island in the McNary Reservoir. *Washington State University. Laboratory of Archaeology and History. Project Report* 19. Pullman.

1983a   Cultural Resource Investigations for the Lyons Ferry Fish Hatchery Project, Near Lyons Ferry, Washington. With contributions by Gregory C. Cleveland, Robert R. Mierendorf, Deborah L. Olson, and Roderick Sprague. *Washington State University. Laboratory of Archaeology and History. Project Report* 8. Pullman.

1984   The Columbia Plateau Salmon Fisheries: Archaeological Evidence for Intensification. (Paper presented at the Annual Meeting of the Society for American Archaeology, Portland, Oreg., April, 13, 1984.)

1986   Estimating Salmon and Steelhead Usage in the Columbia Basin Before 1850: The Anthropological Perspective. *Northwest Environmental Journal* 2(2):1–29. Seattle.

Schalk, Randall F., and Gregory C. Cleveland
1983   A Chronological Perspective on Hunter-Gatherer Land Use Strategies in the Columbia Plateau. Pp. 11–56 in Cultural Resource Investigations for the Lyons Ferry Fish Hatchery Project, Near Lyons Ferry, Washington. Randall F. Schalk, ed. *Washington State University. Laboratory of Archaeology and History. Project Report* 8. Pullman. (Title of article in Table of Contents varies: A Sequence of Adaptations in the Columbia-Fraser Plateau.)

Schalk, Randall F., et al. 1983 *see* Schalk, Randall F. 1983a

Scheuerman, Richard D., ed.
1982   The Wenatchi Indians: Guardians of the Valley. Fairfield, Wash.: Ye Galleon Press.

Schlegel, Alice
1977   Toward a Theory of Sexual Stratification. Pp. 1–40 in Sexual Satisfaction: A Cross-Cultural View. Alice Schlegel, ed. New York: Columbia University Press.

Schlick, Mary D.
1979   A Columbia River Indian Basket Collection by Lewis and Clark in 1805. *American Indian Basketry Magazine* 1(1):10–13.

_____
1980   Art Treasures of the Columbia Plateau Indians. *American Indian Basketry Magazine* 1(2):12–21.

_____
1984   Cedar Bark Baskets. *American Indian Basketry* 4(3):26–29.

_____
1988   An American Tradition: Columbia River Basketmakers. *Fiberarts* 15(1):44–46.

_____
1994   Columbia River Basketry: Gift of the Ancestors, Gift of the Earth. Seattle and London: University of Washington Press.

Schmidt, John L., and Douglas L. Gilbert, comps. and eds.
1978   Big Game of North America: Ecology and Management. Harrisburg, Pa.: Stackpole Books.

Schoning, Robert W., T.R. Merrell, Jr., and D.R. Johnson
1951   The Indian Dip Net Fishery at Celilo Falls on the Columbia River. *Oregon Fish Commission Contributions* 17. Portland.

Schoolcraft, Henry Rowe
1847   Inquiries, Respecting the History, Present Condition and Future Prospects of the Indian Tribes of the United States. Washington, D.C.: [Indian Office and War Department.] (Issued also as an Appendix to Vol. 1 of the author's Historical and Statistical Information, [etc.]. 6 vols., Lippincott, Grambo, Philadelphia, 1851–1857.)

_____, comp. and ed.
1851–1857 Historical and Statistical Information Respecting the History, Condition and Prospects of the Indian Tribes of the United States. 6 vols. Philadelphia: Lippincott, Grambo. (Reprinted: AMS Press, New York, 1969.)

Schroedl, Gerald L.
1973   The Archaeological Occurrence of Bison in the Southern Plateau. *Washington State University. Laboratory of Anthropology. Reports of Investigations* 51. Pullman. (Originally presented as the Author's Thesis in Anthropology, Washington State University, Pullman, 1972, under title: The Association of Bison Remains with Cultural Assemblages of Post-Altithermal Age in the Columbia Plateau of Washington.)

Schulting, Rick J.
1994   An Investigation of Mortuary Variability and Socioeconomic Status Differentiation on the Northwest Plateau. (M.A. Thesis in Archaeology, Simon Fraser University, Burnaby, B.C.)

Schultz, John L.
1968   Deprivation, Revitalization, and the Development of the Shaker Religion. *Northwest Anthropological Research Notes* 2(1):92–119. Moscow, Idaho.

_____
1971   Acculturation and Religion on the Colville Indian Reservation. (Ph. D. Dissertation in Anthropology, Washington State University, Pullman. Photocopy: University Microfilms International, Ann Arbor, Mich., 1984.)

Schultz, John L., and Deward E. Walker, Jr.
1967   Indian Shakers on the Colville Reservation. *Washington State University. Research Studies* 35(2):167–172. Pullman.

Schumm, Stanley A., and G.R. Brakenridge
1987   River Responses. Pp. 221–240 in The Geology of North America Volume K-3: North America and Adjacent Oceans During the Last Deglaciation. W.F. Ruddiman and Herbert E. Wright, Jr., eds. Boulder: Geological Society of America.

Schuster, Helen H.
1965   Implications of the Use of Children's Drawings for Cross-Cultural Research: A Survey and Evaluation. (M.A. Thesis in Anthropology, University of Washington, Seattle.)

_____
1965–1985 [Ethnographic notes from approximately three years' fieldwork among the Yakima and related people in Washington State.] (Fieldnotes and manuscripts in H. Schuster's possession.)

_____
1975   Yakima Indian Traditionalism: A Study in Continuity and Change. 2 vols. (Ph.D. Dissertation in Anthropology, University of Washington, Seattle. Microfilm: Xerox University Microfilms, Ann Arbor, Mich., 1975.)

_____
1978   Children's Drawing and Perceptions of 'Indianness'. *Ethos* 6(3):159–174.

_____
1982   The Yakimas, A Critical Bibliography. *The Newberry Library Center for the History of the American Indian Bibliographical Series*. Bloomington: Indiana University Press.

_____
1989   Political Structure in Historic Perspective: The Yakima Indian Nation. (Paper presented at the American Society for Ethnohistory Conference, Nov. 2–5, 1989, Chicago.)

_____
1990   The Yakima. New York: Chelsea House.

Schwantes, Carlos A.
1989   The Pacific Northwest: An Interpretive History. Lincoln: University of Nebraska Press.

Schwede, Madge L.
1966   An Ecological Study of Nez Perce Settlement Patterns. (M.A. Thesis in Anthropology, Washington State University, Pullman.)

_____
1970   The Relationship of Aboriginal Nez Perce Settlement Patterns to Physical Environment and to Generalized Distribution of Food Resources. *Northwest Anthropological Research Notes* 4(2):129–136. Moscow, Idaho.

Science News
1991   How to Date a Rock Artist. *Science News* 139(3):45.

Scott, Leslie M.
1928   Indian Diseases as Aids to Pacific Northwest Settlement. *Oregon Historical Quarterly* 29(2):144–161.

Scott, William B., and E.J. Crossman
1973   Freshwater Fishes of Canada. *Fisheries Research Board of Canada Bulletin* 184. Ottawa.

Scouler, John
1848   On the Indian Tribes Inhabiting the North-West Coast of America. *Journal of the Ethnological Society of London* 1:228–252. Edinburgh: Neill and Company. (Reprinted in: *Northwest Anthropological Research Notes* 25(2):139–154. Moscow, Idaho, 1991.)

_____
1905   Dr. John Scouler's Journal of a Voyage to N.W. America [1824]. F.G. Young, ed. *Oregon Historical Quarterly* 2(1):159–205.

Scrimsher, Leda Scott
1967   Native Foods Used by the Nez Perce Indians of Idaho. (M.S. Thesis in Anthropology, University of Idaho, Moscow.)

Seaburg, William R.
1982   Guide to the Pacific Northwest Native American Materials in the Melville Jacobs Collection and in Other Archival Collections in the University of Washington Libraries. *University of Washington Libraries Communications in Librarianship* 2. Seattle.

Seaman, Norma G.
1940   An Amateur Archaeologist's 50 years in Oregon. *Oregon Historical Quarterly* 41(2):147–159.

————
1946   Indian Relics of the Pacific Northwest. [1st ed.] Portland, Oreg.: Binfords and Mort. (Reprinted in 1967 and 1974.)

————
1967   Indian Relics of the Pacific Northwest. 2d ed. Portland, Oreg.: Binfords and Mort. (Reprinted in 1974.)

Secrist, Kenneth G.
1960   Pictographs in Central Montana. Part I: Fergus County. Carling Malouf, ed. *Montana State University, Anthropology and Sociology Papers* 20. Missoula.

Secwepemc Cultural Education Society
1996   K'wséltktens Re Secwsecwépemc. (Adapted from a previous book, *The Shuswap Family*, trans. by Brigett Dan in 1985.) Kamloops, B.C. : Secwepemc Cultural Education Society, Language Department.

Seeger, Anthony, and Louise S. Spear, eds.
1987   Early Field Recordings: A Catalogue of Cylinder Collections at the Indiana University Archives of Traditional Music. Bloomington: Indiana University Press.

Seifried, Richard D.
1968   Early Administration of the Flathead Indian Reservation, 1855 to 1893. (M.A. Thesis in History, University of Montana, Missoula.)

Seymour, Peter J.
1985   The Golden Woman: The Colville Narrative of Peter J. Seymour; Translated by Anthony Mattina and Madeline deSautel. Anthony Mattina, ed. Tucson: University of Arizona Press.

Shane, Ralph M.
1950   Early Explorations Through Warm Springs Reservation Area. *Oregon Historical Quarterly* 51(4):273–309.

Shapard, Jeffrey
1980   Interior Salishan (Di)Transitive Systems. Pp. 229–282 in *15th International Conference on Salish Languages*. Vancouver, B.C.

Sharkey, Margery Ann Beach
1984   Revitalization and Change: A History of the Wanapum Indians, Their Prophet Smohalla, and the Washani Religion. (M.A. Thesis in Anthropology, Washington State University, Pullman.)

Shawley, Stephen D.
1975   Nez Perce Dress: A Study in Culture Change. (M.A. Thesis in Anthropology, University of Idaho, Moscow.)

Sheller, Roscoe
1965   The Name Was Olney. Yakima, Wash.: Franklin Press.

Sheppard, John C., Peter E. Wigand, Carl E. Gustafson, and Meyer Rubin
1987   A Reevaluation of the Marmes Rockshelter Radiocarbon Chronology. *American Antiquity* 52(1):118–125.

Sherzer, Joel
1973   Areal Linguistics in North America. Pp. 749–795 in Current Trends in Linguistics, 10. Thomas A. Sebeok, ed. The Hague: Mouton. (Reprinted: Plenum Press, New York, 1976.)

————
1976   An Areal-Typological Study of American Indian Languages North of Mexico. Amsterdam: North-Holland Publishing Co.

Shiner, Joel L.
1950   Archaeological Resources in the Libby and Kataka Reservoirs, Northern Idaho and Northwestern Montana. *Smithsonian Institution. River Basin Surveys. Columbia Basin Project.* Washington.

————
1961   The McNary Reservoir: A Study in Plateau Archeology. *Bureau of American Ethnology Bulletin 179; River Basin Surveys Paper* 23. Washington.

Shipley, William F.
1966   The Relation of Klamath to California Penutian. *Language* 42(2):489–498.

Shuswap Nation Tribal Council
1989   The Shuswap: One People With One Mind, One Heart, and One Spirit. Kamloops, B.C.: Shuswap Nation Tribal Council.

Shuttleworth, Josephine
1936–1938 [Okanagan Legends, As Told to Isabel Christie.] *The Penticton Herald*. Penticton, B.C.

Silar, Jan
1969   Groundwater Structures and Ages in the Eastern Columbia Basin, Washington. *Washington State University. College of Engineering. Bulletin* 315. Pullman.

Silverstein, Michael
1965   Penutian: The Grammatical Dimensions of Sapir's Hypothesis. (A.B. Honors Thesis, Harvard College, Cambridge, Mass.; publ. in vol. 2 of Papers from the Seminar in American Indian Linguistics. Karl V. Teeter, ed. Harvard University, Cambridge.)

————
1966–1974 [Upper Chinookan linguistic and ethnographic notes, from fieldwork on the Yakima Reservation, Wash., the Warm Springs Reservation, Oreg., and Points on the Columbia River; also unpublished papers on Chinookan.] (Manuscripts in Silverstein's possession.)

————
1972   Chinook Jargon: Language Contact and the Problem of Multi-Level Generative Systems. *Language* 48(2):378–406, (3)596–625.

————
1974   Dialectal Developments in Chinookan Tense-Aspect Systems, an Areal-Historical Analysis. *International Journal of American Linguistics, Memoir* 29. (=IJAL 40(4), Pt. 2). Bloomington.

————
1976   Hierarchy of Features and Ergativity. Pp. 112–171 in Grammatical Categories in Australian Languages. R.M.W. Dixon, ed. *Australian Institute of Aboriginal Studies. Linguistic Series* 22. Canberra.

————
1977   Person, Number, Gender in Chinook: Syntactic Rule and Morphological Analogy. Pp. 143–156, in *Proceedings of the Third Annual Meeting of the Berkeley Linguistics Society*. Berkeley, Calif.

————
1978   Deixis and Deducibility in a Wasco-Wishram Passive of Evidence. Pp. 238–253 in *Proceedings of the Fourth Annual Meeting of the Berkeley Linguistics Society*. Berkeley, Calif.

————
1979   Penutian: An Assessment. Pp. 650–691 in The Languages of Native America: Historical and Comparative Assessment. Lyle Campbell and Marianne Mithun, eds. Austin: University of Texas Press.

————
1981   The Limits of Awareness. *Southwest Educational Devlopment. Sociolinguistic Working Papers* 84. Austin, Tex.

————
1984   The 'Value' of Objectual Language. (Paper presented at the 83d Annual Meeting of the American Anthropological Association, Denver, Colo., Nov. 14–18.) (Manuscript in Silverstein's possession.)

————
1984a   Wasco-Wishram Lexical Derivational Processes vs Word-Internal Syntax. Pp 270–288 in Papers from the Parasession on Lexical Semantics: Proceedings of the 20th Regional Meeting, Chicago Linguistic Society. David Testen, Veena Mishra, and Joseph Drogo, eds. Chicago: Chicago Linguistic Society.

1993   The Secret Life of Texts. (Manuscript in Silverstein's posses-sion.)

1994   Relative Motivation in Denotational and Indexical Sound Sybolism of Wasco-Wishram Chinookan. Pp. 40–60 in Sound Symbolism. Leanne Hinton, Johanna Nichols, and John J. Ohala, eds. Cambridge: Cambridge University Press.

Silverstein, Michael, [David H. French,] Katherine S. French, and Robert E. Moore
[1976–1996] [Wasco-Wishram (and Cascades) Dictionary.] (Manuscript in preparation, in the authors' possession.)

Simms, John 1875, 1876 *see* ARCIA for 1875, 1876

1877   [Letter from John Simms to Father Joseph Giorda, 30 June, 1877.] (Manuscripts in Joset Papers, File 84, Foley Library Archives, Gonzaga University, Spokane, Wash.)

1877a   [Letter of August 23, 1877, Fort Colville, Wash. Terr.] Pp. 582–583 in *45th Congress. 2d Session. House Executive Doc-ument* 1, Pt. 5. (Seiral No. 1800). Washington. (See also pp. 186–187 in ARCIA for 1877.)

Simpson, (Sir) George
1847   Narrative of a Journey Round the World, During the Years 1841 and 1842. 2 vols. London: Henry Colburn.

1931   Fur Trade and Empire. George Simpson's Journal; Remarks Connected with the Fur Trade in the Course of a Voyage from York Factory to Fort George and Back to York Factory, 1824–1825; Together with Accompanying Documents. Fred-erick Merk, ed. Cambridge, Mass.: Harvard University Press. (Reprinted: Belknap Press, Cambridge, Mass., 1968.)

1947   Part of Dispatch from George Simpson ... Governor of Rupert's Land to the Governor & Committee of the Hudson's Bay Company, London: March 1, 1829. Continued and com-pleted March 24 and June 5, 1829. E.E. Rich, ed. Toronto: The Champlain Society.

1968   Fur Trade and Empire. George Simpson's Journal. Frederick Merk, ed. Cambdrige, Mass.: Belknap Press.

Sims, Cort
1979   The Centennial Mountains: A Cultural Resource Overview. (Manuscript on file, U.S. Forest Service, Targhee National Forest, St. Anthony.)

Sisson, David A.
1980   Cultural Resourse Evaluation of the Russell Bar Facilities Construction Project, Idaho County, Idaho. (Manuscript on file, Bureau of Land Management, Coeur d'Alene District, Cottonwood, Idaho.)

1983   Lower Salmon Cultural Resource Management Plan. (Manu-script on file, Bureau of Land Management, Coeur d'Alene District, Cottonwood, Idaho.)

1984   Cottonwood-Divide Creek: A New Upland Site. (Manuscript on file, Bureau of Land Management, Coeur d'Alene District, Cottonwood, Idaho.)

1984a   Lower Salmon River Cultural Resource Management Plan, 1984 Annual Report. (Manuscript on file, Bureau of Land Management, Coeur d'Alene District, Cottonwood, Idaho.)

1985   Lone Pine Bar Site Stabilization Plan. (Manuscript on file, Bureau of Land Management, Coeur d'Alene District, Cot-tonwood, Idaho.)

1985a   Lower Salmon River Cultural Resource Management Plan, 1985 Annual Report. (Manuscript on file, Bureau of Land Management, Coeur d'Alene District, Cottonwood, Idaho.)

Sisson, David A., and David Conca
1988   Archaeology of the Russell Bar Ponderosa Pine Seed Orchard 19-IH-58. (Manuscript on file, Bureau of Land Management, Coeur d'Alene District, Cottonwood, Idaho.)

Skinner, Mark, and Stanley A. Copp
1986   The Nicoamen River Burial Site (EbRi 7) Near Lytton, British Columbia. (Manuscript on file, Archaeology Branch, Victoria, B.C.)

Slickpoo, Allen P., Sr., and Deward E. Walker, Jr.
1972   Nu Mee Poom Tit Wah Tit (Nez Perce Legends). Leroy L. Seth., illus. Lapwai, Idaho: Nez Perce Tribe of Idaho.

1973   Noon Nee-me-poo (We, the Nez Perces): Culture and History of the Nez Perces. Lapwai, Idaho: Nez Perce Tribe of Idaho.

Sloat, Clarence
1966   Phonological Redundancy Rules in Coeur d'Alene. (Ph.D. Dissertation in Linguistics, University of Washington, Seattle. Photocopy: University Microfilms International, Ann Arbor, Mich., 1971.)

1968   A Skeleton Key to Reichard's Coeur d'Alene Transcriptions. *Anthropological Linguistics* 10(5):8–11.

1971   The Phonetics and Phonology of Coeur d'Alene /r/. Pp. 123–127 in Studies in Northwest Indian Languages. James E. Hoard and Thomas M. Hess, eds. *Sacramento Anthropologi-cal Society Paper* 2. Sacramento, Calif.

1972   Vowel Harmony in Coeur d'Alene. *International Journal of American Linguistics* 38(4):234–239.

1980   Vowel Alternations in Coeur d'Alene. *International Journal of American Linguistics* 46(1):14–20.

Sloss, Geraldine
1995   A Perspective of Archaeology in Oregon and Idaho. *Tebiwa: Journal of the Idaho Museum of Natural History* 25(1):70–79. Pocatello.

Smally, Eugene V.
1885   The Kalispel Country. *The Century Illustrated Monthly Mag-azine* 29:447–455.

Smead, William H.
1901   [Letter of September 18, 1901, Joco, Mont.] Pp.259–260 in *57th Congress. 1st Session. House Executive Document* 5. (Serial No. 4290). Washington.

1905   Land of the Flatheads: A Sketch of the Flathead Reservation, Montana, Its Past and Present; Its Hopes and Possibilities for the Future. Missoula, Mont.: Press of the Daily Missoulian.

Smet, Pierre Jean *see* de Smet, Pierre-Jean

Smith, Allan H.
1950   [Kalispel ethnography.] (Manuscript, Exhibit 65, Docket 94, Indian Claims Commission, Washington.)

1953   The Indians of Washington. *Research Studies of the State Col-lege of Washington* 21:85–113.Pullman.

1957   Archaeological Survey of the Pend d'Oreille River Valley from Newport to Jared, Washington. [Pullman]: Washington State Department of Conservation, Washington State College.

1983   The Native Peoples. Pp. 135–334 in Cultural Resources of the Rocky Reach of the Columbia River, Vol.1. Randall F. Schalk and Robert R. Mierendorf, eds. *Washington State University. Center for Northwest Anthropology. Project Report* 1. Pullman.

1988   Ethnography of the North Cascades. *Washington State University. Center for Northwest Anthropology. Project Report* 7. Pullman.

Smith, Asa Bowen *see* Drury, Clifford, ed. 1958

Smith, Burton M.
1979   The Politics of Allotment: The Flathead Reservation as a Test Case. *Pacific Northwest Quarterly* 70(3):131–140.

Smith, Clyde
1991   Word Stress in Montana Salish. (M.A. Thesis in Linguistics, University of Pittsburgh, Pittsburgh, Penn.)

Smith, Craig S.
1983   A 4300-Year History of Vegetation, Climate, and Fire from Blue Lake, Nez Perce County, Idaho. (M.A. Thesis in Anthropology, Washington State University, Pullman.)

Smith, Harlan I.
1899   Archaeology of Lytton, British Columbia. *Memoirs of the American Museum of Natural History* 1(3); *Publications of the Jesup North Pacific Expedition* 1(3). New York. (Reprinted: AMS Press, New York, 1975.)

1900   Archaeology of the Thompson River Region. *Memoirs of the American Museum of Natural History* 2; *Publications of the Jesup North Pacific Expedition* 2(6). New York. (Reprinted: AMS Press, New York, 1975.)

1903   Shell-heaps of the Lower Fraser River, British Columbia. *Memoirs of the American Museum of Natural History* 3(4); *Publications of the Jesup North Pacific Expedition* 2(4). New York. (Reprinted: AMS Press, New York, 1975.)

1907   Archaeology of the Gulf of Georgia and Puget Sound. *Memoirs of the American Museum of Natural History* 4(6); *Publications of the Jesup North Pacific Expedition* 2(6). New York. (Reprinted: AMS Press, New York, 1975.)

1910   The Archaeology of the Yakima Valley. *American Museum of Natural History, Anthropological Papers* 6:1–171. New York.

1923   An Album of Prehistoric Canadian Art. *Canada. Department of Mines. Geological Survey. Victoria Memorial Museum Bulletin* 37; *Anthropological Series* 8. Ottawa.

Smith, Jedediah
1934   The Travels of Jedediah Smith: A Documentary Outline Including the Journal of the Great American Pathfinder. Maurice S. Sullivan, comp. and ed. Santa Ana, Calif.: The Fine Arts Press.

Smith, Marian W.
1940   The Puyallup-Nisqually. *Columbia University Contributions to Anthropology* 32. New York. (Reprinted: AMS Press, New York, 1969.)

1946   Petroglyph Complexes in the History of the Columbia-Fraser Region. *Southwestern Journal of Anthropology* 2(3):306–322.

1950   Archaeology of the Columbia-Fraser Region. *Society for American Archaeology Memoir* 6. [New York.]

Smith, William C.
1977   Archaeological Explorations in the Columbia Basin: A Report on the Mesa Project. Ellensburg, Wash.: Central Washington University, Department of Anthropology, Central Washington Archaeological Survey.

Smith, William C., M.L. Uebelacker, T.E. Eckert, and L.J. Nickel
1977   An Archaeological-History Survey of the Proposed Transmission Power Line Corridor from Ashe Substation, Washington to Pebble Springs Substation, Oregon. *Washington Archaeological Research Center. Project Report* 42. Pullman.

Sneed, Paul G.
1971   Of Salmon and Men: An Investigation of Ecological Determinants and Aboriginal Man in the Canadian Plateau. Pp. 229–242 in Aboriginal Man and Environments on the Plateau of Northwest America. Arnoud H. Stryd and Rachel A. Smith, eds. Calgary, Alta.: Students' Press.

Snyder, Warren A.
1956   "Old Man House" on Puget Sound. Pp. 17–37 in Northwest Archaeology Number, by Richard D. Daugherty et al. *Research Studies of the State College of Washington* 24(1). Pullman, Wash.

Somday, James B.
1980   Colville Indian Language Dictionary. 2 vols. (Ph.D. Dissertation in Education, University of North Dakota, Grand Forks. Photocopy: University Microfilms International, Ann Arbor, Mich., 1985.)

Sorensen, M.
1974   The Hudson Bay Company and Its Currency. Pp. 219–222 in Canadian Tokens and Medals. An Anthology ed. by A.D. Hoch. Lawrence, Mass.: Quarterman Publications. (Orig. publ. between 1895 and 1968 in *The Numismatist*.)

Southard, Michael D.
1973   A Study of Two Northwest Housepit Populations. *Northwest Anthropological Research Notes* 7(1):61–83. Moscow, Idaho.

Spafford, James G.
1991   Artifact Distributions on Housepit Floors and Social Organization in Housepits at Keatley Creek. (M.A. Thesis in Archaeology, Simon Fraser University, Burnaby, B.C.)

Spalding, Henry Harmon
1836   [Narrative of an Overland Journey to Fort Vancouver and Lapwai in 1836.] (Manuscript in Coe Collection, Yale University Library, New Haven, Conn.)

1839   Nez-Percés First Book: Designed for Children and New Beginners. Clear Water, [Oreg. Terr./Idaho]: Oregon Mission Press. (Reprinted: Boise State University, Boise, Idaho, 1994.)

1840   Numipuain Shapahitamanash Timash: Primer in the Nez Percés Language. Lapwai, [Oreg. Terr./Idaho]: Oregon Mission Press. (Compiled by A.B. Smith and Cornelius Rogers, according to H.M. Ballou 1922:50–51.)

1842   [Letter of February 18, 1842.] (Manuscript in Henry Spalding Papers, Washington State University Archives, Pullman.)

1842–1843 Talapusapaiain Wanipt Timas. Lapwai, [Oreg. Terr./Idaho]: Oregon Mission Press.

1845   Matthewnim Taaiskt. Clear Water, [Oreg. Terr./Idaho]: Oregon Mission Press; M.G. Foisy, Printer.

1851   [Report on Indians West of the Willamette River, 1851.] (Letter Book B. 10:68–71, MF 68, Reel 3, in Oregon Superintendency of Indian Affairs.)

Spaulding, Kenneth A., ed. 1953 *see* Stuart, Robert 1953
————, ed. 1956 *see* Ross, Alexander 1956

Speck, Brenda J.
1980   An Edition of Father Post's Kalispel Grammar. *University of Montana Occasional Papers in Linguistics* 1. Missoula.

741

Spencer, Robert F.
1952   Sklaven und Sklavenbesitz unter den Klamath-Indianern. *Zeitschrift für Ethnologie* 77:1–6.

1952a   Native Myth and Modern Religion among the Klamath Indians. *Journal of American Folklore* 65(257):217–226.

1956   Exhortation and the Klamath Ethos. *Proceedings of the American Philosophical Society* 100(1):77–86. Philadelphia.

Spencer, Robert F. and Jesse D. Jennings
1977   The Native Americans. New York: Harper and Row.

Spicer, Edward
1962   Cycles of Conquest. Tucson: University of Arizona Press.

Spier, Leslie
1927   The Ghost Dance of 1870 among the Klamath of Oregon. *University of Washington Publications in Anthropology* 2(2):39–55. Seattle.

1930   Klamath Ethnography. *University of California Publications in American Archaeology and Ethnology* 30. Berkeley. (Reprinted: Kraus Reprint, New York, 1965; Millwood, N.Y., 1976.)

1935   The Prophet Dance of the Northwest and Its Derivatives: The Source of the Ghost Dance. *General Series in Anthropology* 1. Menasha, Wis.: George Banta. (Reprinted: AMS Press, New York, 1979.)

1936   Tribal Distribution in Washington. *General Series in Anthropology* 3. Menasha, Wis.: George Banta.
           , ed.
1938   The Sinkaietk or Southern Okanagon of Washington. By Walter Cline, Rachel S. Commons, May Mandelbaum, Richard H. Post, and L.V.W. Walters. *General Series in Anthropology* 6; *Contributions from the Laboratory of Anthropology* 2. Menasha, Wis.: George Banta.

Spier, Leslie, and Edward Sapir
1930   Wishram Ethnography. *University of Washington Publications in Anthropology* 3(3):151–300. Seattle.

Spier, Leslie, Melville J. Herskovits, and Wayne Suttles
1959   [Comment on Aberle's Thesis of Deprivation.] *Southwestern Journal of Anthropology* 15(1):84–88.

Spinden, Herbert J.
1908   The Nez Percé Indians. *Memoirs of the American Anthopological Association* 2(3). Lancaster, Penn. (Reprinted: Kraus Reprint, New York and Millwood, 1964, 1974.)

1917   Nez Percé Tales. Pp. 180–201 in Folk-Tales of Salishan and Sahaptin Tribes. Franz Boas, ed. *Memoirs of the American Folk-Lore Society* 11. Lancaster, Penn., and New York.

Splawn, Andrew J.
1917   Ka-mi-akin, the Last Hero of the Yakimas. [1st ed.] Portland, Oreg.: Kilham Stationary & Print Co. (Reprinted: Binfords and Mort, Portland, Oreg., 1944; also, Caxton Printers, Caldwell, Idaho, 1980.)

1944   Ka-mi-akin, the Last Hero of the Yakimas. 2d ed. Portland, Oreg.: Binfords and Mort for the Oregon Historical Society. (Reprinted: Caxton Printers, Caldwell, Idaho, 1980.)

Spokesman-Review and Spokane Daily Chronicle
1991   [Salmon fisheries.] *The Spokesman-Review and Spokane Daily Chronicle*, May 12–14: A1, A8, A9, B10. Spokane, Wash.

Sprague, Roderick
1959   A Comparative Cultural Analysis of an Indian Burial Site in Southeast Washington. (M.A. Thesis in Anthropology, Washington State University, Pullman.)

1965   The Descriptive Archaeology of the Palus Burial Site, Lyons Ferry, Washington. *Washington State University, Laboratory of Anthropology, Report of Investigations* 32. Pullman.

1967   Aboriginal Burial Practices in the Plateau Region of North America. (Ph.D. Dissertation in Anthropology, University of Arizona, Tucson.)

1967a   A Preliminary Bibliography of Washington Archaeology. *Northwest Anthropological Research Notes* 1(1). Moscow, Idaho.

1968   The Meaning of Palouse. *Idaho Yesterdays* 12(2):22–27. Boise.

1970   George L. Howe and *The Antiquarian. Northwest Anthropological Research Notes* 4(2):166–222. Moscow, Idaho.

1971   Field Notes and Correspondence of the 1901 Field Colombian Museum Expedition by Merton L. Miller to the Colombian Plateau. *Northwest Anthropological Research Notes* 5(2):201–232. Moscow, Idaho.

1973   The Pacific Northwest. Pp. 250–285 in The Development of North American Archaeology: Essays in the History of Regional Traditions. J.E. Fitting, ed. New York: Anchor Books.

1975   The Development of Historical Archaeology in the Pacific Northwest. *Northwest Anthropological Research Notes* 9(1):6–19. Moscow, Idaho.

1983   Rock Art Studies on the Colombia River. *Quarterly Review of Archaeology* 4(3):2. (Reprinted: Pp. 146–148 in The Interpretation of Prehistory. Peabody Museum of Salem, Salem, Mass., 1989.)

1984   A Check List of Columbia Basin Project Papers. *Northwest Anthropological Research Notes* 18(2):256–259. Moscow, Idaho.

1987   Plateau Shamanism and Marcus Whitman. *Idaho Yesterdays* 31(1–2):55–56. Boise.

1991   [Direct testimony of Roderick Sprague, 1991.] (Yakima vs. Oregon, Civil No. 68–513, United States District Court, District of Oregon, Portland.)

1991a   A Bibiography of James A. Teit. *Northwest Anthropological Research Notes* 25(1):103–115. Moscow, Idaho.

1992   *Northwest Anthropological Research Notes* Contents by Title and Author, First 25 Years (1967–1991). *Northwest Anthropological Research Notes* 26(1). Moscow, Idaho.

1993   American Indian Burial and Repatriation in the Southern Plateau with Special Reference to Northern Idaho. *Idaho Archaeologist* 16(2):3–13.

1994   Bead Typology: The Development of a Concept. Pp. 85–100 in Pioneers in Historical Archaeology, Breaking New Ground. Stanley Smith, ed. New York: Plenum Press.

Sprague, Roderick, and Walter Birkby
1970   Miscellaneous Columbia Plateau Burials. *Tebiwa: Journal of the Idaho State University Museum* 13(1):1–26. Pocatello.

Spritzer, Donald E.
1979   Waters of Wealth: The Story of the Kootenai River and Libby Dam. 1st ed. Boulder, Colo.: Pruett Pub. Co. (Originally issued as a typescript prepared for the U.S. Army Corps of Engineers, Libby Dam Visitor Center, Mont., 1973.)

Sproat, Gilbert M.
1868   Scenes and Studies of Savage Life. London: Smith, Elder. (Reprinted: Sono-Nis Press, Victoria, B.C., 1987.)

Spurling, Brian E.
1986   Archaeological Resource Management in Western Canada: A Policy Science Approach. (Ph.D. Dissertation in Anthropology, Simon Fraser University, Burnaby, B.C.)

Squier, Robert J.
1956   Recent Excavations and Survey in Northwestern California. *University of California Archaeological Survey Reports* 33, *Papers in California Archaeology* 39. Berkeley.

Squier, Robert J., and Gordon L. Grosscup
1953   Archaeological Survey, Lava Beds National Monument, California, 1953. *Annual Report to the President, University of California Archaeological Survey* 182. Berkeley.

Stallard, Bruce
1958   Archaeology in Washington. *State of Washington. Department of Conservation. Division of Mines and Geology. Information Circular* 30. Olympia.

Stanley, John Mix
1847   [Letter of December 31, 1847.] (Manuscript No. 1204, Folder 10, in Elkanah and Mary Walker Papers, Oregon Historical Society, Portland.)

1862   Portraits of North American Indians, with Sketches of Scenery, etc., Painted by J.M. Stanley. *Smithsonian Institution Miscellaneous Collections* 2(3). Washington.

Stanwell-Fletcher, John F., and Theodora C. Stanwell-Fletcher
1940   Naturalists in the Wilds of British Columbia. 3 Pts. I.: Our Wilderness Home and Life in Winter. II.: The Ending of Winter and the Coming of Spring. III.: The Summer and Preparations for Our Second Winter. *Scientific Monthly* 50(January): 17–32; (February): 125–137; (March): 210–224. New York: The Science Press.

Statham, Dawn S.
1975   A Biogeographic Model of Camas and Its Role in the Aboriginal Economy of the Northern Shoshone in Idaho. *Tebiwa: Journal of the Idaho State University Museum* 18:59–80. Pocatello.

1982   Camas and the Northern Shoshoni: A Biographic and Socioeconomic Analysis. *Boise State University. Archaeological Reports* 2. Boise, Idaho.

Steedman, Elsie Viault, ed.
1930   Ethnobotany of the Thompson Indians of British Columbia. Based on Field Notes by James A. Teit. Pp. 441–522 in *45th Annual Report of the Bureau of American Ethnology for 1927–1928*. Washington.

Stein, Ben
1949   Nuggets from the Files. *The Western News*, Nov. 10. Hamilton, Mont.

Steinberger, Justus
1897   Letter from Justus Steinberger to Headquarters, District of Oregon, Fort Vancouver, Washington Territory; 23 June 1862. Pp. 1154–1155 in War of the Rebellion, Series 1, Vol. 50, Pt. 1. *55th Congress. 1st Session. House Document* 13(59, Pt. 1). (Serial No. 3583). Washington.

Stenholm, Nancy A.
1985   Botanical Assemblage. Pp. 421–453 in Summary of Results, Chief Joseph Dam Cultural Resources Project, Washington. Sarah K. Campbell, ed. Seattle: Office of Public Archaeology, Institute for Environmental Studies. University of Washington.

Steptoe, George
1858   Report of Colonel Steptoe. Pp. 60-62 in Report of the Secretary of War for 1858. *35th Congress. 2d. Session. Senate Executive Document* 33. (Serial No. 984); and, *House Executive Document* 2: 346–348. (Serial No. 998). Washington.

Stern, Theodore
1953   The Trickster in Klamath Mythology. *Western Folklore* 12:158–174.

1953–1968   [Fieldnotes; incl. notes from members of the 1953 Field School: Ann Chowning, Andrea Wilcox, Michael Horowitz, Donald Hogg, and Robert Oller.] (Manuscripts in Stern's possession.)

1953–1974   [Ethnographic and linguistic notes, together with those of students, from fieldwork on the Umatilla Indian Reservation, Oreg., particularly in the summers of 1953, 1957, 1961, 1963, and 1968.] (Manuscripts in Stern's possession.)

1954   [Klamath Indian Reservation fieldnotes.] (Manuscript in Stern's possession.)

1956   The Klamath Indians and the Treaty of 1864. *Oregon Historical Quarterly* 57(3):229–273.

1956a   Some Sources of Variability in Klamath Mythology. 3 Pts. *Journal of American Folklore* 69(271):1–12, (272):135–146, (274):377–386.

1957   [Klamath fieldnotes.] (Manuscripts in Stern's possession.)

1960   A Umatilla Prophet Cult: an Episode in Culture Change. Pp. 346–350 in Men and Cultures: Selected Papers of the Fifth International Congress of Anthropological and Ethnological Sciences, Philadelphia, September 1–9, 1956. Anthony F.C. Wallace, ed. Philadelphia: University of Pennsylvania Press.

1961–1962   Livelihood and Tribal Government on the Klamath Indian Reservation. *Human Organization* 20(4):172–180.

1963   Ideal and Expected Behavior as Seen in Klamath Mythology. *Journal of American Folklore* 76(299):21–30.

1963a   Klamath Myths Abstracts. *Journal of American Folklore* 76(299):31–41.

1965   The Klamath Tribe: A People and Their Reservation. *American Ethnological Society, Monograph* 41. Seattle: University of Washington Press. (Reprinted in 1970, 1972.)

1993   Chiefs & Chief Traders: Indian Relations at Fort Nez Percés, 1818–1855. [Vol. 1.] Corvallis: Oregon State University Press.

1996   Chiefs & Change in the Oregon Country: Indian Relations at Fort Nez Percés, 1818–1855. [Vol. 2.] Corvallis: Oregon State University Press.

Stern, Theodore, and James P. Boggs
1971   White and Indian Farmers on the Umatilla Indian Reservation. *Northwest Anthropological Research Notes* 5(1):37–76. Moscow, Idaho.

Stern, Theodore, Martin Schmitt, and Alphonse F. Halfmoon
1980   A Cayuse-Nez Percé Sketchbook. *Oregon Historical Quarterly* 81(4): 341–376.

Stevens, Hazard
1901   The Life of Isaac Ingalls Stevens; by His Son, Hazard Stevens. 2 vols. Boston and New York: Houghton, Mifflin.

Stevens, Isaac Ingalls 1854 *see* ARCIA for 1854

1855   Explorations and Surveys for a Railroad Route from the Mississippi River to the Pacific Ocean. Washington: U.S. War Department.

1860   Narrative and Field Report of Exploration for a Pacific Railroad near the Forty-seventh and Forty-ninth Parallels of North Latitude from St. Paul to Puget Sound 1855. In Explorations and Surveys for a Railroad Route from the Mississippi River to the Pacific Ocean, Vol. 12, Book 1. *36th Congress. 1st Session. House Executive Document* 11 (1, No. 56). (Serial No. 1054); and, *Senate Executive Document* 78. Washington.

Stevens, Isaac Ingalls, et al.
1855–1860   Reports of Explorations and Surveys to Ascertain the Most Practicable and Economical Route for a Railroad from the Mississippi River to the Pacific Ocean. 12 vols. [Commonly referred to as "Pacific Railroad Reports".] Washington: [Various printers for the U.S. Congress.]

Stevens, Rebecca A., and Jerry R. Galm
1991   Archaeological Investigations Near Rock Island Rapids: The Excavations at 45CH309. *Eastern Washington University. Archaeological and Historical Services. Reports in Archaeology and History* 100–63. Cheney.

Stevenson, Robert
1914   "A Pioneer of '59." Pp. 243–257 in Stories of Early British Columbia. Wymond Walkem, ed. Vancouver: News-Advertiser.

Steward, Julian H.
1927   A New Type of Carving from the Columbia Valley. *American Anthropologist* 29(2):255–261.

1928   A Peculiar Type of Stone Implement. *American Anthropologist* 30(2):314–316.

1936   Petroglyphs of the United States. Pp. 405–426 in *Annual Report of the Smithsonian Institution for 1936*. Washington.

1938   The Lemhi Indians of the Northwest Washington. *Columbia University Contributions to Anthropology* 17. New York.

1941   Culture Element Distributions, XIII: Nevada Shoshone. *University of California Anthropological Records* 4(2):209–359. Berkeley.

Stewart, Omer C.
1939   The Northern Paiute Bands. *University of California Anthropological Records* 2(3). Berkeley. (Reprinted: Kraus Reprint, Millwood, N.Y., 1976.)

1941   Culture Element Distributions, XIV: Northern Paiute. *University of California Anthropological Records* 4(3):361–446. Berkeley.

1965   The Shoshoni: Their History and Social Organization. *Idaho Yesterdays* 9(3):2–5, 28. Boise.

1987   Peyote Religion: A History. Norman: University of Oklahoma Press.

Stirling, Matthew W.
1943   Report on the Bureau of American Ethnology. Pp. 49–60 (Appendix 5) in *Annual Report of the Smithsonian Institution for the Year 1942*. Washington.

Stoffle, Richard W., David B. Halmo, Michael J. Evans, and John E. Olmsted
1990   Calculating the Cultural Significance of American Indian Plants: Paiute and Shoshone Ethnobotany at Yucca Mountain, Nevada. *American Anthropologist* 92(2): 416–432.

Stone, Arthur L.
1913   Following Old Trails. Missoula, Mont.: M.J. Elrod.

Stone, Buena Cobb
1964   Fort Klamath: Frontier Post in Oregon, 1863–1890. Dallas, Tex.: Royal Publishing Company.

Stowell, Cynthia D.
1987   Faces of a Reservation: A Portrait of the Warm Springs Indian Reservation. [Portland]: Oregon Historical Society Press.

Stratton, David H., and Glen W. Lindeman
1978   A Study of Historical Resources of the Hells Canyon National Recreation Area. Volume 1: Narrative. Pullman, Wash.: National Heritage, Inc.

Strickland, Rennard, and Charles F. Wilkinson, eds.
1982   Felix S. Cohen's Handbook of Federal Indian Law. Charlottesville, Va.: The Michie Company.

Strong, Emory
1959   Stone Age on the Columbia River. Portland: Binfords and Mort. (Reprinted in 1967.)

1960   Phoenix Buttons. *American Antiquity* 24(3):418–419.

1961   Prehistoric Sculpture from the Columbia River. *Archaeology* 14(2):131–137. New York.

Strong, William Duncan
1945   The Occurrence and Wider Implications of a "Ghost Cult" on the Columbia River Suggested by Carvings in Wood, Bone and Stone. *American Anthropologist* 47(2):244–261.

1961   Knickerbocker Views of the Oregon Country: Judge William Strong's Narrative (1878). *Oregon Historical Quarterly* 62(1):57–87.

Strong, William Duncan, and W. Egbert Schenck
1925   Petroglyphs near The Dalles of the Columbia River. *American Anthropologist* 27(1):76–90.

Strong, William Duncan, W. Egbert Schenck, and Julian H. Steward
1930   Archaeology of The Dalles-Deschutes Region. *University of California Publications in American Archaeology an Ethnology* 29(1). Berkeley. (Reprinted: Kraus Reprint, New York, 1965.)

Stryd, Arnoud H.
1972   Housepit Archaeology at Lillooet, British Columbia : the 1970 Field Season. *BC Studies* 14:17–46. Vancouver.

1973   The Later Prehistory of the Lillooet Area, British Columbia. (Ph.D. Dissertation in Archaeology, University of Calgary, Calgary, Alta.)

1974   Lillooet Archaeological Project: 1974 Field Season. *Cariboo College Papers in Archaeology* 1. Kamloops, B.C.

1976   Prehistoric Mobile Art from the Mid-Fraser and Thompson River Areas. Pp. 167–182 in Indian Art Traditions of the Northwest Coast. Roy L. Carlson, ed. Burnaby B.C.: Simon Fraser University Archaeology Press.

1978   An Introduction to the Lillooet Archaeological Project. Pp. 1–21 in Reports of the Lillooet Archaeological Project, Number 1: Introduction and Setting. Arnoud H. Stryd and Steven A. Lawhead, eds. *Archaeological Survey of Canada. Mercury Series. Paper* 66. Ottawa.

1983   Prehistoric Mobile Art from the Mid-Fraser and Thompson River Areas. Pp. 167–181 in Indian Art Traditions of the Northwest Coast. Roy L. Carlson, ed. Burnaby, B.C.: Simon Fraser University Archaeology Press.

1983a   An Overview of Lillooet Prehistory: The Last 4500 Years. (Paper presented at the 11th International Congress of Anthropological and Ethnological Sciences, Vancouver.)

Stryd, Arnoud H., and Stephen Lawhead
1983   Bethlehem Copper Corporation Lake Zone Development Heritage Mitigation Study. (Manuscript on file, Archaeology Branch, Victoria, B.C.)

Stryd, Arnoud H., and Michael K. Rousseau
1996   The Early Prehistory of the Mid Fraser-Thompson River Area. Pp. 177–204 in Early Human Occupation in British Columbia. Roy L. Carlson and Luke Dalla Bona, eds. Vancouver: UBC Press. (Originally a paper presented to the 21st Annual Meeting of the Canadian Archaeological Association, Whistler, B.C., 1988.)

Stuart, Robert
1953   On the Oregon Trail: Robert Stuart's Journey of Discovery [1812–1813]. Kenneth A. Spaulding, ed. Norman: University of Oklahoma Press.

Stuart, Robert, and Wilson Price Hunt
1935   The Discovery of the Oregon Trail; Robert Stuart's Narratives of His Overland Trip Eastward from Astoria in 1812–13;...and Wilson Price Hunt's Diary of His Overland Trip Westward to Astoria in 1811–12. Philip Ashton Rollins, ed. New York: Charles Scribner's Sons. ([Hunt's diary] trans. from: Nouvelles annales des voyages, Paris, 1821.) (Reprinted: University of Nebraska Press, Lincoln, 1995.)

Stubbs, Ron D.
1966   An Investigation of the Edible and Medicinal Plants Used by the Flathead Indians. (M.A. Thesis in Anthropology, University of Montana, Missoula.)

Suckley, George
1854   [Letter of January 4, 1854.] Pp. 123–125 in Report of Exploration of a Route for the Pacific Railroad. 33d Congress. 1st Session. House Executive Document 129. Washington.

Sugden, Henry L., ed.
1972   Seventy Five Years Presbyterian Camp Meetings of the Nez Perce Indians, 1897–1972. Spalding, Idaho: Spalding Presbyterian Church, Camp Meeting Association.

Suphan, Robert J.
1974   Ethnological Report of the Wasco and Tenino Indians; Ethnological Report on the Umatilla, Walla Walla, and Cayuse Indians Relative to Socio-Political Organization and Land Use. Pp. 9–84 and pp. 85–180 in Oregon Indians II. (Commission Findings, pp. 181–534). American Indian Ethnohistory: Indians of the Northwest. New York: Garland.

Suttles, Wayne
1957   The Plateau Prophet Dance among the Coast Salish. Southwestern Journal of Anthropology 13(4): 352–396.

1987   Coast Salish Essays. Vancouver, B.C.: Talonbooks.

Suttles, Wayne, and William W. Elmendorf
1963   Linguistic Evidence for Salish Prehistory. Pp. 42–52 in Symposium on Language and Culture. Proceedings of the 1962 Annual Spring Meeting of the American Ethnological Society. Viola E. Garfield and Wallace L. Chafe, eds. Seattle: University of Washington Press.

Swadesh, Morris
1949   The Linguistic Approach to Salish Prehistory. Pp. 161–171 in Indians of the Urban Northwest. Marian W. Smith, ed. Columbia University Contributions to Anthropology 36. New York.

1950   Salish Internal Relationships. International Journal of American Linguistics 16(4):157–167.

1952   Salish Phonologic Geography. Language 28(2):232–248. (Reprinted: Pp. 293–248 in The Origin of Diversification of Language. Joel Sherzer, ed. Aldine, Chicago, 1971.)

1954   On the Penutian Vocabulary Survey. International Journal of American Linguistics 20(2):123–133.

1955   Toward Greater Accuracy in Lexicostatistic Dating. International Journal of American Linguistics 21(2)121–137.

1956   Problems of Long-Range Comparison in Penutian. Language 32(1):17–41.

1958   Some New Glottochronological Dates for Amerindian Linguistic Groups. Pp. 671–674 in Proceedings of the 32d International Congress of Americanists, Copenhagen, 1956. Copenhagen: Munkgaard.

1959   Linguistics as an Instrument of Prehistory. Southwestern Journal of Anthropology 15(1):20–35.

1964   Comparative Penutian Glosses of Sapir. Pp. 182–191 in Studies in California Linguistics. William Bright, ed. University of California Publications in Linguistics 34. Berkeley.

Swan, James G.
1857   The Northwest Coast; or, Three Years' Residence in Washington Territory. New York: Harper and Row. (Reprinted: University of Washington Press, Seattle, 1972.)

Swanson, Earl H., Jr.
1958   Archaeological Survey of the Crevice Reservoir, Idaho. (Manuscript on file at Idaho State University Museum, Pocatello.)

1958a   Archaeological Survey of the Freedom Reservoir, Idaho. (Manuscript on file at Idaho State University Museum, Pocatello.)

1958b   Archaeological Survey of the Ririe Reservoir, Idaho. (Manuscript on file at Idaho State University Museum, Pocatello.)

1958c   Archaeological Explorations in Central and Southern Idaho-1958. (Manuscript on file at Idaho State University Museum, Pocatello.)

1958d   The Archaeological Survey System of the Museum. Occasional Papers of the Idaho State College Museum 1. Pocatello.

1958e   Archaeological Survey of the Middle Fork Salmon River, Idaho. (Manuscript on file at Interagency Archaeological Services, U.S. Department of Interior, San Francisco.)

1959   Preliminary Appraisal of Archaeological Resources in the Lower Canyon Reservoir of the Salmon River, Idaho. (Manuscript on file at Idaho State University Museum, Pocatello.)

1962   The Emergence of Plateau Culture. Occasional Papers of the Idaho State College Museum 8. Pocatello.

1962a   Early Cultures in Northwestern America. American Antiquity 28(2):151–158.

1962b   Historic Archaeology at Fort Okanogan, Washington, 1957. *Tebiwa: Journal of the Idaho State University Museum* 5(1):1–10. Pocatello.

1966   Prehistoric Idaho: A Report of Recent Archaeological Discoveries. *Idaho State Historical Society. Historical Services* 14. Boise.

1970   Sources for Plateau Prehistory. *American Antiquity* 35(4):495–496.

1972   Birch Creek: Human Ecology in the Cool Desert of the Northern Rocky Mountains 9000 B.C-A.D. 1850. Pocatello: Idaho State University Press.

1972a   Ancient Camps and Villages of the Middle Fork. *Naturalist* 23(2):29.

Swanson, Earl H., Jr., and Alan L. Bryan
1964   Birch Creek Papers No. 1: An Archaeological Reconnaissance in the Birch Creek Valley of Eastern Idaho. *Occasional Papers of the Idaho State University Museum* 13. Pocatello.

Swanson, Earl H., Jr., and Paul G. Sneed
1966   Birch Creek Papers No. 3: The Archaeology of the Shoup Rockshelters in East Central Idaho. *Occasional Papers of the Idaho State University Museum* 17. Pocatello.

1967   An Archaeological Reconnaissance of Railroad Ranch in Eastern Idaho, 1966. *Tebiwa: Journal of the Idaho State University Museum* 10(1):53–59. Pocatello.

1971   Jacknife Cave. *Tebiwa: Journal of the Idaho State University Museum* 14(1):4–32. Pocatello.

Swanson, Earl H., Jr., Chester King, and James Chatters
1969   A Settlement Pattern in the Foothills of East-Central Idaho. Tebiwa: Journal of the Idaho State University Museum 12(1):31–38. Pocatello.

Swanson, Earl H., Jr., Donald Tuohy, and Alan L. Bryan
1959   Archaeological Explorations in Central and South Idaho - 1958: Types of Distributions of Site Features and Stone Tools. *Occasional Papers of the Idaho State University Museum* 2. Pocatello.

Swanson, Guy E.
1973   The Search for the Guardian Spirit: A Process of Empowerment in Simple Societies. *Ethnology* 12(3):359–378.

Swanton, John R.
1952   The Indian Tribes of North America. *Bureau of American Ethnology Bulletin* 145. Washington. (Several reprints, incl.: Smithsonian Institution Press, Washington, 1968, 1974, 1979, 1984; Scholarly Press, St. Clair Shores, Mich., 1976; Native American Book Publishers, Brighton, Mich., 1990.)

Swartz, Benjamin K., Jr.
1960   A Bibliography of Klamath Basin Anthropology; with Excerpts and Annotations. *Klamath County Museum, Research Papers* 3. Klamath Fall, Oreg. (Reprinted, rev. ed.: University of Idaho, Moscow, 1967.)

1961   A Preliminary Archaeological Survey along the Proposed Highway, Lava Beds National Monument, California. Lava Beds National Monument. Tulelake, Calif.

1964.   Archaeological Investigations at Lava Beds National Monument, California. (Ph.D. Dissertation in Anthropology, University of Arizona, Tucson.)

1967   A Bibliography of Klamath Basin Anthropology, with Excerpts and Annotations. Rev. ed. *Northwest Anthropological Research Notes* 1(2). Moscow, Idaho.

Swindell, Edward G., Jr.
1942   Report on Source, Nature, and Extent of the Fishing, Hunting and Miscellaneous Related Rights of Certain Indian Tribes in Washington and Oregon [etc.]. Los Angeles: U.S. Department of the Interior, Office of Indian Affairs, Division of Forestry and Grazing.

Swisher, Lawrence A.
1973   The 1972 Salmon River Archaeological Survey, Final Report. (Manuscript on file at Idaho State Museum, Idaho State University, Pocatello.)

Taggart, S.L.
1905   [Report of Special Indian Agent S.L. Taggart, Riparia, Washington to Commissioner of Indian Affairs, 30 August, 1905.] (Manuscript in Commissioner of Indian Affairs, Letters Received 1905/71108, Records of the Bureau of Indian Affairs, Record Group 75, National Archives, Washington.)

Tanimoto, Kazuko
1994   Elders and Enculturation on the Nez Perce Reservation. (M.A. Thesis in Anthropology, Washington State University, Pullman.)

Tanner, Adrian
1979   Bringing Home Animals: Religious Ideology and Mode of Production of the Mistassini Cree Hunters. New York: St. Martins Press.

Tax, Sol, et al.
1960   The North American Indians: 1950 Distribution of Descendants of the Aboriginal Population of Alaska, Canada, and the United States. Map, 5th printing. Chicago: University of Chicago: University of Chicago, Department of Anthropology.

Taylor, Alexander S.
1862   The Indianology of California. *The California Farmer and Journal of Useful Sciences*, July 19, 1862. San Francisco.

Taylor, Dee C.
1973   Archaeological Investigations in the Libby Reservoir Area, Northwestern Montana. *University of Montana Contributions to Anthropology* 3. Missoula.

Taylor, Graham D.
1980   The New Deal and American Indian Tribalism: The Administration of the Indian Reorganization Act, 1934–1945. Lincoln: University of Nebraska Press.

Taylor, Herbert C., Jr.
1956   Survey of Eastern Vancouver Island. Pp. 53–55 in Northwest Archaeology Number, by Richard D. Daugherty et al. *Research Studies of the State College of Washington* 24(1). Pullman, Wash.

1974   An Anthropological Investigation of the Medicine Creek Tribes Relative to Tribal Identity and Aboriginal Possession of Land. Pp. 401–473 in Coast Salish and Western Washington Indians, II. *American Indian Ethnohistory: Indians of the Northwest*. New York: Garland.

Taylor, Herbert C., Jr., and Wilson Duff
1956   A Post-contact Movement of the Kwakiutl. Pp. 56–66 in Northwest Archaeology Number, by Richard D. Daugherty et al. *Research Studies of the State College of Washington* 24(1). Pullman, Wash.

Taylor, J.M., W. Bokman, and I.N.M. Wainwright
1979   Rock Art Conservation: Some Realities and Practical Considerations. Pp. 293–324 in Papers of the Fourth Biennial Con-

ference of the Canadian Rock Art Research Associates. Doris Lundy, ed. *British Columbia Provincial Museum Heritage Record* 8. Victoria.

Taylor, J.M., R.M. Myers, and I.N.M. Wainwright
1974   Scientific Studies of Indian Rock Paintings in Canada. *Bulletin of the American Institute for Conservation* 14(2):28–43.

Tchakmakian, Pascal
1976   The Great Retreat: The Nez Perces War in Words and Pictures. San Francisco: Chronicle Books.

Teit, James A.
1896   A Rock Painting of the Thompson River Indians, British Columbia. *American Museum of Natural History Bulletin* 8(12):227–230. New York

1896–1918 [Plant names of the Thompson Indians.] (Manuscript No. 30[S1b3] [Freeman No. 2483] in American Philosophical Society Library, Philadelphia.)

1898   Traditions of the Thompson River Indians of British Columbia. *Memoirs of the American Folk-Lore Society* 6:1–137. Boston and New York. (Reprinted: Kraus Reprint, New York, 1969.)

1898–1910 [Salish ethnographic notes.] (Manuscripts in the American Philosophical Society Library, Philadelphia. Microfilm copy A-239 in Provincial Archives of British Columbia, Victoria.)

1900   The Thompson Indians of British Columbia. Franz Boas, ed. *Memoirs of the American Museum of Natural History* 2, *Anthropology* 1(4); *Publications of the Jesup North Pacific Expedition* 1(4). New York. (Reprinted: AMS Press, New York, 1975; also, Nicola Valley Museum Archives Association, Merritt, B.C., 1997, from a volume originally owned and annotated by James A. Teit.)

————— 1900a *see* 1900

1900–1921 [Thompson ethnographic notes.] (Manuscripts in the American Philosophical Society Library, Philadelphia.)

1904   [Fieldnotes on Thompson and neighboring Salish languages.] (Manuscript No. 30(Slb.7)[Freeman No. 2492] in the American Philosophical Society Library, Philadelphia.)

1905   [Ntlakyapamuk relationship terms and terms applied to persons.] (Manuscript 497.3, B63c[30(S1b.91]. Boas Collection, American Philosophical Society Library, Philadelphia.)

1906   The Lillooet Indians. Franz Boas, ed. *Memoirs of the American Museum of Natural History* 4(5); *Publications of the Jesup North Pacific Expedition* 2(5). Leiden and New York. (Reprinted: AMS Press, New York, 1975.)

1907–1910 [Salish tribal names and distributions.] (Manuscript No. 30(S.3)[Freeman No. 3207] in the American Philosophical Society Library, Philadelphia.)

1908   [Vocabulary in Okanagon and related dialects.] (Manuscript No. 30(S1d.2)[Freeman No. 2552] in the American Philosophical Society Library, Philadelphia.)

1908–1920 [Salish ethnographic materials.] (Boas Collection 372 Roll 16, Item S.7 in the American Philosophical Society Library, Philadelphia; microfilm copy in British Columbia Archives and Records Service, Victoria.)

1909   The Shuswap. Franz Boas, ed. *Memoirs of the American Museum of Natural History* 4(7); *Publication of the Jesup North Pacific Expedition* 2(7). New York. (Reprinted: AMS Press, New York, 1975.)

1910   [Thompson materials.] (Manuscript No. 30(Slb.13.5)[Freeman No. 2495] in the American Philosophical Society Library, Philadelphia.)

1910–1913 [Notes to maps of the Pacific Northwest.] (Manuscript in Boas Collection 372, Roll 4, No. 1, Item 59, Library of the American Philosophical Society, Philadelphia.)

1912   Mythology of the Thompson Indians. Franz Boaz, ed. *Memoirs of the American Museum of Natural History* 12; *Publications of the Jesup North Pacific Expedition* 8(2). New York. (Reprinted: AMS Press, New York, 1975.)

1912–1921 [Notes on the early history of the Nicola Valley.] (Typescript copy transcribed by Joyce Kirk, Dec. 13, 1972; Manuscript No. 7079 in National Anthropological Archives, Smithsonian Institution, Washington.)

1912a   Traditions of the Lillooet Indians of British Columbia. *Journal of American Folk-Lore* 25(98):287–371.

1912b   [Letter to the Superintendent General of Indian Affairs, May 16th, 1912.] (Manuscript in Record Group 10, Volume 4047, File 356, 200–1, National Archives of Canada, Ottawa.)

1914   Indian Tribes of the Interior. Franz Boas, ed. Pp. 283–314 in Canada and Its Provinces, Volume XXI. Adam Shortt and Arthur G. Dought, eds. Toronto: Edinburgh University Press.

1915–1921 [Fieldnotes on Interior Salish groups.] (Manuscripts in Ethnology Division, National Museum of Man, Ottawa, Canada.)

1916   [Letter to Mr. Scholefield, 1916.] (Manuscript in Provincial Archives of British Columbia, Victoria.)

1917   Thompson Tales; Okanagon Tales; Pend d'Oreille Tales; Coeur d'Alène Tales; Tales from the Lower Fraser River. Pp. 1–64 [Thompson];65–97 [Okanagon]; 114–118 [Pend d'Oreille]; 119–128 [Coeur d'Alène]; 129–134 [Lower Fraser River], in Folk-Tales of Salishan and Sahaptin Tribes. Franz Boas, ed. *Memoirs of the American Folk-Lore Society* 11. Lancaster, Pa., and New York.

1928   The Middle Columbia Salish. Franz Boas, ed. *University of Washington Publications in Anthropology* 2(4). Seattle.

1930   The Salishan Tribes of the Western Plateaus. Franz Boas, ed. Pp. 23–396 in *45th Annual Report of the Bureau of American Ethnology for 1927–1928*. Washington. (Reprinted: Shorey Book Store, Seattle Wash., 1973.)

1930a   Tattooing and Face and Body Painting of the Thompson Indians, British Columbia. Pp. 397–439 in *45th Annual Report of the Bureau of American Ethnology for 1927–1928*. Washington. (Reprinted: Shorey Book Store, Seattle, 1972.)

1930b   Traditions and Information Regarding the Tona´xa. Franz Boas, ed. *American Anthropologist* 32(4):625–632.

1979   Yakima and Klickitat Basketry. *American Indian Basketry Magazine* 1(1):14–17.(Original: H.K. Haeberlin, James A.

Teit, and Helen H. Roberts, Coiled Basketry in British Columbia and Surrounding Region; Pp. 353–357 in *41st Annual Report of the Bureau of American Ethnology for 1919–1924*, Washington, 1928.)

Teit, James A., et al. 1917 *see* Boas, Franz, ed. 1917

Tennant, Paul
1990 Aboriginal Peoples and Politics: The Indian Land Question in British Columbia, 1849–1989. Vancouver: University of British Columbia Press.

Tepper, Leslie H.
1984 Thompson Indian Painted Clothing: An Analysis of Clothing and Art as Visual Communication. (M.A. Thesis in Anthropology, Carleton University, Ottawa, Ont.)

————
1987 The Interior Salish Tribes of British Columbia: A Photographic Collection. *Canadian Museum of Civilization. Mercury Series. Ethnology Service Paper* 111. Ottawa.

————
1994 Earth Line and Morning Star: NLaka'pamux Clothing Traditions. Hull, Que.: Canadian Museum of Civilization.

Terry James
1891 Sculptured Anthropoid Ape Heads Found in or Near the Valley of the John Day River, a Tributary of the Columbia River, Oregon. New York: Press of J.J. Little.

Thomas, Bryn, Lynn L. Larson, and Marilyn G. Hawkes
1984 Archaeological Investigations at 30 Historic Sites, Chief Joseph Dam Project, Washington. Sarah K. Campbell, ed. Seattle: Office of Public Archaeology, Institute for Environmental Studies. University of Washington.

Thomas, David Hurst
1978 Arrowheads and Atlatl Darts: How the Stones Got the Shaft. *American Antiquity* 43(3): 461–472.

————
1981 How to Classify the Projectile Points of Monitor Valley, Nevada. *Journal of California and Great Basin Anthropology* 3(1): 7–43.

Thomas, Frederick
1988 Mountain Sheep Hunters. (M.A. Thesis in Anthropology, University of Idaho, Moscow.)

Thomas, Jack W., and Dale E. Toweill
1982 Elk of North America: Ecology and Management. Harrisburg, Pa.: Stackpole Books.

Thomason, Sarah Grey
1983 Chinook Jargon in Areal and Historical Context. *Language* 59(4):820–870.

Thomison, Patrick
1987 When Celilo Was Celilo: An Analysis of Salmon Use During the Past During the Past 11,000 Years in the Columbia Plateau. (M.A. Thesis in Anthropology, Oregon State University, Corvallis.)

Thompson, Albert W.
1971 The Early History of the Palouse River and Its Name. *Pacific Northwest Quarterly* 62(2):69–76.

————
1978 Coeur d'Alene: The Names Applied to Tribe and Lake. *Idaho Yesterdays* 21(4):11–15. Boise.

Thompson, David
1813–1814 [Map of the North-west Territory of the Province of Canada, from Actual Survey during the Years 1792 to 1812.] (Original in Provincial Archives of Ontario, Toronto.)

————
1914 Journal of David Thompson. T.C. Elliott, ed. *Oregon Historical Quarterly* 15(2):104–125.

1916 David Thompson's Narrative of His Explorations in Western America, 1784–1812. Joseph B. Tyrrell, ed. *Publications of the Champlain Society* 12. Toronto. The Champlain Society. (Reprinted: Richard Glover, ed., 1962; also, Greenwood Press, New York, 1968.)

————
1917 David Thompson's Journeys in Spokane Country. T.C. Elliott, ed. *Washington Historical Quarterly* 8(4):261–264.

————
1920 David Thompson's Journeys in Idaho. T.C. Elliott, ed. *Washington Historical Quarterly* 11(2):97–103, (3):163–173.

————
1950 David Thompson's Journals Relating to Montana and Adjacent Regions, 1808–1812. Transcribed from a Photostatic Copy of the Original Manuscripts and edited with an Introduction by M. Catherine White. *Montana State University Studies* 1. Missoula.

————
1962 David Thompson's Narrative of His Explorations in Western America, 1784–1812. A new ed. with added material [...]. Richard Glover, ed. *Publications of the Champlain Society* 40. Toronto: The Champlain Society. (Orig. pub.: Joseph B. Tyrrell, ed., The Champlain Society, Toronto, 1916.)

————
1994 Columbia Journals. Barbara Belyea, ed. Montreal and Buffalo: McGill-Queen's University Press.

Thompson, Erwin N.
1971 Modoc War; Its Military History and Topography. With a Preface by Keith A. Murray. Sacramento, Calif.: Argus Books.

Thompson, Laurence C.
1973 The Northwest. Pp. 979–1045 in Current Trends in Linguistics, 10: Linguistics in North America (Pt. 2). Thomas a. Sebeok, ed. The Hague and Paris: Mouton. (Reprinted: Plenum Press, New York, 1976.)

————
1979 Salishan and the Northwest. Pp. 692–765 in The Languages of Native America: Historical and Comparative Assessment. Lyle Campbell and Marianne Mithun, eds. Austin: University of Texas Press.

————
1985 Control in Salish Grammar. Pp. 391–428 in Relational Typology. Frans Plank, ed. (*Trends in Linguistics. Studies and Monographs* 28). The Hague and Berlin: Mouton.

Thompson, Laurence C., and M. Terry Thompson
1992 The Thompson Language. *University of Montana Occasional Papers in Linguistics* 8. Missoula.

————
1996 Thompson River Salish Dictionary: Nłeʔkepmxcín. *University of Montana Occasional Papers in Linguinstics* 12. Missoula.

Thompson, M. Terry, and Steven M. Egesdal
1993 Annie York's Push-Back-Sides-of-His-Hair (nʔikʼʔikʼnʼincút): A Traditional Thompson River Salish Legend with Commentary. Pp. 279–302 in American Indian Linguistics and Ethnography in Honor of Laurence C. Thompson. Anthony Mattina and Timothy Montler, eds. *University of Montana Occasional Papers in Linguistics* 10. Missoula.

Thompson, Nile, and Carolyn Marr
1983 Crow's Shells: Artistic Basketry of Puget Sound. Seattle: Dushuyay Publications.

Thompson, Robert S.
1985 Paleoenvironmental Investigations at Seed Cave (Windust Cave H-45FR46), Franklin County, Washington. *Eastern Washington University. Reports in Archaeology and History* 100–41. Cheney.

748

Thoms, Alston V., ed.
1983   Archaeological Investigations in Upper McNary Reservoir, 1981–1982. With Contributions by Sheila V. Bobalik...[et al.]. *Washington State University. Laboratory of Anthropology and History. Project Report* 15. Pullman.

1984   Cultural Resources Investigations for Libby Reservoir, Northwest Montana. Vol. 1: Environment, Archaeology, and Land Use Patterns in the Middle Kootenai River Valley. *Washington State University. Center for Northwest Anthropology. Project Report* 2(1). Pullman.

1987   Adaptive Strategies in the Northern Rockies: Land Use and Archaeological Assemblage Variation. (Manuscript in Thoms's possession.)

1989   The Northern Roots of Hunter-Gatherer Intensification: Camas and the Pacific Northwest. (Ph.D. Dissertation in Anthropology, Washington State University, Pullman. Photocopy: University Microfilms International, Ann Arbor, Mich., 1991.)

1990   Root Foods and Hunter-Gatherer Intensification: The Role of Camas in the Pacific Northwest. (Paper presented at the 43d Annual Northwest Anthropological Conference, Eugene. Abstract in *Northwest Anthropological Research Notes* 24(1):84. Moscow, Idaho.)

Thoms, Alston V., and Greg C. Burtchard, eds.
1987   Prehistoric Land Use in the Northern Rocky Mountains: A Perspective from the Middle Kootenai River Valley. *Washington State University. Center for Northwest Anthropology. Project Report* 4. Pullman.

Thoms, Alston V., and Randall F. Schalk
1984   Prehistoric Land Use in the Middle Kootenai Valley. Pp. 363–377 in Cultural Resources Investigations for Libby Reservoir, Northwest Montana. Vol. 1: Environment, Archaeology, and Land Use Patterns in the Middle Kootenai River Valley. Alston V. Thoms, ed. *Washington State University. Center for Northwest Anthropology. Project Report* 2(1).

Thomson, Duane
1978   Opportunity Lost: A History of Okanagan Reserves in the Colonial Period. Pp. 43–52 in *42d Annual Report of the Okanagan Historical Society*. Vernon, B.C.

1985   A History of the Okanagan: Indians and Whites in the Settlement Era, 1860–1920. (Ph.D. Dissertation in History, University of British Columbia, Vancouver.)

1990   The Missionaries. Jean Webber and The En'owkin Centre, eds. Penticton B.C.: Theytus Books.

Thornton, Russell
1987   American Indian Holocaust and Survival: a Population History Since 1492. Norman: University of Oklahoma Press.

Thwaites, Reuben G., ed.
1904–1905   Original Journals of the Lewis and Clark Expedition, 1804–1806. 8 vols. New York: Dodd, Mead. (Reprinted: Antiquarian Press, New York, 1959; also, Arno Press, New York, 1969.)

1904–1907   Early Western Travels, 1748–1846: A Series of Annotated Reprints of Some of the Best and Rarest Contemporary Volumes of Travel, Descriptive of the Aborigines and Social and Economic Conditions in the Middle and Far West, during the Period of Early American Settlement. 38 vols. Cleveland, Ohio: Arthur H. Clark. (Reprinted: AMS Press, New York, 1966.)

Tiller, Veronica E. Velarde, comp. and ed.
1996   American Indian Reservations and Trust Areas. Washington: U.S. Department of Commerce, Economic Development Administration. (Published also under title: Tiller's Guide to Indian Country—Economic Profiles of American Indian Reservations. BowArrow Publishing Company, Albuquerque, N.M., 1996.)

Titmus, Gene L.
1987   Clovis and Folsom in Idaho: Where, How, and Why. (Paper presented at the 14th Annual Conference of the Idaho Archaeological Society, Boise, Idaho.)

Todd, C.C.
1933   Origin and Meaning of the Geographical Name Palouse. *Northwest Historical Quarterly* 23(3):190–192.

Toepel, Kathryn Anne
1991   The Western Interior. Pp. 15–20 in The First Oregonians: An Illustrated Collection of Essays on Traditional Lifeways, Federal- Indian Relations, and the State's Native People Today. Carolyn M. Buan and Richard Lewis, eds. Portland: Oregon Council for the Humanities.

Toepel, Kathryn Anne, William F. Willingham, and Rick Minor
1980   Cultural Resource Overview of BLM Lands in North-Central Oregon: Ethnography, Archaeology, History. *University of Oregon Anthropological Papers* 17. Eugene.

Togler, Kim J.
1993   Excavations at Dagger Falls (10-VY-70). D. Sammons, ed. *Idaho State University. Department of Anthropology. Center for Ecological and Environmental Anthropology. Reports of Investigations* 93–1. Pocatello.

Tokle, John F.
1970   Motif Categorization of Idaho Indian Mythology. (M.A. Thesis in Anthropology, University of Idaho, Moscow.)

Tolan, Sister Providentia
1980   A Shining from the Mountains. Montreal: Sisters of Providence, Providence Mother House.

Tolmie, William Fraser, and George M. Dawson
1884   Comparative Vocabularies of the Indian Tribes of British Columbia, with a Map Illustrating Distribution. Montreal: Dawson Brothers.

Torrence, Gaylord
1994   The American Indian Parfleche: A Tradition of Abstract Painting. Seattle, Wash.: University of Washington Press in association with the Des Moines Art Center.

Toups, Polly A.
1969   The Early Prehistory of the Clearwater Valley, North Central Idaho. (Ph.D. Dissertation in Anthropology, Tulane University, New Orleans.)

Towner, Ronald H.
1986   The Basin Creek Site: A Biface Lithic Technology from Central Idaho. (M.A. Thesis Anthropology, Washington State University, Pullman.)

Townsend, Alfred
1857   [Letter of June 30, 1857.] Pp. 636–637 in *35th Congress. 1st Session. Senate Executive Document* 2. (Serial No. 919.) Washington.

Townsend, John K.
1839   Narrative of a Journey across the Rocky Mountains, to the Columbia River, and a Visit to the Sandwich Islands, Chili, &c.; with a Scientific Appendix. Philadelphia: H. Perkins; Boston: Perkins and Marvin. (Reprinted: Pp. 107–369 in Vol. 21 of Early Western Travels, 1748–1846. Reuben G. Thwaites, ed., Arthur H. Clark, Cleveland, 1904–1907; also Ye Galleon Press, Fairfield, Wash., 1970; and under title "Across the Rockies to the Columbia", with an Introduction by Donald Jackson, University of Nebraska Press, Lincoln, 1987.)

Trafzer, Clifford E.
1986   Indians, Superintendents, and Councils: Northwestern Indian Policy, 1850–1855. Lanham, Md.: University Press of America.

1992   The Nez Perce. (*Indians of North America*). New York and Philadelphia: Chelsea House.

1992a   Yakima, Palouse, Cayuse, Umatilla, Walla, Walla, and Wanapum Indians: An Historical Bibliography. *Native American Bibliography Series* 16. Metuchen, N.J.: The Scarecrow Press.

1994   Modoc. P. 352 in Native America in the Twentieth Century: An Encyclopedia. Mary B. Davis, ed. *(Garland Reference Library of Social Science* 452). New York: Garland.

Trafzer, Clifford E., and Richard D. Scheuerman
1986   Renegade Tribe: The Palouse Indians and the Invasion of the Inland Pacific Northwest. Pullman: Washington State University Press.

Treide, Dietrich
1965   Die Organisiering des indianischen Lachsfangs im westlichen Nordamerika. *Veröffentlichungen des Museums für Völkerkunde zu Leipzig* 14. Berlin: Akademie-Verlag.

Trepp, John M.
1966   Music at St. Ignatius Mission 1854–1900. (M.M. Thesis in Music Education, University of Montana, Missoula.)

Trosper, Ronald L.
1974   The Economic Impact of the Allotment Policy on the Flathead Indian Reservation. (Ph.D. Dissertation in Economics, Harvard University, Cambridge, Mass.)

Turnbull, Christopher J.
1971   Recent Archaeological Field Work in the Arrow Lakes, British Columbia. Pp. 44–55 in Aboriginal Man and Environments on the Plateau of Northwest America. Arnoud H. Stryd and Rachel A. Smith, eds. Calgary: The University of Calgary Student's Press.

1977   Archaeology and Ethnohistory in the Arrow Lakes, Southeastern British Columbia. *Mercury Series. Archaeological Survey of Canada. Paper* 65. Ottawa.

Turner, Nancy J.
1974   Plant Taxonomic Systems and Ethnobotany of Three Contemporary Indian Groups of the Pacific Northwest (Haida, Bella Coola, and Lillooet). *Syesis* 7 (Suppl. 1):1–104. Victoria, B.C. (Title on cover page varies: Plant Taxonomies of Haida, Bella Coola, and Lillooet Indians.)

1977   Economic Importance of Black Tree Lichen (*Byroria fremontii*) to the Indians of Western North America. *Economic Botany* 31(4): 461–470.

1978   Food Plants of British Columbia Indians. Part 2: Interior Peoples. *British Columbia Provincial Museum. Handbook* 36. Victoria.

1979   Plants in British Columbia Indian Technology. *British Columbia Provincial Museum. Handbook* 38. Victoria. (Reprinted in 1992.)

1981   Indian Use of *Shepherdia canadensis*, Soapberry, in Western North America. *Davidsonia* 12(1):1–14, Vancouver: Botanical Garden of the University of British Columbia.

1982   Traditional Use of Devil's Club (*Oplopanax horridus*; Araliaceae) by Native Peoples in Western North America. *Journal of Ethnobiology* 2(1):17–38.

1984   Counter-Irritant and Other Medicinal Uses of Plants in Ranunculaceae by Native Peoples in British Columbia and Neighbouring Area. *Journal of Ethnopharmacology* 11(2):181–201.

1987   General Plant Categories in Thompson and Lillooet, Two Interior Salish Languages of British Columbia. *Journal of Ethnobiology* 7(1):55–82.

1988   Ethnobotany of Coniferous Trees in Thompson and Lillooet Interior Salish of British Columbia. *Economic Botany* 42(2):177–194.

1988a   "The Importance of a Rose": Evaluating Cultural Significance of Plants in Thompson and Lillooet Interior Salish. *American Anthropologist* 90(2):272–290.

1989   "All Berries Have Relations": Midlevel Folk Plant Categories in Thompson and Lillooet Interior Salish. *Journal of Ethnobiology* 9(1):60–110.

1991   Burning Mountain Sides for Better Crops: Aboriginal Landscape Burning in British Columbia. Archeology in Montana 32(2):57–74.

1992   Plant Resources of the *Stl'átl'imx* (Fraser River Lillooet) People: A Window into the Past. Pp. 405–469 in A Complex Culture of the British Columbia Plateau: Traditional *Stl'átl'imx* Resource Use. Brian Hayden, ed. Vancouver: UBC Press.

1997   Food Plants of Interior First Peoples. Vancouver: University of British Columbia Press; Victoria: Royal British Columbia Museum.

Turner, Nancy J., and Marianne Boelscher Ignace
1991–1992   [Fieldnotes on Secwepemc (Shuswap) ethnobotany, 1991–1992.] (Manuscript in N.J. Turner and M.B. Ignace's possession.)

Turner, Nancy J., and Harriet V. Kuhnlein
1983   Camas (*Camassia* spp.) and Riceroot (*Fritillaria* spp): Two Liliaceous "Root" Foods of the Northwest Coast Indians. *Ecology of Food and Nutrition* 13:199–219.

Turner, Nancy J., Randy Bouchard, and Dorothy I.D. Kennedy
1980   Ethnobotany of the Okanagan-Colville Indians of British Columbia and Washington. *British Columbia Provincial Museum. Occasional Paper* 21. Victoria.

Turner, Nancy J., Marianne Boelscher Ignace, and Brian D. Compton
1997   Secwepemc (Shuswap) Tree Names: Key to the Past? Pp. 387–417 in Salish Languages and Linguistics: Theoretical and Descriptive Perspectives. Ewa Czaykowska-Higgins and M. Dale Kinkade, eds. (*Trends in Linguistics. Studies and Monographs* 107). Berlin and New York: Mouton de Gruyter.

Turner, Nancy J., Harriet V. Kuhnlein, and Keith N. Egger
1987   The Cottonwood Mushroom (*Tricholoma populinum*): A Food Resource of the Interior Salish Indian Peoples of British Columbia. *Canadian Journal of Botany* 65(5):921–927.

Turner, Nancy J., Randy Bouchard, Dorothy I.D. Kennedy, and Jan P. van Eijk
1987   [Ethnobotany of the *Stl'átl'imx* (Lillooet) People of British Columbia.] (Manuscript in Nancy J. Turner's possession, Environmental Studies Program, University of Victoria, B.C.)

Turner, Nancy J., Laurence C. Thompson, M. Terry Thompson, and Annie Z. York
1990   Thompson Ethnobotany: Knowledge and Usage of Plants by the Thompson Indians of British Columbia. *Royal British Columbia Museum. Memoir* 3. Victoria.

Turney-High, Harry H.
1933   The Bluejay Dance. *American Anthropologist* 35(1):103–107.

———
1935   The Diffusion of the Horse to the Flatheads. *Man: A Monthly Record of Anthropological Science* 35(200):183–185. London.

———
1937   The Flathead Indians of Montana. *Memoirs of the American Anthropological Association* 48. Menasha, Wis. (Reprinted: Kraus Reprint, New York, 1969.)

———
1941   Ethnography of the Kutenai. *Memoirs of the American Anthropological Association* 56. Menasha, Wis. (Reprinted: Kraus Reprints, New York, 1974.)

Tyhurst, Robert
1992   Traditional and Contemporary Land and Resource Use by *Ts'kw'ayláxw* and *Xáxli'p* Bands. Pp. 355–404 in A Complex Culture of the British Columbia Plateau: Traditional *Stl'átl'imx* Resource Use. Brian Hayden, ed Vancouver, B.C.: UBC Press.

Tylor, Edward B., et al.
1889   Fourth Report of the Committee...Appointed for the Purpose of Investigating and Publishing Reports on the Physical Characters, Languages, and Industrial and Social Condition of the North-Western Tribes of the Dominion of Canada. Pp. 233–255 in *58th Annual Report of the British Association for the Advancement of Science for 1888.* London.

Tyrrell, J.B., ed. 1916 *see* Thompson, David 1916

U.S. Bureau of Indian Affairs *see* Bureau of Indian Affairs

U.S. Bureau of the Census
1894   Report on Indians Taxed and Indians Not Taxed in the United States (Except Alaska) at the Eleventh Census: 1890. (With map.) *52d Congress. 1st Session. House Miscellaneous Documents* 50(Pt.6), No. 340(15). (Serial No. 3016). Washington: Government Printing Office. (Reprinted: Norman Ross Publishing, New York, 1994.)

———
1915   Indian Population in the United States and Alaska, 1910. Washington: Government Printing Office.

———
1937   Indian Population in the United States and Alaska. Washington: Government Printing Office.

———
1989   Characteristics of American Indians by Tribes and Selected Areas: 1980. (PC80–2–1C.) Washington: Government Printing Office.

———
1991   Age by Race and Hispanic Origin: 1990. Government Units. (Idaho, Montana, Oregon and Washington; preliminary figures.) Seattle: Bureau of the Census.

———
1991a   American Indian and Alaska Native Areas: 1990. Prepared by Edna Paisano, Joan Greendeer-Lee, June Cowels, and Debbie Carroll. Washington: Racial Statistics Branch, Population Division, Bureau of the Census.

U.S. Congress
1886   [Letter from the Acting Secretary of the Interior.] *49th Congress. 1st Session. Senate Executive Document* 122 (April 8–9, 1886). Washington.

1890   [Ratification of Coeur d'Alene Indian Treaties in Idaho.] *51st Congress. 1st Session. Report* 1109 (March 28, 1890). Washington.

U.S. Congress. House
1856   *34th Congress. 1st Session. House Executive Document* 1. Washington: Government Printing Office.

———
1856a   *34th Congress. 1st Session. House Executive Document* 93. Washington: Government Printing Office.

———
1856b   *34th Congress. 1st Session. House Executive Document* 118. Washington: Government Printing Office.

———
1887   Reduction of Indian Reservations and Report of Northwest Indian Commission. *50th Congress. 1st Session. House Executive Document* 63. Washington.

———
1954–1988 [Executive Documents.] Washington: Government Printing Office.

U.S. Congress. House. Committee on Interior and Insular Affairs
1953   Report with Respect to the House Resolution Authorizing the Committee on Interior and Insular Affairs To Conduct an Investigation of the Bureau of Indian Affairs; Pursuant to H. Res. 698 (82d Cong.). *82d Congress. 2d Session. House Report* 2503. (Union Calendar 790. Serial No. 11582). Washington: Government Printing Office.

U.S. Congress. Senate
1855   Reports of Explorations and Surveys, to Ascertain the Most Practicable and Economic Route for a Railroad from the Mississippi River to the Pacific Ocean. Made Under the Direction of the Secretary of War, in 1853–4, According to Acts of Congress of March 3, 1853, May 31, 1854, and August 5, 1854. *33d Congress 2d Session. Senate Executive Document* 78. (Serial No. 758). Washington.

U.S. Congress. Senate. Committee on Interior and Insular Affairs
1954   Termination of Federal Supervision Over Certain Tribes of Indians; Part 7: Flathead Indians, Montana, Feb. 25–27, 1954. Pt. 7 in *83d Congress. 2d Session:* Joint Hearings before the Subcommittees of the Committees on Interior and Insular Affairs on S. 2750 and H.R. 7319. Washington.

U.S. Congress. Senate. Committee on Public Lands
1947–1948 Klamath Indians, Oregon. Hearings Before the Subcommittee of the Committee on Public Lands. *80th Congress. 1 Session. Senate Hearings on S. 1222.* 2 Pts. Washington.

U.S. Department of Health, Education, and Welfare. Public Health Service. Division of Indian Health
1958   Indians on Federal Reservation in the United States—A Digest. Portland Area: Idaho, Oregon, Washington. *Public Health Service Publication* 615, Pt. 1. Washington.

U.S. Department of Health, Education, and Welfare. Public Health Service. Indian Health Service
1974   Indian Health Trends and Services. *DHEW Publication* (HSA) 74–12.009. Washington.

U.S. Geological Survey
1968   Mean Monthly Average Temperature; compiled by U.S. Geological Survey in 1965. 13 maps on 1 sheet. *National Atlas, Separate Sales Ed., Sheet* 106. Washington: The Survey.

U.S. Hydrographic Office
1882   [Chart of the] North Pacific Ocean, West Coast of North America; from Juan de Fuca Strait to Queen Charlotte Islands, Including Vancouver Island; from British and United States Surveys to 1882.

U.S. National Archives
1857   [Map to accompany Treaty negotiated by Isaac Stevens in 1855.] (Map 187, Tube 1033, Records of the Bureau of Indian Affairs, National Archives, Washington.)

U.S. Public Health Service *see* U.S. Department of Health, Education, and Welfare. Public Health Service. Division of Indian Health

U.S. War Department
1860   Enumeration of Indians in Oregon and Washington Territories. Pp. 139–140 in Report of the Secretary of War for 1860. *36th Congress. 2d Session. Senate Executive Documents* 2. (Serial No. 1079). Washington.

Ubelaker, Douglas H.
1976   The Sources Methodology for Mooney's Estimates of North American Indian Populations. Pp. 243–288 in The Native Population of the Americas in 1492. William M. Denevan, ed. Madison: University of Wisconsin Press. (Reprinted, 2d ed., 1992.)

Udvardy, Miklos D.F.
1977   The Audubon Society Field Guide to North American Birds: Western Edition. Visual key dev. by Susan Rayfield. New York: Alfred A. Knopf; distrib. by Random House.

————
1997   National Audubon Society Field Guide to North American Birds: Western Region. 2d ed., rev. by John Farrand, Jr.; visual key by Amanda Wilson and Lori Hogan. New York: Alfred A. Knopf; distrib. by Random House.

Uebelacker, Morris L.
1984   Time Ball: A Story of the Yakima People and the Land. A Cultural Resource Overview [...]; with Research and Graphics by Jeffrey S. Wilson. Yakima, Wash.: The Yakima Nation.

Uhlenbeck, Christian C., and R.H. van Gulik
1934   A Blackfoot-English Vocabulary; Based on Material from the Southern Peigans. *Verhandelingen der Koninklijke Akademie van Wetenschappen te Amsterdam, Afdeeling Letterkunde*, n.r. 33(2). Amsterdam. (Reprinted: AMS Press, New York, 1984.)

Ulrich, Roberta
1994   Making Good on a Pledge. *The Oregonian*, August 30. Portland, Oreg.

Union of British Columbia Indian Chiefs
1974   The Land We Lost: A History of Cut-off Lands and Land Losses from Indian Reserves in British Columbia. Prepared by Reuben Ware. Victoria, B.C.: Union of B.C. Indian Chiefs, Land Claims Research Centre.

Unruh, John D., Jr.
1979   The Plains Across: The Overland Emigrants and the Trans-Mississippi West, 1840–60. Urbana: University of Illinois Press.

van Eijk, Jan P. *see* Eijk, Jan P. van

Van Kirk, Sylvia
1980   Many Tender Ties: Women in Fur-Trade Society, 1670–1870. Norman: University of Oklahoma Press.

Vannote, Robin L., and G.W. Minshall
1982   Fluvial Processes and Local Lithology Controlling Abundance, Structure, and Composition of Mussel Beds. *Proceedings of the National Academy of Sciences, U.S.A.* 79(13):4103–4107. Washington.

Van Vuren, Dirk
1987   Bison West of the Rocky Mountains: An Alternative Explanation. *Northwest Science* 61(2):65–69. Pullman, Wash.

Velten, Harry V.
1943   The Nez Perce Verb. *Pacific Northwest Quarterly* 34(3):271–292.

Verma, Bihari
1954   [Head-of-the-Lake Okanagan ethnographic fieldnotes.] (Manuscripts in Harry Hawthorn Papers, Special Collections Division, University of British Columbia Library, Vancouver.)

Vernon, Stivers
1934   Saga of the Molalla Hills. *Sunday Oregonian*, Magazine Section, Pt. 1: April 29; Pt. 2: May 5. Portland.

Victor, Frances Fuller
1894   The Early Indian Wars of Oregon: Compiled from the Oregon Archives and Other Original Sources; with Muster Rolls. Salem, Oreg.: Frank C. Baker, State Printer.

Voegelin, Charles F.
1946   Notes on Klamath-Modoc and Achumawi Dialects. *International Journal of American Linguistics* 12(2):96–101.

Voegelin, Charles F., and Florence M. Voegelin
1964   Languages of the World: Native America Fascicle One. *Anthropological Linguistics* 6(6):1–149.

————
1966   Map of North American Indian Languages. *American Ethnological Society. Revised Publication* 20. [New York]: Prepared and printed by Rand McNally.

Voegelin, Erminie Wheeler
1942   Culture Element Distributions, XX: Northeast California. *University of California Anthropological Records* 7(2). Berkeley.

1955–1956 The Northern Paiute of Central Oregon: A Chapter in Treaty-Making. 3Pts. *Ethnohistory* 2(2):95–132, (3):241–272, 3(1):1–10.

Vogt, Hans K.
1940   The Kalispel Language: An Outline of the Grammar with Texts, Translations, and Dictionary. Oslo: Det Norske Videnskaps-Akademi i Oslo.

————
1940a   Salishan Studies: Comparative Notes on Kalispel, Spokan, Colville and Coeur d'Alene. *Skrifter utgitt av Det Norske Videnskaps-Akademi i Oslo*, II, Hist.-Filos. Klasse No. 2. Oslo.

Von Krogh, Henning
1978   Archaeological Investigations in the Spences Bridge Locality, British Columbia. (Manuscript on file, Archaeology Branch, Victoria, B.C.)

Vowell, A.W.
1905   [Letter to the Secretary of Indian Affairs, dated June 9th, 1905.] (Manuscript in National Archives of Canada, Department of Indian Affairs, RG 10, File 29, 58–9, Ottawa.)

Wade, Mark S.
1931   The Overlanders of '62. *Archives of British Columbia. Memoir* 9. Victoria. (Reprinted: Heritage House, Surrey, B.C., 1981.)

Wainwright, Ian N.M.
1985   Rock Art Conservation Research in Canada. *BCSP: Bollettino del Centro Camuno di Studi Preistorici* 22. Capo di Ponte (Brescia), Italy.

Waitt, Richard B., Jr.
1980   About Forty Last-Glacial Lake Missoula Jökulhlaups through Southern Washington. *Journal of Geology* 88(6):653–679. Chicago.

Waldbauer, Richard C., Ruthann Knudson, and Thomas Dechert
1981   The East Kamiah Site, Clearwater River Valley, Idaho, as Known from Test Excavations. *University of Idaho. Laboratory of Anthropology. Anthropological Research Manuscript Series* 64. Moscow.

Walder, Joseph, and Bernard Halet
1985   A Theoretical Model of the Fracture of Rock During Freezing. *Geological Society of America Bulletin* 96(3):336–346.

Waldman, Carl
1985   Atlas of the North American Indian. Molly Brown, illus. New York: Facts on File Publications.

Walker, Deward E., Jr.
1958–1964 [Nez Perce fieldnotes.] (Manuscripts in D. Walker's possession.)

1963–1964   [Ethnographic fieldnotes.] (Manuscripts in D. Walker's possession.)

1964   A Survey of Nez Perce Religion. New York: Board of National Missions, United Presbyterian Church in the U.S.A.

1964a   Schismatic Factionalism and the Development of Nez Perce Pentecostalism. (Ph.D. Dissertation in Anthropology, University of Oregon, Eugene. Microfilm: University Microfilms International, Ann Arbor, Mich., 1965.)

1965   Some Limitations of the Renascence Concept in Acculturation: The Nez Perce Case. *Midcontinent American Studies Journal* 6(2):135–148. Lawrence: University of Kansas.

1966   The Nez Perce Sweat Bath Complex: An Acculturational Analysis. *Southwestern Journal of Anthropology* 22(2):133–171.

1966a   A Nez Perce Ethnographic Observation of Archaeological Significance. *American Antiquity* 31(3):436–437.

1967   Mutual Cross-Utilization of Economic Resources in the Plateau: An Example from Aboriginal Nez Perce Fishing Practices. *Washington State University. Laboratory of Anthropology. Report of Investigations* 41. Pullman.

1967a   Nez Perce Sorcery. *Ethnology* 6(1):66–96.

1967b   Measures of Nez Perce Outbreeding and the Analysis of Cultural Change. *Southwestern Journal of Anthropology* 23(2):141–158.

1967c   [Letter to Richard Halfmoon, Chairman, Nez Perce Tribal Executive Committee, Lapwai, 23 October 1967.] (Copy in Department of Sociology/Anthropology, University of Idaho, Moscow.)

1967d   An Examination of American Indian Reaction to Proposals of the Commissioner of Indian Affairs for General Legislation, 1967. *Northwest Anthropological Research Notes, Memoir* 1. Moscow, Idaho.

1968   Conflict and Schism in Nez Perce Acculturation: A Study of Religion and Politics. Pullman: Washington State University Press. (Reprinted, with a Foreword by Robert A. Hackenberg: University of Idaho Press, Moscow, 1985.)

———, ed.

1968a   Proceedings of: American Anthropological Association Symposium on American Indian Fishing and Hunting Rights, Seattle, November 1968. *Northwest Anthropological Research Notes* 2(2):1–43. Moscow, Idaho.

1969   New Light on the Prophet Dance Controversy. *Ethnohistory* 16(3):245–255.

———, ed.

1970   Systems of North American Witchcraft and Sorcery; by Keith H. Basso, et al. *University of Idaho. Department of Sociology/Anthropology. Anthropological Monographs* 1. Moscow, Idaho.

1970a   Stage and Statistical Models in Plateau Acculturation. *Northwest Anthropological Research Notes* 4(2): 153–164. Moscow, Idaho.

1970b   Ethnology and History. *Idaho Yesterdays* 4(1):24–69. Boise.

———, ed.

1971   An Exploration of the Reservation System in North America. *Northwest Anthropological Research Notes* 5(1):1–143. Moscow, Idaho.

1973   American Indians of Idaho. Volume 1: Aboriginal Cultures. *University of Idaho. Department of Sociology/Anthropology. Anthropological Monographs* 1. Moscow, Idaho.

1980   Myths of Idaho Indians. Moscow: University of Idaho Press. (Orig. publ.: Washington State University, Pullman, 1968.)

1985   Conflict and Schism in Nez Perce Acculturation: A Study of Religion an Politics. 2d ed. Foreword by Robert A. Hackenberg. Moscow: University of Idaho Press. (Orig. publ.: Washington State University Press, Pullman, 1968.)

1985a   The Kutenai Fishery: Part I. (Unpublished manuscript in D. Walker's possession.)

1987   Native Americans and Cultural Impact Analysis: The Proposed Nuclear Waste Repository at Hanford. Pp. 123–124 in Vol. 1 of Proceedings of the Symposium on Waste Management: Session on Economic and Social Effects of High Level Waste Repository Management. University of Arizona, College of Engineering and Mines (Board of Regents), Tucson, March 1–5. (Library of Congress No. 87–70501.)

1989   Witchcraft and Sorcery of the American Native Peoples. Preface by David Carrasco. Moscow: University of Idaho Press.

1991   Protection of American Indian Sacred Geography. Pp. 100–115 in Handbook of American Religious Freedom. Christopher Vecsey, ed. New York: The Crossroad Publishing Company.

1991a   The Moorhouse Collection: A Window on Umatilla History. Pp. 109–114 in The First Oregonians: An Illustrated Collection of Essays on Traditional Lifeways, Federal-Indian Relations, and the State's Native People Today. Carolyn M. Buan and Richard Lewis, eds. Portland: Oregon Council for the Humanities.

1992   Productivity of Tribal Dipnet Fishermen at Celilo Falls: Analysis of the Joe Pinkham Fish Buying Records. *Northwest Anthropological Research Notes* 26(2):123–135. Moscow, Idaho.

1993   The Shoshone-Bannock: An Anthropological Reassessment. *Northwest Anthropological Research Notes* 27(2):139–160. Mowcow, Idaho.

1994   Anthropologists and Native Americans. Pp. 41–43 in Native Americans in the Twentieth Century: An Encyclopedia. Mary B. Davis, ed. (*Garland Reference Library of Social Science* 452). New York and London: Garland.

1994a   Coeur d'Alene. Pp. 122–123 in Native Americans in the Twentieth Century: An Encyclopedia. Mary B. Davis, ed. (*Garland Reference Library of Social Science* 452). New York and London: Garland.

1994b   Confederated Tribes of the Colville Reservation. Pp. 132–133 in Native Americans in the Twentieth Century: An Encyclopedia. Mary B. Davis, ed. (*Garland Reference Library of Social Science* 452). New York and London: Garland.

1994c   Confederated Tribes of the Umatilla Indian Reservation. Pp. 139–140 in Native Americans in the Twentieth Century: An Encyclopedia. Mary B. Davis, ed. (*Garland Reference Library of Social Science* 452). New York and London: Garland.

1994d   Kutenai at Bonners Ferry. Pp. 296–297 in Native Americans in the Twentieth Century: An Encyclopedia. Mary B. Davis, ed. (*Garland Reference Library of Social Science* 452). New York and London: Garland.

1994e   Nez Perce. Pp. 389–390 in Native Americans in the Twentieth Century: An Encyclopedia. Mary B. Davis, ed. (*Garland Reference Library of Social Science* 452). New York and London: Garland.

1996   Durkheim, Eliade, and Sacred Geography in Northwestern North America. Pp. 63–68 in Chin Hills to Chiloquin: Papers Honoring the Versatile Career of Theodore Stern. Don E. Dumond, ed. *University of Oregon Anthropological Papers* 52. Eugene.

1997   Estimated Radiation Doses to Yakima Tribal Fishermen. Boulder, Co.: Walker Research Group, Ltd.

1997a   A CTUIR Study of the Population of the Umatilla Reservation and Umatilla County. Boulder, Co.: Walker Research Group, Ltd.

1997b   The Yakama System of Trade and Exchange. *Northwest Anthropological Research Notes* 31(1). Moscow, Idaho.

Walker, Deward E., Jr., with Frank L. Halfmoon
1995   Transport Factors in Fish: A Review and Evaluation of the HEDR Project Columbia River Pathway Modeling and Dose Calculation Procedures. Final Report. Richland, Wash.: Battelle PNL.

Walker, Deward E., Jr., and Lawrence Johnson
1994   Hatiya "Wind". Film on the Confederated Tribes of the Umatilla Indian Reservation. Portland, Oreg.: Oregon Council on the Humanities in coop. with the CTUIR.

Walker, Deward E., Jr., and Sylvester H. Lahren, Jr.
1977   Anthropological Guide for the Coulee Dam National Recreation Area. *University of Idaho. Anthropological Research Manuscript Series* 3. Moscow, Idaho.

Walker, Deward E., Jr., and Daniel N. Matthews
1994   Blood of the Monster: The Nez Perce Coyote Cycle. Illus. by Marc Seahmer. Worland, Wyo.: High Plains Publishing.

Walker, Deward E., Jr., and John L. Schultz
1967   Indian Shakers on the Colville Reservation. *Washington State University. Research Studies* 35(2):167–172. Pullman.

Walker, Elkanah
1847   [Unabridged diary.] (Typescript in Clifford Drury Papers, Washington State University Archives, Pullman.)

————— 1976 *see* Drury, Clifford M., ed. 1976

Walker, Elkanah, and Cushing Eells
1842   Etshiit thlu sitskai thlu siais thlu Sitskaisitlinish. Lapwai, [Oreg. Terr./Idaho]: Oregon Mission Press.

Walker, Phillip, Patricia Lambert, and Michael DeNiro
1989   The Northern Roots of Hunter Gatherer Intensification: Camas and the Pacific Northwest, by Alston Thomas. (Ph.D. Dissertation in Anthropology, Washington State University, Pullman.)

Wallmo, Olof C., comp. and ed.
1981   Mule and Black-tailed Deer of North America. Lincoln: University of Nebraska Press.

Walter, Edward
1969   Picture Trees, Indian Picture Trees of Mystery. (Nomination form to the National Register of Historic Places, on file, State Historic Preservation Office, Olympia, Wash.)

Walters, L.V.W.
1938   Social Structure. Pp. 71–99 in The Sinkaietk or Southern Okanagon of Washington. Leslie Spier, ed. *General Series in Anthropology* 6, *Contributions from the Laboratory of Anthropology* 2. Menasha, Wis.: George Banta.

Ware, Reuben M.
1983   Five Issues, Five Battlegrounds: An Introduction to the History of Indian Fishing in British Columbia, 1850–1930. Sardis, B.C.: Coqualeetza Education Centre.

Warre, Sir Henry James
1848   Sketches in North America and the Oregon Territory. London: Dickinson. (Reprinted, with an Introduction by Archibald Hanna, Jr.: Imprint Society, Barre, Mass., 1970.)

Warren, Claude N.
1968   The View from Wanas: A Study in Plateau Prehistory. *Idaho State University Museum Occasional Papers* 24. Pocatello.

Warren, Claude N., and Robert Fitzwater
1963   Estimate of Archaeological Salvage on Highway Project F 4113(29). (Manuscript on file at Pacific Northwest Regional Office, National Park Service, Seattle.)

1963a   Archaeological Survey of the Nez Perce Region White Bird Hill, Idaho. (Manuscript on file at Pacific Northwest Regional Office, National Park Service, Seattle.)

Warren, Claude N., Cort Sims, and Max G. Pavesic
1968   Cultural Chronology in Hells Canyon. *Tebiwa: Journal of the Idaho State University Museum* 11(2):1–37. Pocatello.

Warren, Claude N., Kent S. Wilkinson, and Max G. Pavesic
1971   The Midvale Complex. *Tebiwa: Journal of the Idaho State University Museum* 14(2):39–71. Pocatello.

Washington Archaeological Society
1969   The Marmes Year, April 1968 – April 1969. *Washington Archaeologist* 13(2–3).

Waterman, Thomas T.
1914   The Explanatory Element in the Folk-Tales of the North-American Indians. *Journal of American Folk-Lore* 27(103):1–54.

1923   Some Conundrums in Northwest Coast Art. *American Anthropologist*, n.s. 25(4):435–451.

Watkins, Donald
1970   A Description of the Phonemes and Position Classes in the Morphology of Head of the Lake Okanagan Salish. (Ph.D. Dissertation in Linguistics, University of Alberta, Edmonton. Microfilm: *Canadian Theses on Microfilm* 6766, National Library of Canada, Ottawa, 1971.)

1970a   The Practice of Medicine among the Indians. Pp. 30–32 in *34th Annual Report of the Okanagan Historical Society*. Vernon, B.C.

1971   History of Words. Pp. 157–159 in *35th Annual Report of the Okanagan Historical Society*. Vernon, B.C.

Weatherford, Claudine
1971   Trade Bells of the Southern Plateau: Their Use and Occurrence Through Time. (M.A. Thesis in Anthropology, Washington State University, Pullman.)

Webster, Gary S.
1978   Dry Creek Rockshelter: Cultural Chronology in the Western Snake River Region of Idaho, ca. 4150 B.P.–1300 B.P. *Miscellaneous Papers of the Idaho State University Museum of Natural History* 15. Pocatello.

Wegars, Priscilla, and Roderick Sprague
1981   Archaeological Salvage of the Joso Trestle Construction Camp, 45–FR–51, Lower Monumental Project. *University of Idaho Anthropological Research Manuscript Series* 65. Moscow.

Weil, Peter M.
1965   Political Modernization on the Nez Perce Indian Reservation: 1940–1963. (M.A. Thesis in Anthropology, University of Oregon, Eugene.)

Weisel, George F.
1951   The Ram's Horn Tree and Other Medicine Trees of the Flathead Indians. *Montana Magazine of History* 1(3):5–14.

———
1952   Animal Names, Anatomical Terms, and Some Ethnozoology of the Flathead Indians. *Journal of the Washington Academy of Science* 42(11):345–355. Washington.

———
1954   Ten Animal Myths of the Flathead Indians. (Mimeographed.) *University of Montana. Anthropology and Sociology Papers* 18. Missoula.

———
1955   Men and Trade on the Northwest Frontier, as Shown by the "Fort Owen Ledger." *Montana State University Studies* 2. Missoula.

Welch, Debora, and Michael Striker
1994   A Bibliography of Plateau Ethnobotany. *Northwest Anthropological Research Notes* 28(2):211–240. Moscow, Idaho.

Wellmann, Klaus F.
1979   A Survey of North American Indian Rock Art; with 750 Photographs by the Author ... and 200 Line Drawings by Ursula Arndt. Graz, Austria: Akademische Druck- u. Verlagsanstalt.

Wenger, Patrick M.
1968   Phonotactical Indices: A Test Case in Macro-Penutian Classification. (M.A. Thesis in Anthropology, University of Oregon, Eugene.)

Wheeler, Olin D.
1904   The Trail of Lewis and Clark, 1804–1904. 2 vols. New York: G.P. Putnam's Sons.

Wheeler, Richard P.
1952   A Note on the Mckean Lanceolate Point. *Plains Archaeological Conference Newsletter* 4(4):45–50.

———
1954   Two Projectile Point Types: Duncan and Hanna Points. *Plains Anthropologist* 1(May):7–14.

Whitaker, Sylvia McAleer
1992   A Refined Chronology of the Clearwater Region of North Central Idaho Based on Radiocarbon Dates and Associated Projectile Points. (M.A. Thesis in Anthropology, University of Idaho, Moscow.)

White, Elijah *see* Allen, A.J., comp. 1848, and ARCIA 1824–1848

White, Elizabeth L.
1990   Adult Education and Cultural Invasion: A Case Study of the Salish and Jesuits. (Ph.D. Dissertation in Education, Montana State University, Bozeman.)

———
1996   Worlds in Collision: Jesuit Missionaries and Salish Indians on the Columbia Plateau, 1841–1850. *Oregon Historical Quarterly* 97(1):26–45.

White, Eugene E.
1965   Experiences of a Special Indian Agent. With an Introduction of Edward Everett Dale. New ed. *Western Frontier Library* 29. Norman: University of Oklahoma Press. (Originally publ. under title: Service on the Indian Reservations. Arkansas Democrat Company, Little Rock, 1893.)

White, Kris A., and Janice St. Laurent
1996   Mysterious Journey: The Catholic Ladder of 1840. *Oregon Historical Quarterly* 97(1):70–88.

White, M. Catherine
1942   Saleesh House: The First Trading Post Among the Flathead. *Pacific Northwest Quarterly* 33(3):251–263.

——— , ed. 1950 *see* Thompson, David 1950

Whitehead, Margaret
1981   Christianity, a Matter of Choice: The Historic Role of Indian Catechists in Oregon Territory and British Columbia. *Pacific Northwest Quarterly* 72(3):98–106.

———
1981a   The Cariboo Mission: A History of the Oblates. Victoria: Sono Nis Press.

Whitehouse, Joseph *see* Thwaites, Reuben G., ed. 1904–1905

Whitlam, Robert G.
1976   Archaeology in the Williams Lake Area, British Columbia. *Occasional Papers of the Archaeological Sites Advisory Board of British Columbia* 1. Victoria. (Cover title: The Descriptive Analysis of Three Sites—The FaRm 8 Symap Project.)

Whitman, Narcissa
1893   Letters Written by Mrs. Whitman from Oregon to Her Relatives in New York. Pp. 79–179 in *Transactions of the 19th Annual Reunion of the Oregon Pioneer Association for 1891*.

Whitner, Robert L.
1959   Grant's Indian Peace Policy on the Yakima Reservation, 1870–82. *Pacific Northwest Quarterly* 50(4):135–143.

Wickwire, Wendy C.
1978   Songs of the Canadian Interior Salish Tribes: An Anthology and Ethnography. (M.A. Thesis in Interdisciplinary Studies, York University, Toronto.)

———
1982   Cultures in Contact: Music, the Plateau Indian, and the Western Encounter. (Ph.D. Dissertation in Ethnomusicology, Wesleyan University, Middletown, Conn. Microfilm: University Microfilms International, Ann Arbor, Mich., 1985.)

———
1985   Theories of Ethnomusicology and the North American Indian: Retrospective and Critique. *Canadian University Music Review* 6:186–221.

———
1988   James A. Teit: His Contribution to Canadian Ethnomusicology. *Canadian Journal of Native Studies* 8(2):183–204.

———
1992   Women in Ethnography: The Research of James A. Teit. (Manuscript in Wickwire's possession.)

Wigand, Peter E.
1985   Diamond Pond, Harney County, Oregon: Man and Marsh in the Eastern Oregon Desert. (Ph.D. Dissertation in Anthropology, Washington State University, Pullman.)

———
1989   Vegetation, Vegetation History, and Stratigraphy. Pp. 37–85 in Prehistory and Paleoenvironments of the Silvies Plateau, Harney Basin, Southeastern Oregon. K.C. Reid, J.A. Draper, and P.E. Wigand, eds. *Washington State University. Center for Northwest Anthropology. Project Report* 8. Pullman.

Wight, E.L., Mary Mitchell, and Marie Schmidt, comps.
1960   Indian Reservations of Idaho, Oregon, and Washington. Portland, Oreg.: Bureau of Indian Affairs, Portland Area Office.

Wilbur, James
1867   [Letter of June 30, 1867.] Pp. 45–47 in *40th Congress. 2d Session. House Executive Document* 1. Washington.

———
1874   [Letter of September 2, 1874.] Pp. 647–648 in *43d Congress. 2d Session. House Executive Document* 1. (Serial No. 1639). Washington.

1881   [Letter of August 15, 1881.] Pp. 231–234 in *47th Congress. 1st Session. House Executive Document* 1. (Serial No. 2018). Washington.

Wildesen, Leslie E.
1982   The Farthest Frontier of All: A Cultural Resource Overview of the River of No Return Wilderness, Idaho. *USDA Forest Service Intermountain Region. Cultural Resource Report* 8. Ogden, Utah.

Wilfong, Cheryl
1990   Following the Nez Perce Trail: A Guide to the Nee-Me-Poo National Historic Trail with Eyewitness Accounts. [Corvallis]: Oregon State University Press.

Wilkes, Charles
1845   Narrative of the United States Exploring Expedition, During the Years 1838, 1839, 1840, 1841, 1842. 5 vols. and Atlas. Philadelphia: Lea and Blanchard.

Wilkes, George
1845   History of Oregon, Geographical, Geological, and Political. New York: Colyer. (Reprinted: *Washington Historical Quarterly* 4(1):60–80, (2):139–160, (3):207–224, (4):300–312, 5(1):72–80, 1913.)

Wilkinson, M.C.
1877   [Official Report of M.C. Wilkinson, 1st Lieut. 3d Inf. ... made in accordance with the following order: S.O. 167, Hdqs. Dept. of the Columbia.] (Manuscript in Records of the War Department, U.S. Army Commands, Department of the Columbia, No. 2473, 1877, National Archives, Washington.)

Willard, Helen
1990   Pow-Wow and Other Yakima Indian Traditions. Prosser, Wash.: Rosa Run Publishing.

Willey, Gordon W., and Philip Phillips
1958   Method and Theory in American Archaeology. Chicago: University of Chicago Press.

Williams, Chuck
1980   Bridge of the Gods, Mountains of Fire: A Return to the Columbia Gorge. Introd. by David R. Brower. New York and San Francisco: Friends of the Earth; White Salmon, Wash., [and] Petaluma, Calif.: Elephant Mountain Arts.

Williams, Lorna, ed.
1979   Cuystwí malh Ucwalmícwts / Ucwalmícwts Curriculum for Intermediates. Mount Currie, B.C.: The Tŝzil Publishing House.

Williams, Melda Ann
1967   Historical Background and Musical Analysis of Thirty Selected Nez Perce Songs. (M.A. Thesis in Music, University of Idaho, Moscow.)

Willoughby, Charles C.
1905   Textile Fabrics of the New England Indian. *American Anthropologist*, n.s. 7(1):85–93.

Wilmeth, Roscoe
1977   Chilcotin Archaeology: The Direct Historic Approach. Pp. 97–101 in Problems in Prehistory of the North American Subarctic: The Athapaskan Question. J.W. Helmer, S. Van Dyke, and F.J. Kense, eds. Calgary: University of Calgary Archaeological Association.

1977a   Pit House Construction and the Disturbance of Stratified Sites. *Canadian Journal of Archaeology* 1:135–140. Ottawa.

1978   Anahim Lake Archaeology and the Early Historic Chilcotin Indians. *Archaeological Survey of Canada. Mercury Series. Paper* 77. Ottawa.

1979   An Athabaskan Hypothesis. *Canadian Journal of Archaeology* 3:33–40. Ottawa.

1980   Excavations at the Nakwantlun Site (FdSi 11) in 1980. (Manuscript on file, Archaeology Branch, Victoria, B.C.)

Wilson, Charles W.
1866   Report on the Indian Tribes Inhabiting the Country in the Vicinity of the 49th Parallel of North Latitude. *Transactions of the Ethnological Society of London*, n.s. 4:275–332. London.

1970   Mapping the Frontier: Charles Wilson's Diary of the Survey of the 49th Parallel, 1858–1872. George F.G. Stanley, ed. Toronto: Macmillan of Canada.

Wilson, Ian R.
1991   Excavations at EdQx 41 and 42 and Site Evaluation of EdQx43, Monte Creek, B.C. (Manuscript on file, Archaeology Branch, Victoria, B.C.)

1992   Excavations at the Baker Site (EdQx 43), Monte Creek. (Manuscript on file, Archaeology Branch, Victoria, B.C.)

Wilson, Renate
1964   Basket Makers of Mount Currie. *The Beaver* Autumn(295):26–33. Winnipeg, Man.

Wilson, Robert L.
1980   Archaeological Investigation near Kamloops. Pp. 1–86 in The Archaeology of Kamloops. Robert L. Wilson and Catherine Carlson, eds. *Simon Fraser University. Department of Archaeology. Publication* 7. Burnaby, B.C.

Winans, William P.
1870   [Census roster.] (Winans Papers 44, Washington State University Library Archives, Pullman.)

1871   [Letter to Judge Kennedy, April 3d, 1871.] (Winans Papers, Cage 147, W48a, Washington State University Library Archives, Pullman.)

Wingert, Paul S.
1952   Prehistoric Stone Sculpture of the Pacific Northwest; Exhibition, March 11th through April 16th, 1952, at the Portland Art Museum. Portland: Portland Art Museum.

Winter, Barbara J.
1996   Out of Sight, Out of Mind: The Reposition of Archaeological Collections in Canada. (Ph.D. Dissertation in Anthropology, Simon Fraser University, Burnaby, B.C.; Microfiche: *Canadian Theses on Microfiche* AS 044–4871. Ottawa, 1997.)

Winthrop, Theodore
1862   The Canoe and the Saddle; or, Klalam and Klickatat. New York: Dodd, Mead. (Reprinted: John H. Williams, Tacoma, Wash., 1913.)

Wishart, David J.
1979   The Fur Trade of the American West, 1807–1848: A Geographical Synthesis. Lincoln: University of Nebraska Press.

Wissler, Clark
1914   Material Cultures of the North American Indians. *American Anthropologist*, n.s. 16(3):447–505. (Reprinted: Pp. 76–134 in Anthropology in North America, by Franz Boas, et al. G.E. Stechert, New York, 1915.)

1914a   The Influence of the Horse in the Development of Plains Culture. *American Anthropologist*, n.s. 16(1):1–25.

1917   The American Indian: An Introduction to the Anthropology of the New World. New York: Douglas C. McMurtrie. (Reprinted: 2d ed., 1922; 3d ed., 1938.)

1922   The American Indian: An Introduction to the Anthropology of the New World. 2d ed. New York: Oxford University Press.

1938   The American Indian: An Introduction to the Anthropology of the New World. 3d ed. New York: Oxford University Press.

1938a   Indian Cavalcade: or, On the Old-Time Indian Reservation. New York: Sheridan House.

Womack, Bruce R.
1977   An Archaeological Investigation and Technological Analysis of the Stockhoff Basalt Quarry, Northeastern Oregon. (M.A. Thesis in Anthropology, Washington State University, Pullman.)

Wood, W. Raymond
1972   Contrastive Features of Native North American Trade Systems. Pp. 153–169 in For the Chief: Essays in Honor of Luther S. Cressman; by Some of His Students. Fred W. Voget and Robert L. Stephenson, eds. Foreword by Theodore Stern. *University of Oregon Anthropological Papers* 4. Eugene.

Woodcock, Clarence
1983   A Brief History of the Flathead Tribes. St. Ignatius, Mont.: Flathead Culture Committee.

1996   Salish Tradition. *Oregon History Magazine* 39(3–4):8–9. Portland.

Woods, James C., and Gene L. Titmus
1985   A Review of the Simon Clovis Collection. *Idaho Archaeologist* 8(21):3–8. Caldwell.

Woodward, John A.
1982   The Ancient Painted Images of the Columbia Gorge. Ramona, Calif.: Acoma Books.

Woolums, Christy A.
1972   The History of Indian Education. (M.A. Thesis in Anthropology, University of Idaho, Moscow.)

Work, John
1823   [Journal: July 18th–October 28th, 1823, York Factory to Spokan House.] (Typescript A/B/40/W89, British Columbia Archives and Record Service, Victoria.)

1829   [Answers to queries on natural history, April 1, 1829, Fort Colvile.] (Manuscript B.45/e/2, Hudson's Bay Company Archives, Provincial Archives of Manitoba, Winnipeg.)

1830   [Some informations relative to the Colville District, Fort Colvile Report, 1830.] (Manuscript B.45/e/3, Hudson's Bay Company Archives, Provincial Archives of Manitoba, Winnipeg.)

1909   Journal of John Work, April 30th to May 31st, 1830. T.C. Elliott, ed. *Oregon Historical Quarterly* 10(3):296–313.

1912   Journal of John Work's Snake Country Expedition of 1830–31. T.C. Elliott, ed. *Oregon Historical Quarterly* 13(4):363–371.

1912a   Journal of John Work, November and December, 1824. T.C. Elliott, ed. *Washington Historical Quarterly* 3(3):198–228.

1913   Journal of John Work's Snake Country Expedition of 1830–31. T.C. Elliott, ed. *Oregon Historical Quarterly* 14(3):280–314.

1914   Journal of John Work, June-October, 1825. T.C. Elliott, ed. *Washington Historical Quarterly* 5(2):85–115.

1914a   Journal of John Work, September 7th - Dec. 14th, 1825. T.C. Elliott, ed. *Washington Historical Quarterly* 5(3):163–191.

1914b   Journal of John Work, December 15, 1825 to June 12, 1826. T.C. Elliott, ed. *Washington Historical Quarterly* 5(4):258–287.

1915   The Journal of John Work, July 5, - September 15, 1826. T.C. Elliott, ed. *Washington Historical Quarterly* 6(1):26–49.

1920   John Work's Journal of a Trip from Fort Colville to Fort Vancouver and Return in 1828. W.S. Lewis and Jacob A. Meyers, eds. *Washington Historical Quarterly* 11(2):104–114.

1923   The Journal of John Work, a Chief-Trader of the Hudson's Bay Co., during His Expedition from Vancouver to the Flatheads and Blackfeet of the Pacific Northwest. Edited with an Account of the Fur Trade in the Northwest, and Life of Work. William S. Lewis and Paul C. Phillips, eds. (*Northwest Historical Series* 1). Cleveland: Arthur H. Clark.

1971   The Snake River Country Expedition of 1830–1831: John Work's Field Journal. Francis D. Haines, Jr., ed. *American Exploration and Travel Series* 59. Norman: University of Oklahoma Press.

Workman, William B.
1974   The Cultural Significance of a Volcanic Ash Which Fell in the Upper Yukon about 1400 Years Ago. Pp. 239–261 in International Conference on the Prehistory and Palaeoecology of Western North American Arctic and Subarctic. S. Raymond and P. Schlederman, eds. Calgary, Alta.: Archaeological Association, University of Calgary.

1979   The Significance of Volcanism in the Prehistory of Subarctic Northwest North America. Pp. 339–371 in Volcanic Activity and Human Ecology. P.D. Sheets and D.K. Grayson, eds. New York: Academic Press.

Wormington, Hanna Marie, and Richard G. Forbis
1965   An Introduction to the Archaeology of Alberta, Canada. (With Appendix, pp. 209–248: Prehistoric Pottery from Southern Alberta, by James B. Griffin.) *Proceedings of the Denver Museum of Natural History* 11. Denver.

Wright, George
1857   Camp on the Na-chass River, Washington Territory, June 11, 1856. Pp. 160–162 in *34th Congress. 3d Session. House Executive Document* 5. (Serial No. 876). Washington: A.O.P. Nicholson.

1859   Expedition Against the Northern Indians. General Orders of 4 July 1858, Report of the War Department, Department of the Pacific, for 1855–1859. Pp. 363–364 in *35th Congress. 2d Session. House Executive Document* 2. (Serial No. 998). Washington.

1859a   Topographic Memoirs and Map of Colonel Wright's Late Campaign against the Indians in Oregon and Washington Territories. *35th Congress. 2d Session. Senate Executive Document* 10(32). (Serial No. 984). Washington.

Wright, Muriel H.
1951   A Guide to the Indian Tribes of Oklahoma. Norman: University of Oklahoma Press. (Reprinted in 1957, 1965, 1968, 1971, and 1986.)

Wright, Robin K.
1989   The Collection of Native Art in Washington: New Georgia Through Statehood. *American Indian Art Magazine* 14(3):62–74.

1991   Masterworks of Washington Native Art. Pp. 43–151 in A Time of Gathering: Native Heritage in Washington State. Robin K. Wright, ed. (*Thomas Burke Memorial Washington State Museum, Monograph* 7). Seattle: Burke Museum [and] University of Washington Press.

Writers' Project. Oregon
1940   Oregon: End of the Trail. Portland, Oreg.: Binford and Mort. (Reprinted: Somerset Publishers, St. Clair Shores, Mich., 1973.)

Wyatt, David J.
1971   An Outline of Nicola Valley Prehistory. Pp. 60–72 in Aboriginal Man and Environments on the Plateau of Northwest America. Arnoud H. Stryd and Rachel A. Smith, eds. Calgary: The University of Calgary Student's Press.

1972   The Indian History of the Nicola Valley, British Columbia. (Ph.D. Dissertation in Anthropology, Brown University, Providence, R.I.)

1992   [Fieldnotes.] (Manuscript in Wyatt's possession.)

Wydoski, Richard S., and Richard R. Whitney
1979   Inland Fishes of Washington. Seattle: University of Washington Press.

Wyeth, Nathaniel J.
1853   Indian Tribes of the South Pass of the Rocky Mountains. The Salt Lake Basin. ... Pp. 204–228 in Pt. 1 of Historical and Statistical Information, Respecting the History, Conditions and Prospects of the Indian Tribes of the United States, by Henry Rowe Schoolcraft. Philadelphia: Lippincott, Grambo.

1899   The Correspondence and Journals of Captain Nathaniel J. Wyeth, 1831–6. Frederick George Young, ed. *Sources of the History of Oregon* 1 (Pts. 3–6). Eugene, Oreg.: University Press. (Reprinted: Ye Galleon Press, Fairfield, Wash., 1984.)

Wylie, Henry G., and Darlene Flynn
1977   Cultural Resource Investigations: Payette, Boise, Salmon, Challis, Sawtooth, Targhee, and Caribou National Forests, 1975–1976. Preliminary Summary. (Manuscript on file, USDA Forest Service, Intermountain Region, Ogden, Utah.)

Wylie, Henry G., and Susan Ketchum
1978   A Summary of U.S. Forest Service Cultural Activities in South and Central Idaho, 1978. (Manuscript on file, USDA Forest Service, Intermountain Region, Boise, Idaho.)

Wylie, Henry G., T. Scott, and Joseph C. Gallagher
1981   Test Excavations in the River of No Return Wilderness: Preliminary Report on Waterfall Village and Big Creek Cave. (Manuscript on file, USDA Forest Service, Intermountain Region, Ogden, Utah.)

Wynecoop, David
1969   Children of the Sun: A History of the Spokane Indians. Wellpinit, Wash.: [The Author.]

YIRRA = Yakima Indian Reservation Redevelopment Area
1962   Overall Economic Development Plan. Toppenish, Wash.: Yakima Indian Agency.

YNR = *Yakima Nation Review*
1970–   *Yakima Nation Review.* [Official Yakima Indian Nation biweekly newspaper. Toppenish, Wash.]

Yakima Indian Nation. Education Division (and Consortium of Johnson O'Malley Committees)
1978   'Mamashat Sinwit' (Language) Teacher's Guide. Toppenish, Wash.: Yakima Indian Nation.

Yakima Indian Nation. Education Division (and Fort Wright College)
1979   Multi-Cultural Early Childhood Curriculum for the Yakima Indian Nation. Toppenish, Wash.: Kamiakin Research Institute.

Yakima Tribal Council
1955   The Yakimas: Treaty Centennial, 1855–1955. Click Relander, ed. Yakima, Wash.: The Republic Press.

Yale, J. Murray
1838–1839 [Census of Indian Population, 1838–1839.] (Manuscript B.223/z/1 in Hudson's Bay Company Archives, Provincial Archives of Manitoba, Winnipeg.)

Yanan, Eileen, comp.
1971   Coyote and the Colville. Omak, Wash.: St. Mary's Mission.

Yent, Martha E.
1976   The Cultural Sequence at Wawawai (45WT39), Lower Snake River Region, Southeastern Washington. (M.A. Thesis in Anthropology, Washington State University, Pullman.)

York, Annie, Richard Daly, and Chris Arnett
1993   They Write Their Dream on the Rock Forever: Rock Writings of the Stein River Valley of British Columbia. Vancouver, B.C.: Talonbooks.

York, Geoffrey
1989   The Dispossessed: Life and Death in Native Canada. 1st ed. Toronto: Lester & Orpen Dennys.

Zakoji, Hiroto
1953   Klamath Culture Change. (M.A. Thesis in Anthropology, University of Oregon, Eugene.)

[1961]   Termination and the Klamath Education Program, 1955–1961. Salem, Oreg.: [Oregon] State Department of Education.

Zenk, Henry
1988   Chinook Jargon in the Speech Economy of Grand Ronde Reservation, Oregon: An Ethnography of Speaking Approach to an Historical Case of Creolization in Process. Pp. 107–124 in Sociolinguistics and Pidgin-Creole Studies. John R. Rickford, ed. Joshua A. Fishman, gen. ed. *International Journal of the Sociology of Language* 71. Amsterdam, The Netherlands: Mouton de Gruyter.

1992   [Battle of the Mountains. With comments and revisions by Howard Berman.] (Manuscript from Leo J. Frachtenberg's Molale Text Notebooks, Notebook 4, National Anthropological Archives, Smithsonian Institution, Washington; copy in Zenk's possession.)

Zimmerman, Larry J.
1992   Archaeology, Reburial, and the Tactics of a Discipline's Self-Delusion. *American Indian Culture and Research Journal* 16(2):37–56.

Zontek, Kenneth S.
1993   Saving the Bison: The Story of Samuel Walking Coyote. (M.A. Thesis in History, New Mexico State University, Las Cruces.)

Zucker, Jeff, Key Hummel, and Bob Høgfoss
1983   Oregon Indians: Culture, History and Current Affairs: An Atlas and Introduction. [Portland, Oreg.]: Western Imprints, The Press of the Oregon Historical Society.

Zwicky, Arnold M.
1971   More on Nez Perce: On Alternative Analyses. *International Journal of American Linguistics* 37(2):122–126.

BIBLIOGRAPHY

Index

Italic numbers indicate material in figure captions; roman numbers, material in the text.

All variant names of groups are indexed, with the occurrences under synonymy *discussing the equivalences. Variants of group names that differ from those cited only in their capitalization, hy-phenation, or accentuation have generally been omitted; variants that differ only in the presence or absense of one (noninitial) letter or compound element have been collapsed into a single entry with that letter or element in parentheses.*

The entry Indian words *indexes, by language, all words appearing in the standard orthographies and some others.*

nal: 235, 416, 418, 462, 464, 465, 468, 470–472. age of: 477, 483. band: 400, 496–497, 501. birth statistics: 478, 479, 483. blood quantum statistics: 479. censuses: 477–478. children: 477. decline: 470, 472–477, 478, 500, 501, 636. densities: 526. 18th century: 343, 472. environmental limits on: 467–468. health status: 478–479, 482–483. mortality statistics: 468, 470, 472, 474, 476–479, 483. nadir: 478. 19th century: 151, 216, 393, 469–470, 474, 476–477, 480. postcontact: 235. prehistoric: 73, 76, 79, 80, 81, 103, 113, 124, 129, 131, 134, 137, 216, 374. reservation and reserve: 190, 201, 216, 267–269, 281, 296, 312, 358, 418, 433, 444, 464, 476–480, 496–497, 498. residence statistics: 479. sex ratios: 470, 477, 483. 20th century: 174, 216, 479–483, 481, 482. White admixture: 479

Porter, Roger: *580*

Port Pemberton: 186

Post, John: 556

Potato Mountain locality: *82*

potlatches: 148, 160, 185, 199, 211, 214, 549, 552, 553

Potlatch site: *82, 91*

pottery: 134, 232, 501, 600. prehistoric: 135

Powell, John Wesley: 9

power: 265, 303–304, 337, 371, 388, 406, 410–411, 426, 459, 499, 512, 523, 546, 557, 584. acquisition: 372, 410, 426, 455, 457, 459–460, 557, 581. loss of: 499. songs: 342, 373, 410, 426, 459, 546–547, 551, 555, 556, 571, 572. sources of: 519–521, 535–537, 548–549, 580. transfers: 426–427. uses of: 411, 427. *wáptipas* complex: 426. *See also* dreams and visions; shamans, power acquisition

póxolokáti; synonymy: 419

ppegáząźe; synonymy: 438

ppílyaʔqn; synonymy: 312

prehistory: 1, 18, 21, 25, 73–80, 81–102, 103–119, 120–137, 220. adornment: 74, 75, 77, 78, 86, 94, 100, *108*, 115, 118. art: 78, 79, 88. basketry: 74, 111, 118, 134. ceremonies: 103. clothing: 74, 114. death practices: 74, 75, 77, 78–79, 83, 89, 94, 95, 100, 103, 116, 117–118, 129, 134, 135. environment: 73–74, 76, 77–78, 79, 96, 113, 120–122, 123, 125, 130, 131–132, 136, 137. language: 67–69. migrations: 98–99, 100, 137. political organization: 302. population: 76, 79, 80, 81, 103, 113, 124, 129, 131, 134, 137. regional connections: 118–119. religion: 103. sculpture: 88, *115*, 116. settlement pattern: 76, 79, 80, 81, 85, 86, 93, 98, 101, 106, 110, 113, 114. settlements: 74, 76, 77, 78, 91, 113, 114, 124, 128–129, 129, 130, 134, 137. social organization: 79, 87, 134. structures: 74, 75, 76, *77*, 78, 79, *79*, 80, 85, 86, 87, 89, 91–94, 96, 99–100, 101, 106, 107, *107, 108*, 109, 111, 112, 113, 115, 116, 117, 129, 134. subsistence: 74–81, 83, 84, 85, 87, 88, 92, 93, 98, 101, 103, 105, 107, 108, 110, 113, 114, 117, 120, 122, 124, 125, 128–133, 136. technology: 74, 75, 77, *77*, 78, 83–86, *84*, 85, *86*, 88, 89, 91–98, *95*, 100, 103, 106, 107, 109, 110, 113, *115*, 117, 127, 131. textiles: 111. trade: 76, 77, 78, 80, 110, 113, 115, *118*, 118–119, 134, 136. warfare: 79. *See also* archeology

Presbyterians. *See* missionaries

Preston, Charley: 492

Price, Hiram: 152

Priest Rapids Longhouse: 329

Priest Rapids Reservoir: 20, 114, 115, *621*

projectile points: 22, 25, 116, 117, 126–127, 258, 274, 300. classification: 123. prehistoric: 74, 75, 77, 79, 80, 82–89, *84, 85, 86, 87, 91*, 91–96, *95*, 98, 103–104, *105*, 106–119, *108, 114*, 122–128, *124, 126, 128, 130*, 130–136, *133, 134*, 220. *See also* bows and arrows

property: 6, 182–183, 423, 521. ownership: 171, 199, 208, 211, 361, 435, 454, 505, 538. rights: 149, 285. taxation: 171, 307. wealth: 99, 139, 160–162, 261, 300, 368–369, *398–399*, 399, 402, 403, 427, 443, 453, 454, 579, *644*, 646

prostitution: 157, 294

Protestants. *See* missionaries

protoagriculture; burning: 46, 48, 78

Proto-Athapaskans: 220

Protohistoric period: 86

Proto–Interior Salish language: 57

Proto-Sahaptian language: 14, 59

Proto-Salishan language: 56, 58, 68, 69

Pshawanwappam; synonymy: 349

puberty: 213–214, 277–278, 337, 546. boys': 5, 6, 183–184, 186, 196, 213, 214, 247, 262, 277, 290, 292, 321, 337, 372, 388, 423, 457, 459, 553, 616, 617. ceremonies: 423, 444, 555, 556, 558. girls': 5, 6, 180, 183, 196–197, *198*, 209, 213–214, 221, 247, 249, 262, 277, 290, 321, 337, 372, 388, 396, 423, 444, 457, 459, 555, 556, 558, 616–617, *617*. ritual observances: 221, 535, 536. training: 198–199. *See also* menstrual practices

Public Law 83–280: 390, 488

Public Law 93–638: 7

Puck Hyah Toot: 26, *502*, 505

Pueblo Indians; synonymy: 438

Pueblo Revolt of 1680: 138

Puget Sound Agricultural Company: 149

Pumshawis: *506*

punches: 301

Q

Qamĭl-`lĕma; synonymy: 394

qayús; synonymy: 417

Qematspelu: 402, 414

qeṁéʿspelúʿ; synonymy: 296

qemúynu; synonymy: 437

qlispél; synonymy: 296

qlspílx; synonymy: 296

q̇miłáma; synonymy: 394

Quaaout; synonymy: 218

Qualchin: 154, 344

Quapaw; synonymy: 438

Quath-la-poh-tle; population: 469

Queahpama: *387*, 499, 552

Queahpama, Frank: 507

Queahpama, Nettie: 507

Quequesah, Eneas: *639*

Quiarlpi; synonymy: 251

Quib quarlse: *212*

Quiggley Holes site: *82*, 99

Quilix: *285*

Quillatose: 357

Quilomene band. *See* Middle Columbia River Salishans

Quiltanton complex: 89, 97

Quinn, Mac: 513

Quintasket, Charles: *250, 590*

Quintasket, Christine: 269

quirts: *4–5, 227, 234, 291, 356, 543*

qʷʔewt; synonymy: 218

R

Rabbit Island stemmed points: 112

raiding. *See* warfare, raids

railroads: 151, 152, 156, 158, *172*, 187, 200, 307–308, 345, 356, 474, 484, *487*, 637, 639

Rainbow trout people; synonymy: 538

rattles. *See* musical instruments

Rattlesnake Hill site: *82, 83, 84, 84, 85, 85, 86*

Ravalli, Anthony: 286, 322

Red Elk, Wenix: *416*

Red Feather: *147, 155*

Redfish Overhang site: *121*, 124–125

Red Horn: *488, 594*

Red River Mission School: 556, 557

Red Shirt: *285*

Red Thunder: *436–437*

Red Thunder, Joe: *432*

Red Thunder, Keith Soy: *432*

Red Thunder, Kenneth: *432*

Red Wolf, Josiah: *172*

religion: 3, 15, 197–199, 213, 230–231, 233–234, 235, 267, 278–279, 292–293, 303–304, 306, 318–319, 339–342, 354, 373, 388–389, 410–411, 425–427, 434, 462, 499–514, 521–523, 524, 526. Bluejay: 279. charms and amulets: 275, 384, 412, 460, 512, 537, 544. cults: 6, 412, 433, 434, 499, 500, 501. Dreamer cult: 280, 434, 499, 501, 502, 551. Eagle: 319. Earth-lodge cult: 551, 558. Feather cult: 6, 342, 346, 373, 389, 390, 499, 501, 511–513, *512*, 551, 552, 556, 557, 560. Ghost cult: 500. Hunting Horse: 513. Indian Shaker Church: 6, 140, 267, 342, 346, 347, 373, 389, 499, 501, 507–511, *508, 509, 511*, 513, 524, 549, 551, 552, 556, 558, 559, 560, 567. *ʔipnúʿcililpt* cult: 499, 505, 507. jumping: 507. Long Hair: 342, 502. Longhouse: 342, 501–507, 556, 557. Native American Church: 6, 267, 501, 513. nativistic movements: 280, 462, 504. Peyote: 6, 267, 501, 513. Pom-Pom: 502. priests: 141, 551. Prophet Dance: 140, 233, 280, 342, 413, 429, 499–501, 551, 556. prophets: 140, 373, 389, 407, 412, 499, 500, 501, 507, 521, 524, 549, 551–552, 557. protohistoric: 6, 140, 429, 499–501, 557. purification: 499. Seven Drum: 267, 342, 354, 499, 501–507, 506, 551, 558. Spinner cult: 511. Sun Dance: 6, 11, 279, 318, 319, 514. Sunday Dance: 342, 502, 503, 504. Sweatlodge: 231, 278, 340–341, 499, 565. Thunder: 319. *tulím* cult: 507. Washat: 6, 10, 27, 162, 342, 345, 347, 354, 373, 389, 410, 415, 416, 499, 501–507, *502–507*, 509, 511, *512*, 513, 547, *548*, 549, 551, 552, 556, 557, 558, 560, 561. *See also* afterlife; ceremonies; cosmology; shamans; supernatural beings

reservations and reserves: 152, 155–156, 159, 171, 484–498, *485*, 551, 636. acreage: 486, 487, 496–497. Adams Lake Reserve: 218, *485*, 496. administration: 415. agriculture: 491, *493*. Alexandria Reserve: *485*. Alkali Lake Reserve: *485*, 496. allotments: 160, 484, *485*. Anaham Reserve: *485*. Anderson Lake Reserve: 190, *485*, 497. Ashcroft Reserve: *485*, 497. Bitterroot: 306–307. Blackfeet: 573. Bonaparte Reserve: *485*, 496. Boothroyd Reserve: *485*, 497. Boston Bar Reserve: *485*, 497. Bridge River Reserve: 190, *485*, 497. Canim Lake Reserve: *485*, 496. Canoe Creek Reserve: *485*, 496. Cayoosh Creek Reserve: 190, *485*, 497. Chase: 56. checkerboard effect: *485*, 487, 489, 494. Chu Chua: 218. Clinton

787

ISBN 0-16-049514-8